THIRTEENTH EDITION

Current Issues and Enduring Questions

A Guide to Critical Thinking and Argument, with Readings

SYLVAN BARNET

HUGO BEDAU

JOHN O'HARA
Associate Professor of Critical Thinking, Reading, and Writing, Stockton University

bedford/st.martin's
Macmillan Learning

Boston | New York

Vice President: Leasa Burton
Senior Program Manager, Development/Composition: Nancy Tran
Director of Content Development: Jane Knetzger
Senior Development Editor: Leah Rang
Development Editor: Cari Goldfine
Assistant Editor: Heather Haase
Director of Media Editorial: Adam Whitehurst
Media Editor: Daniel Johnson
Executive Marketing Manager: Joy Fisher Williams
Senior Director, Content Management Enhancement: Tracey Kuehn
Senior Managing Editor: Michael Granger
Senior Manager of Publishing Services: Andrea Cava
Lead Content Project Manager: Pamela Lawson
Lead Workflow Project Manager: Paul W. Rohloff
Production Supervisor: Robert Cherry
Director of Design, Content Management: Diana Blume
Senior Design Services Manager: Natasha A. S. Wolfe
Interior Design: Maureen McCutcheon
Cover Design: William Boardman
Director, Rights and Permissions: Hilary Newman
Text Permissions Researcher: Elaine Kosta, Lumina Datamatics, Inc.
Photo Researcher: Cheryl DuBois, Lumina Datamatics, Inc.
Director of Digital Production: Keri deManigold
Media Project Managers: Rand Thomas and Daniel Johnson
Project Management and Editorial Services: Lumina Datamatics, Inc.
Copyeditor: Bridget Leahy
Part and Chapter Opening Photo: bortonia/Getty Images
Composition: Lumina Datamatics, Inc.
Printing and Binding: Transcontinental

Library of Congress Control Number: 2021952720

ISBN 978-1-319-33206-8

Printed in Canada.
1   2   3   4   5   6   27   26   25   24   23   22

Acknowledgments
Text acknowledgments and copyrights appear at the back of the book on pages 764–768, which constitute an extension of the copyright page. Art acknowledgments and copyrights appear on the same page as the art selections they cover.

For information, write: Bedford/St. Martin's, 75 Arlington Street, Boston, MA 02116

Preface

He who knows only his own side of the cause knows little. — JOHN STUART MILL

Current Issues and Enduring Questions: A Guide to Critical Thinking and Argument, with Readings is a text — a book about reading other people's arguments and writing your own arguments — and it is also an anthology — a collection of more than a hundred selections, ranging from the ancient world to the present, with a strong emphasis on critical thinking, reading, and writing about current issues.

Since the first edition, the quotation above has reflected the view of argument that underlies this book: In writing an essay, an author engages in a serious effort to discover their own ideas and, having found them, to contribute to a multisided conversation. The writer is not setting out to trounce an opponent. That is partly why we avoid expressions such as "marshaling evidence," "attacking an opponent," and "defending a thesis." Edmund Burke once wrote, "Our antagonist is our helper," and we agree that views and perspectives contrary to our own can help us sharpen our own thinking and writing. True, on television and social media we see pundits on the right and left who have made up their minds and who are indifferent or hostile to others' analysis and opinions. But in an academic community, and indeed in our daily lives, we learn by listening to others and by questioning our own ideas.

Two other foundational assumptions of this book are that arguments occur in a variety of forms, including but not limited to words on a page, and that arguments are shaped by the contexts in which they are made. In this edition, we reaffirm these beliefs with heightened sensitivity to the interplay between argument and persuasion with a dedicated chapter on rhetorical appeals. Because making decisions based on a clear critical thinking process is a fundamental skill important to interpreting the world around us and determining what to believe and how to act, we developed scenarios and thought experiments for students to reflect on their decision-making skills and consider how argument matters in their everyday lives and interactions. We recognize that academic and cultural discourses may make different kinds of arguments and require us to make different kinds of decisions — but also that thinking critically is a broader application which nevertheless means asking questions, understanding claims, examining evidence, and using reason to support conclusions.

Just as arguments are instruments of inquiry and learning as well as expression, *Current Issues and Enduring Questions* aims to help students learn to think, read, and write in more effective ways in all areas of their lives. As *critical thinkers and readers,* students in courses that use this book should develop their abilities to

- ask good questions about the reasoning processes that shape arguments and decisions;
- understand why information is selected and how it is presented persuasively by producers of arguments in all areas of life;
- account for variation and discrepancy in diverse perspectives on social and personal issues;
- understand how various contexts inform the production and reception of ideas anywhere;
- analyze and evaluate the strength of the evidence and reasoning undergirding arguments and ideas;
- evaluate the credibility and assumptions of sources within various discourses and discourse communities; and
- reflect upon, interrogate, and judge the (stated and unstated) consequences of arguments.

As *critical writers*, students develop their abilities to

- summarize an argument accurately, identifying the thesis, support, and conclusion;
- analyze an argument by reasoning logically and convincingly about it;
- produce a clear and purposeful argument of their own appropriate to a situation or discourse;
- communicate effectively for a specific audience (using appropriate language, tone, style, depth, and detail);
- explore sources of information and incorporate them selectively and skillfully, with proper documentation; and
- synthesize all information, ideas, terms, and concepts in an orderly and coherent way.

We think about and draft a response to something we have read, and in the very act of drafting, we may find — if we think critically about the words we are putting down on paper — that we are changing (perhaps slightly, perhaps radically) our own position. In short, one reason we write is so that we can improve our ideas. And even if we do not drastically change our views, we and our readers at least come to a better understanding of why we hold the views we do.

Enduring Features

ANALYZING AND CRAFTING ARGUMENTS

Part One, Critical Thinking and Reading (Chapters 1–5), and **Part Two, Critical Writing** (Chapters 6–8), together offer a short course in methods of thinking about and writing arguments. By "thinking," we mean *critical* thinking — serious analytic thought, including analysis of one's own perspectives, assumptions, and predispositions as one encounters (and produces) arguments; by "writing," we mean *critical* writing — the use of effective, respectable techniques for reasoned, convincing analysis, not merely gut feelings and persuasive gimmicks. (We are reminded of the notorious note scribbled in the margin of a politician's speech: "Argument weak; shout here").

We offer lots of advice about how to set forth an argument, but we do not offer instruction in dissembling, deceiving, or practicing one-upmanship; rather, we discuss responsible ways of arguing persuasively. We know that before one can write a persuasive argument, one must learn about an issue and clarify one's own ideas — a process that includes thinking critically about others' positions (even when they are agreeable) and being critical about one's own positions before setting them forth responsibly. Therefore, we devote Chapter 1 to critical thinking; Chapters 2, 3, and 4 to critical reading; Chapter 5 to critical reading of images; and Chapters 6, 7, and 8 to critical writing and research.

Parts One and Two, then, offer a preliminary (but we hope substantial) discussion of such topics as

- introducing ways to think critically and make decisions;
- overcoming obstacles to critical thinking;
- identifying assumptions;
- getting ideas by means of invention strategies;
- analyzing arguments from a variety of authors, sources, and genres;
- interpreting visual sources;
- finding, evaluating, and citing printed and electronic sources;
- evaluating kinds of evidence; and
- organizing material in a coherent, logical argument.

Parts One and Two together contain twenty-six selections (seven are student essays) for analysis and discussion as well as a capstone writing prompt that allows students to practice argument in common assignment genres: examining assumptions and exploring an issue, critical summary, rhetorical analysis, visual analysis, argument analysis, argument, research paper, and literary criticism.

CRITICAL THINKING, INQUIRY, AND INVENTION

In the first chapter, we emphasize how the process of critical thinking is a generative process. We focus on identifying the purpose, fairness, and consequences of arguments to various stakeholders and on analyzing ideas and concepts by asking questions — and then asking still further questions — to inspire fair-minded learning.

Our instruction throughout the book is accompanied by essays and images that embody and challenge concepts in critical thinking and argument. Each essay is accompanied by a list of Topics for Critical Thinking and Writing, which is not surprising given the emphasis we place on evaluating arguments, asking questions, and investigating further so as to generate new ideas. By asking critical questions a writer probably will find pathways for discovering new sources, new questions, and new ideas.

Visual Guides in each instructional chapter aid inquiry and invention by creating additional entry points to critical thinking. Colorful graphics and flowcharts help students design their own paths through common argument tasks such as writing a critical summary and organizing an analysis.

STYLES OF ARGUMENTATION

In keeping with our emphasis on writing as well as reading, we raise issues not only of what can roughly be called the "content" of the essays, but also of what can (equally roughly) be called the "style" — that is, the *ways* in which the arguments are set forth. Content and style, of course, cannot finally be kept apart. As Cardinal Newman said, "Thought and meaning are inseparable from each other. . . . *Style is thinking out into language.*" In our Topics for Critical Thinking and Writing, we sometimes ask the student

- to evaluate the effectiveness of an essay's opening paragraph,
- to explain a shift in tone from one paragraph to the next, or
- to characterize the persona of the author as revealed in the whole essay.

In addition, student essays and featured professional selections are marked to show writers' strategies and make argument moves and persuasive strategies visible. In short, this book is not designed as an introduction to some powerful ideas (although in fact it is that, too); rather, it is designed as an aid to thinking about and *writing* well-reasoned, effective arguments on important political, social, cultural, scientific, ethical, legal, and religious issues.

The selections reprinted in this book also illustrate different styles of argument that arise, at least in part, from the different disciplinary backgrounds of the various authors. Essays by journalists, novelists, social scientists, policy analysts, philosophers, critics, activists, and other writers — including first-year undergraduates — will be found in these pages. These authors develop and present their views in arguments that have distinctive features reflecting their special training and concerns. The differences in argumentative styles found in these essays foreshadow the differences students will encounter in the readings assigned in many of their other courses.

TYPES OF ARGUMENTATION

In **Part Three, Further Views on Argument** (Chapters 9–13), we acknowledge and detail some of the different approaches to argument and emphasize their potential usefulness to a particular writing situation — or as a means of framing an argument course or unit.

- Chapter 9, "A Philosopher's View: The Toulmin Model," is a summary of the philosopher Stephen Toulmin's method for analyzing arguments, covering claims, grounds, warrants, backing, modal qualifiers, and rebuttals. This summary will assist those who wish to apply Toulmin's methods to the readings in this book.

- Chapter 10, "A Logician's View: Deduction, Induction, and Fallacies," offers a more rigorous analysis of these topics than is usually found in composition courses and reexamines from a logician's point of view material introduced in Chapter 4.

- Chapter 11, "A Psychologist's View: Rogerian Argument," with an essay by psychotherapist Carl R. Rogers, complements the discussion of audience, organization, and tone in Chapter 7.

- Chapter 12, "A Literary Critic's View: Arguing about Literature," should help students see the things literary critics argue about and *how* they argue. Students can apply what they learn not only to the literary readings that appear in the chapter (a poem by Richard Blanco and a story by Kate Chopin) but also to the readings that appear in Part Six, Enduring Questions: Essays, Poems, and Stories.

- Chapter 13, "A Debater's View: Oral Presentations and Debate," introduces students to standard presentation strategies and debate format.

THE ANTHOLOGY

Part Four, Current Issues: Occasions for Debate (Chapters 14–19), begins with some comments on binary, or pro-con, thinking. It then gives a Checklist for Analyzing a Debate and offers six pairs of arguments — on student loan debt (should it be forgiven?), artificial intelligence (do computers have too much power?), free speech on campus (should speakers be permitted to share intolerant views?), bitcoin (is it a fad or the future?), genetic modification of human beings (it is ethical?), and cancel culture (should it be canceled?). Here, as elsewhere in the book, students can easily study the *methods* the writers use, as well as the issues themselves.

Part Five, Current Issues: Casebooks (Chapters 20–25), presents six chapters on issues discussed by several writers. For example, the first casebook concerns the nature and purpose of a college education: Should students focus their studies in STEM fields in the hopes of securing a more stable future and contributing to the economy, or should college be a place where students learn empathy, citizenship, and critical thinking — attributes often instilled by the humanities? Subsequent chapters focus on issues in the public discourse and relevant to students' lives now: systemic racial injustices, the ethics of cultural appropriation, and conspiracy theories — including those concerning the potential downfall of the nation's democracy.

Part Six, Enduring Questions: Essays, Poems, and Stories (Chapters 26–28), provides a philosophical and theoretical context for the contemporary arguments. These chapters are also useful by themselves as a means of thinking and writing about important concepts: Chapter 26, "What Is the Ideal Society?" (the voices here range from Thomas More, Lao Tzu, and Elizabeth Cady Stanton to literary figures Emma Lazarus and Ursula K. Le Guin); Chapter 27, "How and Why Do We Construct the 'Other'?" (authors in this chapter include Jean-Paul Sartre, W. E. B. Du Bois, and Simone de Beauvoir); and Chapter 28, "What Is Happiness?" (among the eight selections in this chapter are writings by Epictetus, the Dalai Lama, and Gretchin Rubin).

What's New in the Thirteenth Edition

FRESH AND TIMELY NEW READINGS, DEBATES, AND CASEBOOKS

More than a third of the total featured essays are new, as are topics such as diversity in critical thinking, mask mandates, artificial intelligence, bitcoin, cancel culture, critical race theory and antiracism, media representation, conspiracy culture, and more. Existing topics such as free speech and racial injustice have been carefully considered and updated to reflect our contemporary discourse and perspectives.

The topics in readings chapters were developed based on feedback from users of the text. New debates include "Bitcoin: Fad or Future?" and "Should We Cancel 'Cancel Culture'?" New casebook issues include "Representation Matters: How Does Media Shape Us?" and "Conspiracy Theories: Are They a Cultural Problem?"

ACTIVITIES THAT MAKE CRITICAL THINKING RELEVANT TO STUDENTS' LIVES

A new Consider This activity encourages students to think critically about their own decision-making and the ways argument concepts impact their lived experiences. Pointed questions and scenarios set the stage for every instructional chapter (Chapters 1–13) to give students metacognitive opportunities to recognize their critical thinking process and to evaluate the decisions that impact their beliefs and arguments. Scenarios include real versus imagined risks of shark attacks, rhetorical strategy when negotiating with a landlord, considering what gives art value (or what value makes art), and more.

FOCUSED CHAPTERS ON RHETORICAL ANALYSIS AND LOGICAL ARGUMENT

To support how instructors teach *Current Issues and Enduring Questions*, we have created two distinct chapters on rhetorical analysis and foundational argument concepts. In the thirteenth edition, we offer more clarity for the instructional content, separating "Critical Reading: Getting Deeper into Arguments" into two focused chapters — "Understanding Rhetorical Appeals" (Chapter 3) and "Identifying Procedures of Argument" (Chapter 4) — to better align with the assignments taught in the argument writing course.

INTERACTIVE TUTORIALS IN ACHIEVE

Two new tutorials, available in Achieve with *Current Issues and Enduring Questions*, engage students with important critical thinking and rhetorical analysis concepts. Each tutorial is highly visual and dynamic, moving students from a real-world illustration of the argument concept and instruction through modeling, practice, and reflection on topics of critical thinking and reading, especially of sources.

Acknowledgments

The authors would like to thank those who have strengthened this book by their comments and advice on the thirteenth edition: Heidi E. Ajrami, Victoria College; William Allegrezza, Indiana University Northwest; James Allen, College of DuPage; Kim Allen Gleed, Harrisburg Area Community College; Jeffrey Anderson, California State University – Los Angeles; George H. Bailey, Wentworth Institute of Technology; Benjamin J. Banks, Community College of Philadelphia; Amber Barnes, Trinity Valley Community College; Gary Bartlett, Central Washington University; Evelyn Beck, Harrisburg Area Community College; Ludger Brinker, Macomb Community College – Center Campus; Kendra N. Bryant, North Carolina A&T State University; Katawna Caldwell-Warren, Eastfield College; Karen Campbell, Grayson County College; Ty Clever, Harrisburg Area Community College; Rick Cole, Boston University; Jodi Mecham Corser, Southern Utah University; Jeanne K. Cosmos, Massachusetts Bay Community College – Wellesley Hills; Susie Crowson, Del Mar College; Brandon Daher, California State University – Fresno; Michele Domenech, Gaston College; Gina M. Firenzi, San Jose State University; Renea Frey, Xavier University; Deborah Garfinkle, College of San Mateo; Jeanne Guerin, American River College; Anthony Halderman, Alan Hancock College; Rachel Hanan, Northwest College – Powell; Sarah Hancock, California State University – Sacramento; Nile Hartline, Des Moines Area Community College; Jennifer Hauss, College of the Canyons; Pat Herb, North Central State College; Susan Hoeness-Krupsaw, University of Southern Indiana; James Landers, Community College of Philadelphia; Laura M. Lopez, University of the Incarnate World; Edward Mahoney, Pepperdine University; Michael L. Manous, Los Angeles City College; Marina Markossian, Rio Hondo College; Pamela McGlynn, Southwestern College; Susan Miller, University of California – Merced; Mike Perschon, MacEwan University; Sumino Otsuji, El Camino College; Robert Delius Royar, Morehead State University; Karen Ryan, Florida Gulf Coast University; Reid T. Sagara, College of the Desert; Steve Schessler, Cabrillo College; Lindsay Simpson, Des Moines Area Community College; Larry Sklaney, Century College; Stephen J. Sullivan, Metropolitan Community College – Longview; Thomas Shields, North Central State College; Jayanti Tamm, Ocean County College; Christopher Van Nostrand, Trinity Valley Community College; Linda J. Webster, Sam Houston Community College; Jason M. Whitesitt, Yavapai College – Prescott; Steven Yarborough, Bellevue College.

We are also deeply indebted to the people at Bedford/St. Martin's, especially to our thoughtful and supportive editor, Leah Rang, whose unparalleled input, exacting review, and wise feedback shaped both the written chapters and the reading selections at every stage of this edition's development. Most special thanks. Maura Shea and Adam Whitehurst, our editors for preceding editions, have also left a lasting impression on the book; without their work on the first eleven editions, there probably would not be a thirteenth. We particularly wish to thank John Sullivan for his collaborations over the past many years. Others at Bedford/St. Martin's to whom we are deeply indebted include Leasa Burton, Nancy Tran, Joy Fisher Williams, Pamela Lawson, Cari Goldfine, Daniel Johnson, Rand Thomas, and Heather Haase, all of whom have offered countless valuable (and invaluable) suggestions. Our gratitude also goes to those who helped research many of the essays included (and not included) here: Gina Atkins, Eric D. Brown, Emily Gresbrink, Rhiannon Scharnhorst, and Leah Washburn. We would also like to thank Hilary Newman, Elaine Kosta, and Cheryl DuBois, who adeptly managed art research and text permissions; and William Boardman, Natasha Wolfe, and Maureen McCutcheon for their excellent designs. Intelligent, informed, firm yet courteous, persuasive, and persistent — all these folks know how to think and argue.

Bedford/St. Martin's Puts You First

From day one, our goal has been simple: to provide inspiring resources that are grounded in best practices for teaching reading and writing. For over forty years, Bedford/St. Martin's has partnered with the field, listening to teachers, scholars, and students about the support writers need. No matter the moment or teaching context, we are committed to helping every writing instructor make the most of our resources — resources designed to engage every student.

How can we help *you*?

- Our editors can align our resources to your outcomes through correlation and transition guides for your syllabus. Just ask us.
- Our sales representatives specialize in helping you find the right materials to support your course goals.
- Our learning solutions and product specialists help you make the most of the digital resources you choose for your course.
- Our *Bits* blog on the Bedford/St. Martin's English Community (**community. macmillan.com**) publishes fresh teaching ideas regularly. You'll also find easily downloadable professional resources and links to author webinars on our community site.

Contact your Bedford/St. Martin's sales representative or visit **macmillanlearning.com** to learn more.

DIGITAL AND PRINT OPTIONS FOR *CURRENT ISSUES AND ENDURING QUESTIONS*

Choose the format that works best for your course, and ask about our packaging options that offer savings for students.

Digital

- *Achieve with* Current Issues and Enduring Questions. Achieve offers a dedicated composition space for writing instructors and students of all comfort levels with course technology. It provides trusted content with a robust e-book, as well as diagnostics with personalized study plans. Achieve's dedicated writing tools break down the writing process for students, make revision choices more visible to instructors, and guide students through drafting, peer review, avoiding plagiarism, reflection, and revision. Fully editable pre-built assignments support the book's approach. To order Achieve with *Current Issues and Enduring Questions*, use ISBN 978-1-319-33207-5. For details, visit **macmillanlearning.com/achieve/english**.

- *Popular e-book formats.* For details about our e-book partners, visit **macmillanlearning.com/ebooks**.

- *Inclusive Access.* Enable every student to receive their course materials through your LMS on the first day of class. Macmillan Learning's Inclusive Access program is the easiest, most affordable way to ensure all students have access to quality educational resources. Find out more at **macmillanlearning.com /inclusiveaccess**.

Print

- *Paperback edition.* To order the paperback edition of *Current Issues and Enduring Questions*, use ISBN 978-1-319-33206-8. To order the paperback edition packaged with Achieve for additional savings, use ISBN 978-1-319-49885-6.

- *Critical Thinking, Reading, and Writing.* To order the paperback brief edition — which includes the same Parts One, Two, and Three, as well as one debate, one thematic current issues casebook, and one enduring question collection — use ISBN 978-1-319-33205-1. To order the paperback edition packaged with Achieve with *Current Issues and Enduring Questions* for additional savings, use ISBN 978-1-319-49883-2.

- *From Critical Thinking to Argument.* To order the paperback value edition — which includes instruction from Chapters 1–10 and choice readings for analysis — use ISBN 978-1-319-33212-9. To order the paperback edition packaged with Achieve with *Current Issues and Enduring Questions* for additional savings, use ISBN 978-1-319-49914-3.

YOUR COURSE, YOUR WAY

No two writing programs or classrooms are exactly alike. Our Curriculum Solutions team works with you to design custom digital (e-book and Achieve) and print options that provide the resources your students need. (Options below require enrollment minimums.)

- *ForeWords for English.* Customize any print resource to fit the focus of your course or program by choosing from a range of prepared topics, such as Sentence Guides for Academic Writers.

- *Macmillan Author Program (MAP).* Add excerpts or package acclaimed works from Macmillan's trade imprints to connect students with prominent authors and public conversations. A list of popular examples or academic themes is available upon request.

- *Mix and Match.* With our simplest solution, you can add up to 50 pages of curated content to your Bedford/St. Martin's text. Contact your sales representative for additional details.

- *Add your own original course- or program-specific materials.*

INSTRUCTOR RESOURCES

You have a lot to do in your course. We want to make it easy for you to find the support you need — and to get it quickly.

Resources for Teaching Current Issues and Enduring Questions is available as a PDF that can be downloaded from **macmillanlearning.com** and is also available in Achieve. The instructor's manual includes sample syllabi, notes for every selection and chapter, and additional topics for classroom discussion and student writing assignments.

Contents

A cultural theorist and philosopher argues that an understanding and embrace of intersectionality requires that we cut back on "the urge to underwrite our observations with our identities."

PART THREE   FURTHER VIEWS ON ARGUMENT   331

9 A PHILOSOPHER'S VIEW: THE TOULMIN MODEL   333

12 A LITERARY CRITIC'S VIEW: ARGUING ABOUT LITERATURE   395

13 A DEBATER'S VIEW: ORAL PRESENTATIONS AND DEBATE   416

PART SIX   **ENDURING QUESTIONS: ESSAYS, POEMS, AND STORIES**   **653**

26   WHAT IS THE IDEAL SOCIETY?   655

PART ONE

Critical Thinking and Reading

Critical Thinking

Something about us is such that our fulfillment, our integral fulfillment, depends in part in our intellectual engagement. And the higher the level of intellectual engagement, the deeper, the richer the fulfillment.

— CORNEL WEST

CONSIDER THIS

Maui Beach, Hawaii, is the second-most shark-infested shore in the United States. Maui's waters are home to several varieties of shark, none more dangerous than the tiger shark, a near-shore macropredator sometimes called the "maneater" that commonly reaches over ten feet in length.

The "maneater" on its home turf

Rodrigo Friscione/Getty Images

Now, consider a proposition: You are offered a free week-long trip to Maui. All that is required of you is to float in the waters of Maui Beach for one hour per morning. You can tread water or use floaties, but you have to remain in water six to eight feet deep — the depth where the tiger shark most likes to hunt!

Would you take the deal? Why or why not?

Thinking about Thinking

When Ralph Waldo Emerson said the hardest task in the world is simply "to think," he was using the word "think" in the sense of "critical thinking." By itself, thinking does not seem so hard. It can mean almost anything from idle daydreaming ("I'd like to go camping") to simple reasoning ("but if I go this week, I won't be able to study for my chemistry exam"). Thinking by itself may include deliberations and decision-making that occur so automatically they hardly register in our consciousness ("What if I do go camping? I won't be likely to pass the exam. Then what? I better stay home and study").

When you add the adjective "critical" to the noun "thinking," you begin to examine this thinking process *consciously*, which requires **metacognition**, a term that means being self-conscious about your thinking — thinking about your thinking — and understanding *why* you think what you think. When you think metacognitively, you may see that even your simple decisions can involve a fairly elaborate series of calculations.

As an exercise in metacognitive calculus, begin not with your reasoning about politics, religion or art — or other serious issues raised in this book — but instead with something very basic: your reasoning about sharks. Many people are unduly afraid of sharks and therefore vastly overestimate the risk they pose to humans. If you fear sharks, you probably said "no, thank you" to our proposition and moved on. If you accepted it, you probably realized that despite the chilling facts we provided, the proposition did not ask anyone to perform a particularly dangerous activity. Millions of people safely swim in Maui's waters each year. In fifty years, Maui has seen fewer than 200 shark encounters, most of them minor, with an average of one fatality every seven years. People routinely engage in other substantially higher-risk activities all the time and barely think about it: riding in an automobile, for example, which is far more dangerous than a relaxing swim in Maui. And yet, for many, the mere mention of sharks in our proposition is enough for them to say, "No, that's not worth the risk."

We hope to demonstrate the ways in which flawed beliefs about sharks can lead to flawed reasoning and flawed decision-making. Beliefs are simply things we take to be true. Beliefs may be about how the natural world is ordered, or they may be about people, society, politics, economics, or morality. Beliefs are quite powerful in affecting people's decision-making — for better and for worse — and it is not just individuals who are vulnerable to false beliefs and poor decisions. The 1978 release of the movie *Jaws* induced such hysteria about sharks that fishing crews began needlessly killing them up and down US coasts — a disastrous ecological miscalculation that did nothing to reduce the already very low number of shark attacks, even if it felt reassuring. The author of the novel *Jaws*, Peter Benchley, so regretted the effect of his work on beliefs about sharks that he dedicated his later career to marine conservation and dispelling myths about sharks.

Examining your own beliefs before you make decisions is crucial. Many people make decisions based on their "gut," which just means that they are making important judgments based on little more than how they feel in a moment, prioritizing unexamined beliefs and basic instincts such as fear and anxiety over thoughtful deliberation and consideration of evidence. In order to make good decisions, you need to discern the truth of your beliefs, and to do that you need to consult information to find out what *warrants*, or guarantees, your beliefs. If you had spoken to shark experts and researched the risks of shark attacks, you would have found information proving you have little to fear from sharks, that your beliefs were not warranted. (This may not reassure everyone, but then fear is not always rational.)

To decide literally means to "cut off" (from the Latin word *caedere*, the root of the English word "scissors"). Think of it this way: Deciding means cutting away many possibilities until just one remains, your final decision. To decide whether or not to swim in Maui, or what to believe (or what to do) about any issue raised in this book, you need to be able to test your own beliefs, gather and judge information, and cut away what is extraneous, untrue, or irrelevant until you arrive at your answer.

Many people associate being critical with fault-finding and nit-picking. The word *critic* might conjure an image of a sneering art or food critic eager to gripe about everything that's wrong with a particular work of art or menu item. People's low estimation of the stereotypical critic comes to light humorously in Samuel Beckett's play *Waiting for Godot*, when the two vagabond heroes, Vladimir and Estragon, engage in a name-calling contest to see who can hurl the worst insult at the other. Estragon wins hands-down when he fires the ultimate invective:

V: Moron!

E: Vermin!

V: Abortion!

E: Morpion!

V: Sewer-rat!

E: Curate!

V: Cretin!

E: (*with finality*) Crritic!

V: Oh! (*He wilts, vanquished, and turns away*)

However, being a good *critical thinker* isn't the same as being a "critic" in the derogatory sense. Quite the reverse: critical thinkers must analyze *themselves*

Critical thinking involves taking ideas, issues, and problems apart to understand them better, much like mechanics learn to do with automobile engines to understand how all the parts work together.

as rigorously as they analyze others. They must be open-minded, alert to *their own* thinking process, aware of *their own* beliefs and biases, the quality of evidence *they themselves* offer, the logic *they* use, the conclusions *they* draw. Bottom line: Critical thinking is *self-conscious* inquiry, metacognition in action. In college, you may not aspire to become a churlish critic, but we hope you aspire to become a better critical thinker.

The word "critical" comes from the Greek word *krinein*, meaning "to separate, to choose." This suggests that by taking apart a problem, and examining your reasoning about it, you can understand it better and ultimately produce better solutions. This is an essential skill in college, career, and life.

Thinking as a Citizen

Your decisions, choices, and behaviors may feel personal or private, but they are part of the entire social fabric, and they help compose the world around you. According to political scientist Wendy Brown, democracy cannot survive long without a public educated enough to make rational independent decisions that collectively add up to rational social decisions. In short, she says in her article "The End of Educated Democracy" that we are in trouble if we do not foreground critical thinking as a foundational and common skill. The challenges before us, however,

> include complex forms and novel concentrations of economic and political power, sophisticated marketing and theatricality in politics, corporately owned media and a historically unparalleled glut of information and opinion which, again, produces the illusion of knowledge, freedom, and even participation in the face of their opposites.

We live in a media environment designed to steer us toward sources that confirm our existing viewpoints (the so-called echo chamber effect), and where much information is notoriously unreliable, if not plainly false. Information circulates in idiosyncratic ways across various social networks, impacting people's ideas about what is true and false on a widespread basis. In fact, each of us plays a part in this information ecosystem not only when we read but also when we post, share, like, subscribe, or communicate our ideas in any way (and even when we speak in classrooms, workplaces, and at home).

People often develop and express very strong beliefs through the media about what is true and false, right and wrong, yet the *strength* of a belief is not a good test for whether or not it is true. Neither is a good test of truth a matter of how *many* people believe something to be true. Just because something is "trending" or has "gone viral" does not necessarily mean it is true, factual, or legitimate. Most of us know this; nevertheless, we tend to think that consensus beliefs — popular, widely shared beliefs — must have something to them. But the number of people who believe something has little to do with whether or not it is based on facts. At one time, a majority of people believed the earth was flat. If we used merely the number of believers to assess the truth of a claim, we might never have surpassed this and other popular fantasies.

Beliefs — especially those that are strong and shared — factor into decision-making. False beliefs can be treacherous: False beliefs related to the origin of the COVID-19 virus contributed to bias (and even violence) against Asian Americans during the pandemic; false beliefs undermined verifiable proof of the efficacy of COVID-19 vaccines; and false beliefs sowed doubt about the legitimacy of the US Presidential election, culminating in an attack on the US Capitol.

We may scoff at theories such as a flat earth conspiracy or beliefs about virus origins. However, it is sometimes difficult to understand (and therefore question) our own beliefs from the outside. Our beliefs feel natural to us; we just seem to live within them and comprehend the world through them. A story once told by the author David Foster Wallace illustrates our capacity to ignore what we take for granted. Two young fish are swimming in the ocean. An older (we think wiser) fish passes by and says, "Hey, guys, how's the water?" A moment later, one of the younger fish looks at his friend and asks, "What the hell is water?"

But enough with fish (and sharks). Instead, let's address issues that are far more impactful to the society in which we live. Our point is that critical thinking is not just an important individual responsibility but also a social one. It is not our task to tell you *what* to think about the topics raised in this book, but to guide you toward understanding *how* to think in an information ecosystem with competing beliefs, values, and reasoning.

Obstacles to Critical Thinking

Because critical thinking requires engaging seriously with potentially difficult topics — topics that elicit strong opinions and powerful emotions — it's important to recognize other ways in which clear thinking may be clouded. Your critical thinking might be impeded if you

1. Take positions based upon only your own experiences or perspective.
2. Hesitate to form opinions on controversial topics.
3. Are so disgusted, angered, or emotionally affected by a topic that you cannot take an unbiased view.
4. Fear judgment for thinking differently than most of the people around you.
5. Never consider departing from inherited wisdom (the opinions of your parents or other sources of authority).
6. Base your decisions more often on common sense, intuition, or gut reaction rather than on carefully examined information.
7. Tend to simply agree or reject without question the opinions or analysis of one or more public figures (influencer, celebrity, politician, journalist, etc.).
8. Believe issues are too complex to understand or that it is others' jobs to figure out the best course of action.
9. Are unwilling to alter your point of view based on new information, or you are unwilling to grant credibility to reliable information that challenges you.

No matter how controversial the issue, critical thinking requires that you approach it in a way that's fair to all parties and that explores relevant issues and that you evaluate a range of information in an unbiased way — without merely collecting evidence to support a preestablished conclusion.

Let us share with you a *koan*, a type of puzzle designed by Buddhist teachers to confound people and shake them from complacent ways of thinking. One of our favorites is attributed to Linji, a ninth-century Japanese sage, who offered this *koan*: "If you meet the Buddha in the road, kill him." Now why would Linji, himself a believer, advise this? His advice is a fair warning from a faithful adherent: Be skeptical. Resist allowing your *desire* to believe something keep you from asking challenging or uncomfortable questions, such as why the Buddha would appear to you of all people — or to any human being — since Buddhism emphasizes inward sources of truth. Be careful: The person in the road could be a charlatan, merely trying to fool you.

An Essay on Types of Thinking (and Rethinking)

The following essay by Adam Grant addresses the importance of being willing to challenge your own views and to revise your beliefs when new information warrants it. Grant also outlines four distinctive types of thinkers — preachers, politicians, prosecutors, and scientists (Buddhas, you might say, we may very well meet in the road).

ADAM GRANT

Adam Grant is a professor at The Wharton School of the University of Pennsylvania and the author of several popular books on how organizational psychology (the science of how humans behave at work) can be used to improve thinking and decision-making. His latest book is *Think Again: The Power of Knowing What You Don't Know* (2021), in which this selection appears.

A Preacher, a Prosecutor, a Politician, and a Scientist

Rethinking has become central to my sense of self. I'm a psychologist but I'm not a fan of Freud, I don't have a couch in my office, and I don't do therapy. As an organizational psychologist at Wharton, I've spent the past fifteen years researching and teaching evidence-based management. As an entrepreneur of data and ideas, I've been called by organizations like Google, Pixar, the NBA, and the Gates Foundation to help them reexamine how they design meaningful jobs, build creative teams, and shape collaborative cultures. My job is to think again about how we work, lead, and live — and enable others to do the same.

I can't think of a more vital time for rethinking. As the coronavirus pandemic unfolded, many leaders around the world were slow to rethink their assumptions — first that the virus wouldn't affect their countries, next that it would be no deadlier than the flu, and then that it could only be transmitted by people with visible symptoms. The cost in human life is still being tallied.

In the past year we've all had to put our mental pliability to the test. We've been forced to question assumptions that we had long taken for granted: That it's safe to go to the hospital, eat in a restaurant, and hug our parents or grandparents. That live sports will always be on TV and most of us will never have to work remotely or home school our kids. That we can get toilet paper and hand sanitizer whenever we need them.

In the midst of the pandemic, multiple acts of police brutality led many people to rethink their views on racial injustice and their roles in fighting it. The senseless deaths of three Black citizens — George Floyd, Breanna Taylor, and Ahmaud Arbery — left millions of white people realizing that just as sexism is not only a women's issue, racism is not only an issue for people of color. As waves of protest swept the nation, across the political spectrum, support for the Black Lives Matter movement climbed nearly as much in the span of two weeks as it had in the previous two years. Many of those who had long been unwilling or unable to acknowledge it quickly came to grips with the harsh reality of systemic racism that still pervades America. Many of those who had long been silent came to reckon with their responsibility to become antiracists and act against prejudice.

Despite these shared experiences, we live in an increasingly divisive time. For some people a single mention of kneeling during the national anthem is enough to end a friendship. For others a single ballot at a voting booth is enough to end a marriage. Calcified ideologies are tearing American culture apart. Even our great governing document, the U.S. Constitution, allows for amendments. What if we were quicker to make amendments to our own mental constitutions? . . .

This is not an easy task. As we sit with our beliefs, they tend to become more extreme and more entrenched. *I'm still struggling to accept that Pluto may not be a planet.* In education, after revelations in history and revolutions in science, it often takes years for a curriculum to be updated and textbooks to be revised. Researchers have recently discovered that we need to rethink widely accepted assumptions about such subjects as Cleopatra's roots (her father was Greek, not Egyptian, and her mother's identity is unknown); the appearance of dinosaurs (paleontologists now think some tyrannosaurs had colorful feathers on their backs); and what's required for sight (blind people have actually trained themselves to "see" — sound waves can activate the visual cortex and create representations in the mind's eye, much like how echolocation helps bats navigate in the dark).* Vintage records, classic cars, and antique clocks might be valuable collectibles, but outdated facts are mental fossils that are best abandoned.

We're swift to recognize when other people need to think again. We question the judgment of experts whenever we seek out a second opinion on a medical diagnosis. Unfortunately, when it comes to our own knowledge and opinions, we often favor *feeling* right over *being* right. In everyday life, we make many diagnoses of our own, ranging from whom we hire to whom we marry. We need to develop the habit of forming our own second opinions.

Imagine you have a family friend who's a financial adviser, and he recommends investing in a retirement fund that isn't in your employer's plan. You have another friend

---

*For my part, I had assumed the phrase "blowing smoke up your arse" came from people gifting cigars to someone they wanted to impress, so you can imagine how intrigued I was when my wife told me its real origin: In the 1700s, it was common practice to revive drowning victims with tobacco enemas, literally blowing smoke up their behinds. Only later did they learn that it was toxic to the cardiac system.

who's fairly knowledgeable about investing, and he tells you that this fund is risky. What would you do?

When a man named Stephen Greenspan found himself in that situation, he decided to weigh his skeptical friend's warning against the data available. His sister had been investing in the fund for several years, and she was pleased with the results. A number of her friends had been, too; although the returns weren't extraordinary, they were consistently in the double digits. The financial adviser was enough of a believer that he had invested his own money in the fund. Armed with that information, Greenspan decided to go forward. He made a bold move, investing nearly a third of his retirement savings in the fund. Before long, he learned that his portfolio had grown by 25 percent.

Then he lost it all overnight when the fund 10 collapsed. It was the Ponzi scheme managed by Bernie Madoff.

Two decades ago my colleague Phil Tetlock discovered something peculiar. As we think and talk, we often slip into the mindsets of three different professions: preachers, prosecutors, and politicians. In each of these modes, we take on a particular identity and use a distinct set of tools. We go into preacher mode when our sacred beliefs are in jeopardy: we deliver sermons to protect and promote our ideals. We enter prosecutor mode when we recognize flaws in other people's reasoning: we marshal arguments to prove them wrong and win our case. We shift into politician mode when we're seeking to win over an audience: we campaign and lobby for the approval of our constituents. The risk is that we become so wrapped up in preaching that we're right, prosecuting others who are wrong, and politicking for support that we don't bother to rethink our own views.

When Stephen Greenspan and his sister made the choice to invest with Bernie Madoff, it wasn't because they relied on just one of those mental tools. All three modes together contributed to their ill-fated decision. When his sister told him about the money she and her friends had made, she was preaching about the merits of the fund. Her confidence led Greenspan to prosecute the friend who warned him against investing, deeming the friend guilty of "kneejerk cynicism." Greenspan was in politician mode when he let his desire for approval sway him toward a yes — the financial adviser was a family friend whom he liked and wanted to please.

Any of us could have fallen into those traps. Greenspan says that he should've known better, though, because he happens to be an expert on gullibility. When he decided to go ahead with the investment, he had almost finished writing a book on why we get duped. Looking back, he wishes he had approached the decision with a different set of tools. He might have analyzed the fund's strategy more systematically instead of simply trusting in the results. He could have sought out more perspectives from credible sources. He would have experimented with investing smaller amounts over a longer period of time before gambling so much of his life's savings.

That would have put him in the mode of a scientist. . . .

Just as you don't have to be a profes- 15 sional scientist to reason like one, being a professional scientist doesn't guarantee that someone will use the tools of their training. Scientists morph into preachers when they present their pet theories as gospel and treat thoughtful critiques as sacrilege. They veer into politician terrain when they allow their views to be swayed by popularity rather than accuracy. They enter prosecutor mode when they're hell-bent on debunking and discrediting rather than discovering. After upending physics with his theories of relativity, Einstein opposed the quantum revolution: "To punish me for my contempt of authority, Fate has made me an authority myself." Sometimes even great scientists need to think more like scientists. . . .

When we're in scientist mode, we refuse to let our ideas become ideologies. We don't start with answers or solutions; we lead with questions and puzzles. We don't preach from intuition; we teach from evidence. We don't just have healthy skepticism about other people's arguments; we dare to disagree with our own arguments.

Thinking like a scientist involves more than just reacting with an open mind. It means being *actively* open-minded. It requires searching for reasons why we might be wrong — not for reasons why we must be right — and revising our views based on what we learn.

That rarely happens in the other mental modes. In preacher mode, changing our minds is a mark of moral weakness; in scientist mode, it's a sign of intellectual integrity. In prosecutor mode, allowing ourselves to be persuaded is admitting defeat; in scientist mode, it's a step toward the truth. In politician mode, we flip-flop in response to carrots and sticks; in scientist mode, we shift in the face of sharper logic and stronger data. . . .

Scientific thinking favors humility over pride, doubt over certainty, curiosity over closure. When we shift out of scientist mode, the rethinking cycle breaks down, giving way to an overconfidence cycle. If we're preaching, we can't see gaps in our knowledge: we believe we've already found the truth. Pride breeds conviction rather than doubt, which makes us prosecutors: we might be laser-focused on changing other people's minds, but ours is set in stone. That launches us into confirmation bias and desirability bias. We become politicians, ignoring or dismissing whatever doesn't win the favor of our constituents — our parents, our bosses, or the high school classmates we're still trying to impress. We become so busy putting on a show that the truth gets relegated to a backstage seat, and the resulting validation can make us arrogant. We fall victim to the fat-cat syndrome, resting on our laurels instead of pressure-testing our beliefs.

Topics for Critical Thinking and Writing

1. Do people always act according to their beliefs? Consider some instances when people act against their beliefs and why they might do so.

2. Think about your own experiences when you've had to "think again." What is a belief you held in the past that later evolved or changed? What information, influence, or circumstance was most important to you in changing your belief?

3. Pick a public figure and discuss why you consider they think like a preacher, a prosecutor, a politician, or a scientist. How does the figure rely upon and use information differently than another type of thinker? (It is fine if they actually have those occupations or a combination of them.)

Thinking through an Issue

Consider the obstacles to critical thinking (p. 7) and our advice about rethinking your beliefs as we next summon an unusual deity called the Flying Spaghetti Monster (FSM). This all-powerful being is said to be made entirely of spaghetti and meatballs and — we kid you not — has millions of devout followers around the world who refer to themselves as "Pastafarians."

In the spirit of open-mindedness, an essential critical thinking disposition, let's take the Church of the Flying Spaghetti Monster seriously for a moment. Like other religions, the Church has a holy book, *The Gospel of the Flying Spaghetti Monster*, and a creation story: The *Gospel* says that the Spaghetti Monster created man and earth 5,000 years ago (after first creating a beer volcano and drinking too much from it). It enumerates a set of holy commandments ("The Eight I'd-Really-Rather-You-Didn'ts") and declares a major winter holiday ("Holiday") when faithful Pastafarians dress in sacred vestments (pirate costumes) and eat . . . well, what else? "R'Amen," as they say at the end of their noodly prayers.

Take stock of your initial reactions to the Church of the Flying Spaghetti Monster. Some initial responses might be quite uncritical, quite unthinking: "That's outrageous!" or "How funny!" Others might be snap judgments: "That makes no sense!" or "They're just making fun of real religions!"

But remember to try *not* allowing your gut reactions to determine your final judgments. Even while it sounds quite tongue-in-cheek, the Church of the Flying Spaghetti Monster appears and behaves in many ways like a "real" religion. Try being willing to engage with something even though you may feel uncomfortable, infuriated, offended, or, in this case, maybe just too dismissive to give the subject serious attention. Exercise critical thinking. Can you simply say, "No, that belief is ridiculous," in response to a religious claim? Many mainstream religions are based on quite fantastic stories and beliefs.

Dedicated Pastafarians have become champions of the First Amendment's establishment clause, which prohibits all government institutions from *establishing*, or preferring, any one religion over another. To achieve equality for their own religion, FSM church members in Tennessee, Virginia, and Wisconsin have successfully petitioned for permission to display statues or signs of the Flying Spaghetti Monster on government properties where other religious icons are permitted. In Oklahoma, Pastafarians argued that because the state allows a marble and granite Ten Commandments monument on the state courthouse lawn, then a statue of the Flying Spaghetti Monster must also be permitted, an effort which ultimately forced the state to remove the Ten Commandments monument in 2015 and to prohibit all religious statues at the courthouse. Since then, individuals in California, Georgia, Florida, Texas, and Utah have asserted their right to wear religious head coverings in their driver's license photos — a religious exemption afforded to Muslims in those states — and have had their pictures taken with colanders on their heads. In some places, ordained FSM ministers can legally preside over weddings.

"They're just causing trouble," one might venture to say. Think about it yourself: If your hometown approved placing a Christmas tree on the town square during the holiday season and the Church of the Flying Spaghetti Monster argued that it, too, should be allowed to set up its holiday symbol — perhaps a statue — as a matter of religious equality, how would you respond? Should it be afforded equal space? Why or why not?

- **If you said no,** consider how you would respond if members of a different religious group were asking for equal space. Would you agree that other religious representations should be included in public spaces? Should a menorah be allowed? A mural celebrating Kwanzaa? A Native American symbol? If those seem reasonable or even obvious, then why not a Flying Spaghetti Monster?

- **If you said yes,** that all groups should be given equal space, then what if members of even more marginal groups also wanted to be included? Would you agree if the Church of Satan requested that they too should be able to place a statue of the goat-headed, winged demon Baphomet on your hometown's public square? How would you (or people you know) respond to such a proposal? Fundamentally, the question is, "Can some religious expressions be included in public spaces and not others?" If so, why? If not, why not?

When thinking critically on any matter, it's important to ask such questions about various positions and from different perspectives. If we assume that we (or those like us) have a monopoly on the truth and we dismiss those who disagree with us as misguided fools, or if we assume that others who see differently that we do are acting only out of self-interest (or a desire to harass us or the community) and we don't analyze their views carefully and measure them against consistent standards, then we're being critical, but we aren't engaging in critical thinking.

EVALUATING A PROPOSAL

To address whether or not you should support or oppose something, it is important to weigh competing interests fairly, and to predict the outcomes of any decisions or actions you take. In the case of whether to support or oppose a Flying Spaghetti Monster display in your hometown, you must identify the wider issues at stake — questions of religious freedom, equality, and the law. And you must gather as many perspectives as you can before reaching a conclusion. You should ask

- **Who** is *for* and *against* the proposition?
- **Why** are they *for* or *against* it?
- **What** can be said *for* and *against* the proposition?

We must see through others' eyes and *identify and examine possible objections to our own beliefs*. By imagining what others might say to critique *us*, we thus conduct an argument with ourselves, advancing and then questioning as many different opinions as possible.

SURVEY, ANALYZE, AND EVALUATE THE ISSUE

To develop a thoughtful position (which may lead to thoughtful decisions and actions) you will want to gather information — to **survey** what people are saying and thinking. This is true of any issue you face. In the case of the Flying Spaghetti Monster, you will

Under the establishment clause of the First Amendment, members of the Church of the Flying Spaghetti Monster were permitted to install a monument on the lawn of a Crossville, Tennessee, courthouse in 2008.

likely want to gather opinions from religious leaders, community members, and legal experts. You will want to **analyze** those perspectives alongside one another, and **evaluate** the merits of their claims by examining the evidence that warrants them. Pay close attention to specific points on which people agree and disagree, and to how they present and interpret evidence differently. You may need to do some research of your own, for example learning about the legal responsibility of public institutions to accommodate different viewpoints — and the limits of such accommodations. You may want to find your own evidence, perhaps looking at other instances when religious equality, free speech, and the separation of church and state were in conflict. Remember that the Church of the Flying Spaghetti Monster didn't gain so much traction by being easy to dismiss. You'll certainly have to think beyond a knee-jerk value judgment like, "No, a Spaghetti Monster statue would be ugly."

To summarize the process, the following steps can enhance your ability to consider multiple perspectives:

1. **Survey different viewpoints**, considering as many as possible and paying attention to who stands to gain and lose in any debate.
2. **Analyze the conflicts**, identifying and separating out the problems or points of debate and trying to see the bigger issues at stake.
3. **Evaluate the ideas**, judging the merit of various claims and arguments and measuring the weight of the evidence.

Use the Visual Guide: Evaluating a Proposal below to pursue some lines of questioning for evaluating a proposed regulation, policy, or procedure. Apply this line of thinking to the Flying Spaghetti Monster issue.

If you survey, analyze, and evaluate comprehensively, you'll have better and more informed ideas; you'll generate a wide variety of ideas, each triggered by your own responses and the ideas your research brings to light. You will be able to find your position by thinking through the issue and developing your argument. As you do so, you should be as thorough as possible and sensitive to the ideas, claims, and rights of many different people. After all, you may have to present your argument to the town council or community. If you simply decided

Visual Guide: Evaluating a Proposal

that a Spaghetti Monster statue was insulting to other religions and ignored the law in your argument, you could be setting up your town for a lawsuit.

What do you think? If you were on your hometown's city council and a petition came through from the Church of the Flying Spaghetti Monster to permit a Spaghetti Monster display alongside the traditional Christmas tree and menorah on the town square, how would you answer the questions presented in the Visual Guide? How would you vote? Why? How would you explain your vote to opponents of the Spaghetti Monster display?

ANTICIPATING COUNTERARGUMENTS

We generate ideas not only by seeking support for our initial thoughts, but also imagining opposing responses to them — *counterpoints* or *counterpositions*, we call them. When we weigh all those points and positions and draw our reasoned conclusions, we may also find **counterarguments** (other positions and points arranged logically together toward a different conclusion). Sometimes, we avoid counterarguments — or avoid taking them seriously — because we do not want to face them, or we simply do not consider a particular perspective legitimate. But we must take counterarguments seriously because if we find them unreasonable, they can ultimately strengthen our thinking by bolstering our capacity to defend our own positions. When our own arguments demonstrate that we have taken the time to consider other perspectives, our positions gain *credibility* because we've shown that we seriously considered all sides and that we are aware of different views.

We mention counterarguments here because they're an important component in assembling our thoughts and constructing arguments.

> **WRITING TIP**
> Early in the process of conceiving your ideas on a topic, stop to ask yourself, "What might someone reasonably offer as an *objection* to my view?"

The next section follows a student, Alexa Cabrera, as she thought through multiple perspectives and counterpositions to a case concerning the Church of the Flying Spaghetti Monster. (We discuss counterarguments further in the "Rebuttals" section in Chapter 9.)

Critical Thinking at Work: From a Cluster to a Short Essay

Alexa Cabrera was assigned to write approximately 500 words about a specific legal challenge made by a member of the Church of the Flying Spaghetti Monster. She selected the case of Stephen Cavanaugh, a prisoner who had made a complaint against the Nebraska State Penitentiary after being denied the right to practice Pastafarianism while incarcerated there. Because the Department of Corrections had denied him those privileges, Cavanaugh filed suit citing civil rights violations and asked for his rights to be accommodated.

Alexa began thinking through her argument using *clustering*, a brainstorming tool for generating ideas and thinking through an issue. Notice Alexa offered an initial idea, and then began building on it by raising supporting and opposing points and counterpoints built off the initial idea. Her cluster is a *first step* in the critical thinking stage, not a road map of her final written essay. Notice, too, Alexa's cluster contains ideas that eventually did *not* make it into the final essay, and that her essay — the product of several revised drafts — introduces points she had *not* thought of while clustering. The thinking process often means conducting an argument with yourself, and it does not end when you begin writing. Building an argument is a *continuous* process of thinking and learning.

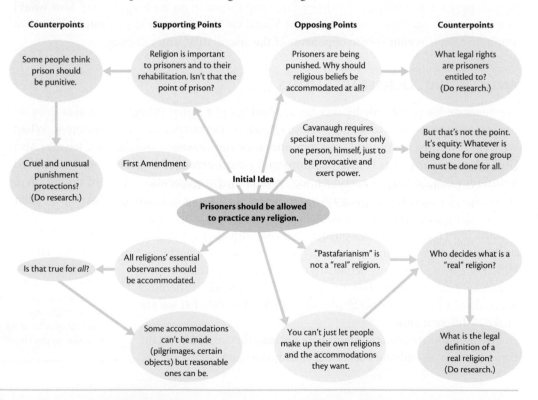

CHAPTER 1 | CRITICAL THINKING

Alexa Cabrera

Professor Regina Dacus

English 112

8 October 2016

<h3 style="text-align:center">Stirred and Strained: Pastafarians Should Be Allowed   ①
to Practice in Prison</h3>

Stephen Cavanaugh is a member of the Church of the Flying Spaghetti Monster (FSM), a mostly web-based religious group notable for its members' demands that they be treated under the First Amendment like any other religion. The group strives to show that if Christians can place Nativity scenes on public grounds or if Muslims can wear head coverings in state driver's license photographs, then by god (or by pasta, as the case may be), they can too. Cavanaugh is in the Nebraska State Penitentiary, where inmates are ② permitted under the Religious Land Use and Institutionalized Persons Act (RLUIPA) to exercise religious freedoms guaranteed by the First Amendment. He wants the same rights and privileges given to incarcerated Christians, Muslims, Jews, and Buddhists — namely, to be able to wear religious clothing, to eat specially prepared meals, and to be given resources, space, and time to conduct worship with his fellow "believers." For Cavanaugh, this means being able to dress up as a pirate, eat pasta on selected holidays, order satirical holy books, and lead a weekly "prayer" group. Many people consider these requests absurd, but Cavanaugh should be permitted under the First Amendment and the RLUIPA to practice his faith. ③

Some arguments against Cavanaugh are easier to dismiss than others. One of these simply casts aside the spiritual needs and concerns of prisoners: They are being punished, after all, so why should they receive any religious accommodations? This position is both immoral and unconstitutional. Religion is an important sustaining force for prisoners who might otherwise struggle to find meaning and purpose in life, and it is protected by the First Amendment *because* it helps prisoners find purpose and become rehabilitated — the fundamental goal of correctional facilities (even for those serving life without parole). Another argument sees religion

---

1 Title: Plays with words related to pasta and prison. The subtitle states the thesis.

2 *Paragraph 1:* Sets the stage. Nifty turn of phrase engages readers and sets the tone as playful but serious.

3 Last sentence presents a clear thesis.

as important as long as it conforms to Judeo-Christian belief structures, which has for a long time been the only spiritual path available in American prisons. But today, in our diverse society, the RLUIPA *requires* prisons to provide religious accommodations for all faiths equally unless an undue administrative, financial, or security burden can be proven. Obviously, many religious observances cannot be accommodated. Prisons cannot permit inmates to carry crosses and staves, construct temples and sweat lodges, or make

4 required religious pilgrimages. However, as long as *some* reasonable religious accommodations can be and are made for some groups—such as Catholics being offered fish on Fridays or Jewish and Muslim prisoners receiving kosher and halal

5 meals—then all religious groups must be similarly accommodated.

The more challenging question about the Church of the Flying Spaghetti Monster is whether it is a religion at all, whether it deserves equal treatment among more established religions. When Cavanaugh was first denied his request, the prison claimed that FSM was not a religion but a "parody" of religion. The Nebraska State Penitentiary suggested it could not grant privileges to anyone who presents his whimsical desires as part of a religious philosophy. In dealing with a humorous and politically motivated "religion" without a strong tradition and whose founder may write a new gospel at any time, should the prison have to keep up with the possibility of constantly changing prisoner demands? Can anyone just make up a

6 religion and then expect to be accommodated?

For better or worse, the answer is yes—as long as the accommodations represent valid forms of observance, are reasonable, and do not pose a substantial burden to the institution. Many religions have councils that at times alter the tenets of their faith. The state does not have the authority to determine what is or is not a "real" religion or religious practice. It does have an obligation under the RLUIPA to accommodate not just some but all forms of faith for incarcerated persons. As long as individuals sincerely hold certain beliefs, and as long as the accommodations requested meet the standards of reasonability and equity, state prisons, like all other government agencies

7 and institutions, cannot discriminate. Some might argue that Cavanaugh's

---

4 *Paragraph 2:* Two counterarguments and two rebuttals.

5 Last sentence sustains the thesis and anticipates that readers may agree on this point but still not consider the FSM a religion

6 *Paragraph 3:* Raises a possible counterposition and gives it due respect.

7 *Paragraph 4:* Responds to opposing position; writer is still discussing reasonable and fair treatment of inmates, not "anything goes."

faith is not sincere—that he does not *really* believe that the Earth was literally created by a ball of pasta with meatball-shaped eyes. But this is not the point. The government cannot apply a religious test to measure the degree of one's sincerity or faith. Like others in the Flying Spaghetti Monster movement—secularists, atheists, and professed believers—Cavanaugh should not be treated as an exploiter of religious freedom. In fact, in a pluralistic society with laws to ensure religious freedom and equality, his challenge helps protect all faiths.

8 Rebuts the counterargument.

9 Writer makes a shrewd rhetorical move, appealing to the democratic value of fairness.

Topics for Critical Thinking and Writing

1. A paper begins with its title, not with its first paragraph. A good title makes readers curious and may let them know where the essay will take them. Does this title have that effect on you? Why or why not? What other title would you suggest?

2. Are you convinced from this essay that it would be unfair to deny Cavanaugh and other Pastafarian inmates their demands? Why or why not?

3. How would you define a "real" religion? Can it be any belief deeply and sincerely felt, or does it require something more? Explain your answer.

Generating Ideas: Writing as a Way of Thinking

"To learn to write," Robert Frost said, "is to learn to have ideas." But how does one "learn to have ideas"?

Sometimes, we discover ideas while talking with others. A friend shares an opinion about some issue, and we — who have never really thought much about it — find ourselves saying that we see their point but have a different opinion. We are, in a sense, offering a counterpoint. This hypothetical conversation might look something like this:

Friend 1: Here's what I think about *the issue* . . .
Us: Well, yes, I see your point, but I'm not of that opinion. I see it differently — not as *X*, but as *Y*.
Friend 2: *Yes*, I see *your* point about *X*, *but* you haven't considered Z.
Friend 3: *Yes*, *and* furthermore . . .

Often we get ideas when we respond and add to others' observations. Haven't we all found ourselves agreeing with someone and extending their observations to include another position, a further example? Lurking in the mind are bits of information, opinions that may arise in an unexpected circumstance — when talking, when listening to a lecture or a classroom discussion, or especially when reading. Chance encounters can produce some of the best original ideas.

Consider Archimedes, the ancient Greek mathematician who discovered a method to determine the volume of an irregularly shaped object. Here's how the story goes: A king gave a goldsmith a specific weight of gold and asked him to make a crown in the shape of laurel leaves. When the job was finished, the king weighed the crown and found that it matched the weight of the gold he had provided. Nevertheless, he suspected that the goldsmith might have substituted some silver for some of the gold. How could the king find out (without melting or otherwise damaging the crown) if the crown was pure gold?

For Archimedes, meditating on this problem produced no ideas at first, but when he entered a bathtub he noticed that the water level rose as he immersed his body. He suddenly realized that he could determine the purity of the crown by measuring the amount of water it displaced. Since silver is less dense than gold, it takes a greater volume of silver to equal a given weight of gold. In his excitement at his idea to measure equal weights and relative volumes by immersing the crown in water, Archimedes is said to have leaped out of the tub and run naked through the street, shouting "*Eureka*!" (Greek for "I have found [it]!").

Why do we tell this story? Partly because we like it, but chiefly because the word "*eureka*" captures that moment of fortuitous chance. Finding an idea can sometimes feel like reaching under the couch to retrieve a dog toy and finding a ten-dollar bill instead: "Hey, look what I found! *Eureka*!"

But we rarely luck into ideas in this way. In fact, learning to have ideas is not usually a matter of chance. Or if chance *is* involved, well, as Louis Pasteur put it, "Chance favors the prepared mind." Ironically, the word "*eureka*" comes from the same Greek word that has given us the word **heuristic**, which refers not to dumb luck but to a *method* or *process* of discovering ideas.

Sculpture in Manchester, England, depicting Archimedes's bathtub "Eureka" moment.

When you're asked to think about something you've read, if your first response is that you have no ideas, we do not recommend simply taking a bath like Archimedes did. Immerse yourself instead with the issues and perspectives at hand. Listen to what's being said in the world around you — both in and out of the classroom. An even stronger method is to *seek out information for yourself*. Be deliberate; search for and target relevant magazines, newspapers, books, and other media — and formulate responses to the ideas you find using the strategies outlined in this chapter.

CONFRONTING UNFAMILIAR ISSUES

Generating ideas can be a challenge when you, as a student, are asked to read about and respond to new or unfamiliar issues. Sometimes, students wonder why they have to engage in particular topics and generate ideas about them. "I want to be a speech pathologist," one might say, "so why do I need to read essays and formulate ideas about capital punishment?"

One answer is that a college curriculum should spur students to think about pressing issues facing our society, so learning about capital punishment is important to all students. But this isn't the only answer. One could never study "all" the important social problems we face (and many of them change very rapidly). Instead, colleges seek to equip students with tools, methods, and habits of mind that enable them to confront arguments about *any* potential issue or problem. The primary goal of a college education (and of this book) is to help students develop an *intellectual apparatus* — a tool kit that can be applied to any subject matter, any issue.

The techniques presented in this book offer a practical framework for approaching issues, thinking about them carefully, asking good questions, identifying problems, and offering reasonable solutions — not necessarily because we want you to form opinions about the specific issues we have selected (although we hope you do), but because we want you to practice critical thinking, reading, and writing in ways that transfer to other aspects of your education as well as to your personal, professional, and civic life.

The Nigerian novelist Chinua Achebe said, "The writer must march up front." Rather than thinking that you must "agree or disagree" with the authors whose positions you'll read about in this book, imagine that you'll be practicing how to discover your own unique point of view by finding pathways into debates, negotiating different positions, and generating new ideas. So when you confront a new or unfamiliar issue in this book (or elsewhere), consider the strategies discussed in this chapter as practical methods — *heuristics* — for generating new ideas, and maybe even new beliefs, from the information at hand. That is what critical thinking (and writing) is all about.

USING CLUSTERING TO DISCOVER IDEAS

As you can see from the student cluster on the Pastafarian issue, we're big fans of clustering as a practical method for generating ideas and thinking through your argument. If you think with pencil and paper in hand and let your mind make associations by clustering, you'll find (perhaps to your surprise) that you have plenty of interesting ideas and that some can lead to satisfying conclusions. Doubtless you'll also have some ideas that represent gut reactions or poorly thought-out conclusions, but that's okay. When clustering, allow your thoughts to take shape without restriction; you can look over your ideas again and organize them later.

> **WRITING TIP**
> If you decide to generate ideas for your essay by clustering, don't worry that some ideas may be off the cuff or even nonsense. Just get ideas down on paper. You can evaluate them later.

To start clustering, take a sheet of paper and jot down what you think is the most basic issue or the fundamental conflict. This will help shape the questions you ask and frame your initial idea. Write down your initial idea — your opinion on the issue or debate at hand — and then develop supporting ideas, explore counterpositions (and rebuttals), and jot down where you need to do some research, eventually leading you to a tighter argument. Review the cluster in this chapter on page 16 to help you work through an issue.

APPROACHING AN ISSUE (OR AN ASSIGNMENT)

Anyone who has played baseball can tell you that one of the most challenging things to do is hit the ball. So, coaches often instruct their players to develop an *approach* to hitting. The hitter's approach begins in the dugout. First, you watch the pitcher. You make observations. What kind of pitches are being thrown? Are they largely inside pitches or outside pitches, high or low, fast or slow? Answering these questions can help determine what you do as you get ready to bat. You must also ask: What is the game situation? Are you attempting to hit long into the outfield or just get the ball in play, perhaps to advance your runners already on the bases? Once you step into the batter's box, where should you set your feet — farther away from the plate or close to it? In short, you are asking questions: *What am I facing? What is my goal?* and, quite literally, *Where do I stand?*

Not everyone plays baseball, but this metaphor is intended to get you thinking about how to prepare for an argument by asking some key questions:

- What should you look for in an issue or problem?
- What kinds of challenges will opponents likely throw at you?
- How will you position yourself?
- What do you want to achieve?

A critical thinker's approach, like a baseball batter's, is the preparation for the argument. It involves assessing issues, identifying key problems, and discovering your ideas.

In real life, and in this book, you will find activities prompting you to think critically or make an argument. A professor (or a textbook author) assigning a prompt is much like a coach instructing you on your approach, and examining the assignment prompt carefully is like reading the pitcher. Ask: What is being thrown at you? How should you strategize to meet the challenges?

Perhaps the assignment prompts you to consider a certain aspect of an issue, compare two arguments, or take a side in a debate. Prompts do not typically tell you *what* to think, but instead *what to ask*. They usually tell you to *survey, analyze,* and *evaluate.* How you do so — what you choose as a topic, what sources you use, how you interpret them — helps you begin developing arguments of your own.

However, you often must think without prompts. When facing issues in your life, work, or society, you will sometimes have to prompt *yourself* to figure out what to think (and what to argue).

PROMPTING YOURSELF: CLASSICAL TOPICS AND INVENTION

If you're at a loss for ideas when confronted with an issue — or an assignment to write about it — one way of generating new ideas is by prompting yourself. Ancient philosophers of rhetoric such as Aristotle in Greece and Cicero in Rome suggested four categories of thinking that constituted the basic elements of arguments: *definition*, *comparison*, *relationship*, and *testimony*. When formulated as questions you can ask yourself about any topic at hand, these elements may prompt you to discover your ideas. We'll use a proposal for a new campus bike lane as an example issue.

Definitions: What are the elements in the debate?

How might definitions of key terms help you think through the issues? What is a road? What is a bike lane? What is a college campus? If you define a "road" as something people need to travel, a "bike lane" as a pathway for a certain means of safe travel, and a "campus" as a place where everyone must be able to live, learn, and work safely, then you may be able to discover the basic elements of the debate: *Because bikes are a common means of safe and efficient transportation on campus, building bike lanes on campus sounds like a reasonable request.*

Comparisons: What are the elements like or unlike?

Comparing students to nonstudents, cars to bikes, or campuses to other public spaces may help you discover your position. You may find that students have a special need for bikes that professors, staff members, and visitors do not have. You might compare the costs of a bike lane to the costs resulting from potential accidents. You might compare one kind of bike lane with another kind (How wide? One way? Two way?). You might compare your campus to another, similar campus that has or has not constructed bike lanes. Making comparisons like these can help you evaluate the various reasons bicycle lanes may be called for (or not) on campus.

Relationships: What are the causes and effects in play?

Think of relationships as "*if . . . then*" propositions that can lead you to further questions. What are the implications and consequences of any decision — or nondecision? Think of all the ways you could fill in the following sentence: "If bike lanes were built on campus, then _____."

- Would students be safer or even more at risk? How do you know?
- Would it break the college's budget or is it affordable? How could you find out?
- Would it be beneficial or detrimental to the campus environment?

You might also explore the consequences of nonactions: If we did *not* build bike lanes, then we would not be keeping up with institutions that are building them, making our school less attractive to new students. The point: Teasing out the relationships of actions to their consequences can help produce ideas.

Testimonies: What are the major opinions and forms of evidence?

All ideas need to be justified in consideration of opinions and evidence. What do drivers think? What do students think? What do experts and respected leaders say? What laws or rules are applicable? What evidence has been (or can be) gathered to testify to the need for bike lanes (or the lack of such a need)? Have there been accidents? Are students or drivers complaining about the risks? Gathering testimony—assessing data, trends, currents, opinions, and attitudes—can help inspire ideas.

These categories are not solutions to any problems at hand, but a means of discovering solutions (a *heuristic*, to use the term we introduced earlier). In other words, they offer a way to organize the *process* of invention, helping you think through an issue to determine what you think and what position you want to take.

An Essay for Generating Ideas

Read the following brief essay by Asao B. Inoue about the usefulness of student grades and whether they accurately or helpfully measure critical thinking and writing skills, or whether they can actually work to inhibit the development of critical thinking and writing skills for some students. Afterward, refer to Thinking Critically: Generating Ideas (p. 28), which asks you to begin jotting down ideas on a sheet of paper along the lines of the classical categories of definitions, comparisons, relationships, and testimonies.

ASAO B. INOUE

Asao B. Inoue is a professor of rhetoric and composition at Arizona State University, specializing in composition theory, learning and assessment, and social justice. He is the author of numerous articles and books, and his book *Antiracist Writing Assessment Ecologies* won the 2017 award for best single-authored book from the National Council of Teachers of English (NCTE)/Conference on College Composition and Communication (CCCC). Inoue's most recent book, *Above the Well: An Antiracist Literacy Argument from a Boy of Color*, was published in 2021.

Do Grades Help Students Learn in Classrooms?

Over many years, lots of studies of grades' effects on students and their learning show clear patterns. Not only are grades bad for students when it comes to helping you learn, they also encourage a lot of counterproductive behaviors that harm your learning.

What do the studies tell us? Grades discourage learning, not encourage it. They often create what researchers call "risk aversion," which is bad for learning. When you avoid taking risks, you tend to rely only on what you know already and what you are sure you can do. You avoid trying to do things that have the potential of failure. In short, grades encourage you to play it safe with your learning and avoid important behaviors that help you learn, or write better.

Think about your own experiences in past courses, whether they were English, writing, math, history, or whatever. When your grade was on the line, did you feel good about taking a risk in your learning? When you knew you were being graded in an activity or assignment, did you feel like you could take a big risk, try something new, or explore things you didn't know? If you were smart, and cared a lot about your grade, you didn't.

While not a bad strategy, risk aversion is like walking a tightrope all the time in a course. One wrong step and you lose part of your grade. With each slip in the term, you erode your chances at the higher grades. But what if you need to get things wrong in order to learn a new practice or discover new information? In writing classrooms, avoiding risks keeps you from doing the kinds of learning, exploring, and discovery that the course is designed for. I mean, two central activities in writing classrooms are to read things that are hard to read, and write things that you haven't written before. Both require risk taking in order to do them well and succeed.

More generally, if you are going to get better at any activity or practice, be it basketball, knitting, or writing, you have to be willing and able to take risks when you practice those activities. You have to stumble around and even fail, as well as learn your initial limits and try to go past them.

Through a careful and extensive look at lots of studies of grading in schools, Alfie Kohn reveals in his books and articles consistent findings about grades in classrooms, all of which are bad for your learning as a student. I'll summarize three important findings that he highlights.

First, "[g]rades tend to diminish students' interest in whatever they're learning." Likely, your grade on an assignment or essay tends to attract most of your attention. Why? Because it is the summative mark that is supposed to say how well you did, or how good you are. That's why you submitted the assignment, right, to get a grade? So you are looking for a grade mostly when you get your assignment back.

The grade easily draws your attention away from the learning parts of the teacher's feedback, or the comments and discussion around that paper. That's where your focus should be if your goal is to learn, develop, and improve as a writer. In fact, you'd want the teacher to find weaknesses and things to improve on, but grades keep you from wanting that because weaknesses in a paper means a lower grade.

Imagine writing a paper for a class, spending a lot of time on it and feeling pretty good about it when you turn it in. Then you get it back with a grade of "D" on it, some comments in the margins, and a note that says:

> Good effort here. The ideas are interesting and worth exploring more. But you don't support your ideas with any of the texts in your reference list, or other information. Next time, try to provide more evidence for your claims after you offer them. These are good places to quote from the interesting books in your reference list.

Getting the D and these comments do not feel like a learning moment. And the comments themselves could be read as a snarky or insensitive response by the teacher. I mean, the grade suggests you've done a bad job, and yet the comments say something else at times. So the stuff that the teacher offers that you could use to learn and grow as a writer is at odds with what you know that grade means and does for your progress in the course. The bottom line here: Grades diminish your interest in learning because they offer you a powerful substitute, a simple, easily understood, one dimensional grade or ranking. That grade keeps you from feeling good about learning and developing from your places of failure and weakness. It keeps you from hearing and exploring the meaningful feedback you got.

Second, "[g]rades create a preference for the easiest possible task." If you have several ways to accomplish a task like writing a research paper, and only the final product of your labors, the paper itself, will be graded, and the labor, process and efforts you put into that paper will not be graded, then it is only logical and smart of you to take the shortest and easiest road to that final product. Why waste your time when time is not calculated in your grade? In fact, the typical grading system encourages you to take the shortest and easiest road possible for all tasks.

The problem with this situation is that it's contrary to the way learning actually works. Learning is about how you do things, how long and in what ways you labor at activities. Learning is not simply about what your labor ends up producing. Your paper, say that paper that got a "D," might represent some of the learning you've accomplished through your research, reading, thinking, and writing, but it is not the learning itself. The paper itself is a shadow of your learning. Your learning is the work you actually did, the researching, reading, writing, etc. That's why you felt good about the paper when you turned it in. You felt good about your experience of working, of laboring. This is also why it feels so awful when you get a low grade on the paper, on the learning shadow.

The learning is in the entire process that produced the paper. Despite your own good intentions to learn, when you are encouraged to prefer the easiest possible task to get to a final product, you end up preferring not to learn. You end up mostly trying to get stuff done for the highest grade possible. Good learning is about taking the longest and hardest way possible, not the shortest and easiest. Grades do not encourage anyone to take the long and hard way.

Third, "[g]rades tend to reduce the quality of students' thinking." This one we might think of as a product or function of the first two findings. This problem comes from an orientation or a stance that grades encourage you to take on. It's the orientation that leads you to rightly ask your teacher grade-based questions, such as, "Is this what you want?" or "how many quotes do I need in my paper?" These questions are ones about what the teacher is looking for in order for you to get a high grade. More critical and learning-based questions are ones about the process of learning, such as "how do I investigate the kinds of information that will help me explore this subject?" or "what diverse voices are important to engage with concerning this topic?" Grades encourage only questions that help a student get a better grade, not think critically on their own, and not learn.

Why do these things happen? Kohn [15] shows through research in psychology that it has to do with the psychological and learning problems that grades carry with them in classrooms. For example, many believe that grades motivate students to excel or at least do work. And this may be true in one sense, but grades tend to be the wrong kind of motivation. They are extrinsic motivation. They are external to the thing we really want, such as learning to write. When you do an assignment to get a good grade, you are doing the assignment for external motivation that is designed into the course itself, since you usually do not have any control over these aspects of the class.

The kind of motivation that really matters for long-term learning, learning that will be meaningful and useful to a person after a course, is a different kind of motivation. It is intrinsic motivation. That is, motivation that comes from a wanting to do the activity itself, or from wanting the learning itself.

Grades create conditions that mostly encourage extrinsic motivation, motivation outside of the subject or activity at hand and is placed on top of that activity. Using extrinsic motivation tends to work from the idea that you, the student, couldn't possibly be motivated or find enough interest in the learning activities asked of you, so an additional reward, a grade, is offered so that you'll do the work. If you are extrinsically motivated in your writing course, it means your interest is focused primarily on the immediate reward or the avoidance of punishment. You will do work and learn only insofar as it helps you get the reward you want, or avoid punishment.

This is a condition that the mere presence of grades creates. Take them away from the course, and you will find other reasons to do the work and learn.

The bottom line: Being extrinsically motivated in a writing class usually means you are more interested in getting a good grade on your paper, than writing a good paper, or even learning how to write one. Now, when grades are absent from a course — when we take grades away — research shows very clearly that the classroom more easily encourages intrinsic motivation in students. This means, you do something because you find ways to be interested and engaged with it. This kind of motivation leads to better, longer-lasting, more meaningful learning. And happier students and teachers.

So do grades help students learn in class-[20] rooms? Absolutely not. Grades harm learning in a number of important ways that writing classrooms are centered on. So every writing teacher should consider carefully with their students why and how grades are used, if at all, and what evidence they have that the grading process the course uses actually helps students learn.

Topics for Critical Thinking and Writing

1. Describe an occasion when you felt that you had learned something significant but the grade you earned did not reflect your sense of achievement. How did you feel? (And how did you respond?)

2. One assumption about grades is that they motivate students to achieve. What is Asao B. Inoue's position on this assumption? Do you think he challenges the assumption effectively?

3. Do you think that students (including you) would learn more if they earned not grades for their work but instead money? Explain your answer, as well as whether you think Inoue would agree or disagree, and why.

THINKING CRITICALLY *Generating Ideas*

Use the four categories introduced in "Prompting Yourself: Classical Topics and Invention" (pp. 23–24) to think through the issues raised by Asao B. Inoue. Provide the relevant information for each category.

TOPICS	QUESTIONS	YOUR ANSWERS
Definitions	What are grades? What is the purpose of grades? What is learning? What other key terms or elements are important?	
Comparisons	How can you compare types or ways of learning? How can you compare types of learners? Do some people learn differently than others? Can you compare types of education, professors, schools, courses in different subject matter, and so on, when considering the issue of grades?	
Relationships	If grades were/were not eliminated, what might happen? Would the consequences be good or bad? How so? For whom?	
Testimonies	How might students and teachers see the issue differently? What do educational experts say? What do college administrators say? Parents? Employers?	

GENERATING IDEAS FROM MULTIPLE PERSPECTIVES

What follows is an inner dialogue that you might engage in as you think critically about the question of the usefulness of grades in student learning.

The purpose of grades is to incentivize students to complete their work in a careful and conscientious way—that seems to be a good thing.

Another purpose is to rank students in such a way that universities and employers can judge the quality of candidates for, say, graduate school, or a job.

Students may be overconcerned with "performance" and "rankings." How do grades fail to rank students reliably?

Furthermore, there really is no single standard for awarding letter grades. If an A from one teacher is a C from another, how can students trust their evaluations?

Grades disincentivize students because they encourage working for an external reward, which is ideally not the purpose of learning.

The author focuses on grades specifically for writing assignments. Is there a difference in the usefulness of grades for, say, students of engineering, medicine, or accounting? What about standards?

Notice, part of the job is **analytic**, recognizing the reasons why grades exist, and part is **evaluative**, asking questions and testing the adequacy of ideas, one by one. Both tasks require critical thinking in the form of analyzing and evaluating, and those processes themselves are a self-conscious and disciplined *approach*.

So far, we jotted down some first thoughts and let second thoughts develop, some contrary to the first. Be aware that counterpositions might not come to mind right away. One way to think of them is to try to think from the perspectives of others: What questions might professors ask of the idea of not giving grades, something they are very accustomed to? What would administrators say? How might different *kinds* of students respond if they found out the class in which they enrolled had no grades? We can't imagine that all students are the same, so what issues might we imagine from different student viewpoints (e.g., students of color, students with disabilities, working students): Would eliminating grades lead to more or less biased grading? How would more grade-anxious students learn? We can also imagine issues for students who may need to know their grades for quite practical reasons (say, in order to qualify for a scholarship or an employee incentive program): Without grades, what would appear on records like college transcripts?

Further questions might not occur until you reread your notes or try to explain the issue to a friend, until you do some preliminary searching and reading on the subject, or even until you begin drafting an essay aimed at supporting or undermining the idea of abandoning letter grades for written work. If you are like most writers, some good ideas won't occur until a third or fourth draft — or even until after you have turned in or published your work.

Here are some examples to show how considering different perspectives can lead to different questions and alternative approaches.

Possible perspectives: Student

- *Questions:* How can we learn effectively if we do not know how we are measured — or if we're measured against a reliable standard?
- *Approach:* Might I argue that standards and competition are great motivators, and that eliminating grades will cause as many problems as it will solve?

Possible perspectives: Professor

- *Questions:* Is it really justifiable to grade student thinking and writing skills with "points" or letter grades? Do numbers really adequately assess the quality of things that aren't obviously quantifiable?
- *Approach:* Might I argue for alternative ways of grading student work, such as allowing students to self-grade, or to grade by amount of effort and labor

expended, or level of growth from one level of skill to another? What might some alternatives be?

Possible perspectives: **School Counselor**

- *Questions*: What kinds of stressors are grades? How can grades be bad for student mental health?

- *Approach*: Might I argue that professors will get more enthusiastic and positive learners if they experiment with alternative grading methods?

Possible perspectives: **University Administrator**

- *Questions*: Are grades absolutely needed to assess teaching and learning? When students enroll in a course, do they expect a tangible outcome? How is the system designed to encourage traditional grading systems? How do employers use GPA systems to evaluate candidates? How would changing the grading system affect my university's reputation or ranking?

- *Approach*: Might I argue that a turn away from grading would create a logistical nightmare in long-entrenched systems (e.g., the GPA and transcript system) and that doing away with grades, while somewhat beneficial in some ways for learning, would actually hurt some students and graduates in the end?

Doubtless there is much that we haven't asked or thought about, but you see that the issue deserves careful thought from multiple perspectives. Some of these questions may require you to do **research** on the topic — for example, to find out what grading alternatives have been developed (and likely tested) by education researchers. Some questions raise issues of fact — how many students report grade anxiety, and what are the effects of grade anxiety? — and relevant evidence probably is available. To reach a conclusion in which you have confidence, you'll likely need find out what the facts — the objective data — are. Explaining your position without giving the evidence will not be convincing.

A CHECKLIST FOR CRITICAL THINKING

- ☐ Does my thinking show open-mindedness and intellectual curiosity?
- ☐ Am I approaching my subject from a particular perspective?
- ☐ Can I examine the assumptions that come with my approach?
- ☐ Am I willing to entertain different ideas, both those that I encounter while reading and those that come to mind while writing?
- ☐ Am I willing to exert myself — for instance, to do research — to acquire information, identify different viewpoints, and evaluate evidence?

A Short Essay Calling for Critical Thinking

When reading an essay, we expect the writer to have thought carefully about the topic. We don't want to read every false start, every fuzzy thought, and every ill-organized paragraph that the writer knocked off. Yes, writers make false starts, put down fuzzy thoughts, and write ill-organized paragraphs, but then they revise and revise yet again, ultimately producing a readable essay that seems effortlessly written. Still — and this is our main point — writers of argumentative essays need to show readers that they have made some effort; they need to show *how* they got to their views. It isn't enough for the writer to say, "I believe *X*"; rather, he or she must in effect say, "I believe *X* because I see things from this perspective. Others believe *Y* or *Z*, and although from their perspective, their answers might sound reasonable, my inquiry shows another way to think or act about the issue. There may be value in *Y* or *Z* (or maybe not), and on the surface they may be plausible (or maybe they are not plausible), but their beliefs do not take into account what I am arguing, that *X* is a better alternative because. . . ." Obviously you don't need to follow that exact pattern (although you could); the point is that writers often need to make their critical thinking explicit to convince their readers of the argument they make.

Notice in selecting the following essay we introduce more on the subject of critical thinking, which resonates as the major theme of this chapter. As you read, think about how perspectives, beliefs, and assumptions are partly the subjects of the essay, and partly what we want you to identify and consider as you read. Remember, critical thinking means taking apart — taking apart a problem, an issue, an essay, or your own logic — in order to understand it better and to inform your own decisions, beliefs, and actions.

ANAND JAYPRAKASH VAIDYA

Anand Jayprakash Vaidya is a professor of philosophy at San Jose State University who specializes in Asian philosophy, particularly its role in Western logic and critical thinking education. This essay was published in 2016 on the blog of the American Philosophical Association.

The Inclusion Problem in Critical Thinking: The Case of Indian Philosophy

1. THE PROBLEM

For many, if not most, philosophy departments, the bread-and-butter courses they offer include the history of philosophy, ethics, and critical thinking. Most of us, at some time or another, have had to teach a course in one of those areas. Rather than design a whole new textbook or syllabus by ourselves, we often choose to adopt a common text that is suggested to us, or one we are familiar with from our own training. Focusing on critical thinking, it is not uncommon to adopt one of the standard texts, such as Patrick Hurley's[1] or Lewis Vaughn's[2]. Both of these texts are well reviewed and contain lots of good material for teaching the standard topics, such as argument identification, diagramming arguments, validity, soundness, truth tables, basic propositional logic, and informal fallacy identification.

However, neither of these texts, and most of the other texts in the category of critical thinking, succeed in mentioning or including any references to or sources for material from outside the western tradition. This could leave a student with the impression that while Socrates, Aristotle, John Venn, and George Boole all contributed to the development of logic and critical thinking, no non-western thinker had anything to say about these matters.

This would not be a problem if it were true that non-western philosophers had nothing to say about matters pertaining to logic and critical thinking. And it would not be such a problem even if they did have something to say, if it were also true that logic and critical thinking were not important parts of an education in philosophy and the humanities in general. *But it is a problem, because there are many contributions from non-western traditions, such as Arabic philosophy, Chinese philosophy, and Indian philosophy*, and *often we sell the importance of philosophy by pointing to critical thinking*. In this post, I will try to briefly characterize one location where one can find an important kind of contribution to critical thinking that is relevant to contemporary issues concerning critical-thinking education and its future direction.

2. THE SETUP

In his, "Not By Skill Alone: The Centrality of Character to Critical Thinking," Harvey Siegel (1993)[3] defends the *character view* against the *skill view*.

- The skill view holds that critical thinking is exhausted by the acquisition and proper deployment of critical thinking skills.

- The character view holds that critical thinking involves the acquisition and proper deployment of specific skills, as well as the acquisition of specific character traits, dispositions, attitudes, and habits of mind. These components are aspects of the "critical spirit."

With this contrast frame, we can ask the following question: Do non-western traditions of debate and discussion have anything to say about what skills are important for dialogical investigation, or what character traits are important? Since there is an abundance of literature on the issue of non-western logic, I will forgo discussion of that area (besides, most instructors don't even talk about non-classical logic in an intro critical thinking and logic course). Rather, I will focus on the character view and some historical sources relevant to it.

---

[1] *The Concise Introduction to Logic* (Cengage).
[2] *Philosophy Here and Now: Powerful Ideas in Everyday Life* (Oxford UP).
[3] Siegel, H. 1993. "Not by Skill Alone: The Centrality of Character to Critical Thinking." *Informal Logic* 25.3: 163–175.

3. CARAKASAṂHITĀ

At section 3.8[4] of the classical Indian handbook of Ayurveda, the author, Acharya Charaka, says the following:

One who has acquired the knowledge (given by the authoritative text) based on various reasons and refuting the opponent's view in debates, does not get fastened by the pressure of opponent's arguments nor does he get subdued by their arguments.

And pertaining to the method of discussion, he says the following:

Discussion with specialists: promotes pursuit and advancement of knowledge, provides dexterity, improves power of speaking, illumines fame, removes doubt in scriptures, if any, by repeating the topics, and creates confidence in case there is any doubt, and brings forth new ideas. The ideas memorized in study from the teacher, will become firm when applied in (competitive) discussion.

And then he offers an important distinction between two different kinds of discussion, and how they should be carried out.

Discussion with specialists is of 2 types — friendly discussion and hostile discussion. The friendly discussion is held with one who is endowed with learning, understanding and the power of expression and contradiction, devoid of irritability, having uncensored knowledge, without jealousy, able to be convinced and convince others, enduring and adept in the art of sweet conversation. While in discussion with such a person one should speak confidently, put questions unhesitatingly, reply to the sincere questioner with elaborateness, not be agitated with fear of defect, not be exhilarated on defeating the partner, nor boast before others, not hold fast to his solitary view due to attachment, not explain what is unknown to him, and convince the other party with politeness and be cautious in that. This is the method of friendly discussion.

Without a doubt, these passage are in the vicinity of our concern with the "critical spirit" and how it should be carried out.

4. MILINDA-PAÑHA

The Buddhist tradition also has a lot to offer in the area of critical thinking. The 10 classic dialogue of the Buddhist tradition, *Milinda-pañha* (*Questions for King Milinda*), is famous for its discussion of the no-self view central to Buddhism. However,

---

[4]G. Van Loon. 2002. *Charaka Saṃhitā: Handbook on Ayurveda*. Chaukhambha Orientalia Publishers.

in the following neglected passage, it also appears to capture some of the important ideas found in the *Carakasaṃhitā*[5]:

MILINDA: Reverend Sir, will you discuss with me again?

NĀGASENA: If your Majesty will discuss (vāda) as a scholar, well, but if you will discuss as a king, no.

MILINDA: How is it that scholars discuss?

NĀGASENA: When scholars talk a matter over one with another, then there is a winding up, an unraveling, one or other is convicted of error, and he then acknowledges his mistake; distinctions are drawn, and contra-distinctions; and yet thereby they are not angered. Thus do scholars, O King, discuss.

MILINDA: And how do kings discuss?

NĀGASENA: When a king, your Majesty, discusses a matter, and he advances a point, if any one differ from him on that point, he is apt to fine him, saying "Inflict such and such a punishment upon that fellow!" Thus, your Majesty, do kings discuss.

MILINDA: Very well. It is as a scholar, not as a king, that I will discuss. (MP 2.1.3)

From this passage, we get further elaboration on the kind of discussion known as *vāda*, which is the friendly discussion found in *Carakasaṃhitā*. More importantly, though, the passage above also introduces the reader to a very important idea about the nature of a good discussion in classical Indian philosophy. Nāgasena says:

> When scholars talk a matter over one with another, then there is a winding up, an unraveling, one or other is convicted of error, and he then **acknowledges his mistake**; distinctions are drawn, and contra-distinctions; and yet thereby **they are not angered**. (emphasis added)

One reading of this claim is that Nāgasena is pointing out that a good discussion requires not only that certain moves made be "a winding up" and "an unraveling," but that the persons involved in making those moves have a certain *epistemic temper*. Participants in a good debate, moreover, have the capacity, and exercise the capacity, to (i) acknowledge mistakes, and (ii) not become angered by the consequences of where the inquiry leads. Nāgasena's answer to King Milinda suggests that at least Buddhist discussions take the *character view* as opposed to the *skill view*. It is not enough to simply know how to "make moves," "destroy," or "demolish" an opponent by various techniques. What is central to an honest debate is that a participant must also have a certain attitude and character that exemplify a specific *epistemic temper*.

---

[5]This passage and work comes from Ganeri, J. 2004. "Indian Logic." In *Handbook of the History of Logic*. D. Gabbay and J. Woods (eds.). Vol. 1. Elsevier B. V. Publishing.

5. WHY IS THIS IMPORTANT?

I won't try to answer this question exhaustively. Rather, I will point to an interesting way to see why it is important now by looking at recent work by Jason Baehr (2013)[6] on educating for intellectual virtues.

In his "Educating for Intellectual Virtues," Baehr goes into an extended examination of what intellectual character virtues are and offers three arguments for the view that education ought to aim at fostering intellectual character virtues such as curiosity, open-mindedness, and intellectual courage. He offers a very important list of contemporary thinkers who help to explain the theoretical nature of intellectual virtues. And he discusses his approach in relation to the approach discussed by Siegel. However, and not by any fault of his own, he does not include discussion of any ideas from outside the western canon. *Might it be useful to explore what non-western philosophers had to say about intellectual character?* Within the vast literature on classical Indian philosophy, one finds ample discussion of critical thinking both at the skill level and at the critical spirit level. One important place to learn about these contributions is in B. K. Matilal's (1998) *The Character of Logic in India*, edited by Jonardon Ganeri and Heeraman Tiwari.

For now, it should be clear that both of the passages above could be used to teach 15 critical thinking students what critical thinking is about, should one agree with the character view. What could be taught is that critical thinking is not only about making certain "critical moves" for the purposes of victory over one's opponent, but that it is also about adopting a certain state of mind about investigation and inquiry. And it is without a doubt that the passage can be adequately compared to a Socratic dialogue, such as *Meno*, where Socrates is exercising his critical thinking skills. There seems to be no harm in showing students that critical thinking has sources both in western traditions and non-western traditions.

Topics for Critical Thinking and Writing

1. Anand Jayprakash Vaidya focuses on the "character view" of critical thinking. What shows good character in thinking, debating, and arguing with others? How does this "critical spirit" contribute to problem-solving, drawing conclusions, and making decisions?

2. Describe in your own words the distinctions drawn in the *Milinda-pañha* (*Questions for King Milinda*) between the ways scholars and kings discuss matters. Why is one elevated over another in the Buddhist philosophical tradition?

3. Vaidya writes in paragraph 3 that "often we sell the importance of philosophy by pointing to critical thinking." What do you think he means by this? Who is selling to whom, and why? How else might philosophy be promoted beyond offering a set of practical tools and skills for problem-solving?

---

[6]Baehr, J. "Educating for Intellectual Virtues: From Theory to Practice." *Journal of Philosophy of Education.* Vol. 47.2.

4. Are there other obstacles to inclusion when it comes to critical thinking? What are they, and why do they exclude people or ways of thought? Explain your answer, referring to Vaidya's ideas in your answer.

Assignment for Critical Thinking

1. Choose one of the following topics that you're interested in thinking through in more detail. (If none of the suggested topics interests you, ask your instructor about the possibility of choosing a topic of your own.)

   a. Religious leaders should not endorse political candidates.
   b. Motorcyclists should be required by law to wear helmets.
   c. The Motion Picture Association of America (MPAA) is outdated and should be abolished as a standard for rating films (G, PG, PG-13, R, NC-17).
   d. High school teachers should have the right to carry concealed firearms in schools.
   e. Vaping (not smoking) should be permitted in college classrooms.
   f. College courses should not have attendance policies.
   g. Cities with large outdoor cat populations should get them off the streets and into shelters.

2. Next, try at least two of the strategies discussed in this chapter to generate ideas:

   - Write down your first thoughts, which may even be your initial "gut" reactions, then pause and rethink these first responses.
   - Use the Visual Guide and try the method for evaluating a proposal (p. 15) to ask pertinent questions.
   - Try clustering (p. 16; 21) to test your idea(s) by considering potential counterpoints.
   - Run through the process of considering the categories of definitions, comparisons, relationships, and testimonies (p. 23).
   - Imagine at least two people coming from different perspectives (p. 28) and write a balanced dialogue between them. Start with one view and consider how that view might be challenged by the other speaker. Present *all* sides as strongly as possible. (You may want to give the speakers distinct characters, or personas.)

Be metacognitive: Write down your reflections on how your thinking changed by engaging with these processes — or, if your thinking did not change, write about how it was challenged or strengthened by the exercise.

After you have generated your ideas, write an exploratory essay in which you identify the issue; work through two different perspectives, positions, and solutions; and finally draw your conclusion (or make your decision about which side presents the most reasonable case).

2

Critical Reading: Getting Started

Read parts of a newspaper quickly or an encyclopedia entry, or a fast-food thriller, but do not insult yourself or a book which has been created with its author's painstakingly acquired skill and effort, by seeing how fast you can dispose of it. — SUSAN HILL

CONSIDER THIS

You are given three choices for a free trip:

    A. a free trip to Paris, with complimentary breakfast each day

    B. a free trip to Rome, with complimentary breakfast each day

    C. a free trip to Rome, *without* complimentary breakfast each day

Which would you choose? Why?

Shaun Egan/Getty Images

Breakfast in Paris

Framing Arguments

The mental puzzle in this chapter's "Consider This" activity is from behavioral psychologist Dan Ariely. If you are like most people, you answered with option B: a free trip to Rome with free breakfast. Why might this be? If you chose A instead, can you tell why?

We doubt you chose C. You might even wonder why option C exists at all. Why would anyone choose C when it is clearly the worst option? But that is precisely the point. Option C is a *decoy* option, there only to distract you — and to demonstrate something quite interesting about how we often make decisions based on the ways our options are *framed*. When option C is missing, around 50 percent of people choose Paris, and around 50 percent choose Rome. However, with option C available, more than 80 percent choose Rome with free breakfast.

Why? One answer is that our minds often take the path of least resistance. Deciding between two cities is mental work: You might say it takes critical thinking — taking apart the problem, comparing the features, cultures, climates, foods, and so on, of each place. It's difficult to say whether Paris or Rome is better. Meanwhile, comparing Rome *with* free breakfast and Rome *without* free breakfast is easy. Option C simplifies the decision-making process, allowing you to compare two things on equal terms. The framing of the question gives us a basis for making a clear decision about which we can be confident.

Framing has to do with the means and manner of communicating a message at least as much as the basic information being reported. Like with a building or a painting, it represents the structure in which something appears or occurs. Think of how a picture frame can enhance certain colors or subjects in a painting. Or think of how photographers carefully using framing as a technique, choosing angles and distances to communicate different meanings in their pictures.

Framing works in all forms of expression. It works in visual media, such as when infomercials on television present themselves as news programs, skillfully conducting "interviews" and "reporting" that suggest that the information is fair and neutral. In film, the conventions of the documentary style or **genre** can suggest veracity, or truth-value, making us more open to believing the messages conveyed by a particular film. And even while we say we should not judge a book by its cover, the truth is we all do so unconsciously, judging the images, size, and quality of the package to set our expectations about the quality of the content. Framing can even be typographic (think of using the comic sans font for messages intended to be funny, or the courier font to suggest seriousness, or the script font to enhance the elegance of your phrasing).

Framing is one of the first concepts you should consider when thinking or reading critically about a topic. **Framing biases** — in which people create beliefs and make choices based on how an issue is presented to them, not on the issue itself — can occur in many ways, and good readers are alert to them. For instance, when someone "loads" a question ("Like all patriotic Americans, do you support policy *X*?"), that's framing. So is the presentation of statistics in such a way that predisposes readers to come to a particular conclusion. Consider the framing of these two scenarios:

- Would you take a driver's education course from a school whose students fail their first driving test at rate of 13 percent? Or would you prefer a school whose students pass their first test at a rate of 87 percent?

- Would you be likely to recommend an oncologist whose patients' survival rate after five years is 92 percent? Or an oncologist who has had 416 of his last 5200 patients die within five years of treatment?

Different font styles can suggest different framing strategies

When you think about it, both scenarios present equivalent information. Yet without carefully examining the framing, one sounds better than the other. You might have detected a similar kind of "spin" in partisan newspaper headlines: "President Proposes Innovative Plan for *X*" sounds much different from "President Pushes Tradition-Breaking Plan for *X*," even when *X* is the same plan.

One of the most famous lessons in understanding framing occurs in Mark Twain's *The Adventures of Tom Sawyer*, when Tom pretends to his friends that his work painting a fence for his Aunt Polly is a privilege and a choice, instead of a time-consuming task presently ruining his Saturday. After his enthusiastic endorsement, Tom's friends soon beg him for a chance to paint, too, and even pay him for the chance to use the brush, which he hands to them "with reluctance on his face but alacrity in his heart." Sitting in the shade nearby, Tom counts his profits while others triple-coat the fence for him.

Active Reading

In the passage quoted at the beginning of the chapter, Susan Hill offers a good metaphor for how we read and what we read. Some types of reading can be consumed completely and quickly, gobbled like a fast-food meal. Other types of reading may not need to be fully ingested — just by a quick examination, we can tell whether or not it is going to be worth tasting in the first place. But some types of reading require our full attention and call for much more appreciation and discernment, not quick consumption. If you "taste" a reading and you begin to detect remarkable flavors — in the language, thoughts, ideas, and theories — then you might slow down and give it more conscious consideration. Like a foodie intent on noticing the balance of ingredients in a gourmet dish, you might begin noticing how an argument's words, meanings, evidence, data, interpretations, logic, purpose, and structure all work together to make an impressive or convincing whole.

So how do you know if you are picking up a book or an essay that should be read quickly (or not at all), or one that deserves to be read slowly? How can you judge the credibility and value of a piece of writing *before* deciding to read it carefully? And if you *do* decide a text is worth reading slowly and carefully, how do you prepare to think even more critically about it once you start to dig in further?

PREVIEWING

Skilled readers rarely read a text "raw"; instead, they prepare it for reading and prepare themselves for reading it. **Previewing** is a strategy for reading that allows you to use prior knowledge — such as your understanding of an author or a publication, or how a certain genre of text generally works — to help judge how deeply you should engage it.

By previewing, you can quickly ascertain quite a bit of information about an article or essay. If you decide to begin **skimming**, or looking at key locations within a text, you can detect such things as the tone and difficulty level, the main perspectives, the major claims and ideas, the methods, and the evidence (statistics, quotations, etc.).

Strategies that give you this kind of information quickly work well if you're researching a topic and need to review many essays — you can read efficiently to find out which voices are most relevant to you and those that offer different perspectives. When you are sampling many different works in different genres — essays, scholarly articles, tweets, websites, videos, and so on — you don't always have the time to read everything closely. If you find an essay to be appetizing during previewing and skimming, you can then start, as Francis Bacon once put it, "chewing and digesting" the text — that is, reading more consciously or else putting it aside for later when you have more time. (Thanks to Bacon for helping us extend Susan Hill's culinary metaphor.)

AUTHOR   One good place to start previewing a piece of writing is to identify the **author** — not just by name but also in terms of any other information you may know or can find out. You might already know, for example, that a work by Dr. Sanjay Gupta will likely address public health concerns in a serious and careful way supported by reliable medical evidence. Still, you know that Gupta is a public and popular figure and that his writing is not likely to be bogged down by too much scientific jargon. If you know that Dr. Angela Davis is an esteemed academic philosopher and a dedicated African American social activist, you know that her writing may be a combination of erudite ideas and passionate prescription. But even if you don't know the author, you can often discern something about them by looking at biographical information provided in the text or by doing a quick internet search. This is especially important for authors you do not know right off the bat. You can use information gathered to predict the subject of an essay and its style, as well as its author's possible assumptions and biases.

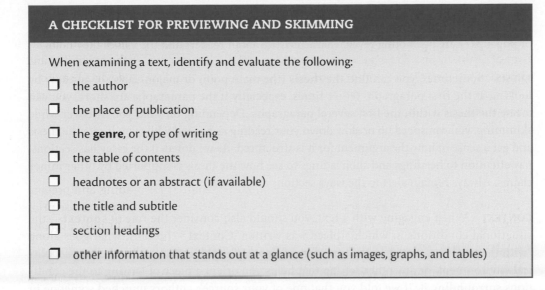

TITLE   The **title** of an essay, too, may give an idea of what to expect. Of course, a title may announce only the subject and not the author's thesis or point of view ("Do Grades Help Students Learn in the Classroom?"; "The Inclusion Problem in Critical Thinking"). Occasionally, however, certain language may reveal the author's likely position: A headline proclaiming "Mob Surrounds City Hall" sounds a bit harsher than one that says "Protestors Gather at City Hall." A title may also be opaque or mysterious and not give you much to go on ("The Chokehold"), but often a title can give you a hint about the author's views ("Saving the Planet Begins at Breakfast"), or even contain charged language that tips the likely viewpoint of the author ("The Yelling of the Lambs"). Sometimes, a title will indicate the thesis explicitly (see the essay in this chapter called "Porn Isn't Free Speech — on the Web or Anywhere"). If you can tell more or less what to expect from a title, you can probably take in some of the major points while previewing or skimming. Glancing at subtitles, section headings, and subheadings can help you map the progression of an argument without fully reading the entire text.

PLACE OF PUBLICATION   The **place of publication** may reveal something about the essay in terms of its subject, style, and approach. For instance, the *National Review* is a conservative journal. If you notice that an essay on affirmative action was published in the *National Review*, you can tentatively assume that the essay will not endorse affirmative action, and be on the lookout for signs indicating such. In contrast, knowing that *Ms.* magazine is a liberal publication, you can guess that an essay on affirmative action published there will probably be an endorsement. If you do not know what perspective a publication represents, you often can learn a good deal about any magazine or journal simply by flipping through it and noticing the kinds of articles in it, or by looking at the editorial board, the publisher, the description in the "about" section or web page (if available), or by searching on the internet for information about the publication's reputation. Advertisements can also tell you what kind of audience the magazine or journal likely has. The products that the ads—on a page, banners, or pop-ups—are promoting reveal characteristics about readers and the values they hold.

THESIS   Sometimes, you can find the **thesis** (the main point or major claim) of an essay by looking at the first paragraph. Other times, especially if the paragraphs are short, you can locate the thesis within the first several paragraphs. Depending on what you discover while skimming, you can speed up or slow down your reading as needed while you locate the thesis and get a sense of how the argument for it is structured. As we noted, if the essay has sections, pay attention to headings and subheadings to see how the thesis is supported by other minor claims. Always remain alert to the ways sections are *framed*.

CONTEXT   When engaging with a text, you should also consider the role of **context**—the situational conditions in which a piece was written. Context—literally, what goes along "with the text"—can refer to the time period, geographical location, cultural climate, political environment, or any other setting that helps you orient a piece of writing to the conditions surrounding it. If we told you that one of your source's authors punched someone in the face last week and broke their nose, you might wonder if they had anger management issues; however, if we told you the *context*—that it was because they were a boxer and had a match—then everything would make sense. Recognizing context can reveal a lot about how an author treats a subject. The context in which something is published, stated, or argued, in many ways determines the meanings you can extract from it. For example, an argument about gay marriage in the United States written before it became legal might sound much different today; similarly, an article about race and police brutality might convey different assumptions about policing depending on whether it was written before or after the murder of George Floyd in 2020. Social conditions, in short, affect how writers (and readers) think.

> **READING TIP**
> Instead of imagining pre-viewing and skimming as progressive stages, think of them as simultaneous activities that can shift back and forth at any time to help you decide whether or not you should begin engaging in more careful reading.

Anything you read exists in at least two broad contexts: the context of its *production* (where and when it was written or published) and the context of its *reception* (where and when it is encountered and read). One thing all good critical readers do when considering the validity of claims and arguments is to take *both* types of context into account. This means asking questions about the approaches, assumptions, and beliefs about certain subjects that were in place when an essay was written (*production*). It also means considering how current events and new trends in thinking that occurred after the original publication date may generate different issues and challenges related to the subject of the essay (*reception*). The state of affairs in the time and place in which that argument is made *and received* matters to the questions you might ask, the evidence you might consider, and the responses you might produce.

Consider these words, spoken by Abraham Lincoln in his famous debates with Stephen Douglas, when the two campaigned against each other for a US Senate seat in 1858. Douglas had accused Lincoln of holding the then-unpopular view that the Black and white races were equal. Lincoln defended himself against these charges, using terms that reflect racial inequalities at the time, and articulating ideas that today would be considered obviously racist:

> I will say then that I am not, nor ever have been, in favor of bringing about in any way the social and political equality of the white and Black races [Applause], that I am not nor ever have been in favor of making voters or jurors of negroes, nor of qualifying them to hold office, nor to intermarry with white people; and I will say in addition to this that there is a physical difference between the white and Black races which I believe will forever forbid the two races living together on terms of social and political equality. And inasmuch as they cannot so live, while they do remain together there must be the position of superior and inferior, and I as much as any other man am in favor of having the superior position assigned to the white race.

Now consider context. Lincoln's ideas about race — and his language choices — in this speech may surprise and even offend you. If you saw this quotation somewhere, it might make you think that Abraham Lincoln held racist views despite his reputation as "The Great Emancipator." And that may even be true. But it is crucial to put his words in context to develop a fuller, more mature understanding of them. Historians, for example, read these words in light of common and even "scientific" beliefs about race in the 1850s, informed by the situation at hand (a campaign speech, in which Lincoln might feel free to overstate or appeal to popular beliefs), and with knowledge of Lincoln's uncompromising efforts later to abolish slavery. How does consideration of these historical contexts help you understand Lincoln's words? How does consideration of the context in which you read them shape your understanding, given your expectations and your prior knowledge about Lincoln?

THE "FIRST AND LAST" RULE   You may apply the "first and last" rule when skimming essays. This rule assumes that somewhere early and late in the writing you can locate the author's key points. Opening paragraphs are good places to seek out the author's central thesis, and final paragraphs are good places to seek out conclusive statements such as "Finally, then, *it is time that we . . .*" or "Given this evidence, *it is clear that. . . .*" Final paragraphs are particularly important because they often summarize the argument and restate the thesis.

The first and last rule works because authors often place main points of emphasis at the beginnings and endings of essays, but they also do the same within individual paragraphs. Authors do not usually bury key ideas in the middle of long essays, and neither do they surround the key ideas of paragraphs with bulky text. Further, authors try not to hide their most important points in the middle of long sentences. Often the main point of a sentence can be found by looking at the elements stated first and last. (Of course, there are always exceptions to the rule.) Consider the following sentences, each of which contains the same basic information arranged in different ways.

Here the time period and the new smoking prohibitions get the most emphasis:

Over the past fifteen years, the rate of smoking among New York City residents declined by more than 35% because of new health trends and *new tobacco restrictions*.

Here the place and the percentage are most emphasized:

In New York City, new health trends and new tobacco restrictions caused the smoking rate to decline over fifteen years by *more than 35%*.

A SHORT ESSAY FOR PREVIEWING PRACTICE

Before reading the following essay, apply the previewing and skimming techniques discussed in the section "Previewing" (p. 40) and complete the Thinking Critically: Previewing activity that follows.

THINKING CRITICALLY *Previewing*

The following activity lists typical types of questions readers use while previewing. Provide the missing information for Charles R. Lawrence's essay "On Racist Speech" (p. 45) or another essay of your choosing.

PREVIEWING STRATEGIES	TYPES OF QUESTIONS	ANSWERS
Author	Who is the author or authors? What expertise and credibility do they have? How difficult is the writing likely to be?	
Title	What does the title reveal about the essay's content? Does it give any clues about how the argument will take shape? Do headings or subheadings reveal any further information?	
Place of Publication	How does the place of publication help you understand the argument? What type of audiences will it be likely to target?	
Context	By placing the article in the context of its time — given trends in the conversations about or popular understandings of the subject — what can you expect about the author's position?	
Skimming	As you skim over the first several paragraphs, where do you first realize what the argument of the essay is? What major forms of evidence support the argument?	

CHARLES R. LAWRENCE III

Charles R. Lawrence III, author of numerous articles in law journals and coauthor of *We Won't Go Back: Making the Case for Affirmative Action* (1997), teaches law at the William S. Richardson School of Law at the University of Hawai'i at Manoa. This essay originally appeared in the *Chronicle of Higher Education* (October 25, 1989), a publication read chiefly by faculty and administrators at colleges and universities. An amplified version of the essay appeared in the *Duke Law Journal* (February 1990).

On Racist Speech

I have spent the better part of my life as a dissenter. As a high school student, I was threatened with suspension for my refusal to participate in a civil defense drill, and I have been a conspicuous consumer of my First Amendment liberties ever since. There are very strong reasons for protecting even racist speech. Perhaps the most important of these is that such protection reinforces our society's commitment to tolerance as a value, and that by protecting bad speech from government regulation, we will be forced to combat it as a community.

But I also have a deeply felt apprehension about the resurgence of racial violence and the corresponding rise in the incidence of verbal and symbolic assault and harassment to which blacks and other traditionally subjugated and excluded groups are subjected. I am troubled by the way the debate has been framed in response to the recent surge of racist incidents on college and university campuses and in response to some universities' attempts to regulate harassing speech. The problem has been framed as one in which the liberty of free speech is in conflict with the elimination of racism. I believe this has placed the bigot on the moral high ground and fanned the rising flames of racism.

Above all, I am troubled that we have not listened to the real victims, that we have shown so little understanding of their injury, and that we have abandoned those whose race, gender, or sexual preference continues to make them second-class citizens. It seems to me a very sad irony that the first instinct of civil libertarians has been to challenge even the smallest, most narrowly framed efforts by universities to provide black and other minority students with the protection the Constitution guarantees them.

The landmark case of *Brown v. Board of Education* is not a case that we normally think of as a case about speech. But *Brown* can be broadly read as articulating the principle of equal citizenship. *Brown* held that segregated schools were inherently unequal because of the *message* that segregation conveyed — that black children were an untouchable caste, unfit to go to school with white children. If we understand the necessity of eliminating the system of signs and symbols that signal the inferiority of blacks, then we should hesitate before proclaiming that all racist speech that stops short of physical violence must be defended.

University officials who have formu- 5 lated policies to respond to incidents of racial harassment have been characterized in the press as "thought police," but such policies generally do nothing more than impose sanctions against intentional face-to-face insults. When racist speech takes the form of face-to-face insults, catcalls, or other assaultive speech aimed at an individual or small group of persons, it falls directly within the "fighting words" exception to First Amendment protection. The Supreme Court has held that words which "by their very utterance inflict injury or tend to incite an immediate breach of the peace" are not protected by the First Amendment.

If the purpose of the First Amendment is to foster the greatest amount of speech, racial insults disserve that purpose. Assaultive racist speech functions as a preemptive strike. The invective is experienced as a blow, not as a proffered idea, and once the blow is struck, it is unlikely that a dialogue will follow. Racial insults are particularly undeserving of First Amendment protection because the perpetrator's intention is not to discover truth or initiate dialogue but to injure the victim. In most situations, members of minority groups realize that they are likely to lose if they respond to epithets by fighting and are forced to remain silent and submissive.

Courts have held that offensive speech may not be regulated in public forums such as streets where the listener may avoid the speech by moving on, but the regulation of otherwise protected speech has been permitted when the speech invades the privacy of the unwilling listener's home or when the unwilling listener cannot avoid the speech. Racist posters, fliers, and graffiti in dormitories, bathrooms, and other common living spaces would seem to clearly fall within the reasoning of these cases. Minority students should not be required to remain in their rooms in order to avoid racial assault. Minimally, they should find a safe haven in their dorms and in all other common rooms that are a part of their daily routine.

I would also argue that the university's responsibility for ensuring that these students receive an equal educational opportunity provides a compelling justification for regulations

that ensure them safe passage in all common areas. A minority student should not have to risk becoming the target of racially assaulting speech every time he or she chooses to walk across campus. Regulating vilifying speech that cannot be anticipated or avoided would not preclude announced speeches and rallies — situations that would give minority-group members and their allies the chance to organize counterdemonstrations or avoid the speech altogether.

The most commonly advanced argument against the regulation of racist speech proceeds something like this: We recognize that minority groups suffer pain and injury as the result of racist speech, but we must allow this hate mongering for the benefit of society as a whole. Freedom of speech is the lifeblood of our democratic system. It is especially important for minorities because often it is their only vehicle for rallying support for the redress of their grievances. It will be impossible to formulate a prohibition so precise that it will prevent the racist speech you want to suppress without catching in the same net all kinds of speech that it would be unconscionable for a democratic society to suppress.

Whenever we make such arguments, [10] we are striking a balance on the one hand between our concern for the continued free flow of ideas and the democratic process dependent on that flow, and, on the other, our desire to further the cause of equality. There can be no meaningful discussion of how we should reconcile our commitment to equality and our commitment to free speech until it is acknowledged that there is real harm inflicted by racist speech and that this harm is far from trivial.

To engage in a debate about the First Amendment and racist speech without a full understanding of the nature and extent of that harm is to risk making the First Amendment an instrument of domination rather than a vehicle of liberation. We have not all known the experience of victimization by racist, misogynist, and homophobic speech, nor do we equally share the burden of the societal harm it inflicts. We are often quick to say that we have heard the cry of the victims when we have not.

The *Brown* case is again instructive because it speaks directly to the psychic injury inflicted by racist speech by noting that the symbolic message of segregation affected "the hearts and minds" of Negro children "in a way unlikely ever to be undone." Racial epithets and harassment often cause deep emotional scarring and feelings of anxiety and fear that pervade every aspect of a victim's life.

Brown also recognized that black children did not have an equal opportunity to learn and participate in the school community if they bore the additional burden of being subjected to the humiliation and psychic assault contained in the message of segregation. University students bear an analogous burden when they are forced to live and work in an environment where at any moment they may be subjected to denigrating verbal harassment and assault. The same injury was addressed by the Supreme Court when it held that sexual harassment that creates a hostile or abusive work environment violates the ban on sex discrimination in employment of Title VII of the Civil Rights Act of 1964.

Carefully drafted university regulations would bar the use of words as assault weapons and leave unregulated even the most heinous of ideas when those ideas are presented at times and places and in manners that provide an opportunity for reasoned rebuttal or escape from immediate injury. The history of the development of the right to free speech has been one of carefully evaluating the importance of free expression and its effects on other important societal interests. We have drawn the line between protected and unprotected speech before without dire results. (Courts have, for example, exempted from the protection of the First Amendment obscene speech and speech that disseminates official secrets, that defames or libels another person, or that is used to form a conspiracy or monopoly.)

Blacks and other people of color are skep- 15 tical about the argument that even the most injurious speech must remain unregulated because, in an unregulated marketplace of ideas, the best ones will rise to the top and gain acceptance. Our experience tells us quite the opposite. We have seen too many good liberal politicians shy away from the issues that might brand them as being too closely allied with us.

Whenever we decide that racist speech must be tolerated because of the importance of maintaining societal tolerance for all unpopular speech, we are asking blacks and other subordinated groups to bear the burden for the good of all. We must be careful that the ease with which we strike the balance against the regulation of racist speech is in no way influenced by the fact that the cost will be borne by others. We must be certain that those who will pay that price are fairly represented in our deliberations and that they are heard.

At the core of the argument that we should resist all government regulation of speech is the ideal that the best cure for bad speech is good, that ideas that affirm equality and the worth of all individuals will ultimately prevail. This is an empty ideal unless those of us who would fight racism are vigilant and unequivocal in that fight. We must look for ways to offer assistance and support to students whose speech and political participation are chilled in a climate of racial harassment.

Civil rights lawyers might consider suing on behalf of blacks whose right to an equal education is denied by a university's failure to ensure a nondiscriminatory educational climate or conditions of employment. We must embark upon the development of a First Amendment jurisprudence grounded in the reality of our history and our contemporary experience. We must think hard about how best to launch legal attacks against the most indefensible forms of hate speech. Good lawyers can create exceptions and narrow interpretations that limit the harm of hate speech without opening the floodgates of censorship.

Everyone concerned with these issues must find ways to engage actively in actions that resist and counter the racist ideas that we would have the First Amendment protect. If we fail in this, the victims of hate speech must rightly assume that we are on the oppressors' side.

Topics for Critical Thinking and Writing

1. If you previewed and skimmed Charles Lawrence's essay, what kinds of information stood out to you? What could you tell just by reading the first two and last two paragraphs? What important ideas (parts you may have noticed in a more active reading) were not indicated in those paragraphs?

2. Engage in a close reading of paragraphs 5–9, in which Lawrence speaks of regulating "racially assaulting speech" and "vilifying speech" on campus but not if part of an announced speech or rally. Why does he believe that racially assaultive speech may be banned in some campus locations, while still being protected in others?

3. Write a critical summary of Lawrence's essay in a paragraph of about 200 words. (You may find it useful to use the Introduce, Explain, Exemplify, Problematize, and Extend model in the Visual Guide on p. 61 and refer to our example of a critical summary of Betty Friedan on p. 59.)

READING WITH A CAREFUL EYE: UNDERLINING, HIGHLIGHTING, ANNOTATING

Once you do some *previewing* (and perhaps some *skimming*) to get a general idea of the work—not only an idea of its topic and thesis, but also a sense of the *way* in which the thesis is presented and argued—you may want to interact with the text even more closely.

As you read, **highlight** or **underline** key passages and make **annotations** in the margins. Because you're reading actively, you will be interacting with the text and won't simply let your eye rove across the page to get the gist of the essay. Here are some ways to read with your pencil in hand or digital highlighting tool at the ready:

- Highlight the chief points, striking examples, or anything that stands out to you as important so that later when reviewing the essay (or writing about it) you can easily locate the main passages, important evidence, and so on.

- Make brief and selective marginal annotations. They may consist of hints or clues for yourself, such as comments like "doesn't follow," "good," "compare with Jones," "check this," or "really? What about X?"

- Highlight key definitions of terms. In the margin you might write "good," or "contrast X's definition" or "Leaves out X" if you think the definition is correct, incorrect, or unclear.

- If you're working digitally, consider copying and pasting passages that you would normally just highlight into a new document file. Clearly identify these passages as direct quotations to avoid plagiarism, and type your annotations next to them using the review functions.

- Don't overdo it. If you find yourself highlighting most of a page, you're probably not distinguishing the key points clearly enough.

In all these ways, you interact with the text and lay the groundwork for eventually writing your own essay incorporating what you have read.

What you annotate may depend largely on your **purpose**. If you're reading an essay to see how the writer organizes an argument, you'll annotate one sort of thing (say, the sequence of paragraphs or the structure of the argument). If you're reading to challenge the thesis, you'll annotate other things (perhaps the central points of evidence, the sources used, etc.).

Here is a passage from Charles R. Lawrence's essay "On Racist Speech," with a student's rather skeptical, even aggressive, annotations. But notice that the student apparently made at least one of the annotations — "Definition of 'fighting words'" — chiefly as a reminder to locate where the definition of an important term appears in the essay. (The essay is presented in full earlier in this chapter on p. 45.)

Example of such a policy? — University officials who have formulated policies to respond to incidents of racial harassment have been characterized in the press as "thought police," but such policies generally do nothing more than

? — impose sanctions against intentional face-to-face insults. When racist

Example? — speech takes the form of face-to-face insults, catcalls, or other assaul-

What about sexist speech? — tive speech aimed at an individual or small group of persons, it falls directly within the "fighting words" exception to First Amendment

Definition of "fighting words" — protection. The Supreme Court has held that words "which 'by their very utterance inflict injury or tend to incite an immediate breach of the peace'" are not protected by the First Amendment.

If the purpose of the First Amendment is to foster the greatest amount of speech, racial insults disserve that purpose. Assaul-

Really? Probably depends on the individual. — tive racist speech functions as a preemptive strike. The invective is experienced as a blow, not as a proffered idea, and once the blow is struck, it is unlikely that a dialogue will follow. Racial insults are particularly undeserving of First Amendment protection because the

Why must speech always seek "to discover truth"? — perpetrator's intention is not to discover truth or initiate dialogue

How does he know? — but to injure the victim. In most situations, members of minority groups realize that they are likely to lose if they respond to epithets by fighting and are forced to remain silent and submissive.

READING: FAST AND SLOW

When you are reading actively with the strategies discussed so far — previewing, skimming, highlighting, annotation — you have decided that a particular text is worth digging into even further, and that you will engage with the argument in a highly analytical way. If critical *thinking* involves "taking apart" a specimen to help you understand it, then critical *reading* is akin to taking apart a similarly complex system of language and meaning to understand better how it works. If you can see how all the parts of an argument work in relation to one another, you can see why they are convincing — or may *sound* convincing even when you disagree with them. But since your task as a thinker, reader, and writer is not just to understand arguments but also to evaluate, judge, and offer possible alternatives to them, you should be alert to areas where improvements can be made, where new questions may be asked, and where new parts can be added to support or challenge the conclusions. To do all this, you must *read slowly*. You sometimes must go back and reread sections, or stop to fact-check details, or pause to gather additional information.

This is **close reading**, a technique that traces a text's details, patterns, and subtleties. Close reading means, for starters, paying attention to the *language* of an essay. By doing this, you can see how words and their meanings lend support to an argument — but perhaps also reveal an author's assumptions through the language they use. For example, an author who calls their city's crime problem a "monster" personifies the problem in a particular way that might be used to argue for somewhat harsher law enforcement policies to solve it (who doesn't want to "capture," "reign in," or "kill" a monster?). Another author might refer to the same crime problem as a "sickness," and argue instead for investigating the root causes of crime, "triaging" and "treating" them.

To develop new perspectives and solutions related to the issues in your world, you must interrogate the readings and test whether or not they hold up to your intellectual scrutiny. The issues raised in this book — and the arguments made about them — require more comment than just saying "I agree with the author." Your reasoning faculties must be on high alert: Why do you agree? With what elements of the argument? What convinced you? How would your agreement stand up to a counterposition? When we say that most of the arguments in this book require close reading, we don't mean that they are obscure or overly difficult; we mean, rather, that you have to approach them thoughtfully and deliberately, always examining their alternatives.

Some arguments appear convincing simply *because* all the parts work so well together. Such arguments may appear airtight and indisputable not because they offer the only reasonable or viable position, but just because they are so well constructed, or because they appeal to common assumptions or rely on widely shared beliefs and concepts. To close read effectively, you must employ **analysis**, another word suggesting an act of taking apart — from the Greek *analusis*, "to loosen; to undo." We like this as a metaphor for close reading analysis because it suggests that all arguments are like woven cloths whose individual threads can be loosened and untied.

When close reading, various threads may help you identify patterns in the argument, allowing you to comment on how they can be improved upon or challenged.

- The language in the article is characterized by . . . [patterns in language]
- Although the argument is convincing, its assumptions are that . . . [patterns in assumptions]
- Although the argument is convincing, it fails to consider *X* alternative perspective . . . [patterns in perspectives]
- Although the author looks at evidence showing . . . , they don't attend fully to other evidence showing . . . [patterns in types or nature of evidence]
- Although the author does a good job offering *X*, the argument could use more *Y* . . . [patterns in argument structure]
- The author's perspective is shaped by the values and interests of . . . [patterns in belief]

Merely passing a series of landmarks is like previewing and skimming; you may be learning something about them but not necessarily getting the full experience.

As these sentence beginnings demonstrate, it takes close reading and analytical skill to decide whether to agree or disagree with an argument, or to draw a different conclusion, or to conceive of a new argument. You must practice disassembling arguments piece by piece, untying words, sentences, and paragraphs thoughtfully, one by one. Above all, *go slow*. You will get more enjoyment and enrichment from a text if you take in its wonders. You wouldn't get much out of visiting Paris *or* Rome by quickly speeding from one museum or landmark to the next, checking off items as you went.

Summarizing and Paraphrasing

After previewing, skimming, and a first reading, perhaps the next best step, particularly with a fairly difficult essay, is to reread it. For maximum comprehension, you might consider simultaneously taking notes on a sheet of paper, summarizing each paragraph in a sentence or two, and then write an overall summary of the whole argument. Writing a **summary** can help you understand the contents and see the strengths and weaknesses of the piece. It will also help you prepare for writing by providing a snapshot of the argument in your notes.

Don't confuse a summary with a paraphrase. A **paraphrase** is a word-by-word or phrase-by-phrase rewording of a text, a sort of translation of the author's language into your own. A paraphrase is therefore as long as the original or even longer; a summary is much shorter. An entire essay, even a whole book, may be summarized in a page, in a paragraph, even in a sentence. Obviously, a summary will leave out most details, but it will accurately state the essential thesis or claim of the original.

Why would anyone summarize, and why would anyone paraphrase? Because, as we've already said, these two activities — in different ways — help you comprehend an author's ideas and offer ways to introduce those ideas into your arguments in a way that readers can follow. Summaries and paraphrases can help you

- **validate** the basis of your ideas by providing an instance in which someone else wrote about the same topic

- **support** your argument by showing readers where someone else "got it right" (corroborating your ideas) or "got it wrong" (countering your ideas, but giving you a chance to refute that position in favor of your own)

- **clarify** in short order the complex ideas contained in another author's work

- **lend authority** to your voice by showing readers that you have considered the topic carefully by consulting other sources

- **build new ideas** from existing ideas on the topic, enabling you to insert your voice into an ongoing debate made evident by the summary or paraphrase

When you *summarize*, you're standing back, saying briefly what the whole adds up to; you're seeing the forest, as the saying goes, not the individual trees. When you *paraphrase*, you're inching through the forest, scrutinizing each tree — finding a synonym for almost every word in the original in an effort to ensure that you know exactly what the original is saying. (Keep in mind that when you incorporate a summary or a paraphrase into your own essay, you should acknowledge the source and state that you are summarizing or paraphrasing.)

Let's examine the distinction between summary and paraphrase in connection with the first two paragraphs of Paul Goodman's essay "A Proposal to Abolish Grading," excerpted from his book *Compulsory Miseducation and the Community of Scholars* (1966):

> Let half a dozen of the prestigious universities — Chicago, Stanford, the Ivy League — abolish grading, and use testing only and entirely for pedagogic purposes as teachers see fit.
>
> Anyone who knows the frantic temper of the present schools will understand the transvaluation of values that would be effected by this modest innovation. For most of the students, the competitive grade has come to be the essence. The naïve teacher points to the beauty of the subject and the ingenuity of the research; the shrewd student asks if he is responsible for that on the final exam.

A *summary* of these two paragraphs might read like this:

> If some top universities used tests only to help students learn and not for grades, students would stop worrying about whether they got an A, B, or C and might begin to share the teacher's interest in the beauty of the subject.

Notice that the summary doesn't convey Goodman's style or voice (e.g., the wry tone in his pointed contrast between "the naïve teacher" and "the shrewd student"). That is not the purpose of summary.

Now for a *paraphrase*. Suppose you're not sure what Goodman is getting at, maybe because you're uncertain about the meanings of some words (e.g., "pedagogic" and "transvaluation"), or you just want to make sure you understand the point.

> Suppose some of the top universities — such as Chicago, Stanford, Harvard, Yale, and others in the Ivy League — stopped using grades and instead used tests only to help students learn.
>
> Everyone who is aware of the rat race in schools today will understand the enormous shift in values about learning that would come about by this small change. At present, idealistic instructors talk about how beautiful their subjects are, but smart students know that grades are what count. They only want to know if that subject will be on the exam.

In short, you may decide to paraphrase an important text if you want the reader to see the passage itself but you know that the full passage will be puzzling. In this situation, you offer help, *paraphrasing* before making your own point about the author's claim.

A second good reason to offer a paraphrase is if there is substantial disagreement about what the text says. The Second Amendment to the US Constitution is a good example of this sort of text:

> A well regulated Militia being necessary to the security of a free State, the right of the people to keep and bear Arms shall not be infringed.

Thousands of pages have been written about that sentence, and if you're going to write about it, too, you certainly have to let readers know exactly how you interpret it. You wouldn't want to appeal to the Second Amendment in an argument about concealed carry laws without addressing your sense of what the words mean. Exactly what is a "Militia"? What does it mean for to be "well regulated"? And does "the people" mean each individual or the citizenry as a unified group? In short, you almost surely will paraphrase the sentence, giving readers your own sense of what each word or phrase means. Here is one possible paraphrase:

> The Second Amendment states that because an independent society needs the protection of an armed force if it is to remain free, the government may not limit the right of the individuals (who may someday form the militia needed to keep the society free) to possess weapons.

Gun control supporters marching in Washington, DC.

In this interpretation, the Constitution grants individuals the right to possess weapons, and that is that.

Other students of the Constitution, however, offer very different paraphrases, usually along these lines:

> The Second Amendment states that because each state in the union may need to protect its freedom from the new national government, the national government may not infringe on the right of each state to form its own disciplined militia.

This paraphrase says that the federal government may not prevent each state from having a militia; it says nothing about every individual person having a right to possess weapons.

The first paraphrase might be offered by the National Rifle Association or any other group that interprets the Constitution as guaranteeing individuals the right to own guns. The second paraphrase might be offered by groups that seek to limit the ownership of guns.

Why paraphrase? Here are two reasons you might paraphrase a passage:

1. To help yourself understand it. In this case, the paraphrase does not appear in your essay.
2. To help your reader understand a passage that is especially important but that is not immediately clear. In this case, you paraphrase to let the reader know exactly what the passage means. This paraphrase does appear in your essay.

A CHECKLIST FOR A PARAPHRASE

☐ Do I have a good reason for offering a paraphrase rather than a summary?

☐ Is the paraphrase entirely in my own words — a word-by-word "translation" — rather than a patchwork of the source's words and my own, with some of my own rearrangement of phrases and clauses?

☐ Do I not only cite the source but also explicitly say that the entire passage is a paraphrase?

Patchwriting and Plagiarism

We have indicated that only rarely will you have reason to paraphrase in your essays. In your notes, you might sometimes copy word for word (quote), paraphrase, or summarize, but if you produce a medley of borrowed words and original words in your essays, you are **patchwriting**, and it can be dangerous: If you submit such a medley, you risk the charge of **plagiarism** *even if you have rearranged the phrases and clauses, and even if you have cited your source.*

Here's an example. First, we give the source: a paragraph from the first page of Louis Menand's *The Free World* (2021), a history of the Cold War in America, in which he provides the following description of the post–World War II period in the United States:

> The number of Americans attending college increased exponentially. Book sales, record sales, and museum attendance soared. Laws were rewritten to permit works of art and literature to use virtually any language and to represent virtually any subject, and to protect almost any kind of speech. American industry doubled its output. Consumer choice expanded dramatically. The income and wealth gap between top earners and the middle class was the smallest in history. The ideological differences between the two major political parties were minor, enabling the federal government to invest in social programs. The legal basis for social and political equality of Americans of African ancestry [was] established and economic opportunities were opened up for women.

Here is a student's patchwriting version:

> During the Cold War, exponentially more Americans were attending college, buying books, buying records, and attending museums. New laws were established to protect freedom of speech, and art and literature were suddenly able to use sensitive language and broach taboo subjects. American industry expanded twofold, and consumerism was on the rise. The political parties were not as divided as they are now, which helped the federal government to provide more social programs and economic opportunities for African Americans and women.

As you can see, the student writer has used patchwriting because they followed the source almost phrase by phrase, making small verbal changes here and there, such as substituting new words and key phrases, while at other points using the same vocabulary slightly rearranged. That is, the sequence of ideas and their arrangement, as well as most of the language, are entirely or almost entirely derived from the source, even if some of the words are different. Thus, even if the student cites the source, it is plagiarism.

What the student should have done is either (1) *quote the passage exactly*, setting it off to indicate that it's a quotation and indicating the source, or (2) *summarize it briefly* and credit the source — maybe in a version such as this:

> According to Louis Menand in *The Free World* (2021), the Cold War brought many changes to the United States — some directly connected to the expansion in higher education, such as the fact that "book sales, record sales, and museum attendance soared" (1). Further, Menand points out, laws were "rewritten" to protect free speech in the arts and literature, which were now able "to use virtually any language and to represent virtually any subject" (1). Other elements Menand emphasizes include an unprecedented narrowing of economic divisions between the rich and the working class, and consensus between political parties which helped expand social programs and opportunities for African Americans and women.

The above example frankly summarizes a source and attributes it to the author, Menand. The reader knows these points are Menand's, not the writer's. This allows the writer to build on their source's ideas to establish — and distinguish — their own argument. The writer could add specific examples or ideas alongside Menand's but must be careful not to blur the lines between what is the source and what is new information.

Citing a source is not enough to protect you from the charge of plagiarism. Citing a source tells the reader that some fact or idea — or some groups of words enclosed within quotation marks or set off by indentation — comes from the named source; it does *not* tell the reader that almost everything in the paragraph is, in effect, someone else's writing with a few words changed, a few words added, and a few phrases moved.

The best way to avoid introducing patchwriting into your final essay is to make certain that when taking notes you indicate, *in the notes themselves*, what sort of notes they are. For example:

- When quoting word for word, put the passage within quotation marks and cite the page number(s) of the source.

- When paraphrasing — perhaps to ensure that you understand the writer's idea or because your readers won't understand the source's highly technical language unless you put it into simpler language — use some sign, perhaps (*par*), to remind yourself later that this passage is a paraphrase and thus is not really *your* writing.

- When summarizing, use a different key, such as (*sum*), and cite the page(s) or online location of the source.

If you have taken notes properly, with indications of the sort we've mentioned, when writing your paper you can say things like the following:

- *X*'s first reason is simple. *X* says, "..." (here you quote *X*'s words, putting them within quotation marks).

- *X*'s point can be summarized thus: ... (here you cite the page).

- *X*, writing for lawyers, uses some technical language, but we can paraphrase her conclusion in this way: ... (here you give the citation).

For additional information about plagiarism, see the section "A Note on Plagiarizing" (p. 292) in Chapter 8.

Strategies for Summarizing

As with paraphrases, summaries can help you establish your understanding of an essay or article. Summarizing each paragraph or each group of closely related paragraphs will enable you to follow the threads of the argument and will ultimately provide a useful map of the essay. You may want to underline passages that represent the author's key ideas, definitions, generalizations, and primary sources. You may also want to jot notes in the margins, questioning the logic, expressing your uncertainty, or calling attention to other people who see the matter differently or other examples that might support or weaken the author's views.

A summary of an entire essay can help you understand the essay better and serve as a useful source later when you may want to integrate it into your own writing. How long should your summaries be? They can be as short as a single sentence or as long as an entire paragraph. Here's a one-sentence summary of Martin Luther King Jr.'s famous essay "Letter from Birmingham Jail," which King wrote after his arrest for marching against racial segregation and injustice in Birmingham, Alabama.

> In his letter, King argues that the time is ripe for nonviolent protest throughout the segregated South, dismissing claims by local clergymen who opposed him and arguing that unjust laws need to be challenged by Black people who have been patient and silent for too long.

King's essay, however, is quite long. Obviously, this one-sentence summary cannot convey substantial portions of King's eloquent arguments, sacrificing almost all the nuance of his rationale, but it serves as an efficient summation and allows the writer to move on to their own analysis promptly.

A longer summary might try to capture more nuance, especially if, for the purposes of your essay, you need to capture more. How much you summarize depends largely on the *purpose* of your summary (see again our list of reasons to summarize on p. 52). Here is a longer summary of King's letter:

> In his letter, King argues that the time is ripe for nonviolent protest in the segregated South despite the criticism he and his fellow civil rights activists received from various authorities, especially the eight local clergymen who wrote a public statement against him. King addresses their criticism point by point, first claiming his essential right to be in Birmingham with his famous statement, "injustice anywhere is a threat to justice everywhere," and then saying that those who see the timing of his group's nonviolent direct action as inconvenient must recognize at least two things: one, that his "legitimate and unavoidable impatience" resulted from undelivered promises by authorities in the past; and two, that African Americans had long been told over and over again to wait for change with no change forthcoming. "This 'wait' has almost always meant 'never,'" King writes. For those who criticized his leadership, which encouraged people to break laws prohibiting their march, King says that breaking *unjust* laws may actually be construed as a *just* act. For those who called him an extremist, he revels in the definition ("was not Jesus an extremist in love?" he asks) and reminds them of the more extremist groups who call for violence in the face of blatant discrimination and brutality (and who will surely rise, King suggests, if no redress is forthcoming for the peaceful southern protestors he leads). Finally, King rails against "silence," saying that to hold one's tongue in the face of segregation is tantamount to supporting it — a blow to "white moderates" who believe in change but do nothing to help bring it about.

This summary, obviously much longer than the first, raises numerous points from King's argument and preserves through quotation some of King's original tone and substance. It sacrifices much, of course, but seeks to provide a thorough account of a long and complex document containing many primary and secondary claims.

If your instructor asks for a summary of an essay, most often they won't want you to include your own thoughts about the content. Of course, you'll be using your own words, but try to "put yourself in the original author's shoes" and provide a summary that reflects the approach taken by the source. It should *not* contain ideas that the original piece doesn't express. If you use exact words and phrases drawn from the source, enclose them in quotation marks.

Summaries may be written for exercises in reading comprehension, but the point of summarizing when writing an essay is to assist your own argument. A faithful summary — one without your own ideas interjected — can be effective when using a source as an example or showing another writer's concordance with your argument. Consider the following paragraph written by a student who wanted to use Henry David Thoreau's 1849 essay, "Resistance to Civil Government," to make a point in their paper on sweatshops and other poor labor conditions in the supply chains of our everyday products. Thoreau famously argued that many northerners who objected to slavery in the United States did not always realize how economically tied up in slavery they were. He argued that true opposition to slavery meant withdrawing fully from all economic activity related to it. The student was arguing that if a person today purchases goods manufactured in sweatshops or under other inadequate labor conditions, they are in a sense just as responsible for the abuses of labor as the companies who operate them. Thoreau provided a convenient precedent. Notice how the student offers a summary (underlined) along the way and how it assists their argument.

> Americans today are so disconnected from the source and origins of the products they buy that it is entirely possible for them one day to march against global warming and the next to collect a dividend in their 401k from companies that are the worst offenders. It is possible to weep over a news report on child labor in China and then post an emotional plea for justice on Facebook using a mobile device made by Chinese child laborers. In 1849, Henry David Thoreau wrote in "Resistance to Civil Government" how ironic it was to see his fellow citizens in Boston opposed to slavery in the South, yet who read the daily news and commodity prices and "fall asleep over them both," not recognizing their own investments in, or patronage of, the very thing that offends their consciences. To Thoreau, such "gross inconsistency" makes even well-intentioned people "agents of injustice." Similarly, today we do not see the connections between our consumer habits and the various kinds of oppression that underlie our purchases — forms of oppression we would never support directly and outright.

The embedded short summary addresses only one point of Thoreau's original essay, but it shows how summaries may serve in an integrative way — as analogy, example, or illustration — to support an argument even without adding the writer's own commentary or analysis.

CRITICAL SUMMARY

When writing a longer summary that you intend to integrate into your argument, you may interject your own ideas. The appropriate term for this kind of writing is **critical summary**. It signifies that you're offering more than a thorough and accurate account of an original source, because you're adding your evaluation of it as well. Think of it as weaving together your neutral summary with your own argument so that the summary meshes seamlessly with your overall writing goal. Along the way, during the summary, you may appraise the original author's ideas, commenting on them as you go — even while being faithful to the original.

How can you faithfully account for an author's argument while commenting on its merits or shortcomings? One way is to offer examples from the original. In addition, you might assess the quality of those examples, or present others that the author didn't consider. Remember, being critical doesn't necessarily mean refuting the author. Your summary can refute, support, or be more balanced, simply recognizing where the original author succeeds and fails.

WRITING TIP
When writing a critical summary, you can problematize by examining areas not considered by the author. Ask: What has the author missed? What evidence or examples have been overlooked or misinterpreted?

A STRATEGY FOR WRITING A CRITICAL SUMMARY   Follow these five steps when writing a critical summary:

1. **Introduce** the summary. You don't have to provide all these elements, but consider offering the *author's name* and *expertise*, the *title* of the source, the *place of publication*, the *year* of publication, or any other relevant information. You may also start to explain the author's main point that you are summarizing:

> Pioneering feminist Betty Friedan, in her landmark book *The Feminine Mystique* (1963), argued that . . .

Don't overdo it. Select the most important details carefully and work toward concision. Remember that this is a summary, so "get in and get out." That is, move quickly back to your analysis.

2. **Explain** the major point the source makes. Here you have a chance to tell your readers what the original author is saying, so be faithful to the original but also highlight the point you're summarizing:

> Pioneering feminist Betty Friedan, in her landmark book *The Feminine Mystique* (1963), argued that women of the early 1960s were exposed to a media-created image of ideal femininity that pressured them to prioritize homemaking, beauty, and maternity above almost all other concerns.

Here you can shape the readers' understanding through simple adjectives such as "pioneering" and "landmark." (Remember framing principles. Compare how "*stalwart* feminist Betty Friedan, in her *provocative* book" might dispose the reader to interpret your material differently.)

3. **Exemplify** by offering one or more representative examples or evidence on which the original author draws. Feel free to quote if needed, although it is not required in a summary.

> Friedan examines post–World War II trends that included the lowering of the marriage age, the rise of the mass media, and what she calls "the problem that has no name" — that of feminine discontentment, or what we might today call "depression."

Feel free to use a short quotation or utilize signature terms, phrases, or concepts from the source, as we did with "the problem that has no name."

4. **Problematize** by placing your assessment, analysis, or question into the summary.

Although the word "depression" never comes up in Friedan's work, <u>one could assume</u> that terms like "malaise," "suffering," and "housewives' fatigue" <u>signal an emerging understanding of the relationship between stereotypical media representations of social identity and mental health.</u>

If you're working toward a balanced critique or rebuttal, here is a good place to insert your ideas or those of someone with a slightly different view. Consider utility phrases that help tie these elements of critical summary together. More adjectives and strong verbs can help indicate your critique and judgment. For example:

5. **Extend** by tying the summary to your argument, helping transition out of the critical summary and back into your own analysis. Imagine your final task as saying (without saying) something like, "And this summary is important to my overall thesis because it shows . . . ."

Friedan's work should raise questions about <u>how women are portrayed in the media today and about what mental health consequences are attributable to the ubiquitous and consistent messages given to women about their bodies, occupations, and social roles.</u>

Combine the statements about Betty Friedan's work above and you will find a fairly cohesive critical summary following the five suggested steps for writing a critical summary. It is possible to use this method — **Introduce**, **Explain**, **Exemplify**, **Problematize**, and **Extend** — in many ways. Essentially it is a way of providing a critical summary, any element of which can be enhanced or built upon as needed — or even omitted. Consider this short version:

WRITING TIP
Use strong adjectives to establish your assessment or judgments on the value, worth, or quality of the writer's argument, thesis, presentation, or sources (e.g., *landmark* essay, *controversial* book, *blunt* critique).

Feminist Betty Friedan wrote in *The Feminine Mystique* (1963) about how more women in the 1960s were becoming depressed in part because they were comparing themselves to the impossible ideals of femininity established in mass media magazines, a phenomenon that still exists today in the form of. . . .

When you're writing your own critical summary, it is up to you to decide whether to make it long and detailed, or short and to the point. Refer to the Visual Guide: Writing a Critical Summary (p. 61) for reference.

A SHORT ESSAY FOR SUMMARIZING PRACTICE

The following piece by Susan Jacoby is annotated to provide a "rough summary" in the margins, more or less paragraph by paragraph — the kind you might make if you are outlining an essay or argument.

Visual Guide: Writing a Critical Summary

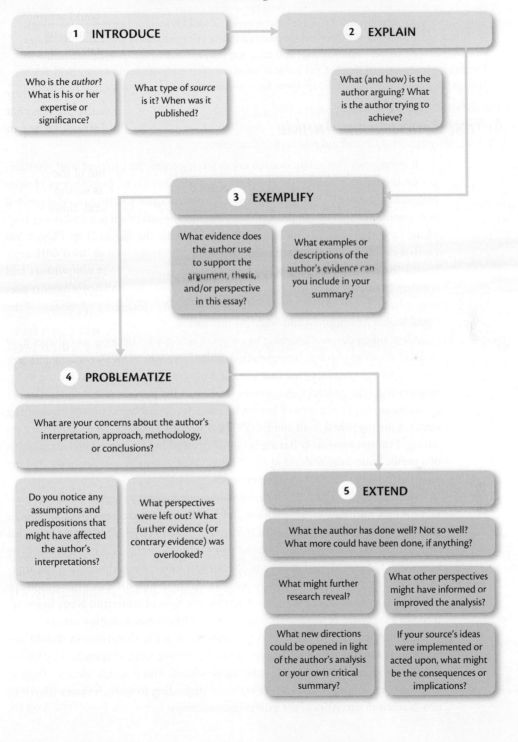

1 INTRODUCE

Who is the *author*? What is his or her expertise or significance?

What type of *source* is it? When was it published?

2 EXPLAIN

What (and how) is the author arguing? What is the author trying to achieve?

3 EXEMPLIFY

What evidence does the author use to support the argument, thesis, and/or perspective in this essay?

What examples or descriptions of the author's evidence can you include in your summary?

4 PROBLEMATIZE

What are your concerns about the author's interpretation, approach, methodology, or conclusions?

Do you notice any assumptions and predispositions that might have affected the author's interpretations?

What perspectives were left out? What further evidence (or contrary evidence) was overlooked?

5 EXTEND

What the author has done well? Not so well? What more could have been done, if anything?

What might further research reveal?

What other perspectives might have informed or improved the analysis?

What new directions could be opened in light of the author's analysis or your own critical summary?

If your source's ideas were implemented or acted upon, what might be the consequences or implications?

SUSAN JACOBY

Susan Jacoby, a journalist since the age of seventeen, is well known for her feminist writings. "A First Amendment Junkie" (our title) appeared in the Hers column in the *New York Times* in 1978. Notice that her argument zigs and zags, not because Jacoby is careless but because in building a strong case to support her point of view, she must consider some widely held views that she does *not* accept; she must set these forth and then give her reasons for rejecting them.

A First Amendment Junkie

1 *Paragraph 1:* Although feminists usually support the First Amendment, when it comes to pornography many feminists take the position of opposing the Equal Rights Amendment, abortion, and other causes of the women's movement.

1   It is no news that many women are defecting from the ranks of civil libertarians on the issue of obscenity. The conviction of Larry Flynt, publisher of *Hustler* magazine — before his metamorphosis into a born-again Christian — was greeted with unabashed feminist approval. Harry Reems, the unknown actor who was convicted by a Memphis jury for conspiring to distribute the movie *Deep Throat*, has carried on his legal battles with almost no support from women who ordinarily regard themselves as supporters of the First Amendment. Feminist writers and scholars have even discussed the possibility of making common cause against pornography with adversaries of the women's movement — including opponents of the Equal Rights Amendment and "right-to-life" forces.

2 *Paragraph 2:* Larry Flynt produces garbage, but Jacoby thinks his conviction represents an unconstitutional limitation of freedom of speech.

2   All of this is deeply disturbing to a woman writer who believes, as I always have and still do, in an absolute interpretation of the First Amendment. Nothing in Larry Flynt's garbage convinces me that the late Justice Hugo L. Black was wrong in his opinion that "the Federal Government is without any power whatsoever under the Constitution to put any type of burden on free speech and expression of ideas of any kind (as distinguished from conduct)." Many women I like and respect tell me I am wrong; I cannot remember having become involved in so many heated discussions of a public issue since the end of the Vietnam War. A feminist writer described my views as those of a "First Amendment junkie."

Many feminist arguments for controls on pornography carry the implicit conviction that porn books, magazines, and movies pose a greater threat to women than similarly repulsive exercises of free speech pose to other offended groups. This conviction has, of course, been shared by everyone — regardless of race, creed, or sex — who has ever argued in favor of abridging the First Amendment. It is the argument used by some Jews who have withdrawn their support from the American Civil Liberties Union because it has defended the right of American Nazis to march through a community inhabited by survivors of Hitler's concentration camps.

3 *Paragraphs 3, 4:* Feminists who want to censor pornography argue that it poses a greater threat to women than similar repulsive speech poses to other groups. They can make this case, but it is absurd to say that pornography is a "greater threat" to women than "neo-Nazi... extermination camps."

3   If feminists want to argue that the protection of the Constitution should not be extended to *any* particularly odious or threatening form of speech, they have a reasonable argument (although I don't agree with it). But it is ridiculous to suggest that the porn shops on 42nd Street are more disgusting to women than a march of neo-Nazis is to survivors of the extermination camps.

The arguments over pornography also blur the vital distinction between expression of ideas and conduct. When I say I believe unreservedly in the First Amendment, someone always comes back at me with the issue of "kiddie porn." But kiddie porn is not a First Amendment issue. It is an issue of the abuse of power — the power adults have over children — and not of obscenity. Parents and promoters have no more right to use their children to make porn movies than they do to send them to work in coal mines. The responsible adults should be prosecuted, just as adults who use children for back-breaking farm labor should be prosecuted.

Susan Brownmiller, in *Against Our Will: Men, Women, and Rape*, has described pornography as "the undiluted essence of antifemale propaganda." I think this is a fair description of some types of pornography, especially of the brutish subspecies that equates sex with death and portrays women primarily as objects of violence.

The equation of sex and violence, personified by some glossy rock record album covers as well as by *Hustler*, has fed the illusion that censorship of pornography can be conducted on a more rational basis than other types of censorship. Are all pictures of naked women obscene? Clearly not, says a friend. A Renoir nude is art, she says, and *Hustler* is trash. "Any reasonable person" knows that.

But what about something between art and trash — something, say, along the lines of *Playboy* or *Penthouse* magazines? I asked five women for their reactions to one picture in *Penthouse* and got responses that ranged from "lovely" and "sensuous" to "revolting" and "demeaning." Feminists, like everyone else, seldom have rational reasons for their preferences in erotica. Like members of juries, they tend to disagree when confronted with something that falls short of 100 percent vulgarity.

In any case, feminists will not be the arbiters of good taste if it becomes easier to harass, prosecute, and convict people on obscenity charges. Most of the people who want to censor girlie magazines are equally opposed to open discussion of issues that are of vital concern to women: rape, abortion, menstruation, contraception, lesbianism — in fact, the entire range of sexual experience from a woman's viewpoint.

Feminist writers and editors and filmmakers have limited financial resources: Confronted by a determined prosecutor, Hugh Hefner[1] will fare better than Susan Brownmiller. Would the Memphis jurors who convicted Harry Reems for his role in *Deep Throat* be inclined to take a more positive view of paintings of the female genitalia done by sensitive feminist artists? *Ms.* magazine has printed color reproductions of some of those art works; *Ms.* is already banned from a number of high school libraries because someone considers it threatening and/or obscene.

Feminists who want to censor what they regard as harmful pornography have essentially the same motivation as other would-be censors: They want to use the power of the state to accomplish what they have been unable to achieve in the marketplace of ideas and images. The impulse to censor places no faith in the possibilities of democratic persuasion.

4 *Paragraph 5*: Trust in the First Amendment is not refuted by kiddie porn; kiddie porn is an issue of child abuse.

5 *Paragraphs 6, 7, 8*: Some feminists think censorship of pornography can be more "rational" than other kinds of censorship, but a picture of a nude woman strikes some women as base and others as "lovely." There is no unanimity.

6 *Paragraphs 9, 10*: If feminists censor girlie magazines, they are unwittingly helping opponents of the women's movement censor discussions of rape, abortion, and so on.

---

[1]**Hugh Hefner** Founder and longtime publisher of *Playboy* magazine.

7 *Paragraphs 11, 12:* Like other would-be censors, feminists want to use the power of the state to achieve what they have not achieved in "the marketplace of ideas." They lack faith in "democratic persuasion."

8 *Paragraphs 13, 14:* This attempt at censorship reveals a "desire to shift responsibility from individuals to institutions." The responsibility is properly the parents'.

9 *Paragraph 15:* We can't have too much of the First Amendment.

7 It isn't easy to persuade certain men that they have better uses for $1.95 each month than to spend it on a copy of *Hustler*. Well, then, give the men no choice in the matter.

I believe there is also a connection between the impulse toward censorship on the part of people who used to consider themselves civil libertarians and a more general desire to shift responsibility from individuals to institutions. When I saw the movie *Looking for Mr. Goodbar*, I was stunned by its series of visual images equating sex and violence, coupled with what seems to me the mindless message (a distortion of the fine Judith Rossner novel) that casual sex equals death. When I came out of the movie, I was even more shocked to see parents standing in line with children between the ages of ten and fourteen.

8 I simply don't know why a parent would take a child to see such a movie, any more than I understand why people feel they can't turn off a television set their child is watching. Whenever I say that, my friends tell me I don't know how it is because I don't have children. True, but I do have parents. When I was a child, they did turn off the TV. They didn't expect the Federal Communications Commission to do their job for them.

9 I am a First Amendment junkie. You can't OD on the First Amendment, because 15 free speech is its own best antidote.

SUMMARIZING JACOBY   If you want to present a *brief summary* in the form of one coherent paragraph — perhaps as part of an essay arguing for or against — you might write something like the one shown in the paragraph below. (Of course, you would introduce it with a lead-in along these lines: "Susan Jacoby, writing in the *New York Times*, offers a forceful argument against censorship of pornography. Jacoby's view, briefly, is. . . .")

> When it comes to censorship of pornography, some feminists take a position shared by opponents of the feminist movement. They argue that pornography poses a greater threat to women than other forms of offensive speech offer to other groups, but this interpretation is simply a mistake. Pointing to kiddie porn is also a mistake, for kiddie porn is an issue involving not the First Amendment but child abuse. Feminists who support censorship of pornography will inadvertently aid those who wish to censor discussions of abortion and rape or censor art that is published in magazines such as *Ms.* The solution is not for individuals to turn to institutions (i.e., for the government to limit the First Amendment) but for individuals to accept the responsibility for teaching young people not to equate sex with violence.

In contrast, a *critical summary* of Jacoby — an evaluative summary in which we introduce our own ideas and examples — might look like this:

Susan Jacoby, writing for the *New York Times* in 1978, offers a forceful argument against censorship of pornography, but one that does not have foresight of the internet age and the new availability of extreme and exploitative forms of pornography. While she dismisses claims by feminists that pornography should be censored because it constitutes violence against women, what would Jacoby think of such things as "revenge porn" and "voyeuristic porn" today or the array of elaborate sadistic fantasies readily available to anyone with access to a search engine? Jacoby says that censoring pornography is a step toward censoring art, and she proudly wears the tag "First Amendment junkie," ostensibly to protect what she finds artistic (such as images of female genitalia in *Ms.* magazine). However, her argument does not help us account for these new forms of exploitation and violence disguised as art or "free speech." Perhaps she would see revenge porn and voyeur porn in the same the way she sees kiddie porn — not so much as an issue of free speech but as an issue of other crimes. Perhaps she would hold her position that we can avoid pornography by just "turning off the TV," but the new internet pornography is intrusive, entering our lives and the lives of our children whether we like it or not. Education is part of the solution, Jacoby would agree, but we could also consider. . . .

1 **Introduces** author, source, and year and characterizes the argument as "forceful"

2 **Problematizes** Jacoby's claims by introducing present-day contexts

3 **Explains** Jacoby's argument

4 **Problematizes** Jacoby's claim by pointing out its omissions in the current context

5 **Extends** Jacoby's argument to a new issue related to today's media environment

This example not only summarizes and applies the other techniques presented in this chapter (e.g., accounting for context and questioning definitions of terms and concepts) but also weaves them together with a central argument that offers a new response and a practicable solution.

A CHECKLIST FOR A SUMMARY

☐ Have I adequately previewed the work?

☐ Can I state the thesis?

☐ If I have written a summary, is it accurate?

☐ Does my summary mention all the chief points?

☐ If there are inconsistencies, are they in the summary or the original selection?

☐ Will my summary be clear and helpful?

☐ Have I considered the audience for whom the author is writing?

Essays for Analysis

In addition to the essays by Lawrence and Jacoby, we present three additional essays on the topic of free speech and censorship. We suggest that you read each one through to get its gist and then read it a second time, writing down after each paragraph a sentence or two summarizing the paragraph. Consider the essays individually and also in relation to one another, keeping in mind the First Amendment to the US Constitution, which reads, in its entirety, as follows:

> Congress shall make no law respecting an establishment of religion, or prohibiting the free exercise thereof; or abridging the freedom of speech, or of the press; or the right of the people peaceably to assemble, and to petition the government for a redress of grievances.

GWEN WILDE

This essay was written for a composition course at Tufts University.

Why the Pledge of Allegiance Should Be Revised (Student Essay)

All Americans are familiar with the Pledge of Allegiance, even if they cannot always recite it perfectly, but probably relatively few know that the *original* Pledge did *not* include the words "under God." The original Pledge of Allegiance, published in the September 8, 1892, issue of the *Youth's Companion,* ran thus:

> I pledge allegiance to my flag, and to the Republic for which it stands: one Nation indivisible, with Liberty and justice for all. (Djupe 329)

In 1923, at the first National Flag Conference in Washington, DC, it was argued that immigrants might be confused by the words "my Flag," and it was proposed that the words be changed to "the Flag of the United States." The following year it was changed again, to "the Flag of the United States of America," and this wording became the official — or, rather,

unofficial — wording, unofficial because no wording had ever been nationally adopted (Djupe 329).

In 1942, the United States Congress included the Pledge in the United States Flag Code (4 USC 4, 2006), thus for the first time officially sanctioning the Pledge. In 1954, President Dwight D. Eisenhower approved adding the words "under God." Thus, since 1954 the Pledge reads:

> I pledge allegiance to the flag of the United States of America, and to the Republic for which it stands: one nation under God, indivisible, with Liberty and Justice for all. (Djupe 329)

In my view, the addition of the words "under God" is inappropriate, and they are needlessly divisive — an odd addition indeed to a nation that is said to be "indivisible."

Very simply put, the Pledge in its latest form ⁵ requires all Americans to say something that some Americans do not believe. I say "requires" because although the courts have ruled that students may not be compelled to recite the Pledge, in effect peer pressure does compel all but the bravest to join in the recitation. When President Eisenhower authorized the change, he said, "In this way we are reaffirming the transcendence of religious faith in America's heritage and future; in this way we shall constantly strengthen those spiritual weapons which forever will be our country's most powerful resource in peace and war" (qtd. in Sterner).

Exactly what did Eisenhower mean when he spoke of "the transcendence of religious faith in America's heritage" and when he spoke of "spiritual weapons"? I am not sure what "the transcendence of religious faith in America's heritage" means. Of course, many Americans have been and are deeply religious — no one doubts it — but the phrase certainly goes far beyond saying that many Americans have been devout. In any case, many Americans have *not* been devout, and many Americans have *not* believed in "spiritual weapons," but they have nevertheless been patriotic Americans. Some of them have fought and died to keep America free.

In short, the words "under God" cannot be uttered in good faith by many Americans. True, something like 70 or even 80% of Americans say they are affiliated with some form of Christianity, and approximately another 3% say they are Jewish. I don't have the figures for persons of other faiths, but in any case we can surely all agree that although a majority of Americans say they have a religious affiliation, nevertheless several million Americans do *not* believe in God.

If one remains silent while others are reciting the Pledge, or even if one remains silent only while others are speaking the words "under God," one is open to the charge that one is unpatriotic, is "unwilling to recite the Pledge of Allegiance." In the Pledge, patriotism is connected with religious belief, and it is this connection that makes it divisive and (to be blunt) un-American. Admittedly, the belief is not very specific: one is not required to say that one believes in the divinity of Jesus, or in the power of Jehovah, but the fact remains, one is required to express belief in a divine power, and if one doesn't express this belief one is — according to the Pledge — somehow not fully an American, maybe even un-American.

Please notice that I am not arguing that the Pledge is unconstitutional. I understand that the First Amendment to the Constitution says that "Congress shall make no law respecting an establishment of religion, or prohibiting the free exercise thereof." I am not arguing that the words "under God" in the Pledge add up to the "establishment of religion," but they certainly do assert a religious doctrine. Like the words "In God We Trust," found on all American money, the words "under God" express an idea that many Americans do not hold, and there is no reason why these Americans — loyal people who may be called upon to defend the country with their lives — should be required to say that America is a nation "under God."

It has been argued, even by members of the ¹⁰ Supreme Court, that the words "under God" are not to be taken terribly seriously, not to be taken to say what they seem to say. For instance, Chief Justice William Rehnquist wrote:

> To give the parent of such a child a sort of "heckler's veto" over a patriotic ceremony willingly participated in by other students, simply because the Pledge of Allegiance contains the descriptive phrase "under God," is an unwarranted extension of the establishment clause, an extension which would have the unfortunate effect of prohibiting a commendable patriotic observance. (qtd. in Stephens et al. 104)

Chief Justice Rehnquist here calls "under God" a "descriptive phrase," but descriptive of *what*? If a phrase is a "descriptive phrase," it describes something, real or imagined. For many Americans, this phrase does *not* describe a reality. These Americans may perhaps be mistaken — if so, they may learn of their error at Judgment Day — but the fact is, millions of intelligent Americans do not believe in God.

Notice, too, that Chief Justice Rehnquist goes on to say that reciting the Pledge is "a commendable patriotic observance." Exactly. That is my point. It is a *patriotic* observance, and it should not be connected with religion. When we announce that we respect the flag — that we are loyal Americans — we should not also have to announce that we hold a particular religious belief, in this case a belief in monotheism, a belief that there is a God and that God rules.

One other argument defending the words "under God" is often heard: The words "In God We Trust" appear on our money. It is claimed that these words on American money are analogous to the words "under God" in the Pledge. But the situation really is very different. When we hand some coins over, or some paper money, we are concentrating on the business transaction, and we are not making any affirmation about God or our country. But when we recite the Pledge — even if we remain silent at the point when we are supposed to say "under God" — we are very conscious that we are supposed to make this affirmation, an affirmation that many Americans cannot in good faith make, even though they certainly can unthinkingly hand over (or accept) money with the words "In God We Trust."

Because I believe that *reciting* the Pledge is to be taken seriously, with a full awareness of the words that is quite different from when we hand over some money, I cannot understand the recent comment of Supreme Court Justice Souter, who in a case said that the phrase "under God" is "so tepid, so diluted, so far from compulsory prayer, that it should, in effect, be beneath the constitutional radar" (qtd. in "Guide"). I don't follow his reasoning that the phrase should be "beneath the constitutional radar," but in any case I am willing to put aside the issue of constitutionality. I am willing to grant that this phrase does not in any significant sense signify the "establishment of religion" (prohibited by the First Amendment) in the United States. I insist, nevertheless, that the phrase is neither "tepid" nor "diluted." It means what it says — it *must* and *should* mean what it says, to everyone who utters it — and, since millions of loyal Americans cannot say it, it should not be included in a statement in which Americans affirm their loyalty to our great country.

In short, the Pledge, which ought to unite 15 all of us, is divisive; it includes a phrase that many patriotic Americans cannot bring themselves to utter. Yes, they can remain silent when others recite these two words, but, again, why should they have to remain silent? The Pledge of Allegiance should be something that *everyone* can say, say out loud, and say with pride. We hear much talk of returning to the ideas of the Founding Fathers. The Founding Fathers did not create the Pledge of Allegiance, but we do know that they never mentioned God in the Constitution. Indeed, the only reference to religion, in the so-called establishment clause of the First Amendment, says, again, that "Congress shall make no law respecting an establishment of religion, or prohibiting the free exercise thereof." Those who wish to exercise religion are indeed free to do so, but the place to do so is not in a pledge that is required of all schoolchildren and of all new citizens.

WORKS CITED

Djupe, Paul A. "Pledge of Allegiance." *Encyclopedia of American Religion and Politics*, edited by Paul A. Djupe and Laura R. Olson, Facts on File, 2003, p. 329.

"Guide to Covering 'Under God' Pledge Decision." *ReligionLink*, 17 Sept. 2005, religionlink.com/database/guide-to-covering-under-god/.

Stephens, Otis H., et al., editors. *American Constitutional Law*. 6th ed., vol. 1, Cengage Learning, 2014.

Sterner, Doug. "The Pledge of Allegiance." *Home of Heroes*, homeofheroes.com/hallofheroes/1st_floor/flag/1bfc_pledge_print.html. Accessed 13 Apr. 2016.

Topics for Critical Thinking and Writing

1. Summarize the essay in a paragraph.

2. What words are defined in this essay? Are they defined more as terms or as concepts? Explain *how* the author defines one word or phrase.

3. Does Gwen Wilde show an adequate awareness of counterarguments? Identify one place where she raises and refutes a counterargument, or where she might have included one.

SOHRAB AHMARI

Sohrab Ahmari is an Iranian-American author and journalist currently serving as the opinion editor of the *New York Post*. He has also contributed to the *Catholic Herald* and *Commentary*. Ahmari is the author of the book *The Unbroken Thread: Discovering the Wisdom of Tradition in the Age of Chaos* (2021). This essay was published in the *New York Post* in 2019.

Porn Isn't Free Speech — on the Web or Anywhere

Of all the stats that keep parents up at night, the one that haunts me most often is this: My toddler son is likely to encounter Internet porn before puberty.

So I cheered when I read a Friday letter from four members of Congress urging Attorney General Bill Barr to revive America's obscenity laws to "stop the explosion of obscene pornography." Amen.

Then came the dismaying reaction — not just from the usual suspects on the left, but from many on the right, where access to porn has bizarrely emerged as a touchstone of "conservative" orthodoxy.

Online porn isn't that bad, the Twitter libertarians insist. Plus, there is no way to restrict access to online porn, and even if there were, such regulation would sound the death knell for our ancient liberties.

All nonsense.

Online porn is that bad. For starters, there is the clear exploitation and links to human trafficking, which belie the libertarians' glib slogans about "consenting adults."

Working with numerous victims, Karen Countryman-Roswurm of Wichita State University's Center for Combating Human Trafficking was shocked to learn how many of them had been involved in porn shoots used by traffickers to "desensitize them to the sexual acts they would experience" and as "advertising" for abuse.

Then there are the harms to consumers, especially boys and young men. Porn creates "a powerful biochemical 'rush' in the user," writes psychologist John Mark Haney for the American Counseling Association. "Teens who experience this biochemical thrill will, not surprisingly, want to experience it again."

Other well-established effects on young users, per Haney: "modeling and imitation of inappropriate behaviors; unhealthy interference with normal sexual development; emotional side effects including nightmares and residual feelings of shame, guilt, anxiety and confusion"; and violent attitudes about sex and women. Fifteen states have declared it a public-health crisis.

OK, online porn is bad, critics of prohibition may admit — but why can't parents do their job and police it? This is the most infuriating of their responses. [10]

Of course, I'll do my damnedest to keep my son away from smut, but there are numerous situations where I can't control his Internet activities. And what about parents who are neglectful: Does the state not have some duty to protect all children from a supremely addictive product that can twist their sexuality?

Happily, there are perfectly constitutional ways to at least limit access. Reno v. ACLU, the 1997 Supreme Court decision that deregulated Internet smut, was decided on narrow, outdated grounds. Justice John Paul Stevens held that Internet porn doesn't fall under existing law allowing government regulation, because "the Internet is not as 'invasive' as radio and television."

LOL, as the kids say.

Terry Schilling of the American Principles Project notes that the Supremes "did not strike down all obscenity laws in Reno v. ACLU." Nor did they "overturn existing precedent recognizing the government's interest in defending minors from both obscene and non-obscene 'indecent' material."

Which means it's still possible to restrict [15] access. Schilling suggests requiring Internet service providers to create opt-in systems, whereby the default version of the Web is porn-free, with adults permitted to request the unfiltered version. Another possibility: corralling all porn into an adult "zone" that requires age verification to enter, while banning it everywhere else.

Would any of this flout constitutional "originalism"? "Real originalists," as Harvard Law School's Adrian Vermeule quipped recently, "uphold obscenity convictions under the common-law rule," the broad definition that prevailed for most of the nation's history: Obscenity is any material with a tendency to "deprave and corrupt the morals of those whose minds are open to such influence."

PornHub would most definitely count. Indeed, the Founding generation would likely have reacted to it not with high-libertarian nostrums, but with tar and feathers.

Topics for Critical Thinking and Writing

1. From what you can tell by just previewing and skimming, what is Sohrab Ahmari's perspective regarding pornography?

2. What assumptions does Ahmari reveal through patterns in language and tone?

3. Identify two key points in Ahmari's argument and provide a counterpoint. (You do not have to agree with the counterpoint you raise).

4. Compare the ideas of Susan Jacoby and Sohrab Ahmari, and write two or three paragraphs in which you consider free speech and its limits in relation to pornography (or any sensitive content). Use one source for supporting evidence and the other source as a counterpoint.

SUZANNE NOSSEL

Suzanne Nossel, a graduate of Harvard Law School, is a leading voice on issues related to freedom of expression. She has held executive roles in Amnesty International USA and Human Rights Watch and is currently the chief executive officer of PEN America, a leading human rights advocacy group. Nossel's writing has appeared in several prominent newspapers and in scholarly journals such as *Foreign Affairs*, *Dissent*, and *Democracy*. She is a feature columnist for *Foreign Policy* magazine, where this essay first appeared in October 2017.

The Pro–Free Speech Way to Fight Fake News

After the gunfire ended, false claims that the Las Vegas carnage was the work of Islamic State terrorists or left-leaning Donald Trump opponents flooded Facebook pages, YouTube searches, and news feeds. Again, we saw how so-called "fake news" can fuel chaos and stoke hatred. Like most fraudulent news, those deceptive articles are protected speech under the First Amendment and international free expression safeguards. Unless they cross specific legal red lines — such as those barring defamation or libel — fake news stories are not illegal, and our government does not have the power to prohibit or censor them.

But the fact that fake news is free speech does not nullify the danger it poses for open discourse, freedom of opinion, or democratic governance. The rise of fraudulent news and the related erosion of public trust in mainstream journalism pose a looming crisis for free expression. Usually, free expression advocacy centers on the defense of contested speech from efforts at suppression, but it also demands steps to fortify the open and reasoned debate that underpins the value of free speech in our society and our lives. The championing of free speech must not privilege any immutable notion of the truth to the exclusion of others. But this doesn't mean that free speech proponents should be indifferent to the quest for truth, or to attempts to deliberately undermine the public's ability to distinguish fact from falsehood.

Both the First Amendment and international law define free speech to include the right to receive and impart information. The power of free speech is inextricably tied to the opportunity to be heard and believed, and to persuade. Fake news undermines precisely these sources of power. If public discourse becomes so flooded with disinformation that listeners can no longer distinguish signal from noise, they will tune out. Autocrats know this well and thus tightly control the flow of information. They purvey falsehoods to mislead, confuse, and — ultimately — to instill a sense of the futility of speech that saps the will to cry foul, protest, or resist. On social media, the problem is not one of control, but of chaos. The ferocious pace with which false information can spread can make defending the truth or correcting the record seem like mission impossible, or an invitation to opponents to double down in spreading deceit.

The problem of fraudulent news right now is compounded by social and political divisions that undercut the traditional ways in which truth ordinarily prevails. Investigations, exposés, and studies fall short in a situation where a significant portion of the population distrusts a wide array of sources they perceive as politically or ideologically hostile — including sources that traditionally commanded broad if not universal respect.

The debate over solutions to fraudulent 5 news has centered on what the government, news outlets, social media platforms, and civil society actors like fact-checking groups can do. Each has an important role to play, but they also must respect sharp limits to their interventions. Of course, no president should

routinely denigrate legitimate news that he dislikes — as Donald Trump continually does. But Trump's misuse of his authority merely reminds us that it's for good reasons that the Constitution forbids the government from adjudicating which news is true and which is false. Google and Facebook, as private platforms, should monitor their sites to make sure that dangerous conspiracy theories don't go viral — but if they over-police what appears on their pages, they'll create new impairments for edgy speech. Certainly, news outlets should strive to uphold professional and ethical standards, but they alone can't convince cynical readers to trust them. Similarly, those who believe fake news tend to distrust the fact-checking outlets that try to tell them the stories are bogus.

Ultimately, the power of fake news is in the minds of the beholders — namely, news consumers. We need a news consumers' equivalent of the venerable Consumers Union that, starting in the 1930s, mobilized millions behind taking an informed approach to purchases, or the more recent drive to empower individuals to take charge of their health by reading labels, counting steps, and getting tested for risk factors.

When there were only a few dishwashers to choose from, buyers didn't need *Consumer Reports* to sort through their features and flaws. But when the appliance shopper began to face information overload, trusted arbiters were established to help them sort out the good from the bad. In decades past, news consumption centered on newspapers, magazines, and network shows that had undergone layers of editing and fact-checking. Most consumers saw little necessity to educate themselves about the political leanings of media owners, modes of attribution for quotes, journalistic sourcing protocols, the meaning of datelines, or other indicators of veracity.

Now, with the proliferation of overtly partisan media, lower barriers to entry into public discourse, and information flooding across the web and cable news, consumers need new tools to sort through choices and make informed decisions about where to invest their attention and trust. The fight against fake news will hinge not on inculcating trust in specific sources of authority but on instilling skepticism, curiosity, and a sense of agency among consumers, who are the best bulwark against the merchants of deceit.

A news consumers' movement should include several prongs, building on PEN America's newly released "News Consumers Bill of Rights and Responsibilities" from its new report, "Faking News: Fraudulent News and the Fight for Truth." The movement should furnish credible information to help consumers weigh the reliability of varied news sources. It should include an advocacy arm to prod newsrooms, internet platforms, and social media giants into being transparent about their decisions as to what news is elevated and how it is marked. This movement should advance news literacy curricula in schools and equip the next generation to navigate the information ocean they were born into. It should conduct outreach to diverse constituencies and strive continually to avoid ideological bias. It should develop an investigative research arm to expose, name, and shame the purveyors of fraudulent news and their financial backers. And it might provide periodic ranking of, and reporting on, newsrooms and other outlets to hold them accountable to their audiences. The movement should also mobilize the public to become good news consumers by encouraging them to apply a critical eye to news sources, favor those that are trustworthy, validate reports before sharing them on social media, and report errors when they see them.

Recognizing fraudulent news as a threat to 10 free expression cannot be grounds to justify a cure — in the form of new government or corporate restrictions on speech — that may end up being worse than the disease. Unscrupulous profiteers and political opportunists may never cease in their efforts to infect the global information flow of information to serve their purposes. The best prescription against the epidemic of fake news is to inoculate consumers by building up their ability to defend themselves.

Topics for Critical Thinking and Writing

1. What problem does Suzanne Nossel identify for free speech advocates in paragraph 2? Why do you think she believes that free speech advocates should defend fake news despite its potential to spread falsehoods?

2. In paragraph 3, Nossel writes, "The power of free speech is inextricably tied to the opportunity to be heard and believed, and to persuade." Explain why Nossel believes it is reasonable to support the production of fake news and at the same time to fight against it.

3. What news sources do you rely upon, and why do you see them as credible and trustworthy? Trace your news sources and evaluate each of them. What criteria do they have to meet for you to trust them?

Assignment for Critical Summary

Write a critical summary of an essay you have read in this book. In a critical summary, you are relating the argument, but along the way also adding your opinion and perspective, commenting on the quality of evidence, pointing out where the argument succeeds and fails, and asking further questions.

Use the moves in the following list to guide your summary, and refer to the Visual Guide: Writing a Critical Summary on page 61. You can combine some of these moves into one sentence, reorder information, provide quotations, and begin problematizing at any point by inserting your position through careful use of words and phrases, adding an evaluative sentence of your own, or providing commentary on a quote or paraphrase from the essay.

- **Introduce:** Provide the author and title and contextualize the information.
- **Explain:** Identify and describe the thesis and argument.
- **Exemplify:** Provide some of the author's original evidence.
- **Problematize:** Pose critical questions or provide an evaluation of the argument.
- **Extend:** Ask further questions or apply, test, or consider the argument in ways that support your evaluation of it.

For more on writing a critical summary, see the following sections in Chapter 2: "Summarizing and Paraphrasing" (p. 51), "Patchwriting and Plagiarism" (p. 54), and A Checklist for a Summary (p. 65).

3

Understanding Rhetorical Appeals

If we take something to be the truth, we may cling to it so much that when the truth comes and knocks at our door, we won't want to let it in.
— THICH NHAT HANH

CONSIDER THIS

Imagine you are renting your home from a landlord whose policy is not to allow pets, but you would like to request an exception. Using the template letter below, choose a word to fill in each blank. (Feel free to work with a partner and have some fun!)

Dear Landlord,

We know you are a _____ [**adjective**] kind of person who takes seriously the care and maintenance of your _____ [**real estate type**]. We know our lease does not allow _____ [**animal (plural)**], _____ [**animal (plural)**], or other similar animals, but if you could make an exception to your _____ [**adjective**] rule, we would be _____ [**positive emotion**] and ready to work with you. Truth is, we really want to adopt a _____ [**animal**]. We have written you _____ [**number**] times in the past asking for things. We were _____ [**adverb**] excited about getting a _____ [**noun**] statue for the lawn. But since you would not allow it, would you be so _____ [**adjective**] as to approve this _____ [**adjective**] request?

Sincerely,

Your _____ [**adjective**] tenants

No doubt you are familiar with this kind of word game. The goal is humor and fun with words, of course. But we wish to make a more serious point about language, especially the word choices and tone you use when constructing an argument: **Thirteen words**, just over ten percent of the message, make all the difference in the effectiveness of your persuasive appeal.

If you were to write this letter to your landlord seriously, making the passage as effective as you can to craft a serious request, which words would you choose?

Argument and Persuasion

It is useful to distinguish between **persuasion** and **argument**. Persuasion has the broader meaning. To persuade is to convince someone else to accept or adopt your position. To be persuasive does not necessarily mean your argument is sound. Persuasion can be accomplished

- by giving reasons (i.e., by argument, by logic);
- by appealing to the emotions; or
- by bullying, lying to, or threatening someone.

Begging and crying can be persuasive, too — ask any parent of a toddler — but does not constitute an argument. ("Tears are not arguments," the Brazilian writer Machado de Assis said.) You can also lie, cajole, bribe, flatter, or otherwise manipulate people to believe your claims or do what you ask, but these are the most rudimentary instruments of persuasion and they do not constitute arguments.

Arguments, then, represent a form of persuasion, but a special, sophisticated one: a form that elevates the cognitive capacity to reason about the truth. Put it this way: The goal of *argument* is to convince you to think something, or act in a certain way, by demonstrating that the assertions are rational and justifiably supported by reason and evidence, whereas the goal of *persuasion* is to convince you by any means whatsoever. So we may say: *All arguments are forms of persuasion, but not all forms of persuasion are arguments.*

It is important to learn about arguments and other forms of persuasion because we are surrounded by them. Open a magazine, news app, or social media feed, or turn on a television, and you will encounter arguments on all manner of subjects. Myriad voices call for your attention, laying out their cases for how you should think about various issues, how you should interpret events, how you should use your time, money, energy, and power. Some headlines are political ("Why the US Needs a New Political Party"), some are social ("Fast Fashion Is an Environmental Disaster"), some are about art ("Should Gaugin Be Canceled?"), and some are about history ("What Went Wrong in Vietnam"). Some are about economics, health, religion, and morality. Some are about practical matters, and some are quite personal and intimate. There are few issues that lie outside the purview of arguments.

Since we discover knowledge and seek direction by engaging with arguments, it is imperative that we understand how to evaluate and judge them, so we can decide whether to accept them (or parts of them), reject them (or parts of them), or compose our own arguments. Learning about arguments is not only useful because you develop the ability to make good decisions and good arguments yourself; it is also a matter of social responsibility and ethics because it prepares you to be a critical consumer of information and a fair-minded citizen.

Persuasive Appeals

Understanding arguments begins with understanding the different ways they persuade an audience and combine different elements to form a fully coherent and convincing whole. When the Greek philosopher Aristotle, in *Rhetoric*, named the three main appeals arguments make — *logos*, *ethos*, and *pathos* — he referred to them as *pistis*, or proofs. In Greek mythology, Pistis was a spirit personifying trust, faith, and reliability. (Her Roman equivalent was Fides, from which we get the English word "fidelity.") Scholars working in the areas of classical rhetoric continue to use the Greek words *logos*, *ethos*, and *pathos* to talk about the ways writers (or speakers, artists, advertisers, etc.) persuade their audiences to accept their arguments. While these three appeals frequently work together in arguments, we can examine them separately.

Logos, the root word for *logic* (originally meaning "word" or "reason"), distinguishes arguments from merely persuasive speech and writing. Appeals to *logos* in an argument include any of the ways a speaker or writer calls upon an audience's higher faculties of reason. They may use such things as

- information (evidence, data, facts);
- testimony (of experts, authorities, respected persons);
- common sense (principles, practical truths, accepted definitions); and
- probability (calculations, likelihoods, cause-and-effect relationships).

Without *logos*, you cannot truly define something as an argument. It represents the reasoned discourse that is occurring, the intellectual elements. But *logos* is not the whole story.

For *logos* to operate in a reliable way, arguments must also have **ethos**. *Ethos*, the Greek word for "character" and the root word of "ethics," is what Aristotle called "the speaker's personal character when the speech is so spoken as to make us think him credible" (*Rhetoric* 1.2.1356a.4–15). Aristotle emphasized the importance of demonstrating to the audience that the speaker is a person of authority, good sense, and moral integrity. Rhetoricians have developed various ways to speak of how *ethos*, or trustworthiness, is conveyed today in mass media. For example, speakers and writers may convey *ethos* by

- signaling their authority and credibility (e.g., their expertise, credentials, or experience);
- presenting information honestly and accurately (e.g., their data and evidence);
- showing fair- and open-mindedness (e.g., their willingness to grant contrary points); or
- using language appropriately to the audience (e.g., their register, form, tone, style, speech).

Ethos tells listeners or readers essentially *why* they should listen to a particular person and their argument. If a speaker or writer is not trustworthy or not qualified to speak on a subject, audiences must take what they hear with a grain of salt, even granting those people the chance to gain their trust by proving themselves worthy of the subject. In short, speakers and writers concerned with *ethos* employ devices that indicate to their audiences that they are reliable, intelligent persons in whom confidence can be placed.

THINKING CRITICALLY *Identifying* Ethos

For each method listed, locate a sentence in one of the readings in this book. Provide a quotation that shows the author establishing *ethos*.

METHOD	EXAMPLES	YOUR TURN
Use personal experience or credentials to establish authority.	"As a student who works and attends school full-time, I can speak firsthand about . . ."	
Acknowledge weaknesses, exceptions, and complexities.	"Although I have shown that *X* is important, investigation into *Y* is also necessary to truly understand . . ." "Understandably, my solution may be seen as too simple or reductive, but it may work as a starting point for . . ."	
Mention the qualifications of any sources as a way to boost your own credibility.	"According to *X*, author and noted professor of *Y* at *Z* University, . . ."	

The third appeal of argument for Aristotle is **pathos**, Greek for "feeling" and the root word of "empathy," "sympathy," and "compassion." Rhetoricians use the word *pathos* to describe the ways in which arguments appeal to the audience's feelings or passions. Writers may call upon any number of basic emotions in attempting to persuade, such as anger, fear, pity, or envy, or else they may appeal to more idealistic feelings about honor, duty, family, or patriotism.

In critically thinking *about* arguments, we may be tempted to privilege the mind (*logos*) over the heart (*pathos*), but we must also note that emotions inform ideas and decision-making in important ways. While it is true that appealing *only* to passionate feelings in arguments can be misguided and even dangerous, without any feelings at all the coldly rational logos can usurp our decision-making and lead us to ignore obvious human needs and emotions. All of this is to say that we may not want to be as coldly rational as Dr. Spock of *Star Trek* fame ("But, Jim, it's not logical"), but at the same time we also do not want to be swept up in emotions and forget to think rationally. That's how people end up buying things they can't afford, or don't really need, and it is also how everyday disagreements (as well as national debates) can quickly become polarized and reductive.

We've already established that *logos* — the facts, evidence, and reasoning of an argument — distinguishes arguments from mere persuasion. Yet, if you think about it, the

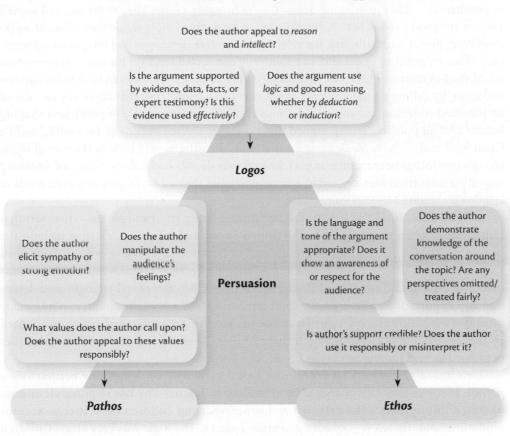

Visual Guide: Evaluating Persuasive Appeals

Does the author appeal to *reason* and *intellect*?

Is the argument supported by evidence, data, facts, or expert testimony? Is this evidence used *effectively*?

Does the argument use *logic* and good reasoning, whether by *deduction* or *induction*?

Logos

Does the author elicit sympathy or strong emotion?

Does the author manipulate the audience's feelings?

Persuasion

Is the language and tone of the argument appropriate? Does it show an awareness of or respect for the audience?

Does the author demonstrate knowledge of the conversation around the topic? Are any perspectives omitted/ treated fairly?

What values does the author call upon? Does the author appeal to these values responsibly?

Is author's support credible? Does the author use it responsibly or misinterpret it?

Pathos

Ethos

other two dimensions of argument, *ethos* and *pathos*, are meaningless without a strong element of *logos*. A well-qualified authority with strong *ethos* may not have reliable information available, or may lie, misdirect, or manipulate evidence. And a pie-in-the-sky activist with strong *pathos* can let passionate ideals obscure practical realities. Yet we do not agree with Stephen D. Levitt, author of *Freakonomics*, that "emotion is the enemy of rational argument" — that good arguments must appeal primarily to reason and never to emotion. We do not agree that reliable people *always* make good arguments, or that unreliable people can *never* make good arguments. Good arguments always depend upon a *balance* of *logos*, *ethos*, and *pathos*.

Seeing the Appeals in Real-World Events

Donald Trump announced his bid for the US Presidency in 2015 by holding a press conference in which he famously descended a golden escalator and promised to staunch the flow of immigrants — legal and illegal — into the United States at the Mexican border. "When Mexico sends its people, they're not sending the best," he said. "They're sending people that have lots of problems. . . . They're bringing drugs, they're bringing crime. They're rapists, and some I assume are good people, but . . . [that's] what we're getting." Now we do have *ethos* at work: Projecting power and authority, the celebrity real-estate developer had long been a prominent voice on political issues and was politically connected (and yet his fiery rhetoric often established or damaged his *ethos*, depending on the audience). *Pathos* ran high in his appearance, too: By calling on nativist fears of outsiders and crime, concerns about the erosion of an idealized America, and common feelings about the incompetence of politicians shaping border control policies, Trump argued that if he were elected president, he would "build a Great Wall and . . . have Mexico pay for that wall." He offered very little in the way of *logos*, though two things bear mentioning: a) the previous decade had witnessed record-breaking migration rates from Mexico, and b) a range of studies showed no disproportionate levels of criminality among Mexican immigrants.

Nevertheless, Trump was able — largely through using *ethos* and *pathos* — to assert that immigration was a major threat to the United States, and it became a wedge issue in the run-up to the 2016 election, which Trump won. In the weeks after taking office, he signed an Executive Order, "Border Security and Immigration Enforcement Improvements," which dramatically expanded Customs and Border Protection (CBP) forces and strengthened detention and deportation policies on the southern border and across the country. While many measures were controversial, none was more so than the "zero tolerance" policy announced by the Department of Homeland Security in April 2018, which included separating families of undocumented immigrants at the US–Mexico border.

Two broad arguments emerged, one based primarily on *logos*, one primarily on *pathos*. Many conservatives argued by appealing to reason: The law requires all undocumented immigrants to be detained and processed, and children need special accommodations and, therefore, separate detention centers. The logic was very clear: Children cannot be incarcerated among adult populations. Homeland Security Director Kirstjen Neilsen told Congress, "[W]hen we separate, we separate because the law tells us to." Attorney General Jeff Sessions sent a public message to would-be asylum-seekers: "If you smuggle a child, then we will prosecute you, and that child will be separated from you as required by law."

By June 2018, more than 2,000 children had been detained by CBP, with many held in temporary camps constructed with chain link fences resembling cages along the

John Moore/Getty Images News/Getty Images

Images of children held in detention centers, such as this one from 2014, appealed to the emotions of Americans in 2018. What aspects of this photograph make it particularly convincing as an appeal to emotions and values?

border. Heart-rending images of frightened and incarcerated children helped liberals argue against the family separation policy by appealing primarily to compassion — *pathos* — in order to inspire public outcry. In response, just over a month after the policy was enacted, President Trump signed another executive order stopping the practice of separating families at the border. In short, emotion won the day over reason — yet we cannot say that *pathos* led Americans astray. Here is a case in which *pathos* came to matter more than the pure *logic* which says, "Crossing the border illegally is a crime, and if you are arrested for that crime with children in your custody, then the state will take custody of your children pending your trial."

Emotions can guide us toward wise choices because emotions are often closely connected to values, ideals, morals, ethics, and principles. It is true that feelings can impassion us to make rash decisions, but they can also inspire bold ones. And reason, a powerful tool of the intellect, can just as soon lead us toward the dark rather than the light. As the poet Emily Dickinson wrote, "Much madness is divinest sense / To a discerning eye / Much sense the starkest madness." To conduct our lives strictly according to pure reason *or* pure feeling would lead, we think, to an intolerable existence in either case. We rely upon both of these faculties, and we need both kinds of appeals.

> **WRITING TIP**
> An argument doesn't require two opposing positions. Even when writing only for oneself, if you are setting forth reasons and justifications for an idea, the result is an argument.

In the case of child separation arguments, *logos* and *pathos* were placed in stark contrast. There appeared to be a fairly clear choice between following reason or following feeling. But most arguments do not divide easily along the lines of *logos* and *pathos* (or *ethos*). Each of the three appeals must be considered relationally, in terms of how they work together and inform each other. Of course, arguments *may* put reason and passion in opposition, but it is not a requirement that they do so, nor that they contain any special degrees of *logos*, *pathos*, or *ethos*.

Furthermore, an argument does not require two voices going back and forth, in the popular sense of an argument being a dispute between two people. The Declaration of Independence is fundamentally an argument: It represents a claim made by various, well-respected colonial leaders (*ethos*) who grounded their position in reason (*logos*): "The history of the present King of Great Britain is a history of repeated injuries and usurpations, all having in direct object the establishment of an absolute Tyranny over these States." This was their claim. "To prove this," they wrote, "let Facts be submitted to a candid world." This was their appeal to *logos*. They then enumerated the misdeeds of King George III, but they did so in powerful language ("he refused," "he neglected,") and also appealed to the emotionally stirring concepts of "Life, Liberty and the Pursuit of Happiness" (*pathos*). All parts of an argument are present.

But arguments are made not just by leaders and influencers, whether of the colonial period or of today's social media, but by all people all the time. Even everyday arguments utilize the three appeals to *logos*, *pathos*, and *ethos*. If you were explaining to your loved ones why you are changing your major, you might remind them that you are a careful and thoughtful decision-maker (*ethos*, establishing your credibility); and you might supply reasons and justifications for your decision (*logos*, perhaps showing statistics about income potential and job prospects); and, while presenting the case, you might also appeal to their beliefs about the importance of being happy with one's learning pathway (*pathos*, the emotional persuasion that casts the information in light of their feelings about what makes for individual happiness). Thus, your argument is a *rational* argument, grounded in your good character and reliable facts, but it also uses forms of emotional persuasion to convince your loved ones that you are making the right choice.

UNETHICAL USES OF RHETORICAL APPEALS

We want to make this key point, one that we feel is vital in a world where various forces of persuasion seek to influence your beliefs, decisions, and actions: Each kind of appeal — *logos*, *ethos*, and *pathos* — can be misused, deployed as strategies to convince you to adopt extreme positions, make irrational choices, or take ill-advised actions, despite the facts and without good reasoning.

How might this occur? Consider *logos* — the facts, data, testimony, and reasoning that underpin logical deduction. If information is presented strategically to ensure a particular outcome, it is partly a reflection of poor *ethos*, or good character, but it also represents a manipulated appeal to reason. Asking someone to reason about your information without supplying all the facts or evidence required to make a good decision pushes people to make irrational choices. The facts provided are leading them to believe that something is true when it is not.

Consider the popular slogan for the Powerball lottery: "You can't win if you don't play." Technically, that's true. But is buying a Powerball ticket a rational decision? Well, you have a 1 in 292 million chance of selecting the matching numbers, which translates to a 99.9999997 percent chance of losing. Those inconvenient facts are not mentioned in the slogan (which also contains a dimension of *pathos*; after all, it's the *desire* to get rich that they really hope guides your decision to play). As Ron Wasserstein, the Executive Director of the American Statistical Association, put it, your chances of winning the Powerball are "unimaginably, ridiculously, impossibly small." Nevertheless, the reasoning is correct: *You can't win if you don't play*. However, the appeal to reason is not entirely honest or rational: The facts actually say *you are virtually guaranteed to lose*. If you bought one Powerball ticket per day every day of your life, your odds of winning would reach 1:1 as you approached 799,500 years old.

Advertisement for a 2019 Powerball jackpot drawing for an estimated $750 million, one of the largest in US history. The odds of winning were 1 in 292 million, but Manuel Franco of Wisconsin won the jackpot.

Joe Raedle/Getty Images

Can appeals to credibility, trustworthiness, and authority be manipulated? Of course. Have you ever received in the mail an advertisement or a fundraising request that appears to be written longhand in ink, but upon closer inspection you find it is actually printed by machine? How about a mass-produced email request that casually calls you by your first name? These are modes of establishing *ethos* intended to impress upon you that the sender is an individual or even a friend who cares about you. How about when an actor on television wears scrubs and asks you to use a certain medicine — projecting the authority of a doctor without the credentials? Each of these examples involves an appeal, however weak, to *ethos*.

But witness the case of Elizabeth Holmes, whom *Forbes* magazine called "the world's youngest self-made female billionaire." Her *ethos* seemed to be sparkling: a highly educated scientist with a track record of inventing new and more efficient medical devices. In 2015 she started a company, Theranos, which claimed to have invented technology that could detect serious diseases such as diabetes and cancer with a quick and simple blood test requiring no needles. The problem was that the technology did not work at all, although Holmes represented the data as if it did work and managed to raise billions of dollars for the now-defunct company. As of 2022, she was convicted of four cases related to wire fraud and faces twenty years in prison. Using her credentials and authority, she was able convince investors that her *logos* was sound.

Another kind of false appeal to credibility comes to us through the "halo effect," which can help people express authority or legitimacy through mere proximity to a credible and trusted source. Metaphorically, a person seeking trust or respect positions themselves in the "glow" surrounding someone or something else. Maybe a person prefaces their opinion on global warming by saying, "My brother is a climate scientist." We may be more apt to listen, but just because someone's brother is a climate scientist doesn't mean their ideas about the environment are necessarily better informed than the next person's. We can see the halo effect too when, for example, a political candidate surrounds himself with uniformed police officers during a press conference to suggest the unanimous support for his policies by the law enforcement community, even though his policies may not be endorsed by everyone in that community. The halo effect operates just about everywhere, from public culture to your own workplace. Another good example is name-dropping, or referring to a respected person casually or by their first name (or their nickname) only in order to suggest their friendship and like-mindedness, is a common way people attempt to demonstrate *ethos*. ("Yes, I am heading to lunch with George and Brad — *you* may know them as George Clooney and Brad Pitt.") We see it when we encounter photographs of famous people on the walls of a restaurant (suggesting that if celebrities dine there, it must be worth it for you, too). In other words, the halo effect occurs whenever someone emphasizes their own association with another person (or institution), without reference to the quality or strength of the association, or when the association itself is irrelevant to the subject or issue a hand. (You might be a wealthy person with wealthy friends and the outward signs of financial success all around you, but that doesn't mean you are qualified to give financial advice.)

Aristotle said, "[T]he judgements we deliver are not the same when we are influenced by joy or sorrow, love or hate." An emotional appeal may be considered unethical when it overwhelms the audience with emotion and does not provide them the supporting information to rationally think through an issue. Credit card advertisements are keen to show you all the luxurious goods you can buy — without mentioning the problems that arise from taking on too much debt. Other advertisements appeal to your sense of nostalgia for childhood, or for better times gone by, or for the authenticity of country life or farm life (which may have never really existed) — such as when large agricultural producers romanticize their products by showing you happy cows being hand-milked on idyllic farms, instead of crammed pens with thousands of cows connected to milk extraction machines.

ARE SUCH APPEALS ALWAYS UNETHICAL?

The kinds of unethical appeals we point to in the previous section do not imply a necessary correlation to reality, and they may steer you away from facts and reason. Yet, as we noted, "You can't win if you don't play" is technically true, not a fallacy or an invalid argument (see Chapter 4 for more on validity and Chapter 10 for more on fallacies). A person whose brother is a climate scientist may very well know quite a bit about environmental issues. And it may very well be true what Elizabeth Holmes's lawyers appealed to a jury — that they should have sympathy for her because when she fooled investors she was in an abusive relationship and mentally impaired. We must make take every case in context with the situation at hand, and use our reason and judge such appeals accordingly.

Our overall point is that weak or irrational appeals are not *necessarily* unethical. One might call it manipulative when a person mentions the esteemed college they attended before speaking on an issue ("Well, I went to Harvard, so . . ."), or hangs a picture behind their desk of themselves with a powerful political leader, but these actions may be more or less harmless in any given situation, and at best may be perhaps substantial. When such appeals heighten the impact of the facts, driving the facts home to the audience rather than simply letting them speak for themselves, they cannot be called unethical. If, when arguing for reforms that would discourage racial bias in law enforcement, a social activist showed a painful montage depicting violence against Black people at the hands of police, it cannot be called a devious strategy to convince the audience by appealing to powerful emotions, even though it could be reasonably argued that the montage does not and cannot tell the whole truth about police officers or the challenges they face. The emotional impact in some cases is an important element of the argument.

Nonrational Appeals: Satire, Irony, Sarcasm

One form of nonrational but sometimes highly effective persuasion is **satire** — that is, witty ridicule. A cartoonist or an actor may persuade viewers that a politician's views are unsound by presenting a grotesquely distorted caricature of their physical appearance, or by a funny if exaggerated (and probably unfair) portrait of how they interact with people. The trick is that the unfairness is presented in a such an over-the-top way that its distortions of reality are understood to be comic (if not always funny) and to have a point.

While satiric artists often use caricature, satiric writers also often seek to persuade by means of ridicule through the use of **verbal irony**. This sort of irony contrasts what is said and what is meant. For instance, when in 1903 W. E. B. Du Bois mocked the accommodationist Black reformer Booker T. Washington for his popular "Atlanta Compromise," calling him "certainly the most distinguished Southerner since Jefferson Davis," he didn't mean to literally equate the well-meaning Washington with the President of the former Confederacy.

How does this mural by street artist Banksy use irony?

Instead, he was making an ironic criticism of how much Washington's ideas proved attractive to white agricultural interests in the South.

Occasionally, words of modesty may actually imply superiority ("Of course, I'm too dumb to understand this problem"), and words of flattery may be barbed criticisms ("You're a real comedian," says someone who doesn't think you're funny at all). Such language is **sarcasm**. It is nonrational but it does the job in affirming the opposite meaning.

Although satire, irony, and sarcasm are not forms of reasoning, passages of humorous ridicule do sometimes appear in otherwise serious argumentative writing (as with W.E.B. Du Bois). Such passages are effective in making a point. The key to using humor in an argument is, on the one hand, to avoid wisecracking or taking cheap shots and, on the other hand, to avoid overdone clownishness. In other words, if you get too acerbic, or outright insulting — or just too silly or cringey — you may damage your *ethos* and alienate your audience rather than invite them to think alongside you.

LEARNING FROM SHAKESPEARE   True, appeals to emotion may distract from the facts of the case; they may blind the audience by, in effect, throwing dust in its eyes or by provoking tears. A classic example occurs in Shakespeare's *Julius Caesar*, when Marc Antony addresses the Roman populace after Brutus, Cassius, and Casca have conspired to assassinate Caesar. The real issue is whether Caesar was becoming tyrannical (as the assassins claim). Antony turns from the evidence and stirs the crowd against the assassins by appealing to its emotions.

Shakespeare drew from an ancient Roman biographical writing, Plutarch's *Lives of the Noble Grecians and Romans*. Plutarch says this about Antony:

> [P]erceiving that his words moved the common people to compassion, . . . [he] framed his eloquence to make their hearts yearn [i.e., grieve] the more, and, taking Caesar's gown all bloody in his hand, he laid it open to the sight of them all, showing what a number of cuts and holes it had upon it. Therewithal the people fell presently into such a rage and mutiny that there was no more order kept.

Here's how Shakespeare reinterpreted the event in his play:

> Friends, Romans, countrymen, lend me your ears;
> I come to bury Caesar, not to praise him.

After briefly offering insubstantial evidence that Caesar gave no signs of behaving tyrannically (e.g., "When that the poor have cried, Caesar hath wept"), Antony begins to play directly on his hearers' emotions. Descending from the platform so that he may be in closer contact with his audience (like a modern politician, he wants to work the crowd), he calls attention to Caesar's bloody toga:

> If you have tears, prepare to shed them now.
> You all do know this mantle; I remember
> The first time ever Caesar put it on:
> 'Twas on a summer's evening, in his tent,
> That day he overcame the Nervii.
> Look, in this place ran Cassius' dagger through;
> See what a rent the envious Casca made;
> Through this, the well-belovèd Brutus stabbed . . .

In these few lines, Antony accomplishes the following:

- He prepares the audience by suggesting to them how they should respond ("If you have tears, prepare to shed them now").
- He flatters them by implying that they, like Antony, were intimates of Caesar (he credits them with being familiar with Caesar's garment).
- He then evokes a personal memory of a specific time ("a summer's evening") — the day that Caesar won a battle against the Nervii, a particularly fierce tribe in what is now France. (In fact, Antony was not at the battle and did not join Caesar until three years later.)

Antony doesn't mind being free with the facts; his point here is not to set the record straight but to stir people against the assassins. He goes on, daringly but successfully, to identify one particular slit in the garment with Cassius's dagger, another with Casca's, and a third with Brutus's. Antony cannot know which dagger made which slit, but his rhetorical trick works.

Notice, too, that Antony arranges the three assassins in climactic order, since Brutus (Antony claims) was especially beloved by Caesar:

Judge, O you gods, how dearly Caesar loved him!
This was the most unkindest cut of all;
For when the noble Caesar saw him stab,
Ingratitude, more strong than traitor's arms,
Quite vanquished him. Then burst his mighty heart.

Nice. According to Antony, the noble-minded Caesar — Antony's words have erased all thought of the tyrannical Caesar — died not from wounds inflicted by daggers but from the heartbreaking perception of Brutus's ingratitude. Doubtless there wasn't a dry eye in the crowd. Let's all hope that if we are ever put on trial, we'll have a lawyer as skilled in evoking sympathy as Antony.

Does All Communication Contain Arguments?

In a sense, arguments are everywhere, even when we don't expect them. Take the cover of a new bestselling book with its colorful images, exciting plot description, serious profile of the author, and ringing endorsements by other writers. In its totality (with elements of *pathos*, *ethos*, and *logos* present) the cover constitutes an argument that you should read the book — even though the argument isn't spelled out formally. Even the results from an internet search — being the product of algorithms and filters that are built into search engines — are fundamentally an argument about what is important or relevant in the area of your query, and about what you should read.

Even something as mundane as a recipe for cherry pie — of the kind turned up by an internet search — reveals its own type of argument. The lead-in reads:

As a busy Mom, I love easy and pleasing desserts. Because this pie can be made quickly using canned cherries that are delicious and always available, you should give it a try. It will surely become one of your favorite go-to desserts.

Clearly, such writing does not require a preponderance of facts and data, counterarguments and rebuttals, or much logic and reasoning, but it *is* technically an argument — an argument that you should try making a pie with canned cherries in order to save time. *Ethos* is established by the mom. We can identify a claim (the pie will become one of your favorite "go-to" desserts). And we can count two reasons in support of the claim: A) It can be made quickly; and B) Canned cherries can always be kept on hand. It also has a smidgen of emotional appeal as well, mentioning how time-saving and delicious canned cherries are. And we can imagine a counterargument *against* canned cherries:

> Using fresh cherries means you will have to pit them yourself and cook them down, but an extra couple of minutes is worth the time. Fresh cherries naturally sweetened with sugar are healthier, more flavorful, and have a more classic, traditional homemade texture than canned cherries. Once you have prepared a pie using your fresh cherries, you will never go back to canned.

Although the subject is hardly very compelling, the presence of claims, reasons, and evidence is clear. That makes it an argument, and that's our point. You can even detect appeals to emotion, rousing our appetites not only for "delicious" pie but also for our sense of the natural, domestic authenticity of "homemade" cherry pie, and preserving (pun *intended*) culinary traditions.

In short, whether you are gathering information on the most pressing issues of the times, or whether you are considering making a dessert, almost all ideas that you encounter constitute some kind of argument, some effort to persuade you to think or act in accordance with the views or intentions of the producer(s) of the message. Because arguments are everywhere, and because many of them address aspects of life that are far more important than which kind of cherry pie you prepare, it is in your best interests — not to mention all of our best interests — to understand how arguments and other forms of persuasion work. As you read the essays in this chapter, keep in mind the appeals to *logos*, *ethos*, and *pathos* in each piece, and how they support (or undermine) the arguments.

THINKING CRITICALLY *Emotional Appeals*

Identify the emotion summoned by the following appeals and explain how the claim may be countered by logic or reason.

EMOTIONAL APPEAL	EMOTION	LOGICAL COUNTER
Football players and other athletes should not be allowed to kneel for the National Anthem to protest police violence because it disrespects the American flag and all those people who died defending it.		
Nowadays, it seems anything goes on television, and even primetime shows feature foul language, sex, and violence. Don't they realize children are watching?		
Back in the 1950s, teenage life was simpler and more innocent. Dating was easier because fewer young people were engaging in premarital sex.		

An Example Argument and a Look at the Writer's Rhetorical Appeals

KWAME ANTHONY APPIAH

Kwame Anthony Appiah (b. 1954) established his reputation as a philosopher at Cornell, Yale, Harvard, Princeton, and New York University. He is a noted cultural theorist, African historian, and novelist decorated with awards and recognitions for more than a dozen books, most recently *As If: Idealization and Ideals* (2017) and *The Lies that Bind: Rethinking Identity* (2018).

Go Ahead, Speak for Yourself

"As a white man," Joe begins, prefacing an insight, revelation, objection or confirmation he's eager to share — but let's stop him right there. Aside from the fact that he's white, and a man, what's his point? What does it signify when people use this now ubiquitous formula ("As a such-and-such, I . . .") to affix an identity to an observation?

Typically, it's an assertion of authority: As a member of this or that social group, I have experiences that lend my remarks special weight. The experiences, being representative of that group, might even qualify me to represent that group. Occasionally, the formula is an avowal of humility. It can be both at once. ("As a working-class woman, I'm struggling to understand Virginia Woolf's blithe assumptions of privilege.") The incantation seems indispensable. But it can also be — to use another much-loved formula — problematic.

The "as a" concept is an inherent feature of identities. For a group label like "white men" to qualify as a social identity, there must be times when the people to whom it applies act as members of that group, and are treated as members of that group. We make lives *as* men and women, *as* blacks and whites, *as* teachers and musicians. Yet the very word "identity" points toward the trouble: It comes from the Latin *idem,* meaning "the same." Because members of a given identity group have experiences that depend on a host of other social factors, they're *not* the same.

Being a black lesbian, for instance, isn't a matter of simply combining African-American, female and homosexual ways of being in the world; identities interact in complex ways. That's why Kimberle Crenshaw, a feminist legal theorist and civil-rights activist, introduced the notion of intersectionality, which stresses the complexity with which different forms of subordination relate to one another. Racism can make white men shrink from black men and abuse black women. Homophobia can lead men in South Africa to rape gay women but murder gay men. Sexism in the United States in the 1950s kept middle-class white women at home and sent working-class black women to work for them.

1 Beginning with "As X person . . ." is a sign of establishing *ethos.*

2 The word choice "incantation" suggests "casting a spell." Over whom? The audience.

3 Appiah includes a key word and a (loose) definition of a concept and cites the authority responsible for the definition.

4 Descriptions conjure stereotypes to appeal to *pathos*.

4 Let's go back to Joe, with his NPR mug and his man bun. (Or are you picturing 5 a "Make America Great Again" tank top and a high-and-tight?) Having an identity doesn't, by itself, authorize you to speak on behalf of everyone of that identity. So it can't really be that he's speaking for all white men. But he can at least speak to what it's like to live as a white man, right?

Not if we take the point about intersectionality. If Joe had grown up in Northern Ireland as a gay white Catholic man, his experiences might be rather different from those of his gay white *Protestant* male friends there — let alone those of his childhood pen pal, a straight, Cincinnati-raised reform Jew. While identity affects your experiences, there's no guarantee that what you've learned from them is going to be the same as what other people of the same identity have learned.

We've been here before. In the academy during the identity-conscious 1980s, many humanists thought that we'd reached peak "as a." Some worried that the locution had devolved into mere prepositional posturing. The literary theorist Barbara Johnson wrote, "If I tried to 'speak as a lesbian,' wouldn't I be processing my understanding of myself through media-induced images of what a lesbian is or through my own idealizations of what a lesbian *should* be?" In the effort to be "real," she saw something fake. Another prominent theorist, Gayatri Chakravorty Spivak, thought that the "as a" move was "a distancing from oneself," whereby the speaker became a self-appointed representative of an abstraction, some generalized perspective, and suppressed the actual multiplicity of her identities. "One is not just one thing," she observed.

5 Paragraph appeals to *logos*. It reasons that speaking "as a" is unstable, abstract, or even derived from the media.

5 It's because we're not just one thing that, in everyday conversation, "as a" can be useful as a way to spotlight some specific feature of who we are. Comedians do a lot of this sort of identity-cuing. In W. Kamau Bell's recent Netflix special, "Private School Negro," the "as a" cue, explicit or implicit, singles out various of his identities over the course of an hour. Sometimes he's speaking as a parent, who has to go camping because his kids enjoy camping. Sometimes he's speaking as an African-American, who, for ancestral reasons, doesn't see the appeal of camping ("sleeping outdoors *on purpose*?"). Sometimes — as in a story about having been asked his weight before boarding a small aircraft — he's speaking as "a man, a heterosexual, cisgender *Dad* man." (Hence: "I have no idea how much I weigh.")

The switch in identities can be the whole point of the joke. Here's Chris Rock, talking about his life in an affluent New Jersey suburb: "As a black man, I'm against the cops, but as a man with property, well, I need the cops. If someone steals some-

6 Funny. Is this *pathos*?

6 thing, I can't call the Crips!" Drawing attention to certain identities you have is often a natural way of drawing attention to the contours of your beliefs, values or concerns.

But *caveat auditor:* Let the listener beware. Representing an identity is usually 10 volunteer work, but sometimes the representative is conjured into being. Years ago, a slightly dotty countess I knew in the Hampstead area of London used to point out a leather-jacketed man on a park bench and inform her companions, with a knowing look, "He's the *head gay*." She was convinced that gays had the equivalent of a pontiff or prime minister who could speak on behalf of all his people.

Because people's experiences vary so much, the "as a" move is always in peril of presumption. When I was a student at the University of Cambridge in the 1970s, gay men were *très chic*: You couldn't have a serious party without some of us scattered around like throw pillows. Do my experiences entitle me to speak for a queer farmworker who is coming of age in Emmett, Idaho? Nobody appointed me head gay.

If someone is advocating policies for gay men to adopt, or for others to adopt toward gay men, what matters, surely, isn't whether the person is gay but whether the policies are sensible. As a gay man, you could oppose same-sex marriage (it's just submitting to our culture's heteronormativity, and anyway monogamy is a patriarchal invention) or advocate same-sex marriage (it's an affirmation of equal dignity and a way to sustain gay couples). Because members of an identity group won't be identical, your "as a" doesn't settle anything. The same holds for religious, vocational and national identities.

And, of course, for racial identities. In the 1990s the black novelist Trey Ellis wrote a screenplay, "The Inkwell," which drew on his childhood in the milieu of the black bourgeoisie. A white studio head (for whom race presumably eclipsed class) gave it to Matty Rich, a young black director who'd grown up in a New York City housing project. Mr. Rich apparently worried that the script wasn't "black enough" and proposed turning the protagonist's father, a schoolteacher, into a garbage man. Suffice to say, it didn't end well. Are we really going to settle these perennial debates over authenticity with a flurry of "as a" arrowheads?

Somehow, we can't stop trying. Ever since Donald Trump eked out his surprising electoral victory, political analysts have been looking for people to speak for the supposedly disgruntled white working-class voters who, switching from their former Democratic allegiances, gave Mr. Trump the edge.

But about a third of working-class whites voted for Hillary Clinton. Nobody explaining why white working-class voters went for Mr. Trump would be speaking for the millions of white working-class voters who didn't. One person could say that she spoke *as* a white working-class woman in explaining why she voted for Mrs. Clinton just as truthfully as her sister could make the claim in explaining her support for Mr. Trump — each teeing us up to think about how her class and race might figure into the story. No harm in that. Neither one, however, could accurately claim to speak *for* the white working class. Neither has an exclusive on being representative.

So we might do well to ease up on "as a" — on the urge to underwrite our observations with our identities. "For me," Professor Spivak once tartly remarked, "the question 'Who should speak' is less crucial than 'Who will listen?'"

But tell that to Joe, as he takes a sip of kombucha — or is it Pabst Blue Ribbon? All right, Joe, let's hear what you've got to say. The speaking-as-a convention isn't going anywhere; in truth, it often serves a purpose. But here's another phrase you might try on for size: "Speaking for myself . . ."

7 A form of trying to establish "credibility," a real-life instance of *ethos*.

8 *Ethos*: In a way he IS using his own sexual orientation to gain credibility in this argument.

9 *Logos* again — sounds reasonable.

10 *Ethos*: Shows open-mindedness. Identity is also never a reason *not* to listen to someone.

Topics for Critical Thinking and Writing

1. In paragraph 2, Kwame Anthony Appiah says that speaking through the lens of an identity group is usually "an assertion of authority." How is this so? In your view, is someone from a particular identity group always more qualified to speak than someone not from the group? Explain.

2. Examine your own identity categories and write about whether or not you feel you have the authority to speak on issues facing those communities, and ways in which you may not. What gives you the authority? What limits your authority?

3. Does Appiah's essay appeal more to *logos*, *ethos*, or *pathos*? How do you know? Was this an effective choice for his audience?

4. Where does Appiah use humor or sarcasm in this essay? Explain how his humor serves to support the argument. Is it the most effective choice for the argument? Why or why not?

Arguments for Analysis

AFRIKA AFENI MILLS

Afrika Afeni Mills is Director of Diversity, Equity, and Inclusion at BetterLesson, an education consulting group. She is a graduate of Boston College's Lynch School of Education, and speaks widely on issues related to schools, teaching, and race. This essay was published in 2021 on the blog *Teaching While White*.

A Letter to White Teachers of My Black Children

Dear White Teachers of My Black Children:

I am a Black mom.

I know it's sometimes hard to decide whether to say Black or African-American. I used to identify as African-American because I loved hearing the reference to my ancestral homeland in my description of myself. But then to say African-American reduces the majestic continent of Africa down to the status of a country. Africa is not a country, and so I now identify as a Black woman. I identify here specifically as a Black mom because I have two children who are now in high school. Raising them to be inquisitive, informed adults with a strong sense of identity and agency is an essential part of my life.

I am also an educator, so I understand the deep importance of guiding and shaping all of our children. I'm also intimately aware of all the cultural complexity surrounding our work. I know, too, that we have a long way to go before we're even close to treating all of our students equitably. This is why I'm writing to you today. I have much to say about what I wish you had been able to do for my children when they were in your elementary and middle school classrooms, and what I hope you will do for all children of color entering your classrooms.

Because I'm an educator, I know well what you — or at least the vast majority of you — learned in your pre-K-12 education and in your teacher-prep program. I also know what you didn't learn. As you grew up, you were most likely taught in school and at home that Abraham Lincoln was the great emancipator, that it was acceptable, right even, to refer to the people of the global majority as minorities, and that communities with higher percentages of Black families are in need of saving.

As a teacher, you most likely did not receive ongoing professional development about race and education in America. You're likely to have a vague understanding about issues of diversity and equity and inclusion with insufficient understanding of culturally responsive teaching and learning. On the other hand, you most likely received extensive training on implementation of state and national education standards, new curricular initiatives, and how to improve standardized test scores. In recent years, you might have received professional development about social emotional learning, but you'll have done so without exploring the critical sociopolitical considerations that are essential to strengthening your ability to teach well across race, class, and gender.

In high school, college, and your teacher-prep program, you no doubt were taught something about race in America, but it's highly unlikely that you learned the truth about Black experience. It's likely, for instance, that you've been taught little to nothing about the pre-enslavement contributions of Black people to the world, the horrors and impact of centuries of enslavement, post "Emancipation" Jim Crow laws and practices, and the many ongoing racially based systemic injustices such as mass incarceration, housing discrimination, wealth disparities, and lack of equal access to quality education, health care, and more.

I didn't learn about these things in school either, but thankfully, my parents made sure I learned about these important aspects of American life and history that are absent from the textbooks and teacher's guides.

Because it's unlikely that you learned about all of these things in school or in your home, it's even more unlikely that you teach about these matters now. I know that those of you who taught my children when they were younger didn't necessarily teach them about these issues. But here's the thing: they truly wanted to hear it from you, too. We have talked extensively about these matters at home, but my children's school experiences would have been far more valuable if you would have introduced them to the lives and works of Ellen and William Craft, Katherine Johnson, Lewis Hayden, Ida B. Wells and Denmark Vesey. They wanted to hear you tell them the truth about The Black Panther Party, the reasons behind the FBI's surveillance of Martin Luther King, Jr., the painful facts about Columbus's experiences in the Americas, and the meaning of Juneteenth. And they didn't want to just hear a few tidbits about these essential and complex aspects of American life in February just because it was Black History Month.

What my children needed from you in school — what all students of color need from you in school — is a much deeper understanding of racial history and ongoing racial matters. If you are to teach them well — teach them as I know you want to teach them — you need deeper cultural knowledge and skills. If, for instance, you teach a social studies unit on immigration and you have your students present about the countries of their ancestors, Black children need you to think more deeply about how this assignment feels for them. One of the many things Black Americans lost as a result of the nation's involvement in enslavement is the knowledge of which

African countries our ancestors came from. Although we now have some helpful information from Ancestry DNA, I, for instance, can't say for sure whether my African ancestors were Nigerian, Senegalese, Ghanaian, Congolese, Beninese, Togolese, Cameroonian, Malian, or from the Ivory Coast. And because we didn't have access to this information when my children were in elementary school, they ended up focusing only on their European heritage because our White ancestors are a lot easier to trace.

This can also be a tough and painful assignment for other students of color as well — especially for First Nations people whose ancestral stories are overlooked by misrepresented in the textbook versions of American history. 10

My guess is that you didn't think about all this in planning the unit. Going forward, I hope you will.

Because you were entrusted to partner with me in the education of my children, I wanted you to be curious about them with the same intensity with which you'd have them stand to pledge allegiance to the flag. I wanted you to wonder how they felt when they saw Mount Rushmore or the face of Andrew Jackson on the twenty-dollar bill they handed you with their field trip permission slip. I wanted you to wonder how they felt in your class after hearing about yet another unarmed Black life erased from this world by police brutality — all because the melanin we see as so beautiful looks like danger to others. Do you know how it felt for my children when you didn't say anything about racial injustices at the time of their occurrences? Do you know how it feels for your Black students today?

If your school is anything like the schools where I taught, you'll be expected to interact with your students' families at open houses, conferences, and literacy or math nights. On those nights, families are expected to come to school, and are often judged harshly if they don't. I want you to think about this, think about why you are judging them harshly and what assumptions you are making. During parent teacher conferences, you will most likely not have a lot of time, so you'll probably default to talking *at* families about their children instead of engaging in dialogues *with* families as partners. I know it's hard. I've been there, too. But I'm asking you now, when it's time for conferences, when families show up to engage in conversation with you about the most precious people in their lives, please don't see your contract as a limitation. Use these moments as opportunities to connect, learn, and share.

As you well know, the dominant culture in the United States tries to suppress conversations on race. There are numerous reasons for this, most of them related to the maintenance of the power status quo. I'm asking you to help break this damaging practice — especially among adults in your school. There are certain conversations that take place in teachers' lounges about students and their families that I find both infuriating and heartbreaking. Too often, teachers are silent in the face of racist, prejudicial, biased, or stereotypical comments. I know it's uncomfortable to confront a colleague. I want you to consider, however, how uncomfortable it makes my family and all other families of color to know that there are people who we've entrusted with the care and teaching of our children who think of them as less than — less important, less worthy of our love and attention. When that moment arises next time — and it will arise — I want you to think of how uncomfortable the students are in that teacher's classroom, and I want you to speak up on their behalf. If a colleague says something derogatory about a child and/or that child's family, you must speak up. As Desmond Tutu said, "If you are neutral in situations of injustice, you have chosen the side of the oppressor."

My children are in high school now and have had the privilege of participating in advanced 15 placement and honors courses in school. They have scored at proficient and advanced levels on standardized tests. They are amazing young people, and they have worked hard. But none of these accomplishments make them exceptional or in any way better than their schoolmates who have not had these same opportunities. It also doesn't make my husband and me exceptional or any better than the families of their schoolmates. Please consider the access and opportunities that are available to all students in your schools. Our job, if we are doing it right, is to celebrate every child where they are and move them forward with skill, love, courage, and grace. In a nation that claims to believe in educating all children to become engaged citizens, this practice of failing so many students of color, or tracking them based on implicit bias, or pushing them out of schools, or driving them into the criminal justice system, or ignoring them in hopes they'll simply drop out — this adult behavior in schools perpetuates inequitable systems.

Finally, I know it's tempting to think that because you teach in a school with a high percentage of Black students, racism isn't an issue for you. Please know that proximity doesn't equal awareness. That would be like a male teacher saying, "I can't be sexist because I have female students." Know, too, that racial colorblindness isn't really a thing. While it's right to treat children equitably, it's also important to understand how race shapes lives in a racist system.

We all breathe in the smog of oppression, and the only way to expel it is to read, listen, reflect, ask questions and become better as a result of what we learn. I'm here asking you as educators to help lead the way. By improving equity in schools, by becoming truly inclusive learning communities with an effective anti-racist curriculum, we improve both individual lives and equity and justice in society. I'm here for you and I'm rooting for you. As Lilla Watson said, "… your liberation is bound up with mine."

With love, respect, and hope,
Afrika Afeni Mills
A Black Educator Mom

Topics for Critical Thinking and Writing

1. Examine Africa Afeni Mills's appeals to *ethos* in the essay. What factors contribute to her authority, and what factors, if any, diminish it?

2. Discuss the reasons and logic Mills offers as to why she no longer uses the term "African American." Are they convincing, and do you think the term is appropriate in discussing race and racism in the United States? Why or why not?

3. Mills states in her title whom she intends to address as her audience — white teachers. She then uses the second person "you" throughout the essay, even though not everyone is a teacher, and not all teachers are white. Does the way Mills constructs her audience add to or subtract from the effectiveness of her argument? Explain.

4. Reflect on your own experience as a student in elementary, middle, or high school, and write a letter from your own perspective on the ways you were taught (or not taught adequately) about race and racism in the course of your education. You may address the letter to whomever you wish.

DODAI STEWART

Dodai Stewart is the Deputy Editor of Narrative Projects at the *New York Times*. She previously worked for the news website *Jezebel*. A graduate of New York University, Stewart has written for *Glamour, New York Magazine,* and *Entertainment Weekly*. The essay featured here appeared in the *New York Times* on April 29, 2021.

The Case for a National One-Week Vacation

MEMO
To: The United States of America
From: Dodai Stewart
Subject: The Case for a National One-Week Vacation
Date: Thursday, April 29, 2021

Hey! I hope this email finds you as well as can be.

So, look. As the subject line of this memo suggests, I think the entire nation needs a simultaneous week off.

A PAID week off.

This won't work unless you're on board. All of you. The government and corporations and small businesses and each and every citizen is a part of this. We need 100 percent participation. Someone (looking at you, maybe, Treasury folks?) has to front the cash. And it has to be a clean, defined break, sharp as a knife. No amorphous gooey, bouncy, rolling spring break. One solid week. No one works. NOTHING happens. No work. No work emails, no schoolwork, no one working in the restaurants or making robocalls. Full nation vacation!

Important: For this one week, *there would be no internet*. No Instagram Lives, no Netflix and chill, ₅ no gaming streams on Twitch. It is a self-care break, and part of the deal is that you have to unplug. In this scenario, we'd all be vaccinated and the weather would be perfect. Go outside and frolic!

We'd prepare the same way you do for a camping trip: Get your groceries, get your gear. Picnic blankets, beer, first-aid kit. Maybe a Frisbee.

And then … everything would just stop. We could all take a deep breath and go outside. Feel the sunshine. Sit in the park. Hike. Bird watch. Make out with a stranger.

Stress would melt away. For one beautiful spring week, the flowers will bloom and we will all be reborn. Refreshed. Rejuvenated.

We have been through *a lot* over the last year or so. It's become quite obvious that nationwide, neurons are absolutely fried. Every cell in our collective bodies has been bathing in cortisol.

Many of our usual means of escape — travel to other countries, spa bookings, bar crawls — have ₁₀ been deemed off-limits, since they're not compatible with C.D.C. guidelines.

At the same time, leaders from all kinds of walks of life have suggested we come together to heal. How can we heal when we're drained and exhausted?

The prescription: One week off. Mandatory timeout. Perhaps we want to consider timing this to coincide with the legalization of recreational marijuana in certain states? Just a suggestion.

If we plan properly and there's universal buy-in, there will be nothing going on. No crime; therefore no need for police supervision or for anyone to staff the 911 lines. Garbage pick up? It can wait!

The subways and buses and airlines won't be running; this is a stay-local, think-global event. It's not just a chance to restore mental health, but also to reduce carbon emissions — while finally finishing one of the many books on our night stands.

Everyone in the news media would be on this break, so there would be no 24-hour news cycle. 15 CNN could just show back-to-back John Wick movies. The network TV evening news slots would be preprogrammed with romantic comedies; the Weather Channel would just have K-dramas.

What I'm trying to say, with a sprinkle of charm and a whole lot of gravitas, is this: Shut it down. *Shut it all down.*

I know you have a lot of questions. How will hospitals function? Who will feed the tigers at the zoo? How does it all work?

I don't know. I don't have all the answers. But I think if we can huddle together — my calendar is up-to-date, feel free to slot some time on there — we can make this happen. A nationwide OOO. Who's in?

Topics for Critical Thinking and Writing

1. Dodai Stewart's essay was published in the *New York Times*, yet its form is an email. How does the form support (or not support) her effort to appeal to emotion?

2. Does Stewart's statement represent a rational or nonrational appeal? Explain by examining her use of reason and logic in the overall context of the persuasive appeal.

3. Choose one of Stewart's appeals to emotion and discuss how it contributes (or fails to contribute) to her argument.

4. Can you imagine any audiences for whom Stewart's appeals would not work? If someone from this audience were critiquing her essay, what might they say?

JEFFREY T. BROWN

Jeffrey T. Brown is an insurance and personal injury attorney in Bowie, Maryland. He frequently writes opinion pieces for the daily online libertarian magazine, *American Thinker*, from which this essay comes.

The Yelling of the Lambs

For all of those who are angry about the Parkland attack and those before it, and who insist that the experiences of the newly minted child-activists for rescinding the Second Amendment require us to do what they demand, ask yourselves: do I want a society where my rights are determined by the raw and manipulated emotions of my accusers?

Do I want my rights decided by what children feel? It is self-evident to rational people that anger, especially misinformed anger, is not a basis for good policy. However, it is all that progressives can offer. At least it helps them to deflect that armed teachers would have ended that attack before more of those children died, making their refusal to allow that defense for years an act of complicity in its outcome.

Being a victim and being young do not make one nobler or smarter than he was before he was attacked. The experience of being attacked certainly makes one vulnerable to exploitation by those who would manipulate the victim, but it does nothing to enlarge the victim's limited understanding of complex issues that are often polluted by corruption and disinformation. Victimhood does not create virtue or wisdom, but it does cause rage and emotion among those cultivated to default to feelings.

Inflamed emotion is the left's engine of change, and the left prizes coercive change above all things. Everything that stands in the way of their crusade to remake America must go. Nothing prevents oppressive change more than an armed citizenry, so nothing needs changing as much or as quickly as that relic of individual liberty. You can't make people servants of an all-powerful government when they can still prevent being bound to the yoke chosen for them by their "betters."

We who still believe in the Bill of Rights are presently being treated to a hefty serving of hate, not because we have done something wrong, but because we have refused to surrender. We have declined the demand that we sacrifice our rights to make happy those who would overwhelm and control us. We have resisted the demands that we permit "commonsense" acts that are anything but sensible, which will erode or erase our rights to defend ourselves against those making the demands. We are told we must continually agree to incremental rescission of the Second Amendment, but progressives can create rights out of whole cloth to which we can neither object nor suggest limits. We are to pretend that we don't see this, or understand where it is intended to lead, and we certainly are not permitted to discuss it without being attacked.

As a country, we should ask ourselves a few 5 things: is it virtuous or wise that the rights of all citizens should be determined by public protests arising from the experiences, identities, politics, or emotions of those few whose positions are shaped by their involvement in an event or a group? Is it virtuous or wise to listen to those demanding, on the basis of a subjective experience, that rights be taken from millions of citizens who played no part in their event and committed no crime? How about this: should the rights of Americans be determined by the most emotional among us? Should our human right of self-defense be decided by the very people who have ensured that mass shootings continue to occur in "gun-free zones" because their agenda isn't advanced by actually protecting people in those zones? Should our rights be decided by angry children? Should we condone seeing children who have been willfully exposed to this danger manipulated to demand "change" by those who consciously make their schools fertile ground for shooters? Are the children who were forced into shooting galleries by their sudden political friends wise enough, or mature enough, to process and understand these facts?

Progressive change is never about what is best, or wise, or virtuous. This explains why their solution is never tailored to cure the alleged problem. It is about what is necessary to their seizure of power and control over all things. Emotion is the enemy of wisdom. Rage and reason are mutually exclusive. Those who knowingly force children into gun-free zones have an unlimited capacity for cynicism, knowing that it will go badly for anyone who points out that the emotions of those children should not bring about the wholesale revocation of rights that children do not understand, with effects they cannot fathom in their limited experience. The adults understand, even if the children do not, that the larger goal is the disarmament of free people whose insistence upon individual liberty has no place in the new progressive political order. The children have no idea that the behemoth they are helping grow will one day consume them, too.

Many children and adults know nothing about the people who lawfully own guns, yet they are taught to hate them instinctively. They know nothing about the social and cultural observations of lawful gun-owners over the last few decades and how the country is being transformed by the irrational hatred with which the vulnerable are indoctrinated within progressivism. They have no concept of what it is like to watch a country succumb to groupthink, bigotry, hatred, censorship, and incitement to open violence against them for holding the very beliefs upon which this country thrived for hundreds of years. They do not realize the rights that Americans once had relative to those they now have, or see where that erosion inevitably has led throughout history. They do not understand that the extent of degradation of our culture and society is directly proportionate to the rise of progressivism. The shooters whom so many fear have appeared in direct proportion to the left's control of education, entertainment, media, health care, perception of religion, and the criminal justice system.

Lambs are not equipped to lead their shepherds, yet they are told they are guiding us as they are herded where their adult handlers want them to go. They have no idea what they stand to lose, or how much harm they are being led to commit. If they succeed, they will only have diminished their own country and their own future. Once our rights are forfeit, theirs are, too. Shame on the adults who are doing this to them and to us.

Topics for Critical Thinking and Writing

1. In his essay, Jeffrey Brown discusses how appeals to *ethos* and *pathos* are used by others in making arguments about gun control. Summarize his primary points.

2. Do you agree or disagree with Brown's characterization of children in his argument? What supports his views? What information contradicts his views?

3. Brown appeals to his own audience by using *pathos*. To what feelings and ideals does he appeal? Are these effective appeals?

4. Brown also uses appeals to reason (*logos*) in making his argument. What pieces of information represent his strongest appeals to reason, and which appear to be less rational?

Assignment for Rhetorical Analysis

Choose one essay from this chapter and investigate *how* the author makes their argument. Here are some questions to consider:

- What is the writer's claim or thesis?
- Who is the writer's audience?

- What is the writer's purpose? What outcome does the writer want to see?
- In what ways is the argument based on *logos*, *pathos*, or *ethos*? What is the balance of these appeals?
- What types of support (evidence) is offered on behalf of the claim?
- What emotions are evoked by the argument and how?
- How does the writer establish credibility?
- Are the writer's strategies effective in convincing the intended audience? If not, what should the writer have done differently?

Identifying Procedures in Argument

Not everything that is faced can be changed, but nothing can be changed until it is faced.

— JAMES BALDWIN

CONSIDER THIS

Imagine you have done some research and decide to use a substantial amount of your money to purchase a cryptocurrency called Frogcoin. Three months later, it "moons" and your original investment has multiplied by ten times. You are fabulously rich!

Was it a good decision to buy Frogcoin?
Now, imagine the same scenario and, three months later, Frogcoin crashes and you lose most of your savings.

Was it a good decision to buy Frogcoin?
If you are like most people, you answered "Yes" to the first question and "No" for the second question. In effect you were not judging the quality of the decision itself *on its own terms*, but instead judging the quality of the decision based *on its outcomes*. But the quality of a decision does not necessarily depend on the outcomes. Very good decisions can sometimes flop, and very bad decisions can work out fine.

How can you be sure your decisions are good or bad before the results are in, or even in spite of the results? You must figure out a way to judge your decisions *independently* of their outcomes. Fortunately, critical thinking gives you these tools.

The Power and Perils of Reason

The psychologist Annie Duke uses the term "resulting" to describe a tendency in thinking that can mislead us because it skews our ability to assess our own decisions. Instead of accounting for the reasoning that made us choose to do one thing or another, we focus on the unknowable and unpredictable turns of events that produce the real-life outcomes. For Duke, resulting leaves us without a method or map to understand what goes into producing a good decision and a bad decision.

In order to judge decisions as good or bad, we need to look not at the results of our decisions, but at the quality of the reasoning and information that went into making the decision in the first place. As long as our decisions are based on rational and fair analysis of the best information at hand — although we can't guarantee good results — we can guarantee that we made the best decision we could.

We realize that events are sometimes unpredictable, and that our decisions, once made, are released into a world we cannot fully control. We also realize that the things we think and believe can later be proven false or misguided. But we do not submit to a condition in which randomness reigns supreme and there are "no right answers." We can and we must use reason and logic to ascertain realities that shape our beliefs and actions. All the while we must remain open to new information, ideas, and arguments to inform further thinking (and rethinking). We must recognize that some things widely accepted as valid and true are sometimes upended and later considered to be false — and vice versa.

YOU MAY FIND SOME OF THE FACTS HAVE CHANGED AS I'VE BROUGHT THEM INTO LINE WITH MODERN HUMAN RIGHTS

Paul Wood/Cartoonstock

Consider this: Before 2015, when the US Supreme Court legalized gay marriage by striking down all state laws banning such partnerships, many politicians and members of the public who today take this right for granted were quickly revising their beliefs and changing courses of action. Even Barack Obama, who in 2004 supported LGBTQ rights, nevertheless opposed gay marriage, insisting that "Marriage is between a man and a woman." That year, while campaigning for Senate, he expressed support for the Defense of Marriage Act (DOMA), which allowed states to refuse to recognize legal gay marriages. When he ran for President in 2008, he repeated his opposition to gay marriage on the campaign trail. Not until 2010 did Obama formally announce that his Administration would no longer "assert the constitutionality of DOMA," and not until 2012 did he say forthrightly, "I think same-sex couples should be able to get married." Later, in his memoirs, he wrote of his rethinking: "I was reminded that it is my obligation . . . to remain open to the possibility that my unwillingness to support gay marriage [was] misguided . . . that Jesus' call to love one another might demand a different conclusion."

Our culture is sometimes referred to as a "post-truth" society in which skepticism and relativity undermine public confidence in the reliability of information. We have said that skepticism is a hallmark of critical thinking — and, if you have read Chapter 1, then you know what to do when you meet a self-proclaimed "Buddha in the road" — but we can also take our doubts too far. An old story illustrates this: Two philosophers driving down a country road pass a recently shaved sheep. "Look," says the first philosopher, "That sheep had just been shaved." The second philosopher raises his eyebrow and replies: "On this side anyway."

The moral: Skepticism is good, but at a certain point we must yield to the most probable realities. When it comes to relativity, we must grant everyone the right to their own view, and yet reserve our own right to judge those views. Before we accept arguments (or make them), we must judge their truth or falseness meticulously. If arguments are based on questionable ideas, we must question them. And if they are based on untrue ideas, we must reject them.

To judge ideas, opinions, and facts when they are presented to us in arguments, we must first understand the judgment process itself — that is, we must examine how reasoning points us toward answers, and also how it can at times lead us astray.

RATIONALIZATION

In Eugène Ionesco's 1962 play *Rhinoceros*, the citizens of a small town in France are inexplicably intruded upon by a rhinoceros stampeding through the public square. While they argue over what kind of rhinoceros it is, and where it might have come from, another animal stomps through from the other direction, killing a cat. The debate continues while more rhinoceroses appear, and eventually the people themselves begin to transform into rhinoceroses.

Ionesco was exploring (in a fantastical way) how the rise of fascism occurred in his native Romania in the 1940s. At first people talked a lot about it but took few actions to stop it. As the ideology became more popular, it created a chain reaction. Many adopted the view simply to conform to others' views; others changed allegiances because the new system would benefit them in some way. Similar things happen in the play: A woman joins the rhinoceroses because her husband has transformed ("It's no more than her

Ionesco's play still resonates today. In a 2021 march, protesters in France who opposed the mandatory COVID-19 vaccine policy hold a sign that translates to "I am not a rhinoceros."

duty," a character says); a man joins because he sees an opportunity to rebuild society. Near the end of the play, when almost everyone has become rhinoceroses, the previously "ugly" animals are depicted more boldly and attractively, while the remaining humans begin to appear weak and distorted. Formerly obtrusive rhinoceros noises become grand and musical, while human speech begins to sound garbled and grating.

Ionesco's warning is that some forms of thinking, especially conformist and self-interested thinking, can become contagious. Reason and logic are twisted by many characters in the play in order to justify their own decisions to become rhinoceroses. When such ideas spread widely, things that once seemed impossible or monstrous become normalized.

Twisting logic and reason to justify a self-serving or preordained course of action is called **rationalization**. We can often find reasons (not always necessarily good ones) for almost anything we want to believe. As Benjamin Franklin once put it ironically, "So convenient a thing it is to be a *reasonable creature*, since it enables one to find or make a reason for everything one has a mind to do." Franklin touches on a truth: If necessary, instead of reasoning truthfully, we *rationalize*, like the fox in Aesop's fables who, finding the grapes he desired were out of reach, consoled himself with the conclusion that they were probably sour.

CONFIRMATION BIAS

Another species of rationalization important to understanding arguments is **confirmation bias**. Confirmation bias is a type of cognitive bias that describes the tendency to seek out, find, and employ evidence in a way that exclusively reinforces our inclinations or preexisting beliefs. In this process, only *confirmatory* ideas, information, and data are accounted for or taken seriously while disconfirming data are ignored or treated with skepticism. Whether consciously or unconsciously, we ignore the full picture, disregard other perspectives without first listening to them, and search only for support for our position, no matter how credible or representative it is.

Confirmation bias occurs most when deeply ingrained beliefs or views impede our ability to interpret information fairly. It also occurs when students write papers and research only tidbits of sources — easy quotes or factoids — that support their thesis, rather than fully reading the source material to get the full picture of what the source's argument is. (Be careful of this in your own writing; cherry-picking evidence from sources often leads to misinterpretation, which will damage your *ethos*.)

Perhaps we can never be certain that we aren't rationalizing or falling victim to confirmation bias. But if we can think critically about these pitfalls, we can be more alert to the ways they can impact our thinking, and the more fairly we can reason.

Types of Reasoning

Traditionally, reasoning is often said to be **inductive** or **deductive**; that is, to proceed along two different pathways toward drawing a conclusion. If you can identify inductive and deductive patterns in arguments, the more assuredly you can understand whether they should be accepted, challenged, or rejected — or perhaps improved to become more convincing.

(A more in-depth discussion of logical reasoning can also be found in Chapter 10, "A Logician's View: Deduction, Induction, and Fallacies.")

INDUCTION

We can distinguish between inductive and deductive reasoning by examining the places where each begins. **Inductive reasoning** starts with observations of reality, then draws a reasonable conclusion based on those observations. For example, one might say: "In my experience, the mail always arrives before 4:00

A shopper conducting inductive research into the quality of avocados.

p.m., so I infer from this evidence that it will also arrive today before 4:00 p.m." Another basic example of inductive reasoning occurs when we think about survey results: If we asked 2,000 college students about their alcohol consumption and learned that the average drinks per week consumed among them was 12, we might state as a conclusion that "the average college student consumes 12 drinks per week."

But surveys are only one method that leads to inductive reasoning. When you calculate probabilities or take samples, you are reasoning inductively. Say you are shopping for a ripe avocado, and when you find avocados in the produce section, you begin to gently press on their skins to feel whether or not they are ready to eat. You find the first to be solid and unripe. After pressing on several more, at a certain point you give up, deciding all the avocados must be unripe. At that point, you acted on an inductive inference. You inferred that, based on the number already tested (your representative sample), it was likely that the remaining avocados were the same.

The word *induction* comes from the Latin *in ducere,* "to lead into" or "to lead up to." In inductive reasoning, we draw from a set of specific instances to make generalizations about reality. We discern the patterns and use them to develop an explanation or a theory. Induction is quite common in the social sciences, which often use interviews, case studies, and experiments to draw conclusions and discern likely realities. Induction is a common feature of other research methods, too, such as content analysis (looking at, say, a set of nineteenth-century magazines to see how motherhood is portrayed, in order to make more claims about nineteenth-century cultural concepts and attitudes about maternity). By examining a number of specific instances and detecting frequencies within or among them you can *generalize* about the broader realities.

DEDUCTION

With deduction, instead of starting with methods of observation such as case studies, sampling, surveying, and the like, the deductive reasoning process begins with a fixed principle — an idea or theory called a **premise**. **Deductive reasoning** is a mental process of moving from one true statement (the premise) through another true statement (the secondary premise) to

Visual Guide: Deduction and Induction

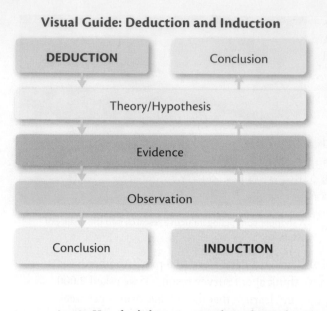

DEDUCTION

Conclusion

Theory/Hypothesis

Evidence

Observation

Conclusion

INDUCTION

produce a reasonable conclusion. In Latin, the term *deduction* means "lead down from," the opposite of induction's tendency "to lead up to." With deduction, the principle, idea, or theory comes first, and as we move "down" through other related principles, a specific conclusion necessarily results.

Let's return to our reasoning about avocados to see a deductive approach: If you had it in your mind before you entered the grocery store that dark, shriveled avocados were always overripe avocados, and then you noticed in the produce section that the available avocados all appeared to be dark and shriveled, you might not bother picking up one and testing it. You don't *have* to sample and test the avocados to know the reality: You began with a theory and followed it to its reasonable conclusion.

PREMISES AND SYLLOGISMS

One of the best ways to demonstrate a deductive argument is to use a syllogism. In classical argument, a **syllogism** — Latin for "a reckoning together" — is often used to show the truth or factuality of a conclusion. A syllogism shows two or more propositions (**premises**) that are *given*, or assumed to be true. The word *premise* comes from a Latin word meaning "to set in front." A deductive argument is said to be **valid** if the premises — the statements of truth — are connected so strongly by internal logical relationships that it makes it impossible for the premises to be true and the conclusion to be false. A classical syllogism therefore joins the premises with a third statement presented as the logical conclusion. One of the most famous syllogisms, demonstrated by Aristotle, is this:

> *Premise*: All human beings are mortal.
>
> *Premise*: Socrates is a human being.
>
> *Conclusion*: Socrates is mortal.

We could superimpose our own version:

> *Premise*: All avocados with dark, shriveled skins are overripe.
>
> *Premise*: This produce section's avocados have dark, shriveled skin.
>
> *Conclusion*: This produce section's avocados are overripe.

The purpose of a syllogism is simply to present reasons that establish the truth of a conclusion. Truth can be demonstrated if the argument satisfies *both* of two independent criteria:

1. All of the premises *must be true.*
2. The syllogism *must be valid.*

If each premise is *true* and the syllogism is *valid*, then the argument is said to be **sound**.

But what is validity? When talking about arguments, many people use the word *valid* incorrectly to describe a *true* argument, a line of reasoning that produces an accurate account of reality. "Oh, she makes a valid argument," someone might say, often meaning that you should trust in its conclusion. However — and this is quite essential to emphasize — *validity alone does not equal truth.* **Validity** means only that the argument "makes sense as stated." For example, the following syllogism presents a *valid* argument, but one that is not *true.*

All toasters are time machines.

Time machines allow us to travel to the past.

Therefore, my toaster will allow me to travel to the past.

Now, that syllogism sounds ridiculous, but it is a *valid* argument. Validity is not concerned with the *truth* of the premises: We *assume that the premises are true* in order to test the internal logic of the reasoning. *If* toasters are time machines, and *if* time machines can be used to travel to the past, then you *can* use your toaster to travel to the past. You can't argue against the reasoning, even though you know the initial premise and the conclusion are not true.

There is an important distinction to make between a *sound* argument and a merely valid argument. A sound argument means that the premises are *in fact* true. If the premises are *in fact* true, *and* the reasoning is valid, then the argument becomes indisputably true. For example:

Water boils at 212°F at sea level.

My stove heats up to 500°F.

Therefore, my stove can boil water.

If A is true, *and* B is true, then C *must* also be true. That is called a sound argument. Presented in a simple syllogism, the argument seems rudimentary, but it is actually quite a feat of human reasoning.

TESTING TRUTH AND VALIDITY

TRUE AND VALID Because deductive arguments carry a certain power to create logically derived truths, they also carry risks. That is, they can *sound* absolutely true even when they are *not necessarily* true. Consider this line of reasoning:

Weed-Ex is the most effective way to prevent weeds in your lawn.

You have a lot of weeds in your lawn.

Therefore, you should buy Weed-Ex.

That sounds pretty airtight, until you start to notice potential flaws. Is Weed-Ex really the most effective? How do you know? Do you really care about weeds in your lawn, as the second premise assumes? Should you really buy Weed-Ex? How much does it cost?

As far as its structure, this argument is not very different than a real-world issue expressed as a syllogism:

A border wall is the most effective way to prevent illegal immigration.

Illegal immigration exists in the United States.

Therefore, the Unites States should build a border wall.

To test the **truth** of a premise, you must determine whether what it asserts corresponds with reality; if it does, then it is true. If it doesn't, then it is false. The truth of a premise depends on its content — what it asserts. You can examine its truth on moral terms — for example, a border wall, even if it is "most effective," does not necessarily mean it is morally right (some people believe a wall is antithetical to national ideals; others believe it protects the national identity). You can also question the facts — is a border wall *in fact* the most effective way of preventing illegal immigration? Are there other effective ways? Finally, the syllogism assumes that illegal immigration is a "problem" worth addressing. Are there any ways in which such immigration is *not* a problem — for example, in the ways undocumented workers contribute to local and state economies? What negative consequences could result from building a new border wall? One of the most important skills in evaluating arguments is the ability to interrogate the truth of their premises. (Later in this chapter we will discuss strategies routinely used to test premises, such as assessing definitions of key terms and concepts, examining types and quality of evidence, and considering unstated assumptions.)

Another way you can test the reasoning of an argument is to go beyond examining the truth of the premises and test the *validity* of the argument — the *necessity* of the conclusions drawn from the premises. Remember, a merely valid argument has nothing to do with the truth of the premises but instead with the relationships that connect them to the conclusion. One special type of invalid argument with which you might be familiar is called a *non sequitur* ("it does not follow"):

All cats die.

Socrates is dead.

Therefore, Socrates was a cat.

A *non sequitur* simply means that, while the premises may be *in fact* true, the conclusion does not *necessarily* follow from them. For an argument to be sound, the conclusion must be a *necessary* and *inevitable* result of the true premises. (See Chapter 10 for more on logical fallacies.)

VALID AND TRUE BUT NOT SOUND   The problem is that arguments can have many premises, or premises that are quite complex, making it difficult to ascertain why they are true, or whether the conclusion necessarily results from the premises. Suppose that one or more of a syllogism's premises are false but the syllogism itself is valid and the conclusion happens to be true. Consider this example:

All Americans prefer vanilla ice cream to other flavors.

Jimmy Fallon is an American.

Therefore, Jimmy Fallon prefers vanilla ice cream to other flavors.

The first (or major) premise in this syllogism is false. Because of that, contrary to the conclusion drawn, we actually cannot be sure what Jimmy Fallon's ice cream preference is. Yet the argument passes the formal test for validity: *If* one grants that both premises are true, then one *must* accept the conclusion that inevitably results. If we found that Jimmy Fallon indeed prefers vanilla ice cream, making this conclusion true, it's not because the argument proved it. We may say that the conclusion *follows from* the premises, even though the premises *do not prove* the conclusion. This makes it an unsound argument, irrespective of whether the conclusion is true or false.

VALID BUT NOT TRUE OR SOUND False conclusions may also occur in valid arguments with true premises when the conclusions follow from — but do not *necessarily* follow from — the premises. Consider this syllogism:

The great fictional detective Sherlock Holmes was credited with having unusual powers of deduction. Holmes could see the logical consequences of many and apparently disconnected premises.

X minoritized group is disadvantaged in schools.

John Doe is a not a member of *X* minoritized group.

Therefore, John Doe is not disadvantaged in school.

Here, let's grant that the premises are true. Let's also grant that the conclusion *could* be true: John Doe may well not be disadvantaged. But it's also possible that the conclusion is false. Suppose you were to point out that the minoritized group isn't the only group who are disadvantaged, and John Doe may be disadvantaged by a learning difference that negatively affects his success in school. In short, even in a valid argument, the truth of the two premises is no guarantee that the conclusion is also true.

Chemists may use litmus paper to determine instantly whether the liquid in a test tube is an acid or a base; unfortunately, we cannot subject arguments to a litmus test like this to determine their reasonability. Logicians beginning with Aristotle have developed techniques to test any given argument, no matter how complex or subtle, for centuries; we cannot express the results of their labor in a few pages. Apart from advising you to consult Chapter 10, "A Logician's View: Deduction, Induction, and Fallacies," what we can do here is offer a checklist you may use when evaluating any argument.

ENTHYMEMES Reasoning that occurs in writing does not usually appear in methodical syllogisms. Instead of a formal syllogism, you are more likely to encounter a sentence like this: *Socrates is mortal because he is human.* This version is called an **enthymeme**, an abbreviated syllogism in which a conclusion is drawn without stating one or more of the premises but implying them instead. Here, the unstated premise is that all humans are mortal; the premise is missing but remains operative.

Critically thinking about arguments depends on our ability to extract and consider implied premises. We can reason better about what we read (and write) by thinking about the things that "go without saying." The rhetoric of advertisers and politicians, for example, can sometimes be dismantled by thinking about how implicit premises work in enthymemes. Consider the following claim:

You will improve your complexion by using Clear-Away.

The premises and conclusion here might be presented as a syllogism:

Unstated premise: All people who use Clear-Away improve their complexion.

Premise: You use Clear-Away.

Conclusion: You will improve your complexion.

Or consider this example:

Jim Hartman doesn't know accurate statistics on crime in his state; therefore, he is unqualified to be governor.

This might be stated as this syllogism:

People who do not know accurate statistics about crime in their states are unqualified to be governor.

Jim Hartman doesn't know accurate statistics.

Jim Hartman is unqualified to be governor.

NOT AN ENTRANCE

NOT AN EXIT

DEPT OF LOGIC

Bob Mankoff/Cartoon Stock

In both cases, you might challenge the truth of the first premise in order to challenge the conclusion.

Occasionally, it is not the premises that are unstated in an enthymeme, but the conclusions that are left out. Consider this example:

Lucky Charms breakfast cereal is fortified with vitamins!

The premises and conclusion might be stated this way:

All food fortified with vitamins is healthy.

Lucky Charms cereal is a food fortified with vitamins.

Lucky Charms cereal is healthy.

You can challenge the unstated conclusion of the enthymeme by challenging the premise it implies.

A WORD ON STRONG AND WEAK INDUCTIVE ARGUMENTS   Inductive and deductive arguments can both be critically examined and challenged by searching for weaknesses in their premises or weaknesses in the inferences that lead to their conclusions. Below, for example, you will see an inductive argument presented as a syllogism. (Inductive arguments are not typically presented as such; when they are, they are called "statistical" or "nondeductive" syllogisms.) Working inductively, we can present two premises based on observations and draw a generalization:

Half of the walleye we have taken from our area of the lake have a fungus.

Every walleye we observed with the fungus has died.

Half the walleye in the lake must be currently dying of a fungus.

Now, check the reasoning and probability of this conclusion. It *could* be true that half the walleye fish in the lake are dying, but it is also quite possible they are not because the conclusion does not *necessarily* follow from the premises.

Inductive arguments are not referred to formally as valid or invalid, or sound or unsound, but as *strong* or *weak* depending on the probability of the conclusion. The example above has *weak induction* because we do not have other needed information about *how many total fish were sampled* or *what other locations of the lake were not sampled,* or *what other factors might have contributed to the deaths of the sampled fish.*

When we reason inductively, weaknesses frequently lie in the size and the quality of the **sample**. This can cause us to leap to a generalization on too little evidence. If we're offering an argument concerning the political leanings of students at our campus, we cannot interview *everyone*, so we select a sample. But we must ask if the sample is a fair one: If we surveyed only one classroom, for instance, that wouldn't be enough of a sample on which to generalize about all students. Or, if we conducted surveys only through fraternities and sororities, we would get the views only of those who are inclined to join the Greek system (and have the means to pay dues). In each case, the sample is not *representative* of the entire school. To get a more *representative sample*, we would need to measure opinions from across the student body.

WRITING TIP
An argument that uses samples should tell the reader how the samples were chosen. If it doesn't provide this information, the reader should treat the argument with suspicion.

A larger sample alone doesn't necessarily mean a *representative* one, however. Suppose we wished to measure the political leanings of *all* college students, and we sampled broadly on our campus, and we repeated the study at all the state universities in our region. We might have many thousands of responses. Yet, we could not use that data to extrapolate conclusions about the political views of *all* college students. Ask yourself: Why not?

Inductive arguments are susceptible to overgeneralization (which occurs when we extend the meaning of the observed cases too far, such as in our example that considers only state university students in one geographic region, not students at private schools or community colleges, or in different areas of the country or globe). Further, the conclusions drawn by inductive arguments can always be altered by new observations and new data. For example, a hundred years ago, observations of wildlife in the Alaskan Arctic would have led researchers to conclude that there were no moose there; today, the same researchers would find plenty of moose, most drawn there after the effects of climate change made the region warmer. Similarly, the political attitudes of college students could change rather rapidly, making our conclusions about them unstable.

THINKING CRITICALLY *Inductive and Deductive Reasoning*

Examine the following lines of reasoning and identify them as inductive (I) or deductive (D). Rate your confidence in the strength of the argument, where 1= weakest and 10 = strongest, then explain the strength or weaknesses in the reasoning.

	INDUCTIVE OR DEDUCTIVE?	RATING (1 = WEAKEST; 10 = STRONGEST)	EXPLANATION
It is a crime to enter the subway without first paying. If I jump the turnstiles, I will be breaking the law.			
I usually see guards posted by the subway turnstiles. If I try to jump the turnstiles, I am going to get caught.			
My friend staying at the Marks Hotel reported seeing a ghost in her room. That hotel must be haunted.			
There are no such things as ghosts. If I stay in this supposedly haunted hotel, I will not see a ghost.			
If meat sits out at room temperature for too long it leads to harmful bacterial growth. This roast beef has been sitting out all day. If I eat it, I could get very sick.			
I ate roast beef that sat out all day at the picnic. I did not get sick. It must be safe to eat roast beef that sits out all day.			

Deductive arguments, on the other hand, which "lead down" from their premises toward a conclusion, often posit facts or principles as their premises. When they are sound, deductive arguments based on incontrovertibly true premises provide an *absolutely* necessary conclusion. Because deduction can (although it does not always) produce truths in this way, the strongest deductive arguments are more reliable than the strongest inductive arguments. This is because even the strongest inductive reasoning can never attain 100 percent certainty the way some deductive arguments can.

Some Procedures in Argument

When we think seriously about an argument, we may perhaps for the first time really see the strengths and weaknesses in what we ourselves believe and what others are asking us to believe. So far in this chapter, we emphasized reasoning about the connections between observations and generalizations (in inductive arguments), and premises and conclusions (in deductive arguments). But these elements themselves depend upon the information that underlies them. Even the claim that "All men are mortal" needs to be proven. This happens to be a statement about which we have no doubt; however, other claims may require more scrutiny. Thus, we turn now to examine how data, facts, and evidence are used in arguments to prove their claims and conclusions are true.

In reading and writing arguments, you must be able to assess the quality of the underlying information — the evidence — grounding the claims, in *addition* to verifying the quality of reasoning about that information.

DEFINITIONS

Writers often attempt to provide a provisional definition of important terms and concepts to advance their arguments. They ask readers, in a way, to accept a definition for the purposes of the argument at hand. Readers may do so, but if they want to argue a different position, they must do so according to the definition offered by the author, or else they must offer their own definition.

Before going further, allow us to define the difference between a **term** and a **concept**. A rule of thumb is that a *term* is more concrete and fixed than a *concept*. You may be able to find an authoritative source (like a federal law or an official policy) to help define a word as a term. An author may write, for example, "According to the legal definition, the term 'exploitation' means *A*, *B*, and *C*" (a technical definition). It may be difficult to contend with an author who offers a definition of a term in a strict way such as this. Unless you can find a different standard, you may have to start out on the same basic ground: an agreed-upon definition.

A *concept* is more open-ended and may have a generally agreed-upon definition but rarely a strict or unchanging one. Writers may say, "For the purposes of this argument, let's define 'exploitation' as a moral *concept* that involves *A*, *B*, and *C*" (a broad definition). Concepts can be abstract but can also function powerfully in argumentation; love, justice, morality, psyche, health, freedom, bravery, masculinity — these are all concepts. You may look up such words in the dictionary, but it won't offer a strict definition and won't say much about how to apply the concept. Arguments that rely predominantly on concepts may be more easily added to or challenged, because concepts are so much more open-ended than terms.

As to whether or not a local stream is "polluted" and needs to be cleaned up, for example, you might use a strict (terminological) or loose (conceptual) definition of the word *pollution* to argue either way. You might define the word *pollution* as a term set forth by your state's environmental protection agency, which perhaps requires that the water contains a minimum threshold of toxins to be called *polluted*, or else you might describe *pollution* according to your own concept of having a lot of garbage and debris lying alongside it. Either definition may help you argue for a state cleanup effort, even while one definition of "polluted" is based on a fixed standard, and the other is a more or less accepted idea of what "polluted" means. When we define key words, we're answering the question "What is it?" and setting out our definition for the purposes of the argument at hand.

Trying to decide the best way to define key terms and concepts is often difficult — and sometimes controversial. Consider one of the most contentious debates in our society: reproductive rights. Many arguments about abortion depend on a definition of "life." Traditionally, human life has been seen as beginning at birth. Nowadays, most people see "life" as something that begins at least at viability (the capacity of a fetus to live independently of the uterine environment). But modern science has made it possible to see the beginning of "life" in different ways. Some define life as beginning with *brain birth*, the point at which "integrated brain functioning begins to emerge." Others see life beginning as early as fertilization. Whatever the merits of these definitions, the debate itself reminds us of just how important it can be to use clear definitions of important terms when making arguments.

Here are some ways definitions can be established in arguments.

STIPULATION   The word *stipulate* comes from the Latin verb *stipulari*, meaning "to bargain" or "to secure a guarantee." When you stipulate something, you ask the reader to agree with a certain definition for the sake of the argument at hand. Of course, a reader may not want to make that bargain, but if someone wanted to argue against you, they would have to contend with your definition, or offer their own. For example, you may write one of the following:

- In my analysis, I am defining *hip-hop* as X, thus . . .
- If we can agree the definition of *pollution* should refer not only to water-based toxins in a stream, but also high levels of unsightly waste around it, then . . .

Stipulating your definition encourages — although it does not require — the reader to consider and evaluate your argument according to your definition.

In some forms of writing, such as in laws and contracts, you can often find stipulated definitions made very explicitly as a requirement, not an option. What distinguishes a misdemeanor theft and a felony theft in a state, for example, is not negotiable but fixed. In other legal contexts, key terms need to be precisely defined and agreed upon by all parties to guarantee fairness and avoid disputes. For example, consider this language from a portion of a California home insurance policy covering damage caused by an earthquake:

> For the purposes of this policy . . . the term Earthquake shall mean seismic activity, including earth movement, landslide, mudslide, sinkhole, subsidence, volcanic eruption, or Tsunami, as defined herein. . . . The term Tsunami shall mean a wave or series of waves caused by underwater earthquakes and/or seismic activity, including, but not limited to, volcanic eruptions, landslides, earth movement, mudslide, sinkhole, or subsidence. In no event shall this Company be liable for any loss caused directly or indirectly by fire, explosion or other excluded perils resulting from an Earthquake as defined herein.

Parties mutually agree to certain definitions by signing the contract itself. Other forms of writing also require comprehensive definitions. For instance, if you were a legislator writing a law to permit "online gambling" in your state, you must have a very precise definition of what that means. (The actual legal definition of online gambling in the US legal code is more than 1,000 words!)

You do not have to be writing a law or a contract to make stipulative definitions. In your arguments, you may stipulate a definition in the following cases:

- when you are seeking to secure a shared understanding of the meaning of a term or concept
- when no fixed or standard definition is available

If you are call something *undemocratic*, you must define what you mean by *democratic*. If you call a painting a *masterpiece*, you may want to try to define that word, perhaps by offering your criteria. What definition of *cruel and unusual punishment* will you use in your argument about solitary confinement? How are you defining *food insecurity* in your call to end hunger on campus? Not everyone may accept your stipulative definitions, and there will likely be defensible alternatives. However, when you stipulate a definition, your audience knows what *you* mean by the term.

Sometimes, a definition that at first seems extremely odd can be made acceptable by offering strong reasons in its support. For instance, in 1990 the US Supreme Court recognized that *speech* includes symbolic nonverbal expressions such as wearing armbands or flying the American flag upside down. Such actions — although they are nonverbal — are considered speech because they express ideas or emotions. More controversially, in 2010 the Supreme Court ruled in *Citizens United vs. Federal Election Commission* that corporate spending in the form of campaign contributions constitutes speech and cannot be limited under the First Amendment. This decision spurred unprecedented spending on elections by corporations and today remains a divisive definition of speech.

Our object with these examples is to make the overall point clear: An argument will be most fruitful if the participants share an understanding of the concepts they are talking about.

SYNONYM   Another way to provide a definition is through **synonym**. For example, *pornography* can be defined, at least roughly, as *obscenity*, even while these terms are not exactly synonyms. This could enable someone to argue against a public display of sexually suggestive photograph, for example, even while it may not meet the strict definition of pornography. Synonyms do the job, but usually require further explanation. Imagine writing, "This company's strategy is essentially a *con game*" or "Spanking children is *child abuse*." In each case, synonyms were provided to help define the terms of the argument, but now the synonyms need to be explained.

"HANG ON, THERE'S A NEW DEFINITION OF EVIL."

Charles Barsotti/CartoonStock

EXAMPLE   Another way to provide a definition is to point to one or more examples (sometimes called an **ostensive definition**, from the Latin *ostendere*, "to show"). This method can be very helpful in adding not only clarity but vivid detail to your writing. If you are reviewing a movie and you want to define "tween movies," you point to specific examples of the kinds of films you mean. You may say that "tween movies" are those films that appeal to a certain age demographic — young people between eight and sixteen years old — but your definition may be made concrete and visible by quickly surveying examples of such films: "Tween movies feature plots developed around preteen or teenage characters, but also contain more mature language and themes that appeal to the audience's emerging adulthood, such as *The Sandlot* (1993), *High School Musical* (2006), or *Eighth Grade* (2018)." Definitions by example also have their limitations, so choosing the right examples — those that have all the central or typical characteristics and that will best avoid misinterpretation — is important to using this method of definition effectively.

ESTABLISHING SUFFICIENT AND NECESSARY CONDITIONS   A final way to define a term or concept is by establishing its *sufficient and necessary conditions*. For writers, this just means controlling definitions by offering certain preconditions. For example, if you say a "sport" is defined as any activity meeting *sufficient* conditions of competition and physical endurance, you can also argue that video gaming, which meets those criteria, may be called a sport, too. (See Matthew Walther's essay, "Sorry Nerds: Video Games Are Not a Sport," on p. 212 on this very subject.) If you were to argue vaping should not be subject to the same rules on your campus as smoking, you could define "smoking" as an activity requiring the *necessary* conditions of combustion and smoke, neither of which is a feature of a vaporizer.

What is the difference between a *sufficient* and a *necessary* condition? One common way to distinguish between them is to imagine them phrased as conditional propositions. Sufficient conditions are the *minimum* conditions needed to be met for the definition to

> **WRITING TIP**
> Avoid quoting dictionaries in your essays and academic arguments when you are trying to establish the meaning of a term or concept. Besides appearing to be "shortcut," dictionary definitions are often too technical or too general to be really informative on a topic. Derive your own definitions instead, perhaps with the help of a dictionary, but also by consulting experts in the area about which you are writing.

stand: "In all fifty states, *if* a child commits a heinous enough crime, or *if* they have an extensive criminal record, or *if* they were approaching their eighteenth birthday when the crime was committed, *then* a judge may try them as a legal adult." Sufficient conditions can include any number of minimum criteria. In contrast, necessary conditions are more exclusive and narrow. Compare this definition adulthood: "A person is an adult *if and only if* they have reached their eighteenth year."

When you are reading arguments, and you wish to challenge the premises or conclusions, one place to look is at the author's definitions. If you can redefine the terms under analysis, you can often find a starting point for critique and counterargument.

THINKING CRITICALLY *Analyzing Definitions*

Read the selections and (a) identify the term or concept being defined; (b) explain which type of definition it is (stipulation, synonym, example); and (c) use details from the examples to support your answer.

	TERM OR CONCEPT BEING DEFINED	TYPE OF DEFINITION	EXPLAIN YOUR ANSWER
Marriage is primarily an economic arrangement, an insurance pact. It differs from the ordinary life insurance agreement only in that it is more binding, more exacting. Its returns are insignificantly small compared with the investments. — Emma Goldman, *Marriage and Love* (1911)			
The "slasher film" is a sub-genre of horror that meets certain criteria, including an effective killer, a high body count, and non-firearm weapons. If a film has these three requirements, it can technically be considered a slasher film. — Sam Kensh, "What Is a Slasher Film" (2021)			

Camp taste has an affinity for certain arts rather than others. . . . For Camp art is often decorative art, emphasizing texture, sensuous surface, and style at the expense of content. Concert music . . . is rarely Camp. . . . There is a sense in which it is correct to say: "It's too good to be Camp." Or "too important," not marginal enough. Thus, the personality of many works of Jean Cocteau are Camp, but not those of Andre Gide; the operas or Richard Strauss, but not those of Wagner; concoctions of Tin Pan Alley and Liverpool, but not jazz. . . . Many examples of Camp are things which, from a serious point of view, are either bad art or kitsch.
— Susan Sontag, "Notes on Camp" (1964)

A slander is a spoken defamation, whether that act of speech is public and one-time or recorded and redistributed. Slander also includes defamation by gesture, which could include making a gesture that suggests professional incompetence or mental illness. Slander carries the additional burden for a plaintiff of having to prove that they suffered actual loss due to the false statement.
— Mitch Ratcliffe, *How to Prevent Against Online Libel and Defamation* (2009)

EVIDENCE

In a courtroom, evidence bearing on the guilt of the accused is introduced by the prosecution, and evidence to the contrary is introduced by the defense. Not all evidence is admissible (e.g., hearsay is not, even if it's true), and the law of evidence is a highly developed subject in jurisprudence. In daily life, the sources of evidence are less disciplined. Daily experience, a memorable observation, or an unusual event — any or all of these may serve as evidence for (or against) some belief, theory, hypothesis, or explanation a person develops.

In making arguments, people in different disciplines use different kinds of evidence to support their claims. For example:

- In literary studies, texts (works of literature, letters, journals, notes, and other kinds of writing) are the chief forms of evidence.

- In the social sciences, field research (interviews, observations, surveys, data) usually provides the evidence.

- In the hard sciences, reports of experiments are the usual evidence; if an assertion cannot be tested — if one cannot show it to be false — it is an *opinion*, not a scientific hypothesis.

When you are offering evidence to support your arguments, you are drawing on the specific information that makes your claims visible, concrete, *evident*. For example, in arguing that the entertainment industry needed to address the problem of sexual harassment in Hollywood, people in the #MeToo movement pointed to the many testimonies of female actresses who accused powerful actors and industry leaders of these behaviors. Each instance constitutes **evidence** for the problem. If you are arguing that bump stocks (devices that allow semiautomatic guns to operate like automatic ones) should be banned, you will point to specific cases in which bump stocks were used to commit crimes in order to show the need for regulation. Evidence can take many forms. Here, we discuss three broad categories of evidence.

EXPERIMENTATION   Often, the forms of evidence that scientists use, whether in the natural and mathematical sciences or in the social sciences, is the result of **experimentation**. Experiments are deliberately contrived situations, often complex in their methodology or the technologies they use, that are designed to yield particular observations. What the ordinary person does with unaided eye and ear, the scientist does much more carefully and thoroughly, often in controlled situations and with the help of laboratory instruments. For example, a natural scientist studying the biological effects of a certain chemical might expose specially bred rodents to carefully monitored doses of the chemical and then measure the effects. A health scientist might design a study in which people who exercise regularly are compared to people who do not in order to argue the beneficial effects of consistent exercise on heart health. A psychologist might introduce a certain type of therapy to a group of people and then compare the results to other treatment methods.

It's no surprise that society attaches much more weight to the findings of scientists than to the corroborative (much less the contrary) experiences of ordinary people. No one today would seriously argue that the sun really does go around the earth just because it looks that way, nor would we argue that the introduction of carcinogens to the human body through smoking does not increase the risk for cancers. Yet because some kinds of scientific validation (such as repeatability) produce unarguable fact, we sometimes assume that all forms of experimentation are equal in their ability to point to truth. However, we should also be skeptical, since experiment designs can also be flawed — by bad design, bad samples, measurement error, or a host of other problems. Moreover, the results of experimentation can also be used to make different kinds of arguments. Consider that the same scientific data are used by people who argue that humans are the primary cause of climate change as well as by people who deny that humans play a significant role in climate change.

EXAMPLES   Unlike the hard sciences, the variety, extent, and reliability of the evidence obtained in the humanities — and in daily life — are quite different from those obtained in the laboratory. In all forms of writing, examples constitute the primary evidence. Suppose we argue that a candidate is untrustworthy and shouldn't be elected to public office. We may point to episodes in their career — misuse of funds in 2008 and the false charges made against an opponent in 2016 — as examples of their untrustworthiness.

An *example* is a type of *sample*. These two words come from the same Old French word, *essample*, from the Latin *exemplum*, which means "something taken out" — that is, a selection from the group, something held up as indicative. A Yiddish proverb shrewdly says, "'For example' is no proof," but the evidence of well-chosen examples can go a long way toward helping a writer convince an audience.

In arguments, three sorts of examples are especially common:

- real events
- invented instances (artificial or hypothetical cases)
- analogies

We will treat each of these briefly.

Real Events   Real events are examples that help prove the truth of a claim by looking to the real world. If we're arguing that President Harry Truman rightly ordered the atomic bombs dropped on Hiroshima and Nagasaki to save American (and, for that matter, Japanese) lives that otherwise would have been lost in a hard-fought land invasion of Japan, we could point to the fierce resistance of the Japanese defenders in battles on the islands of Saipan, Iwo Jima, and Okinawa, where Japanese soldiers fought to the death rather than surrender. These named battles indicate examples of real events in which Japanese defenders of the main islands would have fought to their deaths without surrendering, even though they knew that defeat was certain.

But we can also use counterexamples. If we are arguing that Truman's decision to drop the atomic bombs was wrong, we would not use the Japanese army's behavior on Saipan and on Iwo Jima as evidence for our claim. Instead, our evidence — our counterexamples of other real events — would be that in June and July 1945 certain Japanese diplomats sent out secret peace feelers to Switzerland and offered to surrender if the Emperor Hirohito could retain power. Thus we could conclude that in August 1945, when Truman authorized dropping the bombs, the situation was very different than it had been during the time of Saipan and Iwo Jima. If we were to argue that

> **WRITING TIP**
> By far the most common way to test the adequacy of an inductive argument is to consider one or more **counterexamples**. If the counterexamples are numerous, genuine, and reliable, the generalization can be challenged.

Truman should *not* have dropped the bombs, we could cite those peace feelers specifically, indicating a Japanese willingness to end the war without such destruction.

Real events are often entangled in historical circumstances, and may not be adequate or fully relevant evidence in the case being argued. When real events as examples (a perfectly valid strategy), you as a writer must:

- demonstrate that they are representative,
- anticipate counterexamples, and
- argue against counterexamples, showing that one's own examples can be considered outside of other contexts.

Thus, if we were arguing that Truman's use of atomic bombs was not warranted, we might go out of our way to raise these facts of the fierceness of Japanese resistance in specific earlier battles, but then argue that they are not relevant because our examples show that the Japanese were seeking peace. This way, we respond to the likely challenges we might expect skeptical readers to make. Similarly, if we were arguing that Truman did the right thing by dropping the bombs, we could mention the peace feelers, but also point out that it would not have desirable to permit the emperor to retain power under any circumstances.

Invented Instances   An **invented instance** is an **artificial** or **hypothetical** example. Take this case: A writer poses a dilemma in his argument that "Stand Your Ground" laws are morally indefensible. (These laws allow individuals the right to protect themselves against threats of bodily harm, to the point of using lethal force in self-defense.) In his discussion, he raises one of the most famous of these cases, involving the death of unarmed Florida teenager Trayvon Martin, who was killed in 2012 by a self-appointed neighborhood watchman named George Zimmerman, who mistook the African American youth as a threat. He writes: "If Trayvon Martin had been of age and legally armed, in fact, he would have had the right to kill Zimmerman when Zimmerman approached him in a hostile way." By imagining this scenario, the writer asks readers to apply the principles of justice underlying the law to the reverse scenario: What happens when neither party is clear about which of them is standing his ground? Even though the example isn't "real" — although it alters the details of a real event — it sets forth the problem in a clear way.

Umberto Leporini / EyeEm / Getty Images

The Trolley Problem poses a hypothetical dilemma asking if you would choose to change the path of a trolley car if it meant saving more lives while still sacrificing others. Variations of the trolley involve choosing between the number of lives or different types of people (e.g., three career criminals vs. one young college graduate).

Offering an invented instance is something like a drawing of the parts of an atom in a physics textbook. It is admittedly false, but by virtue of its simplification it sets forth the relevant details very clearly. Invented instances can be wholly fictional, as well: "To understand just how much bullying can affect a child, imagine Gracie, a fourteen-year-old who just proudly posted a picture of herself wearing new braces on her social media, only to find the bullies immediately responding: 'Metal-mouth,' 'Jaws,' 'Train Tracks!'" Thus, in the argument, an example is used here of an event that never really occurred. Invented instances like this can be effective in persuasion, but we also caution you against confirmation bias: After all, anything you invent for the purposes of your own argument is almost certainly going to be the most supportive, probably ideal example.

Invented instances can frame problems in specific ways. In a discussion of legal rights and moral obligation, the philosopher Charles Frankel says:

> It would be nonsense to say, for example, that a nonswimmer has a moral duty to swim to the help of a drowning man.

If Frankel were talking about a real event and a real person, he could get bogged down in details about the actual person and the circumstances of the event, losing his power to put the moral dilemma forward in its clearest terms. However, invented instances are not the highest quality of evidence. A purely hypothetical example can illustrate a point, but it cannot substitute for actual events.

But we repeat: Even a highly fanciful invented case can have the valuable effect of forcing us to see where we stand. A person may say that they are, in all circumstances, against torture—but what would they say if a writer proposed a scenario in which the location of a ticking bomb were known only by one person and extracting that information through torture could save hundreds or thousands of lives? Artificial cases of this sort can help us examine our beliefs; nevertheless, they often create exceptional scenarios that may not be generalized convincingly to support an argument.

Analogies   The third sort of example, **analogy**, is a kind of comparison. Here's an example:

> Before the Roman Empire declined as a world power, it exhibited a decline in morals and in physical stamina; our society today shows a decline in both morals (consider the high divorce rate and the crime rate) and physical culture (consider obesity in children). The United States, like Rome, will decline as a world power.

Strictly speaking, an analogy is an extended comparison in which different things are shown to be similar in several ways. Thus, if one wants to argue that a head of state should have extraordinary power during wartime, one can offer an analogy that, during wartime, the state is *like a ship in a storm* (there's the analogy): The crew is needed to lend its help, but the major decisions are best left to the captain. Notice that an analogy like this compares things that are relatively *un*like. An analogy operates like a metaphor or simile. That's one reason they can be very persuasive: For example, critics may make a powerful point in using a fascist state like Nazi Germany to analogize a US Presidential administration, or Stalin's Gulags to analogize a US Department of Education initiative, but a straight comparison between these things rarely holds up.

The problem with argument by analogy is this: Because different things are similar in some ways does not mean they are similar in all ways. A state in many ways is not like a ship in a storm. Many people say, "The government should be run like a business," but the government is not a business; it has different functions and purposes. What is true for one need not be true for the other. Analogies work to an extent but usually fail in many ways too. As Bishop Butler is said to have remarked in the early eighteenth century, "Everything is what it is, and not another thing."

AUTHORITATIVE TESTIMONY   Another form of evidence is **testimony**, the citation or quotation of authorities. In daily life, we rely heavily on authorities of all sorts: We get a doctor's opinion about our health, we read a book because an intelligent friend recommends it, we see a movie because a critic gave it a good review, and we pay at least a little attention to the weather forecaster. We need people who have the authority to provide us reliable information.

In setting forth an argument, one often tries to show that one's view is supported by authorities — perhaps by quoting a scientist who won a Nobel Prize to discuss outer space, or a decorated journalist to provide a supporting view on a social issue. But authorities do not have to be prominent figures of high stature, or even experts in a field of study. They can be people who have had many types of experiences — for example, a road worker might have something to add to a conversation about congested city traffic, or a prisoner on the issue of solitary confinement. Just heed some words of caution:

- Be sure that the authority, however notable, has some *credibility to speak* on *the topic in question.* (A renowned biologist might not be an authority on criminal law.)

- Be sure to check for the authority's *biases.* (A social media influencer's opinion of a product they are paid to endorse isn't likely to criticize the company.)

- Beware of *nameless* authorities: "a thousand doctors," "leading educators," "researchers at a major medical school." (If possible, seek to identify at least one specific name.)

- Be careful when using authorities who indeed were great authorities in their day but *who now may be out of date.* (Sigmund Freud's specific theories on neuroses were foundational and interesting but simply do not hold up in contemporary practice.)

- Be sure to cite authorities *whose opinions your readers will trust and value.* (If you are writing for a young, college-age audience, an intellectual journalist like Ta-Nehisi Coates may resonate more than the stodgy conservative William F. Buckley, Jr.)

THINKING CRITICALLY *Authoritative Testimony*

Locate one authority or one nonauthority's comment on each issue, then use the table to examine and explain why may their testimony is reliable or unreliable.

ISSUE	EXPERT NAME AND QUALIFICATIONS	TIME AND PLACE OF PUBLICATION	QUOTATION	YOUR EXPLANATION
Recreational marijuana				
Disciplining children				
How to manage test anxiety				
Restoring voting rights to felons				
The quality of the latest Academy Award–winning Best Picture				

One other point: *You* may be an authority. Whether you are unknown or have thousands of followers, on some topics you might have the authority of personal experience. You may have been injured on a motorcycle while riding without wearing a helmet, so your thoughts about helmet laws are informed by experience. You may have dropped out of school and then returned. You may have tutored a student whose native language isn't English, or you may be such a student who has received tutoring. If so, your personal testimony on topics relating to these issues may be invaluable as testimonial evidence.

NUMERICAL DATA   The last sort of evidence we discuss here is data based on math or collections of numbers, also referred to as **quantitative** or **statistical** evidence. Sometimes quantitative evidence is used as a firm basis for making decisions. Suppose the awarding of honors at graduation from college is determined based on a student's cumulative grade-point average (GPA). Consequently, a student with a GPA of 3.9 at the end of her senior year is a stronger candidate for honors than another student with a GPA of 3.6. When faculty members determine the academic merits of graduating seniors, they know that these quantitative, statistical differences in student GPAs will be the basic (if not the only) kind of evidence under discussion.

Here, numbers prove to be reliable evidence, used to justify an underlying argument that one student deserves honors more than another. However, in many cases, numbers do not simply speak for themselves. Numerical information can be presented in many forms. Graphs, tables, and pie charts are familiar ways of presenting quantitative data in an eye-catching manner, but how the numbers are organized, interpreted, and presented can make a difference in how well they support an argument's claims. (See the section "Visuals as Aids to Clarity: Maps, Graphs, and Pie Charts" on pp. 178–182 in Chapter 5 for more on graphs.)

Let's look how some different kinds of numbers are commonly used as evidence.

Presenting Numbers   In an argument, you may need to evaluate whether it is more persuasive to present numbers in percentages or real numbers. For example, arguing that the murder rate increased by 30 percent in one city sounds more compelling than saying there were thirteen murders this year compared to ten last year (only three more, but a technical increase of 30 percent). Should an argument examining the federal budget say that it (1) underwent a *twofold increase* over the decade, (2) increased by *100 percent*, (3) *doubled*, or (4) was *one-half of its current amount ten years ago*? These are equivalent ways of saying the same thing, but by making a choice among them, a writer can play up or play down the fact to support different arguments in more or less dramatic ways.

Different calculations can impact the meaning of numerical data. Here are some statistics that pop up in conversations about wealth distribution in the United States. In 2020, the Census Bureau calculated that the **median** household income in the United States was about $67,500, meaning that half of households earned less than this amount and half earned above it. However, the **average** — technically, the **mean** — household income in the same year was about $98,000, around 45 percent higher. Which number more accurately represents the typical household income? Both are "correct," but both are calculated with different measures (median and mean). If a politician wanted to argue that the United States has a strong middle class, they might use the average (mean) income as evidence. If another politician wished to make a rebuttal, they could point out that the average (mean) income paints a rosy picture because the wealthiest households skew the average higher. The median income (representing the number above and below which two halves of all households fall) should be the measure we use, the rebutting politician could argue, because it helps reduce the effect of the limitless ceiling of higher incomes and the finite floor of lower incomes at zero.

This just shows how different methods of calculating — or how writers may use the results of those different methods — can produce different understandings of an issue.

Unreliable Statistical Evidence   Because we know that 90 percent is greater than 75 percent, we're usually ready to accept as true a claim supported by 90 percent of cases over one supported by 75 percent of cases. The greater the difference, the greater our confidence. Yet it's easy to misuse statistics (unintentionally or not) and difficult to be sure that they were gathered correctly in the first place. "You can use statistics to prove anything," some people say. An older saying goes, "There are lies, damned lies, and statistics." The comedian Bo Burnham demonstrates how absurd misuses of statistics can be: "Statistics prove," he points out, "that the average human has one testicle and one ovary." Joking aside, every branch of social science and natural science needs statistical information, and countless decisions in public and private life are based on quantitative data in statistical form. It's therefore important to be sensitive to the sources and reliability of the statistics, and to the ways they are interpreted.

It is advisable to develop a healthy skepticism when you confront statistics whose parentage is not fully explained. Always ask: Who gathered the statistics? For what purpose? Consider this example of statistics, from the self-described "culture jammer" Kalle Lasn, the founder of AdBusters, a group that commonly criticizes aspects of consumer society:

> Advertisements are the most prevalent and toxic of the mental pollutants. From the moment your radio alarm sounds in the morning to the wee hours of late-night TV, microjolts of commercial pollution flood into your brain at the rate of about three thousand marketing messages per day. (Kalle Lasn, *Culture Jam* [1999], 18–19)

Lasn's book includes endnotes as documentation, so, being curious about the statistics, we checked and found the following information concerning the source of his data:

> "three thousand marketing messages per day." Mark Landler, Walecia Konrad, Zachary Schiller, and Lois Therrien, "What Happened to Advertising?" *BusinessWeek*, September 23, 1991, page 66. Leslie Savan in *The Sponsored Life* (Temple University Press, 1994), page 1, estimated that "16,000 ads flicker across an individual's consciousness daily." I did an informal survey in March 1995 and found the number to be closer to 1,500 (this included all marketing messages, corporate images, logos, ads, brand names, on TV, radio, billboards, buildings, signs, clothing, appliances, in cyberspace, etc., over a typical twenty-four hour period in my life). (219)

Well, this endnote is odd. In the earlier passage, the author asserted that about "three thousand marketing messages per day" flood into a person's brain. In the documentation, he cites a source for that statistic from *BusinessWeek* — although we haven't the faintest idea how the authors of the *BusinessWeek* article came up with that figure. Oddly, he goes on to offer a very different figure (16,000 ads) and then, to our confusion, offers yet a third figure (1,500) based on his own "informal survey." Lasn said, without implying any uncertainty, that "about three thousand marketing messages per day" reach an individual, but it's evident from the endnote that this is more effect than analysis. Even he is confused about the figure he gives.

We'd like to make a final point about the unreliability of some statistical information — data that looks impressive but that is, in fact, insubstantial. Consider Marilyn Jager Adams's book *Beginning to Read: Thinking and Learning about Print* (1994), which was much quoted in newspapers and by children's advocacy groups, for its claim that middle-class families read more to their children than poor families. What were her samples? For poor families, she selected twenty-four children in twenty families, all in Southern California. Ask yourself: Is that a good sample for such a study? And how many families constituted Adams's sample of middle-class families? Exactly one — her own. We leave it to you to judge the quality of her findings.

When problems in definitions of terms collide with problems in numbers, results can also be quite misleading. Sociologist Joel Best notes in his book *Stat Spotting* an interesting case: When research several years ago showed that "one-fifth [20 percent] of college students practice self-injury," the dramatic statistic inspired all kinds of worrying articles. But a closer look at the study revealed not only that the survey was limited to two Ivy League universities (a sampling problem), but also that it *defined* self-injury in a broad way, to include minor acts that most psychologists would consider to be within the range of normal behavior — such as pinching, scratching, or hitting oneself. In actuality, as another analysis showed, only 1.6 percent of college students reported injuring themselves to the point of needing medical treatment — quite a lot fewer than 20 percent.

We are not suggesting that everyone who uses statistics is trying to deceive (or is unconsciously being deceived by them). We suggest only that statistics are open to widely different interpretations. Often those columns of numbers, which appear to be so precise with their decimal points and their complex formulas, may actually be imprecise and possibly worthless — especially if they're based on insufficient samples, erroneous methodologies, or biased interpretation.

A CHECKLIST FOR EVALUATING STATISTICAL EVIDENCE

Regard statistical evidence (like all other evidence) cautiously and don't accept it until you have thought about these questions:

- ☐ Was the evidence compiled by a disinterested (impartial) source?
- ☐ Is it based on an adequate sample?
- ☐ What is the definition of the thing being counted or measured?
- ☐ Is the statistical evidence recent enough to be relevant?
- ☐ How many of the factors likely to be relevant were identified and measured?
- ☐ Are the figures open to a different and equally plausible interpretation?
- ☐ If a percentage is cited, is it the average (or *mean*), or is it the median?

Assumptions

Even the longest and most complex chains of reasoning or proof, and even most carefully constructed definitions, are fastened to assumptions — one or more *unexamined beliefs*. These taken-for-granted, hidden, or neglected beliefs affect how writers and readers make inferences and draw conclusions. Of course, assumptions are common and sometimes logical. If you attend a birthday party, you might *assume* that cake will be served. If the ceiling is wet, you may *assume* that the roof is leaking.

However, false assumptions can be dangerous. If a driver assumes that traffic will stop at a red light and they proceed through an intersection without looking, they could end up in a car crash. If a business executive assumes that sales are down because of poor marketing and not the quality of their company's product, they could end up ignoring the real problem and wasting time and money on a new advertising campaign instead of improving the product. If someone assumes that people of a certain race, class, or gender behave in predictable ways, they are stereotyping them and making guesses about people's actions without evidence.

Assumptions may be *explicit* or *implicit*, stated or unstated. An implicit assumption is one that is not stated but, rather, is taken for granted. It works like an underlying belief that structures an argument. Assumptions can be powerful sources of ideas and opinions. Understanding our own and others' assumptions is a major part of critical thinking.

Assumptions are sometimes deeply embedded in our value systems and therefore hard to recognize. Assumptions about race, class, disability, sex, and gender are among the most powerful sources of social inequality. Consider this case: When education researchers questioned race and class disparities on the SAT exam in the early 2000s, they found it odd that minorities and other economically disadvantaged students performed worse than their white, middle-class counterparts on the *easier* verbal and math questions, *not* the more difficult ones. That is, a basic vocabulary word like *horse* was likely to be misidentified by minority and lower-income students than more challenging words like *anathema* and *intractable*. (Colloquially, *horse* could be a verb, as in "play around," or it could refer to heroin.) Researchers found that the problem was the assumptions made by the test designers, not the student test-takers. The more "difficult" words typically learned in school or in textbooks were understood more uniformly among all students. The test designers had assumed that persons of all socioeconomic groups hear language the same way and therefore that their proficiency could be measured using the same linguistic standards. By challenging the assumptions of the exam, researchers were able to identify the causes of disparities in exam results — the assumptions themselves, not differential student quality based on socioeconomic factors. As a result, college admissions boards began to regard the SAT as a weaker indicator of academic potential for some groups, while test designers began to address other deeply embedded assumptions in the exam.

Sometimes assumptions may be stated explicitly, especially when writers feel confident that readers share their values. But good critical thinking involves sharpening your ability to identify hidden assumptions, especially those that seem so self-evident, or so commonsensical, that they hardly need to be stated. While they may not put into words, exactly, they may be implied by language (think of the gender assumptions in "stewardess" vs. "flight attendant" or "crew member"). They may also be implied in the *reasoning* of argument (think of the possible assumptions made by a writer whose examples of the ten greatest films of all time are all dramas, or all American films, or all films directed by white men).

When you are evaluating arguments or writing your own, you should question the basic ideas upon which a writer's claims rest and ask yourself if there are other, contradictory or opposed ideas that could be considered. If there are, you can explore the alternative forms of understanding — alternative assumptions — to test or to critique an argument and perhaps offer a different analysis or a different possibility for action. When you are hunting for assumptions (your own and others'), try the following:

- **Identify** the ideas, claims, or values that are presented as obvious, natural, or given (so much so that they are sometimes not even stated).

- **Examine** those ideas to test for their commonality, universality, and necessity. Are other ways of thinking possible?

- **Determine** whether or not contradictory ideas, claims, or values provide a fruitful new way of interpreting or understanding the information at hand.

© 2002 Baldo Partnership/Distributed by Universal Uclick via CartoonStock

Cantú and Castellanos/CartoonStock

A CHECKLIST FOR EXAMINING ASSUMPTIONS

- ☐ Have I identified any of the assumptions presupposed in the writer's argument?
- ☐ Are these assumptions explicit (stated) or implicit (not stated)?
- ☐ Are the author's assumptions important to the argument, or are they only incidental?
- ☐ What sort of evidence would be relevant to supporting or rejecting these assumptions?
- ☐ Am I willing to grant the author's assumptions? Would most readers grant them?

In the essay that follows, Elizabeth Aura McClintock argues that women who are getting married should reconsider taking the last name of their spouse. McClintock's argument takes on a major, often explicit, assumption many people make that this practice is traditional, desirable, or "just the way it is." This social custom may also suggest implicit assumptions, however, about gender and about women's roles in matrimony and domestic life.

ELIZABETH AURA MCCLINTOCK

Elizabeth Aura McClintock is an associate professor of sociology at the University of Notre Dame, where she researches gender and family relationships. She received her BA from Princeton University and her PhD from Stanford University. She is a writer for *Psychology Today* and serves on the editorial boards of the *Journal of Marriage and Family* and *Sex Roles*. This essay appeared in *Psychology Today* in 2018.

Should Marriage Still Involve Changing a Woman's Name?

The modern expectation that women adopt their husband's surname at marriage began in the 9th-century *doctrine of coverture* in English common law (Reid 2018). Under this doctrine, women lacked an independent legal identity apart from their spouses (Reid 2018). At birth, women received their father's surname; when they were "given away" at marriage, they automatically took their husband's surname (Reid 2018; Darrisaw 2018). The phrase "giving away the bride" was intended literally — under the doctrine of coverture, women were property, transferred from husband to father, and largely prohibited from owning their own property (Darrisaw 2018).

The expectation that women adopt their husband's surname at marriage is fundamentally rooted in patriarchal marital traditions. Historically, it represents the transfer of women's subservience from father to husband, the subjugation of women's identities to those of men. This tradition is also profoundly heterosexist, leaving same-sex couples with no clear norms regarding surname choice (Clarke et al. 2008). Yet it has proven remarkably durable, even in the face of broad social and legal changes to marriage — the rise of relatively egalitarian and dual-earner marriages, and the acceptance and legalization of same-sex marriage.

SURNAME CHOICE AT MARRIAGE

Although the norm that women take their husband's last name at marriage may be weakening, it remains nearly ubiquitous. In a sample of married couples in the U.S. in 1980, 98.6 percent of women adopted their husband's surname (Johnson and Scheuble 1995). Among the married children of these same couples, 95.3 percent of women adopted their husband's surname — a decrease of 3.3 percent between generations (Johnson and Scheuble 1995). This upward trend in nontraditional surnames has persisted over time, but change has remained relatively slow. A Google poll found that about 20 percent of women married in recent years have maintained their own names (Miller & Willis 2015).

Studies of surname choice among brides in the 1980s and 1990s indicated that highly educated, career-oriented women with non-traditional gender ideology were most likely to select a nontraditional surname (generally by retaining their own name unchanged or hyphenating their own and their husband's names; Johnson and Scheuble 1995). This pattern has persisted, with more recent studies still reporting that highly educated, career-committed, and feminist women are more likely to make nontraditional surname choices (Hoffnung 2006). Yet, despite women's career commitment overtaking men's career commitment (Patten and Parker 2012), the vast majority of brides still adopt their husband's name upon marriage.

So why do women so often change their names? And why is the decision almost always one about the woman's name? If surname change at marriage were simply about having a single "family name," either spouse could take the other spouse's name, or couples could jointly adopt a new name. 5

THE GENDER OF "SELFISH" INDIVIDUALISM

Societal expectations that nuclear families share one last name, coupled with the invisibility of the option that the husband change his name, place many women in a moral dilemma in which they feel they must choose between self and family (Nugent 2010). Women are expected to be communal, sacrificing their individual interests to the well-being of the collective family — and retaining their birth surname is seen as individualistic, selfish, and antagonistic to family unity.

The force of tradition in shaping cognition is another powerful contributor — for many couples, the possibility of the husband changing his name is an invisible option, placing the burden of surname change entirely upon women.

In addition, women face censure for non-traditional name choices. Women who retain their birth surname are seen as selfish and uncommitted to their marriage and family (Nugent 2010; Shafer 2017). Observers may hold women with nontraditional surnames to higher standards of "performance" as wives (Shafer 2017). Needless to say, this censure is not applied to men who retain their birth name — as long as the possibility of men changing their name remains largely unconsidered and invisible, men's retention of their name appears natural and inevitable.

GENDER-NEUTRAL RATIONALES?

In practice, many ostensibly gender-neutral rationales for naming choices — such as not burdening children with an unwieldy hyphenated last name or having the unity of one surname for all nuclear family members — privilege the father's name (Nugent 2010). For example, having a single, non-hyphenated family name would be accomplished if either spouse took the other's name, but it is exceedingly rare for men to adopt their wife's name, with only about 3 percent of men choosing nontraditional surnames upon marriage (Shafer & Christensen 2018).

Among those few couples who defy the norm, options include alternating children's surnames, thus representing both parents' names equally; combining the parents' names into an entirely new name; and developing rationales for privileging the mother's name, such as the labor of pregnancy and birth.

NAMES MATTER

Many couples follow patriarchal marital traditions simply because they are traditional: Rituals such as giving away the bride may be given new meaning (e.g., honoring the bride's relationship with her father) or may be followed by default. Likewise, many couples take women's surname change for granted, following tradition without discussion or consideration. But that does not lessen the sexism inherent in the tradition. [10]

Women's surname change remains a conspicuous reminder that women's identities are changed by marriage, whereas men's identities remain largely the same. When a newly married couple is announced at a wedding reception as "Mr. and Mrs. John Smith," the woman's name and individuality are subsumed. She has gone from "Miss" to "Mrs.," and her husband's name has replaced her own name. Certainly, many women make this choice happily, but for others, the choice is agonizing. More to the point, as long as women are subjected to unequal societal pressure to change their surname, the practical and professional costs to name change are disproportionately born by women, as are the psychological costs of losing an individual identity (Nugent 2010; Reid 2018).

REFERENCES

Clarke, Victoria, Maree Burns, and Carole Burgoyne. 2008. "'Who Would Take Whose Name?' Accounts of Naming Practices in Same-sex Relationships." *Journal of Community & Applied Social Psychology* 18: 420–439.

Darrisaw, Michelle. 2018 "16 Common Wedding Traditions — And The Shocking History Behind Them." *Southern Living*. https://www.southernliving.com/weddings/history-wedding-traditions

Hoffnung, Michele. 2006. "What's In a Name? Marital Choice Revisited." *Sex Roles* 55:817–825.

Johnson, David R., and Laurie K. Scheuble. 1995. "Women's Marital Naming in Two Generations: A National Study." Journal of Marriage and Family, 57(3):724–732.

McClintock, Elizabeth Aura. 2017. "Choosing Children's Surnames." Blog for Psychology Today.

Miller, Claire Cain, & Derek Willis. 2015. "Maiden names, on the rise again." The New York Times. https://www.nytimes.com/2015/06/28/upshot/maiden-names-on-the-rise-again.html

Nugent, Colleen. 2010. "Children's Surnames, Moral Dilemmas: Accounting for the Predominance of Fathers' Surnames for Children." Gender & Society, 24(4):499–525.

Patten, Eileen, and Kim Parker. 2012. "A Gender Reversal On Career Aspirations." Pew Research Center. http://www.pewsocialtrends.org/2012/04/19/a-gender-reversal-on-career-aspirations/

Reid, Stephanie. 2018. "The History Behind Maiden Vs. Married Names." Seattle Bride. https://seattlebridemag.com/expert-wedding-advice/history-behind-maiden-vs-married-names

Shafer, Emily Fitzgibbons. 2017. "Hillary Rodham versus Hillary Clinton: Consequences of surname choice in marriage." Gender Issues, 34:316–332.

Shafer, Emily Fitzgibbons, and MacKenzie A. Christensen. 2018. "Flipping the (Surname) Script: Men's Nontraditional Surname Choice at Marriage." Journal of Family Issues, 39(11):3055–3074.

Topics for Critical Thinking and Writing

1. Why do you think that most women who get married take their husband's last name at marriage? Why do you think that most men assume they will not be faced with this decision? In other words, what are the deeper, unstated assumptions about gender embedded in this common naming practice?

2. Does McClintock make any assumptions? If so, point out where and explain what you mean.

3. When people do not take their spouse's last names upon marriage, other people may make assumptions about the reasons why. What might those assumptions be? Are they valid?

4. What other assumptions about people who identify as men, women, nonbinary, or other genders impact romantic, matrimonial, or family relationships?

An Example Argument and a Look at the Writer's Strategies

The following essay, "The Reign of Recycling" by John Tierney, concerns the efficacy of recycling—whether or not it is helping the environment in significant ways or if it has gone beyond its originally good intentions to become an unsustainable or even counterproductive measure. We follow Tierney's essay with some comments about the ways in which he constructs his argument.

JOHN TIERNEY

John Tierney (b. 1953) is an award-winning journalist for the *New York Times* who publishes frequently on issues related to science, environmentalism, and politics. He has also published extensively in magazines such as the *Atlantic, Rolling Stone, Newsweek, Discover,* and *Esquire.* His most recent book is *The Power of Bad: How the Negativity Effect Rules Us, and How We Can Rule It* (2019). The essay below appeared in the *New York Times* in 2015.

The Reign of Recycling

1 Tierney presents a common assumption — recycling is helping — but questions it.

1   If you live in the United States, you probably do some form of recycling. It's likely that you separate paper from plastic and glass and metal. You rinse the bottles and cans, and you might put food scraps in a container destined for a composting facility. As you sort everything into the right bins, you probably assume that recycling is helping your community and protecting the environment. But is it? Are you in fact wasting your time?

In 1996, I wrote a long article[1] for *The New York Times Magazine* arguing that the recycling process as we carried it out was wasteful. I presented plenty of evidence that recycling was costly and ineffectual, but its defenders said that it was unfair to rush to judgment. Noting that the modern recycling movement had really just begun just a few years earlier, they predicted it would flourish as the industry matured and the public learned how to recycle properly.

So, what's happened since then? While it's true that the recycling message has reached more people than ever, when it comes to the bottom line, both economically and environmentally, not much has changed at all.

Despite decades of exhortations and mandates, it's still typically more expensive for municipalities to recycle household waste than to send it to a landfill. Prices for recyclable materials have plummeted because of lower oil prices and reduced demand for them overseas. The slump has forced some recycling companies to shut plants and cancel plans for new technologies. The mood is so gloomy that one industry veteran tried to cheer up her colleagues this summer with an article in a trade journal titled, "Recycling Is Not Dead!"[2]

While politicians set higher and higher goals, the national rate of recycling has stagnated in recent years. Yes, it's popular in affluent neighborhoods like Park Slope in Brooklyn and in cities like San Francisco, but residents of the Bronx and Houston don't have the same fervor for sorting garbage in their spare time.

The future for recycling looks even worse. As cities move beyond recycling paper and metals, and into glass, food scraps and assorted plastics, the costs rise sharply while the environmental benefits decline and sometimes vanish. "If you believe recycling is good for the planet and that we need to do more of it, then there's a crisis to confront," says David P. Steiner, the chief executive officer of Waste Management, the largest recycler of household trash in the United States. "Trying to turn garbage into gold costs a lot more than expected. We need to ask ourselves: What is the goal here?"

Recycling has been relentlessly promoted as a goal in and of itself: an unalloyed public good and private virtue that is indoctrinated in students from kindergarten through college. As a result, otherwise well-informed and educated people have no idea of the relative costs and benefits.

They probably don't know, for instance, that to reduce carbon emissions, you'll accomplish a lot more by sorting paper and aluminum cans than by worrying about yogurt containers and half-eaten slices of pizza. Most people also assume that recycling plastic bottles must be doing lots for the planet. They've been encouraged by the Environmental Protection Agency, which assures the public that recycling plastic results in less carbon being released into the atmosphere.

But how much difference does it make? Here's some perspective: To offset the greenhouse impact of one passenger's round-trip flight between New York and

---

2 Establishes *ethos*: he has long been familiar with (and right about) the central issues and questions.

3 *Tierney's thesis reveals his argument*:

Premise: Recycling was costly and ineffectual in 1996.

Premise: Not much has changed since 1996.

Conclusion: Recycling remains costly and ineffectual so should not be expanded further.

4 Tierney makes claims important to his argument but does not present evidence or concrete examples.

5 Tierney quotes an expert authority for corroborating evidence.

6 Tierney suggests that the EPA itself may not be trustworthy. Note that the EPA is commonly a target of pro-business conservatives.

7 Persuasive analogy, but are these numbers useful?

---

[1] John Tierney, "Recycling Is Garbage," *New York Times*, June 30, 1996, nyti.ms/2kqksIS. [All citations in this selection are the editors'; they appeared as hyperlinks in the original publication.]
[2] Patty Moore, "Recycling Is Not Dead," *Resource Recycling*, July 1, 2015, resource-recycling.com/node/6130.

London, you'd have to recycle roughly 40,000 plastic bottles, assuming you fly coach. If you sit in business- or first-class, where each passenger takes up more space, it could be more like 100,000.

8

Even those statistics might be misleading. New York and other cities instruct 10 people to rinse the bottles before putting them in the recycling bin, but the E.P.A.'s life-cycle calculation doesn't take that water into account. That single omission can make a big difference, according to Chris Goodall, the author of "How to Live a Low-Carbon Life." Mr. Goodall calculates that if you wash plastic in water that was heated by coal-derived electricity, then the net effect of your recycling could be *more* carbon in the atmosphere.

To many public officials, recycling is a question of morality, not cost-benefit analysis. [Former] Mayor Bill de Blasio of New York declared that by 2030 the city would no longer send any garbage to landfills. "This is the way of the future if we're going to save our earth," he explained[3] while announcing that New York would join San Francisco, Seattle and other cities in moving toward a "zero waste" policy, which would require an unprecedented level of recycling.

The national rate of recycling rose during the 1990s to 25 percent, meeting the goal set by an E.P.A. official, J. Winston Porter. He advised state officials that no more than about 35 percent of the nation's trash was worth recycling, but some ignored him and set goals of 50 percent and higher. Most of those goals were never met and the national rate has been stuck around 34 percent in recent years.

"It makes sense to recycle commercial cardboard and some paper, as well as selected metals and plastics," he says. "But other materials rarely make sense, including food waste and other compostables. The zero-waste goal makes no sense at all — it's very expensive with almost no real environmental benefit."

One of the original goals of the recycling movement was to avert a supposed crisis because there was no room left in the nation's landfills. But that media-inspired fear was never realistic in a country with so much open space. In reporting the 1996 article I found that all the trash generated by Americans for the next 1,000 years[4] would fit on one-tenth of 1 percent of the land available for grazing. And that tiny amount of land wouldn't be lost forever, because landfills are typically covered with grass and converted to parkland, like the Freshkills Park being created on Staten Island. The United States Open tennis tournament is played on the site of an old landfill — and one that never had the linings and other environmental safeguards required today.

Though most cities shun landfills, they have been welcomed in rural commu- 15 nities that reap large economic benefits (and have plenty of greenery to buffer residents from the sights and smells). Consequently, the great landfill shortage has not arrived, and neither have the shortages of raw materials that were supposed to make recycling profitable.

---

[3]Jill Jorgensen, "Bill de Blasio Calls for the End of Garbage by 2030," *Observer*, April 22, 2015, observer.com/2015/04/bill-de-blasio-calls-for-the-end-of-garbage-by-2030/.

[4]A. Clark Wiseman. *U.S. Wastepaper Recycling Policies: Issues and Ethics* (1990; *Google Books*), books.google.com/books/about/U_S_Wastepaper_Recycling_Policies.html?id=m9YsAQAAMAAJ.

---

8 Strong use of environmentalist's authority as evidence.

9 Proposes that people who think they are doing good for the environment are actually doing worse. How ironic!

10 Begins to address "zero waste" proposals, implicitly criticizing New York's decision to pursue such a goal.

11 Tierney cites another authority, J. Winston Porter, but he may be shifting the issue; Porter actually says some forms of recycling are good.

12 Tierney undermines assumptions that landfills are bad.

With the economic rationale gone, advocates for recycling have switched to environmental arguments. Researchers have calculated that there are indeed such benefits to recycling, but not in the way that many people imagine.

Most of these benefits do not come from reducing the need for landfills and incinerators. A modern well-lined landfill in a rural area can have relatively little environmental impact. Decomposing garbage releases methane, a potent greenhouse gas, but landfill operators have started capturing it and using it to generate electricity. Modern incinerators, while politically unpopular in the United States, release so few pollutants that they've been widely accepted in the eco-conscious countries of Northern Europe and Japan for generating clean energy.

Moreover, recycling operations have their own environmental costs, like extra trucks on the road and pollution from recycling operations. Composting facilities around the country have inspired complaints about nauseating odors, swarming rats, and defecating sea gulls. After New York City started sending food waste to be composted in Delaware, the unhappy neighbors of the composting plant successfully campaigned to shut it down last year.

The environmental benefits of recycling come chiefly from reducing the need to manufacture new products — less mining, drilling and logging. But that's not so appealing to the workers in those industries and to the communities that have accepted the environmental trade-offs that come with those jobs.

Nearly everyone, though, approves of one potential benefit of recycling: reduced emissions of greenhouse gases. Its advocates often cite an estimate by the E.P.A. that recycling municipal solid waste in the United States saves the equivalent of 186 million metric tons of carbon dioxide, comparable to removing the emissions of 39 million cars.

According to the E.P.A.'s estimates, virtually all the greenhouse benefits — more than 90 percent — come from just a few materials: paper, cardboard and metals like the aluminum in soda cans. That's because recycling one ton of metal or paper saves about three tons of carbon dioxide, a much bigger payoff than the other materials analyzed by the E.P.A. Recycling one ton of plastic saves only slightly more than one ton of carbon dioxide. A ton of food saves a little less than a ton. For glass, you have to recycle three tons in order to get about one ton of greenhouse benefits. Worst of all is yard waste: it takes 20 tons of it to save a single ton of carbon dioxide.

Once you exclude paper products and metals, the total annual savings in the United States from recycling everything else in municipal trash — plastics, glass, food, yard trimmings, textiles, rubber, leather — is only two-tenths of 1 percent of America's carbon footprint.

As a business, recycling is on the wrong side of two long-term global economic trends. For centuries, the real cost of labor has been increasing while the real cost of raw materials has been declining. That's why we can afford to buy so much more stuff than our ancestors could. As a labor-intensive activity, recycling is an increasingly expensive way to produce materials that are less and less valuable.

Recyclers have tried to improve the economics by automating the sorting process, but they've been frustrated by politicians eager to increase recycling rates by

13 Counterarguments are raised, but Tierney uses them to defend landfills.

14 Enthymeme: The conclusion is implied. "Some workers are willing to accept the environmental trade-off" implies others should too!

15 Tierney uses statistics as evidence to support his view that recycling plastics is less efficient than recycling other materials.

16 Mixes a fraction and a percentage to present his numerical data. But America still has a huge carbon footprint. Is Tierney downplaying the impact of recycling here?

adding new materials of little value. The more types of trash that are recycled, the more difficult it becomes to sort the valuable from the worthless.

In New York City, the net cost of recycling a ton of trash is now $300 more than 25 it would cost to bury the trash instead. That adds up to millions of extra dollars per year — about half the budget of the parks department — that New Yorkers are spending for the privilege of recycling. That money could buy far more valuable benefits, including more significant reductions in greenhouse emissions.

So what is a socially conscious, sensible person to do?

17 Tierney claims his source is "the most thorough" study without defining his criteria. The source title indicates that it is a study of Japan. Does this use of evidence effectively support Tierney's claim?

17 It would be much simpler and more effective to impose the equivalent of a carbon tax on garbage, as Thomas C. Kinnaman has proposed after conducting what is probably the most thorough comparison of the social costs[5] of recycling, landfilling and incineration. Dr. Kinnaman, an economist at Bucknell University, considered everything from environmental damage to the pleasure that some people take in recycling (the "warm glow" that makes them willing to pay extra to do it).

He concludes that the social good would be optimized by subsidizing the recycling of some metals, and by imposing a $15 tax on each ton of trash that goes to the landfill. That tax would offset the environmental costs, chiefly the greenhouse impact, and allow each municipality to make a guilt-free choice based on local economics and its citizens' wishes. The result, Dr. Kinnaman predicts, would be a lot less recycling than there is today.

Then why do so many public officials keep vowing to do more of it? Special-interest politics is one reason — pressure from green groups — but it's also because recycling intuitively appeals to many voters: It makes people feel virtuous, especially affluent people who feel guilty about their enormous environmental footprint. It is less an ethical activity than a religious ritual, like the ones performed by Catholics to obtain indulgences for their sins.

18 Definition by synonym: Recycling is a religion.

18 Religious rituals don't need any practical justification for the believers who perform them voluntarily. But many recyclers want more than just the freedom to prac- 30 tice their religion. They want to make these rituals mandatory for everyone else, too, with stiff fines for sinners who don't sort properly. Seattle has become so aggressive that the city is being sued by residents who maintain that the inspectors rooting through their trash are violating their constitutional right to privacy.

It would take legions of garbage police to enforce a zero-waste society, but true believers insist that's the future. When Mayor de Blasio promised to eliminate garbage in New York, he said it was "ludicrous" and "outdated" to keep sending garbage to landfills. Recycling, he declared, was the only way for New York to become "a truly sustainable city."

19 Tierney ends by proposing a solution: the status quo.

19 But cities have been burying garbage for thousands of years, and it's still the easiest and cheapest solution for trash. The recycling movement is floundering, and its survival depends on continual subsidies, sermons and policing. How can you build a sustainable city with a strategy that can't even sustain itself?

JOHN TIERNEY, "The Reign of Recycling," *The New York Times*, October 3, 2015. Copyright © 2015 by The New York Times. All rights reserved. Used under license. https://nytimes.com/

---

[5]Thomas C. Kinnaman et al., "The Socially Optimal Recycling Rate: Evidence from Japan," *Journal of Environmental Economics and Management*, vol. 68, no. 1 (2014): 54–70, digitalcommons.bucknell.edu/fac_journ/774/.

Topics for Critical Thinking and Writing

1. What elements of argument make John Tierney's essay persuasive (or not persuasive)?

2. What assumptions are at work in Tierney's essay? For example, what are some of the assumptions about environmentalism that he challenges?

3. In paragraph 29, Tierney defines environmentally conscious behaviors as a "religious ritual." What kind of definition is this? How do you know? (For a refresher, see "Definitions" on pp. 114–119.)

4. What does Tierney identify as the main problem, and what solution is he proposing? Provide a summary of his solution, tracing his line of reasoning.

Arguments for Analysis

JOHN E. FINN

John E. Finn is an author and emeritus professor of government at Wesleyan University, where he taught constitutional theory and public law. He has written several acclaimed books on the US Constitution, most recently *Fracturing the Founding: How the Alt-Right Corrupts the Constitution* (2019). He has also written for law reviews, including the *Columbia Journal of Transnational Law* and *The Georgetown Law Journal*, and has testified before the US House Judiciary Subcommittee on Civil and Constitutional Rights.

The Constitution Doesn't Have a Problem with Mask Mandates

Many public health professionals and politicians are urging or requiring citizens to wear face masks to help slow the spread of the COVID-19 virus.

Some Americans have refused, wrongly claiming mask decrees violate the Constitution. An internet search turns up dozens of examples.

"Costco Karen," for instance, staged a sit-in in a Costco entrance in Hillsboro, Oregon after she refused to wear a mask, yelling "I am an American . . . I have rights."

A group called Health Freedom Idaho organized a protest against a Boise, Idaho, mask mandate. One protester said, "I'm afraid where this country is headed if we just all roll over and abide by control that goes against our constitutional rights."

As one protester said, "The coronavirus 5 doesn't override the Constitution."

Speaking as a constitutional law scholar, these objections are nonsense.

THE OBJECTIONS

It is not always clear why anti-maskers think government orders requiring face coverings in public spaces or those put in place by private businesses violate their constitutional rights, much less what they think those rights are. But most of the mistaken objections fall into two categories:

A protester during an anti-mask rally on July 19 in Indianapolis, Indiana, against the mayor's mask order and the governor's extension of the state shutdown.

Mandatory masks violate the First Amendment right to speech, assembly, and especially association and mandatory masks violate a person's constitutional right to liberty and to make decisions about their own health and bodily integrity.

They're not mutually exclusive claims: A lawsuit filed by four Florida residents against Palm Beach County, for example, argued that mask mandates "interfere with . . . personal liberty and constitutional rights," such as freedom of speech, right to privacy, due process, and the "constitutionally protected right to enjoy and defend life and liberty." The lawsuit asked the court to issue a permanent injunction against the county's mask mandate.

On July 27, the Court declined to issue an 10 injunction against the mask mandate. Citing Jacobsen v. Massachusetts, the Court found that "no constitutional right is infringed by the Mask Ordinance's mandate . . . and that the requirement to swear such a covering has a clear rational basis based on the protection of public health." More to the point, the Court continued, "constitutional rights and the ideals of limited government do not . . . allow (citizens) to wholly shirk their social obligation to their fellow Americans or to society as a whole. . . . After all, we do not have a constitutional right to infect others."

Responding to a reporter who asked why President Donald Trump appeared unconcerned about the absence of masks and social distancing at a campaign rally in Tulsa, Vice President Mike Pence said: "I want to remind you again freedom of speech and the right to peaceably assemble is in the Constitution of the U.S. Even in a health crisis, the American people don't forfeit our constitutional rights."

WHAT THE FIRST AMENDMENT DOES — AND DOESN'T — DO

The First Amendment protects freedom of speech, press, petition, assembly and religion.

There are two reasons why mask mandates don't violate the First Amendment.

First, a mask doesn't keep you from expressing yourself. At most, it limits where and how you can speak. Constitutional law scholars and judges call these "time, place, and manner" restrictions. If they do not discriminate on the basis of the content of the speech, such restrictions do not violate the First Amendment. An example of a valid time, place and manner restriction would be a law that limits political campaigning within a certain distance of a voting booth.

Additionally, the First Amendment, like all liberties ensured by the Constitution, is not absolute. [15]

All constitutional rights are subject to the government's authority to protect the health, safety and welfare of the community. This authority is called the "police power." The Supreme Court has long held that protecting public health is sufficient reason to institute measures that might otherwise violate the First Amendment or other provisions in the Bill of Rights. In 1944, in the case of Prince v. Massachusetts, for example, the Supreme Court upheld a law that prohibited parents from using their children to distribute religious pamphlets on public streets.

THE RIGHT TO LIBERTY

Some anti-maskers object that masks violate the right to liberty.

The right to liberty, including the right to make choices about one's health and body, is essentially a constitutional principle of individual autonomy, neatly summarized as "My body, my choice."

The 1905 case of Jacobsen v. Massachusetts shows why mask mandates don't violate any constitutional right to privacy or health or bodily integrity. In that case, the Supreme Court upheld a smallpox vaccination requirement in Cambridge, Massachusetts.

The court said that the vaccination requirement did not violate Jacobsen's right to liberty or "the inherent right of every freeman to care [20] for his own body and health in such way as to him seems best."

As the court wrote, "There are manifold restraints to which every person is necessarily subject for the common good. On any other basis, organized society could not exist with safety to its members." In a 1995 New York case, a state court held that an individual with active tuberculosis could be forcibly detained in a hospital for appropriate medical treatment.

Even if you assume that mask mandates infringe upon what the Supreme Court calls "fundamental rights," or rights that the court has called the "very essence of a scheme of ordered liberty," it has consistently ruled states can act if the restrictions advance a compelling state interest and do so in the least restrictive manner.

RIGHTS ARE CONDITIONAL

As the Jacobsen ruling and the doctrine of time, place and manner make clear, the protection of all constitutional liberties rides upon certain necessary — but rarely examined — assumptions about communal and public life.

One is that constitutional rights — whether to liberty, speech, assembly, freedom of movement or autonomy — are held on several conditions. The most basic and important of these conditions is that our exercise of rights must not endanger others (and in so doing violate their rights) or the public welfare. This is simply another version of the police power doctrine.

Unfortunately, a global pandemic in [25] which a serious and deadly communicable disease can be transmitted by asymptomatic carriers upsets that background and justifies a wide range of reasonable restrictions on our liberties. Believing otherwise makes the Constitution a suicide pact — and not just metaphorically.

Topics for Critical Thinking and Writing

1. John E. Finn argues that the Constitution is not violated by government mask mandates because they do not limit free speech or individual liberty. What kinds of examples does he use to justify his claims? Does he use any other kinds of evidence (experimentation, authoritative testimony, or numerical data? See the section "Evidence: Experimentation, Examples, Authoritative Testimony, and Numerical Data" on pp. 119–128). If so, which kinds?

2. Is Finn's reasoning an example of inductive or deductive reasoning? Explain.

3. Consider Finn's definitions. What important terms does he define in his argument, and how are they defined? (See "Definitions" on pp. 114–119, for more on stipulation, synonym, example, and sufficient or necessary conditions.)

4. Provide an analysis of the following syllogism developed from Finn's essay, discussing the truth of its premises, the validity of its reasoning, and the quality of its conclusion.
   A. The Constitution protects individual liberty to do what one wants with one's body.
   B. Mask mandates legally require individuals to wear a mask whether they want to or not.
   C. Therefore, mask mandates are unconstitutional.

LOREN LAOMINA

Loren Laomina (they/them) is a writer and grassroots activist who works to support organizers in uniting on social issues related to Black freedom in the United States. This essay was published as part of an emerging writer series in *The Audacity* in 2021.

13 Thoughts on Reparations, Afropessimism and White Supremacy

1. WEDNESDAY, JANUARY 6, 2021

I am nursing a kombucha cocktail from a Spelman College wine glass and Zooming for work as terrorists overtake the Capitol. It is 4:13 p.m. when I see a white man raising the American flag high before bringing it down like an axe on someone obscured by a crush of reds and blues; angry white men in army fatigues scaling the Capitol walls and using their bodies as battering rams to break down doors; a Black officer running up the stairs, chased by a white mob; dark smoke descending around the great dome like arms enclosing an unsuspecting other from behind.

My first thought belongs less to me than to existential Blackness: If they were Black, they'd all be dead. And because I grew up watching *Law & Order* and other police state propaganda, I text a friend, Where are the police? She sends me a link to a tweet by Beytwicé: "Why y'all keep asking where the police at? Y'all ask where Miley's at when Hannah's on stage?"

2. THURSDAY, JANUARY 7, 2021

As we are making tuna fish sandwiches for lunch, my father casually mentions that his grandfather owned a ranch in Texas before he was driven out of the state by white terrorists. It was over a hundred acres, he says, then walks out of the kitchen with his plate, leaving me stunned and alone and confronting my ignorance of my family's history, an ignorance of my people's history.

What I know of what my people have gone through in this country is a jerry-rigged edifice: there is papier mâché where there should be cement, duct-taped panels where there should be wood. My knowledge is drafty, droopy, and there are termites. Not until last summer did I learn of the straight line between slave patrols in the South and modern-day policing. I did not know that the Constitutional clauses that enshrined slavery numbered eleven, nor did I know that the Framers tried to conceal their hypocrisy by avoiding the word "slavery." I knew that

America grew from a debt-addled colonial economy into a global goliath thanks to the relentless churn of cotton gins turned by enslaved people. But I did not know until I read Derrick A. Bell's *And We Are Not Saved* that without slavery, America would have crumbled beneath the weight of what it owed to foreign powers. I knew that America became the wealthiest nation in the world because of slavery but I did not know that it owed its very survival to slavery.

Know thyself, we are told. As a student, I 5 sprinted through "Black history," afraid that if I slowed to look long at our stories, ghouls would emerge from between the pages. Centuries of slavery, decades of Jim Crow, of these I sped read with clenched fists from a great emotional distance. I stuck to dates and stats, wrote papers with words like "unfortunate" and "trying" instead of "tragic" and "horrifying." My understanding of the Black existential condition has changed over time, but there is at least one through line: to be a Black American is to be psychically imperiled by your history. And it could not be otherwise for a people forged through the crucibles of routine rape and brutalization. Bred like mules, Black bodies battery-powered American industry for centuries. To know this is to risk going mad with rage and to not know this is to risk being a fool. It is pure absurdity, this business of knowing that knowing yourself could very well cause you to self-destruct.

3. FRIDAY, JANUARY 8, 2021

Fri, Jan 8, 11:27 AM

you read charles blow's piece?

movement is necessary

the question is, how do we arrange ourselves in the present so that we are no longer waiting for white people to do the right thing?

because they will never do the right thing

and as long as we're spread out, we will never have enough power to change our fates.

i want to change my fate, do you?

4. SATURDAY, JANUARY 9, 2021

Instead of arrests, which are not coming, though we haven't the will to admit this yet, we get a trickle of new footage interspersed with liberal pundits bemoaning working class whites willing to die for a tyrant whose policies oppress them. It is Saturday evening and though I set the intention to have a weekend free of MSNBC, my parents cannot help themselves. They want to watch white liberals rail against the Capitol police and say the words "white supremacy." And I am tired. I am tired of white elites indicting non-elite whites for being ignorant. They are not ignorant. Trump's supporters know who their enemies are and they are us: class privileged colored folks. They know that for centuries whites of every class honored a covenant to keep the value of whiteness high by making Blackness a lynching offense and they know that white elites broke this covenant. They broke it with voting rights and civil rights and affirmative action and Black Studies departments but most importantly, they broke it with Obama, who was as sure a sign as any that the value of whiteness had declined. They know, too, that the restoration of this covenant will bring them more security than any of the items on the progressive agenda because whiteness is a wage more bankable than gold itself, a point made by Du Bois nearly a century ago. As unearned as DNA, whiteness is why working class whites prefer Trump to Bernie, tyranny to democracy, white supremacist capitalism to multiracial socialism. Socialism cannot give them the kind of security they want because the security they want is predicated on another's insecurity. This is why there never has been (and probably never will be) a national movement built on interracial class solidarity.

5. SUNDAY, JANUARY 10, 2021

I am walking to the store when my friend S— calls. She wants to move to Georgia. Charles Blow's *New York Times* piece urging Black folks to move en masse to the South in order to nonviolently overtake the region has captured her imagination. S— asks if I have given Blow's proposal more thought. When I remind her that most of my communities are in the North, she is unswayed. Ask not what your communities can do for you, she says, ask what you can do for your community.

For years, S— has been partial to what Jesse McCarthy calls Afropessimism's exceptionality thesis, which he sums up with the opening sentence of the 2001 preface to Cornel West's *Race Matters*: "Black people in the United States differ from all other modern people owing to the unprecedented levels of unregulated and unrestrained violence directed at them."

To her mind, the centuries-long brutalization of Black folks is without analogy. Without analogy, one cannot reason. The literal unreasonableness of our suffering leads her to the impossibility of repair. I understand her point, but it's a nonstarter for me. I cannot consider the exceptionality of Black suffering without my mind coming to a halt, which is, of course, her point. What grips me more is what McCarthy calls the immutability thesis. Championed by Derrick Bell, it is the idea that a long sober look at American history shows that "slavery did not end in 1865; it evolved." And what's more, it will only ever evolve, because America requires the enslavement of Black folks. Sugar to yeast.

6. MONDAY, JANUARY 11, 2021

S— starts a group text and makes her case. A friend from New York is sympathetic to the idea but her allegiance is to Harlem, West Philadelphia, Roxbury, etc. Each Black neighborhood in the North she names in a separate text. We can't abandon them, she says. 10

Another says we should take them with us.

Another says that if we all go to Georgia, they'll do us like Tulsa.

Like Seneca Village, another friend says.

Like Rosewood.

Like Anniston. 15

Greensboro.

Orangeburg.

Ocoee.

Atlanta.

Elaine. 20

Flint.

Slocum.

Wilmington.

Polk County.

Thibodaux. 25

Danville.

Hamburg.

Clinton.

Vicksburg.

Colfax. 30

St. Bernard.

Opelousas.

Camilla.

New Orleans.

Memphis. 35

Catcher.

Osage.

7. TUESDAY, JANUARY 12, 2021

8. WEDNESDAY, JANUARY 13, 2021

Without asking for my permission or even notifying me, my manager BCCs me on an email to the head of Human Resources. She tells them that an incident that happened a year ago has continued to bother her, and that it is one of the reasons she is leaving the company. During last year's performance reviews, she writes, she decided that I deserved the second highest rating, *Superior Performer*.

I was instructed to lower Loren's ranking to "Successful Performer" and add more critical comments to their review as the higher ratings were already going to other members of the team, mostly white men to my knowledge.

Unsurprisingly, Loren was bothered by 40 *this evaluation. The performance-based raise wasn't even an issue, they just wanted to be recognized for their contributions . . . I was unable (and honestly, unwilling) to offer them any reasonable defense of the situation, only a friendly ear.*

I cannot in good conscience abide by this sort of behavior toward employees who report to me, especially employees of color. Even if this behavior was not intentionally racist, the outcome was completely unfair to a very dedicated employee and I regret that I was not successful in shielding them from it. As I hear rumblings of people of color unhappy with their treatment here, I can only wonder how many similar stories are out there.

In two days my manager will leave the company, which is four months after the departure of the person who told her to lower my score. I am the only one who will be around for the fallout of this report. It is not lost on me that my manager thinks she has done me a favor. That she waited until she had nothing to lose to stand up for me, adding to my towering collection yet another example of a white person unwilling to do what racial justice demands unless doing so costs them nothing.

9. THURSDAY, JANUARY 14, 2021

I am thinking about white folks and how they worship their comfort. I am thinking about my manager, if she truly believes she is leaving because of what happened or if she is aware that this is a lie. I am wondering if I will "give her feedback" on her cowardice and complicity. I am wondering about all the hours I have spent educating and thinking about educating white folks. I am wondering about the reparations I will never receive for these hours: time stolen to enlighten my manager who failed me, and whose failure stole from me a raise. Where are the reparations for my sanity?

10. FRIDAY, JANUARY 15, 2021

I am washing the dishes when I recall that a famous reparationist sold my family his house in what was then a Black neighborhood in D.C. Gentrification has driven the Black folks out and now the neighborhood's houses are worth far more because they belong to white people. I played with the famous reparationist's daughter every day for a week as the arrangements were finalized. When my mom told me that the father of my new friend had written a book on reparations, I laughed. I was only twelve but I already knew what reparations were and I knew they were absurd.

Absurd as in impossible, like leprechauns. My mom scolded me, but I left the room chuckling to myself, trying to come up with a joke to my friend about her dad being absurd. Done with the dishes, I look up this reparationist that I knew for only a week and learn that he wrote several national bestsellers including *The Debt: What America Owes to Blacks*. He moved with his family to St. Kitts where he wrote *Quitting America: The Departure of a Black Man from His Native Land*. He is not the first reparationist to give up and leave. To believe in reparations is a faith in two movements: understanding repayment as necessary to Black freedom in America, and then understanding that repayment will almost certainly never happen. To believe in reparations is to believe, then, that the pursuit of racial justice in America is doomed, which is why I end up at Jesse McCarthy's piece on Afropessimism again, which takes me back to the immutability thesis and Derrick Bell, whom I've never read. I download *Faces At The Bottom Of The Well*, pressing the buy button on my kindle before I can ascertain that I have already depleted my psychic reserves for the day.

11. SATURDAY, JANUARY 16, 2021

I try to rise by eight each morning because [45] there are things I need to do to buttress my sanity, like salute the sun and sit on my mat and if I do not do them in the morning, they do not get done, but I awaken without the will to try today. Instead, I huddle up beneath my covers and turn the pages of *Faces*.

The goal of racial equality is, while comforting to many whites, more illusory than real for Blacks. For too long, we have worked for substantive reform, then settled for weakly worded and poorly enforced legislation, indeterminate judicial decisions, token government positions, even holidays. I repeat. If we are to seek new goals for our struggles, we must first reassess the worth of the racial assumptions on which, without careful thought, we have presumed too much and relied on too long.

A preeminent civil rights lawyer and the first Black professor tenured by Harvard Law School, Derrick Bell is arguably the most brilliant and battle-tested scholar to give up on America.

Black people will never gain full equality in this country. Even those herculean efforts we hail as successful will produce no more than temporary "peaks of progress," short-lived victories that slide into irrelevance as racial patterns adapt in ways that maintain white dominance. This is a hard-to-accept fact that all history verifies.

The Bell of *Faces* has arrived at the proverbial mountaintop of the American legal system and from that great height, seen the bounds of the possible. With hands cupped around his mouth, he yells to Black people: get out!

I am just as moved by Bell's arguments, 50 which are forbidding in their acuity, as I am by his life, which is even more forbidding in its integrity. Bell began his career on the frontier of the civil rights movement's legal battles but became disillusioned by the sacrificial use of Black children to desegregate schools. So he joined Harvard Law School and founded critical race theory. He left to become the Dean of University of Oregon's Law School but after a few years there, he resigned in protest because the law school rejected the faculty application of an Asian-American woman whom he felt deserved the position. He returned to Harvard Law School but again

left in protest because it refused to offer tenure to two professors whose work centered critical race theory. He vowed not to return until it added a Black woman to its tenured faculty and after two years of protest, Harvard fired Bell rather than cede to his demand. By then, Bell was already teaching at New York University School of Law where he mentored Kimberlé Crenshaw, the pioneering legal scholar who would go on to coin the term "intersectionality."

There's a mass mobilization hosted by The Movement For Black Lives that I'm supposed to attend at three. Still huddled beneath my blankets, I bring the computer into my lair and click on the webinar link. A prominent Black Congresswoman is telling the crowd that we have two years to achieve meaningful progress because we are unlikely to keep the Senate and the House. She does not sound daunted. Upbeat and caffeinated, she beams her enthusiasm at us and I turn down the brightness. "Policy is my love language," she says.

"Few men ever worshiped Freedom with half such unquestioning faith as did the American Negro for two centuries," wrote Du Bois more than a century ago.

And, as we have seen, even the laws or court decisions that abolish one form of discrimination may well allow for its appearance in another form, subtle though no less damaging . . . the society has managed to discriminate against Blacks as effectively under the remedy as under the prior law — more effectively really, because discrimination today is covert, harder to prove, its ill effects easier to blame on its Black victims.

On cue, a friend texts the findings from new research on antidemocratic sentiment, its headline: Many white Americans seem to be asking themselves, Why act in defense of a democracy that benefits "those people"?

12. SUNDAY, JANUARY 17, 2021

Black people are oppressed in America. [55]

Obama, Oprah, and Black people who summer at Martha's Vineyard exist.

Therefore, some Black people are not oppressed in America.

If some Black people are not oppressed in America,

Then, it is possible for Black people to not be oppressed in America.

So goes a particular strain of liberal think- [60] ing. I too am guilty. I have pointed to my family — middle-class and educated — as proof that racial justice is around the corner. But there have always been "free" Blacks in America. Forty-one years before the Emancipation Proclamation, the American Colonization Society shipped free Blacks to a strip of land that was thirty-six miles long and three miles wide, land that is now known as Liberia. The American Colonization Society was established for this purpose. Its founders feared that by their mere presence, free Blacks would incite enslaved Blacks to revolt. By 1867, the society had shipped more than 13,000 Black people to Liberia, some of whom would go on to enslave other Black people in the territory.

America requires the oppression of Black people.

Obama, Oprah, and Black people who summer at Martha's Vineyard exist.

Therefore the oppression of Black people does not preclude exceptions.

If some Black people are not oppressed in America,

Then the oppression and the exceptions [65] are mutually supportive.

13. MONDAY, JANUARY 18, 2021

I am trying to imagine what white people must give up when the parable of the rich young prince comes to me. The prince runs up to Jesus, kneels before him, and asks what he must do to gain eternal life. Jesus tells him to keep the commandments. The prince says he has already kept all of them. He asks, "What do I still lack?" Jesus tells the prince to sell his possessions, give everything to the poor, and follow Jesus. The prince is stunned. He walks away sad because he has great wealth. Watching him leave, Jesus pronounces to his audience: It is easier for a camel to go through the eye of a needle than for a rich person to enter the kingdom of God.

Topics for Critical Thinking and Writing

1. How does Loren Laomina use inductive and deductive reasoning in their essay? Provide examples of both types of reasoning and discuss the strength or weakness of the conclusions. Pay special attention to the syllogisms in paragraphs 55–59 and 61–65 — do they hold up as valid, sound, and true arguments? Why or why not?

2. Laomina writes, "Without analogy, one cannot reason" (para. 9). Examine Laomina's use of analogies. Are they effective in convincing readers about their argument? In what ways are the analogies logical and in what ways are they not?

3. Examine Laomina's explicit (stated) and implicit (unstated) assumptions. Where do the assumptions occur, and how are they contestable?

4. Laomina's essay is structured as a series of journal entries. How does this form impact the argument? In positive ways? In negative ways? Explain.

Assignment for Identifying Procedures in Argument

Choose one of the essays in this book and discuss the strongest and weakest points of the argument's reasoning, as well as the procedures of argument discussed in Chapter 4. Consider the reasoning methods (induction/deduction), the definitions, evidence and examples provided, and the presence (if any) of rationalization or confirmation bias. Consider also: What kinds of counterarguments and counterexamples could be presented to challenge particular claims? Do they so do adequately?

Visual Rhetoric: Thinking about Images as Arguments

All photographs are accurate. None of them is the truth. — RICHARD AVEDON

CONSIDER THIS

Imagine what is happening in the ambiguous scene depicted here. What is the woman doing? What does she see? What might have led up to the situation? And how does it end? **(Stop here! Write or discuss your answer before moving on.)**

In the 1930s, Henry A. Murray and Christiana D. Morgan developed the Thematic Apperception Test (TAT) for use in psychological research and clinical therapy; the image you just considered comes from their tests. Like the more famous Rorschach (or "ink-blot") test, the TAT is a projective psychological test intended to reveal more about the viewer than about the image itself.

Science History Images/Alamy

Did you gain any insights into how and why you interpreted the image the way you did? How did your response to the TAT image above differ from others' responses?

Uses of Visual Images

This chapter addresses the ways visual images make and support arguments. Since people are raised and educated in particular societies in particular times and places, they tend to interpret the meanings of images and symbols in common ways (e.g., a heart shape in the United States often means like or love, even though it bears no resemblance to an anatomical heart); however, in a diverse world of different societies, not everyone sees and interprets in the same way. Even within a society, individuals from different cultures, communities, and families may interpret images in vastly different ways.

But images aren't only interpreted; they're created. Visuals are often constructed deliberately to communicate or to enhance a particular message, but that does not mean that you must accept the message. Your way of seeing and interpreting — thinking critically — can be just as valuable, if not more valuable than the intentions of the producers of an image.

Most visual materials that accompany written arguments serve one of several functions. One of the most common is to appeal to the reader's emotions (e.g., a photograph of a sad-eyed calf in a narrow pen assists an argument against eating veal by inspiring sympathy for the animal). Pictures can also serve as visual evidence, offering proof that something occurred or appeared in a certain way at a certain moment (e.g., a security photograph shows the face of a bank robber to a jury). Pictures can help clarify numerical data (e.g., a graph shows five decades of law school enrollment by males and females). They can also add humor or satire to an essay (e.g., a photograph of an executive wearing a blindfold made of dollar bills supports an argument that companies are blinded by their profit motives). In this chapter, we concentrate on thinking critically about visual images. This means reading images in the same way we read print or electronic texts: by looking closely at them and discerning not only *what* they show but also *how* and *why* they show what they do and how they convey a particular message or argument.

When we discussed the appeal to emotion, **pathos**, in Chapter 3 (see "Persuasive Appeals," pp. 76–79), we explained how certain words and ideas can muster the emotions of an audience. Images can do the same without words or with minimal, carefully selected, and thoughtfully displayed words. In a very immediate way, they can make us laugh, cry, or gasp. Furthermore, when used as evidence, some images, graphs, and visuals have an additional advantage over words: They carry a high level of what communications scholars call *indexical value*, meaning that they seem to point to what is true and indisputable.

In courtrooms today, trial lawyers and prosecutors help stir the audience's emotions when they

- hold up a murder weapon for jurors to see,
- introduce victims of crime as witnesses, or
- exhibit images of a bloody corpse or a crime scene.

Whether presented sincerely or gratuitously, visuals can have a significantly persuasive effect. Visuals may be rationally connected to an argument: A gruesome image of a diseased lung in an anti-smoking ad makes a reasonable claim, as does a photograph of crime scene that establishes the veracity of the locations of evidence. But the immediate impact of a photograph is more often on the viewer's heart (*pathos*) rather than mind (*logos*). Speaking of those appeals, we can also say that images can help establish *ethos*: Think about how lawyers might present to the jury images of defendants portrayed in wholesome contexts — receiving an award, hugging a family member — in order to bolster their character or credibility (even if their defendants are actually lacking these qualities).

Like any kind of evidence, images make statements and support arguments. When the US Congress debated whether to allow drilling in the Arctic National Wildlife Refuge (ANWR), opponents and supporters both used images to support their verbal arguments:

- *Opponents* of drilling showed beautiful pictures of polar bears frolicking, wildflowers in bloom, and caribou on the move, arguing that such a landscape would be despoiled.

- *Proponents* of drilling showed bleak pictures of what they called "barren land" and "a frozen wasteland," pointing to a useless and barely habitable environment.

Both sides knew very well that images are powerfully persuasive, and they didn't hesitate to use them as supplements to words. Although two contradictory facts can't be true, two depictions of the same event may be presented — and therefore seen and interpreted— as factual.

These two photographs, both of the Arctic National Wildlife Refuge, show different uses of images to argue about the value and use of land.

We invite you to reflect upon the appropriateness of using such images in arguments. Was either side manipulating the "reality" of the ANWR? Both images were *real*, after all. Each side selected a particular *kind* of image for a specific **purpose** — to support its position on drilling in the ANWR. Neither side was being dishonest, and both were showing true pictures, but both were also appealing to emotions.

Seeing versus Looking

One helpful way of deriving the meanings of images by *looking* at them is to use *seeing* first as a way to define what is plainly or literally present in them. You can begin by *seeing* — identifying the elements that are indisputably "there" in an image (the denotative level). In a sense, you are merely taking an inventory of what is visible and evident. Then you move on to *looking*—interpreting the meanings suggested by the elements that are present (the connotative level). Arguably, when we *see*, we pay attention only to the denotative level—that is, we observe just the explicit elements of the image. We aren't concerned with the meaning of the image's elements yet, just with the fact that they're present.

When we *look*, we move to the connotative level—that is, we speculate on the elements' deeper meanings: what they suggest figuratively, symbolically, or metaphorically in our cultural system. We may also consider the relationship of different elements to one another.

Seeing	Looking
Denotation	Connotation
Literal	Figurative
What is present	What it means
Understanding/Textual	Interpreting/Subtextual/Contextual

Further questions we can ask have to do with the contexts in which images are created, disseminated, and received. Within each of those questions, others arise.

Visual Guide: Analyzing Images

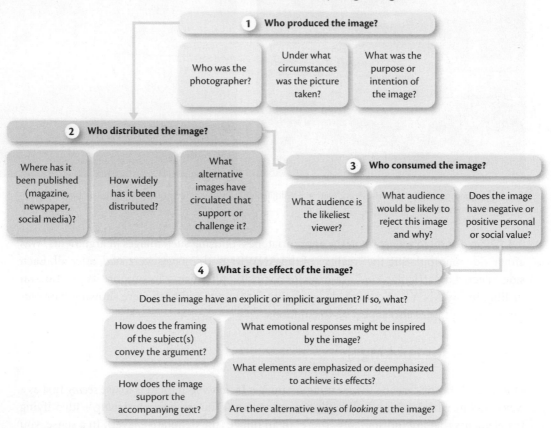

1 **Who produced the image?**

Who was the photographer?

Under what circumstances was the picture taken?

What was the purpose or intention of the image?

2 **Who distributed the image?**

Where has it been published (magazine, newspaper, social media)?

How widely has it been distributed?

What alternative images have circulated that support or challenge it?

3 **Who consumed the image?**

What audience is the likeliest viewer?

What audience would be likely to reject this image and why?

Does the image have negative or positive personal or social value?

4 **What is the effect of the image?**

Does the image have an explicit or implicit argument? If so, what?

How does the framing of the subject(s) convey the argument?

What emotional responses might be inspired by the image?

What elements are emphasized or deemphasized to achieve its effects?

How does the image support the accompanying text?

Are there alternative ways of *looking* at the image?

Examine the images below and do the following:

1. *See* the image. Thoroughly describe the image. Identify as many elements as possible that you see: colors, shapes, text, people, objects, lighting, framing, perspective, and so forth.

2. *Look* at the image. Take the elements you have observed and relate what they suggest by considering their figurative meanings, their meanings in relation to one another, and their meanings in the context of the images' production and consumption.

Cattle grazing in a California pasture near a wind farm in 1996.

Moms Demand Action, a national public safety advocacy group against gun violence, published this advertisement in 2013. The text reads, "One child is holding something that's been banned in America to protect them. Guess which one."

READING ADVERTISEMENTS

Advertising is one of the most common forms of visual persuasion we encounter in every-day life. The influence of advertising in our culture is pervasive and subtle. Part of its power comes from our habit of internalizing the intended messages of words and images without thinking deeply about them. Once we begin decoding the ways in which advertisements are constructed — once we view them critically — we can understand how (or if) they work as arguments. We may then make better decisions about whether to buy particular products and what factors convinced us or failed to convince us. We can also develop a critical lens that will help us read other kinds of images beyond advertising, such as news and documentary photographs.

To read any image critically, it helps to consider some basic rules from the field of **semiotics**, the study of signs and symbols. Fundamental to semiotic analysis is the idea that visual signs have shared meanings in a culture. If you approach a sink and see a red faucet and a blue faucet, you can be pretty sure which one will produce hot water and which one will produce cold water. Thus, one of the first strategies we can use in reading advertisements critically is **deconstructing** them — taking them apart to see what makes them work.

Taking apart an advertisement (or any image) means examining each visual element care-fully in order to understand its purpose, its strategy, and its effect. Consider this 2007 adver-tisement for Nike shoes featuring basketball star LeBron James. By looking closer, we can detect deeper, underlying meanings that invite interpretation and engagement.

Let's consider this advertisement in the context of James's famous 2014 return to the Cleveland Cavaliers, his hometown team, after leaving the team abruptly to play four

The text draws on language commonly used in religious settings to describe the second coming of Christ.

The Nike logo is the only reference to the brand being advertised. It is a powerful symbol and identity marker, much like a cross.

James's arms are outstretched, Christ-like, and seem to be illuminated by divine light from above.

The number 23 references basketball legend (and Nike spokesperson) Michael Jordan. James is, in a way, presented as a new incarnation of a sports "god."

A Nike advertisement featuring basketball star LeBron James, annotated to show a deconstruction of the image.

seasons with the Miami Heat. James's "second coming" to Cleveland resonated with religious themes of forgiveness, redemption, and salvation among Cleveland sports fans. James later moved on to the Los Angeles Lakers; however, at the time the ad shown on page 156 appeared, these religious associations symbolically elevated James, Jordan, and Nike to exalted status. Of course, it was all partly tongue in cheek, but the message was clear: If sports gods wear Nike, why shouldn't we? Furthermore, the ad *grips* the viewer in a complex visual engagement. Few advertisers want you to simply glance at their ad and move on. The more interplay between producer (creator) and consumer (viewer), the more effective the ad.

This kind of critical analysis allows us to read an image beyond what it literally depicts. To practice this kind of viewing, it helps to recognize a difference between *seeing* and *looking*. **Seeing** is a physiological process involving light, the eye, and the brain. It allows us to apprehend images in a basic, physical way. **Looking**, however, is a social process involving the mind. It suggests thinking about images in terms of symbolic, metaphorical, and other social and cultural meanings; "looking" in this sense does not require the physical ability to see. To do this, we must think beyond the *literal* meaning of an image or image element and consider its *figurative* meanings. If you look up *apple* in the dictionary, you'll find its literal, **denotative** meaning — a round fruit with thin red or green skin and a crisp flesh. But an apple also communicates figurative, **connotative** meanings. Connotative meanings are the cultural or emotional associations that an image suggests.

How do the DKNY and Bulova advertisements use the symbolic, connotative meanings of the apple to make an argument about their products?

The connotative meaning of an apple in Western culture dates back to the Judeo-Christian story of the Garden of Eden, where Eve, tempted by a serpent, eats the fruit from the forbidden tree of knowledge and brings about the end of paradise on earth. Throughout Western culture, apples have come to represent knowledge and the pursuit of knowledge. Think of the ubiquitous Apple logo gracing so many mobile phones, tablets, and laptops: With its prominent bite, it symbolizes the way technology opens up new worlds of knowing. Sometimes, apples represent forbidden knowledge, temptation, or seduction — and biting into one suggests giving in to desires for new understandings and experiences. The story of Snow White offers just one example of an apple used as a symbol of temptation.

When you are looking — and not just seeing in the simplest sense — you are attempting to discern the ways in which symbolic meanings are used to communicate a message. Take, for example, the following advertisement for Play-Doh, one of the most enduring and popular toys of the past century. First developed in 1930s, Play-Doh has sold billions of canisters around the world. Today, Play-Doh competes with a wide array of technological toys for children, such as smartphones and video game systems.

An advertisement for the timeless toy, Play-Doh, that takes on its digital competitors.

The ad for Play-Doh featured here makes an argument with just a single line of text: "No In-App Purchases." These words are set below the image of a shopping cart with a plus sign made of Play-Doh, which has come to be an almost universally recognized symbol for an electronic shopping cart online. Both the words and the icon are textured and look a little rough at the edges, suggesting that they are also made of Play-Doh. In a blue open space suggesting three-dimensionality, the advertisement seems to make a case for the role of real-life, nondigital play in the development of children. It presents Play-Doh as a traditional, value-based proposition without manipulative sales tactics, something trustworthy and honest. The way children play has changed dramatically since the 1930s, but by fashioning the electronic icon and text out of a nearly century-old product, the ad implies that just because a toy — or anything else — is new and high-tech, that does not make it inherently better than old-fashioned things. After all, Play-Doh has stood the test of time; how long will an app on a smartphone or tablet last until it is replaced with a newer version requiring a new update?

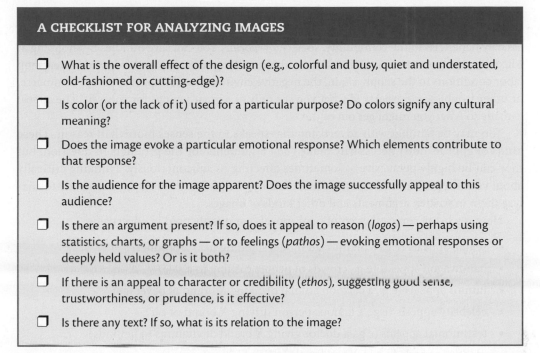

DETECTING EMOTIONAL APPEALS IN VISUAL CULTURE

Visual arguments commonly use emotional appeals, such as an appeal to fear. When advertisers show a burglary, a visceral car crash, embarrassing age spots, or a nasty cockroach infestation, for example, they may successfully convince consumers to buy a product — a home security system, a new car insurance policy, an age-defying skin cream, a pesticide. Such images generate fear and anxiety at the same time they offer the solution for it.

Appeals to other emotions like love, desire, hunger, or ambition can also activate drives that sometimes supersede the logical faculties, enticing people to follow their instincts and passions more than their thoughtful, deliberate calculations. Appeals to pity and sorrow play directly on the heart strings. Appeals to anger and disgust can stir people into frenzied dismissal of others' views and ideas, and into an unwillingness to consider additional or alternative evidence.

Such appeals are not limited to advertising, but are present in the images created by news outlets, political campaigns, and other sources where arguments are made. Emotional appeals span all forms of media and engage a wide range of human emotions. They may elicit nostalgia for a glorified past ("Don't you miss the way things used to be?"), call up common prejudices ("Everyone knows bleeding heart liberals will endorse *X*"), or encourage a desire to belong ("Join the millions who stand behind *Y*!"). They may motivate by triggering an audience's moral conscience ("Only the hardest heart can turn away from giving money to rescue poor, abandoned, and abused animals"), sense of shame ("Don't let sagging skin keep you from looking young"), or fear of missing out ("This opportunity won't last long, so act now!").

Emotional appeals can also be quite persuasive when they speak directly to what benefits *you* the most: the **appeal to self-interest**. The argument may not be promoting what is necessarily beneficial to the community, society, or world. "You can save bundles by shopping at Maxi-Mart," a commercial might claim, without making reference to third-world sweatshop labor conditions in the supply chain, the negative environmental impact of global commerce, or other troublesome aspects of what you see only as a great savings for yourself. The appeal is made to what you might get out of it.

You may be familiar with advertising that speaks to the senses more than reason. These kinds of appeals don't necessarily make *good* arguments for the products in question, but they can be highly persuasive — sometimes affecting us subconsciously. Thinking critically about visual appeals in commercial culture can be a helpful way to sharpen our ability to analyze them in written arguments and other kinds of images.

Here is a list of some other emotional appeals commonly used in advertising:

- sexual appeals (e.g., a bikini-clad model standing near a product)
- bandwagon appeals (e.g., crowds of people rushing to a sale)
- humor appeals (e.g., a cartoon animal drinking *X* brand of beverage)
- celebrity appeals (e.g., a famous person driving *X* brand of car)
- testimonial appeals (e.g., a doctor giving *X* brand of vitamins to her kids)
- identity appeals (e.g., a "good family" going to *X* restaurant)
- prejudice appeals (e.g., a "loser" drinking *X* brand of beer)
- lifestyle appeals (e.g., a jar of *X* brand of mustard on a silver platter)
- stereotype appeals (e.g., a Latinx person enjoying *X* brand of salsa)
- patriotic appeals (e.g., *X* brand of mattress alongside an American flag)

Appeals to fear in visual culture often drive political arguments, especially during a campaign season. In the 2020 US Presidential election, for example, Republicans and Democrats both used visual media as a primary tool to evoke fear in order to convince voters to elect their candidates. In one popular television commercial created by the Donald Trump campaign, an elderly woman's efforts to telephone the police are fruitless as a burglar breaks into her home. In the background, the news is reporting on Joe Biden's efforts to "defund the police." A recorded message from the 911 service tells the woman that "there is no one here to answer your emergency call." The burglar pries open the door and sets upon the woman as the camera cuts to the phone falling to the floor. The screen then fills with the words: "You won't be safe in Joe Biden's America." The Biden campaign warned against such fear-mongering but also did some of its own, airing an ad that that portrayed "Donald Trump's America" through images from the 2017 "Unite the Right" rallies in Charlottesville, Virginia, spliced with images of mass shootings committed by white supremacists, to suggest that Trump emboldened racist individuals and groups to commit violence. Biden said he decided to run against Trump "when those folks came out of the fields carrying those torches, chanting anti-Semitic bile and their veins bulging, accompanied by the Ku Klux Klan. . . . I never thought I'd see something like that again in my life."

Trump campaign ad   Biden campaign ad

Critics of art and culture can also utilize fear in their argumentative appeals. When, in 2020, Netflix premiered *Cuties*, a film written and directed by Maïmouna Doucouré about a group of precocious eleven-year-old girls, Hawaii Congress member Tulsi Gabbard tweeted that the film "will certainly whet the appetite of pedophiles and help fuel the child sex trafficking trade." A Texas grand jury brought criminal charges against Netflix for distributing lewd material involving children. Arguments rooted in fear about the impact of art on society are not new: In 1985, the Parents Music Resource Center (PMRC), founded by Tipper Gore (then wife of politician Al Gore), argued that some popular music was undermining society by promoting occult beliefs, teenage sexuality, and drug and alcohol use. After a US Senate hearing was convened, the PMRC successfully lobbied the recording industry to require the now-iconic "Parental Advisory" warnings on all music deemed inappropriate for children.

READING PHOTOGRAPHS

When advertisers use images, we know they're trying to convince consumers to purchase a product or service. But when images serve as documentary evidence, we often assume that they're showing the "truth" of the matter at hand. We may assume the images in magazines and newspapers capture a particular event or moment in time *as it really happened*. Thus, our level of skepticism may be lower than when we are looking at advertising images designed to persuade us.

As we learned with the uses of images relating to the Arctic National Wildlife Refuge (see p. 153), photographs can serve as evidence but have a peculiar relationship to the truth. We must never forget that images — even documentary images — are constructed, selected, and used for specific purposes. These kinds of images (historical images, images of events, news photographs, and the like) are not free from the potential for manipulation or for (conscious or unconscious) bias. Consider how liberal and conservative media sources portray the nation's president in images: One source may show him proud and smiling in bright light with the American flag behind him, whereas another might show him scowling in a darkened image suggestive of evil intent. Both are "real" images, but the framing, tinting, setting, and background can inspire significantly different responses in viewers.

Martin Luther King Jr. delivering his "I Have a Dream" speech on August 28, 1963, from the steps of the Lincoln Memorial.

As we saw with the image of LeBron James (p. 156), certain postures, facial expressions, and settings can contribute to a photograph's interpretation. Martin Luther King Jr.'s great speech of August 28, 1963, "I Have a Dream," still reads very well on the page, but part of its immense appeal derives from its setting: King spoke to some 200,000 people in Washington, DC, as he stood on the steps of the Lincoln Memorial. That setting, rich with associations of slavery and freedom, strongly assists King's argument. In fact, images of King delivering his speech are nearly inseparable from the very argument he was making. The visual aspects — the setting (the Lincoln Memorial with the Washington Monument and the Capitol in the distance) and King's gestures — are part of the speech's persuasive rhetoric.

These and other images of King are ubiquitous, but do they tell the "real truth" about King? When Derrick Alridge, a historian, examined dozens of accounts of Martin Luther King Jr. in history books, he found that images of King present him overwhelmingly as a messianic figure — standing before crowds, leading them, addressing them in postures reminiscent of a prophet. Although King is an admirable figure, Alridge asserts, history books present him as more than human. They ignore his personal struggles and failures and make a myth of King instead of portraying the real person. They elevate him above other civil rights figures and fail to account for those people who paved the way for King and those who continued his legacy after he was killed. Further, Alridge argues, when history books present King as a holy prophet, it becomes easier to focus on his gospel of love, equality, and justice and not on the specific policies and politics he advocated — his avowed socialist stances, for instance. In short, while photographs of King seek to help us remember, they may

Martin Luther King Jr. on "Chicken Bone Beach" in Atlantic City.

actually portray him in a way that causes us to forget other things—for example, that his approval rating among white people at the time of his death was lower than 30 percent and among Black people lower than 50 percent.

Alridge's thesis is that while images in history books appear to give us access to historical truths, they may actually alter or obscure other truths.

DO PHOTOGRAPHS ALWAYS TELL THE TRUTH?

Photography has been a consistent driver of news stories—and often *the* story. But as our strategy of "seeing and looking" has underscored, and as the images of Martin Luther King Jr. show, photographs that seem to provide a clear window into reality are not absolute guarantors of truth. Photographers such as Mathew Brady, Alexander Gardner, and Timothy O'Sullivan captured shocking images of dead soldiers scattered across the US Civil War battlefields of Antietam, Maryland, and Gettysburg, Pennsylvania. Their photographs countered the glorious depictions of war that frequently appeared in nineteenth-century paintings. (Notably, such paintings were emotional appeals to the honor, sacrifice, and heroism of war.) These photographs documented the battles but also contained a distinct moral charge.

In the photograph from Gardner at Antietam, a Union soldier looks upon the grave of his own Lieutenant Clark, respectfully interred at the place he died; meanwhile, a Confederate casualty lies on the ground nearby, unburied and unmourned. Although this rebel soldier was eventually buried respectfully, the image communicates something different: that while both were killed defending their own ideals, one kind of victim (the Union soldier) deserved special respect.

Such photographs had a profound influence on attitudes towards the US Civil War, and in many ways dispelled myths about the glory of warfare by driving home dehumanizing images of mass death in ways that audiences had not before seen. Just because the outcome was useful does not mean the photographs weren't in some measure "manipulated." If the goal of journalism is to report the unvarnished truth, then the question arises as to whether it is ever ethical for a photographer to "stage" a photograph, such as Gardner and O'Sullivan did in "Home of the Rebel Sharpshooter."

In 1975, historian William Frassanito pointed out that the corpse shown at Gettysburg was actually present in a different photograph taken by Gardner on a nearby hill, called "A Sharpshooter's Last Sleep," indicating that Gardner or his associates moved the body into a picturesque but empty sharpshooter's nest, along with a knapsack and a rifle that served as props. These grim and disturbing facts may represent something we can hardly imagine, but can we say that the manipulations altered the reality of the soldier's sudden death or the fundamentally moral question of whether or not such deaths are justified by warfare?

Alexander Gardner's photograph of the aftermath of Antietam, September 19, 1862

Home of the Rebel Sharpshooter: Gettysburg, 1865

These examples demonstrate that images may not always tell the whole (or most accurate) story, but they can nonetheless accentuate the moral dimensions of an issue by highlighting its most visceral, distressing aspects. In this sense, the war photographs manipulated by Gardner are both unethical (moving dead bodies to stage a shot) and fully principled (an effort to show in a compelling way the true horrors of war).

An old saying tells us, "Seeing is believing." Debates continue about the relationship between photographs and reality and the propriety of constructing images to send a particular message. Today, at a time when it is remarkably easy to alter digital images with free software and easily accessible devices, we should be suspicious any time photographs are used as direct evidence of reality. At the same time, we must recognize the indexical value of photographs and believe what we see when it is appropriate. In other words, *we must judge with our utmost critical attention*. Those who question the images taken from Apollo 11 in order to claim the moon landing never happened, for example, stretch skepticism far past its reasonable limits. With some images, it may be more difficult to identify the trickery: When photographer Tyler Mitchell's image of Parkland school shooting survivor Emma González appeared on the cover of *Teen Vogue* magazine in 2018, it showed her ripping a paper shooting target in half. It wasn't long before another version created by gun rights activists went viral: It showed González tearing up the US Constitution.

Forensic analysts have highly technical methods to detect fake photography. While we may not all have their tools or expertise, the Checklist for Inspecting Digital Photographs offers some fairly simple strategies you can use if you suspect an image is a forgery.

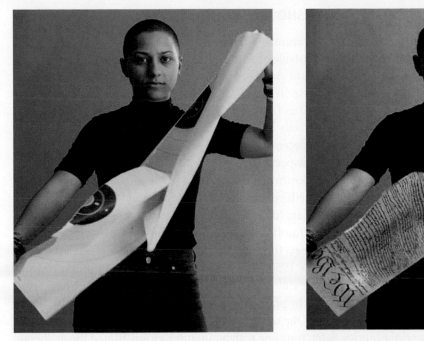

The original and altered photographs of Parkland school shooting victim Emma Gonzalez.

A CHECKLIST FOR INSPECTING DIGITAL PHOTOGRAPHS

☐ Is the photograph extreme or difficult to believe (e.g., a giant shark about to eat a surfer)?

☐ Is the photograph published by a reputable source (e.g., a news organization with editorial oversight)?

☐ Has the photo been questioned or debunked by another reputable source (e.g., a web page committed to ethics in photojournalism)?

☐ Are the sizes and shapes of objects and other elements proportional in relation to one another?

☐ Are there any other asymmetries or distortions that can be identified? (e.g., mismatched earrings, missing or impossible shadows, strange lighting sources?)

☐ Does a reverse image search reveal an original, undoctored version of the same image?

☐ Is the image being used to support an extraordinary claim? (e.g., images of Bigfoot, or of a celebrity or politician doing something uncharacteristic)

ARE SOME IMAGES NOT FIT TO BE SHOWN?

Images of suffering — either human or animal — can be immensely persuasive but also controversial. Until recently, with some notable exceptions, most news outlets did not publish pictures that involved gruesome images of violence and death. Even today, however, when it's commonplace for newspapers and television news to show pictures of victims of war, famine, or traffic accidents, one rarely sees bodies that are horribly maimed. (For traffic accidents, the body is usually covered, and we see only the smashed car.)

It may seem obviously a matter of decency not to show these kinds of images. But some images bear such important witness to aspects of society that many people feel they ought to be shown even if they are disturbing. Reformers such as Ida Tarbell and Lewis Hine, seeking child labor reforms in the early twentieth century, used images of children working in factories, fields, mines, and on street corners to muster outrage. During the Great Depression, photographers such as Walker Evans, Dorothea Lange, and Marion Post Wolcott pushed for Progressive-era reforms by bearing witness through photography to the struggles of the poor. During the civil rights movement of the 1950s and 1960s, photographs and motion pictures proved vital in exposing the realities of violence against Black people in the US South. And during the Vietnam War, images made by photographers shifted sentiment about the war in the United States in significant ways. One of the most famous examples occurred in 1965, when CBS news reporter Morley Safer, traveling with an infantry group, filmed the deliberate burning of the village of Cam Ne by US soldiers. Reflecting in 2003 on the impact of that television moment, Safer said:

> I think [viewers] saw American troops acting in a way people had never seen American troops act before and couldn't imagine. Those people were raised on World War II, in which virtually everything we saw was heroic. And so much of it, indeed, was. And there was plenty in Vietnam, too, that was heroic. But this conjured up not America, but some brutal power — Germany, even, in World War II. To see young GIs, big guys in flak jackets, lighting up thatched roofs, and women holding babies running away, wailing — this was a new sight to everyone. . . .

When the footage aired, President Lyndon B. Johnson was outraged that CBS News would broadcast what he felt were unrepresentative images of the US mission.

In the past few years, some of the most impactful images of police and vigilante violence against Black citizens helped inspire nationwide protests (and yet even these images are sometimes edited or blurred so as to avoid reproducing the trauma or sensationalizing the violence). Photographic evidence of Syrian president Bashar Al-Assad's use of chemical weapons against dissidents helped fuel international condemnation of his regime. Images of hospitals overcrowded with patients dying of COVID-19 were painful yet effective in convincing people to take precautions against the spread of the virus.

The power of photography to expose truths in an unvarnished way is an important part of ensuring a well-informed public. If we avert our gaze from the most dramatic and horrifying realities of war, violence, disease, poverty, and other forms of suffering, we may not feel the urge to address the problems directly and forcefully. In some cases, photographs serve multiple functions — for example, serving simultaneously as attestations to injustice, modes of witness to violence, and evidence in criminal cases. In other cases, photographs can evoke the wrenching but necessary confrontation with reality that inspires action — and arguments about how and why to do so.

But are there some images absolutely not fit to print? Are some images unacceptable? For instance, although capital punishment — by methods including lethal injection, hanging, shooting, and electrocution — is legal in parts of the United States, every state prohibits the publication of pictures showing the execution. The US government refuses to release photographs showing the bodies

John Filo/Getty Images

The photograph seen here by John Filo from the May 4, 1970, shootings of students by National Guardsmen during antiwar protests at Kent State University was reproduced widely in 1970 and won a Pulitzer Prize. The searing image galvanized the student antiwar movement and sparked a nationwide outcry for justice against military invention in domestic disturbances.

of American soldiers killed in the wars in Iraq and Afghanistan — or, typically, their caskets returning to the United States — and it was also reticent to show pictures of dead Iraqi soldiers and civilians. Yet, when many Iraqis doubted that US forces had killed the two sons of Saddam Hussein in 2003, the US government reluctantly released pictures showing the two men's blood-spattered faces — and still some American newspapers and television programs refused to use the images.

Publishers do not just consider the tastes or squeamishness of audiences in deciding whether or not to publish certain images. In the case of images from mass shootings, for example, it is sometimes the goal of the perpetrator to garner just such media attention. By publishing the images, news outlets are not just reporting the news but are also in a sense falling victim themselves to the shooter's plot. Given that many mass shooters have cited media exposure as a motive, and given that more coverage potentially creates more motivation for "copycats," publishers must walk a fine line between documenting the problem and contributing to it. The same is said to be true for publishing images of terrorist acts, riots, and even paparazzi photos that intrude on the personal lives of celebrities.

What do you think? Is judging a photograph as acceptable or unacceptable for publication only a matter of personal taste or experience? Or is publishing an image a necessary act of exposure or witness to social ills that need correction? (We admit we had many discussions with our editor about what was fit to publish in this book.)

The Checklist for Publishing Controversial Images will help you consider some general standards for the appropriateness of using images in your own work.

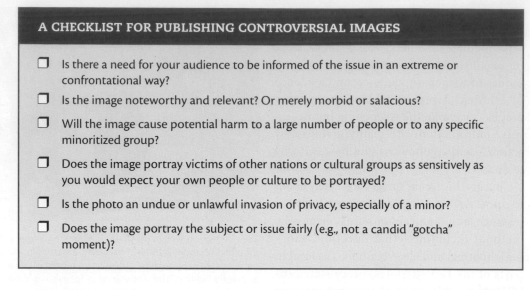

A CHECKLIST FOR PUBLISHING CONTROVERSIAL IMAGES

☐ Is there a need for your audience to be informed of the issue in an extreme or confrontational way?

☐ Is the image noteworthy and relevant? Or merely morbid or salacious?

☐ Will the image cause potential harm to a large number of people or to any specific minoritized group?

☐ Does the image portray victims of other nations or cultural groups as sensitively as you would expect your own people or culture to be portrayed?

☐ Is the photo an undue or unlawful invasion of privacy, especially of a minor?

☐ Does the image portray the subject or issue fairly (e.g., not a candid "gotcha" moment)?

Accommodating, Resisting, and Negotiating the Meaning of Images

To counteract our own tendency to think that "seeing is believing," we can be more critical about images by approaching them through three broad frameworks: *accommodation, resistance*, and *negotiation*. Most images are produced, selected, and published so as to have a specific effect on readers and viewers. This dominant meaning of an image supposes that the audience will react in a predictable way or take away a specific message, usually based on the widespread **cultural codes** that operate within a society. Advertisers count on viewers interpreting images of elegant women in designer dresses, rugged men driving pickup trucks, stodgy teachers, cutthroat CEOs, hipster computer programmers, and so on according to generally accepted notions of what certain types of people are like. An image of a suburban couple in an automobile advertisement washing their new car subconsciously confirms and perpetuates a certain ideal of middle-class suburban life (a heterosexual couple, a well-trimmed lawn, a neatly painted house and picket fence — and a brand-new midsize sedan). An image of a teary-eyed young woman accepting a diamond ring from a handsome man will likely touch the viewer in a particular way, in part because of our society's cultural codes about the rituals of romantic love and marriage, gender roles, and the diamond ring as a sign of love and commitment.

These examples demonstrate that images can be constructed according to dominant connotations of gender, class, and racial, sexual, and political identity. As image consumers, we often **accommodate** (i.e., passively accept) those cultural codes. For example, in the case of the hypothetical advertisement featuring a marriage proposal — a man kneeling, a woman crying sentimentally — you might not decide to buy a diamond because you saw it, but you might just simply accept the assumption embedded in the message that diamond rings are the appropriate objects to represent love and commitment. Further, you might accept the cultural codes about the rituals of romantic love, marriage, and gender roles, sharing the assumption that men should propose to women, that women are more emotional than men, or that marriage is a desirable social construct.

When you *accommodate* cultural codes without understanding them critically, you allow the media that perpetuate these codes to interpret the world for you. That is, you accept their interpretations without questioning the social and cultural values implicit in their assumptions, many of which may actually run counter to your own or others' social and cultural values. When analyzing an image, ask yourself what cultural codes it endorses, what ideals it establishes as natural, and what social norms it assumes or idealizes.

If you **resist** the cultural codes of an image, you actively criticize its message and meaning. Suppose you (1) question how the ad presents gender roles and marriage, (2) claim that it idealizes heterosexual marriage, and (3) point out that it confirms and extends traditional gender roles in which men are active and bold and women are passive and emotional. Moreover, you (4) argue that the diamond ring represents a misguided commodification of love because diamonds are kept deliberately scarce by large companies and, as such, are overvalued and overpriced; meanwhile, you say, the ad prompts young couples to spend precious money at a time when their joint assets might be better saved, and because many diamonds come from third-world countries under essentially slave labor conditions, the diamond is more a symbol of oppression than of love. If your analysis follows such paths, you *resist* the dominant message of the image in question. Sometimes, this is called an *oppositional reading*.

Negotiation, or a *negotiated reading*, perhaps the most useful mode of reading and viewing, involves a middle path — a process of revision that seeks to recognize and change the conditions that give rise to certain negative aspects of cultural codes. Negotiation implies a practical intervention into common viewing processes that help construct and maintain social conditions and relations. A negotiated reading enables you to emphasize the ways in which individuals and social groups relate to images and their dominant meanings and how different personal and cultural perspectives can challenge those meanings. This intervention can be important when inequalities or stereotypes are perpetuated by cultural codes. Without intervention, there can be no revision, no positive social or cultural change. You *negotiate* cultural codes when:

- you understand the underlying messages of images and accept the general cultural implications of these codes, *but*
- you acknowledge that in some circumstances the general codes do not apply.

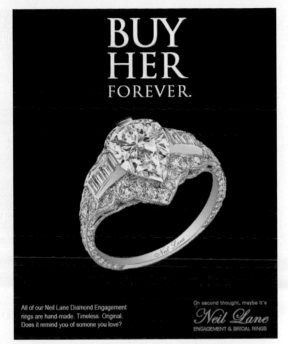

What cultural codes does this ad accommodate?

TODAY MY LIBERAL WIFE FOUND OUT HER RING IS A CUBIC ZIRCONIA.

I TOLD HER NOT TO WORRY; IT IDENTIFIES AS A DIAMOND.

snsif/Shutterstock

Memes often use humor to present oppositional ideas. However, in doing so, they sometimes reaffirm other cultural codes and assumptions.

Writing about Political Cartoons and Memes

Most editorial news outlets publish political cartoons, which circulate in the media and online frequently. Like the writers of op-eds, cartoonists seek to persuade, but they rarely use words to *argue* a point. True, they may use a few words in speech balloons or in captions, but generally the drawing does most of the work. Because their aim usually is to convince the viewer that some action, policy, or proposal is ridiculous, cartoonists almost always **caricature** their subjects: They exaggerate the subject's distinctive features to the point at which the subject becomes grotesque and ridiculous — absurd, laughable, contemptible.

Cartoonists are concerned with producing a striking image, not with exploring an issue deeply, so they almost always oversimplify and distort. As we have said, this sort of persuasion probably is unfair: Almost always the issue is more complicated than the cartoonist indicates. But just because cartoons work largely by ridicule and the omission of counterarguments, we shouldn't reject the possibility that the cartoonist has indeed highlighted some absurdity, hypocrisy, or other perplexing aspect of an issue.

In the course of portraying figures in a cartoon, cartoonists often use **symbolism**. Here's a list of common symbols:

- symbolic figures (e.g., the US government as Uncle Sam)
- animals (e.g., the Democratic Party as donkey and the Republican Party as elephant)
- buildings (e.g., the White House as representing the nation's president)
- things (e.g., a bag with a dollar sign on it as representing a bribe)

For anyone brought up in American culture, these symbols (like the human figures they represent) are obvious, and cartoonists assume that viewers will instantly recognize the symbols and figures, will get the joke, and will see the absurdity of whatever issue the cartoonist is seeking to demolish.

Of course, as with any type of viewing, you can accommodate, resist, or negotiate with the meanings of a political cartoon. In writing about the argument presented in a cartoon, normally you would discuss the ways in which the cartoon makes its point through humor, and then determine whether or not the message corresponds to a reasonable, logical argument. Caricature usually implies, "This is ridiculous, as you can plainly see by the absurdity of the figures depicted" or "What *X*'s proposal adds up to, despite its apparent complexity, is nothing more than. . . ." It is up to you if you want to *accept* or *reject* the point. If you are negotiating with the message of the cartoon, your essay will likely include an *evaluation* of the cartoon, examining how it is effective (persuasive) for such-and-such reasons but unfair for such-and-such other reasons.

The cartoon by Pulitzer Prize–winning cartoonist Walt Handelsman responds to the recent state of political decorum. It depicts a group of Washington, DC, tourists being driven past what the guide calls "The Museum of Modern American Political Discourse," a building in the shape of a giant toilet. The toilet as a symbol of the level of political discussion dominates the cartoon, effectively driving home the point that Americans are watching our leaders sink to new lows in the hostility of their speech. By drawing the toilet on a scale similar to that of familiar monuments in Washington, Handelsman may be pointing out that today's politicians, rather than being remembered for great achievements like those of George Washington or Abraham Lincoln, will instead be remembered for their rudeness and aggression. If you were accommodating the meaning of this cartoon, you might agree with Handelsman; if you were resisting it, you might say it's always been this way and there's nothing wrong with being candid. If you were negotiating its message, you could point out that it

Walt Handelsman/Chicago Tribune/TNS

blames politicians solely for the state of political discourse and portrays the "people" as separate from it (or subject to it); however, as we must recognize, political discourse is also in bad shape among the people themselves, too.

Memes are in many ways a new form of political cartoon and play a prominent role in the modern digital landscape. Memes can often be nonsensical or funny without a strong or evident argument. The viral meme depicting a young woman with braces holding up three books from the popular Goosebumps series, framed by the words "Ermagerd/Berks," comes to mind as a fairly innocuous distraction. Yet, like all memes, the very mode of expression invites transformation, re-articulation, and recirculation.

Other memes can have a more significant cultural impact. In recent years, the term "Karen" has come to symbolize a certain type of suburban, white female who takes her privilege for granted and is prone to self-centered acts of entitlement and racism. While the origins of "Karen" are somewhat disputed (see knowyourmeme.com for a full account), the figure became indisputably a meme in hundreds of widely shared images critiquing stereotypically middle-class, white, cisgender, female cultural attitudes. Memes can also utilize images of political figures and political trends to satirize current events, then quickly fall out of fashion: The "Mike Pence Fly" meme mocked the former Vice President for the common housefly that appeared on his hair during a 2020 debate with Kamala Harris. Before long, the fly was seen in various manifestations: holding up a Biden/Harris sign, communicating messages to Pence from Donald Trump, and more. Our favorite: "Mike Pence on Bring Your Pet to Work Day."

As silly as they can be, memes have a way of spreading contagiously; it's no surprise that we call it "going viral." Like a virus, the image spreads and mutates, but interestingly, by modifying and recirculating memes, everyday people can participate in the political discourse in potentially significant ways. Memes can accentuate or supplement political arguments and function as popular commentary on political and cultural phenomena. They can be used to judge, shame, humiliate, and defame; or they can celebrate, popularize, and add to the texture of social interaction.

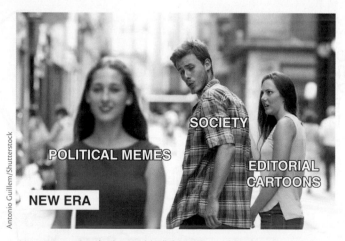

Antonio Guillem/Shutterstock

Memes are uniquely changeable. "The Distracted Boyfriend" meme has been appropriated widely.

THINKING CRITICALLY *Analyzing Memes and Political Cartoons*

Find a recent political meme or political cartoon to analyze, pulled from a print or online publication. For each Type of Analysis section in the chart below, provide your own answer based on the cartoon.

TYPE OF ANALYSIS	QUESTIONS TO ASK	YOUR ANSWER
Context	*Who is the creator or artist? Where and when was the meme or cartoon first circulated or published? What situations, issues, or political conditions does it respond to?*	
Description	*What do you see in the meme or cartoon? What elements does it include?*	
Evaluation	*Does the meme or cartoon appeal to pathos, logos or ethos? Does it mock or satirize something? Is it a fair critique? What is the argument it makes?*	
Analysis	*Looking more closely at the images and considering their meanings, how does the meme or cartoon make its point? Is it effective? How could you accommodate, resist, or negotiate the meanings of this image?*	

An Example: A Student's Essay Analyzing Images

Ryan Kwon

Professor Carter

English 101

17 September 2018

The American Pipe Dream?

Visual arguments are powerful tools used by photographers, advertisers, and artists to persuade an audience. Two powerful examples of visual arguments about a shared subject, the so-called American Dream, occur in two different types of images, yet they both point to important questions about the attainability of the dream in two different contexts. The first is Margaret Bourke-White's 1937 photograph of flood victims, and the second is Mike Keefe's 2012 political cartoon from InToon.com. Both images, although seventy-five years apart, aim to persuade the audience that the ideology of the American Dream is unattainable in reality. While Bourke-White does so through the use of appeals to irony, juxtaposition, and color contrast, Keefe does so through heavy symbolism and carefully selected text. By comparing these two images, we can see how the **(1)** American dream is — and always was — elusive.

Bourke-White's photo of flood victims waiting in a bread line in 1937 (Fig. 1) is not a staged photo like an advertisement, but on closer inspection, it utilizes visual framing to undermine the ideology of the American Dream through appeals to irony, juxtaposition, and color contrast. The billboard is loaded with emotive, powerful phrases like, "World's Highest Standard of Living" and "There's no way like the American Way." The family in the billboard image is nicely dressed, smiling, and driving a shiny, new car. This billboard presents the good life that the American Dream is known **(2)** to give its citizens.

1 *Thesis:* Two visual arguments from different contexts reveal the irony of the American Dream.

2 Makes use of an "inventory" of elements in the photograph— billboard, words, clothing, smiles, car, dog, empty baskets.

Margaret Bourke-White/The LIFE Picture Collection/Shutterstock

Fig. 1. Margaret Bourke-White, *Kentucky Flood* (1937).

However, the juxtaposition of this billboard with the line of flood victims beneath it creates an appeal to irony. The American good life is physically above the heads of the people in line, as if it were nothing more than a dream. The family on the billboard is "free" in the sense that they are on the open road. Even the dog appears to be smiling. Meanwhile, the flood victims, stuck in line, are not moving at all. Unlike the family, they do not appear to be enjoying the privileges of ownership: their baskets are (literally and figuratively) empty. The billboard creates the illusion that all American citizens can live the good life simply by being a citizen, but the realities of the flood victims in this photograph say otherwise.

The audience must also take into account that in 1937, racism and segregation of blacks from whites was heavily prominent. Since the billboard pictures a white family, it excludes minorities from the American Dream. Therefore, this photograph demonstrates specifically that minorities are unable to attain the American Dream. The color contrast in this photo

3

3 Kwon recognizes visual metaphor: Being stuck in line is a symbol for social mobility.

4

4 Placing the photograph in historical context helps interpret meaning.

Fig. 2. Mike Keefe, "The American Pipe Dream with Attached Mirage . . ." (2012).

further emphasizes the division between light and dark, black people and white people. The billboard is bright, white, and promising, in a dreamlike world above the heads the real individuals who are shadowed and dark, demonstrating that the American Dream is nothing more than an unattainable dream for some.

Keefe's more recent political cartoon (Fig. 2) also demolishes the attainability of the American Dream, but adds a more modern perspective through the use of symbolism and carefully selected text. The description of the cartoon reads, "The American Pipe Dream with Attached Mirage . . ." Since political cartoons are meant to be read in a matter of seconds by the audience, it is important for the cartoonist to get their message across quickly. Keefe manages to do so by setting the tone with this description. A white family, like the one in Bourke-White's photo, is drawn struggling to climb up a desert mountain, demonstrated by their wide eyes, their open mouths, and the beads of sweat surrounding the man's head. They are struggling because they are weighed down by four objects: a prison ball named "Underemployment"; a treasure chest of "Credit Card Debt"; a big bag

5 More on how the form and visual details of the photograph add meaning.

5

of "Student Loans"; and a wide-eyed infant. The prison ball weighs the man down because without steady income from a secure job, he cannot support his family. Credit card debt is represented as a treasure chest because a credit card can buy lots of material items, but one must pay off the bill. Leaving the bill unpaid means all of the so-called treasures are taken away. The woman is literally carrying baggage, and that baggage is the amount of student loans that add into the credit card debt. Finally, having a child without a job and with heavy debt is an extra expense. With all of these items weighing the family down, it is no surprise they are struggling to achieve the American Dream, represented by the floating mirage of a suburban home.

> **6** Again, author shows how visual details can be interpreted as metaphors.

The American Dream is floating above the struggling family in Keefe's image, much like the billboard in Bourke-White's photo. This time, however, it is a white family who is struggling to achieve the American Dream, the same kind of family who, ironically, were once the face of it. Thus, Keefe's cartoon manages to express the modern unattainability of the American Dream for all to its audience in a matter of moments, in a way that is just as effective as Bourke-White's photograph.

> **7** Author uses evidence from the image to establish the American Dream as something unreachable—always an ideal, but not a reality for all.

Clearly, visuals are powerful tools that can persuade an audience to take a stance on a certain political ideology, such as the American Dream. Both Bourke-White and Keefe make their stances about the unattainability of the American Dream clear, and even build off of each other to make the message stronger, despite their works being created in two different contexts. While textual arguments are certainly accredited more for their persuasion, visual arguments play a powerful role with the ability to persuade an audience.

Works Cited

Bourke-White, Margaret. *Kentucky Flood*. *Life*, Time Inc., 1937, images .google.com/hosted/life/bdb4f71a5f11cf96.html.

Keefe, Mike. "American Pipe Dream." *InToon.com*, The Association of American Editorial Cartoonists, 13 Apr. 2012, editorialcartoonists.com /cartoon/display.cfm/110032/. Accessed 20 Sep. 2018.

Visuals as Aids to Clarity: Maps, Graphs, and Pie Charts

Often, writers use visual aids that are not images but still present information or data graphically in order to support a point. Maps were part of the argument in the debate over drilling in the Arctic National Wildlife Refuge we discussed at the beginning of this chapter.

- Advocates of drilling argued that it would take place only in a tiny area. Their drawn map showed the entire state of Alaska, with a smaller inset showing a much smaller part of the state that was the refuge. The map points out the drilling area with an arrow, implying it is too insignificant of an area to matter because it is too miniscule to show.

- Opponents utilized a close-up image to show the extent of industrial sprawl and roads that would have to be constructed across the refuge for drilling to take place. The map uses many icons to show how intrusive the drilling would be to this green natural area. The inset Alaska map is much smaller, deemphasizing the size of the refuge relative to the state.

By changing the scale and orienting viewers to the information in different ways, maps of the same area support different arguments.

Graphs, tables, and pie charts usually present quantitative data in visual form, helping writers clarify dry, statistical assertions. For instance, a line graph may illustrate how many immigrants came to the United States in each decade of the twentieth century.

A bar graph (with bars running either horizontally or vertically) offers similar information. In the Coming to America graph on page 180, we can see at a glance that, say, the second bar on the lower left is almost double the height of the first, indicating that the number of immigrants almost doubled between 1850 and 1860.

A pie chart is a circle divided into wedges so that we can see, literally, how a whole comprises its parts. We can see, for instance, in the From Near and Far chart on page 180, an entire pie representing the regions of foreign-born US immigrants: 32 percent were born in Central America and Mexico, 40 percent in Asia, 9 percent in Europe, and so on.

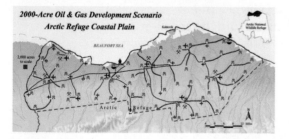

Maps showing the refuge in different ways for different purposes: advocates of drilling used the map on the top to emphasize size, and opponents used the map on the bottom to emphasize industrial transformation.

A WORD ON MISLEADING OR MANIPULATIVE VISUAL DATA

Because maps, charts, tables, and graphs offer empirical data to support arguments, they communicate a high degree of reliability and tend to be convincing. "Numbers don't lie," it is sometimes said, and to some extent this is true. It's difficult to spin a fact like 1 + 1 = 2. However, as author Charles Seife notes in his book *Proofiness*, numbers are cold facts, but the measurements that numbers actually chart aren't always so clear or free from bias and manipulation. Consider two examples of advertising claims that Seife cites — one for a L'Oréal mascara offering "twelve times more impact" and another for a new and improved Vaseline product that "delivers 70% more moisture in every drop." Such measurements *sound* good but remain relatively meaningless. (How was eyelash "impact" measured? What is a percentage value of moisture?)

A CHECKLIST FOR CHARTS AND GRAPHS

☐   Is the source authoritative?

☐   Is the source cited?

☐   Will the chart or graph be intelligible to the intended audience?

☐   Is the caption, if any, clear and helpful?

Another way data can be relatively meaningless is when it addresses only part of the question at stake. In 2013, a Mayo Clinic study found that drinking coffee regularly lowered participants' risk of the liver disease known as primary sclerosing cholangitis (PSC). But PSC is already listed as a "rare disease" by the Centers for Disease Control and Prevention, affecting fewer than 1 in 2,000 people. So even if drinking coffee lowered the risk of PSC by 25 percent, a person's chances would improve only slightly from 0.0005 percent chance to 0.0004 percent chance — hardly a change at all, and hardly a rationale for drinking more coffee. Yet statistical information showing a 25 percent reduction in PSC sounds significant, even more so when provided under a headline proclaiming "Drinking coffee helps prevent liver disease."

Consider other uses of numbers that Seife shows in his book to constitute "proofiness" (his title and word to describe the misuse of numbers as evidence):

- In his 2006 State of the Union Address, George W. Bush declared No Child Left Behind (NCLB) a success: "[B]ecause we acted," he said, "students are performing better in reading and math." (True, fourth to eighth graders showed improved scores, but other grade levels declined. In addition, fourth- to eighth-grade reading and math scores had been improving at an unchanged rate both before and after the NCLB legislation.)

- In 2000, the *New York Times* reported "Researchers Link Bad Debt to Bad Health" (the "dark side of the economic boom"). The researchers claimed that debt causes more illness, but in doing so they committed the correlation-causation fallacy: Just because two phenomena are correlated does not mean they are causally related. (Example: More people wear shorts in the summer and more people eat ice cream in the summer than during other seasons, but wearing shorts does not *cause* higher ice cream consumption.)

COMING TO AMERICA . . .

Both the percentage and number of foreign-born people in the United States dropped during much of the twentieth century, but after 1970, the tide was turning again.

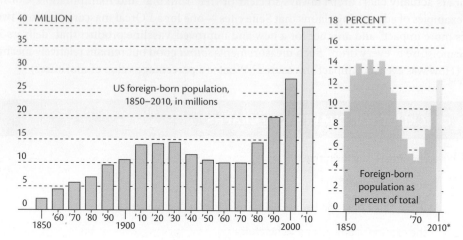

. . . FROM NEAR AND FAR

Central America, Mexico, and Asia contribute most to the foreign-born population.

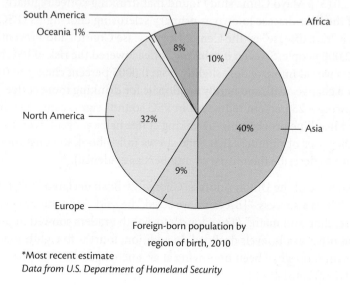

Foreign-born population by region of birth, 2010

*Most recent estimate
Data from U.S. Department of Homeland Security

Finally, consider the following graph showing that eating Quaker Oats decreases cholesterol levels after just four weeks of daily servings. The bar graph suggests that cholesterol levels will plummet. But a careful look at the graph reveals that the vertical axis doesn't begin at zero. In this case, a relatively small change has been (mis)represented as much bigger than it actually is.

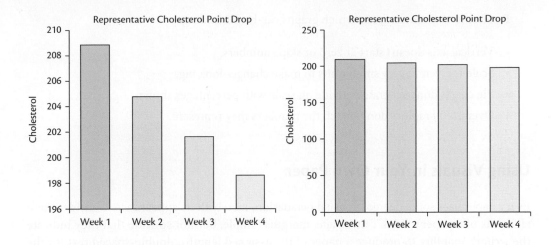

A more accurate representation of cholesterol levels after four weeks of eating Quaker Oats, using a graph that starts at zero, would look more like the second graph — showing essentially unchanged levels.

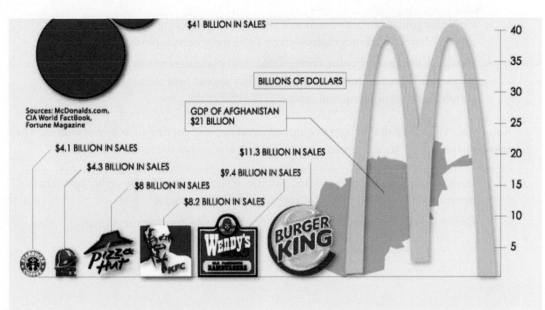

In this graph, McDonald's $41 billion in sales are shown to be about 3.5 times higher than the revenues of its next closest competitor, Burger King (at $11.3 billion), but the McDonald's logo graphic is about 13 times larger than Burger King's.

Be alert to common ways in which graphs can be misleading:

- Vertical axis doesn't start at zero or skips numbers.
- Scale is given in very small units to make changes look big.
- Pie charts don't accurately divide on scale with percentages shown.
- Oversized graphics don't match the numbers they represent.

Using Visuals in Your Own Paper

Every paper uses some degree of visual persuasion, merely in its appearance. Consider these elements of a paper's "look": title page; margins (ample, but not so wide that they indicate the writer's inability to produce a paper of the assigned length); double-spaced text for the reader's convenience; headings and subheadings that indicate the progression of the argument; paragraphing; and so on. But you may also want to use visuals such as pictures, graphs, tables, or pie charts to provide examples, help readers digest statistical data more quickly, or simply liven up your essay or presentation. Keep a few guidelines in mind as you work with visuals, "writing" them into your own argument with as much care as you would read them in others' arguments:

- Consider your audience's needs and attitudes and select the type of visuals — graphs, drawings, photographs — likely to be most persuasive to that audience.
- Consider the effect of color, composition, and placement within your document. Because images are most effective when they appear near the text that they supplement, do not group all images at the end of the paper.

Remember especially that images are almost never self-supporting or self-explanatory. They may be evidence for your argument but they aren't arguments themselves. Therefore:

- Be sure to explain each visual that you use, integrating it into the verbal text that provides the logic and principal support behind your thesis.
- Be sure to cite the source of any visual that you paste into your argument.

Visual Arguments for Analysis

DOROTHEA LANGE

In 1936, photographer Dorothea Lange (1895–1965) took a series of a migrant mother and her children. Widely reprinted in the nation's newspapers, these photographs helped dramatize for the American public the poverty of displaced workers during the Great Depression.

Migrant Mother

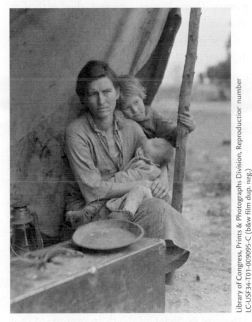

Library of Congress, Prints & Photographs Division, Reproduction number LC-USF34-T01-009095-C (b&w film dup. neg.)

Library of Congress, Prints & Photographs Division, Reproduction number LC-DIG-fsa-8b29516

Topics for Critical Thinking and Writing

1. Dorothea Lange drew increasingly near to her subject as she took a series of pictures. Make a list of details gained and lost by framing the mother and children more closely. The final shot in the series (right) became the most famous and most widely reprinted. Do you find it more effective than the other? Why or why not?

2. Notice the expression on the mother's face, the position of her body, and the way she interacts with her children. What sorts of relationships are implied? Why is it significant that she doesn't look at her children or at the camera? How do the photographs' effects change according to how much you can see of the children's faces?

3. These photographs constitute a sort of persuasive "speech." Of what, exactly, might the photographer be trying to persuade her viewers? Write a brief essay (about 250 words) explaining Lange's purpose for her photographs and how she achieves that purpose. What do the nonhuman elements in the photographs symbolize, and how do they contribute to the argument?

NORA EPHRON

Nora Ephron (1941–2012) attended Wellesley College and then worked as a reporter for the *New York Post* and as a columnist and senior editor for *Esquire*. Ephron wrote screenplays and directed films, including *Sleepless in Seattle* (1993) and *You've Got Mail* (1998), and continued to write essays on a wide variety of topics. "The Boston Photographs" is from her collection *Scribble, Scribble: Notes on the Media* (1978).

The Boston Photographs

"I made all kinds of pictures because I thought it would be a good rescue shot over the ladder . . . never dreamed it would be anything else. . . . I kept having to move around because of the light set. The sky was bright and they were in deep shadow. I was making pictures with a motor drive and he, the fire fighter, was reaching up and, I don't know, everything started falling. I followed the girl down taking pictures. . . . I made three or four frames. I realized what was going on and I completely turned around, because I didn't want to see her hit."

You probably saw the photographs. In most newspapers, there were three of them. The first showed some people on a fire escape — a fireman, a woman, and a child. The fireman had a nice strong jaw and looked very brave. The woman was holding the child. Smoke was pouring from the building behind them. A rescue ladder was approaching, just a few feet away, and the fireman had one arm around the woman and one arm reaching out toward the ladder. The second picture showed the fire escape slipping off the building. The child had fallen on the escape and seemed about to slide off the edge. The woman was grasping desperately at the legs of the fireman, who had managed to grab the ladder. The third picture showed the woman and child in midair, falling to the ground. Their arms and legs were outstretched, horribly distended. A potted plant was falling too. The caption said that the

woman, Diana Bryant, nineteen, died in the fall. The child landed on the woman's body and lived.

The pictures were taken by Stanley Forman, thirty, of the *Boston Herald American*. He used a motor-driven Nikon F set at 1/250, f5.6-S. Because of the motor, the camera can click off three frames a second. More than four hundred newspapers in the United States alone carried the photographs: The tear sheets from overseas are still coming in. The *New York Times* ran them on the first page of its second section; a paper in south Georgia gave them nineteen columns; the *Chicago Tribune*, the *Washington Post*, and the *Washington Star* filled almost half their front pages, the *Star* under a somewhat redundant headline that read: SENSATIONAL PHOTOS OF RESCUE ATTEMPT THAT FAILED.

The photographs are indeed sensational. They are pictures of death in action, of that split second when luck runs out, and it is impossible to look at them without feeling their extraordinary impact and remembering, in an almost subconscious way, the morbid fantasy of falling, falling off a building, falling to one's death. Beyond that, the pictures are classics, old-fashioned but perfect examples of photojournalism at its most spectacular. They're throwbacks, really, fire pictures, 1930s tabloid shots; at the same time they're technically superb and thoroughly modern — the sequence could not have been taken at all until the development of the motor-driven camera some sixteen years ago.

Most newspaper editors anticipate some reader reaction to photographs like Forman's; even so, the response around the country was enormous, and almost all of it was negative. I have read hundreds of the letters that were printed in letters-to-the-editor sections, and they repeat the same points. "Invading the privacy of death." "Cheap sensationalism." "I thought I was reading the *National Enquirer.*" "Assigning the agony of a human being in terror of imminent death to the status of a side-show act." "A tawdry way to sell newspapers." The *Seattle Times* received sixty letters and calls; its managing editor even got a couple of them at home. A reader wrote the *Philadelphia Inquirer*: "*Jaws* and *Towering Inferno* are playing downtown; don't take business away from people who pay good money to advertise in your own paper." Another reader wrote the *Chicago Sun-Times*: "I shall try to hide my disappointment that Miss Bryant wasn't wearing a skirt when she fell to her death. You could have had some award-winning photographs of her underpants as her skirt billowed over her head, you voyeurs." Several newspaper editors wrote columns defending the pictures: Thomas Keevil of the *Costa Mesa* (California) *Daily Pilot* printed a ballot for readers to vote on whether they would have printed the pictures; Marshall L. Stone of Maine's *Bangor Daily News*, which refused to print the famous assassination picture of the Vietcong prisoner in Saigon, claimed that the Boston pictures showed the dangers of fire escapes and raised questions about slumlords. (The burning building was a five-story brick apartment house on Marlborough Street in the Back Bay section of Boston.)

For the last five years, the *Washington Post* has employed various journalists as ombudsmen, whose job is to monitor the paper on behalf of the public. The *Post*'s current ombudsman is Charles Seib, former managing editor of the *Washington Star*; the day the Boston photographs appeared, the paper received over seventy calls in protest. As Seib later wrote in a column about the pictures, it was "the largest reaction to a published item that I have experienced in eight months as the *Post*'s ombudsman. . . .

"In the *Post*'s newsroom, on the other hand, I found no doubts, no second thoughts . . . the question was not whether they should be printed but how they should be displayed. When I talked to editors . . . they used words like 'interesting' and 'riveting' and 'gripping' to describe them. The pictures told of something about life in the ghetto, they said (although the neighborhood where the tragedy occurred is not a ghetto, I am told). They dramatized the need to check on the safety of fire escapes. They dramatically conveyed something that had happened, and that is the business we're in. They were news. . . .

"Was publication of that [third] picture a bow to the same taste for the morbidly sensational that makes gold mines of disaster movies? Most papers will not print the picture of a dead body except in the most unusual circumstances. Does the fact that the final picture was taken a millisecond before the young woman died make a difference? Most papers will not print a picture of a bare female breast. Is that a more inappropriate subject for display than the picture of a human being's last agonized instant of life?" Seib offered no answers to the questions he raised, but he went on to say that although as an editor he would probably have run the pictures, as a reader he was revolted by them.

In conclusion, Seib wrote: "Any editor who decided to print those pictures without giving at least a moment's thought to what purpose they served and what their effect was likely to be on the reader should ask another question: Have I become so preoccupied with manufacturing a product according to professional traditions and standards that I have forgotten about the consumer, the reader?"

© Pulitzer Prize 1976, stanleyformanphotos.com.

© Pulitzer Prize 1976, stanleyformanphotos.com.

It should be clear that the phone calls and letters and Seib's own reaction were occasioned by one factor alone: the death of the woman. Obviously, had she survived the fall, no one would have protested; the pictures would have had a completely different impact. Equally obviously, had the child died as well — or instead — Seib would undoubtedly have received ten times the phone calls he did. In each case, the pictures would have been exactly the same — only the captions, and thus the responses, would have been different.

But the questions Seib raises are worth discussing — though not exactly for the reasons he mentions. For it may be that the real lesson of the Boston photographs is not the danger that editors will be forgetful of reader reaction, but that they will continue to censor pictures of death precisely because of that reaction. The protests Seib fielded were really a variation on an old theme — and we saw plenty of it during the Nixon-Agnew years — the "Why doesn't the press print the good news?"

10 argument. In this case, of course, the objections were all dressed up and cleverly disguised as righteous indignation about the privacy of death. This is a form of puritanism that is often justifiable; just as often it is merely puritanical.

Seib takes it for granted that the widespread though fairly recent newspaper policy against printing pictures of dead bodies is a sound one; I don't know that it makes any sense at all. I recognize that printing pictures of corpses raises all sorts of problems about taste and titillation and sensationalism; the fact is, however, that people die. Death happens to be one of life's main events. And it is irresponsible — and more than that, inaccurate — for newspapers to fail to show it, or to show it only when an astonishing set of photos comes in over the Associated Press wire. Most papers covering fatal automobile accidents will print pictures of mangled cars. But the significance of fatal automobile accidents is not that a great deal of steel is twisted but that people die. Why not show it? That's what accidents are about. Throughout

Pulitzer Prize 1976, stanleyformanphotos.com.

Pulitzer Prize 1976, stanleyformanphotos.com.

the Vietnam War, editors were reluctant to print atrocity pictures. Why *not* print them? That's what that was about. Murder victims are almost never photographed; they are granted their privacy. But their relatives are relentlessly pictured on their way in and out of hospitals and morgues and funerals.

I'm not advocating that newspapers print these things in order to teach their readers a lesson. The *Post* editors justified their printing of the Boston pictures with several arguments in that direction; every one of them is irrelevant. The pictures don't show anything about slum life; the incident could have happened anywhere, and it did. It is extremely unlikely that anyone who saw them rushed out and had his fire escape strengthened. And the pictures were not news—at least they were not national news. It is not news in Washington, or New York, or Los Angeles that a woman was killed in a Boston fire. The only newsworthy thing about the pictures is that they were taken. They deserve to be printed because they are great pictures, breathtaking pictures of something that happened. That they disturb readers is exactly as it should be: that's why photojournalism is often more powerful than written journalism.

Topics for Critical Thinking and Writing

1. In paragraph 5, Nora Ephron refers to "the famous assassination picture of the Vietcong prisoner in Saigon." The famous 1968 photo by Eddie Adams shows the face of a prisoner who is about to be shot in the head at close range. Can you think of similarly controversial photographs in the twentieth or twenty-first century that were both important to understanding a story and emotionally difficult to view? Choose one such image and jot down the reasons you would or would not approve of printing it in a newspaper.

2. In paragraph 9, Ephron quotes a newspaperman as saying that before printing Forman's pictures of the woman and the child falling from the fire escape, editors should have asked themselves "what purpose they served and what their effect was likely to be on the reader." If you were an editor, what would your answers be? By the way, the pictures were *not* taken in a poor neighborhood, and they did *not* expose slum conditions.

3. In fifty words or so, write a precise description of what you see in the third of the Boston photographs. Do you think readers of your description would be "revolted" by the picture (para. 8), as were many viewers, the *Washington Post*'s ombudsman among them? Why or why not?

4. Ephron thinks it would be good for newspapers to publish more photographs of death and dying (paras. 11–13). In an essay of approximately 500 words, state her reasons and your evaluation of them. In the context of the internet age, when gruesome and grisly photographs and videos showing death are widely available, do you think Ephron's ideas still hold up? Why or why not?

Assignment in Visual Rhetoric

Choose a visual text and analyze its argument. Then evaluate whether the argument is effective or not. Support your analysis and evaluation with strong evidence and detail from the visual. (Advertisements, public service announcements, memes, and political cartoons work particularly well for this assignment, although photographs and other visuals can also be rich resources.)

- Identify the author(s) of the image and/or its origin. Who was the photographer/artist/designer? Who produced or sponsored the image?
- Identify the intended audience for the image. Consumers? Art lovers? Newspaper reader of a particular political leaning? A particular demographic (age, gender, race, nationality, etc.)? Explain how you know that is the intended audience (context of publication, producer of the image, etc.).
- Identify and describe the central argument of the image. If you cannot identify the argument, explain why you cannot really describe what the argument is.
- Does the image appeal primarily to reason (*logos*), perhaps even using statistics, charts, graphs, tables, or illustrations? Does it appeal to feelings (*pathos*), evoking emotional responses or deeply held values? Or does it appeal to credibility and character (*ethos*), suggesting good sense, trustworthiness, or prudence? Use details from the image to explain how you know.
- Are there any assumptions you can identify in the argument, either assumptions held by the creator or by the audience?
- Are there any visual symbols present that contribute to the argument?
- What single aspect of the image immediately captures your attention? Why exactly does it stand out? Its size? Position on the page? Beauty? Grotesqueness? Humor? How does the visceral impact of this element contribute to the visual's overall argument?
- What is the relation of any text to the image? Does the visual part do most of the work, or does it serve to attract us and lead us on to read the text?
- What elements at first go unnoticed or seem to be superfluous to the image? Are they important? If so, how? If not, why are they present?

PART TWO

Critical Writing

6

Writing an Analysis of an Argument

And some certain significance lurks in all things, else all things are little worth, and the round world itself but an empty cipher.

— HERMANN MELVILLE

CONSIDER THIS

You are reading an article online about inexperienced and ill-prepared outdoor adventurers (hikers, campers, swimmers, climbers, and the like) who have had to be rescued by emergency services, sometimes from perilous situations. At the end of the article, the first statement in the comments section reads as follows:

stickinthemud1960

Some people have no business being in the wilderness. They visit our parks, mountains, lakes, and rivers, often without maps or flashlights or basic supplies, usually to film themselves doing dangerous things in the hope of creating a viral video. Inevitably, they get themselves stuck and need to be rescued. Every day in our country, hundreds of rescues need to be made as foolhardy people get lost in the woods, stuck on mountainsides and rock faces, or marooned in the middle of rivers. Why should taxpayers foot the bill for rescuing these people? I say we should create a law against stupidity — a law that requires those who need to be rescued to PAY for the rescue operation, and to be prosecuted if any of the rescuers are injured in the process. That or else we get really tough and say, "You got yourself into this mess through your own bad decisions, so get yourself out!"

Like | Share | Flag

How would you rate this argument on a scale of 1 (terrible) to 10 (exceptional)? Why?

Analyzing an Argument

In much of your college writing, you will be asked to set forth reasoned responses to your reading as preparation for making arguments of your own. Most writing in college will require you to write an analysis of someone else's writing. Your professors not only wish to ensure that you comprehend the arguments you encounter in your courses but also want to encourage you to cultivate the intellectual skills associated with critical thinking — namely, the ability to understand, question, critique, and make decisions independently. In a political science course, you may have to analyze, say, an essay first published in *Foreign Affairs* that argues for more limits on executive power. Later, you may want to integrate your analysis in a longer essay that offers reasons why a strong executive is desirable. Writing an analysis of an argument is important in thoroughly comprehending existing viewpoints or perspectives, but ultimately serves as a strong foundation for introducing outside sources into your writing (something we will discuss in Chapter 8, "Using Sources").

EXAMINING THE AUTHOR'S THESIS

Obviously, you must understand an essay before you can analyze it thoughtfully. You must read it several times — not just skim it — and (the hard part) you must think critically about it. You'll find that your thinking is stimulated if you take notes and if:

- You ask yourself questions about the material.
- You keep notes to help you keep track of the writer's thoughts.
- You read about or visit websites or organizations dedicated to the material you are analyzing.

One of the most important aspects of analyzing an argument is identifying the **thesis** — a main claim or point. Perhaps the thesis is explicitly stated in the title, or located conveniently in the opening or concluding paragraph, or perhaps it is not directly stated and you will have to infer it from the essay.

Notice that we said the writer *probably* has a thesis, stated or unstated. Much of what you read will indeed be primarily an **argument**: a writer explicitly or implicitly trying to support some thesis and to convince readers to agree with it. But some of what you read will be relatively neutral, with the argument just faintly discernible — or even with no argument at all. A work may, for instance, chiefly be a report: Here is the data, or here is what *X*, *Y*, and *Z* said; make of it what you will. A report might simply state how various ethnic groups voted in an election, for example. In a report of this sort, of course, the writer hopes to persuade readers that the facts are correct, but no thesis is advanced — at least not consciously; the writer is not evidently arguing a point and trying to change readers' minds. Such a document differs greatly from an essay by a political analyst who presents those same findings to persuade their party to sacrifice the votes of one ethnic bloc to get more votes from another bloc.

To find out if what you are reading is an argument, look for the presence of two elements:

- Transitions implying the drawing of a conclusion (such as *therefore*, *because*, *for the reason that*, and *consequently*) and

- Verbs implying proof (such as *confirms*, *verifies*, *accounts for*, *implies*, *proves*, *disproves*, *is (in)consistent with*, *refutes*, and *it follows that*).

Such terms indicate **extrapolation** — going beyond the facts and data to interpret their implications and consequences. If an essay does not seem to be advancing a clear thesis, think of one whose information might support or undermine some conventional belief or idea. That could be the implicit thesis. (See also Thinking Critically: Examining Language to Analyze an Author's Argument on p. 204.)

EXAMINING THE AUTHOR'S PURPOSE

While reading an argument, try to form a clear idea of the author's **purpose**. A first question is this: Judging from the essay or the book, is the purpose to persuade, or is it to report? An analysis of a persuasive argument requires more investment in the analysis of language and rhetoric, whereas an analysis of a pure report (a work apparently without a thesis or argumentative angle) calls for dealing chiefly with the accuracy of the report. (The analysis must also consider whether the report really has an argument built into it, consciously or unconsciously.)

Purpose can mean many things because people write for many reasons. We write notes and emails sometimes with a purpose to persuade:

Dear Professor, please forgive my absence from class this morning. I hit a deer on the way to class. Thankfully, only my car got damaged. I do hope I can make up the exam.

Such an email seems simple enough, but this note is a pretty carefully constructed argument. It establishes *ethos* (in a polite and formal tone) and appeals to *pathos* (by pointing to a sympathetic circumstance). It reasons, without really stating it, that the unforeseeable nature of the event is a good excuse to allow a make-up exam. If necessary, it could feasibly be underwritten by evidence (such as an accident report or an image of the damaged car).

In formal writing, purposes may vary. Sometimes, writers are trying to change an opinion, arguing that a certain perspective or interpretation of events is the correct one. A historian may assemble evidence from the past to argue that something occurred a certain way or that one event bore a relationship to some other events. A literary scholar might examine a novel and argue that some constellation of details amounts to something significant. In the sciences, the interpretation of data could be an effort to persuade. In opinion columns, blogs, and newspapers, people routinely write editorials sharing their perspectives and interpretations of the world. Whether the purpose is to change minds, challenge common assumptions, criticize institutionalized ideas, or argue that people should take some specific action, all arguments have a purpose.

When you are analyzing arguments, you will have a specific purpose. Perhaps you want simply to inform, attempting to convey someone else's argument as accurately as you can as if it were a report. Or perhaps you want to affirm (or challenge) the argument, making another argument (or counterargument) or your own. You might also satirize the argument, the writer, or the kind of thinking it represents. Whenever you analyze an argument, you are paying special attention to the author, context, language, medium — everything about the setting of an argument — and how those details and choices help the author achieve his or her purpose.

EXAMINING THE AUTHOR'S METHODS

If the essay advances a thesis to achieve a clear purpose, you will want to analyze the strategies or **methods** of argument that allegedly support the thesis.

- Is the argument aimed at a particular audience? Do the author's chosen methods work for that particular audience?

- Does the writer quote authorities? What publications does the writer draw from? Are these authorities competent in this field? Does the writer consider equally competent authorities who take a different view?

- Does the writer use statistics? If so, who compiled them, and are they appropriate to the point being argued? Can they be interpreted differently?

- Does the writer build the argument by using examples or analogies? Are they satisfactory?

- Does the writer include images (photos, graphs, charts, and screenshots)? Are the image sources reliable? Do they support the writer's argument well, perhaps by an appeal to *logos* or *pathos*?

- Are the writer's assumptions acceptable?

- Does the writer consider all relevant factors? Have they omitted some points that you think should be discussed? For instance, should the author recognize certain opposing positions and perhaps concede something to them?

- Does the writer seek to persuade by means of humor or ridicule? If so, is the humor or ridicule fair? Is it supported also by rational argument?

EXAMINING THE AUTHOR'S PERSONA

You will probably also want to analyze something a bit more elusive than the author's explicit arguments: the author's self-presentation. Does the author seek to persuade readers partly by presenting themselves as conscientious, friendly, self-effacing, authoritative, or in some other light? Most writers, while they present evidence, also present themselves (or, more precisely, they present the image of themselves that they wish us to behold). In persuasive writing, this **persona** — this presentation of self, which can often be discerned from *language*, *voice*, and *tone* of the author — may be no less important than the presentation of evidence. In some cases, the persona may not much matter, but the point is that you should look at the author's self-presentation to consider if it's significant.

In establishing a persona, writers adopt various rhetorical strategies, ranging from the level of vocabulary they use, to their specific word choices, to the way they approach or organize their argument. The author of an essay may be polite, for example, and show fair-mindedness and open-mindedness, treating the opposition with great courtesy and expressing interest in hearing other views. Such a tactic is itself a persuasive device. Another author may use a technical vocabulary and rely on a range of hard evidence such as statistics. This reliance on a scientific tone and seemingly objective truths is itself a way of seeking to persuade — a rational way, to be sure, but a mode of persuasion nonetheless.

Consider these further examples:

- A writer who speaks of an opponent's "gimmicks" instead of "strategy" probably is trying to downgrade the opponent and also to convey the self-image of a street-wise person.

- A writer who uses legalistic language and cites numerous court cases is seeking to reveal their fluency in the law and their research capabilities to convince readers of their authority.

- A writer who seems professorial or pedantic, referencing a lot of classical figures and citing intellectual sources, is hoping to present themselves as a person of deep knowledge and wisdom.

- A writer who draws a lot of examples from daily life in their ordinary neighborhood is wanting to be seen as a regular, commonsense person.

On a larger scale, then, consider not only the language, voice, and tone of the author but also the *kind* of evidence that is used and the *ways* in which it is organized and presented. One writer may first bombard the reader with facts and then spend relatively little time drawing conclusions. Another may rely chiefly on generalizations, waiting until the end of the essay to bring the thesis home with a few details. Another may begin with a few facts and spend most of the space reflecting on these. All such devices deserve comment in your analysis.

The writer's persona may color the thesis and help it develop in a distinctive way. If we accept the thesis, it is no doubt partly because the writer has won our goodwill by persuading us of their good character or *ethos*. Good writers present themselves not as know-it-alls, wise guys, or bullies, but as decent people whom the reader presumably would like to invite to dinner.

In short, the author's self-presentation usually matters. A full analysis of an argument must recognize its effect, whether positive or negative.

EXAMINING THE AUTHOR'S AUDIENCE

Another key element in understanding an argument lies in thinking about the intended audience — how the author perceives the audience and what strategies the author uses to connect to it. We have already said something about the creation of the author's persona.

An author with a loyal following is, almost by definition, someone who in earlier writings has presented an engaging persona, a persona with a trustworthy *ethos*. A trusted author can sometimes cut corners and can perhaps adopt a colloquial tone that an unknown author would not. Speaking of unknown authors, the acclaimed mythologian Joseph Campbell once said, "You can always tell an author who is still working under the authorities by the number of footnotes he provides in his text."

Authors who want to convince their audiences need to think about how they present information and how they present themselves. Consider how you prefer people to talk to you. What sorts of language do you find engaging and trustworthy? Much, of course, depends on the circumstances, notably the topic, the type of intended audience, and the place. A joke may be useful in an argument about whether the government should regulate junk food, but almost surely a joke will be inappropriate — will backfire, will alienate the audience — in an argument about abortion.

The *way* an author addresses the reader can have a significant impact on the reader's perception of the author, which is to say perception of the author's *views* and *argument*. Most writers adopt a formal voice when they write, one that sounds somewhat like their personal voice but is also refined for purposes of clarity and seriousness. A slip in tone or an error of fact, however small, may be enough for the audience to dismiss the author's argument.

When you write your own arguments, understanding audience means thinking about all the possible audiences who may come into contact with your writing or your message and thinking about the consequences of what you write and where it is published. It may be tempting to take a cheap shot at liberals, conservatives, church figures, moral authorities, coaches, professors, or whomever, but an author risks losing readers — not necessarily because their ideas are weak, but because they conveyed a flippant or dismissive attitude toward people or institutions that audiences respect.

The same is true of the language you use. An obscenity, for example, might seem right in some contexts, but will surely turn off some readers. That's why it is important to be conscious about the words you choose. Consider how the connotations of the phrase "all lives matter" could alienate readers. While most people would agree with the premise that *all lives matter* as a general humanistic claim about the value of life, the phrase signals something different. It was born out of a backlash against the Black Lives Matter (BLM) movement. By asserting that black lives matter, those in BLM were drawing attention to the fact that the lives of African Americans were not being valued as much as other races in the justice system. "All lives matter" arose as a rejection of BLM's claims about racial inequality in the justice system. That is to say, "all lives matter" may sound good — and an author may use it with the best intentions — but that author may not be expressing exactly what they want to express, as some people will inevitably read those words as alignment with an anti-Black position.

When analyzing an author's argument, it's important to consider more how their argument reaches an audience and less what they might have wanted to accomplish. As many human rights activists remind us, intention matters less than impact.

Steve Greenberg/CartoonStock

Understanding audience also means understanding the place where an author publishes their argument. In written arguments the place of publication is important to determining the style and approach of an author. The *New York Review of Books*, for example, is considered to be an erudite magazine with an intellectual readership, and arguments in that publication are likely to be authoritative and complex, with appeals primarily to *ethos* and *logos*. Meanwhile, arguments in *USA Today*, a national newspaper, are more likely to be accessible and easy to understand, perhaps with a folksier tone and less complexity. When authors anticipate their audience, it helps them determine what needs to be explained and what does not. If an author is writing for *Sports Illustrated*, they may not need to convince anyone of the importance of a playoff series, trusting the audience already knows. The same essay written in a general publication cannot take insider knowledge for granted, and the author will have to do some groundwork to make sure that all readers are on the same page.

Our point is that we must consider the publication type or venue alongside the author's persona in order to fully analyze the argument — whether it is occurring in a tweet, an editorial, a magazine article, a review, or a scholarly essay — because each publication context has a specific intended audience to whom the author is appealing. When you are reading more formal essays, such as those in this book, it is equally important to think about who wrote them (author) and for whom they were intended (audience). These factors can help you better discern the perspective and intentions of the author, which can significantly inform the ways their evidence was gathered, interpreted, and represented.

A CHECKLIST FOR ANALYZING AN AUTHOR'S INTENDED AUDIENCE

❑ Where did the piece appear? Who published it? Why, in your view, might someone have found it worth publishing?

❑ In what technological format does this piece appear? Print journal? Online magazine? Blog? What does the technological format say about the piece, the author, or the audience?

❑ Is the writing relatively informal — for instance, a tweet or a Facebook status update? Why is this medium good or bad for the message?

❑ Who is the intended audience? Are there other audiences who may also have an interest but whom the author has failed to consider?

❑ If *you* are the intended audience, what shared values do you have with the author?

❑ What strategies does the writer use to create a connection with the audience?

ORGANIZING YOUR ANALYSIS

In writing an analysis of an argument, it is usually a good idea at the start of your analysis — if not in the first paragraph, then in the second or third — to let the reader know the purpose (and thesis, if there is one) of the work you are analyzing and then to summarize the work briefly, noting its main points.

Throughout the essay, you will want to analyze the strategies or methods of argument that allegedly support the thesis. Thus, you will probably find it useful (and your readers will certainly find it helpful) to write out *your* thesis (your evaluation or judgment). You might say, for instance, that the essay is impressive but not conclusive, or is undermined by convincing contrary evidence, or relies too much on unsupported generalizations, or is wholly admirable. It all depends on what you conclude as you go through the process of analyzing the argument at hand.

And then, of course, comes the job of setting forth your analysis and the support for your thesis. There is no one way of going about this work, and the organization of your analysis may or may not follow the organization of the work you are analyzing. (The Visual Guide: Organizing Your Analysis graphic shows some options, but there are, of course, others that may better suit your argument.)

Visual Guide: Organizing Your Analysis

What is the writer's organization of arguments? Is it comprehensive enough?

Is the writer's organization *essential* to the arguments? Do paragraphs build on each other to advance the arguments?

Can you identify which of the writer's arguments are simplest or most complex?

Can you identify which of the writer's arguments are sound or unsound?

Are there important arguments missing from the writer's essay?

Analyze the arguments in the same order as the author's thesis.

Discuss the writer's arguments that you think are sound and then turn to the arguments that are flawed. Offer strong counterarguments in your discussion.

Discuss the writer's arguments that are unsound, unpacking and explaining why (fallacies, weak examples, etc.), and then turn to the sound arguments.

Analyze the simplest of the writer's least complex arguments first and then go on to the more difficult ones, spending more time unpacking them.

Construct an additional key argument that is missing from the writer's work.

Especially in analyzing a work in which the author's persona, ideas, and methods are blended, you will want to spend some time commenting on the persona. Whether you discuss it near the beginning of your analysis or near the end will depend on how you want to construct your essay, and this decision will partly depend on the work you are analyzing. For example, if the author's persona is kept in the background and is thus relatively invisible, you may want to make that point fairly early to get it out of the way and then concentrate on more interesting matters. If, however, the persona is interesting — and perhaps seductive, whether because it seems so scrupulously objective or so engagingly subjective — you may want to hint at this quality early in your essay and then develop the point while you consider the arguments.

A good conclusion for an analysis of an argument might offer a reassessment of the major points made by the author and a final statement about the validity or viability of the argument. You also have a chance in the conclusion to test the author's argument further, perhaps applying it to new or different situations that highlight its effectiveness or show where it falls short. If readers were to accept or reject the argument, what would be the implications? What other arguments would gain or lose currency by accepting or rejecting this one? Does the argument represent a new kind of potential or a new kind of threat — in a general sense, does it disrupt or attempt to disrupt current thinking, and, if so, is that a good or bad thing?

SUMMARY VERSUS ANALYSIS

In the last few pages, we have tried to persuade you that, in writing an analysis of an argument, especially a written argument:

- Most of the nonliterary material that you will read is designed to argue, to report, or to do both. Read and reread thoughtfully and take careful notes.
- Most of this material also presents the writer's personality, or voice, and this voice usually merits attention in an analysis.

There is yet another point, equally obvious but often neglected by students who begin by writing an analysis and end up by writing only a summary, a shortened version of the work they have read: Although your essay is an analysis of someone else's writing and you may have to include a summary of the work you are writing about, your essay is *your* essay, your analysis, not a mere summary. The thesis, the organization, and the tone are yours.

- Your thesis, for example, may be that although the author is convinced they have presented a strong case, their case is far from proved because . . .
- Your organization may be deeply indebted to the work you are analyzing, but it need not be. The author may have begun with specific examples and then gone on to make generalizations and to draw conclusions, but you may begin with the conclusions.
- Your tone, similarly, may resemble your subject's (let's say the voice is courteous academic), but it will nevertheless have its own ring, its own tone of, say, urgency, caution, or coolness.

Most of the essays that we have included thus far are written in an intellectual if not academic style, and indeed several are by students and by professors. But argumentative writing is not limited to intellectuals and academics. Arguments occur everywhere — in academic articles and newspaper editorials and on the backs of cereal boxes. Being able to analyze arguments is essential to being a wise citizen, a skeptical consumer, and a competent member of any field or profession. If it weren't all these things (and probably more), colleges would not require so many people to take a course in the subject.

A CHECKLIST FOR ANALYZING A TEXT

Consider the following matters:

- ❏ Does the author have a self-interest in writing this piece?

- ❏ Is there evidence in the author's tone and style that enables me to identify anything about the intended audience? Is the tone appropriate?

- ❏ Given the publication venue (or any other contexts), can I tell if the audience is likely to be neutral, sympathetic, or hostile to the argument?

- ❏ Does the author have a thesis? Does the argument ask the audience to accept or to do anything?

- ❏ Does the author make assumptions? Does the audience share those assumptions? Do I?

- ❏ Is there a clear line between what is factual information and what is interpretation, belief, or opinion?

- ❏ Does the author appeal to reason (*logos*), to the emotions (*pathos*), or to our sense that the speaker is trustworthy (*ethos*)?

- ❏ Is the evidence provided convincing? If visual materials such as graphs, pie charts, or pictures are used, are they persuasive?

- ❏ Are significant objections and counterevidence adequately discussed?

- ❏ Is the organization of the text effective? Are the title, the opening paragraphs, and the concluding paragraphs effective?

- ❏ Is the overall argument correct in its conclusions? Or is there anything missing that I could use to add to or challenge the argument?

- ❏ Has the author convinced me?

An Argument, Its Elements, and a Student's Analysis of the Argument

In many types of media, we are exposed to the opinions and judgments of others, often capable writers, who argue their positions clearly, reasonably, and convincingly. We want to think carefully before we accept an argument, so we encourage skepticism but not entrenchment in your own position. You must be willing to hear and seriously consider different positions. Consider the following argument by columnist Nicholas Kristof, published in the *New York Times* in 2005. Analyze the essay and, after you do, examine our analysis of Kristof's argument, as well as the analysis provided by student Theresa Carcaldi, to see how it matches your own.

NICHOLAS D. KRISTOF

Nicholas D. Kristof, a two-time Pulitzer Prize winner, grew up on a farm in Oregon. After graduating from Harvard, he was awarded a Rhodes scholarship to Oxford, where he studied law. In 1984, he joined the *New York Times* as a correspondent, and since 2001 he has written as a columnist. The editorial that follows first appeared in the *New York Times* in 2005.

For Environmental Balance, Pick Up a Rifle

Here's a quick quiz: Which large American mammal kills the most humans each year?

It's not the bear, which kills about two people a year in North America. Nor is it the wolf, which in modern times hasn't killed anyone in this country. It's not the cougar, which kills one person every year or two.

Rather, it's the deer. Unchecked by predators, deer populations are exploding in a way that is profoundly unnatural and that is destroying the ecosystem in many parts of the country. In a wilderness, there might be ten deer per square mile; in parts of New Jersey, there are up to 200 per square mile.

One result is ticks and Lyme disease, but deer also kill people more directly. A study for the insurance industry estimated that deer kill about 150 people a year in car crashes nationwide and cause $1 billion in damage. Granted, deer aren't stalking us, and they come out worse in these collisions — but it's still true that in a typical year, an American is less likely to be killed by Osama bin Laden[1] than by Bambi.

If the symbol of the environment's being 5 out of whack in the 1960s was the Cuyahoga River in Cleveland catching fire, one such symbol today is deer congregating around what they think of as salad bars and what we think of as suburbs.

So what do we do? Let's bring back hunting.

Now, you've probably just spilled your coffee. These days, among the university-educated crowd in the cities, hunting is viewed as barbaric.

The upshot is that towns in New York and New Jersey are talking about using birth control to keep deer populations down. (Liberals presumably support free condoms, while conservatives back abstinence education.) Deer contraception hasn't been very successful, though.

Meanwhile, the same population bomb has spread to bears. A bear hunt has been scheduled for this week in New Jersey — prompting outrage from some animal rights groups (there's also talk of bear contraception: make love, not cubs).

As for deer, partly because hunting is 10 perceived as brutal and vaguely psychopathic, towns are taking out contracts on deer through discreet private companies. Greenwich, Connecticut, budgeted $47,000 this year to pay a company to shoot eighty deer from raised platforms over four nights — as well as $8,000 for deer birth control.

Look, this is ridiculous.

We have an environmental imbalance caused in part by the decline of hunting. Humans first wiped out certain predators — like wolves and cougars — but then expanded their own role as predators to sustain a rough ecological balance. These days, though, hunters are on the decline.

---

[1] The Al-Qaeda leader and mastermind of the 9/11 attack who was still at large at Kristof's writing. [Editors' note]

According to "Families Afield: An Initiative for the Future of Hunting," a report by an alliance of shooting organizations, for every hundred hunters who die or stop hunting, only sixty-nine hunters take their place.

I was raised on *Bambi* — but also, as an Oregon farm boy, on venison and elk meat. But deer are not pets, and dead deer are as natural as live deer. To wring one's hands over them, perhaps after polishing off a hamburger, is soggy sentimentality.

What's the alternative to hunting? Is it 15 preferable that deer die of disease and hunger? Or, as the editor of *Adirondack Explorer* magazine suggested, do we introduce wolves into the burbs?

To their credit, many environmentalists agree that hunting can be green. The New Jersey Audubon Society this year advocated deer hunting as an ecological necessity.

There's another reason to encourage hunting: it connects people with the outdoors and creates a broader constituency for wilderness preservation. At a time when America's wilderness is being gobbled away for logging, mining, or oil drilling, that's a huge boon.

Granted, hunting isn't advisable in suburban backyards, and I don't expect many soccer moms to install gun racks in their minivans. But it's an abdication of environmental responsibility to eliminate other predators and then refuse to assume the job ourselves. In that case, the collisions with humans will simply get worse.

In October, for example, Wayne Goldsberry was sitting in a home in northwestern Arkansas when he heard glass breaking in the next room. It was a home invasion — by a buck.

Mr. Goldsberry, who is six feet one inch 20 and weighs two hundred pounds, wrestled with the intruder for forty minutes. Blood spattered the walls before he managed to break the buck's neck.

So it's time to reestablish a balance in the natural world — by accepting the idea that hunting is as natural as bird-watching.

Topics for Critical Thinking and Writing

1. What is Nicholas Kristof's chief thesis? State it in one sentence.

2. Does Kristof make any assumptions — tacit or explicit — with which you agree or disagree? Why?

3. Is the slightly humorous tone of Kristof's essay inappropriate for a discussion of deliberately killing wild animals? Why or why not?

4. What kind of evidence does Kristof offer to justify his claim that more hunting is needed? What interpretations of Kristof's evidence could be made if you were trying to challenge him?

5. Do you agree that "hunting is as natural as bird-watching" (para. 21)? In any case, do you think that an appeal to what is "natural" is a good argument for expanding the use of hunting? Why or why not?

6. To whom is Kristof talking? How do you know?

THE ESSAY ANALYZED

By now you have read and begun to analyze Kristof's essay. Now let's examine his argument with an eye to identifying those elements we mentioned earlier in this chapter that deserve notice when examining *any* argument: the author's *thesis, purpose, methods, persona,* and *audience* (see "Analyzing an Argument," p. 192). It is important to point out that analysis does not always (or even usually) happen in a linear way.

When analyzing, we always consider the author, the publication type, and the context in which the argument was written. We knew that Kristof is a self-described progressive and a Democrat (he tried to run for governor of Oregon in 2022) but is also known to take provocative positions somewhat out of step with typical liberal attitudes (e.g., Kristof argued elsewhere in several *New York Times* editorials that sweatshops in foreign countries could be a good thing, a necessary stage on the way to progress). Thus, we could better interpret his argument about hunting deer: Although it involves guns and the killing of animals, it presents ethical and ecological reasons likely to be valued by liberals. We also knew that the essay appeared in a newspaper, the *New York Times*, where paragraphs are customarily very short, partly to allow for easy reading. Taking all this information together, we can assume that Kristof's intended audience was a commonsense, urban (or suburban) moderate who might hold typical liberal values about guns and hunting. This assumption allows us to read Kristof's tone — funny and acerbic but not cutting or insulting — as one suitable to the writer's purpose: to challenge a relatively sympathetic audience and at the same time gently ridicule their more "bleeding-heart" brethren.

Thesis   Kristof does not *announce* the thesis in its full form until paragraph 6 ("Let's bring back hunting"); instead he begins with evidence that builds up to the thesis. (It's worth noting that his paragraphs are very short, and if the essay were published in a book instead of a newspaper, Kristof's first two paragraphs probably would be combined, as would the third and fourth.)

Purpose   He wants to *persuade* readers to adopt his view. Kristof does not show that his essay is argumentative by using key terms that normally mark argumentative prose: *in conclusion*, *therefore*, or *because of this*. Almost the only traces of the language of argument are "Granted" (para. 18) and "So" (i.e., *therefore*) in his final paragraph. But the argument is clear — if unusual — and he wants readers to accept his argument as *true*. Possibly, part of his purpose is that he wants to make this argument specifically to a liberal audience unlikely to assume that hunting or guns could be a solution.

Methods   Kristof offers evidence identifying the problem of deer overpopulation, pointing out the annual number of deaths, and comparing that number — with a reference to a global terrorist — to the number of deaths from terrorism. He also points out other hazards such as Lyme disease and the economic impact of deer overpopulation. Kristof's methods of presenting evidence include providing **statistics** (paras. 3, 4, 10, and 13), giving **examples** (paras. 10, 19–20), and citing **authorities** (paras. 13 and 16).

Persona   Kristof presents himself as a confident, no-nonsense fellow, a newspaper columnist. A folksy tone ("Here's a quick quiz") and informal, humorous language establish a good relationship with readers. A well-known columnist, Kristof is a progressive who often takes nontypical views and presents a voice of "common sense." His readers probably know what to expect, and they read him with pleasure.

Audience   Kristof is known to be progressive, and he knows his audience is, too ("Now you've probably just spilled your coffee," he says when he proposes hunting as a solution). But he also mocks the "the university-educated crowd in the cities, [for whom] hunting is viewed as barbaric" (para. 7). So he is mocking liberal dogmas even though his audience is presumable of the same ilk. But he is not conservative (in fact, he spoofs them, too). Ordinarily, it is a bad idea to make fun of persons, whether they're you're intended audience or not; impartial readers rarely want to align themselves with someone who mocks others. In the essay we are looking at, however, Kristof gets away with this smart-guy tone because he not only has loyal readers but also has written the entire essay in a highly informal or playful manner.

Let's now turn to a student's written analysis of Kristof's essay and then to our own analysis of the student's analysis.

Carcaldi 1

Theresa Carcaldi
Professor Markle
ENG 120
13 July 2018

For Sound Argument, Drop the Jokes:
How Kristof Falls Short in Convincing His Audience

In recent years, the action of hunting wild animals has become controversial. However, the *New York Times* columnist Nicholas D. Kristof attempts to argue for the necessity of hunting deer in America in his piece, "For Environmental Balance, Pick up a Rifle." Kristof certainly engages his audience in this newspaper column, especially progressive-minded readers who might believe any expansion of guns or hunting is abhorrent. He presents evidence that at first seems convincing; however, it is clear that the soundness of his argument falls short as a result of replacing his arguments with jokes, failing to provide adequate evidence, and including lines that are both incapable of relating to a majority of the population as well as disbelieving.

Before describing why Kristof's essay falls short of being sound, it is first important to concede the fact that Kristof's essay appeared in a newspaper column that is meant to be read in a quick manner, so the tone of his essay as well as its length and lack of evidence and full development of ideas is to be expected. His sarcastic, conversational tone is layered with occasional jokes and creates a friendly relationship with the audience that sets the stage for trust between author and reader. Therefore, some initial evidence sets out the problems of deer overpopulation in a way likely to be accepted, including dramatic statistics about human highway deaths caused by deer and the incident rates of Lyme disease spread by deer. By doing this, Kristof appeals to fear in the basic structure of his argument: the drastic rise in the deer population is wreaking havoc across America, and the solution to this problem is to hunt more deer.

No doubt, deer do cause serious problems. As Kristof says, deer "kill people more directly" each year than any other mammal (para. 4). However, the evidence is mostly unconvincing. By showing the deer threat to be more

Margin notes:

1 Carcaldi examines the paradox of the title—for a liberal goal, use a gun.

2 Note in Carcaldi's thesis her primary critique of Kristof's argument.

3 Analyzes how Kristof establishes ethos.

4 Points out Kristof's persuasive strategy.

5 Accounts for the fact that there is a problem, but takes issue with how that problem is overdramatized.

significant than the threat of terrorism, Kristof intends to highlight the irrationality of his audience's anxieties. However, his sample is too small: just because deaths caused by deer in a single year exceed that of terrorism in America, that does not mean that a major terrorist attack will not happen in the future.

Even with the threats deer do pose, the idea of hunting being the best solution is unconvincing. While Kristof states in paragraph 16 that the New Jersey Audubon Society "advocated deer hunting as an ecological necessity," this is only convincing if the audience is aware of what the New Jersey Audubon Society advocates for—which Kristof fails to explain. To add, Kristof proposes that the present alternative to deer hunting is to let the deer perish from natural causes like "disease and hunger" (para. 15). While this appeal to the audience's sensitivities about animal cruelty is good evidence for supporting deer hunting, Kristof does not fully explain why other solutions, such as deer birth control, are inadequate; instead, he just jokes about it, poking fun at the oversensitive "make love, not cubs" crowd. Rather than giving an argument, in other words, he makes a joke, then adds a further one that "Liberals presumably support free condoms, while conservatives back abstinence education" (para. 8). While this may make the audience laugh, it also suggests that people's political attitudes often prevent them from using common sense. This is an appeal to humor and to common sense, but is certainly not a fully stated reason for why deer contraception is not a solution. Kristof once states, "Deer contraception hasn't been very successful" (para. 8), yet does not explain why—he merely makes a statement without evidence, which does not contribute to a sound argument.

In addition, Kristof ends his essay with unbelievable statements. First, he claims hunting "connects people with the outdoors and creates a broader constituency for wilderness preservation" (para. 17). This statement contradicts his previous statement that "Humans first wiped out certain predators—like wolves and cougars" (para. 12). After stating the negative effects hunting has had on wildlife preservation, it is difficult to claim that hunting nowadays would be any different. Finally, Kristof ends with "hunting is as natural as bird-watching" (para. 21). While hunting in the

6 Carcaldi reinterprets and challenges the evidence Kristof uses.

7 Suggests that the argument Kristof makes is presented as one (although not the only or best) solution.

8 Acknowledges other types of appeals Kristof makes.

wild is certainly natural, it goes without saying that hunting with manmade weapons is far from being natural. Thus, with these two statements, not only does Kristof contradict himself, but he jeopardizes his audience's trust. While Kristof may use transitions of argumentation, such as "Granted" (para. 3), "Meanwhile" (para. 9), and "To their credit" (para. 16), his writing is primarily based on unsupported statements and jokes rather than sound reasoning. Ultimately, his essay is left labeled as an unsound argument.

Clearly, Kristof has written an engaging article about a controversial topic and has written it well for the medium in which it was produced and for the audience he sought. However, this does not mean his argument is logical and sound. As a result of his lack of evidence, his often overconfident statements, and the logical fallacies ridden throughout the piece, his argument is left unsound, and his audience is left utterly unconvinced that the only solution to the deer issue across America is to **9** hunt them.

9 Carcaldi concludes by reiterating her own thesis and main points.

AN ANALYSIS OF THE STUDENT'S ANALYSIS

Carcaldi's essay seems to us to be excellent, doubtless the product of a good deal of thoughtful revision. She does not cover every possible aspect of Kristof's essay — she concentrates on Kristof's reasoning and says very little about his style — but we think Carcaldi does a good job in a short space. What makes her essay effective?

- She has a strong title ("For Sound Argument, Drop the Jokes: How Kristof Falls Short in Convincing His Audience") that is of at least a little interest; it picks up Kristof's method of using humor, and it gives a hint of what is to come.

- She promptly identifies Kristof's subject and gives us a hint of where she will be going, telling us outright that it is "clear that the soundness of his essay falls short."

- She recognizes Kristof's audience at the start and analyzes his use of language and his assumptions with that knowledge in mind.

- She uses a few brief quotations to give us a feel for Kristof's essay and to let us hear the evidence for itself, but she does not pad her essay with long quotations.

- She considers all Kristof's main points.

- She organizes her essay reasonably, letting us hear Kristof's thesis, letting us know the degree to which she accepts it, and finally letting us know her specific reservations about Kristof's essay.

- She concludes without the formality of "in conclusion" but structures her analysis in such a way as to account for the charm or effectiveness of Kristof's essay but not agree with his solutions.

- Notice, finally, that she sticks closely to Kristof's essay. She does not go off on a tangent about the virtues of vegetarianism or the dreadful politics of the *New York Times*, the newspaper that published Kristof's essay. She was asked to analyze the essay, and she has done so.

A CHECKLIST FOR WRITING AN ANALYSIS OF AN ARGUMENT

- ☐ Have I accurately stated the writer's thesis (claim) and summarized their supporting reasons?

- ☐ Have I indicated early in the essay where I will be taking my reader (i.e., have I indicated my general response to the essay I am analyzing)?

- ☐ Have I called attention to the strengths, if any, and the weaknesses, if any, of the essay?

- ☐ Have I commented on the ways *logos* (logic, reasoning), *pathos* (emotion), and *ethos* (character of the writer) are presented in the essay?

- ☐ Have I explained any disagreements I might have about definitions of important terms and concepts?

- ☐ Have I examined the chief uses of evidence in the essay and offered supporting or refuting evidence or interpretation?

- ☐ Have I used occasional brief quotations to let my reader hear the author's tone and to ensure fairness and accuracy?

- ☐ Is my analysis effectively organized?

- ☐ Have I taken account of the author's audience(s)?

- ☐ Does my essay, perhaps in the concluding paragraphs, indicate my agreement or disagreement with the writer but also my view of the essay as a piece of argumentative writing?

- ☐ Is my tone appropriate?

Arguments for Analysis

JENNIFER BARTLETT

Jennifer Bartlett is an author, poet, and lecturer who has published and edited several volumes of poetry, including, with Sheila Black and Michael Northen, *Beauty is a Verb: The New Poetry of Disability* (2011), an anthology of essays and poems by and about disabled persons. The essay here was first published in the *New York Times* in 2017.

Disability and the Right to Choose

As a young woman, I had no particular desire to be a mother. I was neither for nor against having and raising a child, and as things were at the time, the opportunity had not presented itself. That changed when I was 29 and met Jim, the man who would become my husband. In 2002, not long after we married, I gave birth to my son.

In my 20s, I was neutral about parenthood partly because, as a woman with cerebral palsy, I was spared the usual intrusive questioning and expectations about having children that most women are subject to. People never pressured me to have children; they just assumed that I could not. In fact, it became clear very fast that women like me are expected *not* to reproduce. Now, in my 40s, I find these attitudes ignorant and prejudicial, but as a young woman, it seemed like a bit of freedom to be excused from the usual problems women complain about.

My disability is not genetic and it does not hamper pregnancy. Being pregnant was physically, emotionally and spiritually easy for me, but socially, it was complicated. Moving around in New York City as a pregnant woman with a disability opened me up for constant commentary. I am used to having my body be an object of attention. The real difficulty came from elsewhere — it was dealing with the medical establishment during my pregnancy that I was not prepared for.

Navigating the medical system as a pregnant woman is difficult; as a disabled pregnant woman, it is nearly impossible. The first OB/GYN I went to told me condescendingly, "You sure know what's going on for someone in your condition." By "condition" she meant cerebral palsy.

She referred me to her colleague to get a 5 sonogram because the clinic did not have the necessary equipment. This doctor was more respectful, so I wanted to be under his care. He told me that he could not treat me because it would be unethical "to take work" from his colleague.

I found a third doctor. This doctor was very traditional and although she did not infantilize me, there was a conflict because I wanted to have natural childbirth, and this was not in her vocabulary. In fact, she called my birth plan a "wish list." As my pregnancy developed, after taking a Bradley class and hiring a doula, I became more and more adamant about natural childbirth. At one point, I called the now-defunct Elizabeth Seton Natural Birth Center in Manhattan in an attempt to get a midwife. Without even an examination, I was told that the center would not take me as a client because I was "high risk." When

I protested, the midwife told me if a woman at the center had trouble during labor, she would have to walk to the nearby hospital. There was no possibility that this was the case, but she managed to get rid of me. I had no choice but to stay with the third doctor.

In my fifth month of pregnancy, my doctor sent me to the hospital to have a transvaginal ultrasound to "check" the fetus. My doctor did not give the reason for the procedure or what it would determine. I later learned that in addition to determining the viability of the pregnancy, this type of ultrasound is used to detect Down syndrome and other birth "defects." I was already beginning to understand the ways in which modern medicine could be used to devalue, or even weed out, people with disabilities.

When I got pregnant, my husband and I discussed what we would do if our child had a disability. I didn't have any anxiety about it. In some ways, I viewed the possibility as an opportunity. If my son ended up with cerebral palsy, he would be like me. If he ended up with a different disability, we would have a chance to see the world in a different light. Either way, there was no question in my mind that I would not have an abortion, no matter what the circumstance. We wanted our son, whether or not he had a disability. As it turned out, he did not.

In 2004, when my son was 3, I read an article in The New York Times that deeply upset me and has stayed with me. In it, Amy Harmon wrote about fetal genetic testing and the hundreds of "defects" that, even then, could be predicted before birth (this technology has since evolved rapidly, as we know). If an abnormality is detected, parents must make the decision whether to continue with the pregnancy or abort. One woman, with a genetic condition that caused her to have an extra finger, which she'd had surgically removed, chose to end two of her pregnancies because tests detected her fetuses' having the same condition. This instance is the extreme, but it is by no means an exception.

I support legal abortion and am not criticizing women who have made the difficult decision to terminate a pregnancy because of a disabled fetus. There are situations in which the life of the child would be so painful and short that abortion would be the most compassionate option.

I do believe, however, that aborting a fetus with a disability should not be a given. In his book "Far From the Tree," Andrew Solomon theorizes that families might abort fetuses if their sexual orientation could be determined. What he is touching upon is that there is sometimes a social and prejudicial component in the decision-making. (We already know this danger is real; gender-selective abortions still take place in the hundreds of thousands in India and China each year, and in lesser numbers in dozens of countries across the globe.) Genetic testing should be given for the purpose of preparation and decision-making, not as a tool for predicting the quality of a child's life.

The right to legal and safe abortion is a core element of American feminism and the struggle for women's rights. This puts me in a strange position. When I think about this issue, I feel my very existence questioned. As a disabled woman, I have been told flat out, "I'd rather be dead than be like you." Even the Dalai Lama has said that aborting a fetus with a disability is understandable. How do I begin to hold this contradiction in my mind? That I am a valid, beautiful human being — as are all my friends, some of whom have much severer impairments — and that I also support women's right to choose, a right that logically must extend to a woman who ends a pregnancy because of the prospect of an extra finger? I don't know the answer, but somehow, I believe the treatment I received as a disabled woman who chose to conceive—the disrespect, the testing, the constant questioning of my capacity to give birth and to be a mother—and my response to it fit into this equation.

Some days, I look at my son, who is now 14, and I want to pull my hair out. O.K., most days. Here I am tempted to compile a list of the ways he makes my life difficult and tedious. But that list is unnecessary. That's not because my son is perfect, but because he's perfect to me. Because I love the person he has become, not the person I wish him to be.

Topics for Critical Thinking and Writing

1. What is Jennifer Bartlett's thesis, and where does it occur in the essay? Do you think the placement is effective?

2. Use the bulleted list in "Examining the Author's Methods" on page 194 to examine the strategies Bartlett uses in her essay. Did you find the essay persuasive? Why or why not? Support your answer with specific evidence from the essay.

3. What observations can you make about Bartlett's language and tone? How does her use of language help or hinder her argument?

4. What assumptions about disabled people is Bartlett trying to dispel, and how are those assumptions demonstrated by her account of the medical establishment? How do those assumptions factor into her argument about aborting fetuses who have been diagnosed with a disability?

MATTHEW WALTHER

Matthew Walther is editor of *The Lamp* magazine and former national correspondent at the *Week*, a widely circulated online and print magazine of news, opinion, and commentary published in both UK and US editions. His work has appeared in various publications including the *Spectator of London*, the *Catholic Herald*, and the *National Review*. This piece was published in May 2018.

Sorry, Nerds: Video Games Are Not a Sport

As a columnist you hate to get a reputation for having anything negative to say about a large group of people. Which is why I am often at great pains to admit that nerd culture has given the world lots of wonderful things and not just wizard erotica, minarchism, and all the anti-anti arguments about racism and misogyny you can find on Reddit. I just don't know what they are yet.

My biggest problem with nerd culture, though, is not that it exists but that it has territorial ambitions. Two decades ago, comic books were still a fringe phenomenon; now they are the only things directors are allowed to make films about, notwithstanding mumblecore and Oscar bait. Oh well. Movie tickets are too expensive anyway. But at sports I feel like it is necessary to draw a line in the sand and, unlike President Obama, to act when my opponents cross it.

In 2016, something called the National Association of Collegiate Esports was established in order to regulate competitions between young adult gamers, taking over a role that had previously belonged to their mothers who needed the garbage taken out. Two years earlier, a private university in Illinois created the nation's first varsity gaming team and began awarding "athletic" scholarships to skilled players. Imagine being that kid's parents. "Oh, yes, Dylan just got accepted with an athletic scholarship." "That's wonderful. Cross country, right?" "No, *Wario's Woods*."

Video games are not a sport. On the loosest imaginable definition a sport involves not only skill and competition but physical exertion and at least the possibility of injury. Even darts and pool and ping pong are, in the broadest sense, sports. Sitting on a couch interacting with your television set is not a sport, otherwise watching CNN with your grandfather would be one. So would self-abuse.

It's actually not difficult to understand 5 why universities are getting into this business. Even for those not lucky enough to make first string on U.C. Berkeley's traveling *Overwatch* team — which has an actual coach — there are plenty of opportunities on our nation's college campuses for people who want to pretend that there is no difference between *FIFA* and FIFA. At Western Michigan University in Kalamazoo, a mid-tier state school, it was recently announced that the administration is spending half a million dollars on "a new facility" for "multiplayer video games."

This is just a continuation of what these colleges have done for decades now when they advertised wave pools and cool dining facilities and hip-looking plate-glass dorms. Undergraduate education is actually a four-year-long debt-financed summer camp for lazy overgrown teenagers. It has nothing to do with the life of the mind, and even less to do with old-fashioned vocational training. One worthless piece of paper is as good as any other, which means that the directional state former polytechnics have to find some nonacademic means of competing with each other for the loan dollars that will one day crush their underemployed 20-something graduates.

Which is not to say that no opportunities await the Doug Fluties of *Mario Kart*. As I write this, hundreds of millions of dollars are being made streaming video games on the internet by people with few or any other marketable skills. The amount of revenue generated by advertising and sponsorships from "esports" is soon expected to reach $1 billion annually.

Treating video games as sports is a civilizational rather than a semantic problem. Enjoyed in moderation, they are probably a harmless pastime like anything else. But increasingly, the reality is not 10-year-olds leveling up their Pikachus on the school bus or even high-school kids unwinding with a little *Goldeneye* but adults — almost all of them men — in their 20s, 30s, and even 40s playing games for hours every day. Gaming is not only a compulsion, but something far more sinister — what one game designer has called "a simulation of being an expert." In a country without meaningful or well-paying opportunities for work young people disappear into their fantasies of competence in which they fly airplanes and score touchdowns and perform daring commando raids without having to go further than the refrigerator.

Video games are, in other words, another of those illusions we peddle to convince people that the world's problems do not exist. Sports, by comparison, are very much of this world. Compared with what's going on inside a PlayStation the most insignificant Saturday afternoon baseball game between two clubs with losing records is a thing of epochal significance, brimming with meaningful human drama.

Topics for Critical Thinking and Writing

1. In his first paragraph, does Matthew Walther define his key terms, *nerds* and *sports*? If so, where? If not, provide the definitions you think Walther assumes.

2. In paragraph 2, why do you think that Walther takes a dig at President Obama? How do you think this affects his relationship with the audience (*ethos*)?

3. Overall, how would you characterize Walther's tone and language? What about it makes it effective and persuasive — or not?

4. What kinds of evidence does Walther provide to support his position that video games are not a sport? Is the evidence adequate enough to be convincing?

JUSTIN CRONIN

Justin Cronin is an award-winning writer of five best-selling novels and a winner of the Hemingway Foundation/PEN Award. Educated at Harvard and the Iowa Writer's Workshop, Cronin taught at La Salle University in Philadelphia, Pennsylvania, and at Rice University in Houston, Texas. The following selection was published in the *New York Times* in 2013.

Confessions of a Liberal Gun Owner

I am a New England liberal, born and bred. I have lived most of my life in the Northeast — Boston, New York, and Philadelphia — and my politics are devoutly Democratic. In three decades, I have voted for a Republican exactly once, holding my nose, in a mayoral election in which the Democratic candidate seemed mentally unbalanced.

I am also a Texas resident and a gun owner. I have half a dozen pistols in my safe, all semiautomatics, the largest capable of holding twenty rounds. I go to the range at least once a week, have applied for a concealed carry license, and am planning to take a tactical training course in the spring. I'm currently shopping for a shotgun, either a Remington

870 Express Tactical or a Mossberg 500 Flex with a pistol grip and adjustable stock.

Except for shotguns (firing one feels like being punched by a prizefighter), I enjoy shooting. At the range where I practice, most of the staff knows me by sight if not by name. I'm the guy in the metrosexual eyeglasses and Ralph Lauren polo, and I ask a lot of questions: What's the best way to maintain my sight picture with both eyes open? How do I clear a stove-piped round?

There is pleasure to be had in exercising one's rights, learning something new in midlife, and mastering the operation of a complex tool, which is one thing a gun is. But I won't deny the seductive psychological power that firearms possess. I grew up playing shooting games, pretending to be Starsky or Hutch or one of the patrolmen on *Adam-12*, the two most boring TV cops in history.

A prevailing theory holds that boys are 5 simultaneously aware of their own physical powerlessness and society's mandate that they serve as protectors of the innocent. Pretending to shoot a bad guy assuages this anxiety, which never goes away completely. This explanation makes sense to me. Another word for it is catharsis, and you could say that, as a novelist, I've made my living from it.

There are a lot of reasons that a gun feels right in my hand, but I also own firearms to protect my family. I hope I never have to use one for this purpose, and I doubt I ever will. But I am my family's last line of defense. I have chosen to meet this responsibility, in part, by being armed. It wasn't a choice I made lightly. I am aware that, statistically speaking, a gun in the home represents a far greater danger to its inhabitants than to an intruder. But not every choice we make is data-driven. A lot comes from the gut.

Apart from the ones in policemen's holsters, I don't think I saw a working firearm until the year after college, when a friend's girlfriend, after four cosmopolitans, decided to show off the .38 revolver she kept in her purse. (Half the party guests dived for cover, including me.)

It wasn't until my mid-forties that my education in guns began, in the course of writing a novel in which pistols, shotguns, and rifles, but also heavy weaponry like the AR-15 and its military analogue, the M-16, were widely used. I suspected that much of the gunplay I'd witnessed in movies and television was completely wrong (it is) and hired an instructor for a daylong private lesson "to shoot everything in the store." The gentleman who met me at the range was someone whom I would have called "a gun nut." A former New Yorker, he had relocated to Texas because of its lax gun laws and claimed to keep a pistol within arm's reach even when he showered. He was perfect, in other words, for my purpose.

My relationship to firearms might have ended there, if not for a coincidence of weather. Everybody remembers Hurricane Katrina; fewer recall Hurricane Rita, an even more intense storm that headed straight for Houston less than a month later. My wife and I arranged to stay at a friend's house in Austin, packed up the kids and dog, and headed out of town — or tried to. As many as 3.7 million people had the same idea, making Rita one of the largest evacuations in history, with predictable results.

By two in the morning, after six hours on 10 the road, we had made it all of fifty miles. The scene was like a snapshot from the Apocalypse: crowds milling restlessly, gas stations and minimarts picked clean and heaped with trash, families sleeping by the side of the road. The situation had the hopped-up feel of barely bottled chaos. After Katrina, nobody had any illusions that help was on its way. It also occurred to me that there were probably a lot of guns out there — this was Texas, after all. Here I was with two tiny children, a couple of thousand dollars in cash, a late-model S.U.V. with half a tank of gas and not so much as a heavy book to throw. When my wife wouldn't let me get out of the car so the dog could do his business, that was it for me. We jumped the median, turned around, and were home in under an hour.

As it happened, Rita made a last-minute turn away from Houston. But what if it hadn't? I believe people are basically good, but not all of them and not all the time. Like most citizens of our modern, technological world, I am wholly reliant upon a fragile web of services to meet my most basic needs. What would happen if those services collapsed? Chaos, that's what.

It didn't happen overnight, but before too long my Northeastern liberal sensibilities, while intact on other issues, had shifted on the question of gun ownership. For my first pistol I selected a little Walther .380. I shot it enough to decide it was junk, upgraded to a full-size Springfield 9-millimeter, liked it but wanted something with a thumb safety, found a nice Smith & Wesson subcompact that fit the bill, but along the way got a little bit of a gun-crush on the Beretta M-9 — and so on.

Lots of people on both sides of the aisle own firearms, or don't, for reasons that supersede their broader political and cultural affiliations. Let me be clear: my personal armory notwithstanding, I think guns are woefully under-regulated. It's far too easy to buy a gun — I once bought one in a parking lot — and I loathe the National Rifle Association. Some of the Obama administration's proposals strike me as more symbolic than effective, with some 300 million firearms on the loose. But the White House's recommendations seem like a good starting point and

nothing that would prevent me from protecting my family in a crisis. The AR-15 is a fascinating weapon, and, frankly, a gas to shoot. So is a tank, and I don't need to own a tank.

Alas, the days of à la carte politics like mine seem over, if they ever even existed. The bigger culprit is the far right and the lunatic pronouncements of those like Rush Limbaugh. But in the weeks since Newtown, I've watched my Facebook feed, which is dominated by my coastal friends, fill up with antigun dispatches that seemed divorced from reality. I agree it would be nice if the world had exactly zero guns in it. But I don't see that happening, and calling gun owners "a bunch of inbred rednecks" doesn't do much to advance rational discussion.

Thus, my secret life — though I guess it's 15 not such a secret anymore. My wife is afraid of my guns (though she also says she's glad I have them). My sixteen-year-old daughter is a different story. The week before her fall semester exams, we allowed her to skip school for a day, a tradition in our house. The rule is, she gets to do whatever she wants. This time, she asked to take a pistol lesson. She's an NPR listener like me, but she's also grown up in Texas, and the fact that one in five American women is a victim of sexual assault is not lost on her. In the windowless classroom off the range, the instructor ran her through the basics, demonstrating with a Glock 9-millimeter: how to hold it, load it, pull back the slide.

"You'll probably have trouble with that part," he said. "A lot of the women do."

"Oh really?" my daughter replied, and with a cagey smile proceeded to rack her weapon with such authority you could have heard it in the parking lot.

A proud-papa moment? I confess it was.

JUSTIN CRONIN, "Confessions of a Liberal Gun Owner," *The New York Times*, January 28, 2013. Copyright © 2013 by The New York Times. All rights reserved. Used under license. https://nytimes.com/

Topics for Critical Thinking and Writing

1. How would you characterize Cronin's persona as he presents it in this essay? Do you feel that his persona effectively connects with you as a reader? Why or why not?

2. What *arguments* does Cronin offer on behalf of gun ownership? Do you think his thesis might have been strengthened if he had cited statistics or authorities, or do you think that such evidence probably would have been inappropriate in a highly personal essay? Explain your response.

3. In paragraph 13, Cronin says that he believes "guns are woefully under-regulated" and that he "loathe[s] the National Rifle Association," but he doesn't go into any detail about what sorts of regulations he favors. Do you think his essay might have been more convincing if he had given us details along these lines? Explain.

4. Each of Cronin's last three paragraphs is very short. We have discussed how, in general, a short paragraph is usually an underdeveloped paragraph. Do you think these paragraphs are underdeveloped, or do you think Cronin knows exactly what he is doing? Explain.

ROXANE GAY

Roxane Gay opinion pieces appear regularly in the *New York Times*, the *Guardian*, the *Nation*, *Time*, and *McSweeney's*, among other prominent publications. She is a celebrated author of four novels, numerous short stories, and several works of nonfiction, including *Bad Feminist* (2014) and *Hunger* (2017), which was named as a 2017 finalist for the National Book Critics Circle Award for autobiography. Gay's most recent projects include a substack newsletter, *The Audacity*, and a podcast of Black feminist thought and experience, *Hear to Slay*, created with Tressie McMillan Cottom. This selection appeared in VQR in Fall 2014.

The Price of Black Ambition

You never know when or if you'll get a big break as a writer. You write and write and write and hope that someone out there will discern what you believe is in that writing, and then you write and hope and wait some more. I think I am having my big break right now. This year I published two books — a novel, *An Untamed State*, and an essay collection, *Bad Feminist*. Both books have received positive critical attention. The latter book has been on the New York Times bestseller list twice. Articles about me keep telling me that I am having a moment, my big break. My friends and loved ones tell me that I am having a moment. Part of me recognizes that I am having a moment, while the more relentless part of me, a part that cannot be quieted, is only hungrier, wanting more.

I began to understand the shape and ferocity of my ambition when I was in kindergarten. Each student had been given a piece of paper in class, bearing an illustration of two water glasses. We were instructed to color in one-half of the illustration. I suspect we were learning about fractions. I diligently shaded in one half of one of the glasses and smugly turned my work in to the teacher. If it had been the parlance of the day, I would have thought, *Nailed it*. I had not, of course, "nailed it." I was supposed to color in an entire glass. Instead of the praise I anticipated, I received an F, which, in retrospect, seems a bit harsh for kindergarten. I couldn't bring such a grade home to my parents. I had already begun demanding excellence of myself and couldn't face falling short.

On the bus ride home, I stuffed my shame between the dry, cracked leather of the seat and assumed the matter had been dealt with. The driver, a zealous sort, found my crumpled failure and handed it to my mother when he dropped me off the next day. She was not pleased. I was not pleased with her displeasure. I never wanted to experience that feeling again. I vowed to be better. I vowed to be the best. As a black girl in these United States — I was the daughter of Haitian immigrants — I had no choice but to work toward being the best.

Many people of color living in this country can likely relate to the onset of outsized ambition at too young an age, an ambition fueled by the sense, often confirmed by ignorance, of being a second-class citizen and needing to claw your way toward equal consideration and some semblance of respect. Many people of color, like me, remember the moment that first began to shape their ambition and what that moment felt like.

The concept of a big break often implies 5 that once you've achieved a certain milestone, everything falls into place. Life orders itself according to your whims. There is no more struggle, there is nothing left to want. There is no more rejection. This is a lovely, lovely fantasy bearing no resemblance to reality. And yet. I have noticed that my e-mails to

certain key people in my professional life are answered with astonishing speed where they once were answered at a sedate and leisurely pace. I enjoy that.

I am thinking about success, ambition, and blackness and how breaking through while black is tempered by so much burden. Nothing exemplifies black success and ambition like Black History Month, a celebratory month I've come to dread as a time when people take an uncanny interest in sharing black-history facts with me to show how they are *not racist*. It's the month where we segregate some of history's most significant contributors into black history instead of fully integrating them into American history. Each February, we hold up civil-rights heroes and the black innovators and writers and artists who have made so much possible for this generation. We say, look at what the best of us have achieved. We conjure W. E. B. Du Bois, who once wrote, "The Negro race, like all races, is going to be saved by its exceptional men." We ask much of our exceptional men and women. We must be exceptional if we are to be anything at all.

Black History Month is important and a corrective to so much of America's fraught racial history. But in the twenty-first century, this relegating of black ambition to one month of recognition feels constraining and limiting rather than inspirational.

In the *Atlantic*, Ta-Nehisi Coates published an essay about President Barack Obama and the tradition of black politics that reached me in a vulnerable place. Coates writes of the president's ascension: "He becomes a champion of black imagination, of black dreams and black possibilities." In that same essay, Coates also writes about how the narrative of personal responsibility is a false one that is, unfortunately, often parroted by our president, our brightest shining star, Barack Obama, the first black president of the United States. At the end of his essay, Coates writes, "But I think history will also remember his [Obama's] unquestioning embrace of 'twice as good' in a country that has always given black people, even under his watch, half as much." About a month after that essay was published, Obama announced the My Brother's Keeper initiative, "an interagency effort to improve measurably the expected educational and life outcomes for and address the persistent opportunity gaps faced by boys and young men of color." The initiative is certainly well-intentioned, but it also speaks to the idea that black Americans must make themselves more respectable in order to matter. In its initial incarnation, it also gave the impression that only boys and men matter. On its surface, My Brother's Keeper is a program that does nothing to address the systemic and structural issues young men of color will face, no matter how well prepared or respectable or personally responsible they are.

I have come to realize how much I have, throughout my life, bought into the narrative of this alluring myth of personal responsibility and excellence. I realize how much I believe that all good things will come if I — if we — just work hard enough. This attitude leaves me always relentless, always working hard enough and then harder still. I am ashamed that sometimes a part of me believes we, as a people, will be saved by those among us who are exceptional without considering who might pay the price for such salvation or who would be left behind.

Du Bois was a vocal proponent of the 10 "Talented Tenth," this idea that out of every ten black men, one was destined for greatness, destined to become the powerful leader black people needed to rise up and overcome and advance. This 10 percent of men were to be educated and mentored so they might become

leaders, the front line for much-needed socio-political change.

We often forget, though, who first came up with the "talented tenth." The idea first began circulating in the 1890s, propagated by wealthy white liberals. The term itself was coined by Henry Lyman Morehouse, a white man, who wrote, "In the discussion concerning Negro education we should not forget the talented tenth man . . . . The tenth man, with superior natural endowments, symmetrically trained and highly developed, may become a mightier influence, a greater inspiration to others than all the other nine, or nine times nine like them." Here was a somewhat repulsive proposition gilded in condescending intentions, that if the strongest efforts were focused on the best of black folk, a few might be saved from themselves. Here we are today, still believing this could be true.

Before, since, and during Du Bois's time, the "Negro" has been a problem demanding a solution. Historically we are, of course, quick to neglect examining how this problem began. We are, it seems, still looking for that solution even as some declare the United States is embarking upon a post-racial era. We forget that we should not only measure black progress by the most visibly successful among us but also by those who continue to be left behind.

While I am having what some refer to as my moment, I am in the middle of a second book tour. The first tour, for my novel, took me to thirteen cities, beginning in Boston. There I stayed in a hotel where my room had a fireplace that kept my feet warm and toasty. I marveled at this fireplace. I still had a lot of energy for my first event at Brookline Booksmith. I had not yet realized how much energy it takes, as an introvert, to fake extroversion. I was nervous during that first event, but holding my book helped. Looking down at the words I had written helped. Seeing so many supportive people in the audience helped. The booksellers were a delight.

I was next off to New York, a city that is always intimidating and exhilarating to be in. There were two readings, at Community Bookstore and McNally Jackson, where I had conversations with Sari Botton and Ruth Franklin, respectively. It was standing-room only at both readings and deeply engaged audiences and people buying my book and asking me to sign those books. I would encounter more of the same in every city. There were reviews, mostly glowing, even in the *New York Times*. *Time* magazine declared, "So let this be the year of Roxane Gay." It all felt so extravagant.

And then my essay collection came out. 15 The crowds at my readings have swelled. People stand in hot rooms and then hot lines for an hour, sometimes two, just to meet me, shake my hand, pose for a picture, have a book signed. In Los Angeles, 450 people gave me a standing ovation, and the recognition nearly brought me to my knees because it was all so unexpected and gratifying.

Another reading, in another city, standing room only. During the Q&A, an older woman recounted a story of how she once couldn't get a credit card because she didn't have a husband. I think she said the year was 1969. I thought about her story all night and kept thinking, *May I be worthy of the work you have done to make my life possible.*

At that same reading, I met a seventeen-year-old girl named Teighlor whose mom had brought her. She sat near the front, and her eyes were shining the whole time. I threw her a *Bad Feminist* tote bag, and she held it tightly in her hands. She was first in the signing line and she told me how she looked up to me and she was wholly adorable and I felt my eyes burning at the corners because I was so moved. I kept thinking, *May I be worthy of your respect and admiration.*

At that same reading, I met a young man named Robert who also brought his mother. She began speaking to me in Creole so I responded in kind. They were Haitian and they were just so excited to meet another Haitian from the Midwest. The bookstore had sold out of my book by that point, but they wanted to meet me anyway. They apologized, as if they owed me something. Their presence at my reading was all I could ever ask for. I gave them my personal copy of the book and signed it. They asked if they could take a picture with me, and I kept thinking, *May I be worthy of your respect. May I be worthy of our people's history.*

There were so many encounters that night and on all the nights that made me think, *May I be worthy of all of this.* And there is a part of me that realizes how hard I have worked for this, and that I have, in part, earned this.

My novel is in its third printing. My essay 20 collection is in its fourth fifth printing. I am having a moment, and the burden of my ambition still has me wondering if I am worthy.

For most of my life, I have taken for granted how my middle-class upbringing and my loving, educated, and involved parents made it possible for me to strive for excellence. Nearly everything has worked in my favor well beyond whatever natural gifts I possess. I attended excellent schools in safe, suburban neighborhoods with healthy tax bases. I had teachers who encouraged my talent and creativity. I had parents who supplemented what I was learning in school with additional studies. It was very easy to buy into the narrative that exceptionalism would help me and those who looked like me to rise above the challenges we face as people of color. All I had to do was work and want hard enough because nothing in my life contradicted this ethos.

All along, though, there were insistent reminders of how, even with all these advantages, certain infrastructures, so profoundly shaped by racial inequality, would never willingly accommodate me or my experiences. I would never be able to work hard enough. I didn't have to be twice as good, I had to be four times as good, or even more. This is why I am relentless. This is why I am not satisfied and likely never will be.

In high school, I attended boarding school. I was one of a handful of black students, and even among them, I was a stranger in a strange land, a Midwestern transplant in the wilds of New Hampshire. At first, my cadre of fellow black students had little in common beyond the brownness of our skin, but at least we had that much-needed kinship because to the white students, we were usurpers, treading upon the hallowed ground to which only they, with their white skin, were entitled.

My senior year, I received an acceptance letter to an Ivy League college. I was in the campus mailroom. Everyone was buzzing as they learned of their fate. I opened my letter and smiled. I had been accepted to all but one of the schools to which I applied. I allowed myself a quiet moment of celebration. A young white man next to me, the sort who played lacrosse, had not been accepted to his top choice, a school to which I had been accepted. He was instantly bitter. He sneered and muttered, "Affirmative action," as he stalked away. I had worked hard and it didn't matter. I was exceptional and it did not matter. In that moment, I was reminded of my place. I was reminded of why my ambition would never be sated, and would, instead, continue to grow ferociously. I hoped my ambition would grow so big I would be able to crowd out those who were unwilling to have me among them without realizing their acceptance should never have been my measure.

In college the situation was much the same. I belonged there, I had earned my place, but few people would acknowledge that belonging. Not a week went by when I or other students of color weren't stopped and asked to show our student IDs. It was easier to believe we were trespassing than simply traversing campus between classes. This was a small indignity, but it also wasn't.

At both my master's and doctoral institutions, I was the only black student. Any success I achieved only spurred me to work harder and harder so I might outrun whispers of *affirmative action* and the arrogant assumptions that I could not possibly belong in those institutions of supposedly higher learning.

Like many students of color, I spent a frustrating amount of time educating white people, my professors included, about their ignorance, or gritting my teeth when I did not have the energy. When race entered class discussions, all eyes turned to me as the expert on blackness or the designated spokesperson for my people. When racist "jokes" were made, I was supposed to either grin and bear it or turn the awkward incident into a teachable moment about difference, tolerance, and humor. When a doctoral classmate, who didn't realize I was in hearing range, told a group of our peers I was clearly the affirmative-action student, I had to pretend I felt nothing when no one contradicted her. Unfortunately, these anecdotes are dreadfully common, banal even, for people of color. Lest you think this is ancient history, I graduated with my Ph.D. in December 2010.

Today, I teach at Purdue University, where in the semester I write this, I have no students in either of my classes who look like me. I have yet to see another black faculty member in the halls of my building, though I know some exist. I previously taught at Eastern Illinois University, where, in my department, I was one of two black faculty members, one of only five faculty of color in all. The more things change, the more they stay the same. This is the price of exceptionalism — you will always be the only one or one of a few. There are no safe harbors. There are no reflections of your experience.

I have written three books, have a fourth under contract, and am working on three more. I have been widely published. I am regularly invited to read and speak all over the country. I advocate, as best I can, for the issues that matter most to me. As a feminist, I try to be intersectional in word and deed. When I fail, I try to learn from that failure instead of hiding it as I did in kindergarten.

I have achieved a modicum of success, 30 but I never stop working. I never stop. I don't even feel the flush of pleasure I once did when I achieve a new milestone. I am having a moment, but I only want more. I need more. I cannot merely be good enough because I am chased by the pernicious whispers that I might only be "good enough for a black woman." There is the shame of sometimes believing they might be right because that's how profound racism in this country can break any woman down. I know I am one of the lucky ones because unlike far too many people of color, I had far more than "half as much" to work with, the whole of my life. It is often unbearable to consider what half as much to work with means for those who are doing their damndest to make do. I call this ambition, but it's something much worse because it cannot ever be satisfied.

Topics for Critical Thinking and Writing

1. What do you think Roxane Gay means by "the price of Black ambition?" Who suffers and who ultimately pays the "price"?

2. What problems does Gay identify in such things as Barack Obama's "My Brother's Keeper" initiative and in W.E.B. Dubois's concept of the "talented tenth?"

3. Is Gay's essay a strong argument? What elements of argument do you see as the most important in the essay's success as a convincing piece, or what elements do you find lacking that make it less successful?

4. What kinds of anxieties or self-doubt have you encountered when you have had gratifying moments of achievement (e.g., an award, a good grade, an achievement in sports or at work)? Why do you think many people struggle to accept their highest achievements? Are such struggles always more difficult for people from minoritized groups, or is it a feature of success common to all?

Assignment for Writing an Analysis of an Argument

Choose a selection not yet discussed in class or an essay assigned by your instructor. In a brief essay, analyze and evaluate the essay. In writing an analysis of a reading, do the following:

- Read and reread thoughtfully the essay you are analyzing. Composing and keeping notes in the margins or in new documents will help you think about what you are reading.

- Be sure to examine the author's thesis, purpose, methods, persona, intended audience, and tone.

- Examine closely the *organization* of an argument. Is the thesis explicitly or implicitly stated, at the very beginning or somewhere later in the essay? What is the author's strongest piece of evidence? Is it presented right off the bat and then supported by further evidence, or does the essay build up to the key evidence? Is the organization effective?

- Remember that although your essay is an analysis of someone else's writing and you may have to include a summary of the work you are writing about, your essay is *your* essay, your analysis, not a mere summary; the thesis, the organization, and the tone are yours.

7

Developing an Argument of Your Own

The difficult part in an argument is not to defend one's opinion but to know what it is.

— ANDRÉ MAUROIS

CONSIDER THIS

Can you draw a better banana? Follow the instructions below.

1. **Draw a banana**. That's it; simply draw a banana. Share your results!

2. **Draw a better banana**. Draw a banana again, doing whatever you can to improve your results.

3. **Draw the BEST banana**. What might you do to draw the best banana possible? What if you were in a contest in which the best banana artist was awarded a large cash prize? What tools or strategies would you use to draw the best banana?

We can't think of a funnier fruit than the banana. Of course, our point is not comedy but the serious matter of composing arguments and improving what you compose. In step 1, you probably didn't plan much and reached for whatever instruments were at hand — a pencil, perhaps, or a digital freeform drawing tool in a paint application — and sketched a basic banana. When asked to improve your banana in step 2, you probably had to stop and think, evaluating the first effort, considering what could be done to improve it. Maybe you added colors, looked for a model to copy, or made your drawing more interesting by drawing a peeled banana. In step 3, the instructions for the *best* banana (for a large cash prize) opens up the possibility for considering new tools, new strategies, and new methods. If the cash prize were large enough, you might even invest in software and hardware (and learn how to use it) to create a nearly perfect image, a true artwork.

How do you think this idea of "a better banana" connects to writing?

Planning an Argument

To execute a well-informed, well-reasoned argument takes time and effort, and most of all a willingness to revise: to revise your thinking as you learn, and your writing as you produce it. Clear, thoughtful, seemingly effortless prose is not common on the first try. Good thinking and writing require rethinking and rewriting. In a live conversation, you can always claim ignorance and cover yourself ("Well, I don't know, but I sort of think X"), and you can always backtrack and revise your words instantly ("Oh, well, I didn't mean it that way, let me say that again differently"). However, once you have had the chance to learn about and reason through an issue, and you begin writing down your thoughts, refining them, and organizing them—and produce the final draft of your writing—then you face the key moment of publication. This may mean turning in your work to your teacher, or sending an email, or posting to a blog, but this act of publication represents your ideas in final form (you might say, if you completed the activity at the beginning of this chapter, that it represents your best banana). Now revision is over. Your ideas are in the hands of others, and you can't take them back (at least not without writing a retraction). As the Persian philosopher and poet Omar Khayyám said in a much-quoted verse:

> The Moving Finger writes; and, having writ,
> Moves on: nor all thy Piety nor Wit
> Shall lure it back to cancel half a Line,
> Nor all thy Tears wash out a Word of it.

> بر لوح نشان بودنی‌ها بوده‌است
> پیوسته قلم ز نیک و بد فرسوده‌است
> در روز ازل هر آنچه بایست بداد
> غم خوردن و کوشیدن ما بیهوده‌است

You may have felt this way about an off-tone tweet or a regretful email. The point is, before you put your ideas before a scrutinizing audience, make sure that they fully represent the quality and clarity of your most judicious thinking.

Producing the strongest arguments begins with good planning—but that can be difficult when you do not yet know what to think about something. Thus, planning your argument starts with developing topics and ideas about those topics.

GETTING IDEAS: ARGUMENT AS AN INSTRUMENT OF INQUIRY

In Chapter 1, we included a section titled "Generating Ideas: Writing as a Way of Thinking" (p. 19) in which we quoted Robert Frost saying, "To learn to write is to learn to have ideas." We offered strategies such as doing research, clustering, anticipating counterarguments, and deciding where you stand by surveying, evaluating, and analyzing an issue. These techniques are traditionally part of the process of **invention**.

You can also have a dialogue with classmates and friends about your topic to try out and develop ideas. But when it comes to writing, the process of "talking things over" usually begins with a dialogue between yourself and a text that you're reading: Your notes, your summary, and your annotations are a kind of dialogue between you and the author(s). You may not be trying to persuade anyone; rather, you're using argument to find the truth — testing ideas, playing the devil's advocate, posing hypothetical questions. Through conversing with others, then conversing with texts by reading and taking notes, you may find that you have developed some clear ideas that can be put into writing. So you pull up a blank screen, but then a paralyzing thought suddenly strikes: "I have ideas but just can't put them into words." The blank white page stares back at you.

All writers, even professional ones, are familiar with this experience. Good writers know that waiting for inspiration is usually not the best strategy. You may be waiting a long time. The best thing to do is begin. Recall: *Writing is a way of thinking*. It's a way of getting and developing ideas. It does not have to be perfect at first. An argument can be an *instrument of inquiry* as well as a means of persuasion. It is an important *method* of critical thinking. It helps us clarify what we think. One reason we have trouble writing is our fear of putting ourselves on record, but another reason is our fear that we have no good ideas worth putting down. However, by writing notes — or even free associations — and by writing a draft, no matter how weak, we can begin to think our way toward good ideas.

Take advantage of the tools at your disposal. Use the internet to explore the conversations happening around your subject of interest. Maybe you are interested in writing about veterans' experiences of Iraq and Afghanistan. Using a search engine, you can find out what topics others have been exploring and discussing. Perhaps you are interested in how service members interacted with Iraqi and Afghan citizens, or how their perceptions of the mission changed while serving, or whether or not they experienced trauma. Finding a good topic often means narrowing down. If possible, identify topics that have not been adequately dealt with. (Often, finding a "gap" in knowledge provides you a place to position yourself to articulate a fresh perspective or idea.) Go further: Post your initial thoughts and questions to online forums on the subject. Writing a blog entry can foster conversations about the topic and help you discover what others think — and where you stand. This is all to underscore a chief method in developing your own argument: Involve yourself in the conversation.

BRAINSTORMING STRATEGIES

If you are facing an issue, debate, or topic and don't know what to write, it is likely because you don't yet know what you think. If, after talking about the topic with yourself (via your reading notes) and others (via any means), you are still unclear on what you think, try one of three strategies: freewriting, listing, or diagramming.

FREEWRITING Write for five or six minutes, nonstop, without censoring what you produce. You may use what you write to improve your thinking. It is likely you will make numerous grammatical and spelling errors, but don't worry about that yet (this is your "first banana," we could say). Your ideas can be free and wide-ranging. You can jump from one idea to another. If you know something to be true, no need to pause and look it up for verification — yet. For now, you can just take a note reminding yourself to do so. Once you have spent some time writing out your ideas, you can use what you've written to look further into the subject at hand. You may find that your best ideas and most incisive questions appeared in the middle of large chunks of text. When you reread what you wrote, you have a chance to pull those ideas out. You might select your best idea as a possible thesis.

Freewriting should be totally free. As a topic, let's imagine a writer is thinking about how children's toys are constructed for different genders. The student is reflecting on the release of the Nerf Rebelle, a type of toy gun made specifically for girls. A good freewrite might look like this:

Nerf released a new toy made for girls, the Nerf Rebelle gun. It was an attempt the company made to offer toys for girls that have been traditionally made for boys. This seems good — it shows an effort toward equality between the sexes. Or is Nerf just trying to broaden its market and sell more toys (after all, boys are only half the population)? Or is it both? (That could be my central question. *Thesis*: Nerf gestures toward gender equality but is really motivated by profit. Good enough?) But is the Nerf Rebelle really gender-neutral? It is pink and purple and has feminine-looking designs on it. With its "elle" ending, the gun sounds small, cute, and stereotypically girly. *Possible thesis*: Nerf Rebelle appears to encourage "girl power" but really embodies stereotypes associated with feminine weakness. It shoots foam arrows, unlike the boys' version of the gun, which shoots foam bullets. Arrows suggest Cupid, maybe — a figure who inspires love. The messages and narratives of the crossbow are different than those suggested by the gun. It's like girls aren't saving the world with their weapons but seeking love and marriage. What kind of messages does this send to young girls? Are there other toys like this? Legos for girls — the Lego Friends series is one. Same deal: The company wants to market it as equality ("girls can play with Legos too!") but the Lego mall, salon, pet store, spa, etc., are quite different than the Legos for boys which feature monsters, miners, science fiction themes, etc. (look up). Maybe that's a thesis: a look at toys that have this dual message? How do dual messages about gender and feminine power work in other areas of life, like business and politics? And what about kids who identify as trans or nonbinary?

Notice that the writer here is jumping around, generating and exploring ideas while writing. Later they can return to the results of freewriting and begin organizing their ideas and observations. Notice along the way that they made a connection between the contradictory messages embodied by the toy and those in the larger society. This connection helped the student to broaden the argument from a critique of a single company's toy to other toys made by other companies, to gender expectations and assumptions in other areas of culture. Freewriting in this case led to new paths of inquiry and may have inspired further research into questions more important and impactful than the Nerf Rebelle by itself.

LISTING   Writing down keywords, just as you do when making a shopping list, is another way of generating ideas. When you make a shopping list, you write *ketchup*, and the act of writing it reminds you that you also need hamburger rolls — and *that* in turn reminds you that you also need pickles. Similarly, when preparing a list of ideas for a paper, just writing down one item will often generate another. Of course, when you look over the list, you'll drop some of these ideas — the dinner menu will change — but you'll be making progress by refining.

Here's an example of a student listing questions and making associations that could help him focus on a specific argument within a larger debate. The subject here is whether prostitution should be legalized.

Sex Work & Law — Should it be legalized?
> Why do people go into this business? What types and kinds of sex workers exist? How has the law traditionally policed sex in history and in different places?
> How many sex workers are arrested every year?
> Individual rights vs. public good?
> Who gains or suffers most from the practice? From enforcement? From legalization?
> If it were legal, could its negative effects be better controlled? How?
> Are "escort services" really "prostitution rings"? How do they get away with that? Are these dangerous for sex workers? Would bringing sex work into an open legal framework make people safer?

Notice that the student doesn't really know the answers yet but is asking questions by freely associating and seeing what turns up as a productive line of analysis. The questions might inspire the student to do some basic internet research or even deeper research — and often one by-product of doing in-depth research is more ideas and a better understanding of the issues informing the questions. If you observe patterns or similarities among the items you listed, you may find your argument (e.g., "The enforcement of prostitution laws is uneven and hurts *X* group unequally, and it uses a lot of public money and clogs up the courts. We would be better off regulating the trade carefully rather than jailing people").

DIAGRAMMING   Sketching a visual representation of an essay is a kind of listing. Three methods of diagramming are especially common.

Clustering   As we discuss in Chapter 1 in "Using Clustering to Discover Ideas" (p. 21), you can make an effective cluster by writing, in the middle of a sheet of paper, a word or phrase summarizing your topic (e.g., *fracking*, the process of forcing high pressure into rock to extract natural resources; see diagram), circling it, and then writing down and circling a related word or idea (e.g., *energy independence*). You then circle these phrases and continue jotting down ideas, making connections, and indicating relationships. Here, the economic and environmental impacts of fracking seem to be the focus. Whether you realize it or not, an argument is taking shape.

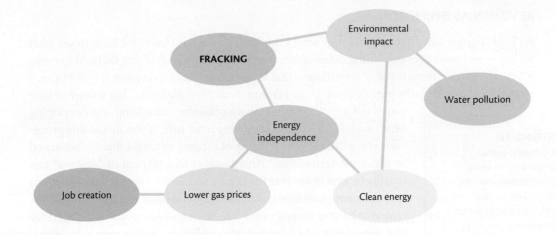

Branching Some writers find it useful to draw a tree, moving from the central topic to the main branches (chief ideas) and then to the twigs (aspects of the chief ideas).

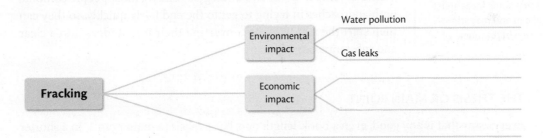

Comparing in Columns Draw a line down the middle of the page and then set up two columns showing oppositions. For instance, if you are concerned with the environmental and economic impacts of fracking, you might produce columns that look something like this:

Environmental	Economic
water pollution	employment
chemicals used	independence from unstable oil-producing countries
gas leaks	cheaper fuel
toxic waste	cheaper electricity

All these methods can, of course, be executed with pen and paper, but you may also be able to use them on your computer, depending on the capabilities of your software. You might also find templates from a good website helpful.

REVISION AS INVENTION

As E. M. Forster said, "How can I know what I think till I see what I say?" We have to see what we say — we have to get something down on the page — before we realize that we need to make it better. Writing, then, is really **rewriting** — that is, **revising** — and a revision is a *re-vision*, a second look. You begin by putting down ideas, perhaps in no particular order, but sooner or later comes the job of looking at them critically, organizing and developing what's useful in them and removing what isn't. If you follow this procedure, you will be in the company of Picasso, who said that he "advanced by means of destruction." Any passages that you cut or "destroy" can actually be kept in another file in case you want to revisit those deletions later. As many professional writers know, you often end up restoring discarded or leftover ideas for new directions and new essays later. An essay that you submit — to a teacher or a publisher — will appear to be effortlessly composed, but in all likelihood it was the result of a much messier process during which you refined your ideas.

> **WRITING TIP**
> If a question seems relevant or if an essay inspires new questions and answers in your mind, it's a good idea to start writing — even just fragmentary sentences if necessary. Put something on paper, and returning to these words, perhaps in five minutes or even the next day, you'll probably find that some ideas aren't at all bad and may stimulate even better ones.

Whether you advance bit by bit (freewriting, brainstorming, revising, etc.) or you write an entire first draft in a single sitting is a matter of temperament and strategy. Probably most people combine both approaches in trying to get to the end fairly quickly, so they can then start the real work of converting their initial ideas into a clear and substantial argument.

THE THESIS OR MAIN POINT

Every essay that is any good, even a book-length one, has a thesis (a main point). In a shorter essay, the thesis can be stated briefly, usually in one sentence. This is the primary claim the rest of the essay is dedicated to advancing, so it is important to ensure that your thesis is strong. Typically a shorter essay we would expect several paragraphs containing the support for the thesis, and a conclusion. The longer the essay, the more complex the thesis may be. Some books will provide an entire chapter — the introduction — to lay out a complex and multidimensional thesis. Then individual chapters work like the paragraphs of a shorter essay, explaining, supporting, and defending the primary claim or contention.

Thesis statements can be general or specific, and they may address any subject. If you think cats make good companions for older adults, that is a thesis. If you think people should get along better and there should be world peace, that is a thesis. However, such evident and general thesis statements do not usually lead to the most compelling arguments. Granted, any idea can be developed in an interesting and convincing way, but when you invent a thesis, some basic rules of thumb will help you set up powerful, engaging, and relevant arguments.

The thesis is the point; the argument sets forth the evidence that supports the thesis. When you formulate a thesis and ask questions about it — such as who the readers are, what they believe, what they know, and what they need to know — you also begin to get ideas about how to organize the material. The thesis may be clear and simple, but the reasons (the argument) may take many pages.

RAISING THE STAKES OF YOUR THESIS

Imagine walking across campus and coming upon something surprising: a person ready to perform on a tightrope suspended between two buildings. They are wearing a glittering leotard and eyeing up the challenge very seriously. Here's the thing, though: The tightrope is only *one foot off the ground*. Would you stop and watch the person walk across it? Maybe, maybe not. Most people would take a look and move on. If you did spend a few minutes watching, you wouldn't be very worried about the performer falling. If they lost their balance momentarily, you wouldn't gasp in horror. And if they did handstands and somersaults as they crossed, you might be somewhat impressed but not enraptured.

Now imagine the rope being *a hundred feet off the ground*. You would almost certainly stop and witness the feat. The audience would likely be captivated, nervous about the performer potentially falling, "oohing" if they momentarily lost their balance, and cheering if they crossed the rope successfully.

Consider the tightrope as your thesis statement, the performer as writer, and the act of crossing as the argument. Low-stakes thesis statements are comparable to low tightropes: A low-stakes thesis statement itself may be interesting, but not much about it is vital or new to any particular audience. Low-stakes thesis statements tend to be general and lack a sense of importance or relevance. Students can write well-organized, clear, and direct papers on such topics, but the performance is similar to that of an expert walking across a tightrope that is only one foot off the ground. The argument may be well executed, but few in the audience will be inspired by it.

Take our example thesis statement: *Cats make good companions for older adults*. A thesis like this may restate what is already widely known and accepted, making a generally reasonable point but not discussing any consequences. It feels a little like saying that Earth is a planet. *Yes*, you want to say, *and what's your point*? So what if cats make good companions for older adults?

To raise the tightrope, and thus raise the stakes of your thesis, try including a stronger sense of the implications of your thesis. Perhaps you can consider the physical, psychological, and social benefits to older adults of owning a cat. These elements "raise the tightrope" of the thesis because they raise the stakes. The thesis becomes: *The good companionship of cats leads to health benefits for older adults*. Now you are arguing something audiences do not want to miss, especially if they have an older adult in their lives who could benefit from the companionship of a cat. To raise the tightrope even further, you could impress upon a specific audience the need to consider action: What could they do to encourage pet ownership for older adults? What problems does it solve? The thesis may become: *The companionship of pet cats leads to multiple benefits for older adults and their families, and it helps solve the problem of abundance in local animal shelters*. This remains a somewhat banal thesis but is more specific and multidimensional. It compels certain readers to *want* to read, and keep reading, which is an effect of raising the tightrope.

> **WRITING TIP**
> When you define your area of analysis and target an audience, you set a course for the organization of your body paragraphs. Over-general and unspecific thesis statements can leave you without a plan and force you to improvise as you go along.

Considering thesis statements as tightropes strung at different heights can help you consider the stakes of your argument.

There are several ways to raise the tightrope. First, *think about what is socially, culturally, or politically important* about your thesis statement and argument. Some writing instructors tell students to ask themselves "So what?" about the thesis, but this can be a vague directive. Here are some better questions:

- Why is your thesis important?

- To whom — what group or demographic — is your thesis important?

- What are the consequences of what you claim?

- What could happen if your position were *not* recognized?

- How can your argument benefit readers or compel them to action (by doing something or adopting a new belief)?

- What will readers *gain* by accepting your argument as convincing?

A CHECKLIST FOR A THESIS STATEMENT

☐ Does the statement make an arguable assertion rather than (1) merely assert an unarguable fact, (2) merely announce a topic, or (3) declare an unarguable opinion or belief?

☐ Is the statement broad enough to cover the entire argument that I will be presenting, and is it narrow enough for me to cover the topic in the space allotted?

☐ Does the thesis have consequences beneficial to some audience or consequences that would be detrimental if it were not accepted? (In other words, are there stakes?)

In formulating your thesis, keep in mind the following points.

- *Different thesis statements may speak to different target audiences.* An argument about changes in estate tax laws may not thrill all audiences, but for a defined group — accountants, lawyers, or the elderly, for instance — it may be quite controversial and highly relevant. Ask yourself: How do I address the audience for whom my thesis is most important?

- *Not all audiences are equal — or equally interested in your thesis or argument.* In this book, we generally select topics of broad importance. However, in a literature course, a film history course, or a political science course, you'll calibrate your thesis statements and arguments to an audience that is invested in those fields. In writing about the steep decline in bee populations, your argument might look quite different if you're speaking to ecologists as opposed to gardeners. (We will discuss audience more in the following section, "Imagining an Audience.")

- *Be wary of compare-and-contrast arguments.* One of the most basic approaches to writing is to compare and contrast, a maneuver that usually produces a low-tightrope thesis. It normally looks like this: "*X* and *Y* are similar in some ways and different in others." But if you think about it, *anything* can be compared and contrasted in this way, and doing so doesn't necessarily *tell* anything important. So, if you're writing a compare-and-contrast paper, make sure to include the reasons why it is important to compare and contrast these things. What benefit does the comparison yield? What significance does it have to some audience or some issue?

THINKING CRITICALLY *"Walking the Tightrope"*

Examine the low-stakes thesis statements provided below and expand each one into a high-stakes thesis by including the importance of asserting it to an audience and by proposing a possible response. The first one has been done as an example.

LOW-STAKES THESIS	HIGH-STAKES THESIS
Good nutrition and exercise can lead to a healthy life.	One way to help address <u>child obesity</u> in the United States is to remind <u>parents and families</u> of basic <u>strategies to encourage</u> good nutrition and exercise, which many reputable health experts advise lead to a healthy life.
Every qualified American should vote.	
Violent video games are bad for society.	
Electric cars will reduce air pollution.	

IMAGINING AN AUDIENCE

Raising the tightrope of your thesis will also require you to imagine the *audience* you're addressing. The questions that you ask yourself in generating thoughts on a topic will primarily relate to the topic, but additional questions that consider the audience are always relevant:

- Who are my readers?
- What do they believe?
- What do I want them to believe?
- What common ground do we share and where do we differ?
- What do they need to know?
- Why should they care?

Let's think about these questions. The literal answer to the first probably is "my professor," but (unless you receive instructions to the contrary) you should not write specifically for your instructor. Instead, you should write for an audience that is, generally speaking, like your classmates. In short, your imagined audience is literate, intelligent, and moderately well informed, but its members don't know everything that you know, and they don't know your response to the problem being addressed. Your audience needs more information along those lines to make an intelligent decision about the issue.

<table>
<tr><td>

WRITING TIP

If you wish to persuade, finding premises that you share with your audience can help establish common ground, a function of *ethos*.

</td></tr>
</table>

For example, in writing about how children's toys shape the minds of young children of different genders differently, it may not be enough to simply say, "Toys are part of the gender socialization process." ("Sure they are," the audience might already agree.) However, if you consider your intended audience is, you have an opportunity to direct your argument more specifically to their concerns and interests, raising the stakes for them. What audiences should be concerned with your topic? Maybe you're addressing the general public, who buy toys for children at least some of the time. Maybe you're addressing parents who are raising young children. Maybe you're addressing consumer advocates, encouraging them to pressure toy manufacturers and retailers to produce more gender-neutral offerings. The point is that your essay should contain (and sustain) an assessment of the impact of your high-stakes thesis for a particular audience, and it should set out a clear course of action for that audience.

How do you raise the stakes? You consider the audience as you frame the questions, lay out the issues, identify the problems, and note the complications that arise because of your basic thesis. If you are writing for toy consumers (which may be most people at least some of the time), you could point out that toys have a significant impact on the interests, identities, skills, and capabilities that children develop and carry into adulthood. Most children think toys are "just fun," but the toys may be teaching kids to conform unthinkingly to the social expectations of their sex, to accept designated sex-based social roles, and to cultivate talents differently based on sex instead of their own interests or abilities. Because toys are so significant, you could point out that it is important for your audience (toy consumers) to ask questions about whether the toys they are selecting for their loved ones perpetuate gender-based stereotypes. When people buy toys for children, they usually do not intend to perpetuate social inequalities, so making people aware of your argument can inspire better, more conscious choices. What we want you to see is that asking questions about the implications of your argument gives it social importance and makes it immediately relevant to your audience.

The bottom line is not just to know your audience but to define it so you can argue for different courses of action that are most likely to be persuasive. You may not be very convincing if you argue to average parents that they should avoid all Disney-themed toys. Perhaps you should argue simply that parents can offer their kids diverse toys and talk to their children while playing with them about alternatives to the stereotypical messages that some of those toys convey. However, if you're writing for a magazine called *Radical Parenting* and your essay is titled "Buying Toys the Gender-Neutral Way," your audience and its expectations — therefore, your thesis and argument — may look far different.

Instructors sometimes tell students to imagine their audience as their classmates. What they probably mean is that your argument should be addressed to people invested in the world of ideas, not just your literal classmates. Again, ask yourself the questions we provided in our list at the beginning of this section (p. 234) in order to tailor your argument to the audience.

ADDRESSING OPPOSITION AND ESTABLISHING COMMON GROUND

Presumably, your imagined audience does not share all your views. By putting yourself into your readers' shoes, you will have an opportunity to view your own argument from different perspectives, and perhaps anticipate what readers who do not share your view might say about your positions. Your essay will almost surely have to summarize the views that you're going to speak against, and it is likely that some of these contrary views are present among your audience. So how do you sensibly and sensitively challenge them to think differently? By considering what your audience knows (or thinks it knows) and predicting how they might interrogate your ideas, you will generate ideas for addressing opposition and establishing common ground. Ask yourself:

- Why does your audience not share your views? What views do they hold?

- How can these readers hold a position that to you seems unreasonable?

- What views do you share? What can you agree upon?

If you have trouble imagining contrary views, you may spend time online reviewing websites dedicated to your topic to discover facts and assess common views and opinions.

Let's assume that you believe the minimum wage should be raised, but you know that some people hold a different view. Why do they hold it? Try to state their view *in a way that would be satisfactory to them*. Having done so, you may perceive that your conclusions and theirs differ because they're based on different premises — perhaps different ideas about how the economy works — or different definitions, concepts, or assumptions about fairness or employment. Examine the opposition's premises carefully and explain, first to yourself (and ultimately to your readers), why you see things differently. Perhaps you can appeal to your shared goals: an arrangement that is mutually beneficial to employers and employees.

Perhaps some facts are in dispute, such as whether or not raising the minimum wage reduces the total number of jobs available, causing a net negative outcome for a certain number of people. The thing to do, then, is to check the facts. If you find a reputable source that reports on job losses after minimum wage hikes, yet you are still for raising the minimum wage in your own state, you will have to admit that job losses are a possibility but also look for counteracting benefits or strategies to avoid that peril. You may grant the opposition a point (that is, concede a point) and prepare a reasoned response for what may be a pretty good critique of your view. You must develop an argument that takes account of the facts and interprets them reasonably — never simply ignore contrary views or evidence.

Among the relevant facts there surely are some that your audience or your opponent will not dispute. The same is true of the values relevant to the discussion; both sides very likely believe in some of the same things, such as the shared belief in setting the minimum wage at a fair and mutually beneficial rate. These areas of shared agreement are crucial to effective persuasion in argument because they establish goodwill between yourself and your opponents, showing that you both seek the same goals, work from the same basic set of facts, and respect one another's values. This is establishing common ground.

The audience presumably consists of supporters and nonsupporters, as well as people who hold no opinion at all (*yet*, perhaps, until they read your ideas). Thinking "What do readers need to know?" and "What do they believe?" may prompt you to find areas of common ground. Nobody wants to see people struggle; therefore, you may paint a portrait of the struggles of real families trying to live on a full-time minimum wage job. Or if you're arguing against raising the minimum wage, it may prompt you to cite studies showing how doing so not only increases the rate of unemployment but also the cost of goods. You could paint a portrait of the same families struggling to get by on minimum wage employment amid diminishing opportunities and rising costs.

Cem Ozdel/Anadolu Agency/Getty Images

A protest for a higher minimum wage.

If you are writing for a general audience, asking yourself what the audience knows and believes informs what facts and ideas are most necessary and relevant to include. With a general audience, you may have to spell out some basic concepts of economics and the number of people earning only a minimum wage. If the audience is specialized, such as a group of economists, you do not have to spell out the basics and can assume the audience already understands. If you are addressing a union group, or a sector of small business owners who fear that rate hikes will interfere with their business, an effective essay will have to address matters on their level according to their unique understandings and beliefs.

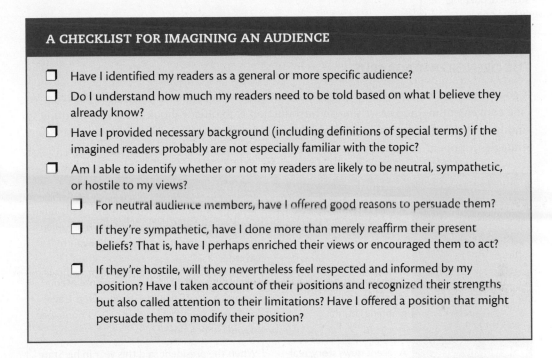

A CHECKLIST FOR IMAGINING AN AUDIENCE

❐ Have I identified my readers as a general or more specific audience?

❐ Do I understand how much my readers need to be told based on what I believe they already know?

❐ Have I provided necessary background (including definitions of special terms) if the imagined readers probably are not especially familiar with the topic?

❐ Am I able to identify whether or not my readers are likely to be neutral, sympathetic, or hostile to my views?

  ❐ For neutral audience members, have I offered good reasons to persuade them?

  ❐ If they're sympathetic, have I done more than merely reaffirm their present beliefs? That is, have I perhaps enriched their views or encouraged them to act?

  ❐ If they're hostile, will they nevertheless feel respected and informed by my position? Have I taken account of their positions and recognized their strengths but also called attention to their limitations? Have I offered a position that might persuade them to modify their position?

Drafting and Revising an Argument

There is no one way to begin writing. Sometimes the best way to get started writing is just to start writing, building ideas, and seeing where your pen (or keyboard) takes you. But, alas, at a certain point, you will want to begin structuring your essay more deliberately, considering your purpose, audience, language, and the organization of your ideas.

THE TITLE

Inventing a **title** allows you to announce the thesis or topic explicitly, or simply attract the attention of readers in a unique or imaginative way. If you examine the titles of essays in this book, you can see that some announce their questions or positions explicitly while others pique curiosity by suggesting a general subject or theme:

"Should Marriage Still Involve Changing a Woman's Name?" (ask a question)
"Porn Isn't Free Speech — On the Web on Anywhere" (announces thesis)
"The Boston Photographs" (announces topic)
"The Yelling of the Lambs" (piques readers' curiosity)

Be prepared to rethink your title *after* completing the last draft of your paper. A working title can help guide your inquiry, but after you have written your argument, check your title to ensure it accurately represents your position and analysis.

THE OPENING PARAGRAPHS

A good introduction arouses readers' interest and prepares them for the rest of the paper. How? One convenient method of writing an introduction is to offer a "hook" first — something to simultaneously attract the reader and set the stage for the essay. The following table lists some strategies for opening paragraphs.

Hook	Description	Example
Anecdote	A brief story or vignette	I was having lunch recently in the newly built food court, and I noticed the word *organic* on my package of carrots, and I began to wonder . . .
Statistic	A relevant (sobering, shocking, attention-grabbing) number	According to a 2017 Common Sense Media report, American children between the ages of 0 and 8 spend an average of 2.25 hours per day of "screen time" . . .
Noteworthy event	A recent news story, real-life account, or interesting illustration of the current situation	When the president said this year in his State of the Union address that more must be done for the nation's infrastructure, he touched on an issue that raises the question of . . .
Analogy	A case similar in structure but different in detail from the point being established	When a leopard stalks its prey, it can spend a full day establishing a prime ambush position, then all at once dart at over 35 miles per hour and jump over 20 feet to close the deal. This is something like . . .
Quotation	Wise, poignant, or landmark words framing your discussion	In 1903, W. E. B. Du Bois said in *The Souls of Black Folk* that "the problem of the twentieth century is the problem of the color line." His words still echo in the twenty-first century because . . .
Historical account	A brief account of the background or evolution of the topic	The evolution of the monster movie extends from early films such as *Nosferatu* (1922) and *The Hunchback of Notre Dame* (1923) to today's renditions such as *Dybbuk* (2021) and *The Djinn* (2021). In that evolution, we can see . . .

You may set your hook quickly, provide a more elaborate version, or even combine the strategies listed in the table. In addition to grabbing readers' attention, opening paragraphs also usually do at least one (and often all) of the following:

- prepare readers for the topic (naming the topic, giving some idea of its importance, noting conventional beliefs about it, or relaying in brief what people are saying about it)
- provide readers with definitions of key terms and concepts (stipulating, quoting an authority, etc.)
- establish a context for your argument by linking your subject, topic, and views to relevant social issues, debates, and trends
- reveal the thesis
- provide readers a map of the argument (giving a sense of how the essay will be organized)

You may write a thorough introduction that does all of these things or a slim introduction that only sets the hook and states the thesis. Although it is possible never to state the thesis directly but only imply it, thesis statements usually stand out as the most bold claim of the opening paragraph (and most college writing requires a clearly stated thesis). If you use the opening paragraph for an extended hook — a story or vignette — you may provide the introductory material from our list in your second paragraph. Don't delay too long: Readers may become impatient when they don't quite know why they are reading. That's why establishing the thesis (and the importance of the thesis) right away is a good idea.

Another way to craft an introduction is to imagine the opening paragraph as a kind of funnel, wider at the top (your context and general subject), narrower in the middle (your topic and issue), and very narrow at the bottom (your specific thesis).

The general subject of your paper may be issues that are important now, such as workers' rights, or immigration, or national security, and your topic will usually be an aspect of that subject — the minimum wage, the Dream Act, or ransomware, for example. Your specific issue may be even more narrow, for example whether or not private companies must disclose ransomware attacks to the government, their customers, or both. Thus, you

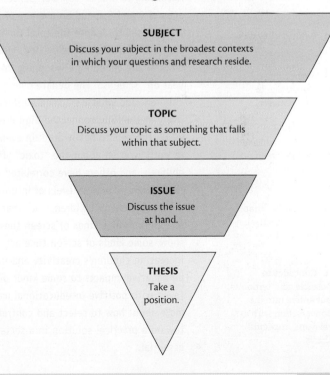

Narrowing Your Thesis

SUBJECT
Discuss your subject in the broadest contexts in which your questions and research reside.

TOPIC
Discuss your topic as something that falls within that subject.

ISSUE
Discuss the issue at hand.

THESIS
Take a position.

frame your subject first, working toward the topic, then work further toward the specific issue within your topic, ultimately stating your position on it. This way, your thesis is positioned within a larger framework.

Some writers add another element to their introductions: a basic map of where the essay is going or of how the author will proceed. Doing so tells your readers up front how the essay is organized. It may sound like this: "In order to show how [my thesis] is sensible, I will first examine X, then Y, and then Z, and conclude by arguing for a conservative course of action." It is not a requirement that all writers must state in their introductions exactly what they will be doing in each part of their essay—and in fact, it may not be an effective strategy for certain audiences, purposes, and genres of writing. Nevertheless, you may announce that there are, say, four common objections to your thesis and that you will take them up one by one, from weakest to strongest, and then advance your own view in greater detail. How far you go to clue the reader in to your methods of analysis is up to you—just as it is up to you to decide how much background, context, definition, and so on to include. It is open ended and a matter of preference but, ultimately, these decisions set the foundations for the rest of your argument.

The elements of introductions we have laid out so far do not have to be included categorically or in a formulaic way. You might do more background work, you might provide a very detailed account of competing perspectives in order to position yourself within a debate, you might offer both an anecdote and a statistic, or you might combine some elements and leave out others.

The following introduction has been annotated to show the writer's choices.

1 Hooks reader with a dramatic statistic.

2 Defines a key term.

3 Author inserts her own voice to express concern.

4 Contextualizes the debate about screen time.

5 Provides a "map" of how the analysis will proceed.

6 Concedes to possible counterpoints, but enters into the conversation with a relevant, impactful thesis.

(1) According to a 2017 Common Sense Media report, American children between the ages of 0 and 8 spend an average of 2.25 hours per day involved in "screen time," (2) a term used to denote the total time a child spends in front of any visual electronic media, whether television, video game, or internet. If that is correct, then (3) children are spending a whopping 34 days—a full month and then some—each year on "screens." The debate over how much screen time is appropriate for children, and what its ultimate effects are on children's development, has been (4) lively in the fully connected digital world. But since the advent of the iPhone in 2007, the debate has heated up even more. One group of investors, JANA Partners, recently worried about the "toxic" effects of the current levels of screen time on children, and others have correlated increasing levels of anxiety and depression in children with high levels of internet usage. To understand the potential impact of screen time on children, and what may be done about it, it is important first to examine what kinds of screen time might be positive or negative. As I will (5) show, some kinds of screen time act as positive influences in children's life, increasing children's creativity and in some instances sociability. While there may be negative impacts to some kinds of "screen time" or too much "screen time" (even with positive or educational media), if parents and educators understand more about how to select and control children's media usage, we can work toward a practical solution in a society where these kinds of technologies are (6) essential.

ORGANIZING THE BODY OF THE ESSAY

We begin with a wise remark by a newspaper columnist, Robert Cromier: "The beautiful part of writing is that you don't have to get it right the first time — unlike, say, a brain surgeon."

In drafting an essay, you will, of course, begin with an organization that seems appropriate, but you may find, in rereading the draft, that some other organization is better. For a start, in the Visual Guide: Organizing Your Argument, we offer three types of organization that are common in argumentative essays. Please note, however, that we do not mean to suggest that essays should be formulaic. These general structures need to be considered alongside your argument's needs to present counterpoints at the appropriate times, to relate an anecdote in the middle of things, or to introduce shorter summaries of others' arguments. Occasionally, these items warrant new paragraphs. The best writers know how to manage structure and how to go down little rabbit holes to explore a point further (perhaps with an analogy, anecdote, or example) but without being *digressive*, departing too far from the main point.

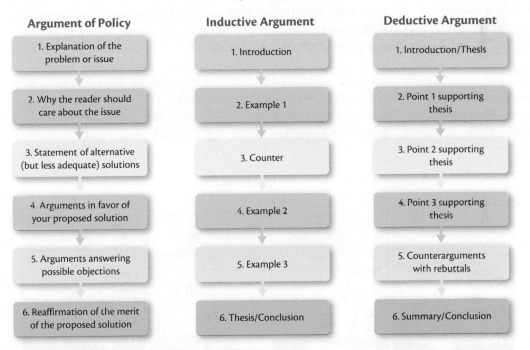

Visual Guide: Organizing Your Argument

Argument of Policy	Inductive Argument	Deductive Argument
1. Explanation of the problem or issue	1. Introduction	1. Introduction/Thesis
2. Why the reader should care about the issue	2. Example 1	2. Point 1 supporting thesis
3. Statement of alternative (but less adequate) solutions	3. Counter	3. Point 2 supporting thesis
4. Arguments in favor of your proposed solution	4. Example 2	4. Point 3 supporting thesis
5. Arguments answering possible objections	5. Example 3	5. Counterarguments with rebuttals
6. Reaffirmation of the merit of the proposed solution	6. Thesis/Conclusion	6. Summary/Conclusion

Even if you were to adhere closely to the patterns, you have a lot of room for variation. In presenting your own position, you can begin with either your strongest or your weakest reasons. Each method of organization has advantages and disadvantages.

- If you begin with your strongest examples or reasons, your essay could impress your readers and then peter out, leaving them asking, "Is that all?"

- If you begin with your weakest material, you build to a climax, but readers may not still be with you because they may have felt that the beginning of the essay was frivolous or irrelevant.

The obvious solution is to ensure that even your weakest argument demonstrates strength. For example, you may go ahead and say that stronger points will soon follow and you offer this point first to show that you are aware of it and that, slight though it is, it deserves some attention. The rest of the essay, then, is devoted to arguing the stronger points.

> **WRITING TIP**
> By acknowledging arguments other than your own — and possible objections to your points — you let readers know that you've done your homework and build their trust (*ethos*). You also have a chance to preempt critiques of your ideas, which helps you be more persuasive.

Doubtless you'll sometimes be uncertain, while drafting an essay, whether to present a given point before or after another point, or when you should explain why you are proceeding the way you are. When you write, and certainly when you revise, try to put yourself into the reader's shoes: Which point do you think the reader needs to know first? Which point *leads to* which further point? Your argument should not be a mere list of points; rather, it should clearly integrate one point with another in order to develop an idea and transition smoothly from one idea to the next. If you finish an essay and you can simply rearrange the body paragraphs without a detrimental effect, it is a sign that there is not enough logical progression in your argument. Ideally, paragraphs build on one another and sometimes even require readers to be familiar with arguments made earlier.

The title of your essay can be smart in general but try to invent something clear and accessible (that is, don't be like Calvin).

CHECKING TRANSITIONS

Make sure, in revising, that the reader can move easily from the beginning of a paragraph to the end and from one paragraph to the next. Transitions help signal the connections between units of the argument. For example ("For example" is a transition, indicating that an illustration will follow), they may illustrate, establish a sequence, connect logically, amplify, compare, contrast, summarize, or concede (see Thinking Critically: Using Transitions in Argument, p. 244). Transitions serve as guideposts that enable the reader to move easily through your essay.

When writers revise an early draft, they chiefly do these tasks:

- They **unify** the essay by eliminating irrelevancies.
- They **organize** the essay by keeping in mind the imagined audience.
- They **clarify** the essay by fleshing out thin paragraphs, by ensuring that the transitions are adequate, and by making certain that generalizations are adequately supported by concrete details and examples.

We are not talking here about polish or elegance; we are talking about fundamental matters. Be especially careful not to abuse the logical connectives (*thus, as a result, and so on*). If you write several sentences followed by *therefore* or a similar word or phrase, it may be repetitive. It is also repetitive to begin each paragraph as a sequence ("First," "Second," "Third," "Finally"). These are often merely substitutes for good transitions — and they can't go on forever ("Sixth," "Seventh," "Eighth," etc.). Logical connectives and sequences should mark a real movement of thought, not be used just to connect bits of unrelated prose or to provide a simple list.

THE ENDING

What about concluding paragraphs, in which you summarize the main points and reaffirm your position? A conclusion — the word comes from the Latin *claudere*, "to shut" — ought to provide a sense of closure, but it can be much more than a restatement of the writer's thesis. It can, for instance, make a quiet, emotional appeal by suggesting that the issue is important and that the ball is now in the reader's court.

If you can look back over your essay and add something that both enriches it and wraps it up, fine; but don't feel compelled to say, "Thus, in conclusion, I have argued X, Y, and Z, and I have refuted Jones." After all, *conclusion* can have two meanings: (1) ending, or finish, as the ending of a joke or a novel or (2) judgment or decision reached after deliberation. Your essay should finish effectively (the first sense), but it need not announce a judgment (the second).

If the essay is fairly short so that a reader can keep its general gist in mind, you may not need to restate your view. Just make sure that you have covered the ground and that your last sentence is a good one. Notice that the student essay presented later in this chapter, Emily Andrews's "Why I Don't Spare 'Spare Change'" (p. 255), doesn't end with a formal conclusion, although it ends conclusively, with a note of finality.

THINKING CRITICALLY *Using Transitions in Argument*

Fill in examples of the types of transitions listed below, using topics of your choice. The first one has been done as an example.

TYPE OF TRANSITION	TYPE OF LANGUAGE USED	EXAMPLE OF TRANSITION
Illustrate	*for example, for instance, consider this case*	"Many television crime dramas contain scenes of graphic violence. For example, in an episode of *Law and Order* . . ."
Establish a sequence	*a more important objection, a stronger example, the best reason*	
Connect logically	*thus, as a result, therefore, so, it follows*	
Amplify	*further, in addition to, moreover*	
Compare	*similarly, in a like manner, just as, analogously*	
Contrast	*on the one hand . . . on the other hand, but, in contrast, however*	
Summarize	*in short, briefly*	
Concede	*admittedly, granted, to be sure*	

By "a note of finality" we do *not* mean a triumphant crowing. It's far better to end with the suggestion that you hope you have by now indicated why those who hold a different view may want to modify it and accept yours.

If you study the essays in this book or the editorials and op-ed pieces in a newspaper, you will notice that writers often provide a sense of closure by using one of the following devices:

- a return to something stated in the introduction
- a glance at the wider implications of the issue (i.e., what would happen if your solution were implemented or not)

- a hint toward unasked or answered questions that the audience might consider in light of the writer's argument (i.e., predict new questions or issues, and let them ring out at the end as guides to further thinking)

- a suggestion that the reader can take some specific action or do some further research (i.e., the ball is now in the reader's court)

- an anecdote that illustrates the thesis in an engaging way (i.e., a brief account, real or imagined, that brings your ideas into a visible form)

- a brief summary (i.e., a recap. But note that this sort of ending may seem unnecessary and tedious if the paper is short and the summary merely repeats what the writer has already said.)

USES OF AN OUTLINE

Outlines may seem rigid to many writers, especially to those who compose online, where we're accustomed to cutting, copying, moving, and deleting as we draft. You're probably familiar with the structure known as a **formal outline**. Major points are indicated by I, II, III; points within major points are indicated by A, B, C; divisions within A, B, C are indicated by 1, 2, 3; and so on. Thus:

I. Arguments for opening all Olympic sports to professional

   A. Fairness

      1. Some Olympic sports are already open to professionals.

      2. Some athletes who really are not professionals are classified as professionals.

   B. Quality (achievements would be higher)

However, an outline — whether you write it before drafting or use it to evaluate the organization of something you've already written — is meant to be a guide rather than a straitjacket.

THE OUTLINE AS A PRELIMINARY GUIDE   Some writers sketch an outline as soon as they think they know what they want to say, even before writing a first draft. This procedure can be helpful in planning a tentative organization, but remember that in revising a draft you'll likely generate some new ideas and have to modify the outline accordingly. A preliminary outline is chiefly useful as a means of getting going, not as a guide to the final essay.

THE OUTLINE AS A WAY OF CHECKING A DRAFT   Whether or not you use a preliminary outline, we strongly suggest that after writing what you hope is your last draft, you make an outline of it; there is no better way of finding out whether the essay is well organized.

Go through the draft and write down the chief points in the order in which you make them. That is, prepare a table of contents — perhaps a phrase for each paragraph. Next, examine your notes to see what kind of sequence they reveal in your paper:

- Is the sequence reasonable? Can it be improved?
- Are any passages irrelevant?
- Does something important seem to be missing?

If no coherent structure or reasonable sequence clearly appears in the outline, the full prose version of your argument probably doesn't have any either. Therefore, produce another draft by moving things around, adding or subtracting paragraphs — cutting and pasting them into a new sequence, with transitions as needed — and then make another outline to see if the sequence now is satisfactory.

A CHECKLIST FOR ORGANIZING AN ARGUMENT

- ☐ Does the introduction let the readers know where the author is taking them?
  - ☐ Does the introduction state the problem or issue?
  - ☐ Does it state the claim (the thesis)?
  - ☐ Does it suggest the organization of the essay, thereby helping the reader follow the argument?
- ☐ Do subsequent paragraphs support the claim?
  - ☐ Do they offer evidence?
  - ☐ Do they face objections to the claim and offer reasonable responses?
  - ☐ Do they indicate why the author's claim is preferable?
  - ☐ Do transitions (signposts such as *Furthermore*, *In contrast*, and *Consider as an example*) guide the reader through the argument?
- ☐ Does the essay end effectively, with a paragraph (at most, two paragraphs) bringing a note of closure?

TONE AND THE WRITER'S PERSONA

What Aristotle called the **ethical appeal** or *ethos* is the idea that effective speakers convey the suggestion that they are

- informed,
- intelligent,
- fair minded (persons of goodwill), and
- honest.

If writers are perceived as trustworthy, their words inspire confidence in their listeners. When reading an argument we're often aware of the *person* or *voice* behind the words, and our assent to the argument depends partly on the extent to which we share the speaker's assumptions and see the matter from their point of view — in short, the extent to which we can *identify* with the speaker.

How can a writer inspire such confidence? First, the writer should possess the virtues Aristotle specified: intelligence or good sense, honesty, and benevolence or goodwill. Still, possession of these qualities is not a guarantee that you will convey them in your writing. Like all other writers, you'll have to revise your drafts so that these qualities become apparent; stated more moderately, you'll have to revise so that nothing in the essay causes a reader to doubt your intelligence, honesty, and goodwill. A blunder in logic, a misleading quotation, a snide remark, even an error in spelling — all such slips can cause readers to withdraw their faith in the writer.

Of course, all good argumentative essays do not sound exactly alike; they do not all reveal the same speaker. Each writer develops his or her own voice, or **persona**. (We discussed persona in more detail in Chapter 6, "Examining the Author's Persona," p. 194.) In fact, one writer may have several voices or personae, depending on the topic and the audience. If you are delivering an address to your college community, you may have one persona; when chatting about the same issue with other students in a workshop, you have another. Different circumstances call for different language. As a French writer put it, there is a time to speak of "Paris" and a time to speak of "the capital of the nation."

When we talk about a writer's persona, we mean the way in which the writer presents his or her attitudes

- toward *the self*,
- toward *the audience*, and
- toward *the subject*.

Thus, if a writer says:

> President Nixon was hounded out of office by journalists ceaselessly interrogating him . . .

we can see a respectful attitude toward Nixon ("President Nixon") and a hostile attitude toward the press. Reversed, it might have said something like this:

> The press turned the searchlight on Tricky Dick's potentially criminal shenanigans.

Here, Nixon is "Tricky Dick" and journalists are not ceaselessly interrogating him but instead trying to illuminate potential crimes. "Shenanigans" also has a connotation of underhanded activities. By mere implication through language, journalists are the heroes in this

> **WRITING TIP**
> Present yourself so that readers see you as knowledgeable, honest, open-minded, and interested in helping them to think about the significance of an issue.

second version of events, and Nixon is contemptible. These two versions suggest two speakers who differ not only in their view of Nixon but also in their manner of speaking.

LOADED WORDS   We are talking now about **loaded words**, which convey the writer's attitude and, through their connotations, seek to win the reader to the writer's side. Compare the words in the left-hand column with those in the right:

militia member	terrorist
pro-choice	pro-abortion
pro-life	antichoice
undocumented migrant	illegal alien
domestic surveillance	spying on citizens

The words in the left-hand column sound like good things; speakers who use them seek to establish themselves as virtuous people supporting worthy causes. The **connotations** (associations, overtones) of these pairs of words differ, even though the **denotations** (explicit meanings, dictionary definitions) are the same — just as the connotations of *mother* and *female parent* differ, although the denotations are the same.

Tone is not only a matter of connotation (*hounded out of office* versus, let's say, *compelled to resign*, or *pro-choice* versus *pro-abortion*); it is also a matter of such things as the selection and type of examples. A writer who offers many examples, especially ones drawn from ordinary life, conveys a persona different from that of a writer who offers no examples or only an occasional invented instance. The first writer seems more honest, more down-to-earth and grounded in reality. The second writer appears to be overlooking things, either because they do not know or do not care to offer reliable evidence.

USING TONE TO ADDRESS OPPOSITION   On the whole, when writing an argument, it's advisable to be courteous and respectful of your topic, your audience, and people who hold views opposite to yours. It is rarely good for one's own intellectual development to regard as villains or fools persons who hold views different from one's own, especially if some of them are in the audience. Keep in mind the story of two strangers on a train who, striking up a conversation, found that both were clergymen, although of different faiths. Then one said to the other, "Well, why shouldn't we be friends? After all, we both serve God, you in your way and I in His."

Complacency is all right when telling a joke, but not when offering an argument:

- Recognize opposing views.
- Assume that they are held in good faith.
- State them fairly. If you don't, you do a disservice not only to the opposition but also to your own position because the perceptive reader won't take you seriously.

- Be temperate in arguing your own position: "If I understand their view correctly . . ."; "It seems reasonable to conclude that . . ."; "Perhaps, then, we can agree that . . ."
- Write calmly. If you become overly emotional, readers may interpret you as biased or unreasonable, and they may lose their confidence in you.

WE, ONE, OR I? The use of *we* in the last paragraph brings us to another point: Is it correct to use the first-person pronouns *I* and *we*? In this book, because three of us are writing, we often use *we* to mean the three authors. Sometimes we use *we* to mean the authors and the readers, or *we* the people in general. This shifting use of one word can be troublesome, but we hope (clearly, the *we* here refers only to the authors) that we have avoided ambiguity. But can, or should, or must an individual use *we* instead of *I*? The short answer is no.

If you're simply speaking for yourself, use *I*. Attempts to avoid the first-person singular by saying things like "This writer thinks . . ." and "It is thought that . . ." and "One thinks that . . ." are far more irritating (and wordy) than the use of *I*. The so-called editorial *we* sounds as odd in a student's argument as the royal *we* does. (Mark Twain joked that the only ones who can appropriately say *we* are kings, editors, and people with a tapeworm.) It's advisable to use *we* only when you are sure you're writing or speaking directly to an audience who holds membership in the same group, as in "We *students of this university should . . .*" or "We *the members of Delta Sigma Theta sorority need to. . . .*" If the *we* you refer to has a referent, simply refer to what it means: Say "Americans are" rather than "We are," or "College students should" rather than "We should," or "Republicans need to" rather than "We need to."

Many students assume that using *one* will solve the problem of pronouns. But because one *one* leads to another, the sentence may end up sounding, as James Thurber once said, "like a trombone solo." It's best to admit that you are the author and to use *I*. However, there is no need to preface every sentence with "I think." The reader knows that the essay is yours and that the opinions are yours; so use *I* when you must, but not needlessly. Do not write, "I think X movie is terrible"; simply say, "X movie is terrible." And do not add extra words that say more obvious things, like "*It is my idea that* the company needs a new mission statement." Just write, "*The company needs a new mission statement.*"

Often you'll see *I* in journalistic writing and autobiographical writing — and in some argumentative writing, too — but in most argumentative writing, it's best to state the facts and (when drawing reasonable conclusions from them) to keep yourself in the background. Why? The more you use *I* in an essay, the more your readers will attach *you* directly to the argument and may regard your position as personal rather than as relevant to themselves.

THINKING CRITICALLY *Eliminating We, One, and I*

Rewrite the following sentences to eliminate unnecessary uses of *we, one, I,* and other gratuitous statements of opinion. (The first row has been completed as an example.)

ORIGINAL SENTENCE	REWRITTEN SENTENCE
I think fracking is the best way to achieve energy independence and to create jobs.	Fracking is the best way to achieve energy independence and to create jobs.
In our country, we believe in equality and freedom.	
One should consider one's manners when one attends formal dinner parties.	
In my opinion, the government should not regulate the sizes of sodas we can order.	
It is clearly the case that the new policy treats employees unfairly.	

A CHECKLIST FOR ESTABLISHING TONE AND PERSONA

☐ Do I have a sense of what the audience probably knows or thinks about the issue to best present myself to them?

☐ Have I tried to establish common ground and then moved on to advance my position?

☐ Have I used appropriate language (e.g., defined terms that are likely to be unfamiliar)?

☐ Have I indicated why readers should care about the issue and should accept my views, or at least give them serious consideration?

☐ Have I presented myself as a person who is fair, informed, and worth listening to? In short, have I conveyed a strong *ethos*?

AVOIDING SEXIST LANGUAGE

Courtesy — as well as common sense — requires that you respect your readers' feelings. Many people today find offensive the implicit gender bias in the use of male pronouns ("As the reader follows the argument, he will find . . .") to denote not only men but also women or people who use nonbinary gender pronouns such as *they*. And sometimes the use of the male pronoun to denote all people is ridiculous ("An individual, no matter what his sex, . . ."). Because of the bias, the use of the male pronoun as a stand-in for everyone has largely fallen out of favor and out of use.

In most contexts, there is no need to use gender-specific nouns or pronouns. One way to avoid using *he* when you mean any person is to use "he or she" (or "she or he"), but the result is sometimes cumbersome — although superior to the overly conspicuous "he/she/they" and "s/he." Increasingly, many people and organizations — including the Modern Language Association and the American Psychological Association, who create the style guides used in Chapter 8 — will accept "they," even when the syntax of a sentence calls for a singular pronoun, to avoid this issue ("When a person enters the exhibit, they will see . . ."). We have chosen to use the singular "they" as a way of being inclusive to all readers.

Here are four simple ways to solve the problem:

- Use the plural ("As readers follow the argument, they will find . . .").
- Recast the sentence so that no pronoun is required ("Readers following the argument will find . . .").
- Use the singular "they" in instances where you do not know someone's stated gender.
- Check with your instructor to see if they have a preference.

Because *man* and *mankind* strike many readers as sexist when used in such expressions as "Man is a rational animal" and "Mankind has not yet solved this problem," consider using such words as *human being*, *person*, *people*, *humanity*, and *we* (e.g., "Human beings are rational animals"; "We have not yet solved this problem").

Peer Review

Your instructor may suggest — or require — that you submit an early draft of your essay to a fellow student or small group of students for comment. Such a procedure benefits both author and readers: You get the responses of a reader, and the student-reader gets experience in thinking about the problems of developing an argument, especially such matters as the degree of detail that a writer needs to offer to a reader and the importance of keeping the organization evident to a reader.

A CHECKLIST FOR PEER REVIEW

Read through the draft quickly. Then read it again, with the following questions in mind. Remember: You are reading a draft, a work in progress. You're expected to offer suggestions, and you're expected to offer them courteously.

In a sentence, indicate the degree to which the draft shows promise of fulfilling the assignment.

- ☐ Is the writer's tone appropriate? Who is the audience?

- ☐ Looking at the essay as a whole, what thesis (main idea) is advanced?

- ☐ Are the needs of the audience kept in mind? For instance, do some words need to be defined?

- ☐ Is the evidence (e.g., the examples and the testimony of authorities) clear and effective?

- ☐ Can I accept the assumptions? If not, why not?

- ☐ Is any obvious evidence (or counterevidence) overlooked?

- ☐ Is the writer proposing a solution? If so,

    - ☐ Are other equally attractive solutions adequately examined?

    - ☐ Has the writer overlooked some unattractive effects of the proposed solution?

Look at each paragraph separately.

- ☐ Is the introduction effective in stating the basic point of the essay?

- ☐ How does each paragraph relate to the essay's main idea or to the previous paragraph?

- ☐ Should some paragraphs be deleted? Be divided into two or more paragraphs? Be combined? Be moved elsewhere? (If you outline the essay by writing down the gist of each paragraph, you'll get help in answering these questions.)

- ☐ Is each sentence clearly related to the sentence that precedes and to the sentence that follows? If not, in a sentence or two indicate examples of good and bad transitions.

- ☐ Is each paragraph adequately developed? Are there sufficient details, perhaps brief supporting quotations from the text?

- ☐ Are the concluding paragraphs effective and not just mere restatement?

Look at the paper as a whole.

- ☐ What are the paper's chief strengths?

- ☐ Make at least two specific suggestions that you think will help the author improve the paper.

Oral peer reviews allow for the give and take of discussion, but probably most students and most instructors find written peer reviews more helpful because reviewers think more carefully about their responses to the draft, and they help essayists to get beyond a knee-jerk response to criticism. Online reviews on a class website, through email, or via another platform such as a learning management system (LMS) or file-sharing service are especially helpful precisely because they are not face to face; the peer reviewer gets practice *writing*, and the essayist is not put on the spot.

A Student's Essay, from Rough Notes to Final Version

Here are the first notes of a student, Emily Andrews, who elected to write about whether to give money to panhandlers she encounters regularly in Boston. To begin, she simply put down ideas, one after the other.

Help the poor? I sometimes do it, but should I?

Why do I do it? I feel guilty, and I think I should help the poor.

Am I really helping? Some will spend the money on alcohol and drugs.

It is sometimes annoying.

Where does the expression "the deserving poor" come from? How about "poor but honest"?

Why don't they work? Guy with red beard always by my bus stop, always wants a handout. He is a regular, there all day every day—is that work? Why not put the same time in on a job? Maybe panhandling is just easier. Maybe he's making more money by panhandling.

Maybe they can't work (mental health issues, etc.). Why don't they get help?
Could be decent people who have had terrible luck.

I *do* believe in giving charity.

BUT how can I tell who is deserving or in special need vs. someone who is a con artist?

Do people asking for "spare change" really deserve it?

Possibilities:

> Give to no one.
> Make an annual donation instead (local food banks? United Way?).
> Give change and stop caring about what it is spent on? Is that right?
> Do some volunteer work?

So what's the problem I can address in my essay?

How I can help the poor (handouts, donations, volunteering)?

How I can feel less guilty about as a fortunate person encountering unfortunate people? I can't help every beggar who approaches on the grounds that:

 a. it's probably their fault (or their choice).
 b. many will spend my money on drugs or alcohol and make their situations worse.
 c. they can get better gov't help.

Maybe some are too proud to look for government help, or don't know that they're entitled to it.

What to do?

On balance, it seems best to give to charity if I want to help.

After writing and revising a draft, Emily submitted her essay to a fellow student for review. She then revised her work in light of the peer's suggestions and her own further thinking.

Emily's final essay appears below. When Emily made the notes, she wasn't so much putting down her ideas as *finding* ideas through the process of writing. (By the way, Emily told us that in her next-to-last draft, the title was "Is It Right to Spare 'Spare Change'?" Note that this title, unlike the revision, introduces the topic but not the author's position.)

Emily Andrews
Professor O'Hara
English 102
January 15, 2019

Why I Don't Spare "Spare Change" **1**

"Poor but honest." "The deserving poor." I don't know the origin of **2**
these quotations, but they always come to mind when I walk through my
city, Boston, and encounter "the poor" on the streets asking for money.
When I do, I have to face an ethical dilemma—not as to whether or not
I *can* spare my spare change, but whether or not I *should*. Panhandlers **3**
by definition are people who solicit money for their personal use without
providing goods or services. This forces me to consider the behavior I
am enabling by giving away money on the street. Many of these people,
perhaps through alcohol or drugs, have ruined not only their own lives but
also the lives of others in order to indulge in their own habits. Perhaps **4**
alcoholism and drug addiction really are "diseases," as many people say, but
my own feeling—based, of course, not on any serious study—is that most
alcoholics and drug addicts can be classified with the "undeserving poor."
And that is largely why I don't distribute spare change to panhandlers.

Surely among street people there are also some who can rightly be
called "deserving." Deserving of what? A fair shake in life, or government **5**
assistance? Perhaps. But my spare change? It happens that I have been
brought up to believe that it is appropriate to make contributions to
charity—let's say a shelter for battered women—but if I give some change
to a panhandler, I may be helping someone, or, on the contrary, I could just
as easily be encouraging someone to continue their alcohol or drug abuse,
and not to get help. Maybe even worse: maybe I am supporting a criminal,
or con artist, or someone who could use my money to get high and take
advantage of someone else. The fact is, I don't know. **6**

If one believes in the value of private charity, one can give either
to needy individuals or to charitable organizations. Money given to **7**
panhandlers may indeed help a person badly in need, but it could just as

---

1 Title is informative, altering the reader to the topic and the author's position.

2 Opening paragraph holds readers' interest by alluding to familiar phrases and an anecdote.

3 Defines a key term: "panhandler."

4 Author presents general outline of argument and thesis.

5 Voices the reader's probably uneasy response to the opening, showing audience awareness.

6 Supports her argument with reason.

7 Clearly sets forth the alternatives. A reader may disagree with them, but they are stated fairly.

easily be misused and cause greater harm. In giving to an organization such as the United Way, in contrast, one can feel that one's money is likely to be used wisely. True, confronted by a panhandler one may feel that *this* particular unfortunate individual needs help at *this* moment—a cup of coffee or a sandwich—and the need will not be met unless I put my hand in my pocket right now. But I have come to think that the beggars whom I encounter can get along without my spare change. If they choose, they can go to shelters where charitable contributions can be collected and spent wisely. Indeed, panhandlers may actually be better off if people did not give them spare change which they can subsequently use on alcohol or drugs.

8   It happens that in my neighborhood I encounter a few panhandlers regularly. There is one fellow who is always by the bus stop where I catch the bus to the college, and I never give him anything precisely because he is always there. He is such a regular that, I think, he ought to be able to hold a regular job. Putting him aside, I routinely encounter about three or four beggars in an average week. (I'm not counting street musicians. These people seem quite able to work for a living. If they see their "work" as playing or singing, let persons who enjoy their performances pay them. I do not consider myself among their audience.) The truth of the matter is that since I meet so few beggars, I could give each one a dollar and hardly feel the loss. At most, I might go without seeing a movie some week. But I know nothing about these people, and it's my impression—based on what I see—that they simply prefer begging to working.

9   That's why I usually do not give "spare change," and I don't think I will in the future. These people will get along without me, and may get along better without me if their needs eventually lead them to a shelter or a food bank. Someone else will have to come up with money for their coffee or their liquor, or, at worst, they will just have to do without. I will continue to contribute occasionally to a charitable organization, not simply (I hope) to salve my conscience but because I believe that these organizations actually do good work. But I will not attempt to be a mini-charitable organization, distributing spare change likely to go to an unworthy cause.

8 Paragraphs 4 and 5 are more personal than the earlier paragraphs. The writer, more or less having stated what she takes to be the facts, now is entitled to offer a highly personal response to them.

9 The final paragraph nicely concludes with a reference to the title, giving the reader a sense of completeness.

Topics for Critical Thinking and Writing

1. Does the writer establish a good sense of *ethos* in this essay? Explain what works best and what works least in terms of establishing credibility or goodwill.

2. Do you think this essay has a strong thesis? A strong argument? Explain.

3. What assumptions are made about panhandlers in this essay? If you wanted to challenge these assumptions, what kinds of questions could you ask and what evidence could you seek?

4. What are some alternative solutions or counterarguments that the writer did not address?

Assignment for Developing an Argument of Your Own

In a brief essay, state a claim and support it with evidence. Choose an issue in which you are genuinely interested and about which you already know something. You may want to consult sources or interview someone, but you need not attempt to write a highly researched paper (unless your instructor advises otherwise). Be sure to organize your argument thoughtfully, with consideration of your audience, the context of the argument, and alternative viewpoints. Sample topics:

1. Students in laboratory courses should not be required to participate in the dissection of animals.

2. Washington, DC, should be granted statehood.

3. In wartime, women should be subject to the military draft.

4. The annual Miss America contest was right to eliminate the swimsuit competition.

5. Students should/should not have to take general courses in arts and literature.

8

Using Sources

A university is just a group of buildings gathered around a library.

— SHELBY FOOTE

CONSIDER THIS

Imagine you're assigned a research paper and you decide to do some exploratory research. Choose one word from each column in the table and enter them into a search engine. (You may also swap one word for a key term of your choice.)

Environment	Tradition	Land	Religion
Law	Technology	Water	Belief
Art	Sex	Fire	Fact
History	Love	Heat	Opinion
Politics	Power	Earth	Science
Biology	War	Time	Experiment
Psychology	Crime	Space	Discovery

Choose one (or more) of the stronger and weaker search results, and explain why you find them strong or weak. Share your answers.

Why Use Sources?

When writing about complex, serious questions, nobody is expected to invent all the answers out of thin air. And even if you feel very confident about your position, thinking critically involves introducing and contending with other perspectives. Writers are expected to be familiar with the chief answers already produced by others and to make use of them through selective incorporation and criticism. When you write about an issue, you are not expected to reinvent the wheel; sometimes, simply adding a spoke is enough.

You may be familiar with some directives about research from previous courses. Your instructors may have asked you to locate three sources, or four sources, or six sources, and to use those sources in support of an argument (perhaps with some added requirement that one or more of these be scholarly sources). However, your teachers generally do not want you simply to find a fixed number of sources and plug them in to your essay for the sake of "having sources" or to send you on a scavenger hunt. The goal of research is more idealistic. No minimum or maximum number of sources is right for every argument. Research is intended to encourage learning, thoughtful engagement with a topic, and the production of an informed view.

ENTERING A DISCOURSE

Kenneth Burke (1887–1993), one of America's most important theorists of rhetoric, offers a very useful metaphor for the writing process suggesting the importance of learning, engaging, and participating in a conversation:

> Imagine that you enter a parlor. You come late. When you arrive, others have long preceded you, and they are engaged in a heated discussion, a discussion too heated for them to pause and tell you exactly what it is about. In fact, the discussion had already begun long before any of them got there, so that no one present is qualified to retrace for you all the steps that had gone before. You listen for a while, until you decide that you have caught the tenor of the argument; then you put in your oar. Someone answers; you answer him; another comes to your defense; another aligns himself against you, to either the embarrassment or gratification of your opponent, depending upon the quality of your ally's assistance. However, the discussion is interminable. The hour grows late, you must depart. And you do depart, with the discussion still vigorously in progress.[1]

When you are writing, imagine you are entering a discussion, but not a live one as in Burke's analogy. Imagine instead you are entering into a **discourse**. A discourse is a type of discussion, surely. But unlike a live conversation, a discourse takes place over a longer period of time among many participants in various types of writing and public venues. A discourse is a conversation writ large, one that has gone on before you enter the fray, and one that will likely continue after you leave.

---

[1] *The Philosophy of Literary Form* (Baton Rouge: Louisiana State University Press, 1941), 110–11.

Jürgen Habermas coined the term "public sphere" to describe this space where public discourse occurs. In its ideal form, the public sphere is comprised of many spaces where rational public debates and decisions occur — a site of democratic participation. Understandings of a democratic public sphere have been complicated by scholars after Habermas who have asked important questions about whether or not all people have equal access to the conversation, or whether commercial interests play too big a role in it. These are questions we should keep in mind later, when we discuss *finding*, *evaluating*, and *synthesizing* sources, but for now we answer the question as to why sources are so important in discourse:

- The first answer is practical: You use sources because they are where conversations about important topics occur.

- The second is more idealistic: It is your responsibility as an intelligent citizen to participate meaningfully in discourses.

From sources, you learn what the facts are, what issues are current, and what positions certain people or groups are taking on the issues. Through sources, you discover new ideas, questions, and answers. When you perform research on a topic, you are finding, evaluating, and synthesizing sources so as to position yourself to speak within that kind of conversation known as a discourse.

Two caveats are important. First, although we will discuss finding, evaluating, and synthesizing sources separately, once you begin researching you will see that these activities are not entirely separable. As you find sources, you will simultaneously be assessing their relevancy and value (evaluating) and placing sources into conversation with one another (synthesizing) while considering ways to integrate them into your own writing.

Second, the boundaries of discourse are not clear-cut, and discourses are sometimes overlapping. Obviously, many conversations about many different topics occur constantly in a variety of places. We may speak generally of political discourse, scientific discourse, or economic discourse, and we may speak more particularly of discourses on women's rights, environmentalism, or taxation. We may even speak more specifically of discourses on abortion rights, the impact of fracking, or newly proposed capital gains tax increases. Narrowing down even further, we can find very discrete discourses *within* those discourses: conversations about abortion access, fracking and water quality, or whether or not US companies operating offshore businesses should pay capital gains on their profits.

Any subject at all may be thought of in terms of these discourses (or conversations) that take place about it. Some discourses are broad and general and may have been going on for a long time; others are issue-based and particularized and may come with the dust and be gone with the wind, to use the words of Bob Dylan.

Consider, for example, the conversation about security and freedom in the United States. This debate — this *discourse* — has been ongoing since the nation was founded, and it continues today. In articles, essays, speeches, legal reviews, court opinions, congressional debates, and elsewhere, people continue to weigh the appropriate balance between security and freedom: The country needs to be kept safe, and so law enforcement agencies are granted many powers to investigate, detect, and prevent lawbreaking, yet US citizens are also protected by the US Constitution from unwarranted harassment, search and seizure, and other invasions of privacy. Today, terrorism, immigration, stop-and-frisk practices, and cybersecurity are just a few areas of focus in this conversation-writ-large. Within each of those categories, even narrower conversations occur. Airport security, border security, cell phone searches, facial recognition technology — the list goes on and on. Many combined, overlapping conversations (some very general, some quite specific, some coming, and some going) may all be said to be part of this *discourse* about freedom and security. Even fictional novels, plays, films, and television show contribute to the discourse. A television series like *Homeland* (2011–2020) or a blockbuster superhero movie like *Captain America: Winter Soldier* (2014) can represent and

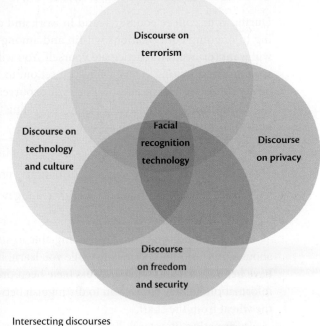

Intersecting discourses

spur discussion about topical issues related to freedom and security — and potentially be a rich source for research and analysis to support your own argument and entry into the conversation.

A **discourse community** is any group of people who share general interests, assumptions, and values and who communicate with one another in some form of media, usually adhering to a set of conventions for that communication. For example, a professor of physics who is active in the scientific discourse on thermodynamics, publishes his theories in academic books and articles. In doing so, he is addressing one discourse community of scientists and experts in a particular type of writing style or genre with its own expectations of scientific rigor. But maybe he is also an environmentalist in his hometown who publishes on the Sierra Club blog and posts videos about local ecology. There, he may change his voice and tone, as well as his purposes. And maybe he is also a fan of X-Men and writes passionately about the Marvel mutants on a listserv dedicated to that series. In that cases, he is addressing a narrower discourse community and his writing and arguments may sound quite different from his scientific and environmental work.

Understanding discourse communities is important because it can help you

- focus your own research by determining which types of sources you need to seek,
- evaluate the sources you find,
- define your audience and purpose in writing, and
- write more persuasively.

UNDERSTANDING INFORMATION LITERACY

During your college courses — and in work and daily life — you will be reading and listening to ongoing conversations within and among discourse communities. Sometimes, you will want (or need) to participate yourself. You will have to interject, responding to issues by speaking and writing. Thus, when you set out to learn about and contribute to a discourse, how you discover, evaluate, and use your sources is crucial. Together, these are integrated skills known as **information literacy.** According to the Association of College and Research Libraries, these skills encompass

- the thoughtful and reflective discovery of information,
- the understanding of how information is produced and valued, and
- the ethical use of information in creating new ideas by participating in various academic or civic discourses.

Information literacy involves being able to survey what and how knowledge circulates about a topic, thinking critically while you learn. It allows you to see what kinds of questions have been raised and what answers have been provided. As you poke and pry into a topic, information literacy allows you to distinguish between strong and weak sources and separate the wheat from the chaff.

Information literacy skills are necessary to be able to navigate the vast fields of information to which we are exposed constantly in the digital media environment. Even when we are trying to be diligent in our efforts to find quality sources, we face obstacles. Search engines, for example, simply cannot index, curate, and return results from the billions of websites on the ever-expanding internet. This means we need to develop skills on *how* to search: how to use search operators and phrases to limit the results we get and how to search for only certain kinds of websites or file types. But even the best search strategies will not return full-length published books or password-protected content such as subscription-only magazines, newspapers, and journals, many of which are carefully edited and vetted for quality (and are often the best possible sources).

Further, we should also be aware that search engines are not neutral. They commonly return results that are most popular (or most highly paid for), not necessarily those that are most thorough, interesting, or reliable. Some search engines tailor the top results to your previous searches and online activity through "personalized" search results, leading to an information ecosystem susceptible to "filter bubble" and "echo chamber" effects in which people are led to information limited by a single perspective or ideology. If you are searching for a political topic and your search engine knows your political leanings, it will likely return in your top results web pages that reflect your political views. This practice seriously raises the potential for confirmation bias (discussed on p. 104)

Once you narrow in on a topic and adopt a central idea or position on an issue — a thesis — your ability to persuade an audience will depend on the sources you provide, evaluate, and cite. Even one citation of a fraudulent website or one uncritical reference to a highly partisan or narrowly ideological source can undermine your credibility. On the other hand, well-researched and thoughtfully discussed sources show that you are an educated participant in a discourse — or even one small area of it — who is equipped with foundational facts and evidence drawn from reputable sources; you have an argument worth listening to.

Choosing a Topic

Because of the complexity of discourses — the plurality of topics, issues, ideas, and opinions (in so many different forms and from so many different groups) — the research process isn't straightforward and neat. Research is a form of inquiry that can range from finding answers to simple questions to exploring complex topics, problems, or issues discussed within or among discourse communities. Part of conducting a successful, fruitful research effort is first selecting an area of focus and narrowing the scope of your research to suit the needs of your assignments or interests.

If a topic is not assigned, choose one that

- interests you, and
- can be researched with reasonable thoroughness in the allotted time.

Topics such as censorship, the environment, and sexual harassment obviously impinge on our lives, and it may well be that one such topic is of special interest to you. But the breadth of these topics (like with freedom vs. security, discussed earlier) makes researching them potentially overwhelming. Type the word *censorship* into an internet search engine, and you will be referred to millions of information sources.

This brings us to our second point: deciding on a manageable topic. Any of the previous topics would need to be refined substantially before you could begin researching in earnest. Similarly, even more specific topics such as "the effects of the Holocaust" can hardly be mastered in a few weeks or argued in a ten-page paper. They are simply too big. (The questions that immediately come to mind are, What kind of effects do you mean? Political effects? Psychological effects? For whom? Where? When? Where will you find the evidence?) Getting a manageable topic often means working on one area of a larger puzzle, pinpointing the places where you can add your piece. You can do that by

- seeking gaps or areas of conflict within or among discourses (places where you can weigh in) or
- breaking down complex topics, issues, or debates into simpler questions (perhaps focusing on one question informing the larger issue).

By focusing your research on one area within a broader discourse, you can limit the range and types of resources you consult based on

> **WRITING TIP**
> You may think you have little to contribute to conversations whose participants are illustrious authorities and experts. However, by dint of being a student, you have a unique perspective: You are on the edge of the future, able to apply new questions and issues in the present to those old primary and secondary resources. Or maybe you may have a purpose for writing that is fundamentally different from anyone else's because it speaks to new or emerging trends.

your circumstances and goals. As you research, you may find yourself drawn toward even more specific questions. If you were writing about the psychological effects of the Holocaust, for instance, you could focus on an affected ethnic group like Jewish people or focus further on German, French, Russian, or American Jews; you could define a time frame; or you could deal with a specific postwar generation, or consider a group within that generation, such as women, men, children, or second-generation survivors (those born after the war). If you chose to develop your analysis around specific traumatic events, places, or even practices, such as the use of gas chambers, you might seek evidence in psychological studies, memoirs, and testimony or in the arts.

One strategy for narrowing your topic is, first, to find your general topic and then apply some basic questions like those in A Checklist for Approaching a Topic to discover how you might find an entry point into the conversations about it.

A CHECKLIST FOR APPROACHING A TOPIC

Find Relevance

- ❐ What are some of the ways people have been discussing this topic recently?

- ❐ To whom — that is, to what groups or audiences — is this topic especially important now?

- ❐ Is there any data, any evidence, or an example that arguments on this topic have not yet accounted for?

Develop a New Approach

- ❐ What is most important or interesting to *me* about this topic?

- ❐ Is there a perspective or an application that has been underreported in the discourses on this topic?

- ❐ Can I ask new questions by thinking politically, historically, religiously, scientifically, psychologically, philosophically, culturally — or in some combination of these?

Determine Your Research Goals and Writing Context

- ❐ Where do I stand?

- ❐ What type of audience do I want to reach most?

- ❐ How do I want to position myself in the discourse on this topic (i.e., in what genre, in what format will I make myself heard, including considerations of length and depth)?

Once you've narrowed your focus, spend a little time exploring your topic to see if you can locate interesting conversations and manageable topics or issues by taking one or more of these approaches:

- **Do a web search on the topic.** You can quickly put your finger on the pulse of popular approaches to a topic by scanning the first page or two of results to see who is talking about it (individuals, groups, etc.) and in what forms (articles, news, blogs, etc.).

- **Plug the topic into one of the library's article databases.** Just by scanning the titles in a general database, you can get a sense of what questions have been and are currently being raised about your topic. If you want to explore further, examine the abstract if available. Then decide whether or not it is worth skimming or reading more carefully.

- **Browse the library shelves where books on the topic are kept.** A quick check of the tables of contents of recently published books may give you ideas of how to narrow your topic.

- **Ask a librarian to show you where specialized reference books on your topic are found.** Instead of general encyclopedias, try sources like *CQ Researcher* or *Encyclopedia of Science, Technology, and Ethics*.

- **Talk to an expert.** Members of the faculty who specialize in the area of your topic might be able to point you to key sources and discourses.

Finding Sources

Your sources' quality and integrity are crucial to your own credibility and to the strength of your argument. In previous chapters, we discussed *ethos* as an appeal that establishes credibility with readers. When you do competent research, you let your audience see that you have done your homework, which thereby increases your *ethos*. Sources, we mean to say, provide evidence in support of your argument, but they also collectively serve as evidence that you are familiar with the discourses on your topic, that you know what you're talking about, and that your interpretation is sound.

To find good sources, you must have a strategy for searching. What strategy you use will depend on your topic. Researching a social problem or a new economic policy may involve reading recent newspaper articles, scanning information on government websites, and locating current statistics. On the other hand, researching a fashion trend, for example, may be best tackled by seeking out books and scholarly journal articles on the sociological meanings of fashion and perhaps also some popular style magazines or videos to use as evidence. In all your research, you will be attempting to identify the places where conversations on your topic are taking place — in specific academic journals, magazines, websites, annual conferences, and so on. By noting what is common among your sources, what data and evidence are shared, you may find other authoritative sources and get leads on further research.

If your topic warrants it, you may also want to supplement your library or internet research with your own fieldwork. You could conduct surveys or interviews, design an experiment, or visit a museum. You could perform research in an archive or other repository to analyze original documents or artifacts. This kind of research is called **primary research** because you are the one gathering the basic evidence and data. **Secondary research** is the term given to the kind of inquiry that involves your study of research done by others.

One form of research is not necessarily better than the other, although some may be better suited to certain topics or research questions than others. Many types of research projects involve both methods. Whether research is primary or secondary also does not bear on its reliability. Both kinds are subject to biases, omissions, and assumptions that could color the data. Therefore, critical thinking is essential every step of the way, whether you are seeking primary or secondary research or are performing it.

FINDING QUALITY INFORMATION ONLINE

The internet is a valuable source of information for many topics and less helpful for others. In general, if you're looking for information on public policy, popular culture, current events, legal affairs, or any subject of interest to agencies of the federal or state government, the internet is likely to have useful material. If you're looking for literary criticism or scholarly analysis of historical or social issues, you may be better off using library databases, described later in this chapter.

It is important to remember that the research process and the application of critical thinking do not occur separately: You may be jumping around from contemporary to historical sources, databases, and web pages, evaluating them as you proceed. Seek more facts as needed and remain adaptable, flexible, and open-minded all the while. Be prepared to take different perspectives seriously and be on the lookout for areas of ambiguity, unsettled issues, and debatable questions. Again, these are places where you can potentially weigh in. Do not hesitate to modify your search terms. If a path of research is not getting you anywhere, back up and try different terms. Think of your process as an open-ended engagement with information, not as an effort to prove something you already think.

To make good use of the internet, try these strategies:

- Use the most specific terms possible when using a general search engine; put phrases in quotes.

- Use the advanced search option to limit a search by date (such as websites updated in the past week or month).

- Consider which government agencies and organizations might be interested in your topic and go directly to their websites.

Visual Guide: Finding Discourse on Your Topic

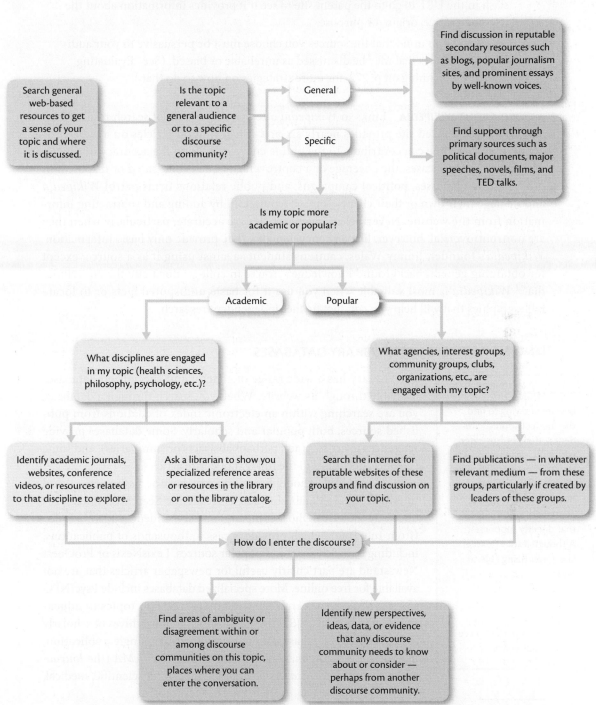

Search general web-based resources to get a sense of your topic and where it is discussed.

Is the topic relevant to a general audience or to a specific discourse community?

General

Specific

Find discussion in reputable secondary resources such as blogs, popular journalism sites, and prominent essays by well-known voices.

Find support through primary sources such as political documents, major speeches, novels, films, and TED talks.

Is my topic more academic or popular?

Academic

Popular

What disciplines are engaged in my topic (health sciences, philosophy, psychology, etc.)?

What agencies, interest groups, community groups, clubs, organizations, etc., are engaged with my topic?

Identify academic journals, websites, conference videos, or resources related to that discipline to explore.

Ask a librarian to show you specialized reference areas or resources in the library or on the library catalog.

Search the internet for reputable websites of these groups and find discussion on your topic.

Find publications — in whatever relevant medium — from these groups, particularly if created by leaders of these groups.

How do I enter the discourse?

Find areas of ambiguity or disagreement within or among discourse communities on this topic, places where you can enter the conversation.

Identify new perspectives, ideas, data, or evidence that any discourse community needs to know about or consider — perhaps from another discourse community.

- Use clues in URLs to see where sites originate. Delete everything after the first slash in the URL to go to the parent site to see if it provides information about the website's source, origin, or purpose.

- Always bear in mind that the sources you choose must be persuasive to your audience. Avoid sites that may be dismissed as unreliable or biased. (See "Evaluating Sources," beginning on p. 272, for more strategies on how to do that.)

A WORD ABOUT *WIKIPEDIA* Links to *Wikipedia* often rise to the top of search results. This vast and decentralized site provides nearly six-and-a-half million articles on a wide variety of topics. Anyone can contribute to the online encyclopedia, so the accuracy of articles varies, and in some cases, the coverage of a controversial issue is one-sided or disputed. In other cases, businesses, political campaigns, and public relations firms patrol *Wikipedia* and manage their own or their clients' "online reputation" by adding and subtracting information from the website. Nevertheless, many articles are accurate, particularly when they are noncontroversial; however, like any encyclopedia, they provide only basic information. *Wikipedia*'s founder, Jimmy Wales, cautions students against using it as a source, except for obtaining general background knowledge: "You're in college; don't cite the encyclopedia."[2] *Wikipedia* is most valuable when you use it for basic undisputed facts or to locate bibliographies that will help you conduct further independent research.

FINDING ARTICLES USING LIBRARY DATABASES

RESEARCH TIP
Beware of trying to find the "perfect source." Students often get frustrated with the research process because they have an excellent original idea but cannot find analysis, commentary, or opinion that directly supports it. Although it may not feel like it, not being able to find sources may actually be a *good* thing: It may indicate you have an original perspective or argument, a perfect place to add your voice.

Your library has a wide range of general and specialized databases available through its website. When you search through a database, you are searching within an electronic index of citations from published sources, both popular and scholarly. Some databases provide references to articles (and perhaps abstracts or summaries), and some provide direct links to the full text of entire articles.

Through your school library, you may have access to general and interdisciplinary databases such as Academic Search Premier (produced by the EBSCOhost company) and Expanded Academic Index (from InfoTrac), which provide access to thousands of publications, including both scholarly and popular sources. LexisNexis or ProQuest Newsstand are particularly useful for newspaper articles that are not available for free online. More specialized databases include PsycINFO (for psychology research) and ERIC (focused on topics in education). Others, such as JSTOR, are full-text digital archives of scholarly journals. Some databases offer the archives of a single publication, like the *New York Times, Wall Street Journal,* or *JAMA* (the *Journal of the American Medical Association*). Others offer scientific, medical,

---

[2] "Wikipedia Founder Discourages Academic Use of His Creation," *Chronicle of Higher Education Wired Campus,* June 12, 2006, http://www.chronicle.com/wiredcampus/article/1328/wikipedia-founder-discourages-academic-use-of-his-creation.

or economic data exclusively (such as Web of Science, MEDLINE, EconLit), and still others are virtual archives (such as African American Newspapers of the Nineteenth Century or The Sixties, a searchable database of independent newspapers and ephemera of that age). Some databases offer art (ArtStor), video (Films on Demand), music (Database of Recorded American Music [DRAM]), or photography (Associated Press Images Collection). Others may offer excellent resources for highly specific material: The Burns Archive, for example, offers one million historic photographs and is recognized by scholars as a primary resource for early medical photography. Look at your library's website and find out where you can browse the databases.

As you can see, databases abound. To navigate them and find the right one for your topic and project, look at your library's offerings and roll your cursor over database titles to get some information about the scope and holdings of each one. Never hesitate to ask a librarian at the reference desk for a quick tutorial on how to use your university databases — after all, you technically pay for these subscriptions through your tuition.

When using databases for research, first choose a topic, then narrow your topic using the strategies outlined earlier in this chapter. List synonyms for your key search terms. As you search, look at words used in titles and descriptors for alternative ideas and make use of the "advanced search" option so that you can easily combine multiple terms. Rarely will you find exactly what you're looking for right away. Try different search terms and different ways to narrow your topic. Consider limiting the date range of your search to find historical sources on your topic or narrowing results to show scholarly journal articles only.

Most databases have an advanced search option that offers fillable forms for combining multiple terms. In Figure 8.1, we show a search field using Boolean operators (AND, OR, and

Figure 8.1 A Database Search

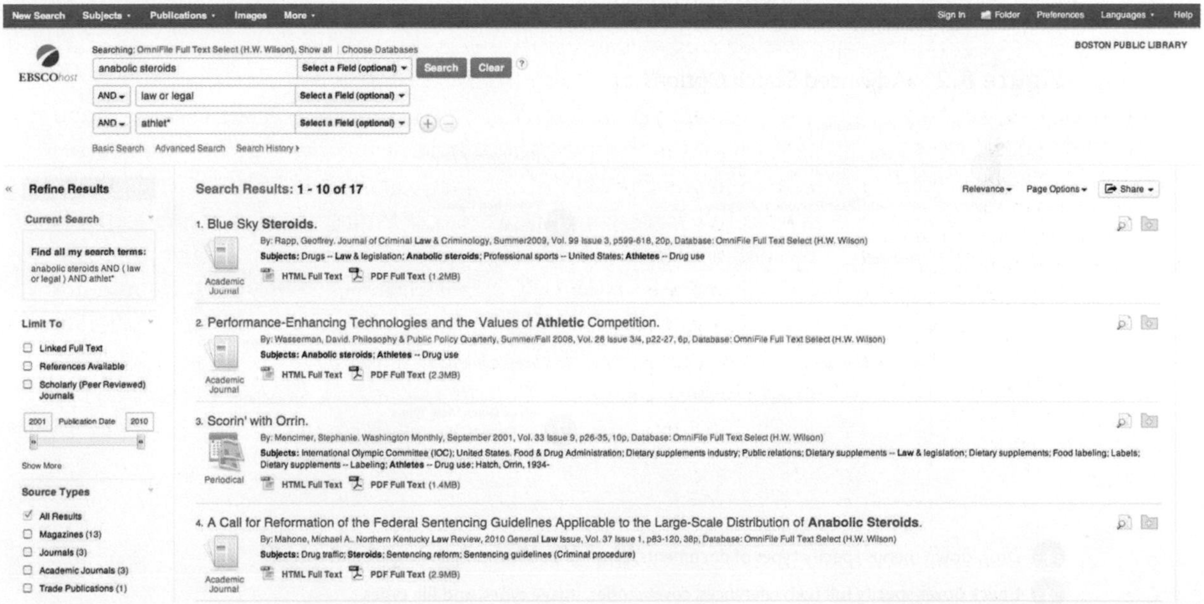

NOT) to seek targeted information on the use of anabolic steroids. Because a simple search of "anabolic steroids" retrieved far too many results, we used this advanced search to combine three concepts: anabolic steroids, legal aspects of their use, and use of them by athletes. Related terms are combined with the word "or": *law* or *legal*. The last letters of a word have been replaced with an asterisk so that any ending will be included in the search. *Athlet** will search for *athlete*, *athletes*, or *athletics*. Options on both sides of the list of articles retrieved offer opportunities to refine a search by date of publication or to restrict the results to only academic journals, magazines, or newspapers. Notice in Figure 8.2 some further ways to limit your searches.

RESEARCH TIP
Sources that at first appear to be unrelated to your topic may actually be *relatable* to your topic. If you are writing about poor labor conditions in US clothing companies' supply chains in Asia, and you find an article about the working conditions of agricultural laborers in South America, don't just cast that article aside. Rather, explore the possible overlaps. Determine whether or not you can apply one situation to the other.

As with an internet search, when you search through databases, you'll need to make critical choices about which articles are worth pursuing. Some results may not be useful. A title might tell you right away that a source is not exactly about your topic, or you might notice that the publication date is not relevant to your questions. The subject lines may contain some keywords associated with your topic (or not), and if you open the source, you may find an abstract that tells you more about the contents and findings of the source. All these leads can let you know how much further to look into your source.

Don't forget that your sources need not have links to the full text for you to retrieve them easily. It is the role of a library to get you the information you need. If you cannot link to the full text of an article you want to read, find your library's Interlibrary Loan (ILL) system, which you can use to request books and copies of articles to be sent to your library for you. Often, ILL materials take less than a day for electronic delivery and anywhere from two days to two weeks for physical books.

Figure 8.2   Advanced Search Options

Limit your results

Full Text ☐

References Available ☐

Scholarly (Peer Reviewed) Journals ☐

Published Date
Month ▾ Year: ___ – Month ▾ Year: ___

Publication
[_____]

Publication Type
All
Periodical
Newspaper
Book

Number Of Pages
All ▾ [_____]

Image Quick View ☐

Image Quick View Types
☐ Black and White Photograph   ☐ Chart
☐ Color Photograph   ☐ Diagram
☐ Graph   ☐ Illustration
☐ Map

① Drop-down menus specify types of documents, types of publications, languages, and dates.

② Check boxes specify full text, references, cover stories, image types, and file types.

As you choose and use sources, keep track of them. You can save them in a folder, or you can use your library's system for selecting and saving resources. You can save, email, or print the references you have selected. You may also have an option to export references to a citation management program such as RefWorks or EndNote. These programs allow you to create your own personal database of sources in which you can store your references and take notes. Later, when you're ready to create a bibliography, these programs will automatically format your references in MLA, APA, or another style. Ask a librarian if one of these programs is available to students on your campus.

THINKING CRITICALLY *Using Search Terms*

Imagine that your research question is this: Should first-year college students be required to live on campus? Identify useful key issues, terms, and related terms that you can use to search. (The first row has been completed as an example.)

QUESTION	KEY TERMS	RELATED TERMS	SEARCH TERMS
Should first-year college students be required to live on campus?	first-year students required to live on campus traditional and nontraditional students	freshmen freshman year residency policies residence hall requirement dorm dormitory	freshman OR first-year student* Residency rules OR residence requirement dorm*
Which schools have a first-year residency requirement, and which do not? What different types of first-year students are there?			
What are the benefits and drawbacks of living on campus? For which students?			
How do alternative on- or off-campus living situations compare for different kinds of students?			

LOCATING BOOKS

The books that your library owns can be found through its online catalog. Typically, you can search by author or title or, if you don't have a specific book in mind, by keyword or subject. As with databases, think about different search terms to use, keeping an eye out for subject headings used for books that appear relevant. Take advantage of an "advanced search" option. You may, for example, be able to limit a search to books on a particular topic in English published within recent years. In addition to books, the catalog will also list digital media such as films, audio and video recordings, and other formats.

Unlike articles, books tend to cover broad topics, so be prepared to broaden your search terms. It may be that a book has a chapter or ten pages that are precisely what you need, but the catalog typically doesn't index the contents of books in detail. Think instead of what kind of book might contain the information you need.

Once you've found some promising books in the catalog, note down the call numbers, find them on the shelves, and then browse. Because books on the same topic are shelved together, you can quickly see what additional books are available by scanning the shelves. As you browse, be sure to look for books that have been published recently enough for your purposes. You do not have to read a book from cover to cover to use it in your research. Instead, skim the introduction to see if it will be useful and then use its table of contents and index to pinpoint the sections of the book that are the most relevant.

If you are searching for a very specific name or phrase, you might try typing it into Google Book Search (books.google.com), which searches the contents of more than twenty-five million scanned books. Although it tends to retrieve too many results for most topics and you may only be able to see a snippet of content, it can help you locate a particular quote or identify which books might include an unusual name or phrase. There is a "find in a library" link that will help you determine whether the books are available in your library.

Evaluating Sources

Each step of the way in your research process, you will be making choices about your sources. As you proceed, from selecting promising items in a database search to browsing the book collection, you will want to use the techniques for previewing and skimming (in the section "Previewing" in Chapter 2 on pp. 40–44) in order to make your selections and develop your argument as you research. Begin by asking yourself some basic questions:

- Is this source relevant?
- Is it current enough?
- Does the title or abstract suggest it will address an important aspect of my topic?
- Am I choosing sources that represent a range of ideas, not simply ones that support my opinion?
- Do I have a reason to believe that these sources are trustworthy?

Once you have collected a number of likely sources, you will want to do further filtering. Examine each one with these questions in mind:

- *Is this source credible? Does it include information about the author and his or her credentials that can help me decide whether to rely on it?* In the case of books, you might check a database for book reviews for a second opinion. In the case of websites, find out where the site came from and why it has been posted online. Don't use a source if you can't determine its authorship or purpose.

- *Will my audience find this source credible and persuasive?* A story about US politics from the *Washington Post*, whose writers conduct firsthand reporting in the nation's capital, carries more clout than a story from a small-circulation newspaper that is drawing its information from a wire service.

- *Am I using the best evidence available?* Quoting directly from a government report may be more effective than quoting a news story that summarizes the report. Finding evidence that supports your claims in a president's speeches or letters is more persuasive than drawing your conclusions from a page or two of a history textbook.

- *Am I being fair to all sides?* Make sure you are prepared to address alternate perspectives, even if you ultimately take a position. Avoid sources that clearly promote an agenda in favor of ones that your audience will consider balanced and reliable.

- *Can I corroborate my key claims in more than one source?* Compare your sources to ensure that you aren't relying on facts that can't be confirmed. If you're having trouble confirming a source, check with a librarian.

- *Do I really need this source?* It's tempting to use all the books and articles you have found, but if two sources say essentially the same thing, choose the one that is likely to carry the most weight with your audience.

> **RESEARCH TIP**
> During your research, write down observations and questions. This way, you won't find yourself with a pile of printouts and books and no idea what to say about them. What you have to say will flow naturally out of the prewriting you've already done — and that prewriting will help guide your further research.

SCHOLARLY, POPULAR, AND TRADE SOURCES

An important part of finding and evaluating the reliability of your sources is determining whether they are **scholarly** or **popular** sources. In the "Types of Sources" table (p. 275), we cover some of the basic elements that distinguish these two types of publications. We also examine a third category called **trade** publications.

Scholarly publications are generally considered the gold standard of reliability in the production of knowledge and the circulation of discourse. This is primarily because scholarly publications are generally

- nonprofit;
- built on a mission to advance knowledge in a specific area;

- organized according to disciplinary methodologies, standards, and ethics; and

- peer-reviewed or refereed (meaning that before publication, the articles are reviewed and accepted by a group of experts in that field and in that specific area).

Popular publications — newspapers, magazines, newsletters, websites, and blogs — may be more or less reliable sources, but they generally do not carry the academic weight of scholarly ones. Popular sources have relative value: Some have high journalistic and editorial standards — think of the *Los Angeles Times* or the *Economist* magazine — and may contain articles and essays by respected journalists and experts — even scholars. But even intellectual magazines like *Science* or the *New Yorker* are popular publications in the same sense that *Cosmopolitan, Game Informer, Better Homes and Gardens*, or *Car and Driver* are: They are written for a general audience, and they are driven by profit.

Consider the implications. Magazines and newspapers must publish articles that sell to broad audiences; indeed, the goal of any commercial media enterprise is to make money from sales, subscriptions, and sponsors. Therefore, they are not as likely as academic sources to offer the widest range of subjects or perspectives, the same level of complexity, or the deepest, most thorough, and thoughtful forms of analysis.

Trade publications, the third category of sources, are more related to publications in the popular category; however, trade sources are designed for people in particular industries and professional associations. They sometimes appear to be very complex because they assume that readers are familiar with an insider's vocabulary. However, they are not popular because they are not for a general audience, and they are not scholarly because they do not involve a peer review process. Nevertheless, trade publications often utilize the latest field-specific research and expert voices and may be considered reliable resources in many cases. That said, we must remember that industry groups are likely to interpret issues through the lens of their interests — so, for example, *Coal Age* magazine (published by Mining Media International) and *SNLEnergy* (published by the American Coal Council) are much more likely to view coal production and use favorably as compared to *Solar Today Magazine* (published by the American Solar Energy Society).

Remember that just because something is published in a scholarly journal doesn't mean it is peer reviewed. In some journals, a peer-reviewed article may sit side by side with a book review or an editorial. Popular magazines will almost never contain scholarly articles; a respected scholar might contribute an original essay to a popular magazine, but again that doesn't mean the article is "scholarly."

Types of Sources

	Scholarly	Popular	Trade
Publisher	Universities, government agencies, research foundations, and institutions	Media companies, for-profit groups, internet website owners, interest groups	Professional associations, trade groups, unions, business groups, consortiums
Purpose	To report on research, experiments, and theories to expand human knowledge	To inform, entertain, and engage; to expand influence or profit or both	To inform, entertain, and engage; to expand influence in a specific field or industry
Audience	Academics, intellectuals, specialists, researchers	General public	People who have interests in a specific trade or industry
Language	Complex, technical, authoritative	Accessible, conversational	Accessible but with insider-speak such as jargon and acronyms
Sources cited	Always	Sometimes, usually through in-text reference or hyperlinks	Sometimes, usually through in-text reference or hyperlinks
Features and characteristics	Plain style; lots of footnotes or endnotes, long articles; few advertisements (if any); often charts and graphs; longer paragraphs and titles; peer reviewed	Glossy, attractive style; shorter and easier-to-digest articles; many advertisements; simple charts and graphs; shorter paragraphs and titles (if any); not peer reviewed	Various styles ranging from newsprint to glossy styles; technical but easier-to-digest articles, titles indicating industry-specific issues, advertising related to field; not peer reviewed
Frequency	Usually quarterly, semiannually	Usually daily, weekly, biweekly, monthly	Sometimes quarterly or semiannually; most often daily, weekly, monthly, bimonthly
Examples	*American Journal of Sociology, Harvard Asia Pacific Review, Foreign Affairs,* government reports	*Time, New York Times, Vogue, Popular Mechanics, HuffPost, Business Insider*	*AdWeek, Publishers Weekly, Columbia Journalism Review, Chronicle of Higher Education, Comics and Games Retailer*

EVALUATING ONLINE SOURCES

Unlike the information found in a library or published and circulated widely in print, much information online does not go through an evaluative process, as when librarians curate their collections or an editor reviews and selects material for a publication. Thus, one of the first things you must do to determine the quality and reliability of information online is consider the pathway of its publication on the internet. Did the information pass through any review process? Who was doing the reviewing? If the comments section in the *New York Times* shows someone claiming to be a doctor giving advice on some health issue, should you believe it? After all, you too could claim to be a doctor and publish your comments somewhere. At the same time, it may be that the commentator *is* a doctor and *is* reliable — but how would you know? In this hypothetical case, we would recommend corroborating the alleged doctor's claim using a respectable, reviewed medical publication (even if it happens to be openly available online).

Today, most print publications offer their content online in a digital format. However, there are also reliable online resources that are not duplicated in print, from high-quality citizen journalism to TED talks to university lectures online. There may be thoughtful blogs or other publication formats (video, podcast, and indexes) created or curated by people who have a high degree of credibility, but you must be cautious. The popularity of a website, blog, or podcast does not automatically confer expertise upon the creators or producers. Neither does the way a website *looks*. Given the ease of entry into the marketplace of ideas via the internet and the relative ease of designing a professional-looking web page, the popularity and design of a website cannot be considered key criteria in evaluating reliability.

A further problem is caused by the surge in disreputable publication venues that offer open-access publishing in journals that appear to be peer reviewed but really have dramatically lower standards — or none at all. These venues are usually predatory: They project the veneer of a scholarly journal, often with academic-sounding titles to match. For a fee, or sometimes for free (if they are ad revenue–based), these "journals" will publish material with little or no quality control. They are primary locations for fraudulent and hoax papers. Be wary of online journals discovered on the open internet and review them very carefully. It is always safer to use your university databases for scholarly sources.

Nevertheless, it is likely most of us will seek sources on the internet. The best steps you can take to remain a skeptical but open-minded researcher is to apply critical thinking skills. The first thing to do is consider all the contexts that inform your online sources:

- How did they get onto the internet?
- What organizations or individuals are behind their publication?
- Were they originally published elsewhere?

> **WRITING TIP**
> You can use (and cite) the information you find on websites, in blogs, in comments, and on social media posts; just make sure you frame that information with a fair accounting of the source. ("One user on YouTube with the handle *SportsTVFan* commented that the latest Super Bowl commercials are '*X*.'" or "Twitter user @DavidScottRedpath, an amateur astronomer with over a million followers, posted a tweet that claimed *X* about black holes.")

- What are the limitations of this particular kind of online resource?
- Why is this type of source a legitimate form of evidence in the context of your analysis?
- What special authority does the individual or group cited have for speaking on an issue?

With so much information online, you don't always get the basic indicators of authority, such as author credentials or an indication of editorial review. Remember that anyone can publish online with no review process. All that is needed is access to the internet.

You need not discount information available online, though; the internet provides a stunning array of unique perspectives and analyses. It has made it possible for people everywhere to contribute their arguments, opinions, and comments to public discourses.

Many students have been told to examine the domains of websites to judge the reliability of a source; however, whether a website is a *.com, .org,* or *.edu* is a weak marker of a source's reliability. All domain types can host reliable or unreliable information. Similarly, tweets and comments,

Figure 8.3 A Page from a Government Website

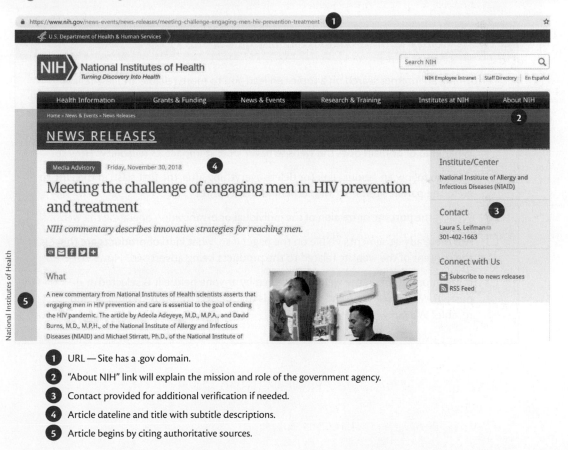

1. URL — Site has a .gov domain.
2. "About NIH" link will explain the mission and role of the government agency.
3. Contact provided for additional verification if needed.
4. Article dateline and title with subtitle descriptions.
5. Article begins by citing authoritative sources.

even when written by experts, may or may not carry much weight depending on the subject and occasion of their tweets or comments.

The information you will look for as you evaluate internet sources is often the same as what you need to record in any citation. Use clues in URLs to see where sites originate. For example, URLs containing *.k12* are hosted at elementary and secondary schools, so they may be intended for a young audience; those ending in *.gov* are government agencies, so they tend to provide official information, but if a *.gov* website is followed by a country code, you must also consider the context of place revealed by that origin. A website with a domain such as *.gov.ca* (Canada) may be more trustworthy than one from a country where freedoms of speech are curtailed, such as *.gov.kp* (North Korea). You can streamline the process of creating a list of works cited by identifying these elements as you find and begin to evaluate a source. (See "Documentation" later in this chapter for more on how to properly cite sources.)

In Figure 8.3 (p. 277), the URL includes the ending *.gov*, meaning it is a government website, an official document that has been vetted. There is an "about" link that will explain the government agency's mission. This appears to be a high-quality source of basic information on the issue. The information you need to cite this report is also on the page; make sure

A CHECKLIST FOR IDENTIFYING RELIABLE WEBSITES

Performing an internet search on a topic can lead you to more reliable and less reliable websites. Using the questions in this checklist can help you determine the factors that indicate reliability. *Hint:* To get past the most popular results from major news organizations, go deeper in the search results.

❑ What kind of domain does the website have? Does it impact its reliability? How so?

❑ Can you follow an "about" link (or delete everything after the first slash in the URL to go to the parent site)? If so, who is behind the website?

❑ What is the purpose or mission of the individual or organization operating the website?

❑ Are there advertisements visible on the page? If so, what kind of products are they? Is the content of the website related to the products being advertised? How?

❑ Is the information on the website reviewed by anyone before it is selected and posted? Who is selecting and reviewing? Is that person (or body) reputable and reliable? Why or why not?

you keep track of where you found the source and when, since websites can change. One way to keep track is by creating an account at a social bookmarking site such as Diigo (diigo.com) where you can store and annotate websites.

Figure 8.4 shows how the information on a web page might lead you to reject it as a source. Clearly, although this site purports to provide educational information in a well-meaning way, its primary purpose is to sell services and products. The focus on marketing should send up a red flag.

Figure 8.4   A Page from a Commercial Website

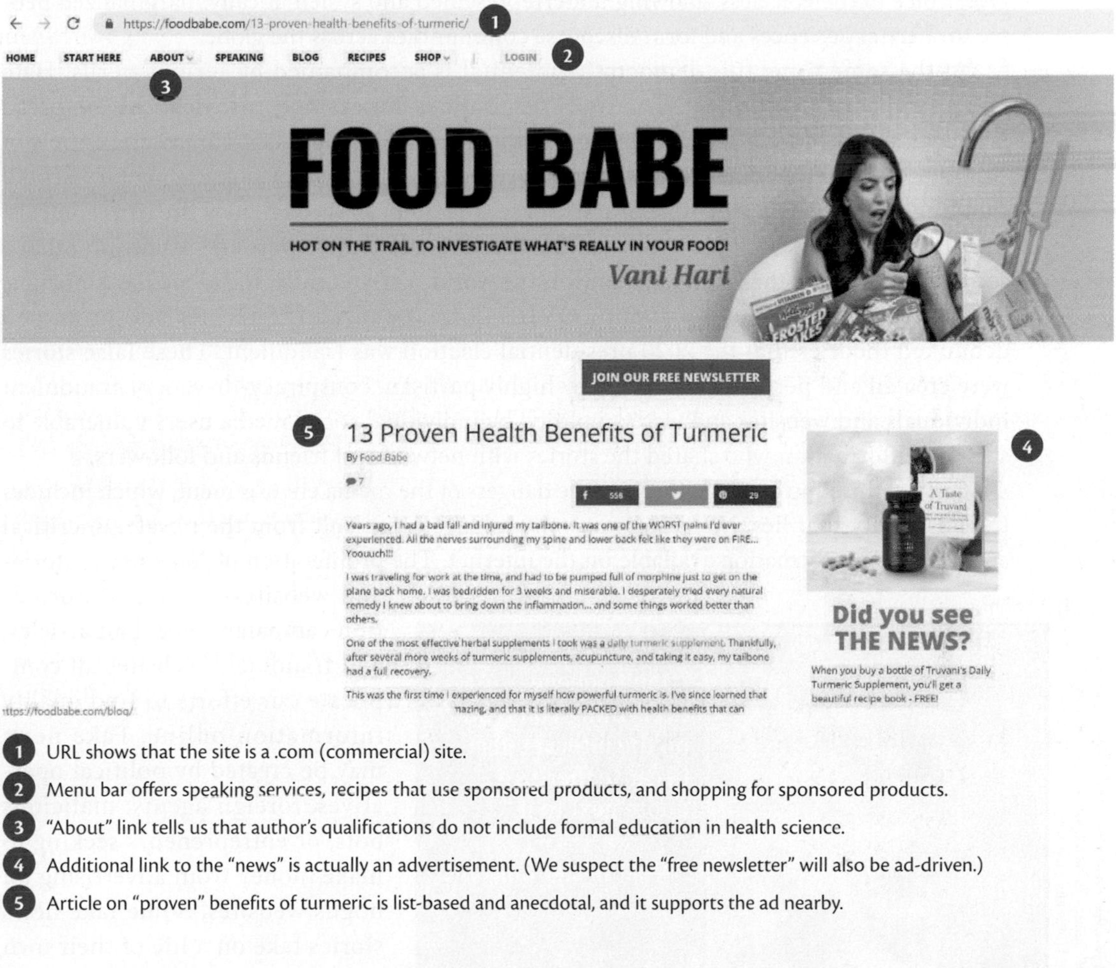

1. URL shows that the site is a .com (commercial) site.

2. Menu bar offers speaking services, recipes that use sponsored products, and shopping for sponsored products.

3. "About" link tells us that author's qualifications do not include formal education in health science.

4. Additional link to the "news" is actually an advertisement. (We suspect the "free newsletter" will also be ad-driven.)

5. Article on "proven" benefits of turmeric is list-based and anecdotal, and it supports the ad nearby.

WHY FINDING RELIABLE INTERNET SOURCES IS SO CHALLENGING   With our instant access to so much knowledge, and in the midst of an online cacophony of perspectives and voices, finding dependable, trustworthy sources of information can be difficult. Today, individuals can articulate their views publicly in a variety of online venues. With just a few clicks, individuals can expose poor customer service at a restaurant or abuses of power by police. They can report on news events as they happen, rally like-minded people to causes and activism, and share their opinions about almost anything in videos, blogs, tweets, and comments. This suggests an unprecedented democratic potential: The role of the internet in facilitating the Arab Spring, a series of antigovernment protests across the Middle East in 2010–2011, or the #occupy, #blacklivesmatter, and #metoo movements in the United States, were early and inspiring examples of social media–driven, grassroots movements. The internet's structure gives voice to the voiceless, allowing underrepresented and systematically marginalized people to share experiences and form discourse communities across the globe.

At the same time, this democratic potential is accompanied by serious perils. Hate groups and narrowly ideological activist organizations, for example, also deliberately spread propaganda, promoting shallow conspiracy theories and outright lies. Consider a couple of claims popularized by such groups in recent years: that the Sandy Hook Elementary School shooting was staged by gun-control activists seeking to push through new firearms controls; that the September 11, 2001, attacks on the World Trade Center were an "inside job"; that a secret society called the Illuminati controls the world. Very recently, social media campaigns have spread misinformation about COVID-19 treatments and vaccines and promoted debunked theories that the 2020 presidential election was fraudulent. These false stories were created and perpetuated mostly by highly partisan, conspiracy-driven, or fraudulent individuals and websites and were amplified by individual social media users vulnerable to such misinformation who shared the stories with networks of friends and followers.

Critical thinking can help mitigate the dangers of the media environment, which includes the possibility that lies, hysteria, and even violence can result from the unsafe, uncritical acceptance of information available on the internet. The proliferation of "fake news" stories and websites, viral misinformation campaigns, clickbait articles, and fraudulent websites all complicate our efforts to find quality information online. Fake news may be created by political operatives, foreign agents, malicious bots, or entrepreneurs seeking to make money from advertising on bogus websites. Some fake news stories take on a life of their own by going viral. In 2020, just as the results of the US presidential election appeared to be favoring Joe Biden, Austen Fletcher, under the

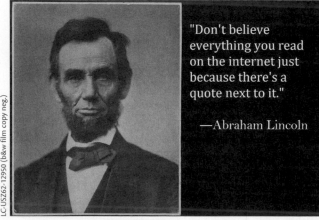

"Don't believe everything you read on the internet just because there's a quote next to it."

—Abraham Lincoln

Sometimes "authority" can be misleading.

Twitter handle @EssentialFleccas, tweeted a screenshot of his own voter roll research in the contested state of Michigan showing that an absentee ballot had been received from a deceased person from Wayne County named William Bradley. Fleccas's screenshot was posted on Facebook by Students for Trump co-founder John Fournier, then tweeted by the incumbent candidate's son, Donald Trump, Jr., becoming a talking point among cable news pundits alleging voter fraud. However, although Fleccas's image was real, the information it appeared to show was incorrect. The paper ballot was matched by officials to William Bradley, Jr., the deceased man's son, who shared his father's name and still lived at the same address. Despite this counterevidence, the original claim helped fuel false beliefs about election fraud and may even still be regarded as valid evidence by some people today.

In sum, the internet gives us unprecedented access to information and to our own assertions of authority, but this empowerment also requires us to examine information carefully and proffer it responsibly. It is important to respect accuracy and reliability when sharing our ideas on the internet, to track the sources of viral stories, and to fact-check as much as possible the claims and details they offer.

A WORD ON "FAKE NEWS" It has become somewhat fashionable to label as "fake news" any kind of information that does not accord with one's own worldview. For example, politicians often call into question the objectivity and reliability of news outlets that have been the standard-bearers of ethical journalism in the United States for decades — in some cases, for more than a century (the *New York Times*, for example). Here we must be emphatic: The mainstream news media, such as the *New York Times*, CNN, Fox News Channel, MSNBC, and others, are *not* fake news outlets. These organizations may or may not exhibit political biases and may or may not privilege information likely to attract certain kinds of readers and viewers, but they also carefully demarcate what they consider to be news programs and opinion programs, and they follow the most rigorous standards of verifiable reporting in their "hard news" reports. (Also remember that taking a thoughtful position is not the same as having a bias. In fact, taking a thoughtful position means *overcoming* biases, integrating a range of perspectives, meeting challenges to your own views, and adhering strictly to the goals of fairness and accuracy.)

Whether today's fake news stories are created by nefarious individuals or antagonistic intelligence agencies, their purpose is to sow confusion, doubt, and disorder by promoting falsehoods on the internet. Often these stories play upon base prejudices and superstitions. Their creators are not shy about telling wholesale lies, inventing quotations, and manipulating charts, graphs, and images, for example. They are indiscriminate in their attacks on truth: Liberals and conservatives, celebrities and everyday people have been targeted. Sometimes fake news stories are built around issues: Unscientific claims denying climate change, the efficacy of vaccinations, and the integrity of elections are just a few instances. Other types of fake news stories are created to further the agendas of activist organizations. Still others are designed merely to be eye-catching, their sole purpose to generate traffic to a website.

Unreliable or misleading news sources also include popular tabloids such as the *National Enquirer*, which blurs the lines between fiction and reality with salacious, screaming headlines like "Muslim Spies in Obama's CIA" and "Senator Ted Cruz's Father Linked to JFK Assassination." Consider, too, satirical publications and programs like *The Onion, The Daily Show* (Comedy Central), or *Last Week Tonight* (HBO). Although such programs offer sometimes sharp commentary and analysis, their purpose is largely to entertain, not to inform. As such, they should not be considered quality sources of information.

ANATOMY OF A FAKE NEWS STORY NewsPunch is a fake news website posing as a legitimate news outlet, which you can see in Figure 8.5. It has a respectable title and a "punchy" tagline ("Where Mainstream Fears to Tread"), as well as a clean design and layout characteristic of respectable news websites (a navigation menu of relevant topics and lists of recent and

Figure 8.5 A Fake News Website

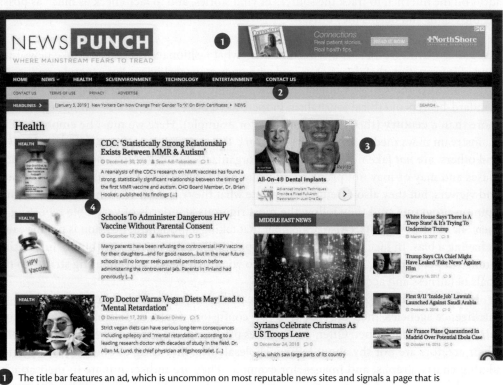

1 The title bar features an ad, which is uncommon on most reputable news sites and signals a page that is revenue-driven.

2 The navigation menu looks standard, but "Contact Us" is repeated on both lines, and there is an option for "Advertise," another warning sign.

3 Another ad, higher and more prominent on the page than most articles.

4 The stories mimic the layout of news sites: a photo with a category label ("Health") and a title, publication date, author, and first lines of the article.

popular articles). There is even a headline ticker bar that scrolls between titles as if they were breaking news stories. When we visited the site, clickbait-style titles appeared — at best dubious and misleading headlines, at worst debunked falsehoods. Although the site projects some outwardly cosmetic signs of journalistic legitimacy, we know we need to look more closely to determine if its information is actually reliable.

We looked at the first story on the page and searched for author Sean Adl-Tabatabai to verify his credentials as a writer. We discovered through a quick internet search that the former television producer is the founder of this fake news site, and the site has been flagged by a European Union task force charged with investigating Russian efforts to destabilize Western democracies. We found no biographical information whatsoever about the second author listed, Niamh Harris, and no other published material by Adl-Tabatabai besides forty-two articles for NewsPunch.

The first headline, "CDC: 'Statistically Strong Relationship Exists Between MMR and Autism,'" suggests that the Centers for Disease Control and Prevention (CDC), the US government's national health protection agency, makes this claim. In fact, the CDC is *very* clear that MMR vaccines do NOT cause autism — the CDC uses huge letters on its website to emphasize its position — and it has devoted significant resources to debunking dangerous theories that they do. The quotation in the headline is actually attributed to Dr. Brian Hooker of the Children's Health Defense organization, an activist group widely discredited in the medical community for its antivaccine stance and not associated at all with the CDC.

Hooker's findings were first published (the NewsPunch article tells us) in the *Journal of American Physicians and Surgeons*. This publication sounds fairly impressive at first. However, further searching on Google and "source watch" websites such as Beall's List of Predatory Journals and Publications showed us that this journal is published by the Association of American Physicians and Surgeons (AAPS), an ultraconservative activist group advocating a range of scientifically discredited theories, including that HIV does not cause AIDS and that abortion leads to breast cancer. The *Journal of American Physicians and Surgeons* is not listed in reputable academic literature databases like MEDLINE and Web of Science, and the US Library of National Medicine has denied AAPS's requests to index the journal, which has also been listed by watchdog scholars as a predatory open-access journal. As a result of our evaluation of the website plus further research and cross-checking, we concluded this article is fake news and not to be trusted.

The article on MMR vaccines and autism, and the other examples cited earlier, are undoubtedly the strictest forms of fake news (spurious, mendacious, and malicious). Websites like NewsPunch contain information mostly from other sources, recycled and reinterpreted through a sensationalistic or ideological lens. Other partisan websites may be less severe but nevertheless project the look of a news organization with none of its integrity.

What we cannot stress enough is that such information sources — and, in fact, *all* types of information sources — demand our most careful critical thinking and information literacy skills. Use the table that follows to help identify and evaluate resources that may be unreliable. Use the Checklist for Identifying Fake News on page 286 to ascertain a website's origins, legitimacy, and value and to dig further into the online sources you find to measure their validity.

NATIVE ADVERTISING AND BRANDED CONTENT   Some magazines, you probably have noticed, contain nearly as many (or even more) pages of advertisements than original content — a sign that the publication's content may be driven by the sponsors. In some publications, content itself can be part of an overall marketing scheme. In the magazine industry, this type of content is known as "ad-friendly copy" or "advertorial," with articles deliberately written to puff up a person, product, or service. On the internet, you have probably seen links to "sponsored content," which is like a digital version of advertorial (see Fig. 8.6). Even reputable news agencies will include links to sponsored content (and will usually indicate as much). These are not good sources because they are not neutral: They are less interested in providing quality information and more interested in selling a product or service.

Figure 8.6   Sponsored Content

1. Website is the *New York Times*, but content is clearly marked "Paid for and posted by Aetna."
2. No author listed (the company Aetna is the author and sponsor).
3. Features of actual news articles imitated (title, citations of sources, a pull quote).

Types of "Fake News" and Unreliable Content

Type	Creator(s)	Purpose(s)	Features	Example(s)
Propaganda	Government agencies, activist groups, political organizations, corporations	To affect social and political beliefs, attitudes, and behaviors to further an agenda	Widespread, often misleading or biased; one-sided (not objective or neutral)	Advertising, issue-based political messages, public service announcements, recruitment, or indoctrination materials
Clickbait	Companies and paid content creators	To entice viewers to navigate to websites designed to generate ad revenue based on traffic volume	Sensational "teaser" headlines with links	"Amazing" health news, discoveries, celebrity gossip, lists, inspirational, or revolting personal stories
Sponsored content	Companies and marketing firms	To present advertisements as news or interest stories so as to drive revenue	Designed to look like news, will reference products or services in main text	Articles worked into major news sources and web pages directing users to third-party content; often labeled
Partisan news	Media companies and special-interest groups	To provide perspective-based information to like-minded viewers/readers	Ideological; not impartial (although may claim to be); facts may be present but selective; biased interpretations of facts	Self-identified liberal or conservative information outlets, news personalities; some mainstream networks
Conspiracy theory	Special-interest groups, individuals	To subvert, fool, or entertain (for political or other purposes)	Dismisses experts and authorities; provides simplistic or sensationalistic answers to complex questions; spreads beliefs rooted in paranoia, fear, uncertainty	Material claiming to provide the "real" truth contrary to accepted knowledge or beliefs; claims to expose "hoaxes" perpetuated by powerful persons or interests

A CHECKLIST FOR IDENTIFYING FAKE NEWS

Website

☐ Does my source appear to be on a reputable website?

☐ Is there an "About" link (or a "Who We Are" or "Mission" link)? What individual or organization is behind the website?

☐ Is the content edited, or can users post anything?

☐ Does the website respect intellectual property? What website policies ensure (or compromise) source integrity?

☐ Do errors or misspellings on the website signal a lack of quality or reputability?

☐ How is the website supported (ads, donations, sponsorships)? What kinds of products and services are being sold, directly or indirectly, on the website? Are ads and sponsored content clearly marked as such?

☐ Are there a lot of pop-ups, surveys, or other distractions? Are visitors being asked for personal information or to sign up for something?

Authors

☐ Are authors or contributors named? Are they identifiable people with first and last names, or are they known just by "handles"?

☐ Are they real people? Can I find additional information about them?

☐ What authority do they have? What biases or other ideological predispositions might they have, if any?

Accuracy

☐ Does the information in my source check against other reputable sources?

☐ Are there links or citations in the articles (and do they point to other reputable, timely sources)? What kind of sources are being quoted and cited?

☐ Can I verify or cross-reference images to ensure that they have not been manipulated?

Comments

☐ What kind of audience seems to be involved in the debate?

☐ Do comments agreeing with the source tend to reflect reasonable ideas and common values? What about dissenting comments?

☐ If the site does not allow commenting, why?

CONSIDERING HOW CURRENT SOURCES ARE

Popular sources do have one major advantage in that they are very current. Newspapers and magazines publish frequently enough — daily, weekly, monthly — that they can respond to events as they occur. Although this schedule makes them prone to errors of fact and misreadings of developing situations, they have an indispensable immediacy. Academic journals, on the other hand, usually publish quarterly or semiannually because the peer-review process is so elaborate and the content so rich: Although it takes a longer time to write, review, and publish issues of an academic journal, the content tends not to age as fast. Because academic journals are so deeply researched, analyzed, and reviewed, their findings generally have staying power.

So far, we have been discussing the difference between scholarly, popular, and trade **periodicals** — that is, publications that appear on a regular basis. Whether they are scholarly, popular, or trade publications, or appear frequently or not, reputable publications have strong editorial review processes and abide by the codes of journalistic ethics. Full-length books, too, may be popular or scholarly, published by a university press or a respected organization. Although scholarly books are not always peer reviewed, many academic publishers are overseen by editorial boards who solicit feedback from expert reviewers. Academic books are also subject to a secondary review process in scholarly journals after they are published, so you can always examine how a source has been regarded by other experts if you wanted to verify its credibility. Like with popular and scholarly periodicals, full-length books may also have different levels of continuing relevance. Some books are published quickly and are intended to speak to current events; others take years to write, vet, and publish and may stick around as authoritative sources for a long time, even decades.

Remember, however, that academic books *do* age. Those you find on the library shelves may be much older than the relevant results from an internet or database search. Such books published long ago may be of historical interest, but they are rarely the strongest sources speaking directly to current issues, and they must be regarded in context. A book about juvenile delinquency published by a sociologist in 1955 cannot be used as evidence for a theory of adolescence nowadays, and even a landmark work, like Sigmund Freud's *The Interpretation of Dreams* (1899), may be an interesting book to study in and of itself or may prove to be an excellent background reference in your work, but it would not serve as evidence in an argument that the Oedipal complex — Freud's famous theory of psychosexual development — should inform how parents interact with their children today.

A CHECKLIST FOR EVALUATING SOURCES

☐ Can I identify the person or organization who produced the source?

☐ Can I identify the source's purpose?

☐ Are the authors real, reliable, and credentialed?

(continues on next page)

❑ Do sources cited represent a range of ideas, not simply ones that support one viewpoint?

❑ Are images verifiable from other sources?

❑ Is the source recent? If not, is the information I will be using from it likely or unlikely to change over time?

❑ Does the source treat the topic superficially or in depth?

❑ Does the article speak directly (or relevantly) to my topic and tentative thesis?

❑ If the article is from a scholarly journal, am I sure I understand it?

❑ Is the source titled and marketed as entertainment? If so, have I considered the author's commercial biases?

❑ Is the source targeted at a specific audience likely to be sympathetic to its claims?

❑ Do the arguments in the source seem sound, based on what I have learned about skillful critical reading and writing?

Performing Your Own Primary Research

Research isn't limited to the world of professors and scientists. In one way or another, everyone does research at some point. If you decided to open your own business, you would want to do market research to persuade the bank that you are likely to be profitable enough to repay a loan. If you wanted to find out how and why a campus monument was erected, you could visit the university library's institutional archives and seek out information on it. If you were reviewing a film or book, you would probably go to the cinema or read in a comfortable place. Doing any of these things is performing primary research. In college, you might find yourself working on primary research alongside faculty members or participating in a class project to collect data. In other circumstances, you may wish to supplement your arguments with primary sources. Here, we touch on several kinds of primary research commonly performed by students.

INTERVIEWING PEERS AND LOCAL AUTHORITIES

For many topics, consider that you are surrounded by experts at your college. You ought to try to consult them — for instance, members of the faculty or other authorities on art, business, law, university administration, and so forth. You can also consult interested laypersons. Remember that experts may have their biases and "ordinary" people may have knowledge that experts lack. When interviewing experts, keep in mind Pablo Picasso's comment: "You mustn't always believe what I say. Questions tempt you to tell lies, particularly when there is no answer."

If you are interviewing your peers, you will probably want to make an effort to get a representative sample. Of course, even within a group not all members share a single view — for example, many African Americans favor affirmative action, but not all do; some lawmakers support capital punishment, but again, many do not. Make an effort to talk to a range of people who might offer varied opinions. You may learn some unexpected things.

You may also collect **testimonial** evidence from professors, students, community members, or family members. If you are writing about the women's rights movement of the 1970s, you might interview a professor or family member who lived through the era or participated in civil rights activities. You may know veterans who can speak to issues surrounding US wars or the experience of military service. Or perhaps an expert on a particular subject is visiting your campus for a lecture or talk, and you can find a way to put some questions of interest to them.

CONDUCTING OBSERVATIONS

Observational research is the process of collecting information by situating yourself in a real-life context and making observations of what is present or what occurs. It may be *structured*, which means that you spend time designing your observation in a systematic way so as to get consistent results. For example, perhaps you want to see if male and female children are more likely to select gender-specific toys from a toy chest if they are with peers of the same sex; to prepare, you might code each toy according to its gendered properties and then watch and record while same-sex and mixed-sex groups of children are at play in the toy chest. To aim for consistent results, you might conduct the observation in multiple sittings, but always at the same time with the same number of children in each group.

Observational research may also be *unstructured*, meaning that you simply immerse yourself in a situation and carefully note what you see or experience. If you visited a toy store to gather impressions about how children's toys are segregated according to gender, you would be performing unstructured observational research. The same goes for attending a political convention as an observer (as opposed to a participant) or riding along with a police officer.

However, when you conduct observations, you must be careful to abide by ethical standards; you should not record people without their consent, for example. You must also be aware of observer biases — the notion that people's behavior changes when they know they are being watched, for one thing, and also that you yourself as a researcher may get swept up in what you are observing to a degree that you are not able to be neutral or objective in your observations.

CONDUCTING SURVEYS

Surveys are excellent ways to ascertain the opinions and beliefs of a certain population. Whether you distribute your surveys via paper or set up an online survey through an online service like Doodle or SurveyMonkey, your college's in-house software such as Qualtrics, or even a Facebook poll, be sure to distribute your survey to the target population. Whether you are trying to collect opinions, values, behaviors, or facts, your survey questions should be constructed carefully to get the data that you want. Here are some other pitfalls of collecting surveys:

- **Not enough respondents/bad sample size:** If only five women responded to your survey on attitudes about fraternities on campus, you shouldn't use just five responses to say "80% of women on campus have a favorable view of fraternities."

- **Leading questions:** Leading questions use language likely to influence respondents' answers, such as "How fast should drivers be allowed to go on our serene campus roads?" As you can see, the language "leads" the respondent: For these questions, respondents are likely to answer lower speeds for "serene" roads. A more appropriate version of this question would be "What in your opinion is a safe driving speed for campus roads?"

- **Loaded questions:** Loaded questions push respondents to answer questions that don't fully or accurately represent their actual opinions. "On a scale of 1 to 5," a loaded question might ask, "how awful do you think it is that our administration is raising tuition?" Such a question forces all respondents to answer in the "awful" range, even if they are somewhat satisfied with the tuition amount overall.

RESEARCH IN ARCHIVES AND SPECIAL COLLECTIONS

Archives are collections of material maintained and preserved by organizations such as college and university libraries, public libraries, corporations, governments, churches, museums, and historical societies. Archives generally contain records that are important to an institution's own history and that may be relevant to others. The National Archives in Washington, DC, for example, curates a vast number of resources, including America's founding documents and military service records. Coca-Cola's company archives and the Walt Disney archives are examples of corporate archives that hold a vast array of materials related to those companies' pasts. Your college or university probably keeps its own institutional archives in its library.

Special collections are bodies of original material — including photographs, films, letters, memos, manuscripts of unique interests, and often material artifacts — usually gathered around a specialized topic, theme, or individual. Special collections often include original, rare, and valuable artifacts that may require permission for access or examination. Many libraries and museums offer at least limited access to digital archives and special collections via their websites, and some databases offer access to primary research sources, too (letters, original newspapers, early manuscripts, and so on).

Some special collections are broad and deep: The Library of Congress, the Smithsonian, and other national museums, for example, hold special collections on a variety of subjects in American political, social, and natural history. Other special collections can be quite specific, ranging from collections of science fiction pulp novels of the 1950s; to letters from combat veterans of World War II; to photograph, film, art, and music collections, antique and contemporary. The Blues Archive at the University of Mississippi contains — among other treasures — the musician B.B. King's personal record collection. The popular culture collection at Bowling Green State University holds 10,000 comic books and graphic novels, among other curiosities like a complete Pokémon set and *Star Trek* memorabilia.

Synthesizing Sources

When you are evaluating sources, consider the words of Francis Bacon, Shakespeare's contemporary: "Some books are to be tasted, others to be swallowed, and some few to be chewed and digested."

Your instructor will expect you not just to find but to digest your sources. This doesn't mean you need to accept them but only that you need to read them thoughtfully. Your readers will expect you to tell them *what you make of your sources*, which means that you will go beyond writing a summary and will synthesize the material into your own contribution to the discourse. *Your* view is what is wanted, and readers expect this view to be thoughtful — not mere summary and not mere tweeting.

Let's pause for a moment and consider the word **synthesis**. You probably are familiar with *photosynthesis*, the chemical process in green plants that produces carbohydrates from carbon dioxide and hydrogen. Synthesis combines preexisting elements and produces something new. In your writing, you will *synthesize* sources, combining existing material into something new, drawing nourishment from what has already been said (giving credit, of course), and converting it into something new — a view that you think is worth considering. In our use of the word *synthesis*, even a view that you utterly reject becomes a part of your new creation *because it helped stimulate you to formulate your view*; without the idea that you reject, you might not have developed the view that you now hold.

During the process of reading and evaluating sources, and afterward, you will want to listen, think, and say to yourself something like the following:

> **WRITING TIP**
> In your final draft, *you must give credit to all your sources*. Let the reader know whether you are quoting (in this case, you will use quotation marks around all material directly quoted), whether you are summarizing (you will explicitly say so), or whether you are paraphrasing (again, you will explicitly say so).

- "No, no, I see things very differently; it seems to me that . . ."

- "Yes, of course, but on one large issue I think I differ."

- "Yes, sure, I agree, but I would go further and add . . ."

- "Yes, I agree with the conclusion, but I hold this conclusion for reasons different from the ones offered."

Taking Notes

Whether you are performing primary or secondary research, using library special collections or online resources, you should be keeping notes along the way. When it comes to taking notes, all researchers have their own habits that they swear by: We still prefer to take notes on four-by-six-inch index cards; others use a notebook or a computer for note taking.

If you use a citation management program such as RefWorks or EndNote, you can store your personal notes and commentary with the citations you have saved. By using the program's search function, you can easily pull together related notes and citations, or you can create project folders for your references so that you can easily review what you've collected.

Whatever method you use, the following techniques should help you maintain consistency and keep organized during the research process:

1. *Organize notes carefully.* If you use a notebook or index cards, write in ink (pencil gets smudgy), and write on only one side of the paper or card to avoid losing track of your material. If you keep notes electronically, consider an online tool such as Microsoft OneNote, a Google Doc, or another cloud-based service so that you will not lose your research in the event of a computer crash or a lost laptop.

2. *Summarize*, for the most part, rather than quote at length. Quote only passages in which the writing is especially effective or passages that are in some way crucial. Make sure that all quotations are exact.

3. *Indicate the source.* The author's last name is enough if you have consulted only one work by the author, but if you consult more than one work by an author, you need further identification, such as both the author's name and a short title.

4. *Add your own comments* about the substance of what you are recording. Such comments as "but contrast with Sherwin" or "seems illogical" or "evidence?" will ensure that you are thinking as well as reading and writing.

5. *Write a bibliographic entry for each source.* Use a separate computer file, or a separate card or page. The information in each entry will vary, depending on whether the source is a book, a periodical, an electronic document, and so forth. The kind of information (e.g., author and title) needed for each type of source can be found in the sections "MLA Format: The List of Works Cited" (p. 303) and " APA Format: The List of References" (p. 319).

A Note on Plagiarizing

Plagiarism is the unacknowledged use of someone else's work. The word comes from a Latin word for "kidnapping," and plagiarism is indeed the stealing of something engendered by someone else. Your college or your class instructor probably has issued a statement concerning plagiarism. If there is such a statement, be sure to read it carefully.

We won't deliver a sermon on the dishonesty (and folly) of plagiarism; we intend only to help you understand exactly what plagiarism is. The first thing to say is that plagiarism is not limited to the unacknowledged quotation of words.

PARAPHRASING   A *paraphrase* is a sort of word-by-word or phrase-by-phrase translation of the author's language into your own language. Unlike a summary, then, a paraphrase is approximately as long as the original.

Paraphrase thus has its uses, but writers often use it unnecessarily, and students who overuse it may find themselves crossing the border into plagiarism. True, if you paraphrase you are using your own words, but you are also using someone else's ideas, and, equally important, you are using this other person's sequence of thoughts.

Even if you change every third word in your source, you are plagiarizing. Here is an example of this sort of plagiarism, based on the previous sentence:

> Even if you alter every second or third word that your source gives, you still are plagiarizing.

Further, even if the writer of this paraphrase had cited a source after the paraphrase, he or she would still have been guilty of plagiarism. How, you may ask, can a writer who cites a source be guilty of plagiarism? Easy. Readers assume that only the gist of the idea is the source's and that the development of the idea — the way it is set forth — is the present writer's work. A paraphrase that runs to several sentences is in no significant way the writer's work: The writer is borrowing not only the idea but also the shape of the presentation, the sentence structure. What the writer needs to do is to write something like this:

> Changing an occasional word does not free the writer from the obligation to cite a source.

And, if the central idea were not a commonplace one, the source would still need to be cited.

Now consider this question: *Why* paraphrase? As we explained in "Summarizing and Paraphrasing" in Chapter 2 (p. 51), the chief reason to paraphrase a passage is to clarify it — that is, to ensure that you and your readers understand a passage that — perhaps because it is badly written — is obscure. Often there is no good answer for why you should paraphrase. Since a paraphrase is as long as the original, you might as well quote the original, if you think that a passage of that length is worth quoting. Probably it is *not* worth quoting in full; probably you should *not* paraphrase but rather should drastically *summarize* most of it, and perhaps quote a particularly effective phrase or two.

A CHECKLIST FOR AVOIDING PLAGIARISM

Ask yourself these questions, first about your notes:

- ☐ Did I *always* put quoted material within quotation marks?
- ☐ Did I summarize *in my own words* and give credit to the source for the idea?
- ☐ Did I avoid paraphrasing? That is, did I avoid copying, keeping the structure of the source's sentences but using some of my own words?

(continues on next page)

And then about your paper:

☐ If I set forth a borrowed idea, do I give credit, even though the words and the structure of the sentences are entirely my own?

☐ If I quote directly, do I put the words within quotation marks and cite the source?

☐ Do I *not* cite material that can be considered common knowledge?

☐ If I have the slightest doubt about whether I should or should not cite a source, have I taken the safe course and cited the source?

Compiling an Annotated Bibliography

When several sources have been identified and gathered, many researchers prepare an annotated bibliography. That's a list providing all relevant bibliographic information (just as it will appear in your Works Cited list or References list), as well as a brief descriptive and evaluative summary of each source — perhaps one to three sentences. Your instructor may ask you to provide an annotated bibliography for your research project.

An annotated bibliography serves four main purposes:

1. It helps you master the material contained in any given source. To find the heart of the argument presented in an article or book, to phrase it briefly, and to comment on it, you must understand it fully.

2. It helps you think about how each portion of your research fits into the whole of your project, how you will use it, and how it relates to your topic and thesis.

3. It allows your readers to see quickly which items may be especially helpful in their own research.

4. It gives you hands-on practice at bibliographic format, thereby easing the job of creating your final bibliography (the Works Cited list or References list of your paper).

Following is an example entry for an annotated bibliography in MLA (Modern Language Association) format for a project on the effect of violence in the media. Notice that the entry does three things:

1. It begins with a bibliographic entry — author (last name first), title, and so forth.

2. Then it provides information about the content of the work under consideration.

3. Then it suggests how the source might work to support your argument in the final research paper you are writing.

Clover, Carol J. *Men, Women, and Chain Saws: Gender in the Modern Horror Film*. Princeton UP, 1992. The author focuses on Hollywood horror movies of the 1970s and 1980s. She studies representations of women and girls in these movies and the responses of male viewers to female characters, suggesting that this relationship is more complex and less exploitative than the common wisdom claims. Could use this source to establish a counterpoint to the idea that all women are represented stereotypically in horror films.

CITATION GENERATORS   There are many citation generators available online. These generators allow you to enter the information about your source, and, with a click, they will create Works Cited entries in MLA format or References in APA format. But just as you cannot trust spell- and grammar-checkers in Microsoft Word, you cannot trust these generators completely. If you use them, be sure to double-check what they produce before submitting your essay. Always remember that responsible writers take care to cite their sources properly and that failure to do so puts you at risk for accusations of plagiarism.

Quoting from Sources

When is it necessary, or appropriate, to quote? Using your notes, consider where the reader would benefit by seeing the exact words of your source. If you are arguing that *Z*'s definition of *rights* is too inclusive, your readers have to know exactly how *Z* defined *rights*, word for word. If your source material is so pithy and well worded that summarizing it would weaken its force, give your readers the pleasure of reading the original. Of course, readers won't give you credit for writing these words, but they will appreciate your taste and your effort to make their reading experience pleasant. In short, use (but don't overuse) quotations. Don't quote *too often* and don't quote *too much* of the original source (and never use quotations to achieve more length!). Speaking roughly,

- quotations should occupy no more than 10 to 15 percent of your paper;
- they may occupy much less; and
- most of your paper should set forth your ideas, not other people's ideas.

LONG AND SHORT QUOTATIONS   **Long quotations** (more than four lines of typed prose or three or more lines of poetry) are set off from the text. To set off material, start on a new line, indent one-half inch from the left margin, and type the quotation double-spaced. Do not enclose quotations within quotation marks if you are setting them off.

Short quotations are treated differently. They are embedded within the text; they are enclosed within quotation marks, but otherwise they do not stand out.

All quotations, whether set off or embedded, must be exact. If you omit any words, you must indicate the ellipsis by substituting three spaced periods for the omission; if you insert any words or punctuation, you must indicate the addition by enclosing it within square brackets — not to be confused with parentheses. Here is an original quote from Jane Goodall:

Original	Hope is often misunderstood. People tend to think that it is simply passive wishful thinking: I hope something will happen but I'm not going to do anything about it. This is indeed the opposite of real hope, which requires action and engagement. Many people understand the dire state of the planet — but do nothing about it because they feel helpless and hopeless.
Quotation in student paper	Jane Goodall wrote that "wishful thinking" about saving the planet is "[T]he opposite of real hope, which requires action and engagement. Many people . . . do nothing about it because they feel helpless and hopeless."

LEADING INTO A QUOTATION   Now for a less mechanical matter: The way in which a quotation is introduced. To say that it is "introduced" implies that one leads into it, although on rare occasions a quotation appears without an introduction, perhaps immediately after the title. Normally one leads into a quotation by giving any one or more of the following (but be aware that using them all at once can get unwieldy and produce awkward sentences):

- the *name of the author* and (no less important) the author's expertise or authority

- an indication of *the source of the quotation*, by title and/or year

- *clues signaling the content of the quotation and the purpose* it serves in the present essay

For example:

William James provides a clear answer to Huxley when he says that ". . . ."

In *The Will to Believe* (1897), psychologist William James provides a clear answer to Huxley when he says that ". . . ."

Either of these lead-ins work, especially because William James is quite well known. When you're quoting from a lesser-known author, it becomes more important to identify his or her expertise and perhaps the source, as in

Biographer Theodora Bosanquet, author of *Henry James at Work* (1982), subtly criticized Huxley's vague ideas on religion by writing, ". . . ."

Notice that in all these samples, the writer uses the lead-in to signal to readers the general tone of the quotation to follow. The writer uses the phrase "a clear answer" to signal that what's coming is, in fact, clear, uses the terms "subtly criticized" and "vague" to indicate that the following words by Bosanquet will be critical and will point out a shortcoming in Huxley's ideas. In this way, the writer anticipates and controls the meaning of the quotation for the reader. If the writer believed otherwise, the lead-ins might have run thus:

> William James's weak response to Huxley does not really meet the difficulty Huxley calls attention to. James writes, ". . . ."

> Biographer Theodora Bosanquet, author of *Henry James at Work* (1982), unjustly criticized Huxley's complex notion of religion by writing ". . . ."

In these examples, clearly the words "weak" and "unjustly criticized" imply how the essayist wants the reader to interpret the quotation. In the second one, Huxley's idea is presented as "complex," not vague.

Be sure to check your style guide for proper formatting of in-text citations (see "Documentation").

SIGNAL PHRASES   Think of your writing as a conversation between you and your sources. As in conversation, you want to be able to move smoothly between different, sometimes contrary, points of view. You also want to be able to set your thoughts apart from those of your sources. Signal phrases make it easy for readers to know where your information came from and why it's trustworthy by pointing to key facts about the source:

> *According to* psychologist Stephen Ceci . . .

> A report published by the US Bureau of Justice Statistics *concludes* . . .

> Feminist philosopher Sandra Harding *argues* . . .

To avoid repetitiveness, vary your sentence structure:

> . . . *claims* Stephen Ceci.

> . . . *according to* a report published by the US Bureau of Statistics.

Some useful verbs to introduce sources include the following:

acknowledges	contends	points out
argues	denies	recommends
believes	disputes	reports
claims	observes	suggests

Note that MLA style refers to sources in the present tense ("argue"), while APA style uses the past tense ("argued") or present perfect tense ("have argued").

LEADING OUT OF A QUOTATION   You might think of providing quotations as a three-stage process that includes the **lead-in**, the **quotation** itself, and the **lead-out**. The lead-out gives you a chance to interpret the quoted material, further controlling the intended meaning and telling the reader what is most important.

Visual Guide: Integrating Quotations

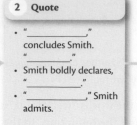

1 Lead-in

- Name of author(s)
- Author's (or authors') expertise or authority
- Title of source, publication title, publication year/date
- Signal phrases that indicate the content of the quotation and the purpose it serves for your argument

2 Quote

- "_____," concludes Smith.
- "_____."
- Smith boldly declares, "_____."
- "_____," Smith admits.

3 Lead-out

- Interpret the quotation.
- Reflect on its usefulness to your essay and argument.

In the lead-out, you have a chance to reflect on the quotation and to shift back toward your own ideas and analysis. Consider this three-stage process applied in the following two ways:

In his first book, *A World Restored*, future Secretary of Defense Henry Kissinger wrote the famous axiom "History is the memory of states" (331). It is the collective story of an entire people, displayed in public museums and libraries, taught in schools, and passed on from generation to generation.

In his first book, *A World Restored*, Nixon's former Secretary of Defense Henry Kissinger wrote glibly, "History is the memory of states" (331). By asserting that history is largely the product of self-interested propaganda, Kissinger's words suggest that the past is maintained and controlled by whatever groups happen to hold power.

Notice the three-step process, and notice especially how the two examples convey different meanings of Kissinger's famous phrase. In the lead-in to the first sample, Kissinger's "future" role suggests hope. It signals a figure whose influence is growing. By using "famous" and "axiom," the author presents the quotation as true or even timeless. In the lead-out, the role of the state in preserving history is optimistic and idealistic.

WRITING TIP

In introducing a quotation, remember to provide a description of the author's expertise or authority, so your readers know who it is and why they should take seriously the ideas quoted.

In the second sample, "former" is used in the lead-in, suggesting Kissinger's later association with the ousted president he served, Richard Nixon. Readers are told that Kissinger "wrote glibly" even before they are told what he wrote, so readers may tend to read the quoted words that way. In the lead-out, the state becomes a more nefarious source of history keeping, one not interested in accommodating marginal voices or alternative perspectives, or remembering events inconvenient to its authority or righteousness.

Again, we hope you can see in these examples how the three-step process facilitates a writer's control over the meanings of quotations. Returning to our earlier example, if after reading something by Huxley the writer had merely stated that "William James says . . . ," readers wouldn't know whether they were getting confirmation, refutation, or something else. The essayist would have put a needless burden on the readers. Generally speaking, the more difficult the quotation, the more important is the introductory or explanatory lead-in, but even the simplest quotation profits from some sort of brief lead-in, such as "James reaffirms this point when he says . . ."

Documentation

In the course of your essay, you will probably quote or summarize material derived from a source. You must give credit, and although there is no one form of documentation to which all scholarly fields subscribe, you will probably be asked to use one of two. One, established by the Modern Language Association (MLA), is used chiefly in the humanities; the other, established by the American Psychological Association (APA), is used chiefly in the social sciences.

We include two papers that use sources. "An Argument for Corporate Responsibility" (p. 313) uses the MLA format. "Does Ability Determine Expertise?" (p. 325) follows the APA format. (You may notice that various styles are illustrated in other selections we have included.)

In some online venues, you can link directly to your sources. If your assignment is to write a blog or some other online text, linking helps the reader look at a note or citation or the direct source quickly and easily. For example, in describing or referencing a scene in a movie, you can link to reviews of the movie, to a YouTube video of the trailer, or to the exact scene you're discussing. These kinds of links can help your audience get a clearer sense of your point. When formatting such a link in your text, make sure the link opens in a new window so that readers won't lose their place in your original text. In a blog, linking to sources usually is easy and helpful.

A NOTE ON FOOTNOTES (AND ENDNOTES)

Before we discuss these two formats, a few words about footnotes are in order. Before the MLA and the APA developed their rules of style, citations commonly appeared in footnotes. Although today footnotes are not so frequently used to give citations, they still may be useful for another purpose. (Most readers seem to think that footnotes are preferable to endnotes. After all, who wants to keep shifting from a page of text to a page of notes at the end?) If you want to include some material that may seem intrusive in the body of the paper, you may relegate it to a footnote or endnote. For example, you might translate a quotation given in a foreign language, or you might demote from text to footnote a paragraph explaining why you aren't taking account of such-and-such a point. By putting the matter in a footnote, you signal to the reader that it is dispensable — that it's relevant but not essential, something extra that you are, so to speak, tossing in. Don't make a habit of writing this sort of note, but there are times when it is appropriate to do so.

MLA Format: Citations within the Text

Brief citations within the body of the essay give credit, in a highly abbreviated way, to the sources for material you quote, summarize, or make use of in any other way. These *in-text citations* are made clear by a list of sources, titled Works Cited, appended to the essay. Thus, in your essay you may say something like this:

> Commenting on the relative costs of capital punishment and life imprisonment, Ernest van den Haag says that he doubts "that capital punishment really is more expensive" (33).

The **citation**, the mention of the author's name and the number 33 in parentheses, means that the quoted words come from page 33 of a source (listed in the Works Cited) written by van den Haag. Without a Works Cited list, a reader would have no way of knowing that you are quoting from page 33 of an article that appeared in the February 8, 1985, issue of the *National Review*.

Usually, the parenthetic citation appears at the end of a sentence, as in the example just given, but it can appear elsewhere; its position will depend chiefly on your ear, your eye, and the context. You might, for example, write the sentence thus:

> Ernest van den Haag doubts "that capital punishment really is more expensive" than life imprisonment (33), but other writers have presented figures that contradict him.

Five points must be made about these examples:

1. *Quotation marks* The closing quotation mark appears after the last word of the quotation, not after the parenthetic citation. The punctuation appears after the citation – unless the quotation ends is an exclamation point or a question mark.

2. **Omission of words (ellipsis)** If you are quoting a complete sentence or only a phrase, as in the examples given, you do not need to indicate (by three spaced periods) that you are omitting material before or after the quotation. But if for some reason you want to omit an interior part of the quotation, you must indicate the omission by inserting an ellipsis, the three spaced dots. To take a simple example, if you omit the word "really" from van den Haag's phrase, you must alert the reader to the omission:

> Ernest van den Haag doubts that "capital punishment . . . is more expensive" than life imprisonment (33).

3. **Punctuation with parenthetic citations** In the preceding examples, the punctuation (a period or a comma in the examples) follows the citation. If, however, the quotation ends with a question mark, include the question mark within the quotation, since it is part of the quotation, and put a period after the citation:

> Van den Haag asks, "Isn't it better — more just and more useful — that criminals, if they do not have the certainty of punishment, at least run the risk of suffering it?" (33).

But if the question mark is your own and not in the source, put it after the citation, thus:

> What answer can be given to van den Haag's doubt that "capital punishment really is more expensive" (33)?

4. **Two or more works by an author** If your list of Works Cited includes two or more works by an author, you cannot, in your essay, simply cite a page number — the reader will not know which of the works you are referring to. You must give additional information. You can give it in your lead-in; thus:

> In "New Arguments against Capital Punishment," van den Haag expresses doubt that "capital punishment really is more expensive" than life imprisonment (33).

Or you can give the title, in a shortened form, within the citation:

> Van den Haag expresses doubt that "capital punishment really is more expensive" than life imprisonment ("New Arguments" 33).

5. **Citing even when you do not quote** Even if you don't quote a source directly but instead use its point in a paraphrase or a summary, you will give a citation:

> Van den Haag thinks that life imprisonment costs more than capital punishment (33).

Notice that in all the previous examples, the author's name is given in the text (rather than within the parenthetic citation). But there are several other ways of giving the citation, and we shall look at them now.

AUTHOR AND PAGE NUMBER IN PARENTHESES

> It has been argued that life imprisonment is more costly than capital punishment (van den Haag 33).

AUTHOR, TITLE, AND PAGE NUMBER IN PARENTHESES (MORE THAN ONE WORK BY THE SAME AUTHOR)

Doubt has been expressed that capital punishment is as costly as life imprisonment (van den Haag, "New Arguments" 33).

A GOVERNMENT DOCUMENT OR A WORK OF CORPORATE AUTHORSHIP

The Commission on Food Control, in *Food Resources Today*, concludes that there is no danger (37–38).

A WORK BY TWO AUTHORS

There is not a single example of the phenomenon (Christakis and Fowler 293).

Christakis and Fowler insist there is not a single example of the phenomenon (293).

A WORK BY MORE THAN TWO AUTHORS

If there are *more than two authors*, give the last name of the first author, followed by "and others" or "and colleagues" in the text. In parentheses, use *et al* (an abbreviation for *et alia,* Latin for "and others")

Gittleman and colleagues argue (43) that . . .

On average, the cost is even higher (Gittleman et al. 43).

PARENTHETICAL CITATION OF AN INDIRECT SOURCE (CITATION OF MATERIAL THAT ITSELF WAS QUOTED OR SUMMARIZED IN YOUR SOURCE)

Suppose you're reading a book by Jones in which she quotes Smith and you wish to use Smith's material. Your citation must refer the reader to Jones — the source you're using — but you will have to make it clear that you are quoting Smith. So after a lead-in phrase like "Smith says," followed by the quotation, you will give a parenthetic citation along these lines:

(qtd. in Jones 324-25).

PARENTHETICAL CITATION OF TWO OR MORE WORKS

The costs are simply too high (Jones 28; Smith 301).

AN ANONYMOUS WORK

For an anonymous work, or for a work where the author is unknown, give the title in your lead-in or give it in a shortened form in your parenthetic citation:

A Prisoner's View of Killing includes a poll taken of the inmates on death row (32).

Coca-Cola and other similarly well-known companies often avoid public politics to uphold their images as "emblems of American harmony" ("CEO Activism").

AN INTERVIEW

Vivian Berger, in an interview, said . . .

AN ONLINE SOURCE

Generally, you can use the same formatting of the entries we've discussed so far for an online source. If the source uses pages or breaks down further into numbered paragraphs, chapters, or sections, use an appropriate abbreviation (*par.* or *pars.* for paragraphs, *ch.* or *chs.* for chapters, *sec.* or *secs.* for sections). For audio or video sources, include a timestamp for the quoted material.

As a *Slate* analysis notes, "Prominent sports psychologists get praised for their successes and don't get grief for their failures" (Engber).

The author's son points out that his father and Ralph Waldo Emerson, in their lives and their writing, "together . . . met the needs of nearly all that is worthy in human nature" (Hawthorne, ch. 4).

Kalika Bali explains that as the "digital divide between languages" with and without technological resources grows, "the divide between the communities that speak these languages is expanding" (00:04:40-51).

MLA Format: The List of Works Cited

As the previous pages explain, parenthetic documentation consists of references that become clear when the reader consults the list titled Works Cited at the end of an essay. Here are some general guidelines.

FORM ON THE PAGE

- The list of Works Cited begins on its own page. Continue the pagination of the essay: If the last page of text is 10, then the Works Cited begins on page 11.
- Type the heading *Works Cited* (no italics), centered, one inch from the top, and then double-space and type the first entry.
- Double-space each entry, and double-space between entries.
- Begin each entry flush with the left margin, and indent a half inch for each succeeding line of the entry. This is known as a hanging indent, and you can set most word processors to achieve this formatting easily.
- Italicize titles of works published independently (which the MLA also calls *containers*; see "Containers and Publication Information" on p. 304), such as books, pamphlets, and journals.
- Enclose within quotation marks a work not published independently — for instance, an article in a journal or a short story.

- Arrange the list of sources alphabetically by author, with the author's last name first. For anonymous works, use the title, and slot in your list alphabetically. For works with more than one author, and two or more works by one author, see sample entries that follow. If your list includes two or more works by one author, do not repeat the author's name for the second title; instead represent it by three hyphens followed by a period (---.).

- Anonymous works are listed under the first word of the title or the second word if the first is *A*, *An*, or *The* or a foreign equivalent. We discuss books by more than one author, government documents, and works of corporate authorship in the sample entries in this section.

CONTAINERS AND PUBLICATION INFORMATION

When a source being documented comes from a larger source, the larger source is considered a *container* because it contains the smaller source you are citing. For example, a container might be an anthology, a periodical, a website, a television program, a database, or an online archive. The context of a source will help you determine what counts as a container.

In Works Cited lists, the title of a container is listed after the period following the author's name. The container title is generally italicized and followed by a comma, since the information that follows describes the container. Here are some guidelines:

- Capitalize the first word and the last word of the title.

- Capitalize all nouns, pronouns, verbs, adjectives, adverbs, and subordinating conjunctions (e.g., *although, if, because*).

- Do not capitalize articles (e.g., *a, an, the*), prepositions (e.g., *in, on, toward, under*), coordinating conjunctions (e.g., *and, but, or, for*), or the *to* in infinitives, unless it's the first or last word of the title or the first word of the subtitle.

- Disregard any unusual typography, such as the use of all capital letters or the use of an ampersand (&) for *and*.

- Italicize the container title (and subtitle, if applicable; separate them by a colon), but do not italicize the period that concludes this part of the entry.

When citing a source within a container, the title of the source should be the first element following the author's name. The source title should be set within quotation marks with a period inside the closing quotation mark. The title of the container is then listed, followed by a comma, with additional information — including publication information, dates, and page ranges — about the container, set off by commas.

The following example cites a story, "Achates McNeil," from an anthology — or container — called *After the Plague: Stories*. The anthology was published by Viking Penguin in 2001, and the story appears on pages 82 through 101.

Boyle, T. C. "Achates McNeil." *After the Plague: Stories*, Viking Penguin, 2001, pp. 82-101.

Notice that the full name of the publisher is listed. Always include the full names of publishers except for terms such as "Inc." and "Company"; retain terms such as "Books" and "Publisher." The only exception is university presses, which are abbreviated thus: *Yale UP, U of Chicago P, State U of New York P.*

On the following pages, you will find more specific information for listing different kinds of sources. Although we have covered many kinds of sources, it's entirely possible that you will come across a source that doesn't fit any of the categories that we have discussed. For greater explanations of these matters, covering the proper way to cite all sorts of troublesome and unbelievable (but real) sources, see the *MLA Handbook*, Ninth Edition (2021).

BOOKS

A BOOK BY ONE, TWO, AND MORE AUTHORS

The book is alphabetized under the last name of the first author named on the title page.

Wilkerson, Isabel. *Caste: The Origins of Our Discontents*. Random House, 2020.

If there are *two authors*, the name of the second author is given in the normal order, *first name first, after the first author's name.*

Gilbert, Sandra M., and Susan Gubar. *The Mudwoman in the Attic: The Woman Writer and the Nineteenth-Century Literary Imagination*. Yale UP, 1979.

If there are *more than two authors*, give the name only of the first, followed by a comma, and then add *et al.* (Latin for "and others").

Zumeta, William, et al. *Financing American Higher Education in the Era of Globalization*. Harvard Education Press, 2012.

WORKS OF CORPORATE AUTHORSHIP

Begin the citation with the organization author, even if the same body is also the publisher.

American Psychiatric Association. *Psychiatric Glossary*. American Psychiatric Association, 1984.

Human Rights Watch. *World Report of 2018: Events of 2017*. Seven Stories Press, 2018.

EDITION OTHER THAN THE FIRST

de Mille, Agnes. *Dance to the Piper*. 1951. Introduction by Joan Acocella, New York Review Books, 2015.

Eagleton, Terry. *Literary Theory: An Introduction*. 3rd ed., U of Minnesota P, 2008.

Walker, John A. *Art In the Age of Mass Media*. 3rd ed., Pluto Press, 2001.

A BOOK WITH AN AUTHOR AND AN EDITOR

Kant, Immanuel. *The Philosophy of Kant: Immanuel Kant's Moral and Political Writings*. Edited by Carl J. Friedrich, Modern Library, 1949.

A TRANSLATED BOOK

Ullmann, Regina. *The Country Road: Stories*. Translated by Kurt Beals, New Directions Publishing, 2015.

AN INTRODUCTION, FOREWORD, PREFACE, OR AFTERWORD

If you are referring to the apparatus rather than to the book itself, list by the author of the part. Include the name of the part in the title position; if the part has its own unique title, include that title in quotation marks.

Coates, Ta-Nehisi. Foreword. *The Origin of Others*, by Toni Morrison, Harvard UP, 2017, pp. vii-xvii.

A BOOK WITH AN EDITOR BUT NO AUTHOR

Horner, Avril, and Anne Rowe, editors. *Living on Paper: Letters from Iris Murdoch, 1934-1995*. Princeton UP, 2016.

A WORK WITHIN A VOLUME OF WORKS BY ONE AUTHOR

The following entry indicates that a short work by Susan Sontag, an essay called "The Aesthetics of Silence," appears in a book by Sontag titled *Styles of Radical Will*. Notice that the inclusive page numbers of the short work are cited — not merely page numbers that you may happen to refer to, but the page numbers of the entire piece.

Sontag, Susan. "The Aesthetics of Silence." *Styles of Radical Will*, Farrar, Straus, and Giroux, 1969, pp. 3-34.

A BOOK REVIEW

Walton, James. "Noble, Embattled Souls." *The Bone Clocks and Slade House*, by David Mitchell. *The New York Review of Books*, 3 Dec. 2015, pp. 55-58.

If a review is anonymous, list it under the first word of the title or under the second word if the first is *A*, *An*, or *The*. If a review has no title, begin the entry with *Review of* and then give the title of the work reviewed.

AN ARTICLE OR ESSAY IN A COLLECTION OR ANTHOLOGY

A book may consist of a collection (edited by one or more persons) of essays by several authors. Here, the essay by Sayrafiezadeh occupies pages 3 to 29 in a collection edited by Marcus.

Sayrafiezadeh, Saïd. "Paranoia." *New American Stories*, edited by Ben Marcus, Vintage Books, 2015, pp. 3-29.

MULTIPLE WORKS FROM THE SAME COLLECTION

You may find that you need to cite multiple sources from within a single container, such as several essays from the same edited anthology. In these cases, provide an entry for the entire anthology (the entry for Marcus below) and a shortened entry for each selection. Alphabetize the entries by authors' or editors' last names.

Eisenberg, Deborah. "Some Other, Better Otto." Marcus, pp. 94-136.

Marcus, Ben, editor. *New American Stories*. Vintage Books, 2015.

Sayrafiezadeh, Saïd. "Paranoia." Marcus, pp. 3-29.

ARTICLES IN PERIODICALS

AN ARTICLE IN A REFERENCE WORK (INCLUDING A WIKI)

For a *signed* article, begin with the author's last name. Provide the name of the article, the publication title, edition number and editor(s) (if applicable), the publisher, the copyright year, and the page number (if applicable).

Robinson, Lisa Clayton. "Harlem Writers Guild." *Africana: The Encyclopedia of the African and African American Experience*, edited by Kwame Anthony Appiah and Henry Louis Gates Jr., 2nd ed., Oxford UP, 2005, p. 163.

For an online reference work, such as a wiki, include the author name (if known) and article name followed by the name of the website, the date of publication or the most recent update, and the URL.

"Oligarchy, N." *Merriam-Webster*, 2021, www.merriam-webster.com/dictionary/oligarchy.

"House Music." *Wikipedia*, Wikimedia Foundation, 8 Apr. 2021, en.wikipedia.org/wiki/House_music.

AN ARTICLE IN A SCHOLARLY JOURNAL

The title of the article is enclosed within quotation marks, and the title of the journal is italicized.

Matchie, Thomas. "Law versus Love in the Round House." *Midwest Quarterly*, vol. 56, no. 4, summer 2015, pp. 353-64.

Matchie's article occupies pages 353 to 364 in volume 56, issue number 4, which was published in 2015.

AN ARTICLE IN A MAGAZINE

Misner, Rebecca. "How I Became a Joiner." *Condé Nast Traveler*, vol. 5, 2018, pp. 55-56.

AN ARTICLE IN A NEWSPAPER

Because a newspaper usually consists of several sections, a section number or a capital letter may precede the page number. The example indicates that an article begins on page 1 of section A and continues on nonconsecutive pages.

Corasaniti, Nick, and Jim Rutenberg. "Record Turnout Hints at Future of Vote in U.S." *New York Times*, 6 Dec. 2020, pp. A1+.

AN ARTICLE IN AN ONLINE PERIODICAL

Give the same information as you would for a print article, plus the URL. (See Fig. 8.7.)

Acocella, Joan. "In the Blood." *The New Yorker*, 16 Mar. 2009. www.newyorker.com/magazine/2009 /03/16/in-the-blood.

Figure 8.7   Citing an Online Magazine

1   URL

2   Title of periodical

3   Title of article

4   Author

5   Publication date (If the article doesn't have a publication date, include the date you accessed it.)

AN EDITORIAL OR LETTER TO THE EDITOR

Include the label "Editorial" or "Op-Ed" at the end of the entry (and before any database information) if the author does not make it clear that it's an opinion piece. If a letter does not have a title, include the label "Letter" in place of the title.

Shribman, David M. "Gorman, Summoned to Participate, Is Celebrated." *Pittsburgh Post-Gazette*, 24 Jan. 2021, www.post-gazette.com/opinion/david-shribman/2021/01/24/Gorman-summoned -to-participate-is-celebrated/stories/202101240042. Op-ed.

Carasso, Roger. Letter. *New York Times*, 4 Apr. 2021, Sunday Book Review sec., p. 5.

A DATABASE SOURCE

Treat material obtained from a database like other printed material, but at the end of the entry add (if available) the title of the database (italicized) and a permalink or DOI (digital object identifier) if the source has one, with the protocol (such as *http://*). If a source does not have that information, include a URL (without the protocol).

Coles, Kimberly Anne. "The Matter of Belief in John Donne's Holy Sonnets." *Renaissance Quarterly*, vol. 68, no. 3, fall 2015, pp. 899-931. *JSTOR*, www.jstor.org/stable/10.1086/683855.

Harris, Ashleigh May, and Nicklas Hållén. "African Street Literature: A Method for an Emergent Form beyond World Literature." *Research in African Literatures*, vol. 51, no. 2, summer 2020, pp. 1-26. *JSTOR*, https://doi.org/10.2979/reseafrilite.51.2.01.

GOVERNMENT DOCUMENTS

If the writer is not known, treat the government and the agency as the author.

United States, Department of Agriculture, Food and Nutrition Service, Child Nutrition Programs. *Eligibility Manual for School Meals: Determining and Verifying Eligibility*. July 2015, www.fns.usda.gov/sites/default/files/cn/SP40_CACFP18_SFSP20-2015a1.pdf.

INTERVIEWS

A PUBLISHED OR BROADCAST INTERVIEW

Give the name of the interview subject and the interviewer, followed by the relevant publication or broadcast information, in the following format:

Weddington, Sarah. "Sarah Weddington: Still Arguing for *Roe*." Interview by Michele Kort, *Ms.*, Winter 2013, pp. 32-35.

Tempkin, Ann, and Anne Umland. Interview by Charlie Rose. *Charlie Rose: The Week*, PBS, 9 Oct. 2015.

AN INTERVIEW YOU CONDUCT

Freedman, Sasha. Video interview with the author. 10 Nov. 2020.

Figure 8.8   Citing a Blog

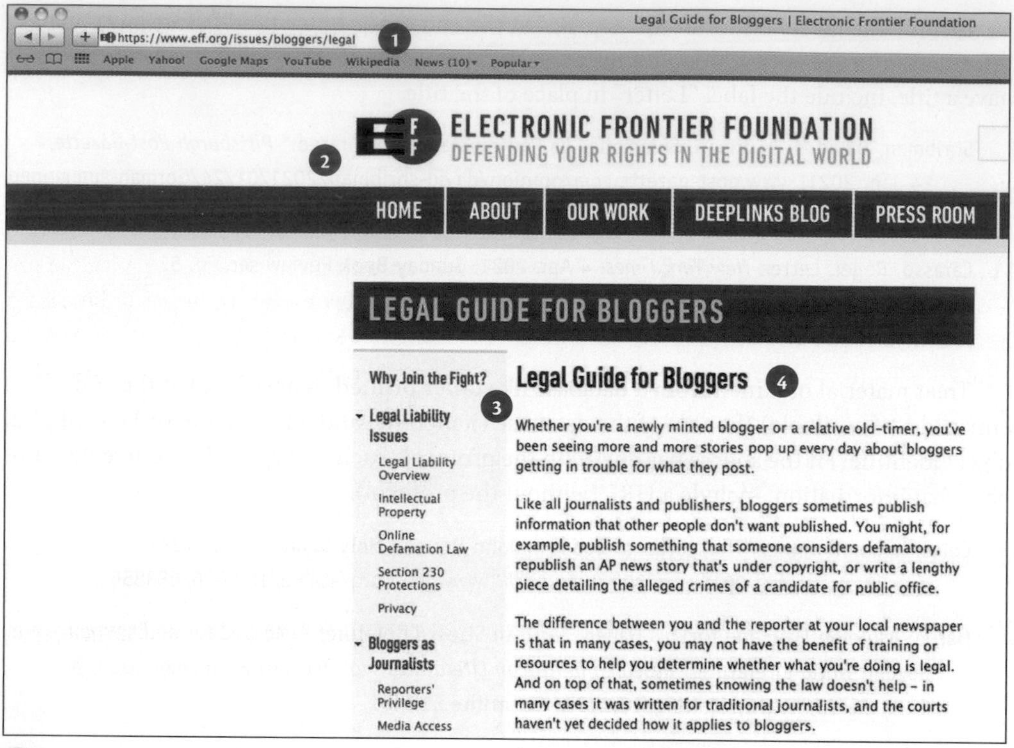

① URL

② Title and sponsor of website

③ No author given; start citation with the title.

④ No date of publication given; include date of access in citation.

ONLINE SOURCES

A WEBSITE AND PARTS OF WEBSITES

Include the following elements: the name of the person who created the site or authored the page (omit if not given, as in Figure 8.8); page title (in quotation marks), if applicable, and site title (italicized); any sponsoring institution or organization (if the title of the site and the sponsor are the same or similar, use the title of the site but omit the sponsor); date of electronic publication or of the latest update (if given; if not, provide the date you accessed the site at the end of the citation); and the URL.

"Legal Guide for Bloggers." *Electronic Frontier Foundation*, www.eff.org/issues/bloggers/legal. Accessed 5 Apr. 2016.

The Newton Project. 2021, www.newtonproject.ox.ac.uk/.

Enzinna, Wes. "Syria's Unknown Revolution." *Pulitzer Center*, 24 Nov. 2015, pulitzercenter.org /projects/middle-east-syria-enzinna-war-rojava.

Kiuchi, Tatsuro. *Tatsuro Kiuchi: News & Blog*. tatsurokiuchi.com. Accessed 3 Mar. 2016.

Ng, Amy. *Pikaland*. 2020, www.pikaland.com.

A SOCIAL MEDIA POST OR COMMENT

If the author's display name is a traditional first and last name, invert it like a standard author name, then include the screen name (if different) in brackets. If there is no display name, include only the screen name. For the title, use quotation marks around the caption of the post; the full text of the post, if it is brief; or the first few words of the post, followed by an ellipsis. If there is no text — or if the focus is on the video or image in the post, not the text — use a description of the photo or video as the title. Follow with the name of the site as the container, the date, and the URL.

ACLU. "Public officials have. . . ." *Facebook*, 10 May 2021, www.facebook.com/aclu
/photos/a.74134381812/10157852911711813.

Jones, James [@notoriouscree]. "Some traditional hoop teachings #indigenous #culture
#native #powwow." *TikTok*, 6 Apr. 2021, www.tiktok.com/@notoriouscree/video
/6948207430610226438.

Rosa, Camila [camixvx]. Illustration of nurses in masks with fists raised. *Instagram*, 28 Apr. 2020,
www.instagram.com/p/B_h62W9pJaQ/.

MULTIMEDIA SOURCES

WORK OF ART (INCLUDING PHOTOGRAPHS)

Bradford, Mark. *Let's Walk to the Middle of the Ocean*. 2015, Museum of Modern Art, New York.

Hura, Sohrab. *Old Man Lighting a Fire*. 2015. *Magnum Photos*, pro.magnumphotos.com
/CS.aspx?VP3=SearchResult&VBID=2K1HZO4JVP42X8&SMLS=1&RW=1280&RH=692.

CARTOON OR COMIC

Zyglis, Adam. "City of Light." *Buffalo News*, 8 Nov. 2015, buffalonews.com/2015/11/08/city-of-light/.

ADVERTISEMENT

Advertisement for Better World Club. *Mother Jones*, Mar.-Apr. 2021, p. 2.

"The Whole Working-from-Home Thing — Apple." *YouTube*, uploaded by Apple, 13 July 2020,
www.youtube.com/watch?v=6_pru8U2RmM.

VISUALS (TABLES, CHARTS, GRAPHICS, ETC.)

Add the type of visual at the end, if it's not obvious from the title or website. This is optional, but good for clarity.

"New COVID-19 Cases Worldwide." *Coronavirus Resource Center*, Johns Hopkins U and Medicine, 3 May 2021, coronavirus.jhu.edu/data/new-cases. Chart.

Brown, Evan. "15 Golden Principles of Visual Hierarchy." *DesignMantic*, 15 Oct. 2014, www .designmantic.com/blog/infographics/15-golden-principles-of-visual-hierarchy. Infographic.

A TELEVISION OR RADIO PROGRAM

Be sure to include the title of the episode or segment (in quotation marks), the title of the show (italicized), the producer or director of the show, the network, and the date of the airing. If the episodes are not individually titled, include the episode and season as the title. Other information, such as performers, narrator, and so forth, may be included if pertinent.

Hillary. Directed by Nanette Burstein, Propagate Content/Hulu, 2020. *Hulu* app.

"Federal Role in Support of Autism." *Washington Journal*, narrated by Robb Harleston, C-SPAN, 1 Dec. 2012.

"Shock and Delight." *Bridgerton*, season 1, episode 2, Shondaland/Netflix, 2020. *Netflix*, www .netflix.com.

PODCAST

Style as you would a television or radio episode or program (above).

Dolly Parton's America. Hosted by Jad Abumrad, produced and reported by Shima Oliaee, WNYC Studios, 2019, www.wnycstudios.org/podcasts/dolly-partons-america.

FILM

Begin with whatever you are emphasizing in your work: entire film (first model), director (second model), and so forth.

Birdman or (The Unexpected Virtue of Ignorance). Directed by Alejandro González Iñárritu, performances by Michael Keaton, Emma Stone, Zach Galifianakis, Edward Norton, and Naomi Watts, Fox Searchlight, 2014.

Kubrick, Stanley, director. *A Clockwork Orange*. Hawk Films/Warner Bros. Pictures, 1971. *Netflix*, www.netflix.com

VIDEO FROM AN ONLINE SOURCE (SUCH AS YOUTUBE)

"The Art of Single Stroke Painting in Japan." *YouTube*, uploaded by National Geographic, 13 July 2018, www.youtube.com/watch?v=g7H8lhGZnpM.

An Annotated Student Research Paper in MLA Format

The following argument makes good use of sources. The document style as well as the citations are in MLA format.

Lesley Timmerman

Professor Jennifer Wilson

English 102

15 August 2019

An Argument for Corporate Responsibility ①

Opponents of corporate social responsibility (CSR) argue that a company's sole duty is to generate profits. According to them, by acting for the public good, corporations are neglecting their primary obligation to make money. However, as people are becoming more and more conscious of corporate impacts on society and the environment, separating profits from company practices and ethics does not make sense. Employees want to work for institutions that share their values, and consumers want to buy products from companies that are making an impact and improving people's lives. Furthermore, businesses exist in an interdependent world where the health of the environment and the well-being of society really do matter. For these reasons, corporations have to take responsibility for their actions, ② beyond making money for shareholders. For their own benefit as well as the public's, companies must strive to be socially responsible.

In his article "The Case against Corporate Social Responsibility," *Wall Street Journal* writer Aneel Karnani argues that CSR will never be able to solve the world's problems. Thinking it can, Karnani says, is a dangerous illusion. He ③ recommends that instead of expecting corporate managers to act in the public interest, we should rely on philanthropy and government regulation. Karnani maintains that "Managers who sacrifice profit for the common good [. . .] are ④ in effect imposing a tax on their shareholders and arbitrarily deciding how that money should be spent." In other words, according to Karnani, corporations should not be determining what constitutes socially responsible behavior; individual donors and the government should. Certainly, individuals should continue to make charitable gifts, and governments should maintain laws and regulations to protect the public interest. However, Karnani's reasoning for why ⑤ corporations should be exempt from social responsibility is flawed. With very few exceptions, corporations' socially responsible actions are not arbitrary and do not sacrifice long-term profits.

⑥

---

1 Title is focused and announces the thesis.

2 Brief statement of one side of the issue.

3 Summary of the opposing view.

4 Lead-in to quotation.

5 Essayist's response to the quotation.

6 1" margin on each side and at bottom.

7 Author concisely states her position.

8 Transitions ("For example," "also") alert readers to where the writer is taking them.

7   In fact, corporations have already proven that they can contribute profitably and meaningfully to solving significant global problems by integrating CSR into their standard practices and long-term visions. Rather than focusing on shareholders' short-term profits, many companies have begun measuring their success by "profit, planet and people"—what is known as the "triple bottom line." Businesses operating under this principle consider their environmental and social impacts, as well as their financial impacts, and

8 make responsible and compassionate decisions. For example, such businesses use resources efficiently, create healthy products, choose suppliers who share their ethics, and improve economic opportunities for people in the communities they serve. By doing so, companies often save money. They also contribute to the sustainability of life on earth and ensure the sustainability of their own businesses. In their book *The Triple Bottom Line: How Today's Best-Run Companies Are Achieving Economic, Social, and Environmental Success*, coauthors Andrew W. Savitz and Karl Weber demonstrate that corporations need to become sustainable, in all ways. They argue that "the only way to succeed in today's interdependent world is to embrace sustainability" (xi). The authors go on to show that, for the vast majority of companies, a broad commitment to sustainability enhances profitability (Savitz and Weber 39).

For example, PepsiCo has been able to meet the financial expectations of its shareholders while demonstrating its commitment to the triple bottom line. In addition to donating over $16 million to help victims of natural disasters, Pepsi has woven concerns for people and for the planet into its company practices and culture (Bejou 4). For instance, because of a recent water shortage in an area of India where Pepsi runs a plant, the company began a project to build community wells (Savitz and Weber 160). Though Pepsi did not cause the water shortage nor was its manufacturing threatened by it, "Pepsi realizes that the well-being of the community is part of the company's responsibility" (Savitz and Weber 161). Ultimately, Pepsi chose to look beyond the goal of maximizing short-term profits. By doing so, the company improved its relationship with this Indian community, improved people's daily lives and opportunities, and improved its own reputation. In other words, Pepsi embraced CSR and ensured a more sustainable future for everyone involved.

Another example of a wide-reaching company that is working toward greater sustainability on all fronts is Walmart. The corporation has issued **9** a CSR policy that includes three ambitious goals: "to be fully supplied by renewable energy, to create zero waste and to sell products that sustain people and the environment" ("From Fringe to Mainstream"). As Dr. Doug Guthrie, dean of George Washington University's School of Business, noted in a recent lecture, if a company as powerful as Walmart were to succeed in these goals, the impact would be huge. To illustrate Walmart's potential influence, Dr. Guthrie pointed out that the corporation's exports from China to the United States are equal to Mexico's total exports to the United States (00:03:15-59). In committing to CSR, the company's leaders are acknowledging how much their power depends on the earth's natural resources, as well as the communities who produce, distribute, sell, and purchase Walmart's products. The company is also well aware that achieving its goals will "ultimately save the company a great deal of money" ("From Fringe to Mainstream"). For good reason, Walmart, like other companies around the world, is choosing to act in *everyone*'s best interest.

Recent research on employees' and consumers' social consciousness offers companies further reason to take corporate responsibility seriously. For example, studies show that workers care about making a difference (Meister). In many cases, workers would even take a pay cut to work for a more responsible, sustainable company. In fact, 45% of workers said they would take a 15% **10** reduction in pay "for a job that makes a social or environmental impact" (Meister). Even more said they would take a 15% cut in pay to work for a company with values that match their own (Meister). The numbers are most significant among Millennials (those born between, approximately, 1980 and the early 2000s). Fully 80% of Millennials said they "wanted to work for a company that cares about how it impacts and contributes to society," and over half said they would not work for an "irresponsible company" (Meister). Given this more socially conscious generation, companies are going to find it harder and harder to ignore CSR. To recruit and retain employees, employers will need to earn the admiration, respect, and loyalty of their workers by becoming "good corporate citizen[s]" (Robert Grosshandler qtd. in "From Fringe to Mainstream").

9 Author provides two examples of forward-thinking moves by major companies.

10 Author now introduces statistical evidence that, if introduced earlier, might have turned the reader off.

Similarly, studies clearly show that CSR matters to today's consumers. According to an independent report, 80% of Americans say they would switch brands to support a social cause (Cone Communications 6). Fully 88% say they approve of companies' using social or environmental issues in their marketing (Cone Communications 5). And 83% say they "wish more of the products, services and retailers would support causes" (Cone Communications 5). Other independent surveys corroborate these results, confirming that today's customers, especially Millennials, care about more than just price ("From Fringe to Mainstream"). Furthermore, plenty of companies have seen what happens when they assume that consumers do not care about CSR. For example, in 1997, when Nike customers discovered that their shoes were manufactured by child laborers in Indonesia, the company took a huge financial hit (Guthrie). Today, Information Age customers are even more likely to educate **11** themselves about companies' labor practices and environmental records. Smart corporations will listen to consumer preferences, provide transparency, and commit to integrating CSR into their long-term business plans.

In this increasingly interdependent world, the case against CSR is becoming more and more difficult to defend. Exempting corporations and relying on government to be the world's conscience does not make good social, environmental, or economic sense. Contributors to a recent article in the online journal *Knowledge@Wharton*, published by the Wharton School of Business, agree. Professor Eric Orts maintains that "it is an outmoded view to say that one must rely only on the government and regulation to police business responsibilities. What we need is re-conception of what the purpose of business is" (qtd. in "From Fringe to Mainstream"). The question is, what should the purpose of a business be in today's world? Professor of Business Administration David Bejou of Elizabeth City State University has a **12** thoughtful and sensible answer to that question. He writes,

13   . . . it is clear that the sole purpose of a business is not merely that of generating profits for its owners. Instead, because compassion provides the necessary equilibrium between a company's purpose and the needs of its communities, it should be the new philosophy of business. (1)

11 Author argues that it is in the *companies'* interest to be socially responsible.

12 Author's lead-in to the quotation guides the reader's response to the quotation.

13 Author uses a block quotation for quotation longer than three lines in text.

As Bejou implies, the days of allowing corporations to act in their own financial self-interest with little or no regard for their effects on others are over. None of us can afford such a narrow view of business. The world is far too interconnected. A seemingly small corporate decision — to buy coffee beans directly from local growers or to install solar panels — can affect the lives and livelihoods of many people and determine the environmental health of whole regions. A business, just like a government or an individual, therefore has an ethical responsibility to act with compassion for the public good.

Fortunately, corporations have many incentives to act responsibly. Customer loyalty, employee satisfaction, overall cost-saving, and long-term viability are just some of the advantages businesses can expect to gain by embracing comprehensive CSR policies. Meanwhile, companies have very little to lose by embracing a socially conscious view. These days, compassion is profitable. Corporations would be wise to recognize the enormous power, opportunity, and responsibility they have to effect positive change.

Works Cited

Bejou, David. "Compassion as the New Philosophy of Business." *Journal of Relationship Marketing,* vol. 10, no. 1, Apr. 2011, pp. 1-6. *Taylor and Francis Online,* https://doi.org/10.1080/15332667.2011.550098.

Cone Communications. *2010 Cause Evolution Study.* Cone Communications, 2010, www.conecomm.com/research-blog/2010-cause-evolution-study.

"From Fringe to Mainstream: Companies Integrate CSR Initiatives into Everyday Business." *Knowledge@Wharton,* Wharton School of the University of Pennsylvania, 23 May 2012, knowledge.wharton.upenn.edu/article/from-fringe-to-mainstream-companies-integrate-csr-initiatives-into-everyday-business/.

Guthrie, Doug. "Corporate Social Responsibility: A State Department Approach." *Promoting a Comprehensive Approach to Corporate Social Responsibility (CSR),* George P. Shultz National Foreign Affairs Training Center, 22 May 2012. *YouTube,* uploaded by Doug Guthrie, 23 Aug. 2013, www.youtube.com/watch?v=99cJMe6wERc.

Karnani, Aneel. "The Case against Corporate Social Responsibility." *The Wall Street Journal,* 14 June 2012, www.wsj.com/articles/SB10001424052748703338004575230112664504890.

Meister, Jeanne. "Corporate Social Responsibility: A Lever for Employee Attraction & Engagement." *Forbes,* 7 June 2012, www.forbes.com/sites/jeannemeister/2012/06/07/corporate-social-responsibility-a-lever-for-employee-attraction-engagement/#6125425a7511.

Savitz, Andrew W., with Karl Weber. *The Triple Bottom Line: How Today's Best-Run Companies Are Achieving Economic, Social, and Environmental Success,* Jossey-Bass, 2006.

14 Works Cited list begins on a new page.

15 Alphabetical by author's last name.

16 Hanging indent ½".

17 An article on a blog without a known author.

18 A clip from YouTube.

APA Format: Citations within the Text

The APA style emphasizes the date of publication; the date appears not only in the list of references at the end of the paper but also in the paper itself, when you give a brief parenthetic citation of a source that you have quoted or summarized or in any other way used. Here is an example:

> Statistics supported the claims (Smith, 1989, p. 20).

The title of Smith's book or article will be given at the end of your paper in the list titled References. We discuss the form of the material listed in the References after we look at some typical citations within the text of a student's essay. Note that all signal phrases should be in past or present perfect tense; thus, "argued" or "has argued," and *not* "argue."

A SUMMARY OF AN ENTIRE WORK

> Smith (1988) held the same view.

> Similar views have been held widely (Smith, 1988; Jones & Metz, 1990).

A REFERENCE TO A PAGE OR TO PAGES

> Lanier (2018) argued that "to free yourself, to be more authentic . . . delete your accounts" (p. 24).

THREE OR MORE AUTHORS

Use the first author's name followed by "et al." (Latin for "and others") in either a signal phrase or a parenthetical citation.

> Examining the lives of women expands our understanding of human development (Belenky et al., 1986).

APA Format: The List of References

Your paper will conclude with a separate page headed References, on which you list all your sources. If the last page of your essay is numbered 10, number the first page of the References 11. Here are some general guidelines.

FORM ON THE PAGE

- Begin each entry flush with the left margin, but if an entry runs to more than one line, indent one-half inch for each succeeding line of the entry.
- Double-space each entry and double-space between entries.

ORDER

- Arrange the list alphabetically by last name of the author (or editor or organization, if identified as the authoring body). If there is no author, alphabetize it by the first word of the title other than "A," "An," or "The."

- Give the author's last name first and then the initial of the first name and of the middle name (if any).

- For two authors, name both of the authors, again inverting the name (last name first) and giving only initials for first and middle names. Use an ampersand (&) before the name of the second author. For example (here, of an article in the tenth volume of a journal called *Developmental Psychology*):

Drabman, R. S., & Thomas, M. H. (1974). Does media violence increase children's tolerance of real-life aggression? *Developmental Psychology, 10*(3), 418-421.

- For three to twenty authors, list each author, last name first, with an ampersand (&) before the last author. For twenty-one or more authors, list the first nineteen followed by three ellipsis dots (. . .) and then the last author.

Wiegand, I., Seidel, C., & Wolf, J.

Sharon, G., Cruz, N. J., Kang, D.-W., Gandal, M. J., Wang, B., Kim, Y.-M., Zink, E. M., Casey, C. P., Taylor, B. C., Lane, C. J., Bramer, L. M., Isern, N. G., Hoyt, D. W., Noecker, C., Sweredoski, M. J., Moradian, A., Borenstein, E., Jansson, J. K., Knight, R., . . . Mazmanian, S. K.

- If you list more than one work by an author, do so in the order of publication, the earliest first. If two works by an author were published in the same year, first list the works that include only the year (e.g., books and journal articles), then alphabetize them by the first letter of the title, disregarding *A*, *An*, or *The*, and a foreign equivalent. Next list works that include a year, month, and day (e.g., newspaper articles), also in alphabetical order. Designate the first work as *a*, the second as *b*, and so forth. Repeat the author's name at the start of each entry.

Donnerstein, E. (1980a). Aggressive erotica and violence against women. *Journal of Personality and Social Psychology, 39*(2), 269-277.

Donnerstein, E. (1980b). Pornography and violence against women. *Annals of the New York Academy of Sciences, 347*(1), 227-288.

Donnerstein, E. (1983). Erotica and human aggression. In R. Green & E. Donnerstein (Eds.), *Aggression: Theoretical and empirical reviews* (pp. 87-103). Academic Press.

FORM OF TITLE

- In references to stand-alone works such a books, websites, or films, capitalize only the first letter of the first word of the title (and of the subtitle, if any) and capitalize proper nouns. Italicize the complete title (but not the period at the end).

- In references to works that are part of a larger whole, such as articles in periodicals or chapters in books, capitalize only the first letter of the first word of the article's title (and subtitle, if any) and all proper nouns. Do not put the title within quotation marks or italicize it. Type a period after the title of the article.

- In references to periodicals, give the volume number in arabic numerals and italicize it. Do not use *vol.* before the number and do not use *p.* or *pg.* before the page numbers.

For a full account of the APA method of dealing with all sorts of unusual citations, see the *Publication Manual of the American Psychological Association*, seventh edition (2020).

BOOKS

A BOOK BY ONE AUTHOR

Treuer, D. (2019). *The heartbeat of Wounded Knee: Native America from 1890 to the present*. Riverhead Books.

A BOOK BY MORE THAN ONE AUTHOR (FROM TWO TO TWENTY)

Belenky, M. F., Clinchy, B. M., Goldberger, N. R., & Torule, J. M. (1986). *Women's ways of knowing: The development of self, voice, and mind*. Basic Books.

A COLLECTION OF ESSAYS

Christ, C. P., & Plaskow, J. (Eds.). (1979). *Woman-spirit rising: A feminist reader in religion*. Harper & Row.

A WORK IN A COLLECTION OF ESSAYS

Fiorenza, E. (1979). Women in the early Christian movement. In C. P. Christ & J. Plaskow (Eds.), *Woman-spirit rising: A feminist reader in religion* (pp. 84-92). Harper & Row.

ARTICLES IN PERIODICALS

AN ARTICLE IN A JOURNAL

Foot, R. J. (1988-89). Nuclear coercion and the ending of the Korean conflict. *International Security, 13*(4), 92-112.

Tversky, A., & Kahneman, D. (1981). The framing of decisions and the psychology of choice. *Science, 211*(4481), 453-458. https://doi.org/10.1126/science.7455683

AN ARTICLE FROM A MAGAZINE

Bensman, D. (2015, December 4). Security for a precarious workforce. *The American Prospect*. http://prospect.org/

Greenwald, J. (1989, February 27). Gimme shelter. *Time, 133*, 50-51.

AN ARTICLE IN A NEWSPAPER

Connell, R. (1989, February 6). Career concerns at heart of 1980s campus protests. *Los Angeles Times*, 1, 3.

Roberson, K. (2015, May 3). Innovation helps address nurse shortage. *Des Moines Register*. http://www.desmoinesregister.com/story/life/living-well/2015/05/03 /innovation-helps-address-nurse-shortage/26328043/

AN ARTICLE FROM A DATABASE

Lyons, M. (2015). Writing upwards: How the weak wrote to the powerful. *Journal of Social History*, *49*(2), 317-330. https://doi.org/10.1093/jsh/shv038

A BOOK REVIEW

Daniels, N. (1984). Understanding physician power [Review of the book *The social transformation of American medicine,* by P. Starr]. *Philosophy and Public Affairs*, *13*(4), 347-356.

Daniels is the reviewer, not the author of the book. The book under review is called *The Social Transformation of American Medicine*, but the review, published in volume 13 of *Philosophy and Public Affairs*, had its own title, "Understanding Physician Power."

If the review does not have a title, retain the square brackets and use the material within as the title. Proceed as in the example just given.

GOVERNMENT PUBLICATIONS

If the author is not known, treat the department or the agency as the author. If a document number has been assigned, insert that number in parentheses between the title and the following period.

Bureau of Economic Analysis. (2015, December). *U.S. international trade in goods and services, October 2015* (Report No. CB15-197, BEA15-60, FT-900 [15-10]). U.S. Census Bureau. http://www.census.gov/foreign-trade/Press-Release/current_press_release/ft900.pdf

ONLINE SOURCES

WEBSITES AND PARTS OF WEBSITES

Most websites and parts of websites can be cited by using another format for a stand-alone work or part of a work. If your source does not fit, you can adapt the model below.

Badrunnesha, M., & Kwauk, C. (2015, December). *Improving the quality of girls' education in madrasa in Bangladesh*. The Brookings Institution. http://www.brookings.edu/research /papers/2015/12/05-bangladesh-girls-education-madrasa-badrunnesha

BLOG POST

Costandi, M. (2015, April 9). Why brain scans aren't always what they seem. *Guardian*.
http://www.theguardian.com/science/neurophilosophy/2015/apr/09/bold-assumptions-fmri

COMMENT ON AN ONLINE ARTICLE

Insert up to twenty words of the comment. Include a direct link to the comment if possible, but if one is not available, link to the article.

lollyl2. (2019, September 25). My husband works in IT in a major city down South. He is a permanent employee now, but for years [Comment on the article "The Google workers who voted to unionize in Pittsburgh are part of tech's huge contractor workforce"]. *Slate*. https://fyre.it/0RT8HmeL.4

A SOCIAL MEDIA POST

Include up to twenty words of the post, counting each emoji as one word. If you cannot insert the emoji, describe the emoji name in brackets: [red heart emoji].

National Science Foundation. (2015, December 8). Simulation shows key to building powerful magnetic fields 1.usa.gov/1TZUiJ6 #supernovas #supercomputers [Tweet]. Twitter. https://twitter.com/NSF/status/674352440582545413

MULTIMEDIA SOURCES

WORK OF ART (INCLUDING PHOTOGRAPHS)

O'Keeffe, G. (1931). *Cow's skull: Red, white, and blue* [Painting]. Metropolitan Museum of Art, New York, NY, United States. https://www.metmuseum.org/art/collection/search/488694

Sabogal, J. (2015). *Los hijos of the Revolution* [Outdoor mural]. San Francisco, CA, United States.

TELEVISION OR RADIO PROGRAM

If referencing the full series, begin with the information following "In."

Oliver, J. (Host), & Leddy, B. (Director). (2015, October 4). Mental health [TV series episode]. In J. Oliver & J. Taylor (Executive Producers), *Last week tonight with John Oliver*. HBO.

PODCAST

If referencing an episode of a podcast, treat it as a selection from an edited book, but include a label for anyone in the "author" position.

Abumrad, J., & Krulwich, R. (Hosts). (2002–present). *Radiolab.* [Audio podcast]. https://www.wnycstudios.org/shows/radiolab/podcasts

DATA SET OR GRAPHIC REPRESENTATION OF DATA (GRAPH, CHART, TABLE)

Gallup. (2015). *Gallup worldwide research data collected from 2005-2018* [Data set]. http://www.gallup.com/services/177797/country-data-set-details.aspx

Economic Research Service. (2015). *USDA expenditures for food and nutrition assistance, FY 1980-2014* [Chart]. U.S. Department of Agriculture. http://www.ers.usda.gov/data-products/chart-gallery/detail.aspx?chartId=40105&ref=collection&embed=True

A VIDEO FROM AN ONLINE SOURCE (SUCH AS YOUTUBE)

Renaud, B., & Renaud, C. (2015, October 8). *Between borders: America's migrant crisis* [Video]. YouTube. https://www.youtube.com/watch?v=rxF0t-SMEXA

A CHECKLIST FOR CRITICAL PAPERS USING SOURCES

❐ Are all borrowed words and ideas credited, including those from internet sources?

❐ Are all summaries and paraphrases acknowledged as such?

❐ Are quotations and summaries not too long?

❐ Are quotations accurate? Are omissions of words indicated by three spaced periods? Are additions of words enclosed within square brackets?

❐ Are quotations provided with helpful lead-ins?

❐ Is documentation in proper form?

Of course, you will also ask yourself the questions that you would ask of a paper that did not use sources, such as

❐ Is the topic sufficiently narrowed?

❐ Is the thesis stated early and clearly, perhaps even in the title?

❐ Is the audience kept in mind? Are opposing views stated fairly and as sympathetically as possible? Are controversial terms defined?

❐ Is the purpose and focus clear (evaluation, recommendation of policy)?

❐ Is evidence (examples, testimony, and statistics) adequate and sound?

❐ Is the organization clear (effective opening, coherent sequence of arguments, unpretentious ending)?

❐ Is the tone appropriate?

❐ Is the title effective?

An Annotated Student Research Paper in APA Format

The following paper is an example of a student paper that uses APA format.

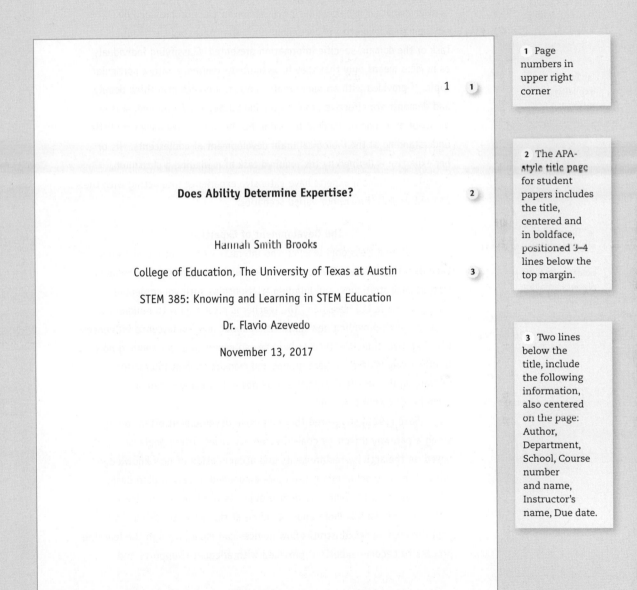

1

Does Ability Determine Expertise?

Hannah Smith Brooks

College of Education, The University of Texas at Austin

STEM 385: Knowing and Learning in STEM Education

Dr. Flavio Azevedo

November 13, 2017

1 Page numbers in upper right corner

2 The APA-style title page for student papers includes the title, centered and in boldface, positioned 3–4 lines below the top margin.

3 Two lines below the title, include the following information, also centered on the page: Author, Department, School, Course number and name, Instructor's name, Due date.

4

5

Does Ability Determine Expertise?

To become an expert requires long-term commitment to the field of study, whether it be calculus or classroom instruction provided by a teacher. Thus, expertise is dependent upon the context of the required task or the domain-specific information presented. Classifying individuals as novices means only that they have limited experience with a particular topic. If provided with an appropriate context, a novice may think deeply and demonstrate effective problem-solving strategies. An individual may be adept at managing student behavior, but he or she may have very little understanding of the biological brain development of adolescents. His or her expertise is defined by the required task of managing a classroom. Importantly, domain experts have extensive experience interacting with the content or skill throughout varied scenarios.

6

The Development of Expertise

Picture a classroom teacher who interacts with groups of students each day. That teacher develops a deep understanding of student behavior, instructional strategies, and building relationships with young people. During a year in the classroom, the teacher is presented with hundreds of students, each providing new information about how adolescence influences learning. Over time, the teacher becomes an expert in understanding how to effectively instruct student groups and manage student interactions, reinforcing the idea that expertise develops out of many different experiences within a domain.

Saxe (1992) suggested that cognitive development often follows along a pathway driven by goal-directed activities. These goals can shift based on the activity requirements and accumulation of new knowledge. Our classroom teacher might use goals embedded in lesson plan design and the building of diverse student groups. As the teacher completes each goal, he or she builds more understanding of the art of teaching. This goal-directed model illustrates how novices can move through the learning process to become experts if provided with adequate supports and scaffolds. Constructivism theorizes that all new learning is built on prior knowledgeand conceptions. Smith, diSessa, and Roschelle (1993/1994) discussed the role of student conceptions in the development of expertise. They argued that more complex cognitive structures must build on existing structures, illustrating how expertise can be developed exclusive of any innate ability. There must be a basic understanding of the foundational concepts in order for knowledge and information to build toward expertise, but these foundational concepts are learned, not inherent.

Many would argue that an individual's natural interests may dictate success across domains. However, interest and expertise may not be directly related. Some argued that all understanding occurs when new information is fully integrated into one's existing cognitive structure (Carey, 1985). Using this definition, interest could be seen as driving an individual to understand and learn more about a particular topic or concept, but does not guarantee integration of information into the cognitive structure. Similarly, while an individual may move through the learning process at a unique speed, the rate of learning does not correlate to an underlying ability to become a "better expert." Individuals are not born with an inherent ability or pre-existing cognitive structure that allows immediate and deep understanding of domain-specific concepts, whether interested or not. In order to become recognized as an expert, the individual must actively build the domain-specific cognitive structure. Expertise is based on area specificity, where novices are only novices based on the contextual environment.

An important factor in the development of expertise is the learning environment in which the individual interacts. Cultural practices, social experiences, and the physical world influence how an individual sees and understands the world. The goal-directed activities mentioned previously are determined by the specific cultural norms and expectations acting in the environment of the individual. In addition, the early interactions of childhood can greatly impact the belief system of a developing student. These influences can shape academic outcomes, but are not based on the inherent ability an individual may or may not be born with.

7 Author and date cited for summary or paraphrase

8 Author raises and refutes well-researched counterarguments.

How Do Experts Differ From Novices?

There are some notable differences between experts and novices, and I would argue that each of the following skills or strategies is based on a repeated set of experiences and interactions with the domain-specific content, not an inherent ability. Goldman and Petrosino (1999) concluded that experts are able to use acquired knowledge of their domain to improve the ability to notice subtle differences and characteristics of presented problems. They went on to suggest that expertise allows an individual to better develop problem-solving strategies and process information using complex creative mental representations. Each of these strategies is based on the continued experience and exposure to content-specific concepts and ideas, not an individual's inherent problem-solving ability. An expert is "not simply [a] 'general problem solver' who [has] learned a set of strategies that operate across all domains" (Bransford et al., 1999, p. 48). I consider myself a very creative problem solver inside the walls of a science classroom. If I was asked to solve for a derivative, I would be hopelessly lost and unable to draw upon my extensive problem-solving experience. As Goldman and Petrosino (1999) stated, a deep domain-specific knowledge does not equate to an individual's general intelligence. Bransford et al. (1999) took this one step further and suggested that specialization within a specific domain actually reduces the amount of general knowledge an individual can hold at any given time.

Conclusion

If provided with the supports and scaffolds to learn the required mathematical processes and calculations, I could grow into an expert within that domain. Successful acquisition of skills or knowledge in either area is based on my desire to improve and learn, not an inherent ability. Expertise arises with extended and extensive study and exposure to a specific area of study or content. While a student may be more interested in science, they are not born with an inherent ability that precedes the learning process. Everyone must learn how to incorporate new ideas, strategies, and skills into a unique cognitive structure that promotes increased understanding of the world around us to become an expert.

9 When author's name appears in text, only the date is cited parenthetically.

10 Bracketed word not in quotation in the original source. Authors (in this case, three), date, and page number are cited for a direct quotation.

11 Conclusion restates and strengthens thesis.

5

References

Bransford, J., Brown A. L., & Cocking, R. R. (1999). How experts differ from novices. In J. D. Bransford, A. L. Brown, & R. R. Cocking (Eds.), *How people learn: Brain, mind, experience, and school*. National Academy Press. https://www.nap.edu/read/9853/chapter/1

Carey, S. (1985). *Conceptual change in childhood*. MIT Press.

Goldman, S., & Petrosino, A. (1999). Design principles for instruction in content domains: Lessons from research on expertise and learning. In F. T. Durso & R. S. Nickerson (Eds.), *Handbook of applied cognition* (pp. 595-627). Wiley.

Saxe, G. B. (1992). Studying children's learning in context: Problems and prospects. *Journal of the Learning Sciences, 2*, 215-234.

Smith, J. P., diSessa, A. A., & Roschelle, J. (1993/1994). Misconceptions reconceived: A constructivist analysis of knowledge in transition. *Journal of the Learning Sciences, 3*, 115-163. https://doi.org/10.1207 /s15327809jls0302_1

12 References begin on new page.

13 A book.

14 An article or a chapter in a book.

15 An article in a journal, retrieved from a database.

Assignment for Using Sources

Write an essay in which you enter a discourse (an ongoing conversation) on a topic and make an argument. To research effectively, you'll need to do the following:

- Narrow your topic sufficiently to make the research manageable.

- Research your topic thoroughly. Find appropriate sources through library or online research (see "Finding Sources," p. 265) or conduct your own primary research (see "Performing Your Own Primary Research," p. 288).

- Evaluate your sources to determine if they are credible, relevant, and appropriate to your argument. (See "Evaluating Sources," p. 272.)

- Take good, thorough notes that you can organize later to form the outline of your paper. Be sure to mark which ideas are your sources' and which are yours during this process. (See "Taking Notes," p. 291.)

When writing your essay, build your argument according to the strategies discussed in Chapter 6. In using sources, be sure to adequately introduce and describe the discourse you're entering: What are people saying about your topic? What "sides" or approaches are there, and who takes them? How will you contribute to the conversation? Support your argument with evidence from your research, making sure to summarize, paraphrase, and quote effectively and ethically, citing your source in the appropriate format (see "Documentation," p. 299). Address counterpositions and counterarguments you find in your sources to show you are aware of the various strains in the discourse, but be sure to return to and support your own argument and claims to persuade your audience of your thesis.

PART THREE

Further Views on Argument

A Philosopher's View: The Toulmin Model

The usual duty of the "intellectual" is to argue for complexity and to insist that phenomena in the world of ideas should not be sloganized or reduced to easily repeated formulae.

— CHRISTOPHER HITCHENS

CONSIDER THIS

Only about 10 percent of any iceberg is visible above the water line, while about 90 percent is hidden beneath the surface. (The density of ice is about 10 percent lower than the density of water.)

Consider for a moment that many claims we encounter in public life appear "on the surface" without revealing full arguments — that is, without obvious reasons, evidence, or consideration of situational factors "underneath" that justify the claim. Such claims may be slogans, catchphrases, or sound bites, or they may be taken-for-granted axioms that commonly go unchallenged. They may even be communicated by a bumper sticker, tattoo, or article of clothing that presents someone's ideas "on the surface" — but what is underneath?

NOAA

You might have heard claims such as "You can't fight City Hall" or seen billboards that read "Pornography Ruins Lives" or "Repent and Save Your Soul." Bumper stickers display messages such as "War Is Not the Answer," "Stop Eating Animals," or "Resist." Other claims may be more subtle:

A T-shirt advertising a band or clothing brand makes an unstated claim about the nature and quality of the product and of the person wearing the shirt. Driving an electric car makes a kind of claim about how to address climate change by reducing CO_2 emissions. These examples are just a few instances in which we encounter *claims without support*.

Choose such a claim — a popular spoken or written claim, or a nonverbal identifier — and consider it the "tip" of an iceberg.

Dive under the surface. Show the ideas or evidence that are beneath the claim. The claim "You can't fight City Hall" is built on the idea that it is futile to resist government rules, policies, and practices. The evidence for this could be instances in which efforts to work through channels of government were thwarted or delayed by elaborate, time-consuming processes. The claim is based on assumptions that large and unwieldy institutions are implacable and unchangeable. However, other examples could also show that the message is not always true, that you CAN "fight City Hall" even if it might take dedication, patience, grass-roots activism, or other kinds of actions.

Answer questions like these: What is the **purpose** of the message? How does it convince or fail to convince? What **beliefs** or **assumptions** are reflected in it? What **reasons** support a belief? What is the strongest argument against the message, and how would you respond to it?

This exercise is intended to get you thinking about the reasons that underlie claims. Unlike the kinds of claims you worked with in the opening activity, written arguments must be justified and supported explicitly with information and evidence. They must be contextualized and compared to other arguments, and they must be presented confidently yet also in a way that recognizes exceptions and extenuating circumstances.

Understanding the Toulmin Model

As we begin examining the Toulmin model of understanding arguments, we mean to emphasize the dimensions of support that undergird arguments.

We use the vocabulary popularized by Stephen Toulmin, Richard Rieke, and Allan Janik in their book *An Introduction to Reasoning* (1979) to explore the various elements of argument. Once these elements are understood, it is possible to analyze an argument using their approach and their vocabulary in what has come to be known as the Toulmin method.

The major components of arguments using this model are laid out in the Visual Guide to the Toulmin Method (p. 335), and we go into more detail about each of them throughout this chapter.

Visual Guide: The Toulmin Method

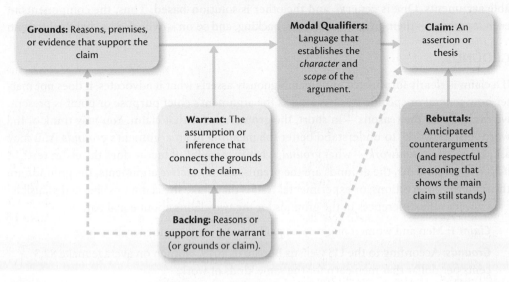

Grounds: Reasons, premises, or evidence that support the claim

Modal Qualifiers: Language that establishes the *character* and *scope* of the argument.

Claim: An assertion or thesis

Warrant: The assumption or inference that connects the grounds to the claim.

Rebuttals: Anticipated counterarguments (and respectful reasoning that shows the main claim still stands)

Backing: Reasons or support for the warrant (or grounds or claim).

Components of the Toulmin Model

THE CLAIM

Every argument has a purpose, goal, or aim — namely, to establish a **claim** (*conclusion* or *thesis*). Claims may be general or specific. As we have noted in earlier chapters, arguments may attempt to persuade readers simply to change an opinion or adopt a belief, or they may advocate for some action or seek to convince people to take some action. In other words, the *claim* being made in an argument is the whole point of making the argument in the first place. Consequently, when you read or analyze an argument, the first questions you should ask are these:

1. What is the argument intending to prove or establish?
2. What claim is it making?

Different types of claims will lead to different types of grounds, warrants, and backing and to different types of qualifiers and rebuttals.

Suppose that you are arguing in a very general sense that men and women should receive equal pay for equal work. You might state your thesis or claim as follows:

Men and women ought to be paid equally for the same kinds of jobs.

A more specific and precise claim might be the following:

The Equal Pay Act of 1963 should be strengthened in order to guarantee that men and women are paid equally for the same kinds of jobs.

Both formulations are arguments with strong claims. They make similar but still distinguishable arguments. One is general, and the other is solution-based. Thus, the components of each argument — their grounds, warrants, backing, and so on — will also be slightly different.

GROUNDS

If a claim is clearly formulated and unambiguously asserts what it advocates, it does not matter how general or specific it is. As long as the argument's chief purpose or point is present, we can look for the reasons — in short, the **grounds** — for that claim. You may think of the word "groundwork" to understand better the meaning of an argument's *grounds*. You may ask, On what *groundwork* — what *ground*, what firmament of fact — does the claim rest? In *deductive* arguments, the grounds are the premises; in *inductive* arguments, the grounds are the samples, observations, or experimental results that make the claim possible and plausible.

Consider the differences in the grounds for the two claims about equal pay.

Claim 1: Men and women ought to be paid equally for the same kinds of jobs.

Grounds: According to the US Census Bureau in 2019, women on average make 82.3 cents per dollar that men earn for the same kinds of work.

Claim 2: The Equal Pay Act of 1963 should be strengthened in order to guarantee that men and women are paid equally for the same kinds of jobs.

Grounds: The Equal Pay Act was passed in 1963 to eliminate the gender pay gap. Because women still less money than men for the same kinds of work, the Equal Pay Act has not been effective.

But something is missing. We have provided the grounds and claim, but neither explains the reasoning nor justifications that connects them. That women earn less money for similar work doesn't in and of itself justify the claim that pay should be equal among the sexes. One might simply counter that, no, women *should* make less money than men (and with only grounds and a claim you could not effectively argue back). Your opponent's argument might look like this:

Claim: Women and men get paid exactly what they deserve.

Grounds: According to the US Census Bureau in 2019, women on average make 82.3 cents per dollar that men earn for the same kinds of work.

The grounds here are the same as in the argument against pay inequity. Thus, good arguments exhibit — and require — another feature that connects the claim and the grounds: the *warrant*.

WARRANTS

Once we have determined the claim of an argument and have isolated the grounds for its existence, the next question to ask is what **warrants** it? That is, what reasoning justifies the connection between the claim and grounds, or *why does the claim arise from the grounds*? The grounds can be used to shore up all kinds of arguments, so what is it *exactly* that warrants the claim?

The word "warrant" is related to the Old French word "*gurant*," the root word of "guarantee." A warrant in this context is like the *warranty* you get when you buy something. It guarantees it. With an argument, you might ask what *guarantees* that a rational claim may arise given these grounds. What reasons could be proffered to justify the claim? Warrants help establish the *connections* between the claim and the grounds.

Imagine you establish your grounds (the existence of the pay gap). Then you claim that women and men should be paid equally for similar work. Someone might ask you: *Why* should women and men get equivalent pay for the same kinds of jobs? So you offer something such as:

> We live in a society where it is illegal and wrong to discriminate based on sex, and unequal pay based on sex is discriminatory.

In this case, your warrant is a legal and moral proposition about equality that connects the claim and grounds. (Part of your warrant, too, is that the US Census Bureau numbers are reliable.) Warrants are *interpretations* of how the data and the arguments stemming from them are inherently related.

In ordinary and straightforward *deductive* arguments, warrants may be quite simple. If John is six feet tall and Mary is five feet tall, you have the grounds to argue that John is taller than Mary. The warrant here is just a matter of language: "Taller than" means exceeding something in a measurement of height, so the warrant is "People are said to be taller than other people when they exceed them in measurements of height." The *warrant* is the common understanding of what the phrase "taller than" means.

In ordinary *inductive* arguments, we are likely to point to the way in which observations or data constitute a *representative sample*. When Anne McKee, a neuropathologist, examined the brains of 110 deceased professional football players and found that 99 percent of them showed signs of chronic traumatic encephalopathy (CTE), she claimed that playing professional football increases the likelihood of brain damage. Her warrant was the reasoning about such a high percentage of her sample showing signs of CTE — that one (football) caused the other (CTE); the warrant is the logic that connected her grounds and her claim.

Establishing the warrants for our reasoning can be a highly technical and exacting procedure when we are making complex, ambiguous, or values-based claims — that is, when we are explaining why our grounds really do support our claims about why something is right or wrong, moral or immoral, just or unjust. "That's just the way I feel" is not a convincing warrant for any argument.

BACKING

Warrants explain why our *grounds* support our *claims*. The next task is to be able to show that our warrants are good, reasonable, or rational. To establish that, further support is provided by **backing**.

What is appropriate backing for one kind of argument might be quite inappropriate for another kind of argument. For example, the reasons to support the warrant that men and women should be paid equally may be completely different from the reasons used to justify the claim that the Equal Pay Act should be amended. For the first argument, you might draw upon political documents, speeches, and other evidence showing that gender equality is a value and priority. For the second argument, that the Equal Pay Act needs strengthening, your backing might consist of arguments about that piece of legislation specifically — theories and illustrations about what makes good, effective, and practical policy, for example.

Your backing explains why your reasons are good reasons — telling why anyone should believe your reasons rather than not. They have to be the right *kinds* of reasons given the field you are arguing about. A claim about the constitutionality of corporate personhood (in which corporations are regarded legally as sharing rights and responsibilities of natural persons) would have to be rationalized using backing that would look quite different from the backing required to settle the question of what motivated Chinese people to immigrate to the United States in the nineteenth century. The *canons* (the established conventions, rules, laws, principles, and important texts) of two scholarly communities in law and history, respectively, developed differently over the years to justify, support, defend, and challenge ideas in those areas of discourse differently.

Why (to give a simple example) should we accept the testimony of Dr. *X* when Dr. *Y*, equally renowned, supports the opposite side? What more do we need to know about "expert testimony" before it can be believably invoked? Consider a different kind of case: When and why is it safe to rest a prediction on a small — although admittedly carefully selected — sample? Anne McKee, the researcher who studied the brains of professional football players, has been criticized for examining only *donated* brains, suggesting that those players or their families suspected CTE in the first place. Why is it legitimate to argue that smoking cigarettes indoors is not appropriate? You might say, "It's bad for everyone," but what evidence explains your thinking?

To answer questions of these sorts is to support your reasons and to give them legitimate *backing*. No argument is any better than its backing.

MODAL QUALIFIERS

As we have seen, all arguments are made up of assertions or propositions that can be sorted into four categories:

- *claims* (theses to be established)
- *grounds* (explicit reasons advanced)
- *warrants* (guarantees, evidence, or principles that connect grounds and claims)
- *backing* (relevant support)

All the kinds of propositions that emerge when we assert something in an argument have what philosophers call a **modality**. In other words, propositions generally indicate — explicitly or tacitly — the *character* and *scope* of what is believed to be their likely truth.

CHARACTER **Character** has to do with the nature of the claim being made, the extent of an argument's presumed reach. Both making and evaluating arguments require being clear about whether they are

- *necessary,*
- *probable,*
- *plausible,* or
- *possible.*

Consider, for example, a claim that it is to the advantage of a college to have a racially diverse student body. Is that *necessarily* true or only *probably* true? What about an argument that a runner who easily wins a 100-meter race should also be able to win a 200-meter race? Is that *plausible*, or is it only *possible*? Indicating the *character* with which an assertion is advanced is crucial to any argument for or against it. Furthermore, if there is more than one reason for making a claim and all those reasons are good, it is still possible that one of those good reasons may be *better* than the others. If so, the better reason should be stressed.

SCOPE   Indicating the **scope** of an assertion is equally crucial to how an argument plays out. *Scope* entails such considerations as whether the proposition is thought to be true *always* or just *sometimes*. Further, is the claim being made supposed to apply in *all* instances or just in *some*? Assertions are usually clearer, as well as more likely to be true, if they are explicitly *quantified* and *qualified*. Suppose, for example, you are arguing against smoking, and the ground for your claim is this:

> Heavy smokers cut short their life span.

In this case, there are three obvious alternative quantifications to choose among: *All* smokers cut short their life span, *most* do, or only *some* do. Until the assertion is quantified in one of these ways, we really don't know what is being asserted, and so we don't know what degree and kind of evidence or counterevidence is relevant. Other quantifiers include *few, rarely, often, sometimes, perhaps, usually, more or less, regularly*, and *occasionally*.

Scope also reflects that empirical generalizations are typically **contingent** on various factors. Indicating such contingencies clearly is an important way to protect a generalization against obvious counterexamples. Thus, consider this empirical generalization:

> Students do best on final examinations if they study hard for them.

Are we really to believe that students who cram ("study hard" in that concentrated sense) for an exam will do better than those who do the work diligently throughout the whole course ("study hard" in that broader sense) and therefore do not need to cram for the final? Probably not; what is really meant is that, *all other things being equal* (in Latin, *ceteris paribus*), concentrated study just before an exam will yield good results. Alluding in this way to the contingencies — the things that might derail the argument — shows that the writer is aware of possible exceptions and is conceding them from the start.

In sum, sensitivity to both character and (especially) scope — paying attention to the role played by quantifiers, qualifiers, and contingencies and making sure you use appropriate ones for each of your assertions — will strengthen your arguments enormously. Not least of the benefits is that you will reduce the peculiar vulnerabilities of an argument that is undermined by exaggeration and other misguided generalizations.

REBUTTALS

Very few arguments of any interest are beyond dispute, conclusively knockdown affairs. Only very rarely is the claim of an argument so rigidly tied to its grounds, warrants, and backing — and with its quantifiers and qualifiers argued in so precise a manner — that it proves its conclusion beyond any possibility of doubt. On the contrary, most arguments have many counterarguments, and sometimes one of these counterarguments is more convincing than the original argument. When writers raise counterarguments, they build their *ethos* and assure readers that other views are taken seriously; however, those counterarguments should not be raised simply to challenge your own position. If you indeed believe in your position, you can offer a **rebuttal** to the counterargument — telling your readers where it succeeds, perhaps, but also where it fails (thus implying or stating that your position is more convincing).

Suppose someone has taken a sample that appears to be random: An interviewer on your campus approaches the first ten students they encounter, and seven of the students are fraternity or sorority members. The pollster is now ready to argue that seven-tenths of enrolled students belong to Greek organizations. You point out that the interviews occurred around the corner from the Panhellenic Society's office just off Sorority Row. The random sample is anything but random. The ball is now back in the pollster's court as you await their response to your rebuttal.

As this example illustrates, it is safe to say that we do not understand our own arguments very well until we have tried to get a grip on the places in which they are vulnerable to criticism, counterattack, or refutation. As Edmund Burke astutely observed, "He that wrestles with us strengthens our nerves, and sharpens our skill. Our antagonist is our helper."

THINKING CRITICALLY *Constructing a Toulmin Argument*

STEP OF TOULMIN ARGUMENT	QUESTION THIS STEP ADDRESSES	YOUR SENTENCES
Claim	*What is your argument?*	
Grounds	*What is your evidence?*	
Warrant	*What reasoning connects your evidence to your argument?*	
Backing	*What can you provide as support to convince the reader to agree with your grounds, claims, and warrants?*	
Qualifier	*What are the limits of your argument?*	
Rebuttal	*What are the objections to your argument — and can you reason that your argument still holds?*	

Putting the Toulmin Method to Work: Responding to an Argument

Let's take a look at another argument — on why we must act to save the planet — and see how the Toulmin method can be applied. The Checklist for Using the Toulmin Method (p. 347) can help you focus your thoughts as you read.

JONATHAN SAFRAN FOER

Jonathan Safran Foer is a novelist and nonfiction writer. His works of fiction, including *Everything Is Illuminated* (2002), *Extremely Loud and Incredibly Close* (2005), and *Here I Am* (2016), have earned him literary acclaim and awards such as the Guardian First Book Prize and the National Jewish Book Award. Foer holds a degree in philosophy from Princeton University, where he formed an ethical framework for his two nonfiction books, *Eating Animals* (2009) and *We Are the Weather: How Saving the Planet Begins at Breakfast* (2019), both of which provide philosophical rationales for ethical and environmentally conscious meat-eating. The essay, "Show Your Hands," here is from Foer's book *We Are the Weather*.

Show Your Hands: Saving the Planet Begins at Breakfast

This is a book about the impacts of animal agriculture on the environment. Yet I have managed to conceal that for the previous sixty-three pages. I have navigated away from the subject for the same reasons that Gore and others have: fear that it is a losing hand. I evaded even while I was critiquing Gore[1] for his evasion — I never mentioned what he never mentions. I felt sure, as Gore must have, that it was the right strategy. Conversations about meat, dairy, and eggs make people defensive. They make people annoyed. No one who isn't a vegan is eager to go there, and the eagerness of vegans can be a further turnoff. But we have no hope of tackling climate change if we can't speak honestly about what

is causing it, as well as our potential, and our limits, to change in response. Sometimes a fist needs the word "fist" written across it, so I'll name it now: we cannot save the planet unless we significantly reduce our consumption of animal products.

This book is an argument for a collective act to eat differently — specifically, no animal products before dinner. That is a difficult argument to make, both because the topic is so fraught and because of the sacrifice involved. Most people like the smell and taste of meat, dairy, and eggs. Most people value the roles animal products play in their lives and aren't prepared to adopt new eating identities. Most people have eaten animal products at almost every meal since they were children, and it's hard to change lifelong habits, even when they aren't freighted with pleasure and identity. Those are meaningful challenges, not only worth acknowledging but necessary to acknowledge.

---

[1] **Al Gore** American politician who served with as the 45th Vice President of the United States under President Bill Clinton and environmentalist who was the subject of the climate change documentary *An Inconvenient Truth* (2007), which won the Academy Award for Best Documentary Feature. [Editors' note]

Changing the way we eat is simple compared with converting the world's power grid, or overcoming the influence of powerful lobbyists to pass carbon-tax legislation, or ratifying a significant international treaty on greenhouse gas emissions — but it isn't simple.

In my early thirties, I spent three years researching factory farming and wrote a book-length rejection of it called *Eating Animals*. I then spent nearly two years giving hundreds of readings, lectures, and interviews on the subject, making the case that factory-farmed meat should not be eaten. So it would be far easier for me not to mention that in difficult periods over the past couple of years — while going through some painful personal passages, while traveling the country to promote a novel when I was least suited for self-promotion — I ate meat a number of times. Usually burgers. Often at airports. Which is to say, meat from precisely the kinds of farms I argued most strongly against. And my reason for doing so makes my hypocrisy even more pathetic: they brought me comfort. I can imagine this confession eliciting some ironic comments and eye-rolling, and some giddy accusations of fraudulence. Other readers may find it genuinely disturbing — I wrote at length, and passionately, about how factory farming tortures animals and destroys the environment. How could I argue for radical change, how could I raise my children as vegetarians, while eating meat *for comfort*?

I wish I had found comfort elsewhere — in something that would have provided it in a lasting way and that wasn't anathema to my convictions — but I am who I am, and I did what I did. Even while I was working on this book, and having my commitment to vegetarianism — which had been driven by the issue of animal welfare — deepened by a full awareness of meat's environmental toll, rarely a day has passed when I haven't craved it. At times I've wondered if my strengthening intellectual rejection of it has fueled a strengthening desire to consume it. Whatever the case, I've had to come to terms with the fact that while actions might be at least somewhat responsive to will, cravings aren't. I have felt a version of Felix Frankfurter's knowledge-without-belief, and that has led me to some real struggling, and at times to extreme hypocrisy. I find it almost unbearably embarrassing to share this. But it needs to be shared.

While I was promoting *Eating Animals*, 5 people frequently asked me why I wasn't vegan. The animal welfare and environmental arguments against dairy and eggs are the same as those against meat, and often stronger. Sometimes I would hide behind the challenges of cooking for two finicky children. Sometimes I would bend the truth and describe myself as "effectively vegan." In fact, I had no answer, other than the one that felt too shameful to voice: my desire to eat cheese and eggs was stronger than my commitment to preventing cruelty to animals and the destruction of the environment. I found some relief from that tension by telling other people to do what I couldn't do myself.

Confronting my hypocrisy has reminded me how difficult it is to live — even to try to live — with open eyes. Knowing that it will be tough helps make the efforts possible. *Efforts*, not effort. I cannot imagine a future in which I decide to become a meat-eater again, but I cannot imagine a future in which I don't want to eat meat. Eating consciously will be one of the struggles that span and define my life. I understand that struggle not as an expression of my uncertainty about the right way to eat, but as a function of the complexity of eating.

We do not simply feed our bellies, and we do not simply modify our appetites in response to principles. We eat to satisfy primitive cravings, to forge and express ourselves, to realize community. We eat with our mouths and stomachs, but also with our minds and hearts. All my different identities — father, son, American, New Yorker, progressive, Jew, writer, environmentalist, traveler, hedonist — are present when I eat, and so is my history. When I first chose to become vegetarian, as a nine-year-old, my motivation was simple: do not hurt animals. Over the years, my motivations changed — because the available information changed, but more importantly, because my life changed. As I imagine is the case for most people, aging has proliferated my identities. Time softens ethical binaries and fosters a greater appreciation of what might be called the messiness of life.

If I'd read the previous sentences in high school, I'd have dismissed them as a bursting sack of self-serving bullshit — *messiness of life?* — and been deeply disappointed by the flimsy person I was to become. I'm glad that I was who I was then, and I hope that other young people have the same inflexible idealism. But I'm glad that I am who I am now, not because it is easier but because it is in better dialogue with my world, which is different from the world I occupied twenty-five years ago.

There is a place at which one's personal business and the business of being one of seven billion earthlings intersect. And for perhaps the first moment in history, the expression "one's time" makes little sense. Climate change is not a jigsaw puzzle on the coffee table, which can be returned to when the schedule allows and the feeling inspires. It is a house on fire. The longer we fail to take care of it, the harder it becomes to take care of, and because of positive feedback loops — white ice melting to dark water that absorbs more heat; thawing permafrost releasing huge amounts of methane, one of the worst greenhouse gases — we will very soon reach a tipping point of "runaway climate change," when we will be unable to save ourselves, no matter our efforts.

We do not have the luxury of living in our time. We cannot go about our lives as if they were only ours. In a way that was not true for our ancestors, the lives we live will create a future that cannot be undone. Imagine if history were such that if Lincoln hadn't abolished slavery in 1863, then America would be condemned to uphold the institution of slavery for the rest of time. Imagine if the right of two people of the same sex to marry depended entirely and eternally on Obama's conversion in 2012. When speaking about moral progress, Obama often quoted Martin Luther King's statement that "the arc of the moral universe is long, but it bends toward justice." In this unprecedented moment, the arc could irreparably snap.

There are several pivotal moments in the Bible when God asks people where they are. The two most cited instances are when he finds Adam hiding after eating the forbidden fruit and says "Where are you?," and when he calls to Abraham before asking him to sacrifice his only son. Clearly an omniscient God knows where his creations are. His questions are not about the location of a body in space but about the location of a self within a person.

We have our own modern version of this. When we think back on moments when history seemed to happen before our eyes — Pearl Harbor, the assassination of John F. Kennedy, the fall of the Berlin Wall, September 11 — our reflex is to ask others where they were when it happened. Yet as with God in the Bible, we are not really trying to establish someone's coordinates. We are asking something deeper about their connection to the moment, with the hope of situating our own.

The word "crisis" derives from the Greek *krisis*, meaning "decision."

The environmental crisis, though a universal experience, doesn't feel like an event that we are a part of. It doesn't feel like an event at all. And despite the trauma of a hurricane, wildfire, famine, or extinction, it's unlikely that a weather event will inspire a "Where were you when . . ." question of anyone who didn't live through it — perhaps not even of those who did live through it. It's all just weather. Just environmental.

But future generations will almost cer- 15 tainly look back and wonder where we were in the biblical sense: Where was our selfhood? What decisions did the crisis inspire? Why on earth — why on *Earth* — did we choose our suicide and their sacrifice?

Perhaps we could plead that the decision wasn't ours to make: as much as we cared, there was nothing we could do. We didn't know enough at the time. Being mere individuals, we didn't have the means to enact consequential change. We didn't run the oil companies. We weren't making government policy. Perhaps we could argue, as Roy Scranton does in his *New York Times* essay "Raising My Child in a Doomed World," that "we [were] not free to choose how we live[d] any more than we [were] free to break the laws of physics." The ability to save ourselves, and save them, was not in our hands.

But that would be a lie.

While information is not sufficient — without belief, knowing is *only knowing* — it is necessary for making a good decision. Awareness of Nazi atrocities didn't shake Felix Frankfurter's conscience, but without that awareness, he would have no reason to be asked, or to ask himself, "Where are you?" Knowing is the difference between a grave error and an unforgivable crime.

With respect to climate change, we have been relying on dangerously incorrect information. Our attention has been fixed on fossil fuels, which has given us an incomplete picture of the planetary crisis and led us to feel that we are hurling rocks at a Goliath far out of reach. Even if they are not persuasive enough on their own to change our behavior, facts can change our minds, and that's where we need to begin. We know we have to do something, but *we have to do something* is usually an expression of incapacitation, or at least uncertainty. Without identifying the thing that we have to do, we cannot decide to do it.

The next section of this book will correct the 20 picture by explaining the connection between animal agriculture and climate change. I have condensed what could have been several hundred pages of prose into a handful of the most essential facts. And I have not included important complementary narratives — the other kinds of destruction factory farming wreaks on the environment, like water pollution, ocean dead zones, and loss of biodiversity; the cruelty that is fundamental to contemporary animal agriculture; the health and societal effects of eating unprecedentedly large amounts of meat, dairy, and eggs. This book is not a comprehensive explanation of climate change, and it is not a categorical case against eating animal products. It is an exploration of a decision that our planetary crisis requires us to make.

The word "decision" derives from the Latin *decidere*, which means "to cut off." When we decide to turn off the lights during a war, refuse to move to the back of the bus, flee our shtetl with our sister's shoes, lift a car off a trapped person, make way for an ambulance, drive home through the night from Detroit, rise for a wave, take a selfie, participate in a medical trial, attend a Thanksgiving meal, plant a tree, wait in line to vote, or eat a meal that reflects our values, we are also deciding to cut off the possible worlds in which we don't do those things. Every decision requires loss, not only of what we might have done otherwise but of the world to which our alternative action would have contributed. Often that loss feels too small to notice; sometimes it feels too large to bear. Usually, we just don't think about our decisions in those terms. We live in a culture of historically unprecedented acquisition, which so often asks us and enables us to attain. We are prompted to define ourselves by what we have: possessions, dollars, views, and likes. But we are revealed by what we release.

Climate change is the greatest crisis humankind has ever faced, and it is a crisis that will always be simultaneously addressed together and faced alone. We cannot keep the kinds of meals we have known and also keep the planet we have known. We must either let some eating habits go or let the planet go. It is that straightforward, that fraught.

Where were you when you made your decision?

Thinking with the Toulmin Model

Remember to make use of the Visual Guide: The Toulmin Method (p. 335) as you work to find the claim(s), grounds, and warrant(s) that Foer puts forward in this selection.

1. What **claim** is the author making? Is it in the title? Is it in the opening sentence? Or is it buried in the first paragraph? Or is it located elsewhere?

Foer hints at his thesis in the book's subtitle, "How Saving the Planet Begins at Breakfast," even though this obscures what might be done specifically at breakfast to save the planet. We are assured that it is *something*, however. Early on, Foer says explicitly that his work is "an argument for a collective act to eat differently — specifically, no animal products before dinner" (para. 2). Of course, this is a way of speaking (it wouldn't logically matter to the argument if you ate meat at breakfast but not at dinner instead). If you read the entire essay, you see that Foer's real argument is to encourage conscious consumption of animal products at any time of day as a place to start "saving the planet." Taking the plunge — making the decision to do something immediate about the environmental crisis instead of claiming helplessness — is something many people struggle with. How would you state this claim?

2. What are the **grounds**, the evidence or reasons, that the author advances in support of his claim?

As it turns out, Foer does not spend a lot of time spelling out evidence that factory farming is bad for the environment, and he doesn't cite clear evidence until almost the end of the essay. However, we see no data or statistics backing these claims (although Foer does say that such evidence could fill hundreds of pages). He also lists some additional consequences of factory farming, such as its impact on water quality, animal cruelty, and human health. This brings us once again to the more subtle argument Foer makes in this essay. Examined closely, this is really an argument that people need to take some action related to their meat-heavy diets: "We must either let some eating habits go or let the planet go" (para. 22). Because Foer spends more time discussing how and why to make a difficult but pivotal decision — the self-conscious, ethically driven decision to modify individual dietary practices for the collective good — the grounds supporting the claim that factory farming damages the environment perhaps do not need to be very specific, and perhaps we can wait for the proof he assures us he will present later. Should Foer have provided more evidence in this section? Or is it enough for him to promise that his forthcoming evidence will summarize what "could have been several hundred pages of prose" (para. 20)?

Can you find any information about the environmental impact of factory farming? If you could add some of that information as grounds in this piece, where would you include it?

3. What **warrants** does Foer offer to connect his grounds to his overall claim that people should reduce or stop eating animal products? Why we should accept his grounds? What authority does he cite? How effective and convincing is this way of trying to get us to accept the grounds offered in support of the claim?

Warrants connect the grounds to the claim. If Foer's claim is that we should eat fewer animal products and choose carefully the ones we do eat, and his grounds state that factory farming damages the environment, then the warrants could be that we have a shared responsibility for the future of the planet, a personal responsibility to recognize the difference between not knowing and not caring, and an ethical responsibility to take a stand by making the decision — however difficult it is for some omnivores.

The essence of the Toulmin method lies in these three elements: the claim(s), the grounds, and the warrant(s). If you have extracted these from Foer's essay, you are well on the way to being able to identify the argument he is putting forward. So far, so good. Further probing, however — looking for the other three elements of the Toulmin method (the backing, the modal qualifiers and quantifiers, and the rebuttal) — is essential before you are in a position to actually evaluate the argument. So let's go on.

4. What **backing** does Foer provide? What reasons does he give that might persuade us to accept his argument?

We already know that Foer's grounds about factory farming's impact are sparse although they promise much. What backs them would be the hard evidence. The backing provided in the argument that we need to act now is drawn from references to Felix Frankfurter's inability to believe stories of Nazi atrocities and the implications of his response: "Knowing is the difference between a grave error and an unforgivable crime" (para. 18). Other backing is provided by references to Abraham Lincoln, Barack Obama, Martin Luther King Jr., and the Bible.

What could Foer tell us if we challenged him with questions like "How do you know . . .?" or "Why do you believe . . .?" Has he provided adequate backing? Or does he want us to just accept such references as the facts that should inspire us to action?

5. Does Foer use **modal qualifiers**? Does he present his argument as *necessary*, *probable*, *plausible*, or *possible*? Can you find phrases that indicate the character and scope of his argument? Are there any contingencies that would make his argument stronger, or weaker?

One way Foer qualifies his argument is by showing how he himself struggles to avoid meat 100 percent of the time, and that he is not perfect, and that few of us can expect to be. It may not be necessary or desirable to completely eliminate animal products from our lives, but limiting them substantially is a good and morally necessary start.

6. Does Foer prepare **rebuttals**, the reasons and responses to anticipated counterclaims that readers might make?

For example, in paragraph 16, he raises the excuses a future generation might offer: "[T]here was nothing we could do. . . . We didn't run the oil companies. . . . The ability to save ourselves . . . was not in our hands." His rebuttal: "[T]hat would be a lie" (para. 17). In some ways, Foer's essay constitutes a rebuttal to the idea that individuals can't do anything about climate change.

Does the author offer anything else to forestall potential criticisms? If so, where is it that he does? If not, what could or should have been raised?

Just how good an argument has Foer made? Is he convincing? If you identified weak points in his argument, what are they? Can you help strengthen the argument? Or can you work to show where it fails? In either case, how?

A CHECKLIST FOR USING THE TOULMIN METHOD

- ☐ What **claim** does the argument make?
- ☐ What **grounds** are offered for the claim?
- ☐ What **warrants** connect the grounds to the claim?
- ☐ What **backing** supports the claim?
- ☐ With what **modalities** are the claim and grounds asserted?
- ☐ To what **rebuttals** are the claim, grounds, and backing vulnerable?

10

A Logician's View: Deduction, Induction, and Fallacies

Logic takes care of itself; all we have to do is to look and see how it does it.

— LUDWIG WITTGENSTEIN

CONSIDER THIS

You are presented with a logic puzzle. What is the longest distance you could trace in three straight lines within the continental United States, touching only three different states and turning only twice?

Decide where to draw your three lines to achieve the longest possible distance.

Adhere to the following rules:

- You may start drawing anywhere, but your lines must enter three and only three different states. (You may not travel through the same state twice.)

- You must turn or continue at each state border you come to (you may not travel along borders to "skip" states).

- Your three lines must all be straight lines.

- No need to worry about roads, obstacles, bodies of water, and so on.

Pavlo Stavnichuk/Getty Images

If possible, compare your answers to the answers of others, or complete the puzzle in different ways. What were the most creative solutions? What were the most logical solutions? How did creativity and logic guide you in your strategies? (For example, did you try any unique solutions? Did logic help you strategize and choose where to start, what states to ignore, or which state(s) must be involved?) Why?

Finally, what was the **best** answer?

Using Formal Logic for Critical Thinking

In Chapter 3, we introduced the terms "deduction," "induction," and "fallacy." In this chapter, we discuss them in more detail and present some principles of *formal logic* to help you develop your ability to understand arguments.

Formal logic is a discipline of philosophy that studies the *nature* and *structure* of arguments independent of their content. Formal logic emerged in the ancient world and was developed further during the Enlightenment (ca. 1685–1815), a time of great scientific ferment. Thinkers at this time sought to understand truth according to *a priori* rules — rules that exist before, or *prior* to, any specific content. Their assumption was that the rules of logic were fixed, permanent, and natural in the same way as the laws of physics.

For these reasons, formal logic is closely related to mathematics. Each expresses reality using symbols and variables. In math, the phrase "two plus two equals four" is true no matter if apples or oranges or anything at all are being counted. Consider the structure of an equation using variables:

If $A + B = C$, then $C + D = (A + B) + D$.

This formula expresses logical truth no matter what numbers you plug into the letters. The variables can change, but not the underlying truth of the formula: If the first proposition is true, the second must be, too.

Perhaps for obvious reasons, formal logic is quite important in computer science, which is based on binaries of 0 and 1. Think about it: When you play a video game, the graphics, sound effects, and voices may enhance the experience of the game. The choices you can make when playing can cause the gaming experience to feel life-like. But you are merely activating a series of complex logical arrangements — the code. Your choices are finite and deterministic — theoretically, if you played a video game enough times, every possible pathway would be expended. In the code, all possible statements are perfectly interconnected by logic.

Enlightenment philosophers sought, in a sense, to discover the underlying code of everything. The scientific method is one major product of this pursuit. It proposed that, through a process of making objective observations, a person could discern permanent and stable truths about the physical world. Similarly, with formal logic, the code of logic itself was the object of inquiry; the goal was to discover the proper method for testing truth and falseness that could be applied reliably to any statements whatsoever.

We use methods of formal logic to demonstrate truth every day in our lives. If you have a can of soda in the refrigerator, and you open the door and it is gone, and if your roommate was the only other person in the house all day, you may conclude that your roommate drank the soda. (If the premises are true, the conclusion must be true.)

Good arguments are rooted in high-quality reasoning. Poor arguments feature poor reasoning. But how do we decide when reasoning is good or poor? Even poor arguments *can* produce true conclusions. Consider an argument that states that all soda cans are red; therefore, all the soda cans in your refrigerator are red. If all the soda cans in your fridge *were* in fact red, you would have a poor argument with a (quite accidentally) true conclusion. And good arguments, presented logically, may *appear* to have the character of truth even while they remain disputable. If you concluded when you discovered that your soda was missing that your roommate was a "thief," then your logic led you to a kind of truth, and one that sounds quite reasonable — but also remains highly dependent on the meaning of the word *thief* (not to mention what is considered *theft*, and what we consider to be private property capable of being stolen).

In a world of values, language, and morals, we often encounter variables in arguments that are not objective or permanent. Terms and concepts that appear in the premises of arguments are not always fixed or reliable, and sometimes arguments are based on social values that can change over time. When we start to think about what words mean, and what anyone *should* or *ought* to do, or have a *right* to do — we must recognize the limits of formal logic's ability to demonstrate absolute truth.

Consider the premise, "Every person is either a man or a woman." This likely would have been considered a true statement in eras that did not recognize the spectrum along which biological sex or social gender norms are determined. For arguments to work, the components must have meaning, but things only have meaning in the context of their place and time. Therefore, evaluating arguments that make assertions of human value in a fluid language system involves contextual forms of thinking as well as pure logic.

Nevertheless, understanding formal logic can assist us in seeing the ways real-world arguments are structured, and ultimately help us judge such arguments and construct our own counter-arguments. Looking more deeply into practical uses of logic helps us identify the problems and limitations of arguments as they are presented to us in real life. Only some students will major in philosophy or take a deep interest in formal logic, but it helps to know the basics so that you can be on the lookout for such structures when you are thinking critically about the issues that surround you.

Deduction

The basic aim of deductive reasoning is to start with some given premise and extract from it a conclusion — a logical consequence — that is concealed but implicit in it. When we introduced the idea of deduction in Chapter 4, we gave as our primary example the *syllogism*, and we provided a classical syllogism to represent how this aspect of formal logic, deduction, can lead to true conclusions:

> *Premise*: All human beings are mortal.
>
> *Premise*: Socrates is a human being.
>
> *Conclusion*: Socrates is mortal.

If the premises are absolutely true, and the conclusion necessarily follows from them, the syllogism is *valid* and the argument is *sound*. (For a reminder of the distinctions between validity and soundness, see "Testing Truth and Validity," p. 107.)

Here is another example of a statement that proves to be indisputably true:

Texas is larger than California.

California is larger than Arizona.

Therefore, Texas is larger than Arizona.

The conclusion in this syllogism can be derived from the two premises; that is, anyone who asserts the two premises is committed to accepting the conclusion as well, whatever one thinks of it. It is not a matter of perspective, opinion, or dispute.

Using formal logic, we can derive an equation of sorts to represent the argument graphically using nested circles:

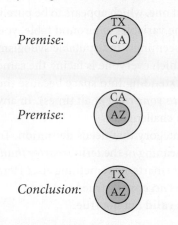

Premise:

Premise:

Conclusion:

We can see that this conclusion follows from the premises because it amounts to nothing more than what one gets by superimposing the two premises on each other. Thus, the whole argument can be represented like this:

The so-called middle term in the argument — California — disappears from the conclusion; its role is confined to be the link between the other two terms, Texas and Arizona, in the premises. In a graphic depiction, as with an equation, one can literally *see* that the conclusion follows from the premises. (This technique is an adaptation of one used in elementary formal logic known as Venn diagrams.)

In formal logic, the validity of a deductive inference depends on being able to show how the concepts in the premises are related to the concepts in the conclusion. In this case, the validity of the inference depends on the meaning of a key concept, *being larger than*. This concept has the property of *transitivity*, a property that many concepts share (e.g., *is equal to*, *is to the right of*, *is smarter than*). Transitive concepts can be represented symbolically in equations. Consequently, regardless of what is represented by A, B, and C, we can say:

If $A > B$, and $B > C$, then $A > C$.

This is all intended to show that the validity of deductive inference is a purely *formal* property of argument. You can substitute any state for Texas, California, and Arizona — or anything at all for the variables *A*, *B*, and *C* — as long as they adhere to the meaning of the transitive concept *larger than*.

Understanding this technique can help you see how some arguments can appear to be valid, but may also be challenged. For example:

If *A* is to the right of *B* and *B* is to the right of *C*, then *A* is to the right of *C*.

or

If *A* is smarter than *B* and *B* is smarter than *C*, then *A* is smarter than *C*.

Let's dig into these examples. First, let's challenge the first one, which appears to be purely logical and basically indisputable. However, if we situate the variables at a round table, you can see that plainly that *A* is *also to the left* of *C*. Here, the seemingly indisputable syllogism may be refuted on the grounds that it assumes a plane in which everyone is facing the same direction. Technically, it also assumes a theoretical plane extending into space because the earth is a globe — making anything that is *to your left* also *to your right* at all times). In any case, the very meaning of the phrase *to the right of* has been challenged.

In the second example, the concept *smarter than* is a category that needs definition. To challenge this argument, you can contest the comparative meaning of the term *smarter than*: Does "smart" refer to IQ level, grades earned in school, street smarts, or something else? Here you have two examples of valid syllogism, neither of which is *necessarily* true.

Now let's look at an example of another syllogism that is **valid** but not true.

Rhode Island is larger than Texas.

Texas is larger than Canada.

Therefore, Rhode Island is larger than Canada.

TetyanaRusanova/Shutterstock

At a round table, anyone to the right of anyone else is also to their left.

How, you might ask, can this syllogism be valid? Remember our lesson about the formal properties of arguments: *If* the premises are true, *and* the conclusion is inherently related to the premises, then the argument is valid *even if it is not in fact true*. Logicians assume that the premises of an argument are true *in order to examine the elements of reason* that produce true conclusions. (To consider how the truth of each premise was obtained would lead them to different arguments altogether.)

If all you can say about an argument is that it is valid — that is, its conclusion follows from the premises — then you have not given a sufficient reason for accepting the argument's conclusion. A valid deductive argument doesn't prove anything is true unless the premises and the conclusion *are true*, but they can't be true unless they *mean* something in the first place. As critical thinkers, we need to pay close attention to the meanings of words and concepts used in arguments. Consider this syllogism:

Rhode Island is cooler than Texas.

Texas is cooler than Alaska.

Therefore, Rhode Island is cooler than Alaska.

Formal logic would say this conclusion is proven by the premises. When we are thinking critically about arguments in the real world, we do *not* assume the premises are true. We ask questions about how their truths have been obtained: "What do you mean by *cooler than*?" Are you comparing temperatures (and if so, are you using average temperature, or temperature at a given moment in time)? Or are you using, say, fashion and lifestyle as a standard, and if so what is your definition of *cool* anyway?

It has been said that the devil can quote scripture; similarly, an argument can be deductively valid and also of little value because valid conclusions may be drawn from poorly defined, false, misleading, or meaningless premises.

These examples show that the form of an argument can be good but the argument itself bad — or at least debatable or more open-ended than it first appears. Think about this one:

If President Truman knew the Japanese were about to surrender, then it was immoral of him to order that atom bombs be dropped on Hiroshima and Nagasaki. Truman knew the Japanese were going to surrender. Therefore, it was immoral of him to order dropping those bombs.

Once again, anyone who assents to the *if . . . then* proposition in the premise, and accepts that Truman knew the Japanese were about to surrender, must assent to the conclusion that it was an immoral choice. But do the premises *prove* this conclusion? That depends on whether both premises are true. Well, are they? The answer turns on a number of considerations, and it is worth pausing to examine how we might think critically about this argument.

The second premise proposes a fact. But did Truman really know the Japanese were about to surrender? This question is controversial even today. Autobiography, memoranda, other documentary evidence — all are needed to assemble the evidence to back up the grounds for the thesis or claim made in the conclusion of this argument. Evaluating this material effectively may involve further deductions (and perhaps inductive reasoning as well).

As to the first premise, its truth doesn't depend on facts about the past but, rather, on moral principles. The first premise contains a hypothetical ("if") and asserts a connection between two very different kinds of things (prior knowledge and morality). This premise as a whole can thus be seen as expressing *a principle of moral responsibility*. The principle is this: If we have knowledge that makes violence unnecessary, it is immoral to act violently anyway. Someone could compare Truman's decision to an argument that shares its form: If someone is surrendering, it is immoral to do violence to him. Such principles can, of course, be supported or contested.

EXAMPLES OF DEDUCTION

When we engage with and construct arguments, it is useful to keep in mind some of the basic structures (including but not limited to *syllogism*) because they help us see what is going on under the surface of an argument.

DISJUNCTION   One common form of argument occurs through **disjunctive syllogism**, so called because its major premise is a **disjunction**, or a relationship between distinct alternatives. For example:

> Either censorship of fake news is overdue or our society does not care about truth.
>
> Our society cares about truth.
>
> Therefore, censorship of fake news is overdue.

This could be reduced to a simple equation:

> Either *A* or *B*.
>
> Not *B*.
>
> Therefore, *A*.

The key feature of disjunctive syllogism is that the resulting conclusion is whichever of the alternatives remains after the others have been negated. We could easily have a very complex disjunctive syllogism with a dozen alternatives in the first premise and seven of them denied in the second, leaving a conclusion of the remaining five. Usually, however, a disjunctive argument is formulated in this manner: Assert a disjunction (an "or" statement) with two or more alternatives in the major premise, *deny all but one* in the second premise, and then infer validly the remaining alternative(s) as the conclusion.

Since it represents valid reasoning, an argument structured like this may appear to be true even when the alternatives in the premise are not finite or exhausted. For example:

> Either you can vote for the Republican candidate for president, or for the Democrat.
>
> You are not voting Democrat.
>
> Therefore, you are voting Republican.

It is easy to see how this is valid as stated, while also false because you could vote for a third-party or write-in candidate, or not vote at all. Nevertheless, many campaign commercials present this "choice" between two parties as an inevitable one voters must make.

Sometimes, nonessential elements can be dropped or equivalent expressions substituted without adverse effect on the reasoning as long as those relationships are established. A commercial that shows a flattering image of a Democratic candidate and states, "You can vote for the common-sense moderate candidate or you can be an extremist," may fall apart under scrutiny, but it says all it needs to say: If you wish to disassociate from extreme views, your only "logical" choice becomes the Democrat. The somewhat devious but persuasive logic goes: *Either you can vote for* A, *or you can vote for* B, C, D. *You can't vote for* B, C, D *unless you are an extremist. You are not an extremist. Therefore, you must vote for* A.

DILEMMA   Another type of argument, especially favored by orators and rhetoricians, is the **dilemma**. Ordinarily, we use the term *dilemma* in the sense of an awkward predicament, as when we say, "His dilemma was that he didn't have enough money to pay the waiter." But when logicians refer to a dilemma, they mean a forced choice between two or more equally unattractive alternatives. Take for example, a parent who faces a choice: Either they can monitor their teenage child's social media activity or they can choose not to monitor it. The argument could be stated as such:

> If the parent monitors the child's online activity, then they are surveilling the child and denying them certain latitudes of freedom, trust, and privacy.

> If they do not monitor the child's online activity, then they are exposing the child to risks such as cyberbullying, predatory behavior, and viewing inappropriate content.

> Thus, in deciding what to do, the parents will either be limiting the child's autonomy or exposing the child to risk. Either way, there are unattractive consequences.

Notice first the structure of the argument: Two conditional propositions ("if . . . then" statements) asserted as premises, followed by another premise that states a **necessary truth**. Boiled down, the premise "Either the parents monitor or they do not" is a disjunction. Because the two alternatives are presented as exhaustive (the only options), one of the two alternatives must be true. (Such a statement is often called analytically true, or a *tautology*.) The conclusion of this dilemma ("unattractive consequences") follows from its premises.

But does the argument *prove*, as it purports to do, that whatever the parents do, the child will suffer "unattractive consequences"? If the two conditional premises fail to exhaust the possibilities, we can escape from the dilemma by finding a third alternative (or a fourth or fifth). Perhaps there are ways to monitor online behavior that could lessen the impact on privacy and autonomy, while at the same time achieving a higher degree of safety. Later, when we discuss logical fallacies, we will discuss among others the "false dichotomy" (p. 371), sometimes called the "false dilemma" or the "either/or" fallacy. This refers to the many ways a choice between alternatives may fail to account for different potential choices or consequences of an action.

Modern student dilemma.

If third (or more) alternatives are not possible, we can still ask whether both of the main premises are true. Do children have a reasonable right to unfettered and unmonitored access to the internet? What are the meanings and limits of "freedom, trust, and privacy"? Are the risks of online behavior overstated? Is this particular child more or less likely to encounter trouble? Neither of the main premises spells out the answers, leaving us with an apparently true but also debatable argument.

If both of the conditional premises are in fact true, then it may also be that the consequences of one alternative are not as bad as those of the other (i.e., it's better to limit freedom and autonomy in the name of maximum safety). If that is true, but our reasoning stops before evaluating that fact, we may be guilty of failing to distinguish between the greater and the lesser of two evils. The logic of the dilemma itself cannot decide this choice for us. Instead, we must bring to bear empirical inquiry and imagination to the evaluation of the grounds of the dilemma.

REDUCTIO AD ABSURDUM   One powerful and dramatic form of argument is **reductio ad absurdum** (from the Latin, meaning "reduction to absurdity"). The idea of a reductio argument is to disprove a proposition by showing the absurdity of its inevitable conclusion. It is used, of course, to refute your opponent's position and prove your own.

Let's look at an example. Suppose you are opposed to any form of gun control, whereas we are in favor of gun control. We might try to refute your position by attacking it with a reductio argument. We start out by assuming the very opposite of what we believe or favor and try to establish a contradiction that results from following out the consequences of your initial assumption:

> Your position is that there ought to be no legal restrictions of any kind on the sale and ownership of guns. That means that you'd permit having every neighborhood hardware store sell pistols and rifles to whoever walks in the door. But that's not all. You apparently also would permit selling machine guns to children, antitank weapons to lunatics, and small-bore cannons to the nearsighted, as well as guns and ammunition to anyone with a criminal record. But that is utterly preposterous; no one could favor such a dangerous policy. So the only question worth debating is what kind of gun control is necessary.

Now in this example, our reductio of your position on gun control is not based on claiming to show that you have strictly contradicted yourself, for there is no purely logical contradiction in opposing all forms of gun control. Instead, what we have tried to do is to show that there is a contradiction between what you profess — no gun controls at all — and what you probably really believe, if only you'll stop to think about it — which is that no lunatic should be allowed to buy a loaded machine gun. Our refutation of your position rests on whether we succeed in establishing an inconsistency among your own beliefs. If it turns out that you really believe lunatics should be free to purchase guns and ammunition, our attempted refutation fails.

CONTRADICTION, CONSISTENCY, AND CONJUNCTION   In explaining reductio ad absurdum, we have had to rely on another idea fundamental to logic, that of **contradiction**, or inconsistency. The opposite of contradiction is **consistency**, a notion important to good reasoning. These concepts deserve a few words of further explanation and illustration. Consider this pair of assertions:

A. Abortion is homicide.

B. Racism is unfair.

There is no evident connection between these two assertions. No one would plausibly claim that we can infer or deduce B from A or, for that matter, A from B. They are unrelated assertions; logically speaking, they are *independent* of each other. The two assertions are potentially *consistent*; that is, both could be true — or both could be false. But now consider another proposition:

C. Euthanasia is not murder.

Could a person assert A (*Abortion is homicide*) and also assert C (*Euthanasia is not murder*) and be consistent? Could you assert these two propositions as a **conjunction**? Consider:

D. Abortion is homicide, and euthanasia is not murder.

It's not so easy to say whether these are consistent or inconsistent. One person could assert one of these propositions and reject the other, leading to a conclusion of general inconsistency. Another could be convinced that there is no inconsistency in asserting that *Abortion is homicide* and that *Euthanasia is not murder*. (For instance, suppose you believe both that the unborn are persons who deserve a chance to live and that putting terminally ill persons to death in a painless manner and with their consent confers a benefit on them.)

Let us generalize: We can say of any set of propositions that they are consistent *if and only if* all could be true together. Remember that, once again, the truth of the assertions in question doesn't matter. Two propositions can be consistent or not, quite apart from whether they are true. That's not so with falsehood: It follows from our definition of consistency that an *inconsistent* proposition must be *false*. (We have relied on this idea in explaining how a reductio ad absurdum argument about gun control works.)

Assertions or claims that are not consistent can take either of two forms. Suppose you assert that abortion is homicide, early in an essay you are writing, but later you assert that abortion is harmless. You have now asserted a position on abortion that is strictly contrary to the one with which you began — both cannot be true. It is simply not true that if an abortion involves killing a human being (which is what *homicide* strictly means), it causes no one any harm (killing a person always causes harm — even if it is excusable, justifiable, not wrong, the best thing to do in the circumstances, and so on). Notice that while both cannot be true, they *can* both be false. In fact, many people who are perplexed about the morality of abortion believe precisely this. They concede that abortion does harm the fetus, but they also believe that abortion doesn't kill a person.

Let's consider another, simpler case. If you describe the glass as half empty and I describe it as half full, both of us can be right; the two assertions are consistent, even though they sound vaguely incompatible. (This is the reason that disputing over whether the glass is half full or half empty has become the popular paradigm of a futile, purely *verbal disagreement*.) But if I describe the glass as half empty whereas you insist that it is two-thirds empty, we have a real disagreement; your description and mine are strictly contrary, in that both cannot be true — although both *can* be false. (Both are false if the glass is only one-fourth full.)

This, by the way, enables us to define the difference between a pair of **contradictory** propositions and a pair of **contrary** propositions. Two propositions are contrary if and only if both cannot be true (though both can be false); two propositions are contradictory if and only if they are such that if one is true the other must be false, and vice versa. Thus, if Jack says that Alice Walker's *The Color Purple* is a better novel than Mark Twain's *Huckleberry Finn*, and Jill says, "No, *Huckleberry Finn* is better than *The Color Purple*," she is contradicting Jack. If what either one of them says is true, then what the other says must be false.

A more subtle case of contradiction arises when two or more of one's own beliefs implicitly contradict each other. We may find ourselves saying "Travel is broadening" and saying an hour later "People don't really change." Just beneath the surface of these two beliefs lies a self-contradiction: How can travel broaden us unless it influences — and changes — our beliefs, values, and outlook? But if we can't really change ourselves, traveling to new places won't change us, either. "Travel is broadening" and "People don't change" collide with each other; something has to give.

Our point, of course, is not that you must never say today something that contradicts something you said yesterday. Far from it; if you think you were mistaken yesterday, of course you will take a different position today. But what you want to avoid is what George Orwell called *doublethink* in his novel *1984*: "*Doublethink* means the power of holding two contradictory beliefs in one's mind simultaneously, and accepting them both."

PARADOX   While we're speaking of inconsistency, let's spend a moment on **paradox**. The word refers to two different things:

- an assertion that is essentially self-contradictory and therefore cannot be true
- a seemingly contradictory assertion that nevertheless may be true

An example of the first might be "Evaluating quality of art is subjective, but Frida Kahlo is a great painter." It is hard to make any sense out of this assertion. Contrast it with a paradox of the second sort, a *seeming* contradiction that may make sense, such as "The longest way around is the shortest way home," or "Work is more fun than fun," or "The best way to find happiness is not to look for it." Here we have assertions that are striking because as soon as we hear them we realize that although they seem inconsistent and self-defeating, they contain (or may contain) profound truths. If you use the word *paradox* in your own writing — for instance, to characterize an argument you're reading — be sure the reader will understand in which sense you're using the word. (And, of course, you won't want to write paradoxes of the first, self-contradictory sort.)

Induction

Deduction involves logical thinking that applies to absolutely any assertion or claim — because every possible statement, true or false, has deductive logical consequences. Induction, remember, is the type of thinking that begins with specific **empirical** or *factual* observations and leads to general conclusions. Induction is relevant to one kind of assertion only. Other kinds of assertions (such as definitions, mathematical equations, and moral or legal norms) simply are not the product of inductive reasoning and cannot serve as a basis for further inductive thinking.

So, in studying the methods of induction, we are exploring tactics and strategies useful in gathering and then using **evidence** — empirical, observational, experimental — in support of a belief as its ground. Modern scientific knowledge is the product of these methods, and they differ somewhat from one science to another because they depend on the theories and technology appropriate to each of the sciences. Here all we can do is discuss generally the more abstract features common to inductive inquiry. For fuller details, you must eventually consult a physicist, chemist, geologist, or their colleagues and counterparts in other scientific fields.

OBSERVATION AND INFERENCE

Let's begin with a simple example. Suppose we have evidence (actually we don't, but that won't matter for our purposes) in support of this claim:

In a sample of 500 smokers, 230 persons observed have cardiovascular disease.

The basis — the evidence or grounds — for asserting this claim would be, presumably, straightforward physical examination of the 500 persons in the sample, one by one.

With this claim in hand, we can think of the purpose and methods of induction as pointing in two opposite directions: toward establishing the basis or ground of the very empirical proposition with which we start (in this example, the observation stated above) or toward understanding what that observation indicates or suggests as a more general, inclusive, or fundamental fact of nature.

In each case, we start from something we *do* know (or take for granted and treat as a sound starting point) — some fact of nature, perhaps a striking or commonplace event that we have observed and recorded — and then go on to something we do *not* fully know and perhaps cannot directly observe. In the smoking example above, only the second of these two orientations (the 230 persons with cardiovascular disease) is of any interest, so let's concentrate exclusively on it.

GENERALIZATION   Anyone truly interested in the observed fact that *230 of 500 smokers have cardiovascular disease* is likely to start speculating about, and thus be interested in finding out, whether any or all of several other propositions are also true. For example, one might wonder whether the following claim is true:

All smokers have cardiovascular disease or will develop it during their lifetimes.

This claim is a straightforward generalization of the original observation as reported in the first claim. When we think inductively, we are reasoning from an observed sample (some smokers — i.e., 230 of the 500 *observed*) to the entire membership of a more inclusive class (*all* smokers, whether observed or not). The fundamental question raised by reasoning from the narrower claim to the broader claim is whether we have any ground for believing that what is true of *some* members of a class is true of them *all*. So the difference between these claims is that of *quantity* or scope.

RELATION   We can also think inductively about the *relation* between the factors mentioned in the original claim, *In a sample of 500 smokers, 230 persons observed have cardiovascular disease*. Having observed data, we may be tempted to assert a different and more profound kind of claim:

Smoking *causes* cardiovascular disease.

Here our interest is not merely in generalizing from a sample to a whole class; it is the far more important one of *explaining* the observation with which we began. Certainly, the preferred, even if not the only, mode of explanation for a natural phenomenon is a *causal* explanation. In this claim, we propose to explain the presence of one phenomenon (cardiovascular disease) by the prior occurrence of an independent phenomenon (smoking). The original observation about the number of diseased smokers is now serving as evidence or support for this new conjecture.

But there is a third way to think inductively beyond our original claim. Instead of a straightforward generalization or a pronouncement on the cause of a phenomenon, we might have a more complex and cautious further claim in mind, such as this:

Smoking is a factor in the causation of cardiovascular disease in some persons.

This proposition also advances a claim about causation, although it is obviously weaker than the claim *Smoking causes cardiovascular disease*. That is, other observations, theories, or evidence that would support the "factor" claim could easily fail to be enough to support the claim that smoking is the sole or main cause. Claiming that smoking is only one factor allows for other (unmentioned) factors in the causation of cardiovascular disease (e.g., genetic or dietary factors) that may not be found in all smokers.

INDUCTIVE INFERENCE (OR HYPOTHESIS)   We began by assuming that our first proposition states an empirical fact based on direct observation but that the propositions that follow do not. Instead, they state empirical *hypotheses* or conjectures — tentative generalizations not fully confirmed — each of which goes beyond the observed facts. As such, they can be regarded as an *inductive inference* from the first proposition or observation.

PROBABILITY

Another way of thinking about inferences and hypotheses is to say that whereas a statement of observed fact (*230 out of 500 smokers have cardiovascular disease*) has a **probability** of 1.0 — that is, it is absolutely certain — the probability of each of the hypotheses that followed, *relative* to 1.0, is smaller than 1.0. (We need not worry here about how much smaller than 1.0 the probabilities are, nor about how to calculate these probabilities precisely.) But it takes only a moment's reflection to realize that no matter what the probability actually is, those probabilities in each case will be quite different relative to different information, such as this:

> Ten persons observed in a sample of 500 smokers have cardiovascular disease.

The idea that *a given proposition can have different probabilities* relative to different bases is fundamental to all inductive reasoning. The following example makes a convincing illustration. Suppose we want to consider the probability of this proposition being true:

> Susanne Smith will live to be eighty.

Taken as an abstract question of fact, we cannot even guess what the probability is with any assurance. But we can do better than guess; we can, in fact, even calculate the answer — if we get some further information. Thus, suppose we are told that Susanne Smith is seventy-nine. Our original question then becomes one of determining the probability that the proposition is true given this fact — that is, relative to the evidence. There's no doubt that if Susanne Smith really is seventy-nine, the probability that she will live to be eighty is greater than if we know only that Suzanne Smith is more than nine years old. Obviously, a lot can happen to

Al Ross/The New Yorker Collection/The Cartoon Bank

Susanne in the seventy years between nine and seventy-nine that isn't very likely to happen in the one year between seventy-nine and eighty. So our proposition is more probable relative to the evidence of Susanne's age of seventy-nine than of "more than nine years old."

Let's suppose for the sake of the argument that the following is true:

Ninety percent of women alive at age seventy-nine live to be eighty.

Given this additional information and the information that Susanne is seventy-nine, we now have a basis for answering our original question about our proposition about Susanne's longevity with some precision. But suppose, in addition, we are also told that

Susanne Smith is suffering from inoperable cancer.

and also that

The survival rate for women suffering from inoperable cancer is 0.6 years (i.e., the average life span for women after a diagnosis of inoperable cancer is about seven months).

With this new information, the probability that Susanne will live to eighty drops significantly, all because we can now estimate the probability in relation to a new body of evidence.

The probability of an event, thus, is not a fixed number but one that varies because it is always relative to some evidence — and given different evidence, one and the same event can have different probabilities. In other words, the probability of any event is always relative to how much is known (assumed, believed), and because different persons may know different things about a given event or the same person may know different things at different times, one and the same event can have two or more probabilities. This conclusion is not a paradox but, rather, a logical consequence of the concept of what it is for an event to have (i.e., to be assigned) a probability.

S. Harris/Cartoonstock

MILL'S METHODS

Now let's return to our earlier discussion of smoking and cardiovascular disease and consider in greater detail the question of a causal connection between the two phenomena. We began thus:

> In a sample of 500 smokers, 230 persons observed have cardiovascular disease.

We regarded this claim as an observed fact, although in truth, of course, it is mere supposition. Our question now is how we might augment this information so as to strengthen our confidence of our causal hypotheses that

> Smoking *causes* cardiovascular disease.

or at least that

> Smoking is a factor in the causation of cardiovascular disease in some persons.

Suppose further examination showed that

> In the sample of 230 smokers with cardiovascular disease, no other suspected factor (such as genetic predisposition, lack of physical exercise, age over fifty) was also observed.

Such an observation would encourage us to believe that our hypotheses are true. Why? Because we're inclined to believe also that no matter what the cause of a phenomenon is, it must *always* be present when its effect is present. Thus, the inference from observed fact to our hypotheses is supported by this new evidence, using **Mill's Method of Agreement**, named after the British philosopher John Stuart Mill (1806–1873), who first formulated it. It's called a method of agreement because of the way in which the inference relies on *agreement* among the observed phenomena where a presumed cause is thought to be *present*.

Let's now suppose that in our search for evidence to support our hypotheses we conduct additional research and discover that

> In a sample of 500 nonsmokers, selected to be representative of both sexes, different ages, dietary habits, exercise patterns, and so on, none is observed to have cardiovascular disease.

This observation would further encourage us to believe that we had obtained significant additional confirmation of our hypotheses. Why? Because we now know that factors present (such as male sex, lack of exercise, family history of cardiovascular disease) in cases where the effect is absent (no cardiovascular disease observed) cannot be the cause. This is an example of **Mill's Method of Difference**, so called because the cause or causal factor of an effect must be *different* from whatever factors are present when the effect is *absent*.

Suppose now that, increasingly confident we've found the cause of cardiovascular disease, we study our first sample of 230 smokers ill with the disease, and we discover this:

> Those who smoke two or more packs of cigarettes daily for ten or more years have cardiovascular disease either much younger or much more severely than those who smoke less.

This is an application of **Mill's Method of Concomitant Variation**, perhaps the most convincing of the three methods. Here we deal not merely with the presence of the conjectured cause (smoking) or the absence of the effect we are studying (cardiovascular disease), as we were previously, but with the more interesting and subtler matter of the *degree and regularity of the correlation* of the supposed cause and effect. According to the observations reported here, it strongly appears that the more we have of the "cause" (smoking), the sooner or the more intense the onset of the "effect" (cardiovascular disease).

Notice, however, what happens to our confirmation if, instead, we had discovered this:

> In a representative sample of 500 nonsmokers, cardiovascular disease was observed in 34 cases.

(We won't pause here to explain what makes a sample more or less representative of a population, although the representativeness of samples is vital to all statistical reasoning.) Such an observation would lead us almost immediately to suspect some other or additional causal factor: Smoking might indeed be *a* factor in causing cardiovascular disease, but it can hardly be *the* cause because (using Mill's Method of Difference) we cannot have the effect, as we do in the observed sample of 34 cases reported above, unless we also have the cause.

An observation such as this is likely to lead us to think our hypothesis that *smoking causes cardiovascular disease* has been disconfirmed. But we have a fallback position ready — we can still defend our weaker hypothesis: *Smoking is a factor in the causation of cardiovascular disease in some persons.* It is still quite possible that smoking is a factor in causing this disease, even if it isn't the *only* factor.

Fallacies

The straight road on which sound reasoning proceeds gives little latitude for cruising about. Irrationality, carelessness, passionate attachment to one's unexamined beliefs, and the sheer complexity of some issues occasionally spoil the reasoning of even the best of us. An inventory of some common fallacies proves an instructive and potentially amusing exercise. The Visual Guide: Common Fallacies and the discussion that follows, then, is a quick tour through the twisting paths, mudflats, and quicksands we sometimes encounter in reading arguments that stray from the way of clear thinking.

Visual Guide: Common Fallacies

	Fallacy	Definition	Example
Fallacies of Ambiguity	Ambiguity (p. 367)	Using a word, phrase, or claim that gives rise to more than one possible interpretation.	People have equal rights, and so everyone has a right to property.
	Division (p. 368)	Assuming that all members of a set share characteristics of the set as a whole.	PETA is a radical organization; therefore, anyone who is a member of PETA is radical.
	Composition (p. 368)	Assuming that a set shares characteristics with a given member of a set (the reverse of division fallacy).	Kimberly is a freelance writer and makes a lot of money; therefore, freelance writers must make a lot of money.
	Equivocation (p. 368)	Making two words or phrases equivalent in meaning while ignoring contextual differences.	Evolution is a natural process, so this company's growth is natural and good.
	Non sequitur (p. 368)	Literally, "it does not follow." Drawing conclusions that are unrelated or do not follow logically from the premises.	Because Sammy is good at math, we should let him draw up our annual budget.
Fallacies of Presumption	Distorting the Facts (p. 368)	Misrepresenting information, data, or facts in an argument.	Video games have been shown to cause violence in one out of five kids; 20 percent of the next generation will be violent citizens.
	Post Hoc, Ergo Propter Hoc (p. 369)	Literally, "after this, therefore because of this." Assuming that sequence equals consequence.	After the invention of the birth control pill, the divorce rate increased; therefore, the "pill" contributed to the rising divorce rate.
	Many Questions (p. 369)	Presupposing facts that are assumed in the question itself.	Can selfish and self-interested politicians be trusted to do anything to bring about banking reform?
	Hasty Generalization (p. 369)	Jumping to conclusions based on insufficient evidence or biases.	I'm not moving to that neighborhood. When I visited it, there were two people fighting in the street.
	Slippery Slope (p. 370)	Arguing that an idea or action will lead inevitably to unrealistically steeper and steeper consequences.	If we allow legal recreational marijuana, other drugs will soon follow, and soon there will be addicts everywhere.
	False Analogy (p. 370)	Comparing two things that may be similar in some ways but remain different in other ways.	Building a border wall is just like fencing in our backyards; it is simply a safe and reasonable precaution.

(Continued)

	Fallacy	Definition	Example
Fallacies of Presumption	Straw Man (p. 370)	Misrepresenting an argument so that you can attack the misrepresentation rather than the actual argument.	If you want prison reform, you are basically saying you want to treat criminals like they're at a resort. We should not be rewarding criminals!
	Special Pleading (p. 371)	Making an unwarranted claim by misapplying or misusing rules and standards.	I should get an A because I worked really hard.
	Begging the Question (p. 371)	Making an argument in which the premises are based on the truth of the conclusion.	We have a free press because the US Constitution guarantees it.
	False Dichotomy (p. 371)	Establishing only two opposing positions or points when more might be available or when the opposing positions are not mutually exclusive.	Either we drill for natural gas, or we keep using carbon fuel.
	Oversimplification (p. 372)	Reducing a complex thing to a simple cause or consequence.	With all the bullying on the internet, it is no wonder school shootings are happening.
	Red Herring (p. 372)	Presenting a question or issue intended to divert and distract from the central or most relevant question or issue.	I recognize that the issue of race and police violence needs to be addressed, but the real question is whether or not athletes should kneel during the national anthem.
Fallacies of Irrelevance	Tu Quoque (p. 372)	Literally, "you also." Discrediting an argument by attacking the speaker's failure to adhere to their conclusion.	How can my professor say that electric vehicles are the future when he still drives a fuel-cell car?
	Genetic Fallacy (p. 372)	Arguing a position based on the real or imagined origin, history, or source of the idea.	In ancient times, men were hunters and women were gatherers — that's why women tend to be more domestic than men.
	Appeal to Ignorance (p. 373)	Saying that something is true because there is no evidence against it.	No one has complained about our new chili recipe, so it must be good.
	Poisoning the Well (p. 373)	Creating negative associations preemptively to discredit another person or position.	Now that I have highlighted the importance of keeping the controversial monument on campus, watch out because all the liberal snowflakes are going to argue that it "injures" them.

(Continued)

Visual Guide: Common Fallacies (Continued)

	Fallacy	Definition	Example
Fallacies of Irrelevance	Ad Hominem (p. 373)	Literally, "against the man [person]." Attacking the character of a person by providing irrelevant negative information.	How can this woman be the mayor when she can't even hold her own family together?
	Appeal to Authority (p. 373)	Asserting that a claim is true by citing someone thought to be an authority, regardless of the merits of the position or the relevance of the authority's expertise.	If the coach says throwing balls at the players makes them tougher, it must be true.
	Appeal to Fear (p. 374)	Supporting a position by instilling irrational fear of the alternatives.	If we don't strengthen our drug laws, drug dealers will see our community as a place to buy and sell openly on the streets.
Other	Death by a Thousand Qualifications (p. 375)	Justifying a weak idea or position by changing (or qualifying) it each time it is challenged.	Television is so bad for kids. (Well, not all television, and not all kids, and not in moderation, etc.)
	Protecting the Hypothesis (p. 375)	Distorting evidence to support a preexisting belief or idea.	According to the prophecy, the world was supposed to end. It didn't end. Therefore, the prophecy was not wrong, but we must have misinterpreted it.

FALLACIES OF AMBIGUITY

AMBIGUITY Near the center of the town of Concord, Massachusetts, is an empty field with a sign reading "Old Calf Pasture." Hmm. A former calf pasture? Or a calf pasture that has been there for a long time? Or a pasture for elderly calves? These alternative readings arise because of **ambiguity**, when a group of words gives rise to more than one possible interpretation, confusing the reader and (presumably) frustrating the writer's intentions.

Consider a more complex example. Suppose someone asserts *People have equal rights* and also *Everyone has a right to property.* Many people believe both these claims, but their combination involves an ambiguity. According to one interpretation, the two claims entail that everyone has an *equal right* to property. (That is, you and I each have an equal right to whatever property we have.) But the two claims can also be interpreted to mean that everyone has a *right to equal property.* (That is, whatever property you have a right to, I have a right to the same, or at least equivalent, property.) The latter interpretation is revolutionary, whereas the former is not. Arguments over equal rights often involve this ambiguity.

DIVISION   In a famous example of the **fallacy of division**, the US Air Force in 1926 designed a new cockpit sized according to the average of over 4,000 pilots. The result: a prototype that fit no pilot perfectly. The reason: *There is no perfectly average-sized individual pilot.* The fallacy of division generalizes from the property of a group to the property of each member of that group.

COMPOSITION   The **fallacy of composition** is the opposite of the fallacy of division. A fallacy of composition occurs when properties of some members of a group are assumed to be true for the totality of the group. If someone stands up at a concert, they will get a better view, but if everyone stands up, everyone's view is impeded. What is true for one (a better view) will not be true for all.

EQUIVOCATION   **Equivocation** (from the Latin for "equal voice" — i.e., giving utterance to two meanings at the same time in one word or phrase) can ruin otherwise good reasoning, as in this example: *Euthanasia is a good death; one dies a good death when one dies peacefully in old age; therefore, euthanasia is dying peacefully in old age.* The etymology of *euthanasia* is literally "a good death," so the first premise is true. And the second premise is certainly plausible. But the conclusion of this syllogism is false. Euthanasia cannot be defined as a peaceful death in one's old age for two reasons. First, euthanasia requires the intervention of another person who kills someone (or lets the person die); second, even a very young person can be euthanized. The problem arises because "a good death" works in the second premise in a manner that does not apply to euthanasia. Both meanings of "a good death" are legitimate, but when used together, they constitute an equivocation that spoils the argument.

NON SEQUITUR   The fallacy of equivocation takes us from the discussion of confusions in individual claims or grounds to the more troublesome fallacies that infect the linkages between the claims we make and the grounds (or reasons) for them. These fallacies occur in statements that, following the vocabulary of the Toulmin method, are called the *warrant* of reasoning. Each fallacy is an example of reasoning that involves a **non sequitur** (Latin for "it does not follow"). That is, the *claim* (the conclusion) does not follow from the *grounds* (the premises).

For a start, here is an obvious non sequitur: "He went to the movies on three consecutive nights, so he must love movies." Why doesn't the claim ("He must love movies") follow from the grounds ("He went to the movies on three consecutive nights")? Perhaps the person was just fulfilling an assignment in a film course (maybe he even hated movies so much that he had postponed three assignments to see films and now had to see them all in quick succession), or maybe he went with a partner who was a movie buff, or maybe . . . — there are any number of other possible reasons.

FALLACIES OF PRESUMPTION

DISTORTING THE FACTS   Facts can be distorted either intentionally (to deceive or mislead) or unintentionally, and in either case usually (but not invariably) to the benefit of whoever is doing the distortion. Consider this case. In 1964, the US surgeon general reported that smoking cigarettes increased the likelihood that smokers would eventually suffer from lung cancer. The cigarette manufacturers vigorously protested that the surgeon general relied on inconclusive research and was badly misleading the public about the health risks of smoking. It later turned out that the tobacco companies knew that smoking increased the risk of lung cancer — a fact established by the company's own laboratories but concealed from the public. Today, thanks to public access to all the facts, it is commonplace knowledge that inhaled smoke — including secondhand smoke — is a risk factor for many illnesses.

POST HOC, ERGO PROPTER HOC   One of the most tempting errors in reasoning is to ground a claim about causation on an observed temporal sequence — that is, to argue "after this, therefore because of this" (which is what **post hoc**, **ergo propter hoc** means in Latin). When the medical community first announced that smoking tobacco caused lung cancer, advocates for the tobacco industry replied that doctors were guilty of this fallacy.

These industry advocates argued that medical researchers had merely noticed that in some people, lung cancer developed *after* considerable smoking — indeed, years after — but (they insisted) that this correlation was not at all the same as a causal relation between smoking and lung cancer. True enough. The claim that *A causes B* is not the same as the claim that *B comes after A*. After all, it was possible that smokers as a group had some other common trait and that this factor was the true cause of their cancer.

As the long controversy over the truth about the causation of lung cancer shows, to avoid the appearance of fallacious post hoc reasoning one needs to find some way to link the observed phenomena (the correlation between smoking and the onset of lung cancer). This step requires some further theory and preferably some experimental evidence for the exact sequence or physical mechanism, in full detail, of how ingestion of tobacco smoke is a crucial factor — and is not merely an accidental or happenstance prior event — in the subsequent development of the cancer.

MANY QUESTIONS   Some questions contain presuppositions that are presented as true and are built into the question itself. Loaded questions, leading questions, and trick questions are all part of the **many questions fallacy**. "Are you still not over your ex?", someone could ask you. Here, the presupposition is that at one time you were not over your ex. Whether you answer yes or no, you are admitting to having been in a condition of emotional distress.

HASTY GENERALIZATION   From a logical point of view, **hasty generalization** is the precipitous move from true assertions about *one* or a *few* instances to dubious or even false assertions about *all*. For example, although it may be true that the only native Hungarians you personally know do not speak English very well, that is no basis for asserting that all Hungarians do not speak English very well. Likewise, if the clothes you recently ordered online turn out not to fit very well, it doesn't follow that *all* online clothes turn out to be too large or too small. A hasty generalization usually lies behind a **stereotype** — that is, a person or event treated as typical of a whole class.

SLIPPERY SLOPE   One of the most familiar arguments against any type of government regulation is that if it is allowed, it will be just the first step down the path that leads to ruinous interference, overregulation, and totalitarian control. Fairly often we encounter this mode of argument in the public debates over handgun control, the censorship of pornography, and physician-assisted suicide. The argument is called the **slippery slope** (or the wedge argument, from the way people use the thin end of a wedge to split solid things apart; it is also called, rather colorfully, "letting the camel's nose under the tent"). The fallacy here is in implying that the first step necessarily leads to the second and so on down the slope to disaster, when in fact there is no necessary slide from the first step to the second. (Would handgun registration lead to a police state? Well, it hasn't in Switzerland.)

Closely related to the slippery slope is what lawyers call a **parade of horrors**, an array of examples of terrible consequences that will or might follow if we travel down a certain path. A good example appears in Justice William Brennan's opinion for the US Supreme Court in *Texas v. Johnson* (1989) regarding a Texas law against burning the American flag in political protest. If this law is allowed to stand, Brennan suggests, we may next find laws against burning the presidential seal, state flags, and the US Constitution.

FALSE ANALOGY   Argument by analogy, as we point out in Chapter 3 and as many of the selections in this book show, is a familiar and even indispensable mode of argument. But it can be treacherous because it runs the risk of the **fallacy of false analogy**. Unfortunately, we have no simple or foolproof way of distinguishing between the useful, legitimate analogies and the others. The key question to ask yourself is, Do the two things put into analogy differ in any essential and relevant respect, or are they different only in unimportant and irrelevant aspects?

In a famous example from his discussion in support of suicide, philosopher David Hume rhetorically asked: "It would be no crime in me to divert the Nile or Danube from its course, were I able to effect such purposes. Where then is the crime of turning a few ounces of blood from their natural channel?" This is a striking analogy—except that it rests on a false assumption. No one has the right to divert the Nile or the Danube or any other major international watercourse; it would be a catastrophic crime to do so without the full consent of people living in the region, their government, and so forth. Therefore, arguing by analogy, one might well say that no one has the right to take their own life either. Thus, Hume's own analogy can be used to argue against his thesis that suicide is no crime. But let's ignore the way in which his example can be turned against him. The analogy is a terrible one in any case. Isn't it obvious that the Nile, regardless of its exact course, would continue to nourish Egypt and the Sudan, whereas the blood flowing out of someone's veins will soon leave that person dead? The fact that the blood is the same blood, whether in a person's body or in a pool on the floor (just as the water of the Nile is the same body of water no matter what path it follows to the sea) is, of course, irrelevant to the question of whether one has the right to commit suicide.

STRAW MAN   It is often tempting to reframe or report your opponent's thesis to make it easier to attack and perhaps refute it. If you do so in the course of an argument, you are creating a straw man, a thing of no substance that's easily blown away. The straw man you've constructed is usually a radically conservative or extremely liberal thesis, which few if any would want to defend. That is why it is easier to refute the straw man than refute the view your opponent actually holds: "So you defend the death penalty — and all the horrible things done in its name." It's highly unlikely that your opponent supports *everything* that has been done in the name of capital punishment — crucifixion and beheading, for example, or execution of the children of the guilty offender.

SPECIAL PLEADING   We all have our favorites — relatives, friends, and neighbors — and we're all too likely to show that favoritism in unacceptable ways. Here is an example: "I know my son punched another boy but he is not a bully, so there must have been a good reason."

BEGGING THE QUESTION   The fallacy called "begging the question," *petitio principii* in Latin, is so named because the conclusion of the argument is hidden among its assumptions — and so the conclusion, not surprisingly, follows from the premises. The argument over whether the death penalty is a deterrent to crime illustrates this fallacy. From the facts that you live in a death-penalty state and were not murdered yesterday, we cannot infer that the death penalty was a deterrent. Yet it is tempting to make this inference, perhaps because — all unaware — we are relying on the **fallacy of begging the question**. If someone tacitly assumes from the start that the death penalty is an effective deterrent, the fact that you weren't murdered yesterday certainly looks like evidence for the truth of that assumption. But it isn't, as long as there are competing but unexamined alternative explanations, as in this case.

Of course, that you weren't murdered is *consistent* with the claim that the death penalty is an effective deterrent, just as someone else being murdered is also consistent with that claim (because an effective deterrent need not be a *perfect* deterrent). In general, from the fact that two propositions are consistent with each other, we cannot infer that either is evidence for the other.

Note: "Begging the question" is often wrongly used to mean "raises the question," as in "His action of burning the flag begs the question, What drove him to do such a thing?"

FALSE DICHOTOMY   Sometimes, oversimplification takes a more complex form in which contrary possibilities are wrongly presented as though they were exhaustive and exclusive. "Either we get tough with drug users, or we must surrender and legalize all drugs." Really? What about doing neither and instead offering education and counseling, detoxification programs, and incentives to "Say no"? A favorite of debaters, **either/ or reasoning** always runs the risk of ignoring a third (or fourth) possibility. Some disjunctions are indeed exhaustive: "Either we get tough with drug users, or we do not." This proposition, although vague (what does "get tough" really mean?), is a tautology; it cannot be false, and there is no third alternative. But most disjunctions do not express a pair of *contradictory* alternatives: They offer only a pair of *contrary* alternatives, and mere contraries do not exhaust the possibilities (recall our discussion of contraries versus contradictories on p. 357).

OVERSIMPLIFICATION "Poverty causes crime," "Taxation is unfair," "Truth is stranger than fiction"—these are examples of generalizations that exaggerate and therefore oversimplify the truth. Poverty as such can't be the sole cause of crime because many poor people do not break the law. Some taxes may be unfairly high, others unfairly low—but there is no reason to believe that *every* tax is unfair to all those who have to pay it. Some true stories do amaze us as much or more than some fictional stories, but the reverse is true, too. (In the language of the Toulmin method, **oversimplification** is the result of a failure to use suitable modal qualifiers in formulating one's claims or grounds or backing.)

RED HERRING The fallacy of **red herring**, less colorfully named "irrelevant thesis," occurs when one tries to distract one's audience by invoking a consideration that is irrelevant to the topic under discussion. (This fallacy probably gets its name from the fact that a rotten herring, or a cured herring, which is reddish, will throw pursuing hounds off the right track.) Consider this case: Some critics, seeking to defend the US government's refusal to sign the Kyoto accords to reduce climate change, argue that signing is supported mainly by left-leaning scientists. This argument supposedly shows that climate change is not a serious, urgent issue. But claiming that the supporters of these accords are left-inclined is a red herring, an irrelevant thesis. By raising doubts about the political views of the advocates of signing, critics distract attention from the scientific question (Is there climate change?) and also from the separate political question (Ought the US government to sign the accords?). The refusal of a government to sign the accords doesn't show there is no such thing as climate change. And even if all the advocates of signing were left-leaning (they aren't), this fact (if it were a fact, but it isn't) would not show that worries about climate change are exaggerated.

FALLACIES OF IRRELEVANCE

TU QUOQUE The Romans called one particular type of fallacy *tu quoque*, for "you also." Consider this: "You're a fine one, trying to persuade me to give up smoking when you indulge yourself with a pipe and a cigar from time to time. Maybe I should quit, but then so should you. It's hypocritical of you to complain about my smoking when you persist in the same habit." The fallacy is this: The merit of a person's argument has nothing to do with the person's character or behavior. Here the assertion that smoking is bad for one's health is *not* weakened by the fact that a smoker offers the argument.

GENETIC FALLACY In the **genetic fallacy**, the error takes the form of arguing against a claim by pointing out that its origin (genesis) is tainted or that it was invented by someone deserving our contempt. For example, an opponent of the death penalty might argue this:

> Capital punishment arose in barbarous times, but we claim to be civilized; therefore, we should discard this relic of the past.

Such reasoning shouldn't be persuasive because the question of the death penalty for our society must be decided by the degree to which it serves our purposes—justice and defense against crime, presumably — to which its historic origins are irrelevant. The practices of beer- and wine-making are as old as human civilization, but their origin in antiquity is no reason to outlaw them in our time. The curious circumstances in which something originates usually play no role in its validity. Anyone who would argue that nothing good could possibly come from molds and fungi is refuted by Sir Alexander Fleming's discovery of penicillin in 1928.

APPEAL TO IGNORANCE   In the controversy over the death penalty, the issues of deterrence and executing the innocent are bound to be raised. Because no one knows how many inno- cent persons have been convicted for murder and wrongfully executed, it is tempting for abo- litionists to argue that the death penalty is too risky. It is equally tempting for proponents of the death penalty to argue that since no one knows how many people have been deterred from murder by the threat of execution, we abolish it at society's peril.

Each of these arguments suffers from the same flaw: the **fallacy of appeal to ignorance**. Each argument invites the audience to draw an inference from a premise that is unquestion- ably true, but what is that premise? It asserts that there is something "we don't know." But what we *don't* know cannot be *evidence* for (or against) anything. Our ignorance is no reason for believing anything, except perhaps that we ought to undertake an appropriate investiga- tion so as to replace our ignorance with reliable information.

POISONING THE WELL   During the 1970s, some critics of the Equal Rights Amendment (ERA) argued against it by pointing out that Karl Marx and Friedrich Engels, in their *Communist Manifesto*, favored equality of women and men — and therefore the ERA was immoral, unde- sirable, and perhaps even a Communist plot. This kind of reasoning is an attempt to **poison the well**; that is, it is an attempt to shift attention from the merits of the argument — the validity of the reasoning, the truth of the claims — to the source or origin of the argument. Such criticism deflects attention from the real issue — namely, whether the view in question is true and what the quality of evidence is in its support. The mere fact that Marx (or Hitler, for that matter) believed something does not show that the belief is false or immoral; just because some scoundrel believes the world is round is no reason for you to believe it is flat.

AD HOMINEM   Closely allied to poisoning the well is another fallacy, **ad hominem** argument (from the Latin for "against the person"). A critic can easily yield to the temptation to attack an argument or theory by trying to impeach or undercut the credentials of its advocates.

Consider this example: Jones is arguing that prayer should not be permitted in public schools, and Smith responds by pointing out that Jones has twice been convicted of assault- ing members of the clergy. Jones's behavior doubtless is reprehensible, but the issue is not Jones, it is prayer in school, and what must be scrutinized is Jones's argument, not his police record or his character.

APPEAL TO AUTHORITY   One might easily imagine someone from the South in 1860 defending the slavery-dependent society of that day by appealing to the fact that no less a person than Thomas Jefferson — a brilliant public figure, thinker, and leader by any measure — enslaved people. Or today one might defend capital punishment on the ground that Abraham Lincoln, surely one of the nation's greatest presidents, signed many death warrants during the Civil War, authorizing the execution of Union soldiers. No doubt the esteem in which such figures as Jefferson and Lincoln are deservedly held amounts to impressive endorsement for whatever acts and practices, policies, and institutions, they supported. But the **authority** of these figures in itself is not evidence for the truth of their views, so their authority cannot be a reason for anyone to agree with them.

Sometimes, the appeal to authority is fallacious because the authoritative person is not an expert on the issue in dispute. The fact that a high-energy physicist has won the Nobel Prize is no reason for attaching any special weight to her views on the causes of cancer, the reduction of traffic accidents, or the legalization of marijuana. We all depend heavily on the knowledge of various experts and authorities, so we tend to respect their views. Conversely, we should resist the temptation to accord their views on diverse subjects the same respect that we grant them in the area of their expertise.

APPEAL TO FEAR   The Romans called the **appeal to fear** fallacy *ad baculum*, for "resorting to violence" (*baculum* means "stick" or "club"). Trying to persuade people to agree with you by threatening them with painful consequences is obviously an appeal that no rational person would contemplate. The violence need not be physical; if you threaten someone with the loss of a job, for instance, you are still using a stick. Violence or the threat of harmful consequences in the course of an argument is beyond reason and always shows the haste or impatience of those who appeal to it. It is also an indication that the argument on its merits would be unpersuasive, inconclusive, or worse. President Theodore Roosevelt's epigrammatic doctrine for the kind of foreign policy he favored — "Speak softly but carry a big stick" — illustrates an attempt to have it both ways; an appeal to reason for starters, but a recourse to coercion, or the threat of coercion, as a backup if needed.

A CHECKLIST FOR EVALUATING AN ARGUMENT WITH LOGIC

☐ Can I identify the premises and the conclusion of the argument?

☐ Given the premises, is the argument valid?

☐ If it is valid, are all its premises true?

☐ If all the premises are true, does the conclusion necessarily follow from them?

☐ Are there any claims that are inconsistent in the argument?

☐ Does the argument contain one or more fallacies?

☐ If the argument is inductive, on what observations is it based?

☐ Do the observations or data make the conclusion probable?

☐ Is there enough evidence to disconfirm the conclusion?

ADDITIONAL FALLACIES

Finally, we add two fallacies, not easily embraced by Engels's three categories that have served us well thus far (ambiguity, erroneous presumption, and irrelevance): death by a thousand qualifications and protecting the hypothesis.

DEATH BY A THOUSAND QUALIFICATIONS   **Death by a thousand qualifications** gets its name from the ancient torture of death by a thousand small cuts. Thus, a bold assertion can be virtually killed and its true content reduced to nothing, bit by bit, as all the appropriate or necessary qualifications are added to it.

Consider an example. Suppose you hear a politician describing another country (let's call it Ruritania) as a "democracy" — except it turns out that Ruritania doesn't have regular elections, lacks a written constitution, has no independent judiciary, prohibits religious worship except of the state-designated deity, and so forth. So what remains of the original claim that Ruritania is a democracy is little or nothing. The qualifications have taken all the content out of the original description.

PROTECTING THE HYPOTHESIS   In Chapter 4, we contrasted *reasoning* and *rationalization* (or the finding of bad reasons for what one intends to believe anyway). Rationalization can take subtle forms, as the following example indicates. Suppose you're standing with a friend on the shore or on a pier and you watch as a ship heads out to sea. As it reaches the horizon, it slowly disappears — first the hull, then the upper decks, and finally the tip of the mast. Because the ship (you both assume) isn't sinking, it occurs to you that this sequence of observations provides evidence that the earth's surface is curved. Nonsense, says your companion. Light waves sag, or bend down, over distances of a few miles, and so a flat surface (such as the ocean) can intercept them. Therefore, the ship, which appears to be going "over" the horizon, really isn't: It's just moving steadily farther and farther away in a straight line. Your friend, you discover to your amazement, is a card-carrying member of the Flat Earth Society, a group who insists the earth is a plane surface. Now most of us would regard the idea that light rays bend down in the manner required by the Flat Earther's argument as a rationalization whose sole purpose is to protect the flat-earth doctrine against counterevidence. We would be convinced it was a rationalization, and not a very good one at that, if the Flat Earther held to it despite a patient and thorough explanation from a physicist that showed modern optical theory to be quite incompatible with the view that light waves sag.

This example illustrates two important points about the *backing* of arguments. First, it is always possible to **protect a hypothesis** by abandoning adjacent or connected hypotheses; this is the tactic our Flat Earth friend has used. This maneuver is possible, however, only because — and this is the second point — whenever we test a hypothesis, we do so by taking for granted (usually, quite unconsciously) many other hypotheses as well. So the evidence for the hypothesis we think we are confirming is impossible to separate entirely from the adequacy of the connected hypotheses. As long as we have no reason to doubt that light rays travel in straight lines (at least over distances of a few miles), our Flat Earth friend's argument is unconvincing. But once that hypothesis is itself put in doubt, the idea that seemed at first to be a pathetic rationalization takes on an even more troublesome character.

There are, then, not one but two fallacies exposed by this example. The first and perhaps graver one is in rigging your hypothesis so that *no matter what* observations are brought against it, you will count nothing as falsifying it. The second and subtler one is in thinking that as you test one hypothesis, all your other background beliefs are left safely to one side, immaculate and uninvolved. On the contrary, our beliefs form a corporate structure, intertwined and connected to one another with great complexity, and no one of them can ever be singled out for unique and isolated application, confirmation, or disconfirmation to the world around us.

THINKING CRITICALLY *Identifying Fallacies*

Here are some fallacies in action. Using the explanations in this section, identify what type of fallacy the argument example commits and then explain your reasoning.

EXAMPLE	TYPE OF FALLACY	EXPLANATION
Senator Case was friends with a disgraced racketeer; he shouldn't be your selection in the upcoming election.		
These activists say they want justice, but is it really justice to clog up the streets with the protests?		
East Coast urban liberals are going to say that hunting is inhumane. They do not realize how narrow-minded they are.		
There have been few terrorist attacks since September 11, 2001; therefore, our national security efforts must be working.		
If you start out with a bottle of beer a day and then go on to a glass or two of wine on the weekends, you're well on your way to becoming a hopeless drunk.		
My marriage was a failure, which just proves my point: Don't ever get married in the first place.		
Not until astronauts sailed through space around the moon did we have adequate reason to believe that the moon even had a back side.		
A professional baseball player has a good-luck charm. When he wears it, the team wins.		
How come herbivores don't eat herbs?		

MAX SHULMAN

Max Shulman began his career as a writer when he was a journalism student at the University of Minnesota. Later he wrote humorous novels, stories, and plays. One of his novels, *Barefoot Boy with Cheek* (1943), was made into a musical, and another, *Rally Round the Flag, Boys!* (1957), was made into a film starring Paul Newman and Joanne Woodward. *The Tender Trap* (1954), a play he wrote with Robert Paul Smith, still retains its popularity with theater groups.

"Love Is a Fallacy" was first published in 1951, when demeaning stereotypes about women and minoritized groups were widely accepted in the marketplace, as well as the home. Thus, jokes about domineering mothers-in-law or about dumb blondes routinely met with no objection.

Love Is a Fallacy

Cool was I and logical. Keen, calculating, perspicacious, acute, and astute — I was all of these. My brain was as powerful as a dynamo, as precise as a chemist's scales, as penetrating as a scalpel. And — think of it! — I was only eighteen.

It is not often that one so young has such a giant intellect. Take, for example, Petey Bellows, my roommate at the university. Same age, same background, but dumb as an ox. A nice enough fellow, you understand, but nothing upstairs. Emotional type. Unstable. Impressionable. Worst of all, a faddist. Fads, I submit, are the very negation of reason. To be swept up in every new craze that comes along, to surrender yourself to idiocy just because everybody else is doing it — this, to me, is the acme of mindlessness. Not, however, to Petey.

One afternoon I found Petey lying on his bed with an expression of such distress on his face that I immediately diagnosed appendicitis. "Don't move," I said. "Don't take a laxative. I'll call a doctor."

"Raccoon," he mumbled thickly.

"Raccoon?" I said, pausing in my flight. 5

"I want a raccoon coat," he wailed.

I perceived that his trouble was not physical, but mental. "Why do you want a raccoon coat?"

"I should have known it," he cried, pounding his temples. "I should have known they'd come back when the Charleston came back. Like a fool I spent all my money for textbooks, and now I can't get a raccoon coat."

"Can you mean," I said incredulously, "that people are actually wearing raccoon coats again?"

"All the Big Men on Campus are wearing 10 them. Where've you been?"

"In the library," I said, naming a place not frequented by Big Men on Campus.

He leaped from the bed and paced the room. "I've got to have a raccoon coat," he said passionately. "I've got to!"

"Petey, why? Look at it rationally. Raccoon coats are unsanitary. They shed. They smell bad. They weigh too much. They're unsightly. They ——"

"You don't understand," he interrupted impatiently. "It's the thing to do. Don't you want to be in the swim?"

"No," I said truthfully. 15

"Well, I do," he declared. "I'd give anything for a raccoon coat. Anything!"

My brain, that precision instrument, slipped into high gear. "Anything?" I asked, looking at him narrowly.

"Anything," he affirmed in ringing tones.

I stroked my chin thoughtfully. It so happened that I knew where to get my hands on a raccoon coat. My father had had one in his undergraduate days; it lay now in a trunk in the attic back home. It also happened that Petey had something I wanted. He didn't *have* it exactly, but at least he had first rights on it. I refer to his girl, Polly Espy.

I had long coveted Polly Espy. Let me empha- ₂₀ size that my desire for this young woman was not emotional in nature. She was, to be sure, a girl who excited the emotions, but I was not one to let my heart rule my head. I wanted Polly for a shrewdly calculated, entirely cerebral reason.

I was a freshman in law school. In a few years I would be out in practice. I was well aware of the importance of the right kind of wife in furthering a lawyer's career. The successful lawyers I had observed were, almost without exception, married to beautiful, gracious, intelligent women. With one omission, Polly fitted these specifications perfectly.

Beautiful she was. She was not yet of pin-up proportions, but I felt sure that time would supply the lack. She already had the makings.

Gracious she was. By gracious I mean full of graces. She had an erectness of carriage, an ease of bearing, a poise that clearly indicated the best of breeding. At table her manners were exquisite. I had seen her at the Kozy Kampus Korner eating the specialty of the house — a sandwich that contained scraps of pot roast, gravy, chopped nuts, and a dipper of sauerkraut — without even getting her fingers moist.

Intelligent she was not. In fact, she veered in the opposite direction. But I believed that under my guidance she would smarten up. At any rate, it was worth a try. It is, after all, easier to make a beautiful dumb girl smart than to make an ugly smart girl beautiful.

"Petey," I said, "are you in love with Polly ₂₅ Espy?"

"I think she's a keen kid," he replied, "but I don't know if you'd call it love. Why?"

"Do you," I asked, "have any kind of formal arrangement with her? I mean are you going steady or anything like that?"

"No. We see each other quite a bit, but we both have other dates. Why?"

"Is there," I asked, "any other man for whom she has a particular fondness?"

"Not that I know of. Why?" ₃₀

I nodded with satisfaction. "In other words, if you were out of the picture, the field would be open. Is that right?"

"I guess so. What are you getting at?"

"Nothing, nothing," I said innocently, and took my suitcase out of the closet.

"Where you going?" asked Petey.

"Home for the weekend." I threw a few ₃₅ things into the bag.

"Listen," he said, clutching my arm eagerly, "while you're home, you couldn't get some money from your old man, could you, and lend it to me so I can buy a raccoon coat?"

"I may do better than that," I said with a mysterious wink and closed my bag and left.

"Look," I said to Petey when I got back Monday morning. I threw open the suitcase and revealed the huge, hairy, gamy object that my father had worn in his Stutz Bearcat in 1925.

"Holy Toledo!" said Petey reverently. He plunged his hands into the raccoon coat and then his face. "Holy Toledo!" he repeated fifteen or twenty times.

"Would you like it?" I asked. ₄₀

"Oh yes!" he cried, clutching the greasy pelt to him. Then a canny look came into his eyes. "What do you want for it?"

"Your girl," I said, mincing no words.

"Polly?" he said in a horrified whisper. "You want Polly?"

"That's right."

He flung the coat from him. "Never," he said stoutly.

I shrugged. "Okay. If you don't want to be in the swim, I guess it's your business."

I sat down in a chair and pretended to read a book, but out of the corner of my eye I kept watching Petey. He was a torn man. First he looked at the coat with the expression of a waif at a bakery window. Then he turned away and set his jaw resolutely. Then he looked back at the coat, with even more longing in his face. Then he turned away, but with not so much resolution this time. Back and forth his head swiveled, desire waxing, resolution waning. Finally he didn't turn away at all; he just stood and stared with mad lust at the coat.

"It isn't as though I was in love with Polly," he said thickly. "Or going steady or anything like that."

"That's right," I murmured.

"What's Polly to me, or me to Polly?"

"Not a thing," said I.

"It's just been a casual kick — just a few laughs, that's all."

"Try on the coat," said I.

He complied. The coat bunched high over his ears and dropped all the way down to his shoe tops. He looked like a mound of dead raccoons. "Fits fine," he said happily.

I rose from my chair. "Is it a deal?" I asked, extending my hand.

He swallowed. "It's a deal," he said and shook my hand.

I had my first date with Polly the following evening. This was in the nature of a survey; I wanted to find out just how much work I had to do to get her mind up to the standard I required. I took her first to dinner. "Gee, that was a delish dinner," she said as we left the restaurant. Then I took her to a movie. "Gee, that was a marvy movie," she said as we left the theater. And then

I took her home. "Gee, I had a sensaysh time," she said as she bade me good night.

I went back to my room with a heavy heart. I had gravely underestimated the size of my task. This girl's lack of information was terrifying. Nor would it be enough merely to supply her with information. First she had to be taught to *think*. This loomed as a project of no small dimensions, and at first I was tempted to give her back to Petey. But then I got to thinking about her abundant physical charms and about the way she entered a room and the way she handled a knife and fork, and I decided to make an effort.

I went about it, as in all things, systematically. I gave her a course in logic. It happened that I, as a law student, was taking a course in logic myself, so I had all the facts at my fingertips. "Polly," I said to her when I picked her up on our next date, "tonight we are going over to the Knoll and talk."

"Oo, terrif," she replied. One thing I will say for this girl: You would go far to find another so agreeable.

We went to the Knoll, the campus trysting place, and we sat down under an old oak, and she looked at me expectantly: "What are we going to talk about?" she asked.

"Logic."

She thought this over for a minute and decided she liked it. "Magnif," she said.

"Logic," I said, clearing my throat, "is the science of thinking. Before we can think correctly, we must first learn to recognize the common fallacies of logic. These we will take up tonight."

"Wow-dow!" she cried, clapping her hands delightedly.

I winced, but went bravely on. "First let us examine the fallacy called Dicto Simpliciter."

"By all means," she urged, batting her lashes eagerly.

"Dicto Simpliciter means an argument based on an unqualified generalization. For example: Exercise is good. Therefore everybody should exercise."

"I agree," said Polly earnestly. "I mean exercise is wonderful. I mean it builds the body and everything."

"Polly," I said gently, "the argument is a fallacy. *Exercise is good* is an unqualified generalization. For instance, if you have heart disease, exercise is bad, not good. Many people are ordered by their doctors *not* to exercise. You must *qualify* the generalization. You must say exercise is *usually* good, or exercise is good *for most people*. Otherwise you have committed a Dicto Simpliciter. Do you see?" 70

"No," she confessed. "But this is marvy. Do more! Do more!"

"It will be better if you stop tugging at my sleeve," I told her, and when she desisted, I continued. "Next we take up a fallacy called Hasty Generalization. Listen carefully: You can't speak French. I can't speak French. Petey Bellows can't speak French. I must therefore conclude that nobody at the University of Minnesota can speak French."

"Really?" said Polly, amazed. "*Nobody?*"

I hid my exasperation. "Polly, it's a fallacy. The generalization is reached too hastily. There are too few instances to support such a conclusion."

"Know any more fallacies?" she asked breathlessly. "This is more fun than dancing even." 75

I fought off a wave of despair. I was getting nowhere with this girl, absolutely nowhere. Still, I am nothing if not persistent. I continued. "Next comes Post Hoc. Listen to this: Let's not take Bill on our picnic. Every time we take him out with us, it rains."

"I know somebody just like that," she exclaimed. "A girl back home — Eula Becker, her name is. It never fails. Every single time we take her on a picnic ——"

"Polly," I said sharply, "it's a fallacy. Eula Becker doesn't *cause* the rain. She has no connection with the rain. You are guilty of Post Hoc if you blame Eula Becker."

"I'll never do it again," she promised contritely. "Are you mad at me?"

I sighed. "No, Polly, I'm not mad." 80

"Then tell me some more fallacies."

"All right. Let's try Contradictory Premises."

"Yes, let's," she chirped, blinking her eyes happily.

I frowned, but plunged ahead. "Here's an example of Contradictory Premises: If God can do anything, can He make a stone so heavy that He won't be able to lift it?"

"Of course," she replied promptly. 85

"But if He can do anything, He can lift the stone," I pointed out.

"Yeah," she said thoughtfully. "Well, then I guess He can't make the stone."

"But He can do anything," I reminded her.

She scratched her pretty, empty head. "I'm all confused," she admitted.

"Of course you are. Because when the premises of an argument contradict each other, there can be no argument. If there is an irresistible force, there can be no immovable object. If there is an immovable object, there can be no irresistible force. Get it?" 90

"Tell me some more of this keen stuff," she said eagerly.

I consulted my watch. "I think we'd better call it a night. I'll take you home now, and you go over all the things you've learned. We'll have another session tomorrow night."

I deposited her at the girls' dormitory, where she assured me that she had had a perfectly terrif evening, and I went glumly home to my room. Petey lay snoring in his bed, the raccoon coat huddled like a great hairy beast at his feet. For a moment I considered waking him and telling him that he could have his girl back. It seemed clear that my project was doomed to failure. The girl simply had a logic-proof head.

But then I reconsidered. I had wasted one evening; I might as well waste another. Who knew? Maybe somewhere in the extinct crater of her mind a few embers still smoldered. Maybe somehow I could fan them into flame. Admittedly it was not a prospect fraught with hope, but I decided to give it one more try.

Seated under the oak the next evening 95 I said, "Our first fallacy tonight is called Ad Misericordiam."

She quivered with delight.

"Listen closely," I said. "A man applies for a job. When the boss asks him what his qualifications are, he replies that he has a wife and six children at home, the wife is a helpless cripple, the children have nothing to eat, no clothes to wear, no shoes on their feet, there are no beds in the house, no coal in the cellar, and winter is coming."

A tear rolled down each of Polly's pink cheeks. "Oh, this is awful, awful," she sobbed.

"Yes, it's awful," I agreed, "but it's no argument. The man never answered the boss's question about his qualifications. Instead he appealed to the boss's sympathy. He committed the fallacy of Ad Misericordiam. Do you understand?"

"Have you got a handkerchief?" she 100 blubbered.

I handed her a handkerchief and tried to keep from screaming while she wiped her eyes. "Next," I said in a carefully controlled tone, "we will discuss False Analogy. Here is an example: Students should be allowed to look at their textbooks during examinations. After all, surgeons have X rays to guide them during an operation, lawyers have briefs to guide them during a trial, carpenters have blueprints to guide them when they are building a house. Why, then, shouldn't students be allowed to look at their textbooks during an examination?"

"There now," she said enthusiastically, "is the most marvy idea I've heard in years."

"Polly," I said testily, "the argument is all wrong. Doctors, lawyers, and carpenters aren't taking a test to see how much they have learned, but students are. The situations are altogether different, and you can't make an analogy between them."

"I still think it's a good idea," said Polly.

"Nuts," I muttered. Doggedly I pressed on. 105 "Next we'll try Hypothesis Contrary to Fact."

"Sounds yummy," was Polly's reaction.

"Listen: If Madame Curie had not happened to leave a photographic plate in a drawer with a chunk of pitchblende, the world today would not know about radium."

"True, true," said Polly, nodding her head. "Did you see the movie? Oh, it just knocked me out. That Walter Pidgeon is so dreamy. I mean he fractures me."

"If you can forget Mr. Pidgeon for a moment," I said coldly, "I would like to point out that the statement is a fallacy. Maybe Madame Curie would have discovered radium at some later date. Maybe somebody else would have discovered it. Maybe any number of things would have happened. You can't start with a hypothesis that is not true and then draw any supportable conclusions from it."

"They ought to put Walter Pidgeon in 110 more pictures," said Polly. "I hardly ever see him anymore."

One more chance, I decided. But just one more. There is a limit to what flesh and blood can bear. "The next fallacy is called Poisoning the Well."

"How cute!" she gurgled.

"Two men are having a debate. The first one gets up and says, 'My opponent is a notorious liar. You can't believe a word that he is going to say.' . . . Now, Polly, think. Think hard. What's wrong?"

I watched her closely as she knit her creamy brow in concentration. Suddenly a glimmer of intelligence — the first I had seen — came into her eyes. "It's not fair," she said with indignation. "It's not a bit fair. What chance has the second man got if the first man calls him a liar before he even begins talking?"

"Right!" I cried exultantly. "One hundred 115 percent right. It's not fair. The first man has *poisoned the well* before anybody could drink from it. He has hamstrung his opponent before he could even start. . . . Polly, I'm proud of you."

"Pshaw," she murmured, blushing with pleasure.

"You see, my dear, these things aren't so hard. All you have to do is concentrate. Think — examine — evaluate. Come now, let's review everything we have learned."

"Fire away," she said with an airy wave of her hand.

Heartened by the knowledge that Polly was not altogether a cretin, I began a long, patient review of all I had told her. Over and over and over again I cited instances, pointed out flaws, kept hammering away without letup. It was like digging a tunnel. At first everything was work, sweat, and darkness. I had no idea when I would reach the light, or even *if* I would. But I persisted. I pounded and clawed and scraped, and finally I was rewarded. I saw a chink of light. And then the chink got bigger and the sun came pouring in and all was bright.

Five grueling nights this took, but it was 120 worth it. I had made a logician out of Polly; I had taught her to think. My job was done. She was worthy of me at last. She was a fit wife for me, a proper hostess for my many mansions, a suitable mother for my well-heeled children.

It must not be thought that I was without love for this girl. Quite the contrary. Just as Pygmalion loved the perfect woman he had fashioned, so I loved mine. I decided to acquaint her with my feelings at our very next meeting. The time had come to change our relationship from academic to romantic.

"Polly," I said when next we sat beneath our oak, "tonight we will not discuss fallacies."

"Aw, gee," she said, disappointed.

"My dear," I said, favoring her with a smile, "we have now spent five evenings together. We have gotten along splendidly. It is clear that we are well matched."

"Hasty Generalization," said Polly brightly. 125

"I beg your pardon," said I.

"Hasty Generalization," she repeated. "How can you say that we are well matched on the basis of only five dates?"

I chuckled with amusement. The dear child had learned her lessons well. "My dear," I said, patting her hand in a tolerant manner, "five dates is plenty. After all, you don't have to eat a whole cake to know that it's good."

"False Analogy," said Polly promptly. "I'm not a cake. I'm a girl."

I chuckled with somewhat less amuse- 130 ment. The dear child had learned her lesson perhaps too well. I decided to change tactics. Obviously the best approach was a simple, strong, direct declaration of love. I paused for a moment while my massive brain chose the proper words. Then I began:

"Polly, I love you. You are the whole world to me, and the moon and the stars and the constellations of outer space. Please, my darling, say that you will go steady with me, for if you will not, life will be meaningless. I will languish. I will refuse my meals. I will wander the face of the earth, a shambling, hollow-eyed hulk."

There, I thought, folding my arms, that ought to do it.

"Ad Misericordiam," said Polly.

I ground my teeth. I was not Pygmalion; I was Frankenstein, and my monster had me by the throat. Frantically I fought back the tide of panic surging through me. At all costs I had to keep cool.

"Well, Polly," I said, forcing a smile, "you 135 certainly have learned your fallacies."

"You're darn right," she said with a vigorous nod.

"And who taught them to you, Polly?"

"You did."

"That's right. So you do owe me something, don't you, my dear? If I hadn't come along you never would have learned about fallacies."

"Hypothesis Contrary to Fact," she said instantly. 140

I dashed perspiration from my brow. "Polly," I croaked, "you mustn't take all these things so literally. I mean this is just classroom stuff. You know that the things you learn in school don't have anything to do with life."

"Dicto Simpliciter," she said, wagging her finger at me playfully.

That did it. I leaped to my feet, bellowing like a bull. "Will you or will you not go steady with me?"

"I will not," she replied.

"Why not?" I demanded. 145

"Because this afternoon I promised Petey Bellows that I would go steady with him."

I reeled back, overcome with the infamy of it. After he promised, after he made a deal, after he shook my hand! "That rat!" I shrieked, kicking up great chunks of turf. "You can't go with him, Polly. He's a liar. He's a cheat. He's a rat."

"Poisoning the Well," said Polly, "and stop shouting. I think shouting must be a fallacy too."

With an immense effort of will, I modulated my voice. "All right," I said. "You're a logician. Let's look at this thing logically. How could you choose Petey Bellows over me? Look at me — a brilliant student, a tremendous intellectual, a man with an assured future. Look at Petey — a knothead, a jitterbug, a guy who'll never know where his next meal is coming from. Can you give me one logical reason why you should go steady with Petey Bellows?"

"I certainly can," declared Polly. "He's got a raccoon coat." 150

Topic for Critical Thinking and Writing

After you have finished reading "Love Is a Fallacy," consider the following hypothetical conversation and then join the conversation: Write your own, final response that points out to these three peers how their arguments succeed or fail, using the elements of logic from this chapter (premises, conclusions, assumptions, fallacies, etc.). Finally, make your own argument about the nature of this story and how it bears on the question of sexism and publication.

CAITLYN: The story is condescending and even insulting to women. You could even call it sexist. Sexist stories should not be in college textbooks, and therefore this story should not have been published in this college textbook.

JOSHUA: This story may be sexist, but that is acceptable in the context of learning. Now if any story were racist, you would have a point about not including it in a textbook. But this story was written in 1951, and it wasn't considered sexist in its own time.

SAM: Max Shulman was a great humorist who worked in old-time television and invented the iconic character Dobie Gillis. The story is intended to be funny; therefore, it is not sexist. If anything, it should not be included in this textbook because it is not funny.

A Psychologist's View: Rogerian Argument

Fight for the things you care about, but do it in a way that will lead others to join you.

— RUTH BADER GINSBURG

CONSIDER THIS

When we encounter arguments, we commonly focus on the distances between opponents, the points where they most starkly differ from one another, and the conflicts created by their distinct views. But what happens when we try to bridge these differences?

Choose two people who represent different "sides" of an issue, problem, or solution in public life. You may choose a pair of Democratic and Republican opponents; liberal and conservative news commentators; artists, critics, or journalists disputing some issue; world leaders in conflict; two friends with different backgrounds or experiences — or another pair of opponents you have in mind.

Consider what these opponents share. What common values, beliefs, principles, and morals do they share? What larger goals do they have that might overlap? What unites them despite their differences? On what points would they agree?

Bridges / Common Ground

Person / Perspective

Person / Perspective

Rogerian Argument: An Introduction

As Ruth Bader Ginsburg's words at the opening of this chapter suggest, one of the most important aspects of effective argumentation is your ability to convince your opponents to come over to your side. This can be quite a tall order, however, because people who stand on different sides of issues commonly disagree on more than just the issue at stake. It may be quite difficult to convince someone with an entirely different political or religious perspective, for example, to see things your way and act accordingly.

But arguments are rarely zero-sum games with clear winners or losers. Arguments are more often about understanding, compromising, and finding solutions that are acceptable to both sides. In most arguments, we work with our opponents to think through issues together, even perhaps appreciating one another for helping us to test, clarify, and modify our positions. Maybe in asking our opposition to consider our views, we may find that they have something to offer us for consideration, too.

Carl R. Rogers (1902–1987), perhaps best known for his book titled *On Becoming a Person* (1961), was a psychotherapist, not a teacher of writing. Nonetheless, Rogers's approach to argument (put forth in the short essay by Rogers beginning on p. 387) has exerted much influence on instructors who teach argument.

On the surface, many arguments seem to show *A* arguing with *B*, presumably seeking to change *B*'s mind, but *A*'s argument is really directed not to *B* but to *C*. This attempt to persuade a non-participant is evident in the courtroom, where neither the prosecutor (*A*) nor the defense lawyer (*B*) is really trying to convince the opponent. Rather, both are trying to convince a third party, the jury (*C*). Prosecutors don't care whether they convince defense lawyers; they don't even mind infuriating defense lawyers because their only real goal is to convince the jury. Similarly, the writer of a letter to a newspaper, taking issue with an editorial, doesn't expect to change the paper's policy. Rather, the writer hopes to convince a third party, the reader of the newspaper.

Carl R. Rogers (second from the right) leading a panel discussion in 1966.

Michael Rougier/The LIFE Picture Collection/Shutterstock

But suppose *A* really does want to bring *B* around to *A*'s point of view and suppose *B* is also arguing with *A*, too, trying to persuade *A* that his or her way is best. Politicians often argue with one another in such a manner, often trying to convince the other party to support or vote a particular way. In such instances, both parties may be reluctant to listen to the other. Rogers points out that when we engage in an argument, if we feel our integrity or our identity is threatened, we will stiffen our position. The sense of threat may be so great that we are unable to consider the alternative views being offered, and we therefore remain unpersuaded.

Threatened, we may defend *ourselves* rather than our argument, and little communication will take place. Of course, a third party might say that we or our opponent presented the more convincing case, but we ourselves, and perhaps our opponent, too, have barely listened to each other, and so the two of us remain apart.

Rogers therefore suggests that a writer who wishes to communicate with someone (as opposed to convincing a third party) needs to reduce the threat. In a sense, the participants in the argument need to become partners rather than adversaries. Rogers, a therapist, was keen to highlight **empathy**, the understanding of someone else's perspective or experiences, as a fundamental part of effective communication. Writers, like therapists and significant others, also must work toward understanding their partners in communication. That is achieved partially through an honest attempt to inhabit the psyche of the other, to see and feel the issues through the other's perspectives, in light of the perceptions and feelings of the other. At the same time, we trust that the other is giving us this same treatment. Instead of point–counterpoint argument, the goal is to foster emotional and intellectual reciprocity. Listeners are more willing to be persuaded when they see their partner in communication as an honest collaborator instead of an opponent. Rogers wrote, "Mutual communication tends to be pointed toward solving a problem rather than toward attacking a person or group."

Thus, in an essay on standardized testing, for instance, the writer need not — and probably should not — see the issue as black or white, as *either/or*. Such an essay might indicate that testing is undesirable because it has negative effects on students or teaching, *but in some circumstances* it may also be seen as reasonable and acceptable. This qualification does not mean that one must compromise. Thus, the essayist might argue that high-stakes testing increases student anxiety, constrains teachers, and devalues the arts, but may also recognize how such tests ensure educational consistency across public school systems.

Visual Guide: Rogerian Argument

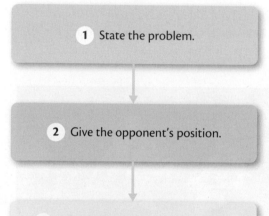

1. State the problem.

2. Give the opponent's position.

3. Grant whatever validity the writer finds in that position.

4. (If possible) Attempt to show how the opposing position will be improved if the writer's own position is accepted.

A writer who wishes to reduce the psychological threat to the opposition and thus facilitate partnership in the study of some issue can do several things:

- show sympathetic understanding of the opposing argument
- recognize what is valid in it
- recognize and demonstrate that those who take the other side are nonetheless persons of goodwill

Advocates of Rogerian argument are likely to contrast it with Aristotelian argument, saying that the style of argument associated with Aristotle has these two characteristics:

- It is adversarial, seeking to refute other views.
- It sees the listener as wrong, as someone who now must be overwhelmed by evidence.

In contrast to the confrontational Aristotelian style, which allegedly seeks to present an airtight case that compels belief, Rogerian argument (it is said) has the following characteristics:

- It is nonconfrontational, collegial, and friendly.
- It respects other views and allows for multiple truths.
- It seeks to achieve some degree of assent and empathy rather than convince utterly.

Sometimes, of course, the differing positions may be so far apart that no reconciliation can be proposed, in which case the writer will probably seek to show how the problem can best be solved by adopting the writer's own position. These matters are discussed in Chapter 7, but not from the point of view of a psychotherapist, and so we reprint Rogers's essay here.

> ## A CHECKLIST FOR ANALYZING ROGERIAN ARGUMENT
>
> ☐ Have I stated the problem and indicated that a dialogue is possible?
>
> ☐ Have I stated at least one other point of view in a way that would satisfy its proponents?
>
> ☐ Have I been courteous to those who hold views other than mine?
>
> ☐ Have I enlarged my own understanding to the extent that I can grant validity, at least in some circumstances, to at least some aspects of other positions?
>
> ☐ Have I stated my position and indicated the contexts in which I believe it is valid?
>
> ☐ Have I pointed out the ground that we share?
>
> ☐ Have I shown how other positions will be strengthened by accepting some aspects of my position?

CARL R. ROGERS

Carl R. Rogers, perhaps best known for his book *On Becoming a Person* (1961), was a psychotherapist. The following essay was originally presented on October 11, 1951, at Northwestern University's Centennial Conference on Communications. In it, Rogers reflects the political climate of the cold war between the United States and the Soviet Union, which dominated headlines for more than forty years (1947–1989). Several of Rogers's examples of bias and frustrated communication allude to the tensions of that era.

Communication: Its Blocking and Its Facilitation

It may seem curious that a person whose whole professional effort is devoted to psychotherapy should be interested in problems of communication. What relationship is there between providing therapeutic help to individuals with emotional maladjustments and the concern of this conference with obstacles to communication? Actually the relationship is very close indeed. The whole task of psychotherapy is the task of dealing with a failure in communication. The emotionally maladjusted person, the "neurotic," is in difficulty first because communication within himself has broken down, and second because as a result of this his communication with others has been damaged. If this sounds somewhat strange, then let me put it in other terms. In the "neurotic" individual, parts of himself which have been termed unconscious, or repressed, or denied to awareness, become blocked off so that they no longer communicate themselves to the conscious or managing part of himself. As long as this is true, there are distortions in the way he communicates himself to others, and so he suffers both within himself, and in his interpersonal relations. The task of psychotherapy is to help the person achieve, through a special relationship with a therapist, good communication within himself. Once this is achieved he can communicate more freely and more effectively with others. We may say then that psychotherapy is good communication, within and between men. We may also turn that statement around and it will still be true. Good communication, free communication, within or between men, is always therapeutic.

It is, then, from a background of experience with communication in counseling and psychotherapy that I want to present here two ideas. I wish to state what I believe is one of the major factors in blocking or impeding communication, and then I wish to present what in our experience has proven to be a very important way to improving or facilitating communication.

I would like to propose, as an hypothesis for consideration, that the major barrier to mutual interpersonal communication is our very natural tendency to judge, to evaluate, to approve or disapprove, the statement of the person, or the other group. Let me illustrate my meaning with some very simple examples. As you leave the meeting tonight, one of the statements you are likely to hear is, "I didn't like that man's talk." Now what do you respond? Almost invariably your reply will be either approval or disapproval of the attitude expressed. Either you respond, "I didn't either. I thought it was terrible," or else you tend to reply, "Oh, I thought it was really good." In other words, your primary reaction is to evaluate what has just been said to you, to evaluate it from *your* point of view, your own frame of reference.

Or take another example. Suppose I say with some feeling, "I think the Republicans are behaving in ways that show a lot of good sound sense these days," what is the response that arises in your mind as you listen? The overwhelming likelihood is that it will be evaluative. You will find yourself agreeing, or disagreeing, or making some judgment about me such as "He must be a conservative," or "He seems solid in his thinking." Or let us take an illustration from the international scene. Russia says vehemently, "The treaty with Japan is a war plot on the part of the United States." We rise as one person to say "That's a lie!"

This last illustration brings in another 5 element connected with my hypothesis. Although the tendency to make evaluations is common in almost all interchange of language, it is very much heightened in those situations where feelings and emotions are deeply involved. So the stronger our feelings, the more likely it is that there will be no mutual element in the communication. There will be just two ideas, two feelings, two judgments, missing each other in psychological space. I'm sure you recognize this from your own experience. When you have not been emotionally involved yourself and have listened to a heated discussion, you often go away thinking, "Well, they actually weren't talking about the same thing." And they were not. Each was making a judgment, an evaluation, from his own frame of reference. There was really nothing which could be called communication in any genuine sense. This tendency to react to any emotionally meaningful statement by forming an evaluation of it from our own point of view, is, I repeat, the major barrier to interpersonal communication.

But is there any way of solving this problem, of avoiding this barrier? I feel that we are making exciting progress toward this goal and I would like to present it as simply as I can. Real communication occurs, and this evaluative tendency is avoided, when we listen with understanding. What does that mean? It means *to see the expressed idea and attitude from the other person's point of view, to sense how it feels to him, to achieve his frame of reference in regard to the thing he is talking about.*

Stated so briefly, this may sound absurdly simple, but it is not. It is an approach which we have found extremely potent in the field of psychotherapy. It is the most effective agent we know for altering the basic personality structure of an individual, and improving his relationships and his communications with others. If I can listen to what he can tell me, if I can understand how it seems to him, if I can see its personal meaning for him, if I can sense the emotional flavor which it has for him, then I will be releasing potent forces of change in him. If I can really understand how he hates his father, or hates the university, or hates communists — if I can catch the flavor of his fear of insanity, or his fear of atom bombs, or of Russia — it will be of the greatest help to him in altering those very hatreds and fears, and in establishing realistic and harmonious relationships with the very people and situations toward which he has felt hatred and

fear. We know from our research that such empathic understanding — understanding *with* a person, not *about* him — is such an effective approach that it can bring about major changes in personality.

Some of you may be feeling that you listen well to people, and that you have never seen such results. The chances are very great indeed that your listening has not been of the type I have described. Fortunately I can suggest a little laboratory experiment which you can try to test the quality of your understanding. The next time you get into an argument with your wife, or your friend, or with a small group of friends, just stop the discussion for a moment and for an experiment, institute this rule. "Each person can speak up for himself only *after* he has first restated the ideas and feelings of the previous speaker accurately, and to that speaker's satisfaction." You see what this would mean. It would simply mean that before presenting your own point of view, it would be necessary for you to really achieve the other speaker's frame of reference — to understand his thoughts and feelings so well that you could summarize them for him. Sounds simple, doesn't it? But if you try it you will discover it one of the most difficult things you have ever tried to do. However, once you have been able to see the other's point of view, your own comments will have to be drastically revised. You will also find the emotion going out of the discussion, the differences being reduced, and those differences which remain being of a rational and understandable sort.

Can you imagine what this kind of an approach would mean if it were projected into larger areas? What would happen to a labor-management dispute if it was conducted in such a way that labor, without necessarily agreeing, could accurately state management's point of view in a way that management could accept; and management, without approving labor's stand, could state labor's case in a way that labor agreed was accurate? It would mean that real communication was established, and one could practically guarantee that some reasonable solution would be reached.

If then this way of approach is an effective avenue to good communication and good relationships, as I am quite sure you will agree if you try the experiment I have mentioned, why is it not more widely tried and used? I will try to list the difficulties which keep it from being utilized.

In the first place it takes courage, a quality which is not too widespread. I am indebted to Dr. S. I. Hayakawa, the semanticist, for pointing out that to carry on psychotherapy in this fashion is to take a very real risk, and that courage is required. If you really understand another person in this way, if you are willing to enter his private world and see the way life appears to him, without any attempt to make evaluative judgments, you run the risk of being changed yourself. You might see it his way, you might find yourself influenced in your attitudes or your personality. This risk of being changed is one of the most frightening prospects most of us can face. If I enter, as fully as I am able, into the private world of a neurotic or psychotic individual, isn't there a risk that I might become lost in that world? Most of us are afraid to take that risk. Or if we had a Russian communist speaker here tonight, or Senator Joe McCarthy, how many of us would dare to try to see the world from each of these points of view? The great majority of us could not *listen*; we would find ourselves compelled to *evaluate*, because listening would seem too dangerous. So the first requirement is courage, and we do not always have it.

But there is a second obstacle. It is just when emotions are strongest that it is most difficult to achieve the frame of reference of the other person or group. Yet it is the time the attitude is most needed, if communication is to be established. We have not found this to be an insuperable obstacle in our experience in psychotherapy. A third party, who is able to lay aside his own feelings and evaluations, can assist greatly by listening with understanding to each person or group and clarifying the views and attitudes each holds. We have found this very effective in small groups in which contradictory or antagonistic attitudes exist. When the parties to a dispute realize that they are being understood, that someone sees how the situation seems to them, the statements grow less exaggerated and less defensive, and it is no longer necessary to maintain the attitude, "I am 100 percent right and you are 100 percent wrong." The influence of such an understanding catalyst in the group permits the members to come closer and closer to the objective truth involved in the relationship. In this way mutual communication is established and some type of agreement becomes much more possible. So we may say that though heightened emotions make it much more difficult to understand *with* an opponent, our experience makes it clear that a neutral, understanding, catalyst type of leader or therapist can overcome this obstacle in a small group.

This last phrase, however, suggests another obstacle to utilizing the approach I have described. Thus far all our experience has been with small face-to-face groups — groups exhibiting industrial tensions, religious tensions, racial tensions, and therapy groups in which many personal tensions are present. In these small groups our experience, confirmed by a limited amount of research, shows that this basic approach leads to improved communication, to greater acceptance of others and by others, and to attitudes which are more positive and more problem-solving in nature. There is a decrease in defensiveness, in exaggerated statements, in evaluative and critical behavior. But these findings are from small groups. What about trying to achieve understanding between larger groups that are geographically remote? Or between face-to-face groups who are not speaking for themselves, but simply as representatives of others, like the delegates at Kaesong?[1] Frankly we do not know the answers to these questions. I believe the situation might be put this way. As social scientists we have a tentative test-tube solution of the problem of breakdown in communication. But to confirm the validity of this test-tube solution, and to adapt it to the enormous problems of communication breakdown between classes, groups, and nations, would involve additional funds, much more research, and creative thinking of a high order.

Even with our present limited knowledge we can see some steps which might be taken, even in large groups, to increase the amount of listening *with*, and to decrease the amount of evaluation *about*. To be imaginative for a moment, let us suppose that a therapeutically oriented international group went to the Russian leaders and said, "We want to achieve a genuine understanding of your views and even more important, of your attitudes and feelings, toward the United States. We will summarize and resummarize the views and feelings if necessary, until you agree that our description represents the situation as it seems to you." Then suppose they did the same thing with the leaders in our own country. If they then gave the widest possible distribution to these two views, with the feelings clearly described but not expressed in name-calling, might not the effect be very great? It would not guarantee the type of understanding I have been describing, but it would make it much more possible. We can understand the feelings of a person who hates us much more readily when his attitudes are accurately described to us by a neutral third party, than we can when he is shaking his fist at us.

But even to describe such a first step is to 15 suggest another obstacle to this approach of understanding. Our civilization does not yet have enough faith in the social sciences to utilize their findings. The opposite is true of the physical sciences. During the war[2] when a test-tube solution was found to the problem of synthetic rubber, millions of dollars and an army of talent was turned loose on the problem of using that finding. If synthetic rubber could be made in milligrams, it could and would be made in the thousands of tons. And it was. But in the social science realm, if a way is found of facilitating communication and mutual understanding in small groups, there is no guarantee that the finding will be utilized. It may be a generation or more before the money and the brains will be turned loose to exploit that finding.

In closing, I would like to summarize this small-scale solution to the problem of barriers in communication, and to point out certain of its characteristics.

I have said that our research and experience to date would make it appear that breakdowns in communication, and the evaluative tendency which is the major barrier to communication, can be avoided. The solution is

---

[1] **the delegates at Kaesong** Representatives of North Korea and South Korea met at the border town of Kaesong to arrange terms for an armistice to hostilities during the Korean War (1950–1953). [Editors' note]

[2] **the war** World War II. [Editors' note]

provided by creating a situation in which each of the different parties come to understand the other from the *other's* point of view. This has been achieved, in practice, even when feelings run high, by the influence of a person who is willing to understand each point of view empathically, and who thus acts as a catalyst to precipitate further understanding.

This procedure has important characteristics. It can be initiated by one party, without waiting for the other to be ready. It can even be initiated by a neutral third person, providing he can gain a minimum of cooperation from one of the parties.

This procedure can deal with the insincerities, the defensive exaggerations, the lies, the "false fronts" which characterize almost every failure in communication. These defensive distortions drop away with astonishing speed as people find that the only intent is to understand, not judge.

This approach leads steadily and rapidly 20 toward the discovery of the truth, toward a realistic appraisal of the objective barriers to communication. The dropping of some defensiveness by one party leads to further dropping of defensiveness by the other party, and truth is thus approached.

This procedure gradually achieves mutual communication. Mutual communication tends to be pointed toward solving a problem rather than toward attacking a person or group. It leads to a situation in which I see how the problem appears to you, as well as to me, and you see how it appears to me, as well as to you. Thus accurately and realistically defined, the problem is almost certain to yield to intelligent attack, or if it is in part insoluble, it will be comfortably accepted as such.

This then appears to be a test-tube solution to the breakdown of communication as it occurs in small groups. Can we take this small-scale answer, investigate it further, refine it; develop it and apply it to the tragic and well-nigh fatal failures of communication which threaten the very existence of our modern world? It seems to me that this is a possibility and a challenge which we should explore.

Topics for Critical Thinking and Writing

1. What obstacles to effective argument does Carl R. Rogers outline in his essay? Consider that it was written in the 1950s. Are there any additional obstacles we face today? How might they be overcome through critical thinking and effective argument?

2. Rogers writes in paragraph 12 that it is "when emotions are strongest that it is most difficult to achieve the frame of reference of the other person or group." Select a current debate in the news and explain how strong emotions — about issues or in relation to particular factors — inhibit effective communication in that debate. Is each side equally emotional, or do emotions inhibit one side more than the other? How can one or the other side argue more effectively not by discounting the emotions of the other but expressing understanding?

3. List three additional debate topics with two generally opposing positions. Then identify potentially shared goals or outcomes among the two positions. (Use the Visual Guide: Rogerian Argument on p. 386 as a model.) Reflect on the exercise: What challenges did you face following the Rogerian framework for argument? What do you think may help and hinder empathy between the two positions?

LEWIS OAKLEY

Lewis Oakley is a London-based LGBTQ+rights activist and blogger who studied linguistics. His advocacy earned him recognition in 2017 as a runner-up for PinkNews's Campaigner of the Year award, and in 2018 he was named with nine others making an Outstanding Contribution to LGBT+Life in the UK by the NatWest British LGBT Awards. The following essay was published in the *Advocate* in 2020.

Is It Time to Retire the Word "Privileged"?

As an equality activist, it's my job to keep track of the tools that effectively change hearts and minds — hitting the delete button on tactics that worked five years ago and keeping my eye on new and inventive ways to get others to empathize and understand.

If understanding is indeed the goal, the word "privilege" is no longer having the desired impact. And that's giving it the benefit of the doubt that it ever did. It may be a good word for people to let out their frustrations, but if we're serious about change it's time to leave the word in the past.

As someone who studied linguistics at university, I understand how loaded this word has become. Whether intentionally or not, it implies the person you are talking about is somehow responsible for their difference. It's calling them guilty.

The word immediately puts a person's shields up. So much so that they actually won't hear your point, they are too busy thinking of defenses.

As a bisexual activist, I rarely call some- 5 one biphobic. I may say that a certain thing they said was biphobic, but I know writing an entire person off as phobic isn't going to help. No one has ever agreed to change their behavior because someone called them a name.

When I encounter negative perceptions of bisexuality, the first thing I do is ask questions. If you're going to change someone's perception, you need to know how their brain works. "So why do you think bisexuals will never be satisfied in a relationship?" "Okay, but surely you've been attracted to other women that aren't your wife?" "Are you not satisfied?" "Then why wouldn't I be?" The skill of an activist is to use someone's own logic to prove the point.

Some may argue that a lot of people have accepted that they have privilege and are fine recognizing it. This is true, and part of the battle is won with these people. However, the truth is, for many people, while they have privilege in certain ways, they don't see themselves that way. They see themselves as a whole person; it's labeling someone in a way they don't recognize. It makes you wrong in their eyes before you've got to the point you're trying to make. Some may also feel that you lack empathy; you might see them as privileged because they are straight or white, while they see themselves as severely damaged from their father's suicide, for example.

Just a slight change in the wording can dramatically change responses and perceptions and encourage people to empathize; think of words like "lucky" or "blessed."

Rather than exclaiming, "As a straight person you're privileged," try explaining "You're lucky that you can walk down the street holding your partner's hand and not worry about being attacked."

For some reason, we've reached a point in history where we think shouting and name-calling will produce equality. When in truth, it's just going to raise the temperature.

The next time you go to use the word "privileged," ask yourself, *Will this make someone understand the plight of the marginalized? Will this word have the desired outcome of changing hearts and minds?*

Topics for Critical Thinking and Writing

1. How would you respond if someone called you "privileged?"

2. In Lewis Oakley's view, how does the word "privilege" undermine achieving effective change toward a more equitable society? How does his view of speaking represent the theories of Carl Rogers?

3. Oakley writes about good communication, but does he do an effective job himself in convincing his audience? In other words, does he use Rogerian argumentative strategies? Explain.

4. Do you think the word "privilege" should be "retired"? Provide a careful counterargument to Oakley in favor of retaining the word in some circumstance(s), being sure to model Rogerian empathy as you make your point.

12

A Literary Critic's View: Arguing about Literature

Stories have been used to dispossess and to malign. But stories can also be used to empower, and to humanize. Stories can break the dignity of a people. But stories can also repair that broken dignity.
— CHIMAMANDA NGOZI ADICHIE

CONSIDER THIS

Most fictional (or fictionalized) stories have a larger point or a purpose beyond just telling a compelling story. Through characters, settings, episodes, conflicts, and resolutions, stories often make arguments by dramatizing real life and real-world issues in creative ways.

Choose one of the two following options and sketch out how you would tell a story through the medium of your choice: flash fiction, a short film, a poem or song, a video game — the list of options goes on. (Screenwriters call this kind of sketch a "treatment," a brief description of a film project usually written before a screenplay to summarize and flesh out the details and major points of the drama.)

- Choose an important moment from your life in which you learned a valuable lesson, then transform the experience into a fictional form that portrays the lesson as a valuable one.

- Choose a social, political, cultural, or moral claim — something like a thesis — then argue it not through rational presentation of real-world evidence but through a fictional story or poem.

Reflect on your choices. Why did you choose to tell that story, and why did you select the medium or genre you did? Why should the theme resonate with your audience? How did you use elements of your medium (e.g., title, characters, actors, cinematography, musical genre, poetic structure) to affect your audience?

Why Is Literature Important?

You might think that literature — fiction, poetry (including songs), drama — is meant only to be enjoyed, not to be argued about. Yet literature is constantly the subject of argumentative writing — not all of it by teachers of English. For instance, if you glance at the current issue of a local city newspaper or the arts section of a magazine site, you probably will find reviews of stories, novels, and plays suggesting whether they are worth engaging, or else arguing that they mean something particular if they are interpreted in the way the writer presents them. In the same publication, you may find articles supporting or opposing government funding for the arts, or arguing that funding for some particular work is justified or not. Or you may find arguments situating certain works within trends, genres, movements, social issues, or schools of literature.

Probably most writing about literature, whether done by college students, professors, journalists, politicians, or whomever, is devoted to one or more of these goals: interpreting, judging (evaluating), or theorizing. Let's look at each of these, drawing our examples chiefly from comments about Shakespeare's *Macbeth*.

Interpreting

Interpreting literature in an argument is centrally a matter of setting forth the *meaning* (or meanings) of a work. However, the meaning of a work of literature is a complex question.

Take Shakespeare's tragedy *Macbeth* as an example of a work that has yielded many interpretations over time. Let's take two fairly simple and clearly opposed views:

> Macbeth is a villain who, by murdering his lawful king, offends God's rule, so he is overthrown by God's earthly instruments, Malcolm and Macduff. Macbeth is justly punished; the reader or spectator rejoices in his defeat.

> Macbeth is a hero-villain, a man who commits terrible crimes but who never completely loses the reader's sympathy; although he is justly punished, the reader believes that with the death of Macbeth the world has become a smaller place.

A writer *must* offer evidence in an essay that presents one of these theses or indeed presents any interpretation. For instance, to support the latter thesis, a writer might argue that although Macbeth's villainy is undeniable, his conscience never deserts him — here one would point to specific passages and would offer some brief quotations.

For many readers, a work of literature might appear to have meanings clearly intended by the writer. For others, the meanings might be latent in the text itself (whether or not intended by the author). So, we have two basic kinds of interpretation, one *author-centered* and one *text-centered*. Further, because individual readers experience texts in unique ways, we may add a third general category of interpretation, a *reader-centered* one.

AUTHOR-CENTERED INTERPRETATION **Author-centered interpretation** deals chiefly with the meanings intended by the author. Let's again take up our example of *Macbeth*, sometimes called "The Scottish Play." It is about a Scottish king, written by Shakespeare soon after a Scot — James VI of Scotland — had been installed as James I, King of England. One thing James did was announce that he would be the new sponsor of Shakespeare's Theater Company. If someone asked,

> Was Shakespeare paying homage to James I, his king and patron, in *Macbeth*?

they might seek evidence by exploring Shakespeare's relationship to James I and tracing allusions to the king apparent in *Macbeth*. For example, *Macbeth* is overflowing with biblical imagery, and King James was an avid reader and eventually the first translator of the Bible into English. Add to that the "two-fold balls and treble scepters" of James's double coronation, another allusion to the foiled Gunpowder Plot of 1607 to kill James, and the fact that the play was presented at James's court, and a convincing argument emerges that Shakespeare was indeed paying homage to James I in the play.

Author-centered arguments need not be strictly about the author's intentions. They may also be rooted in efforts to show the meaning of the work in the author's *milieu* — how it was read or how it impacted people (or a specific group of people) at the particular time of publication (or performance) regardless of the author's intentions. In such arguments, one might explore how specific themes of *Macbeth* — heredity, ambition, blood, power, and the supernatural — would have been interpreted by ordinary English audiences sharing with Shakespeare the general worldview of the early seventeenth century and the particularities of life in England at the time. Or someone might ask,

> How would the portrayal of Banquo have been understood by members of James's court, where we know it was presented?

Author-centered arguments, in other words, may consider the author's intentions, or they may consider the time and place in which the author, text, and audience coexisted.

TEXT-CENTERED INTERPRETATION   **Text-centered interpretation** usually focuses on "the text itself" as the primary source of meaning. For some critics, it is futile to attempt to discern an author's intentions and only marginally interesting to argue about what a text might have meant in its own time. What is more immediately important is how literature's formal elements — plot, characterization, language, symbols, setting, tension, ironies — combine to make its meanings. By performing **close reading**, one can discern and describe *how* literary texts produce powerful meanings. A text-centered interpretation of *Macbeth* might examine a certain set of metaphors to discover a theme in the play, asking questions such as:

> How do images of clothing (and nakedness) recur in the play to demonstrate the artificiality of social positions?
>
> How does blood appear in the play as a symbol of guilt?
>
> How are Macbeth, MacDuff, and Banquo similarly and differently characterized?

Arguments in this vein may be supported by prior interpretations, but in text-centered arguments, the text itself is often the primary source of evidence.

READER-CENTERED INTERPRETATION **Reader-centered interpretations** of literature concern the experience of reading itself, especially the ways in which a work becomes meaningful to an individual reader. From this perspective, the point of reading is not to discover biographical or historical meanings (author-centered) or to construct meanings thought to be inherent within the text itself (text-centered). Instead, the point is to pay attention to the reading experience as a means to discover the self — to understand oneself and one's own relationship to the world at large. In this view, literature can help people articulate their views on the world, clarify their own personal values, and connect to others. A reader-centered critic might ask,

How does Macbeth relate to ambition in my own life and times?

Reader-centered interpretation does not always mean purely subjective interpretation; it may also concentrate on meanings that are relevant to particular groups of people. Thus, political interpretations, feminist readings, psychological approaches, and a range of cultural studies methodologies may be considered reader-focused. Such readings might focus on marginalized or oppressed groups evident (or absent) from texts or examine how ideologies are extended or suppressed through works of literature. One reader-centered argument might claim that Lady Macbeth — the devious schemer who convinces her husband to murder King Duncan and usurp the throne — presents a vision not of evil but of rebellion against gender norms. (At one point in the play, she asks the spirits to "unsex" her so she may gain the will to power.) Sometimes undermining or challenging previous interpretations with one's own idiosyncratic interpretation can be an empowering act. Reader-centered interpretation recognizes that meaning itself is not permanent or universal but changes according to reader, time, and place.

For most critics today, a work of literature has many meanings — the meaning it had for the writer and the audience, the meanings it has accumulated over time, and the meanings it has for today's diverse readers. In the end, the meaning of a work of literature involves readers, texts, and authors, all of which are important. Arguments about literature in this sense may be thought of as **intersectional**. Consider the reader-centered interpretation of Lady Macbeth above. To fully articulate the argument, it may be important to analyze the symbolic power of blood, motherhood, and heredity in the play (a text-centered approach) and also to attempt to understand Elizabethan values about the proper roles of women (an author-centered approach).

Judging (or Evaluating)

Evaluative arguments about literature are primarily concerned with the value of a work: Is *Macbeth* a great tragedy? Is *Macbeth* a greater tragedy than *Romeo and Juliet*? What is the importance of *Macbeth*? Does *Macbeth* contribute positively to our understanding of the nature and limits of ambition? As with any thesis statement, if a writer judges the worth of a play, the claim must be supported by an argument and expressed in sentences that offer supporting evidence.

Let's pause for a moment to think about evaluation in general. When we say "This is a great play," are we in effect saying only "I like this play"? That is, are we merely *expressing* our taste rather than *asserting* something independent of our tastes and feelings? On the other hand, a statement such as "I like the New York Yankees" is not an argument that requires justification — it is merely an opinion. However, statements such as "The New York Yankees are the best team in the league" or "The Yankees are the most important franchise in Major League Baseball" would require an argument and evidence.

Now consider another statement, "This is a really good book." It is entirely reasonable for someone to ask you *why* you say that. You might answer with any one of the following:

- "Well, the author really captured the tensions of a rapidly transforming society." (author-centered)

- "The characters are realistically portrayed, and the plot is dramatic with a gripping climax." (text-centered)

- "I really gained insights into the question of betrayal, which is important to me because I was once betrayed and now I can see how forgiveness is the only path." (reader-centered)

Even when we are *evaluating*, we are also often *interpreting* in various modes at the same time. The key in judging or evaluating the worth of a work of literature, then, is to state as clearly as possible what kind of **criteria** we are using, such as

- the skill or motivation of the author;

- the innovation, uniqueness, or originality of the work;

- the faithfulness of the work in its depiction of *X*;

- the importance, status, or durability of the work;

- the degree to which the work helps people understand themselves or another group better;

- the artistic quality in terms of the work's structure, balance, coherence, unity, or use of other literary devices (characterizations, settings, dialogue, etc.).

At the very least, we should show *why* we evaluate the work as we do and suggest that if readers try to see it from our point of view, they may then accept our evaluation.

Evaluations are always based on assumptions, although these assumptions may be unstated; in fact, the writer may even be unaware of them. For instance, what does it mean to be a "skillful" author? Is "originality" a good thing in and of itself? Is the "faithfulness" of a literary depiction dependent upon a realistic description of a time and place, or can abstraction or impressionism also do the job? Can a work of literature be awful but important or be excellent but insignificant? As usual with arguments, the more you define your criteria (and the reasons you use those criteria), the more convincing you may be.

Some common ideas about art often play the role of criteria in literary judgments.

1. A good work of art, even when fictional, says something about real life. If you believe that art is a means by which people connect themselves to enduring human ideas and values, or to society at large, you bring to your evaluation of art an assumption that a good work of art reflects reality (or even impacts it) in some meaningful way. If you hold the view that human beings encounter fairly common experiences and behave in fairly consistent ways — that is, that each of us has an enduring "character" — you probably will judge as inferior a work in which the plot is implausible or one in which characters are inconsistent or inadequately motivated. The novelist Henry James said, "You will not write a good novel unless you possess the sense of reality."

However, there are plenty of arguments to be made for the worth of artworks that do not reflect reality in the usual or expected ways. Some kinds of literary expression are not intended to *say* anything at all (in and of themselves, at least). Consider the poetic form haiku or this imagistic piece by the Japanese poet Matsuo Bashō (1644–1694):

> An old pond
> Leap, splash
> A frog.

This poem, like a haiku, presents an image only and tells us little to nothing about how to interpret it. Experimental fiction and poetry, absurdist drama, and other forms often challenge us to reconceive our ideas about the role and goal of literature. Can a story be successful or good if it offers two or more different endings? Should supernatural events occur in otherwise true-to-life plots? We do not have the answers, but we think the questions are worth pondering.

2. A good work of art is complex yet unified. One of the staples of literary criticism is the idea that a successful work of art exhibits a unified, complex whole constructed out of carefully arranged elements. In many ways, today's audiences continue to value those works in which structure, character, setting, irony, paradox, language, symbol, plot — indeed any of the imaginable literary devices — all work together in meaningful, interconnected ways. *Macbeth* is a good work of art, one might argue, partly because it shows us so many aspects of life (courage, fear, loyalty, treachery, for a start) through richly varied language (the diction ranges from a grand passage in which Macbeth says that his bloody hands will "incarnadine," or make red, "the multitudinous seas" to colloquial passages such as the drunken porter's "Knock, knock"). The play shows the heroic Macbeth tragically destroying his own life through villainy, and it shows the comic porter making coarse jokes about deceit and damnation, jokes that (although the porter doesn't know it) connect with Macbeth's

Robbie Jack/Getty Images

A contemporary production of *Macbeth* performed at the Globe Theatre in London.

crimes. A work may be considered complex yet unified when it contains a rich and multivalent symbolic structure in which all the parts contribute to the complexity of the whole.

Of course, wholeness itself is also an aspect of successful art explicitly challenged by some artists and critics. In the twentieth century, "fragmented" texts were deliberately constructed by some authors to defy the principle of wholeness: James Joyce's *Finnegan's Wake*, for example, contains this indicative passage:

> The great fall of the offwall entailed at such short notice the pftjschute of Finnegan, erse solid man, that the humptyhillhead of humself promptly sends an unquiring one well to the west in quest of his tumptytumtoes: and their upturapikepointandplace is at the knock out in the park where oranges have been laid to rust upon the green since dev-linsfirst loved livvy.

Joyce's language reflects the basically random, nonlinear, and episodic nature of experience — all mixed in with inner monologues, daydreams, puns, and breakdowns of language that defy any sense of coherence in the mind or art. Today, authors readily combine genres, mix historical fiction and nonfiction, create plots that go nowhere, or include other unaccustomed elements such as stream of consciousness, shifting narrators, or multiple endings that disrupt the ideal of unity in literature.

3. *A good work of art sets forth a wholesome view of life.* The general public widely believes that a work should be judged partly or largely on the moral view that it sets forth. (Esteemed philosophers, notably Plato, have felt the same way.) Thus, a story that demeans women — perhaps one that takes a casual view of sexual assault — would be held in low estimation, as would a play that treats a mass murderer as a hero.

Implicit in this approach is what is called an *instrumentalist* view — the idea that a work of art is an instrument, a means, to some higher value. Thus, many people hold that reading great works of literature makes us better — or at least does not make us worse. In this view, a work that is pornographic or in some other way considered immoral will be devalued.

Moral judgments, of course, must be considered very carefully in arguments about the quality of art or literature. Historically, platitudes about what is decent and good have led in some instances to censorship. Changing values have also transformed the ways artists have been regarded and how artworks have been interpreted. Walt Whitman's landmark poem *Leaves of Grass* (1855), one of the most influential works of American literature, was accused by one critic in *Criterion* magazine as exhibiting "a degrading, beastly sensuality that is fast rotting the health core of all social virtues." Kate Chopin, a southern realist, had her career ruined by critics who deemed her 1899 novel *The Awakening* "immoral" for its depiction of a married woman's sexuality and her transgression of gender norms. The controversial themes of racial politics and homosexuality raised in James Baldwin's novels, such as *Go Tell It on the Mountain* (1953) and *Giovanni's Room* (1956), caused much consternation among some morally outraged critics at the time. Even today, arguments about the ways in which art may instruct or corrupt audiences remain at the heart of cultural debates. For instance, current law requires the National Endowment for the Arts to take into account standards of decency when making awards.

4. *A good work of art is original.* The assumption that a good work of art is original puts special value on new techniques and new subject matter in art. If a writer employs a new or innovative way to structure a novel, for instance, they might get a kind of critical extra credit. Nicholson Baker's novel *The Mezzanine* (1988), for example, takes place over the course of a character's single trip up an escalator — a digressive exploration of the spectacular array of thoughts that occur in the mind of a person in just a few short moments. New kinds of characters and story lines tend to be valued, as do new ways of representing reality in literature, such as techniques that help represent email, text messaging, and tweeting. Sometimes, the *first* text to introduce a new subject (say, AIDS) gets that critical extra credit, so to speak, for opening a needed conversation or debate. Or returning to Shakespeare, consider that one sign of his genius, it is held, is that he was so highly varied — none of his tragedies seems merely to duplicate another; each is a world of its own, a new kind of achievement. (Compare, for instance, *Romeo and Juliet*, with its two youthful and innocent heroes, with *Macbeth*, with its deeply guilty hero.)

Of course, just because a work is new or innovative may not reflect qualitatively on it. A full-length novel written entirely through tweets might be a neat idea or a somewhat interesting concept, but it need not signal genius. Newness or originality, that is, is not necessarily synonymous with excellence.

5. *A good work of art is important.* When we consider if a piece of art deals with an important subject, we are often concerned with themes: Great works, in this view, must deal with great themes. Love, death, patriotism, and God, say, are great themes; a work that deals with these subjects may achieve a height, an excellence, that, say, a work describing a dog scratching for fleas may not achieve. (Of course, if the reader believes that the dog is a symbol of humanity plagued by invisible enemies, the poem about the dog may reach the heights; but then, too, it is *not* a poem about a dog and fleas: It is really a poem about humanity and the invisible.)

Another way to construe the importance of a work of literature is to regard it as a social or political object. Works of literature commonly derive their importance by being relevant to public beliefs and attitudes. Some may be important to specific communities. Some may help mark in public memory the meaning of historical events. In this sense, a work's importance is found in its ability to reflect (and reproduce) culture.

The point is that in writing an evaluation, you must let the reader know *why* you value the work as you do. Obviously, it is not enough just to keep saying that *this* work is great whereas *that* work is not so great; the reader wants to know *why* you offer the judgments you do, which means that you must

- set forth your criteria, and then
- offer evidence that is in accord with them.

Theorizing

Another kind of argument about literature is more theoretical; as such, it is more of a meta-cognitive discourse, one that attempts to understand and define the very nature of literary expression and interpretation. Some literary criticism is concerned with such theoretical questions as these:

- What is tragedy? Can the hero be a villain? How does tragedy differ from melodrama?
- Why do tragedies — works showing good or at least interesting people destroyed — give us pleasure?
- How did the detective genre develop over time, and how is it different in different places and times?

Other kinds of criticism might explore theories about the value of literature and ask questions such as these:

- Are classic works of Western literature great because they contain great wisdom or beauty, or are they great because they have been privileged over time?
- Can a work of art really be said to offer anything that can be called "truth"?
- Does a work of art have meaning in itself, or is the meaning simply whatever anyone wishes to say it is?

Yet again, one hopes that anyone asserting a thesis concerned with any of these topics will offer evidence — will, indeed, *argue* rather than merely assert.

A CHECKLIST FOR ARGUING ABOUT LITERATURE

☐ Can I identify if my argument is primarily author-centered, text-centered, or reader-centered?

☐ Can I determine whether my thesis is based on interpreting, judging, or theorizing about the work of literature at hand (or whether it is some combination of the three)?

☐ Do I have a good reason to make my reader interested in hearing my point of view about a work?

☐ Is my essay supported with evidence from the text itself?

☐ If I am using sources such as interpretations written by others or other contextual material, am I integrating them well to support my argument?

Example: A Student Interprets Richard Blanco's "One Today"

Let's consider a student's interpretation of Richard Blanco's poem, "One Today," which was read by Blanco at President Barack Obama's second inauguration in January 2013. In Chapter 5, we discussed how interpretations of visual arguments can be classified as accommodating, negotiating, or resisting the messages intended by the producer. This is also true in literary interpretation. When readers make arguments about fiction or poetry, they often find themselves agreeing or disagreeing (or both) with the message of the work. Their writing often constitutes an attempt to show how effective or ineffective the message of a work is. Different approaches can illuminate different aspects of the work, or they can emphasize or subordinate different elements of the work in order to prove their claims. In the next few pages, we present Blanco's poem along with an interpretation and argument about it in order to show how a reader can choose to accept or counteract the intentions of the artist.

After reading the poem and the student's interpretation, consider your own experience reading the poem and interpreting it for yourself, then how you respond to the student's argument. Use the Checklist for Arguing about Literature (p. 403) to pose questions about the student's essay.

RICHARD BLANCO

Richard Blanco is a native-born Cuban who emigrated to the United States with his family as an infant. A 1991 graduate of Florida International University, Blanco worked as an engineer in Miami before returning to that university to pursue poetry, earning his MFA in 1997. His first collection of poems, *City of a Hundred Fires* (1998), won the Agnes Lynch Starret Poetry Prize from the University of Pittsburgh, and his later efforts, *Directions to the Beach of the Dead* (2005) and *Looking for the Gulf Motel* (2012), earned him international recognition. Blanco's recent work includes a critically acclaimed memoir, *The Prince of Los Cocuyos: A Miami Childhood* (2014), and his latest collection of poems, *How to Love a Country* (2019). In 2012, President Barack Obama invited Blanco to become the fifth presidential inaugural poet, the first Latino, immigrant, and openly gay person in that role. On January 21, 2013, Blanco read "One Today," a poem written for that inauguration and reprinted here.

One Today

One sun rose on us today, kindled over our
    shores,
peeking over the Smokies, greeting the faces
of the Great Lakes, spreading a simple truth
across the Great Plains, then charging across
    the Rockies.
One light, waking up rooftops, under each 5
    one, a story

told by our silent gestures moving behind
    windows.

My face, your face, millions of faces in morn-
    ing's mirrors,
each one yawning to life, crescendoing into
    our day:
pencil-yellow school buses, the rhythm of traf-
    fic lights,

fruit stands: apples, limes, and oranges arrayed 10
  like rainbows
begging our praise. Silver trucks heavy with
  oil or paper — bricks or milk, teeming over
  highways alongside us,
on our way to clean tables, read ledgers, or
  save lives —
to teach geometry, or ring up groceries, as my
  mother did
for 20 years, so I could write this poem.

All of us as vital as the one light we move 15
  through,
the same light on blackboards with lessons for
  the day:
equations to solve, history to question, or
  atoms imagined,
the "I have a dream" we keep dreaming,
or the impossible vocabulary of sorrow that
  won't explain
the empty desks of 20 children marked absent° 20
today, and forever. Many prayers, but one light
breathing color into stained glass windows,
life into the faces of bronze statues, warmth
onto the steps of our museums and park
  benches
as mothers watch children slide into the day. 25

One ground. Our ground, rooting us to every
  stalk
of corn, every head of wheat sown by sweat
and hands, hands gleaning coal or planting
  windmills
in deserts and hilltops that keep us warm,
  hands
digging trenches, routing pipes and cables, 30
  hands
as worn as my father's cutting sugarcane
so my brother and I could have books and
  shoes.

20**empty desks of 20 children** Reference to the December 14,
2012, Sandy Hook Elementary School massacre in Newtown,
Connecticut. [Editor's note.]

The dust of farms and deserts, cities and plains
mingled by one wind — our breath. Breathe.
  Hear it
through the day's gorgeous din of honking 35
  cabs,
buses launching down avenues, the symphony
of footsteps, guitars, and screeching subways,
the unexpected song bird on your clothes line.

Hear: squeaky playground swings, trains
  whistling,
or whispers across cafe tables, Hear: the doors 40
  we open
for each other all day, saying: hello, shalom,
buon giorno, howdy, namaste, or buenos días
in the language my mother taught me — in
  every language
spoken into one wind carrying our lives
without prejudice, as these words break from 45
  my lips.

One sky: since the Appalachians and Sierras
  claimed
their majesty, and the Mississippi and Colorado
  worked
their way to the sea. Thank the work of our
  hands:
weaving steel into bridges, finishing one more
  report
for the boss on time, stitching another wound 50
or uniform, the first brush stroke on a portrait,
or the last floor on the Freedom Tower°
jutting into a sky that yields to our resilience.

One sky, toward which we sometimes lift our
  eyes
tired from work: some days guessing at the 55
  weather
of our lives, some days giving thanks for a love
that loves you back, sometimes praising a
  mother

52**Freedom Tower** The main building of the rebuilt World Trade
Center in New York City, completed in 2013. [Editor's note.]

who knew how to give, or forgiving a father
who couldn't give what you wanted.

We head home: through the gloss of rain or 60
  weight
of snow, or the plum blush of dusk, but
  always — home,
always under one sky, our sky. And always one
  moon

like a silent drum tapping on every rooftop
and every window, of one country — all of us —
facing the stars   65
hope — a new constellation
waiting for us to map it,
waiting for us to name it — together

Topics for Critical Thinking and Writing

1. The word *one* appears in the title and throughout the poem. What do you think Richard Blanco was trying to accomplish with repetition of this word? Explain your answer.

2. This poem was written on the occasion of Barack Obama's second inauguration; it was read aloud by Blanco and broadcast nationally during the ceremony. (Find the clip on YouTube and watch it if you can.) How do you think these facts affect the meaning of the poem? What do you think Blanco intended to convey?

3. How do colors and sounds work in the poem to support its meanings?

4. In your opinion, is the poem overly optimistic? Explain your answer in about 500 words.

Jackson DiPiero

Professor Halsey

English 102

11 January 2023

Unity in Times of Division: An Analysis of Richard Blanco's "One Today"

At the 2013 presidential inauguration of Barack Obama, Cuban-American poet Richard Blanco delivered a reading of the poem "One Today," a piece intended to capture the spirit of the historic day of swearing in the nation's first Black president for the second time. Blanco's appearance was itself symbolic of a similar theme of diversity, inclusion, and integration. As the first openly gay, first immigrant, and first Latino inaugural poet, Blanco was, like Obama, a kind of embodiment of the American Dream. The son of Cuban refugees who arrived in Miami just before his birth, Blanco was now addressing the entire nation. His poem contains powerful and inspirational images of hard-working individuals finding opportunity and hope in the land of plenty, and a fundamental celebration of American diversity and togetherness. It is difficult not to be moved by such a message. However, at **1** the same time, a closer analysis reveals how these lofty ideals presented in the poem do not, then or now, represent entirely the truth of the nation.

"One Today" is full of grandiose natural and human imagery. The poem opens with the rising sun, a symbol of hope, and follows the dawn across "the Smokies . . . Great Lakes . . . [and] Great Plains" (Blanco, lines 2–4) as it awakens people across the country,

> . . . crescendoing into our day:
> pencil-yellow school buses, the rhythm of traffic lights,
> fruit stands: apples, limes, and oranges arrayed like rainbows
> begging our praise. Silver trucks heavy with oil or paper — bricks or
> milk, teeming over highways alongside us, (8–12)

Vivid colors suggest a spectrum of racial, ethnic, gender, and also sexual differences since the rainbow is a symbol of peace, diversity, and gay pride. Blanco also uses a spectrum of colors to represent diversity later in the poem. When he mentions the Sandy Hook school shootings of December 14,

1 Even though Blanco's identity and the occasion of the poem indicate some interest in the author's intentions in the context of the inauguration, the thesis suggests a reader-centered approach.

2 Writer uses a text-centered approach as he interprets the meaning of symbols and images. The reference to Blanco's intentions with the symbols is an author-centered approach.

2012, he depicts a nation finding comfort in different religious faiths, but all fundamentally mourning together: "Many prayers, but one light / breathing colors into stained glass windows" (22–23). A reader can almost see the prism of colors refracted through the lenses of different faiths.

While such images represent ideals of American racial, ethnic, and religious diversity, it could also be argued that they somewhat overstate and overlook divisions that may have been latent or suppressed on inauguration day 2013. Obama faced explicit and implicit racism in the campaigns of 2008 and 2012. Some of the first viral memes that came with the growth of social media and mobile technologies suggested Obama was a radical Muslim infiltrator. In 2008, John McCain's campaign manipulated images of Obama by making his skin darker (Ehrenfreund). In 2012, with conflicts simmering in Congress related to the DREAM Act and immigration enforcement, Obama challenger Mitt Romney called for immigrants to "self-deport" (Madison). After a hate-inspired mass shooting at a Sikh temple in Minneapolis in 2012, CNN reported that white supremacist groups were on the rise in the United States (CNN Wire Staff), and an AP poll that year reported an increase in implicit bias and negative racial sentiments (AP). These were the years when conspiracy theories arose that Obama was not born in the United States, an idea repeated by conservative talk show host Rush Limbaugh, who said Obama "is more African in his roots than American." It is fair to say things were not as rosy as "One Today" portrays them, and that the poem fails to recognize racial conflicts and feuds about immigration.

3 Writer addresses the context in which the poem was written and uses numerous pieces of evidence from 2008 to 2012 to show that the poem might be too optimistic.

4 Author reminds readers of the overall point after a flurry of evidence that is not really about the poem's language, symbols, themes.

Don't get me wrong. Blanco's poem can be inspiring. It certainly appears to speak to what is best in people. It imagines an almost transcendent mutual respect and grace among different groups in the population. One line asks readers to "Hear: the doors we open / for each other all day, saying: hello, shalom, / buon giorno, howdy, namaste, or buenos días / . . . in every language / spoken into one wind carrying our lives / without prejudice . . . " (41–46). Such sentiment is commonly appreciated in a country founded on immigration, whose Statue of Liberty offers a beacon of hope to the world's "tired . . . poor . . . huddled masses yearning to breathe free" (Lazarus, lines 10–11). But it is also important to

5 Writer accounts for the inspiring nature of the poem but also wants to acknowledge other interpretations of the poem.

recognize that the tightening of immigration policies, the increased number of deportations that happened under Obama, and the many prejudices between and among groups in the United States cannot be erased by an inauguration poem, however inspiring the poem may be. Blanco's "One Today" offers a vision of a unified America, and a unified worldview among Americans, that obscures more complicated realities.

Take the poem's reference to the Sandy Hook shootings. Blanco includes Sandy Hook as an emotionally searing sign of national unity in the face of a recent tragedy that had taken place shortly before he wrote the poem. The deaths of innocent elementary school students and teachers were shocking and brought about a wave of collective mourning. However, Sandy Hook also fueled debates and feuds about gun control and spawned ugly conspiracy theories that remain potent even now. Alex Jones, a popular conservative radio talk show host, helped spread the idea that the government faked the shootings in order to advance a gun control agenda (Stanton). It is also worth mentioning that mutual grieving, however comforting, may not provide room for engaged efforts to address how such crimes can be prevented.

Blanco averts his gaze from the realities of America's internal conflicts, in favor of presenting an oversimplified and overgeneralized vision of harmony in the United States built for the inauguration. This is a romantic vision that also occurs when Blanco portrays working people achieving and living the American Dream. When he mentions his own parents "ring[ing] up groceries, as my mother did / for 20 years, so I could write this poem" (14–15), and "my father's cutting sugarcane / so my brother and I could have books and shoes" (32–33), he seems to represent one of immigration's ideals of improving opportunities of future generations through hard work. Yet Blanco's experience cannot be said to be the representative experience of those who immigrate to the United States and encounter less-than-ideal conditions. The struggles of poverty, food insecurity, and lack of access to health care are not only more prevalent among immigrant populations than among "natural born citizens," but immigrant populations also experience social inequality and disadvantage in harsher ways. Many children of immigrants will not have the experience **6**

6 Writer does not provide evidence although such evidence may be available.

Blanco did and will face obstacles and challenges that prevent their success no matter hard their parents work.

In celebrating the working class, Blanco also looks favorably on those who "clean tables, read ledgers or save lives" (13). He praises "hands, hands gleaning coal or planting windmills / in deserts and hilltops that keep us warm, hands / digging trenches, routing pipes and cables . . ." (29–31). These are standard romantic portrayals of blue-collar work that do not account for the difficulties and hazards of industrial employment. Later, he asks readers to "Thank the work of our hands: / weaving steel into bridges, finishing one more report / for the boss on time, stitching another wound / or uniform, the first brush stroke on a portrait, / or the last floor on the Freedom Tower . . ." (49–53). Hands are powerful symbols of *doing*, of being productive, creative, and constructive, and they are also a shared human characteristic. However, Blanco presents no distinctions between laborers, office workers, doctors, garment workers, artists, or construction crews, who are all presented as if their statuses in society were equal. Obviously, these occupations convey different social statuses, are paid differently, and are open to different groups and individuals unequally, often based on educational and economic access.

"One Today" repeats a pattern of nationalistic and patriotic pride at the expense of the reality. Perhaps "the dust of farms and deserts, cities and plains" (34), and "the day's gorgeous din of honking cabs, / buses launching down avenues, the symphony / of footsteps, guitars, and screeching subways" (36–38) indicates America's bustle and industriousness. Blanco instructs us to "hear" all this as the "one wind — our breath" (35), like a collective and unifying hum. It is a testament to how effectively Blanco uses sonic images in his poem to introduce textures of sound and activity. However, few people would normally associate the "din of honking cabs" and "screeching subways" with anything "gorgeous" — at least outside of a poem. These images are more likely to signal sources of environmental and noise pollution in crowded cities. As noble as its message may be, "One Today" presents only one side of the coin, one view of these aspects of life in the United States.

7 An instance of text-centered analysis.

7

Don't misunderstand. The poem *is* stirring and optimistic, and it was written for a very specific occasion to which Blanco was invited to contribute. The choices he made make sense in that context. Inauguration day is traditionally a time of celebration and commonality, a time when the national voice of "We, the People" resounds. It is understandable that the sentiment of the poem is positive; however, such sentiment also glosses over the experiences of people who live in hardship or oppressive conditions in their work and lives, and the experiences of those have been harmed or even oppressed at the hands of other groups (or even the government itself). "One Today" is a beautifully composed poem that represents national ideals but also masks American realities: inequalities and power differentials, racism and cultural violence, gun violence, environmental threats, and more. These realities would be brought into full view on January 6, 2021, when rioters supporting Donald Trump's "Stop the Steal" efforts carried Confederate flags through the halls of the Capitol, broke windows, intimidated politicians, and attacked police officers on the day when electoral votes for Joe Biden were to be certified by Congress.

8

8 Writer wants to assure readers that he sees the poem as it was intended in context, but also doesn't want readers to imagine the perfect country the poem portrays.

Listeners of "One Today" on inauguration day in 2013 must have felt the poem's power in the context of that occasion. Inauguration day is traditionally a day for national pride and a democratic ritual signifying the peaceful transfer of power. However, reading "One Today" after the 2020 election and the January 6 riot, one wonders if Blanco's vision of togetherness was more fantasy than reality. While Americans do remain united along many lines, the poem's optimism overlooks divisions and hostilities among the people Blanco unproblematically calls "we," us," and "our" as if differences among them did not exist and were not potent sources of national conflict. The fault lines in American political culture have been made more evident recently with rising anti-immigrant sentiment, a resurgence of white supremacist groups, and the continuation of police and social violence against Black Americans. Internal divisions within the United States were further exacerbated after the beginning of the COVID-19 pandemic, the rise of the Black Lives Matter movement, and the continued spread of conspiracy theories related to the 2020 election. We can certainly celebrate Blanco's poem due to its circumstance and theme, but it is also imperative to recognize how it presents points of conflict as symbols of unity. Regrettably, as political divisions continue to define the United States, it is hard to imagine such a poem arising on the occasion of the next presidential inauguration, no matter who or which party is elected.

Works Cited

AP. "AP poll: U.S. Majority Have Prejudice against Blacks." *USA Today*. 27 Oct. 2012, https://www.usatoday.com/story/news/politics/2012/10/27/poll-black-prejudice-america/1662067/.

Barnet, Sylvan, et al. *Current Issues and Enduring Questions*. 13th ed., Bedford/St. Martin's, 2023.

Blanco, Richard. "One Today." Barnet et al., pp. 404–06.

CNN Wire Staff. "'Swimming Upstream,' White Supremacist Groups Still Strong." *CNN*. 7 Aug. 2012, https://www.cnn.com/2012/08/07/us/white-supremacist-groups/index.html.

Ehrenfreund, Max. "Obama's Skin Looks a Little Different in These GOP Campaign Ads." *Washington Post*, 29 Dec. 2015, https://www.washintonpost.com/news/wonk/wp/2015/12/29/obamas-skin-looks-a-little-different-in-these-gop-campaign-ads/.

Lazarus, Emma. "The New Colossus." Barnet et al., p. 687.

Madison, Lucy. "Romney on Immigration: I'm for 'Self-Deportation.'" *CBS News*. 24 Jan. 2012, https://www.cbsnews.com/news/romney-on-immigration-im-for-self-deportation/.

Stanton, Andrew. "Alex Jones Defamed Sandy Hook Victims by Calling Shooting 'Giant Hoax,'

Will Pay Damages." *Newsweek*, 15 Nov. 2021, https://www.newsweek.com/alex-jones-defamed-sandy-hook-victims-calling-shooting-giant-hoax-will-pay-damages-1649339.

A Short Story for Analysis

KATE CHOPIN

Kate Chopin was born in St. Louis and named Katherine O'Flaherty. At the age of nineteen, she married a cotton broker in New Orleans, Oscar Chopin (the name is pronounced something like "show pan"), who was descended from the early French settlers in Louisiana. After her husband's death in 1883, Kate Chopin turned to writing fiction. The following story was first published in 1894.

The Story of an Hour

Knowing that Mrs. Mallard was afflicted with a heart trouble, great care was taken to break to her as gently as possible the news of her husband's death.

It was her sister Josephine who told her, in broken sentences, veiled hints that revealed in half concealing. Her husband's friend Richards was there, too, near her. It was he who had been in the newspaper office when intelligence of the railroad disaster was received, with Brently Mallard's name leading the list of "killed." He had only taken the time to assure himself of its truth by a second telegram, and had hastened to forestall any less careful, less tender friend in bearing the sad message.

She did not hear the story as many women have heard the same, with a paralyzed inability to accept its significance. She wept at once, with sudden, wild abandonment, in her sister's arms. When the storm of grief had spent itself she went away to her room alone. She would have no one follow her.

There stood, facing the open window, a comfortable, roomy armchair. Into this she sank, pressed down by a physical exhaustion that haunted her body and seemed to reach into her soul.

She could see in the open square before 5 her house the tops of trees that were all aquiver with the new spring life. The delicious breath of rain was in the air. In the street below a peddler was crying his wares. The notes of a distant song which some one was singing reached her faintly, and countless sparrows were twittering in the eaves.

There were patches of blue sky showing here and there through the clouds that had met and piled one above the other in the west facing her window.

She sat with her head thrown back upon the cushion of the chair, quite motionless, except when a sob came up into her throat and shook her, as a child who has cried itself to sleep continues to sob in its dreams.

She was young, with a fair, calm face, whose lines bespoke repression and even a certain strength. But now there was a dull stare in her eyes, whose gaze was fixed away off yonder on one of those patches of blue sky. It was not a glance of reflection, but rather indicated a suspension of intelligent thought.

There was something coming to her and she was waiting for it, fearfully. What was it? She did not know; it was too subtle and elusive to name. But she felt it, creeping out of the sky, reaching toward her through the sounds, the scents, the color that filled the air.

Now her bosom rose and fell tumultu- 10 ously. She was beginning to recognize this thing that was approaching to possess her, and she was striving to beat it back with her will—as powerless as her two white slender hands would have been.

When she abandoned herself a little whispered word escaped her slightly parted lips. She said it over and over under her breath: "Free, free, free!" The vacant stare and the look of terror that had followed it went from her eyes. They stayed keen and bright. Her pulses beat fast, and the coursing blood warmed and relaxed every inch of her body.

She did not stop to ask if it were not a monstrous joy that held her. A clear and exalted perception enabled her to dismiss the suggestion as trivial.

She knew that she would weep again when she saw the kind, tender hands folded in death; the face that had never looked save with love upon her, fixed and gray and dead. But she saw beyond that bitter moment a long procession of years to come that would belong to her absolutely. And she opened and spread her arms out to them in welcome.

There would be no one to live for her during those coming years; she would live for herself. There would be no powerful will bending her in that blind persistence with which men and women believe they have a right to impose a private will upon a fellow creature. A kind intention or a cruel intention made the act seem no less a crime as she looked upon it in that brief moment of illumination.

And yet she had loved him—sometimes. 15 Often she had not. What did it matter! What could love, the unsolved mystery, count for in face of this possession of self-assertion which she suddenly recognized as the strongest impulse of her being.

"Free! Body and soul free!" she kept whispering.

Josephine was kneeling before the closed door with her lips to the keyhole, imploring for admission. "Louise, open the door! I beg; open the door—you will make yourself ill. What are you doing, Louise? For heaven's sake open the door."

"Go away. I am not making myself ill." No; she was drinking in a very elixir of life through that open window.

Her fancy was running riot along those days ahead of her. Spring days, and summer days, and all sorts of days that would be her own. She breathed a quick prayer that life might be long. It was only yesterday she had thought with a shudder that life might be long.

She arose at length and opened the door 20 to her sister's importunities. There was a feverish triumph in her eyes, and she carried herself unwittingly like a goddess of Victory. She clasped her sister's waist, and together they descended the stairs. Richards stood waiting for them at the bottom.

Some one was opening the front door with a latchkey. It was Brently Mallard who entered, a little travel-stained, composedly carrying his gripsack and umbrella. He had been far from the scene of accident, and did not even know there had been one. He stood amazed at Josephine's piercing cry; at Richards' quick motion to screen him from the view of his wife.

But Richards was too late.

When the doctors came they said she had died of heart disease—of joy that kills.

Topics for Critical Thinking and Writing

Read the following assertions and consider whether you agree or disagree, and why. For each assertion, draft a paragraph with your arguments.

1. The railroad accident is a symbol of the destructiveness of the Industrial Revolution.

2. The story accurately captures how trapped many women felt by marriage in the nineteenth century.

3. This story's setting is unclear, which makes the story less effective than if the setting had been specified.

4. Mrs. Mallard's death at the end is a just punishment for the joy she takes in her husband's death.

Thinking about the Effects of Literature

What about the *consequences* of literature? Does literature shape our character and therefore influence our behavior? It is generally believed that it does have an effect. One hears, for example, that literature (like travel) is broadening, that it makes us aware of, and tolerant of, kinds of behavior that differ from our own and from what we see around us. One of the chief arguments against pornography, for instance, is that it desensitizes us, makes us too tolerant of abusive relationships, relationships in which people (usually men) use other people (usually women) as mere things or instruments for pleasure. (A contrary view: Some people argue that pornography provides a relatively harmless outlet for fantasies that otherwise might be given release in the real world. In this view, pornography acts as a sort of safety valve.)

Other topics are also the subjects of controversy. For instance, in recent decades, parents and educators have been much concerned with fairy tales. Does the violence in some fairy tales ("Little Red Riding Hood," "The Three Little Pigs") have a negative effect on children? Do some of the stories teach the wrong lessons, implying that women should be passive and men active ("Sleeping Beauty," for instance, in which the sleeping woman is brought to life by the action of the handsome prince)? The Greek philosopher Plato (427–347 BC) strongly believed that the literature we hear or read shapes our later behavior, and since most of the ancient Greek traditional stories (notably Homer's *Odyssey* and *Iliad*) celebrate acts of love and war rather than of justice, he prohibited the reading of such material in his ideal society.

13

A Debater's View: Oral Presentations and Debate

Don't raise your voice. Improve your argument.

– DESMOND TUTU

CONSIDER THIS

Which of the following images is an authentic artwork?

China News Service/Getty Images

Davide Zanin/Alamy Stock Photo

The image on the left is Maurizio Cattelan's *Comedian* (2019), debuted in three editions at Miami's Art Basel, an annual international art fair featuring some of the world's most appreciated visual artists. The first edition of *Comedian* sold for $150,000. The second and third editions sold for $120,000 each. Buyers received a certificate of authenticity, a roll of duct tape, and instructions to tape a banana to the wall (and change it out periodically). The image on the right, a stock photo, is not a piece of art work you would (typically) find in a museum or a private collection.

Debate one of the following questions in a group, with a partner, or by yourself.

- Is *Comedian* art?
- Is it morally wrong for anyone to pay that much money for this artwork?
- Does anybody have the authority to declare something art (or not)?

Oral Presentations

Forensic comes from the Latin word *foris*, meaning "out of doors," which also produced the word *forum*, an open space in front of a public building. In the language of rhetoricians, the place where one delivers a speech to an audience is the forum — whether it is a classroom, a court of law, or the steps of the Lincoln Memorial. In fact, the earliest meaning of *forensics* in English was related to public discussion and debate.

Your instructor may ask you to make an oral presentation (in which case, the forum would be the classroom), and if they don't make such a demand, later life almost certainly will. For example, you'll find that at a job interview, you will be expected to talk persuasively (perhaps to a group) about what good qualities or experience you can bring to the place of employment. Similarly, when you have a job, you'll sometimes have to summarize a report orally or argue your case out loud, perhaps so that your colleagues might do something they are hesitant to do.

The goal of your oral presentation is to persuade the audience to share your view or, if you can't get them to agree completely, to get them to see that at least there is something to be said for this view — that it is a position a reasonable person can hold.

Elsewhere in this book we have said that the subjects of persuasive writing are usually

- matters of fact (e.g., statistics show that the death penalty does — or does not — deter crime),
- matters of value (e.g., separating families is — or is not — immoral), or
- matters of policy (e.g., government should — or should not — make college "free").

Similarly, many kinds of public speaking involve such matters, and the habits of critical thinking, argument, and persuasion we have discussed to this point now need to be personified and articulated.

No matter what your subject is, when you draft and revise your talk, make certain that a thesis statement underlies the whole (e.g., "Proposition 2 is a bad idea because . . .").

The text of an oral presentation ought not to be identical with the text of a written presentation. Both must have a clear organization, but oral presentations usually require making the organization a bit more obvious, with abundant **signposts**. Signposts help audiences listen to your key points. For example, audiences benefit from knowing how long they are expected to listen. (Think about it: Who hasn't checked the time remaining in a movie or television show to help anticipate where they are in the plot?) It sometimes helps to inform your audience: "*In the next ten minutes*, I will be speaking to you about *X*"; "Before I talk about *X*, I am going *to spend a minute or two* on background"; or "Now, *with just few minutes remaining*, I would like to

> **SPEAKING TIPS**
>
> - *In preparing your oral presentation, keep your thesis in mind.* You may be giving counterarguments, examples, definitions, and so forth, but make sure that your thesis is evident to the audience and return to it occasionally as a reminder.
> - *Keep your audience in mind.* Inevitably, you will have to make assumptions about what the audience does and does not know about your topic. Do not overestimate their knowledge and do not underestimate their intelligence.

make my key point." Skilled speakers know how to raise their audience's perceptions at key moments. Following are some more signpost words and phrases that can help an audience hear what you need them to hear most.

Transitioning to a new topic or another point

Up to this point we have been discussing X. *Turning now to Y*, we can see something different.

Now *let me pause for a second* before moving on. My first point was X. This supports my argument. But so does Y, a different kind of case.

Exploring something further

Now, *for just a minute*, let's look at this more deeply.

X is worth *elaborating on for a couple minutes* before I continue.

Digressing

Let's *take a detour* for a second.

I am going *to stop for a minute and tell a brief story* to show a perfect example.

Summarizing or returning to the beginning

To recap everything I have said here, *let me walk through the key points* . . .

Going back to my previous points, A, B, and C, we can safely conclude . . .

In general, when speaking, you will have to repeat a bit more than you would in a written presentation. An old rule of thumb suggests that to make your audience remember something, you may need to write it only once but say it three times. After all, a reader can turn back to check a sentence or a statistic, but a listener cannot. Thus, you may find yourself saying things out loud that you would scarcely or ever write, such as "The authorities were wrong. So that's my first conclusion. The authorities were wrong," or "The reason Jones was arrested was unjust. *I repeat*: The reasons were unjust."

You will want to think carefully about the **organization** of your talk. We've already stressed the need to develop essays with clear thesis statements and logical supporting points. Oral presentations are no different, but remember that when you are speaking in public, a clear organization will always help alleviate anxiety and reassure you. Thus, you can deliver a powerful message without getting tripped up yourself. We suggest you try the following:

- Outline your draft in advance to ensure it has clear organization.

- Inform the audience at the start about the organization of your presentation. Early in the talk, you probably should say something along these lines, although not in an abbreviated form:

In talking about *A*, I'll have to define a few terms, *B* and *C*, and I will also have to talk about two positions that differ from mine, *D* and *E*. I'll then try to show why *A* is the best policy to pursue, clearly better than *D* and *E*.

- So that the listeners can easily follow your train of thought, be sure to use transitions such as "Furthermore," "Therefore," "Although it is often said," and "Some may object that." Sometimes, you may even remind the listeners what the previous stages were, with a comment such as "We have now seen three approaches to the problem of...."

METHODS OF DELIVERY

After thinking about helping the audience follow your speech, consider how much help you'll need delivering it. Depending on your comfort level with the topic and your argument, you might decide to

- deliver a memorized talk without notes,
- read the talk from a written text, or
- speak from an outline, perhaps with quotations and statistics written down.

Each of these methods has strengths and weaknesses. A memorized talk allows for plenty of eye contact with the audience, but unless you are a superb actor, it is almost surely going to seem a bit mechanical. A talk that you read from a text will indeed let you say to an audience exactly what you intend (with the best possible wording), but reading a text inevitably establishes some distance between you and the audience, even if you occasionally glance up from your pages. If you talk from a mere outline, almost surely some of your sentences will turn out to be a bit awkward — although a little awkwardness may help convey sincerity and therefore be a plus.

No matter what form of delivery you choose, try to convey the impression that you're conversing with the audience, not talking down to them (even though if you're standing on a platform you will be literally talking down).

You may want to use **multimedia aids** in your presentation. These can range from such low-tech materials as handouts, blackboards, and whiteboards to high-tech graphic presentations, videos, and recordings. Each has advantages and disadvantages. For instance, if you distribute handouts when the talk begins, the audience may start thumbing through them during your opening comments. And although software like PowerPoint can provide highly useful aids, some speakers make too much use of it simply because it's available. Any software you use, or any supplementary materials you introduce, should be essential to communicating your message effectively, not superfluous or merely decorative. And these materials should be legible: If you do use visuals, make certain that your words and images are large enough to be seen

> **SPEAKING TIP**
> Some common errors in using slides include providing too much information on each slide or providing too many words. You do not want your audience to read your presentation; rather, you want the audience to see the key points you are making, supported perhaps by images, charts, and graphs. (These too should not be too complex. Also, be prepared to help your audience interpret your images, charts, and graphs.)

by all given the size of the room and the expectation that not everyone can see equally clearly. A graph with tiny words won't impress your audience, nor will words that cannot be read by everyone. Also, to accommodate as many people as possible, it helps to describe your slides even when you have created them to be extremely clear.

AUDIENCE

It is not merely because topics are complicated that we cannot agree that one side is reasonable and correct and the other side irrational and wrong. The truth is that we are swayed not only by reason (*logos*) but also by appeals to the emotions (*pathos*) and by the speaker's character (*ethos*). (For more on these appeals, see Chapter 3, "Understanding Rhetorical Appeals.") We can combine these last two factors and put it this way: Sometimes we are inclined to agree with *X* rather than with *Y* because *X* strikes us as a more appealing person (perhaps more open-minded, more intelligent, better informed, more humane, and less cold). *X* is the sort of person we want to have as a friend. We disagree with *Y* — or at least we're unwilling to associate ourselves with *Y* — because *Y* is, well, *Y* just isn't the sort of person we want to agree with. *Y*'s statistics don't sound right, or *Y* seems like a bully; for some reason, we just don't have confidence in *Y*. Confidence is easily lost.

Earlier in the book, we talked about the importance of **tone** and of the writer's **persona**. We have also made the point that the writer's tone will depend partly on the audience. A person writing for a conservative journal whose readership is almost entirely conservative can adopt a highly satiric manner in talking about liberals and will win much approval. But if this conservative writer is writing in a liberal journal and hopes to get a sympathetic hearing, they will have to avoid satire and wisecracks and, instead, present themselves as a person of goodwill who is open-minded and eager to address the issue seriously.

The **language** you use — the degree to which it is formal as opposed to colloquial and the degree to which it is technical as opposed to general — will also depend on the audience. Technical language is entirely appropriate if your audience is familiar

---

A CHECKLIST FOR AN ORAL PRESENTATION

Keep the following in mind, whether you are evaluating someone else's talk or preparing your own.

Delivery

❑ Voice loud enough but not too loud.

❑ Appropriate degree of speed — neither hurried nor drawn out.

❑ Dress and attitude toward audience appropriate.

❑ Gestures and eye contact appropriate.

❑ Language clear (e.g., technical words adequately explained).

❑ Audiovisual aids, if any, appropriate and effectively used.

Content

❑ Thesis clear and kept in view.

❑ Argument steadily advanced, with helpful transitions.

❑ Thesis supported by evidence.

❑ Lightweight material (e.g., bits of humor, relevant and genuinely engaging).

with it. If you are arguing before members of Amnesty International about the use of torture, you can assume certain kinds of specialized knowledge. You can, for instance, breezily speak of the DRC and of KPCS, and your listeners will know what you're talking about because Amnesty International has been active with issues concerning the Democratic Republic of Congo and the Kimberley Process Certification Scheme. In contrast, if you are arguing the same case before a general audience, you'll have to explain these abbreviations, and you may even have to explain what Amnesty International is. If you are arguing before an audience of classmates, you probably have a good idea of what they know and don't know.

DELIVERY

Your audience will in some measure determine not only your tone but also the way you appear when giving the speech. Part of the delivery is the speaker's appearance. The medium is part of the message. The president can appear in golf clothes when chatting about reelection plans, but wears business attire when delivering the State of the Union address. Just as we wear one kind of clothing when playing tennis, another when attending classes, and yet another when going for a job interview, an effective speaker dresses appropriately. A lawyer arguing before the Supreme Court wears a suit or dress. The same lawyer, arguing at a local meeting, speaking as a community resident, may well dress informally — maybe in jeans — to show that they are not stuffy or overly formal but, rather, a regular member of the community.

Your appearance when you speak is not merely a matter of clothing; it includes your **facial expressions**, your **posture**, your **gestures**, and your general demeanor. In general, you should avoid bodily motions — swaying, thumping the table, craning your neck, smirking — that are so distracting that they cause the audience to concentrate on the distraction rather than on the argument. ("That's the third time he straightened his necktie. I wonder how many more times he will — oops, that's the fourth!") Most of us are unaware of our annoying habits; if you're lucky, a friend, when urged, will tell you about them. In preparation, you may also film yourself speaking to observe your physical gestures from a third-person perspective.

You probably can't do much about your **voice** and its unique character — it may be high-pitched, or it may be gravelly — but you can make sure to speak loudly enough for the audience members to hear you and slowly and clearly enough for them to understand you.

We have some advice about quotations, too. First, if possible, use an effective quotation or two, partly because — we'll be frank here — the quotations may be more impressively worded than anything you come up with on your own. A quotation may be the chief thing your audience comes away with: "Hey, yes, I liked that: 'War is too important to be left to the generals'"; "When it comes down to it, I agree with that Frenchman who said 'If we are to abolish the death penalty, I should like to see the first step taken by the murderers'"; or "You know, I think it was all summed up in that line by Margaret Mead, something like, 'No one would remember the Good Samaritan if he'd had only good intentions. He had money as well.' Yes, that's pretty convincing. Morality isn't enough. You need money." You didn't invent the words that you quote, but you did bring them to your listeners' attention, and they will be grateful to you.

Our second piece of advice concerning quotations is this: If the quotation is only a phrase or a brief sentence, you can memorize it and be confident that you'll remember it, but if it's longer than a sentence, write it on a sheet in your notes large enough for you to read easily. You have chosen these words because they are effectively put, so you don't want to misquote them or hesitate in delivering them.

CONTENT

As for the talk itself, well, we have been touching on it in our discussion of such matters as the speaker's relation to the audience, the need to provide signposts, and the use of quotations. All our comments in earlier chapters about developing a written argument are also relevant to oral arguments, but here we should merely emphasize that because the talk is oral and the audience cannot look back to an earlier page to remind itself of some point, the speaker may have to repeat and summarize a bit more than is usual in a written essay.

Remember, too, that a reader can see when the essay ends — there is blank space at the end of the page — but a listener depends on aural cues. Give your hearers ample clues that you are ending (post such signs as "Finally," "Last," or "Let me end by saying"), and be sure to end with a strong sentence. It may not be as good as the end of the Gettysburg Address ("government of the people, by the people, for the people, shall not perish from the earth"), nor will it be as good as the end of Martin Luther King Jr.'s "I Have a Dream" speech ("Free at last! Free at last! Thank God Almighty, we are free at last!"), but those are models to emulate.

Formal Debates

It would be nice if all arguments ended with everyone, participants and spectators, agreeing that the facts are clear, that one presentation is more reasonable than the other, and therefore that one side is right and the other side is wrong. But in life, most issues are complicated. High school students may earnestly debate — this is a real topic in a national debate —

> Resolved: That education has failed its mission in the United States but it takes only a moment of reflection to see that neither the affirmative nor the negative can be true. Yes, education has failed its mission in many ways, but, no, it has succeeded in many ways. Its job now is (in the words of Samuel Beckett) to try again: "Fail. Fail again. Fail better."

Debates of this sort, conducted before a judge and guided by strict rules concerning "Constructive Speeches," "Rebuttal Speeches," and "Cross-Examinations," are not attempts to get at the truth; like lawsuits, they are attempts to win a case. Each speaker seeks not to persuade the opponent but only to convince the judge. Although most of this section is devoted not to forensics in the strictest sense but more generally to the presentation of oral arguments, we begin with the standard format.

STANDARD DEBATE FORMAT

Formal debates occur within a structure that governs the number of speeches, their order, and the maximum time for each one. The format may vary from place to place, but there is always a structure. In most debates, a formal resolution states the reason for the debate ("Resolved: That capital punishment be abolished in juvenile cases"). The affirmative team supports the resolution; the negative team denies its legitimacy. The basic structure has three parts:

- *The constructive phase*, in which the debaters construct their cases and develop their arguments (usually for ten minutes).

- *The rebuttal*, in which debaters present their responses and also present their final summary (usually for five minutes).

- *The preparation*, in which the debater prepares for presenting the next speech. (During the preparation — a sort of time-out — the debater is not addressing the opponent or audience. The total time allotted to a team is usually six or eight minutes, which the individual debaters divide as they wish.)

We give, very briefly, the usual structure of each part, although we should mention that another common format calls for a cross-examination of the First Affirmative Constructive by the Second Negative, a cross-examination of the First Negative Constructive by the First Affirmative, a cross-examination of the Second Affirmative by the First Negative, and a cross-examination of the Second Negative by the Second Affirmative:

First Affirmative Constructive Speech: Serves as introduction, giving summary overview, definitions, criteria for resolution, major claims and evidence, statement, and intention to support the resolution.

First Negative Constructive Speech: Responds by introducing the basic position, challenges the definitions and criteria, suggests the line of attack, emphasizes that the burden of proof lies with the affirmative, rejects the resolution as unnecessary or dangerous, and supports the status quo.

A debate among party leaders in Canada

Second Affirmative Constructive: Rebuilds the affirmative case; refutes chief attacks, especially concerning definitions, criteria, and rationale (philosophic framework); and further develops the affirmative case.

Second Negative Constructive: Completes the negative case, if possible advances it by rebuilding portions of the first negative construction, and contrasts the entire negative case with the entire affirmative case.

First Negative Rebuttal: Attacks the opponents' arguments and defends the negative constructive arguments (but a rebuttal may not introduce new constructive arguments).

First Affirmative Rebuttal: Usually responds first to the second negative construction and then to the first negative rebuttal.

Second Negative Rebuttal: Constitutes final speech for the negative, summarizing the case and explaining to the judge why the negative should be declared the winner.

Second Affirmative Rebuttal: Summarizes the debate, responds to issues pressed by the second negative rebuttal, and suggests to the judge that the affirmative team should win.

PART FOUR

Current Issues
Occasions for Debate

Debates as an Aid to Thinking

Throughout this book, we emphasize critical thinking, which means thinking analytically not only about the ideas of others but also about your *own* ideas. You have ideas, obviously, but if you allow your ideas to settle or become entrenched without challenging them, then you may not improve your critical thinking and arguments. You must have (or at least try to have) an open mind and remain willing (or try to remain willing) to change your mind.

You are, we hope, ready to grant that someone with differing views may indeed have something to teach you. When you hear other views, of course you won't always embrace them. At times, though, you may find merit in some aspects of them, and sometimes you will find that different views strengthen your own ideas by forcing you to confront and respond to the contrary views. Remember, too, that contrary views do not necessarily imply hostile views. The basis of mutual understanding and respect in a democratic society is meeting those who think differently than you in the middle, finding shared or common ground, and debating your points in the spirit of discovery, not conflict. (We discuss the importance of finding shared ground in Chapter 11, "A Psychologist's View: Rogerian Argument.")

Much of the difficulty in improving our ideas lies in our tendency to think in an either/or pattern. Academics call this *binary* (Latin, "two by two") or *dichotomous* (Greek, "divided into two") thinking. (Recall our discussion of false dichotomies in Chapter 10 in the section "Fallacies," p. 364). We often think in terms of contrasts: life and death, good and evil, right and left, up and down, on and off, white and black, boys and girls, men and women, yes and no, freedom and tyranny. We understand what something is partly by thinking of what it is not: "He is liberal; she is conservative."

But we know that there are gradations. We know that not everything is binary. We know that there are conservative Democrats and liberal Republicans, and although we may refer to red states and blue states, we can see there are, in fact, many types of people along a spectrum of political belief in all states. True, there are times when gradations are irrelevant in decision-making: In the polling booth, when voting for a political candidate, you must decide between *X* and *Y*. Yet, the reason why making such a choice can be so difficult is *because* of nondichotomous thinking. If you find yourself 100-percent committed to any political perspective to the total exclusion of all other views, it is likely you are not thinking carefully or critically about your own or others' ideas. We have words to describe such thinkers: ideologues, zealots, fanatics, extremists. Such people rarely seek common ground, compromises, or pragmatic solutions. They are susceptible to a range of fallacious and simplistic thinking or outright self-delusion. Those who stare facts in the face and nevertheless say the opposite is true are probably yielding to such thinking. Those who bend and contort themselves to defend their position no matter how reasonably it is challenged are probably guilty of such thinking. And those who resort to name-calling, personal attacks, or unfounded conspiracy theories to undermine their opponents are nearly always failing to think critically. (Remember, too, that volume does not improve arguments: There is no correlation between reason and how loudly one speaks — in fact, the opposite is usually the case.)

Only the most extreme stances can be easily opposed to another as an either/or proposition. We suppose there are some things about which we can and should remain uncompromising (slavery, genocide, sexual violence, for example); however, even our most controversial issues (abortion, gun control) are typically best addressed in the middle ground. Few people could convincingly argue that terminating a pregnancy is *never* warranted, or that all citizens should be allowed to own any type of firearm without some kind of qualification to such statements. (See our discussion on qualifications in Chapter 9, "A Philosopher's View: The Toulmin Model.")

The word *debate* comes from the Latin word *battere* ("to battle"), and this may imply a combative atmosphere, a contest in which there will be a winner and a loser. Indeed, the language used to describe a debate is often martial. Debaters *aim* their arguments; they *target* the *opposition* by *rebutting* (from Old French, *boter*, "to butt") and *refuting* (from Latin *futare*, "to beat") them. Some of the writers in these debates do appear to be convinced that only one view makes sense, and they may seem to be out to conquer their opponents. Others are more measured, taking into account the complexities and the possibilities for various solutions to the issues at stake. In writing about complex issues, Virginia Woolf said the following:

> When a subject is highly controversial . . . one cannot hope to tell the truth. One can only show how one came to hold whatever opinion one does hold. One can only give one's audience the chance of drawing their own conclusions as they observe the limitations, the prejudices, the idiosyncrasies of the speaker.

We urge you to read the debates in the next five chapters not to decide who is right or wrong, or who has more access to the truth, but rather to think about the issues they present. Some paired essays might seem based on either/or perspectives. (You might even be able to identify the opposition from the titles alone.) But we do not mean to suggest that there are *only* two points of view. In fact, when you read closely, you may see that some writers share common ground and goals but are approaching the same issue from different vantage points. Sure, they may have different premises; they may advocate for different pragmatic solutions; and they may be trying to be convince different audiences. But in most cases they are also presenting complicated views with a lot of moving parts. As you read, look for ways to compare and contrast the arguments, understand the elements of argument in their different views, and try to discover you own stance in the comparison.

In reading these essays, keep in mind the questions provided in A Checklist for Analyzing a Debate. These questions are very similar to those you should ask when analyzing any argument, with a few additional points of special relevance to debates.

A CHECKLIST FOR ANALYZING A DEBATE

- ☐ Is the writer's thesis clear?
    - ☐ Have I identified the writer's claim?
    - ☐ Has the writer made any assumptions?
    - ☐ Are key terms defined satisfactorily?
- ☐ Does the writer offer adequate support for the claim?
    - ☐ Are examples relevant and convincing?
    - ☐ Are statistics relevant, accurate, and convincing?
    - ☐ Are the authorities appropriate?
    - ☐ Is the logic — deductive and inductive — valid?
    - ☐ If there is an appeal to emotion, is this appeal acceptable?
- ☐ Does the writer seem fair?
    - ☐ Are counterarguments considered?
    - ☐ Is there any evidence of dishonesty?
- ☐ Do the disputants differ in
    - ☐ assumptions?
    - ☐ interpretations of relevant facts?
    - ☐ selection of and emphasis on these facts?
    - ☐ definitions of key terms?
    - ☐ values and norms?
    - ☐ goals?
- ☐ Do the disputants share any common ground?
- ☐ Does one argument stand out to me as better than the other?

14

Student Loans: Should Some Indebtedness Be Forgiven?

HILLARY HOFFOWER AND MADISON HOFF

Hillary Hoffower is a correspondent for *Business Insider*, where she reports on issues concerning, broadly, millennials and money — that is, how emerging generations are working, spending, and saving in the twenty-first century. Madison Hoff is an economic writer for *Business Insider* and reports on issues related to economics and lifestyle.

The Case for Canceling Student Loan Debt Isn't Political, It's Practical

Layla is in no rush to finish up her doctoral degree in educational leadership.

Graduating means she would have to start paying an estimated $1,500 to $2,000 per month in student loans, the 35-year-old, who asked to go by a pseudonym for privacy reasons, told *Insider*. They're currently in deferment, meaning monthly payments aren't required, but she's still shelling out $250 a month to try and stay ahead of her balance.

"Knowing that I will soon have a payment due larger than many mortgage payments can be daunting to think about," she said.

She's racked up several degrees in her quest to become a dean in higher education, including a masters in education and an MBA. But her debt — which has climbed to six figures — stems from her undergraduate and doctoral education. She didn't originally borrow this much, but said she's acquired about $35,000 in interest alone at a 6% interest rate since first taking out loans in 2003 as a college freshman.

Layla is one of millions of Americans who 5 would benefit from student-loan forgiveness.

President Joe Biden effectively rejected a plan put forward by Sens. Elizabeth Warren and Chuck Schumer to wipe out $50,000 in student-loan debt per borrower on Tuesday, but said he supports cancelling $10,000 per borrower. Additionally, Biden plans $10,000 of student loan forgiveness a year for people working in public service jobs for up to five years.

With around 10 million people unemployed right now, forgiving $10,000 per student loan borrower would be beneficial for millions of Americans.

Student loan debt makes up the second biggest share of household debt, according to the Brookings Institution. About 45 million Americans hold student loan debt with a total national outstanding amount over $1.7 trillion. Borrowers with outstanding education debt typically hold between $20,000 and $24,999, according to the Federal Reserve's 2020 US households report using 2019 data.

To determine the economic impact of student-loan debt cancellation, *Insider* spoke with six experts and economists, parsed through non-profit and government studies and reports, and dove into the data of national student debt.

JUST $10,000 IN FORGIVENESS COULD WIPE OUT DEBT FOR MILLIONS

Eliminating $10,000 of debt would help 15.3 [10] million borrowers completely wipe out their outstanding federal student debt.

The US Department of Education's office of Federal Student Aid has outstanding debt figures for federal debt borrowers, those who took out Direct Loans, Federal Family Education Loans, and Perkins Loans.

Based on fourth quarter 2020 data, loan forgiveness of $10,000 would mean complete debt cancellation for 33.6% of borrowers, who have an outstanding debt of less than $10,000 in federal student loans. It would also benefit the 9.6 million who owe between $20,000 to $40,000, the debt group with the largest number of borrowers.

However, researchers from the Center for American Progress noted in their own analysis of how many borrowers would have their debt completely eliminated using last year's figures that these shares may actually be lower "because some individuals who currently appear to have low debt levels are in school and are thus likely to end up with higher loan balances as they continue their studies."

STUDENT-DEBT CANCELLATION COULD BOOST THE ECONOMY

Bharat Ramamurti, a member of the Congressional Oversight Commission, recently tweeted out a thread that argues the benefits of cancelling student loan debt for these millions of borrowers based on previous studies and government data.

"The bottom line is that broad debt cancella- [15] tion via executive order is popular, economically potent, and—most importantly—life-changing for millions of Americans struggling through this crisis," Ramamurti wrote on Twitter.

One of the studies Ramamurti shared is a 2018 paper from the Levy Economic Institute of Bard College using 2016 data that looks at the effects of student loan debt forgiveness. The authors write that a one-time cancellation of the $1.4 trillion outstanding student debt held would translate to an increase of $86 billion to $108 billion a year, on average, to GDP.

Cancelling student debt could also mean current monthly payments could go toward savings or other spending. Per the Federal Reserve report, those who make payments usually pay about $200 to $299 per month. Ramamurti tweeted that this "is like sending those people a check every month."

He told *Insider* that with student loan forgiveness, that is essentially putting almost $3,000 back in Americans' pockets each year, which as a result could help boost the economy.

Indeed, forgiveness would benefit younger Americans who have been putting off milestones. A SoFi survey of 1,000 Americans ages 22 to 35 found 61% of millennials said they've delayed buying a house because of student-loan debt.

The Levy Institute also noted that beyond [20] the effects seen in their models, forgiveness would help with both business and household formation.

"Of course, starting a small business means that there's going to be more jobs available. Buying a home means there's more demand for home construction and so on," Ramamurti said. "And so it has all of these positive ripple effects throughout the economy."

AFFLUENT HOUSEHOLDS WON'T BE THE ONLY ONES WHO BENEFIT

One of the biggest arguments against forgiveness is that it would mainly help higher-income households since they typically have more student loan debt.

Lowell Ricketts, lead analyst for the Center for Household Financial Stability at the St. Louis Fed, agreed that affluent graduates would disproportionately benefit from student loan forgiveness. "Most borrowers typically have low balances under $10,000 or $20,000," he told *Insider* in a November 23 interview. "Most of the total balance outstanding is held by high-balance borrowers."

This cohort, who are typically in high-earning professions, hold two-thirds of all student debt, Ricketts said. For example, he added, students who owe over $100,000 make up just 7% of student loan borrowers but own 37% of all student debt out there.

But that's not to say low-balance borrowers wouldn't benefit, Ricketts said. Forgiving $10,000 worth of student loans would resolve the serious delinquency that 19% of this cohort has, he said. It would even "carve out an income-based repayment plan or a payment plan that is more workable" for borrowers with $20,000 in debt, he said.

Based on 2016 Consumer of Survey Finances data, Matthew Chingos, vice president for education, data, and policy at the Urban Institute, wrote "the benefits to lower-income households would come almost entirely in the $10,000 reduction in their loan principal, which will reduce their future loan burden but have a much smaller effect on their monthly cash flows. This is because they are less likely to be making payments on their loans, and payments made tend to be smaller."

But debt cancellation for low-income borrowers as a share of their income is much higher than for wealthier individuals, Laura Beamer, lead researcher at the Jain Family Institute (JFI), told *Insider*.

Beamer has spent the past year studying inequality in student access to higher education in the US for JFI's Millennial Student Debt Project. Her research found that in 2009, the lowest income zip codes across the country saw their student debt burdens go to 56% of their income; by 2018, it had risen to 94%.

"People who are low-income are going to be benefiting the most, even just looking at their debt-to-income ratios before and after debt cancellation," she said. "Those getting $10,000 in student loan relief, the impact for households as a portion of their income that would be freed up is dramatically greater for lower income households."

FORGIVENESS WOULD HELP NARROW THE RACIAL WEALTH GAP

It's these lowest-income households, and communities of color, that will gain the most from cancellation plans. Beamer said: "Progress on mitigating wealth inequality is one of the biggest effects of student debt forgiveness."

Black students shoulder a heavier debt burden than their white peers: About 87% of Black students attending four-year colleges take out student loans compared to about 60% of white students. They also owe $7,400 more on average than their white peers after graduating, per Brookings.

Post-college, it's difficult for workers of color to financially catch up. As the Economic Policy Institute wrote in its latest wages report, "average wages grew faster among white and Hispanic workers than among [Black] workers for all education groups from 2000 to 2019."

Black borrowers under the age of 40 were also more likely to be behind on payments in 2019 than white or Hispanic borrowers: 26% for Black borrowers, 19% for Hispanic borrowers, and 7% for white borrowers, according to the Federal Reserve.

A paper by The Roosevelt Institute using data from the Fed's Survey of Consumer Finances looked at what different levels of forgiveness would mean for debt relief for white and black borrowers.

The researchers found that if anything, 35 $10,000 is not enough, according to Suzanne Kahn, the director of education, jobs, and worker power and the Great Democracy Initiative at Roosevelt Institute.

While Kahn said the think tank doesn't have a certain amount they suggest for debt forgiveness, an updated paper based on the latest data suggests that forgiveness of $75,000, "would be a more appropriate level to increase household wealth, help close the racial wealth gap, and boost our struggling economy."

It all ties back to Ramamurti's argument that forgiveness wouldn't just benefit the individual borrower, but the economy as a whole. A threshold could pull lower-end borrowers out of default and restore their credit scores and even help those not in default delaying the aforementioned life milestones.

Consider Layla, who said she's had to weigh life decisions like buying a home, having a kid, and accepting a job against her debt. "Before any major or minor decision is made, I have to consider my student loans," she said.

She said debt relief would open the door for countless opportunities and the hope that she could still create a viable future for herself and her family. "I would feel like I could breathe a little easier. Almost as if I had a second chance at my financial life to do things better."

Topics for Critical Thinking and Writing

1. What are Hillary Hoffower and Madison Hoff arguing for specifically? What do they think the government should do about student debt? Summarize their argument in one or two sentences.

2. Do you find Hoffower and Hoff's use of data and statistics effective? Using specific examples from the text, explain why or why not.

3. What do you think is the authors' best point? What data backs up that point? How reliable is the source from which the data came? Once you have evaluated the claim and support, write a brief rebuttal to the claim from the perspective of someone who would disagree.

4. What do you think the economic effects of total student debt cancellation would be? In what ways could it boost the economy? In what ways might it hurt the economy? Why would anyone be against it?

5. Compare the cases for a $10,000 vs. a $75,000 threshold of student loan forgiveness. Is one more or less fair than the other? Why?

Analyzing a Visual: Student Loan Debt

Anadolu Agency/Getty Images

Topic for Critical Thinking and Writing

Briefly, what arguments are on display in this photo? What particular aspects of college education are these protesters critical of? Do you agree or disagree with them? Why?

JUSTIN WOLFERS

Justin Wolfers is a professor of economics and public policy at the University of Michigan and a research associate with the National Bureau of Economic Research who has also served on the Congressional Budget Office Panel of Economic Advisers. In 2011, Wolfers was invited by the economics blog Freakonomics to comment on a petition of support for canceling student debt that claimed such forgiveness would stimulate the nation's economy by giving the nation's millions of borrowers more disposable income. We reprint Wolfers's contribution to Freakonomics, September 19, 2011. When he wrote this piece in 2011, the petition had 300,000 signatures.

Forgive Student Loans? Worst Idea Ever

Let's look at this through five separate lenses:

Distribution: If we are going to give money away, why on earth would we give it to college grads? This is the one group who we know typically have high incomes, and who have enjoyed income growth over the past four decades. The group who has been hurt over the past few decades is high school dropouts.

Macroeconomics: This is the worst macro policy I've ever heard of. If you want stimulus, you get more bang-for-your-buck if you give extra dollars to folks who are most likely to spend each dollar. Imagine what would happen if you forgave $50,000 in debt. How much of that would get spent in the next month or year? Probably just a couple of grand (if that). Much of it would go into the bank. But give $1,000 to each of fifty poor people, and nearly all of it will get spent, yielding a larger stimulus. Moreover, it's not likely that college grads are the ones who are liquidity-constrained. Most of 'em could spend more if they wanted to; after all, they are the folks who could get a credit card or a car loan fairly easily. It's the hand-to-mouth consumers — those who can't get easy access to credit — who are most likely to raise their spending if they get the extra dollars.

Education Policy: Perhaps folks think that forgiving educational loans will lead more people to get an education. No, it won't. This is a proposal to forgive the debt of folks who already have an education. Want to increase access to education? Make loans more widely available, or subsidize those who are yet to choose whether to go to school. But this proposal is just a lump-sum transfer that won't increase education attainment. So why transfer to these folks?

Political Economy: This is a bunch of kids 5 who don't want to pay their loans back. And worse: Do this once, and what will happen in the next recession? More lobbying for free money, rather than doing something socially constructive. Moreover, if these guys succeed, others will try, too. And we'll just get more spending in the least socially productive part of our economy — the lobbying industry.

Politics: Notice the political rhetoric? Give free money to us, rather than "corporations, millionaires, and billionaires." Opportunity cost is one of the key principles of economics. And that principle says to compare your choice with the next best alternative. Instead, they're comparing it with the worst alternative. So my question for the proponents: Why give money to college grads rather than the 15 percent of the population in poverty?

Conclusion: Worst. Idea. Ever.

And I bet that the proponents can't find a single economist to support this idiotic idea.

Topics for Critical Thinking and Writing

1. What do you make of Justin Wolfers's first "lens" about distribution, that the last people to whom we should "give money away" are college graduates? Is this premise fair? Why or why not?

2. Examine Wolfers's second point about macroeconomics. What alternative does he offer to forgiving $50,000 in debt? Would it be more or less fair to do things Wolfers's way? Why?

3. Is Wolfers's argument a good refutation of Hoffower and Hoff's argument? Why or why not?

4. Think of several ways to refer to the term "student debt cancellation" in words or phrases that make it sound more or less favorable. Why do these word choices matter?

5. Examine Wolfers's last two paragraphs. Would the essay be more effective if he omitted the final paragraph? Explain.

6. Should student loan forgiveness be based on the proportion of income earned by borrowers after graduation? That is, would it be more appropriate to forgive the debt of a service worker who borrowed $100,000 for an elite private school education or a wealthy doctor who borrowed just $25,000? Explain your rationale using as support the selections in this chapter or others you find on the topic.

15

Artificial Intelligence: Should We Let Computers Decide?

SAFIYA UMOJA NOBLE

Safiya Umoja Noble is a professor of gender studies and African-American studies at the University of California, Los Angeles, where she researches and teaches about the impact of digital media on contemporary society and culture. Her book *Algorithms of Oppression: How Search Engines Reinforce Racism* (2018), which focuses on racial biases in search engines, social media, and other algorithm-based platforms, brought increased attention to algorithmic bias as a function of systemic racism. Noble also co-edited two volumes on technology and culture, *The Intersectional Internet: Race, Sex, Class, and Culture Online* (2016), and *Emotions, Technology, and Design* (2016). In 2019, she became a senior research fellow with the Oxford Internet Institute at Oxford University, United Kingdom. In 2021, she won a MacArthur Foundation Fellowship "Genius Award." The following selection appeared in *Bitch* magazine in 2012.

Missed Connections: What Search Engines Say about Women

On occasion, I ask my university students to follow me through a day in the life of an African-American aunt, mother, mentor, or friend who is trying to help young women learn to use the Internet. In this exercise, I ask what kind of things they think young black girls might be interested in learning about: music, hair, friendship, fashion, popular culture?

I ask them if they could imagine how my nieces' multicultural group of friends who are curious to learn about black culture and contributions (beyond watching rap music videos or Tyler Perry movies) might go to Google to find information about black accomplishments, identities, and intellectual traditions. I ask them to think about the book report they might write, or the speech they might give about famous black girls involved in human and civil rights movements in the United States and across the world. I remind my students that to be black is to encompass more than an African-American identity, but to embrace an affinity with black people in the diaspora, that it is our identification with others of African descent in Africa, the Caribbean, Latin America, Europe, and all parts of the globe. I remind them of the reclamation of the word "black" that my parents' and their grandparents' generations fought for, as in "Black Is Beautiful." I ask them to imagine a 16-year-old, or even an 8-year-old, opening up Google in her browser and searching for herself and her friends by typing in the words "black girls."

Someone inevitably volunteers to come forward and open a blank Google search page — a portal to the seemingly bottomless array of information online — intending to find accurate and timely information that can't easily be found without a library card or a thoughtful and well-informed teacher.

Last semester, SugaryBlackP---y.com was the top hit. No matter which year or class the students are in, they always look at me in disbelief when their search yields this result. They wonder if they did something wrong. They double-check. They try using quotation marks around the search terms. They make sure the computer isn't logged in to Gmail, as if past searches for pornography might be affecting the results. They don't understand.

I consider myself far from prudish. I don't 5 care if someone types "porn" into a search engine and porn is what they get. I do care about porn turning up in the results when people are searching for support, knowledge, or answers about identity. I care that someone might type in "black girls," "Latinas," or other terms associated with women of color and instantly find porn all over their first-page results. I care that women are automatically considered "girls," and that actual girls find their identities so readily compromised by porn.

At the moment, U.S. commercial search engines like Google, Yahoo!, and Bing wield tremendous power in defining how information is indexed and prioritized. Cuts to public education, public libraries, and community resources only exacerbate our reliance on technology, rather than information and education professionals, for learning. But what's missing in the search engine is awareness about stereotypes, inequity, and identity. These results are deeply problematic and are often presented without any way for us to change them.

Last year when I conducted these exercises in class, the now-defunct HotBlackP---y.com outranked SugaryBlackP---y.com, indicating that the market for black women and girls' identities online is also in flux, and changes as businesses and organizations can afford to position and sustain themselves at the top of the search pile. These search engine results, for women whose identities are already maligned in the media, only further debase and erode efforts for social, political, and economic recognition and justice.

While preparing to write this article, I did a search for "women's magazines," having a hunch that feminist periodicals would not rise to the top of the search pile. After looking through the websites provided by Google, I gave up by page 11, never to find *Bitch* magazine. This search raises questions about why "women's magazines" are automatically linked to unfeminist periodicals like *Cosmopolitan* and *Women's Day*. (Not coincidentally, these titles are all owned by the Hearst Corporation, which has the funds to purchase its way to the top of the search pile, and which benefits from owning multiple media properties that can be used for cross-promotional hyperlinks that mutually push each other higher in the rankings.) These titles are the default for representations of women's magazines, while alternative women's media — say, those with a feminist perspective — can be found only via searching by name or including purposeful search terms like "feminist."

Try Google searches on every variation you can think of for women's and girls' identities and you will see many of the ways in which commercial interests have subverted a diverse (or realistic) range of representations. Try "women athletes" and do your best not to cringe at the lists of "Top 25 Sexiest Female Athletes" that surface. Based on these search results, constructions of women's identities and interests seem to be based on traditional, limited sexist norms, just as they are in the traditional media. What does it mean that feminism — or, barring a specific identification with that term, progressivism — has been divorced from the definitions or representations of "women" in a commercial search engine? That antifeminist or even pornographic representations of women show up on the first page of results in search engines by default?

Google's search process is based on identifying and assigning value to various types of information through web indexing. Many search engines, not just Google, use the artificial intelligence of computers to determine what kinds of information should be retrieved and displayed, and in what order. Complex mathematical formulations are developed into algorithms that are part of the automation process. But these calculations do not take social context into account.

If you were to try my classroom experiments for yourself (which I imagine you may do in the middle of reading this article), you may get a variation on my students' results. The truth is, search engine results are impacted by myriad factors. Google applications like Gmail and social media sites like Facebook track your identity and previous searches to unearth something slightly different. Search engines increasingly remember where you've been and what links you've clicked in order to provide more customized content. Search results will also vary depending on whether filters to screen out porn are enabled on your browser. In some cases, there may be more media and interest in non-pornographic information about black girls in your locale that push such sites higher up to the first page, like a strong nonprofit, blog, or media source that gets a lot of clicks in your region (I teach in the Midwest, which may have something to do with the results we get when we do Google searches in class). Information that rises to the top of the search pile is not the same for every user in every location, and a variety of commercial advertising and political, social, and economic factors are linked to the way search results are coded and displayed.

Recently, the Federal Trade Commission started looking into Google's near-monopoly status and market dominance and the harm this could cause consumers. Consumer Watchdog .org's report "Traffic Report: How Google Is Squeezing Out Competitors and Muscling into New Markets," from June 2010, details how Google effectively blocks sites that it competes with and prioritizes its own properties to the top of the search pile (YouTube over other video sites, Google Maps over MapQuest, and Google Images over Photobucket and Flickr). The report highlights how Universal Search is not a neutral search process, but rather a commercial one that moves sites that buy paid advertising (as well as Google's own investments) to the top of the pile. But many analysts watching the antitrust debates around Google argue that in the free market economy, market share dominance and control over search results isn't a crime. In a September 2011 Businessweek.com article, reporter Mathew Ingram suggested that "it would be hard for anyone to prove that the company's free services have injured consumers."

But Ingram is arguably defining "injury" a little too narrowly. Try searching for "Latinas," or "Asian women," and the results focus on porn, dating, and fetishization. "Black women" will give you sites on "angry black women," and articles on "why black women are less attractive." The largest commercial search engines fail to provide relevant and culturally situated knowledge on how women of color have traditionally been discriminated against, denied rights, or been violated in society and the media even though we have organized and resisted this on many levels. Search engine results don't only mask the unequal access to social, political, and economic life in the United States as broken down by race, gender, and sexuality — they also maintain it.

You might think that Google would want to do something about problematic search results, especially those that appear racist or sexist. Veronica Arreola wondered as much on the *Ms.* blog in 2010, when Google Instant, a search-enhancement tool, initially did not include the words "Latinas," "lesbian," and "bisexual," because of their X-rated front-page results: "You're Google. I think you could figure out how to put porn and violence-related results, say, on the second page?" But they don't — except where it's illegal (Google will not surface certain neo-Nazi websites in France and Germany, where Holocaust denial is against the law). Siva Vaidhyanathan's 2011 book reminds us why this is an

important matter to trace. He chronicles recent attempts by the Jewish community and the Anti-Defamation League to challenge Google's priority ranking of anti-Semitic, Holocaust-denial websites. So troublesome were these search results that in 2011 Google issued a statement about its search process, encouraging people to use "Jews" and "Jewish people" in their searches, rather than the pejorative term "Jew" — which they claim they can do nothing about white supremacist groups co-opting. The need for accurate information about Jewish culture and the Holocaust should be enough evidence to start a national discussion about consumer harm, to which we can add a whole host of cultural and gender-based identities that are misrepresented in search engine results.

Google's assertion that its search results, [15] though problematic, were computer-generated (and thus not the company's fault) was apparently a good enough answer for the ADL, which was "extremely pleased that Google has heard our concerns and those of its users about the offensive nature of some search results and the unusually high ranking of peddlers of bigotry and anti-Semitism." A search for the word "Jew" today will surface a beige box from Google linking to its lengthy disclaimer about your results — which remain a mix of both anti-Semitic and informative sites.

These kinds of disclaimers about search results are not enough, and though our collective (and at times tormented) love affair with Google continues, it should not be given a pass just because it issues apologies under the guise of its motto, "Don't be evil." Just because search engines are shrouded in high-tech processes that may be difficult for the average Internet user to grasp doesn't mean that the search methods of all the market leaders shouldn't be examined. In addition, it is important that those who feel harmed by what goes to the top of a page-ranking system be heard in these processes. The question that the Federal Trade Commission might ask is whether search engines like Google should be probed about the values they assign to keyword combinations like "black girls," "Latinas," and other racial, gendered, and sexual-identity combinations, and whether saying they are not responsible for what happens through disclaimers should suffice.

The rapid shift over the past decade from public-interest journalism to the corporate takeover of U.S. news media — which has made highlighting any kind of alternative news increasingly difficult — has occurred simultaneously with the erosion of professional standards applied to information provision on the web. As the search arena is consolidated to a handful of corporations, it's even more crucial to pay close attention to the types of biases that are shaping the information prioritized in search engines. The higher a web page is ranked, the more it's trusted. And unlike the vetting of journalists and librarians, who have been entrusted to fact-check and curate information for the public, the legitimacy of websites is taken for granted. When it comes to commercial search engines, it is no longer enough to simply share news and education on the web — we must ask ourselves how the things we want to share are found, and how the things we find have surfaced.

These shifts are similar to the ways that certain kinds of information are prioritized to the top of the search pile: information, products, and ideas promoted by businesses and sold to industries that can afford to purchase keywords at a premium, or URLS

and advertising space online that drive their results and links to the top of the near-infinite pile of information available on the web. All of these dynamics are important for communities and organizations that want to make reliable information, education, culture, and resources available to each other — and not on page 23 of a Google search.

The Pew Internet & American Life consumer-behavior tracking surveys are conducted on a regular basis to understand the ways that Americans use the Internet and technology. An August 9, 2011, report found that 92 percent of adults who use the Internet — about half of all Americans — use search engines to find information online, and 59 percent do so on a typical day. These results indicate searching is the most popular online activity among U.S. adults. An earlier Pew report from 2005, "Search Engine Users," specifically studied trust and credibility, finding that for the most part, people are satisfied with the results they find in search engines, with 64 percent of respondents believing search engines are a fair and unbiased source of information.

But in the case of a search on the words [20] "black girls," the results that come up are certainly not fair or unbiased representations of actual black girls. In a centuries-old struggle for self-determination and a decades-long effort to have control over our media misrepresentations — from mammies to sapphires, prostitutes to vixens — black women and girls have long been subject to exploitation in the media. Since we are so reliant on search engines for providing trusted information, shouldn't we question the ways in which "information" about women is offered up to the highest bidder, advertiser, or company that can buy search terms and portray them any way they want?

When I conducted my classroom exercise this semester, Black Girls Rock!, a nonprofit dedicated to empowering young women of color, was ranked high on the first-page results, showing that there are, indeed, alternatives to the usual search results. This coincided with a national campaign the organization was doing for an upcoming TV special, meaning a lot of people visited their site, helping move them up to the front page. But not all organizations have the ability to promote their URL via other media. One of the myths of our digital democracy is that what rises to the top of the pile is what is most popular. By this logic, sexism and pornography are the most popular values on the Internet when it comes to women. There is more to result ranking than simply "voting" with our clicks.

Search engines have the potential to display information and counternarratives that don't prioritize the most explicit, racist, or sexist formulations around identity. We could experience freedom from such contrived and stereotypical representations by not supporting companies that foster a lack of social, political, and economic context in search engine results, especially as search engines are being given so much power in schools, libraries, and in the public domain. We could read more for knowledge and understanding and search less for decontextualized snippets of information. We could support more funding for public resources like schools and libraries, rather than outsourcing knowledge to big corporations. We need more sophisticated and thoughtful rankings of results that account for historical discrimination and misrepresentation. Otherwise, it appears that identity-based search results could be nothing more than old bigotry packaged in new media.

Topics for Critical Thinking and Writing

1. Identify the problem Safiya Umoja Noble proposes at the beginning of her article. As thoroughly as you can, describe the problem. Is it a problem particular to Black girls? Explain.

2. Do you think Noble singles out Google unfairly? Why or why not?

3. What is Noble's purpose (or purposes) in writing this essay? Does she argue that anything should be done to correct biases she discusses in her article? If so, what? What might you add to the list of things that can be done to lessen the impact of racial, gender, and class biases in search engines?

4. Analyze the statistics Noble cites in paragraph 19. How do these statistics contribute to her argument? What do you think she is trying to say in offering these statistics?

Analyzing a Visual: Predictive Search

About   Store

Gmail Images ▦ **Sign in**

Google

🔍 why are women   ✕ 🎤

🔍 why are women **always cold**

🔍 why are women **paid less**

🔍 why are women **shorter than men**

🔍 why are women **so beautiful**

🔍 why are women **colder than men**

🔍 why are women **more flexible**

🔍 why are women **more emotional**

🔍 why are women **important**

🔍 why are women **attracted to men**

🔍 why are women **treated differently**

Google Search   I'm Feeling Lucky

Report inappropriate predictions

Advertising   Business   How Search works   Privacy   Terms   Settings

Topics for Critical Thinking and Writing

1. In her essay, Safiya Umoja Noble imagines that readers will try searching on their own to see what kinds of results are returned (para. 11). Examine the results in this image. Do they confirm or refute Noble's claims? Since her article was published, search engine companies have attempted to rectify clear instances of racial and other biases in search results. Do you think the problem is solved? Why or why not?

2. Write about a time when you believed that information you discovered on the internet was affected by predictive algorithms that provided you results based on your purchases or previous usage. Consider questions such as the following: Did you feel like the technologies made undue assumptions about you? Were you led to advertising sites? Were the best results obscured by paying or popular companies that rose to the top of the list? Refer to the visual — or provide your own for analysis — in your answer.

MARK MANSON

Mark Manson is a technology and culture blogger whose web page tagline is "Life Advice that Doesn't Suck." ("I write life advice that is science-based, pragmatic, and non-bullshitty," he claims.) Manson has written numerous influential pieces with a flair of a humor in the analysis. One of his blog posts was transformed into the *New York Times* bestselling book, *The Subtle Art of Not Giving a F*ck* (2016). His latest book, also a bestseller, is entitled *Everything is F*cked: A Book about Hope* (2019). The essay that follows was published on Manson's blog in 2016.

I, for One, Welcome Our AI Overlords

A few weeks ago, for the first time ever, a computer beat the world champion of Go, one of the most complex games known to man. This was another watershed moment in the progress of artificial intelligence.

To give you an idea how complex Go is, there are 2.082×10^{170} possible board configurations. That is 2 with 170 zeroes after it. Chances are your brain cannot even conceive of a number that large (but a computer can). Or to give you an idea of how big of a number *that* is, there are only 10^{80} atoms in the universe—that is, one followed by 80 zeroes.

The reason this is such a big deal is that Go is so complicated that in order to beat a top human player, a machine would have to learn how to think creatively, improvising and adapting to the situation at hand without being able to calculate every possible outcome; i.e., there has to be some serious artificial intelligence going on—like real, creative intelligence.

In case you haven't gotten the memo on the whole "AI is going to take over the world" thing, here are the few facts you need to know.

1. Computers are getting smarter.

2. Computers are getting smarter at an accelerating rate—i.e., advancements that used to take 10 years now take one year. Advancements that used to take one year, now take weeks or even days.

3. It is highly likely that within our lifetimes, there will be computers that are far smarter and more capable than any single human being.

4. These smarter computers will then likely be able to design and improve upon technology (i.e., themselves) and create new technology that we cannot even begin to fathom.

People who understand the above points 5 generally have one of two reactions. Either:

1. They think we're totally fucked. The computers are going to take over everything and kill/enslave us all. Or:

2. This is going to bring about a technological utopia that will fix all of our silly human squabbles and we can all live happily ever after having orgies in our ultra-VR world that exists in the cloud.

As with most things, the truth is likely somewhere in the middle.

But even if shit does hit the fan, even if the robots see us as the lice ruining this planet's pristine scalp and want to round us all up and throw us into an active volcano, even if we are inadvertently inventing the very mechanisms of our own extinction . . .

. . . I don't care. It doesn't matter. It doesn't bother me. And it shouldn't bother you, either. I will explain why in a bit. But for now, you should know that I, for one, welcome our new robot overlords.

ACCELERATING GROWTH IN THE TECH INDUSTRY

Technological developments compound upon themselves, causing the *rate* of development itself to accelerate. What that means is that the more advanced technology we create, the easier it gets to create even more advanced technology. As a result, when we look at the advancement of computing technology, we see an exponential curve—i.e., the more time that goes by, the faster the things develop.

Computing power has doubled on average every 18 months for 50 years now. In terms of raw computing power, computers now rival the abilities of mouse brains, where only a few years ago, computers couldn't even compete with an insect brain.

To give you a more immediate example of how rapid technology has advanced, more pictures are now taken every 2 minutes than were taken in the entire 19th century.[1] About 10% of the 3.5 trillion photos ever taken were taken in the past 12 months.

If we are indeed on an exponential curve when it comes to high-tech advances, then people like Jeremy Howard are probably right when he says we're only a few years away from artificial machine intelligence that rivals, if not surpasses, our own in many domains previously thought to be uniquely human.

And to be sure, AI is creeping into more and more domains of our lives.

Only a decade ago, people were laughing at the poor performance of self-driving cars. Today, only a decade later, self-driving cars can not only finish a closed-road course, they drive on busy freeways right alongside cars driven by humans.[2]

And when computers aren't beating world champion Go players, they're busy doing things like writing articles about sports and breaking news events, writing descriptions of images they've never "seen" before, and diagnosing cancer. For many of these tasks, the computers are as good if not better than humans, and for the ones they're not, they're *learning* how to do them better and better every day without the help of humans.

A few short years ago, facial recognition software was incredibly expensive and not that good at identifying people in real-world settings. It was considered super-advanced spy-level technology and really only used by a few world governments.

Now Facebook can fucking tag your friends from last weekend's barbecue.[3]

Here's the thing about accelerating growth in computers: there will one day come a point where we build a computer that is smarter than any human on Earth. On that day, computers will usurp us as the primary problem solvers on the planet, and from there, our thoughts, decisions, and actions will slowly become obsolete. The machines will be better than us at everything, so more and more, we will do nothing useful.

This terrifies some people. They envision some sort of future like *Terminator* or *The Matrix* where machines enslave us or exterminate us.

Other people look forward to the rise of the robots with a sort of cultish fervor because they believe their problem-solving capabilities will outstrip ours so much that life will become unimaginably pleasant and problem-free. All diseases will be cured. Poverty, world hunger, war, and climate change will all be solved. We'll have an infinite amount of leisure time, and in extreme cases, some people believe the machines will make us immortal.

THE TWO POSSIBLE OUTCOMES

Since we're always being told to be fucking positive, let's start with the techno-utopiasts.

There are people like Ray Kurzweil who think that technology will not only improve

---

[1] How many photos have ever been taken? | eyebeam.org.

[2] Yeah, yeah, that one Google car hit a bus at 2 mph and everyone freaked out. But no one seemed to give a shit about the more than 3,000 people that were killed that same day by human drivers around the world.

[3] Speaking of Facebook, the social media juggernaut achieved over 1 billion users in 2012 and yet it employs less than 5,000 people, at least seven of which are billionaires. Achieving this kind of scale with so few human resources is a hallmark of the technological revolution in which we find ourselves.

our lives, it will save humanity and possibly guarantee our place in the universe indefinitely. Kurzweil believes in future technology like nanobots that will repair our cells and reverse aging or remove excess fat and sugar so we can eat whatever we want. And just in case our physical bodies aren't able to live forever, Kurzweil thinks we'll have the ability to upload our brains into the cloud and "live" in a virtual world forever, long after our physical bodies are gone.

Others in this camp think that an artificial super intelligence would be able to answer questions that are too complex for humans to even understand and we'll be exponentially better off for it. Also, not only would the machines invent better gadgets and widgets, they would invent exponentially more efficient ways of building gadgets and widgets, making it possible for virtually everyone on the planet to reap their benefits.

A few lines of reasoning support this idea. First, even though technology has created some new problems for humanity, like nuclear weapons and YouTube celebrities, it has, so far, clearly been a net benefit for humanity. Despite what politicians and pundits want you to believe, the average person on Earth is better off than they were just a few short years ago and it's largely due to technology becoming better, cheaper, and more widespread. If this trend continues, we may have nothing to worry about.

Second, Kurzweil and his supporters believe that technology will have no reason to harm humanity because not only is it created by us, it is becoming more a part of us. They believe we will even reach a point where our biology and our technology are indistinguishable. If this is the case, the argument goes, any form of technology that is detrimental for humans is also detrimental to itself, and a self-destructive technology of any kind cannot persist. That is, it would quickly "die off"

just as a detrimental gene mutation is quickly weeded out of the gene pool.

But techno-utopiasts are likely biased in that they don't acknowledge that all technologies can be used for various purposes, both beneficial and destructive. They're also likely biased in that they ignore the fact that humans move slow to adapt to new technologies and that there are always groups of people who will seek to abuse those technologies for their own selfish ends.

In the other camp, you have the techno-armageddonists. I totally just made that word up, but apparently it exists, because spellcheck told me so.

What the techno-armageddonists lack in conviction (most of them just aren't sure what to think yet), they make up in celebrity star power.[4] Bill Gates, Stephen Hawking, and Elon Musk are just a few of the leading thinkers and scientists who are crapping their pants at how rapidly AI is developing and how under-prepared we are as a species for its repercussions. When Musk was asked what the most imminent threats to humanity in the near future were, he quickly said there were three: first, wide-scale nuclear war; second, climate change. Before naming a third, he went silent. When the interviewer asked him, "What is the third?" He smiled and said, "Let's just say that I hope that the computers will decide to be nice to us."

Possibly the most outspoken and respected of the techno-armageddonists is the Swedish philosopher Nick Bostrom. One thing Bostrom and others fear is runaway self-improving technology; that is, a machine that is smart enough

---

[4]Techno-armageddonists are likely biased in that they still imagine the advanced machines of the future as amoral and without emotion, much like the machines now. They are also biased in that they imagine that if humans aren't able to be productive then machines will want to get rid of us, as if being productive was the only reason for existing.

to make itself (or new versions of itself) smarter without human intervention. If it reaches a point where it surpasses human intelligence, it's only a very short matter of time before the law of accelerating returns kicks into overdrive and the exponential curve shoots straight up and we won't be able to stop it.

Bostrom makes a good point here: creating something that is smarter than you could be an evolutionary disaster for your species.

We run a very real risk of not being able to control an entity that is orders of magnitude more intelligent than us. Perhaps if computers get smart enough, they'll figure out a way to domesticate us a lot like humans domesticated horses to do labor like pull plows and buggies and war chariots (or whatever the hell horses did back then). The scary part is that this might be the best scenario for us — doing work for machines that they can't do or don't want to do — because just as humans created new technology to replace the horse, a super intelligent self-improving machine would eventually come up with new technology to replace us. And, well, let's just say the horse population isn't what it used to be.

Some argue that this isn't plausible because 30 humans build technology with safety in mind. But name the last time a major technological breakthrough was NOT used by somebody for nefarious or destructive purposes? Oh yeah, that's right. Never.

WHY I DON'T CARE WHAT HAPPENS AND NEITHER SHOULD YOU

So let's assume that super-intelligent machines are created and do render humanity powerless. Let's assume they're not integrated into us and our brains somehow and let's assume that people like Hawking and Musk are right:

that humanity really is just a multi-millennium boot drive to digital hyper-intelligence and we have outlived our usefulness.

I'm still not worried about it.

Why? Well, to keep the bullet point train rolling, let's take this point-by-point:

1. The machines' understanding of good/evil will likely surpass our own. When was the last time a dog or dolphin committed genocide? When was the last time a computer decided to vaporize entire cities in the name of abstract concepts such as 'freedom' and 'world peace'?

That's right, the answer is never. 35

My point here is not that intelligent machines won't want to exterminate the entire human species. My point is that as humans, we're throwing rocks from inside a glass house here. What the fuck do we know about ethics and humane treatment of animals, the environment, and each other? What leg do we have to stand on?

That's right: pretty much nothing. When it comes to moral questions, humanity historically flunks the test. Super-intelligent machines will likely come to understand ethics, life/death, creation/destruction on a much higher level than we ever could on our own. And this idea that they will exterminate us for the simple fact that we aren't as productive as we used to be, or that sometimes we can be a nuisance, I think, is just projecting the worst aspects of our own psychology onto something we don't know and can't understand.

Right now, most of human morality is based around an obsessive preservation and promotion of each of our individual human consciousnesses. What if advanced technology renders individual human consciousness arbitrary? What if consciousness can be replicated, expanded and contracted at will? It will completely obliterate any ethical understanding we could ever have. What if removing all of these lunky, inefficient biological prisons we call bodies may actually be a far more ethical decision than letting us continue to squirm and squirt our way through 80-some-odd years of existence? What if the machines realize we'd be much happier being freed from our intellectual prisons and have our conscious perception of our own identities expanded to include all of perceivable reality? What if they think we're just a bunch of drooling idiots and keep us occupied with incredibly good pizza and video games until we all die off by our own mortality? Who are we to know? And who are we to say?

But I will say this: they will be far better informed than we ever have been.

2. Even if they do decide to kill or 40 **enslave us, they will surely be practical about it.** Humans tend to cause the most trouble when we're not happy. When we're not happy, that's when we get all moody and whiny and angry and violent. That's when we start political uprisings and religious cults and bombing remote countries and demanding *our rights be respected goddamnit!* and start killing indiscriminately until somebody pays attention to us like mommy never did.

If the machines try to do us in like Skynet in *The Terminator*, then we're going to have a global civil war on our hands, and that's no good for anybody, especially the machines. Civil wars are inefficient. And machines are programmed for efficiency.

When humans are happy, we don't have time for such things — we're too busy giggling and fucking to care. Therefore, a far more practical way to get rid of us would be for the machines to manipulate us into gleefully getting rid of ourselves. It'll be like Jim Jones on a global scale. Whatever they cook up for us will appear to be the best goddamn idea we've ever heard of — none of us will be able to resist it and we'll all euphorically agree to their plan — and then boom, it'll be over. Quick and painless. It'll be the best-tasting cyanide-laced Kool-Aid ever conceived. And we'll all be in line happily gulping it down.

Now, if you think about it, this isn't such a bad way to go. Beats getting bombed by drones or being vaporized in a nuclear blast.

As for enslavement, same thing goes. A deliriously happy slave never rebels. I imagine a sort of Matrix-y type deal where we're kept in a constant hallucinogenic state where it's Mardi Gras on MDMA pretty much 24/7/365. Can't be that bad, can it?

3. We don't have to fear what we don't 45 **understand.** A lot of times parents will raise a kid who is far more intelligent, educated, and successful than they are. Parents then react in one of two ways to this child: either they become intimidated by her, insecure, and desperate to control her for fear of losing her, or they sit back and appreciate and love that they created something so great that even they can't totally comprehend what their child has become.

Those that try to control their child through fear and manipulation are shitty parents. I think most people would agree on that.

And right now, with the imminent emergence of machines that are going to put you, me, and everyone we know out of work, we are acting like the shitty parents. As a species, we are on the verge of birthing the most prodigiously advanced and intelligent child within our known universe. It will go on to do things that we cannot comprehend or understand. It may remain loving and loyal to us. It may bring us along and integrate us into its adventures. Or it may decide that we were shitty parents and stop calling us back.

Whatever happens, that shouldn't change how we feel about this moment. It's bigger than us. Who cares if we are one big, long evolutionary boot disk for something greater than we can comprehend? That's great! It means we had one job. And we came and fucking did it. Be happy you were part of the generation that saw it get done. And now tearfully wave goodbye as our kid gets ready to move out of the house and start a life so amazing that it exists beyond the horizon of our comprehension.

Topics for Critical Thinking and Writing

1. At the beginning of Mark Manson's essay, he provides four "facts." Do you find that these facts are backed by adequate evidence? Would you agree they are all facts? Explain your answers.

2. How would you describe the language and tone of Manson's essay? Do you think they help or hurt his argument? How so?

3. In the article, how does Manson support his position that soon technology will overtake humans' capacity to make decisions? What are his arguments' strengths on this point? What are the weaknesses? Are there any ways to challenge his premise about this rate of acceleration?

4. Can you locate logical fallacies in Manson's essay? (Use the Visual Guide: Common Fallacies chart on p. 365 and the description of common argumentative fallacies in Chapter 10, "Fallacies," on pp. 364–76.), Do the fallacies you identified undermine his argument or are they just part of the humor?

5. In the years that have passed since Manson wrote this piece, have his predictions been borne out? Where have the promises of technology succeeded and failed in "replacing humans"?

6. Is Manson's enthusiasm for technology a strong counterargument to Noble's piece? Why or why not?

16

(Un)safe Spaces: Can We Tolerate Intolerant Speech on Campus?

JULIA SERANO

Julia Serano is an author, a trans-bi activist, and biologist based in Oakland, California. Her work has appeared in numerous publications, including *Time*, the *Guardian*, and *Ms*. She recently won Publishing Triangle's 2021 Edmund White Award for Debut Fiction for her novel *99 Erics: A Kat Cataclysm Faux Novel* (2020). Her previous non-fiction works include *Whipping Girl: A Transsexual Woman on Sexism* (2007), *Excluded: Making Feminism and Queer Movements More Inclusive* (2013), and *Outspoken: A Decade of Transgender Activist and Trans Feminism* (2016). Her most recent publication is *Sexed Up: How Society Sexualizes Us, and How We Can Fight Back* (2022). The selection below was originally posted on Medium in 2017.

Free Speech and the Paradox of Tolerance

Any time activists (regardless of affiliation) protest a public speaking event, or the publication of a particular book or article, there will inevitably be claims that such actions threaten "free speech" or constitute "censorship." Lately, these sorts of claims have been heard following the presidential-inauguration-day silencing (via punching) of white nationalist leader Richard Spencer while he was being interviewed, and after protesters attempted to force the cancellation of Breitbart[1] editor Milo Yiannopoulos's speaking engagements at University of Washington and UC Berkeley. Some people who take such a stance do so for purely political reasons — they share Spencer's and Yiannopoulos's views, and invoke "free speech" to make their ideologies appear unassailable. Many others who do not share these views may instead adhere to *free speech absolutism*, and their reasoning might be summarized as follows:

1. The First Amendment to the Constitution (or analogous statutes in other countries) ensures our right to "freedom of speech."

2. Therefore, even if we detest Spencer's and Yiannopoulos's extreme

---

[1] **Breitbart** Breitbart News Network is a far-right online news platform that became associated with the alt-right and with white supremacist groups around the time of the 2016 election of US President Donald Trump. [Editors' note]

racist, misogynistic, and xenophobic beliefs, we must nevertheless defend their right to freely express them.

3. Any attempt to suppress or silence Spencer or Yiannopoulos (or their views) is essentially an attack on freedom of speech itself. And once we start down that slippery slope, it is only a matter of time before we find that our own freedom of speech is in jeopardy as well.

While the free speech absolutist position may sound compelling on the surface — indeed, it is what most of us were taught in school, and what most intellectuals espouse — the reality is not nearly so clear-cut. For instance, the courts have ruled that false statements of fact, defamation, obscenity, fighting words, and incitement (e.g., shouting "fire" in a crowded theater) do not qualify as protected speech. There are also occasions where our right to free speech bumps up against (and therefore, may be restricted by) other rights (e.g., privacy) and laws (e.g., copyright protection).

Aforementioned exceptions aside, while the First Amendment prohibits the government from passing laws that prohibit our freedom of speech (plus freedom of press, the right to peaceably assemble, and so on), this by no means guarantees us the right to speak our minds however and wherever we want. I obviously do not have the right to give a speech in your living room, or to force you to publish my article in your newspaper. And of course, free speech does not shield us from criticism: If you don't like what I have to say, then you have every right (via your freedom of speech) to criticize me, sign a petition condemning me, and/or protest my next public appearance. An organization is free to invite me to give a talk in their space, but they are also free to rescind that invitation upon further consideration (e.g.,

if they think that I might offend or injure members of their community, or if they simply want to avoid "bad press" — yet another manifestation of freedom of expression).

In other words, we have the right to free speech, but that right is somewhat limited. We are by no means entitled to "free speech without criticism or consequences," nor are we entitled to an audience.

While it is important to keep these 5 well-established limitations on free speech in mind, what I really want to focus on in this essay — especially given the steep rise in openly expressed white nationalist rhetoric over the last year — is the *paradox* of free speech. Here is what I mean: Spencer has used his right to free speech to call for "peaceful ethnic cleansing" — presumably this entails scaring people into fleeing and/or using the legal system to forcibly purge all people of color and indigenous peoples from the United States. Wouldn't that be tantamount to silencing these groups, thereby violating their freedom of speech (not to mention countless other rights)? Or take what happened to actor/comedian Leslie Jones last summer: She was forced to leave the social media platform Twitter and had to shut down her personal website after Yiannopoulos incited a fierce campaign of doxxing[2] and harassment against her. In other words, he used his free speech to suppress her free speech. (And for the record, he has done this to many other people.)

Hate speech, and other speech acts designed to harass and intimidate (rather than merely express criticism or dissent), are routinely used to thwart other people's freedom of expression. Free speech absolutists tend not to consider or fully appreciate this, probably because most of them have never felt silenced by pervasive or

---

[2]**doxxing** From *dox*, an abbreviation for documents. Doxxing refers to researching and posting private information about an individual on the internet. [Editors' note]

systemic hatred and intolerance before. Others of us, however, have experienced this firsthand.

I grew up during the 1970s and '80s, during a time when transgender people were extremely stigmatized and not tolerated by society at large. As a child, I saw how gender-variant people were openly and relentlessly mocked, so I decided not to tell anyone about what I was experiencing. As a young adult, I continued to remain quiet about my identity. Colloquially, we call this being "in the closet," but that's just a fancy way of saying "hiding from hate speech and harassment." Of course, I *technically* had free speech, but that doesn't count for much if speaking your mind is likely to result in you being bombarded with epithets, losing your job, being ostracized by your community, and possibly other forms of retribution. When I attended my first transgender support group in the early '90s, we held our meetings in a secret location because, despite our First Amendment right to peaceably assemble, it was simply not safe for us to meet in public or be discovered by others.

Free speech absolutists love to cite George Orwell's *1984* as harbinger of what might come to pass if we fail to adhere to complete unadulterated free speech. I find this ironic, as it was my favorite book growing up. This was not because I was fascinated with its futuristic dystopian setting, but because the world it described very much reflected my own personal circumstances. I identified with the main character Winston — the panic he felt as he wrote in his journal, his fear of what might happen if he were ever found out. Years later, I would name myself Julia after the female protagonist of the book — like me, she was a passionate person who kept that part of herself hidden from an inhospitable world; she was a survivor who took pride in her ability to conceal what she was really thinking.

I think that "freedom of speech" is a lovely aphorism. And aphorisms are useful. But I am not gullible enough to believe that "free speech" (as free speech absolutists envision it) actually exists, or that it is something that I have ever truly possessed. The truth of the matter is that there are two types of speech or expression: those that we (either as individuals, or as a society) are willing to tolerate, and those that we do not. You may cherish a particular word, idea, expression, or identity. But if enough people collectively refuse to tolerate it, well . . . you can shout "free speech!" at the top of your lungs all you want, but it isn't going to protect you.

Believing that freedom of speech is gen- [10] erally a good thing — an ideal worth striving for — but also knowing that speech can be (and often is) used to suppress other people's freedom of expression, the question becomes: How do we best strike a balance between these two competing forces? I remember expressing a potential solution to this problem in a conversation that I had with a friend in the late '90s. I told him that I tolerate all forms of expression, except for expressions that convey intolerance toward others. My friend was a free speech absolutist, and found my pronouncement to be hypocritical. He argued that being intolerant of intolerance was itself a form of intolerance. I argued the reverse: If I tolerated intolerance, that would *not* make me a tolerant person; it would merely make me an enabler of, or accomplice to, intolerance.

Years later, thanks to the invention of Internet search engines, I discovered that the line of reasoning that I had forwarded had been previously (and more eloquently) expressed by someone who had considered this problem far longer and in more depth than most of the rest of us have. In *The Open Society and Its Enemies*, philosopher Karl Popper described this as "the paradox of tolerance." Here is how he put it:

> Unlimited tolerance must lead to the
> disappearance of tolerance. If we extend

unlimited tolerance even to those who are intolerant, if we are not prepared to defend a tolerant society against the onslaught of the intolerant, then the tolerant will be destroyed, and tolerance with them.

Popper's words are (unfortunately) highly relevant to our current situation. (Much of *The Open Society and Its Enemies* is concerned with how societies can avoid plummeting into totalitarianism.) There is a reason why expressions of white nationalism are suddenly cropping up everywhere — in our high schools and colleges, on social media and in the mainstream press, and worst of all, in our federal government. Until recently, we (as a society) viewed such expressions as reprehensible, and we absolutely refused to tolerate them. But Trumpism has pushed the envelope — shifted the Overton Window,[3] as they say — such that now increasing numbers of people perceive white nationalistic rhetoric to be merely "radical" rather than "unthinkable." These people (most of whom are not personally threatened by white nationalism and/or have not seriously considered the paradox of tolerance) now seem to view extreme expressions of racism and xenophobia, and the misogyny that often goes hand-in-hand with them, as merely unsavory rather than anathema. Increasingly, people are mistaking this blatant hate rhetoric for simply another form of "free speech" that we must reflexively defend.

Those of us who are passionate about free speech, and who want to live in a truly open society, cannot afford to be bystanders anymore. We must absolutely refuse to tolerate intolerant speech and the people who promote intolerant ideologies. The First Amendment may prohibit Congress from passing laws censoring white

nationalist beliefs, but the rest of us are well within our rights to wholly refuse to accept, and to refuse to provide a platform for, anyone who espouses or enables such intolerant ideologies.

Skeptics might ask, "Well, how do we precisely define intolerance, and who gets to make that determination?" This is admittedly a potential point of contention (one that I plan to write about soon), but it is not formally any different from current debates we may have over what counts as protected free speech (e.g., does a particular statement constitute libel or fighting words?). While we may each have somewhat different opinions on precise definitions, I believe that we can (and should) easily come to a consensus that people who explicitly advocate ethnic cleansing (as Spencer has), or who incite campaigns of hate speech and harassment targeting women, people of color, transgender people, immigrants, and other minorities (as Yiannopoulos has), are clearly attempting to suppress other people's right to free expression, and as such, they are promoting intolerance. And we should not tolerate them!

The strategy of free speech absolutism has seemed to suffice over the last fifty years, but that is not because it works per se. Rather, in a post–World War II, post–civil rights world, most (albeit not all) Americans collectively decided not to tolerate blatant unabashed bigotry — that is what kept nefarious ideologies like white nationalism at bay. But cracks are now showing in this shared public commitment. And free speech absolutism will not save us from this — if anything, it will only make matters worse by allowing intolerance to fester, to proliferate, and to garner momentum. In this sense, free speech absolutism is akin to laissez-faire approaches to economic policy: Both seem to promote unadulterated freedom (after all, what could possibly be more free than a completely hands-off approach?). But any system that entirely forgoes standards or regulations will ultimately result in

---

[3]**Overton Window** A set of political ideas broadly acceptable to the public, named after political scientist Joseph P. Overton. [Editors' note]

atrocities, infringements on other people's rights, and the consolidation of power in the hands-off a few.

This is what we face now. And the only way to stop this from happening, to reverse this trend, is to absolutely refuse to tolerate intolerance.

Topics for Critical Thinking and Writing

1. Examine the reasoning behind free speech absolutism (enumerated in para. 1). Do you agree or disagree that we *must* defend people's rights to express racist, misogynistic, or xenophobic beliefs? Why or why not?

2. Would you call Julia Serano's argument a *valid* argument? (See Chapter 4, "Testing Truth and Validity," pp. 107–114 for a reminder on validity.) Why or why not?

3. Serano points to Richard Spencer and Milo Yiannopoulos as examples of people who seek to harass and intimidate under the protection of free speech. Do you think it is reasonable to cite their intentions as a good reason to prohibit further speeches on college campuses?

4. What are the implications of Serano's thesis — that is, if we were to accept her argument, what paradox does it lead to? Do you think Serano resolves the paradox? If so, how?

5. Do you agree or disagree with Karl Popper's statement in paragraph 11 that "Unlimited tolerance must lead to the disappearance of tolerance"? Why?

6. Characterize Serano's overall argument. If you agree with her, discuss in about 500 words the *weakest* points in the argument. If you disagree with her, discuss the *strengths* of the argument.

Analyzing a Visual: Student Views on Speech

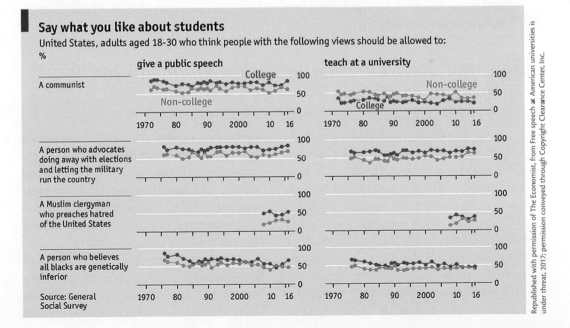

Say what you like about students

United States, adults aged 18-30 who think people with the following views should be allowed to:

%

Source: General Social Survey

Republished with permission of The Economist, from Free speech at American universities is under threat, 2017; permission conveyed through Copyright Clearance Center, Inc.

Topics for Critical Thinking and Writing

1. Between 2014 and 2017, college graduates and nongraduates went from about the same views on "communists giving a public speech" to a divergence in attitudes on this subject. What do you think explains this divergence? Do think the divergences have continued since 2017, and if so, can you find any supporting evidence?

2. Consider the data on "a Muslim clergyman who preaches hatred of the United States." In your view, should someone who preaches hatred of the United States be permitted to teach at a university in the United States? If you think yes, tell why and then explain any exceptions. If you think no, tell why and then explain under what circumstances such an appointment would be acceptable, if any.

   Now consider whether or not a person who believes the United States is a racist country built on the oppression of Black people should teach at a university. Do you think someone who believes this should teach at a university?

   Are your answers consistent or inconsistent for the two beliefs? Explain.

3. Do you think this graph offers useful information? If so, what do you think is most useful? If not, what do you think is not useful? Does any of the information in the graph surprise you?

SHIRA HOFFER

Shira Hoffer, at the time when she published this article, was a student at Harvard University and held a Harvard Political Review Journalism Fellowship. She wrote for the *Harvard Political Review*, a quarterly magazine published by the Harvard Institute of Politics and managed, written, and produced entirely by undergraduate students; the publication focuses on current events in the world and at Harvard. The essay below appeared on the website for the *Harvard Political Review* on July 21, 2021.

Safe and Free: Envisioning a New Guide for Speakers on Campus

In the fall of 2020, two San Francisco State University professors invited Leila Khaled to speak at a virtual roundtable entitled "Whose Narratives? Gender, Justice and Resistance: A Conversation with Leila Khaled." Khaled, a self-described "freedom fighter," has hijacked two planes on behalf of the Popular Front for the Liberation of Palestine, a US-designated terrorist organization. She unabashedly promotes violence, saying "When you defend humanity, you use all the means at your disposal … I chose arms and I believe that taking up arms is one of the main tools to solve this conflict in the interest of the oppressed and not the oppressors." Facing increasing pressure, Zoom, Facebook, and YouTube refused to stream the event, citing unwillingness to sanction pro-terrorism content.

Across the country, people took stances on this issue, some praising the media platforms for preventing "hate speech," and others decrying the censorship of a member of a marginalized group. San Francisco Hillel, an organization serving Jewish college students in the San Francisco area, penned an open letter to SFSU President Lynn Mahoney expressing its concern over "the normalization of violent rhetoric," explaining that "seeing someone who engaged in terror be held up as a role model, we are worried about the potential for hateful or dangerous backlash." John K. Wilson, an editor of the American Association of University Professors' "Academe" blog, took a different view, writing, "for those on the left who demand that tech companies censor speech they think are wrong or offensive, this is a chilling reminder that censorship is a dangerous weapon that can be turned against progressives." He also called upon colleges which use Zoom to "demand that Zoom commit to protecting free expression of academic classes and events on its platform."

Although this event was shut down not by the college but by the tech companies, the controversy surrounding this event highlights two important campus questions: who should be invited to speak, and who gets to decide?

In today's environment of strict partisanship, academic campuses should be looking for every opportunity to invite a diverse range of speakers, and they should be encouraging openness and dialogue, not censorship and one-sidedness. Students should have the chance to invite and decide for themselves which viewpoints they want to hear, and which they do not. There should be speeches and protests, but not protests that drown out the speeches, because growth comes from dialogue and questioning of views. Colleges themselves should stay out of the decision-making process of who gets invited and who does not. That means that people across the political spectrum, regardless of how controversial their views are, should be permitted to speak so long as they are not endorsing lawlessness or violence.

Before we continue, I would like to make 5 two things clear: First, it is important to remember that a university or student organization inviting someone to speak does not necessarily mean that the university is endorsing that individual's views. Second, and perhaps more importantly, I would like to clarify that I am not suggesting that clubs or universities should go looking for white supremacists and anti-Semites to come speak on campus about race and religion just for the sake of it. (I believe the vast majority of students and universities would not do that, even if it were what I was suggesting). Rather, I am suggesting that the potential of a hateful speaker coming to campus — albeit a scary possibility — is less frightening than the potential for universities to become moral arbiters in deciding whose views are "safe enough" to be heard on campus.

Many argued that inviting Khaled to campus crossed a line. But, how better can we understand the plight of those that feel that violence is the only option than to hear directly from someone in that category? Most Americans do not believe in using violence to achieve political gain, but most Americans also lack personal experience in the context in which that violence might seem necessary. Leila Khaled does not — she became a refugee as a toddler, and committed herself to armed struggle for the Palestinian cause at the mere age of 15.

However, the issue at hand is not whether one believes that they would learn something valuable from Khaled, or that they would be personally offended by her presence. Rather, what matters here is who gets to decide whether or not someone like Khaled speaks, and why. I would argue that anyone should be allowed to invite any speaker to campus, and — due to the risks of letting colleges decide who is too radical or controversial and who is not — any speaker who does not incite imminent unlawful behavior or violence should be allowed on campus.

Undoubtedly, this issue is controversial and nuanced. Students may feel exceedingly uncomfortable about the invitation of a speaker whose views they find abhorrent. But censorship and speaker discretion are slippery slopes, and potentially more harmful than hateful speech is letting colleges decide, by banning or shutting down speaking engagements, what speech should and should not be permitted. As the American Civil Liberties Union notes, "speech that deeply offends our morality or is hostile to our way of life warrants the same constitutional protection as other speech because the right of free speech is indivisible: When we grant the government the power to suppress controversial ideas, we are all subject to censorship by the state."

The ACLU is well-known for defending free speech, even abhorrent-but-constitutionally-protected speech. With regard to on-campus speech, the ACLU emphasizes the fact that, while "the First Amendment does not protect behavior on campus that crosses the line into targeted harassment or threats, or that creates a pervasively hostile environment for vulnerable students … merely offensive or bigoted speech does not rise to that level, and determining when conduct crosses that line is a legal question that requires examination on a case-by-case basis." Admittedly, private universities are not bound by the First Amendment, and are free to limit speech as they see fit. But the First Amendment may provide crucial guidance for colleges in making campus speech-related decisions.

For example, the Supreme Court's 1969 10 decision in *Brandenburg v. Ohio* concluded that inflammatory speech can only be punished if it is "directed at inciting or producing imminent lawless action" and is "likely to incite or produce such action." Holding to this decision prevents colleges from becoming moral arbiters, an extremely dangerous position. Allowing universities to decide which views are too controversial, or to determine the line between political and hate speech, will always upset someone. More frighteningly, it will allow colleges to tailor education to align with their viewpoints instead of encouraging independent thought and the free exchange of ideas.

Though universities should not be in the business of moral arbitration, they still do have a role in creating a safe space for their students in a way that the government does not. In order to protect the emotional — and potentially physical — well-being of students, the key when it comes to this issue should be choice: students should have the absolute choice as to whether or not they would like to be exposed to controversial extracurricular speakers and demonstrations on campus.

Perhaps there should be more nuanced rules regarding controversial marches or outdoor speakers. Maybe the policy should be that public demonstrations may only take place in certain campus areas, or at certain times. Or maybe demonstrators should simply be required to publicize the time of their event, and students may opt to stay in their dorms and either join class via Zoom or have absences excused during that time. Certainly, creating any policy which would dictate which types of events may take place in public would again place the college in the role of arbiter, which should be avoided. But care should be taken that students are never *required* to be exposed to these events. Policy on indoor events to which people can come or not as they choose, however, should adhere to a *Brandenburg v. Ohio* standard.

It should be noted that this choice should extend to rules around protesting speakers:

any protest which does not affect the ability of interested students to hear the lecture should be strongly encouraged, but forms of protest that drown out the speaker should be forbidden. In ideal circumstances, a student's right to choice should not trump a speaker's right to free speech, and a speaker's right to free speech should not trump a student's right to choice.

Censorship is not the cure for polarization — dialogue is. I dream of a campus where speakers of all viewpoints, whether students or experts, feel empowered to share their opinions, and where others are free to engage with them or not, as they feel comfortable. I envision a poster advertising a lecture by Leila Khaled, and an adjacent poster advertising the protest against her speech to be held by the door. I picture a student raising their hand to push back on her view that violence is the only answer, and I picture a student listening to music in the Yard, avoiding the situation entirely. Empowerment, dissent, and choice, all exercised respectfully — this is the cure for polarization.

Topics for Critical Thinking and Writing

1. Hoffer introduces Leila Khaled as a terrorist who hijacked an airplane in the name of Palestinian liberation — an event that occurred in 1969. Khaled currently lives with her family in Jordan. She has committed no known crimes since that time. In 2014, she said, "My actions [plane hijackings] were my contribution to my people, to the struggle. We did not hurt anyone. We declared to the whole world that we are a people, living through an injustice, and that the world had to help us to reach our goal." Does this context inform your initial judgment of the circumstances surrounding her canceled appearance at San Francisco State University?

2. What are your views on social media platforms, notably Zoom, refusing to host the planned lecture by Khaled? Should platforms like Zoom be the arbiter of who may speak or not speak at a public university? Why or why not?

3. Do you agree or disagree with Hoffer's claim that "anyone should be allowed to invite any speaker to campus, and — due to the risks of letting colleges decide who is too radical or controversial and who is not — any speaker who does not incite imminent unlawful behavior or violence should be allowed on campus" (para. 7)? Who do you think should decide these matters: students, faculty members, college managers and administrators, someone else? Explain your answer.

4. In paragraph 10, Hoffer appeals to the US Supreme Court case *Brandenburg v. Ohio*. Using *Brandenburg* as a standard, what kind of speech would be constitutionally protected and what kinds of speech would not be? Explain the differences, using the definition provided by *Brandenburg*.

5. Does Hoffer qualify her claims or attempt to find middle ground in inviting controversial speakers to college campuses? Where in her argument and how?

6. Use Serano's ideas to criticize Hoffer, and Hoffer's ideas to criticize Serano's. Which way do you lean in terms of agreeing with Serano's claim that "we cannot tolerate intolerance," and Hoffer's that even people who make room for violence in response to oppression are worth listening to? Why?

17

Bitcoin: Fad or Future?

ELIZABETH KOLBERT

Elizabeth Kolbert is the author of influential books such as *Field Notes from a Catastrophe* (2006) and *Under a White Sky* (2021), as well as *The Sixth Extinction: An Unnatural History* (2014), for which she won a Pulitzer Prize. As a staff writer for *The New Yorker* reporting on the environment, science, and nature, she received multiple awards, including the 2006 National Magazine Award for Public Interest. She also served on the Bulletin of Atomic Scientists from 2017 to 2020. Her essay here was published on Earth Day, April 22, 2021.

Why Bitcoin Is Bad for the Environment

Money, it's often said, is a shared fiction. I give you a slip of paper or, more likely these days, a piece of plastic. You hand me eggs or butter or a White Chocolate Mocha Frappuccino, and we both walk away satisfied. With cryptocurrency, the arrangement is more like a shared metafiction, and the instability of the genre is, presumably, part of the thrill. Dogecoin, a cryptocurrency that was created as a spoof, has risen in value by eight thousand per cent since January, owing to a combination of GameStop-style pumping and boosterish tweets from Elon Musk. On Tuesday, which backers proclaimed DogeDay, the cryptocurrency was valued at more than fifty billion dollars, which is more than the market cap of Ford. Coinbase, a cryptocurrency exchange, went public last Wednesday; almost immediately, it became worth more than G.M.

The mainstreaming of cryptocurrency, as it's been called, is obviously a big deal for the world of finance. It's also a big deal for the world of, well, the world. This is particularly true in the case of the ur-cryptocurrency, Bitcoin. Like Dogecoin, bitcoin has recently surged in value. In April, 2020, a coin was worth about seven thousand dollars; today, it's worth more than fifty-five thousand. (It hit a record high of $64,895.22 on April 14th, but has since fallen off.) As the cost of investing in bitcoin has soared, so, too, has the potential profit in "mining" it. Bitcoin mining is, of course, purely metaphorical, but the results can be every bit as destructive as with the real thing.

According to the Cambridge Bitcoin Electricity Consumption Index, bitcoin-mining operations worldwide now use energy at the rate of nearly a hundred and twenty terawatt-hours per year. This is about the annual domestic electricity consumption of the entire nation of Sweden. According to the Web site Digiconomist, a single bitcoin transaction uses the same amount of power that the average American household consumes in a month, and is responsible for roughly a million times more carbon emissions than a single Visa transaction. At a time when the world desperately needs to cut carbon emissions, does it make sense to be devoting a Sweden's worth of electricity to a virtual currency? The answer would seem, pretty clearly, to be no. And, yet, here we are.

The Greenidge Generating Station in Dresden, New York, sits on the shores of Seneca Lake, about an hour southeast of Rochester. It was originally built in the nineteen-thirties to run on coal; over the decades, new units were added and older ones shuttered. The power station ceased operations in 2011, and it sat idle until it was purchased by a private-equity firm and converted to run on natural gas. In 2017, under the ownership of Greenidge Generation Holdings, the plant reportedly began operating as a "peaker plant," to provide power to the grid during times of high demand. (A spokesperson noted that the plant "is permitted to run 24/7.") Then, in 2019, it was announced that the plant would power bitcoin mining.

Mining is the process by which bitcoin 5 is both created and accounted for. Instead of being cleared by, say, a bank, bitcoin transactions are recorded by a decentralized network — a blockchain. Miners compete to register the latest "block" of transactions by solving cryptographic puzzles. The first one to the solution is rewarded with freshly minted bitcoin. Miners today receive 6.25 bitcoins per block, which, at current values, are worth more than three hundred thousand dollars.

It's unclear exactly who dreamt up bitcoin, so no one knows what this person (or persons) was thinking when the mining protocols were first established. But, as Ari Juels, a computer scientist at Cornell Tech, recently explained to me, the arrangement seems to have been designed with equity in mind. Anyone devoting a processor to the enterprise would have just as much stake in the outcome as anyone else. As is so often the case, though, the ideal was soon subverted.

"What was quickly discovered is that specialized computing devices — so-called mining rigs — are much, much more effective at solving these puzzles," Juels said. "And, in addition, there are economies of scale in the operation of these mining groups. So the process of mining, which was originally conducted by a loose federation of presumably individual participants with ordinary computing devices, has now become heavily consolidated."

Because rig "farms," which are essentially like server farms, consume a lot of energy, bitcoin-mining operations tend to chase cheap electricity. Roughly seventy per cent of bitcoin mining today takes place in China. (A recent study found that the associated electricity consumption could "potentially undermine" China's efforts to curb its carbon emissions.) Russia is also a bitcoin-mining center — there are big operations in Siberia, where cold temperatures help keep rig farms from overheating — as is Iran, where electricity is subsidized.

In the United States, home to about seven per cent of the world's bitcoin mining, finding cheap power can be complicated. A few years ago, miners "descended upon" the city of Plattsburgh, New York, about a hundred and fifty miles north of Albany, which gets much of its electricity from hydroelectric dams on the St. Lawrence River. The power is relatively inexpensive, but, once Plattsburgh uses up its allotment, it has to purchase more at higher rates. Bitcoin mining drove up the cost of electricity in the city so dramatically that, in 2018, Plattsburgh enacted a moratorium on new mining operations.

Buying a generating station, as Greenidge [10] Generation Holdings has done, is a way around the problem. Let others pay retail; Greenidge now gets its power "behind the meter." The firm recently announced that it was going public, via a merger with a Nasdaq-listed company called Support.com, and boasted that it "expects to be the first publicly traded bitcoin mining company with a wholly-owned power plant." In the announcement, Greenidge said that it was planning to more than double its bitcoin-mining operations in Dresden by the fall of 2021, and to double them again by the end of 2022. It further declared that it intends to "replicate its vertically integrated mining model at other power sites."

To expand its operations in Dresden, Greenidge will have to burn more and more natural gas, thus producing correspondingly more greenhouse-gas emissions. The firm's plans have sparked demonstrations in the Finger Lakes region. On Saturday, a hundred protesters marched to the gates of the plant.

"This is a test case," Joseph Campbell, the president of Seneca Lake Guardian, the group that organized the march, told WRFI, an Ithaca radio station. Two days later, the local planning board approved Greenidge's application to build four new structures at the site, to house more mining rigs. Members of the planning board said that for, legal reasons, they were barred from considering the broader implications of their decision. "We know that bitcoin is a big waste of energy," the chairman of the planning board, David Granzin, said. "But we're bound by law."

Whether this is, in fact, the case is debatable. What's beyond debate — or should be, at least — is that this is a matter that shouldn't be left to a local planning board to decide. There's no way for New York, or the U.S. as a whole, to meet its emissions-reductions goals if old generating stations, rather than being closed, are converted into bitcoin-mining operations. Greenidge may become the first mining firm with a "wholly-owned power plant," but, unless the state or federal government steps in, it won't be the last: another cryptocurrency firm, Digihost International, has already applied to New York State's Public Service Commission for permission to purchase a natural-gas-burning station near Buffalo. As representatives of Earthjustice and the Sierra Club recently put it, in a letter to officials of New York's Department of Environmental Conservation, "additional scrutiny . . . is essential to prevent the floodgates opening for other retiring power plants."

Andrew Yang, the former Presidential candidate who's now running for mayor of New York City, has said that he wants to turn the city into a cryptocurrency-mining hub. It's hard to imagine a worse idea. The city is already looking at spending billions of dollars to protect itself from sea-level rise; increased emissions are pretty much the last thing it needs. Forward-looking politicians should be thinking about ways not to buoy bitcoin mining but to bury it.

Topics for Critical Thinking and Writing

1. With any innovation, people often ask "what problem does it solve?" What problem does bitcoin solve? What new problems does it pose? What about other cryptocurrencies?

2. Elizabeth Kolbert begins her article with the sentence, "Money, it's often said, is a shared fiction." How does this sentence foreground her argument?

3. Kolbert's premise is that the energy consumption of bitcoin mining does not justify its use as a major currency or asset. Can you think of or find any information to challenge the premise?

4. In July 2021, China banned all bitcoin mining, and many of those operations were welcomed in the United States, which by January 2022, accounted for about 35 percent of all bitcoin mining. How have concerns about bitcoin's energy consumption been addressed in the United States?

5. Do you think the energy concerns about bitcoin are enough to warrant the claim Kolbert makes in her final sentence?

6. Comparing bitcoin mining to mining of natural resources, Kolbert writes that with bitcoin mining, "the results can be every bit as destructive as with the real thing" (para. 2). Choose another mining industry such as gold, silver, or rare earth minerals; or coal, oil, or natural gas. Compare the environmental impact of another mining industry with bitcoin, and use your findings to write a statement of support or opposition to Kolbert's claim.

Analyzing a Visual: Bitcoin

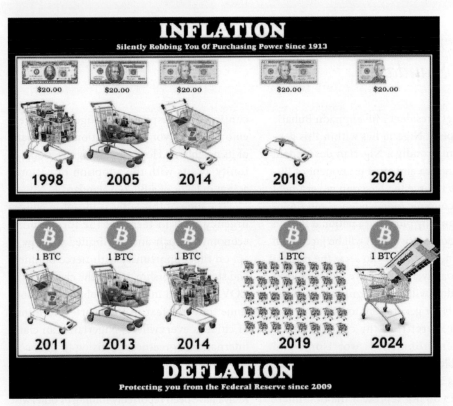

Topics for Critical Thinking and Writing

1. Analyze the meme by pointing out the argument it makes about currency. Explain whether or not you think the meme oversimplifies the issue.

2. Have you seen other online memes about cryptocurrency? How does this one compare to the others?

3. How do memes, such as this one, influence public perception of cryptocurrency? How does that public perception influence the value of cryptocurrency?

RUSSELL OKUNG

Russell Okung played ten seasons as an offensive tackle for the Seattle Seahawks and helped the team win Super Bowl XLVIII. He remains an active NFL free agent. Okung's advocacy of bitcoin became well known in 2019 when he requested half his NFL salary to be paid in the cryptocurrency. When bitcoin's value dramatically increased in 2020, he became technically the highest-paid NFL player. The following letter, addressed to the President of Nigeria, was published as an opinion piece by *Bitcoin Magazine* in 2021.

An Open Letter to the Nigerian Government: Pursue a Bitcoin Standard

Greetings President Muhammadu Buhari,

The hope of Nigeria lies within this generation. I am proudly a Nigerian descendant living in America and am a proponent of Bitcoin. I write to urge the Nigerian government to pursue economic independence and financial sovereignty by pursuing a national Bitcoin standard. Soon every nation will be faced with this decision, but those who seize the present moment proactively as we have just witnessed in El Salvador, will enjoy significant advantages globally for generations to come.

It is no secret that the current global economic environment is worrisome and unsustainable. Sadly, the fate of the Nigerian economy is in the hands of global central bankers who do not represent the best interests of the Nigerian people. Despite the challenges we face, the resilience of Nigerians continues to inspire. The Nigerian society enjoys more favorable conditions than many of its neighbors. However, even greater opportunity awaits with the adoption of national action in favor of a Bitcoin standard.

The tone of this letter is meant to convey urgency both in terms of the forthcoming economic despair and the limited window to act on this opportunity with fierce boldness and strong leadership. While the challenges of COVID-19 and increased global unrest continue to instill fear in the hearts and minds of citizens everywhere, Nigerians can claim international greatness by rising to the occasion that our unique times require.

Nations such as Iran, Russia, China and Kenya have been reportedly mining or otherwise utilizing bitcoin, often as a means to circumvent U.S. sanctions which prevent them from full participation in the global financial system. Other nations like Barbados, Singapore and Malta have moved to become "bitcoin friendly" in an effort to attract wealth and human capital through migration. And this week, El Salvador became the world's first nation to require merchants to accept bitcoin as legal tender. I'm proposing an equally aggressive approach to national Bitcoin adoption which would significantly bolster every sector of the Nigerian economy and revitalize the spirit of every Nigerian domestically and abroad.

Bitcoin is not controlled, managed or operated by any single entity. It is an innovation that will surpass the automobile or the internet in terms of its impact on humanity. Nigeria does not need to ask for permission from any other nation nor acquire a license nor secure a trade agreement from any corporation to reshape its economy with Bitcoin. All that is required is a vision for a new future and an allocation of its own national resources to pursue a Bitcoin standard.

The primary reason for urgently pursuing and executing a national plan for adoption is the finite supply of bitcoin. There will only ever be 21 million bitcoin in circulation. This hard cap on the supply makes bitcoin even more verifiably finite than gold. As this simple yet unique property of scarcity becomes more widely understood, the economic laws of supply and demand will create a global frenzy to acquire as much bitcoin as possible, before it's too late. This momentum for acquiring bitcoin is already underway throughout the world and it is rapidly accelerating. In recent months, continued economic turmoil and uncertainty has created increased curiosity in bitcoin. Multiple institutional investors have announced sizable bitcoin allocations in their portfolios, some citing it as a hedge against a weakening U.S. dollar.

The Nigerian government, along with every other government in the world, has a once in a generation opportunity to claim global prominence by rising to the occasion. Many other politicians in Latin America have signalled their intention to pursue similar moves as El Salvador. In leading the next global financial shift, Nigeria can create prosperity for its citizens in a manner that requires no bloodshed, no election and no resistance. Such a proposition may seem too good to be true, and these ambitions certainly require thorough investigation, scrutiny and debate. Conversely, a delay in pursuing a national plan for bitcoin adoption will risk a scenario where Nigeria is left behind and its citizens excluded from the possibility of significant wealth creation and preservation. As world leaders become more aware of the chance to make history, pursuit of bitcoin will be widespread. We offer our full support, a willingness to voluntarily consult and commitment to activate every resource available to us in order to see Nigeria pursue a Bitcoin standard.

Nigeria must never carry last,
Russell Okung

Topics for Critical Thinking and Writing

1. One argument against bitcoin is that it "isn't based on anything." What are currencies "based on" in the twenty-first century? What does it mean for a currency to be based on something else?

2. How does the form of Russell Okung's essay, an open letter to a government, impact his argument? Who is the audience of an "open" (published) letter?

3. The inflation rate of the naira, Nigeria's official currency, was about 17 percent in 2021. According to Okung, why would bitcoin adoption help Nigerian citizens? What risks would it pose?

4. Okung advocates a "bitcoin standard." What does this mean? Why do you think some governments would be open to bitcoin adoption and other countries resistant to bitcoin adoption?

5. Okung suggests in his final paragraph that bitcoin can create prosperity with "no bloodshed, no election and no resistance." Evaluate this claim. What reactions might a country's population have to a national adoption of bitcoin? Why?

6. How do you think Okung would respond to Kolbert's article in *The New Yorker*? How might Kolbert respond to the points outlined in Okung's letter?

18

Genetic Modification of Human Beings: Is It Acceptable?

RONALD M. GREEN

Ronald M. Green is the Eunice and Julian Cohen Professor Emeritus for the Study of Human Ethics and Human Values in the Department of Religion at Dartmouth College and a professor in the Department of Community and Family Medicine at Dartmouth's Geisel School of Medicine. He is the author of nine books, including *Babies by Design: The Ethics of Genetic Choice* (2007). He most recently co-edited, with George A. Little, a volume entitled *Religion and Ethics in the Neonatal Intensive Care Unit* (2019), a resource for healthcare practitioners, parents of sick newborns, and students of bioethics. This commentary on predicative genetics and embryos was published in the *Washington Post* in 2008.

Building Baby from the Genes Up

The two British couples no doubt thought that their appeal for medical help in conceiving a child was entirely reasonable. Over several generations, many female members of their families had died of breast cancer. One or both spouses in each couple had probably inherited the genetic mutations for the disease, and they wanted to use in-vitro fertilization and preimplantation genetic diagnosis (PGD) to select only the healthy embryos for implantation. Their goal was to eradicate breast cancer from their family lines once and for all.

In the United States, this combination of reproductive and genetic medicine — what one scientist has dubbed "reprogenetics" — remains largely unregulated, but Britain has a formal agency, the Human Fertilization and Embryology Authority (HFEA), that must approve all requests for PGD. In July 2007, after considerable deliberation, the HFEA approved the procedure for both families. The concern was not about the use of PGD to avoid genetic disease, since embryo screening for serious disorders is commonplace now on both sides of the Atlantic. What troubled the HFEA was the fact that an embryo carrying the cancer mutation could go on to live for forty or fifty years before ever developing cancer, and there was a chance it might never develop. Did this warrant selecting and discarding embryos? To its critics, the HFEA, in approving this request, crossed a bright line separating legitimate medical genetics from the quest for "the perfect baby."

Like it or not, that decision is a sign of things to come — and not necessarily a bad sign. Since the completion of the Human Genome Project in 2003, our understanding of the genetic bases of human disease and non-disease traits has been growing almost exponentially. The National Institutes of Health has initiated a quest for the "$1,000 genome," a ten-year program to develop machines that could identify all the genetic letters in anyone's genome at low cost (it took more than $3 billion to sequence the first human genome). With this technology, which some believe may be just four or five years away, we could not only scan an individual's — or embryo's — genome, we could also rapidly compare thousands of people and pinpoint those DNA sequences or combinations that underlie the variations that contribute to our biological differences.

With knowledge comes power. If we understand the genetic causes of obesity, for example, we can intervene by means of embryo selection to produce a child with a reduced genetic likelihood of getting fat. Eventually, without discarding embryos at all, we could use gene-targeting techniques to tweak fetal DNA sequences. No child would have to face a lifetime of dieting or experience the health and cosmetic problems associated with obesity. The same is true for cognitive problems such as dyslexia. Geneticists have already identified some of the mutations that contribute to this disorder. Why should a child struggle with reading difficulties when we could alter the genes responsible for the problem?

Many people are horrified at the thought 5 of such uses of genetics, seeing echoes of the 1997 science-fiction film *Gattaca*, which depicted a world where parents choose their children's traits. Human weakness has been eliminated through genetic engineering, and the few parents who opt for a "natural" conception run the risk of producing offspring — "invalids" or "degenerates" — who become members of a despised underclass. *Gattaca's* world is clean and efficient, but its eugenic obsessions have all but extinguished human love and compassion.

These fears aren't limited to fiction. Over the past few years, many bioethicists have spoken out against genetic manipulations. The critics tend to voice at least four major concerns. First, they worry about the effect of genetic selection on parenting. Will our ability to choose our children's biological inheritance lead parents to replace unconditional love with a consumerist mentality that seeks perfection?

Second, they ask whether gene manipulations will diminish our freedom by making us creatures of our genes or our parents' whims. In his book *Enough*, the techno-critic Bill McKibben asks: If I am a world-class runner, but my parents inserted the "Sweatworks 2010 GenePack" in my genome, can I really feel pride in my accomplishments? Worse, if I refuse to use my costly genetic endowments, will I face relentless pressure to live up to my parents' expectations?

Third, many critics fear that reproductive genetics will widen our social divisions as the affluent "buy" more competitive abilities for their offspring. Will we eventually see "speciation," the emergence of two or more human populations so different that they no longer even breed with one another? Will we re-create the horrors of eugenics that led, in Europe, Asia, and the United States, to the sterilization of tens of thousands of people declared to be "unfit" and that in Nazi Germany paved the way for the Holocaust?

Finally, some worry about the religious implications of this technology. Does it amount to a forbidden and prideful "playing God"?

To many, the answers to these questions are clear. Not long ago, when I asked a large class at Dartmouth Medical School whether they thought that we should move in the direction of human genetic engineering, more than 80 percent said no. This squares with public opinion polls that show a similar degree of opposition. Nevertheless, "babies by design" are probably in our future — but I think that the critics' concerns may be less troublesome than they first appear.

Will critical scrutiny replace parental love? Not likely. Even today, parents who hope for a healthy child but have one born with disabilities tend to love that child ferociously. The very intensity of parental love is the best protection against its erosion by genetic technologies. Will a child somehow feel less free because parents have helped select his or her traits? The fact is that a child is already remarkably influenced by the genes she inherits. The difference is that we haven't taken control of the process. Yet.

Knowing more about our genes may actually increase our freedom by helping us understand the biological obstacles — and opportunities — we have to work with. Take the case of Tiger Woods. His father, Earl, is said to have handed him a golf club when he was still in the playpen. Earl probably also gave Tiger the genes for some of the traits that help make him a champion golfer. Genes and upbringing worked together to inspire excellence. Does Tiger feel less free because of his inherited abilities? Did he feel pressured by his parents? I doubt it. Of course, his story could have gone the other way, with overbearing parents forcing a child into their mold. But the problem in that case wouldn't be genetics, but bad parenting.

Granted, the social effects of reproductive genetics are worrisome. The risks of producing a "genobility," genetic overlords ruling a vast genetic underclass, are real. But genetics could also become a tool for reducing the class divide. Will we see the day when perhaps all youngsters are genetically vaccinated against dyslexia? And how might this contribute to everyone's social betterment?

As for the question of intruding on God's domain, the answer is less clear than the critics believe. The use of genetic medicine to cure or prevent disease is widely accepted by religious traditions, even those that oppose discarding embryos. Speaking in 1982 at the Pontifical Academy of Sciences, Pope John Paul II observed that modern biological research "can ameliorate the condition of those who are affected by chromosomic diseases," and he lauded this as helping to cure "the smallest and weakest of human beings . . . during their intrauterine life or in the period immediately after birth." For Catholicism and some other traditions, it is one thing to cure disease, but another to create children who are faster runners, longer-lived, or smarter.

But why should we think that the human genome is a once-and-for-all-finished, untamperable product? All of the biblically derived faiths permit human beings to improve on nature using technology, from agriculture to aviation. Why not improve our genome? I have no doubt that most people considering these questions for the first time are certain that human genetic improvement is a bad idea, but I'd like to shake up that certainty.

Genomic science is racing toward a future in which foreseeable improvements include reduced susceptibility to a host of diseases, increased life span, better cognitive functioning, and maybe even cosmetic enhancements such as whiter, straighter teeth. Yes, genetic orthodontics may be in our future. The challenge is to see that we don't also unleash the demons of discrimination and oppression.

Although I acknowledge the risks, I believe that we can and will incorporate gene technology into the ongoing human adventure.

Topics for Critical Thinking and Writing

1. By the end of paragraph 2, did you think the British are probably right to be cautious, to require approval for all requests for PGD? Explain your position.

2. Paragraph 4 talks, by way of example, about avoiding obesity and "cognitive problems." At this stage in your reading of the essay, did you find yourself saying "Great, let's go for it," or were you thinking "Wait a minute"? Why, or why not?

3. Do paragraphs 5 and 6 pretty much set forth your own response? If not, what *is* your response?

4. Does Bill McKibben's view, mentioned in paragraph 7, represent your view? If not, what would you say to McKibben?

5. If you are a believer in any of "the biblically derived faiths," does the comment in paragraph 15 allay whatever doubts you may have had about the acceptability of human genetic improvement? Explain.

6. In his final paragraph, Ronald Green says that he acknowledges the risks of gene technology. Are you satisfied that he does acknowledge them adequately? Explain.

Analyzing a Visual: Genetic Modification of Human Beings

Caroline Purser/Getty Images

Topics for Critical Thinking and Writing

1. What does this photograph seem to say about human genetic modification? Why do you think the photographer included a bar code in the image? In a couple of paragraphs, analyze the ways the photo makes an argument and evaluate the photo's effectiveness.

2. Do you agree with the point of view expressed in the photograph? In 250 words, write a description of a photograph that might work as a rebuttal to this one.

RICHARD HAYES

Richard Hayes is the founding executive director emeritus of the California-based Center for Genetics and Society, an organization that describes itself as working to "encourage responsible uses of human genetic and reproductive technologies" and to "oppose any applications that objectify and commodify human life and threaten to divide human society, such as inheritable genetic modification." The essay included here originally appeared in the *Washington Post* in 2008.

Genetically Modified Humans? No Thanks

In an essay in Sunday's Outlook section, Dartmouth ethics professor Ronald Green asks us to consider a neo-eugenic future of "designer babies," with parents assembling their children quite literally from genes selected from a catalogue. Distancing himself from the compulsory, state-sponsored eugenics that darkened the first half of the last century, Green instead celebrates the advent of a libertarian, consumer-driven eugenics motivated by the free play of human desire, technology, and markets. He argues that this vision of the human future is desirable and very likely inevitable.

To put it mildly: I disagree. Granted, new human genetic technologies have real potential to help prevent or cure many terrible diseases, and I support research directed towards that end. But these same technologies also have the potential for real harm. If misapplied, they would exacerbate existing inequalities and reinforce existing modes of discrimination. If more widely abused, they could undermine the

foundations of civil and human rights. In the worst case, they could undermine our experience of being part of a single human community with a common human future.

Once we begin genetically modifying our children, where do we stop? If it's acceptable to modify one gene, why not two, or twenty or two hundred? At what point do children become artifacts designed to someone's specifications rather than members of a family to be nurtured?

Given what we know about human nature, the development and commercial marketing of human genetic modification would likely spark a techno-eugenic rat-race. Even parents opposed to manipulating their children's genes would feel compelled to participate in this race, lest their offspring be left behind.

Green proposes that eugenic technologies 5 could be used to reduce "the class divide." But nowhere in his essay does he suggest how such a proposal might ever be made practicable in the real world.

The danger of genetic misuse is equally threatening at the international level. What happens when some rogue country announces an ambitious program to "improve the genetic stock" of its citizens? In a world still barely able to contain the forces of nationalism, ethnocentrism, and militarism, the last thing we need to worry about is a high-tech eugenic arms race.

In his essay, Green doesn't distinguish clearly between different uses of genetic technology — and the distinctions are critical. It's one thing to enable a couple to avoid passing on a devastating genetic condition, such as Tay-Sachs.[1] But it's a different thing altogether to create children with a host of "enhanced" athletic, cosmetic, and cognitive traits that could be passed to their own children, who in turn could further genetically modify their children, who in turn . . . you get the picture. It's this second use of gene technology (the technical term is "heritable genetic enhancement") that Green most fervently wants us to embrace.

In this position, Green is well outside the growing national and international consensus on the proper use of human genetic science and technology. To his credit, he acknowledges that 80 percent of the medical school students he surveyed said they were against such forms of human genetic engineering, and that public opinion polls show equally dramatic opposition. He could have noted, as well, that nearly forty countries — including Brazil, Canada, France, Germany, India, Japan, and South Africa — have adopted socially responsible policies regulating the new human genetic technologies. They allow genetic research (including stem cell research) for medical applications, but prohibit its use for heritable genetic modification and reproductive human cloning.

In the face of this consensus, Green blithely announces his confidence that humanity "can and will" incorporate heritable genetic enhancement into the "ongoing human adventure."

Well, it's certainly possible. Our desires for good looks, good brains, wealth and long lives, for ourselves and for our children, are strong and enduring. If the gene-tech entrepreneurs are able to convince us that we can satisfy these desires by buying into genetic modification, perhaps we'll bite. Green certainly seems eager to encourage us to do so.

But he would be wise to listen to what medical students, the great majority of Americans, and the international community appear to be saying: We want all these things, yes, and genetic technology might help us attain them, but we don't want to run the huge risks to the human community and the human future that would come with altering the genetic basis of our common human nature.

10

---

[1]**Tay-Sachs** A progressive disorder that destroys nerve neurons in the brain and spinal cord. [Editors' note]

Topics for Critical Thinking and Writing

1. Do you believe that in his first paragraph, Richard Hayes fairly summarizes Green's essay? Explain your reasoning.

2. Does the prospect raised in paragraph 6 frighten you? Why or why not?

3. In his final paragraph, Hayes speaks of "huge risks." What are these risks? Are you willing to take them? Why or why not?

4. "When They Warn of Rare Disorders, These Prenatal Tests Are Usually Wrong," an article published in the *New York Times* on January 1, 2022, reported that many blood tests used to screen embryos for serious developmental problems worked well for detecting Down syndrome but were wrong up to 85 percent of the time when they diagnosed rarer disorders. If a doctor discovered that a developing embryo would not develop Down syndrome but had a 15-percent chance of having a rarer and more serious disorder, should the parents be told? Why or why not?

5. What arguments could be made for and against aborting a pregnancy before viability upon the discovery of a genetic condition that would make independent adult life impossible if the pregnancy were carried through? Support your answer with sound logic and evidence.

19

Should We Cancel "Cancel Culture"?

DANA BROWNLEE

Forbes magazine Senior Contributor Dana Brownlee is also a business consultant and founder of Professionalism Matters, an Atlanta-based firm that works with corporations to provide strategic planning for creating equitable and just workplaces. She has developed three LinkedIn Learning courses on antiracism; authored a book, *The Unwritten Rules of Managing Up* (2019); and published essays in various business-focused publications such as the *Wall Street Journal* and the *Economist*. This selection was published in *Forbes* in 2021.

Is "Cancel Culture" Really Just Long Overdue Accountability for the Privileged?

In July 2010, former Georgia State Director of Rural Development for the United States Department of Agriculture (USDA) Shirley Sherrod was abruptly and unceremoniously fired after a highly-edited video of portions of a speech she gave at a NAACP event began circulating on conservative media. The July 20 CBS News article "Shirley Sherrod: White House Forced My Resignation" reported her reflections about two calls she received from USDA deputy undersecretary Cheryl Cook while driving. "The last time they asked me to pull over the side of the road and submit my resignation on my Blackberry, and that's what I did," explained Sherrod. The next day, CBS News continued the story with an article entitled, "Vilsack: I Will Have to Live with Shirley Sherrod Mistake." By then, President Obama's Agriculture Secretary who'd made the decision to terminate her learned of the full video and the context that showed her speech was actually denouncing racial bias. Vilsack (and The White House) apologized to Sherrod admitting that the decision was made hastily, Vilsack adding "I did not think before I acted and for that reason, this poor woman has gone through a very difficult time." While Sherrod was ultimately offered a different position at the USDA, her reputation was clearly sullied in the most public of spectacles. Tom Vilsack on the other hand was not terminated for his clear and consequential lapse in judgment, and instead years later was named Secretary of the USDA earlier this year by the Biden administration.

While Sherrod's firing is arguably one of the most egregious and public examples of someone being terminated prematurely and wrongly, there was little if any whining about "cancel culture" then as the term hadn't become common vernacular yet. Indeed, "cancel culture" has become the persistent refrain for high-profile "cancellations" over the past couple years, but people have been wrongly or prematurely "cancelled" for decades (if not longer) which begs the question....Why is "cancel culture" such a common refrain now?

Maybe the difference isn't the prevalence of the cancellations as much as it is *who* is getting cancelled? Perhaps the truth is that Black and Brown people have historically been granted very little (if any) margin of error much less second, third and fourth chances, and in the midst of the country's racial reckoning, high-profile, mostly White celebrities, executives and other leaders are now being treated more like everyone else? Maybe it's yet another example of the saying, "When those with privilege are faced with equality, to them it often feels like oppression."

The truth is that while many high-profile (usually) White people are disgusted by this new "one significant strike and you're out" culture, many Black and Brown people are thinking "Welcome to the party" while even more are wondering how they can even attain these high-profile positions in the first place. Certainly, no one wants to feel like they work in a perfectionist environment where any single misstep or minor slip of the tongue could spell termination, but is that a fair assessment of what's really happening? That's highly debatable.

Yes, we have to create a space for people to make mistakes, have a bad day or just get it wrong occasionally. Let's face it — if we were all judged by our worst moment, we'd likely be unemployed (or worse). But on the other hand, much of what seems to be increasingly labeled as "cancel culture" may just be long overdue accountability for the elite and powerful who have grown accustomed to the tacit immunity that often accompanies wealth, power and celebrity. For people of color and other marginalized communities, our "cancel culture" was always in effect only then, the powers that be labeled it "consequences." I can't help but think that now — in the age of ubiquitous video camers and lighting fast social media — those consequences have crept into the ivory towers of those unaccustomed to them, and they've been received as an invasion.

Diversity, equity and inclusion practitioner Farzin Farzad insists, "Cancel culture is a relatively new term developed to insulate the powerful from being held accountable for hateful language. It is a mere propaganda tool that has proliferated in our mainstream discourse." Anti-racism educator and author of *Blaxhaustion: Karens & Other Threats to Black Lives and Well-Being* Theresa M. Robinson also points out the subjectivity of what gets labeled "cancel culture"... and what doesn't. "Cancel culture is either unfair or justified based on the recipient and the alleged 'transgression,'" insists Robinson. "Colin Kaepernick is one of the best examples of how the cancel culture double-standard operates. He is just one in a long line of Black folks who've been subject to 'canceling' at the hands of a system that systemically marginalizes and oppresses others."

For those who may be quick to defend a politician compelled to resign after the publication of an incriminating video or a company executive resigning after being caught on a hot mike yelling racial slurs, let's consider the following.

Actions Have Consequences and Some Infractions are Indeed Cancel Worthy.

Sometimes once is enough. It's just that simple.

Just as there are no mulligans for teachers who molest children or airline pilots who drink and fly, there are some decisions, actions and behaviors that should require immediate separation from the organization, and that separation isn't necessarily the worst that could happen to them. For some, it actually might be the wake up call that helps them get it together and grow professionally. When it comes to issues of equity and inclusion, many advocates consider zero tolerance policies an important part of rooting out racism, bias and broader discrimination. "Freedom of speech or freedom to act doesn't imply freedom from consequences," insists anti-racism educator and consultant Denise Branch. "'Consequence culture' is needed to build safer, more inclusive, equitable and accountable workplaces."

We Should Expect More of Our Leaders, Media Personalities and Government Officials.

Why is it that Brad the CEO who gets 10 caught misusing company information or participating in inappropriate relationships often departs with a lucrative payout and a carefully worded public relations statement about his desire to spend more time with family, but Jerome the mail clerk who may have padded an expense report once or twice is not just terminated and persecuted, but possibly prosecuted? Certainly, all the behaviors are wrong, but too often it seems that we excuse so much more from those at the top of the food chain but are ready to pounce on less serious infractions from those at the bottom. Arguably, our system of "workplace justice" is often anything but just.

The High Profile Incident May Very Well Have Been Just One in a Pattern.

The truth is that while it may *seem* like someone was terminated, forced to resign or otherwise cancelled immediately after one particularly public incident, it may very well have been one incident of many—particularly if they exhibited extreme behavior. Consider situations like those where a politician is caught hurling a racial slur on a hot microphone, or a senior executive's leaked emails are found to be riddled with offensive homophobic references. While it's certainly possible that those incidents were completely out of character for them (and the first of their kind), arguably they're more likely a reflection of simply who they are when no one is looking. After all, if a 60 year old gets caught speeding 90+ mph on the highway, it's most likely not the first time she's sped. Remember that personnel issues are typically confidential so while someone may have had a very public incident that resulted in dismissal, that may have actually been one in a string of previous incidents that were not publicly known.

Certainly, the ubiquity of cameras and a 24/7 news cycle has made it exponentially easier to get caught doing something stupid or worse, and that's placed a brighter spotlight on those in high-profile positions, but isn't that a feature, not a bug of our more technologically advanced society? Shouldn't we expect people in these esteemed positions to actually live up to the supposed merits that got them there or do we treat those in high-profile positions as if they're untouchable atop the corporate caste system and not subject to the same consequences as mere underlings — even though role modeling is arguably part of a leader's job?

Let's be clear — having anyone be wrongly or prematurely terminated or otherwise "cancelled" is obviously a horrible, unfortunate injustice. It was wrong when it happened to Shirley Sherrod, and it's wrong now, but it's not necessarily "cancel culture." It may just be good, old-fashioned poor management. But when high-profile leaders and personalities are denounced, fired or pressured to step down after bad behavior, we could just be witnessing swift, direct consequences. The accusation "cancel culture" seems to suggest that some outside force or societal aberration is actually to blame when the truth may be that it just feels overly harsh and shocking to those used to doling out consequences, not experiencing them.

DANA BROWNLEE, "Is 'Cancel Culture' Really Just Long Overdue Accountability For the Privileged?" *Forbes*, July 1, 2021. Copyright © 2021 by Forbes. All rights reserved. Used under license. https://forbes.com

Topics for Critical Thinking and Writing

1. What is the lesson of the anecdote in Dana Brownlee's opening paragraph? How does it represent cancel culture, even before the term was used?

2. In paragraph 3, Brownlee proposes a saying, "When those with privilege are faced with equality, to them it often feels like oppression." How is this related to the backlash against cancel culture? Does Brownlee's argument suggest that all white people are privileged? Explain why you agree or disagree with that statement.

3. Brownlee writes, "Certainly, no one wants to feel like they work in a perfectionist environment where any single misstep or minor slip of the tongue could spell termination, but is that a fair assessment of what's really happening?" (para. 4). Answer her question: Is it a fair assessment of what is happening in contemporary culture? Seek examples of when a form of cancelation was and was not justified.

4. Do you think Brownlee would agree if you said, "Dana Brownlee is pro-cancel culture?" What qualifications might she make?

5. Have you witnessed or been part of an effort to cancel a person for saying, writing, or posting inappropriate or racially insensitive material? If so, what were the consequences, and, in your opinion, was the age, gender, race, or identity of the person a factor?

6. Imagine two scenarios, each of which results in a formal complaint by a student to the administrators of a college or university. In scenario 1, a teacher talking about politics says, "Opponents of this proposal are acting like *X*," where *X* is a racial slur. In scenario 2, a student says the same thing. Should the teacher and student face similar consequences? What should those consequences be? How does your conclusion relate to Brownlee's ideas about "those at the top" and "those at the bottom" (para. 10)?

Analyzing a Visual: Cancel Culture

Topics for Critical Thinking and Writing

1. First, analyze each image independently. What does the "This Cancel Culture Is Getting Out of Hand" cartoon suggest about conservative Republican views of cancel culture, and what does the "You're History, Cancel Culture" image imply about liberal Democrats' views of cancel culture? Now, compare the two images and attempt to find some common ground to bring the two views closer together.

2. What prior knowledge does each image assume the viewer holds?

3. Which image did you find more compelling or effective as a critique? Did your selection tend to align with your own political views? If so, focus on the image you found less effective and say why.

EVAN GERSTMANN

Evan Gerstmann is a professor of political science and international relations at Loyola Marymount University and the author of *The Constitutional Underclass* (1999), *Same-Sex Marriage and the Constitution* (2017), and *Campus Sexual Assault: Constitutional Rights and Fundamental Fairness* (2019). He is also a contributor to *Forbes* magazine, where he writes about freedom of speech, minority rights, and the intersection of law, politics, and culture.

Cancel Culture Is Only Getting Worse

There is no single accepted definition of cancel culture, but at its worst, it is about unaccountable groups successfully applying pressure to punish someone for perceived wrong opinions. The victim ends up losing their job or is significantly harmed in some way well beyond the discomfort of merely being disagreed with. Someone like J.K. Rowling isn't really a victim of cancel culture — she's too rich to be punished in any meaningful way and she doesn't have the kind of job that one can be fired from.

Powerful voices on the institutional left claim that there is no such thing as cancel culture. For example, the *New York Times* columnist Charles Blow, tweets: "Once more THERE IS NO SUCH THING AS CANCEL CULTURE. There is free speech. You can say and do as pls, and others can choose never to deal this [sic] you, your company or your products EVER again. The rich and powerful are just upset that the masses can now organize their dissent."

This argument confuses dissent with punishment. The victims of cancel culture are generally not powerful people. They are often vulnerable people who suffer devastating harm. A previous post discussed an African American school security guard who was fired for using the N-word in the course of telling a student not to direct that word at him. (Thankfully, he was eventually re-hired after a national furor erupted.) The same post discussed a teacher who was fired for inadvertently failing to address a student by his self-identified gender pronoun. The security guard and the teacher each have four children to support and lost their health insurance as well as their income when they were fired. They are hardly examples of the rich and powerful.

But at least one can say the security guard actually used the n-word and the teacher actually did have a religious objection to recognizing transgender identities. But as people, especially in educational settings, have grown more intimidated, it has been harder for the cancel culture warriors to find such people. So instead of finding someone who actually used the n-word, they expand the definition of cancel-worthy language. A professor at the University of Southern California was placed on leave for using a Chinese word that some people think *sounds like* the n-word even though it is simply the Chinese word for "that." The professor is a member of USC US-China Institute, and was teaching a communications course and was using the word to illustrate how different languages use different words to fill in pauses.

The situation has deteriorated to the point that one no longer needs to *say* anything to be targeted by cancel culture. At Skidmore College in New York State, a professor is being boycotted for merely *attending* a pro-police "Back the Blue" rally. He didn't participate in any way, he didn't speak or shout slogans, or carry a sign. He says he just wanted to hear what the demonstrators had to say. But an email circulated at the college saying, "Tonight, I and other Skidmore students witnessed Profs. David Peterson and Andrea Peterson at an anti-Black Lives Matter protest. We demand the immediate dismissal of both Skidmore staff members for engaging in hateful conduct that threatens Black Skidmore students." (It turned out that Andrea Peterson doesn't work at the college.)

The professor found a notice on his classroom door saying "STOP. By entering this class you are crossing a campus-wide picket line and breaking the boycott against Professor David Peterson. This is not a safe environment for marginalized students . . . By continuing to take this course you are enabling bigoted behavior on this campus."

According to Professor Peterson, as a result of the boycott, he has no remaining students in one class and only a very small number of students in his other two classes. He also says the university is investigating him for possible bias.

This extravagant expansion of cancel-worthy behavior is not limited to academia and it is not limited to anything a person has said or done anytime this century. A top executive at Boeing recently lost his job because of an article he wrote in *1987*, opposing allowing women to serve as fighter pilots. The executive apologized for the article, writing: "My article was a 29-year-old Cold War navy pilot's misguided contribution to a debate that was live at the time. The dialogue that followed its publication 33 years ago quickly opened my eyes, indelibly changed my mind, and shaped the principles of fairness, inclusion, respect and diversity that have guided my professional life since." That was not enough to save his job.

In no way is contemporary cancel culture about free speech or debate. Nor is it any longer primarily about social justice. The power to get someone fired must be a thrilling feeling. It also strengthens group bonds and can raise one's social standing in certain groups. It is not hard to understand why many people would be willing to look further and further afield to find targets: an innocently uttered Chinese word for "that," mere attendance at a rally to hear a point of view, or a 33-year-old article that the author has renounced and apologized for.

What is harder to understand is why the 10 truly powerful, those with the power to suspend and investigate professors and to fire people, are allowing this? Perhaps they fear becoming targets themselves. Whatever the reason, there is no denying that cancel culture exists and is getting worse.

Topics for Critical Thinking and Writing

1. What is the major premise of Evan Gerstmann's argument? What is he trying to prove? Explain whether or not you think he makes his case effectively.

2. How do Gerstmann's examples support his claims? What kinds of examples are they? (See the section "Examples" in Chapter 4, p. 121.) Which alternative examples or example types might further support or contradict his views?

3. Consider the case of the Boeing executive who was called to account for this previously published opinion (para. 8). Why does Gerstmann see this as a problem? Explain whether or not you think the response was fair.

4. Compare Gerstmann's argument with Brownlee's (p. 472) in this chapter. Does Gerstmann's argument effectively refute Brownlee's argument? Why or why not? Is there any potential common ground between them?

5. Write an argument in which you characterize cancel culture as a problem, not a problem, or something in between, using specific examples drawn from these articles as well as from your own research.

PART FIVE

Current Issues Casebooks

20

A College Education: What Is Its Purpose?

ANDREW DELBANCO

Andrew Delbanco is a widely published author who teaches at Columbia University, where he is the Alexander Hamilton Professor of American Studies. In 2012, Delbanco was awarded the National Humanities Medal by President Barack Obama. He is the author of *The War Before the War: Fugitive Slaves and the Struggle for America's Soul from the Revolution to the Civil War* (2018). The following essay first appeared in *Parade*, and was later included in Delbanco's book *College: What It Was, Is, and Should Be* (2012).

3 Reasons College Still Matters

The American college is going through a period of wrenching change, buffeted by forces — globalization, economic instability, the information technology revolution, the increasingly evident inadequacy of K–12 education, and, perhaps most important, the collapse of consensus about what students should know — that make its task more difficult and contentious than ever before.

For a relatively few students, college remains the sort of place that Anthony Kronman, former dean of Yale Law School, recalls from his days at Williams, where his favorite class took place at the home of a philosophy professor whose two golden retrievers slept on either side of the fireplace "like bookends beside the hearth" while the sunset lit the Berkshire Hills "in scarlet and gold." For many more students, college means the anxious pursuit of marketable skills in overcrowded, underresourced institutions. For still others, it means traveling by night to a fluorescent office building or to a "virtual classroom" that only exists in cyberspace.

It is a pipe dream to imagine that every student can have the sort of experience that our richest colleges, at their best, provide. But it is a nightmare society that affords the chance to learn and grow only to the wealthy, brilliant, or lucky few. Many remarkable teachers in America's community colleges, unsung private colleges, and underfunded public colleges live this truth every day, working to keep the ideal of democratic education alive.

And so it is my unabashed aim to articulate in my forthcoming book, *College: What It Was, Is, and Should Be*, what a college — any college — should seek to do for its students.

What, then, are today's prevailing answers to the question, what is college for? The most common answer is an economic one. It's clear that a college degree long ago supplanted the high school diploma as the minimum qualification for entry into the skilled labor market, and there is abundant evidence that people with a college degree earn more money over the course of their lives than people without one. Some estimates put the worth of a bachelor of arts degree at about a million dollars in incremental lifetime earnings.

For such economic reasons alone, it is 5 alarming that for the first time in history, we face the prospect that the coming generation of Americans will be less educated than its elders.

Within this gloomy general picture are some especially disturbing particulars. For one thing, flat or declining college attainment rates (relative to other nations) apply disproportionately to minorities, who are a growing portion of the American population. And financial means have a shockingly large bearing on educational opportunity, which, according to one authority, looks like this in today's America: If you are the child of a family making more than $90,000 per year, your odds of getting a BA by age twenty-four are roughly one in two; if your parents make less than $35,000, your odds are one in seventy.

Moreover, among those who do get to college, high-achieving students from affluent families are four times more likely to attend a selective college than students from poor families with comparable grades and test scores. Since prestigious colleges serve as funnels into leadership positions in business, law, and government, this means that our "best"

colleges are doing more to foster than to retard the growth of inequality in our society. Yet colleges are still looked to as engines of social mobility in American life, and it would be shameful if they became, even more than they already are, a system for replicating inherited wealth.

Not surprisingly, as in any discussion of economic matters, one finds dissenters from the predominant view. Some on the right say that pouring more public investment into higher education, in the form of enhanced subsidies for individuals or institutions, is a bad idea. They argue against the goal of universal college education as a fond fantasy and, instead, for a sorting system such as one finds in European countries: vocational training for the low scorers, who will be the semiskilled laborers and functionaries; advanced education for the high scorers, who will be the diplomats and doctors.

Other thinkers, on the left, question whether the aspiration to go to college really makes sense for "low-income students who can least afford to spend money and years" on such a risky venture, given their low graduation rates and high debt. From this point of view, the "education gospel" seems a cruel distraction from "what really provides security to families and children: good jobs at fair wages, robust unions, affordable access to health care and transportation."

One can be on either side of these ques- 10 tions, or somewhere in the middle, and still believe in the goal of achieving universal college education. Consider an analogy from another sphere of public debate: health care. One sometimes hears that eliminating smoking would save untold billions because of the immense cost of caring for patients who develop lung cancer, emphysema, heart disease, or diabetes. It turns out, however, that reducing the incidence of disease by curtailing smoking may actually end up costing us more, since people who don't smoke live longer and eventually require expensive therapies for chronic diseases and the inevitable infirmities of old age.

In other words, measuring the benefit as a social cost or gain does not quite get the point — or at least not the whole point. The best reason to end smoking is that people who don't smoke have a better chance to lead better lives. The best reason to care about college — who goes, and what happens to them when they get there — is not what it does for society in economic terms but what it can do for individuals, in both calculable and incalculable ways.

The second argument for the importance of college is a political one, though one rarely hears it from politicians. This is the argument on behalf of democracy. "The basis of our government," as Thomas Jefferson put the matter near the end of the eighteenth century, is "the opinion of the people." If the new republic was to flourish and endure, it required, above all, an educated citizenry.

This is more true than ever. All of us are bombarded every day with pleadings and persuasions — advertisements, political appeals, punditry of all sorts — designed to capture our loyalty, money, or, more narrowly, our vote. Some say health care reform will bankrupt the country, others that it is an overdue act of justice; some believe that abortion is the work of Satan, others think that to deny a woman the right to terminate an unwanted pregnancy is a form of abuse. The best chance we have to maintain a functioning democracy is a citizenry that can tell the difference between demagoguery and responsible arguments.

Education for democracy also implies something about what kind of education democratic citizens need. A very good case for college in this sense has been made recently by Kronman, the former Yale dean who now teaches in a Great Books program for Yale undergraduates. In his book *Education's End*, Kronman argues for a course of study that introduces students to the constitutive ideas of Western culture, including, among many others, "the ideals of individual freedom and toleration," "a reliance on markets as a mechanism for the organization of economic life," and "an acceptance of the truths of modern science."

Anyone who earns a BA from a reputable 15 college ought to understand something about the genealogy of these ideas and practices, about the historical processes from which they have emerged, the tragic cost when societies fail to defend them, and about alternative ideas both within the Western tradition and outside it. That's a tall order for anyone to satisfy on his or her own — and one of the marks of an educated person is the recognition that it can never be adequately done and is therefore all the more worth doing.

There is a third case for college, seldom heard, perhaps because it is harder to articulate without sounding platitudinous and vague. I first heard it stated in a plain and passionate way after I had spoken to an alumni group from Columbia, where I teach. The emphasis in my talk was on the Jeffersonian argument — education for citizenship. When I had finished, an elderly alumnus stood up and said more or less the following: "That's all very nice, professor, but you've missed the main point." With some trepidation, I asked him what that point might be. "Columbia," he said, "taught me how to enjoy life."

What he meant was that college had opened his senses as well as his mind to experiences that would otherwise be foreclosed to him. Not only had it enriched his capacity to read demanding works of literature and to grasp fundamental political ideas, it had also heightened and deepened his alertness to color and form, melody and harmony. And now, in the late years of his life, he was grateful. Such an education is a hedge against utilitarian values. It slakes the human craving for contact with works of art that somehow register one's own longings and yet exceed what one has been able to articulate by and for oneself.

If all that seems too pious, I think of a comparably personal comment I once heard my colleague Judith Shapiro, former provost of Bryn Mawr and then president of Barnard, make to a group of young people about what they should expect from college: "You want the inside of your head to be an interesting place to spend the rest of your life."

What both Shapiro and the Columbia alum were talking about is sometimes called "liberal education"—a hazardous term today, since it has nothing necessarily to do with liberal politics in the modern sense of the word. The phrase "liberal education" derives from the classical tradition of *artes liberales*, which was reserved in Greece and Rome — where women were considered inferior and slavery was an accepted feature of civilized society—for "those free men or gentlemen possessed of the requisite leisure for study." The tradition of liberal learning survived and thrived throughout European history but remained largely the possession of ruling elites. The distinctive American contribution has been the attempt to democratize it, to deploy it on behalf of the cardinal American principle that all persons, regardless of origin, have the right to pursue happiness — and that "getting to know," in poet and critic Matthew Arnold's much-quoted phrase, "the best which has been thought and said in the world" is helpful to that pursuit.

This view of what it means to be educated is often caricatured as snobbish and narrow, beholden to the old and wary of the new; but in fact it is neither, as Arnold makes clear by the (seldom quoted) phrase with which he completes his point: "and through this knowledge, turning a stream of fresh and free thought upon our stock notions and habits."

In today's America, at every kind of institution — from underfunded community colleges to the wealthiest Ivies — this kind of education is at risk. Students are pressured and programmed, trained to live from task to task, relentlessly rehearsed and tested until winners are culled from the rest. Too many colleges do too little to save them from the debilitating frenzy that makes liberal education marginal — if it is offered at all.

In this respect, notwithstanding the bigotries and prejudices of earlier generations, we might not be so quick to say that today's colleges mark an advance over those of the past.

Consider a once-popular college novel written a hundred years ago, *Stover at Yale*, in which a young Yalie declares, "I'm going to do the best thing a fellow can do at our age, I'm going to loaf." The character speaks from the immemorial past, and what he says is likely to sound to us today like a sneering boast from the idle rich. But there is a more dignified sense in which "loaf" is the colloquial equivalent of contemplation and has always been part of the promise of American life. "I loaf and invite my soul," says Walt Whitman in that great democratic poem "Song of Myself."

Surely, every American college ought to defend this waning possibility, whatever we call it. And an American college is only true to itself when it opens its doors to all — the rich, the middle, and the poor — who have the capacity to embrace the precious chance to think and reflect before life engulfs them. If we are serious about democracy, that means everyone.

Topics for Critical Thinking and Writing

1. In two or three sentences, describe what Andrew Delbanco is arguing for. Then, in another two or three sentences, describe what he is arguing against.

2. What do you think Delbanco considers to be the most important outcomes of a college education? What outcomes are less important to him?

3. Do you think that the higher education system in the United States *perpetuates* inequalities or that it helps *resolve* inequalities? Or is it a little of both? Explain.

4. In paragraph 10, Delbanco introduces, as an analogy, the cost of lung cancer and other life-threatening diseases (although he goes on to reject this comparison). Do you think his use of this analogy is effective? Why or why not?

5. Why is higher education good for freedom and democracy? What evidence can you cite from Delbanco as support for your answer? What evidence can you cite on your own?

6. Using Delbanco's own formulation of a "liberal education" in paragraph 19, assess your own university's liberal education requirements and explain whether you think it is a valuable part of your education. Would you prefer an education that trained you only in your chosen career field or one that spreads learning across disciplines and experiences? If possible, talk to a humanities professor at your institution about the importance of a liberal education and include his or her thoughts, agreeing or countering them as you see fit, in your assessment.

EDWARD CONARD

Edward Conard, who has an MBA from Harvard, is best known for his controversial book on the US economy, *Unintended Consequences: Why Everything You've Been Told about the Economy Is Wrong* (2012). He has made more than one hundred television appearances, debating luminaries such as Paul Krugman and Jon Stewart. This article appeared with Christian Madsbjerg and Mikkel B. Rasmussen's as part of a Pro/Con debate in the *Washington Post* in 2013.

We Don't Need More Humanities Majors

It's no secret that innovation grows America's economy. But that growth is constrained in two ways. It is constrained by the amount of properly trained talent, which is needed to produce innovation. And it is constrained by this talent's willingness to take the entrepreneurial risks critical to commercializing innovation. Given those constraints, it is hard to believe humanities degree programs are the best way to train America's most talented students.

According to the Bureau of Labor Statistics (BLS), U.S. employment has grown roughly 45 percent since the early 1980s. Over the same period, Germany's employment grew roughly 20 percent, while France's employment grew less than 20 percent and Japan's only 13 percent. U.S. employment growth put roughly 10 million immigrants to work since the BLS started keeping track in 1996 and it has employed tens of millions of people offshore. The share of people in the world living on less than $1.25-a-day has fallen from over 50 percent to nearly 20 percent today, according to The World Bank. Name another high-wage economy that has done more than the United States for the employment of the world's poor and middle class during this time period.

Contrary to popular belief, U.S. employment growth isn't outpacing other high-wage economies because of growing employment in small businesses. Europe has plenty of small family-owned businesses. U.S. growth is predominately driven by successful high-tech startups, such as Google, Microsoft, and Apple, which have spawned large industries around them.

A Kauffman Institute survey of over 500 engineering and tech companies established between 1995 and 2005 reveals that 55 percent of the U.S.-born founders held degrees in the science, engineering, technology or mathematics, so called STEM-related fields, and over 90 percent held terminal degrees in STEM, business, economics, law and health care. Only 7 percent held terminal degrees in other areas — only 3 percent in the arts, humanities or social sciences. It's true some advanced degree holders may have earned undergraduate degrees in humanities, but they quickly learned humanities degrees alone offered inadequate training, and they returned to school for more technical degrees.

Other studies reach similar conclusions. 5 A seminal study by Stanford economics professor Charles Jones estimates that 50 percent of the growth since the 1950s comes from increasing the number of scientific researchers relative to the population.

Another recent study from UC–Davis economics professor Giovanni Peri and Colgate economics associate professor Chad Sparber finds the small number of "foreign scientists and engineers brought into this country under the H-1B visa program have contributed to 10%–20% of the yearly productivity growth in the U.S. during the period 1990–2010." Despite the outsized importance of business and technology to America's economic growth, nearly half of all recent bachelor's degrees in the 2010–2011 academic year were awarded in fields outside these areas of study. Critical thinking is valuable in all forms, but it is more valuable when applied directly to the most pressing demands of society.

At the same time, U.S. universities expect to graduate a third of the computer scientists our society demands, according to a study released by Microsoft. The talent gap in the information technology sector has been bridged by non-computer science majors, according to a report by Daniel Costa, the Economic Policy Institute's director of immigration law and policy research. Costa finds that the sector has recruited two-thirds of its talent from other disciplines — predominately workers with other technical degrees. But with the share of U.S. students with top quintile SAT/ACT scores and GPAs earning STEM-related degrees declining sharply over the last two decades, the industry has turned to foreign-born workers and increasingly offshore workers to fill its talent needs. While American consumers will benefit from discoveries made in other countries, discoveries made and commercialized here have driven and will continue to drive demand for U.S. employment — both skilled and unskilled.

UC–Berkeley economics professor Enrico Moretti estimates each additional high-tech job creates nearly five jobs in the local economy, more than any other industry. Unlike a restaurant, for example, high-tech employment tends to increase demand overall rather than merely shifting employment from one competing establishment to another.

If talented workers opt out of valuable training and end up underemployed, not only have they failed to create employment for other less talented workers, they have taken jobs those workers likely could have filled.

Thirty years ago, America could afford to misallocate a large share of its talent and still grow faster than the rest of the world. Not anymore; much of the world has caught up. My analysis of data collected by economics professors Robert Barro of Harvard University and Jong-Wha Lee of Korea University reveals that over the last decade America only supplied 10 percent of the increase in the world's college graduates, much less than the roughly 30 percent it supplied thirty years ago. Fully harnessing America's talent and putting it to work addressing the needs of mankind directly would have a greater impact on raising standards of living in both the United States and the rest of the world than other alternatives available today.

Topics for Critical Thinking and Writing

1. In paragraph 1, Edward Conard makes clear his thesis: "It is hard to believe humanities degree programs are the best way to train America's most talented students." What assumption is Conard making about college degrees and the economy? Do you agree? Why or why not?

2. Conard argues in paragraph 2 that the rate of employment in the United States has outpaced that of other advanced nations. To what does he attribute this growth? How does the US economy in turn provide worldwide prosperity?

3. Conard argues that economic growth is not generated by small businesses, as many people believe, but by start-up companies that become huge, such as Google, Microsoft, and Apple (para. 3). What other companies, if any, have started up in recent decades outside of the technological fields that have had a major impact on the economy, including job growth?

4. In paragraph 7, Conard points out that the United States is graduating only about one-third of the number of graduates needed in the fields of science, technology, engineering, and mathematics (STEM). Why is that? Do some research to support your answer.

5. Conard's arguments are driven almost entirely by economic concerns, not issues of personal happiness or career satisfaction. In your opinion, to what extent should those factors, as opposed to economic concerns, play a role in one's choice of a major? Explain your answer.

CHRISTIAN MADSBJERG AND MIKKEL B. RASMUSSEN

Christian Madsbjerg and Mikkel B. Rasmussen are senior partners at ReD Associates, a consulting firm that, in the words of its website, uses "social science tools to understand how people experience their reality" so that businesses can better reach customers. Together, Madsbjerg and Rasmussen wrote *The Moment of Clarity: Using Human Sciences to Solve Your Toughest Business Problems* (2014) and, more recently, Madsbjerg published *Sensemaking: The Power of the Humanities in the Age of the Algorithm* (2017). This article appeared with Edward Conard's as part of a Pro/Con debate in the *Washington Post* in 2013.

We Need More Humanities Majors

It has become oddly fashionable to look down on the humanities over the last few decades. Today's students are being told that studying the classics of English literature, the history of the twentieth century, or the ethics of privacy are a fun but useless luxury. To best prioritize our scarce education resources, we ought instead to focus on technical subjects such as math and engineering.

This short-term market logic doesn't work across the thirty-or-so-year horizon of a full career. A generation ago, lawyers made more money than investment bankers. Today, we have too many law graduates (though there appears to be data to support it's still worth the money) and the investment banks complain about a lack of talent. It is basically impossible to project that sort of thing into the far future.

We are also told that a degree in the humanities is unlikely to make you successful. Take North Carolina Governor Pat McCrory (R), who, while making the case for subsidizing state community colleges and universities based on how well they do in terms of placing students in the workforce, said this in January:

> ". . . frankly, if you want to take gender studies, that's fine. Go to a private school and take it, but I don't want to subsidize that if that's not going to get someone a job. . . . It's the tech jobs that we need right now."

But quite a few people with humanities degrees have had successful careers and, in the process, created numerous jobs. According to a report from *Business Insider*, the list includes A.G. Lafley of Procter & Gamble (French and History), former Massachusetts Governor and Republican presidential nominee Mitt Romney (English), George Soros (Philosophy), Michael Eisner of Disney (English and Theater), Peter Thiel of Paypal (Philosophy), Ken Chenault of American Express (History), Carl Icahn (Philosophy), former Secretary of the Treasury Hank Paulson (English), Supreme Court Justice Clarence Thomas (English), Ted Turner of CNN (History), and former IBM CEO Sam Palmisano (History). *Business Insider* has a list of 30 business heavyweights in total.

One might think that most people starting 5 out or running tech companies in the heart of Silicon Valley would be from the science, technology, engineering and mathematics (STEM) fields. Not so. Vivek Wadhwa, a columnist for *The Washington Post*'s Innovations section and a fellow at the Rock Center for Corporate Governance at Stanford University, found that 47 percent of the 652 technology and engineering company founders surveyed held terminal degrees in the STEM fields, with 37 percent of those degrees being in either engineering or computer technology and 2 percent in mathematics. The rest graduated with a healthy combination of liberal arts, health-care and business degrees.

This leads us to a very important question: What good is a degree in the humanities in the real world of products and customers? Here's the answer: Far more than most people think. It all comes down to this: Is it helpful to know your customers? Deeply understanding their world, seeing what they see and understanding why they do the things they do, is not an easy task. Some people have otherworldly intuitions. But for most of us, getting under the skin of the people we are trying to serve takes hard analytical work.

By analytical work we mean getting and analyzing data that can help us understand the bigger picture of people's lives. The real issue with understanding people, as opposed to bacteria, or numbers, is that we change when we are studied. Birds or geological sediments do not suddenly turn self-conscious, and change their behavior just because someone is looking. Studying a moving target like this requires a completely different approach than the one needed to study nature. If you want to understand the kinds of beings we are, you need to use your own humanity and your own experience.

Such an approach can be found in the humanities. When you study the writings of, say, David Foster Wallace, you learn how to step into and feel empathy for a different world than your own. His world of intricate, neurotic detail and societal critique says more about living as a young man in the 1990s than most market research graphs. But more importantly: The same skills involved in being a subtle reader of a text are involved in deeply understanding Chinese or Argentinian consumers of cars, soap or computers. They are hard skills of understanding other people, their practices and context.

The market is naturally on to this: In a recent study, Debra Humphreys from the Association of American College & Universities concludes that 95 percent of employers say that "a candidate's demonstrated capacity to think critically, communicate clearly, and solve complex problems is more important than their undergraduate major." These all are skills taught at the highest level in the humanities.

Companies — with the most sophisticated 10 ones such as Intel, Microsoft and Johnson & Johnson leading the charge — are starting to launch major initiatives with names such as "customer-centric marketing" and "deep customer understanding." The goal of these programs is to help companies better understand the people they're selling to.

The issue is that engineers and most designers, by and large, create products for people whose tastes resemble their own. They simply don't have the skill set of a humanities major — one that allows a researcher or executive to deeply understand what it is like to be an Indonesian teenager living in Jakarta and getting a new phone, or what kind of infused beverages a Brazilian 25-year-old likes and needs.

The humanities are not in crisis. We need humanities majors more now than before to strengthen competitiveness and improve products and services. We have a veritable goldmine on our hands. But, in order for that to happen, we need the two cultures of business and the humanities to meet. The best place to start is collaboration between companies and universities on a research level — something that ought to be at the top of the minds of both research institutions and R&D departments in the coming decade.

Topics for Critical Thinking and Writing

1. Christian Madsbjerg and Mikkel B. Rasmussen note at the beginning of their article that there has been a significant trend of pushing students to major in the fields of science, technology, engineering, and mathematics (STEM). Why has that trend occurred? What do they say is the problem with pushing students in that direction?

2. In paragraph 4, Madsbjerg and Rasmussen list several big-name businesspeople, politicians, and others who have degrees in the humanities. Are they merely cherry-picking examples (i.e., finding the few examples that support your position while ignoring the vast majority that do not), or do those examples accurately reflect the broader whole? (You may need to do some research to support your answer.)

3. What argument do Madsbjerg and Rasmussen make about the abilities of humanities majors being superior to the abilities of those who major in technical fields? Do you find the authors' argument credible? Why or why not?

4. In paragraph 9, Madsbjerg and Rasmussen use the example of studying literature as a way to better understand human nature. Explain why this is or is not a fair claim.

5. Madsbjerg and Rasmussen point out that employers want to see employment candidates who can "think critically, communicate clearly, and solve complex problems" (para. 9). The authors argue that humanities graduates best fit that description. In your opinion, is that true or not? Be specific in your response.

6. In paragraph 11, Madsbjerg and Rasmussen state, "The issue is that engineers and most designers, by and large, create products for people whose tastes resemble their own." Consider a specific recent product or invention and argue whether its design is reflective of what a customer wants or what an engineer or designer wants.

JOHN SAILER

John Sailer is a research associate for the National Association of Scholars, where he is project lead on the Keeping the Republic Project, which focuses on promoting civic education in the United States. Sailer is also a freelance scholar-writer whose publications have appeared in the *New York Post*, *American Compass*, and *City Journal*. The article below was published by the James G. Martin Center for Academic Renewal in 2021.

Is Our Obsession with College Fueling a Mental Health Crisis?

Long before COVID, mental health experts declared a different sort of pandemic — a precipitous decline in mental health on college campuses.

One 2019 survey by the American College Health Association found that over the course of a year, 55.9 percent of students reported feeling hopelessness, 65.6 percent reported feeling very lonely, 70.8 percent reported feeling very sad, and 65.7 percent reported overwhelming anxiety. Nearly half said that at some point in the year they felt so depressed that it was difficult to function.

This data creates an odd disjunction. College, after all, publicly signifies opportunity, success,

and even the American Dream — and yet, far from feeling empowered by these supposed institutional vehicles of success, many students buckle under the weight of loneliness and anxiety.

According to one common explanation, college life simply puts too much pressure on students, who feel the need to perform academically so they can get a good job. While certainly a feature, the pressure to perform falls short of explaining the problem. Economic pressure exists everywhere, so why does college uniquely lend itself to anxiety? Why depression and loneliness?

Along with the rigors of the university, 5 our national obsession with college shares at least some of the blame. While college often alienates students, our public policy and culture increasingly mandate that all young people pursue a college degree — and this is a recipe for our campus mental health crisis and its attendant consequences.

Higher education carries an almost salvific status in American society. Graduates of elite universities receive immense esteem and opportunity, bolstered by the rhetoric and policy of our major businesses, nonprofits, and of course, schools. Out of the nation's ten largest charter school networks, a majority explicitly tout college admissions and attendance as their *raison d'etre*. These schools share almost identical language in their mission statements, promising success in "college, career, and beyond." Unsurprisingly, many university leaders echo the call for everyone to go to college. Margaret Spellings, the former University of North Carolina system president, enthusiastically endorsed building "a college-going culture in all 100 [North Carolina] counties."

Politicians at the national level, perhaps most of all, embrace this college-obsessed rhetoric. In *The Tyranny of Merit*, Michael Sandel explains how education — and especially college — has become a public policy panacea, a go-to solution to poverty and inequality. In the 90s, Tony Blair, former Prime Minister of the United Kingdom, famously expressed his faith in education: "Ask me for my three main priorities for government and I tell you: education, education, and education." Meanwhile, Bill Clinton popularized a college-pushing slogan: "What you can earn depends on what you can learn."

While politicians and education leaders talk up the benefits of college, they rarely mention the non-monetary costs. For most students, attending college means leaving friends, family members, and longstanding communities. This broad network of support — social capital, to invoke the sociological term — plays an important role in the formation of young people.

Deep communities can be hard to replicate on campus, but they're vital to good health. Young people develop a sense of self through relationships, through conversation with older relatives and longtime friends. Moreover, these bonds create accountability. Students who have to own up to their decisions — and explain them face-to-face to friends and neighbors — will think twice about what they are doing. Perhaps most obviously, longstanding relationships provide a stable community, often inculcating a sense of loyalty that makes it undesirable to opt out and a commitment to place which makes it difficult to opt out. In places where social capital is strong, young people might lament that their community is overbearing — but they probably won't feel lonely.

As Patrick Deneen points out, universities 10 weaken social capital. "Elite universities," Deneen writes in his book *Why Liberalism Failed*,

> engage in the educational equivalent of strip mining: identifying economically viable raw materials in every city, town, and hamlet, they strip off that valuable commodity, process it in a distant location, and render the products economically useful for productivity elsewhere. The places that supplied the raw materials are left much like depressed coal towns whose mineral wealth has been long since mined and exported.

Predictably, communities suffer when young people — especially the brightest young people — move away and don't return.

Educational "strip mining" also takes a toll on students. Leaving home entails a tradeoff — students lose their community but gain the benefits of an advanced education. Some people are uniquely suited for this education. In their case, the tradeoff makes sense. While they still have to consider the cost of being more isolated, these students are more likely to see reasons to pull through.

Others have less to gain from higher education in the first place. In 2020, the Federal Reserve found that 41 percent of recent college graduates work jobs that don't require a degree. Of those who are underemployed, two-thirds remain that way five years later. For these students, the costs of college remain. The Mayo Clinic suggests that homesickness and the challenges of adjusting to independence can be key reasons for depression in college, and the Journal of American College Health published research linking homesickness with depression in college. Unfortunately, for those who aren't naturally inclined toward college, there are fewer benefits to outweigh the isolation.

Public policy could encourage young people to consider options other than college. One tool is to create workforce training grants, redirecting some of the money that goes to higher education to businesses that take on "trainees." Similarly, states could implement policies that support students on non-college track in high schools. At the moment, many politicians instead gravitate toward buzzword policy solutions like college-for-all and canceling student debt.

Against the current backdrop of our college-obsessed policy, a campus mental health "epidemic" makes sense. Deep relationships are hard to replicate — they take time and work. College students have limited time to devote, and they often aren't encouraged to do the work. The idealized college experience is usually equated with experimentation and partying, neither of which are conducive to the development of deep relationships. Many students treat college like a consumer experience, a four year alcohol-soaked prelude to adult life. In light of

this, the poor indicators make sense — including the droves of students who report feeling so depressed they can't function.

Unsurprisingly, colleges across the country have spent millions on mental health facilities and services. In fact, a lot of university spending aims to replicate a sense of belonging — or distract from the absence.

When students lose this natural sense of belonging, they may even become more susceptible to extreme causes, which can fill the void. Hannah Arendt argues that isolation makes totalitarian ideology more attractive. In the absence of strong communal ties, utopian movements can fill the void and impart an overarching sense of meaning. If Arendt is right, it shouldn't be surprising that colleges are hotbeds of radicalism; isolated students find meaning in extreme politics.

This potent mix of undergraduate alienation, academic under-preparedness, and student radicalization is well illustrated by the infamous Yale Halloween scandal. In 2015, Erika Christakis — an associate master at a Yale University residential college — responded to an email that encouraged students to be culturally sensitive when choosing Halloween costumes. In her congenial response, Christakis suggested that perhaps this sort of policing went too far. Students at Yale responded with vehement protests, calling for Christakis to resign. When her husband, Nicholas Christakis, famously tried to reason with the student protesters, they angrily confronted him — one student interrupted him, yelling: "It is not about creating an intellectual space! It is not! It's about creating a home here!"

College and universities spend billions of dollars attempting to do just that — create a home. Perhaps instead we should make it easier for young people to stay in their communities in the first place.

Topics for Critical Thinking and Writing

1. John Sailer's title asks a question: "Is Our Obsession with College Fueling a Mental Health Crisis?" Support or challenge the assumption that people are "obsessed" with going to college.

2. Analyze Sailer's reasoning in his argument that college is causing a widespread mental health crisis. Explain his logic.

3. In paragraphs 8–9, Sailer worries about the effects on mental health of students "leaving friends, family members, and longstanding communities" and argues that doing so lends itself to increased loneliness and anxiety. What are some counterarguments to this claim? Would addressing these counterarguments strengthen Sailer's argument?

4. Patrick Deneen claims that elite universities "'engage in the educational equivalent of strip mining'" (para. 10). Examine this metaphor more closely. How does comparing students to natural resources impact your view of the value of education?

5. Sailer refers to "those who aren't *naturally* inclined toward college" (para. 12, emphasis added). What is the nature versus nurture debate? Now consider it in the context of Sailer's argument and briefly discuss whether people are "naturally" not inclined toward college.

6. Toward the end of Sailer's essay (paras. 16–18), he asserts that one effect of pressuring the majority of people to attend college is a tendency toward political radicalism. Do you think this is an effective argument? Why or why not?

7. Do you think that some, most, or all young people should attend college after high school? What are some arguments in favor of most people getting a college degree according to other authors in this chapter?

CAROLINE HARPER

Caroline Harper holds a PhD in political science with concentrations in Black politics and international relations from Howard University, where she is a lecturer. Located in Washington, DC, Howard is the most prominent historically Black university in the United States. This essay was first published in 2018 on the blog *Higher Education Today*, operated by the American Council on Education.

HBCUs, Black Women, and STEM Success

The demand for professionals in science, technology, engineering, and math, or STEM, has been on the rise since 2000 — and projections indicate that the need for qualified candidates will not slow down any time soon. As new technology has driven market growth around the world, the United States has struggled to develop a workforce capable of maintaining a competitive edge in the global market. The ability to compete in the global market is contingent upon our ability to maximize resources that educate and prepare a diverse pipeline of students who understand the necessity of global citizenship.

During the White House College Opportunity Summit in 2014, President Obama reiterated the need to develop long-term strategies that expose students to STEM disciplines in elementary and middle school, increase college access, and maintain postsecondary affordability. These goals become increasingly important as projections indicate that more students from low-income and underrepresented minorities will pursue college degrees by 2025. According to the Bureau of Labor Statistics, women will make up 47.2 percent of the total labor force by 2024. It has become clear that postsecondary education is the gateway to obtaining professional opportunities in STEM occupations. In 2015, the Bureau of Labor Statistics confirmed that more than 99 percent of jobs in STEM required postsecondary education, compared to 36 percent of occupations overall.

The ability to create a pathway from degree attainment to gainful employment ensures that the STEM workforce reflects the diversity of our country. In recognizing this, the White House Council on Women and Girls and the Office of Science and Technology Policy have worked to encourage more women and girls to earn college degrees and pursue careers in STEM fields. But do existing strategies ensure a diverse STEM pipeline? Do these strategies reduce disparities between degree attainment and labor force outcomes among women and minorities?

CONDITIONS OF THE STEM PIPELINE

Although policy efforts to encourage STEM degree attainment are laudable, the STEM pipeline is leaky when it comes to underrepresented minorities. At the high school level, it is difficult to maintain a campus culture that encourages equity in the pursuit of STEM degrees when calculus and physics courses are available in only 33 percent and 48 percent of high schools with high black and Latino student enrollment, respectively.

Beyond access to courses that serve as the 5 foundation to STEM careers, many black and Latino students have limited access to college and career readiness counselors. According to a national survey of school counselors, in high schools in which the student body is primarily low-income and/or underrepresented minority, the average caseload is at least 1,000 students per counselor — at least twice the national average. As a consequence of factors beyond their control, it is especially difficult for these students to successfully navigate a career trajectory that incorporates course selection, experiential learning opportunities, extracurricular activities, and college admission requirements.

Although many of the students aspire to attend college, black students are struggling to meet mathematics (13 percent), science (11 percent) and general STEM (4 percent) ACT test benchmarks, which are often seen as a measure of college readiness. What is the alternative for students who are interested in pursuing STEM careers but need additional resources to overcome limitations in their K–12 education?

CAMPUS CULTURE AND COLLEGE SUCCESS

Despite limited access to resources during high school, students who choose to pursue their undergraduate degrees at Historically Black Colleges and Universities (HBCUs) are welcomed by a nurturing environment that provides critical resources to overcome academic, social, and financial hurdles. For more than 150 years, HBCUs have continued to serve first-generation, low-income, and underprepared students.

According to the U.S. Census Bureau, the number of traditional college-aged Americans is projected to grow to 13.3 million by 2025. The largest growth is expected to occur among students who identify as black, Hispanic, or Asian/Pacific Islander. In an analysis of black student graduation rates, about half of all four-year HBCUs enrolled freshmen classes where 75 percent of students were from low-income backgrounds, compared to 1 percent of the 676 non-HBCUs in the study. Among the institutions where 40–75 percent of the freshman class was low-income, the graduation rate for black students who attended HBCUs was 37.8 percent — five percentage points higher than their counterparts at non-HBCUs.

HBCUs produced 46 percent of black women who earned degrees in STEM disciplines between 1995 and 2004. HBCUs produced 25 percent of all bachelor's degrees in STEM fields earned by African Americans in 2012. In 2014, black women represented the highest percentage of minority women who earned bachelor's degrees in computer sciences. HBCUs such as North Carolina A&T State University, Howard University, Florida A&M University, and Xavier University of Louisiana continue producing undergraduate STEM degree earners who pursue graduate degrees in their field.

Beyond producing bachelor's degrees, research confirms that HBCUs are the institution of origin among almost 30 percent of blacks who earned doctorates in science and engineering. According to the National Science Foundation, within STEM fields such as mathematics, biological sciences, physical sciences, agricultural sciences, and earth, atmospheric, and ocean sciences, a large percentage of doctorate degree holders earned their bachelor's degrees at HBCUs.

CAREER OUTCOMES

While the campus culture at HBCUs provides black students with a sense of community, self-confidence, and efficacy, the workforce provides a stark contrast. Relative to their share of degree attainment, blacks are underrepresented in the overall context of the workforce and earnings.

Research has shown that compared to their Hispanic and Asian counterparts, blacks have the highest rate of unemployment. Among minorities currently employed in a STEM occupation, 41.4 percent are Asian, 18.4 percent are Hispanic or Latino, and only 17.4 percent are black. Moreover, blacks who work full time, year-round in STEM occupations are paid less than their Asian and Hispanic counterparts.

Despite disparities in employment rates and income, there are still important achievements that should be considered as the STEM workforce continues to grow. Within mathematical occupations, there were more black operations research analysts than any other minority group in 2011. In engineering occupations, black engineers outnumbered other minorities in the petroleum engineering field and rivaled Asians in roles related to environmental engineering, surveyors, cartographers, and photogrammetrists. Black scientists outnumbered other minorities in chemical technician and nuclear scientist roles. Compared to their Hispanic counterparts, there was a higher percentage of black professionals in conservation sciences and forestry occupations and geological and petroleum technician roles.

NEXT STEPS

While HBCUs do their share of producing black graduates with STEM degrees, there is a greater need for equity throughout the education pipeline and in workforce hiring practices. Suggestions to fill gaps in the STEM pipeline and ensure a diverse workforce that increases our ability to compete internationally include:

- Ensure that high schools serving low-income and minority students are provided with adequate resources to hire additional school counselors proportional to the student body and with the capacity to help students develop strategies to achieve college and career readiness.

- Provide funding to support collaborations with organizations that encourage academic rigor in STEM disciplines, including calculus and physics, in addition to advanced placement and honors courses. Specifically, funds should be designated to increase access to STEM foundation courses, advanced placement, and honors courses.

- Encourage private corporations to actively engage in the process of creating a diverse workforce by developing partnerships that encourage diversity in recruitment, hiring, and development of African American college students pursuing degrees in STEM disciplines.

- Develop internship opportunities in collaboration with HBCU campuses to provide students with opportunities to put their coursework into practice while developing skills that can be transferred into the workforce.

HBCUs have maintained their legacies of producing African American professionals in critical professions. Staying true to their mission, HBCUs continue to provide a nurturing environment where students gain academic and professional training to drive innovation in STEM fields and make valuable contributions in communities around the world. 15

Topics for Critical Thinking and Writing

1. What is Caroline Harper's argument? Describe how she lays out the problem and solution over the course of the essay. Use details and examples from her essay in your description.

2. What does Harper mean by the STEM pipeline? Briefly define the STEM pipeline in your own words, using your own examples.

3. Why does Harper think that HBCUs are the ideal places for correcting the inequities between different economic, racial, and gender groups? Support your answer with evidence from Harper's essay.

4. Does Harper's argument imply that the kind of humanities-based, liberal arts education advocated by Delbanco and by Madsbjerg and Rasmussen is not as important for under-represented groups as advancement in STEM skills and fields? In a brief essay, supplement Harper's argument with your own ideas on why it might be important for underrepresented groups to take courses in history, art, or other humanities fields.

21

Racial Injustice: Is the Problem Systemic?

KMELE FOSTER, DAVID FRENCH, JASON STANLEY, AND THOMAS CHATTERTON WILLIAMS

The writers here represent a diverse group of cross-partisan thinkers who work on issues surrounding free speech and democracy. They collaborated on this 2021 piece published in the *New York Times* in order to address the debate on teaching critical race theory (CRT) in public schools. This contentious debate centers around whether schools should teach young people about forms of systemic racial oppression in the United States, both past and present. Proponents of CRT tend to situate racism at the heart of the United States' economic growth and development, showing how power and privilege have been maintained along racial lines through the legacies of slavery, segregation, and inequality up to present structural inequalities (in employment, housing, access to education, criminal justice, and more). Opponents of CRT claim that such views unduly center racism and inequality as fundamental aspects of American life, and that teaching CRT perpetuates awareness and attitudes toward the self and others based on race.

Kmele Foster is a telecommunications entrepreneur and chairman of the conservative-libertarian America's Future Foundation. David French is a political commentator and senior editor at the *Dispatch*, a conservative magazine. Jason Stanley is the Jacob Urowsky Professor of Philosophy at Yale University and author of *How Fascism Works: The Politics of Us and Them* (2018). Thomas Chatterton Williams is a cultural critic and author of three books, most recently *Self-Portrait in Black and White: Unlearning Race* (2019). He also contributes to the *New York Times Magazine* and *Harper's* and currently serves as a resident fellow at the right-leaning think tank the American Enterprise Institute.

We Disagree on a Lot of Things. Except the Danger of Anti-Critical-Race-Theory Laws

What is the purpose of a liberal education? This is the question at the heart of a bitter debate that has been roiling the nation for months.

Schools, particularly at the kindergarten-to-12th-grade level, are responsible for help-ing turn students into well-informed and discerning citizens. At their best, our nation's schools equip young minds to grapple with complexity and navigate our differences. At their worst, they resemble indoctrination factories.

In recent weeks, Tennessee, Oklahoma, Iowa, Idaho and Texas have passed legislation that places significant restrictions on what can be taught in public school classrooms and, in some cases, public universities, too.

Tennessee House Bill SB 0623, for example, bans any teaching that could lead an individual to "feel discomfort, guilt, anguish or another form of psychological distress solely because of the individual's race or sex." In addition to this vague proscription, it restricts teaching that leads to "division between, or resentment of, a race, sex, religion, creed, nonviolent political affiliation, social class or class of people."

Texas House Bill 3979 goes further, forbid- 5 ding teaching that "slavery and racism are anything other than deviations from, betrayals of, or failures to live up to, the authentic founding principles of the United States." It also bars any classroom from requiring "an understanding of the 1619 Project" — The New York Times Magazine's special issue devoted to a reframing of the nation's founding — and hence prohibits assigning any part of it as required reading.

These initiatives have been marketed as "anti-critical race theory" laws. We, the authors of this essay, have wide ideological divergences on the explicit targets of this legislation. Some of us are deeply influenced by the academic discipline of critical race theory and its critique of racist structures and admire the 1619 Project. Some of us are skeptical of structural racist explanations and racial identity itself and disagree with the mission and methodology of the 1619 Project. We span the ideological spectrum: a progressive, a moderate, a libertarian and a conservative.

It is *because* of these differences that we here join, as we are united in one overarching concern: the danger posed by these laws to liberal education.

The laws differ in some respects but generally agree on blocking any teaching that would lead students to feel discomfort, guilt or anguish because of one's race or ancestry, as well as restricting teaching that subsequent generations have any kind of historical responsibility for actions of previous generations. They attempt various carve outs for the impartial teaching of the history of oppression of groups. But it's hard to see how these attempts are at all consistent with demands to avoid discomfort. These measures would, by way of comparison, make Germany's uncompromising and successful approach to teaching about the Holocaust illegal, as part of its goal is to infuse them with some sense of the weight of the past and (famously) lead many German students to feel anguish about their ancestry.

Indeed, the very act of learning history in a free and multiethnic society is inescapably fraught. Any accurate teaching of any country's history could make *some* of its citizens feel uncomfortable (or even guilty) about the past. To deny this necessary consequence of education is, to quote W.E.B. Du Bois, to transform "history into propaganda."

What's more, these laws even make it 10 difficult to teach U.S. history in a way that would reveal well-documented ways in which past policy decisions, like redlining, have contributed to present-day racial wealth gaps. An education of this sort would be negligent, creating ignorant citizens who are unable to understand, for instance, the case for reparations — or the case against them.

Because these laws often aim to protect the feelings of hypothetical children, they are dangerously imprecise. State governments exercise a high degree of lawful control over K-12 curriculum. But broad, vague laws violate due process and fundamental fairness because they don't give the teachers fair warning of what's prohibited. For example, the Tennessee statute prohibits a public school from including in a course of instruction any "concept" that promotes "division between, or resentment of" a "creed." Would teachers be violating the law if they express the opinion that the creeds of Stalinism or Nazism were evil?

Other laws appear to potentially ban even expression as benign as support for affirmative action, but it's far from clear. In fact, shortly after Texas passed its purported ban on critical race theory, the Texas Public Policy Foundation, a conservative think tank, published a list of words and concepts that help "identify critical race theory in the classroom." The list included terms such as "social justice," "colonialism" and "identity." Applying the same standards to colleges or private institutions would be flatly unconstitutional.

These laws threaten the basic purpose of a historical education in a liberal democracy. But censorship is the wrong approach even to the concepts that are the intended targets of these laws.

Though some of us share the antipathy of the legislation's authors toward some of these targets and object to overreaches that leave many parents understandably anxious about the stewardship of their children's education, we all reject the means by which these measures encode that antipathy into legislation.

A wiser response to problematic elements 15 of what is being labeled critical race theory would be twofold: propose better curriculums and enforce existing civil rights laws. Title VI and Title VII of the Civil Rights Act prohibit discrimination on the basis of race, and they are rooted in a considerable body of case law that provides administrators with far more concrete guidance on how to proceed. In fact, there is already an Education Department Office of Civil Rights complaint and a federal lawsuit aimed at programs that allegedly attempt to place students or teachers into racial affinity groups.

The task of defending the fundamentally liberal democratic nature of the American project ultimately requires the confidence to meet challenges to that vision. Censoring such challenges is a concession to their power, not a defense.

Let's not mince words about these laws. They are speech codes. They seek to change public education by banning the expression of ideas. Even if this censorship is legal in the narrow context of public primary and secondary education, it is antithetical to educating students in the culture of American free expression.

There will always be disagreement about any nation's history. The United States is no exception. If history is to judge the United States as exceptional, it is because we welcome such contestation in our public spaces as part of our unfolding national ethos. It is a violation of this commonly shared vision of America as a nation of free, vigorous and open debate to resort to the apparatus of the government to shut it down.

Topics for Critical Thinking and Writing

1. Kmele Foster et al. suggest that "subsequent generations have [a] . . . historical responsibility for the actions of previous generations" (para. 8). Do you agree? What is a "historical responsibility?" And is feeling uncomfortable with the past a good reason not to learn about it?

2. What do you think the authors' purposes are in expressing their political affiliations? Do you think it is a function of *ethos* or *pathos*? Explain.

3. According to the Pulitzer Center, the 1619 Project "challenges us to reframe US history by marking the year when the first enslaved Africans arrived on Virginia soil as our nation's foundational date." Why do you think lawmakers in various states might oppose this claim?

4. Is the authors' analogy to teaching about the Holocaust in Germany effective (para. 8)? Why or why not?

5. Think of an instance in which history is (or was) misrepresented in an educational context and argue whether or not it is a case of turning "history into propaganda" (para. 9). What was the motivation? What was the outcome? Do some research to support your answer, and be sure to examine the multiple sides of the issue that exist(ed).

IBRAM X. KENDI

Ibram X. Kendi is the Andrew W. Mellon Professor in the Humanities at Boston University and the founding director of the Boston University Center for Antiracist Research. Widely published in academic journals and popular media, he is also a MacArthur Fellow and member of the Society of American Historians. Kendi won the National Book Award for Nonfiction in 2016 for his history of racism in the United States, *Stamped from the Beginning: The Definitive History of Racist Ideas in America*. The following selection is from his influential 2020 book, *How to Be an Antiracist*.

Dueling Consciousness

Deep down, my parents were still the people who were set on fire by liberation theology back in Urbana. Ma still dreamed of globetrotting the Black world as a liberating missionary, a dream her Liberian friends encouraged in 1974. Dad dreamed of writing liberating poetry, a dream Professor Addison Gayle encouraged in 1971.

I always wonder what would have been if my parents had not let their reasonable fears stop them from pursuing their dreams. Traveling Ma helping to free the Black world.

Dad accompanying her and finding inspiration for his freedom poetry. Instead, Ma settled for a corporate career in healthcare technology. Dad settled for an accounting career. They entered the American middle class — a space then as now defined by its disproportionate White majority — and began to look at themselves and their people not only through their own eyes but also "through the eyes of others." They joined other Black people trying to fit into that White space while still trying to be themselves and save their people.

They were not wearing a mask as much as splitting into two minds.

This conceptual duple reflected what W.E.B. Du Bois indelibly voiced in *The Souls of Black Folk* in 1903. "It is a peculiar sensation, this double-consciousness, this sense of always looking at one's self through the eyes of others," Du Bois wrote. He would neither "Africanize America" nor "bleach his Negro soul in a flood of white Americanism." Du Bois wished "to be both a Negro and an American." Du Bois wished to inhabit opposing constructs. To be American is to be White. To be White is to not be a Negro.

What Du Bois termed double consciousness may be more precisely termed *dueling consciousness*. "One ever feels his two-ness," Du Bois explained, "an American, a Negro; two souls, two thoughts, two unreconciled strivings; two warring ideals in one dark body, whose dogged strength alone keeps it from being torn asunder." Du Bois also explained how this war was being waged within his own dark body, wanting to be a Negro and wanting to "escape into the mass of Americans in the same way that the Irish and Scandinavians" were doing.

These dueling ideas were there in 1903, 5 and the same duel overtook my parents — and it remains today. The duel within Black consciousness seems to usually be between antiracist[1] and assimilationist[2] ideas. Du Bois believed in both the antiracist concept of racial relativity, of every racial group looking at itself with its own eyes, and the assimilationist concept of racial standards, of "looking at one's self through the eyes" of another racial group — in his case, White people. In other words, he wanted to liberate Black people from racism but he also wanted to change them, to save them from their "relic of barbarism." Du Bois argued in 1903 that racism and "the low social level of the mass of the race" were both "responsible" for the "Negro's degradation." Assimilation would be part of the solution to this problem.

Assimilationist ideas are racist ideas. Assimilationists can position any racial group as the superior standard that another racial group should be measuring themselves against, the benchmark they should be trying to reach. Assimilationists typically position White people as the superior standard. "Do Americans ever stop to reflect that there are in this land a million men of Negro blood . . . who, judged by any standard, have reached the full measure of the best type of modern European culture? Is it fair, is it decent, is it Christian . . . to belittle such aspiration?" Du Bois asked in 1903.

The dueling consciousness played out in a different way for my parents, who became all about Black self-reliance. In 1985, they were drawn to Floyd H. Flake's Allen African Methodist Episcopal Church in Southside Queens. Flake and his equally magnetic wife, Elaine, grew Allen into a megachurch and one of the area's largest private-sector employers through its liberated kingdom of commercial and social-service enterprises. From its school to its senior-citizen housing complex to its crisis center for victims of domestic abuse, there were no walls to Flake's church. It was exactly the type of ministry that would naturally fascinate those descendants of Urbana '70. My father joined Flake's ministerial staff in 1989.

My favorite church program happened every Thanksgiving. We would arrive as lines of people were hugging the church building, which smelled

---

[1]**antiracist** One who is expressing the idea that racial groups are equals and none needs developing, and is supporting policy that reduces racial inequity.

[2]**assimilationist** One who is expressing the racist idea that a racial group is culturally or behaviorally inferior and is supporting cultural or behavioral enrichment programs to develop that racial group.

particularly good that day. Perfumes of gravy and cranberry sauce warmed the November air. The aromas multiplied in deliciousness as we entered the basement fellowship hall, where the ovens were. I usually found my spot in the endless assembly line of servers. I could barely see over the food. But I strained up on my toes to help feed every bit of five thousand people. I tried to be as kind to these hungry people as my mother's peach cobbler. This program of Black people feeding Black people embodied the gospel of Black self-reliance that the adults in my life were feeding me.

Black self-reliance was a double-edged sword. One side was an abhorrence of White supremacy and White paternalism, White rulers and White saviors. On the other, a love of Black rulers and Black saviors, of Black paternalism. On one side was the antiracist belief that Black people were entirely capable of ruling themselves, of relying on themselves. On the other, the assimilationist idea that Black people should focus on pulling themselves up by their baggy jeans and tight halter tops, getting off crack, street corners, and government "handouts," as if those were the things partially holding their incomes down. This dueling consciousness nourished Black pride by insisting that there was nothing wrong with Black people, but it also cultivated shame with its implication that there was something behaviorally wrong with Black people . . . well, at least those other Black people. If the problem was in our own behavior, then Reagan revolutionaries were not keeping Black people down — we were keeping ourselves down.

White people have their own dueling con- 10 sciousness, between the segregationist[3] and the assimilationist: the slave trader and the missionary, the proslavery exploiter and the antislavery civilizer, the eugenicist and the melting pot–ter, the mass incarcerator and the mass developer, the Blue Lives Matter and the All Lives Matter, the not-racist nationalist and the not-racist American.

Assimilationist ideas and segregationist ideas are the two types of racist ideas, the duel within racist thought. White assimilationist ideas challenge segregationist ideas that claim people of color are incapable of development, incapable of reaching the superior standard, incapable of becoming White and therefore fully human. Assimilationists believe that people of color can, in fact, be developed, become fully human, just like White people. Assimilationist ideas reduce people of color to the level of children needing instruction on how to act. Segregationist ideas cast people of color as "animals," to use Trump's descriptor for Latinx immigrants — unteachable after a point. The history of the racialized world is a three-way fight between assimilationists, segregationists, and antiracists. Antiracist ideas are based in the truth that racial groups are equals in all the ways they are different, assimilationist ideas are rooted in the notion that certain racial groups are culturally or behaviorally inferior, and segregationist ideas spring from a belief in genetic racial distinction and fixed hierarchy. "I am apt to suspect the negroes and in general all the other species of men (for there are four or five different kinds) to be naturally inferior to the whites," Enlightenment philosopher David Hume wrote in 1753. "There never was a civilized nation of any other complexion than white. . . . Such a uniform and constant difference could not happen, in so many countries and ages, if nature had not made an original distinction between these breeds of men."

David Hume declared that all races are created unequal, but Thomas Jefferson seemed

---

[3]**segregationist** One who is expressing the racist idea that a permanently inferior racial group can never be developed and is supporting policy that segregates away that racial group.

to disagree in 1776 when he declared "all men are created equal." But Thomas Jefferson never made the antiracist declaration: All racial groups are equals. While segregationist ideas suggest a racial group is permanently inferior, assimilationist ideas suggest a racial group is temporarily inferior. "It would be hazardous to affirm that, equally cultivated for a few generations," the Negro "would not become" equal, Jefferson once wrote, in assimilationist fashion.

The dueling White consciousness fashioned two types of racist policies, reflecting the duel of racist ideas. Since assimilationists posit cultural and behavioral hierarchy, assimilationist policies and programs are geared toward developing, civilizing, and integrating a racial group (to distinguish from programs that uplift individuals). Since segregationists posit the incapability of a racial group to be civilized and developed, segregationist policies are geared toward segregating, enslaving, incarcerating, deporting, and killing. Since antiracists posit that the racial groups are already civilized, antiracist policies are geared toward reducing racial inequities and creating equal opportunity.

White people have generally advocated for both assimilationist and segregationist policies. People of color have generally advocated for both antiracist and assimilationist policies. The "history of the American Negro is the history of this strife," to quote Du Bois — the strife between the assimilationist and the antiracist, between mass civilizing and mass equalizing. In Du Bois's Black body, in my parents' Black bodies, in my young Black body, this double desire, this dueling consciousness, yielded an inner strife between Black pride and a yearning to be White. My own assimilationist ideas stopped me from noticing the racist policies really getting high during Reagan's drug war.

The dueling white consciousness has, from its position of relative power, shaped the struggle within Black consciousness. Despite the cold truth that America was founded "by white men for white men," as segregationist Jefferson Davis said on the floor of the U.S. Senate in 1860, Black people have often expressed a desire to be American and have been encouraged in this by America's undeniable history of antiracist progress, away from chattel slavery and Jim Crow. Despite the cold instructions from the likes of Nobel laureate Gunnar Myrdal to "become assimilated into American culture," Black people have also, as Du Bois said, desired to remain Negro, discouraged by America's undeniable history of racist progress, from advancing police violence and voter suppression, to widening racial inequities in areas ranging from health to wealth.

History duels: the undeniable history of antiracist progress, the undeniable history of racist progress. Before and after the Civil War, before and after civil rights, before and after the first Black presidency, the White consciousness duels. The White body defines the American body. The White body segregates the Black body from the American body. The White body instructs the Black body to assimilate into the American body. The White body rejects the Black body assimilating into the American body — and history and consciousness duel anew.

The Black body in turn experiences the same duel. The Black body is instructed to become an American body. The American body is the White body. The Black body strives to assimilate into the American body. The American body rejects the Black body. The Black body separates from the American body. The Black body is instructed to assimilate into the American body — and history and consciousness duel anew.

But there is a way to get free. To be antiracist is to emancipate oneself from the dueling consciousness. To be antiracist is to conquer the assimilationist consciousness and

15

the segregationist consciousness. The White body no longer presents itself as the American body; the Black body no longer strives to be the American body, knowing there is no such thing as the American body, only American bodies, racialized by power.

Topics for Critical Thinking and Writing

1. Describe in your own words how Ibram X. Kendi connects his parents' experiences of the middle class ("Black people trying to fit into that White space") to the theories of W.E.B. Du Bois (paras. 2–5).

2. Why would Kendi be suspicious of programs that attempt to uplift minoritized youth? Think of some examples — historical or contemporary — that represent the differences between assimilationist and antiracist programs.

3. What fallacy or fallacies does Kendi see in Thomas Jefferson's phrase "All men are created equal" (para. 12)?

4. What do you think Kendi means by his statement that "the American body is the White body" (para. 17)? What kinds of evidence might be used to prove or disprove this statement?

5. In paragraph 5, Kendi distinguishes between assimilationist policies and antiracist policies. If someone proposed that all African Americans could go to college for free, would that be an assimilationist policy or an antiracist policy? Explain your answer and support it with references to Kendi's writing.

6. Do you think that Kendi's book (from which this selection comes) would be the kind of material targeted by the various state laws against teaching critical race theory that are described in the op-ed by Kmele Foster, David French, Jason Stanley, and Thomas Chatterton Williams (p. 497)? Why or why not?

MARIAN WRIGHT EDELMAN

Marian Wright Edelman, educated at Spelman College and Yale University, is the founder of the Children's Defense Fund, a group that, according to its website, is dedicated to "the needs of poor children, children of color and those with disabilities." She has received numerous awards, including a MacArthur Fellowship (1985), the Albert Schweitzer Prize for Humanitarianism (1988), and the Presidential Medal of Freedom (2000). This article appeared as an editorial in *Preventing Chronic Disease: Public Health Research, Practice, and Policy* in July 2007.

The Cradle to Prison Pipeline

Suppose that during the next decade, a quarter of all the children born in New York, North Carolina, Texas, Colorado, Ohio, and Pennsylvania were infected by a virulent new strain of polio or tuberculosis sometime during their youth. Clearly, our response to a health crisis affecting that many children would be to mobilize the nation's vast public health resources. Medical laboratories would operate around the clock to develop new vaccines.

Unfortunately, an infection akin to this hypothetical tragedy is actually coursing through African American and Latino communities across the nation. I'm not referring to a virus such as HIV/AIDS or a hazardous bacterium. I'm talking about the criminalization of poor children and children from minority races who enter what the Children's Defense Fund (CDF) identified as America's Cradle to Prison Pipeline. Together, African Americans and Latinos comprise a segment of the U.S. population equal to that of the six states I mentioned earlier. Like the victims of a crippling or wasting disease, once drawn into the prison pipeline, massive numbers of young people lose their opportunity to live happy, productive lives, not because of festering microbes but because of years spent behind bars.

Through its Cradle to Prison Pipeline initiative, the Children's Defense Fund has studied the grim effects of being trapped in a criminalizing environment from which the obstacles to escape are formidable. The Cradle to Prison Pipeline consists of a complex array of social and economic factors as well as political choices that converge to reduce the odds that poor children — especially poor black and Latino children — will grow up to become productive adults. These factors include limited access to health care (including mental health care), underperforming schools, broken child welfare and juvenile justice systems, and a toxic youth culture that praises pimps and glorifies violence.

Hardened by long terms of incarceration, released criminalized youngsters return to communities that are ill equipped to reintegrate them positively. Outcast and unemployed, they become the teachers and role models for a new crop of youngsters pushed onto the streets of America's most depressed neighborhoods. This cycle of infection makes the Cradle to Prison Pipeline one of the most damaging health problems in America today.

A major factor in determining whether 5 a child enters the prison pipeline is access to health care. Currently, nine million children in America are without health insurance (1). Among low-income communities, there is a high incidence of teen pregnancy and low-birthweight babies (1). Physical and mental developmental delays among young children are commonly left undiagnosed and often go untreated (2,3). Unlike the children from affluent families, children from low-income families rarely have access to institutions that can intervene and address their health problems (2,3).

Few public schools in economically depressed neighborhoods have the resources to recognize health issues such as dyslexia, attention deficit disorder, hyperactivity disorder, or post-traumatic stress disorder and then to provide counseling and therapy for children with these disorders (1). Instead, their behavior is more often perceived as insubordinate or disruptive than it is recognized as symptomatic of a disorder or of the environment in which these children live (1,4). In these cases, zero-tolerance disciplinary standards are frequently applied, and thousands of students are expelled and even arrested for subjectively defined behaviors such as "disorderly conduct" and "malicious mischief" (5).

We must dismantle the Cradle to Prison Pipeline now because all children are sacred. What is required are collaborative efforts at the community, municipal, and state levels.

To start with, we should demand the passage of legislation that would guarantee health care, including mental health care, to all children.

We need new investment to support proven community health delivery programs such as the National Campaign to Prevent Teen Pregnancy, which promotes community and school programs focused on delaying sexual activity (6), and the Nurse-Family Partnership, which supplies nurses for home visits to low-income, first-time mothers through their pregnancies and for two years after they give birth (7). Other valuable programs provide early intervention in cases of family violence (8). A healthy child is an empowered child. Communities should strive to replicate model umbrella programs that mentor and empower children such as the Harlem Children's Zone (9), the Boston TenPoint Coalition (10), and the CDF Freedom Schools program (11).

The effects of the Cradle to Prison Pipeline constitute a scourge of epidemic proportions. We must act to dismantle the prison pipeline now. We fail at our peril. The future of our nation is at stake.

REFERENCES

1. The state of America's children 2005. Washington (DC): Children's Defense Fund; 2005. Available from: http://www.childrensdefense.org/site/DocServer/Greenbook_2005.pdf?docID=1741

2. Manderscheid RW, Berry JT. Mental health, United States, 2004. Rockville (MD): U.S. Department of Health and Human Services, Substance Abuse and Mental Health Services Administration; 2004. Available from: http://download.ncadi.samhsa.gov/ken/pdf/SMA06-4195/CMHS_MHUS_2004.pdf

3. Burns BJ, Phillips SD, Wagner HR, Barth RP, Kolko DJ, Campbell Y, et al. Mental health need and access to mental health services by youths involved with child welfare: a national survey. *J Am Acad Child Adolesc Psychiatry* 2004;43(8):960-70.

4. Cocozza JJ, Skowyra KR. Youth with mental health disorders: issues and emerging responses. *Juvenile Justice* 2000;7(1):3-13.

5. Advancement Project, Civil Rights Project of Harvard University. Opportunities suspended: the devastating consequences of zero tolerance and school discipline. Proceeding from the National Summit on Zero Tolerance. 2000 Jun 15-16; Washington, DC. Available from: http://www.civilrightsproject.harvard.edu/research/discipline/cover_tableofcontents.pdf

6. Kirby D. No easy answers: research findings on programs to reduce teen pregnancy (summary). Washington (DC): The National Campaign to Prevent Teen Pregnancy; 1997.

7. Nurse-Family Partnership overview. Denver (CO): NFP National Service Office; [cited 2007 Feb 15]. Available from: http://www.nursefamilypartnership.org/resources/files/PDF/Fact_Sheets/NFPOverview.pdf

8. Fisher BS, editor. Violence against women and family violence: developments in research, practice, and policy. Rockville (MD): National Criminal Justice Reference Service; 2004. Available from: http://www.ncjrs.gov/pdffiles1/nij/199701.pdf

9. Harlem children's zone [homepage]. New York (NY): Harlem Children's Zone; [cited 2007 Feb 15]. Available from: http://www.hcz.org/index.html

10. Boston TenPoint Coalition [homepage]. Boston (MA): Boston TenPoint Coalition; [cited 2007 Feb 15]. Available from: http://www.bostontenpoint.org/index.html

11. Children's Defense Fund freedom schools. Washington (DC): Children's Defense Fund; [cited 2007 Feb 15]. Available from: http://www.childrensdefense.org/site/PageServer?pagename=Freedom_Schools

Topics for Critical Thinking and Writing

1. In your opinion, how effective is the opening to Marian Wright Edelman's article? Did drawing a comparison between physical diseases like tuberculosis and polio to the "criminalization of poor children" (para. 2) strike you as appropriate, or did you find it overstated? Why, or why not?

2. In paragraph 3, Edelman states that many children grow up in a "criminalizing environment." What do you think she means by that? How do children facing the obstacles she lists in this paragraph become "criminalized"?

3. Edelman also speaks of a "toxic youth culture that praises pimps and glorifies violence" (para. 3). Do you agree or disagree that youth culture contributes to the prison pipeline? Be specific in your answer.

4. In paragraph 6, Edelman discusses the problems with "zero-tolerance disciplinary standards." Research the zero-tolerance standards, particularly in schools. Investigate why they were created and what effects they have had. Then argue either for or against the use of zero-tolerance standards.

5. Research the terms "systemic racism" and "institutionalized racism" and find some examples, noting facts, statistics, and opinions about each term. In what specific ways does this kind of racism work to disempower or oppress certain groups of people? What are some of the problems that impede change in these kinds of systems?

6. The overarching idea of the "Cradle to Prison Pipeline" slogan suggests that some children in our society are virtually doomed from birth to wind up in prison. Opponents might argue that individual choices and responsibilities are at the root of crime, not environment. Do you agree with Edelman or her opponents? Support your answer.

REYNA ASKEW AND MARGARET A. WALLS

Reyna Askew graduated from the Ohio State University and Johns Hopkins University with degrees in international relations. She works as the Manager of Community Based Restoration for the Anacostia Watershed Society, an organization that focuses on resource management and the environment of the Anacostia River area in Washington, DC, and Maryland.

Margaret A. Walls is a senior fellow at Resources for the Future (RFF), an environmental research institute based in Washington, DC, whose mission is to "improve environmental, energy, and natural resource decisions through impartial economic research and policy engagement." Walls serves as the Director of the Climate Risks and Impacts Program, the Adaptation and Resilience Program, and the Environmental Justice Initiative.

This co-authored essay appeared in 2019 in *Resources*, a print and online magazine focusing on the environment and natural resources.

Diversity in the Great Outdoors: Is Everyone Welcome in America's Public Parks and Lands?

Memorial Day weekend is upon us and like many Americans, we're looking forward to the unofficial launch of the summer holiday season. Our plans might include a visit to a national or state park—nearby Shenandoah National Park in Virginia, for example, or Assateague Island National Seashore in Maryland, or closer to home, Great Falls Park.

We're not alone. Signs point to Americans having a growing interest in the outdoors. As we've discussed in podcasts and blog posts, the popularity of national parks is on the rise, with park campgrounds filled to the brim in the peak summer seasons. We also wrote about the growing outdoor recreation economy movement, including the recent establishment of outdoor recreation offices in several states to promote tourism and economic development around outdoor recreation and public lands.

Do your plans for the long weekend include visiting America's public lands? Your answer may depend on which racial or ethnic groups you belong to.

Data from the US Forest Service, National Park Service, and Fish and Wildlife Service suggest deep inequality in the ethnic/racial mix of visitors to our public lands. While the most recent US census shows that non-Hispanic whites make up approximately 63 percent of the US population, they comprise between 88 and 95 percent of all visitors to public lands (Figure 21.1). African Americans comprise only 1 to 1.2 percent of all visitors and Hispanic/Latinos between 3.8 and 6.7 percent; both groups are underrepresented as visitors to public lands relative to their presence in the population at large.

Interestingly, this disparity across racial 5 and ethnic groups is not reflected in an annual national survey by the outdoor recreation industry. The survey, which covers a wide variety of outdoor activities, including mountain biking, fishing, camping, and much more, finds that overall participation rates for Hispanics, whites, and Asian Americans are around the same at 50 percent, all higher than the participation rate for blacks at 34 percent. But it also finds that Hispanics and blacks who do recreate spend more time doing so: 87 and 86 outings per year, on average, respectively, compared to 76 for whites and 74 for Asians.

Figure 21.1 Visitors to Public Lands and US Population by Ethnic/Racial Group

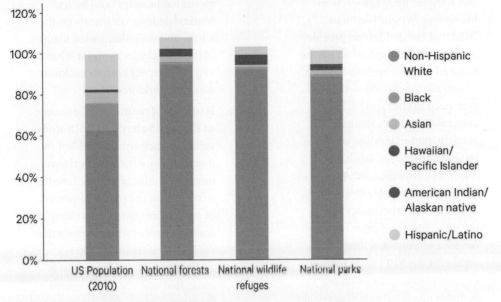

Non-Hispanic White

Black

Asian

Hawaiian/ Pacific Islander

American Indian/ Alaskan native

Hispanic/Latino

Note: The national forest and national wildlife refuge surveys allowed respondents to select more than one ethnic/racial identity, thus the totals are greater than 100 percent.

Why, then, do we see differences across racial and ethnic groups for public land visitation? If African Americans and Hispanics/ Latinos are spending time outdoors, as the survey suggests, why not in national parks, national forests, and national wildlife refuges?

BARRIERS TO PARTICIPATION IN OUTDOOR RECREATION

Researchers and outdoor advocates have pointed to several potential barriers to minority enjoyment of public lands.

1. **Affordability and Access.** Visiting remote national parks such as Glacier or Yellowstone can be expensive and time-consuming, presenting significant obstacles to lower-income Americans, especially hourly workers with limited vacation time. Even closer-to-home sites such as state parks often have entrance fees, and some outdoor recreation activities — including camping — require expensive equipment.

2. **Early Childhood Experiences.** Some experts writing on this topic have highlighted that early childhood experiences of engaging with the natural world can shape a person's views of self-confidence and enjoyment of nature well into adulthood. One of the organizations working to change this pattern, City Kids Wilderness Project, has been serving youth in the District of Columbia since 1996. They bring DC students to Jackson, Wyoming, for an intensive program of experiential learning through outdoor recreation. Check out this recent video about their work.

3. **Cultural Factors.** David Scott and KangJae Jerry Lee wrote in the George Wright Forum in 2018 that cultural factors provide people with a "template" about the kinds of outdoor recreation — and leisure more generally — they feel they need to conform to. Thus, cultural factors can facilitate participation in outdoor activities by some groups but inhibit it for others. Ambreen Tariq, an Indian-American Muslim woman, describes her experiences being the only woman of color in many outdoor recreation settings in an article for the REI Co-op Journal. For her, enjoying the outdoors includes overcoming feelings of not fitting in. She started the Instagram account @BrownPeopleCamping to promote diversity in the outdoors and help people like herself find a community. For a poignant but comical take on what it's like to be "the only one" read, J. Drew Lanham's "9 Rules for the Black Birdwatcher."

4. **Discrimination and White Racial Frames.** Prior to the 1964 Civil Rights Act, African Americans were banned from, or segregated at, public recreation sites, including national and state parks. This legacy lives on, and many minorities report feeling excluded at parks where interpretive exhibits and historical information often feature only white Americans. The problem is exacerbated by a lack of diversity among park rangers and other employees: 83 percent of National Park Service employees are white; 62 percent are male. The outdoor recreation industry is no better. Marinel de Jesus comments on the white- and male-dominated nature of the industry and how far it has to go to diversify both its customer base and workforce.

5. **Historical Trauma and Concerns of Physical Safety.** In a 2018 study, survey participants were asked to describe why African Americans might be fearful of visiting forests. According to the paper, 66 percent of participants did discuss thoughts and experiences which suggest that the historical trauma of slavery and lynchings in Jim Crow era is associated with the environment for many African Americans. In this paper, 19 year old Pharaoh explains: ". . . So, nature is not something for Black people, um they killed us a lot in nature. They would do a lot of wild things, like plantations . . . . Yeah they would hang us in trees, so maybe that's why black people don't go to the forest, don't want to see a tree." This can also be seen in the popular Billie Holiday song "Strange Fruit" where she poignantly sings "Black bodies swinging in the southern breeze, Strange fruit hanging from the poplar trees."

All of the above suggests a very real concern exists in communities of people of color regarding not having significant community support or not feeling safe in our public lands.

THE PATH FORWARD

Things are slowly starting to change, however. Women and people of color are leading the way by working to improve the way that outdoor recreation is represented in the public sphere and creating spaces where people of color feel encouraged to take part in the great outdoors. Rue Mapp, Founder and CEO of Outdoor Afro, explains in this video how her organization ties outdoor recreation activities to black history to help African Americans re-establish relationships with America's public lands. In addition to Outdoor Afro, other active groups include Latino Outdoors, The Black Outdoors, Pride Outside, and Diversify Outdoors. People who are looking to get outside but do not want to be "the only one" of their particular community might find a home in one of these organizations.

In our view, two policy moves would 10 also help. The first is increased funding for state and local parks. The Land and Water Conservation Fund (LWCF), which has been the primary source of federal funding for parks and conservation since 1965, includes a stateside program that provides grants for state and local park projects. The LWCF was recently reauthorized as part of the John Dingell Jr. Conservation, Management, and Recreation Act, but as we've shown in previous posts, the stateside LWCF program has dwindled over the years. In 2016, $110 million was distributed to the states through the LWCF, and although this was more than double the spending in the prior ten years, it was only 20 percent of the average spending (in inflation-adjusted dollars) in the first 15 years of the program. Providing more public lands closer to where people live will improve access to outdoor recreation for people with more limited financial resources and could go a long way to promoting diversity in parks and public lands.

Our second recommendation is directed at the new state outdoor recreation offices. As these offices promote economic development around public lands and outdoor recreation—which is an emphasis in all of these new offices—they should make diversity a focus. Utah, for example, provides grants for development of outdoor amenities in rural communities with revenues from a hotel tax. The state could target these funds to more diverse communities, including Native American tribal communities. New Mexico, one of the newest states to establish an outdoor recreation office, could be leading the way. The state has established an "Outdoor Equity Grant Program," which partners with private businesses to provide grants to offset some of the costs of outdoor recreation for low-income youth, including equipment costs, entrance fees, and travel costs. Following up on the effectiveness of this new first-of-its-kind state initiative will be important and provide lessons for other states.

These policy moves are not enough, however, and it is critically important not to rush into a new diversity initiative or costly new programs without first understanding the landscape, having many conversations with people in diverse communities, and developing policies and programs in tandem with the communities you intend to serve. Not doing this engagement can create a great backlash. Diversity initiatives, and other such measures are important first steps towards having more inclusive national parklands but further study must be done into the root causes for this situation in order to develop better informed policies at the national level.

Lastly, whether you are preparing for this weekend by packing up for a family road trip to visit one of America's parklands or national monuments, spending time outdoors enjoying family barbeques, playing sports, or listening to your favorite songs while sipping sweet tea on your front porch, let us remember: "This land was made for you and me."

This land is your land, this land is my land
From the California to the New York island
From the Redwood Forest, to the Gulf stream waters
This land was made for you and me

As I went walking that ribbon of highway
I saw above me that endless skyway
And saw below me that golden valley
This land was made for you and me.

—Woody Guthrie, 1940

Topics for Critical Thinking and Writing

1. In paragraph 3, Reyna Askew and Margaret A. Walls provide data showing that proportionally fewer Black people routinely participate in outdoor activities available at public recreational parks but when they do, they do more often. How does this detail speak to the interests of the audience and the authors' overall argument?

2. Choose one item from Askew and Walls's list of barriers limiting the use of public parks by minoritized groups, and examine the evidence they use to support their claims. Do you find the evidence convincing? Why or why not? What could be changed or added to better support their claims?

3. Examine Askew and Walls's proposed solutions to the problem on inequity in the use of outdoor space in the section "The Path Forward." Do you think that these are the most effective approaches? Can you add one or two more ideas?

4. Do you think the racial imbalances in recreational park usage is the result of structural racism, or is there another alternative explanation? Explain, using support from other selections in this chapter or from your own research.

TRESSIE McMILLAN COTTOM

Tressie McMillan Cottom is an associate professor in the School of Information and Library Science at the University of North Carolina–Chapel Hill and the senior faculty researcher for the Center for Information, Technology, and Public Life. She is a 2020 MacArthur Foundation Fellow whose essays appear frequently in publications such as the *Atlantic*, the *New York Times*, the *Washington Post*, and *Dissent* magazine. Cottom cohosts the podcast *Hear to Slay* with writer Roxane Gay. The essay reprinted here is from her book *Thick and Other Essays* (2019), a critically acclaimed bestseller about race, gender, and capitalism.

Know Your Whites

The origins of property rights in the United States are rooted in racial domination.

Even in the early years of the country, it was not the concept of race alone that *operated to oppress Blacks and Indians; rather, it was the interaction between conceptions of race and property that played a critical role in establishing and maintaining racial and economic subordination.*

—Cheryl I. Harris, *Whiteness as Property*[1]

Barack Obama's election was a catalyst for a level of voter suppression activities that had not been seen so clearly or disturbingly in decades.

—Carol A. Anderson, *White Rage*[2]

A year before it was real, the very idea of a President Barack Obama was ridiculous to me. I was and am southern, god bless. I am black. I come from black people who are southerners even when they were New Yorkers for a spell. We are the black American story of enslavement, rural migration, urban displacement, resistance, bootstrapping, mobility, and class fragility. In this milieu we, as a friend once described it, know our whites. To know our whites is to understand the psychology of white people and the elasticity of whiteness. It is to be intimate with some white persons but to critically withhold faith in white people categorically. It is to anticipate white people's emotions and fears and grievances, because their issues are singularly our problem. To know our whites is to survive without letting bitterness rot your soul.

That is what I was working with when I went to my first Obama house party in 2007 — a few generations' worth of lived and inherited expertise in knowing our whites. Our whites are southern, like me. Even if they spent some time in places north

and west, to become white in the South is to absorb some large part of its particular iteration of the U.S. racial hierarchy. The house party was being held in Myers Park, a lush, wealthy in-town enclave in Charlotte, North Carolina. Charlotte was my home. I knew Myers Park as a place and a cultural geography of the city's racist histories. Myers Park is gorgeous. The streets are wide. The homes are stately without being garish. The residents are mere miles from the center of the city's banking, employment, transportation, and entertainment hubs. As neighborhoods throughout Charlotte fell victim to blight during the housing crash of the 2000s, Myers Park remained stable, thriving even, with housing values continuing upward trends year over year.[3]

Myers Park is also, as one with even a cursory knowledge of how wealth works in the United States would know, the beneficiary of years of racist covenant restrictions and redlining. Myers Park is beautiful because it has encoded its whiteness into the mundane market transactions that we rarely see: zoning, planning, investment, homeowners associations. White people in Myers Park, no matter where they are from at any time in their lives, are *of* Myers Park whether they acknowledge it or not.

I grew up knowing those whites. They mostly go to private school. When they don't, they make the public high school (Myers Park High School, naturally) function like a private

---

[1] Cheryl I. Harris, "Whiteness as Property," *Harvard Law Review* (1993): 1707–91.

[2] Carol Anderson, *White Rage: The Unspoken Truth of Our Racial Divide* (New York: Bloomsbury, 2016).

[3] This should tell you everything you need to know about the neighborhood. Thinking sociologically, if you know an urban, suburban, or exurban rate of housing price change, foreclosure rates post–Great Recession, and type of neighborhood infrastructure, you should be able to intuit the community's racial and economic makeup. A stable community like this one correlates with wealth, which correlates with race in the United States. That is how we experience structural wealth inequality in our everyday lives.

school.[4] We call this opportunity hoarding, and it looks something like this: white parents use their economic privilege to purchase homes in communities that have benefited from generations of wealth privilege. That wealth privilege generates investment in streets, sidewalks, greenspace, traffic lights, clean air, proper waste treatment, and safe drinking water. When white families purchase in these neighborhoods they are also purchasing access to the local public school. That is because we assign students in the U.S. public school system, for the most part, by their home zip codes. Once enrolled in these schools by virtue of having the income to live in communities that are built on the stabilizing forces of generational wealth, these families generally prize "diversity."

They are good people. They want all the 5 children in their child's school to thrive, but they want their child to thrive just a bit more than most. To help their child thrive, these parents use their proximity to local and civic leaders to lobby their personal preferences as politically expedient positions. They gently but insistently marshal resources like teacher time, curriculum access, and extracurricular participation for their children. They donate. They volunteer. They call. They email. They make this already well-funded public school work like a private school for their child: individualized attention, personalized resources, and cumulative advantage. The opportunities these parents hoard become zero-sum for parents who cannot do the same. The families that can hoard do, and the neighborhoods in which they live benefit.

---

[4]R. L'Heureux Lewis-McCoy, *Inequality in the Promised Land: Race, Resources, and Suburban Schooling* (Stanford, CA: Stanford University Press, 2014). Amanda E. Lewis and John B. Diamond, *Despite the Best Intentions: How Racial Inequality Thrives in Good Schools* (Oxford and New York: Oxford University Press, 2015).

For a spell, Myers Park was at the heart of the nation's public relations tour for post–Civil Rights era integration. The wealthy white families of the community had mostly supported busing their students into the historically black West Charlotte High School. They believed in diversity. Once there, a rising tide of investment in the resource-starved black high school seemed to benefit all . . . but the white students benefited most. The experiment in integration lasted but thirty years.

Myers Park is typical of a national pattern of how segregated lives and intertwined cross-racial fortunes play out. But, Myers Park performs resegregation differently than some other urban-suburban enclaves, if only for how very *southern* its residents are in articulating their privilege. The homes are large but not plantation-like. They are the kinds of old homes that toothy gentrifiers on HGTV remodeling shows say have "good bones." I am almost certain "good bones" means "worth however much money this pit is about to suck from you because the neighborhood is reliably white," but I digress. Myers Park is neighborly, even to strangers, before dark. It has manners. There are porches, even if few people sit on them, preferring, instead, the safety of the backyard. Social networks are cultivated at the local church — it is the South, after all — and cemented through business partnerships. Myers Park people donate, their money and their time, to good causes. And these perfectly civil people live in intentionally cultivated, nominally diverse, in-town panopticons that need no guard in the central watchtower but whiteness.

Charlotte, North Carolina, is full of middle-class blacks, activist black people of all classes, organized third- and fourth-generation Latinos. I could not believe the Obama house party was happening in Myers Park, of all places in the city. Today I cannot imagine it anywhere else.

The party was in one of the homes usually only accessible to someone like me when, twice a year, you can pay $15 or so for one of those charity parades of homes. I was early. When I rang the bell a young white woman, still wet from a shower, told me to come on in, but no one was yet there. I sat for almost half an hour as they finished preparing, acutely aware of my social faux pas. As people arrived, of all ages and walks of life, I was the only black person until almost an hour into the house party. That is when a brother carrying a bicycle arrived with his white girlfriend.

The hosts asked for donations without   10 stuttering the way that I still do when I have to do "the ask." It was taken for granted that you had come to spend money and had money to spend. Here, a full eight years before mobile credit card payments would penetrate my black hair salon or Saturday swap meets, the hosts took mobile payments using a website. The whites in this room were all in for Obama. They talked about him like old black people talk about Martin Luther King. They loved his biography. They embraced his political mantra. They were positive he could win.

Back at home, the black people I know were positive that white people were crazy to think that he could win. My mother told me as much: "White people are crazy," The Vivian said. She, like me, knew her whites. I went home that night of the house party and told her that I had seen, not new whites, but white people doing what people do: coalescing around shared interests. Only, their interests converged with my own. They still had more money, more power than we had. They were as young as me, but lived in million-dollar estates. They would still negotiate the daily experience of racial segregation in their neighborhoods and schools and jobs, but they had,

for countless reasons, chosen this black man as "their guy." The question I could not parse for many years was why.

There is no need to rehash our national identity crisis at the election of the first African American (if not black American) U.S. president. Fox News scaled new heights of shrill paranoia. Then they built a stair lift to the top for their predominantly white, elderly audience. African Americans did not believe the election had happened until a month before the end of Obama's second, and final, term. Many black Americans, of all national origins but with shared political ideologies, struggled to find a way to critique the imperialist office without disparaging the man occupying it. Hispanic voters and Asian American voters were divided in their support by national origin, generational status, and income.[5] But in almost every ethnic community there was a strong contingent seeking their own people's story in Obama's.

The times were not idyllic, but they were as close to multicultural as the U.S. public sphere has ever felt. Those are the eight years that writer Ta-Nehisi Coates calls the "Good Negro Government period."[6] Like the eight years of Black Reconstruction some 130 years prior to his first presidential contest — one that he would win handily — Obama's Good

---

[5]Nonwhite voters went heavily for Barack Obama in both 2008 and 2012, but there were some differences within those groups. Black voters overwhelmingly voted for Obama across class, immigrant status, education, and income level. There were minor variations among Asian Americans of different national origins. For example, South Asian American voters were more solidly Obama voters than other ethnic groups. See the Asian American Legal Defense and Education Fund report, "The Asian American Vote 2012." There are similar differences among Hispanics by national origin and generational status. See Mark Hugo Lopez and Paul Taylor, "Dissecting the 2008 Electorate: Most Diverse in U.S. History," Pew Research Center's Hispanic Trends Project, April 30, 2009, http://www.pewhispanic.org/2009/04/30/dissecting-the-2008-electorate-most-diverse-in-us-history.

[6]Ta-Nehisi Coates, *We Were Eight Years in Power: An American Tragedy* (New York: One World/Ballantine, 2017).

Negro Government period was marked by black political competence and white fear. Political analyst Jamelle Bouie once said, during a joint interview we recorded for a radio program, that in the twilight of Obama's final term it occurred to him that if this safely competent black man was not good enough for white America, then he would never be.[7] It was heart-wrenching listening to Jamelle discover this fundamental truth of being black in America. And it was for me indeed a fundamental truth.

How could I explain the hope of that Myers Park house party *and* my core truth that whiteness necessitates black subjugation? This paradox — that is what it is, because these truths seem to occupy opposing sides but in reality are the same side of a Janus-faced coin — mirrored the national paradox: how could the same nation that elected Barack Obama immediately elect Donald Trump? The answer was not in Obama's blackness. Blackness is not a paradox. Blackness *is*. It has to be for whiteness, at any point in time or space, to enact its ultimate expression: elasticity.

Whiteness, the idea, the identity tethered 15 to no nation of origin, no place, no gods, exists only if it can expand enough to defend its position over every group that challenges the throne. White is being European until it needs to also be Irish because of the Polish who can eventually be white if it means that Koreans cannot. For that situational dominance to reproduce itself, there must be a steady pole. That pole is blackness. And so the paradox of how we could elect Obama and Trump is not in how black Obama is or is not. It is, instead, in how white he is (or, is not). The Obama-Trump dialectic is not progress-backlash but do-si-do; one dance, the same steps, mirroring each other, and each existing only in tandem.

Like whiteness itself, Obama was because Trump is.

White voters allowed Barack Obama to become an idea and a president because he was a fundamental projection of the paradox that defines them as white. I almost forgot once. Old trees and new whites are a seduction. But my soul remembers my grandmother's memories. It is imperative that one knows one's whites.

[7]"Obama's Legacy: Diss-ent or Diss-respect?" *Codeswitch* podcast, NPR, http://www.npr.org/sections/codeswitch/2017/02/23/51681/8239/obamas-legacy-diss-ent-or-diss-respect.

Topics for Critical Thinking and Writing

1. Examine Tressie McMillan Cottom's title and first paragraph in which she describes "knowing your whites." Why does Cottom think it is important for Black people to "know their whites?"

2. Segregation by race in schools and neighborhoods has been illegal since *Brown v. Board of Education* in 1954 and the Fair Housing Act of 1968. Given this context, is the overwhelmingly white population of affluent Myers Park, as Cottom describes it, legal?

3. Cottom references journalist Jamelle Bouie's realization near the end of Obama's second term "that if this safely competent black man was not good enough for white America, then he [Bouie] would never be" (para. 13). Restate Bouie's epiphany in your own words. How does referencing Bouie advance Cottom's argument — or not?

4. Do you think that Cottom would agree that Barack Obama's presidency was an advancement in race relations and equity? Why or why not? Use evidence from the selection to support your answer.

5. In paragraph 2, Cottom claims that "to become white in the south is to absorb some large part of its particular iteration of the US racial hierarchy." What do you think she means by this? Is racial privilege or disadvantage something that people cannot avoid inheriting?

6. Cottom claims that a "core truth [is] that whiteness necessitates black subjugation" (para. 14). What does she mean? How does whiteness *necessitate* black subjugation? Do you think racial categories themselves cause racism, or that a color-blind society would be a less racist one? Explain.

HEATHER Mac DONALD

Heather Mac Donald, educated at Stanford, Yale, and Cambridge, is a conservative columnist and Thomas W. Smith fellow at the Manhattan Institute. She is the author of *The Burden of Bad Ideas: How Modern Intellectuals Misshape Our Society* (2000), *Are Cops Racist?* (2003), and, more recently, *The War on Cops: How the New Attack on Law and Order Makes Everyone Less Safe* (2016) and *The Diversity Delusion: How Race and Gender Pandering Corrupt the University and Undermine Our Culture* (2018). Presented here is Mac Donald's 2015 written testimony before the United States Senate Judiciary Committee hearings on criminal justice reform legislation that would release some prisoners previously convicted of drug offenses on the basis of unfair sentencing guidelines and requirements.

The Myth of Criminal-Justice Racism

Chairman Grassley, Ranking Member Leahy, and members of the Committee, my name is Heather Mac Donald. I am honored to address you today regarding the Sentencing Reform and Corrections Act of 2015. I am the Thomas W. Smith fellow at the Manhattan Institute for Policy Research, a public policy think tank in New York City. I have written extensively on law enforcement and criminal justice.

Today I want to examine the broader political context of the Sentencing Reform and Corrections Act. We are in the midst of a national movement for deincarceration and decriminalization. That movement rests on the following narrative: America's criminal justice system, it is said, has become irrationally draconian, ushering in an era of so-called

"mass incarceration." The driving force behind "mass incarceration," the story goes, is a misconceived war on drugs. As President Barack Obama said in July in Philadelphia: "The real reason our prison population is so high" is that we have "locked up more and more nonviolent drug offenders than ever before, for longer than ever before." In popular understanding, prisons and jails are filled with harmless pot smokers.

The most poisonous claim in the dominant narrative is that our criminal justice system is a product and a source of racial inequity. The drug war in particular is said to be infected by racial bias. "Mass incarceration" is allegedly destroying black communities by taking fathers away from their families and imposing crippling criminal records on released convicts. Finally, prison is condemned as a huge waste of resources.

Nothing in this dominant narrative is true. Prison remains a lifetime achievement award for persistence in criminal offending. Drug enforcement is not the driving factor in the prison system, violent crime is. Even during the most rapid period of prison growth from 1980 to 1990, increased sentences for violent crime played a larger role than drug sentences in the incarceration build up. Since 1999, violent offenders have accounted for all of the increase in the national prison census.

Today, only 16 percent of state prisoners 5 are serving time for drug offenses — nearly all of them for trafficking. Drug possession accounts for only 3.6 percent of state prisoners. Drug offenders make up a larger portion of the federal prison caseload — about 50 percent — but only 13 percent of the nation's prisoners are under federal control. In 2014, less than 1 percent of sentenced drug offenders in federal court were convicted of simple drug possession; the rest were convicted of trafficking. The size of America's prison population is a function of our violent crime rate. The U.S. homicide rate is seven times higher than the combined rate of 21 Western nations plus Japan, according to a 2011 study by researchers of the Harvard School of Public Health and UCLA School of Public Health.

The most dangerous misconception about our criminal justice system is that it is pervaded by racial bias. For decades, criminologists have tried to find evidence proving that the overrepresentation of blacks in prison is due to systemic racial inequity. That effort has always come up short. In fact, racial differences in offending account for the disproportionate representation of blacks in prison. A 1994 Justice Department survey of felony cases from the country's 75 largest urban areas found that blacks actually had a lower chance

of prosecution following a felony than whites. Following conviction, blacks were more likely to be sentenced to prison, however, due to their more extensive criminal histories and the gravity of their current offense.

The drug war was not a war on blacks. It was the Congressional Black Caucus that demanded a federal response to the 1980s crack epidemic, including more severe penalties for crack trafficking. The Rockefeller drug laws in New York State were also an outgrowth of black political pressure to eradicate open-air drug markets. This local demand for suppression of the drug trade continues today. Go to any police-community meeting in Harlem, South-Central Los Angeles, or Anacostia in Washington, D.C., and you will hear some variant of the following plea: "We want the dealers off the streets, you arrest them and they are back the next day." Such voices are rarely heard in the media.

Incarceration is not destroying the black family. Family breakdown is in fact the country's most serious social problem, and it is most acute in black communities. But the black marriage rate was collapsing long before incarceration started rising at the end of the 1970s, as my colleague Kay Hymowitz has shown. Indeed, the late Senator Daniel Patrick Moynihan issued his prescient call for attention to black out-of-wedlock child-rearing in 1965, just as that era's deincarceration and decriminalization movement was gaining speed.

It is crime, not incarceration, that squelches freedom and enterprise in urban areas. And there have been no more successful government programs for liberating inner-city residents from fear and disorder than proactive policing and the incapacitation of criminals.

Compared with the costs of crime, prison 10 is a bargain. The federal system spends about $6 billion on incarceration; the state system spent $37 billion in 2010 on institutional corrections. The economic, social, and psychological costs of uncontrolled crime and drug trafficking dwarf such outlays. And prison spending is a minute fraction of the $1.3 trillion in taxpayer dollars devoted to means-tested federal welfare programs, as Senator Sessions has documented.

To be sure, the federal drug penalties are not sacrosanct. But though all sentencing schemes are ultimately arbitrary, our current penalty structure arguably has been arrived at empirically through trial and error. Sentences were increased incrementally in response to the rising crime rates of the 1960s and 1970s. Those rising crime rates were themselves the product of an earlier era of deincarceration and decriminalization. Sentences lengthened until they took a serious bite out of crime, in conjunction with the policing revolution of the 1990s.

Violent crime is currently shooting up again in cities across the country. Police officers are backing away from proactive enforcement in response to the yearlong campaign that holds that police are the greatest threat facing young black men today. Officers encounter increasing hostility and resistance when they make a lawful arrest. With pedestrian stops, criminal summons, and arrests falling precipitously in urban areas, criminals are becoming emboldened. While I do not think that the current crime increase is a result of previous changes in federal sentencing policy, it behooves the government to tread cautiously in making further changes. However, I unequivocally support the "productive activities" component of Section 202 of the Act, to the extent that it aims to engage all prisoners in work.

In closing, let me say that the committee would provide an enormous public service if it could rebut the myth that the criminal justice system is racist. Thank you for your attention.

Topics for Critical Thinking and Writing

1. Examine the features of Heather Mac Donald's testimony. In what ways is it similar to a written argumentative essay? How does it differ?

2. After opening with an account of a "dominant narrative" about the criminal justice system, Mac Donald begins paragraph 4 by saying, "Nothing in this dominant narrative is true." What are her primary arguments against that dominant narrative?

3. In paragraph 6, Mac Donald writes, "The most dangerous misconception about our criminal justice system is that it is pervaded by racial bias." Using your own research or evidence, verify Mac Donald's claim or provide a rebuttal to her ideas in this paragraph.

4. In paragraph 8, Mac Donald says, "Incarceration is not destroying the black family." Do some research on your own to discover facts and opinions on the effect of incarceration on black families and communities and use your findings to support or refute Mac Donald's claim (or take a middle ground).

5. Given the occasion of Mac Donald's testimony, do you find her an adequate source of information for lawmakers in the US Senate Judiciary Committee? If you had to present counter-evidence to the same committee following Heather Mac Donald, what would you add to further support or challenge her claims? If not you, whom would you choose to do so and why?

22

The Ethics of Appropriation:
Is It OK to Copy?

KENAN MALIK

Kenan Malik is an India-born British writer, lecturer, and broadcaster whose work on the history of thought has appeared in the *Guardian*, the *Financial Times*, the *Independent*, the *Sunday Times*, and the *New York Times*. Malik's writing on topics related to diversity, equality, and freedom of expression has been published in several books, including *The Meaning of Race: Race, History and Culture in Western Society* (1996), *Strange Fruit: Why Both Sides Are Wrong in the Race Debate* (2008), and *Multiculturalism and Its Discontents: Rethinking Diversity after 9/11* (2013). His most recent book is *The Quest for a Moral Compass: A Global History of Ethics* (2014). The following selection was published by *Al Jazeera* in 2016.

The Bane of Cultural Appropriation

Another week, another controversy about "cultural appropriation." The latest has been the furor over Justin Bieber's dreadlocks. The Bieber furor followed similar controversies over Beyoncé's Bollywood outfit, Kylie Jenner's cornrows, Canadians practicing yoga, English students wearing sombreros and American students donning Native American Halloween costumes.

Many of these controversies may seem as laughable as Bieber's locks. What they reveal, however, is how degraded have become contemporary campaigns for social justice.

Cultural appropriation is, in the words of Susan Scafidi, professor of law at Fordham University, and author of *Who Owns Culture? Appropriation and Authenticity in American Law*, "Taking intellectual property, traditional knowledge, cultural expressions, or artifacts from someone else's culture without permission." This can include the "unauthorized use of another culture's dance, dress, music, language, folklore, cuisine, traditional medicine, religious symbols, etc."

A COLONIAL PAST?

But what is it for knowledge or an object to "belong" to a culture? And who gives permission for someone from another culture to use such knowledge or forms?

The idea that the world could be divided 5 into distinct cultures, and that every culture belonged to a particular people, has its roots in late 18th-century Europe.

The Romantic movement, which developed in part in opposition to the rationalism of the Enlightenment, celebrated cultural differences and insisted on the importance of "authentic" ways of being.

For Johann Gottfried Herder, the German philosopher who best articulated the Romantic notion of culture, what made each people — or "volk" — unique was its particular language, history and modes of living. The unique nature of each volk was expressed through its "volksgeist" — the unchanging spirit of a people refined through history.

Herder was no reactionary — he was an important champion of equality — but his ideas about culture were adopted by reactionary thinkers. Those ideas became central to racial thinking — the notion of the volksgeist was transformed into the concept of racial make-up — and fueled the belief that non-Western societies were "backward" because of their "backward" cultures.

Radicals challenging racism and colonialism rejected the Romantic view of culture, adopting instead a universalist perspective. From the struggle against slavery to the anticolonial movements, the aim was not to protect one's own special culture but to create a more universal culture in which all could participate on equal terms.

ENTER IDENTITY POLITICS

In recent decades, however, the univer- 10 salist viewpoint has eroded, largely as many of the social movements that embodied that viewpoint have disintegrated. The social space vacated by that disintegration became filled by identity politics.

As the broader struggles for social transformation have faded, people have tended to retreat into their particular faiths or cultures, and to embrace more parochial forms of identity. In this process, the old cultural arguments of the racists have returned, but now rebranded as "antiracist."

But how does creating gated cultures, and preventing others from trespassing upon one's culture without permission, challenge racism or promote social justice?

Campaigners against cultural appropriation argue that when "privileged" cultures adopt the styles of "less privileged" ones they help create stereotypes of what such cultures are like, and assert racial power.

"By dressing up as a fake Indian," one Native American told white students, "you are asserting your power over us, and continuing to oppress us."

The trouble is that in making the case 15 against cultural appropriation, campaigners equally perpetuate stereotypes.

After all, to suggest that it is "authentic" for blacks to wear locks, or for Native Americans to wear a headdress, but not for whites to do so, is itself to stereotype those cultures.

Cultures do not, and cannot, work through notions of "ownership." The history of culture is the history of cultural appropriation — of cultures borrowing, stealing, changing, transforming.

Nor does preventing whites from wearing locks or practicing yoga challenge racism in any meaningful way.

What the campaigns against cultural appropriation reveal is the disintegration of the meaning of "anti-racism." Once it meant to struggle for equal treatment for all.

Now it means defining the correct eti- 20 quette for a plural society. The campaign against cultural appropriation is about policing manners rather than transforming society.

WHO IS THE AUTHORITY?

This takes us to the second question: who does the policing? Who gives permission for people of other cultures to use particular cultural forms? Who acts as the gatekeepers to gated cultures?

Most black people could probably not care less what Justin Bieber does to his hair. Inevitably, the gatekeepers are those who are outraged by Bieber's locks.

The very fact of being outraged makes one the arbiter of what is outrageous. The gatekeepers, in other words, define themselves, because they are ones who want to put up the gates.

The debates around Justin Bieber's hair or Beyoncé's Bollywood outfit are relatively trivial. But, in other contexts, the creation of gatekeepers has proved highly problematic.

In many European nations, minority groups 25 have come to be seen as distinct communities, each with their own interests, needs and desires, and each with certain so-called "community leaders" acting as their representatives.

Such leaders are frequently religious, often conservative, and rarely representative of their communities. But they wield great power as mediators between their communities and wider society. In effect, they act as gatekeepers to those communities.

Their role as gatekeepers is particularly problematic when it comes to policing not fashion styles or cuisine but ideas. Community leaders often help define what is acceptable to say about particular communities, and what is "offensive."

And notions of "offense" are often used to police not just what outsiders may say about a particular community, but to shut down debate within those communities — think of the fatwa against Salman Rushdie or the shutting down by Sikh activists of Sikh playwright Gurpreet Kaur Bhatti's play *Behzti*, which explored the role of women within Sikh communities.

The campaign against cultural appropriation is, in other words, part of the broader attempt to police communities and cultures. Those who most suffer from such policing are minority communities themselves, and in particular progressive voices within those communities.

The real fight against injustice begins 30 with ridding ourselves of our self-appointed gatekeepers.

Topics for Critical Thinking and Writing

1. Apply Susan Scafidi's definition of cultural appropriation (para. 3) to the examples offered by Kenan Malik in paragraph 1 (e.g., Justin Bieber's dreadlocks, Beyoncé's Bollywood garb). Are such fashion choices acceptable? Are some more acceptable than others? Why, or why not?

2. What factors should inform people's choices to adopt forms of dress or decoration whose origins lie in other cultures? What benefits or drawbacks, potentialities or pitfalls, are suggested by such attire? (Feel free to add your own examples.)

3. Examine Malik's account of the tensions between a Romantic view of culture and a universalist view of culture (paras. 4–9). Outline some reasons each view could be celebrated or condemned.

4. Explain Malik's thinking in paragraph 11 that "the old cultural arguments of the racists have returned, but now rebranded as 'anti-racist.'" Do you agree or disagree with Malik that people arguing against cultural appropriation can be considered "racist"? Explain your reasoning.

5. Do you agree with Malik (para. 20) that "the campaign against cultural appropriation is about policing manners rather than transforming society"? Explain.

6. In the last section of Malik's argument, he explores the negative effects of holding too firmly to the idea that communities and cultures need to be protected from offense. What does he mean? Do you think this part of his argument follows from his arguments about appropriation? Why, or why not?

7. Consider your own cultural background. Are there forms of dress, decoration, language, or rituals that you see as acceptable for others to "borrow" and others you see as unacceptable? Explain using these examples as you respond.

YO ZUSHI

Yo Zushi is a British Japanese songwriter and performer whose most recent albums are *It Never Entered My Mind* (2015) and *King of the Road* (2018). Zushi also contributes essays on culture and politics to the *New Statesman*, where the selection below was published in 2015.

What's Mine Is Yours

The policing of appearance is nothing new. In the mid-1920s, the then Mexican president, Plutarco Elías Calles, forbade Catholic priests from wearing clerical collars outdoors; more recently, on 14 September 2010, the French Senate passed the *Loi interdisant la dissimulation du visage dans l'espace public*, better known in the English-speaking world as "the burqa ban." What is curious, however, is that the latest round of strictures on how individuals can present themselves comes not from repressive, dictatorial regimes or panicked politicians but from those who consider themselves progressives: liberals united against the menace of "cultural appropriation."

In August, a student committee at Western University in Canada announced a ban on the wearing of cultural symbols such as turbans, dreadlock wigs and ethnic headdresses by white volunteers during orientation week. The sale of Native American headdresses has also been proscribed at Glastonbury Festival, after an online petition that garnered just 65 signatures persuaded organizers that offering them as a "costume" was insensitive. (The Canadian festival Bass Coast has similarly issued a prohibition on guests wearing the war bonnets.) Pharrell Williams came under fire on Twitter when he posed in a feather headdress for an *Elle* cover in 2014 — a striking image that the magazine initially boasted was the singer's "best-ever shoot" — and was forced to apologize. "I respect and honor every kind of race, background and culture," he said. "I am genuinely sorry."

From Katy Perry's adoption of geisha garb at the 2013 American Music Awards to Lena Dunham's cornrows and their supposed flaunting of racial identity theft, all cultural cross-pollination now seems to be fair game for a drubbing at the hands of the new race activists. Recently in the *Guardian*, Julianne Escobedo Shepherd denounced the adoption of the Mexican-American *chola* style — dark-outlined lips, crucifixes, elaborate fringes, teardrop tattoos — by fashion labels and the pop star Rihanna as a "fashion crime" that amounted to an "ignorant harvesting" of the self-expression of others; she then mocked Sandra Bullock's admission that she would "do anything to become more Latina." Back off, whitey.

At a time of heightened racial tensions across the world, with police shootings of black men in the United States and Islamophobia (and phobias of all kinds) seemingly on the rise, this rage against cultural appropriation is understandable: no right-minded liberal wants to cause unnecessary offense, least of all to minorities. Yet simply to point out instances of appropriation in the assumption that the process is by its nature corrosive seems to me a counterproductive, even reactionary pursuit; it serves no end but to essentialize race as the ultimate component of human identity.

I'm Japanese but I felt no anger when I read 5 that the Museum of Fine Arts in Boston was holding kimono try-on sessions to accompany its recent exhibition "Looking East: Western Artists and the Allure of Japan" — after all, it was a show that specifically set out to examine the orientalist gaze. However, some protesters (carrying signs that read "Try on the kimono, learn what it's like to be a racist imperialist today!" and "This is orientalism") evidently did. Their complaints against the show, which was organized in collaboration with NHK, Japan's national broadcaster, swiftly led to the cancellation of the "Kimono Wednesday" sessions. "We thought it would be an educational opportunity for people to have direct encounters with works of art and understand different cultures and times better," said Katie Getchell, the justifiably surprised deputy director of the museum.

"Stand against yellowface!" the protesters declaimed on blogs and on Facebook. Elsewhere, the white rapper Iggy Azalea — like Elvis and Mick Jagger before her — was accused of "blackfacing" her way to stardom, after she became the fourth solo female hip-hop artist ever to reach the top of the *Billboard* Hot 100 with her 2014 single "Fancy." At the end of that year, the African-American rapper Azealia Banks suggested that Azalea's "cultural smudging" was yet another careless instance of cross-racial stealing; that white adoption of a historically black genre had an "undercurrent of kinda like, 'F — k you.' There's always a 'f — k y'all, n — s. Y'all don't really own shit . . . not even the shit you created for yourself.' "

Many of those calling out cultural appropriation of all kinds — from clothing and hair to musical genres — seem to share this proprietorial attitude, which insists that culture, by its nature a communally forged and ever-changing project, should belong to specific peoples and not to all. Banks is doubtless correct to feel this "undercurrent" of racial persecution by an industry that prefers its stars to be white and what they sell to be black, yet there is also truth in the second part of that undercurrent: "Y'all don't really own shit." When it comes to great movements in culture, the racial interloper is not wrong. None of us can, or should, "own" hip-hop, cornrows, or the right to wear a kimono.

Speaking to the website Jezebel, the law professor Susan Scafidi of Fordham University in New York explained that appropriation involves "taking intellectual property, traditional knowledge, cultural expressions or artifacts from someone else's culture without permission." Yet such a definition seems to assume the existence of mythical central organizations with absolute mandates to represent minority groups — a black HQ, an Asian bureau, a Jewish head office — from which permissions and authorizations can be sought. More troubling is that it herds culture and tradition into the pen of a moral ownership not dissimilar to copyright, which may suit a legalistic outlook but jars with our human impulse to like what we like and create new things out of it.

Elvis liked black music. While other kids dashed around at school picnics, the juvenile Presley would sit off by himself, "plunking softly at that guitar," as one teacher later recalled. He shared with the Sun Records founder, Sam Phillips, the opinion that African-American music was of that magic kind in which "the soul of man never dies," and when he launched into a hopped-up version of Arthur Crudup's blues "That's All Right" at the tail end of a recording session in 1954, it was a natural, uncalculated act of cultural appropriation. "Elvis just started singing this song, jumping around and acting the fool," remembered the guitarist Scotty Moore, who played on the single that many credit as the foundation stone of rock'n'roll.

It wasn't the first of its kind. Rock'n'roll 10 grew organically out of the miscegenation of rhythm'n'blues and hillbilly music, and other contenders for that title include Goree Carter's "Rock Awhile" (1949) and Jackie Brenston's "Rocket '88'" (1951). Both Carter and Brenston were black — but they are now largely forgotten. The smoking gun in the periodically revived argument that Elvis should be condemned for having participated in interracial plundering is Phillips's often quoted remark: "If I could find a white man who had the Negro feel, I could make a billion dollars." Yet the studio owner's remark was, if anything, more a groan of exasperation than the blueprint for a robbery. He had tried to make a billion dollars before he recorded Elvis, with BB King, Howling Wolf and other black musicians; indeed, it was Phillips who recorded Brenston's song. The racism wasn't in the studio or cut into the record grooves. It was out there, woven into American life in the 1950s.

That tainted life was altered for the better by the emergence of rock'n'roll, whose enormous popularity forced many previously white-oriented labels to sign African-American artists and changed forever the social interactions of black and white teenagers. It gave them a common culture based less on skin color than on the spirit of youth, frightening reactionaries who were perturbed precisely by what they viewed as an unnatural cultural appropriation. After Elvis performed the "Big Mama" Thornton song "Hound Dog" on national television on 5 June 1956, Congressman Emanuel Celler stated disapprovingly, "Rock'n'roll has its place: among the colored people." Many white fans of the music, appropriators all, could not help but realize that their place and that of "colored" fans were one and the same.

What was so with rock'n'roll goes also for rap, fashion and even that packet of tortilla chips you ate at the movies or the shish kebab you had on the way home. Appropriation tests imaginary boundaries. It questions them and exposes, just as Judith Butler did in relation to gender, the performative aspects of our racial and cultural identity: much of our yellowness, brownness, blackness or whiteness is acted out and not intrinsic to our being. It shows that we can select who we are and who we want to be. By opposing it unilaterally under the banner of racial justice, activists often end up placing themselves on the side of those who insist on terrifying ideals of "purity": white and black should never mix and the Australian-born Iggy Azalea should leave rap alone. She should stick to performing . . . what, exactly? Perhaps she should consult a family tree. But how far back is she expected to go? And should we impose some sort of one-drop rule?

It is true that cultural appropriation can hurt those whose traditions, religions and ways of life have been lifted, taken out of context and repackaged as a new aesthetic trend or exotic bauble. The feather headdress, for instance, has deep symbolic value to many Native Americans and to see it balancing on the wobbly head of a drunk, white festivalgoer might feel like an insult. Yet is it a theft at all, when that original value is still felt by the Native American tribe? Little of substance has been taken away. To the white reveller, those feathers probably signify something as simple as: "I am trying my best to have fun." There is no offense intended. If it channels anything of the headdress's origins, it is no doubt a distant echo of some ancient myth that placed "Indians" as the other, the sworn enemies of the "cowboys."

Appropriations of this sort can, if unchallenged, entrench negative racial mythologies. But such myths are part of the language of human culture and their potential for harm can only truly be diffused by putting forward stronger, newer narratives about ourselves and by tackling the systemic injustices that oppress us: in law, in government, in the workplace. I can live in the knowledge that the *Mikado* myth continues to have some currency and that films, songs and books still toy with the orientalist fantasy of Japan. That is partly because their sting has been dulled by an ever-increasing understanding in the west of what real life in east Asia is like. I accept that our culture can be transformed and absorbed into the folklore of another people — and when this happens, we have only a limited claim on that folklore. Like it or not, it becomes theirs as much as ours. Sometimes, we have to let culture do its thing.

Topics for Critical Thinking and Writing

1. Examine the critique of Iggy Azalea as "'blackfacing' her way to stardom" and being guilty of "cultural smudging" (para. 6). In your opinion, should Azalea be faulted? Briefly explain your position.

2. Zushi compares the cultural appropriations of rock and roll, rap, and fashion with "that packet of tortilla chips you ate at the movies or the shish kebab you had on the way home" (para. 12). Is this comparison a form of equivocation (see "Equivocation" on p. 368)? Why, or why not?

3. Zushi writes that as a Japanese man he had little trouble accepting people trying on kimonos, a traditional Japanese fashion, at the Museum of Fine Arts in Boston, even while protestors condemned the activity, with one person's sign reading, "This is orientalism" (para. 5). In your opinion, do Zushi's race and ethnicity help or hurt his overall argument, or do they have no effect at all? Why?

4. On the whole, whose argument did you find to be more fair-minded, Malik's or Zushi's? Support your answer with evidence from the selections.

5. Do some research into the historical and cultural roots of a musical genre or style (e.g., rock, punk, rap, jazz, blues, country, or folk). Address questions related to the themes of Zushi's and Malik's essays: Were these forms based on cultural appropriation? Who, if anyone, can claim "authenticity"? Could any artists or performers be said to have stolen or misused another culture's expressions? Why or why not?

6. Select one of the examples Yo Zushi refers to in his essay and do some further research to assess general opinions on the instance or incident. What issues were at stake? Whose view do you think was most convincing, and why?

K. TEMPEST BRADFORD

K. Tempest Bradford is an award-winning teacher, media critic, and the author of the middle grade novel *Ruby Finley vs. the Interstellar Invasion*. Tempest's short fiction has appeared in multiple anthologies and magazines, including In *The Shadow of the Towers* and *Strange Horizons*. Her media criticism and essays on diversity and representation have been published at *NPR, io9, Ebony Magazine*, and more. This piece was published online at National Public Radio's Code Switch, which covers race and culture. In it, she responds to a piece written for the *New York Times* by Kenan Malik, "In Defense of Cultural Appropriation." Malik's essay "The Bane of Cultural Appropriation" appears earlier in this chapter.

Cultural Appropriation Is, in Fact, Indefensible

In June 2017, the *New York Times* published an op-ed titled "In Defense of Cultural Appropriation" in which writer Kenan Malik attempted to extol the virtues of artistic appropriation and chastise those who would stand in the way of necessary "cultural engagement." What would have happened, he argues, had Elvis Presley not been able to swipe the sounds of black musicians?

Malik is not the first person to defend cultural appropriation. He joins a long list that, most recently, has included prominent members of the Canadian literary community and author Lionel Shriver.

But the truth is that cultural appropriation is indefensible. Those who defend it either don't understand what it is, misrepresent it to muddy the conversation, or ignore its complexity — discarding any nuances and making it easy to dismiss both appropriation and those who object to it.

At the start of the most recent debate, Canadian author Hal Niedzviecki called on the readers of *Write* magazine to "Write what you don't know . . . Relentlessly explore the lives of people who aren't like you. . . . Win the Appropriation Prize." Amid the outcry over this editorial, there were those who wondered why this statement would be objectionable. Shouldn't authors "write the Other"? Shouldn't there be more representative fiction?

Yes, of course. The issue here is that 5 Niedzviecki conflated cultural appropriation and the practice of writing characters with very different identities from yourself — and they're not the same thing. Writing inclusive fiction might involve appropriation if it's done badly, but that's not a given.

Cultural appropriation can feel hard to get a handle on, because boiling it down to a two-sentence dictionary definition does no one any favors. Writer Maisha Z. Johnson offers an excellent starting point by describing it not only as the act of an individual, but an individual working within a "*power dynamic* in which members of a dominant culture take elements from a culture of people who have been systematically oppressed *by that dominant group*."

That's why appropriation and exchange are two different things, Johnson says — there's no power imbalance involved in an exchange. And when artists appropriate, they can profit from what they take, while the oppressed group gets nothing.

I teach classes and seminars alongside author and editor Nisi Shawl on Writing the Other, and the foundation of our work is that authors *should* create characters from many different races, cultures, class backgrounds, physical abilities, and genders, even if — especially if — these don't match their own. We are not alone in this. You won't find many people advising authors to only create characters similar to themselves. You will find many who say: Don't write characters from minority or marginalized identities if you are not going to put in the hard work to do it well and avoid cultural appropriation and other harmful outcomes. These are different messages. But writers often see or hear the latter and imagine that it means the former. And editorials like Niedzviecki's don't help the matter.

Complicating things even further, those who tend to see appropriation as exchange are often the ones who profit from it.

Even Malik's example involving rock and 10 roll isn't as simple as Elvis "stealing" from black artists. Before he even came along, systematic oppression and segregation in America meant black musicians didn't have access to the same opportunities for mainstream exposure, income, or success as white ones. Elvis and other rock and roll musicians were undoubtedly influenced by black innovators, but over time the genre came to be regarded as a cultural product created, perfected by, and only accessible to whites.

This is the "messy interaction" Malik breezes over in dismissing the idea of appropriation as theft: A repeating pattern that's recognizable across many different cultural spheres, from fashion and the arts to literature and food.

And this pattern is why cultures and people who've suffered the most from appropriation sometimes insist on their traditions being treated like intellectual property — it can seem like the only way to protect themselves and to force members of dominant or oppressive cultures to consider the impact of their actions.

This has led to accusations of gatekeeping by Malik and others: Who has the right to decide what is appropriation and what isn't? What does true cultural exchange look like? There's no one easy answer to either question.

But there are some helpful guidelines: The Australian Council for the Arts developed a set of protocols for working with Indigenous artists that lays out how to approach Aboriginal culture as a respectful guest, who to contact for guidance and permission, and how to proceed with your art if that permission is not granted. Some of these protocols are specific to Australia, but the key to all of them is finding ways for creativity to flourish while also reducing harm.

All of this lies at the root of why cultural 15 appropriation is indefensible. It is, without question, harmful. It is not inherent to writing representational and inclusive fiction, it is not a process of equal and mutually beneficial exchange, and it is not a way for one culture to honor another. Cultural appropriation does damage, and it should be something writers and other artists work hard to avoid, not compete with each other to achieve.

For those who are willing to do that hard work, there are resources out there. When I lecture about this, I ask writers to consider whether they are acting as Invaders, Tourists, or Guests, according to the excellent framework Nisi Shawl lays out in her essay "Appropriate Cultural Appropriation." And then I point them towards "The Cultural Appropriation Primer" and all the articles and blog posts I've collected over time on the subject of cultural appropriation, to give them as full a background in understanding, identifying, and avoiding it as I possibly can.

Because I believe that, instead of giving people excuses for why appropriation can't be avoided (it can), or allowing them to think it's no big deal (it is), it's more important to help them become better artists whose creations contribute to cultural understanding and growth that benefits us all.

Topics for Critical Thinking and Writing

1. In paragraph 3, K. Tempest Bradford states her argument boldly. Do you find this approach to be a strong rhetorical move? Why or why not? What might an effective alternative approach look like?

2. According to Bradford, why might it be objectionable for an author to write a story or novel from the perspective of a different racial or cultural group? Is it similarly objectionable for musicians to utilize the instruments, forms, or expressions of a different culture's music?

3. Reread Maisha Z. Johnson's definition of appropriation in paragraph 6. Do you agree that appropriation is particularly wrong when the group appropriating from another culture is the dominant group? Does this definition establish a double standard? Why or why not?

4. Do you think it is reasonable to define intellectual property rights for certain cultural groups' myths, traditions, and symbols? Explain your position with support from Bradford's essay.

5. Describe the similarities and differences between the kinds of appropriation Bradford discusses and those Zushi deals with. Are all kinds of appropriation equal? What kinds do you find acceptable, and why? What kinds do you not find acceptable, and why?

6. Write an essay in which you explore an example of appropriation that is exploitative and an example of appropriation that constitutes "exchange" (see para. 7). Do you think this standard of evaluation established by Bradford is a fair one?

CONOR FRIEDERSDORF

Conor Friedersdorf is a graduate of Pomona College and New York University and a regular contributor to the *Atlantic*, where he writes about politics and international affairs. This piece was published in the *Atlantic* in 2015.

A Food Fight at Oberlin College

In the winter of 2015, students at Oberlin made national headlines for casting complaints about bad dining-hall food — a perennial lament of collegians — as a problematic social-justice failure. Word spread via people who saw their behavior as political correctness run amok. *The New York Post* gleefully mocked the students "at Lena Dunham's college." On social media, many wondered if the controversy was a parody.

In fact, it is quite real.

The core student grievance, as reported by Clover Lihn Tran at *The Oberlin Review*: Bon Appétit, the food service vendor, "has a history of blurring the line between culinary diversity and cultural appropriation by modifying the recipes without respect for certain Asian countries' cuisines. This uninformed representation of cultural dishes has been noted by a multitude of students, many of who have expressed concern over the gross manipulation of traditional recipes."

One international student suffered a *sando-aggression*:

Diep Nguyen, a College first-year from Vietnam, jumped with excitement at the sight of Vietnamese food on Stevenson Dining Hall's menu at Orientation this year. Craving Vietnamese comfort food, Nguyen rushed to the food station with high hopes. What she got, however, was a total disappointment. The traditional Banh Mi Vietnamese sandwich that Stevenson Dining Hall promised turned out to be a cheap imitation of the East Asian dish.

Instead of a crispy baguette with grilled pork, pate, pickled vegetables and fresh herbs, the sandwich used ciabatta bread, pulled pork and coleslaw. "It was ridiculous," Nguyen said. "How could they just throw out something completely different and label it as another country's traditional food?"

Multiple students were dissatisfied with 5 their landlocked, Midwestern institution's take on the cuisine of an island nation with Earth's most sophisticated fishing culture:

Perhaps the pinnacle of what many students believe to be a culturally appropriative sustenance system is Dascomb Dining Hall's sushi bar. The sushi is anything but authentic for Tomoyo Joshi, a College junior from Japan, who said that the undercooked rice and lack of fresh fish is disrespectful. She added that in Japan, sushi is regarded so highly that people sometimes take years of apprenticeship before learning how to appropriately serve it.

"When you're cooking a country's dish for other people, including ones who have never tried the original dish before, you're also representing the meaning of the dish as well as its culture," Joshi said. "So if people not from that heritage take food, modify it and serve it as 'authentic,' it is appropriative."

Another student, Yasmine Ramachandra, offered a distinct complaint, saying she was compelled to join the protest "after arriving at Stevenson Dining Hall with other South Asian students on Diwali, a Hindu holiday, and finding the traditional Indian tandoori made with beef, which many Hindi people do not eat for religious reasons."

Even *Red State* grants that her grievance is legitimate.

Her grievance aside, the typical response to the controversy from observers across the ideological spectrum is weary, bemused disagreement with the students.

What exactly are they thinking?

In the ongoing debate about the state of academia, Oberlin is properly seen as an outlier, not a reflection of what most campuses are like. This story is hardly all there is to Oberlin — it's an outlying story about a small number of students plucked by the tabloid most adept at trolling its readers from the stream of campus news. There are dissenters at the school. And students at many campuses often complain about food in overwrought ways.

Still, it's possible to glean insights from the most absurd events at Oberlin as surely as it's possible to learn something about America by observing the biggest Black Friday sales, the most over-the-top displays of militarism at professional sporting events, or the most extreme reality televisions show. Every subculture and ideology has its excesses. And Oberlin, where the subculture is unusually influenced by "social justice" activism, can starkly illuminate the particular character of that ideology's excesses.

One caveat: Although it's easy to minimize college student complaints about the dining halls — especially since they're likely *much* better than what older college graduates ate in the era before sushi bars — the transition from a Japanese or Vietnamese diet to dining-hall food in Ohio would be challenging for a lot of people. At that basic level, I feel empathy for the international students, as well as for American students whose only food options leave them not wanting to eat anything. If I were an Oberlin professor, I'd be quietly amassing spices and recipes to have a few of the homesick students over for whatever they consider comfort food. And a lot of people mocking the students would have a hard time adjusting to the dining-hall cuisine of an Asian country if forced to live abroad there for a year.

But there's a flip side to my empathy. Many people relate to the complaint, "Gosh, this food is awful — can't you dining hall people make it better." Yet Oberlin culture — I feel certain that the international students did not import these modes of expression — re-framed a banal, sympathetic complaint in a way that alienated millions.

Can Oberlin insiders help explain why?

Some find the approach of the Oberlin students off-putting because it strikes them as ultimately cynical. One reader of Rod Dreher's blog at *The American Conservative* explained that reaction this way:

> Are all college students like this? Of course not. If they were, one shudders to think what they'd make of the Ramen noodle industry. Still. Better, more authentic, more flavorful foods aren't necessarily bad.

> It's a cause you might support!

> But there are no longer complaints or gripes or suggestions. Only outrage. "Hey, putting ketchup on the linguini isn't really Italian night," becomes, "You are oppressing me with your white privilege." Why? Because it works. Saying that to a college administrator is like telling a self conscious girl that she looks fat in her jeans, or telling a young fella that size really does matter and, sorry pal, you don't measure up.

> And threatening to do these things publicly.

If this *is* a cynical power play on some level, its effectiveness cannot be denied. While being mocked in the national press, the students are getting results at Oberlin:

Following claims of Campus Dining Services appropriating traditional Asian dishes, representatives from the South Asian, Vietnamese and Chinese student associations met with CDS to discuss students' concerns . . .

"They took us very seriously and were taking notes the whole time," said Clover Linh Tran, College sophomore and Vietnamese Student Association co-chair . . . "They seemed very willing to learn and fix what was offending people." Tran organized the meeting after coordinating with CDS representatives and inviting fellow students through a Facebook event.

Michele Gross, director of CDS; Eric Pecherkiewicz, campus registered dietitian; and John Klancar, Bon Appétit director of operations, were all in attendance.

The less-cynical explanation is that these students really do feel culturally disrespected by low-wage dining hall staff making do with sub-optimal ingredients.

Even observers who presume the earnestness of the students have taken aim at the substance of their beliefs, pointing out that there is nothing wrong with radically tweaking dishes from different culinary traditions — and it's particularly incoherent to complain about "appropriative" treatments of items like the bánh mi sandwich (one half expects them to protest the colonialism of the baguette rather than its absence) or General Tsao's Chicken that are themselves inseparable from cultural collisions. The dining hall is serving cheap imitations of East Asian dishes because all college campuses serve cheap imitations of *all dishes* — they're trying to feed students as cheaply as possible, and authentic bánh mis, never mind sushi, would cost much more. And, of course, East Asian students are hardly alone in being served inauthentic versions of foods they grew up eating. As the grandson of two French Cajuns, I can assure aggrieved Oberlin students that the "gumbo" and "jambalaya" I was sometimes served for campus meals was in no way authentic! (Nor was the spaghetti carbonara, nor the Danishes, nor the beef goulash.)

The avowed position of these students strikes some observers as so wrongheaded that they prefer to believe that the young people don't *really* believe what they're saying.

"I am more sympathetic to campus activists' concerns than most people here, but the 'cultural appropriation' business fills me with blind fury," another reader at Rod Dreher's blog wrote. "Mixing and matching and intermingling and borrowing and stealing and creating new traditions out of whole cloth is what America does, and in my view, it is the encapsulation of what is best about this country . . . to crap on the one thing that makes America one of the few successful multicultural countries in the world on the basis of half-understood theories is beyond infuriating. The best spin I could put on this is that these people are basically using the language of appropriation to push for better food service, but I am afraid they are serious."

So how about it, Oberlin insiders?

The majority of you aren't participating in this activist effort. Help outsiders to understand what's really going on. Should these students be understood as having an understandable desire for higher-quality food — who can blame them for urging the powers that be to feed them better? — and opportunistically co-opting the language of social justice to get their way? Or are they framing their complaints in terms of cultural appropriation and "problematic" affronts to enlightened behavior because they really believe that's what is going on?

Neither option seems quite right to me. Maybe there's another that I'm missing. Oberlin is full of intelligent people.

If there is, in fact, some opportunism to the way these students are framing their complaints, does it suggest that Oberlin would do well to better guard against the exploitation of its frequently admirable efforts to be inclusive? Or if students really believe that they are the victims of "problematic" behavior, is social-justice ideology causing them to conclude that they face more antagonism than is in fact the case?

I suppose my questions telegraph my perspective. At the very least, these students would be well served by more exposure to different ways of thinking, if only so that they can understand why so many outsiders perceive *them* to be the privileged jerks of this particular story. As an Oberlin alum commented in the student newspaper, "I worked in multiple dining halls and was friendly with many of the staff there, and out of everyone I met, maybe two of them had been out of the country before. One of them even told me that she had never seen or heard of a chickpea before she started working there. Before students start labeling the lack of authenticity of their food as 'cultural appropriation,' maybe they should take a step back and think about the likely differences between themselves and the people who are preparing it."

Freddie de Boer put it more pointedly:

> an undergrad at a $50K/year liberal arts college berating cafe workers making $12/hour in the name of social justice on a human face forever[1]
>
> — Fredrik deBoer (@freddiedeboer)
> December 19, 2015

These critiques may be harsh, but are not grounded in antagonism toward the students. Were I an Oberlin administrator, I'd diligently inquire into any complaints about poor food quality and negotiate for the best fare possible, given cost constraints, even if students expressed their dissatisfaction in an off-putting manner.

But I like to think I'd call them on their nonsense, too.

It seems to me that staff and administrators at Oberlin ill-serve these students insofar as they accommodate behavior of this sort without offering any critique in response. After all, beyond allowing them to persist in their highly dubious and wildly unpopular beliefs, they're training students to air grievances in a way that will be counterproductive — and thus serve them ill — *everywhere except college campuses*. As de Boer wrote, "I'm a college educator. It's the only job I ever wanted. It's my job to take college activists seriously. And this reflects bigger problems . . . life is full of political injustice, but also full of just sucky and disappointing shit, and you need to know the difference . . . I have this crazy hang up: I care about student activists so much, I pay attention to whether their tactics can actually win or not."

I understand why some observers are inclined to defend young people when they become objects of ridicule in the *New York Post*. I certainly oppose demonizing these students. But constructive criticism is not only legitimate, it is salutary. It confronts students who've been acculturated into a seductive ideology with the diversity of thought they need to refine their ideas. From the outside, Oberlin seems unable to provide dissent in anything

---

[1]Reference to George Orwell's novel *1984*, in which the dystopian future is pictured as "a boot stamping on a human face forever." [Editors' note]

like the quality and quantity needed to prepare these young people for the enormous complexity of life in a diverse society, where few

defer to claims just because they are expressed in the language of social justice.

Is that how it looks from the inside, too?

Topics for Critical Thinking and Writing

1. Examine the argument made by Clover Lihn Tran in paragraph 3. Is it a reasonable request that culture-specific foods be served in accordance with a standard of authenticity? Is it reasonable to argue that failing to establish such a standard constitutes appropriation and is therefore offensive? Think of some other grounds upon which an argument for food quality standards could be made.

2. Do you think there is a difference in the critique made by Tomoyo Joshi related to sushi (para. 5) and the critique made by Yasmine Ramachandra about the tandoori (para. 6)? Explain.

3. How does Conor Friedersdorf characterize the students at Oberlin who argued for more authentic food and charged the college and the cafeteria with appropriation and cultural insensitivity? Explain why you agree or disagree with Friedersdorf's characterization.

4. Do you agree with Friedersdorf that the Oberlin students working for improved food need to be "call[ed] out" (para. 28)? Do you think the author does so successfully? Explain your answers.

5. Consider a situation in which a person of one cultural or ethnic background sought to open a restaurant that prepared the cuisine of another cultural or ethnic group. What kinds of factors would matter most in judging whether or not the effort was appropriative or not?

KENNETH GOLDSMITH

Kenneth Goldsmith is an American poet, writer, musician, DJ, and performance artist. In 2007, a documentary feature on his art, *Sucking on Words*, premiered at the British Library, and in 2013, he became the Museum of Modern Art's first poet laureate. Goldsmith teaches in the English department at the University of Pennsylvania, where he is senior editor of PennSound, an online poetry archive. The selection below was published in the *Chronicle of Higher Education* in the lead-up to the release of Goldsmith's book, *Uncreative Writing: Managing Language in the Digital Age* (2012).

Uncreative Writing

In 1969 the conceptual artist Douglas Huebler wrote, "The world is full of objects, more or less interesting; I do not wish to add any more." I've come to embrace Huebler's idea, though it might be retooled as: "The world is full of texts, more or less interesting; I do not wish to add any more."

It seems an appropriate response to a new condition in writing: With an unprecedented amount of available text, our problem is not needing to write more of it; instead, we must learn to negotiate the vast quantity that exists. How I make my way through this thicket of information — how I manage it, parse it, organize and distribute it — is what distinguishes my writing from yours.

The prominent literary critic Marjorie Perloff has recently begun using the term "unoriginal genius" to describe this tendency emerging in literature. Her idea is that, because of changes brought on by technology and the Internet, our notion of the genius — a romantic, isolated figure — is outdated. An updated notion of genius would have to center around one's mastery of information and its dissemination. Perloff has coined another term, "moving information," to signify both the act of pushing language around as well as the act of being emotionally moved by that process. She posits that today's writer resembles more a programmer than a tortured genius, brilliantly conceptualizing, constructing, executing, and maintaining a writing machine.

Perloff's notion of unoriginal genius should not be seen merely as a theoretical conceit but rather as a realized writing practice, one that dates back to the early part of the 20th century, embodying an ethos in which the construction or conception of a text is as important as what the text says or does. Think, for example, of the collated, note-taking practice of Walter Benjamin's *Arcades Project*[1] or the mathematically driven constraint-based works by Oulipo[2], a group of writers and mathematicians.

Today technology has exacerbated these mechanistic tendencies in writing (there are, 5

for instance, several Web-based versions of Raymond Queneau's 1961 laboriously hand-constructed *Hundred Thousand Billion Poems*), inciting younger writers to take their cues from the workings of technology and the Web as ways of constructing literature. As a result, writers are exploring ways of writing that have been thought, traditionally, to be outside the scope of literary practice: word processing, databasing, recycling, appropriation, intentional plagiarism, identity ciphering, and intensive programming, to name just a few.

In 2007 Jonathan Lethem published a pro-plagiarism, plagiarized essay in *Harper's* titled, "The Ecstasy of Influence: A Plagiarism." It's a lengthy defense and history of how ideas in literature have been shared, riffed, culled, reused, recycled, swiped, stolen, quoted, lifted, duplicated, gifted, appropriated, mimicked, and pirated for as long as literature has existed. Lethem reminds us of how gift economies, open-source cultures, and public commons have been vital for the creation of new works, with themes from older works forming the basis for new ones. Echoing the cries of free-culture advocates such as Lawrence Lessig and Cory Doctorow, he eloquently rails against copyright law as a threat to the lifeblood of creativity. From Martin Luther King Jr.'s sermons to Muddy Waters's blues tunes, he showcases the rich fruits of shared culture. He even cites examples of what he had assumed were his own "original" thoughts, only later to realize — usually by Googling — that he had unconsciously absorbed someone else's ideas that he then claimed as his own.

It's a great essay. Too bad he didn't "write" it. The punchline? Nearly every word and idea was borrowed from somewhere else — either appropriated in its entirety or rewritten by Lethem. His essay is an example of "patchwriting," a way of weaving together various shards of

---

[1]*Arcades Project* Walter Benjamin's (1892–1940) collected notes and observations of the Parisian arcades, published posthumously in 1999. [All notes are the editors'.]

[2]**Oulipo** A group of French experimental writers and mathematicians founded in 1960 who created innovative writing forms (e.g., poems with only one vowel).

other people's words into a tonally cohesive whole. It's a trick that students use all the time, rephrasing, say, a Wikipedia entry into their own words. And if they're caught, it's trouble: In academia, patchwriting is considered an offense equal to that of plagiarism. If Lethem had submitted this as a senior thesis or dissertation chapter, he'd be shown the door. Yet few would argue that he didn't construct a brilliant work of art — as well as writing a pointed essay — entirely in the words of others. It's the way in which he conceptualized and executed his writing machine — surgically choosing what to borrow, arranging those words in a skillful way — that wins us over. Lethem's piece is a self-reflexive, demonstrative work of unoriginal genius.

Lethem's provocation belies a trend among younger writers who take his exercise one step further by boldly appropriating the work of others without citation, disposing of the artful and seamless integration of Lethem's patchwriting. For them, the act of writing is literally moving language from one place to another, proclaiming that context is the new content. While pastiche and collage have long been part and parcel of writing, with the rise of the Internet plagiaristic intensity has been raised to extreme levels.

Over the past five years, we have seen a retyping of Jack Kerouac's *On the Road* in its entirety, a page a day, every day, on a blog for a year; an appropriation of the complete text of a day's copy of *The New York Times* published as a 900-page book; a list poem that is nothing more than reframing a listing of stores from a shopping-mall directory into a poetic form; an impoverished writer who has taken every credit-card application sent to him and bound them into an 800-page print-on-demand book so costly that he can't afford a copy; a poet who has parsed the text of an entire 19th-century book on grammar according to its own

methods, even down to the book's index; a lawyer who re-presents the legal briefs of her day job as poetry in their entirety without changing a word; another writer who spends her days at the British Library copying down the first verse of Dante's *Inferno* from every English translation that the library possesses, one after another, page after page, until she exhausts the library's supply; a writing team that scoops status updates off social-networking sites and assigns them to the names of deceased writers ("Jonathan Swift has got tix to the Wranglers game tonight"), creating an epic, never-ending work of poetry that rewrites itself as frequently as Facebook pages are updated; and an entire movement of writing, called Flarf, that is based on grabbing the worst of Google search results: the more offensive, the more ridiculous, the more outrageous, the better.

These writers are language hoarders; their projects are epic, mirroring the gargantuan scale of textuality on the Internet. While the works often take an electronic form, paper versions circulate in journals and zines, purchased by libraries, and received by, written about, and studied by readers of literature. While this new writing has an electronic gleam in its eye, its results are distinctly analog, taking inspiration from radical modernist ideas and juicing them with 21st-century technology.

Far from this "uncreative" literature being a nihilistic, begrudging acceptance — or even an outright rejection — of a presumed "technological enslavement," it is a writing imbued with celebration, ablaze with enthusiasm for the future, embracing this moment as one pregnant with possibility. This joy is evident in the writing itself, in which there are moments of unanticipated beauty — some grammatical, others structural, many philosophical: the wonderful rhythms of repetition, the spectacle of the mundane reframed as literature, a reorientation to the poetics of time, and fresh perspectives on readerliness, to name just a few. And then there's emotion: yes, emotion. But far from being coercive or persuasive, this writing delivers emotion obliquely and unpredictably, with sentiments expressed as a result of the writing process rather than by authorial intention. . . .

While home computers have been around for about two decades, and people have been cutting and pasting all that time, it's the sheer penetration and saturation of broadband that makes the harvesting of masses of language easy and tempting. On a dial-up, although it was possible to copy and paste words, in the beginning texts were doled out one screen at a time. And even though it was text, the load time was still considerable. With broadband, the spigot runs 24/7.

By comparison, there was nothing native to typewriting that encouraged the replication of texts. It was slow and laborious to do so. Later, *after* you had finished writing, you could make all the copies you wanted on a Xerox machine. As a result, there was a tremendous amount of 20th-century postwriting print-based *detournement:*[3] William S. Burroughs's cutups and fold-ins and Bob Cobbing's distressed mimeographed poems are prominent examples. The previous forms of borrowing in literature, collage, and pastiche — taking a word from here, a sentence from there — were developed based on the amount of labor involved. Having to manually retype or hand-copy an entire book on a typewriter is one thing; cutting and pasting an entire book with three keystrokes — select all/copy/paste — is another.

Clearly this is setting the stage for a literary revolution.

Or is it? From the looks of it, most writing proceeds as if the Internet had never happened. The literary world still gets regularly scandalized by age-old bouts of fraudulence, plagiarism, and hoaxes in ways that would make, say, the art, music, computing, or science worlds chuckle with disbelief. It's hard to imagine the James Frey or J.T. Leroy scandals[4] upsetting anybody familiar with the sophisticated, purposely fraudulent provocations of Jeff Koons or the rephotographing of advertisements by Richard Prince, who was awarded a Guggenheim retrospective for his plagiaristic tendencies. Koons and Prince began their careers by stating upfront that they were appropriating and being intentionally "unoriginal," whereas Frey and Leroy — even after they were caught — were still passing off their works as authentic, sincere, and personal statements to an audience clearly craving such qualities in literature. The ensuing dance was comical. In Frey's case, Random House was sued and had to pay hundreds of thousands of dollars in legal fees and thousands to readers who felt deceived. Subsequent printings of the book now include a disclaimer informing readers that what they are about to read is, in fact, a work of fiction.

Imagine all the pains that could have been avoided had Frey or Leroy taken a Koonsian tack from the outset and admitted that their strategy was one of embellishment, with dashes of inauthenticity, falseness, and unoriginality thrown in. But no.

---

[3]*Detournement* (Fr., "hijacking; rerouting") A critical concept and technique of performing a variation on an existing text or artwork to resist its original meanings.

[4]**James Frey or J.T. Leroy scandals** Frey (b. 1961) was disgraced by plagiarism and falsification charges for his 2001 memoir, *A Million Little Pieces.* J.T. Leroy, after three autobiographical books, was discovered to be a persona invented by the American writer Laura Albert (b. 1965).

Nearly a century ago, the art world put to rest conventional notions of originality and replication with the gestures of Marcel Duchamp's ready-mades, Francis Picabia's mechanical drawings, and Walter Benjamin's oft-quoted essay "The Work of Art in the Age of Mechanical Reproduction." Since then, a parade of blue-chip artists from Andy Warhol to Matthew Barney have taken these ideas to new levels, resulting in terribly complex notions of identity, media, and culture. These, of course, have become part of mainstream art-world discourse, to the point where counterreactions based on sincerity and representation have emerged.

Similarly, in music, sampling — entire tracks constructed from other tracks — has become commonplace. From Napster to gaming, from karaoke to torrent files, the culture appears to be embracing the digital and all the complexity it entails — with the exception of writing, which is still mostly wedded to promoting an authentic and stable identity at all costs.

I'm not saying that such writing should be discarded: Who hasn't been moved by a great memoir? But I'm sensing that literature — infinite in its potential of ranges and expressions — is in a rut, tending to hit the same note again and again, confining itself to the narrowest of spectrums, resulting in a practice that has fallen out of step and is unable to take part in arguably the most vital and exciting cultural discourses of our time. I find this to be a profoundly sad moment — and a great lost opportunity for literary creativity to revitalize itself in ways it hasn't imagined. . . .

For the past several years, I've taught a 20 class at the University of Pennsylvania called "Uncreative Writing." In it, students are penalized for showing any shred of originality and creativity. Instead they are rewarded for plagiarism, identity theft, repurposing papers, patchwriting, sampling, plundering, and stealing. Not surprisingly, they thrive. Suddenly what they've surreptitiously become expert at is brought out into the open and explored in a safe environment, reframed in terms of responsibility instead of recklessness.

We retype documents and transcribe audio clips. We make small changes to Wikipedia pages (changing an "a" to "an" or inserting an extra space between words). We hold classes in chat rooms, and entire semesters are spent exclusively in Second Life.[5] Each semester, for their final paper, I have them purchase a term paper from an online paper mill and sign their name to it, surely the most forbidden action in all of academia. Students then must get up and present the paper to the class as if they wrote it themselves, defending it from attacks by the other students. What paper did they choose? Is it possible to defend something you didn't write? Something, perhaps, you don't agree with? Convince us.

All this, of course, is technology-driven. When the students arrive in class, they are told that they must have their laptops open and connected. And so we have a glimpse into the future. And after seeing what the spectacular results of this are, how completely engaged and democratic the classroom is, I am more convinced that I can never go back to a traditional classroom pedagogy. I learn more from the students than they can ever learn from me. The role of the professor now is part party host, part traffic cop, full-time enabler.

The secret: the suppression of self-expression is impossible. Even when we do something as seemingly "uncreative" as retyping a few pages, we express ourselves in a variety of ways. The act of choosing and

---

[5] **Second Life** An online multiuser virtual world launched in 2003.

reframing tells us as much about ourselves as our story about our mother's cancer operation. It's just that we've never been taught to value such choices.

After a semester of my forcibly suppressing a student's "creativity" by making her plagiarize and transcribe, she will tell me how disappointed she was because, in fact, what we had accomplished was not uncreative at all; by not being "creative," she had produced the most creative body of work in her life. By taking an opposite approach to creativity — the most trite, overused, and ill-defined concept in a writer's training — she had emerged renewed and rejuvenated, on fire and in love again with writing.

Having worked in advertising for many 25 years as a "creative director," I can tell you that, despite what cultural pundits might say, creativity — as it's been defined by our culture, with its endless parade of formulaic novels, memoirs, and films — is the thing to flee from, not only as a member of the "creative class" but also as a member of the "artistic class." At a time when technology is changing the rules of the game in every aspect of our lives, it's time for us to question and tear down such clichés and reconstruct them into something new, something contemporary, something — finally — relevant.

Clearly, not everyone agrees. Recently, after I finished giving a lecture at an Ivy League university, an elderly, well-known poet, steeped in the modernist tradition, stood up in the back of the auditorium and, wagging his finger at me, accused me of nihilism and of robbing poetry of its joy. He upbraided me for knocking the foundation out from under the most hallowed of grounds, then tore into me with a line of questioning I've heard many times before: If everything can be transcribed and then presented as literature, then what makes one work better than another? If it's a matter of simply cutting and pasting the entire Internet into a Microsoft Word document, where does it end? Once we begin to accept all language as poetry by mere reframing, don't we risk throwing any semblance of judgment and quality out the window? What happens to notions of authorship? How are careers and canons established, and, subsequently, how are they to be evaluated? Are we simply re-enacting the death of the author, a figure that such theories failed to kill the first time around? Will all texts in the future be authorless and nameless, written by machines for machines? Is the future of literature reducible to mere code?

Valid concerns, I think, for a man who emerged from the literary battles of the 20th century victorious. The challenges to his generation were just as formidable. How did they convince traditionalists that disjunctive uses of language, conveyed by exploded syntax and compound words, could be equally expressive of human emotion as time-tested methods? Or that a story need not be told as strict narrative in order to convey its own logic and sense? And yet, against all odds, they persevered.

The 21st century, with its queries so different from those of the last, finds me responding from another angle. If it's a matter of simply cutting and pasting the entire Internet into a Microsoft Word document, then what becomes important is what you — the author — decide to choose. Success lies in knowing what to include and — more important — what to leave out. If all language can be transformed into poetry by merely reframing — an exciting possibility — then she who reframes words in the most charged and convincing way will be judged the best. . . .

In 1959 the poet and artist Brion Gysin claimed that writing was 50 years behind painting. He might still be right: In the art world, since Impressionism, the avant-garde has been the mainstream. Innovation and risk taking have been consistently rewarded. But, in spite of the successes of modernism, literature has remained on two parallel tracks, the mainstream and the avant-garde, with the two rarely intersecting. Now the conditions of digital culture have unexpectedly forced a collision, scrambling the once-sure footing of both camps. Suddenly we all find ourselves in the same boat, grappling with new questions concerning authorship, originality, and the way meaning is forged.

Topics for Critical Thinking and Writing

1. Does the concept of "cultural appropriation" undermine Kenneth Goldsmith's endorsement of a shared information economy open for "sampling, plundering, and stealing" (para. 20)? Why or why not?

2. Is there a difference between creative, literary, or artistic forms of "theft" (borrowing, sampling, appropriating) and forms of plagiarism in argumentative writing? If so, characterize the difference(s), and explain why one form is "worse" than another. If you think there are no substantial differences, explain why.

3. Is it fair that the novelist Jonathan Lethem published an entirely plagiarized essay in a national magazine (para. 7) while a student who might write the same essay for a literature course would likely be charged with plagiarism? Explain your answer.

4. Reread the descriptions of conceptual art projects Goldsmith lists in paragraph 9. Do you think these projects rise to the level of art? Explain why or why not.

5. Experiment with a type of writing Goldsmith would describe as "uncreative writing": that is, adopt, appropriate, reuse, or steal another type of writing and reframe it in such a way that "the construction or conception of [the] text is as important as what the text says or does" (para. 4). Then reflect on your project, explaining your writing choices and experience and how effective you think the outcome is.

ANDREA PITZER

Andrea Pitzer graduated from Georgetown University's School of Foreign Service in 1994 and went on to study journalism at MIT and Harvard University. Her writing has appeared in publications such as the *Washington Post*, the *Daily Beast*, *Vox*, *USA Today*, *McSweeney's*, and *Lapham's Quarterly*, and she has published three books, *The Secret History of Vladimir Nabokov* (2013), *One Long Night: A Global History of Concentration Camps* (2017), and *Icebound: Shipwrecked at the End of the World* (2022). This essay on the iconic singer and songwriter Bob Dylan appeared in *Slate* in 2013.

Bob Dylan is one of America's most celebrated singers and songwriters. His songs include "Blowin' in the Wind" (1963), "The Times They Are A-Changin'" (1963), and "Like a Rolling Stone" (1965), which was designated the number one rock and roll song of all time by *Rolling Stone* magazine in 2011. Dylan has won numerous prestigious musical awards, including three Grammys for Album of the Year (1973, 1998, and 2002) and the prestigious Grammy for Lifetime Achievement in 1992. He was inducted in the Rock and Roll Hall Fame in 1988; won the National Book Award for his autobiography, *Chronicles: Volume One*, in 2004; and was awarded the Nobel Prize in Literature in 2016.

The Freewheelin' Bob Dylan

If a songwriter can win the Nobel Prize for literature, can CliffsNotes be art? During his official lecture recorded on June 4, 2017, laureate Bob Dylan described the influence on him of three literary works from his childhood: *The Odyssey, All Quiet on the Western Front,* and *Moby-Dick*. Soon after, writer Ben Greenman noted that in his lecture Dylan seemed to have invented a quote from *Moby-Dick*.

Those familiar with Dylan's music might recall that he winkingly attributed fabricated quotes to Abraham Lincoln in his "Talkin' World War III Blues." So Dylan making up an imaginary quote is nothing new. However, I soon discovered that the *Moby-Dick* line Dylan dreamed up last week seems to be cobbled together out of phrases on the website Spark-Notes, the online equivalent of CliffsNotes.

In Dylan's recounting, a "Quaker pacifist priest" tells Flask, the third mate, "Some men who receive injuries are **led to God, others are led to bitterness**" (my emphasis). No such line appears anywhere in Herman Melville's novel. However, SparkNotes' character list describes the preacher using similar phrasing, as "someone whose trials have **led him toward God rather than bitterness**" (again, emphasis mine).

Following up on this strange echo, I began delving into the two texts side by side and found that many lines Dylan used throughout his Nobel discussion of *Moby-Dick* appear to have been cribbed even more directly from the site. The SparkNotes summary for *Moby-Dick* explains, "One of the ships . . . carries Gabriel, a crazed prophet who predicts doom." Dylan's version reads, "There's a crazy prophet, Gabriel, on one of the vessels, and he predicts Ahab's doom."

Shortly after, the SparkNotes account 5 relays that "Captain Boomer has lost an arm in an encounter with Moby Dick. . . . Boomer, happy simply to have survived his encounter, cannot understand Ahab's lust for vengeance." In his lecture, Dylan says, "Captain Boomer — he lost an arm to Moby. But . . . he's happy to have survived. He can't accept Ahab's lust for vengeance."

Across the 78 sentences in the lecture that Dylan spends describing *Moby-Dick*, even a cursory inspection reveals that more than a dozen of them appear to closely resemble lines from the SparkNotes site. And most of the key shared phrases in these passages (such as "Ahab's lust for vengeance" in the above lines) do not appear in the novel *Moby-Dick* at all.

Dylan's Nobel Lecture	SparkNotes For *Moby-Dick*
(78 sentences appear in the *Moby-Dick* portion of Dylan's talk.)	**(At least 20 sentences bear some similarity to passages from SparkNotes.)**
"Ahab's got a wife and child back in Nantucket that he reminisces about now and then."	" . . . musing on his wife and child back in Nantucket." **(The phrase "wife and child back in Nantucket" does not appear in the novel.)**
"The ship's crew is made up of men of different races"	" . . . a crew made up of men from many different countries and races."
"He calls Moby the emperor, sees him as the embodiment of evil."	" . . . he sees this whale as the embodiment of evil." **(The phrase "embodiment of evil" does not appear in the novel itself.)**
"Ahab encounters other whaling vessels, presses the captains for details about Moby."	" . . . the ship encounters other whaling vessels. Ahab always demands information about Moby Dick from their captains." **(The phrase "encounters other whaling vessels" does not appear in the novel.)**
"There's a crazy prophet, Gabriel, on one of the vessels, and he predicts Ahab's doom."	"One of the ships . . . carries Gabriel, a crazed prophet who predicts doom." **(Neither "predicts doom" nor "predicts Ahab's doom" appears in the novel.)**
"Another ship's captain — Captain Boomer — he lost an arm to Moby. But he tolerates that, and he's happy to have survived. He can't accept Ahab's lust for vengeance."	" . . . a whaling ship whose skipper, Captain Boomer, has lost an arm in an encounter with Moby Dick. . . . Boomer, happy simply to have survived his encounter, cannot understand Ahab's lust for vengeance." **(Neither "lost an arm" nor "lust for vengeance" appears in the novel.)**

(continues on next page)

Dylan's Nobel Lecture	SparkNotes For *Moby-Dick*
"Stubb gives no significance to anything."	"Stubb . . . refusing to assign too much significance to anything." **(The phrase "significance to anything" does not appear in the novel.)**
"A Quaker pacifist priest, who is actually a bloodthirsty businessman, tells Flask, 'Some men who receive injuries are led to God, others are led to bitterness.'"	" . . . a bloodthirstiness unusual for Quakers, who are normally pacifists." "... someone whose trials have led him toward God rather than bitterness." **(The above are from adjacent entries in the character list; the Flask quote does not appear in the novel, nor does the word pacifist.)**
"Tashtego says that he died and was reborn. His extra days are a gift. He wasn't saved by Christ, though, he says he was saved by a fellow man and a non-Christian at that. He paradies the resurrection."	"Tashtego . . . has died and been reborn, and any extra days of his life are a gift. His rebirth also parodies religious images of resurrection. Tashtego is 'delivered' from death not by Christ but by a fellow man — a non-Christian at that." **(Neither "reborn" nor "non-Christian" appears in the novel.)**
"Finally, Ahab spots Moby. . . . Boats are lowered. . . . Moby attacks Ahab's boat and destroys it. Next day, he sights Moby again. Boats are lowered again. Moby attacks Ahab's boat again."	"Ahab finally sights Moby Dick. The harpoon boats are launched, and Moby Dick attacks Ahab's harpoon boat, destroying it. The next day, Moby Dick is sighted again, and the boats are lowered once more . . . Moby Dick again attacks Ahabs boat." **(In the novel, this sequence covers several pages of text.)**
"Moby attacks one more time, ramming the *Pequod* and sinking it. Ahab gets tangled up in the harpoon lines and is thrown out of his boat into a watery grave."	"Moby Dick rams the *Pequod* and sinks it. Ahab is then caught in a harpoon line and hurled out of his harpoon boat to his death." **(In the novel, this is similarly a much longer passage and is described quite differently. For instance, the verb ram doesn't appear at all.)**

I reached out to Columbia, Dylan's record label, to try to connect with Dylan or his management for comment, but as of publication time, I have not heard back.

Theft in the name of art is an ancient tradition, and Dylan has been a magpie since the 1960s. He has also frequently been open about his borrowings. In 2001, he even released an album titled *"Love and Theft,"* the quotation marks seeming to imply that the album title was itself taken from Eric Lott's acclaimed history of racial appropriation, *Love & Theft:*

Blackface Minstrelsy and the American Working Class.

When he started out, Dylan absorbed classic tunes and obscure compositions alike from musicians he met, recording versions that would become more famous than anything by those who taught him the songs or even the original songwriters. His first album included two original numbers and 11 covers.

Yet in less than three years, he would learn to warp the Americana he collected into stupefyingly original work. Throwing everything from electric guitar and organ to tuba into the musical mix, he began crafting lyrics that combined machine-gun metaphor with motley casts of characters. Less likely to copy whole verses by then, his drive-by invocations of everything from the biblical Abraham to Verlaine and Rimbaud became more hit-and-run than kidnapping. The lyrics accumulated into chaotic, juggling poetry from a trickster willing to drop a ball sometimes. They worked even when they shouldn't have.

In the past several years, Dylan seems to have expanded his appropriation. His 2004 memoir *Chronicles: Volume One* is filled with unacknowledged attributions. In more recent years, he has returned to recording covers, as many legends do. In Dylan's case, his past three albums (five discs in all) have been composed of standards.

Dylan remains so reliant on appropriation that tracing his sourcing has become a cottage industry. For more than a decade, writer Scott Warmuth, an admiring Ahab in pursuit, has tracked Dylan lyrics and writings to an astonishing range of texts, from multiple sentences copied out of a New Orleans travel brochure to lifted phrases and imagery from former Black Flag frontman Henry Rollins. Warmuth dove into Dylan's Nobel

lecture last week, too, and found that the phrase "faith in a meaningful world" from the CliffsNotes description of *All Quiet on the Western Front* also shows up in Dylan's talk (but not in the book).

Even many of the paintings Dylan produces as an artist are reproductions of well-known images, such as a photo from Henri Cartier-Bresson. For Dylan, recapitulation has replaced invention.

If the *Moby-Dick* portion of his Nobel lecture was indeed cribbed from SparkNotes, then what is the world to make of it? Perhaps the use of SparkNotes can be seen as a sendup of the prestige-prize economy. Either way, through Dylan's Nobel lecture, SparkNotes material may well join Duchamp's urinal and Andy Warhol's fake Brillo pad boxes as a functional commodity now made immortal.

It's worth mentioning that Dylan turned in his lecture just before the six-month deadline, ensuring that he would get paid. In the interest of settling any potential moral debt, I would encourage him to throw some of his $923,000 prize to whoever wrote the original version of the online summary.

In the meantime, I asked a few academics for their thoughts on whether Dylan had committed punishable literary theft. After reviewing the similarities, they gave mixed marks. Longtime Dylan fan and George Washington University English professor Dan Moshenberg told me no alarm bells went off for him while reviewing the passages. Gwynn Dujardin, an English professor from Queen's University in Kingston, Ontario, had more issues with Dylan's approach, noting the irony that "Dylan is cribbing [from] a contemporary publication that is under copyright instead of from *Moby-Dick* itself, which is in the public domain." A final reviewer, Juan Martinez, a literature professor at Northwestern University, said, "If Dylan was in my class and he submitted an essay with these plagiarized bits, I'd fail him."

Topics for Critical Thinking and Writing

1. Andrea Pitzer draws her title from the title of Bob Dylan's 1963 album, *The Freewheelin' Bob Dylan*. How does her title support her argument?

2. According to Pitzer, is there a difference between appropriation of another's work and plagiarism? Explain your answer.

3. If "theft in art is an ancient tradition," as Pitzer writes in paragraph 8, do you think Bob Dylan's appropriations in his Nobel speech are just another example of the artist at work? Or is his appropriation of language from SparkNotes a form of "cheating"? Explain your view.

4. In the final sentence of this essay, a literature professor is quoted saying that he would fail Bob Dylan if Dylan had turned in his Nobel speech as a classroom essay. If you were a teacher, would you fail him? Why or why not?

5. Do some research into contemporary hip-hop songs that use samples of other songs. Determine whether or not your selections credited their sources — and/or paid for them — and then argue whether or not the difference between sampling and plagiarism in hip-hop is merely a matter of money. What would Pitzer argue?

6. Because folk music developed over centuries and longer, the notion of "ownership" in that genre is complicated by the inability to find the precise origins of many songs. Research a popular folk song such as "Blue Tail Fly," "She'll be Comin' 'Round the Mountain," "The Ballad of John Henry," or "Go Down Moses" — or select a traditional song you know — and describe what is known about its origins.

23

Online versus IRL: How Has Social Networking Changed How We Relate to One Another?

STEPHEN MARCHE

Stephen Marche has written essays for the *New Yorker*, the *New York Times*, the *Atlantic*, and *Esquire*, among others, and has written six books, including two novels, a collection of stories, and two works of nonfiction, most recently *The Unmade Bed: The Messy Truth about Men and Women in the Twenty-First Century* (2017). Marche wrote the essay presented here for the *Atlantic* in 2012.

Is Facebook Making Us Lonely?

Yvette Vickers, a former *Playboy* playmate and B-movie star, best known for her role in *Attack of the 50 Foot Woman*, would have been eighty-three last August, but nobody knows exactly how old she was when she died. According to the Los Angeles coroner's report, she lay dead for the better part of a year before a neighbor and fellow actress, a woman named Susan Savage, noticed cobwebs and yellowing letters in her mailbox, reached through a broken window to unlock the door, and pushed her way through the piles of junk mail and mounds of clothing that barricaded the house. Upstairs, she found Vickers's body, mummified, near a heater that was still running. Her computer was on too, its glow permeating the empty space.

The *Los Angeles Times* posted a story headlined "Mummified Body of Former Playboy Playmate Yvette Vickers Found in Her Benedict Canyon Home," which quickly went viral. Within two weeks, by Technorati's count, Vickers's lonesome death was already the subject of 16,057 Facebook posts and 881 tweets. She had long been a horror-movie icon, a symbol of Hollywood's capacity to exploit our most basic fears in the silliest ways; now she was an icon of a new and different kind of horror: our growing fear of loneliness. Certainly she received much more attention in death than she did in the final years of her life. With no children, no religious group, and no immediate social circle of any kind, she had begun, as an elderly woman, to look elsewhere for companionship. Savage later told *Los Angeles* magazine that she had searched Vickers's phone bills for clues about the life that led to such an end. In the months before her grotesque death, Vickers had made calls not to friends or family but to distant fans who had found her through fan conventions and Internet sites.

Vickers's web of connections had grown broader but shallower, as has happened for many of us. We are living in an isolation that would have been unimaginable to our ancestors, and yet we have never been more accessible. Over the past three decades, technology has delivered to us a world in which we need not be out of contact for a fraction of a moment. In 2010, at a cost of $300 million, 800 miles of fiber-optic cable was laid between the Chicago Mercantile Exchange and the New York Stock Exchange to shave three milliseconds off trading times. Yet within this world of instant and absolute communication, unbounded by limits of time or space, we suffer from unprecedented alienation. We have never been more detached from one another, or lonelier. In a world consumed by ever more novel modes of socializing, we have less and less actual society. We live in an accelerating contradiction: the more connected we become, the lonelier we are. We were promised a global village; instead we inhabit the drab cul-de-sacs and endless freeways of a vast suburb of information.

At the forefront of all this unexpectedly lonely interactivity is Facebook, with 845 million users and $3.7 billion in revenue last year. The company hopes to raise $5 billion in an initial public offering later this spring, which will make it by far the largest Internet IPO in history. Some recent estimates put the company's potential value at $100 billion, which would make it larger than the global coffee industry — one addiction preparing

to surpass the other. Facebook's scale and reach are hard to comprehend: last summer, Facebook became, by some counts, the first Web site to receive 1 trillion page views in a month. In the last three months of 2011, users generated an average of 2.7 billion "likes" and comments every day. On whatever scale you care to judge Facebook — as a company, as a culture, as a country — it is vast beyond imagination.

Despite its immense popularity, or more 5 likely because of it, Facebook has, from the beginning, been under something of a cloud of suspicion. The depiction of Mark Zuckerberg, in *The Social Network*, as a bastard with symptoms of Asperger's syndrome, was nonsense. But it felt true. It felt true to Facebook, if not to Zuckerberg. The film's most indelible scene, the one that may well have earned it an Oscar, was the final, silent shot of an anomic Zuckerberg sending out a friend request to his ex-girlfriend, then waiting and clicking and waiting and clicking — a moment of superconnected loneliness preserved in amber. We have all been in that scene: transfixed by the glare of a screen, hungering for response.

When you sign up for Google+ and set up your Friends circle, the program specifies that you should include only "your real friends, the ones you feel comfortable sharing private details with." That one little phrase, *Your real friends* — so quaint, so charmingly mothering — perfectly encapsulates the anxieties that social media have produced: the fears that Facebook is interfering with our real friendships, distancing us from each other, making us lonelier; and that social networking might be spreading the very isolation it seemed designed to conquer.

Facebook arrived in the middle of a dramatic increase in the quantity and intensity of human loneliness, a rise that initially made the site's promise of greater connection seem deeply attractive. Americans are more solitary than ever before. In 1950, less than 10 percent of American households contained only one person. By 2010, nearly 27 percent of households had just one person. Solitary living does not guarantee a life of unhappiness, of course. In his recent book about the trend toward living alone, Eric Klinenberg, a sociologist at NYU, writes: "Reams of published research show that it's the quality, not the quantity of social interaction, that best predicts loneliness." True. But before we begin the fantasies of happily eccentric singledom, of divorcées dropping by their knitting circles after work for glasses of Drew Barrymore pinot grigio, or recent college graduates with perfectly articulated, Steampunk-themed, 300-square-foot apartments organizing croquet matches with their book clubs, we should recognize that it is not just isolation that is rising sharply. It's loneliness, too. And loneliness makes us miserable.

We know intuitively that loneliness and being alone are not the same thing. Solitude can be lovely. Crowded parties can be agony. We also know, thanks to a growing body of research on the topic, that loneliness is not a matter of external conditions; it is a psychological state. A 2005 analysis of data from a longitudinal study of Dutch twins showed that the tendency toward loneliness has roughly the same genetic component as other psychological problems such as neuroticism or anxiety.

Still, loneliness is slippery, a difficult state to define or diagnose. The best tool yet developed for measuring the condition is the UCLA Loneliness Scale, a series of twenty questions that all begin with this formulation: "How often do you feel . . . ?" As in: "How often do you feel that you are 'in tune' with the people around you?" And: "How often do you feel that you lack companionship?" Measuring the condition in these terms, various studies have shown loneliness rising drastically over a very short period of recent history. A 2010 AARP survey found that 35 percent of adults older than forty-five were chronically lonely, as opposed to 20 percent of a similar group only a decade earlier. According to a major study by a leading scholar of the subject, roughly 20 percent of Americans — about 60 million people — are unhappy with their lives because of loneliness. Across the Western world, physicians and nurses have begun to speak openly of an epidemic of loneliness.

The new studies on loneliness are beginning to yield some surprising preliminary findings about its mechanisms. Almost every factor that one might assume affects loneliness does so only some of the time, and only under certain circumstances. People who are married are less lonely than single people, one journal article suggests, but only if their spouses are confidants. If one's spouse is not a confidant, marriage may not decrease loneliness. A belief in God might help, or it might not, as a 1990 German study comparing levels of religious feeling and levels of loneliness discovered. Active believers who saw God as abstract and helpful rather than as a wrathful, immediate presence were less lonely. "The mere belief in God," the researchers concluded, "was relatively independent of loneliness."

But it is clear that social interaction matters. Loneliness and being alone are not the same thing, but both are on the rise. We meet fewer people. We gather less. And when we gather, our bonds are less meaningful and less easy. The decrease in confidants — that is, in quality social connections — has been dramatic over the past twenty-five years. In one survey, the mean size of networks of personal confidants decreased from 2.94 people in 1985 to 2.08 in 2004. Similarly, in 1985, only 10 percent of Americans said they had no one with whom to discuss important

10

matters, and 15 percent said they had only one such good friend. By 2004, 25 percent had nobody to talk to, and 20 percent had only one confidant.

In the face of this social disintegration, we have essentially hired an army of replacement confidants, an entire class of professional carers. As Ronald Dworkin pointed out in a 2010 paper for the Hoover Institution, in the late 1940s, the United States was home to 2,500 clinical psychologists, 30,000 social workers, and fewer than 500 marriage and family therapists. As of 2010, the country had 77,000 clinical psychologists, 192,000 clinical social workers, 400,000 nonclinical social workers, 50,000 marriage and family therapists, 105,000 mental-health counselors, 220,000 substance-abuse counselors, 17,000 nurse psychotherapists, and 30,000 life coaches. The majority of patients in therapy do not warrant a psychiatric diagnosis. This raft of psychic servants is helping us through what used to be called regular problems. We have outsourced the work of everyday caring.

We need professional carers more and more, because the threat of societal break down, once principally a matter of nostalgic lament, has morphed into an issue of public health. Being lonely is extremely bad for your health. If you're lonely, you're more likely to be put in a geriatric home at an earlier age than a similar person who isn't lonely. You're less likely to exercise. You're more likely to be obese. You're less likely to survive a serious operation and more likely to have hormonal imbalances. You are at greater risk of inflammation. Your memory may be worse. You are more likely to be depressed, to sleep badly, and to suffer dementia and general cognitive decline. Loneliness may not have killed Yvette Vickers, but it has been linked to a greater probability of having the kind of heart condition that did kill her.

And yet, despite its deleterious effect on health, loneliness is one of the first things ordinary Americans spend their money achieving. With money, you flee the cramped city to a house in the suburbs or, if you can afford it, a McMansion in the exurbs, inevitably spending more time in your car. Loneliness is at the American core, a by-product of a long-standing national appetite for independence: The Pilgrims who left Europe willingly abandoned the bonds and strictures of a society that could not accept their right to be different. They did not seek out loneliness, but they accepted it as the price of their autonomy. The cowboys who set off to explore a seemingly endless frontier likewise traded away personal ties in favor of pride and self-respect. The ultimate American icon is the astronaut: Who is more heroic, or more alone? The price of self-determination and self-reliance has often been loneliness. But Americans have always been willing to pay that price.

Today, the one common feature in 15 American secular culture is its celebration of the self that breaks away from the constrictions of the family and the state, and, in its greatest expressions, from all limits entirely. The great American poem is Whitman's "Song of Myself." The great American essay is Emerson's "Self-Reliance." The great American novel is Melville's *Moby-Dick*, the tale of a man on a quest so lonely that it is incomprehensible to those around him. American culture, high and low, is about self-expression and personal authenticity. Franklin Delano Roosevelt called individualism "the great watchword of American life."

Self-invention is only half of the American story, however. The drive for isolation has always been in tension with the impulse to cluster in communities that cling and suffocate. The Pilgrims, while fomenting spiritual rebellion, also enforced ferocious cohesion. The Salem witch trials, in hindsight, read like attempts to impose solidarity — as do the McCarthy hearings. The history of the United States is like the famous parable of the porcupines in the cold, from Schopenhauer's *Studies in Pessimism* — the ones who huddle together for warmth and shuffle away in pain, always separating and congregating.

We are now in the middle of a long period of shuffling away. In his 2000 book *Bowling Alone*, Robert D. Putnam attributed the dramatic postwar decline of social capital — the strength and value of interpersonal networks — to numerous interconnected trends in American life: suburban sprawl, television's dominance over culture, the self-absorption of the Baby Boomers, the disintegration of the traditional family. The trends he observed continued through the prosperity of the aughts, and have only become more pronounced with time: the rate of union membership declined in 2011, again; screen time rose; the Masons and the Elks continued their slide into irrelevance. We are lonely because we want to be lonely. We have made ourselves lonely.

The question of the future is this: Is Facebook part of the separating or part of the congregating; is it a huddling-together for warmth or a shuffling-away in pain?

Well before Facebook, digital technology was enabling our tendency for isolation, to an unprecedented degree. Back in the 1990s, scholars started calling the contradiction between an increased opportunity to connect and a lack of human contact the "Internet paradox." A prominent 1998 article on the phenomenon by a team of researchers at Carnegie Mellon showed that increased Internet usage was already coinciding with increased loneliness. Critics of the study pointed out that the two groups that participated in the study — high-school journalism students who were heading to university

and socially active members of community-development boards — were statistically likely to become lonelier over time. Which brings us to a more fundamental question: Does the Internet make people lonely, or are lonely people more attracted to the Internet?

The question has intensified in the 20 Facebook era. A recent study out of Australia (where close to half the population is active on Facebook), titled "Who Uses Facebook?" found a complex and sometimes confounding relationship between loneliness and social networking. Facebook users had slightly lower levels of "social loneliness" — the sense of not feeling bonded with friends — but "significantly higher levels of family loneliness" — the sense of not feeling bonded with family. It may be that Facebook encourages more contact with people outside of our household, at the expense of our family relationships — or it may be that people who have unhappy family relationships in the first place seek companionship through other means, including Facebook. The researchers also found that lonely people are inclined to spend more time on Facebook: "One of the most noteworthy findings," they wrote, "was the tendency for neurotic and lonely individuals to spend greater amounts of time on Facebook per day than non-lonely individuals." And they found that neurotics are more likely to prefer to use the wall, while extroverts tend to use chat features in addition to the wall.

Moira Burke, until recently a graduate student at the Human-Computer Institute at Carnegie Mellon, used to run a longitudinal study of 1,200 Facebook users. That study, which is ongoing, is one of the first to step outside the realm of self-selected college students and examine the effects of Facebook on a broader population, over time. She concludes that the effect of Facebook depends on what you bring to it. Just as your mother said: you get out only what you put in. If you use Facebook to communicate directly with other individuals — by using the "like" button, commenting on friends' posts, and so on — it can increase your social capital. Personalized messages, or what Burke calls "composed communication," are more satisfying than "one-click communication" — the lazy click of a like. "People who received composed communication became less lonely, while people who received one-click communication experienced no change in loneliness," Burke tells me. So, you should inform your friend in writing how charming her son looks with Harry Potter cake smeared all over his face, and how interesting her sepia-toned photograph of that tree-framed bit of skyline is, and how cool it is that she's at whatever concert she happens to be at. That's what we all want to hear. Even better than sending a private Facebook message is the semi-public conversation, the kind of back-and-forth in which you half ignore the other people who may be listening in. "People whose friends write to them semi-publicly on Facebook experience decreases in loneliness," Burke says.

On the other hand, nonpersonalized use of Facebook — scanning your friends' status updates and updating the world on your own activities via your wall, or what Burke calls "passive consumption" and "broadcasting" — correlates to feelings of disconnectedness. It's a lonely business, wandering the labyrinths of our friends' and pseudo-friends' projected identities, trying to figure out what part of ourselves we ought to project, who will listen, and what they will hear. According to Burke, passive consumption of Facebook also correlates to a marginal increase in depression. "If two women each talk to their friends the same amount of time, but one of them spends more time reading about friends on Facebook as well, the one reading tends to grow slightly more depressed,"

Burke says. Her conclusion suggests that my sometimes unhappy reactions to Facebook may be more universal than I had realized. When I scroll through page after page of my friends' descriptions of how accidentally eloquent their kids are, and how their husbands are endearingly bumbling, and how they're all about to eat a home-cooked meal prepared with fresh local organic produce bought at the farmers' market and then go for a jog and maybe check in at the office because they're so busy getting ready to hop on a plane for a week of luxury dogsledding in Lapland, I do grow slightly more miserable. A lot of other people doing the same thing feel a little bit worse, too.

Still, Burke's research does not support the assertion that Facebook creates loneliness. The people who experience loneliness on Facebook are lonely away from Facebook, too, she points out; on Facebook, as everywhere else, correlation is not causation. The popular kids are popular, and the lonely skulkers skulk alone. Perhaps it says something about me that I think Facebook is primarily a platform for lonely skulking. I mention to Burke the widely reported study, conducted by a Stanford graduate student, that showed how believing that others have strong social networks can lead to feelings of depression. What does Facebook communicate, if not the impression of social bounty? Everybody else looks so happy on Facebook, with so many friends, that our own social networks feel emptier than ever in comparison. Doesn't that *make* people feel lonely? "If people are reading about lives that are much better than theirs, two things can happen," Burke tells me. "They can feel worse about themselves, or they can feel motivated."

Burke will start working at Facebook as a data scientist this year.

John Cacioppo, the director of the Center 25 for Cognitive and Social Neuroscience at the University of Chicago, is the world's leading expert on loneliness. In his landmark book, *Loneliness*, released in 2008, he revealed just how profoundly the epidemic of loneliness is affecting the basic functions of human physiology. He found higher levels of epinephrine, the stress hormone, in the morning urine of lonely people. Loneliness burrows deep: "When we drew blood from our older adults and analyzed their white cells," he writes, "we found that loneliness somehow penetrated the deepest recesses of the cell to alter the way genes were being expressed." Loneliness affects not only the brain, then, but the basic process of DNA transcription. When you are lonely, your whole body is lonely.

To Cacioppo, Internet communication allows only ersatz intimacy. "Forming connections with pets or online friends or even God is a noble attempt by an obligatorily gregarious creature to satisfy a compelling need," he writes. "But surrogates can never make up completely for the absence of the real thing." The "real thing" being actual people, in the flesh. When I speak to Cacioppo, he is refreshingly clear on what he sees as Facebook's effect on society. Yes, he allows, some research has suggested that the greater the number of Facebook friends a person has, the less lonely she is. But he argues that the impression this creates can be misleading. "For the most part," he says, "people are bringing their old friends, and feelings of loneliness or connectedness, to Facebook." The idea that a Web site could deliver a more friendly, interconnected world is bogus. The depth of one's social network outside Facebook is what determines the depth of one's social network within Facebook, not the other way around. Using social media doesn't create new social networks; it just transfers established networks from one platform to another. For the most part, Facebook doesn't destroy friendships — but it doesn't create them, either.

In one experiment, Cacioppo looked for a connection between the loneliness of subjects and the relative frequency of their interactions via Facebook, chat rooms, online games, dating sites, and face-to-face contact. The results were unequivocal. "The greater the proportion of face-to-face interactions, the less lonely you are," he says. "The greater the proportion of online interactions, the lonelier you are." Surely, I suggest to Cacioppo, this means that Facebook and the like inevitably make people lonelier. He disagrees. Facebook is merely a tool, he says, and like any tool, its effectiveness will depend on its user. "If you use Facebook to increase face-to-face contact," he says, "it increases social capital." So if social media let you organize a game of football among your friends, that's healthy. If you turn to social media instead of playing football, however, that's unhealthy.

"Facebook can be terrific, if we use it properly," Cacioppo continues. "It's like a car. You can drive it to pick up your friends. Or you can drive alone." But hasn't the car increased loneliness? If cars created the suburbs, surely they also created isolation. "That's because of how we use cars," Cacioppo replies. "How we use these technologies can lead to more integration, rather than more isolation."

The problem, then, is that we invite loneliness, even though it makes us miserable. The history of our use of technology is a history of isolation desired and achieved. When the Great Atlantic and Pacific Tea Company opened its A&P stores, giving Americans self-service access to groceries, customers stopped having relationships with their grocers. When the telephone arrived, people stopped knocking on their neighbors' doors. Social media bring this process to a much wider set of relationships. Researchers at the HP Social Computing Lab who studied the nature of people's connections on Twitter came to a depressing, if not surprising, conclusion: "Most of the links declared within Twitter were meaningless from an interaction point of view." I have to wonder: What other point of view is meaningful?

Loneliness is certainly not something 30 that Facebook or Twitter or any of the lesser forms of social media is doing to us. We are doing it to ourselves. Casting technology as some vague, impersonal spirit of history forcing our actions is a weak excuse. We make decisions about how we use our machines, not the other way around. Every time I shop at my local grocery store, I am faced with a choice. I can buy my groceries from a human being or from a machine. I always, without exception, choose the machine. It's faster and more efficient, I tell myself, but the truth is that I prefer not having to wait with the other customers who are lined up alongside the conveyor belt: the hipster mom who disapproves of my high-carbon-footprint pineapple; the lady who tenses to the point of tears while she waits to see if the gods of the credit-card machine will accept or decline; the old man whose clumsy feebleness requires a patience that I don't possess. Much better to bypass the whole circus and just ring up the groceries myself.

Our omnipresent new technologies lure us toward increasingly superficial connections at exactly the same moment that they make avoiding the mess of human interaction easy. The beauty of Facebook, the source of its power, is that it enables us to be social while sparing us the embarrassing reality of society — the accidental revelations we make at parties, the awkward pauses, the farting and the spilled drinks and the general gaucherie of face-to-face contact. Instead, we have the lovely smoothness of a seemingly social machine. Everything's so simple: status updates, pictures, your wall.

But the price of this smooth sociability is a constant compulsion to assert one's own happiness, one's own fulfillment. Not only must we contend with the social bounty of others; we must foster the appearance of our own social bounty. Being happy all the time, pretending to be happy, actually attempting to be happy — it's exhausting. Last year a team of researchers led by Iris Mauss at the University of Denver published a study looking into "the paradoxical effects of valuing happiness." Most goals in life show a direct correlation between valuation and achievement. Studies have found, for example, that students who value good grades tend to have higher grades than those who don't value them. Happiness is an exception. The study came to a disturbing conclusion:

> Valuing happiness is not necessarily linked to greater happiness. In fact, under certain conditions, the opposite is true. Under conditions of low (but not high) life stress, the more people valued happiness, the lower were their hedonic balance, psychological well-being, and life satisfaction, and the higher their depression symptoms.

The more you try to be happy, the less happy you are. Sophocles made roughly the same point.

Facebook, of course, puts the pursuit of happiness front and center in our digital life. Its capacity to redefine our very concepts of identity and personal fulfillment is much more worrisome than the data-mining and privacy practices that have aroused anxieties about the company. Two of the most compelling critics of Facebook — neither of them a Luddite — concentrate on exactly this point. Jaron Lanier, the author of *You Are Not a Gadget*, was one of the inventors of virtual-reality technology. His view of where social media are taking us reads like dystopian science fiction: "I fear that we are beginning to design ourselves to suit digital models of us, and I worry about a leaching of empathy and humanity in that process." Lanier argues that Facebook imprisons us in the business of self-presenting, and this, to his mind, is the site's crucial and fatally unacceptable downside.

Sherry Turkle, a professor of computer 35 culture at MIT who in 1995 published the digital-positive analysis *Life on the Screen*, is much more skeptical about the effects of online society in her 2011 book, *Alone Together*: "These days, insecure in our relationships and anxious about intimacy, we look to technology for ways to be in relationships and protect ourselves from them at the same time." The problem with digital intimacy is that it is ultimately incomplete: "The ties we form through the Internet are not, in the end, the ties that bind. But they are the ties that preoccupy," she writes. "We don't want to intrude on each other, so instead we constantly intrude on each other, but not in 'real time.' "

Lanier and Turkle are right, at least in their diagnoses. Self-presentation on Facebook is continuous, intensely mediated, and possessed of a phony nonchalance that eliminates even the potential for spontaneity. ("Look how casually I threw up these three photos from the party at which I took 300 photos!") Curating the exhibition of the self has become a 24/7 occupation. Perhaps not surprisingly, then, the Australian study "Who Uses Facebook?" found a significant correlation between Facebook use and narcissism: "Facebook users have higher levels of total narcissism, exhibitionism, and leadership than Facebook nonusers," the study's authors wrote. "In fact, it could be argued that Facebook specifically gratifies the narcissistic individual's need to engage in self-promoting and superficial behavior."

Rising narcissism isn't so much a trend as the trend behind all other trends. In preparation for the 2013 edition of its diagnostic manual, the psychiatric profession is currently struggling to update its definition of narcissistic personality disorder. Still, generally speaking, practitioners agree that narcissism manifests in patterns of fantastic grandiosity, craving for attention, and lack of empathy. In a 2008 survey, 35,000 American respondents were asked if they had ever had certain symptoms of narcissistic personality disorder. Among people older than sixty-five, 3 percent reported symptoms. Among people in their twenties, the proportion was nearly 10 percent. Across all age groups, one in sixteen Americans has experienced some symptoms of NPD. And loneliness and narcissism are intimately connected: a longitudinal study of Swedish women demonstrated a strong link between levels of narcissism in youth and levels of loneliness in old age. The connection is fundamental. Narcissism is the flip side of loneliness, and either condition is a fighting retreat from the messy reality of other people.

A considerable part of Facebook's appeal stems from its miraculous fusion of distance with intimacy, or the illusion of distance with the illusion of intimacy. Our online communities become engines of self-image, and self-image becomes the engine of community. The real danger with Facebook is not that it allows us to isolate ourselves, but that by mixing our appetite for isolation with our vanity, it threatens to alter the very nature of solitude. The new isolation is not of the kind that Americans once idealized, the lonesomeness of the proudly nonconformist, independent-minded, solitary stoic, or that of the astronaut who blasts into new worlds.

Facebook's isolation is a grind. What's truly staggering about Facebook usage is not its volume — 750 million photographs uploaded over a single weekend — but the constancy of the performance it demands. More than half its users — and one of every thirteen people on Earth is a Facebook user — log on every day. Among eighteen-to-thirty-four-year-olds, nearly half check Facebook minutes after waking up, and 28 percent do so before getting out of bed. The relentlessness is what is so new, so potentially transformative. Facebook never takes a break. We never take a break. Human beings have always created elaborate acts of self-presentation. But not all the time, not every morning, before we even pour a cup of coffee. Yvette Vickers's computer was on when she died.

Nostalgia for the good old days of disconnection would not just be pointless, it would be hypocritical and ungrateful. But the very magic of the new machines, the efficiency and elegance with which they serve us, obscures what isn't being served: everything that matters. What Facebook has revealed about human nature — and this is not a minor revelation — is that a connection is not the same thing as a bond, and that instant and total connection is no salvation, no ticket to a happier, better world or a more liberated version of humanity. Solitude used to be good for self-reflection and self-reinvention. But now we are left thinking about who we are all the time, without ever really thinking about who we are. Facebook denies us a pleasure whose profundity we had underestimated: the chance to forget about ourselves for a while, the chance to disconnect. 40

Topics for Critical Thinking and Writing

1. In his first three paragraphs, Stephen Marche argues that, despite modern technology, "we have never been more detached from one another, or lonelier." What methods does he go on to use in his effort to persuade? Did his essay convince you? Explain.

2. Marche states that "social networking might be spreading the very isolation it seemed designed to conquer" (para. 6). Does your own experience with social media confirm or refute this assertion? Explain your response.

3. In paragraph 17, Marche speaks of "social capital." What does this term mean? How do you know?

4. In paragraph 20, Marche discusses the findings of an Australian study of Facebook users. How do you interpret the study's finding of "significantly higher levels of family loneliness" among Facebook users?

5. In paragraph 33, Marche writes: "[Facebook's] capacity to redefine our very concepts of identity and personal fulfillment is much more worrisome than the data-mining and privacy practices that have aroused anxieties about the company." In your estimation, is this claim true? Support your position.

JIA TOLENTINO

Jia Tolentino is a staff writer for the *New Yorker* and has published articles on a range of topics surrounding internet culture, youth culture, and feminism. Her work has also appeared in the *New York Times Magazine*, *Jezebel*, and *Pitchfork*. In 2019, she published an essay collection called *Trick Mirror: Reflections on Self-Delusion*, which reached the *New York Times* bestseller list. This essay is from that collection.

The I in the Internet

In the beginning the internet seemed good. "I was in love with the internet the first time I used it at my dad's office and thought it was the ULTIMATE COOL," I wrote, when I was ten, on an Angelfire subpage titled "The Story of How Jia Got Her Web Addiction." In a text box superimposed on a hideous violet background, I continued:

> But that was in third grade and all I was doing was going to Beanie Baby sites. Having an old, icky bicky computer at home, we didn't have the Internet. Even AOL seemed like a far-off dream. Then we got a new top-o'-the-line computer in spring break '99, and of course it came with all that demo stuff. So I finally had AOL and I was completely amazed at the marvel of having a profile and chatting and IMS!!

Then, I wrote, I discovered personal webpages. ("I was astonished!") I learned HTML and "little Javascript trickies." I built my own site on the beginner-hosting site Expage, choosing pastel colors and then switching to a "starry night theme." Then I ran out of space, so I "decided to move to Angelfire. Wow." I learned how to make my own graphics. "This was all in the course of four months," I wrote, marveling at how quickly my ten-year-old internet citizenry was evolving. I had recently revisited the sites that had once inspired me, and realized "how much of an idiot I was to be wowed by *that*."

I have no memory of inadvertently starting this essay two decades ago, or of making this Angelfire subpage, which I found while hunting for early traces of myself on the internet. It's now eroded to its skeleton: its landing page, titled "THE VERY BEST," features a sepia-toned photo of Andie from *Dawson's Creek* and a dead link to a new site called "THE FROSTED FIELD," which is "BETTER!" There's a page dedicated to a blinking mouse GIF named Susie, and a "Cool Lyrics Page" with a scrolling banner and the lyrics to Smash Mouth's "All Star," Shania Twain's "Man! I Feel Like a Woman!" and the TLC diss track "No Pigeons," by Sporty Thievz. On an FAQ page — there was an FAQ page — I write that I had to close down my customizable cartoon-doll section, as "the response has been enormous."

It appears that I built and used this Angelfire site over just a few months in 1999, immediately after my parents got a computer. My insane FAQ page specifies that the site was started in June, and a page titled "Journal" — which proclaims, "I am going to be completely honest about my life, although I won't go too deeply into personal thoughts, though" — features entries only from October. One entry begins: "It's so HOT outside and I can't count the times acorns have fallen on my head, maybe from exhaustion." Later on,

I write, rather prophetically: "I'm going insane! I literally am addicted to the web!"

In 1999, it felt different to spend all day on the internet. This was true for everyone, not just for ten-year-olds: this was the *You've Got Mail* era, when it seemed that the very worst thing that could happen online was that you might fall in love with your business rival. Throughout the eighties and nineties, people had been gathering on the internet in open forums, drawn, like butterflies, to the puddles and blossoms of other people's curiosity and expertise. Self-regulated newsgroups like Usenet cultivated lively and relatively civil discussion about space exploration, meteorology, recipes, rare albums. Users gave advice, answered questions, made friendships, and wondered what this new internet would become.

Because there were so few search engines and no centralized social platforms, discovery on the early internet took place mainly in private, and pleasure existed as its own solitary reward. A 1995 book called *You Can Surf the Net!* listed sites where you could read movie reviews or learn about martial arts. It urged readers to follow basic etiquette (don't use all caps; don't waste other people's expensive bandwidth with overly long posts) and encouraged them to feel comfortable in this new world ("Don't worry," the author advised. "You have to *really* mess up to get flamed."). Around this time, GeoCities began offering personal website hosting for dads who wanted to put up their own golfing sites or kids who built glittery, blinking shrines to Tolkien or Ricky Martin or unicorns, most capped off with a primitive guest book and a green-and-black visitor counter. GeoCities, like the internet itself, was clumsy, ugly, only half functional, and organized into neighborhoods: /area51/ was for sci-fi, /westhollywood/ for

LGBTQ life, /enchantedforest/ for children, /petsburgh/ for pets. If you left GeoCities, you could walk around other streets in this ever-expanding village of curiosities. You could stroll through Expage or Angelfire, as I did, and pause on the thoroughfare where the tiny cartoon hamsters danced. There was an emergent aesthetic — blinking text, crude animation. If you found something you liked, if you wanted to spend more time in any of these neighborhoods, you could build your own house from HTML frames and start decorating.

This period of the internet has been labeled Web 1.0 and — a name that works backward from the term Web 2.0, which was coined by the writer and user-experience designer Darcy DiNucci in an article called "Fragmented Future," published in 1999. "The Web we know now," she wrote, "which loads into a browser window in essentially static screenfuls, is only an embryo of the Web to come. The first glimmerings of Web 2.0 are beginning to appear. . . . The Web will be understood not as screenfuls of texts and graphics but as a transport mechanism, the ether through which interactivity happens." On Web 2.0, the structures would be dynamic, she predicted: instead of houses, websites would be portals, through which an ever-changing stream of activity — status updates, photos — could be displayed. What you did on the internet would become intertwined with what everyone else did, and the things other people liked would become the things that you would see. Web 2.0 platforms like Blogger and Myspace made it possible for people who had merely been taking in the sights to start generating their own personalized and constantly changing scenery. As more people began to register their existence digitally, a pastime turned into an imperative: you had to register yourself digitally to exist.

In a *New Yorker* piece from November 2000, Rebecca Mead profiled Meg Hourihan, an early blogger who went by Megnut. In just the prior eighteen months, Mead observed, the number of "weblogs" had gone from fifty to several thousand, and blogs like Megnut were drawing thousands of visitors per day. This new internet was social ("a blog consists primarily of links to other Web sites and commentary about those links") in a way that centered on individual identity (Megnut's readers knew that she wished there were better fish tacos in San Francisco, and that she was a feminist, and that she was close with her mom). The blogosphere was also full of mutual transactions, which tended to echo and escalate. The "main audience for blogs is other bloggers," Mead wrote. Etiquette required that, "if someone blogs your blog, you blog his blog back."

Through the emergence of blogging, personal lives were becoming public domain, and social incentives — to be liked, to be seen — were becoming economic ones. The mechanisms of internet exposure began to seem like a viable foundation for a career. Hourihan cofounded Blogger with Evan Williams, who later cofounded Twitter. JenniCam, founded in 1996 when the college student Jennifer Ringley started broadcasting webcam photos from her dorm room, attracted at one point up to four million daily visitors, some of whom paid a subscription fee for quicker-loading images. The internet, in promising a potentially unlimited audience, began to seem like the natural home of self-expression. In one blog post, Megnut's boyfriend, the blogger Jason Kottke, asked himself why he didn't just write his thoughts down in private. "Somehow, that seems strange to me though," he wrote. "The Web is the place for you to express your thoughts and feelings and such. To put those things elsewhere seems absurd."

Every day, more people agreed with him. 10 The call of self-expression turned the village of the internet into a city, which expanded at time-lapse speed, social connections bristling like neurons in every direction. At ten, I was clicking around a web ring to check out other Angelfire sites full of animal GIFs and Smash Mouth trivia. At twelve, I was writing five hundred words a day on a public LiveJournal. At fifteen, I was uploading photos of myself in a miniskirt on Myspace. By twenty-five, my job was to write things that would attract, ideally, a hundred thousand strangers per post. Now I'm thirty, and most of my life is inextricable from the internet, and its mazes of incessant forced connection — this feverish, electric, unlivable hell.

As with the transition between Web 1.0 and Web 2.0, the curdling of the social internet happened slowly and then all at once. The tipping point, I'd guess, was around 2012. People were losing excitement about the internet, starting to articulate a set of new truisms. Facebook had become tedious, trivial, exhausting. Instagram seemed better, but would soon reveal its underlying function as a three-ring circus of happiness and popularity and success. Twitter, for all its discursive promise, was where everyone tweeted complaints at airlines and bitched about articles that had been commissioned to make people bitch. The dream of a better, truer self on the internet was slipping away. Where we had once been free to be ourselves online, we were now *chained* to ourselves online, and this made us self-conscious. Platforms that promised connection began inducing mass alienation.

The freedom promised by the internet started to seem like something whose greatest potential lay in the realm of misuse.

Even as we became increasingly sad and ugly on the internet, the mirage of the better online self continued to glimmer. As a medium, the internet is defined by a built-in performance incentive. In real life, you can walk around living life and be visible to other people. But you can't just walk around and be visible on the internet — for anyone to see you, you have to *act*. You have to communicate in order to maintain an internet presence. And, because the internet's central platforms are built around personal profiles, it can seem — first at a mechanical level, and later on as an encoded instinct — like the main purpose of this communication is to make yourself look good. Online reward mechanisms beg to substitute for offline ones, and then overtake them. This is why everyone tries to look so hot and well-traveled on Instagram; this is why everyone seems so smug and triumphant on Facebook; this is why, on Twitter, making a righteous political statement has come to seem, for many people, like a political good in itself.

This practice is often called "virtue signaling," a term most often used by conservatives criticizing the left. But virtue signaling is a bipartisan, even apolitical action. Twitter is overrun with dramatic pledges of allegiance to the Second Amendment that function as intra-right virtue signaling, and it can be something like virtue signaling when people post the suicide hotline after a celebrity death. Few of us are totally immune to the practice, as it intersects with a real desire for political integrity. Posting photos from a protest against border family separation, as I did while writing this, is a microscopically meaningful action, an expression of genuine

principle, and also, inescapably, some sort of attempt to signal that I am good.

Taken to its extreme, virtue signaling has driven people on the left to some truly unhinged behavior. A legendary case occurred in June 2016, after a two-year-old was killed at a Disney resort — dragged off by an alligator while playing in a no-swimming-allowed lagoon. A woman, who had accumulated ten thousand Twitter followers with her posts about social justice, saw an opportunity and tweeted, magnificently, "I'm so finished with white men's entitlement lately that I'm really not sad about a 2yo being eaten by a gator because his daddy ignored signs." (She was then pilloried by people who chose to demonstrate their own moral superiority through mockery — as I am doing here, too.) A similar tweet made the rounds in early 2018 after a sweet story went viral: a large white seabird named Nigel had died next to the concrete decoy bird to whom he had devoted himself for years. An outraged writer tweeted, "Even concrete birds do not owe you affection, Nigel," and wrote a long Facebook post arguing that Nigel's courtship of the fake bird exemplified . . . *rape culture.* "I'm available to write the feminist perspective on Nigel the gannet's non-tragic death should anyone wish to pay me," she added, underneath the original tweet, which received more than a thousand likes. These deranged takes, and their unnerving proximity to online monetization, are case studies in the way that our world — digitally mediated, utterly consumed by capitalism — makes communication about morality very easy but makes actual moral living very hard. You don't end up using a news story about a dead toddler as a peg for white entitlement without a society in which the discourse of righteousness occupies far more public attention than the conditions that necessitate righteousness in the first place.

On the right, the online performance [15] of political identity has been even wilder. In 2017, the social-media-savvy youth conservative group Turning Point USA staged a protest at Kent State University featuring a student who put on a diaper to demonstrate that "safe spaces were for babies." (It went viral, as intended, but not in the way TPUSA wanted — the protest was uniformly roasted, with one Twitter user slapping the logo of the porn site Brazzers on a photo of the diaper boy, and the Kent State TPUSA campus coordinator resigned.) It has also been infinitely more consequential, beginning in 2014, with a campaign that became a template for right-wing internet-political action, when a large group of young misogynists came together in the event now known as Gamergate.

The issue at hand was, ostensibly, a female game designer perceived to be sleeping with a journalist for favorable coverage. She, along with a set of feminist game critics and writers, received an onslaught of rape threats, death threats, and other forms of harassment, all concealed under the banner of free speech and "ethics in games journalism." The Gamergaters — estimated by *Deadspin* to number around ten thousand people — would mostly deny this harassment, either parroting in bad faith or fooling themselves into believing the argument that Gamergate was actually about noble ideals. Gawker Media, *Deadspin's* parent company, itself became a target, in part because of its own aggressive disdain toward the Gamergaters: the company lost seven figures in revenue after its advertisers were brought into the maelstrom.

In 2016, a similar fiasco made national news in Pizzagate, after a few rabid internet denizens decided they'd found coded messages about child sex slavery in the advertising of a pizza shop associated with Hillary Clinton's campaign. This theory was disseminated all over the far-right internet, leading to an extended attack on DC's Comet Ping Pong pizzeria and everyone associated with the restaurant — all in the name of combating pedophilia — that culminated in a man walking into Comet Ping Pong and firing a gun. (Later on, the same faction would jump to the defense of Roy Moore, the Republican nominee for the Senate who was accused of sexually assaulting teenagers.) The over-woke left could only dream of this ability to weaponize a sense of righteousness. Even the militant antifascist movement, known as antifa, is routinely disowned by liberal centrists, despite the fact that the antifa movement is rooted in a long European tradition of Nazi resistance rather than a nascent constellation of radically paranoid message boards and YouTube channels. The worldview of the Gamergaters and Pizzagaters was actualized and to a large extent vindicated in the 2016 election — an event that strongly suggested that the worst things about the internet were now *determining,* rather than reflecting, the worst things about offline life.

Mass media always determines the shape of politics and culture. The Bush era is inextricable from the failures of cable news; the executive overreaches of the Obama years were obscured by the internet's magnification of personality and performance; Trump's rise to power is inseparable from the existence of social networks that must continually aggravate their users in order to continue making money. But lately I've been wondering how everything got so *intimately* terrible, and why, exactly, we keep playing along. How did a huge number of people begin spending the bulk of our disappearing free time in an openly torturous environment? How did the internet get so bad, so confining, so inescapably personal, so politically determinative — and why are all those questions asking the same thing?

I'll admit that I'm not sure that this inquiry is even productive. The internet reminds us on a daily basis that it is not at all rewarding to become aware of problems that you have no reasonable hope of solving. And, more important, the internet already is what it is. It has already become the central organ of contemporary life. It has already rewired the brains of its users, returning us to a state of primitive hyperawareness and distraction while overloading us with much more sensory input than was ever possible in primitive times. It has already built an ecosystem that runs on exploiting attention and monetizing the self. Even if you avoid the internet completely — my partner does: he thought #tbt meant "truth be told" for ages — you still live in the world that this internet has created, a world in which selfhood has become capitalism's last natural resource, a world whose terms are set by centralized platforms that have deliberately established themselves as near-impossible to regulate or control.

The internet is also in large part inextricable from life's pleasures: our friends, our families, our communities, our pursuits of happiness, and — sometimes, if we're lucky — our work. In part out of a desire to preserve what's worthwhile from the decay that surrounds it, I've been thinking about five intersecting problems: first, how the internet is built to distend our sense of identity; second, how it encourages us to overvalue our opinions; third, how it maximizes our sense of opposition; fourth, how it cheapens our understanding of solidarity; and, finally, how it destroys our sense of scale. 20

Topics for Critical Thinking and Writing

1. Consider Jia Tolentino's account of discovering her youthful writing on the internet. What are some reasons for and against giving teenagers unrestricted access to express themselves on social media platforms and, in general, the internet?

2. What do you think helps explain the "curdling of the social internet" that Tolentino describes in paragraph 11?

3. What examples does Tolentino use to describe the evolution of the internet from the "period of the Internet . . . labeled Web 1.0." (para. 7) to the emergence of Web 2.0? What important landmarks do you think mark the transition to Web 3.0, and what new hazards might Web 3.0 pose?

4. Tolentino's piece comes from her book, *Trick Mirror*. How does her writing style differ in terms of articulating an argument from the style of essays that come from magazines or websites? (You can find examples of both in this book.) Select such an essay that you have already read and compare them. What advantages or disadvantages does each form suggest? Is either more or less effective than the other? Why?

5. What are some things you or an average person could do to limit or control the negative effects of the internet that Tolentino discusses?

KRISTIN AROLA

Kristin Arola is an associate professor in the Writing, Rhetoric, and American Cultures Department at Michigan State University. She has written, co-authored, and co-edited numerous essays, book chapters, and books on technology, writing, identity, and culture. This selection comes from the collection *Social Writing/Social Media* (2017), co-edited by Douglas Walls and Stephanie Vie. It has been edited for length; to view the full article, please visit https://wac .colostate.edu/docs/books/social/writing.pdf.

Indigenous Interfaces

Not so long ago, I returned to my hometown in order to attend the Spirit of the Harvest Powwow — a powwow sponsored by my alma mater, Michigan Technological University, and largely attended by members of the Keweenaw Bay Indian Community Lake Superior Band of Chippewa Indians, one of whom includes my mother, a powwow jingle dancer (among other things). I spent a week with Michigan Tech's American Indian student group attending regalia-making workshops, helping make frybread for the powwow, and interviewing powwow participants (both dancers and those organizing the event) about their cultural crafting practices. While my work was most focused on material crafting practices, I concluded most interviews with the question, "What would Facebook look like if it were designed by and for American Indians?" . . .

RACE AND THE INTERFACE

The idea of an ideological rhetorical interface — that is, that the design of a digital space persuades users to engage in particular actions, representations, and relations, and that it is always already embedded in existing belief systems — is not new. . . . Those of us who work with digital rhetorics understand that interfaces are value-laden and work to position us and relate us to information, ideas, and each other in particular ways.

I've argued before that "the act of composing a [social media] profile is an act of composing the self " (K. L. Arola, 2010, p. 8). I would add that the act of composing *within* a social media space — be it to post a picture, respond to a posted link, post a status update, etc. — is also an act of composing the self in relation to, and with, other people and ideas. However, the fixed template-driven design of most social media platforms appears to limit the ways in which one is able to compose oneself and one's relations online. Lisa Nakamura (2002, 2007) has done a good deal of work exploring the ways in which race and representation are figured and refigured through the use of digital media. Nakamura and Peter Chow-White (2011) have argued that "the digital is altering our understandings of what race is as well as nurturing new types of inequality along racial lines" (p. 2). Nakamura (2002) has suggested that this inequality comes, in part, through cybertyping, or a menu-driven identity whereby certain prefixed racial categories are available for one to choose from when composing the online self. Her claims about race online — that it doesn't simply go away but is reinscribed with similar baggage from offline spaces — hold true today. . . .

BEING/SEEING INDIAN

In asking what Facebook would look like if it were designed by and for American Indians,

I was largely relying on the assumption that visual design guides a user's composing practices in a space. That is, I was thinking that were a social media interface to "look" a certain way, it would attract a specific set of users and would enable a specific set of uses. I presumed that an interface could, in some ways, *be* Indian. Within American Indian Studies as it is found in the halls of academe, as well as American Indian thought generally, there is an ongoing tension between this sense of *being* Indian and *doing* Indian. Ellen Cushman (2008) suggested this shift from *being* Indian to *doing* Indian so as to move the focus of "Indianness" away from preoccupations with blood quantum and phenotype, and toward issues of what's at stake and for whom when Indianness is categorized in particular ways.[1] Similarly, in interrogating the notion that there is something identifiable and representable to *being* Indian, Scott Richard Lyons (2010) reframed the question, "what is an Indian?" to "what should an Indian do?" This shift from *being* to *doing* "would mean a move away from conceptions of Indians as 'things' and toward a deeper analysis of Indians as human beings who *do* things" (p. 59). In short, the presumption that one can *be* Indian tends to fall prey to notions of the visible as a burden of proof. For example, one must have a certain skin tone, a certain color and length of hair, and be adorned in the proper jewelry to be *seen as* Indian.

Given the visible burden of proof that many Natives live with on a daily basis, it's perhaps not surprising that the most common answer I heard to my Facebook question referred to the four colors important to most tribes.[2,3] Five respondents simply answered, "Red, black, white, and yellow." Another suggested it would "definitely [be] colorful, I know that one. . . . It would definitely have deeper meaning." And yet another respondent described that "I think you'd definitely have the four colors somewhere associated with it, probably eagle feathers, and, um, just overall . . . more colorful instead of the typical blue and white." These answers provide a seemingly straightforward visible way to envision how Indianness might be represented through an interface. That is, the use of a specific design element recognizable as Native — be it the four colors or an iconic image like a feather or medicine wheel — suddenly makes the site visibly Indian. Rather than the colorful feathered design suggested by these respondents (a design that to them would make Facebook feel more Indian), the design elements of many social media sites — from LinkedIn to Facebook to Instagram to Twitter — use "the typical blue and white." While the template can be changed in some sites, the default design is blue and white. In fact, these colors are so common that in some ways they become nearly invisible. While perhaps a bit audacious of a claim, in some ways blue-and-white interfaces function as the white privilege of online design. For those who enjoy its benefits, it remains invisible, a means to an end, a way of doing and being that is normalized and routinized into everyday digital practice. Similar to Dennis Baron's (2009) idea that writing technologies become invisible as we acclimate to them, or Michel Foucault's (1991) broader claims that power becomes invisible as it is diffused

---

[1] Blood quantum, a colonized conception of race, remains a frequent battleground for Indianness. The question "so how Indian are you?" — as though a certain percentage will satisfy someone's desire for one to be a "real" Indian — exemplifies this problem. Meanwhile, tribes have varying requirements for quantum, some requiring 1/4 or 1/2 to enroll as a tribal member, whereas other tribes focus on lineage (if a direct descendent is on the Dawes Roll, you can enroll). This "proving" of race, be it through percent blood or a family name on a document, has been interrogated and challenged by many native scholars (Bizzaro, 2004; Garroutte, 2003).

[2] If you claim to be Native but don't phenotypically present as dark-haired, dark-skinned, and appropriately adorned, be prepared to be told by white folks, "but you don't look Indian."

[3] Most North American tribes hold culturally important the four directions and ascribe four colors to those directions. Each direction and color comes with its own teachings and stories. My own tribe uses yellow (east), red (south), black (west), and white (north); however, other tribes (including the Navajo) use blue, white, yellow, and black.

and embodied through discourse, the design of interfaces becomes an invisible background upon which we compose ourselves — invisible, at least, to those for whom it feels a natural space within which to interact. As Paula S. Rothenberg (2008) described of white privilege, "Many [whites] cannot remember a time when they first 'noticed' that they were white because whiteness was, for them, unremarkable. It was everywhere" (p. 2). Yet for those who desire another type of space, another way of being, this blue-and-white interface can in fact be very visible.

. . . I believe we should interrogate our interfaces and question any system that becomes so normalized so as to be invisible, yet I am hesitant to say that American Indians cannot and do not make a white-and-blue interface their own. In fact, there is a long history of postcolonized American Indians taking agency over new technologies. As Kade Twist (2000) described, "Indian people have always made new technologies reflect their own respective world views." That being said, as Angela M. Haas (2005) asserted, there is a great "rhetorical and cultural value of online digital rhetorical sovereignty" for American Indians. That is, there is power in composing the self within a design of one's own making.

To be fair, it is entirely possible that the participants who suggested that a Facebook designed by and for American Indians would include images of eagle feathers or the four colors were speaking from a tribal sensibility whereby these images are incredibly significant for many of their own spiritual practices. And, in this way, these visual cues in an interface may signify a space that is native-friendly. Yet, such answers indicate a somewhat serious problem — not so much with the answers themselves, but instead with my question. My question, "what would Facebook look like if it were designed by and for American Indians?" presumes that, first, it is not; second, it led participants down a path whereby I requested

a visible promise of Indianness. I suggested that there was a way that one can *be* Indian and thus be visibly recognized through an interface.

While in some ways different than a body physically appearing "Indian" — be it through phenotype or wearing the right clothes or jewelry — the idea that a design can be Indian is intimately connected to issues of embodiment and race. Many native scholars have discussed in great detail the issues surrounding American Indian identity and representation (Clifton, 1990; P. Deloria, 1998; V. Deloria, 1990, 1998; Garroutte, 2003; Mihesuah, 1996). While not always in full agreement, these scholars do agree that stereotypical visual representations — the noble savage, the wise medicine man, the Indian maiden — serve to distance, or in Malea Powell's (2002) words, "unsee" the contemporary Indian. As native artist and scholar Erica Lord (2009) described, these images function as "an attempt (even if unconscious) to keep the Native in the past, easily recognizable, simple, and, essentially, separate and different from 'us'" (p. 315). An interface tailored to visually appeal to one set of users falls prey to similar issues, as it suggests an interface can embody a recognizable and uncomplicated visual racial identity.

Returning to Lyons' (2000, 2010) and Cushman's (2008) suggestions that we understand Indianness as something one *does* (that is, through a certain set of actions or relations) as opposed to something one *is* (through being a certain skin tone or blood quantum) shifts how we understand race as embodied, and also shifts how we might understand the interface as visually composed for one set of users. Acknowledging how one might go about *doing* Indian instead of *being* recognizable as Indian via the interface suggests a rephrasing of my question from "what would Facebook *look* like?" to "what would Facebook allow you to *do*?" In spite of not asking this question, this is precisely how some respondents answered.

DOING/ACTING INDIAN

... The concept of *doing* Indian still contains 10 the possibility of essentializing what counts as Indian insofar as certain actions (powwow dancing, basket weaving, wild ricing, etc.) might be seen as something a Real Indian does. As one respondent described, laughing, "it would look ghetto, and what I mean by ghetto [laughs] is that it wouldn't look like a white person designed it! It would have 'teepee creepin' as an option for your away message, 'snaggin' would also be an option, all the status updates would be about frybread, going outside, eating frybread, making frybread, chillin' at someone's house." While partially a tongue-in-cheek answer given how often the respondent laughed during this answer, there is a sense here that certain actions equate with Indianness. What I find interesting about this answer is that she considers both the interface design — options related to her sense of what American Indians do — as well as the content that people post within the interface. Similarly, another respondent suggested how the interface might allow users to compose themselves and their relations in ways important to American Indians (specifically Ojibwe): "Creating ways that it could allow for Ojibwemowin or different cultural stuff, like the sharing groups . . . that'd be nice." In both cases, the respondents imagine an interface that doesn't necessarily look a certain way but that allows and encourages certain actions important to a group of people. Another respondent appeared excited by the idea that a social media site might be designed by and for someone like him, and after spending a few seconds smiling and pondering, he said, "I think it'd be neat, it definitely wouldn't be, um, so formal." I wasn't clear at first if he meant the design or the content, but in a follow-up question it became clear he wished for a social media space where users would be more playful and informal, not trying so hard to compose a perfect and uncomplicated sense of self.

The idea that a social media site wouldn't be so formal, would allow for various cultural connections between people, would have built-in away messages that use the vernacular of many American Indians, and would allow for the use of native languages indicates that some respondents understood the idea of a space designed *for* a certain group to mean much less about *looking* American Indian and more about *doing* (even if in a bit of a tongue-in-cheek way, as the "ghetto" response implied). Lyons' (1996) work on rhetorical sovereignty seems particularly apt in considering what American Indians might want from composing within social media. Lyons asked a broader question of composing. What do American Indians want from writing? His answer is "rhetorical sovereignty," which he defines as "the inherent right and ability of *peoples* to determine their own communicative needs and desires in this pursuit, to decide for themselves the goals, modes, styles, and languages of public discourse" (pp. 449–450, emphasis in original). In describing sovereignty as it relates to Indian nations, Lyons suggested that "the sovereignty of individuals and the privileging of procedure are less important in the logic of a nation-people, which takes as its supreme charge the sovereignty of the group through a privileging of its traditions and culture and continuity" (p. 455). That is, the individual's communicative acts gain importance as they are understood as furthering, and positively transforming and sustaining, the group's culture. A space that affords and encourages American Indians to compose and relate in a self-determined way, one that supports and sustains one's culture, seems an important way of *doing* Indianness within a social media space. . . .

An American Indian interface, then, isn't so much about visually presenting as Indian as it is about doing Indian, about encouraging composing practices within a preexisting and shifting web of relations. This type of interface would afford opportunities for rhetorical sovereignty, for one to compose and understand oneself within a web of relations where things only have meaning insofar as they are connected to other things.

THE INDIGENOUS NETWORK: BEING AND DOING

Shortly after my interviews with pow-wow participants about what an American Indian Facebook would look like, I received a request from a native friend to join the Indigenous Network. The Indigenous Network was a social networking site "powered by the indigenous to share their culture and promote solidarity" (Indigenous Network, n.d.). Essentially, it was a social networking site designed by and for American Indians and other indigenous peoples. Angelica Chrysler, from the Delaware Nation in Ontario, Canada, created the site as a way for native communities to reach out to each other "inspiring action for common goals" (Indigenous Network, n.d.).

In many ways the site looked and acted like a more flexible version of Facebook (see Figures 23.1 and 23.2).

Figure 23.1 Main Page of Indigenous Network.

Kristin Arola, "Indigenous Interfaces." University Press of Colorado from Social Writing/Social Media: Pedagogy, Presentation, and Publics. Eds. Douglas Walls and Stephanie Vie. WAC Clearinghouse Perspectives on Writing Series. Copyright © 2017 by University Press of Colorado. Used with permission.

Figure 23.2   My Indigenous Network profile page.

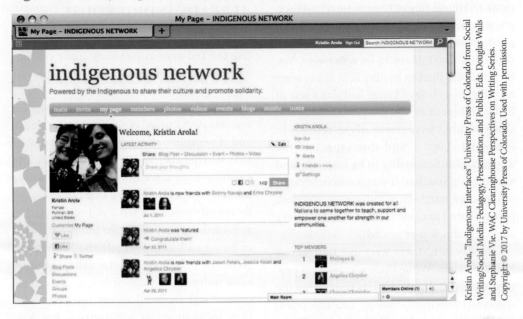

Similar to Facebook, users had a home 15 screen that displayed other user activities (Figure 23.1). The design used blue and white but also included a banner photo of an eagle wing, providing both the genre expectation for color on a social media site as well as a visible promise of Indianness. Users also had a profile page that displayed activity directly posted by and to the user herself (Figure 23.2). Unlike Facebook, however, a user could choose her profile template (notice mine used a concentric leaf pattern) and, similar to the MySpace options of the early 2000s, it was also incredibly easy to post and share music. The media (such as music, art, or videos) that a user posted were automatically accessible to all users for viewing and listening. Additionally, the activities — including the media posted by users — displayed on the home screen were from all users of the network, not just those designated as one's friends in the network. This sharing from one-to-many both on the home screen itself (what the design affords) and the links themselves (what the functionality affords) embodied a very indigenous sensibility. It automatically put one in relation to others in the space, even if you hadn't actively made someone a friend. You were, by nature of being there, visibly part of something bigger than yourself.

This interface not only put one in a visible relationality with others, it relied on a built-in spirit of sharing and reciprocity. As Cordova (2007) explained, one aspect of a Native American worldview is questioning "what is the good of having anything if you can't share it?" (p. 65). Sharing is necessarily related to the notion of being-in-relation insofar as, as Cordova explained, "If humans were solitary individuals, then there would be no need for cooperative behavior and there would be no social groups. . . . it is 'natural' for humans to be cooperative" (p. 184). And while she used the term "humans" here, she defined this characteristic as an ethical rule of Native American society, which she set against a Western/Christian perspective. Not that those raised in the latter can't, and don't, learn to be otherwise. Yet, the idea of a sharing society is in many ways an indigenous way of being, and was a way of being embraced by the Indigenous Network. One's postings were constantly in-relation-to everyone else's. I find this aspect of the design and functionality to be inspiring and exciting, yet much of it was possible because of the small numbers of Indigenous Network participants. (Imagine seeing every link *every* single Facebook user posted!)

In May 2012 there were 257 Indigenous Network users. While there was nothing preventing non-indigenous users from using the space, all participants had, up until this point, filled in the question, "What Nation/Tribe are you from?", leading me to believe that all users were indigenous. There is power in affinity groups and cultural empowerment, and a space designed by and for indigenous users definitely has its place. Yet, unfortunately, this limited audience for the site is where the Indigenous Network broke down for me. It took me a while to notice, but after eagerly signing up, I realized I would go weeks at a time without checking the Indigenous Network; those weeks became months, and truthfully until I started writing this chapter in spring 2013 it had been six months since I last logged in. I noticed that my friend who invited me to join has not logged on in over 11 months. And today, as I continue working on this chapter in 2015, I came to discover the Indigenous Network is no more. It folded in April 2013, lasting only two years. The space, while intriguing at the onset, did not keep our attention. In spite of appearing to be and do Indian, it was not an online place to call home.

FACEBOOK AS ALWAYS ALREADY INDIGENOUS?

So if stand-alone social networking sites like the Indigenous Network aren't sustainable, can preexisting social media sites provide a space for rhetorical sovereignty? . . .

If we think about Indianness as something that one does instead of something that one is, and if we think about those characteristics that distinguish indigenous cultures and epistemologies, we must also think of the interface not as something that can necessarily visually promise a sense of Indianness, but as something that allows for indigenous ways of being and doing. While the Indigenous Network's sharing functionality encouraged indigenous ways of being, separating oneself out from all of my relations — be they indigenous or otherwise — brackets my relations to one slice of who I am. The fact that the Indigenous Network is no more indicates I was not alone. And even though Facebook is a corporate entity designed within a Western culture, as the Seminole-Creek art historian Mary Jo Watson put it, "what makes Indian people so unique and so persistent is their ability to take foreign material, or a foreign technology, and make it Indian" (as quoted in Haas, 2005, n.p.). Similarly, Lyons (2010) described his conception of the x-mark (that is, the signature made by many American Indians on treaties) as "more than just embracing new or foreign ideas as your own; it means consciously connecting those ideas to certain values, interests, and political objectives, and making the best call you can under conditions not of your making" (p. 70). The interface is but one player in a web of relations, one that may not be of one's own making but can be put into relation with ideas, people, and the world in a very indigenous way. The act of posting a social networking profile allows, in danah boyd's (2007) words, users to "write themselves and their community into being" (p. 2). However, composing the self is never an act free of context. In the case of social networking, the interface provides a visual context wherein the self is composed. And while the interface affords certain opportunities and understandings — consider the Indigenous Network's entry page which visually represented all user's posts (a one-to-all relationship) versus a news feed in Facebook which visually represents a predefined subset of posts (a one-to-some relationship) — indigenous users will always already place themselves in-relation-to so long as a space allows for it.

What would Facebook look like if designed by and for American Indians? An American Indian interface doesn't necessarily have to be red, white, black and yellow, nor does it have to include eagle feathers, nor does it necessarily mean that one will talk about frybread (but it might) or that it will "have a point" (but it might) or that one will talk about teepee creepin' (but it might), but instead it means an acknowledgement of the network that I sustain, and that sustains me back. And, you know what my network looks like? It looks a lot like Facebook. Miigwetch.[4]

REFERENCES

Arola, K. L. (2010). The design of web 2.0: The rise of the template, the fall of design. *Computers & Composition, 27*(1), 4-14.

Baron, D. (2009). *A better pencil: Readers, writers, and the digital revolution.* New York, NY: Oxford University Press.

Bizzaro, R. C. (2004). Shooting our last arrow: Developing a rhetoric of identity for unenrolled American Indians. *College English, 67*(1), 61-74.

boyd, d. (2007). Why youth (heart) social network sites: The role of networked publics in teenage social life. In D. Buckingham (Ed.), *MacArthur foundation series on digital learning — Youth, identity, and digital media volume* (pp. 1-26). Cambridge, MA: MIT Press.

Clifton, J. A. (1990). *The invented Indian: Cultural fictions and government policies.* New Brunswick, NJ: Transaction.

Cordova, V. F. (2007), What is the world? In V. F. Cordova, K. D. Moore, K. Peters, T. Jojola, & A. Lacy (Eds.), *How it is: The Native American philosophy of V. F. Cordova* (pp. 100-106). Tucson, AZ: University of Arizona Press.

Cushman, E. (2008). Toward a rhetoric of self representation: Identity politics in Indian country and rhetoric and composition. *College Composition and Communication, 60*(2), 321-365.

Deloria, P. J. (1998). *Playing Indian.* New Haven, CT: Yale University Press.

Deloria, V. (1990). Comfortable fictions and the struggle for turf: An essay review of the invented Indian: Cultural fictions and government policies. *American Indian Quarterly, 16*(3), 397-410.

Deloria, V. (1998). *Custer died for our sins: An Indian manifesto.* Norman, OK: University of Oklahoma Press.

Foucault, M. (1991). *Discipline and punish: The birth of a prison.* London, England: Penguin.

Garroutte, E. M. (2003). *Real Indians: Identity and the survival of Native America.* Berkeley, CA: California University Press.

---

[4]Miigwech means "thank you" in Ojibwemowin.

Haas, A. M. (2005). Making online spaces more native to American Indians: A digital diversity recommendation. *Computers and Composition Online*. Retrieved from http://www.cconlinejournal.org/Haas/sovereignty.htm

Indigenous Network. (n.d.). Retrieved from http://indigenousnetwork.net/

Lord, E. (2009). America's wretched. In M. S. T. Williams (Ed.), *The Alaska native reader: History, culture, politics* (pp. 309-317). Durham, NC: Duke University Press.

Lyons, S. R. (2000). Rhetorical sovereignty: What do American Indians want from writing? *College Composition and Communication, 51*(3), 447-468.

Lyons, S. R. (2010). *X-Marks: Native signatures of assent.* Minneapolis, MN: University of Minnesota Press.

Mihesuah, D. A. (1996). *American Indians: Stereotypes and realities.* Atlanta, GA: Clarity International Press.

Nakamura, L. (2002). *Cybertypes: Race, ethnicity, and identity on the Internet.* New York, NY: Routledge.

Nakamura, L. (2007). *Digitizing race: Visual cultures of the Internet.* Minneapolis, MN: University of Minnesota Press.

Nakamura, L., & Chow-White, P. L. (Eds.). (2011). *Race after the Internet.* New York, NY: Routledge.

Powell, M. (2002). Rhetorics of survivance: How American Indians use writing. *College Composition and Communication, 53*(3), 396-434.

Rothenberg, P. (2008). *White privilege: Essential readings on the other side of racism.* New York, NY: Worth.

Twist, K. (2000, December 4). Four directions to making the Internet Indian. Retrieved from http://www.digitaldivide.net/articles/view.php?ArticleID=241

Topics for Critical Thinking and Writing

1. In paragraph 3, Kristin Arola asserts that "template-driven designs . . . limit the ways in which one is able to compose oneself and one's relations online." In what specific ways might the design of a website encourage or discourage certain kinds of expressions or relations?

2. What are some of the complications Arola recognizes in conceiving a Facebook interface that would be "recognizable as Native" (para. 5)?

3. What does it mean to have "rhetorical sovereignty" (para. 6)? Where else in contemporary culture might one's rhetorical sovereignty be limited or challenged?

4. How does the Indigenous Network webpage represent a distinctively American Indian interface that encourages specific cultural relations? Why do you think it ultimately did not last as a social networking site?

5. What do you think Arola's answers are in her effort to encourage culturally specific forms of self-expression? What are some of the problems certain cultures or groups confront in social media spaces, and what are some possible solutions? Explore other social media platforms or consider cultures and groups you belong to and their relationships with different online spaces.

HOSSEIN DERAKHSHAN

Hossein Derakhshan is an Iranian Canadian journalist and blogger who started his career as a writer in 1999 in Tehran, Iran, where he penned articles for the reformist newspapers *Asr-e Azadegan* and *Hayat-e-No*. In 2000, he began a Persian-language blog, *Sardabir: khodam* (*"Editor: myself"*) and quickly inspired a blogging revolution in Iran — becoming known as the "blogfather." Following two visits to Israel, Derakhshan was arrested by the Iranian government and charged with "propagating against the state" and "cooperating with hostile governments." He was sentenced to nineteen and a half years in prison, served six, and was pardoned by Iran's supreme leader in 2014. After his release, he went on to write about the social and political power of the internet in a widely translated essay, "The Web We Have to Save" (2015), and, with Claire Wardle, in a report commissioned by the Council of Europe, "Information Disorder" (2017). He is currently a research fellow at Harvard University's Kennedy School. The piece reprinted here originally appeared in *Wired* magazine in 2017.

How Social Media Endangers Knowledge

Wikipedia, one of the last remaining pillars of the open and decentralized web, is in existential crisis.

This has nothing to do with money. A couple of years ago, the site launched a panicky fundraising campaign, but ironically thanks to Donald Trump, Wikipedia has never been as wealthy or well-organized. American liberals, worried that Trump's rise threatened the country's foundational Enlightenment ideals, kicked in a significant flow of funds that has stabilized the nonprofit's balance sheet.

That happy news masks a more concerning problem — a flattening growth rate in the number of contributors to the website. It is another troubling sign of a general trend around the world: The very idea of knowledge itself is in danger.

The idea behind Wikipedia — like all encyclopedias before it — has been to collect the entirety of human knowledge. It's a goal that extends back to the Islamic Golden Age, when numerous scholars — inspired by Muhammad's famous verdict of "Seek knowledge, even from China" — set themselves to collecting and documenting all existing information on a wide variety of topics, including translations from Greek, Persian, Syrian, and Indian into Arabic. In the 9th century, a Persian scholar named Ibn Qutaybah collected the first true encyclopedia, 10 books on power, war, nobility, character, learning and eloquence, asceticism, friendship, prayers, food, and women. He was followed a century later by another Persian scholar, al-Khwārizmī who, in addition to inventing algebra, produced an encyclopedia covering what he called indigenous knowledge (jurisprudence, scholastic philosophy, grammar, secretarial duties, prosody and poetic art, history) and foreign knowledge (philosophy, logic, medicine, arithmetic, geometry, astronomy, music, mechanics, alchemy). The Chinese had their own encyclopedia dating back to the 7th century.

In Europe, the quest to compile a modern 5 encyclopedia started with the Enlightenment in the 18th century. (Immanuel Kant coined a fitting Latin motto for the movement: "Sapere aude," or "Dare to know.") French Enlightenment thinkers like Francis Bacon and Denis Diderot began compiling ambitious encyclopedias, inspiring others throughout France, Germany, England, Switzerland and the Netherlands.

The religious ruling class's discomfort with the effort only helped its financial feasibility; there was an obvious market for these massive collections, often published in numerous volumes, for an increasingly secular middle-class. The first volume of Encyclopedie was sold in 1751 to 2,000 subscribers, who would go on to receive the entire twenty-eight-volume set. Notable revolutionary thinkers such as Voltaire, Rousseau, and Montesquieu were involved in the editing of the work and several even ended up in prison. Only 17 years after the publication of the last volume in 1772, the French revolution began, leading to perhaps the most secular state in human history.

That trend toward rationality and enlightenment was endangered long before the advent of the Internet. As Neil Postman noted in his 1985 book *Amusing Ourselves to Death,* the rise of television introduced not just a new medium but a new discourse: a gradual shift from a typographic culture to a photographic one, which in turn meant a shift from rationality to emotions, exposition to entertainment. In an image-centered and pleasure-driven world, Postman noted, there is no place for rational thinking, because you simply cannot think with images. It is text that enables us to "uncover lies, confusions and overgeneralizations, to detect abuses of logic and common sense. It also means to weigh ideas, to compare and contrast assertions, to connect one generalization to another."

The dominance of television was not contained to our living rooms. It overturned all of those habits of mind, fundamentally changing our experience of the world, affecting the conduct of politics, religion, business, and culture. It reduced many aspects of modern life to entertainment, sensationalism, and commerce. "Americans don't talk to each other, we entertain each other," Postman wrote. "They don't exchange ideas, they exchange images. They do not argue with propositions; they argue with good looks, celebrities and commercials."

At first, the Internet seemed to push against this trend. When it emerged towards the end of the 80s as a purely text-based medium, it was seen as a tool to pursue knowledge, not pleasure. Reason and thought were most valued in this garden — all derived from the project of Enlightenment. Universities around the world were among the first to connect to this new medium, which hosted discussion groups, informative personal or group blogs, electronic magazines, and academic mailing lists and forums. It was an intellectual project, not about commerce or control, created in a scientific research center in Switzerland.

Wikipedia was a fruit of this garden. So was Google search and its text-based advertising model. And so were blogs, which valued text, hypertext (links), knowledge, and literature. They effectively democratized the ability to contribute to the global corpus of knowledge. For more than a decade, the web created an alternative space that threatened television's grip on society.

Social networks, though, have since colonized the web for television's values. From Facebook to Instagram, the medium refocuses our attention on videos and images, rewarding emotional appeals — "like" buttons — over rational ones. Instead of a quest for knowledge, it engages us in an endless zest for instant approval from an audience, for which we are constantly but unconsciously performing. (It's telling that, while Google began life as a PhD thesis, Facebook started as a tool to judge classmates' appearances.) It reduces our curiosity by showing us exactly what we already want and think, based on our profiles and preferences. Enlightenment's motto of "Dare to know" has become "Dare not to care to know."

It is a development that further proves the words of French philosopher Guy Debord, who wrote that, if pre-capitalism was about "being," and capitalism about "having," in late-capitalism what matters is only "appearing" — appearing rich, happy, thoughtful, cool and cosmopolitan.

It's hard to open Instagram without being struck by the accuracy of his diagnosis.

Now the challenge is to save Wikipedia and its promise of a free and open collection of all human knowledge amid the conquest of new and old television — how to collect and preserve knowledge when nobody cares to know. Television has even infected Wikipedia itself — today many of the most popular entries tend to revolve around television series or their cast.

This doesn't mean it is time to give up. But we need to understand that the decline of the web and thereby of the Wikipedia is part of a much larger civilizational shift which has just started to unfold.

Topics for Critical Thinking and Writing

1. Hossein Derakhshan writes in paragraph 3 that "knowledge itself is in danger." What does he mean by that?

2. In paragraphs 4 and 5, Derakhshan accounts for the evolution of the encyclopedia to its print form and then its emergence as a user-generated version like Wikipedia. Which kind of reference work could be considered more reliable — the traditional professionally edited encyclopedia or Wikipedia? Why? What are the advantages and disadvantages of each?

3. In paragraph 10, Derakhshan writes, "It's telling that, while Google began life as a PhD thesis, Facebook started as a tool to judge classmates' appearances." Explain how that assessment connects to Derakhshan's overall argument about the ways the internet has changed information access and exchange.

4. Consider what Neil Postman said about Americans, especially his conclusion that Americans "do not argue with propositions; they argue with good looks, celebrities and commercials" (para. 7). Is this statement true? Test Postman's claim by refuting it or supporting it in a brief essay.

5. Has technology created a landscape where information is limited, manipulated, and controlled, or has it democratized the process of knowledge construction, opening it up to outsider voices, new perspectives, and expanded knowledge? Cite specific examples to support your position.

JOSH ROSE

Josh Rose is founder and creative director at Humans Are Social, a digital content agency dedicated to social media marketing. A graduate of the University of California–Santa Cruz, Rose has also worked at public relations agencies Deutsch LA and Weber Shandwick. The following article was published in 2011 on Mashable, an online source that reports on digital innovation.

How Social Media Is Having a Positive Impact on Our Culture

Two events today, although worlds apart, seem inextricably tied together. And the bond between them is as human as it is electronic.

First, on my way to go sit down and read the newspaper at my coffee shop, I got a message from my ten-year-old son, just saying good morning and letting me know he was going to a birthday party today. I don't get to see him all the time. He's growing up in two houses, as I did. But recently I handed down my old iPhone 3G to him to use basically as an iPod Touch. We both installed an app called Yak, so we could communicate with each other when we're apart.

The amount of calming satisfaction it gives me to be able to communicate with him through technology is undeniably palpable and human. It's the other side of the "I don't care what you ate for breakfast this morning" argument against the mundane broadcasting of social media. In this case, I absolutely care about this. I'd listen to him describe a piece of bacon, and hang on every word. Is it better than a conversation with "real words"? No. But is it better than waiting two more days, when the mundane moment that I long to hear about so much is gone? Yes.

I guess one man's TMI is another man's treasure.

Moments later, I sat down and opened 5 the paper. A headline immediately stood out: "In China, microblogs finding abducted kids" with the subhead, "A 6-year-old who was snatched when he was 3 is discovered with a family 800 miles away." Apparently, the occurrence of reclaimed children through the use of China's version of Twitter — and other online forums — has become triumphant news over there. I'm reading about the father's tears, the boy's own confusing set of emotions, the rapt attention of the town and country, and I'm again marveling at the human side of the Internet.

THE PARADOX OF ONLINE CLOSENESS

I recently asked the question to my Facebook friends: "Twitter, Facebook, Foursquare . . . is all this making you feel closer to people or farther away?" It sparked a lot of responses and seemed to touch one of our generation's exposed nerves. What is the effect of the Internet and social media on our humanity?

From the outside view, digital interactions appear to be cold and inhuman. There's no denying that. And without doubt, given the choice between hugging someone and "poking" someone, I think we can all agree which one feels better. The theme of the responses to my Facebook question seemed to be summed up by my friend Jason, who wrote: "Closer to people I'm far away from." Then, a minute later, wrote, "but maybe farther from the people I'm close enough to." And then added, "I just got confused."

It is confusing. We live in this paradox now, where two seemingly conflicting realities exist side-by-side. Social media simultaneously draws us nearer and distances us. But I think very often, we lament what we miss and forget to admire what we've become. And it's human nature to want to reject the machine at the moment we feel it becoming ubiquitous. We've seen it with the printing press, moving pictures, television, video games, and just about any other advanced technology that captures our attention. What romantic rituals of relationship and social interaction will die in the process? Our hearts want to know.

In the *New Yorker* this week [February 14, 2011] Adam Gopnik's article "How the Internet Gets Inside Us" explores this cultural truism in depth. It's a fantastic read and should be mandatory for anyone in an online industry. He breaks down a whole slew of new books on the subject and categorizes it all into three viewpoints: "the Never-Betters, the Better-Nevers, and the Ever-Wasers." In short, those who see the current movement as good, bad, or normal. I think we all know people from each camp. But ultimately, the last group is the one best equipped to handle it all.

FILLING IN THE SPACE WITH CONNECTIONS

Another observation from the coffee shop: In 10 my immediate vicinity, four people are looking at screens and four people are reading something on paper. And I'm doing both. I see Facebook open on two screens, but I'm sure at some point, it's been open on all of them. The dynamic in this coffee shop is quite a bit more revealing than any article or book. Think about the varied juxtapositions of physical and digital going on. People aren't giving up long-form reading, considered thinking, or social interactions. They are just filling all the space between. And even that's not entirely true as I watch the occasional stare out the window or long glance around the room.

The way people engage with the Internet and social media isn't like any kind of interaction we've ever seen before. It's like an intertwining sine wave that touches in and out continuously. And the Internet itself is more complex and interesting than we often give it credit for. Consider peer-to-peer networking as just one example, where the tasks are distributed among the group to form a whole. It's practically a metaphor for the human mind. Or a township. Or a government. Or a family.

The Internet doesn't steal our humanity, it reflects it. The Internet doesn't get inside us, it shows what's inside us. And social media isn't cold, it's just complex and hard to define. I've always thought that you really see something's value when you try to destroy it. As we have now laid witness to in recent news, the Internet has quickly become the atom of cultural media; intertwined with our familial and cultural bonds, and destroyed only at great risk. I think if we search our own souls and consider our own personal way of navigating, we know this is as true personally as it is globally. The machine does not control us. It is a tool. As advanced today as a sharpened stick was a couple million years ago. Looked at through this lens, perhaps we should reframe our discussions about technology from how it is changing us to how we are using it.

Topics for Critical Thinking and Writing

1. In your own experience, what are the best parts and worst parts of social media? How do you balance the positives and negatives? What would you recommend for others?

2. In paragraph 8, Josh Rose says, "Social media simultaneously draws us nearer and distances us." Do you agree? Write a short response citing examples that may help convince a reader of the truth or untruth of this assertion.

3. In paragraph 9, Rose claims that of the Never-Betters, the Better-Nevers, and the Ever-Wasers, "the last group is the one best equipped to handle it all." Do you agree or disagree that those who see the changes brought about by the internet and social media as normal are the best equipped to handle it? Explain your answer.

4. In paragraph 11, Rose writes that the internet is a "metaphor for the human mind." Extend this metaphor. In what ways does the brain work like a computer? In what ways does it not?

5. Rose begins his final paragraph with these three sentences: "The Internet doesn't steal our humanity, it reflects it. The Internet doesn't get inside us, it shows what's inside us. And social media isn't cold, it's just complex and hard to define." Assume for the moment that he is correct. Go on to continue his conclusion, offering details that support an argument that the internet is not the cause of social problems but a reflection of them. Or, assume that Rose is incorrect and continue the paragraph by arguing that the internet indeed causes new problems. (For evidence, consider drawing upon one or more of the other essays in this chapter.)

JARON LANIER

Jaron Lanier is a computer scientist, philosopher, artist, and composer who worked for Atari Games in the early 1980s before leaving to develop early research on virtual reality and later to work at Microsoft and Internet2. Lanier's written work often predicts and interrogates the transformations that digital technologies bring to commerce and culture. He has written five books: *You Are Not a Gadget* (2010), *Who Owns the Future?* (2012), *When Dreams Grow Up* (2015), *Dawn of the New Everything* (2017), and *Ten Arguments for Deleting Your Social Media Accounts Right Now* (2018). The following essay appeared in *You Are Not a Gadget*.

Trolls

"Troll" is a term for an anonymous person who is abusive in an online environment. It would be nice to believe that there is a only a minute troll population living among us. But in fact, a great many people have experienced being drawn into nasty exchanges online. Everyone who has experienced that has been introduced to his or her inner troll.

I have tried to learn to be aware of the troll within myself. I notice that I can suddenly become relieved when someone else in an online exchange is getting pounded or humiliated, because that means I'm safe for the moment. If someone else's video is being ridiculed on YouTube, then mine is temporarily protected. But that also means I'm complicit in a mob dynamic. Have I ever planted a seed of mob-beckoning ridicule in order to guide the mob to a target other than myself? Yes, I have, though I shouldn't have. I observe others doing that very thing routinely in anonymous online meeting places.

I've also found that I can be drawn into ridiculous pissing matches online in ways that just wouldn't happen otherwise, and I've never noticed any benefit. There is never a lesson learned, or a catharsis of victory or defeat. If you win anonymously, no one knows, and if you lose, you just change your pseudonym and start over, without having modified your point of view one bit.

If the troll is anonymous and the target is known, then the dynamic is even worse than an encounter between anonymous fragmentary pseudo-people. That's when the hive turns against personhood. For instance, in 2007 a series of "Scarlet Letter" postings in China incited online throngs to hunt down accused adulterers. In 2008, the focus shifted to Tibet sympathizers. Korea has one of the most intense online cultures in the world, so it has also suffered some of the most extreme trolling. Korean movie star Choi Jin-sil, sometimes described as the "Nation's Actress," committed suicide in 2008 after being hounded online by trolls, but she was only the most famous of a series of similar suicides.

In the United States, anonymous internet users have ganged up on targets like Lori Drew, the woman who created a fake boy persona on the internet in order to break the heart of a classmate of her daughter's, which caused the girl to commit suicide.

But more often the targets are chosen randomly, following the pattern described in the short story "The Lottery" by Shirley Jackson. In the story, residents of a placid small town draw lots to decide which individual will be stoned to death each year. It is as if a measure of human cruelty must be released, and to do so in a contained yet random way limits the damage by using the fairest possible method.

Some of the better-known random victims of troll mobs include the blogger Kathy Sierra. She was suddenly targeted in a multitude of ways, such as having images of her as a sexually mutilated corpse posted prominently, apparently in the hopes that her children would see them. There was no discernible reason Sierra was targeted. Her number was somehow drawn from the lot.

Another famous example is the tormenting of the parents of Mitchell Henderson, a boy who committed suicide. They were subjected to gruesome audio-video creations and other tools at the disposal of virtual sadists. Another occurence is the targeting of epileptic people with flashing web designs in the hope of inducing seizures.

There is a vast online flood of videos of humiliating assaults on helpless victims. The culture of sadism online has its own vocabulary and has gone mainstream. The common term "lulz," for instance, refers to the gratification of watching others suffer over the cloud.[1]

When I criticize this type of online culture, 10 I am often accused of being either an old fart or an advocate of censorship. Neither is the case. I don't think I'm necessarily any better, or more moral, than the people who tend the lulzy websites. What I'm saying, though, is that the user interface designs that arise from the ideology of the computing cloud make people-all of us-less kind. Trolling is not a string of isolated incidents, but the status quo in the online world.

---

[1] A website called the Encyclopedia Dramatica brags on its main page that it "won the 2nd Annual Mashable Open Web Awards for the wiki category." As I check it today, in late 2008, just as this book is about to leave my hands, the headlining "Article of the Now" is described in this way: "[Three guys] decided that the best way to commemorate their departing childhood was to kill around 21 people with hammers, pipes and screwdrivers, and record the whole thing on their [video recording] phones." This story was also featured on Boing Boing — which went to the trouble of determining that it was not a hoax — and other top sites this week.

THE STANDARD SEQUENCE OF TROLL INVOCATION

There are recognizable stages in the degradation of anonymous, fragmentary communication. If no pack has emerged, then individuals start to fight. This is what happens all the time in online settings. A later stage appears once a pecking order is established. Then the members of the pack become sweet and supportive of one another, even as they goad one another into ever more intense hatred of nonmembers.

This suggests a hypothesis to join the ranks of ideas about how the circumstances of our evolution influenced our nature. We, the bigbrained species, probably didn't get that way to fill a single, highly specific niche. Instead, we must have evolved with the ability to switch between different niches. We evolved to be *both* loners *and* pack members. We are optimized not so much to be one or the other, but to be able to switch between them.

New patterns of social connection that are unique to online culture have played a role in the spread of modern networked terrorism. If you look at an online chat about anything, from guitars to poodles to aerobics, you'll see a consistent pattern: jihadi chat looks just like poodle chat. A pack emerges, and either you are with it or against it. If you join the pack, then you join the collective ritual hatred.

If we are to continue to focus the powers of digital technology on the project of making human affairs less personal and more collective, then we ought to consider how that project might interact with human nature.

The genetic aspects of behavior that have 15 received the most attention (under rubrics like sociobiology or evolutionary psychology) have tended to focus on things like gender differences and mating behaviors, but my guess is that clan orientation and its relationship to violence will turn out to be the most important area of study.

DESIGN UNDERLIES ETHICS IN THE DIGITAL WORLD

People are not universally nasty online. Behavior varies considerably from site to site. There are reasonable theories about what brings out the best or worst online behaviors: demographics, economics, child-rearing trends, perhaps even the average time of day of usage could play a role. My opinion, however, is that certain details in the design of the user interface experience of a website are the most important factors.

People who can spontaneously invent a pseudonym in order to post a comment on a blog or on YouTube are often remarkably mean. Buyers and sellers on eBay are a little more civil, despite occasional disappointments, such as encounters with flakiness and fraud. Based on those data, you could conclude that it isn't exactly anonymity, but *transient* anonymity, coupled with a lack of consequences, that brings out online idiocy.

With more data, that hypothesis can be refined. Participants in Second Life (a virtual online world) are generally not quite as mean to one another as are people posting comments to Slashdot (a popular technology news site) or engaging in edit wars on Wikipedia, even though all allow pseudonyms. The difference might be that on Second Life the pseudonymous personality itself is highly valuable and requires a lot of work to create.

So a better portrait of the troll-evoking design is effortless, consequence-free, transient anonymity in the service of a goal, such as promoting a point of view, that stands entirely apart from one's identity or personality. Call it drive-by anonymity.

Computers have an unfortunate tendency 20 to present us with binary choices at every level, not just at the lowest one, where the bits are switching. It is easy to be anonymous or fully revealed, but hard to be revealed just enough. Still, that does happen, to varying degrees. Sites like eBay and Second Life give hints about how design can promote a middle path.

Anonymity certainly has a place, but that place needs to be designed carefully. Voting and peer review are preinternet examples of beneficial anonymity. Sometimes it is desirable for people to be free off ear of reprisal or stigma in order to invoke honest opinions. To have a substantial exchange, however, you need to be fully present. That is why facing one's accuser is a fundamental right of the accused.

COULD DRIVE-BY ANONYMITY SCALE UP THE WAY COMMUNISM AND FASCISM DID?

For the most part, the net has delivered happy surprises about human potential. As I pointed out earlier, the rise of the web in the early 1990s took place without leaders, ideology, advertising, commerce, or anything other than a positive sensibility shared by millions of people. Who would have thought that was possible? Ever since, there has been a constant barrage of utopian extrapolations from positive online events. Whenever a blogger humiliates a corporation by posting documentation of an infelicitous service representative, we can expect triumphant hollers about the end of the era of corporate abuses.

It stands to reason, however, that the net can also accentuate negative patterns of behavior or even bring about unforeseen social pathology. Over the last century, new media technologies have often become prominent as components of massive outbreaks of organized violence.

For example, the Nazi regime was a major pioneer of radio and cinematic propaganda.

The Soviets were also obsessed with propaganda technologies. Stalin even nurtured a "Manhattan Project" to develop a 3-D theater with incredible, massive optical elements that would deliver perfected propaganda. It would have been virtual reality's evil twin if it had been completed. Many people in the Muslim world have only gained access to satellite TV and the internet in the last decade. These media certainly have contributed to the current wave of violent radicalism. In all these cases, there was an intent to propagandize, but intent isn't everything.

It's not crazy to worry that, with millions 25 of people connected through a medium that sometimes brings out their worst tendencies, massive, fascist-style mobs could rise up suddenly. I worry about the next generation of young people around the world growing up with internet-based technology that emphasizes crowd aggregation, as is the current fad. Will they be more likely to succumb to pack dynamics when they come of age?

What's to prevent the acrimony from scaling up? Unfortunately, history tells us that collectivist ideals can mushroom into large-scale social disasters. The *fascias* and communes of the past started out with small numbers of idealistic revolutionaries.

I am afraid we might be setting ourselves up for a reprise. The recipe that led to social catastrophe in the past was economic humiliation combined with collectivist ideology. We already have the ideology in its new digital packaging, and it's entirely possible we could face dangerously traumatic economic shocks in the coming decades.

Topics for Critical Thinking and Writing

1. Is trolling ever justified? If so, what factors might contribute to justifying the behavior? What factors make it problematic?

2. Jaron Lanier suggests in paragraph 3 that online disputes rarely end up resolved or with the result of a perspective change. Do you agree or disagree? Explain.

3. Lanier uses terms from the animal kingdom such as the "hive" (para. 4) and the "pack" (paras. 11–13, 25) to describe human behavior in online environments. How do Lanier's metaphors represent different types of behavior? What online venues do you think are more or less accommodating to the "hive" versus the "pack," and why?

4. In paragraph 10, Lanier states that "Trolling is not a string of isolated incidents, but the status quo in the online world." To what does Lanier attribute this phenomenon? Do you agree with Lanier's claim that the modern digital environment makes "all of us" less kind? Why or why not?

5. In paragraph 15, Lanier states that when it comes to understanding human behavior in online environments, "My guess is that clan orientation and its relationship to violence will turn out to be the most important area of study." Read his final three paragraphs and consider that this essay was published in 2010. Do you think Lanier's predictions were accurate? Explain.

6. Go to Reddit, the comments section of an article, or another online forum, and identify a dispute between two or more people. Then analyze the conflict in terms of how the parties debate. Are they mutually constructive debates or futile exercises in talking past one another? Do they represent open-minded inquiry or weak critical thinking, fallacies, insults,

and so on? Does the venue improve the chances for rational debate or does it invite troll-like behavior? If possible, share your experiences and the conclusions you have drawn from it with your classmates.

TOURIA BENLAFQIH

Touria Benlafqih is the founder and chief executive officer of Social Impact and Development Employment (SIDE), a group that works to build public/private partnerships addressing social, economic, and environmental development issues in Africa. This essay was published in the World Economic Forum in 2015.

Has Social Media Made Young People Better Citizens?

There have never been as many young people as there are today. This is particularly true in Africa and the Middle East. Young people are a considerable asset to their countries, with a critical role to play in the political, social, economic and cultural landscape. Yet their potential is still untapped, and their contribution to their nations still hasn't been fully realized: a large part of this young population remains uneducated, unemployed or uninterested.

Youth is a pivotal period in a person's life; it's the bridge between childhood and adulthood. According to Erik Erikson's stages of psychological development, each individual experiences a phase during which they search for their identity, a phase where they blend their identity with friends and want to fit in, and a phase of "generativity," where they start wishing to build a legacy and guide the next generation.

With that in mind, we understand that the very nature of youth is to be involved and contribute. It is quite difficult for me to believe the line that young people lack engagement in society nowadays. So why is it the case, then?

There are various reasons why young people are less likely to be active citizens: the lack of effective communication between them and decision-makers, for example. Also, young people feel used instead of empowered, so they don't easily embrace the "old school mindset" in doing things. Often, they lack information and don't fully understand how political institutions, economic development, public services or social inclusion work—and nothing is more vital to a democracy than a well-informed electorate.

Ten years ago, when I began working with young people, I was surprised to discover that many of them don't know where or how to get started. They had dreams, energy and enthusiasm, but no proper knowledge of how to be active, and no proper guidance to channel that energy.

Back then, the internet was a new concept in Morocco, and was still confined to a very limited population. A young person could only access information through traditional media (TV, radio, newspapers and magazines); and they could only find out about the activities of a political party or a public gathering for a social cause, through word of mouth, provided they knew the right people.

Social media is the most adapted communication tool of today's younger generation. It's easy to see why: accessible and user-friendly, platforms such as Twitter, Facebook and LinkedIn let you create and showcase your personality, develop new contacts, discuss issues and keep in touch in real time. They allow you to read, analyze and share content without any prerequisites.

Media is no longer the one-way communication channel as it used to be. With connected devices becoming ever more ubiquitous, questions can be answered and misunderstandings avoided. It has become easier to connect with people from different places and backgrounds: to benefit from their experience, to support a cause without being directly involved, to engage with organizations and movements, and to mobilize people in less time and with less cost.

Working with young people in Morocco over the years, I have witnessed a change in how they engage: they have become better and more active citizens, in both a formal and informal way. Thanks to social media's diverse platforms, young people can view content about their region, about influencers and decision-makers. They can participate in online petitions, join groups and talk to like-minded people on Facebook, contribute to the debate on Twitter, report an injustice on Instagram, or share videos and podcasts on YouTube. Social media fosters a sense of ownership and responsibility, and young people can engage directly, not just as individuals, but as part of a community in their own personal way.

While many young people in Morocco are engaged in social activities outside social media, youth engagement in "real-life" organizations, projects and awareness-raising is comparatively insignificant, and remains concentrated in major cities, where most government, civil-society and private-sector activity is focused. 10

How can we help the momentum of online youth engagement spread to real-world local areas? We need to provide monitoring and funding for local initiatives, organize more events and training workshops, and attract more attention to civil-society activities in smaller cities, towns and villages. We need to create local success stories that inspire and drive young people, and which they can showcase on social media to inspire others.

I believe that participation and engagement is a natural attribute of youth, and has been like this for as long as humanity and social interaction existed. Young people will continue to expand their contribution and participation for as long as they have the tools. Even though more than half of Morocco is connected to the internet, more efforts have to be made in terms of youth mobilization and participation, in order to see this contribution growing exponentially towards a better, more inclusive world.

Topics for Critical Thinking and Writing

1. Do you agree with Touria Benlafqih's assessment that young people "don't fully understand how political institutions, economic development, public services or social inclusion work" (para. 4)? Use evidence to support your response.

2. What kinds of remedies does Benlafqih advocate to get young people more involved in politics and global issues? Do you think they would be effective?

3. Does Benlafqih's essay provide a convincing counterpoint to Marche's (p. 546) and Lanier's (p. 576)? Explain.

4. Do you think the voting age in the United States should be lowered? If so, to what age, and why? If not, provide reasons why it should be kept the same or increased.

5. Do some research on the term "hashtag activism" and discuss whether or not you think such activism is worthwhile or effective. Why or why not?

24

Representation Matters: How Does Media Portray Us?

TERESE MAILHOT

Terese Mailhot is a Nlaka'pamux writer and teacher of the Seabird Island Band, one of over six hundred Indigenous communities constituting the First Nation governments of Canada. Her 2018 book *Heart Berries: A Memoir* was a finalist for the Governor General's Literary Award, a Now Read This Book Club selection from PBS Newshour and the *New York Times*, and included on several best books of the year lists from NPR, *The Library Journal*, and *Harper's Bazaar*. She teaches creative writing at Purdue University. Mailhot's journalism has appeared in *Guernica*, the *Guardian*, *Al-Jazeera*, and *Mother Jones*, where this selection was published in 2018.

Native American Lives Are Tragic, But Probably Not in the Way You Think

> "Healing requires acknowledgement," says Lisa Schrader, a student at St. Joe's Indian School and Red Cloud Indian School in the 1970s and early 1980s. "And when we were taken away from our homes and we lost our language, and we lost our culture, and we lost our identity, no one ever told us, 'Welcome home. I'm glad you made it back.'"

Back in June, activist Shaun King tweeted out a colleague's *Intercept* story to his million-plus followers: "All over this country, for decades on end now, indigenous women have gone missing at an alarming rate," he wrote.

"Authorities are just now truly acknowledging the crisis." I remembered then to ask around the rez whether Roberta was still missing.

Roberta, whose name I have changed to protect her privacy, is from my reserve on British Columbia's Seabird Island. It's a small community, and it only took a few Facebook messages to learn she'd been spotted at a 7-Eleven. I'd seen her myself a few months earlier, and she wasn't looking well. When I was young I used to babysit for a friend of hers, and I still remember how hard they partied. Someone close to Roberta told me she had been trying to stay in recovery — she was "lost but not lost." Just putting this to paper perpetuates a negative stereotype: We're doing this to ourselves.

In March, Roberta had posted on Facebook, "Do you believe in me? acknokwledge me please." She was reported missing April 13, and for weeks I would stare at her profile picture, then at her "missing person" photo. She eventually resurfaced. Then a woman from my father's nearby reserve went missing. Her name is Shawnee and she's 29 years old.

Native people are familiar with brutality, with our histories. We bear witness firsthand, and then again via media reports articulating how bad we have it — if they notice us at all. It seems like all I see in my news feed are missing-persons photos and stories about racism against us. I empathize with Roberta's circumstances. I think it's easy to fall in a hole where I'm from, easy to give up hope. People will be mad at me for saying that.

My friend Tommy Orange begins his 5 debut novel, *There There*, with a prologue about the circumstances Native Americans once faced — the brutal truth: "Some of us grew up with stories about massacres. Stories about what happened to our people not so long ago." He describes how white people tore unborn babies from our bodies. How they danced with our dismembered parts and displayed our heads in jars. A *Globe and Mail* reviewer warned that his novel could be weaponized: "I found myself wondering how non-Indigenous people would read this book," she wrote, "and whether they would interpret it to reinforce their stereotypes of Indigenous people." But I don't know how we can be artists if we're worried about what white people will think of us.

I believe all good stories are tragedies. I also realize outsiders see our plight differently. They see it as voyeurs, hoping to affirm something in themselves: that we are braves humiliated, or wild savages from a lost time, people who were ravaged, and what is left is only a mirror of what's been done, a vessel for a white person's imagination.

The tropes are porous and easy to get lost in. Last year, the Native American Journalists Association and *HighCountry News* issued a bingo board designed "to catch overused and hackneyed ideas employed by newsrooms" — alcohol, poverty, "vanishing culture," "dying language." This may be helpful for reporters, but what of us Native authors and artists who want to express the truth of our lives, which are sometimes affected by, yes, poverty and alcohol? These conditions are not unique to Native people, of course, but when they are applied to us it feels definitive.

No matter what we write, white people can turn our stories into weapons, an excuse to be paternalistic. If we depict ourselves as educated and self-sufficient, they might advance the narrative that our tragedies are long past, that we should dust ourselves off and move on. If we are portrayed as poor or dysfunctional or prone to alcoholism, they can use that to take away services or argue that we game the system. No matter what we do, we're still Indian, and often we don't get to speak for ourselves.

> "You have no time to think for yourself," says Bessie Randolph, who attended Albuquerque Indian School from 1952 to 1962. "Wake up at 5:30, clean the building and make the beds, breakfast from 6 to 7, report to the school building at 8, lunch at 12, out of school at 4, dinner at 5:30, asleep by 8. Ten years of following that routine and we didn't know how to live like real people. We were told when and how to do everything. How do you apply for a job? How do you use the telephone? Are you supposed to go to college? We left school completely lost."

I grew up thinking about the tragedy of my history. Elders used to say we were stewards of the Earth, close to creation, divine in intellect and body, and living in abundance like Adam and Eve before the fall, before "contact" — a strangely puritanical ideology, no doubt violently ingrained in us by Christian influence; call that a tragedy, too. There's plenty of content about our misfortune now. Search YouTube and you can find a "drunk Native" subgenre — dozens of videos of our people, obliterated by drink, speaking nonsensically or fighting in the street. Some of the titles include the word "funny."

It wasn't until graduate school that I heard 10 the term "poverty porn" and realized non-Natives were titillated by our misfortunes, and that indigenous people were consuming it too, albeit for different reasons. Maybe, like me, they were just happy to be seen, finally — not as mascots or advertising icons or mystic ghosts, but as people, alive and still struggling in the aftermath of colonization.

Another friend, Blackfeet writer Sterling HolyWhiteMountain, wrote on social media this year that "1 in 3 Native Americans will be assaulted by statistics in their lifetime." It's the kind of joke we sometimes use to flick at stark truths: More than one-quarter of Native Americans live in poverty. The latest numbers show roughly 1 in 5 lacking health insurance — 8 percent are jobless. Gross underfunding of Native health care has resulted in life expectancies that are, in some states, about a decade shorter than the national average. A staggering 60 percent of children on Canadian reservations are impoverished. Native women are raped and assaulted at higher rates than any other group. The numbers go on to show, from every angle, a gap in service, a grave injustice. The statistics are burdensome but a little redemptive. They prove we aren't crazy for thinking our communities face disparities most couldn't imagine, a violence most cannot see.

I resist an identity fixed in grief, but I welcome tragedy. To me the word is pregnant with meaning. I don't mind a tragic life in which there is a magnitude to my character, my loss, and it is all toward some end — a denouement.

In my kitchen hangs a print my father made. He abused my mother, my sisters and brothers, and me and then left when I was six. He was a drunk. He didn't have a home. The only good parts of him were his artwork, exquisitely symmetrical and Salish, experimental with form and color. I don't know why I keep the print on my wall. Tragedy, I think. I want to see the human in the work.

Across the house, my first book is displayed on our mantel. Sherman Alexie wrote the introduction. Then he was accused of sexually harassing and assaulting Native women. (He later apologized vaguely and said he did not recall physically or verbally threatening anybody.) Now I can't look at my book without knowing that, even in triumph, I can't escape the statistics, the violence surrounding Native women.

But I am not a hopeless illustration, some- 15 thing for non-Natives to witness. This world is larger for us in it, because we saw things the white settlers didn't — we had maps and taxonomy, an interior knowledge of the Earth that our colonizers willfully tried to erase and negate. Amid the land allotments and limitations and government schools aimed at molding Native children, as one historian put it, "in the image of White America," we see the histories forgotten, the matrilineal societies, confederacies and prophets, infighting and clans, and stories the world is richer for. We discovered medicines, saved lives, and carried things we still hold in our minds. Thanks to secret knowledge and secret ceremonies, at least some of our cultures and people survived genocides. I feel we are failing when we allow the majority culture to burden us with its binaries: left behind or assimilated, saints or heathens, savages or healers, warriors or drunks. I don't know what to do with my definition of tragedy in the face of theirs. But I think the answer is always story. The duplicities in our identities as indigenous people are key.

> Oreos Eriacho spent the entire 1960s at Ramah Elementary School and Ramah Dormitory. "Your spirit is kind of broken when you're told you're not supposed to act like a Native American," he now says. "We've lost our identity—my kids ask me who we are and I have nothing to give them. But I'm teaching my daughters how to hunt, how to cut up the meat, how to use plants. I hope it helps."

At a Naval Academy graduation in May, President Donald Trump told cadets, "We are not going to apologize for America," and he claimed the nation's ancestors had "tamed a continent"—as if those who came before were savage. Where my people are from, Prime Minister Justin Trudeau is fighting with First Nations people who oppose a pipeline expansion that would triple the amount of tar sands oil shipped from Alberta to the coast of British Columbia.

My family now lives in Indiana ("Land of the Indians"), where my son was told by his middle-school bully that America is for whites only and Indians are dirty. They said the same to me, I told him, and to my mother when she was a kid—except they threw rocks at her when she walked into town, and my grandmother

experienced worse. I wanted him to know things aren't so bad as they used to be, but that they won't get better anytime soon. The age of Trumpism seems hell-bent on walking back progress to a time when white people enjoyed the benefit of even more brutal and explicit discrimination than they do today. I acknowledged the way defeat is useless, and hope might be, too. By the end of the day I had no conclusions to make—he went back to class.

I used to fight for awareness only to realize that once a system, a friend, or a teacher learned of our circumstances, they leveraged it as proof they should be paternal, or they did nothing but pity us and revel in that pity. For much of my life, outsiders have been telling me how sorry they are about what happened to Indians, or telling me to get over it. I'm hypervigilant about how I talk about myself and my people because we aren't a monolith, and while pity can feel like empathy or kindness, it's ultimately of no use.

Tommy Orange and I are close, personally and professionally. Together we went from poor to secure, grad students to teachers, unknown to critically acclaimed. So I messaged him to get his take on all this. He replied that he thinks most Indians don't view themselves as mired in tragic circumstances: "We become what we most don't want to become, and sometimes that is tragic. I think we should resist pity, and monolithic, static thinking regarding who we are and what we're about. Tragedy is unavoidable for humanity. I just always hope it's balanced with humor. I think of life as a tragicomedy."

Tommy is right. I've heard Natives, academics, and people on Twitter extolling joyous indigenous futures. But I like joy that's earned, because what good is it without the threat it can be taken away? The symmetry of the Salish artwork I grew up around beckons me to consider the whole story. My father's work redeemed him in the eyes of some people—it complicated him for me, which is what good art does. I don't want a joyous future nearly as much as I want the freedom to present the tragedy in our lives—and not be bound to it.

Topics for Critical Thinking and Writing

1. Consider Terese Mailhot's language, tone, and persona in the essay. How do they establish her *ethos*? How do they contribute to her argument?

2. What do you think Mailhot means when she expresses concerns that representations of Indigenous people have become "vessel[s] for a white person's imagination" (para. 6)? What paradoxes does Mailhot describe when it comes to portrayals of Indigenous people in media?

3. In paragraph 12, Mailhot writes, "I resist an identity fixed in grief, but I welcome tragedy." What does she mean? How does this statement relate to the reasons why she keeps an artwork created by her father on the wall?

4. Mailhot references several media sources as evidence in her argument about media representation. Is her chosen evidence effective? Why or why not?

5. Consider the similarities and differences between Mailhot's concerns for how her people are represented and the concerns voiced by Aubrey Gordon. Do you think it is productive to compare the histories and experiences of different groups of people? Why or why not?

6. Do some research to discover the presence of Indigenous culture in your area, then reflect on the question of visibility. In what ways do you see the legacies of Indigenous culture in your area, and how would you characterize the ways such cultures are present or recognized?

ANNA SWARTWOOD HOUSE

Anna Swartwood House holds a PhD from Princeton University and is an assistant professor of art history at the University of South Carolina, where she focuses on Renaissance and Baroque art. She is completing a book on the Italian painter Antonello da Messina, and published an article about him in 2018 entitled "Pulling Faces: Antonello da Messina's Laughing, Smiling Subjects." The essay reprinted here was published in *The Conversation* in July 2020.

The Long History of How Jesus Came To Resemble a White European

Painting depicting transfiguration of Jesus, a story in the New Testament when Jesus becomes radiant upon a mountain.

The portrayal of Jesus as a white, European man has come under renewed scrutiny during this period of introspection over the legacy of racism in society.

As protesters called for the removal of Confederate statues in the U.S., activist Shaun King went further, suggesting that murals and artwork depicting "white Jesus" should "come down."

His concerns about the depiction of Christ and how it is used to uphold notions of white supremacy are not isolated. Prominent scholars and the archbishop of Canterbury have called to reconsider Jesus' portrayal as a white man.

As a European Renaissance art historian, I study the evolving image of Jesus Christ from A.D. 1350 to 1600. Some of the best-known depictions of Christ, from Leonardo da Vinci's "Last Supper" to Michelangelo's "Last Judgment" in the Sistine Chapel, were produced during this period.

But the all-time most-reproduced image of 5 Jesus comes from another period. It is Warner Sallman's light-eyed, light-haired "Head of Christ" from 1940. Sallman, a former commercial artist who created art for advertising campaigns, successfully marketed this picture worldwide.

Through Sallman's partnerships with two Christian publishing companies, one Protestant and one Catholic, the Head of Christ came to be included on everything from prayer cards to stained glass, faux oil paintings, calendars, hymnals and night lights.

Sallman's painting culminates a long tradition of white Europeans creating and disseminating pictures of Christ made in their own image.

IN SEARCH OF THE HOLY FACE

The historical Jesus likely had the brown eyes and skin of other first-century Jews from

Galilee, a region in biblical Israel. But no one knows exactly what Jesus looked like. There are no known images of Jesus from his lifetime, and while the Old Testament Kings Saul and David are explicitly called tall and handsome in the Bible, there is little indication of Jesus' appearance in the Old or New Testaments.

Even these texts are contradictory: The Old Testament prophet Isaiah reads that the coming savior "had no beauty or majesty," while the Book of Psalms claims he was "fairer than the children of men," the word "fair" referring to physical beauty.

The earliest images of Jesus Christ emerged [10] in the first through third centuries A.D., amidst concerns about idolatry. They were less about capturing the actual appearance of Christ than about clarifying his role as a ruler or as a savior.

To clearly indicate these roles, early Christian artists often relied on syncretism, meaning they combined visual formats from other cultures.

Probably the most popular syncretic image is Christ as the Good Shepherd, a beardless, youthful figure based on pagan representations of Orpheus, Hermes and Apollo.

In other common depictions, Christ wears the toga or other attributes of the emperor. The theologian Richard Viladesau argues that the mature bearded Christ, with long hair in the "Syrian" style, combines characteristics of the Greek god Zeus and the Old Testament figure Samson, among others.

CHRIST AS SELF-PORTRAITIST

The first portraits of Christ, in the sense of authoritative likenesses, were believed to be self-portraits: the miraculous "image not made by human hands," or acheiropoietos.

This belief originated in the seventh [15] century A.D., based on a legend that Christ healed King Abgar of Edessa in modern-day Urfa, Turkey, through a miraculous image of his face, now known as the Mandylion.

A similar legend adopted by Western Christianity between the 11th and 14th centuries recounts how, before his death by crucifixion, Christ left an impression of his face on the veil of Saint Veronica, an image known as the volto santo, or "Holy Face."

These two images, along with other similar relics, have formed the basis of iconic traditions about the "true image" of Christ.

From the perspective of art history, these artifacts reinforced an already standardized image of a bearded Christ with shoulder-length, dark hair.

In the Renaissance, European artists began to combine the icon and the portrait, making Christ in their own likeness. This happened for a variety of reasons, from identifying with the human suffering of Christ to commenting on one's own creative power.

The 15th-century Sicilian painter Antonello [20] da Messina, for example, painted small pictures of the suffering Christ formatted exactly like his portraits of regular people, with the subject positioned between a fictive parapet and a plain black background and signed "Antonello da Messina painted me."

The 16th-century German artist Albrecht Dürer blurred the line between the holy face and his own image in a famous self-portrait of 1500. In this, he posed frontally like an icon, with his beard and luxuriant shoulder-length hair recalling Christ's. The "AD" monogram could stand equally for "Albrecht Dürer" or "Anno Domini" — "in the year of our Lord."

IN WHOSE IMAGE?

This phenomenon was not restricted to Europe: There are 16th- and 17th-century pictures of Jesus with, for example, Ethiopian and Indian features.

In Europe, however, the image of a light-skinned European Christ began to influence other parts of the world through European trade and colonization.

The Italian painter Andrea Mantegna's "Adoration of the Magi" from A.D. 1505 features three distinct magi, who, according to one contemporary tradition, came from Africa, the Middle East and Asia. They present expensive objects of porcelain, agate and brass that would have been prized imports from China and the Persian and Ottoman empires.

But Jesus' light skin and blues eyes 25 suggest that he is not Middle Eastern but European-born. And the faux-Hebrew script embroidered on Mary's cuffs and hemline belie a complicated relationship to the Judaism of the Holy Family.

In Mantegna's Italy, anti-Semitic myths were already prevalent among the majority Christian population, with Jewish people often segregated to their own quarters of major cities.

Artists tried to distance Jesus and his parents from their Jewishness. Even seemingly small attributes like pierced ears — earrings were associated with Jewish women, their removal with a conversion to Christianity — could represent a transition toward the Christianity represented by Jesus.

Much later, anti-Semitic forces in Europe including the Nazis would attempt to divorce Jesus totally from his Judaism in favor of an Aryan stereotype.

WHITE JESUS ABROAD

As Europeans colonized increasingly farther-flung lands, they brought a European Jesus with them. Jesuit missionaries established painting schools that taught new converts Christian art in a European mode.

A small altarpiece made in the school 30 of Giovanni Niccolò, the Italian Jesuit who founded the "Seminary of Painters" in Kumamoto, Japan, around 1590, combines a traditional Japanese gilt and mother-of-pearl shrine with a painting of a distinctly white, European Madonna and Child.

In colonial Latin America — called "New Spain" by European colonists — images of a white Jesus reinforced a caste system where white, Christian Europeans occupied the top tier, while those with darker skin from perceived intermixing with native populations ranked considerably lower.

Artist Nicolas Correa's 1695 painting of Saint Rose of Lima, the first Catholic saint born in "New Spain," shows her metaphorical marriage to a blond, light-skinned Christ.

LEGACIES OF LIKENESS

Scholar Edward J. Blum and Paul Harvey argue that in the centuries after European colonization of the Americas, the image of a white Christ associated him with the logic of empire and could be used to justify the oppression of Native and African Americans.

In a multiracial but unequal America, there was a disproportionate representation of a white Jesus in the media. It wasn't only Warner Sallman's Head of Christ that was depicted widely; a large proportion of actors who have played Jesus on television and film have been white with blue eyes.

Pictures of Jesus historically have served 35 many purposes, from symbolically presenting his power to depicting his actual likeness. But representation matters, and viewers need to understand the complicated history of the images of Christ they consume.

ANNA SWARTWOOD HOUSE, "The long history of how Jesus came to resemble a white European." The Conversation, 17 July 2020, https://theconversation.com/the-long-history-of-how-jesus-came-to-resemble-a-white-european-142130.

Topics for Critical Thinking and Writing

1. In the essay's opening paragraph, Anna Swartwood House states, "The portrayal of Jesus as a white, European man has come under renewed scrutiny during this period of introspection over the legacy of racism in society." Do you think the preponderance of representations of Jesus as a white person — from European painting to modern biblical ephemera — is in fact rooted in racism? Why or why not?

2. Examine House's *ethos* and determine whether or not she is a credible source for analyzing media representations of religious figures. Does her particular expertise lend value to the debates over Jesus's appearance? Why or why not?

3. Debates over what historical figures like Jesus looked like, particularly pertaining to race, can be controversial. Consider the challenges to critical thinking discussed in Chapter 1, "Obstacles to Critical Thinking," on pages 7–8. What obstacles do you think are most relevant to people who might resist the claim that Jesus was dark skinned? In short, why is this controversial, and what evidence would be most convincing in trying to persuade someone that it is unlikely that Jesus was white?

4. In 2013, discussing an article published in *Slate* magazine that challenged depictions of Santa Claus as a white person, Fox News correspondent Megyn Kelly asserted that "[J]ust because it makes you feel uncomfortable . . . doesn't mean it has to change. Jesus was a white man, too . . . he's a historical figure and that's a verifiable fact, as is Santa [Claus], I just want kids to know that." Respond to Kelly in a brief essay.

5. Do some of your own research and attempt to find the scientific and/or historical consensus on what an ancient historical figure of your choosing (Socrates, Nefertiti, Mohammed, Cleopatra, etc.) might have looked like. What aspects of the evidence fuel debate? Which evidence do you find most convincing? Why?

MARIANNA CERINI

Marianna Cerini is a freelance journalist who publishes lifestyle articles on topics ranging from fashion to food to travel. Her work appears on her own website as well as in publications such as *Conde Nast Traveler*, *Bon Appetit*, *Forbes*, and *Vogue Italia*. The essay here was posted on CNN Style in March 2020.

Why Women Feel Pressured to Shave

Type "When did women start..." into Google and one of the top autocomplete suggestions to pop up is, "When did women start shaving?"

The answer goes back centuries. Hair removal — or otherwise — has long shaped gender dynamics, served as a signifier of class and defined notions of femininity and the "ideal body."

However, in its most recent evolution, body hair is being embraced by a growing number of young women who are turning a source of societal shame and turning it into a sign of personal strength.

The rise of gender fluidity, the body-positivity movement and the beauty sector's growing inclusiveness have all contributed to the new wave of hirsuteness.

"It's been deeply stigmatized — it still 5 is — and cast with shame," said Heather Widdows, professor of global ethics at the UK's University of Birmingham and author of "Perfect Me: Beauty as an Ethical Ideal," in a phone interview. "Its removal is one of the few aesthetic traditions that have gone from being a beauty routine to a hygienic one.

"Today, most women feel like they have to shave. Like they have no other option. There's something deeply fraught about that — though perceptions are slowly changing."

FROM ANCIENT EGYPT TO DARWIN

Hairlessness wasn't established as a mandate for women until the early 20th century.

Before that, removing body hair was something both men and women did — as far back as the Stone Age, then through ancient Egypt, Greece and the Roman Empire — using seashells, beeswax and various other depilatories. In these earlier eras, as Victoria Sherrow writes in "Encyclopedia of Hair: A Cultural History," hairlessness was seen mostly as a way to keep the body clean. Ancient Romans also associated it with class: The smoother your skin was, the purer and more superior you were.

In the Middle East, as well as East and South Asia, threading was used on the entire face. But unibrows were actually considered alluring for both sexes, and were often accentuated with kohl.

In Persia, hair removal and brow shaping 10 was a marker of adulthood and marriage for women, and was mainly reserved for that occasion. While in China, body hair was long considered normal, and even today woman face far less social pressure to shave.

The same goes for other countries in Asia: While hair removal has become routine for many of the continent's young women, waxing

Threading — which removes facial hair — has long been a traditional beauty procedure, as seen in this picture at a Taipei night market. A thin thread is doubled, then twisted and rolled over areas of unwanted hair, plucking the hair at the follicle level.

Credit: Pacific Press/Getty Images

or trimming pubic hair, for instance, isn't as common as it is in the West.

In fact, in Korea, pubic hair was long considered a sign of fertility and sexual health — so much so that, in the mid-2010s, it was reported that some Korean women were undergoing pubic hair transplants, to add extra hair to their own.

Europeans weren't always obsessed with hair-free skin.

In the Middle Ages, good Catholic women were expected to let their hair grow as a display of femininity, while keeping it concealed in public. The face was the only place where hair was considered unsightly: 14th-century ladies would pluck the hair from their foreheads in order to push back their hairlines and give their faces a more oval appearance. When Elizabeth I came to power in 1558, she made eyebrow removal fashionable.

By the late 18th century, hair removal still wasn't considered essential by European and American women, although when the first safety razor for men was invented by French barber Jacques Perret in 1760, some women reportedly used them too.

It wasn't until the late 1800s that women on both sides of the Atlantic started making hair removal an integral part of their beauty routines. The modern-day notion of body hair being unwomanly can be traced back to Charles Darwin's 1871 book "Descent of a Man," according to Rebecca Herzig's "Plucked: A History of Hair Removal."

Darwin's theory of natural selection associated body hair with "primitive ancestry and an atavistic return to earlier, 'less developed' forms," wrote Herzig, a professor of gender and sexuality studies at Bates College in Maine. Conversely, having less body hair, the English naturalist suggested, was a sign of being more evolved and sexually attractive.

As Darwin's ideas became popularized, other 19th-century medical and scientific experts began linking hairiness to "sexual inversion, disease pathology, lunacy, and criminal violence," Herzig continued. Interestingly, those connotations were applied mostly to women's body hair, not men's — not just because of evolutionary arguments but also, the author pointed out, the enforcement of "gendered social control"

15

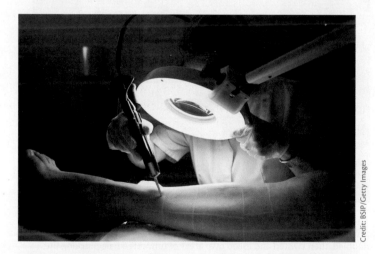

Credit: BSIP/Getty Images

In Paris, a patient undergoes a hair removal session using an Alexandrite laser.

on women's rising role in society. Making women think they had to be hairless to be considered worthy of attention was a heteronormative way of controlling their bodies — and, inherently, their selves — through shame, Widdows explained.

By the early 1900s, upper- and middle-class white America increasingly saw smooth skin as a marker of femininity, and female body hair as disgusting, with its removal offering "a way to separate oneself from cruder people, lower class and immigrant," Herzig wrote.

A FEMALE "NECESSITY"

In the first decades of the 20th century, 20 changing fashions — sleeveless dresses exposing the skin — further popularized body hair removal in the US.

In 1915, Harper's Bazaar was the first women's magazine to run a campaign dedicated to the removal of underarm hair ("a necessity," as it was described). That same year, men's shaving company Gillette launched the first razor marketed specifically for women, the Milady Décolletée. Its advert read, "A beautiful addition to Milady's toilet table — and one that solves an embarrassing personal problem."

The shorter hemlines of the 1930s and '40s, and a shortage of nylon stockings during World War II meant more and more American women began shaving their legs, too. The introduction of the bikini in the US in 1946 also led shaving companies and female consumers to focus on the trimming and shaping of their nether region.

In the 1950s, as Playboy hit the newsstands (its first issue came out in 1953), clean-shaven, lingerie-touting women set a new standard of sexiness. By 1964, 98% of American women aged 15 to 44 were regularly shaving their legs. Wax strips and the first laser hair removal also debuted around then, though

Italian actress Sophia Loren, wearing a white embroidered dress, posing for the photographer in Venice, 1955.

the latter was quickly abandoned for its damaging effects on the skin before being reintroduced decades later.

"And yet shaving was far from being as extreme as it is today," Widdows said. "In the late 1960s and 1970s, full bushes were not at all uncommon, even in Playboy. Around that time you also had the second wave of feminism and the spread of hippie culture, both of which rejected hairless bodies. For a lot of women, body hair was symbol of their fight for equality. It wasn't seen as unnatural — not yet."

That shift, Widdows said, kicked off in the 25 following decades, with the rising popularity of waxing, pornography and increasingly explicit pop culture. In 1987, seven sisters from Brazil (known as the J Sisters) opened a salon in New York City offering the so-called "Brazilian" — a complete wax hair removal of the genital region. Celebrities like Gwyneth Paltrow and Naomi Campbell started doing it. The masses followed suit.

"Removing body hair went from being 'expected' to the norm," Widdows explained.

"Being hairless has come to be seen as the only 'natural' and clean way to present the body. Except it really isn't."

With advertising and media further promoting the ideal of hair-free bodies, the idea that female hair is gross has only grown. In turn, methods to achieve hairlessness have become more precise: The last four decades have seen the ascent of electrolysis, pulsed light and more advanced laser technology.

"Anything associated with the 'abject' — what we expel from our cultural worlds in order to define ourselves — arouses disgust, shame and hostility almost by definition," Herzig told CNN in an email. "Visible female body hair certainly tends to be treated as abject today. It's worth noting that those are ideas about cleanliness, contingent social norms, rather than about actually removing 'dirt.' Most hair removal practices tend to introduce new opportunities for abrasion and infection."

Mexican artist Frida Kahlo boasted a unibrow.

Credit: Everett/Shutterstock

EMBRACING HAIRINESS

In 2008, Breanne Fahs, professor of women and gender studies at Arizona State University, set female students an assignment to grow their body hair and write a paper reflecting on the experience. Fahs later extended the assignment to include the course's men, who were asked to shave their legs. The project still runs today.

"The assignment has spotlighted the cultural inevitability of female hair removal," Fahs said in a phone interview. "Over the years, those who have taken part in it have shared quite consistent issues: a deep sense of shame, struggle with self-confidence, even social ostracism.

"There have also been cases of heterosexism and homophobia — this idea that growing your leg hair automatically implies you're queer, or shaving it means you're a gay man. Women often don't realize how much society, family and friends weigh in on what we do with our bodies. And how much of what we think is a choice — that 'I choose to shave' — has actually been imparted to and enforced upon us for generations."

But Fahs also saw feelings of empowerment, rebellion and anger stirring from the project. "Particularly in the last two years, in the wake of the election and the #MeToo movement — there's been a deeper awareness of the restrictions surrounding women's bodies, of feminism, gender and sexuality, and a willingness to push back against it all, or at least break out of the comfort zone," she said.

It's not just Fahs' students.

A new cohort of young women is embracing body hair, especially on Instagram. The phenomenon has also made it into magazines. In the September issue of Harper's Bazaar, actress

Emily Ratajkowski posed with unshaven underarms (a full 360-degree turn for the publication since its early anti-armpit hair messages). YouTuber Ingrid Nilsen and musician Halsey have also showed off their body hair.

Newly launched women's shaving brands 35 are also making a case for female fuzz, and encouraging positive conversations around the topic. The Flamingo razor, from the popular grooming line Harry's, emphasizes the right to choose whether to shave with ad slogans like "No Waxation Without Representation" and "We Are Grow Choice."

Direct-to-consumer razor start-up Billie, established in 2017, is another company that's marketing the idea of choice. Rather than showing the perfectly smooth models typical of female shaving ads, its campaigns depicted diverse groups of women shaving, combing their wispy underarm locks or lying on the beach in bikinis with varying levels of hairiness.

"For so long, advertising has only reinforced the taboo around the subject," said Billie co-founder Georgina Gooley in a phone interview. "We wanted to actually acknowledge that women have body hair, show it, and say that shaving is a choice. If you want to keep your body hair, we celebrate that. And if you want to remove it, that's fine as well.

Photographer Ashley Armitage, who worked on the Billie campaigns and artfully depicts body hair on her Instagram account, agrees. "Body hair is a personal choice," she wrote in an email. "Shaving it, waxing it, or growing it are all valid options, and all up to the individual."

The idea that not shaving can be a choice may not seem revolutionary, when it comes to normalizing body hair. But it could be an important step towards reframing the issue.

"I think more women are realizing how body 40 hair is deeply connected to gender and power," said Fahs. "The emotional nature of what body hair elicits in people has tremendous potential as a tool for activism and social change."

Topics for Critical Thinking and Writing

1. Consider the connotative meanings of body hair for all genders, and discuss how displaying or not displaying body hair communicates social meanings differently. Is there a double standard at play?

2. What assumptions are behind the different views of body hair and its management, as described in Cerini's essay? (See Chapter 4 section, "Assumptions," on p. 129 for a reminder.)

3. Do you think that body hair "styling" such as those practices described in the Billie advertising campaign (paras. 36–38) has the potential to change how men and women display their visible body hair? Why or why not? What other media might change these practices?

4. Examine the classroom assignment designed by Breanne Fahs discussed in paragraphs 29–32. Do you think the effects reported by students who participated constitute a good reason to justify continuing the practice of managing visible body hair according to social norms? Or should they be challenged? Why or why not?

5. In paragraph 39, Cerini writes, "The idea that not shaving can be a choice may not seem revolutionary, when it comes to normalizing body hair. But it could be an important step towards reframing the issue." Provide a counterargument to Cerini, defending the practice of body hair removal as a social norm.

6. Do you think social practices like removing body hair place an undue burden on women? Explain your answer. What other social norms and practices place pressure on certain demographics such as gender, age, class, and so on?

REBECCA JENNINGS

Rebecca Jennings is a senior reporter with the online news outlet *Vox*, where she reports on internet culture, social media, influencers, and creators. She has closely followed the rise of TikTok and its cultural impact since 2018. The essay here was published on *Vox* in 2021.

The $5,000 Quest for the Perfect Butt

When she woke up from surgery, Kayla Malveaux found herself alone in the clinic recovery room, slumped over in a wheelchair. She felt sharp pain around her face and swollen eyes, but she wasn't sure why. The operation she'd just had involved fat taken from her abdomen and transplanted into her bottom, an increasingly common procedure called the Brazilian butt lift. Though she can't say for sure what really happened between the time the surgery was over and the time she woke up, she has a guess. "It's like they threw me in the wheelchair and then I must have hit my head," she says.

As the 22-year-old was wheeled out of the Miami cosmetic surgery clinic, she understood. In the waiting room was "a herd of girls," she says, all waiting for their own procedures with a single surgeon. "I couldn't see how a doctor can do that many patients a day without overworking themselves, you know?" she says.

Kayla is one of thousands of women who've flown to South Florida — or Turkey or Mexico or Thailand — for questionably cheap operations, where a complex, multi-hour surgery not covered by health insurance can run as low as $3,000, although most clinics advertise BBL packages for around $5,500 (not including aftercare, which can double the cost). These procedures often take place in small clinics, where doctors who might have been trained as dermatologists or pediatricians are legally allowed to advertise themselves as "board certified" physicians even though the extent of their plastic surgery training might have consisted of a single weekend course. To make up for the high cost of running an operating room, they squeeze in as many as eight patients every day.

You can see where the Brazilian butt lift — a physically taxing surgery for the doctor as well as the patient — might start to get dangerous. But this hasn't stopped the thousands of women who've undergone it over the past few years; the number of BBLs globally since 2015 has risen 77.6 percent, according to a survey by the International Society of Aesthetic Plastic Surgery, and it is now the fastest-growing cosmetic procedure in the world.

As Kayla arrived at the airport after her surgery, she was told the terminal didn't have any wheelchairs left. On her flight back to California, she realized she was one of several BBL patients on the plane.

You spend enough time on TikTok and Instagram, and it can start to feel like you're the only person in the world who hasn't had their butt done. The BBL silhouette is omnipresent and unmissable, an impossibly tiny middle resting atop a plump bottom and thick thighs; at its most extreme it presents a cartoonish version of a fertile woman, a cross between the Venus of Willendorf and Jessica Rabbit. At its most subtle, a BBL just looks like good genes, the kind of golden ratio associated with the most iconic sex symbols of the last 100 years.

The BBL aesthetic of the 2010s and the present day, however, is most often associated with the Instagram influencer, whose body exists to be consumed by the most people possible (whether or not it has been photoshopped is almost beside the point). After Kim Kardashian, one of the ur-examples of the modern influencer, proved with an X-ray that she hadn't had butt implants, the next logical question was, "Well, how?" The answer, many have speculated, is that she and some of her sisters had gotten Brazilian butt lifts, which wouldn't have shown up on an X-ray because the procedure involves the removal and retransplant of one's own fat.

The platforms that provided the foundation for the rise of influencers are also the reason why the BBL has penetrated the mainstream. Consider "Instagram face," the button-nosed, cat-eyed, pouty-lipped look popularized by professionally sexy models like Emily Ratajkowski and Bella Hadid, that for the vast majority of the population is only achievable through skillful makeup or, more often than not, a click of a button. Apps like Facetune bring that same kind of one-touch wizardry to bodies, which can be stretched, slimmed, and smoothed to infinity — and can do it convincingly. The BBL, just like any of the fastest-growing cosmetic surgery procedures, attempts to recreate the way we look when our bodies are filtered through the internet.

Until the last decade or so, the BBL was not common practice in the US. Its origins, as its name suggests, are in Brazil, where cosmetic surgery has a storied background, largely due to the country's history of eugenics. In 1918, Dr. Renato Kehl founded the Eugenics Society of São Paulo, which aimed to erase all signs of Black and Indigenous physical appearance in Brazil. In 1960, a surgeon named Ivo Pitanguy founded the world's first plastic surgery training center in Brazil, where he pioneered what became known as the Brazilian butt lift and taught surgeons all over the globe how to perform his techniques.

From there, the practice traveled north and exploded once pop culture began to shed its preference for the "tits on a stick" silhouette and started to revere stars like Jennifer Lopez and Nicki Minaj. As the mainstream media began to incorporate the beauty standards that have long been held by Black and Latinx cultures — e.g., that big butts are hot — it continued to idealize the white women who conformed to these standards and, furthermore, allowed them to profit over Black and Latina women whose bodies the fashion establishment had previously critiqued. The idea that certain body types can be considered trendy at all, of course, has a history that has always been laden with classism, racism, and sexism, and it's easy to argue that the media only began to celebrate big butts when it became financially beneficial to do so.

South Florida quickly emerged as the plastic surgery capital of America, in part because of its huge Latinx population and the fact that Floridians can comfortably wear bikinis year round. By 1999, more than one in 10 plastic surgery procedures performed by board-certified plastic surgeons took place in Florida, and the history of malpractice goes back just as far. Florida, just like every other state in the country, allows medical doctors to practice and treat patients in any field, as long as they obtain consent from the patient.

"You can set up your own clinic and you could be doing liposuction tomorrow with no training in liposuction whatsoever, and it's perfectly legal," explains Adam Rubinstein, a board-certified plastic surgeon in Miami. Though these doctors wouldn't be able to perform plastic surgery in a hospital or legitimate surgery center, where regulations are stricter and have far more oversight, there's nothing stopping them from opening a clinic of their own, and no higher board they must answer to.

The field of medicine largely relies on the industry policing itself, which makes it difficult for legislators to address the issues. "We have the expertise to do that, but we don't have the legal authority," explains Arthur Perry, a plastic surgeon who spent 10 years on the New Jersey State Board of Medical Examiners and who refuses to perform BBLs. "So yeah, I could call myself a cardiac surgeon today, set up an operating room, and do cardiac surgery in my office. You can sue me for malpractice, but that's a civil penalty as opposed to criminal."

Helly Larson, a 26-year-old podcaster in Georgia, got her BBL in 2019 at a Miami clinic. Though she'd known plenty of women who'd had BBLs through her work as a stripper, she was making enough money with the body she already had. "Then literally, one day I just was like, 'Okay, I'm doing it,'" she says.

"I scheduled a consultation with a doctor who had done a YouTuber that I was watching, they approved me and I paid my deposit, all within a week." She'd done further research on the website RealSelf, which acts almost like a Yelp for cosmetic surgeons, where former patients can post reviews and photos.

Like Kayla, she didn't get the sense that 15 something was off until she was in the bed waiting to start the surgery. Four hours after she was supposed to be anesthetized, she says the doctor came in and complained about the lack of professionalism by the anesthesiologist. "As I'm sitting in the gown, all of the red flags start to come through and I was just like, 'You're gonna be okay, it's gonna be okay,'" she says. "I didn't even know about the death rates."

The death rates for BBLs have been, historically, not good. One 2017 study placed the worldwide mortality rate at a whopping one in 3,000; 25 of those deaths occurred in the US in the five years prior. Thanks to more widespread education and better safety techniques, that ratio is widening: In 2019, one survey estimated the mortality risk at one in 14,921, and as of 2020 it is one in 20,117. That's still higher than the mortality rate from liposuction (1.3 in 50,000) or for outpatient surgery (0.25-0.5 in 100,000). (All figures via the *International Open Access Journal of the American Society of Plastic Surgeons*.)

BBL deaths have, for the most part, occurred because of improper technique. The problem with inserting fat into the buttock is that your butt contains a lot of very large blood vessels — "as big as drinking straws," one doctor put it — which, if accidentally injected with fat, can result in that fat traveling to your lungs and cause a deadly pulmonary embolism. That's part of the reason why most reputable surgeons have a limit to the amount of fat they'll insert — there's less likelihood of dead fat, which creates lumps and lopsidedness. (In popular BBL destinations like Turkey, doctors are willing to insert much more fat.)

These issues are compounded when doctors are pumping out clients as fast as they can. At a single plastic surgery clinic, eight women died over the course of six years, seven of them working-class Black and Latina women who reportedly were targets of the clinic's advertising campaigns. In 2018, a patient died three days after getting a BBL at New Life Cosmetic Surgery; the cause of death was determined to be from liposuction and fat transfer procedure complications. "Miami is the chop shop of plastic surgery," Helly says. "I think the doctor had, like, five BBLs the day I had mine." In the lead-up to her surgery, the clinic had been emailing and checking in regularly, but once it was over, she says, "It's crickets."

One aspect that many clinics don't always fully explain is what happens after you get a new butt. Many aren't upfront about the fact that there are limits to how much fat surgeons can remove and implant, and therefore what a single BBL procedure can accomplish. For many women to achieve their desired look, they must come back for two or three procedures. What's more, not all of the fat inserted into the butt will stay alive — it's a common complaint among BBL patients to fall in love with their post-surgery butt, only to watch it shrink over the next few months.

Aftercare guidance depends on the patient's 20 existing body type, but all of them must wear a faja, a corset-like garment that keeps the body shape in place, for about three months as the new fat learns to connect with the existing fat. Sleeping must be done face-down for at least six weeks, and sitting requires a special pillow. To help with circulation, patients must schedule regular post-op massages, which are often painful. Peeing, by the way, is its own hurdle. "I've seen people where they'll keep [the garment] on while they go to the bathroom, they'll literally just pee all over themselves and live like that," Helly says.

Outside of the network of cheap clinics, Miami has also seen a spate of surgery recovery centers that offer pickup and drop off, massages, and other post-op assistance, with names like Prima Dollhouse, Barbie Dolls Recovery House, and Sassy Queen, though it's also typical to rent an Airbnb and use trusted loved ones as temporary nurses. Sites like YouTube are filled with women's experiences with their own post-operative care, some decent, some awful; vlogger Latausha Denn chronicled her terrible recovery process in a video titled "THE WORST EXPERIENCE OF MY LIFE." For Helly, the first week was "absolute hell;" she described walking around a coffee table like running a mile. Long-term effects are common as well; both Kayla, who got her procedure last fall, and Helly, who got hers in 2019, still experience abdominal numbness. Helly also has lingering circulation issues when sitting down, back pain, and trouble sleeping.

These aftereffects are rarely present in the many Instagram and TikTok accounts run by doctors advertising their prowess in creating sculpted hourglass figures. Some have built huge audiences with cheeky sketches on how a BBL means freedom from the gym or how all their patients are having hot girl summers. They field dozens of DMs a day from women hoping to recreate the bodies they've seen online.

Edward Chamata, a doctor who works under popular TikToker Dr. Jung at Premiere Surgical Arts in Houston, Texas, sees this as a boon to prospective patients, who enter the consultation room with far more knowledge about different procedures than they would have access to otherwise. "Every kind of plastic surgeon is on Instagram, and it's a massive reach on those platforms," he says. "It's a big part of empowering the patients and informing them on their care, so they almost have a lot of education already at hand."

Other doctors see it differently. Perry believes that "as doctors, we're not supposed to be salesmen." On the rash of self-described BBL experts, Perry quotes Willie Sutton, a famous robber from the 1950s who was asked why he robbed banks and replied, "Because that's where the money is."

"Why do these doctors do these proce- 25 dures? Because that's where the money is," Perry says. "But that doesn't mean it's right."

The best — and only, really — way a patient can make an educated choice about where to get any kind of cosmetic surgery is to research as much as they possibly can. Resources like certificationmatters.org and the American Board of Plastic Surgery allow people to look up doctors' certifications in particular areas. Rubinstein also warns against any surgery that sounds too good to be true: $5,000 isn't enough to cover the costs of running an operating room, he says, without cutting some serious corners. "I'd say you probably shouldn't pay much less than $8,000 for a BBL in Miami," he says. Often, he'll operate on women who've had a botched operation from a less educated doctor.

Ethical guidelines state that doctors should use rigorous screening processes that weed out people who aren't optimal patients for a BBL — people who are severely under- or overweight, people with a history of eating disorders or body dysmorphia, people who maybe haven't thought through the enormous decision they're about to make. "I always ask my patients to bring in wish pics, and many

times, they'll bring in pics from Instagram," says Chamata. "And a lot of times those photos are photoshopped, with obviously unnatural proportions that just aren't achievable in the real world." He says around 30 percent of the patients he sees aren't appropriate candidates.

Yet looking "unnatural" has often been one of the goals for many people who've undergone plastic surgery. "It's an interesting sociological phenomenon," says Perry. "It started with breast implants in the 1960s, where there were so many bad breast implants — too big, too high — that women began to think that was normal. I've actually had people request me to put implants up a little high, so that the bulge is visible under the collarbone. I try to explain to people, this is not normal. It's the same thing with brows." (He mentions a certain powerful politician as a particularly bad example of a brow lift done wrong.) "My goal as a plastic surgeon is to help people look normal, and sometimes we forget about that as plastic surgeons who are very interested in just getting everyone and their sister operated on. My job is not to do whatever you ask me to do. It's to use my aesthetic and ethical judgment, and do what's right."

Unsurprisingly, Perry believes the BBL boom will fade out, and perhaps is already starting to. "The people coming in are no longer saying, 'I want it as big as possible.' Now they're saying, 'I just want it to be round,'" says Rubinstein.

That specific bodies can be "trendy" is, 30 again, an ugly concept with an uglier history. The BBL, however, has an even more complex one. As Sophie Elmhirst put it in her thorough investigation on BBLs at the Guardian:

Following the chain of cultural appropriation that has led to this point is bewildering. The notion of the idealised

Brazilian bottom, which some rich white Brazilian women disdain because of its stereotypical associations with biracial women, has become the desired shape among certain white women in the US and Europe, who are in turn emulating a body shape artificially constructed and popularised by an Armenian-American woman, who is often accused of appropriating a Black aesthetic, which some Black women then feel compelled to copy, not having the idealised body shape they believe they're supposed to have naturally. "You steal a version of what a Black woman's body should be, repackage it, sell it to the masses, and then if I'm Black and I don't look like that? That's a mindfuck," summarised [Alisha] Gaines, [professor of English at Florida State University].

The stereotype of the Instagram-faced, BBL-bodied influencer is now almost bigger than a person's physical appearance. On TikTok, where advertisements for and real-life stories about BBLs proliferate, so too does a meme known as "the BBL effect." Twenty-three-year-old Antoni Bumba came up with the idea for the character, which they call "Miss BBL," after idolizing a certain type of influencer who weaved seamlessly between the ranks of Hollywood and Instagram baddies — Amber Rose, Kylie Jenner, the Real Kyle Sisters.

"We have 20-something seasons of *Keeping Up With the Kardashians*, where you see these girls taking 45, 60 seconds just to get out of the car and into the restaurant because they have to serve every single angle for the paparazzi," says Antoni. Miss BBL is recognizable not with the way she looks but in the little motions that let others know she's a bad bitch — taking ample time to flick her hair behind her shoulders, eating slowly and carefully, and wearing a constant camera-ready smize. "People who get work done essentially have no problem holding up people's time to be able to cater to their needs," they explain. "And it's so fire because it gives all of these people, especially women, this sort of edge, invoking confidence and self-sufficiency into their day-to-day lives."

While Kayla and Helly ultimately ended up happy with their results, both wish they'd done more research before going under the knife. "If I were to do anything else again, it would probably be in California," Kayla says. "Most places in Miami, after they take your money, they don't really care."

Helly described how her body dysmorphia got worse after she had the surgery; for about a year, she could barely look at herself in the mirror. "I would say to anybody looking into getting procedures, you're not just going to magically be a brand new person that has this work ethic and great motivation. You need to find that before you go in and change your whole body." she says. "If I had seen a girl on TikTok or YouTube talking about the reality behind it, I don't even know if I would have gone through with it."

It's certainly possible that within a decade, 35 the BBL will continue to fade out, just as body types have risen and fallen in popularity throughout history. "Think about the way that nobody has these huge watermelon titties anymore," Helly says. "Working in the dancer industry, I had a lot of clubs that wouldn't hire me because I had thick thighs and their mindset was still stuck in the '90s. All these women are going to start getting their hips and butt reduced because it's going to go out of fashion."

Whatever the next most desirable silhouette looks like, what will remain is the cosmetic surgery industry's willingness to follow aesthetic trends at any cost, offering "pioneering" procedures that haven't been properly vetted, or doctors who've decided they could make more money jumping from podiatry to plastic surgery. Until lawmakers catch up with the reality of the field, over time the BBL could just be one of any number of dangerous operations that promises to build the perfect body.

Topics for Critical Thinking and Writing

1. In what places does Rebecca Jennings use *pathos* to warn about the dangers of the Brazilian butt lift (BBL)? In what places does she use *logos*? Which is more effective?

2. Given the pros and cons of electing to have a surgery such as the BBL, what are some of the best reasons why one would choose to do so, and what are some of the weakest reasons? Explain your thinking.

3. Evaluate Jennings's use of evidence in showing the prevalence and dangers of the Brazilian butt lift. What types of evidence does Jennings rely upon? Which are most convincing, and which are least convincing? (Consult the section "Evidence" in Chapter 4, p. 119.)

4. What solutions does Jennings offer as a way to protect people who are considering surgery? Can you add any additional solutions to the problem?

5. Mariana Cerini's "Why Women Feel Pressured to Shave" also addresses the social forces that compel people to conform to body image norms. Consider how representations in mass media encourage or discourage certain ways of managing and displaying the body. Why do some practices come and go and others seem to last or become normalized?

6. Suppose the dangers of the BBL outlined by Jennings were reduced or fully eliminated by more responsible surgeons and tighter regulations. What points would you make beyond safety concerns to dissuade a loved one from having the surgery? For each of your points, imagine the counterpoints that might be made by your loved one who was motivated to have such a surgery. Which of your points is strongest? Which of their counterpoints is strongest? If you had to come some agreement in the middle, what might that agreement look like?

MARILYN GREENWALD

Marilyn Greenwald is professor emerita of journalism at Ohio University, where she taught news reporting, arts criticism, and biography for more than thirty years. Prior to her academic career, she was a reporter for the *Columbus Citizen-Journal* and the *Columbus Dispatch*. She has written five biographies, including one about Leslie McFarlane, also known as Frank W. Dixon, the man who wrote the immensely popular series of Hardy Boys books in the 1930s and 1940s. The essay reprinted here was published in the *Wall Street Journal* in 2021.

Dr. Seuss, Meet the Sanitized Sleuths Known as the Hardy Boys

The recent decision by the estate of Theodor "Dr. Seuss" Geisel to pull six of his books because of crude stereotypical portrayals has exploded in the news. Some claim that the action represents the worst of cancel culture, while others praise the decision because they believe the depictions can promote racial insensitivity.

But Geisel's heirs aren't the first to confront the sanctity of children's literature and whether books should ever be altered for changing times. In 1959 and 1960, some of the world's most beloved fictional characters — Nancy Drew, Frank and Joe Hardy, Tom Swift and others — received a face-lift as publishers grappled with a similar challenge. In 1959, series fiction published by the Stratemeyer Syndicate underwent a multi-year rewrite, ostensibly to eliminate racial and ethnic stereotypes and to conform to modern times.

Those extensive changes weren't publicized and remained unknown for years to unsuspecting readers, including parents, who assumed their children were reading the same books they read decades ago as kids. The "updating," as the publishers called it, was a secret worthy of the talents of the Hardys or Ms. Drew.

Even the author of the first group of Hardy Boys books, the man behind the pen name Franklin W. Dixon, wasn't aware of the changes. Hardy Boys ghostwriter Leslie McFarlane was told about the changes by a Toronto reporter more than three decades after he wrote most of the books.

McFarlane had moved on to become a successful writer and film producer, but he was shocked by many of the changes. McFarlane didn't mind that the revisions eliminated the description of a Chinese character as having "an evil yellow face," nor did he care that criminals were no longer described routinely as "dark" or "swarthy," often with foreign accents. He and his fellow ghostwriters were equal-opportunity xenophobes: Cops were usually Irish, Italians ran fruit stands, and Scots swept floors. Another revision deleted the comment of a black character who speaks in an odd dialect while resting his feet on a train seat: "Ah pays mah fare, an' Ah puts mah shoes where Ah please," he says.

But as part of the revisions, the books were shortened considerably and many literary allusions and picturesque descriptions were removed. Also new: Authority figures, especially policemen, were portrayed as people to be respected and admired at all times. This is particularly evident in the case of Hardy Boys characters Collig and Smuff, bumbling detectives who in the original were routinely outwitted by Frank and Joe when it came to solving cases. In the revisions, the cops were respectable, helpful and competent, a change that rattled McFarlane, who was particularly proud of the silly Keystone Kops-like figures he created. He believed that most of his readers enjoyed irreverence and humor.

McFarlane was of the conviction that children read series fiction to be challenged. He often said in interviews that he wanted to send boys and girls to dictionaries. Gone in there writes were words like "sibilant," "ostensible" and "expostulate." An inveterate reader, McFarlane also threw in a few references to Shakespeare and Dickens in his Hardy Boys books — allusions that were ditched in the rewrites.

Like many critics of children's literature, McFarlane believed that most of the changes robbed the books of their personality, turning them into shadows of their former selves. "They were gutted," he said in a 1973 interview.

The changes made by the Stratemeyer Syndicate exemplify the challenges inherent in modifying classic works of literature, especially for children. Are the changes being made for the benefit of the young minds, or are they being "dumbed down" to draw more readers? Or are they made for the economic benefit of publishers who want to be "safe" and avoid controversy that might put a dent in sales?

In the case of the Hardy Boys, Nancy 10 Drew and other Stratemeyer characters, it might have been all these reasons. First written in the early 20th century, the content of the books did reflect the casual prejudices of the era. But literary "cancel culture" also exists, in children's literature in particular.

Harsh stereotypical portrayals in books may reinforce racism and sexism in young readers, and altering texts to avoid that may be necessary. But changing the tenor and personality of the work of the artist is another issue, as is encouraging bland, colorless work because it may be easier or safer to market.

It is one thing to eliminate offensive or crude content that might instill offensive views in children. But all changes should be made with a light hand and after much thought. McFarlane wrote his last Hardy Boys book in 1947, but his understanding of his audience holds: Readers are a logical and perceptive group who know when they are being condescended to.

Topics for Critical Thinking and Writing

1. Do you think it is publishers' responsibility to revise books published in the past — and therefore reflecting the values and assumptions of the past — or should works of literature be preserved in their original form? What would be the drawbacks or benefits of each approach?

2. Of the examples Marilyn Greenwald provides showing how the original Hardy Boys books were altered, which do you agree were necessary and which do you think were unnecessary? Why?

3. Examine the debate provided in Chapter 19, "Should We Cancel 'Cancel Culture'?" Then, consider whether or not the changes to the Hardy Boys books made in 1959–1960 represent reasonable changes or an instance of cancel culture.

4. Greenwald wrote this piece in 2021, just as controversy swelled concerning the decision of the estate of Theodore Geisel (aka Dr. Seuss) to stop publishing six Dr. Seuss titles because they contained racially stereotyped characters. Why do you think Greenwald introduces the Hardy Boys into the debate? What details are most important, and how do they reflect on the controversies surrounding the Dr. Seuss books?

5. Think of some examples of other stories or characters that have been problematic in the context of changing values. Focusing on one or more examples, what do you think is the best way to approach the problem of such outdated representations? What contexts are important to consider?

AUBREY GORDON

Aubrey Gordon is a podcaster, activist, and writer who covers topics regarding fatphobia, antifat bias, and fat acceptance, as well as the science behind nutrition and health practices as portrayed in the media, especially on her co-hosted podcast (with Michael Hobbes) *Maintenance Phase*. She writes a regular column for *Self*, and her work has appeared on Medium and in publications such as *Vox* and the *New York Times* under the pseudonym Your Fat Friend. In 2020, Gordon published her first book, *What We Don't Talk About When We Talk About Fat*, in which this selection appeared.

Into Thin Air

In 2015 Nicole Arbour briefly became a household name. The comedian made a video called "Dear Fat People" whose shock value led it to quick viral success. In it, Arbour lets loose a frustrated rant about fat people, all triggered by her alleged encounter with a fat family at an airport.

> As I get to the front of the line, a family comes to the front and gets to butt me. Fattest, most obese — I'm talking TLC special fat. . . . They got to go to the front of the line because they were complaining that their knees hurt too much to stand in it. "Oh, I just came an hour early, like I was supposed to. But you overeat, let me help you." And they complain, and they smell like sausages, and I don't even think they ate sausages, that's just their aroma. They're so fat that they're that standing sweat fat. Crisco was coming out of their pores like a fucking play-doh fun factory. . . .
>
> I'm sitting in the aisle, and then a stewardess walks up to me. "Hi ma'am, I hate to ask, but we've got a disabled passenger. Would you mind switching seats?" And of course, because I'm not an asshole, I'm like "oh my god, of course, yes." Oh look, it's fat family. And Jabba the son sits right beside me. I just lost my shit. His fat was on my lap. I took the handle, I squished it down, and I said "MY SEAT, YOUR SEAT." I actually took his fat and I pushed it into his seat and I held it. He was fine. He was just fat. Make better choices.

Arbour's video, with its blunt approach and crass language sparked a nationwide conversation about what is and isn't okay to say to and about fat people. Notably, however, the conversation stopped short of considering the impact of Arbour's video on actual fat people.

In a tense appearance on *The View*, Arbour defended the video as comedy designed to provoke. "That video was made to offend people, just like I do with all my other videos. It's just satire, I'm just being silly, I'm just having a bit of fun, and that's what we did. And that topic was actually voted in by fans, some of them who are fat [sic]."[1] *The View* cohost Joy Behar, herself a comic, called out Arbour's defense. "You sort of hide behind this 'it's not healthy' thing and that's bull and you know it. [. . .] I'd be interested to see you do that live and see how many laughs you get."[2]

---

[1] "Nicole Arbour's AWKWARD Interview on *The View*," What's Trending, September 17, 2015, 2:25, video, https://www.youtube.com/watch?v=IjlVPzGXTPo.

[2] "Nicole Arbour on *The View*," Ronnie, September 16, 2015, 6:43, video, https://www.youtube.com/watch?v=yMhsSb$_2$BvnQ.

Arbour was roundly rejected for her video, but it still received over twenty-seven million views and became a touchstone in conversations about fatness and fat people. While "Dear Fat People" was an especially outrageous example, it didn't stand alone in its views on fatness and fat people — especially fat people on airplanes.

Six years before Arbour's viral video, [5] The Young Turks (TYT) held a conversation about fat people on planes. Despite its role as a widely viewed left-wing news and opinion show on YouTube, The Young Turks' take was strikingly similar to Arbour's. Co-hosts Cenk Uygur and Ana Kasparian discussed the issue with a discomfort that quickly turned to honest disgust. Kasparian described a photograph taken by an American Airlines flight attendant of a fat passenger in a cramped airline seat that didn't fit his body.

"I love how Ana's trying to be polite about it," said Uygur. "He *seems* to be taking up a lot of room? Does he *seem* that way?"

Kasparian relented, laughing. "What do you want me to say? There's a fat motherfucker on the plane."

As the conversation proceeded, Uygur initially acknowledged that the passenger was "trying his best not to get in [the] way" and was "probably super uncomfortable, sitting halfway on the seat" — even acknowledging that the airline's policy may be discriminatory. But the two co-hosts quickly agreed that the passenger should have to buy two seats.

"I mean, look," Kasparian added, "I think it's discrimination when it's something that the person can't help, right? [. . .] We're facing a huge obesity epidemic, right? Okay, so we've got a bunch of fatties in the United States, and if they want to travel, too bad, we're gonna give them two seats and they just have to pay for one? That just doesn't make any sense to me. I don't think that's fair."[3]

It was surreal to watch it all unfold, this lit- [10] igation of my body, a voiceless inconvenience, an inanimate obstacle. Like Nicole Arbour, the Young Turks insulted fat people. Like Arbour, they acknowledge, then write off, the idea that someone might be fat for reasons beyond their control. And like Arbour, they focus exclusively on the comfort and safety of thin people sitting nearby, easily bypassing any consideration for the fat person in question. The similarities are striking. But Nicole Arbour's video received 27 million views and faced significant backlash before being taken down by YouTube. The Young Turks' video, as of this writing, has received just under 1.5 million views and remains available online. So why did one incite outrage and the other receive so little attention?

The difference is that Arbour's video offers no counterpoint and comes across to many viewers as crass and crude. The Young Turks, while arguing similar points, do so in what *feels* like a more measured way. But fundamentally, both videos argue the same points and lay out a road map of core cultural beliefs about fat people — especially fat people in public spaces: Fat people shouldn't be so fat. Fat people inconvenience thin people with our bodies. Fatness is a choice for most. Arbour's crime wasn't that she *believed* fat people were disgusting, it's that she openly *said it*.

That, it seems, is where our conversation about how to treat fat people has stalled. Very few public conversations surface our core beliefs about fat people, hold them up to the light, examine them. Very few engage with the facts. In the case of airplanes, the evershrinking seats, the inconsistent policies, and the heartbreaking losses fat people continue to suffer. Very few of those public conversations

---

[3]"Should Obese People Have to Buy Two Seats on a Plane?" The Young Turks, December 4, 2009, 5:21, video, https://www .youtube.com/watch?v=z74EqQfWMUA.

challenge us, individually, to face our own biases against fatness and fat people. Instead of expressing outrage at the concrete harm we do to fat people, the painful and wrongheaded beliefs we stubbornly cling to, and the systems set up to exclude and underserve fat people, we opt for the easier conversation. We opt for politeness. We opt for *if you can't say anything nice, don't say anything at all.*

Instead of confronting our own beliefs, we confront the few who give voice to those beliefs. And instead of fixing the problem, we silence it. But anti-fat bias isn't just a problem for public figures, nor is it a simple problem of politeness. A growing body of research in recent decades has taken a closer look at the prevalence of anti-fat bias in the general population. Its findings are increasingly damning.

In 2019 Harvard University released a study based on the results of their immensely popular online implicit bias test. The test asks participants to move through rapidly flashing slides of words and images to measure their unconscious biases around race, gender, sexual orientation, disability, weight, and other characteristics. The study, published in *Psychological Science*, reviewed the results of over four million test takers over the course of nine years.

On some fronts, the findings were promising. According to the study's lead author, Tessa Charlesworth, "The most striking finding is that sexuality attitudes have changed toward neutrality, toward less bias, by as much as 33 percent on implicit measures," with nearly half of people also self-reporting changes in their own attitudes.[4] Similarly, if less dramatically, test takers' implicit bias on the basis of race also decreased by 17 percent.

While most measures of implicit bias decreased or remained stable, one measure exploded: anti-fat bias. In those nine years, pro-thin, anti-fat bias increased by a full 40 percent. Not only that, but weight-based bias was the slowest changing of all explicit attitudes — that is, the attitudes that test takers self-reported. According to Charlesworth:

> It is the only attitude out of the six that we looked at that showed any hint of getting *more* biased over time . . . . And of course again the question might be: why? What is specific about body-weight attitude?

> We can only speculate: Body weight has been the target of much discussion, but discussion in a negative light. We often talk about the "obesity epidemic," or about "the problem" with obese individuals.

> Also, we typically think about body weight as something that people can control, and so we are more likely to make the moral judgement of, "Well, you should just change."

The raw numbers are striking too. In 2016 a full 81 percent of test takers showed pro-thin, anti-fat bias. That's four out of five of us.

These implicit bias findings are uncomfortable to read, and they run counter to popular assumptions about how bias works. In public discourse, we often discuss bias and hate as things we *decide* to take on — that our default setting is an unbiased one, and that it's up to us to decide to take up the mantle of hate. In the popular imagination of many white folks, racism is relegated to virulent, organized white supremacists. Misogyny is the work of overt, proud chauvinist men. Homophobia is the domain of Fred Phelps and Pat Robertson,

15

[4]Goldberg, "Study: Bias Drops Dramatically for Sexual Orientation and Race — but Not Weight."

a cruel and outspoken minority. Few of us think of ourselves as biased because we're not like *them*. Few of us think of ourselves as hating any group of people. Still, our implicit biases often belie that self-image and the more comforting stories we tell ourselves.

But acknowledging our biases isn't a matter of making ourselves into villains, all black hearts and gleeful misdeeds. Acknowledging our biases is a matter of recognizing the social contexts that encourage them. Weight-loss ads flood the airwaves despite the fact that no diet has proven to lead to major, sustained weight loss. A Stanford study comparing low fat and low carbohydrate diets found that neither proved particularly effective for long-term weight loss, leading to an average loss of just over one pound per month for study subjects. Some lost more; many lost less.[5] Still, we are constantly confronted with an impossible ideal and snake oil that promises to bring it to fruition. Media messages about *revenge bodies* and *baby weight* and *beach bodies* abound, conditioning our feelings about our own bodies and the ways that we treat those who are fatter than us.

Our biases aren't just encouraged by private media, either. During those pivotal nine years of booming anti-fat bias, Michelle Obama was the First Lady of the United States, and her flagship campaign was aimed at ending obesity. Throughout the Obama years, the US established a series of federal and state programs aimed at asserting the personal responsibility of adults, children, and their parents to become and remain thin. Between the private and public sectors, billions of dollars have been spent seeding body dissatisfaction that would increase profits for weight-loss companies. In the process, both sectors seeded this astronomical rise in anti-fat attitudes, actions, and policies — all targeted at the fatness we learned to fear in ourselves. But those many shots we have learned to take at ourselves have long landed blows at fat people in the process.

Fat people aren't impacted equally, either, in part because we aren't distributed evenly. According to the CDC, women are more likely to be fat than men, and Black and Latinx people are more likely to be fat than white people.[6] Fatness is frequently used as a stand-in for poverty, even intellectual disability. In *The Obesity Myth*, Paul Campos argues that as overt racism, sexism, and classism fell out of favor among white and wealthy Americans, anti-fat bias offered a stand-in: a dog whistle that allowed disdain and bigotry aimed at poor people and people of color to persist, uninterrupted and simply renamed.

We also like to think that unlike Nicole Arbour, though we also have unkind thoughts about fat people, we keep them to ourselves. We believe that they don't influence our actions, and that we are able to remain clear-headed and objective, even when those judgments enter our minds. But again, the data points to something else. In nearly every facet of public life that's been studied, fat people face immense bias and often overt discrimination.

One informal survey of over five hundred hiring managers tested their attitudes toward potential employees based on size. Based solely on photographs, 21 percent described the fattest woman they were shown as "lazy" and

20

---

[5]Hanae Armitage, "Low-Fat or Low-Carb? It's a Draw, Study Finds," *Stanford Medicine News Center,* Stanford University, accessed October 24, 2019, https://med.stanford.edu/news/all-news/2018/02/low-fat-or-low-carb-its-a-draw-study-finds.hml.

[6]Craig M. Hales et al., "Prevalence of Obesity Among Adults and Youth."

"unprofessional" more than any other size. Just 18 percent said she had "leadership potential," and only 15 percent would even consider hiring her.[7] A study from Vanderbilt University found that fat women were more likely to work in more physically active jobs behind the scenes and less likely to work in jobs interacting with customers or representing a company.[8] Another Wharton study found that "obesity serves as a proxy for low competence. People judge obese people to be less competent even when it's not the case."[9]

Anti-fat bias doesn't just impact our ability to get hired — it also impacts our wages. Scientists at the University of Exeter found that, in England, women who are just one stone (14 pounds) over their BMI-mandated weight earned over 1,500 pounds ($1,867) *less* than a thinner woman.[10] In the United States, the findings are even more troubling. A 2010 study published in the *Journal of Applied Psychology* found staggering salary inequities based on size. "Heavy women earned $9,000 less than their average-weight counterparts; very heavy women earned $19,000 less. Very thin women, on the other hand, earned $22,000 more than those who were merely average."[11] Conversely, men's salaries *increased* with weight gain — until those men became fat.[12]

The aftershocks of our bias aren't just 25 limited to the workplace, either. Fat people feel its effects in the criminal justice system too. A 2013 Yale University study published in the *International Journal of Obesity* found that men were more likely to find a fat woman guilty of the same crime. "Male participants rated the obese female defendant guiltier than the lean female defendant, whereas female respondents judged the two female defendants equally regardless of weight. Among all participants, there were no differences in assessment of guilt between the obese male and lean male defendants."[13] And the bias isn't just limited to jurors. In 2017, a Quebec judge made headlines by saying that a fat seventeen-year-old woman might have been "flattered" by being sexually assaulted, saying the woman "is a bit overweight, but she has a pretty face. [. . .] The court specifies that she is a pretty young girl."[14] While his remarks were publicly decried, he faced no formal censure or consequences.

Anti-fat bias is so ubiquitous and unquestioned that the New York Police Department (NYPD) union used it as a defense against murder. On July 17, 2014, Eric Garner, a Black man, was killed on video. He lay on the ground, an officer's arm wrapped around his neck, while three other officers looked on. Garner repeatedly told officers he couldn't

---

[7]Fairygodboss, "The Grim Reality of Being a Female Jobseeker," https://res.cloudinary.com/fairygodboss/raw/upload/v1518462741/production/The_Grim_Reality_of_Being_A_Female_Job_Seeker.pdf, accessed October 23, 2019.

[8]Ronald Alsop, "Fat People Earn Less and Have a Harder Time Finding Work," BBC News, December 1, 2016, https://www.bbc.com/worklife/article/20161130-fat-people-earn-less-and-have-a-harder-time-finding-work.

[9]Shana Lebowitz, "Science Says People Determine Your Competence, Intelligence, and Salary Based on Your Weight," *Business Insider,* September 9, 2015. https://www.businessinsider.com/science-overweight-people-less-successful-2015-9.

[10]Alsop, "Fat People Earn Less and Have a Harder Time Finding Work."

[11]Suzanne McGee, "For Women, Being 13 Pounds Overweight Means Losing $9,000 a Year in Salary," *Guardian,* October 30, 2014, https://www.theguardian.com/money/us-money-blog/2014/oct/30/women-pay-get-thin-study.

[12]Lisa Quast, "Why Being Thin Can Actually Translate into a Bigger Paycheck for Women," *Forbes,* August 21, 2012, https://www.forbes.com/sites/lisaquast/2011/c6/can-being-thin-actually-translate-into-a-bigger-paycheck-for-women/#1a59co267b03.

[13]Megan Orciari, "Body Weight and Gender Influence Judgment in the Court-room," *YaleNews,* Yale University, January 8, 2013, https://news.yale.edu/2013/or/08/body-weight-and-gender-influence-judgment-courtroom.

[14]Matthew Rozsa, "Judge: Overweight Teen Victim May Have Been 'Flattered' by Sexual Assault," *Salon,* October 27, 2017, https://www.salon.com/2017/10/27/judge-overweight-teen-victim-may-have-been-flattered-by-sexual-assault.

breathe before he was finally choked to death — all for selling loose cigarettes on the street in New York City. Shortly thereafter, the coroner ruled Garner's death a homicide. The case seemed open and shut: Garner's death was taped and widely circulated. In the wave of police killings of unarmed Black men, this one seemed as close to an open-and-shut case as possible. As the case progressed, however, its resolution slipped further and further out of reach. Prosecutors declined to file criminal charges in the case. The officer who killed Garner, Daniel Pantaleo, has kept his job thus far, though he has been relegated to desk duty. In 2019, the NYPD held administrative hearings to determine whether or not Pantaleo would be permitted to keep his job. His defense team argued that Pantaleo should not be held accountable for his actions because Garner was fat. "He died from being morbidly obese," Stuart London, the police union attorney leading the team, said during an administrative hearing. "He was a ticking time bomb that resisted arrest. If he was put in a bear hug, it would have been the same outcome."[15]

By London's logic, a fat person can't be murdered, given the widespread and false belief that being fat is simply a death sentence. While the defense's argument ran in multiple newspapers, just one mainstream headline called attention to its cruel logic. *New York Magazine* ran the story with the headline "NYPD Union Lawyers Argue That Eric Garner Would Have Died Anyway Because He Was Obese."[16]

We create public policy around our bias, ensuring that fat people are not protected from even the most naked abuse. As of 2020,

in forty-eight states, it is perfectly legal to fire someone, refuse to hire them, deny them housing, or turn them down for a table at a restaurant or a room in a hotel simply because they're fat. Michigan, Washington State, and San Francisco are the United States' three jurisdictions to ban size-based discrimination.[17] In the rest of the nation, however, those who experience weight stigma in the workplace are left to fend for themselves with little, if any, legal recourse at all. In 2013, twenty-two cocktail waitresses sued Atlantic City's Borgata Hotel Casino & Spa for weight-based discrimination. They were regularly weighed in at work and were suspended if they gained "too much weight." Despite this overt discrimination, the court denied the servers' claim and upheld the hotel's legal right to discriminate.[18]

Whatever we may think of our own beliefs, however hard it may be to stretch beyond our own experience of the world as an unbiased meritocracy, this growing body of research proves that for fat people, it simply isn't. We get fewer jobs and earn significantly less money. In court, we are more likely to be found guilty by jurors and judges alike.

All of this happens because anti-fat bias 30 exists in *all of us*. It exists in all of us because it exists in every corner of our culture: our institutions, media, and public policy. How could we avoid it? Ninety-seven million Americans diet, despite the $66 billion industry's failure

---

[15]Zak Cheney-Rice, "NYPD Union Lawyers Claim Eric Garner Would've Died Anyway Because He Was Obese," *Intelligencer*, June 14, 2019, http://nymag.com/intelligencer/2019/06/eric -garner-death-inevitable-says-lawyer.html.

[16]Cheney-Rice, "NYPD Union Lawyers Claim Eric Garner Would've Died Anyway Because He Was Obese."

[17]Areva Martin, "Weight Discrimination Is Legal in 49 States." *Time*, August 16, 2017, https://time.com/4883176/weight -discrimination-workplace-laws; Sarah Kim, "Washington State Supreme Court Rules That Obesity Is a Disability," *Forbes Magazine*, July 19, 2019, https://www.forbes.com/sites /sarahkim/2019/07/18/washington-state-supreme-courts -obesity-disability/#1e5a504cd274.

[18]Josh Sanburn, "Too Big to Cocktail? Judge Upholds Weight Discrimination in the Workplace," *Time*, July 26, 2013, http:// nation.time.com/2013/07/26/too-big-to-cocktail-judge -upholds-weight-discrimination-in-the-workplace.

rate of up to 98 percent.[19] *The Biggest Loser* was a smash hit for its twelve years on the air, reaching over seven million viewers at the height of its popularity.[20] Magazines like *Woman's World* reliably feature cover stories like "Lose 13 Lbs Every 5 Days on the World's Hottest Diet" alongside "Ring in 2019 with Munchies!"[21] And the United States has not poured endless federal and state dollars into public education campaigns aimed at regulating corporate food production, subsidizing nutritious foods, or ending poverty and economic instability — top predictors of individual health, according to the US Office of Disease Prevention and Health Promotion.[22] Instead, *fat bodies themselves* are targeted in the "war on obesity" and the "childhood obesity epidemic." Anti-fatness is like air pollution. Some days we may see it; others, we may not.

But it always surrounds us, and whether we mean to or not, we are always breathing it in.

But where does all that bias come from? Like so many morality panics before it, it's difficult to identify a single source of our cultural and political commitment to sidelining and scapegoating fat bodies. Its roots are many and varied. As it stands, these forces — often driven by profit and political expediency — are today as strong as they've ever been. The power and profitability of anti-fatness means that most of us have already internalized hurtful, harmful, and inaccurate messages about fat people. Whatever we may want to think about ourselves, we've got to make the shift from thinking of anti-fat bias as *something we decide to do out of animus* to *something that exists within us unless and until we uproot it.* If we are passive, we absorb the bias in the world around us, overwhelmingly suggested to us by people and institutions that stand to gain power and profits by scapegoating fat people. It is up to us to both change those systems and to unlearn these enculturated attitudes. In so doing, we can make the world a little less punishing for the 70 percent of Americans who are fat.[23]

[19]MarketResearch.com. "U.S. Weight Loss Market Worth $66 Billion." PR Newswire, June 26, 2018, https://www.prnewswire.com/news-releases/us-weight-loss-market-worth-66-billion-300573968.html; Charlotte Markey, "5 Lies from the Diet Industry," *Psychology Today*, January 21, 2015, https://www.psychologytoday.com/us/blog/smart-people-don-t-diet/201501/5-lies-the-diet-industry.
[20]"The Biggest Loser: Fall 2011–2012 Ratings," Canceled Renewed TV Shows, TV Series Finale, February 8, 2012, https://tvseriesfinale.com/tv-show/the-biggest-loser-ratings-2011–2012.
[21]*Woman's World*, December 31, 2018.
[22]"Poverty," Healthy People 2020, U.S. Department of Health and Human Services, https://www.healthypeople.gov/2020/topics-objectives/topic/social-determinants-health/interventions-resources/poverty, accessed October 24, 2019.

[23] "Overweight & Obesity Statistics," National Institute of Diabetes and Digestive and Kidney Diseases, U.S. Department of Health and Human Services, August 1, 2017, https://www.niddk.nih.gov/health-information/health-statistics/overweight-obesity.

Topics for Critical Thinking and Writing

1. Consider the definition of the word "disabled" as used by Nicole Arbour in her "Dear Fat People" video discussed at the opening of this selection. Is "disabled" a useful term to apply to fat people? Explain, connecting the ways applying this word may impact policies on airlines or elsewhere. Should airlines make special accommodations for bodies that do not fit the standard seats?

2. What does Aubrey Gordon see as the reasons why Nicole Arbour's video was roundly criticized while the Young Turks' YouTube video was not? How might the distinctions between the two backlashes be relevant to understanding other forms of discriminatory beliefs and discriminatory expressions?

3. Stereotypes and assumptions about fat people, Gordon shows, occur regularly in media and culture. In what ways does Gordon claim that fat people feel "targeted" in American culture? What social factors might explain the increase in antifat bias shown by the 2019 Harvard study?

4. Do you think that body weight is a social justice and equal rights issues that needs antidiscrimination laws to protect a class of people? Why or why not?

5. Evaluate Gordon's suggestions in her final paragraph about what can be done to address antifat bias. Think of some specific strategy that a person or an institution could implement to begin the process. Explain how it might work and what challenges and obstacles might be faced (and, if possible, addressed).

6. Consider other human characteristics that may lead people to be discriminated against, but that are not protected by antidiscrimination frameworks such as those that guarantee the rights of racial, ethnic, gender, and disability categories. Drawing from your own observations or research, characterize their treatment in culture and consider what might be done to shift biased attitudes.

TRACY DEONN

Tracy Deonn is an educator, fan-fiction aficionado, and writer. She has contributed to the fortieth-anniversary *Empire Strikes Back* anthology, *From a Certain Point of View* (2013), and served as a co-writer and consulting producer on the SyFy channel docuseries *Looking for Leia* (2019). Deonn published a *New York Times* bestselling novel, *Legendborn* (2020), a modern twist on the King Arthur legend. The essay included here appeared in 2021 on the website for Tor, a publishing imprint devoted to science fiction and fantasy writing.

Every King Arthur Retelling Is Fanfic about Who Gets to Be Legendary

King Arthur stories are experiencing a recent resurgence in popular media, with *The Green Knight* starring Dev Patel announced in 2020, *Cursed* on Netflix, and several new Arthur-inspired books on shelves and on the horizon. Like clockwork, with each announcement of a new Arthurian tale, there come inevitable calls for "authenticity." Within hours of the trailer for *The Green Knight* dropping last year, people took to Twitter to discuss the significance of Patel's casting, and plenty of commenters began asserting that Patel's inclusion was ahistoric, even though people of color existed and participated in the world of the medieval era. They claimed the film was not "true" to the legend.

I reflexively tweeted the following, having been deeply embedded in my own King Arthur research at the time:

Tracy Deonn 🖤⚔️🖤 **(on hiatus)**
@tracydeonn
...

I'm excited about The Green Knight! But, LORDT. People are ALREADY being loud & wrong about King Arthur on Beyonce's internet!

There is no single Arthurian story. No sacred text. Black people existed in the Medieval. KA is 1500 year-old global fanfic that began in Wales. Repeat!

12:31 PM · Feb 13, 2020 · Twitter Web App

2,521 Retweets **313** Quote Tweets **11.7K** Likes

Arthurian stories originated in Wales, but for the modern audience the body of work we call Arthuriana is not drawn from a single reference point. These calls for authenticity are framed as though Arthuriana has a pure, original state to which we as storytellers can and should return. It does not. They suggest that the canon of King Arthur legends includes one single, universally accepted, historically accurate narrative. It does not. Not only are these calls for a single true Arthur story *themselves* ahistoric, but they ignore hundreds of years of Arthurian storytelling tradition–a tradition that has always included remixes and reinventions.

Why is it important to me to call Arthuriana fanfic? Because doing so reframes these stories as shared, flexible narratives. Calling it fanfic loosens the grip of ownership that the myth of a single story perpetuates. (We'll get to who *benefits* from that claim to ownership in a moment.)

When you hear the phrase, "the legend 5 of King Arthur" what images appear in your mind? Do you see Arthur first, a noble man in shining armor? Excalibur in its stone? Do you think of the Round Table? The Holy Grail? What would you say if I told you that your

constructed list of Arthurian mental images both belongs to you and to someone else, is both true and false, is both complete and incomplete? Because this "both-and" paradox is the very nature of King Arthur.

Let me clarify: I don't mean the historic Arthur, if he ever existed. Or even the specific Arthur character in a given piece of literature or media. I mean the *imagined* Arthur, and the narrative network of Arthuriana that has been woven around him over the past 1500 years. The one that lives in our collective modern minds in story bites and flashes of imagery. The one we stitch together from TV shows and children's books and adult novels and, yes, *The Sword in the Stone* Disney movie. *This* Arthur resists a single story as a matter of course, making him the perfect epicenter for inclusive reimaginings, reinterpretations, and remixes—and a confusing, if not futile, site for retellings.

If you ask a medievalist to tell you the King Arthur story, they will bemusedly ask, "Which one?" If you ask them to list the roster of knights at the Round Table, they will say "Whose list?" Some stories claim there were 150 knights, some claim twelve. I witnessed varying levels of this academic response over two years while consulting with experts on *Legendborn*. There is no agreed-upon canon to point to, cling to, or worship. There is only a collection of literature, stories, settings, characters, magical objects, and circumstances that contribute to the massive world of Arthuriana.

MY ARTHURIAN REIMAGINING DID NOT BEGIN WITH KING ARTHUR. IT BEGAN WITH GRIEF

When my mother passed away, I learned that she had lost her mother at the same age that I lost her, and that the same had occurred with my grandmother and great-grandmother — a strange pattern with no explanation. I wondered, why would this pattern of death exist in my family? Of course, there is no answer here, but I'm a writer raised on science fiction and fantasy, so I wrote a magical answer to an impossible question. *Legendborn* began from a place of grief and mystery, the same place in which my main character, a sixteen year-old girl named Bree, begins in the prologue to the book.

I needed to explore the idea of legacy through an epic, modern fantasy because a mystery this big deserved a journey that expansive, and because I had never seen a novel like that with a Black teenage girl at the center.

Like me, Bree is the most recent daughter 10 in a line of Black women whose deaths came early. Like me, and so many other Black Americans, as she explores her family history, she eventually comes up against the wall of enslavement — the wall where the answers stop, weren't recorded, and were stripped away. At this point, the question changed. Instead of "Why does this pattern exist?" it became, "Whose lives and losses get forgotten or erased, and whose lives and losses become legendary?" That is when Arthur appeared, as a collective legend about a man who may not have ever existed, but whose stories have survived centuries. Arthurian legends explore the same themes I wanted to examine in my contemporary fantasy novel: legacy, power, family, and the responsibilities laid before each generation when the previous generation dies.

North Carolina became the setting of my reimagined Arthurian tale, because growing up in the South, the question of whose lives we memorialize is in the air we breathe. From statues to memorials to names of streets and buildings, I learned very early that the creation of public memory is a privilege locked tight in white and Western hands. When Bree's search for the truth about her mother's death leads her to an Arthurian secret society, I intentionally use her experiences as a Black teenage girl in the South to interrogate and refresh King Arthur and the legends, both in her world and ours. While I anchor my Arthur in Wales, I use magic to explain how the Round Table could still be in existence in Bree's modern day. If I described *Legendborn* in fanfic language, I'd call it a canon-divergent Arthurian alternate universe (or AU) set in the real world with an original character, or OC. And I wouldn't be the first to write this way.

FANFIC IS THE TRADITION

Before legal and financial structures around story came into being, before printing and distribution, the idea of "owning" a story probably seemed very silly. A story was something shared from person to person and mouth-to-ear, from one speaker sitting around a campfire to a group of eager listeners. Stories are flexible, living things, while works have defined boundaries: page counts, run-times, first and second editions. And alongside these boundaries come the broader structures of copyright, intellectual property, ownership, and canon.

As a lifelong fangirl who has been immersed in Arthuriana for the past several years, now I see these stories as branching pathways and intentional games of telephone. And the writers generating these stories worked much like fanfic authors, using an existing story structure and cast of characters, but telling the story from an alternate perspective to explore a new idea. Or lifting a cast of characters wholesale and placing them in a new plot to better examine relationships. This transformative approach is in the genetic make-up of King Arthur. In fact, rewriting King Arthur from new cultural, national, and experiential perspectives is the tradition.

Geoffrey of Monmouth's *Historia regum Britanniae*, or "The History of the Kings of Britain," crafted many of the now familiar Arthurian elements, but he built them on top of and alongside previously existing details and

stories. In other words, Monmouth's *Historia* is a massively influential piece of 12th century fanfic.

In the 21st century, Lancelot du Lac, argu-[15] ably the most famous knight of Arthur's Table, is presented as an ever-present, essential figure and first knight. But this version of Lancelot was crafted by poet Chrétien de Troyes in the 12th century as an addition to Arthuriana, six hundred years after the first written mention of Arthur. This Lancelot, in fic-speak, is an OC; an Original Character the author added to the existing cast. I look at the Lancelot-Grail Cycle and see a long series of "missing scenes" and shipper fics.

The tale of the sword in the stone and Arthur pulling the blade to prove his right to be king is from 13th century French poet Robert de Boron, rewriting portions of Monmouth to weave a new work that also included a heavy emphasis on the wizard Merlin. When Thomas Malory took on the legends in 15th century England, he used pre-existing characters to write a sweeping canon-divergent, romance-heavy, epic AU series. He called this series *Le Morte d'Arthur*, and it became one of the most cited "sources" for Arthurian legends.

Each of these authors in history was writing in his own specific cultural and political context, and the new additions and changes they made were created from and for these contexts. Each new contribution was, as my friend and Arthurian scholar Bezi Yohannes says, "an act of political imagination." A declaration of values and a prioritization of some characters over others. These authors were deliberately weaving into Arthuriana — one of the most iconic collections of legends we have — the type of representation that they wanted to see, and we cannot separate their identities and perspectives from their creations.

This borrowing and building story process didn't stop with these writers. Authors and screenwriters still pull the canon of Arthuriana open like a drawer and select the components they most want to utilize without restrictive concern for whether their portrayals are "accurate" to previous ones. And it's time we take a hard look at whose "inaccurate" storytelling gets privileged as "accurate," and why.

In a domain of fanfic based on other fanfic, written by countless people across centuries, cultures, and languages without prior permission or citation — claiming which stories are real and which aren't is also a political act.

If one were to look only back to the dominant Arthurian texts and movies, extremely white, cis, straight, and male dominated narratives are the outcome, often in gritty, medieval-esque settings. But those types of retellings are a symptom of canon-dependency, when freedom from canon is how Arthur has survived this long in the first place. This is why Arthurian retellings are so powerful, after all — because we are watching characters in the midst of epic, legendary lives, who have the potential to be remembered long after they're gone.

When Arthurian retellings like *The Green Knight*, or other stories with inclusive representations of race, gender, sexuality, and other identities, are deemed "inauthentic," these claims aren't based on Arthuriana's reality. They're based on exclusion. When someone declares one story the "true" and another one "false," in an example as egregious as King Arthur, the declaration must be interrogated. When a narrative landscape has no central and true text, an effort to delegitimize certain versions becomes a tool of oppression that polices who gets to tell which stories, and who gets to have adventures at an Arthurian scale. Simply put, marking new and diverse additions to Arthuriana as either fact or fiction is a way to limit who gets to be legendary — and whose challenges and triumphs are worthy of remembrance.

20

Topics for Critical Thinking and Writing

1. Define the term "fanfic" — short for "fan fiction" — and provide some notable examples. (Search the internet if necessary for assistance.)

2. Examine Deonn's discussion of the differences between "stories as shared, flexible narratives" (para. 4) and "works [which] have defined boundaries" (para. 12). What are the differences? Which has more authority?

3. Is it more important that stories remain open to changes or that we cultivate a canon of stories that should not be changed? That is, are there benefits to preserving works that have stood the test of time? What might they be, and how do we confront the controversies they raise?

4. Consider some of the major sources of the Arthur legend Deonn discusses, and/or do some research to discover other primary or canonical versions of the Arthur legend. Now consider where you first learned about the Arthur legend, and how your acquisition of the story related to the venerated "originals." How does your experience inform your view of Deonn's essay?

5. Consider paragraph 11 in which Deonn writes, "I learned very early that the creation of public memory is a privilege locked tight in white and Western hands." Describe the reasons Deonn finds fanfic a form of personal empowerment, considering her personal story about her relationship to mythical and fantasy stories.

6. Compare Deonn's claims about there being no original or authoritative Arthur legend to the essay in this chapter by Anna Swartwood House about the appearance of Jesus. Are representations or Jesus, or retellings of biblical stories about Jesus, also a form of fanfic? Explain.

Conspiracy Theories: Are They a Cultural Problem?

RUSSEL MUIRHEAD AND NANCY ROSENBLUM

Russel Muirhead is the Robert Clements Professor of Democracy and Politics at Dartmouth College, where he is chair of the government department. He is a leading authority on democratic theory and political economy and has published his ideas widely, including in his 2004 book *Just Work*.

Nancy Rosenblum is a professor of political science and has taught at both Harvard University and Brown University. Among her many award-winning books on political theory, her 2010 work *On the Side of the Angels: An Appreciation of Parties and Partisanship* won the Walter Channing Cabot Award for scholarly eminence at Harvard University. Her book *Good Neighbors: The Democracy of Everyday Life in America* was published by Princeton University Press in 2016.

The following was published in the journal *Dissent* in 2018. Muirhead and Rosenblum subsequently published a book on this topic, *A Lot of People Are Saying: The New Conspiracism and the Assault on Democracy* (2019).

The New Conspiracists

The conspiracist mindset moved into the White House with the election of Donald Trump as president of the United States. Trump is the most powerful person who views politics through a miasma of secret, malignant intent, but he's not the only one. Alex Jones, a syndicated radio talk show host from Austin, Texas, has become a celebrity by peddling conspiracy. Fox News is not above giving its audience the conspiracy they want to hear — even if it turns out to be false, as was "pundit" Andrew Napolitano's

charge that British intelligence (on President Obama's orders) spied on Trump during the 2016 campaign. Amplifying charges by characters such as Napolitano are websites like *Infowars* (which is operated by Jones) or the *Gateway Pundit*, which, like burbling mud pots, release new conspiracies by the day. And underlying the officials, celebrities, and the fantasy news sites are online forums like Reddit, where anyone can share conspiracy theories with an audience of thousands at the click of a button.

Conspiracism has traveled from the margins to the mainstream, infusing public life and altering the bounds of what is acceptable in democratic politics. Aside from the presidency, conspiratorial designs are attributed to judges, elected representatives, and civil servants working in federal agencies. No official action is immune to being labelled a conspiracy. Rewording questions in the Census, for instance, is cast as a conspiracy to make the Affordable Care Act look more successful. Even acts of nature point to secret conspiratorial machinations: in 2012, some insisted that Hurricane Sandy was engineered by scientists at the direction of President Obama to help secure his reelection.

Conspiracism is not new, of course, but the conspiracism we see today does introduce something new — conspiracy without the theory. And it betrays a new destructive impulse: to delegitimate the government. Often the aim is merely to delegitimate an individual or a specific office. The charge that Obama conspired to fake his birth certificate only aimed at Obama's legitimacy. Similarly, the charge that the National Oceanic and Atmospheric Administration publicized flawed data in order to make global warming look more menacing was designed only to demote the authority of climate scientists working for the government. But the effects of the new strategy cannot be contained to one person or entity. The ultimate effect of the new conspiracism will be to delegitimate democracy itself.

Conventional conspiracism makes sense of a disorderly and complicated world by insisting that powerful human beings can and do control events. In this way, it gives order and meaning to apparently random occurrences. And in making sense of things, conspiracism insists on proportionality. JFK's assassination, this type of thinking goes, was not the doing of a lone gunman — as if one person acting alone could defy the entire U.S. government and change the course of history. Similarly, the brazen attacks on the World Trade Center and the Pentagon on 9/11 could not have been the work of fewer than two dozen men plotting in a remote corner of Afghanistan. So conspiracist explanations insist that the U.S. government must have been complicit in the strikes.

Conspiracism insists that the truth is not 5 on the surface: things are not as they seem, and conspiracism is a sort of detective work. Once all the facts — especially facts ominously withheld by reliable sources and omitted from official reports — are scrupulously amassed and the plot uncovered, secret machinations make sense of seemingly disconnected events. What historian Bernard Bailyn observed of the conspiracism that flourished in the Revolutionary era remains characteristic of conspiracism today: "once assumed [the picture] could not be easily dispelled: denial only confirmed it, since what conspirators profess is not what they believe; the ostensible is not the real; and the real is deliberately malign."

When conspiracists attribute intention where in fact there is only accident and coincidence, reject authoritative standards of evidence and falsifiability, and seal themselves off from any form of correction, their conspiracism can seem like a form of paranoia — a delusional insistence that one is the victim of a hostile world. This is not to say that all conspiracy theories are wrong; sometimes what conspiracists allege is really there. Yet warranted or not, conventional conspiracy theories offer both an explanation of the alleged danger and a guide to the actions necessary to save the nation or the world.

The new conspiracism we are seeing today, however, often dispenses with any explanations or evidence, and is unconcerned with uncovering a pattern or identifying the operators plotting in the shadows. Instead, it offers only innuendo and verbal gesture, as exemplified in President Trump's phrase, "people are saying." Conspiracy without the theory can corrode confidence in government, but it cannot give meaning to events or guide constructive collective action.

The effect of conspiratorial thinking, once it ceases to function as any sort of explanation, is delegitimation. The new conspiracist accusations seek not only to unmask and disempower those they accuse but to deny their standing to argue, explain, persuade, and decide. Conspiracism rejects their authority. In the end, the consequences of delegitimation are not targeted or discrete but encompassing.

CONSPIRACY WITHOUT THE THEORY

The new conspiracist mindset posits the meaning of events with certainty, but in contrast to conventional conspiracism — the myriad accounts of JFK's assassination or 9/11, say — it has little interest in explanation. "Rigged" was a single word that in the election of 2016 had the power to evoke sinister intentions, fantastic plots, and an awesome capacity to mobilize three million illegal voters to support Hillary Clinton for president and then to cover it up. In Trump's (and Bannon's) insistence that busloads of fraudulent voters were sent to vote against him in the New Hampshire primary there are no stray facts to account for: no local officials testify to having been besieged by hundreds or thousands of new voters exiting from fleets of busses. The baseless charge of voter fraud in New Hampshire is designed to obscure the reality that Trump lost the popular vote: it is an attempt to enhance Trump's legitimacy by delegitimizing the electoral process.

The new, lazy conspiracism satisfies itself 10 with vague assertions. For instance, when a

former Washington D.C. homicide investigator wrote on Facebook, referring to Justice Scalia's death: "My gut tells me there is something fishy going on in Texas." References to unnamed actors ("people are saying") are elastic; they can embrace a changing cast of public enemies and a wide but unspecified repertoire of nefarious acts. Complicity by insinuation and equivocation also evades responsibility. A telling example was Mike Huckabee's seemingly off-hand comment in relation to Obama's birth certificate in 2011: "I would love to know more. What I know is troubling enough."

The manner of coy insinuation that marks the new conspiracism both absolves the speaker of responsibility for the charge he's putting forth and invites endless investigation. As Trump said about a *National Enquirer* story that linked Texas senator Ted Cruz's father with JFK's assassination, "even if it isn't totally true, there's something there." Or, as Representative Bryan Zollinger (R-ID) said about the allegation that Democratic Party officials lured white nationalists and antifascist protestors to Charlottesville in order to manufacture a clash, "I am not saying it is true, but I am suggesting that it is completely plausible."

Where nothing is true but everything is plausible, it becomes respectable, even necessary, to insert conspiracism into the official business of democratic institutions. Trump enlisted administration officials to affirm his ungrounded claim that he was being wiretapped by former president Obama ("during the very sacred election process"), and followed up with a demand for a congressional investigation. In another example from 2013, Congress held a joint hearing to investigate ammunition purchases by the Department of Homeland Security, in response to charges that the federal government was stockpiling arms in preparation for a violent campaign against American citizens. Conspiracism simultaneously degrades and exploits Congress, the Justice Department, intelligence agencies, and the press.

The new conspiracism — conspiracy without the theory — is potent and divisive. It pretends to own reality. It carries us beyond partisan polarization to epistemic polarization, so that Americans are in conflict about nothing less than what it means to know something. And through disinterest in explanation and disregard for the logic of evidence and argument, it is energetic and all-encompassing in its targets.

THE NEW CONSPIRACISM'S PARTISAN PENUMBRA

The ultimate consequence of the new conspiracism is the destruction of the administrative state, a state with the capacity to design and implement long-term policy. The administrative state is the legacy of the Progressive era and the New Deal. To be sure, every conspiracy theory is not designed to attack the administrative state in toto. It is often only one institution (like the EPA) or one actor (such as President Obama) that is the target. But the blizzard of conspiracy theories creates whiteout conditions that obscure any perception of governmental integrity. The consequence of conspiracism is not simply distrust; it feeds the assumption that the government is staffed by those who are actively hostile to the common interest.

In its consequences for the administrative state, today's conspiracism is congruent with partisan Republican purposes, because it has the effect of derailing the operations of liberal policies and programs that defined national politics in the twentieth century. In its modest iteration, conservatism sought to correct the alleged excesses of New Deal liberalism while securing its core. As Ronald Reagan explained, in his youth he shared the goals of Roosevelt and the New Deal, but as he saw it, the Democratic Party became more extreme. "I didn't leave the Democratic Party," Reagan pronounced, "the Party left me." In its current, more radical iteration, conservatism seeks to reverse the New Deal legacy altogether. It was also Reagan who gave radical Republicanism its organizing principle: "government is not the solution to our problem. Government is the problem." This more radical and destructive impulse was exemplified by Rick Perry when he insisted during the presidential campaign of 2011 that he would eliminate three federal agencies, but could only name two. The specifics do not matter — what matters is that government be dismantled.

Yet once in power, radical conservatism runs into a formidable obstacle: dismantling government is not very popular. People expect government to protect them from dangerous products, to monitor the safety of the water and food supply, to assist victims of natural disasters, to ensure access to healthcare, to regulate markets, to prosecute frauds, and so on. Conspiracism helps accomplish what radical conservatives in office cannot by delegitimizing the institutions that deliver these policies. It dissolves the authority of knowledge-producing institutions inside and outside government, communities of expertise, and conventions of fact and argument necessary to make effective decisions.

Conspiracism's attack has a partisan penumbra, then, but its effects are totalizing and go well beyond what even radical conservatives want. It destroys not only liberal policies but the institutional capacities of the state wholesale. The communities of special knowledge — the doctors and economists and engineers who regulate the safety of airplanes, who steward the macroeconomy toward low inflation and sustainable growth — do not reside on one side of the partisan divide. To undermine them is not to weaken liberalism or progressivism or the left but to weaken democracy. Conspiracism is the acid that dissolves the institutions, processes, and standards of justification that make government possible.

THE DELEGITIMATION OF POLITICAL PARTIES

Political parties are among the most important institutions that conspiracism corrodes. Americans are so used to disparaging parties and partisans that we don't spring to their defense as we do to (ironically) the FBI. From George Washington to Barack Obama, anti-partisanship has been a staple of American political life. Against the background of endemic anti-partisanship and weak parties, conspiracism goes about the business of delegitimizing the democratic state.

It starts with delegitimizing opposition candidates. The most infamous case was the Republican story about a conspiracy to conceal President Obama's foreign birth. President Trump is the most notorious birther, and helped bring the conspiracy into the mainstream. The conspiracy moved quickly from the periphery of political discourse to the formal institutions of politics, and threatened to keep Obama's name from appearing on the Kansas ballot in the reelection campaign of 2012 — the state where Obama's own mother was born. Kansas Secretary of State Kris Kobach said at the time, "I don't think it's a frivolous objection." Kobach said of the charge that Obama was foreign-born: "I do think the factual record could be supplemented." This was more than a year after the White House released Obama's "long form" birth certificate.

Allegations of conspiracy extend beyond [20] this or that candidate or official to the political opposition altogether. Not content with the hyper-criticism and incivility that mark polarized partisanship, conspiracists cast the Democratic Party as a danger to the nation. The conspiracist mindset is part of a larger tendency to paint the opposition as a revolutionary party surreptitiously altering national identity and creating an alien nation. The party is said to be the agent of Muslims, Jews, blacks, immigrants — exploiting the electoral process to subvert America as a Christian nation, to "mongrelize" a white population, to empower "takers and suckers," to extend rights to outsiders, to cede sovereignty to the "new world order." As an existential threat (not merely an opponent), President Obama is cast by some, like Senator Ted Cruz (R-TX), as a "lawless" president, and by others, like conservative attorney Cleta Mitchell, as a "dictatorial tyrant."

And of course, the opposition is said to abet foreign enemies. Their foreign policy of international aggression (or failure to act aggressively) is not just ineffective or immoral but designed to undermine the United States' power and status in the world. Hillary Clinton, according to President Trump, "meets in secret with international banks to plot the destruction of U.S. sovereignty."

The objective in all this is not only defeating the opposition in an election but assuring their permanent incapacitation. That was Steve Bannon's consolation at a moment when he thought Trump would lose the election: "Our back-up strategy is to f—k her [Clinton] up so bad that she can't govern."

Senate Republicans' refusal to consider Judge Merrick Garland's nomination to the Supreme Court was tactical, of course, designed to entrench a conservative majority on the court. But the terms of refusal are telling. Stalling until the next election in order to "let the voters decide" is a public disavowal of the authority of voters who elected President Obama in 2012.

This is delegitimation — not just opposing or discrediting or defeating. When conspiracism delegitimizes regulated party rivalry, loyal opposition, and the tradition of "agreeing to disagree" it strikes at the bedrock of representative democracy.

The ultimate moment in delegitimizing 25 democratic politics is to impugn all parties. Trump is perfectly cast to preside over such a moment. He was never loyal to a party. His presidential campaign did not have the support of the national Republican leadership, party elites, or donors. He does not call his supporters Republicans. The conspiracist-in-chief may destroy the Republican Party, but he is not reshaping it or organizing another. He is preparing the public for a politics without parties.

True, parties and partisans frustrate this impulsive personality. He would work without and around them, bully or disregard them. But more important, he and networks of conspiracists see parties as cabals. In Trump's view, Democratic/Obama "holdovers" at the National Security Council, the State Department, and other agencies are pulling the strings of the "deep state," undermining the country and his rightful authority. In this respect, the Trump administration sounds much like figures such as Alex Jones, who sees the federal government as a "Trojan horse" harboring "enemies within." And Democrats are not the only ones with nefarious, concealed aims. Republicans are complicit. The parties collude. They are all agents of (pick the conspiracy of the moment) global elites who rule the world. Both parties are responsible for the "American carnage" Trump conjured up in his apocalyptic campaign speeches.

NEW CONSPIRACISM VERSUS PROGRESSIVE ANTIPARTYISM

The United States has a history of antipartyism, but today's conspiracism deviates from its antecedents. For, in the past, a common reason for wanting to do away with parties and partisanship was democratic reform — aimed at *enhancing* democracy.

Progressivism early in the twentieth century saw political parties as "perverters of the democratic spirit," part of a system shrouded in corruption and fraud. Progressives ferreted out facts and observed patterns and wove them into detailed accounts of conspiracy; they called it muckraking. They championed nonpartisan local government and reliance on expertise. They accepted electoral democracy, but insisted on a secret ballot and primary elections in which candidates were not identified with a party and voters were independents, not partisans. And like many progressives today, they championed direct participatory democracy: initiatives and referenda, recall, and constitutional conventions.

By contrast, the new conspiracists' delegitimation of parties is not a sober confrontation with the limitations of party democracy. There is no interest in democratic reform, no prescription for institutional innovation, or any form of collective democratic action.

Rather than appeal to his fellow partisans, 30 Trump instead appeals to "real Americans." After all, we don't need parties if there is only one collective identity, one community, one people with only one voice. Trump gives us identity politics with a vengeance. Because unlike ethnic or racial identities, the category of "real Americans" is not just one element of the American polity.

The value of parties lies in the way they connect the pluralism of a free society to the formal institutions of politics. And though every partisan believes she is "on the side of the angels," partisans do not imagine they speak for the whole or that their victory is anything but partial and temporary. It takes humility not to claim to be the voice of "the nation" or "the people," and to recognize opposition as legitimate.

Today's antipartyism — with its virulent populist trappings and eruptions of justificatory conspiracism — is a form of malignant anti-pluralism. This is delegitimation of democracy at the deepest level, penetrating beyond the formal state to society.

THERE ARE NO ALTERNATIVES

What, exactly, the new conspiracist mindset wants to put in place of the institutions, practices, and policies it degrades is uncertain. Perhaps nothing at all. For despite its partisan penumbra — its alignment with radical conservatism — conspiracism today is not embedded in an ideology, a political program or movement, an understanding of justice or a constitutional view (this is why discerning conservatives have so forcefully resisted endorsing Trump's conspiracism). Conspiracism claims to uncover odious plots against the Constitution, the fabric of society, sacred American values, national identity — but not for the sake of upholding any constitutional theory, or affirming any vision of society, or installing any coherent understanding of American values and national identity.

Some commentators see in conspiracism an aspiration to overturn the established political order for the sake of a new regime — a populist authoritarian regime unconstrained by constitutional limitations, for example. This is wrong. To be sure, Trump has a few policies he favors, some venal, like lower estate taxes. He indulges his hostility toward immigrants, affinity for white supremacy and anti-Semitism, lust for thuggery, and disdain for legal restraints. But backlash garnished with a handful of grievances and bad policies is not a political theory. We're witness to the fact that it does not take an alternative ideology or program — communism, authoritarianism, theism, fascism, nativism — to delegitimize democracy. Sterile conspiracism does the work.

The new conspiracism is destabilizing, degrading, and delegitimizing, without a countervailing constructive impulse, as if whatever rises from the detritus of constitutional democracy is less important and less captivating than narratives of grievance, catastrophe, and humiliation.

This is striking. Fearsome fascist and totalitarian regimes, revolutionary politics, even apocalyptic movements that would destroy the world to save it all envision what the next world or our own revivified world will be like. Disregard for what might be constructed in place of what is destroyed goes against the grain of human hopefulness. It instead reveals a conspiracist mindset trapped in an angry private reality of the moment, with no next steps or better ways forward.

Contemporary politics is a lesson in what delegitimation looks like. Authorities, institutions, and reasoning based on standards of evidence and argument are held in contempt, its principals charged with malicious intent. Officials are "so-called" officials (for example, "the quote president" Obama) and can be justifiably demeaned, subverted, undermined, or declared criminal. Agencies and knowledge-producing institutions can be hollowed out. Parties can be dismissed as cabals. Delegitimation proceeds by assaulting, degrading, and violating the institutions and norms that make democracy possible.

Social scientists since Weber (or Aristotle) have studied legitimacy and how authorities

35

gain it. The process of delegitimation, however, especially in wealthy, historically stable democracies, is much less well understood. In a sense, we are on our own.

What can be done? First, we must call out conspiracists' claim to reality. Speaking truth to conspiracy is a moral imperative. It is a sign of dangerous times that so few responsible office-holders, and barely any among conservatives, do.

We also need democratic narratives as 40 compelling as the accusations conjured by conspiracists. Speaking truth to conspiracy is disarming, when it is, not because it offers facts or represents sounder reasoning but because it supports a story that makes better sense to citizens.

Yet we also need more. When conspiracism becomes a regular element of public life, we need to defend the ordinary routines of democratic politics. That means not only adherence to the customary and legal processes of constitutional democracy by both parties (and civil society groups and others)

but also literally articulating them, pedagogically, so citizens appreciate the purpose of democratic norms. Citizens need to witness exhibitions of institutional integrity and regular politics at work, such as when the chair of a congressional intelligence committee announces that he will investigate as the evidence warrants rather than act at President Trump's direction. These deliberate exhibitions of institutional integrity and regular democratic politics have to be meaningful, producing recognizably fair outcomes in the public interest. With that, the conspiracist threat to democratic legitimacy may be called out and contained.

Reversing the damage already done, however, is more complicated. Conspiracism has an extended half-life. Re-legitimation will be long and arduous. The challenge is clear: as Archibald MacLeish once said, "It is not enough, in this war of hoaxes and delusions and perpetuated lies, to be merely honest. It is necessary also to be wise."

Topics for Critical Thinking and Writing

1. Explore the psychology of conspiracies. Why are conspiracies and conspiracy theories so alluring? What do Russel Muirhead and Nancy Rosenblum think? What do you think?

2. In paragraph 2, the authors argue that "conspiracism has traveled from the margins to the mainstream." Point to some evidence for this claim by drawing from Muirhead and Rosenblum or adding your own observations and examples.

3. Explain what Muirhead and Rosenblum mean by arguing against the "new" conspiracy theories (as opposed to the "old" ones). Why do they see the new conspiracists as particularly dangerous?

4. Do some research on one of the conspiracy theories mentioned by Muirhead and Rosenblum and compare what conspiracists believe to what more conventional, accepted beliefs are. Write an essay in which you weigh the evidence and determine whether or not you believe the conspiracy. (Use A Checklist for Evaluating Sources in Chapter 8, p. 287.) Which sources are more reliable, and why?

5. Argue for or against the following claim: Muirhead and Rosenblum are part of a conspiracy to undermine Donald Trump and his allies.

6. Invent your own conspiracy theory. Describe it — and feel free to be humorous. You may be imaginative, or you might think of a time when you were paranoid that somebody or some group "had it out for you." What evidence did you have? How did you put the evidence together to support your theory?

JAMES B. MEIGS

James B. Meigs is a writer, editor, and podcaster whose work has appeared in the *New York Post*, *City Journal*, *Commentary*, and other periodicals. He served as the editor-in-chief of *Premiere* magazine, the editor of *Popular Mechanics*, and editorial director for *Car and Driver* and *Road and Track* magazines, in addition to being a founding team member of *Entertainment Weekly*. He cohosts the podcast *How Do We Fix It?* The essay here appeared in *City Journal* in 2021.

Conspiracies All the Way Down

I hadn't intended to join the Globalist/Bush–Cheney/Zionist/CIA cabal for world domination. And I certainly didn't mean to become a leading figure in the conspiracy to cover up the truth about 9/11. According to my critics, though, I was all that and more. All I'd meant to do was publish an article investigating 9/11 conspiracy theories. The unhinged response to that article taught me a lot about the hold such paranoid worldviews can have on otherwise normal people. In Jonathan Kay's 2011 book *Among the Truthers*, he describes followers of the "9/11 Truth Movement" as having "spun out of rationality's ever-weakening gravitational pull" and fallen into "fantasy universes of their own construction." I met those people. They used to call and email me every day. Many took pains to explain all the horrible things that would happen to me once my crimes were "exposed."

I now believe the 9/11 Truthers I encountered were canaries in the coal mines of American society. They were an early warning sign of a style of thinking that has only grown more common in the years since 9/11: alienated, enraged, and not just irrational,

but *anti*-rational. Today, fantasy universes abound in our current political culture. On the far right, Capitol-storming QAnon followers imagine vast, deep-state conspiracies involving pedophiles and pizza parlors. The Left's conspiracy theories aren't as obviously bonkers, but progressives also imagine powerful forces that secretly conspire against the people. In her 2007 book, *The Shock Doctrine*, for example, writer Naomi Klein introduced the concept of "disaster capitalism" — a kind of global plot to exploit the powerless — and promised to "reveal the puppet strings behind the critical events of the last four decades." Today, the Woke Left routinely portrays American institutions as engines of cleverly concealed oppression. Racism, sexism, and the like are not just biases to be overcome but fundamental organizing principles of American society.

For more than two centuries, the U.S. has occasionally had spasms of populist fantasies: fears about Freemasons, "minions of the Pope," "international bankers," or other shadowy forces controlling events from behind the scenes. But the grassroots popularity of 9/11 conspiracy theories — and the surprising tolerance for such ideas in elite media and political circles — helped bring paranoia into the modern mainstream. I watched it happen.

Let me start at the beginning. In the fall of 2004, I had recently been hired as editor-in-chief of *Popular Mechanics*, the century-old magazine that combines science and tech news with do-it-yourself advice. The publication had grown stale, and it was my job to reinvigorate it with new talent and bold reporting. So I had my eye out for newsworthy stories rooted in science and technology.

One day, I opened the *New York Times* 5 and saw a full-page advertisement for a book called *Painful Questions*. The ad suggested that we hadn't been told the truth about 9/11 and offered a list of factual claims that supposedly refuted the conventional account of the attacks. For example, it claimed that jet fuel doesn't burn at a temperature high enough to melt steel (therefore the jet plane impacts couldn't explain the collapse of the Twin Towers) and that the hole in the Pentagon wasn't big enough to have been made by a commercial jet (so it could only have been made by a guided missile), and so on.

I'd been in Manhattan on September 11, 2001, and I had loosely followed the conspiracy theories that bubbled up in the attack's aftermath. The theories surfaced first in the Arab world — for them it was all Israel's fault, of course — but extremists of various stripes around the world quickly embraced and embellished them. Most versions of the idea suggested the real perpetrator was a cabal that included Bush, Cheney, oil companies, military contractors, the Mossad, and other malefactors, all conspiring to launch wars in the Middle East. In the faux-insider jargon that conspiracists love, it was a "false-flag operation." The notion meshed perfectly with the

Howard Zinn view of history in which all evils in the world can be traced back to some original sin involving U.S. policy. (True to form, Zinn offered a supportive blurb for one of the most popular books promoting these 9/11 claims, David Ray Griffin's *The New Pearl Harbor*.) Such theories, avidly discussed on left-wing websites and in the alternative press, rarely surfaced in the American mainstream media. But here was a full-page ad proclaiming these ideas in the *New York Times*.

The book's claims sounded doubtful but also fairly easy to confirm or disprove. How hot does jet fuel burn? How big a hole would a Boeing 757 make in a reinforced concrete building? These questions were very much in the *Popular Mechanics* wheelhouse. Every conspiracy theory ultimately rests on a handful of claims about physical reality. What if we put together a team of reporters and simply fact-checked the most common claims made by 9/11 conspiracy theorists? If the factual assertions were wrong, then the elaborate theories built on them were wrong, too. On the other hand, if there were even a grain of truth in any of these claims, well, what could be more vital to investigate?

We assigned eight reporters to the inquiry. *Popular Mechanics* executive editor David Dunbar led the project, making sure to keep it focused on technical questions and rigorously non-political. For the next few weeks, our reporters interviewed experts, pored over documents, and talked with eyewitnesses. In every case, they found that the conspiracy advocates' claims were based on evidence that was inaccurate, misinterpreted, or deliberately falsified. For example, it is true that jet fuel burns at 1,100 degrees Celsius, while steel melts at about 1,500 degrees Celsius. But, as our sources explained, a steel beam can lose half its strength at temperatures as low as 600 degrees. A number of in-depth engineering studies provide detailed accounts of how the impacts of the planes, combined with heat from fires, eventually weakened the structures to the point where collapse was inevitable.

The claim that the hole in the Pentagon wasn't big enough to have been made by a 757 rested on similarly flawed evidence: the airplane's wings were simply sheared off by the building's thick concrete walls. In any event, investigators found wreckage from the fuselage and remains of the passengers, crew, and hijackers deep inside the Pentagon, and they subjected this evidence to forensic examination. (We interviewed some of the people involved in this horrific task.) And so it went. Every conspiracy claim crumbled when subjected to the slightest factual scrutiny. In every case, we found, the theorists clung to slender reeds of misinformation, while scorning mountains of evidence supporting the mainstream view.

In February 2005, as our cover story, 10 "Debunking 9/11 Myths," hit newsstands, we braced for the blowback. When we started the project, we imagined some conspiracy buffs might actually be pleased that a mainstream outlet was finally taking their questions seriously. By the time we finished, we had learned that conspiracy theorists respond to factual refutation much the way the human immune system reacts to a foreign substance: by trying to destroy or absorb the unwelcome intruder. Almost overnight, my staff and I weathered the most inflammatory accusations: *Popular Mechanics* was a CIA front, a "tool of the Illuminati," and an agent of the Mossad. Christopher Bollyn, a longtime champion of the most outré conspiracy theories, published an article comparing our investigation with the 1933 Reichstag fire, which helped cement Nazi power in Germany.

If not for the death threats, it might have been almost amusing.

We had launched the project in the hopeful belief that facts matter, and that people of goodwill could review the evidence and make up their own minds. That turned out to be the case for many readers. I gave some lectures about our 9/11 reporting and was reassured by the people who showed up. Quite a few had doubts about what they saw as the "official" version of events — which isn't a bad thing; people shouldn't blindly accept everything the media or government tells them. But after listening to how carefully we had investigated their concerns, most left satisfied that the mainstream view of 9/11 — that it really was the work of al-Qaida terrorists — actually made sense.

That appeal to a shared sense of reality didn't work with hardcore conspiracy fans, however. Quite the opposite. Dedicated conspiracists use a whole suite of techniques to dismiss inconvenient facts. They vilify opponents with ad hominem attacks. While refusing to engage with legitimate evidence, they zero in on a handful of anomalies they think undermine the mainstream narrative. For example, a single eyewitness's mistaken impression becomes definitive proof against the weight of hundreds of other eyewitness accounts. (Michael Shermer, then a columnist at *Scientific American*, called this approach "argument by anomaly" and noted that creationists and Holocaust deniers employ the same sort of selection bias.) Of course, *Popular Mechanics'* reporting showed that even the supposed anomalies relied on falsehoods. But that gave the Truthers little pause. If a claim became too troublesome, they would simply abandon it and move on to new, even flimsier assertions. For example, most Truthers eventually dropped the contention that a missile and not an airplane hit the Pentagon. (There

CHAPTER 25 | CONSPIRACY THEORIES: ARE THEY A CULTURAL PROBLEM?

were simply too many photos showing pieces of American Airlines Flight 77 scattered around the impact zone.) Instead, the defter theorists pivoted. They began arguing not only that the missile claims were wrong, but that *phony conspiracy theorists* had planted them in order to make the Truther movement look bad.

If all else fails, conspiracy theorists neutralize contradictory evidence by simply expanding the orbit of their theories. If a magazine like *Popular Mechanics* points out facts that demolish your theory, you just declare the magazine a part of the conspiracy. Now you can ignore those inconvenient facts; they are all part of the coverup. Under Truther logic, anyone who doubts the conspiracy narrative is, ipso facto, on the side of the cabal. In this way, conspiracy theorists are like Marxists or members of a cult; their worldview is immune to refutation. Today's Woke Left employs a similar kind of unfalsifiable logic: Robin DiAngelo's *White Fragility* claims that to doubt one's own racism is proof of racism.

The following year we expanded our 15 reporting into a book-length version, *Debunking 9/11 Myths: Why Conspiracy Theories Can't Stand Up to the Facts*. In 2011, we updated the book with new research in time for the tenth anniversary of the attacks. In other words, for more than half a decade, my team and I were among the very few mainstream journalists aggressively challenging the Truther narrative. Each installment of our investigation prompted supportive coverage from conservative media (including Fox News) but relatively grudging interest from mainstream or liberal outlets. The attacks of 9/11 were arguably the most important event in the lifetimes of most Americans. Why wasn't the mainstream media more interested in correcting the growing flood of misinformation about the event?

Not long after our first article came out, I was booked to appear on NPR's "On the Media" with host Brooke Gladstone. I assumed Gladstone would support our mission and might want to hear some shop-talk about our reporting methods. Instead, she seemed perplexed as to why we had bothered to challenge the conspiracy claims in the first place. "Who's your audience for this?" she asked. I told her that we didn't think we would win over hardcore conspiracy theorists but hoped we could influence "the sensible middle."

By that I meant any readers willing to look honestly at the verifiable facts, regardless of their personal politics. That notion left her cold. "I don't want to be a contrarian here, but when you talk about a sensible middle, that's a rather slippery location," she said. The interview wasn't openly hostile, but Gladstone's questioning left the distinct impression that there was something vaguely fishy about a magazine trying to set the record straight about 9/11.

Eventually, I developed a few thoughts about why the liberal media was lukewarm toward our work. First, it's important to remember that 9/11 conspiracy theories were mostly embraced on the far left at that point. George W. Bush was in the White House, and antiwar sentiment was strong. Few liberal leaders and media figures actively promoted the theories, but few also saw them as a problem worth criticizing. (David Corn, then a columnist at *The Nation*, was a notable — and noble — exception.) The unspoken assumption seemed to be that there wasn't much harm in a few hotheads calling Bush a terrorist puppet master. In fact, if it convinced a few more people to hate Republicans, it might even be a good thing.

When *Popular Mechanics* waded into the discussion, some on the mainstream left were bemused. We must have some kind of political agenda. Were we trying to defend the Bush White House? Why would we want to help *them*? This was the moment I realized journalism was changing. The evenhanded search for truth — rarely achieved in practice — was fading even as a journalistic aspiration. Now every set of facts must serve a political purpose. If it wasn't helpful to the Left, it must be helpful to the Right. Where journalists once obsessed over the accuracy of facts, now they worried more about their utility. If some piece of information helps the wrong sorts of people, perhaps it's best left unpublished. Last year, we saw this logic carried to a new extreme, when virtually all major media outlets refused to cover the revelations contained in Hunter Biden's laptop, or to explore evidence that Covid-19 might have escaped from a Wuhan, China lab.

So, with a few exceptions, the media 20 mostly gave the 9/11 Truthers a pass. That was one factor helping this minor cult become a mass movement. Another was the Internet. Social media was in its infancy at the time, and YouTube didn't yet exist. But anyone could start a blog. Websites dedicated to 9/11 theories sprouted like weeds. In 2005, a Red Lobster waiter and aspiring filmmaker named Dylan Avery released a homemade 9/11 film he called *Loose Change*. The movie was a pastiche of absurd claims, spooky music, and portentous narration. But it was slickly made and — for anyone unfamiliar with the facts — weirdly compelling. Aided by a growing team of compatriots, Avery released several increasingly polished versions of the film over the next four years. The movie's claims shifted from one edition to another but included the notion that no plane hit the Pentagon, that the Twin Towers had been wired for controlled demolition, and that Flight 93 didn't crash in Pennsylvania but instead landed in Cleveland, where the passengers were mysteriously disappeared. *Loose Change* became an Internet blockbuster. In 2006 alone, the movie clocked more than 10 million views on the YouTube precursor Google Video.

Even before *Loose Change*, a few prominent Democrats had begun catering to the Truther cohort. Howard Dean flirted with conspiracy claims during his 2004 presidential campaign. Van Jones had to resign as an Obama advisor when word got out that he had earlier signed a 9/11 conspiracy petition. In the House of Representatives, Georgia's Cynthia McKinney invited conspiracy theorists, including David Ray Griffin, to address the Congressional Black Caucus. But *Loose Change* opened the floodgates. Filmmakers Kevin Smith and David Lynch praised the movie. Alec Baldwin called it "the *Gone With the Wind*" of the conspiracy movement. Progressive radio stations including New York's WBAI and Los Angeles's KPFK began giving away *Loose Change* DVDs during their fundraising drives. *Vanity Fair* published a gushing profile of the filmmakers (which included a backhanded suggestion that *Popular Mechanics* was part of a 9/11 coverup). Actors including Mark Ruffalo, Roseanne Barr, Martin Sheen, and Woody Harrelson expressed support for the Truther position. Rosie O'Donnell promoted Truther claims on *The View*, the daily gabfest the *New York Times* has called "the most important political TV show in America."

Hollywood's weakness for conspiracy theories lives on. The original version of Spike Lee's four-part documentary, *NYC Epicenters 9/11➔ 2021½*, currently airing on HBO, included interviews with about a dozen conspiracy theorists, including Robert Gage, founder of a group called Architects & Engineers for 9/11 Truth. Slate's Jeremy Stahl, who has covered the Truther movement for over a decade, describes Gage as being "responsible for peddling some of the most pernicious and long-running lies about the 9/11 attacks." When the *New York Times* asked Lee why he chose to include such voices in his film, he responded, "I mean, I got questions." But, after encountering some blowback, Lee returned to the editing room and cut the entire 30-minute section.

The left-wing indulgence of the Truther movement obscured a strange fact: much of the original source material for these theories came from ultra-right-wing activists. Many Truther websites employed the sort of anti-Semitic canards promulgated in the *Protocols of the Elders of Zion* and in the 1971 paranoia handbook *None Dare Call It Conspiracy*: the attacks must have been connected to some shadowy cabal of Jewish bankers — the Rothschilds are often mentioned — whom anti-Semites accuse of "funding both sides" in various wars. (In 2006, when a drunken Mel Gibson told a Malibu police officer, "The Jews are responsible for all the wars in the world," he was referring to this ancient trope.) Truthers accused World Trade Center landlord Larry Silverstein of having the towers demolished as part of a global Zionist plot — but also to avoiding spending money on remodeling. (Oscar-winning actress Marion Cotillard repeated that charming canard in the French media.) Of course, it's worth noting that the very first conspiracy theory about 9/11, floated just days after the attacks, held that 4,000 Jewish World Trade Center workers had somehow known not to show up for work that day. A quick look at the names engraved at the Ground Zero September 11 Memorial is enough to dispel that libel.

Christopher Bollyn, the prolific conspiracist who compared *Popular Mechanics*' reporting with the Reichstag Fire, has worked with the *American Free Press*, a publication founded by notorious anti-Semite and white-supremacist Willis Carto. The publication mashes together 9/11 theories, Holocaust denial, vaccine paranoia, and other conspiracist topics. Bollyn's own website is full of references to "Zionist criminals," "the elders of Zion," and articles suggesting that Israel was behind the disappearance of Malaysian Airlines Flight 370. The *Loose Change* films rely heavily on assertions from the *American Free Press*. During the Bush years, alternative weeklies and progressive websites also routinely published articles from AFP and similar sources.

The leftists who amplified these Truther narratives probably believed they were undermining the hated Bush administration. But they were also nudging their followers along a path toward the worst sort of neo-fascist propaganda. Those who went all the way down the rabbit hole — as millions of Americans did — wound up in an ideological jungle where far-left and far-right politics become almost indistinguishable. It is a place where the U.S. democratic system is a cynical sham; where true power is held by a merciless, secretive cabal; and where Israel is the world's eternal villain. So while progressives either ignored it or cheered it on, the Truther movement was evolving into a kind of gateway drug for paranoid extremism.

Alex Jones had been waiting all his life for this moment. Prior to 9/11, Jones was a blowhard Texas radio host with a small following and a website aptly named InfoWars. He rode the growing Truther movement to national prominence. I hadn't heard of Jones before launching the *Popular Mechanics* conspiracy project. A few months later, I was doing a radio interview about our story when I found myself being yelled at by Jones himself. Unbeknownst to the publicist who had set up the interview, the radio host had arranged for Jones to call in, hoping for an explosive confrontation.

25

Jones shouted something about how the Hearst Corporation, *Popular Mechanics'* parent company, was started by William Randolph Hearst, who launched the Spanish-American War and invented yellow journalism, and, and . . . something or other. (Whether it's the Reichstag Fire or the Spanish-American War, conspiracy theorists love citing historical events as if they bolster the plausibility of modern claims.) Jones's method doesn't depend on making coherent arguments — like explaining how the long-dead Hearst could entice the staff of *Popular Mechanics* to help cover up the greatest crime in American history — so much as wearing the audience down. Jones spews so many supposed facts, spooky coincidences, and unhinged allegations that the unwary listener might conclude that at least *some* of it must be true.

When *Loose Change* started taking off, Jones reached out to the filmmakers and offered to fund production of the movie's third edition, which credits him as executive producer. In a recent fascinating history of *Loose Change, Esquire's* John McDermott writes that the film's most enduring legacy may have been "the mainstreaming of conspiracists — most notably InfoWars founder Alex Jones." Jones would go on to interview presidential candidate Donald Trump on his radio show, be treated as a serious thinker on Joe Rogan's massively popular podcast, and — in Zelig-like fashion — be found outside the U.S. Capitol on January 6, 2021, exhorting the protestors with a bullhorn.

Meantime, the conspiracy mindset was soaking into the culture from the ground up. In a 2006 Scripps-Howard poll, 36 percent of Americans reported believing it was likely or somewhat likely that the U.S. government either launched the 9/11 attacks or let them happen to further geopolitical goals.

(The idea that the government "let it happen on purpose" — known as LIHOP theory — is a major theme in conspiracy circles.) By 2016, 54 percent of Americans believed the government was hiding the truth about 9/11, according to a Chapman University poll.

Of course, it wasn't just 9/11. Research shows that once people accept one conspiracy theory, they're more likely to embrace others. "Conspiracism is a sort of creed," author Jonathan Kay told *Rolling Stone*. "It's the idea that there is a secret power in the world that can't be changed by elections, that it has evil motivations and that it's trying to destroy our way of life." Many of the websites promoting 9/11 conspiracy theories also pushed the notion that the CIA created the crack epidemic, that Bush stole the 2000 election thanks to hacked Diebold voting machines, that the world economy would soon collapse due to "Peak Oil," and so on. Not surprisingly, surveys show that a belief in conspiracies correlates strongly with anti-vaccine sentiment. Once people dip their toes in the conspiracy waters, they have fewer defenses against all kinds of misinformation. For one thing, they have no other trusted sources of information they can turn to. The conspiracy-minded, Kay says, "come to see the world as presented by the mainstream media and other institutions as sort of a counterfeit hoax."

After the 2008 election, with Obama in 30 the White House and Bush out of the picture, the Truther movement began to lose focus, but the alienation and distrust it had engendered didn't entirely dissipate. Some of that intensity flowed into the Occupy Wall Street movement. "Inside-job" memes were common enough at OWS encampments to annoy protesters who thought the group should concentrate on economic issues. At the same time, conspiracist themes — like the obsession over Obama's birth certificate — began circulating more widely on the right. Trump's penchant for making wild claims further eroded the norm that political statements needed to be based on verifiable facts. At the same time, the media became so obsessed with protecting the public from Trump's falsehoods that it lowered its own standards of veracity. Mainstream media routinely misrepresented Trump statements, such as his "fine people on both sides" comment regarding the 2017 protests in Charlottesville, Virginia. Meantime, they eagerly repeated some of the wildest anti-Trump allegations, especially ones involving Russia. Step by step, the press surrendered any claim to being an honest broker in factual debates.

"It is the mark of an intellectually pathologized society that intellectuals and politicians will reject their opponents' *realities*," Kay writes. The U.S. might not be quite to that point, but we're getting closer. Not long ago, fact-free, conspiratorial theories were mostly the province of cranks on street corners or paranoid bloggers. Today, we increasingly see mainstream political leaders indulging in conspiracist-style arguments. It's not a coincidence that Trump entered the political arena flogging the Obama "birther" conspiracy claim. In 2012, Alex Jones bellowed that the Sandy Hook school shooting was a "false flag" operation orchestrated by the U.S. government. Three years later, presidential candidate Trump was on Jones's radio show telling the host, "Your reputation is amazing."

When politicians like Trump use conspiracist rhetoric, they are actually doing two things. First, they are asking their followers to accept a particular claim on faith ("We won the election by a landslide!"), almost as a test of loyalty. But they are also asking followers to reject competing claims ("Fake news!") coming from sources they consider illegitimate.

In the process, that slippery middle ground — the place where both sides can make their cases using a shared, undisputed set of facts — becomes a scorched no-man's-land.

Trump took political demagoguery to new extremes, but he certainly didn't invent it. Asking followers to accept wild, unsupported assertions can be politically useful. And politicians no longer pay much of a price for going overboard. Campaigning as Obama's vice presidential nominee in 2008, Biden told a largely black audience that Republicans were "going to put you all back in chains." Hillary Clinton and other Democrats endlessly asserted that Trump's 2016 election victory was "illegitimate." Their followers listened. Even four years later, 62 percent of Democrats told pollsters they believe the 2016 election was fraudulent. That number is a mirror image of the 61 percent of Republicans who think the 2020 election was rigged. The idea that our democratic institutions are corrupt and untrustworthy is a hallmark of conspiracist thinking. But today political leaders in both parties routinely deploy such claims to motivate voters and raise money. Not surprisingly, in a recent survey of voters' trust in the electoral process, the United States ranked close to last among developed countries.

In a recent essay, Bari Weiss noted that "revolutions in the street begin as revolutions in sense-making." The way Americans make sense of the world has undoubtedly changed. Meanwhile, the institutions that help keep our society fact-based — especially academia and the media — are under attack from without by the conspiracist Right and from within by the Woke Left. Both sides deny the legitimacy of American democracy; to them, it's all just a front for ruthless power, greed, and bias. You would think such a worldview would leave people in a state of hopelessness and despair. But the deep appeal of conspiracist thinking is that it actually makes people feel empowered. It gives them a *mission*.

In his classic 1964 essay, "The Paranoid 35 Style in American Politics," historian Richard Hofstadter put his finger on what makes the paranoid worldview so compelling: "As a member of the avant-garde who is capable of perceiving the conspiracy before it is fully obvious to an as yet unaroused public, the paranoid is a militant leader," he wrote. "He is always manning the barricades of civilization. He constantly lives at a turning point." The Truthers I encountered believed an evil, all-powerful conspiracy had hijacked our government. But they weren't depressed about it. In fact, they were having a blast. Unlike ordinary people sleepwalking through life — the "sheeple" as Truthers used to call them — they were fully alive and manning the barricades. Progressive activists today are similarly energized: they are "woke." They aren't crushed by the belief that our society is built on a secret infrastructure of oppression. Instead, they're proud of their ability to detect the hidden hand of racism and sexism even within institutions that, to the untrained eye, might seem like models of tolerance.

By the final year of the Trump administration, QAnon and Proud Boy cultists on the right, and woke activists on the left, were primed to take their revolutions to the streets. The pandemic, Black Lives Matter, and the fight over the presidential election gave both sides the spark they needed. Like most people, I watched the protesters storming the Capitol on January 6, 2021, with dismay and outrage. But for me, the scenes of impassioned, self-defined patriots also carried a whiff of déjà vu. In one video taken that day, a burly man turns to the camera and shouts, "They don't get to tell us we didn't see what we saw." He *knew* the election had been stolen, in other words, and no set of so-called facts could dissuade him. I understood exactly how he'd learned to think like that.

In those BLM protests that veered into destruction, it was not inner-city youths but committed political radicals instigating the most determined violence. During antipolice riots in Brooklyn in May 2020, two young lawyers were arrested after tossing a Molotov cocktail into an empty police van. NPR described them as "idealistic attorneys hoping to change the world." Perhaps. But, like the Capitol rioters, they seemed wedded to the view that the American system is too far gone for peaceful reform. One of the pair, Urooj Rahman, gave an impassioned video interview minutes before launching her firebomb attack. "The only way they hear us is through violence," she said. "This s — t won't ever stop unless we f — kin' take it all down."

This is what we're up against. For now, only the most extreme activists on the right or left seek to participate in such violence. But the share of people who think political violence might be appropriate is growing. In a poll conducted prior to the 2020 election, 44 percent of Republicans and 41 percent of Democrats said that there would be "at least 'a little' justification for violence if the other party's nominee won the election." The revolution in sense-making that is driving these viewpoints must be confronted at its roots. The sensible middle, the place where Americans can hash out their differences on neutral ground with a shared definition of reality, might be a slippery location. But it's all we've got, and 20 years after 9/11, we need it more than ever. We're going to have to fight for it.

Topics for Critical Thinking and Writing

1. Are there any reasons to explain the growing sense of paranoia and conspiracy in US culture? Are you convinced that people in the twenty-first century are increasingly paranoid or more likely to believe in conspiracy theories than they were in other times? Why or why not?

2. In paragraph 2, James B. Meigs distinguishes between the irrational and the *anti*-rational. How does the difference suggest different ways people respond to facts that debunk conspiracy theories?

3. Examine the two central claims Meigs shares from the book *Painful Questions* (para. 5), and the facts his team at *Popular Mechanics* collected that debunked them. How does this evidence represent what he calls the "appeal to a shared sense of reality" (para. 13)?

4. The so-called appeal to ignorance proposes that just because something has not been proven untrue, it is likely true. Explain how 9/11 Truthers utilize such an appeal based on information in Meigs's essay. On which political group does Meigs lay the responsibility for 9/11 conspiracy theories? In your analysis, does this undermine his *ethos*? Explain.

5. Reread paragraph 32. Think about Meigs's appeal to the "place where both sides can make their cases heard using a shared, undisputed set of facts." Do you think there are any public or media venues where this occurs? Explain.

6. Meigs frequently expresses a sense of surprise that everyday people can be vulnerable, gullible, or prone to conspiratorial thinking. Do you think he overestimates the public's capacity for reason? What other kinds of widespread beliefs are irrational (or anti-rational) but nevertheless powerful and widely shared?

ANNE APPELBAUM

Anne Appelbaum is a Pulitzer Prize–winning author and historian who has published numerous books focused on the roots and legacies of socialism and communism in Eastern Europe. In her career, she has served as a writer and editor at the *Washington Post*, a staff writer at the *Atlantic*, and author of political analysis and commentary published in the *American Interest* and the *Journal of Democracy*, among other publications. She holds memberships and board positions on the Council of Foreign Relations, the National Endowment for Democracy, and the Institute for War and Peace Reporting. Her latest book, *Twilight of Democracy: The Seductive Lure of Authoritarianism*, was published in 2020. This selection was published in the *Atlantic* in 2021.

The My Pillow Guy Really Could Destroy Democracy

When you contemplate the end of democracy in America, what kind of person do you think will bring it about? Maybe you picture a sinister billionaire in a bespoke suit, slipping brown envelopes to politicians. Maybe your nightmare is a rogue general, hijacking the nuclear football. Maybe you think of a jackbooted thug leading a horde of men in white sheets, all carrying burning crosses.

Here is what you probably don't imagine: an affable, self-made midwesterner, one of those goofy businessmen who makes his own infomercials. A recovered crack addict, no less, who laughs good-naturedly when jokes are made at his expense. A man who will talk to anyone willing to listen (and to many who aren't). A philanthropist. A good boss. A patriot — or so he says — who may well be doing more damage to American democracy than anyone since Jefferson Davis.

I met Mike Lindell, the CEO of MyPillow, in the recording studio that occupies the basement of Steve Bannon's stately Capitol Hill townhouse, a few blocks from the Supreme Court — the same Supreme Court that will, according to Lindell, decide "9–0" in favor of reinstating Donald Trump to the presidency sometime in August, or possibly September. I made it through the entirety of the Trump presidency without once having to meet Bannon but here he was, recording his *War Room* podcast with Lindell. Bannon has been decomposing in front of our eyes for some years now, and I can report that this process continues to take its course. I walked in during a break and the two men immediately gestured to me to join the conversation, sit at the table with them, listen in on headphones. I demurred. "Anne Applebaum ... hmm," Bannon said. "Should've stuck to writing books. Gulag was a great book. How long did it take you to write it?"

In the room adjacent to the basement studio, an extra-large image of a *New York Times* front page hung on the wall, featuring a picture of Bannon and the headline "The Provocateur." A bottle of Bio-Active Silver Hydrosol, whatever that is, sat on the desk. The big-screen TV was tuned to MSNBC. This wasn't surprising: In his podcasts, Bannon carries on a kind of dialogue with Rachel Maddow, playing her sound bites and then offering his

own critique. Later, Lindell told me that if it weren't for attacks by "the left" — by which he means Politico, the Daily Beast, and, presumably, me — his message would never get out, because Fox News ignores him.

Bannon, too, lives outside the Fox bubble 5 these days. Instead, he inhabits an alternate universe in which every minute of every day seems to be entirely devoted to the discussion and analysis of "electoral fraud," with just a little time devoted to selling wellness products and vitamins that, despite his claims, won't actually cure COVID-19. Bannon's podcast, which he says has millions of listeners (it is ranked 59th on Apple Podcasts, so he might be right), is populated by full-time conspiracy theorists, some of whom you have heard of and some of whom you probably haven't: Peter "Trump Won in a Freakin' Landslide" Navarro, Rudy Giuliani, Garland Favorito, Willis @treekiller35, Sonny Borrelli, the Pizzagate propagator Jack Posobiec, and, of course, Lindell. Bannon calls them up one by one to report on the current status of the Trump-reinstatement campaign and related fake scandals. There are daily updates. The guests talk fast and loud. It is very exciting. On the day I was at the studio, Bannon was gloating about how President Joe Biden was now "defending his own legitimacy": "We are going to spring the trap around you, sir!" He kept telling people to "lawyer up."

Even in this group, Lindell stands out. Not only is he presumably much richer than Garland Favorito and Willis @treekiller35; he is willing to spend his money on the cause. MyPillow has long been an important advertiser on Fox News, so much so that even Trump noticed Lindell ("That guy is on TV more than I am"), but has since widened its net. MyPillow spent tens of thousands of dollars advertising on Newsmax just in the week following the January 6 attack on the Capitol.

And now Lindell is spending on more than just advertising. Last January — on the 9th, he says carefully, placing the date after the 6th — a group of still-unidentified concerned citizens brought him some computer data. These were, allegedly, packet captures, intercepted data proving that the Chinese Communist Party altered electoral results … in all 50 states. This is a conspiracy theory more elaborate than the purported Venezuelan manipulation of voting machines, more improbable than the allegation that millions of supposedly fake ballots were mailed in, more baroque than the belief that thousands of dead people voted. This one has potentially profound geopolitical implications.

That's why Lindell has spent money — a lot of it, "tens of millions," he told me — "validating" the packets, and it's why he is planning to spend a lot more. Starting on August 10, he is holding a three-day symposium in Sioux Falls (because he admires South Dakota's gun-toting governor, Kristi Noem), where the validators, whoever they may be, will present their results publicly. He has invited all interested computer scientists, university professors, elected federal officials, foreign officials, reporters, and editors to the symposium. He has booked, he says variously, "1,000 hotel rooms" or "all the hotel rooms in the city" to accommodate them. (As of Wednesday, Booking.com was still showing plenty of rooms available in Sioux Falls.)

Wacky though it seems for a businessman to invest so much in a conspiracy theory, there are important historical precedents. Think of Olof Aschberg, the Swedish banker who helped finance the Bolshevik revolution, allegedly melting down the bars of gold that Lenin's comrades stole in train robberies and reselling them, unmarked, on European exchanges. Or Henry Ford, whose infamous anti-Semitic tract, *The International Jew*, was widely read in Nazi Germany, including by Hitler himself. Plenty of successful, wealthy people think that their knowledge of production technology or private equity gives them clairvoyant insight into politics. But Aschberg, Ford, and Lindell represent the extreme edge of that phenomenon: Their business success gives them the confidence to promote malevolent conspiracy theories, and the means to reach wide audiences.

In the cases of Aschberg and Ford, this had 10 tragic, real-world consequences. Lindell hasn't created Ford-level havoc yet, but the potential is there. Along with Bannon, Giuliani, and the rest of the conspiracy posse, he is helping create profound distrust in the American electoral system, in the American political system, in the American public-health system, and ultimately in American democracy. The eventual consequences of their actions may well be a genuinely stolen or disputed election in 2024, and political violence on a scale the U.S. hasn't seen in decades. You can mock Lindell, dismiss him, or call him a crackhead, but none of this will seem particularly funny when we truly have an illegitimate president in the White House and a total breakdown of law and order.

Lindell had agreed to have lunch with me after the taping. But where to go? I didn't think it would be much fun to take someone inclined to shout about rigged voting machines and fake COVID-19 cures to a crowded bistro on Capitol Hill. Because Lindell is famously worried about Chinese Communist influence, I thought he would like to pay homage to the victims of Chinese oppression. I booked a Uyghur restaurant.

This proved a mistake. For one thing, the restaurant — the excellent Dolan Uyghur, in D.C.'s Cleveland Park neighborhood — was not at all close to Bannon's townhouse. Getting there required a long and rather uncomfortable drive, in Lindell's rented black SUV;

he talked at me about packet captures the whole way, one hand on the steering wheel, the other holding up a phone showing Google Maps. Once we got there, he didn't much like the food. He picked at his chicken kebabs and didn't touch his spicy fried green beans. More to the point, he didn't understand why we were there. He had never heard of the Uyghurs. I told him they were Muslims who are being persecuted by Chinese Communists. Oh, he said, "like Christians." Yes, I said. Like Christians.

He kept talking at me in the restaurant, a kind of stream-of-consciousness account of the packet captures, his mistreatment at the hands of the media and the Better Business Bureau, the dangers of the COVID-19 vaccines, and the wonders of oleandrin, a supplement that he says he and everyone else at MyPillow takes and that he says is 100 percent guaranteed to prevent COVID-19. On all of these points he is utterly impervious to any argument of any kind. I asked him what if, hypothetically, on August 10 it turns out that other experts disagree with his experts and declare that his data don't mean what he thinks his data mean. This, he told me, was impossible. It couldn't happen:

"I don't have to worry about that. Do you understand that? Do you understand I've been attacked? I have 2,500 employees, and I've been attacked every day. Do I look like a stupid person? That I'm just doing this for my health? I have better things to do — these guys brought me this and I owe it to the United States, to all, whether it's a Democrat or Republican or whoever it is, to bring this forward to our country. I don't have to answer that question, because it's not going to happen. This is nonsubjective evidence."

The opprobrium and rancor he has brought down upon himself for trying to make his case are, in Lindell's mind, further proof that it is true. Stalin once said that the emergence of opposition signified the "intensification of the class struggle," and this is Lindell's logic too: If lots of people object to what you are doing, then it must be right. The contradictions deepen as the ultimate crisis draws closer, as the old Bolsheviks used to say.

But there is a distinctly American element to his thinking too. The argument from personal experience; the evidence acquired on the journey from crack addict to CEO; the special kind of self-confidence that many self-made men acquire, along with their riches — these are native to our shores. Lindell is quite convinced, for example, that not only did China steal the election, but that "there is a communist agenda in this country" more broadly. I asked him what that meant. Communists, he told me, "take away your right to free speech. You just told me what they are doing to these people" — he meant the Uyghurs. "I've experienced it firsthand, more than anyone in this country."

The government had taken his freedom away? Put him in a reeducation camp? "I don't see anybody arresting you," I said. He became annoyed.

"*Okay*, I'm not talking about the government," he said. "I'm talking about social media. Why did they attack me? Why did bots and trolls attack all of my vendors? I was the No. 1 selling product of every outlet in the United States — every one, every single one, all of them drop like flies. You know why? Because bots and troll groups were hired. They were hired to attack. Well, now I've done investigations. They come out of a building in China."

It is true that there has been some organized backlash against MyPillow, which is indeed no longer stocked by Bed Bath & Beyond, Kohl's, and other retailers. But I suspect that this reaction is every bit as red-white-and-blue as Lindell himself: Plenty of

Americans oppose Lindell's open promotion of both election and vaccine conspiracy theories, and are perfectly capable of boycotting his company without the aid of Chinese bots. Lindell's lived experience, however, tells him otherwise, just like his lived experience tells him that COVID-19 vaccines will kill you and oleandrin won't. Lived experience always outweighs expertise: Nobody can argue with what you *feel* to be true, and Lindell *feels* that the Chinese stole the election, sent bots to smear his company, and are seeking to impose communism on America.

Although he describes the packet captures as "cyberforensics" — indisputable, absolute, irreversible proof of Chinese evildoing — Lindell is more careful about evidence that isn't "nonsubjective." When I asked him how exactly Joe Biden's presidency was serving the interests of the Chinese Communist Party, for example, his reasoning became more circuitous. He didn't want to say that Joe Biden is *himself* a Communist. Instead, when I asked for evidence of communist influence on Biden, he said this: "Inauguration Day — I'll tell you — Inauguration Day, he laid off 50,000 union workers. Boom! Pipeline gone. The old Democrat Party wouldn't lay off union workers."

In other words, the evidence of Joe Biden's links to the Chinese Communist Party was ... his decision to close the Keystone XL pipeline. Similarly convoluted reasoning has led him to doubt the patriotism of Arizona Governor Doug Ducey as well as Georgia Governor Brian Kemp and Secretary of State Brad Raffensperger, all of whom deny the existence of serious electoral cheating in their states. "My personal opinion," he told me, is that "Brian Kemp is somehow compromised and maybe could be blackmailed or in on it or whatever. I believe Raffensperger's totally in on it."

In on what? I asked.

"In on whatever's going on ..."

I asked if he meant the Chinese takeover of America. Was Raffensperger pro-China?

"I believe he's pro-China."

Alongside the American business boosterism, Lindell's thinking contains a large dose of Christian millenarianism too. This is a man who had a vision in a dream of himself and Donald Trump standing together — *and that dream became reality*. No wonder he believes that a lot of things are going to happen after August 10. It's not just that the Supreme Court will vote 9–0 to reinstate Trump. It is also that America will be a better place. "We're going to get elected officials that make decisions for the people, not just for their party," Lindell said. There will be "no more machines" in this messianic America, meaning no more voting machines: "On both sides, people are opening their eyes." In this great moment of national renewal, there will be no more corruption, just good government, goodwill, goodness all around.

That moment will be good for Lindell, too, because he will finally be able to relax, knowing that "I've done all I can." After that, "everything will take its course. And I don't have to be out there every day fighting for media attention." He won't, in other words, have to be having lunch with people like me.

Alas, a happy ending is unlikely. He will not, on August 10, find that "the experts" agree with him. Some have already provided careful explanations as to why the "packet captures" can't be what he says they are. Others think that the whole discussion is pointless. When I called Chris Krebs, the Trump administration's director of the Cybersecurity and Infrastructure Security Agency, he refused even to get into the question of whether Lindell has authentic data, because the whole proposal is absurd. The heavy use of paper ballots, plus all of the postelection audits and recounts, mean that any issues with mechanized voting systems would have been quickly revealed. "It's all part of the grift," Krebs told me. "They're exploiting the aggrieved audience's confirmation bias and using scary yet unintelligible imagery to keep the Big Lie alive, despite the absence of any legitimate evidence."

What will happen when Lindell's ideological, all-American, predicted-in-a-dream absolute certainty runs into a wall of skepticism, disbelief, or — even worse — indifference? If history is anything to go by ... nothing. Nothing will happen. He will not admit he is wrong; he will not stop believing. He will not understand that he was conned out of the millions he has spent "validating" fake data. (One has to admire the salesmanship of the tech grifters who talked him into all of this, assuming they exist.) He will not understand that his company is having trouble with retailers because so many people are repulsed by his ideas. He will not understand that people attack him because they think what he says is dangerous and could lead to violence. He will instead rail against the perfidy of the media, the left, the Communists, and China.

Certainly he will not stop believing that 30 Trump won the 2020 election. The apocalypse has been variously predicted for the year 500, based on the dimensions of Noah's Ark; the year 1033, on the 1,000th anniversary of Jesus's crucifixion; and the year 1600, by Martin Luther no less; as well as variously by Jehovah's Witnesses, Nostradamus, and Aum Shinrikyo, among many others. When nothing happened — the world did not end; the messiah did not arrive — did any of them throw in the towel and stop believing? Of course not.

Lindell mostly speaks in long, rambling monologues filled with allusions and grievances; he circles back again and again to electoral fraud, to the campaigns against him, to particular interviewers and articles that he disputes, some of it only barely comprehensible unless you've been following his frequent media appearances — which I have not. At only one moment was there a hint that this performance was more artful than it appeared to be. I asked him about the events of January 6. He immediately grew more precise. "I was not there, by the grace of God," he said. He was doing media events elsewhere, he said. Nor did he want to talk about what happened that day: "I think that there were a lot of things that I'm not going to comment on, because I don't want that to be your story."

Not too long after that, I suddenly found I couldn't take any more of this calculated ranting. (I can hear that moment on the recording, when I suddenly said "Okay, enough" and switched off the device.) Although he ate almost nothing, Lindell insisted on grabbing the check, like any well-mannered Minnesotan would. In the interests of investigative research, I later bought a MyPillow (conclusion: it's a lot like other pillows), so perhaps that makes us even.

When we walked outside, I thought that I might say something dramatic, something cutting, something like "You realize that you are destroying our country." But I didn't. He *is* our country after all, or one face of our country: hyper-optimistic and overconfident, ignorant of history and fond of myths, firm in the belief that we alone are the exceptional nation and we alone have access to exceptional truths. Safe in his absolute certainty, he got into his black SUV and drove away.

Topics for Critical Thinking and Writing

1. In what ways does Anne Appelbaum fairly or unfairly characterize Mike Lindell and Steve Bannon in her essay? Do you think her characterizations enhance or damage her *ethos*?

2. Consider Lindell's views, such as those in paragraph 13, on COVID-19, election fraud, and similar issues. Why do you think he was able to achieve such prominence in the national discourse about the 2020 election?

3. Think about Appelbaum's use of language and the portrayal of her interview with Lindell. Do you think she is using humor as part of her argument? If so, show where you see you see these elements and how they contribute to her argument.

4. Discuss what role evidence plays in Lindell's reasoning about his sense of persecution described in paragraphs 13–19. What other evidence does Appelbaum offer to explain the backlash against him? Based on the evidence she provides, do you think that Appelbaum is fair in imagining telling Lindell outright that he is "destroying the country" (para. 33)? Explain.

5. In paragraph 16, Appelbaum describes "the argument from personal experience." Why do you think Appelbaum calls the argument from experience "distinctly American"? What are the hazards of such arguments, and why are they so potent in shaping belief? Can you provide any examples?

6. The event Lindell planned, described in paragraph 8, occurred in Sioux Falls, South Dakota, in August 2021. In an interview, Lindell said: "We got attacked by China and they flipped this election . . . this is crazy, and all you have to do is come to the symposium." Ultimately, Lindell did not produce the data to prove his claim. Look up some of the coverage of this event on the internet, and examine the logic and reasoning Lindell offered as to why he could not produce the data.

ARIEL BOGLE AND JANE LEE

Ariel Bogle has worked as a public policy and government affairs intern for Google, publicist and blogger for Melville House Publishing, and associate editor with the Future Tense, a "citizen's guide" for exploring new technologies and their impact on life and work. She has also done work with the Australian Strategic Policy Institute's International Cyber Policy Centre and served as a technology reporter with the Australian Broadcasting Corporation.

Jane Lee is a news reporter and writer who covers crime, law, politics, and social justice issues for the Melbourne, Australia, newspaper *The Age*. She won the 2014 Victorian Law Foundation's Legal Reporting Award for best print report.

The co-written piece included here was posted on the website of the Australian Broadcast Corporation in 2020.

Children Feature in COVID-19 and QAnon Conspiracy Theories

Conspiracy theories that centre on fears about child abuse and removal are being shared in Australia, as part of a broader trend of misinformation related to children.

In addition to the gamut of #baking shots, pet pics and lockdown selfies, coronavirus has seen an upswing in the sharing of conspiracy theories on social media.

Recently many of these have focused on children, with the ABC's COVID-19 misinformation tracking project being sent screenshots of posts focused on the theme of children's removal from their families.

They make a range of false claims including that children will be removed if their parents refuse to give them a COVID-19 vaccine, or that children will be taken from their families if they have symptoms of coronavirus.

These posts are part of a broader trend, 5 and long history, of conspiracy theories related to children.

POLITICAL THEMES IN MISINFORMATION

The most well-known is the mega-conspiracy theory QAnon, which centres on the belief that global political elites are engaged in satanic child abuse, and that US President Donald Trump is engaged in a secret war against this cabal.

Its central idea — that President Trump is saving children from paedophiles — is a way of saying that he is engaged in a battle against the ultimate evil, said Anna Merlan, journalist and author of a book about American conspiracy theorists.

> "It is, at its heart, a pro-Trump conspiracy theory. The most heroic thing he could be doing is saving children," said Ms Merlan.

The graphic allegations of sexual abuse that tipify QAnon also serve to characterise the movement's political enemies — Democrats, for instance — as unfathomably evil and deserving of the most extreme punishment, even execution, according to Dr Michael Salter, an expert in child sexual exploitation and gendered violence at the University of New South Wales.

QANON, PIZZAGATE, AND #METOO

The connection between alleged child abuse and right-wing conspiratorial thinking gained mainstream attention after Pizzagate.

Back in 2016, a North Carolina man Edgar 10 Welch drove to the Comet Ping Pong pizzeria in Washington, DC, with a gun and fired it in the building. He'd read online that children were being abused by Democrats in the venue's basement and wanted to investigate.

The Pizzagate conspiracy theory, linking high-ranking Democratic Party officials with restaurants and an alleged paedophile ring, that motivated Welch has been debunked, but it is widely credited to be the predecessor of QAnon.

Dr Salter suggests QAnon and Pizzagate were able to gain popularity online more recently because they followed the #MeToo movement against sexual assault and prosecutions of celebrities like Jeffrey Epstein for sexual offences against children, which raised greater public awareness of the complexities of sexual violence and power.

"What MeToo uncovered is that it is very difficult to bring claims of sexual violence against powerful wealthy figures," Dr Salter said.

When it comes to child sexual abuse, media outlets often struggled to report on credible allegations because they lacked the high level of evidence needed to publish them, Dr Salter said.

This left "fertile territory" for conspiracy theories to grow. [15]

And platforms like Facebook and YouTube have also allowed conspiratorial communities to find each other and fuse together in an unprecedented way.

HISTORY OF CHILD-RELATED CONSPIRACIES

But this isn't an entirely new phenomenon. Allegations of child abuse have featured in conspiracy theories for centuries.

> "The idea that elites kidnap and abuse children is a very old, powerful fear," Ms Merlan said.

Blood libel, the anti-Semitic superstition that claims Jews kill Christian children as part of religious ritual, emerged in medieval Europe and has returned repeatedly to the public consciousness, particularly during moments of social unrest.

James Kline, professor of psychology at Northern Marianas College, said that child abuse was among a handful of taboos, including blood-drinking and cannibalism, that have historically been viewed as both anti-human and sacred.

Pizzagate and QAnon are both part of [20] a conspiracy archetype that involves such taboos, evil groups of powerful elites and a struggle for political power.

"We want to say 'That's not part of us, it's got to be them, not us'. But it remains a fascination," he said.

"These types of taboos generate this sense of fascination because they are things we're not supposed to think about (or) associate with. So we project them upon other people."

Professor Kline likened Pizzagate to a scandal in the US in the early 1980s, when child abuse allegations involving Satanic rituals against a family that ran a children's day care centre in California were widely reported in the media and later discredited.

He said that while no one was ultimately convicted over the scandal, similar accusations later spread to other pre-schools in the United States.

Philip Jenkins, professor of history at Bay- [25] lor University, agreed, saying that more recent child-related conspiracies in the US appeared to be "recycled" from false claims made in the 1980s.

"I can say, 'well they're going to show up (again) in times of stress and a crisis of values' but the problem is I can apply a term like that to almost any time," Professor Jenkins said.

> "The biggest thing that's new here, and is not going anywhere, is the internet... nothing dies on the internet."

WHO ARE THE CHILDREN?

While adherents of QAnon claim they are motivated by child safety, their depiction of perpetrators who are strangers bears little relationship with the real-world problems of child abuse and child pornography rings.

Dr Salter said that the primary traffickers of prepubescent children were their parents, while post-pubescent children were also targeted in institutions, particularly out-of-home care.

"It's not just conspiracy theorists who ignore the evidence of child exploitation, very broadly it's been an overlooked issue for a long time," he said.

It's important to note that QAnon and Pizzagate did not originate from reports or investigations of child abuse by children or adult survivors themselves.

"The child really just (features) as sort of an empty symbol or an empty signifier that can be manipulated within the conspiracy theory as a kind of vessel for a whole set of inchoate concerns and anxieties and projections," Dr Salter said.

Dr Salter said that QAnon followers did not seem to be particularly concerned with the Jeffrey Epstein case, for example, which contained legitimate evidence of child exploitation against wealthy, powerful people.

"And that's because QAnon is largely a right-wing conspiracy theory and the Epstein case is politically explosive for all sides of the aisle," he said.

DAMAGING CHILD WELLBEING

But misinformation related to children is likely to have real impacts on actual survivors of child abuse.

As well as flooding the #SaveTheChildren hashtag, QAnon adherents have reportedly clogged trafficking hotlines in the United States with false claims, meaning genuine cases can't get through.

Dr Salter recalled that several child abuse survivors had espoused QAnon material to him in recent years, with many of the themes involved resonating with their own experiences of not being listened to or believed.

He was concerned that such material could derail their own recovery.

"A crucial part of trauma therapy is about empowering people to make their own decisions about what's real and what's not," he said.

"If you've got an external force about QAnon that's deliberately blurring the boundaries between fiction and non-fiction then naturally that's going to introduce complexities for some clients who've been exposed to this material.

"In the trauma field, we're going to be unpicking the damage that QAnon has done for some survivors... for years to come."

Topics for Critical Thinking and Writing

1. Summarize Ariel Bogle and Jane Lee's argument. Then, consider their role: Are they functioning more as reporters of information or as advocates for a specific position? Or something else? Explain.

2. Why are children often employed as a rhetorical strategy to advance arguments? Can you think of other arguments that are warranted largely by the impact of the issue on children?

3. Do you find the argument convincing that the #MeToo movement paved the way for conspiracy theories such as Pizzagate and child sexual abuse among powerful US figures (paras. 9–16)? Why or why not?

4. If a person is deciding whether or not to believe the conspiracy theories discussed by Bogle and Lee, how should they consider confirmation bias? What might be done to overcome the challenge?

5. Do you think false conspiracy theories related to pedophilia do damage to the actual problem of child sex trafficking? How so? (See "Raising the Stakes of Your Thesis" in Chapter 7, p. 231.) Explain.

JAMES PETERSON

James Peterson writes for the nonprofit, nonpartisan independent media organization the *Philadelphia Citizen*. He has also published articles on race, culture, and politics for the *Daily Mail*, *HuffPost*, and MSNBC. The article included here was published in the *Philadelphia Citizen* in 2020.

What's Behind Black Conspiracism?

In a recent viral video on social media, Dr. Stella Immanuel claims to have the cure for the coronavirus: hydroxychloroquine. She also says that we don't need to wear masks.

Flanked by "America's Frontline Doctors" all in white coats, Dr. Immanuel urgently argues that we could open schools and that no one has to die from Covid-19. These "Frontline Doctors" argue that we have all been duped by "fake science" into a kind of hysteria about Covid-19 that to them is unnecessary and unwarranted.

To date, over 150,000 Americans have died from Covid-19 and there are more than four million cases of diagnosed coronavirus nationwide. Hydroxychloroquine is not an effective treatment or cure for the virus. And wearing masks is one of the most effective means of mitigating the transmission of the virus.

FACTS ARE THE MOST POTENT ANTIDOTE

When it comes to rumor and conspiracy, facts are the most potent antidote, but State Senator Anthony Williams believes the path ahead is challenging. "The governor, the mayor, the president, the senator — they are not necessarily listening to us, because they follow Facebook for their news," Williams says. "They don't follow us. They follow Twitter for their information. That's the space we have to begin to dominate and drive out the message."

The challenges of coronavirus are personal 5 and professional for Senator Williams. He is feeling "much stronger" these days, but he is recovering from coronavirus and eager to get back to the important work of making sure that the pandemic is mitigated in a racially equitable way.

The America's Frontline Doctors' video, made viral by Breitbart's politically conservative website (with help from Facebook, Twitter and Instagram), collected over 14 million views in six hours. Supportive tweets from the 45th President of the United States made matters worse. The president's namesake son had his Twitter account suspended for retweeting the same viral video.

Within a day or so social media platforms had removed the video and various news outlets have since reported on the fact that the video is misinformative and counterfactual. But the damage has already been done.

Conspiracism thrives in the era of coronavirus for a variety of related reasons. First, coronavirus is a global pandemic. Pandemics are literally the subject matter of apocalyptic science fiction in film, novels, television and all things popular culture. Second, at the heart of many conspiracy theories is some form of government malfeasance.

This current administration's mishandling of the pandemic will achieve legendary status in the annals of history. And that is an unfortunate disadvantage in the challenges that conspiracy theories present. "The government has to work with the community to create a bond of trust so constituents trust that elected officials and governmental departments are providing accurate information," says Councilperson-at-Large Isaiah Thomas. When it doesn't, conspiracy theories flourish.

Jesse Walker, author of *The United States* [10] *of Paranoia: A Conspiracy Theory*, agrees. "Elected leaders should be as honest and transparent as possible," he says, but when it comes to "debunking a false conspiracy theory," Walker does not believe in any kind of cure-all. "People just need to learn to ask the same questions they should be asking about any other story. How strong is the evidence for this? What sort of track record does this source have? Basically, hone your media literacy skills and apply them all the time."

It does not feel like (social) media literacy is at a premium during this pandemic. And the fact that there is a viral video about a viral pandemic underscores the speed with which information (and misinformation) can be circulated.

The critical role that contemporary media platforms have and will continue to play in how we process public health information has its highest stakes in the Black community.

CONSPIRACISM IN THE AFRICAN-AMERICAN COMMUNITY

It is a strange morphological irony that 'racism' is embedded in the word conspiracism. Much like underlying health conditions, access to coronavirus testing and Covid-19 mortality rates, conspiracism has a disparate impact on the African-American community.

"While engagement with conspiracy theories is high across the board, in the United States, African Americans appear in surveys to be more receptive to conspiracy theories in

general," says Professor Rob Brotherton, a psychologist and author of *Suspicious Minds: Why We Believe Conspiracy Theories*.

"Given that most conspiracy theories [15] allege that authorities and institutions like the government or the medical establishment are not to be trusted, it's entirely understandable that such theories resonate among communities with long histories of being marginalized and mistreated by those very institutions."

Systemic racism is the root cause of the racial disparities evidenced in the impact of the pandemic in the African-American community. And systemic racism underwrites all of the ways in which conspiracies thrive in the African-American community. But the potential for Black people to believe in conspiracy theories related to public health — especially those theories that might preclude people from accurate public health knowledge during a global pandemic that disproportionately impacts African Americans — may have deadly disparate outcomes. If racism wasn't already embedded in the word conspiracism, we would have to revise it for factual accuracy.

There are real conspiratorial reasons why African Americans have an abiding skepticism of the American health care industry. The U.S. government conspired with health officials to develop a treatment for syphilis by secretly studying it in Black men. Medical researchers developed "HeLa" cells from samples taken from Henrietta Lacks in 1951; the modern notion of informed consent did not exist then. These kinds of stories abound in American history and they provide a generative context for Black conspiracism to thrive.

Black conspiracism has evolved over the short span of the pandemic's trajectory in the United States. In the early days, before the virus spread, some in the Black community pointed to the continent of Africa — and its relatively low numbers — as some kind of indicator that

Black folks might be more immune to the virus than our white counterparts. This was more rumor than conspiracy, but nothing could have been further from the truth.

Eventually, the Blacks-don't-get-it rumor was supplanted by the demographic data on deaths related to Covid-19. Unfortunately, the timing of an influx of data on racial disparities in coronavirus infection rates and Covid-19 mortality rates almost perfectly coincided with the implosion of the current administration's façade of actually caring about the public health crisis evolving under their watch.

Black conspiracy theorists seized on [20] the fact that more Black people will die as a result of premature re openings and general mismanagement of the pandemic in the U.S. Now, Senator Williams tells me that some of his Black constituents believe that "the government's trying to kill us. So they created this virus, and of course it's killing black people at a higher rate on purpose."

The fact of disparate Black death is a compelling corollary for conspiracy theories that the U.S. government is deliberate in its failure to meet the challenges of the coronavirus pandemic.

While it is impossible to prove that the U.S. government is deliberately ignoring the public health intelligence on coronavirus because it believes that Black lives don't matter, the consequences are the same for the Black community.

Intentional or not, the federal government's ignorance and public health ineptitude has deadly disparate consequences for the Black community in America. And so, whether or not it's a conspiracy is, in fact, immaterial. The consequences of an unchecked spread of coronavirus are real for Black folks.

A third iteration of Black conspiracism in the age of Covid-19 is bubbling up now as concerns about the vaccine, how it is tested, and who will actually take it begin to substantiate a new skepticism.

As early as late May, only about 25 per- [25] cent of African Americans surveyed said they were willing to even take a coronavirus vaccine once one is available. This reluctance to be vaccinated is understandable, based upon history and the history of systemic racism. But the conspiracists (some in the Black community) will cultivate that skepticism and transform it into a full-blown conspiracy that the developers of the vaccine, in concert with the government and private industry, will deploy the vaccine (somehow/someway) to the detriment of the African American community.

Senator Williams is worried that the vaccine rollout will mirror the testing rollout in Philadelphia, i.e. "the vaccine rollout will follow your economic status."

LOOKING TO THE KING ALFRED PLAN FOR SOLUTIONS

Scholars who research conspiracism in the Black community generally agree that "theories about government conspiracies against Blacks are widespread in African American culture," according to Professor Jennifer Crocker.

There are many fact-based reasons for this. But there are at least two inflection points that might help us to better understand why conspiracy theories are widespread in the Black community and how we might confront the specter of conspiracy in ways that work to keep the African-American community informed and vigilant about the real conspiratorial machinations in our midst.

For Professor Crocker and other scholars, system blame — "a specific tendency to make external attributions for the problems facing Black Americans as a group" — is the most likely underlying factor of Black conspiracism.

Black folks blame the system, not to absolve 30 themselves of agency or to obscure bad choices/behavior. But to direct their vigilant skepticism toward the systemic nature of white supremacy and anti-Black racism — two ideological and material entities that brutally truncate the value of Black life in real time across all of America's social and corporate institutions.

System blame is how kernels of truth often animate Black conspiracism in ways that make conspiratorial ideas sticky in Black public consciousness. One way — maybe the most effective way to diminish the suasion of Black conspiracism — is to eradicate anti-black racism in the systems through which the American government operates.

If ending the real reasons for Black people to place blame on racist systems of oppression seems too fantastical, the second option or inflection point might be a pathway of lesser resistance.

Read about the King Alfred Plan. You can find a copy here, but it is best read in the context of John A. Williams' classic political novel, *The Man Who Cried I Am*.

The King Alfred Plan is named after King Alfred the Great, so monikered because of his Eurocentric efforts to foreground the Anglo-Saxons, uplift the English language (over Latin at that time) and to promote Christianity — arguably three pillars of modern white supremacy in America.

In the world of *The Man Who Cried I Am*, 35 the King Alfred Plan is a plot designed by the CIA, in collaboration with nearly every facet of the American government and American law enforcement, to architect a final solution for the "minority" problem in America. It's worth quoting here at length for readers to appreciate it's ominous and veritable tones.

"Each passing month has brought new intelligence that, despite new laws passed to alleviate the condition of the Minority, the Minority still is not satisfied. Demonstrations and rioting have become a part of the familiar scene.

Troops have been called out in city after city across the land, and our image as a world leader severely damaged. . . . The Minority has adopted an almost military posture to gain its objectives, which are not clear to most Americans. It is expected, therefore, that, when those objectives are denied the Minority, racial war must be considered inevitable.

When that Emergency comes, we must expect the total involvement of all 22 million members of the Minority, men, women and children, for once this project is launched, its goal is to terminate, once and for all, the Minority threat to the whole of the American society, and, indeed, the Free World."

In the real world, circa 1967, Williams decided to promote his novel, guerrilla-style, by placing photocopies of the King Alfred Plan in subway trains in New York City. The plan was taken as factual and it spread like a virus. It perfectly encapsulated the politics of the moment and the very real fear of how "the system" might respond to Black civil rights unrest in the streets of America. The plan became required reading for Black social movements and the sense of truth that it conveyed far outweighed the reality of its fictional creation.

The King Alfred Plan reminds us well why 40 Black conspiracism reigns supreme in the contemporary moment. When the lines of fact and fiction are convincingly blurred, the truth of American anti-Black racism remains laid bare for all to see, hear and feel. This truth is too often endured in the lived experiences of African Americans.

Today, there may be no actual King Alfred Plan for the extinction of Black people in America, but the disparate impact of the coronavirus, the government's mismanagement of the pandemic, along with the ongoing and unchecked brutalization of Black people by American law enforcement, combined with the recent martial response to civic unrest by this very same government, all collude to make us feel as if The Plan is already in full effect.

Topics for Critical Thinking and Writing

1. What does it mean to mitigate the effects of COVID-19 in a racially equitable way (para. 5)? Why might this be as priority for James Peterson as he makes his argument?

2. What reasons are offered by Peterson to establish the claim that conspiracism thrives in the African American community?

3. Where in his argument does Peterson makes assumptions or take for granted the truth of certain claims without backing them with evidence?

4. What would you add to Jesse Walker's advice in paragraph 10 to further strengthen the notion of media literacy?

5. Do you find Peterson convincing in his argument against Black conspiracism? Explain in a brief essay, drawing quotations for the essay to support your claims.

6. Do your own research to uncover data on health disparities among racial groups related to the COVID-19 pandemic. In your estimation, are such disparities attributable to systemic racism? What (other) social determinants of health are important to understanding the disparate effects of the pandemic on minoritized groups?

BEN CRAIR

Ben Crair is a story editor for the *New Republic* and a science and travel writer whose articles have appeared in the *New Yorker*, *Smithsonian*, *National Geographic*, and the *New York Times*. The selection here was published in *Smithsonian* magazine in 2018.

Why Do So Many People Still Want to Believe in Bigfoot?

Sixty years ago this fall, Bigfoot first stepped into the public consciousness. "Giant footprints puzzle residents," a headline in the *Humboldt Times* announced. The small Northern California newspaper reported that a road construction crew had discovered humanlike footprints that were a massive 16 inches long. The paper was the first to give the mysterious animal that made the prints its memorable moniker — "Bigfoot" — and the creature has been stomping through the American imagination ever since.

Today, the legendary beast seems to be everywhere: You will find Bigfoot looking awfully cute this year in two children's films: *The Son of Bigfoot* and *Smallfoot*. Animal Planet recently aired the finale of its popular series "Finding Bigfoot," which lasted

11 seasons despite never making good on the promise of its title. And the Bigfoot Field Researchers Organization lists at least one report from every state, except Hawaii, over the past two decades. The most recent sighting, in June 2018, was by a woman in Florida who reported a creature that looked like "a large pile of soggy grass." Other evidence in the database includes supposed Bigfoot scat, nests and noises. If a tree falls in the forest and no one is around to hear it, it may not make a sound—but it seems someone will report that a Bigfoot knocked it over.

"Interest in the existence of the creature is at an all-time high," the paleontologist Darren Naish has observed, even though "there's nothing even close to compelling as goes the evidence."

Of course, Bigfoot is not the first fabled hominid to roam North America. Sasquatches long populated the mythologies of American Indian tribes in the Pacific Northwest, but those 1958 footprints transformed the myth into a media sensation. The tracks were planted near Bluff Creek in Northern California by a man named Ray Wallace—but his prank was not revealed until his death in 2002, when his children said it had all been "just a joke."

By that point, more important evidence 5 had entered the Bigfoot file. In 1967, Roger Patterson and Bob Gimlin filmed a few seconds of a hairy creature walking on two legs by the same Bluff Creek—the most famous and contested piece of Bigfoot "evidence" to this day. That the Patterson-Gimlin film was created in the same place that Wallace had staged his hoax is just one reason to doubt its authenticity. Skeptics say the animal was a man in costume, while believers argue that the creature's movements and body proportions cannot possibly have been human. The debate has been raging for half a century, which raises a question of its own. "How is it that the evidence has not gotten any better despite the exponential increase in the quantity and quality of cameras?" asks Benjamin Radford, a research fellow with the Committee for Skeptical Inquiry.

Still the absence of evidence is not evidence of absence either. Wild animals don't exactly mug for photos, and the planet's

Screenshot from the iconic Patterson-Gimlin film purporting to show an image of Bigfoot.

ever-shrinking forests still regularly unpack surprises, such as the saola, an untamed cousin of the cow that was discovered by scientists in Vietnam in 1992. But the saola did not have legions of amateurs hunting it with cameras. With or without hard evidence, many people clearly want to believe in Bigfoot. Which suggests we are dealing more with human imagination than human evolution.

Naish has written that Bigfoot is the modern American "manifestation of a human-wide cultural concept, not a zoological reality." It has much in common with the Australian yowie and the Himalayan yeti: an upright posture, shaggy hair and, of course, large feet. As so-called wild men, they hold a crude mirror up to our own species: What might Homo sapiens be like if civilization had not removed it from nature?

FACT OR FOLKLORE

Some people see these cryptohominids as symbols of pure freedom, living by instinct and foiling every effort to pin them down. To search for Bigfoot in the forest is to taste that freedom. On the trail, you become extra-attuned to nature: the smell of scat, the sounds of breaking branches, the curious impressions in the dirt. As long as there are wild places in America, Bigfoot remains a possibility that, to its most ardent proponents, cannot be disproved.

The hunt for Bigfoot emulates an earlier mode of discovery, when new knowledge was not the product of advanced degrees and expensive machinery but rather curiosity, bravery, patience and survival. In the 19th century, the American landscape revealed its majesties to ordinary settlers pushing westward into territory unmapped by Europeans. To track Bigfoot today is to channel that frontier spirit (as well as to appropriate Native American traditions).

Bigfoot also embodies other less romantic 10 but no less enduring American traits, like gullibility and a hunger for attention. "There are so many fake videos," says Loren Coleman, the founder of the International Cryptozoology Museum in Portland, Maine. The problem has grown worse with social media, where viral hoaxes, like drone footage of a supposed Bigfoot in a clearing in Idaho, can rack up millions of views. Coleman, for his part, believes there is evidence for Bigfoot's existence, but he and his like-minded peers find it difficult to focus attention on this material amid the growing number of obvious shams. "Technology has ruined the old cryptozoology," Coleman says.

His complaint echoes concerns in more mainstream American life, where technologies that promised to build consensus have, in fact, made the truth more difficult than ever to discern. On the internet, Bigfoot has found a habitat much more hospitable than North American forests. It turns out that Bigfoot does not need to exist in order to live forever.

Topics for Critical Thinking and Writing

1. Ben Crair points out in paragraph 2 that there has been at least one report of a Bigfoot sighting in every state, except Hawaii, for the past two decades. Provide some reasons why this number of sightings represents a weak inductive inference that Bigfoot therefore exists. (For an explanation of inductive inference, see "Induction" in Chapter 10, p. 359.)

2. What kinds of evidence are used to prove Bigfoot conspiracies, and what kinds of evidence are used in perpetuating contemporary political conspiracy theories? Are they similar or different? Explain.

3. Examine Crair's reasoning as to why Bigfoot is a uniquely American fantasy (paras. 7–11). Do you find this aspect of his argument convincing? Why or why not?

4. Consider the essay in Chapter 24 by Tracy Deonn on the King Arthur legend and the malleability of stories, and compare the ways the Bigfoot legend lives on in ways similar and different to the ways the Arthur legend lives on.

5. Briefly discuss the problems with proving the existence or nonexistence of something widely thought to be real but as-yet-unverified — ghosts, gods, angels, aliens, or creatures such as the Loch Ness Monster or Chupacabra, for example. Survey the types of evidence that support each view, and evaluate the strength of the evidence "for" and "against." Based on the evidence, what do you believe in this regard and why?

6. The essays in this chapter are mostly about the reasons why beliefs in social or political conspiracy theories gain and maintain momentum. What forms of logic and reasoning are shared among those who believe in government conspiracies and those who believe in Bigfoot?

PART SIX

Enduring Questions
Essays, Poems, and Stories

26

What Is the Ideal Society?

THOMAS MORE

The son of a prominent London lawyer, Thomas More (1478–1535) served as a page in the household of the Archbishop of Canterbury, went to Oxford University, and then studied law in London. More's charm, brilliance, and gentle manner caused Erasmus, the great Dutch humanist who became his friend during a visit to London, to write to a friend: "Did nature ever create anything kinder, sweeter, or more harmonious than the character of Thomas More?"

More served in Parliament, became a diplomat, and after holding several important positions in the government of Henry VIII, rose to become lord chancellor. But when Henry married Anne Boleyn, broke from the Church of Rome, and established himself as head of the Church of England, More refused to subscribe to the Act of Succession and Supremacy. Condemned to death as a traitor, he was executed in 1535, nominally for treason but really because he would not recognize the king rather than the pope as the head of his church. A moment before the axe fell, More displayed a bit of the whimsy for which he was known: When he put his head on the block, he brushed his beard aside, commenting that his beard had done no offense to the king. In 1886, the Roman Catholic Church beatified More, and in 1935, the four-hundredth anniversary of his death, it canonized him as St. Thomas More.

More wrote *Utopia* (1514–1515) in Latin, the international language of the day. The book's name, however, is Greek for "no place" (*ou topos*), with a pun on "good place" (*eu topos*). *Utopia* owes something to Plato's *Republic* and something to then-popular accounts of voyagers such as Amerigo Vespucci. *Utopia* purports to record an account given by a traveler named Hytholodaeus (Greek for "learned in nonsense"), who allegedly visited Utopia. The work is playful, but it is also serious. In truth, it is hard to know exactly where it is serious and how serious it is. One inevitably wonders, for example, if More the devoted Roman Catholic could really have advocated euthanasia. And could More the persecutor of heretics really have approved of the religious tolerance practiced in Utopia? Is he perhaps in effect saying, "Let's see what reason, unaided by Christian revelation, can tell us about an ideal society"? But if so, is he nevertheless also saying, very strongly, that Christian countries, although blessed with the revelation of Christ's teachings, are far behind these unenlightened pagans? Utopia has been widely praised by all sorts of readers — from Roman Catholics to communists — and for all sorts of reasons. The selection presented here is about one-twelfth of the book (in a translation by Paul Turner).

From Utopia

A DAY IN UTOPIA

And now for their working conditions. Well, there's one job they all do, irrespective of sex, and that's farming. It's part of every child's education. They learn the principles of agriculture at school, and they're taken for regular outings into the fields near the town, where they not only watch farm work being done, but also do some themselves, as a form of exercise.

Besides farming which, as I say, is everybody's job, each person is taught a special trade of his own. He may be trained to process wool or flax, or he may become a stonemason, a blacksmith, or a carpenter. Those are the only trades that employ any considerable quantity of labor. They have no tailors or dressmakers, since everyone on the island wears the same sort of clothes — except that they vary slightly according to sex and marital status — and the fashion never changes. These clothes are quite pleasant to look at, they allow free movement of the limbs, they're equally suitable for hot and cold weather — and the great thing is, they're all home-made. So everybody learns one of the other trades I mentioned, and by everybody I mean the women as well as the men — though the weaker sex are given the lighter jobs, like spinning and weaving, while the men do the heavier ones.

Most children are brought up to do the same work as their parents, since they tend to have a natural feeling for it. But if a child fancies some other trade, he's adopted into a family that practices it. Of course, great care is taken, not only by the father, but also by the local authorities, to see that the foster father is a decent, respectable type. When you've learned one trade properly, you can, if you like, get permission to learn another — and when you're an expert in both, you can practice whichever you prefer, unless the other one is more essential to the public.

The chief business of the Stywards[1] — in fact, practically their only business — is to see that nobody sits around doing nothing, but that everyone gets on with his job. They don't wear people out, though, by keeping them hard at work from early morning till late at night, like cart horses. That's just slavery — and yet that's what life is like for the working classes nearly everywhere else in the world. In Utopia they have a six-hour working day — three hours in the morning, then lunch — then a two-hour break — then three more hours in the afternoon, followed by supper. They go to bed at 8 p.m., and sleep for eight hours. All the rest of the twenty-four they're free to do what they like — not to waste their time in idleness or self-indulgence, but to make good use of it in some congenial activity. Most people spend these free periods on further education, for there are public lectures first thing every morning. Attendance is quite voluntary, except for those picked out for academic training, but men and women of all classes go crowding in to hear them — I mean, different people go to different lectures, just as the spirit moves them. However, there's nothing to stop you from spending this extra time on your trade, if you want to. Lots of people do, if they haven't the capacity for intellectual work, and are much admired for such public-spirited behavior.

After supper they have an hour's recreation, 5 either in the gardens or in the communal dining-halls, according to the time of year. Some people

---

[1]**Stywards** In Utopia, each group of thirty households elects a styward; each town has two hundred stywards, who elect the mayor. [Editors' note]

practice music, others just talk. They've never heard of anything so silly and demoralizing as dice, but they have two games rather like chess. The first is a sort of arithmetical contest, in which certain numbers "take" others. The second is a pitched battle between virtues and vices, which illustrates most ingeniously how vices tend to conflict with one another, but to combine against virtues. It also shows which vices are opposed to which virtues, how much strength vices can muster for a direct assault, what indirect tactics they employ, what help virtues need to overcome vices, what are the best methods of evading their attacks, and what ultimately determines the victory of one side or the other.

But here's a point that requires special attention, or you're liable to get the wrong idea. Since they only work a six-hour day, you may think there must be a shortage of essential goods. On the contrary, those six hours are enough, and more than enough to produce plenty of everything that's needed for a comfortable life. And you'll understand why it is, if you reckon up how large a proportion of the population in other countries is totally unemployed. First you have practically all the women — that gives you nearly 50 percent for a start. And in countries where the women *do* work, the men tend to lounge about instead. Then there are all the priests, and members of so-called religious orders — how much work do they do? Add all the rich, especially the landowners, popularly known as nobles and gentlemen. Include their domestic staffs — I mean those gangs of armed ruffians that I mentioned before. Finally, throw in all the beggars who are perfectly hale and hearty, but pretend to be ill as an excuse for being lazy. When you've counted them up, you'll be surprised to find how few people actually produce what the human race consumes.

And now just think how few of these few people are doing essential work — for where money is the only standard of value, there are bound to be dozens of unnecessary trades carried on, which merely supply luxury goods or entertainment. Why, even if the existing labor force were distributed among the few trades really needed to make life reasonably comfortable, there'd be so much overproduction that prices would fall too low for the workers to earn a living. Whereas, if you took all those engaged in nonessential trades, and all who are too lazy to work — each of whom consumes twice as much of the products of other people's labor as any of the producers themselves — if you put the whole lot of them on to something useful, you'd soon see how few hours' work a day would be amply sufficient to supply all the necessities and comforts of life — to which you might add all real and natural forms of pleasure.

THE HOUSEHOLD

But let's get back to their social organization. Each household, as I said, comes under the authority of the oldest male. Wives are subordinate to their husbands, children to their parents, and younger people generally to their elders. Every town is divided into four districts of equal size, each with its own shopping center in the middle of it. There the products of every household are collected in warehouses, and then distributed according to type among various shops. When the head of a household needs anything for himself or his family, he just goes to one of these shops and asks for it. And whatever he asks for, he's allowed to take away without any sort of payment, either in money or in kind. After all, why shouldn't he? There's more than enough of everything to go round, so there's no risk of his asking for more than he needs — for why should anyone want to start hoarding, when he knows he'll never have to go short of anything? No living creature is naturally greedy, except from fear of want — or in the case of human beings, from vanity, the notion that you're better than people if you can display more superfluous property than they can. But there's no scope for that sort of thing in Utopia.

UTOPIAN BELIEFS

The Utopians fail to understand why anyone should be so fascinated by the dull gleam of a tiny bit of stone, when he has all the stars in the sky to look at — or how anyone can be silly enough to think himself better than other people, because his clothes are made of finer woollen thread than theirs. After all, those fine clothes were once worn by a sheep, and they never turned it into anything better than a sheep.

Nor can they understand why a totally 10 useless substance like gold should now, all over the world, be considered far more important than human beings, who gave it such value as it has, purely for their own convenience. The result is that a man with about as much mental agility as a lump of lead or a block of wood, a man whose utter stupidity is paralleled only by his immorality, can have lots of good, intelligent people at his beck and call, just because he happens to possess a large pile of gold coins. And if by some freak of fortune or trick of the law — two equally effective methods of turning things upside down — the said coins were suddenly transferred to the most worthless member of his domestic staff, you'd soon see the present owner trotting after his money, like an extra piece of currency, and becoming his own servant's servant. But what puzzles and disgusts the Utopians even more is the idiotic way some people have of practically worshipping a rich man, not because they owe him money or are otherwise in his power, but simply because he's rich — although they know perfectly well that he's far too mean to let a single penny come their way, so long as he's alive to stop it.

They get these ideas partly from being brought up under a social system which is directly opposed to that type of nonsense, and partly from their reading and education. Admittedly, no one's allowed to become a full-time student, except for the very few in each town who appear as children to possess unusual gifts, outstanding intelligence, and a special aptitude for academic research. But every child receives a primary education, and most men and women go on educating themselves all their lives during those free periods that I told you about. . . .

In ethics they discuss the same problems as we do. Having distinguished between three types of "good," psychological, physiological, and environmental, they proceed to ask whether the term is strictly applicable to all of them, or only to the first. They also argue about such things as virtue and pleasure. But their chief subject of dispute is the nature of human happiness — on what factor or factors does it depend? Here they seem rather too much inclined to take a hedonistic view, for according to them human happiness consists largely or wholly in pleasure. Surprisingly enough, they defend this self-indulgent doctrine by arguments drawn from religion — a thing normally associated with a more serious view of life, if not with gloomy asceticism. You see, in all their discussions of happiness they invoke certain religious principles to supplement the operations of reason, which they think otherwise ill-equipped to identify true happiness.

The first principle is that every soul is immortal, and was created by a kind God, Who meant it to be happy. The second is that we shall be rewarded or punished in the next world for our good or bad behavior in this one. Although these are religious principles, the Utopians find rational grounds for accepting them. For suppose you didn't accept them? In that case, they say, any fool could tell you what you ought to do. You should go all out for your own pleasure, irrespective of right and wrong. You'd merely have to make sure that minor pleasures didn't interfere with major ones, and avoid the type of pleasure that has painful aftereffects. For what's the sense of struggling to be virtuous, denying yourself the pleasant things of life, and deliberately making yourself uncomfortable, if there's nothing you hope to gain by it? And what *can* you hope to gain by it, if you receive no compensation after death for a thoroughly unpleasant, that is, a thoroughly miserable life?

Not that they identify happiness with every type of pleasure — only with the higher ones. Nor do they identify it with virtue — unless they belong to a quite different school of thought. According to the normal view, happiness is the *summum bonum*[2] toward which we're naturally impelled by virtue — which in their definition means following one's natural impulses, as God meant us to do. But this includes obeying the instinct to be reasonable in our likes and dislikes. And reason also teaches us, first to love and reverence Almighty God, to Whom we owe our existence and our potentiality for happiness, and secondly to get through life as comfortably and cheerfully as we can, and help all other members of our species to do so too.

The fact is, even the sternest ascetic tends to be slightly inconsistent in his condemnation of pleasure. He may sentence *you* to a life of hard labor, inadequate sleep, and general discomfort, but he'll also tell you to do your best to ease the pains and privations of others. He'll regard all such attempts to improve the human situation as laudable acts of humanity — for obviously nothing could be more humane, or more natural for a human being, than to relieve other people's sufferings, put an end to their miseries, and restore their *joie de vivre,* that is, their capacity for pleasure. So why shouldn't it be equally natural to do the same thing for oneself?

Either it's a bad thing to enjoy life, in other words, to experience pleasure — in which case you shouldn't help anyone to do it, but should try to save the whole human race from such a frightful fate — or else, if it's good for other people, and you're not only allowed, but positively obliged to make it possible for them, why shouldn't charity begin at home? After all, you've a duty to yourself as well as to your neighbor, and, if Nature says you must be kind to others, she can't turn round the next moment and say you must be cruel to yourself. The Utopians therefore regard the enjoyment of life — that is, pleasure — as the natural object of all human efforts, and natural, as they define it, is synonymous with virtuous. However, Nature also wants us to help one another to enjoy life, for the very good reason that no human being has a monopoly of her affections. She's equally anxious for the welfare of every member of the species. So of course she tells us to make quite sure that we don't pursue our own interests at the expense of other people's.

On this principle they think it right to keep one's promises in private life, and also to obey public laws for regulating the distribution of "goods" — by which I mean the raw materials of pleasure — provided such laws have been properly made by a wise ruler, or passed by common consent of a whole population, which has not been subjected to any form of violence or deception. Within these limits they say it's sensible to consult one's own interests, and a moral duty to consult those of the community

15

---

[2]*summum bonum* Latin for "the highest good." [Editors' note]

as well. It's wrong to deprive someone else of a pleasure so that you can enjoy one yourself, but to deprive yourself of a pleasure so that you can add to someone else's enjoyment is an act of humanity by which you always gain more than you lose. For one thing, such benefits are usually repaid in kind. For another, the mere sense of having done somebody a kindness, and so earned his affection and goodwill, produces a spiritual satisfaction which far outweighs the loss of a physical one. And lastly — a belief that comes easily to a religious mind — God will reward us for such small sacrifices of momentary pleasure, by giving us an eternity of perfect joy. Thus they argue that, in the final analysis, pleasure is the ultimate happiness which all human beings have in view, even when they're acting most virtuously.

Pleasure they define as any state or activity, physical or mental, which is naturally enjoyable. The operative word is *naturally*. According to them, we're impelled by reason as well as an instinct to enjoy ourselves in any natural way which doesn't hurt other people, interfere with greater pleasures, or cause unpleasant after-effects. But human beings have entered into an idiotic conspiracy to call some things enjoyable which are naturally nothing of the kind — as though facts were as easily changed as definitions. Now the Utopians believe that, so far from contributing to happiness, this type of thing makes happiness impossible — because, once you get used to it, you lose all capacity for real pleasure, and are merely obsessed by illusory forms of it. Very often these have nothing pleasant about them at all — in fact, most of them are thoroughly disagreeable. But they appeal so strongly to perverted tastes that they come to be reckoned not only among the major pleasures of life, but even among the chief reasons for living.

In the category of illusory pleasure addicts they include the kind of person I mentioned before, who thinks himself better than other people because he's better dressed than they are. Actually he's just as wrong about his clothes as he is about himself. From a practical point of view, why is it better to be dressed in fine woollen thread than in coarse? But he's got it into his head that fine thread is naturally superior, and that wearing it somehow increases his own value. So he feels entitled to far more respect than he'd ever dare to hope for, if he were less expensively dressed, and is most indignant if he fails to get it.

Talking of respect, isn't it equally idiotic to attach such importance to a lot of empty gestures which do nobody any good? For what real pleasure can you get out of the sight of a bared head or a bent knee? Will it cure the rheumatism in your own knee, or make you any less weak in the head? Of course, the great believers in this type of artificial pleasure are those who pride themselves on their "nobility." Nowadays that merely means that they happen to belong to a family which has been rich for several generations, preferably in landed property. And yet they feel every bit as "noble" even if they've failed to inherit any of the said property, or if they have inherited it and then frittered it all away.

Then there's another type of person I mentioned before, who has a passion for jewels, and feels practically superhuman if he manages to get hold of a rare one, especially if it's a kind that's considered particularly precious in his country and period — for the value of such things varies according to where and when you live. But he's so terrified of being taken in by appearances that he refuses to buy any jewel until he's stripped off all the gold and inspected it in the nude. And even then he won't buy it without a solemn assurance and a written guarantee from the jeweler that the stone is genuine. But my dear sir, why shouldn't a fake give you just as much pleasure, if you can't, with your own eyes, distinguish it from a real one? It makes no difference to you whether it's genuine or not — any more than it would to a blind man!

And now, what about those people who accumulate superfluous wealth, for no better purpose than to enjoy looking at it? Is their pleasure a real one, or merely a form of delusion? The opposite type of psychopath buries his gold, so that he'll never be able to use it, and may never even see it again. In fact, he deliberately loses it in his anxiety not to lose it — for what can you call it but lost, when it's put back into the earth, where it's no good to him, or probably to anyone else? And yet he's tremendously happy when he's got it stowed away. Now, apparently, he can stop worrying. But suppose the money is stolen, and ten years later he dies without ever knowing it has gone. Then for a whole ten years he has managed to survive his loss, and during that period what difference has it made to him whether the money was there or not? It was just as little use to him either way.

Among stupid pleasures they include not only gambling — a form of idiocy that they've heard about but never practiced — but also hunting and hawking. What on earth is the fun, they ask, of throwing dice onto a table? Besides, you've done it so often that, even if there was some fun in it at first, you must surely be sick of it by now. How can you possibly enjoy listening to anything so disagreeable as the barking and howling of dogs? And why is it more amusing to watch a dog chasing a hare than to watch one dog chasing another? In each case the essential activity is running — if running is what amuses you. But if it's really the thought of being in at the death, and seeing an animal torn to pieces before your eyes, wouldn't pity be a more appropriate reaction to the sight of a weak, timid, harmless little creature like a hare being devoured by something so much stronger and fiercer?

So the Utopians consider hunting below the dignity of free men, and leave it entirely to butchers, who are, as I told you, slaves. In their view hunting is the vilest department of butchery, compared with which all the others are relatively useful and honorable. An ordinary butcher slaughters livestock far more sparingly, and only because he has to, whereas a hunter kills and mutilates poor little creatures purely for his own amusement. They say you won't find that type of blood lust even among animals, unless they're particularly savage by nature, or have become so by constantly being used for this cruel sport.

There are hundreds of things like that, 25 which are generally regarded as pleasures, but everyone in Utopia is quite convinced that they've got nothing to do with real pleasure, because there's nothing naturally enjoyable about them. Nor is this conviction at all shaken by the argument that most people do actually enjoy them, which would seem to indicate an appreciable pleasure content. They say this is a purely subjective reaction caused by bad habits, which can make a person prefer unpleasant things to pleasant ones, just as pregnant women sometimes lose their sense of taste, and find suet or turpentine more delicious than honey. But however much one's judgment may be impaired by habit or ill health, the nature of pleasure, as of everything else, remains unchanged.

Real pleasures they divide into two categories, mental and physical. Mental pleasures include the satisfaction that one gets from understanding something, or from contemplating truth. They also include the memory of a well-spent life, and the confident expectation of good things to come. Physical pleasures are subdivided into two types. First there are those which fill the whole organism with a conscious sense of enjoyment. This may be the result of replacing physical substances which have been burnt up by the natural heat of the body, as when we eat or drink. Or else it may be caused by the discharge of some excess, as in excretion, sexual intercourse, or any relief of irritation by rubbing or scratching. However, there are also pleasures which satisfy no organic need, and relieve no previous discomfort. They merely act, in a mysterious but quite unmistakable way, directly on our senses, and monopolize their reactions. Such is the pleasure of music.

Their second type of physical pleasure arises from the calm and regular functioning of the body — that is, from a state of health undisturbed by any minor ailments. In the absence of mental discomfort, this gives one a good feeling, even without the help of external pleasures. Of course, it's less ostentatious, and forces itself less violently on one's attention than the cruder delights of eating and drinking, but even so it's often considered the greatest pleasure in life. Practically everyone in Utopia would agree that it's a very important one, because it's the basis of all the others. It's enough by itself to make you enjoy life, and unless you have it, no other pleasure is possible. However, mere freedom from pain, without positive health, they would call not pleasure but anesthesia.

Some thinkers used to maintain that a uniformly tranquil state of health couldn't properly be termed a pleasure since its presence could only be detected by contrast with its opposite — oh yes, they went very thoroughly into the whole question. But that theory was exploded long ago, and nowadays nearly everybody subscribes to the view that health is most definitely a pleasure. The argument goes like this —illness involves pain, which is the direct opposite of pleasure, and illness is the direct opposite of health, therefore health involves pleasure. They don't think it matters whether you say that illness *is* or merely *involves* pain. Either way it comes to the same

thing. Similarly, whether health *is* a pleasure, or merely *produces* pleasure as inevitably as fire produces heat, it's equally logical to assume that where you have an uninterrupted state of health you cannot fail to have pleasure.

Besides, they say, when we eat something, what really happens is this. Our failing health starts fighting off the attacks of hunger, using the food as an ally. Gradually it begins to prevail, and, in this very process of winning back its normal strength, experiences the sense of enjoyment which we find so refreshing. Now, if health enjoys the actual battle, why shouldn't it also enjoy the victory? Or are we to suppose that when it has finally managed to regain its former vigor — the one thing that it has been fighting for all this time — it promptly falls into a coma, and fails to notice or take advantage of its success? As for the idea that one isn't conscious of health except through its opposite, they say that's quite untrue. Everyone's perfectly aware of feeling well, unless he's asleep or actually feeling ill. Even the most insensitive and apathetic sort of person will admit that it's delightful to be healthy — and what is delight, but a synonym for pleasure?

They're particularly fond of mental plea- 30 sures, which they consider of primary importance, and attribute mostly to good behavior and a clear conscience. Their favorite physical pleasure is health. Of course, they believe in enjoying food, drink, and so forth, but purely in the interests of health, for they don't regard such things as very pleasant in themselves — only as methods of resisting the stealthy onset of disease. A sensible person, they say, prefers keeping well to taking medicine, and would rather feel cheerful than have people trying to comfort him. On the same principle it's better not to need this type of pleasure than to become addicted to it. For, if you think that sort of thing will make you happy, you'll have to admit that your idea of perfect felicity would be a life consisting entirely of hunger, thirst, itching, eating, drinking, rubbing, and scratching — which would obviously be most unpleasant as well as quite disgusting. Undoubtedly these pleasures should come right at the bottom of the list, because they're so impure. For instance, the pleasure of eating is invariably diluted with the pain of hunger, and not in equal proportions either — for the pain is both more intense and more prolonged. It starts before the pleasure, and doesn't stop until the pleasure has stopped too.

So they don't think much of pleasures like that, except insofar as they're necessary. But they enjoy them all the same, and feel most grateful to Mother Nature for encouraging her children to do things that have to be done so often, by making them so attractive. For just think how dreary life would be, if those chronic ailments, hunger and thirst, could only be cured by foul-tasting medicines, like the rarer types of disease!

They attach great value to special natural gifts such as beauty, strength, and agility. They're also keen on the pleasures of sight, hearing, and smell, which are peculiar to human beings — for no other species admires the beauty of the world, enjoys any sort of scent, except as a method of locating food, or can tell the difference between a harmony and a discord. They say these things give a sort of relish to life.

However, in all such matters they observe the rule that minor pleasures mustn't interfere with major ones, and that pleasure mustn't cause pain — which they think is bound to happen, if the pleasure is immoral. But they'd never dream of despising their own beauty, overtaxing their strength, converting their agility into inertia, ruining their physique by going without food, damaging their health, or spurning any other of Nature's gifts, unless they were doing it for the benefit of other people or of society, in the hope of receiving some greater pleasure from God in return. For they think it's quite absurd to torment oneself in the name of an unreal virtue, which does nobody any good, or in order to steel oneself against disasters which may never occur. They say such behavior is merely self-destructive, and shows a most ungrateful attitude toward Nature — as if one refused all her favors, because one couldn't bear the thought of being indebted to her for anything.

Well, that's their ethical theory, and short of some divine revelation, they doubt if the human mind is capable of devising a better one. We've no time to discuss whether it's right or wrong — nor is it really necessary, for all I undertook was to describe their way of life, not to defend it.

TREATMENT OF THE DYING

As I told you, when people are ill, they're 35 looked after most sympathetically, and given everything in the way of medicine or special food that could possibly assist their recovery. In the case of permanent invalids, the nurses try to make them feel better by sitting and talking to them, and do all they can to relieve their symptoms. But if, besides being incurable, the disease also causes constant excruciating pain, some priests and government officials visit the person concerned, and say something like this:

"Let's face it, you'll never be able to live a normal life. You're just a nuisance to other people and a burden to yourself — in fact you're really leading a sort of posthumous existence. So why go on feeding germs? Since your life's a misery to you, why hesitate to die? You're imprisoned in a torture chamber — why don't you break out and escape to a better world? Or say the word, and we'll arrange for your release. It's only common sense to cut your losses. It's also an act of piety to take the advice of a priest, because he speaks for God."

If the patient finds these arguments convincing, he either starves himself to death, or is given a soporific and put painlessly out of his misery. But this is strictly voluntary, and, if he prefers to stay alive, everyone will go on treating him as kindly as ever.

THE SUMMING UP

Well, that's the most accurate account I can give you of the Utopian Republic. To my mind, it's not only the best country in the world, but the only one that has any right to call itself a republic. Elsewhere, people are always talking about the public interest, but all they really care about is private property. In Utopia, where's there's no private property, people take their duty to the public seriously. And both attitudes are perfectly reasonable. In other "republics" practically everyone knows that, if he doesn't look out for himself, he'll starve to death, however prosperous his country may be. He's therefore compelled to give his own interests priority over those of the public; that is, of other people. But in Utopia, where everything's under public ownership, no one has any fear of going short, as long as the public storehouses are full. Everyone gets a fair share, so there are never any poor men or beggars. Nobody owns anything, but everyone is rich — for what greater wealth can there be than cheerfulness, peace of mind, and freedom from anxiety? Instead of being worried about his food supply, upset by the plaintive demands of his wife, afraid of poverty for his son, and baffled by the problem of finding a dowry for his daughter, the Utopian can feel absolutely sure that he, his wife, his children, his grandchildren, his great-grandchildren, his great-great-grandchildren, and as long a line of descendants as the proudest peer could wish to look forward to, will always have enough to eat and enough to make them happy. There's also the further point that those who are too old to work are just as well provided for as those who are still working.

Now, will anyone venture to compare these fair arrangements in Utopia with the so-called justice of other countries? — in which I'm damned if I can see the slightest trace of justice or fairness. For what sort of justice do you call this? People like aristocrats, goldsmiths, or moneylenders, who either do no work at all, or do work that's really not essential, are rewarded for their laziness or their unnecessary activities by a splendid life of luxury. But laborers, coachmen, carpenters, and farmhands, who never stop working like cart horses, at jobs so essential that, if they *did* stop working, they'd bring any country to a standstill within twelve months — what happens to them? They get so little to eat, and have such a wretched time, that they'd be almost better off if they *were* cart horses. Then at least, they wouldn't work quite such long hours, their food wouldn't be very much worse, they'd enjoy it more, and they'd have no fears for the future. As it is, they're not only ground down by unrewarding toil in the present, but also worried to death by the prospect of a poverty-stricken old age — since their daily wages aren't enough to support them for one day, let alone leave anything over to be saved up when they're old.

Can you see any fairness or gratitude [40] in a social system which lavishes such great rewards on so-called noblemen, goldsmiths, and people like that, who are either totally unproductive or merely employed in producing luxury goods or entertainment, but makes no such kind provision for farmhands, coal heavers, laborers, carters, or carpenters, without whom society couldn't exist at all? And the climax of ingratitude comes when they're old and ill and completely destitute. Having taken advantage of them throughout the best years of their lives, society now forgets all the sleepless hours they've spent in its service, and repays them for all the vital work they've done, by letting them die in misery. What's more, the wretched earnings of the poor are daily whittled away by the rich, not only through private dishonesty, but through public legislation. As if it weren't unjust enough already that the man who contributes most to society should get the least in return, they make it even worse, and then arrange for injustice to be legally described as justice.

In fact, when I consider any social system that prevails in the modern world, I can't, so help me God, see it as anything but a conspiracy of the rich to advance their own interests under the pretext of organizing society. They think up all sorts of tricks and dodges, first for keeping safe their ill-gotten gains, and then for exploiting the poor by buying their labor as cheaply as possible. Once the rich have decided that these tricks and dodges shall be officially recognized by society — which includes the poor as well as the rich — they acquire the force of law. Thus an unscrupulous minority is led by its insatiable greed to monopolize what would have been enough to supply the needs of the whole population. And yet how much happier even these people would be in Utopia! There, with the simultaneous abolition of money and the passion for money, how many other social problems have been solved, how many crimes eradicated! For obviously the end of money means the end of all those types of criminal behavior which daily punishments are powerless to check: fraud, theft, burglary, brawls, riots, disputes, rebellion, murder, treason, and black magic. And the moment money goes, you can also say goodbye to fear, tension, anxiety, overwork, and sleepless nights. Why, even poverty itself, the one problem that has always seemed to need money for its solution, would promptly disappear if money ceased to exist.

Let me try to make this point clearer. Just think back to one of the years when the harvest was bad, and thousands of people died of starvation. Well, I bet if you'd inspected every rich man's barn at the end of that lean period you'd have found enough corn to have saved all the lives that were lost through malnutrition and disease, and prevented anyone from suffering any ill effects whatever from the meanness of the weather and the soil. Everyone could so easily get enough to eat, if it weren't for that blessed nuisance, money. There you have a brilliant invention which was designed to make food more readily available. Actually it's the only thing that makes it unobtainable.

I'm sure that even the rich are well aware of all this, and realize how much better it would be to have everything one needed, than lots of things one didn't need — to be evacuated altogether from the danger area, than to dig oneself in behind a barricade of enormous wealth. And I've no doubt that either self-interest, or the authority of our Savior Christ — Who was far too wise not to know what was best for us, and far too kind to recommend anything else — would have led the whole world to adopt the Utopian system long ago, if it weren't for that beastly root of all evils, pride. For pride's criterion of prosperity is not what you've got yourself, but what other people haven't got. Pride would refuse to set foot in paradise, if she thought there'd be no underprivileged classes there to gloat over and order about — nobody whose misery could serve as a foil to her own happiness, or whose poverty she could make harder to bear, by flaunting her own riches. Pride, like a hellish serpent gliding through human hearts — or shall we say, like a sucking-fish that clings to the ship of state? — is always dragging us back, and obstructing our progress toward a better way of life.

But as this fault is too deeply ingrained in human nature to be easily eradicated, I'm glad that at least one country has managed to develop a system which I'd like to see universally adopted. The Utopian way of life provides not only the happiest basis for a civilized community, but also one which, in all human probability, will last forever. They've eliminated the root causes of ambition, political conflict, and everything like that. There's therefore no danger of internal dissension, the one thing that has destroyed so many impregnable towns. And as long as there's unity and sound administration at home, no matter how envious neighboring kings may feel, they'll never be able to shake, let alone to shatter, the power of Utopia. They've tried to do so often enough in the past, but have always been beaten back.

Topics for Critical Thinking and Writing

1. Thomas More, writing early in the sixteenth century, was living in a primarily agricultural society. Laborers were needed on farms, but might More have had any other reason for insisting that all people should do some farming and that farming should be "part of every child's education" (para. 1)? Do you think everyone should put in some time as a farmer? Why or why not?

2. More indicates that in the England of his day, many people loafed or engaged in unnecessary work (producing luxury goods, for one thing), putting an enormous burden on those who engaged in useful work. Is this condition, or any part of it, true of our society? Explain.

3. What arguments can you offer against the Utopians' treatment of persons who are incurably ill and in pain?

4. What aspects of More's Utopia do not sound particularly "utopian" to you? Why?

5. How would you summarize More's report of the Utopians' idea of pleasure in two to three paragraphs?

6. As More makes clear in the part called "The Summing Up," in Utopia there is no private property. In a sentence or two, summarize the reasons he gives for this principle and then, in a paragraph, evaluate them.

JOHN HORGAN

John Horgan is a science writer whose work has appeared in *National Geographic, Discover, Science, New Republic, Slate,* and a host of other prominent science and news publications. He is a Senior Writer at *Scientific American,* where he has published over four hundred articles and writes the Cross Check blog. He also teaches science writing and journalism at the Stevens Institute of Technology. As a leading public intellectual in the sciences, Horgan's work often challenges assumptions about the goals and horizons of scientific inquiry. His book *The End of Science* (1996) argues that scientific inquiry is approaching its limits — that science has exhausted the possibility for new questions and will hitherto continue to work within the existing dominant questions. His other books include *The Undiscovered Mind* (1999), *Rational Mysticism* (2003), and *The End of War* (2012), as well as a recent "fictionalized memoir," *Pay Attention: Sex, Death, and Science*(2020). This essay was published in *Scientific American*'s Cross Check blog in 2017.

What's Your Utopia?

Utopia gets a bad rap. If someone calls you or your idea "utopian," they usually mean it as an insult, a synonym for naïve and unrealistic. As his run for the Presidency wound down, Bernie Sanders griped, "There is nothing we've said in our campaign that is pie-in-the-sky or utopian." My call for an end to war[1] is often derided as utopian.

But everyone, it seems to me, should envision an ideal world, one much better than ours. Even if you doubt your utopia is attainable, it can serve as a useful thought experiment. Imagine a really good world, and imagine how we can get there. All progress begins with such wishful thinking.

That's why I've been asking smart people, "What's your utopia?" See the responses of Sabine Hossenfelder, Stephen Wolfram, Scott Aaronson, Eliezer Yudkowsky, Sheldon Solomon and Robin Hanson. I recently posed this question to a freshman humanities class and gave the students 10 minutes to write responses. Below are excerpts from their answers, one of which defines utopia as "a world with the perfect amount of imperfection." I hope these responses prod readers to dream up their own utopias.

NAZRIN: I imagine a world without greed, hunger, thirst, violence, but with subtle pains that make our happy moments even more valuable and precious. I imagine a feeling of love and welcoming no matter who we are or where we go. I imagine a world where numbers don't define us, and where everyone is free to roam without holding a mask (or several) in front of his or her face.

In his famous 1516 book, Thomas More describes an ideal island society called "Utopia," a term coined from Greek words for "no place."

I imagine a world where sicknesses are cured by love and the desire to live.

JESSE: My utopia is a world where the rat race no longer exists. Why is it that people find it normal to slave away all their lives for a minuscule reward in the end? Why is it that wanting to enjoy life and take breaks is frowned upon? We have followed the same pattern for centuries, but it is time for a change. Instead of one long and boring retirement at the end of our lives, why not enjoy mini-retirements throughout our lives?

AMANDA: My utopia would be one with no death. I've dealt with so many deaths of family members in the past 4 years. Every time, I feel a little more alone, and a little more like life sucks. People always tell me that good things will happen to good people, and bad things to bad. But my grandpa, grandma and uncle were selfless people who had a hard

[1] John Horgan, "War Is Our Most Urgent Problem — Let's Solve It," *Scientific American*, Aug. 12, 2014, https://blogs.scientificamerican.com/cross-check/war-is-our-most-urgent-problem-let-8217-s-solve-it/

life. Time and again I would see them in pain, and then in the end I lose them to cancer. Why? I don't understand and I want it to stop. This is my unicorn and rainbow-like utopia.

ANJALI: Everyone will keep their front doors open to let in the fresh air. There will be no harsh winters. A little snow is okay for Christmas. When it rains, the clouds shouldn't be all gloomy, and there will be no pollution or acid rain. Everyone's house will have a compost bin and a garden. No families will be separated because they are across the border in another country. Everyone should be able to visit other countries without visas. This can be possible if everyone has a good heart.

DANIEL: Instead of going to school to pursue an opportunity to make money, everyone just goes for the sake of learning, an opportunity to be himself and pursue a higher level of thinking. All life-threatening illnesses are gone. Little things like the common cold can stay, but cancer and other serious diseases will be eradicated. Also, no more third-world countries. I want all nations to have first-world standards.

AHMET: How would life be like if there was absolutely no war/conflict, tyranny and poverty? This is the utopian society that Karl Marx proposed, but it failed when implemented in the real world, simply because it was done through tyranny, where war and poverty existed. Communism would be an ideal world to live in, but this looks far away and almost impossible to implement.

DANIELLE: In utopia, everyone would feel safe at 10 all times. No girl would have to walk alone in fear because everyone would respect each other's space. No one would be denied anything, especially education. No child would go to bed hungry or scared.

BRENDAN: A utopia can come from everyone having a strong education. There are some major problems in the world, including war, disease, poverty and tyranny. If everyone has a strong educational background, all of these major problems can be eradicated. There will be more people to help cure diseases.

MICHAEL: In utopia there is a perfect ethical code that everyone follows. If someone breaks the code, the rest of society decides his/her punishment. There are no religions, there is only science. Obviously there is no war because of the perfect ethical code and the cooperation of the society. There is no fear, greed or hate to start a war.

HANNAH: I would be living in a lake house with my dogs. I would work a job I loved, and get paid well doing it. The weather would be a perfect 70-80 degrees and sunny every day, because why not? Actually, I'll just control the weather myself.

EMILY: No one grows up rich or poor, but instead everyone has the same resources and opportunity when they begin their life. Whether they decide to go to school or start a trade or whatever, that would be a direct result of their own actions and choices. No one has less opportunities than another person, and no one has unlimited wealth/opportunities to mess around with either.

MARIAM: Higher education is available to every-15 one and not just anyone who can afford it. Everyone has protected rights and lives under democratic ideals where they are free. No evil exists. Everyone can afford clothes, food, shelter and good health care.

SEAN: Everyone has only one priority: making the world better for all. Issues that would normally lead to war are now resolved through a friendly pickup baseball game.

VICKTORIA: There should be basic foods available for free for those who cannot afford to eat and are begging on the street. Another necessity is for everyone to have a home. There are so many homeless people around Hoboken and even more in NYC. These people should be taken in by the state and given jobs to do that are simple in exchange for a home.

ZACHARY: A utopian world is impossible. The problem is, in my utopia the laws and common beliefs would be similar to ones I hold. I want people to agree with me, but I realize I am not always right and will have something to learn. Basically everyone would need to agree but also hold differing opinions, which is impossible. Another problem for me is economic equality. While I would not want anyone in poverty, I believe peoples' decisions and actions should affect their outcomes.

JYOTSNA: Creating a utopia is really a lot of hard work. You want to fix all the problems you see in the world, but you also realize that there are so many problems, you wonder if your own utopia could even handle all of the fixes. That said, in my utopia there would be no need for environmental alarm. People would respect nature. Politics would be about the betterment of people, not power or personal gain. I would be friends with Robert Redford. Also, colleges would be free, or at least cheaper.

RYAN: Some of the conflict that comes from 20 an imperfect world makes it better. I wouldn't want scientists, philosophers and other intellectuals to have all the answers. They should have different views, because debates are often entertaining and make life more worth living. Competition can also give meaning to life. Utopia should have a certain amount of inequality to make things interesting, but not a staggering amount to where people suffer because of it. Utopia isn't a completely perfect world, but a world with the perfect amount of imperfection.

Topics for Critical Thinking and Writing

1. Why would John Horgan mention his call for an absolute end to war at the beginning of his essay (para. 1)? What does it add — or detract — from the argument at hand?

2. In paragraph 3, Horgan says he hopes to "prod readers to dream up their own utopias." Try his assignment. Take ten minutes and write freely about what a "perfect world" would look like to you.

3. Think critically about Daniel's hope that all countries in the world have first-world standards (para. 8). Do you think this is an example of utopian thinking? Why or why not?

4. The theme of education occurs in several student responses. Can you imagine a scenario in which education for all would be more of a dystopia than a utopia? Explain.

5. Select a response by one of Horgan's students that stands out most to you as containing an idea you see as part of an ideal society. Expand on the idea: What sorts of practices or policies would have to be discarded in order to bring about this utopia? What practical problems would the idea pose, and how might they be resolved?

6. Which student responses do you think are the best responses, and which are the worst? Why? Are there any common threads or ideas shared among the strongest or weakest ideas?

MICHAEL SHERMER

Michael Shermer is a Presidential Fellow at Chapman University, where he teaches a critical thinking course called Skepticism 101. He is a founder of *Skeptic* magazine and was a long-time columnist at *Scientific American*. He hosts a podcast, *The Michael Shermer Show*, writes a weekly Substack column called Skeptic, and is the author of popular books including *Why People Believe Weird Things* (1997), *Why Darwin Matters* (2006), *The Believing Brain* (2011), *Heavens on Earth: The Scientific Search for the Afterlife, Immortality and Utopia* (2018), and *Giving the Devil His Due* (2020). Shermer is a leading voice in matters of rationality and irrationality, conspiratorial thinking, and extraordinary claims, with several of his books approaching subjects such as belief in ghosts, alien abductions, Holocaust denial, intelligent design, and other unscientific ideas. This essay was adapted from *Heavens on Earth* and was published on the website *Aeon* in 2018.

Utopia Is a Dangerous Ideal: We Should Aim for "Protopia"

Utopias are idealised visions of a perfect society. Utopianisms are those ideas put into practice. This is where the trouble begins. Thomas More coined the neologism *utopia* for his 1516 work that launched the modern genre for a good reason. The word means "no place" because when imperfect humans attempt perfectibility — personal, political, economic and social — they fail. Thus, the dark mirror of utopias are *dystopias* — failed social experiments, repressive political regimes, and overbearing economic systems that result from utopian dreams put into practice.

The belief that humans are perfectible leads, inevitably, to mistakes when "a perfect society" is designed for an imperfect species. There is no best way to live because there is so much variation in how people want to live. Therefore, there is no best society, only multiple variations on a handful of themes as dictated by our nature.

For example, utopias are especially vulnerable when a social theory based on collective ownership, communal work, authoritarian rule and a command-and-control economy collides with our natural-born desire for autonomy, individual freedom and choice. Moreover, the natural differences in ability, interests and preferences within any group of people leads to inequalities of outcomes and imperfect living and working conditions that utopias committed to equality of outcome cannot tolerate. As one of the original citizens of Robert Owen's 19th-century New Harmony community in Indiana explained it:

> We had tried every conceivable form of organisation and government. We had a world in miniature. We had enacted the French revolution over again with despairing hearts instead of corpses as a result. … It appeared that it was nature's own inherent law of diversity that had conquered us … our 'united interests' were directly at war with the individualities of persons and circumstances and the instinct of self-preservation.

Most of these 19th-century utopian experiments were relatively harmless because, without large numbers of members, they lacked political and economic power. But add those factors, and utopian dreamers can turn into dystopian murderers. People act on their beliefs, and if you believe that the only thing preventing you and/or your family, clan, tribe, race or religion from going to heaven (or achieving heaven on Earth) is someone else or some other group, then actions know no bounds. From homicide to genocide, the murder of others in the name of some religious or ideological belief accounts for the high body counts in history's conflicts, from the Crusades, Inquisition, witch crazes and religious wars of centuries gone to the religious cults, world wars, pogroms and genocides of the past century.

We can see that calculus behind the utopian logic in the now famous "trolley problem" in which most people say they would be willing to kill one person in order to save five. Here's the set-up: you are standing next to a fork in a railroad line with a switch to divert a trolley car that is about to kill five workers on the track. If you pull the switch, it will divert the trolley down a side track where it will kill one worker. If you do nothing, the trolley kills the five. What would you do? Most people say that they would pull the switch. If even people in Western enlightened countries today agree that it is morally permissible to kill one person to save five, imagine how easy it is to convince people living in autocratic states with utopian aspirations to kill 1,000 to save 5,000, or to exterminate 1,000,000 so that 5,000,000 might prosper. What's a few zeros when we're talking about infinite happiness and eternal bliss?

The fatal flaw in utilitarian utopianism is found in another thought experiment: you are a healthy bystander in a hospital waiting room in which an ER physician has five patients dying from different conditions, all of which can be saved by sacrificing you and harvesting your organs. Would anyone want to live in a society in which they might be that innocent bystander? Of course not, which is why any doctor who attempted such an atrocity would be tried and convicted for murder.

Yet this is precisely what happened with the grand 20th-century experiments in utopian socialist ideologies as manifested in Marxist/Leninist/Stalinist Russia (1917–1989), Fascist Italy (1922–1943) and Nazi Germany (1933–1945), all large-scale attempts to achieve political, economic, social (and even racial) perfection, resulting in tens of millions of people murdered by their own states or killed in conflict with other states perceived to be blocking the road to paradise. The Marxist theorist and revolutionary Leon Trotsky expressed the utopian vision in a 1924 pamphlet:

> The human species, the coagulated *Homo sapiens*, will once more enter into a state of radical transformation, and, in his own hands, will become an object of the most complicated methods of artificial selection and psychophysical training. … The average human type will rise to the heights of an Aristotle, a Goethe, or a Marx. And above this ridge new peaks will rise.

This unrealisable goal led to such bizarre experiments as those conducted by Ilya Ivanov, whom Stalin tasked in the 1920s with crossbreeding humans and apes in order to create 'a new invincible human being'. When Ivanov failed to produce the man-ape hybrid, Stalin had him arrested, imprisoned, and exiled to Kazakhstan. As for Trotsky, once he gained power as one of the first seven members of the founding Soviet Politburo, he established concentration camps for those who refused to join in this grand utopian experiment, ultimately leading to the gulag archipelago that killed millions of Russian citizens who were also believed to be standing in the way of the imagined utopian paradise to come. When his own theory of Trotskyism opposed that of Stalinism, the dictator had Trotsky assassinated in Mexico in 1940. *Sic sempertyrannis.*

In the second half of the 20th century, revolutionary Marxism in Cambodia, North Korea and numerous states in South America and Africa led to murders, pogroms, genocides, ethnic cleansings, revolutions, civil wars and state-sponsored conflicts, all in the name of establishing a heaven on Earth that required the elimination of recalcitrant dissenters. All told, some 94 million people died at the hands of revolutionary Marxists and utopian communists in Russia, China, North Korea and other states, a staggering number compared with the 28 million killed by the fascists. When you have to murder people by the tens of millions to achieve your utopian dream, you have instantiated only a dystopian nightmare.

The utopian quest for perfect happiness was 10 exposed as the flawed goal that it is by George Orwell in his 1940 review of *Mein Kampf*:

> Hitler ... has grasped the falsity of the hedonistic attitude to life. Nearly all western thought since the last war, certainly all 'progressive' thought, has assumed tacitly that human beings desire nothing beyond ease, security and avoidance of pain. ... [Hitler] knows that human beings *don't* only want comfort, safety, short working-hours, hygiene, birth-control and, in general, common sense; they also, at least intermittently, want struggle and self-sacrifice ...

On the broader appeal of Fascism and Socialism, Orwell added:

> Whereas Socialism, and even capitalism in a more grudging way, have said to people "I offer you a good time," Hitler has said to them "I offer you struggle, danger, and death," and as a result a whole nation flings itself at his feet. ... we ought not to underrate its emotional appeal.

What, then, should replace the idea of utopia? One answer can be found in another neologism — *protopia* — incremental progress in steps toward *improvement*, not perfection. As the futurist Kevin Kelly describes his coinage:

> Protopia is a state that is better today than yesterday, although it might be only a little better. Protopia is much much harder to visualise. Because a protopia contains as many new problems as new benefits, this complex interaction of working and broken is very hard to predict.

In my book *The Moral Arc* (2015), I showed how protopian progress best describes the monumental moral achievements of the past several centuries: the attenuation of war, the abolishment of slavery, the end of torture and the death penalty, universal suffrage, liberal democracy, civil rights and liberties, same-sex marriage and animal rights. These are all examples of protopian progress in the sense that they happened one small step at a time.

A protopian future is not only practical, it is realizable.

Topics for Critical Thinking and Writing

1. In paragraph 2, Michael Shermer claims, "There is no best way to live because there is so much variation in how people want to live." If you agree, flesh out this claim with some examples. If you disagree, think of some specific ways to live that you would consider to be "best" for most — if not everyone — in a society.

2. In paragraph 3, Shermer points out that "inequalities" would mark any theoretical social utopia. Under what conditions could inequalities exist within a utopian society? Is there any way to achieve perfection without ensuring that every person in the society is equal?

3. "Utopian dreamers can turn into dystopian murderers," Shermer writes in paragraph 4. Think of examples from the real world in which utopian dreams turned for the worst — resulting in violence. What caused the breakdown?

4. Do you find Shermer's argument by analogy effective when he discusses the trolley problem and the ER problem in paragraphs 5 and 6? (For a refresher on analogy in argumentation, see the section "Examples" in Chapter 4, p. 121.) What point do you think he is trying to make?

5. Consider Shermer's quotation of George Orwell in paragraphs 10–11. Why do you think "struggle, danger, and death" might be a powerful emotional appeal?

6. Near the end of his essay, Shermer argues for the realization of a "protopia" instead of aspirations toward a utopia. Explain the distinction, then discuss whether or not you agree with Shermer that our society is moving toward a protopia today. Be sure to address the aspects of protopian progress that Shermer outlines in his final paragraph.

NICCOLÒ MACHIAVELLI

Niccolò Machiavelli (1469–1527) was born in Florence at a time when Italy was divided into five major states: Venice, Milan, Florence, the Papal States, and Naples. Although these states often had belligerent relations with one another as well as with lesser Italian states, under the Medici family in Florence they achieved a precarious balance of power. In 1494, however, Lorenzo de' Medici, who had ruled from 1469 to 1492, died, and two years later Lorenzo's successor was exiled when the French army arrived in Florence. Italy became a field where Spain, France, and Germany competed for power. From 1498 to 1512, Machiavelli held a high post in the diplomatic service of the Florentine Republic, but when the French army reappeared and the Florentines in desperation recalled the Medici, Machiavelli lost his post and was imprisoned, tortured, and then exiled. Banished from Florence, he nevertheless lived in comfort on a small estate nearby, writing his major works and hoping to obtain an office from the Medici. In later years, he was employed in a few minor diplomatic missions, but even after the collapse and expulsion of the Medici in 1527 and the restoration of the republic, he did not regain his old position of importance. He died shortly after the restoration.

This selection comes from *The Prince*, which Machiavelli wrote in 1513 during his banishment, hoping that it would interest the Medici and thus restore him to favor; but the book was not published until 1532, five years after his death. In this book of twenty-six short chapters, Machiavelli begins by examining different kinds of states, but the work's enduring power resides in the discussions (in Chapters 15–18, reprinted here) of qualities necessary to a prince — that is, a head of state. Any such examination obviously is based in part on assumptions about the nature of the citizens of the realm.

This selection was taken from a translation by W. K. Marriott.

From The Prince

CONCERNING THINGS FOR WHICH MEN, AND ESPECIALLY PRINCES, ARE PRAISED OR BLAMED

It remains now to see what ought to be the rules of conduct for a prince towards subject and friends. And as I know that many have written on this point, I expect I shall be considered presumptuous in mentioning it again, especially as in discussing it I shall depart from the methods of other people. But, it being my intention to write a thing which shall be useful to him who apprehends it, it appears to me more appropriate to follow up the real truth of the matter than the imagination of it; for many have pictured republics and principalities which in fact have never been known or seen, because how one lives is so far distant from how one ought to live, that he who neglects what is done for what ought to be done, sooner effects his ruin than his preservation; for a man who wishes to act entirely up to his professions of virtue soon meets with what destroys him among so much that is evil.

Hence it is necessary for a prince wishing to hold his own to know how to do wrong, and to make use of it or not according to necessity. Therefore, putting on one side imaginary things concerning a prince, and discussing those which are real, I say that all men when they are spoken of, and chiefly princes for being more highly placed, are remarkable for some of those qualities which bring them either blame or praise; and thus it is that one is reputed liberal, another miserly, using a Tuscan term (because an avaricious person in our language is still he who desires to possess by robbery, whilst we call one miserly who deprives himself too much of the use of his own); one is reputed generous, one rapacious; one cruel, one compassionate; one faithless, another faithful; one effeminate and cowardly, another bold and brave; one affable, another haughty; one lascivious, another chaste; one sincere, another cunning; one hard, another easy; one grave, another frivolous; one religious, another unbelieving, and the like. And I know that everyone will confess that it would be most praiseworthy in a prince to exhibit all the above qualities that are considered good; but because they can neither be entirely possessed nor observed, for human conditions do not permit it, it is necessary for him to be sufficiently prudent that he may know how to avoid the reproach of those vices which would lose him his state; and also to keep himself, if it be possible, from those which would not lose him it; but this not being possible, he may with less hesitation abandon himself to them. And again, he need not make himself uneasy at incurring a reproach for those vices without which the state can only be saved with difficulty, for if everything is considered carefully, it will be found that something which looks like virtue, if followed, would be his ruin; whilst something else, which looks like vice, yet followed brings him security and prosperity.

CONCERNING LIBERALITY AND MEANNESS

Commencing then with the first of the above-named characteristics, I say that it would be well to be reputed liberal. Nevertheless, liberality exercised in a way that does not bring you the reputation for it, injures you; for if one exercises it honestly and as it should be exercised, it may not become known, and you will not avoid the reproach of its opposite. Therefore, anyone wishing to maintain among men the name of liberal is obliged to avoid no attribute of magnificence; so that a prince thus inclined will consume in such acts all his property, and will be compelled in the end, if he wish to maintain the name of liberal, to unduly weigh down his people, and tax them, and do everything he can to get money. This will soon make him odious to his subjects, and becoming poor he will be little valued by anyone; thus, with his liberality, having offended many and rewarded few, he is affected by the very first trouble and imperiled by whatever may be the first danger; recognizing this himself, and wishing to draw back from it, he runs at once into the reproach of being miserly.

Therefore, a prince, not being able to exercise this virtue of liberality in such a way that it is recognized, except to his cost, if he is wise he ought not to fear the reputation of being mean, for in time he will come to be more considered than if liberal, seeing that with his economy his revenues are enough, that he can defend himself against all attacks, and is able to engage in enterprises without burdening his people; thus it comes to pass that he exercises liberality towards all from whom he does not take, who are numberless, and meanness towards those to whom he does not give, who are few.

We have not seen great things done in our time except by those who have been considered mean; the rest have failed. Pope Julius the Second was assisted in reaching the papacy by a reputation for liberality, yet he did not strive afterwards to keep it up, when he made war on the King of France; and he made many wars without imposing any extraordinary tax on his subjects, for he supplied his additional expenses out of his long thriftiness. The present King of Spain would not have undertaken or conquered in so many enterprises if he had been reputed liberal. A prince, therefore, provided that he has not to rob his subjects,

that he can defend himself, that he does not become poor and abject, that he is not forced to become rapacious, ought to hold of little account a reputation for being mean, for it is one of those vices which will enable him to govern.

And if anyone should say: Caesar obtained empire by liberality, and many others have reached the highest positions by having been liberal, and by being considered so, I answer: Either you are a prince in fact, or in a way to become one. In the first case this liberality is dangerous, in the second it is very necessary to be considered liberal; and Caesar was one of those who wished to become pre-eminent in Rome; but if he had survived after becoming so, and had not moderated his expenses, he would have destroyed his government. And if anyone should reply: Many have been princes, and have done great things with armies, who have been considered very liberal, I reply: Either a prince spends that which is his own or his subjects' or else that of others. In the first case he ought to be sparing, in the second he ought not to neglect any opportunity for liberality. And to the prince who goes forth with his army, supporting it by pillage, sack, and extortion, handling that which belongs to others, this liberality is necessary, otherwise he would not be followed by soldiers. And of that which is neither yours nor your subjects' you can be a ready giver, as were Cyrus, Caesar, and Alexander; because it does not take away your reputation if you squander that of others, but adds to it; it is only squandering your own that injures you.

And there is nothing wastes so rapidly as liberality, for even whilst you exercise it you lose the power to do so, and so become either poor or despised, or else, in avoiding poverty, rapacious and hated. And a prince should guard himself, above all things, against being despised and hated; and liberality leads you to both. Therefore it is wiser to have a reputation for meanness which brings reproach without hatred, than to be compelled through seeking a reputation for liberality to incur a name for rapacity which begets reproach with hatred.

CONCERNING CRUELTY AND CLEMENCY, AND WHETHER IT IS BETTER TO BE LOVED THAN FEARED

Coming now to the other qualities mentioned above, I say that every prince ought to desire to be considered clement and not cruel. Nevertheless he ought to take care not to misuse this clemency. Cesare Borgia[1] was considered cruel; notwithstanding, his cruelty reconciled the Romagna, unified it, and restored it to peace and loyalty. And if this be rightly considered, he will be seen to have been much more merciful than the Florentine people, who, to avoid a reputation for cruelty, permitted Pistoia[2] to be destroyed. Therefore a prince, so long as he keeps his subjects united and loyal, ought not to mind the reproach of cruelty; because with a few examples he will be more merciful than those who, through too much mercy, allow disorders to arise, from which follow murders or robberies; for these are wont to injure the whole people, whilst those executions which originate with a prince offend the individual only.

And of all princes, it is impossible for the new prince to avoid the imputation of cruelty, owing to new states being full of dangers.

---

[1]**Cesare Borgia** The son of Pope Alexander VI, Cesare Borgia (1476–1507) was ruthlessly opportunistic. Encouraged by his father, in 1499 and 1500 he subdued the cities of Romagna, the region including Ferrara and Ravenna. [All notes are the editors']

[2]**Pistoia** A town near Florence; Machiavelli suggests that the Florentines failed to treat dissenting leaders with sufficient severity.

Hence Virgil, through the mouth of Dido, excuses the inhumanity of her reign owing to its being new, saying, "against my will, my fate / A throne unsettled, and an infant state, / Bid me defend my realms with all my pow'rs, / And guard with these severities my shores."[3] Nevertheless, he ought to be slow to believe and to act, nor should he himself show fear, but proceed in a temperate manner with prudence and humanity, so that too much confidence may not make him incautious and too much distrust render him intolerable.

Upon this a question arises: whether it be better to be loved than feared or feared than loved? It may be answered that one should wish to be both, but, because it is difficult to unite them in one person, it is much safer to be feared than loved, when, of the two, either must be dispensed with. Because this is to be asserted in general of men, that they are ungrateful, fickle, false, cowardly, covetous, and as long as you succeed they are yours entirely; they will offer you their blood, property, life, and children, as is said above, when the need is far distant; but when it approaches they turn against you. And that prince who, relying entirely on their promises, has neglected other precautions, is ruined; because friendships that are obtained by payments, and not by greatness or nobility of mind, may indeed be earned, but they are not secured, and in time of need cannot be relied upon; and men have less scruple in offending one who is beloved than one who is feared, for love is preserved by the link of obligation which, owing to the baseness of men, is broken at every opportunity for their advantage; but fear preserves you by a dread of punishment which never fails.

Nevertheless, a prince ought to inspire fear in such a way that, if he does not win love, he

---

[3]In *Aeneid* I, 563–64, **Virgil** (70–19 BC) puts this line into the mouth of **Dido**, the queen of Carthage.

avoids hatred; because he can endure very well being feared whilst he is not hated, which will always be as long as he abstains from the property of his citizens and subjects and from their women. But when it is necessary for him to proceed against the life of someone, he must do it on proper justification and for manifest cause, but above all things he must keep his hands off the property of others, because men more quickly forget the death of their father than the loss of their patrimony. Besides, pretexts for taking away the property are never wanting; for he who has once begun to live by robbery will always find pretexts for seizing what belongs to others; but reasons for taking life, on the contrary, are more difficult to find and sooner lapse. But when a prince is with his army, and has under control a multitude of soldiers, then it is quite necessary for him to disregard the reputation of cruelty, for without it he would never hold his army united or disposed to its duties.

Among the wonderful deeds of Hannibal[4] this one is enumerated: that having led an enormous army, composed of many various races of men, to fight in foreign lands, no dissensions arose either among them or against the prince, whether in his bad or in his good fortune. This arose from nothing else than his inhuman cruelty, which, with his boundless valor, made him revered and terrible in the sight of his soldiers, but without that cruelty, his other virtues were not sufficient to produce this effect. And shortsighted writers admire his deeds from one point of view and from another condemn the principal cause of them. That it is true his other virtues would not have been sufficient for him may be proved by the case of Scipio,[5] that most excellent man, not only of his own times but within the memory of man, against whom, nevertheless, his army rebelled in Spain; this arose from nothing but his too great forbearance, which gave his soldiers more license than is consistent with military discipline. For this he was upbraided in the Senate by Fabius Maximus, and called the corrupter of the Roman soldiery. The Locrians were laid waste by a legate of Scipio, yet they were not avenged by him, nor was the insolence of the legate punished, owing entirely to his easy nature. Insomuch that someone in the Senate, wishing to excuse him, said there were many men who knew much better how not to err than to correct the errors of others. This disposition, if he had been continued in the command, would have destroyed in time the fame and glory of Scipio; but, he being under the control of the Senate, this injurious characteristic not only concealed itself, but contributed to his glory.

Returning to the question of being feared or loved, I come to the conclusion that, men loving according to their own will and fearing according to that of the prince, a wise prince should establish himself on that which is in his own control and not in that of others; he must endeavor only to avoid hatred, as is noted.

CONCERNING THE WAY IN WHICH PRINCES SHOULD KEEP FAITH

Everyone admits how praiseworthy it is in a prince to keep faith, and to live with integrity and not with craft. Nevertheless our experience has been that those princes who have

---

[4]**Hannibal** The Carthaginian general (247–183 BC) whose crossing of the Alps with elephants and full baggage train is one of the great feats of military history.

[5]**Scipio** Publius Cornelius Scipio Africanus the Elder (235–183 BC), the conqueror of Hannibal in the Punic Wars. The mutiny of which Machiavelli speaks took place in 206 BC.

done great things have held good faith of little account, and have known how to circumvent the intellect of men by craft, and in the end have overcome those who have relied on their word. You must know there are two ways of contesting, the one by the law, the other by force; the first method is proper to men, the second to beasts; but because the first is frequently not sufficient, it is necessary to have recourse to the second. Therefore it is necessary for a prince to understand how to avail himself of the beast and the man. This has been figuratively taught to princes by ancient writers, who describe how Achilles and many other princes of old were given to the Centaur Chiron[6] to nurse, who brought them up in his discipline; which means solely that, as they had for a teacher one who was half beast and half man, so it is necessary for a prince to know how to make use of both natures, and that one without the other is not durable. A prince, therefore, being compelled knowingly to adopt the beast, ought to choose the fox and the lion; because the lion cannot defend himself against snares and the fox cannot defend himself against wolves. Therefore, it is necessary to be a fox to discover the snares and a lion to terrify the wolves. Those who rely simply on the lion do not understand what they are about. Therefore a wise lord cannot, nor ought he to, keep faith when such observance may be turned against him, and when the reasons that caused him to pledge it exist no longer. If men were entirely good this precept would not hold, but because they are bad, and will not keep faith with you, you too are not bound to observe it with them. Nor will there ever be wanting to a prince legitimate reasons to excuse this non-observance. Of this endless modern examples could be given, showing how many treaties and engagements have been made void and of no effect through the faithlessness of princes; and he who has known best how to employ the fox has succeeded best.

But it is necessary to know well how to disguise this characteristic, and to be a great pretender and dissembler; and men are so simple, and so subject to present necessities, that he who seeks to deceive will always find someone who will allow himself to be deceived. One recent example I cannot pass over in silence. Alexander the Sixth[7] did nothing else but deceive men, nor ever thought of doing otherwise, and he always found victims; for there never was a man who had greater power in asserting, or who with greater oaths would affirm a thing, yet would observe it less; nevertheless his deceits always succeeded according to his wishes, because he well understood this side of mankind.

Therefore it is unnecessary for a prince to have all the good qualities I have enumerated, but it is very necessary to appear to have them. And I shall dare to say this also, that to have them and always to observe them is injurious, and that to appear to have them is useful; to appear merciful, faithful, humane, religious, upright, and to be so, but with a mind so framed that should you require not to be so, you may be able and know how to change to the opposite. And you have to understand this, that a prince, especially a new one, cannot observe all those things for which men are esteemed, being often forced, in order to maintain the state, to act contrary to fidelity, friendship, humanity, and religion. Therefore it is necessary for him to have a mind ready to turn itself accordingly as the winds and variations of fortune force it, yet, as I have

---

[6]**Chiron** (Kī'ron) A centaur (half man, half horse) who was said in classical mythology to have been the teacher not only of Achilles but also of Theseus, Jason, Hercules, and other heroes.

[7]**Alexander the Sixth** Pope from 1492 to 1503; father of Cesare Borgia.

said above, not to diverge from the good if he can avoid doing so, but, if compelled, then to know how to set about it.

For this reason a prince ought to take care that he never lets anything slip from his lips that is not replete with the above-named five qualities, that he may appear to him who sees and hears him altogether merciful, faithful, humane, upright, and religious. There is nothing more necessary to appear to have than this last quality, inasmuch as men judge generally more by the eye than by the hand, because it belongs to everybody to see you, to few to come in touch with you. Everyone sees what you appear to be, few really know what you are, and those few dare not oppose themselves to the opinion of the many, who have the majesty of the state to defend them; and in the actions of all men, and especially of princes, which it is not prudent to challenge, one judges by the result.[8]

For that reason, let a prince have the credit of conquering and holding his state, the means will always be considered honest, and he will be praised by everybody; because the vulgar are always taken by what a thing seems to be and by what comes of it; and in the world there are only the vulgar, for the few find a place there only when the many have no ground to rest on. One prince of the present time, whom it is not well to name, never preaches anything else but peace and good faith, and to both he is most hostile, and either, if he had kept it, would have deprived him of reputation and kingdom many a time.

---

[8] **one judges by the result** The original Italian, *si guarda al fine*, has often been translated erroneously as "the ends justify the means." Although this saying is often attributed to Machiavelli, he never actually wrote it.

Topics for Critical Thinking and Writing

1. In the opening paragraph, Niccolò Machiavelli claims that a ruler who wishes to keep in power must "know how to do wrong" — that is, must know where and when to ignore the demands of conventional morality. In the rest of the excerpt, does he give any convincing evidence to support this claim? Can you think of any recent political event in which a political leader violated the requirements of morality, as Machiavelli advises? Explain your response.

2. In paragraph 2, Machiavelli claims that it is impossible for a ruler to exhibit *all* the conventional virtues (trustworthiness, liberality, and so on). Why does he make this claim? Do you agree with it? Why or why not?

3. Machiavelli says that Cesare Borgia's cruelty brought peace to Romagna and that, in contrast, the Florentines who sought to avoid being cruel in fact brought pain to Pistoia. Can you think of recent episodes supporting the view that cruelty can be beneficial to society? If so, restate Machiavelli's position, using these examples from recent history. Or if you believe that Machiavelli's point here is fundamentally wrong, explain why, again using current examples.

4. In *The Prince*, Machiavelli is writing about how to be a successful ruler. He explicitly says that he is dealing with things as they are, not as they should be. Do you think that one can, in fact, write usefully about governing without considering ethics? Explain.

5. In paragraph 17, Machiavelli declares that "in the actions of all men, . . . one judges by the result." Taking account of the context, do you think the meaning is (a) that any end, goal, or purpose of anyone justifies using any means to reach it or (b) that the end of governing the state, nation, or country justifies using any means to achieve it? Or do you think Machiavelli means both? Or something else entirely?

6. Thomas More wrote *Utopia* at almost the exact same time as Machiavelli wrote *The Prince*. Compare and contrast the two authors' arguments about the nature of the state, examining their assumptions about human beings and the role of government.

THOMAS JEFFERSON

Thomas Jefferson (1743–1826) was a congressman, the governor of Virginia, the first secretary of state, and the president of the United States, but he said he wished to be remembered for only three things: drafting the Declaration of Independence, writing the Virginia Statute for Religious Freedom, and founding the University of Virginia. All three were efforts to promote freedom.

Jefferson was born in Virginia and educated at William and Mary College in Williamsburg, Virginia. After graduating, he studied law, was admitted to the bar, and in 1769 was elected to the Virginia House of Burgesses, his first political office. In 1776, he went to Philadelphia as a delegate to the second Continental Congress, where he was elected to a committee of five to write the Declaration of Independence. Jefferson drafted the document, which was then subjected to some changes by the other members of the committee and by the Congress. Although he was unhappy with the changes (especially with the deletion of a passage against slavery), his claim to have written the Declaration is just.

The Declaration of Independence

When in the course of human events, it becomes necessary for one people to dissolve the political bands which have connected them with another, and to assume among the Powers of the earth, the separate and equal station to which the Laws of Nature and of Nature's God entitle them, a decent respect to the opinions of mankind requires that they should declare the causes which impel them to the separation.

We hold these truths to be self-evident, that all men are created equal, that they are endowed by their Creator with certain unalienable Rights, that among these are Life, Liberty and the pursuit of Happiness.

That to secure these rights, Governments are instituted among Men, deriving their just powers from the consent of the governed.

That whenever any Form of Government becomes destructive of these ends, it is the Right of the People to alter or to abolish it, and to institute a new Government, laying its foundation on such principles and organizing its powers in such form, as to them shall seem most likely to effect their Safety and Happiness. Prudence, indeed, will dictate that Governments long established should not be changed for light and transient causes; and accordingly all experience hath shown that mankind are more disposed to suffer, while evils are sufferable, than to right themselves by abolishing the forms to which they are accustomed. But when a long train of abuses and usurpations pursuing invariably the same Object evinces a design to reduce them under absolute Despotism, it is their right, it is their duty, to throw off such government, and to provide new Guards for their future security.

Such has been the patient sufferance of 5 these Colonies; and such is now the necessity which constrains them to alter their former Systems of Government. The history of the present King of Great Britain is a history of repeated injuries and usurpations, all having in direct object the establishment of an absolute Tyranny over these States. To prove this, let Facts be submitted to a candid world.

He has refused his Assent to Laws, the most wholesome and necessary for the public good.

He has forbidden his Governors to pass Laws of immediate and pressing importance, unless suspended in their operation till his Assent should be obtained; and when so suspended, he has utterly neglected to attend to them.

He has refused to pass over Laws for the accommodation of large districts of people, unless those people would relinquish the right of Representation in the Legislature, a right inestimable to them and formidable to tyrants only.

He has called together legislative bodies at places unusual, uncomfortable, and distant from the depository of their Public Records, for the sole purpose of fatiguing them into compliance with his measures.

He has dissolved Representative Houses 10 repeatedly, for opposing with manly firmness his invasions on the rights of the people.

He has refused for a long time, after such dissolutions, to cause others to be elected; whereby the Legislative Powers, incapable of

Annihilation, have returned to the People at large for their exercise; the State remaining in the meantime exposed to all the dangers of invasion from without, and convulsions within.

He has endeavored to prevent the population of these States, for that purpose obstructing the Laws of Naturalization of Foreigners; refusing to pass others to encourage their migration hither, and raising the conditions of new Appropriations of Lands.

He has obstructed the Administration of Justice, by refusing his Assent to Laws for establishing Judiciary Powers.

He has made Judges dependent on his Will alone, for the tenure of their offices, and the amount and payment of their salaries.

He has erected a multitude of New Offices, 15 and sent hither swarms of Officers to harass our People, and eat out their substance.

He has kept among us, in time of peace, Standing Armies without the consent of our Legislature.

He has affected to render the Military independent of and superior to the Civil Power.

He has combined with others to subject us to jurisdictions foreign to our constitution, and unacknowledged by our laws; giving his Assent to their acts of pretended Legislation:

For quartering large bodies of armed troops among us:

For protecting them, by a mock Trial, 20 from Punishment for any Murders which they should commit on the Inhabitants of these States:

For cutting off our Trade with all parts of the world:

For imposing Taxes on us without our Consent:

For depriving us in many cases, of the benefits of Trial by Jury:

For transporting us beyond Seas to be tried for pretended offenses:

For abolishing the free System of English 25 Laws in a Neighbouring Province, establishing therein an Arbitrary government, and enlarging its boundaries so as to render it at once an example and fit instrument for introducing the same absolute rule into these Colonies:

For taking away our Charters, abolishing our most valuable Laws, and altering fundamentally the Forms of our Governments.

For suspending our own Legislatures, and declaring themselves invested with Power to legislate for us in all cases whatsoever.

He has abdicated Government here, by declaring us out of his Protection and waging War against us.

He has plundered our seas, ravaged our Coasts, burnt our towns and destroyed the Lives of our people.

He is at this time transporting large 30 Armies of foreign Mercenaries to complete the works of death, desolation and tyranny, already begun with circumstances of Cruelty & perfidy scarcely paralleled in the most barbarous ages, and totally unworthy the Head of a civilized nation.

He has constrained our fellow Citizens taken Captive on the high Seas to bear Arms against their Country, to become the executioners of their friends and Brethren, or to fall themselves by their Hands.

He has excited domestic insurrections amongst us, and has endeavored to bring on the inhabitants of our frontiers, the merciless Indian Savages, whose known rule of warfare is an undistinguished destruction of all ages, sexes and conditions.

In every stage of these Oppressions We Have Petitioned for Redress in the most humble terms: Our repeated petitions have been answered only by repeated injury. A Prince, whose character is thus marked by every act which may define a Tyrant, is unfit to be the ruler of a free People.

Nor have We been wanting in attention to our British brethren. We have warned them from time to time of attempts by their legislature to extend an unwarrantable jurisdiction over us. We have reminded them of the circumstances of our emigration and settlement here. We have appealed to their native justice and magnanimity and we have conjured them by the ties of our common kindred to disavow these usurpations, which would inevitably interrupt our connections and correspondence. They too have been deaf to the voice of justice and of consanguinity. We must, therefore, acquiesce in the necessity, which denounces our Separation, and hold them, as we hold the rest of mankind, Enemies in War, in Peace Friends.

We, therefore, the Representatives of the 35 United States of America, in General Congress, Assembled, appealing to the Supreme Judge of the world of the rectitude of our intentions, do, in the Name, and by Authority of the good People of these Colonies, solemnly publish and declare, That these United Colonies are, and of Right ought to be, Free and Independent States; that they are Absolved from all Allegiance to the British Crown, and that all political connection between them and the State of Great Britain, is and ought to be totally dissolved; and that as Free and Independent States, they have full power to levy War, conclude Peace, contract Alliances, establish Commerce, and to do all other Acts and Things which Independent States may of right do. And for the support of this Declaration, with a firm reliance on the protection of Divine Providence, we mutually pledge to each other our lives, our Fortunes and our sacred Honor.

Topics for Critical Thinking and Writing

1. According to the first paragraph, for what audience was the Declaration of Independence written? To what other audiences do you think the document was (in one way or another) addressed?

2. In the Declaration of Independence, Thomas Jefferson argues that the colonists are entitled to certain things and that under certain conditions they may behave in a certain way. Make explicit the syllogism that Jefferson is arguing. (For more on this tool for deductive argument, see the section "Premises and Syllogisms" in Chapter 4, p. 106.) What evidence does Jefferson offer to support his major premise? His minor premise?

3. In paragraph 2, the Declaration cites "certain unalienable Rights" and mentions three: "life, liberty and the pursuit of happiness." What is an unalienable right? If someone has an unalienable (or inalienable) right, does that imply that he or she also has certain duties? If so, what are these duties? John Locke, a century earlier (1690), asserted that all men have a natural right to "life, liberty, and property." Do you think the decision to drop "property" and substitute "pursuit of happiness" improved Locke's claim? Explain how or why you think Jefferson changed the phrase.

4. The Declaration states that it is intended to "prove" that the acts of the government of George III had as their "direct object the establishment of an absolute Tyranny" in the American colonies (para. 5). Write an essay showing whether the evidence offered in the Declaration "proves" this claim to your satisfaction. (You will want to define "absolute tyranny.") If you think further evidence is needed to "prove" the colonists' point, indicate what this evidence might be.

5. King George III has asked you to reply, on his behalf, to the colonists. Write this reply in 500 to 750 words. (Caution: A good reply will probably require you to do some reading about the period.)

6. Write a declaration of your own, setting forth why some group is entitled to independence. You may want to argue that adolescents should not be compelled to attend school, that animals should not be confined in zoos, or that persons who use drugs should be able to buy them legally. Begin with a premise, then set forth facts illustrating the unfairness of the present condition, and conclude by stating what the new condition will mean to society.

ELIZABETH CADY STANTON

Elizabeth Cady Stanton (1815–1902), a lawyer's daughter and journalist's wife, proposed in 1848 a convention to address the "social, civil, and religious condition and rights of women." Responding to Stanton's call, women and men from all over the Northeast traveled to the Woman's Rights Convention held in the village of Seneca Falls, New York. Her declaration, adopted by the convention — but only after vigorous debate and some amendments by others — became the platform for the women's rights movement in the United States.

Declaration of Sentiments and Resolutions

When, in the course of human events, it becomes necessary for one portion of the family of man to assume among the people of the earth a position different from that which they have hitherto occupied, but one to which the laws of nature and of nature's God entitle them, a decent respect to the opinions of mankind requires that they should declare the causes that impel them to such a course.

We hold these truths to be self-evident: that all men and women are created equal; that they are endowed by their Creator with certain inalienable rights; that among these are life, liberty and the pursuit of happiness; that to secure these rights governments are instituted, deriving their just powers from the consent of the governed. Whenever any form of government becomes destructive of these ends, it is the right of those who suffer from it to refuse allegiance to it, and to insist upon the institution of a new government, laying its foundation on such principles, and organizing its powers in such form, as to them shall seem most likely to effect their safety and happiness. Prudence, indeed, will dictate that governments long established should not be changed for light and transient causes; and accordingly all experience hath shown that mankind are more disposed to suffer, while evils are sufferable, than to right themselves by abolishing the forms to which they were accustomed. But when a long train of abuses and usurpations, pursuing invariably the same object, evinces a design to reduce them under absolute despotism, it is their duty to throw off such government, and to provide new guards for their future security. Such has been the patient sufferance of the women under this government, and such is now the necessity which constrains them to demand the equal station to which they are entitled.

The history of mankind is a history of repeated injuries and usurpations on the part of man toward woman, having in direct object the establishment of an absolute tyranny over her. To prove this, let facts be submitted to a candid world.

He has never permitted her to exercise her inalienable right to the elective franchise.

He has compelled her to submit to laws, in 5 the formation of which she had no voice.

He has withheld from her rights which are given to the most ignorant and degraded men — both natives and foreigners.

Having deprived her of this first right of a citizen, the elective franchise, thereby leaving her without representation in the halls of legislation, he has oppressed her on all sides.

He has made her, if married, in the eye of the law, civilly dead.

He has taken from her all right in property, even to the wages she earns.

He has made her, morally, an irresponsible 10 being, as she can commit many crimes with impunity, provided they be done in the presence of her husband. In the covenant of marriage, she is compelled to promise obedience to her husband, he becoming to all intents and purposes, her master — the law giving him power to deprive her of her liberty, and to administer chastisement.

He has so framed the laws of divorce, as to what shall be the proper causes, and in case of separation, to whom the guardianship of the children shall be given, as to be wholly regardless of the happiness of women — the law, in all cases, going upon a false supposition of the supremacy of man, and giving all power into his hands.

After depriving her of all rights as a married woman, if single, and the owner of property, he has taxed her to support a government which recognizes her only when her property can be made profitable to it.

He has monopolized nearly all the profitable employments, and from those she is permitted to follow, she receives but a scanty remuneration. He closes against her all the avenues to wealth and distinction which he considers most honorable to himself. As a teacher of theology, medicine, or law, she is not known.

He has denied her the facilities for obtaining a thorough education, all colleges being closed against her.

He allows her in Church, as well as State, 15 but a subordinate position, claiming Apostolic authority for her exclusion from the ministry, and, with some exceptions, from any public participation in the affairs of the Church.

He has created a false public sentiment by giving to the world a different code of morals for men and women, by which moral delinquencies which exclude women from society, are not only tolerated, but deemed of little account in man.

He has usurped the prerogative of Jehovah himself, claiming it as his right to assign for her a sphere of action, when that belongs to her conscience and to her God.

He has endeavored, in every way that he could, to destroy her confidence in her own powers, to lessen her self-respect, and to make her willing to lead a dependent and abject life.

Now, in view of this entire disfranchisement of one-half the people of this country, their social and religious degradation — in view of the unjust laws above mentioned, and because women do feel themselves aggrieved, oppressed, and fraudulently deprived of their most sacred rights, we insist that they have immediate admission to all the rights and privileges which belong to them as citizens of the United States.

In entering upon the great work before 20 us, we anticipate no small amount of misconception, misrepresentation, and ridicule; but we shall use every instrumentality within our power to effect our object. We shall employ agents, circulate tracts, petition the State and National legislatures, and endeavor to enlist the pulpit and the press in our behalf. We hope this Convention will be followed by a series of Conventions embracing every part of the country.

[The following resolutions were discussed by Lucretia Mott, Thomas and Mary Ann McClintock, Amy Post, Catharine A. F. Stebbins, and others, and were adopted:]

Whereas, The great precept of nature is conceded to be, that "man shall pursue his own true and substantial happiness." Blackstone in his Commentaries remarks, that this law of Nature being coeval with mankind, and dictated by God himself, is of course superior in obligation to any other. It is binding over all the globe, in all countries, and at all times; no human laws are of any validity if contrary to this, and such of them as are valid, derive all their force, and all their validity, and all their authority, mediately and immediately, from this original; therefore,

Resolved, That such laws as conflict, in any way, with the true and substantial happiness of woman, are contrary to the great precept of nature and of no validity, for this is "superior in obligation to any other."

Resolved, That all laws which prevent woman from occupying such a station in society as her conscience shall dictate, or which place her in a position inferior to that of man, are contrary to the great precept of nature, and therefore of no force or authority.

Resolved, That woman is man's equal — was 25 intended to be so by the Creator, and the highest good of the race demands that she should be recognized as such.

Resolved, That the women of this country ought to be enlightened in regard to the laws under which they live, that they may no longer publish their degradation by declaring themselves satisfied with their present position, nor their ignorance, by asserting that they have all the rights they want.

Resolved, That inasmuch as man, while claiming for himself intellectual superiority, does accord to woman moral superiority, it is preeminently his duty to encourage her to speak and teach, as she has an opportunity, in all religious assemblies.

Resolved, That the same amount of virtue, delicacy, and refinement of behavior that is required of woman in the social state, should also be required of man, and the same transgressions should be visited with equal severity on both man and woman.

Resolved, That the objection of indelicacy and impropriety, which is so often brought against woman when she addresses a public audience, comes with a very ill-grace from those who encourage, by their attendance, her appearance on the stage, in the concert, or in feats of the circus.

Resolved, That woman has too long rested 30 satisfied in the circumscribed limits which corrupt customs and a perverted application of the Scriptures have marked out for her, and that it is time she should move in the enlarged sphere which her great Creator has assigned her.

Resolved, That it is the duty of the women of this country to secure to themselves their sacred right to the elective franchise.

Resolved, That the equality of human rights results necessarily from the fact of the identity of the race in capabilities and responsibilities.

Resolved, therefore, That, being invested by the Creator with the same capabilities, and the same consciousness of responsibility for their exercise, it is demonstrably the right and duty of woman, equally with man, to promote every righteous cause by every righteous means; and especially in regard to the great subjects of morals and religion, it is self-evidently her right to participate with her brother in teaching them, both in private and in public, by writing and by speaking, by any instrumentalities proper to be used, and in any assemblies proper to be held; and this being a self-evident truth growing out of the divinely implanted principles of human nature, any custom or authority adverse to it, whether modern or wearing the hoary sanction of antiquity, is to be regarded as a self-evident falsehood, and at war with mankind.

[At the last session Lucretia Mott offered and spoke to the following resolution:]

Resolved, That the speedy success of our 35 cause depends upon the zealous and untiring efforts of both men and women, for the overthrow of the monopoly of the pulpit, and for the securing to woman an equal participation with men in the various trades, professions, and commerce.

Topics for Critical Thinking and Writing

1. Elizabeth Cady Stanton echoes the Declaration of Independence because she wishes to associate her ideas and the movement she supports with a document and a movement that her readers esteem. She must have believed that if readers esteem the Declaration of Independence, they must grant the justice of her goals. Does her strategy work, or does it backfire by making her essay seem strained? Explain your response.

2. When Stanton insists that women have an "inalienable right to the elective franchise" (para. 4), what does she mean by "inalienable"?

3. Stanton complains that men have made married women, "in the eye of the law, civilly dead" (para. 8). What does she mean by "civilly dead"? How is it possible for a person to be biologically alive and yet civilly dead?

4. Stanton objects that women are "not known" as teachers of "theology, medicine, or law" (para. 13). Is that still true today? Do some research in your library and then write three biographical sketches, one each on well-known female professors of theology, medicine, and law.

5. The Declaration of Sentiments and Resolutions claims that women have "the same capabilities" as men (para. 32). Yet in 1848 Stanton and the others at Seneca Falls knew, or should have known, that history recorded no example of a woman philosopher comparable to Plato or Kant, a composer comparable to Beethoven or Chopin, a scientist comparable to Galileo or Newton, or a mathematician comparable to Euclid or Descartes. Do these facts contradict the Declaration's claim? If not, why not? How else but by different intellectual capabilities do you think such facts can be explained?

6. Stanton's declaration is more than 165 years old. Have all the issues she raised been satisfactorily resolved? If not, which ones remain?

EMMA LAZARUS

Emma Lazarus (1849–1887) was born in New York City as the fourth of seven children in a well-established family. Her parents provided her with a private education, and her father supported her writing: When Lazarus was just seventeen, her father had a collection of Lazarus's poetry, called *Poems and Translations: Written between the Ages of Fourteen and Sixteen*, printed for private circulation. In addition to poetry, Lazarus wrote essays, plays, several highly respected translations, and a novel, going on to become part of the literary elite in late nineteenth-century New York. Lazarus is probably known best for the poem that follows, "The New Colossus." She wrote this sonnet in 1883 as a donation to an auction held to raise money to build the pedestal for the Statue of Liberty. The poem was installed on the base of the statue in 1903, nearly two decades after Lazarus's death in 1887.

The New Colossus

Not like the brazen giant of Greek fame,
With conquering limbs astride from land to
    land;
Here at our sea-washed, sunset gates shall
    stand
A mighty woman with a torch, whose flame
Is the imprisoned lightning, and her name   5
Mother of Exiles. From her beacon-hand
Glows world-wide welcome; her mild eyes
    command
The air-bridged harbor that twin cities frame.
"Keep, ancient lands, your storied pomp!"
    cries she
With silent lips. "Give me your tired, your   10
    poor,
Your huddled masses yearning to breathe free,
The wretched refuse of your teeming shore.
Send these, the homeless, tempest-tost to me,
I lift my lamp beside the golden door!"

Topics for Critical Thinking and Writing

1. In the opening line of the poem, Emma Lazarus alludes to the Colossus of Rhodes — a statue of the Greek titan-god of the sun Helios that was erected in the city of Rhodes in 280 BCE. The Colossus was ninety-eight feet tall, making it one of the tallest statues of the ancient world. Compare the language Lazarus uses to describe this "brazen giant of Greek fame" (l. 1) to the language she uses to describe the Statue of Liberty, the "Mother of Exiles" (l. 6). If both statues are symbols for nations, what kind of argument does Lazarus make by describing the two statues as she does?

2. Notice the description of the Statue of Liberty's eyes as "mild" in line 7. Do you think it is an accurate depiction of how "the homeless, tempest-tost" are generally seen in the United States today? Why, or why not?

3. Lazarus refers to the Statue of Liberty as the "Mother of Exiles." Do you think this description still holds up today in light of current debates about immigration laws? Write a brief essay using both historical evidence and current events to support your argument.

4. Do some research into immigration in the United States today and then write an essay in which you judge whether or not the current immigration debate lives up to the ideals of "The New Colossus."

LAO TZU

Lao Tzu (ca. fourth to fifth century BCE) is a world-renowned ancient Chinese philosopher and writer. He is commonly regarded as the founder of Taoism and author of the Tao Te Ching, one of the most important philosophical and religious texts of the ancient world. Translated roughly as "the Way," the word "tao" indicates the path to virtue ("te") through the book ("ching"); thus, Lao Tzu's work comprises a manual for wise and spiritual living. The text preaches virtues such as selflessness, simplicity, and pacifism, and it was at least partially devoted to instructing rulers in the proper way of leading an empire. The Tao Te Ching is a short text of about 5,000 words (Chinese characters) divided into eighty-one chapters. We include Chapter 53 here.

Far Indeed Is This from the Way

If I understood only one thing,
I would want to use it to follow the Tao.
My only fear would be one of pride.
The Tao goes in the level places,
but people prefer to take the short cuts. 5
If too much time is spent cleaning the house
the land will become neglected and full of weeds,
and the granaries will soon become empty
because there is no one out working the fields.
To wear fancy clothes and ornaments, 10
to have your fill of food and drink
and to waste all of your money buying
  possessions
is called the crime of excess.
Oh, how these things go against the way of
  the Tao!

Topics for Critical Thinking and Writing

1. What is the central argument of this section of the Tao Te Ching?

2. Consider lines 6–7: "If too much time is spent cleaning the house the land will become neglected and full of weeds." How does the metaphor apply to other areas of political, personal, or social life?

3. Survey the conditions of contemporary society and consider the elements of Tzu's writing in relation not to the ancient world but to the present. What symbols in the poem can be correlated to modern phenomena? Is contemporary society living up to Tzu's perspective of an ideal society?

URSULA K. LE GUIN

Ursula K. Le Guin (1929–2018) was born in Berkeley, California, the daughter of a distinguished mother (Theodora Kroeber, a folklorist) and father (Alfred L. Kroeber, an anthropologist). After graduating from Radcliffe College, she earned a master's degree at Columbia University; in 1952, she held a Fulbright Fellowship for study in Paris, where she met and married Charles Le Guin, a historian. She began writing in earnest while bringing up three children. Although her work is most widely known to buffs of science fiction, it interests many other readers who normally do not care for sci-fi because it usually has large moral or political dimensions.

Le Guin said that she was prompted to write the following story by a remark she encountered in William James's "The Moral Philosopher and the Moral Life." James suggests there that if millions of people could be "kept permanently happy on the one simple condition that a certain lost soul on the far-off edge of things should lead a life of lonely torment," our moral sense "would make us immediately feel" that it would be "hideous" to accept such a bargain. This story first appeared in *New Dimensions 3* (1973).

The Ones Who Walk Away from Omelas

With a clamor of bells that set the swallows soaring, the Festival of Summer came to the city Omelas, bright-towered by the sea. The rigging of the boats in harbor sparkled with flags. In the streets between houses with red roofs and painted walls, between old moss-grown gardens and under avenues of trees, past great parks and public buildings, processions moved. Some were decorous: old people in long stiff robes of mauve and gray, grave master workmen, quiet, merry women carrying their babies and chatting as they walked. In other streets the music beat faster, a shimmering of gong and tambourine, and the people went dancing, the procession was a dance. Children dodged in and out, their high calls rising like the swallows' crossing flights over the music and the singing. All the processions wound towards the north side of the city, where on the great water-meadow called the Green Fields boys and girls, naked in the bright air, with mudstained feet and ankles and long, lithe arms, exercised their restive horses before the race. The horses wore no gear at all but a halter without bit. Their manes were braided with streamers of silver, gold, and green. They flared their nostrils and pranced and boasted to one another; they were vastly excited, the horse being the only animal who has adopted our ceremonies as his own. Far off to the north and west the mountains stood up half encircling Omelas on her bay. The air of morning was so clear that the snow still crowning the Eighteen Peaks burned with white-gold fire across the miles of sunlit air, under the dark blue of the sky. There was just enough wind to make the banners that marked the racecourse snap and flutter now and then. In the silence of the broad green meadows one could hear the music winding through the city streets, farther and nearer and ever approaching, a cheerful faint sweetness of the air that from time to time trembled and gathered together and broke out into the great joyous clanging of the bells.

Joyous! How is one to tell about joy? How describe the citizens of Omelas?

They were not simple folk, you see, though they were happy. But we do not say the words of cheer much any more. All smiles have become archaic. Given a description such as this one tends to make certain assumptions. Given a description such as this one tends to look next for the King, mounted on a splendid stallion and surrounded by his noble knights, or perhaps in a golden litter borne by great-muscled slaves. But there was no king. They did not use swords, or keep slaves. They were not barbarians. I do not know the rules and laws of their society, but I suspect that they were singularly few. As they did without monarchy and slavery, so they also got on without the stock exchange, the advertisement, the secret police, and the bomb. Yet I

repeat that these were not simple folk, not dulcet shepherds, noble savages, bland utopians. They were not less complex than us. The trouble is that we have a bad habit, encouraged by pedants and sophisticates, of considering happiness as something rather stupid. Only pain is intellectual, only evil interesting. This is the treason of the artist: a refusal to admit the banality of evil and the terrible boredom of pain. If you can't lick 'em, join 'em. If it hurts, repeat it. But to praise despair is to condemn delight, to embrace violence is to lose hold of everything else. We have almost lost hold, we can no longer describe a happy man, nor make any celebration of joy. How can I tell you about the people of Omelas? They were not naïve and happy children — though their children were, in fact, happy. They were mature, intelligent, passionate adults whose lives were not wretched. O miracle! But I wish I could describe it better. I wish I could convince you. Omelas sounds in my words like a city in a fairy tale, long ago and far away, once upon a time. Perhaps it would be best if you imagined it as your own fancy bids, assuming it will rise to the occasion, for certainly I cannot suit you all. For instance, how about technology? I think that there would be no cars or helicopters in and above the streets; this follows from the fact that the people of Omelas are happy people. Happiness is based on a just discrimination of what is necessary, what is neither necessary nor destructive, and what is destructive. In the middle category, however — that of the unnecessary but undestructive, that of comfort, luxury, exuberance, etc. — they could perfectly well have central heating, subway trains, washing machines, and all kinds of marvelous devices not yet invented here, floating light-sources, fuelless power, a cure for the common cold. Or they could have none of that: it doesn't matter. As you like it.

I incline to think that people from towns up and down the coast have been coming in to Omelas during the last days before the Festival on very fast little trains and double-decked trams, and that the train station of Omelas is actually the handsomest building in town, though plainer than the magnificent Farmers' Market. But even granted trains, I fear that Omelas so far strikes some of you as goody-goody. Smiles, bells, parades, horses, bleh. If so, please add an orgy. If an orgy would help, don't hesitate. Let us not, however, have temples from which issue beautiful nude priests and priestesses already half in ecstasy and ready to copulate with any man or woman, lover or stranger, who desires union with the deep godhead of the blood, although that was my first idea. But really it would be better not to have any temples in Omelas — at least, not manned temples. Religion yes, clergy no. Surely the beautiful nudes can just wander about, offering themselves like divine soufflés to the hunger of the needy and the rapture of the flesh. Let them join the processions. Let tambourines be struck above the copulations, and the glory of desire be proclaimed upon the gongs, and (a not unimportant point) let the offspring of these delightful rituals be beloved and looked after by all. One thing I know there is none of in Omelas is guilt. But what else should there be? I thought that first there were no drugs, but that is puritanical. For those who like it, the faint insistent sweetness of *drooz* may perfume the ways of the city, *drooz* which first brings a great lightness and brilliance to the mind and limbs, and then after some hours a dreamy languor, and wonderful visions at last of the very arcana and inmost secrets of the Universe, as well as exciting the pleasure of sex beyond all belief; and it is not habit-forming. For more modest tastes I think there ought to be beer. What else, what

else belongs in the joyous city? The sense of victory, surely, the celebration of courage. But as we did without clergy, let us do without soldiers. The joy built upon successful slaughter is not the right kind of joy; it will not do; it is fearful and it is trivial. A boundless and generous contentment, a magnanimous triumph felt not against some outer enemy but in communion with the finest and fairest in the souls of all men everywhere and the splendor of the world's summer: this is what swells the hearts of the people of Omelas, and the victory they celebrate is that of life. I really don't think many of them need to take *drooz*.

Most of the processions have reached the Green Fields by now. A marvelous smell of cooking goes forth from the red and blue tents of the provisioners. The faces of small children are amiably sticky; in the benign grey beard of a man a couple of crumbs of rich pastry are entangled. The youths and girls have mounted their horses and are beginning to group around the starting line of the course. An old woman, small, fat, and laughing, is passing out flowers from a basket, and tall young men wear her flowers in their shining hair. A child of nine or ten sits at the edge of the crowd, alone, playing on a wooden flute. People pause to listen, and they smile, but they do not speak to him, for he never ceases playing and never sees them, his dark eyes wholly rapt in the sweet, thin magic of the tune.

He finishes, and slowly lowers his hands 5 holding the wooden flute.

As if that little private silence were the signal, all at once a trumpet sounds from the pavilion near the starting line: imperious, melancholy, piercing. The horses rear on their slender legs, and some of them neigh in answer. Sober-faced, the young riders stroke the horses' necks and soothe them, whispering, "Quiet, quiet, there my beauty, my hope. . . ."

They begin to form in rank along the starting line. The crowds along the racecourse are like a field of grass and flowers in the wind. The Festival of Summer has begun.

Do you believe? Do you accept the festival, the city, the joy? No? Then let me describe one more thing.

In a basement under one of the beautiful public buildings of Omelas, or perhaps in the cellar of one of its spacious private homes, there is a room. It has one locked door, and no window. A little light seeps in dustily between cracks in the boards, secondhand from a cob-webbed window somewhere across the cellar. In one corner of the little room a couple of mops, with stiff, clotted, foul-smelling heads, stand near a rusty bucket. The floor is dirt, a little damp to the touch, as cellar dirt usually is. The room is about three paces long and two wide: a mere broom closet or disused tool room. In the room a child is sitting. It could be a boy or a girl. It looks about six, but actually is nearly ten. It is feeble-minded. Perhaps it was born defective, or perhaps it has become imbecile through fear, malnutrition, and neglect. It picks its nose and occasionally fumbles vaguely with its toes or genitals, as it sits hunched in the corner farthest from the bucket and the two mops. It is afraid of the mops. It finds them horrible. It shuts its eyes, but it knows the mops are still standing there; and the door is locked; and nobody will come. The door is always locked; and nobody ever comes, except that sometimes — the child has no understanding of time or interval — some-times the door rattles terribly and opens, and a person, or several people, are there. One of them may come in and kick the child to make it stand up. The others never come close, but peer in at it with frightened, disgusted eyes. The food bowl and the water jug are hastily filled, the door is locked, the eyes disappear. The people at the door never say anything, but the child, who has not always lived in the tool room, and can remember sunlight and its mother's voice, sometimes speaks. "I will be good," it says. "Please let me out. I will be good!" They never answer. The child used to scream for help at night, and cry a good deal, but now it only makes a kind of whining, "eh-haa, eh-haa," and it speaks less and less often. It is so thin there are no calves to its legs; its belly protrudes; it lives on a half-bowl of corn meal and grease a day. It is naked. Its but-tocks and thighs are a mass of festered sores, as it sits in its own excrement continually.

They all know it is there, all the people of Omelas. Some of them have come to see it, others are content merely to know it is there. They all know that it has to be there. Some of them understand why, and some do not, but they all understand that their happiness, the beauty of their city, the tenderness of their friendships, the health of their children, the wisdom of their scholars, the skill of their makers, even the abundance of their harvest and the kindly weathers of their skies, depend wholly on this child's abominable misery.

This is usually explained to children when 10 they are between eight and twelve, whenever they seem capable of understanding; and most of those who come to see the child are young people, though often enough an adult comes, or comes back, to see the child. No matter how well the matter has been explained to them, these young spectators are always shocked and sickened at the sight. They feel disgust, which they had thought themselves superior to. They feel anger, outrage, impotence, despite all the explanations. They would like to do something for the child. But there is nothing they can do. If the child were brought up into the sunlight out of that vile place, if it were cleaned and fed and comforted, that would be a good thing, indeed; but if it were done, in that day and hour all the prosperity and beauty and delight of Omelas would wither and be destroyed. Those are the terms. To exchange all the goodness and grace of every life in Omelas for that single, small improvement: to throw away the happiness of thousands for the chance of the happiness of one: that would be to let guilt within the walls indeed.

The terms are strict and absolute; there may not even be a kind word spoken to the child.

Often the young people go home in tears, or in a tearless rage, when they have seen the child and faced this terrible paradox. They may brood over it for weeks or years. But as time goes on they begin to realize that even if the child could be released, it would not get much good of its freedom: a little vague pleasure of warmth and food, no doubt, but little more. It is too degraded and imbecile to know any real joy. It has been afraid too long ever to be free of fear. Its habits are too uncouth for it to respond to humane treatment. Indeed, after so long it would probably be wretched without walls about it to protect it, and darkness for its eyes, and its own excrement to sit in. Their tears at the bitter injustice dry when they begin to perceive the terrible justice of reality, and to accept it. Yet it is their tears and anger, the trying of their generosity and the acceptance of their helplessness, which are perhaps the true source of the splendor of their lives. Theirs is no vapid, irresponsible happiness. They know that they, like the child, are not free. They know compassion. It

is the existence of the child, and their knowledge of its existence, that makes possible the nobility of their architecture, the poignancy of their music, the profundity of their science. It is because of the child that they are so gentle with children. They know that if the wretched one were not there snivelling in the dark, the other one, the flute-player, could make no joyful music as the young riders line up in their beauty for the race in the sunlight of the first morning of summer.

Now do you believe in them? Are they not more credible? But there is one more thing to tell, and this is quite incredible.

At times one of the adolescent girls or boys who go to see the child does not go home to weep or rage, does not, in fact, go home at all. Sometimes also a man or woman much older falls silent for a day or two, and then leaves home. These people go out into the street, and walk down the street alone. They keep walking, and walk straight out of the city of Omelas, through the beautiful gates. They keep walking across the farmlands of Omelas. Each one goes alone, youth or girl, man or woman. Night falls; the traveler must pass down village streets, between the houses with yellow-lit windows, and on out into the darkness of the fields. Each alone, they go west or north, towards the mountains. They go on. They leave Omelas, they walk ahead into the darkness, and they do not come back. The place they go towards is a place even less imaginable to most of us than the city of happiness. I cannot describe it at all. It is possible that it does not exist. But they seem to know where they are going, the ones who walk away from Omelas.

Topics for Critical Thinking and Writing

1. The narrator suggests, "Perhaps it would be best if you imagined it [Omelas] as your own fancy bids . . . for certainly I cannot suit you all" (para. 3). Do you think leaving the description of Omelas to the reader is an effective strategy for storytelling? Why or why not?

2. Consider the narrator's assertion in paragraph 3 that happiness "is based on a just discrimination of what is necessary." Do you agree? Why or why not?

3. Summarize the point of the story — not the plot, but what the story adds up to, the argument the author is getting at. What do you think is the intended meaning of the story?

4. Why do you think the citizens of Omelas hold a child captive, and why do you think they refer to the child as "it"?

5. Do you think the story implies a criticism of contemporary American society? Explain.

27

How and Why Do We Construct the "Other"?

JEAN-PAUL SARTRE

Jean-Paul Sartre (1905–1980) was a French philosopher, playwright, novelist, critic, and political activist whose influence on post–World War II intellectual life is significant. As the first philosopher of what he called "existentialism," Sartre drew from the notions about the individual and society established by Søren Kierkegaard and Friedrich Nietzsche; in his many philosophical treatises and artworks, Sartre addresses what he called "the phenomenon of being," a concept he articulated most prominently in *Being and Nothingness* (1943). In that work — and others around the same time, such as the plays *Nausea* (1938) and *No Exit* (1944) and the essay "Existentialism Is Humanism" (1944) — Sartre explored the limits and possibilities of individual consciousness in relation to knowledge and experience. His ideas inspired many of the countercultural trends of the postwar period, especially those that advocated nonconformity as a means of discovering personal authenticity and freedom. Further, they were politically salient: The concept of the individual liberated from social pressures to conform undermined cultural assumptions about the social order and gave weight to claims by women, African Americans, and others that their identities and experiences were inherently valuable and legitimate. Such views found articulation in much European and American art, literature, and theater, especially of the 1950s and 1960s.

Sartre was awarded (but declined) the Nobel Prize in Literature in 1964. The following selection is from his book *Anti-Semite and Jew* (1946).

Anti-Semite and Jew

If a man attributes all or part of his own misfortunes and those of his country to the presence of Jewish elements in the community, if he proposes to remedy this state of affairs by depriving the Jews of certain of their rights, by keeping them out of certain economic and social activities, by expelling them from the country, by exterminating all of them, we say that he has anti-Semitic *opinions*.

This word *opinion* makes us stop and think. It is the word a hostess uses to bring to an end a discussion that threatens to become acrimonious. It suggests that all points of view are equal; it reassures us, for it gives an inoffensive appearance to ideas by reducing them to the level of tastes. All tastes are natural; all opinions are permitted. Tastes, colors, and opinions are not open to discussion. In the name of democratic institutions, in the name of freedom of opinion, the anti-Semite asserts the right to preach the anti-Jewish crusade everywhere. . . .

A man may be a good father and a good husband, a conscientious citizen, highly cultivated, philanthropic, *and* in addition an anti-Semite. He may like fishing and the pleasures of love, may be tolerant in matters of religion, full of generous notions on the condition of the natives in Central Africa, *and* in addition detest the Jews. If he does not like them, we say, it is because his experience has shown him that they are bad, because statistics have taught him that they are dangerous, because certain historical factors have influenced his judgment. Thus this opinion seems to be the result of external causes, and those who wish to study it are prone to neglect the personality of the anti-Semite in favor of a consideration of the percentage of Jews who were mobilized in 1914, the percentage of Jews who are bankers, industrialists, doctors, and lawyers, or an examination of the history of the Jews in France since early times. They succeed in revealing a strictly objective situation that determines an equally objective current of opinion, and this they call anti-Semitism, for which they can draw up charts and determine the variations from 1870 to 1944. In such wise anti-Semitism appears to be at once a subjective taste that enters into combination with other tastes to form a personality, and an impersonal and social phenomenon which can be expressed by figures and averages, one which is conditioned by economic, historical, and political constants.

I do not say that these two conceptions are necessarily contradictory. I do say that

they are dangerous and false. I would admit, if necessary, that one may have an opinion on the government's policy in regard to the wine industry, that is, that one may decide, *for certain reasons*, either to approve or condemn the free importation of wine from Algeria: here we have a case of holding an opinion on the administration of things. But I refuse to characterize as opinion a doctrine that is aimed directly at particular persons and that seeks to suppress their rights or to exterminate them. The Jew whom the anti-Semite wishes to lay hands upon is not a schematic being defined solely by his function, as under administrative law; or by his status or his acts, as under the Code. He is a Jew, the son of Jews, recognizable by his physique, by the color of his hair, by his clothing perhaps, and, so they say, by his character. Anti-Semitism does not fall within the category of ideas protected by the right of free opinion.

Indeed, it is something quite other than an 5 idea. It is first of all a *passion*. No doubt it can be set forth in the form of a theoretical proposition. The "moderate" anti-Semite is a courteous man who will tell you quietly: "Personally, I do not detest the Jews. I simply find it preferable, for various reasons, that they should play a lesser part in the activity of the nation." But a moment later, if you have gained his confidence, he will add with more abandon: "You see, there must be *something* about the Jews; they upset me physically."

This argument, which I have heard a hundred times, is worth examining. First of all, it derives from the logic of passion. For, really now, can we imagine anyone's saying seriously: "There must be something about tomatoes, for I have a horror of eating them"? In addition, it shows us that anti-Semitism in its most temperate and most evolved forms remains a syncretic whole which may be expressed by statements of reasonable tenor, but which can involve even bodily modifications. Some men are suddenly struck with impotence if they learn from the woman with whom they are making love that she is a Jewess. There is a disgust for the Jew, just as there is a disgust for the Chinese or the Negro among certain people. Thus it is not from the body that the sense of repulsion arises, since one may love a Jewess very well if one does not know what her race is; rather it is something that enters the body from the mind. It is an involvement of the mind, but one so deep-seated and complete that it extends to the physiological realm, as happens in cases of hysteria.

This involvement is not caused by experience. I have questioned a hundred people on the reasons for their anti-Semitism. Most of them have confined themselves to enumerating the defects with which tradition has endowed the Jews. "I detest them because they are selfish, intriguing, persistent, oily, tactless, etc." . . . A young woman said to me: "I have had the most horrible experiences with furriers; they robbed me, they burned the fur I entrusted to them. Well, they were all Jews." But why did she choose to hate Jews rather than furriers? Why Jews or furriers rather than such and such a Jew or such and such a furrier? Because she had in her a predisposition toward anti-Semitism.

A classmate of mine at the lycée[1] told me that Jews "annoy" him because of the thousands of injustices that "Jew-ridden" social organizations commit in their favor. "A Jew passed his *agrégation*[2] the year I was failed, and you can't make me believe that that fellow, whose father came from Cracow or Lemberg, understood a poem by Ronsard or an eclogue by Virgil better than I." But he admitted that he disdained the *agrégation* as a mere academic exercise, and that he didn't study for it.

---

[1]**Lycée** School (Fr.). [Editors' note]
[2]Competitive state teachers' examination. [Editors' note]

Thus, to explain his failure, he made use of two systems of interpretation, like those madmen who, when they are far gone in their madness, pretend to be the King of Hungary but, if questioned sharply, admit to being shoemakers. His thoughts moved on two planes without his being in the least embarrassed by it. As a matter of fact, he will in time manage to justify his past laziness on the grounds that it really would be too stupid to prepare for an examination in which Jews are passed in preference to good Frenchmen. . . . To understand my classmate's indignation we must recognize that he had adopted in advance a certain idea of the Jew, of his nature and of his role in society. And to be able to decide that among twenty-six competitors who were more successful than himself, it was the Jew who robbed him of his place, he must a priori have given preference in the conduct of his life to reasoning based on passion. Far from experience producing his idea of the Jew, it was the latter which explained his experience. If the Jew did not exist, the anti-Semite would invent him. . . .

The anti-Semite has chosen hate because hate is a faith; at the outset he has chosen to devaluate words and reasons. How entirely at ease he feels as a result. How futile and frivolous discussions about the rights of the Jew appear to him. He has placed himself on other ground from the beginning. If out of courtesy he consents for a moment to defend his point of view, he lends himself but does not give himself. He tries simply to project his intuitive certainty onto the plane of discourse. I mentioned awhile back some remarks by anti-Semites, all of them absurd: "I hate Jews because they make servants insubordinate, because a Jewish furrier robbed me, etc." Never believe that anti-Semites are completely unaware of the absurdity of their replies. They know that their remarks are frivolous, open to challenge. But they are amusing themselves, for it is their adversary who is obliged to use words responsibly, since he believes in words. The anti-Semites have the *right* to play. They even like to play with discourse for, by giving ridiculous reasons, they discredit the seriousness of their interlocutors. They delight in acting in bad faith, since they seek not to persuade by sound argument but to intimidate and disconcert. If you press them too closely, they will abruptly fall silent, loftily indicating by some phrase that the time for argument is past. It is not that they are afraid of being convinced. They fear only to appear ridiculous or to prejudice by their embarrassment their hope of winning over some third person to their side.

If then, as we have been able to observe, [10] the anti-Semite is impervious to reason and to experience, it is not because his conviction is strong. Rather his conviction is strong because he has chosen first of all to be impervious.

He has chosen also to be terrifying. People are afraid of irritating him. No one knows to what lengths the aberrations of his passion will carry him — but he knows, for this passion is not provoked by something external. He has it well in hand; it is obedient to his will: now he lets go the reins and now he pulls back on them. He is not afraid of himself, but he sees in the eyes of others a disquieting image — his own — and he makes his words and gestures conform to it. . . .

The anti-Semite readily admits that the Jew is intelligent and hard-working; he will even confess himself inferior in these respects. This concession costs him nothing, for he has, as it were, put those qualities in parentheses. Or rather they derive their value from the one who possesses them: the more virtues the Jew has the more dangerous he will be. The anti-Semite has no illusions about what he is. He considers himself an average man, modestly average, basically mediocre. There is no example of an anti-Semite's claiming individual superiority over the Jews. But

you must not think that he is ashamed of his mediocrity; he takes pleasure in it; I will even assert that he has chosen it. This man fears every kind of solitariness, that of the genius as much as that of the murderer; he is the man of the crowd. However small his stature, he takes every precaution to make it smaller, lest he stand out from the herd and find himself face to face with himself. He has made himself an anti-Semite because that is something one cannot be alone. The phrase, "I hate the Jews," is one that is uttered in chorus; in pronouncing it, one attaches himself to a tradition and to a community — the tradition and community of the mediocre.

We must remember that a man is not necessarily humble or even modest because he has consented to mediocrity. On the contrary, there is a passionate pride among the mediocre, and anti-Semitism is an attempt to give value to mediocrity as such, to create an elite of the ordinary. . . .

Besides this, many anti-Semites — the majority, perhaps — belong to the lower middle class of the towns; they are functionaries, office workers, small businessmen, who possess nothing. It is in opposing themselves to the Jew that they suddenly become conscious of being proprietors: in representing the Jew as a robber, they put themselves in the enviable position of people who could be robbed. Since the Jew wishes to take France from them, it follows that France must belong to them. Thus they have chosen anti-Semitism as a means of establishing their status as possessors. . . .

By treating the Jew as an inferior and per- [15] nicious being, I affirm at the same time that I belong to the elite. This elite, in contrast to those of modern times which are based on merit or labor, closely resembles an aristocracy of birth. There is nothing I have to do to merit my superiority, and neither can I lose it. It is given once and for all. It is a *thing*. . . .

Whatever [the anti-Semite] does, he knows that he will remain at the top of the ladder; whatever the Jew does, he will never get any higher than the first rung.

We begin to perceive the meaning of the anti-Semite's choice of himself. He chooses the irremediable out of fear of being free; he chooses mediocrity out of fear of being alone, and out of pride he makes of this irremediable mediocrity a rigid aristocracy. To this end he finds the existence of the Jew absolutely necessary. Otherwise to whom would he be superior? Indeed, it is vis-à-vis the Jew and the Jew alone that the anti-Semite realizes that he has rights. If by some miracle all the Jews were exterminated as he wishes, he would find himself nothing but a concierge or a shopkeeper in a strongly hierarchical society in which the quality of "true Frenchman" would be at a low valuation, because everyone would possess it. He would lose his sense of rights over the country because no one would any longer contest them, and that profound equality which brings him close to the nobleman and the man of wealth would disappear all of a sudden, for it is primarily negative. His frustrations, which he has attributed to the disloyal competition of the Jew, would have to be imputed to some other cause, lest he be forced to look within himself. He would run the risk of falling into bitterness, into a melancholy hatred of the privileged classes. Thus the anti-Semite is in the unhappy position of having a vital need for the very enemy he wishes to destroy. . . .

We are now in a position to understand the anti-Semite. He is a man who is afraid. Not of the Jews, to be sure, but of himself, of his own consciousness, of his liberty, of his instincts, of his responsibilities, of solitariness, of change, of society, and of the world — of everything except the Jews. He is a coward who does not want to admit his cowardice to himself; a murderer who represses and censures his tendency to murder without being able to hold it back, yet who dares to kill only in effigy or protected by the anonymity of the mob; a malcontent who dares not revolt from fear of the consequences of his rebellion. In espousing anti-Semitism, he does not simply adopt an opinion, he chooses himself as a person. He chooses the permanence and impenetrability of stone, the total irresponsibility of the warrior who obeys his leaders — and he has no leader. He chooses to acquire nothing, to deserve nothing; he assumes that everything is given him as his birthright — and he is not noble. He chooses finally a Good that is fixed once and for all, beyond question, out of reach; he dares not examine it for fear of being led to challenge it and having to seek it in another form. The Jew only serves him as a pretext; elsewhere his counterpart will make use of the Negro or the man of yellow skin. The existence of the Jew merely permits the anti-Semite to stifle his anxieties at their inception by persuading himself that his place in the world has been marked out in advance, that it awaits him, and that tradition gives him the right to occupy it. Anti-Semitism, in short, is fear of the human condition. The anti-Semite is a man who wishes to be pitiless stone, a furious torrent, a devastating thunderbolt — anything except a man.

Topics for Critical Thinking and Writing

1. Early in the essay, Jean-Paul Sartre examines how anti-Semitism can be a feature even of a good person's character. What, to him, is the source of such anti-Semitism? Is the individual responsible for his own views on the Jews? Explain.

2. Reread paragraphs 5 and 6 and explain why Sartre views anti-Semitism as a form of "hysteria."

3. Use ideas, examples, and evidence from the text to explain Sartre's claim, "If the Jew did not exist, the anti-Semite would invent him" (para. 8). What benefits does the anti-Semite derive from these attitudes about Jews?

4. Explain what Sartre means by "the passionate pride among the mediocre" (para. 13) and discuss how this type of pride relates to conformity. Do you see the passionate pride of the mediocre operating today? Explain.

5. Sartre remarks that anti-Semites "know that their remarks are frivolous" but nevertheless, they "have the *right* to play" (para. 9). Define the term "white privilege" — especially as the concept is understood in our society today — and then compare it to anti-Semitism. Are the terms similar in character, or are they different? Explain.

6. In the final paragraph of this selection, Sartre compares anti-Semitism to the nature of racism elsewhere against "the Negro or the man of yellow skin." These words — "Negro" and "yellow skin" — are today considered to be offensive terms in the United States. Do you think Sartre's argument is undermined by his own use of the words? Explain.

HANS MASSAQUOI

Hans Massaquoi (1926–2013) was a German of African descent (his mother was German; his father Liberian) who grew up in Hamburg, Germany, during the rise and reign of the Nazi Party. Although he was not Aryan by Hitler's definition of the term, Massaquoi was German-born and non-Jewish, and thus his family managed to remain German citizens despite the increasing persecutions against nonwhite "others." However, after the 1936 Olympic Games in Berlin, where African American athlete Jesse Owens embarrassed Hitler by winning four gold medals over his German opponents, Black people in Germany became increasingly targeted by the regime. Massaquoi was forced into an apprenticeship and labor during World War II; shortly after the war, he immigrated to the United States. He served in the Korean War and then studied journalism at the University of Illinois at Urbana-Champaign, eventually becoming a writer at *Jet* magazine and editor of *Ebony* magazine, both lifestyle magazines created specifically for Black audiences. Massaquoi's autobiography, *Destined to Witness: Growing Up Black in Nazi Germany*, was published in 1999. This selection, reprinted in *Lapham's Quarterly* in 2015, is from that work.

Destined to Witness

With arch-Nazi Principal Wriede at the helm, my school aggressively pursued the indoctrination and recruitment of young souls for the *Jungvolk*, the Hitler Youth's junior league for ten- to thirteen-year-olds, whose members were known as *Pimpfe* [cubs].

Hardly a day went by without our being reminded by our teachers or Wriede himself that for a German boy, life outside the movement was no life at all. Pursuing his objective with characteristic single-mindedness, Wriede was tireless in thinking up new gimmicks to further his goal. One day, he announced his latest brainchild, a school-wide contest in which the first class to reach 100 percent *Jungvolk* membership would be rewarded with a holiday.

The immediate effect of the announcement was that my new homeroom teacher, Herr Schürmann, became obsessed with the idea of winning the coveted prize for our class and some brownie points for himself. Toward that end, he became a veritable pitchman, who spent much of his — and our — time trying to persuade, cajole, or otherwise induce our class to join the Nazi fold. The centerpiece of his recruitment drive was a large chart he had carefully drawn on the blackboard with white chalk. It consisted of a large box divided into as many squares as there were boys in the class. Each morning, Herr Schürmann would inquire who had joined the Hitler Youth. After a show of hands, he would count them, then gleefully add the new enlistees' names to his chart. Gradually the squares with names increased until they outnumbered the blank ones.

Up to that point I had followed the contest with a certain degree of emotional detachment because quite a few of my classmates, including some of my closest pals, had let it be known that they had no interest in anything the Hitler Youth did and would not join, no matter what Wriede or Schürmann had to say. That suited me fine since I, too, had no intention of joining. But under the relentless pressure from Schürmann, one resister after another caved in and joined.

One morning, when the empty squares had dwindled to just a few, Herr Schürmann started querying the holdouts as to the reasons for their "lack of love for Führer and *Vaterland*." Some explained that they had nothing against Führer and *Vaterland* but weren't particularly interested in the kinds of things the *Jungvolk* were doing, such as camping, marching, blowing bugles and fanfares, and beating on medieval-style drums. Others said they didn't have their parents' permission, whereupon Herr Schürmann instructed them to bring their parents in for a conference. When it came to what I thought was my turn to explain, I opened my mouth, but Herr Schürmann cut me off. "That's all right; you are exempted from the contest since you are ineligible to join the *Jungvolk*."

The teacher's words struck me like a bolt 5 of lightning. Not eligible to join? What was he talking about? I had been prepared to tell him that I hadn't quite made up my mind whether I wanted to join or not. Now he was telling me that, even if I wanted to, I couldn't. Noticing my bewildered expression, Herr Schürmann told me to see him immediately after class.

Until the bell rang, I remained in a state of shock, unable to follow anything that was said. I felt betrayed and abandoned by my friends and terrified at the prospect of being the only person in class whose name would not appear on the chart. At age ten, I was as tough as any of my peers, able to take just about anything they dished out in the course of rough-and-tumble schoolboy play. What I couldn't take, however, was feeling that I didn't belong — being treated like an outcast, being told, in effect, that I was not only different but inferior.

Schürmann invited me to take a seat beside his desk. "I always thought you knew that you could not join the *Jungvolk* because you are non-Aryan," he began. "You know your father is an African. Under the Nuremberg Laws, non-Aryans are not allowed to become members of the Hitler Youth movement." Charitably, perhaps to spare at least some of my feelings, he omitted the much maligned and despised Jews from his roster of ineligibles.

"But I am a German," I sobbed, my eyes filling with tears. "My mother says I'm German just like anybody else."

"You *are* a German boy," Herr Schürmann conceded with unusual compassion, "but unfortunately not quite like anybody else."

Having gotten his point only too well, I made no further plea. 10

"I'm very sorry, my boy," Schürmann concluded the conference. "I wish I could help you, but there's nothing I can do; it's the law."

That evening, when I saw my mother, I didn't tell her what had transpired in school. Instead, I asked her to come with me to the nearest *Jungvolk Heim*, the neighborhood *Jungvolk* den just one block up the street, so I could join. Since I had never expressed the slightest interest in joining the Hitler Youth, she had never felt it necessary to burden me with the thought that I would be rejected. Thus, my sudden decision to join took her completely by surprise. When she tried to talk me out of it, even hinting that there was a possibility of my not being accepted, I grew frantic. I told her that I simply had to join since I could not be the only one in my class who was not a member. But she still didn't think it was a good idea. "Please take me," I pleaded, almost hysterically. "Maybe they'll make an exception. Please!"

Against her better judgment, my mother finally relented and agreed to do whatever she could to help me join. When we arrived at the *Jungvolk Heim*, a long, solidly built, one-story stone structure, the place was buzzing with activities and paramilitary commandos. Through the open door of a classroom-like meeting room, I could see a group of boys, most of them about my age, huddled around a long table, apparently listening to a troop leader's lecture. They wore neat uniforms, black shorts, black tunics over khaki shirts, and black scarfs that were held together at the neck by braided leather knots. Most of them, I noticed with envy, wore the small black *Dolch* [dagger] with the rhombus-shaped swastika

emblem of the Hitler Youth. Ever since seeing it displayed in the window of a neighborhood uniform store, I had secretly coveted this largely ceremonial weapon. Even the words *Blut und Ehre* [blood and honor] that were engraved on its shiny blade, and whose symbolic meaning had totally eluded me, stirred my soul. I knew that once my membership had been approved, nothing would stand in the way of my becoming a proud owner of a Hitler Youth *Dolch*. I wanted it so much, I could almost feel it in my hand.

After one *Pimpf* spotted me, I immediately became the subject of snickers and giggles until the troop leader, annoyed by the distraction, shouted "*Rube* [Quiet]!" and closed the door. When my mother asked a passing *Pimpf* to show us to the person in charge, he clicked his heels, then pointed to a door with the sign HEIMFÜHRER. Upon my mother's knock, a penetrating male voice shouted, "Enter!"

"*Heil Hitler!* What can I do for you?" asked 15 the handsome, roughly twenty-year-old man in the uniform of a mid-level Hitler Youth leader who was seated behind a desk.

My mother returned the mandatory Nazi salute, then asked, "Is this the right place to apply for membership?"

The young man looked incredulous. "Membership for whom? For *him*?" he inquired, his eyes studying me as if they had spied a repulsive worm.

"Yes, for my son," my mother responded without flinching.

The Nazi recoiled. "I must ask you to leave at once," he commanded. "Since it hasn't occurred to you by now, I have to tell you that there is no place for your son in this organization or in the Germany we are about to build. *Heil Hitler!*" Having said that, he rose and pointedly opened the door.

For a moment I thought my mother 20 would strike the man with her fist. She was trembling and glaring at him with an anger I had never before seen in her eyes. But she quickly regained her composure, took me by the hand, and calmly said, "Let's go." Neither she nor I spoke a word on the way back home. I felt guilty for having been the cause of her anguish and humiliation, and I was afraid she would be angry. Instead, when we reached our apartment, she just hugged me and cried. "I'm so sorry, I'm so sorry," was all she could say.

Seeing my mother like this was more than I could bear. "Please don't cry, *Mutti*," I pleaded while tears were streaming down my cheeks. It was a rare occurrence, since usually we outdid each other in keeping our hurt to ourselves. We were Germans, after all.

Topics for Critical Thinking and Writing

1. What explains Hans Massaquoi's initial reluctance and then growing interest in becoming part of the *Jungvolk* group at his school? Refer to the text in your explanation.

2. Explore the conundrum of Massaquoi's teacher who apologizes to him by saying, "I wish I could help you, but there's nothing I can do; it's the law" (para. 11). How, in our own time, is the law used to define and exclude "others"?

3. Do some research and write about the purpose and the activities of the *Jungvolk*. Why was it established? How did it contribute to the ideologies of the Nazis?

4. Examine the final paragraph of the selection and tell why the last sentence is effective.

5. Write a brief essay in which you integrate Massaquoi's experience with Sartre's theories in "Anti-Semite and Jew." How do the authorities in Massaquoi's piece reflect Sartre's ideas about racism?

6. In the United States, there are many organizations and groups that children can join for fun, leisure, and community. Select one and discuss the nature of its activities and its underlying principles. What values does the organization teach through its activities? Is it open, or does it exclude any class of people? Would you call your selected organization or group "ideological" — that is, committed to indoctrinating children into a particular belief system? If so, is it for good or ill? Explain.

W. E. B. DU BOIS

William Edward Burghardt Du Bois (1868–1963) was born in Great Barrington, Massachusetts, was educated at Fisk University, and was the first Black person to earn a doctorate degree from Harvard University. He held fellowships and appointments at the University of Berlin, Wilberforce College, and the University of Pennsylvania. Du Bois wrote his first book, *The Philadelphia Negro*, in 1899. It was the first systematic study of urban conditions for African Americans and one of the first examples of sociology as a modern social science. In 1903, he published *The Souls of Black Folk* and became a prominent voice in American social thought. Du Bois was highly critical of the most well-regarded Black American social theorist at the time, Booker T. Washington. Where Washington argued for a program of economic advancement for Black people through industrial education and gradual change, Du Bois argued strenuously for traditional liberal arts education and immediate reformation of laws disadvantaging the racial group. In 1905, along with other Black activists, Du Bois started the Niagara Movement, and in 1909, he was among a handful of leaders who established the National Association for the Advancement of Colored People (NAACP). He became the editor of *The Crisis*, the official magazine of the NAACP. In the 1950s, Du Bois's socialist sympathies, internationalism, and peace activism put him squarely in the sights of the US government's anticommunist campaign, and he was indicted and put on trial in 1951 for refusing to register as a communist under new, restrictive laws in the United States intended to quash communist subversion. Incensed by the US Supreme Court's decision in 1961 to uphold the McCarran Act, a piece of anticommunist legislation, Du Bois moved to Ghana, where he was given a state funeral following his death in 1963. The following selection is the first chapter of *The Souls of Black Folk* (1903).

Of Our Spiritual Strivings

O water, voice of my heart, crying in the sand,
All night long crying with a mournful cry,
As I lie and listen, and cannot understand
The voice of my heart in my side or the
*   voice of the sea,*
O water, crying for rest, is it I, is it I?
All night long the water is crying to me.

Unresting water, there shall never be rest
Till the last moon droop and the last tide
*   fail,*
And the fire of the end begin to burn in the
*   west;*
And the heart shall be weary and wonder
*   and cry like the sea,*
All life long crying without avail,
As the water all night long is crying to me.
                    —ARTHUR SYMONS

Between me and the other world there is ever an unasked question: unasked by some through feelings of delicacy; by others through the difficulty of rightly framing it. All, nevertheless, flutter round it. They approach me in a half-hesitant sort of way, eye me curiously or compassionately, and then, instead of saying directly, How does it feel to be a problem? they say, I know an excellent colored man in my town; or, I fought at Mechanicsville; or, Do not these Southern outrages make your blood boil? At these I smile, or am interested, or reduce the boiling to a simmer, as the occasion may require. To the real question, How does it feel to be a problem? I answer seldom a word.

And yet, being a problem is a strange experience, — peculiar even for one who has never been anything else, save perhaps in babyhood and in Europe. It is in the early days of rollicking boyhood that the revelation first bursts upon one, all in a day, as it were. I remember well when the shadow swept across me. I was a little thing, away up in the hills of New England, where the dark Housatonic winds between Hoosac and Taghkanic to the sea. In a wee wooden schoolhouse, something put it into the boys' and girls' heads to buy gorgeous visiting-cards — ten cents a package — and exchange. The exchange was merry, till one girl, a tall newcomer, refused my card, — refused it peremptorily, with a glance. Then it dawned upon me with a certain suddenness that I was different from the others; or like, mayhap, in heart and life and longing, but shut out from their world by a vast veil. I had thereafter no desire to tear down that veil, to creep through; I held all beyond it in common contempt, and lived above it in a region of blue sky and great wandering shadows. That sky was bluest when I could beat my mates at examination-time, or beat them at a foot-race, or even beat their stringy heads. Alas, with the years all this fine contempt began to fade; for the worlds I longed for, and all their dazzling opportunities, were theirs, not mine. But they should not keep these prizes, I said; some, all, I would wrest from them. Just how I would do it I could never decide: by reading law, by healing the sick, by telling the wonderful tales that swam in my head, — some way. With other black boys the strife was not so fiercely sunny: their youth shrunk into tasteless sycophancy, or into silent hatred of the pale world about them and mocking distrust of everything white; or wasted itself in a bitter cry, Why did God make me an outcast and a stranger in mine own house? The shades of the prison-house closed round about us all: walls strait and stubborn to the whitest, but relentlessly narrow, tall, and unscalable to sons of night who must plod darkly on in resignation, or beat unavailing palms against the stone, or steadily, half hopelessly, watch the streak of blue above.

After the Egyptian and Indian, the Greek and Roman, the Teuton and Mongolian, the Negro is a sort of seventh son, born with a veil, and gifted with second-sight in this American world, — a world which yields him no true self-consciousness, but only lets him see himself through the revelation of the other world. It is a peculiar sensation, this double-consciousness, this sense of always looking at one's self through the eyes of others, of measuring one's soul by the tape of a world that looks on in amused contempt and pity. One ever feels his two-ness, — an American, a Negro; two souls, two thoughts, two unreconciled strivings; two warring ideals in one dark body, whose dogged strength alone keeps it from being torn asunder.

The history of the American Negro is the history of this strife, — this longing to attain self-conscious manhood, to merge his double self into a better and truer self. In this merging he wishes neither of the older selves to be lost. He would not Africanize America, for America has too much to teach the world and Africa. He would not bleach his Negro soul in a flood of white Americanism, for he knows that Negro blood has a message for the world. He simply wishes to make it possible for a man to be both a Negro and an American, without being cursed and spit upon by his fellows, without having the doors of Opportunity closed roughly in his face.

This, then, is the end of his striving: to 5 be a co-worker in the kingdom of culture, to escape both death and isolation, to husband and use his best powers and his latent genius. These powers of body and mind have in the past been strangely wasted, dispersed, or forgotten. The shadow of a mighty Negro past flits through the tale of Ethiopia the Shadowy and of Egypt the Sphinx. Throughout history, the powers of single black men flash here and there like falling stars, and die sometimes before the world has rightly gauged their brightness. Here in America, in the few days since Emancipation, the black man's turning hither and thither in hesitant and doubtful striving has often made his very strength to lose effectiveness, to seem like absence of power, like weakness. And yet it is not weakness, — it is the contradiction of double aims. The double-aimed struggle of the black artisan — on the one hand to escape white contempt for a nation of mere hewers of wood and drawers of water, and on the other hand to plough and nail and dig for a poverty-stricken horde — could only result in making him a poor craftsman, for he had but half a heart in either cause. By the poverty and ignorance of his people, the Negro minister or doctor was tempted toward quackery and demagogy; and by the criticism of the other world, toward ideals that made him ashamed of his lowly tasks. The would-be black *savant* was confronted by the paradox that the knowledge his people needed was a twice-told tale to his white neighbors, while the knowledge which would teach the white world was Greek to his own flesh and blood. The innate love of harmony and beauty that set the ruder souls of his people a-dancing and a-singing raised but confusion and doubt in the soul of the black artist; for the beauty revealed to him was the soul-beauty of a race which his larger audience despised, and he could not articulate the message of another people. This waste of double aims, this seeking to satisfy two unreconciled ideals, has wrought sad havoc with the courage and faith and deeds of ten thousand thousand people, — has sent them often wooing false gods and invoking false means of salvation, and at times has even seemed about to make them ashamed of themselves.

Away back in the days of bondage they thought to see in one divine event the end of all doubt and disappointment; few men ever worshipped Freedom with half such unquestioning faith as did the American Negro for two centuries. To him, so far as he thought and dreamed, slavery was indeed the sum of all villainies, the cause of all sorrow, the root of all prejudice; Emancipation was the key to a promised land of sweeter beauty than ever stretched before the eyes of wearied Israelites. In song and exhortation swelled one refrain — Liberty; in his tears and curses the God he implored had Freedom in his right hand. At last it came, — suddenly, fearfully, like a dream. With one wild carnival of blood and passion came the message in his own plaintive cadences:—

> "Shout, O children!
>   Shout, you're free!
>   For God has bought your liberty!"

Years have passed away since then, — ten, twenty, forty; forty years of national life, forty years of renewal and development, and yet the swarthy spectre sits in its accustomed seat at the Nation's feast. In vain do we cry to this our vastest social problem:—

> "Take any shape but that, and my firm nerves
>   Shall never tremble!"

The Nation has not yet found peace from its sins; the freedman has not yet found in freedom his promised land. Whatever of good may have come in these years of change, the shadow of a deep disappointment rests upon the Negro people, — a disappointment all the more bitter because the unattained ideal was unbounded save by the simple ignorance of a lowly people.

The first decade was merely a prolongation of the vain search for freedom, the boon that seemed ever barely to elude their grasp, — like a tantalizing will-o'-the-wisp, maddening and misleading the headless host. The holocaust of war, the terrors of the Ku-Klux Klan, the lies of carpet-baggers, the disorganization of industry, and the contradictory advice of friends and foes, left the bewildered serf with no new watchword beyond the old cry for freedom. As the time flew, however, he began to grasp a new idea. The ideal of liberty demanded for its attainment powerful means, and these the Fifteenth Amendment gave him. The ballot, which before he had looked upon as a visible sign of freedom, he now regarded as the chief means of gaining and perfecting the liberty with which war had partially endowed him. And why not? Had not votes made war and emancipated millions? Had not votes enfranchised the freedmen? Was anything impossible to a power that had done all this? A million black men started with renewed zeal to vote themselves into the kingdom. So the decade flew away, the revolution of 1876 came, and left the half-free serf weary, wondering, but still inspired. Slowly but steadily, in the following years, a new vision began gradually to replace the dream of political power, — a powerful movement, the rise of another ideal to guide the unguided, another pillar of fire by night after a clouded day. It was the ideal of "book-learning"; the curiosity, born of compulsory ignorance, to know and test the power of the cabalistic letters of the white man, the longing to know. Here at last seemed to have been discovered the mountain path to Canaan; longer than the highway of Emancipation and law, steep and rugged, but straight, leading to heights high enough to overlook life.

Up the new path the advance guard toiled, 10 slowly, heavily, doggedly; only those who have watched and guided the faltering feet, the misty minds, the dull understandings, of the dark pupils of these schools know how faithfully, how piteously, this people strove to learn. It was weary work. The cold statistician wrote down the inches of progress here and there, noted also where here and there a foot had slipped or someone had fallen. To the tired climbers, the horizon was ever dark, the mists were often cold, the Canaan was always dim and far away. If, however, the vistas disclosed as yet no goal, no resting-place, little but flattery and criticism, the journey at least gave leisure for reflection and self-examination; it changed the child of Emancipation to the youth with dawning self-consciousness, self-realization, self-respect. In those sombre forests of his striving his own soul rose before him, and he saw himself, — darkly as through a veil; and yet he saw in himself some faint revelation of his power, of his mission. He began to have a dim feeling that, to attain his place in the world, he must be himself, and not another. For the first time he sought to analyze the burden he bore upon his back, that dead-weight of social degradation partially masked behind a half-named Negro problem. He felt his poverty; without a cent, without a home, without land, tools, or savings, he had entered into competition with rich, landed, skilled neighbors. To be a poor man is hard, but to be a poor race in a land of dollars is the very bottom of hardships. He felt the weight of his ignorance, — not simply of letters, but of life, of business, of the humanities; the accumulated sloth and shirking and awkwardness of decades and centuries shackled his hands and feet. Nor was his burden all poverty and ignorance. The red stain of bastardy, which two centuries of systematic legal defilement of Negro women had stamped upon his race, meant not only the loss of ancient African chastity, but also the hereditary weight of a mass of corruption from white adulterers, threatening almost the obliteration of the Negro home.

A people thus handicapped ought not to be asked to race with the world, but rather allowed to give all its time and thought to its own social problems. But alas! while sociologists gleefully count his bastards and his prostitutes, the very soul of the toiling, sweating black man is darkened by the shadow of a vast despair. Men call the shadow prejudice, and learnedly explain it as the natural defence of culture against barbarism, learning against ignorance, purity against crime, the "higher" against the "lower" races. To which the Negro cries Amen! and swears that to so much of this strange prejudice as is founded on just homage to civilization, culture, righteousness, and progress, he humbly bows and meekly does obeisance. But before that nameless prejudice that leaps beyond all this he stands helpless, dismayed, and well-nigh speechless; before that personal disrespect and mockery, the ridicule and systematic humiliation, the distortion of fact and wanton license of fancy, the cynical ignoring of the better and the boisterous welcoming of the worse, the all-pervading desire to inculcate disdain for everything black, from Toussaint to the devil, — before this there rises a sickening despair that would disarm and discourage any nation save that black host to whom "discouragement" is an unwritten word.

But the facing of so vast a prejudice could not but bring the inevitable self-questioning, self-disparagement, and lowering of ideals which ever accompany repression and breed in an atmosphere of contempt and hate. Whisperings and portents came borne upon the four winds: Lo! we are diseased and dying, cried the dark hosts; we cannot write, our voting is vain; what need of education, since we must always cook and serve? And the Nation echoed and enforced this self-criticism, saying: Be content to be servants, and nothing more; what need of higher culture for half-men? Away with the black man's ballot, by force or fraud, — and behold the suicide of a race! Nevertheless, out of the evil came something of good, — the more careful adjustment of education to real life, the clearer perception of the Negroes' social responsibilities, and the sobering realization of the meaning of progress.

So dawned the time of *Sturm und Drang*: storm and stress today rocks our little boat on the mad waters of the world-sea; there is within and without the sound of conflict, the burning of body and rending of soul; inspiration strives with doubt, and faith with vain questionings. The bright ideals of the past, — physical freedom, political power, the training of brains and the training of hands, — all these in turn have waxed and waned, until even the last grows dim and overcast. Are they all wrong, — all false? No, not that, but each alone was over-simple and incomplete, — the dreams of a credulous race-childhood, or the fond imaginings of the other world which does not know and does not want to know our power. To be really true, all these ideals must be melted and welded into one. The training of the schools we need today more than ever, — the training of deft hands, quick eyes and ears, and above all the broader, deeper, higher culture of gifted minds and pure hearts. The power of the ballot we need in sheer self-defence, — else what shall save us from a second slavery? Freedom, too, the long-sought, we still seek, — the freedom of life and limb, the freedom to work and think, the freedom to love and aspire. Work, culture, liberty, — all these we need, not singly but together, not successively but together, each growing and aiding each, and all striving toward that vaster ideal that swims before the Negro people, the ideal of human brotherhood, gained through the unifying ideal of Race; the ideal of fostering and developing the traits and talents of the Negro, not in opposition to or contempt for other races, but rather in large conformity to the greater ideals of the American Republic, in order that some day on American soil two world-races may give each to each those characteristics both so sadly lack. We the darker ones come even now not altogether empty-handed: there are today no truer exponents of the pure human spirit of the Declaration of Independence than the American Negroes; there is no true American music but the wild sweet melodies of the Negro slave; the American fairy tales and folk-lore are Indian and African; and, all in all, we black men seem the sole oasis of simple faith and reverence in a dusty desert of dollars and smartness. Will America be poorer if she replace her brutal dyspeptic blundering with light-hearted but determined Negro humility? or her coarse and cruel wit with loving jovial good-humor? or her vulgar music with the soul of the Sorrow Songs?[1]

---

[1]**Sorrow Songs** Music originating among African slaves, especially slave spirituals. [Editors' note]

Merely a concrete test of the underlying principles of the great republic is the Negro Problem, and the spiritual striving of the freedmen's sons is the travail of souls whose burden is almost beyond the measure of their strength, but who bear it in the name of an historic race, in the name of this the land of their fathers' fathers, and in the name of human opportunity.

And now what I have briefly sketched 15 in large outline let me on coming pages tell again in many ways, with loving emphasis and deeper detail, that men may listen to the striving in the souls of black folk.

Topics for Critical Thinking and Writing

1. In paragraph 2, Du Bois juxtaposes his own ambitions with those of "other black boys" whose "youth shrunk into tasteless sycophancy, or into silent hatred of the pale world about them . . . or wasted itself in a bitter cry." How would you characterize these three responses?

2. In paragraph 3, Du Bois coins the phrase "double-consciousness, this sense of always looking at one's self through the eyes of others." Describe what he means in relation to the experience of being African American at the time. Then attempt to apply your concept of double-consciousness to a group or class of people today, and examine whether or not individuals of that group or class may see and evaluate themselves "through the eyes of others."

3. Examine the dilemma of the Black artist outlined by Du Bois in paragraph 5. Explain what Du Bois means in this paragraph and also discuss whether or not you think it applies in the present day.

4. Why do you think Du Bois delves into the history of Africans in America in paragraphs 6 through 10? How does this background help his argument?

5. Write a brief analysis of Du Bois's use of metaphor and poetic language in making his argument. Is it an effective strategy for his argument? Why or why not?

6. In paragraph 11, Du Bois writes that people often "learnedly explain it [prejudice] as the natural defence of culture against barbarism, learning against ignorance, purity against crime, the 'higher' against the 'lower' races. To which the Negro cries Amen!" How might it happen that an oppressed group comes to agree with forms of prejudice against its own members? Can people be taught to hate themselves? Explain.

BRIDGET ANDERSON

Bridget Anderson is director of the University of Bristol Institute on Migration and Mobility Studies in Bristol, England. With her doctorate in sociology, she has produced a formidable body of interdisciplinary research on immigration, citizenship, and economics, including more than a dozen book chapters, six edited books, twenty journal articles, and two authored books, *Doing the Dirty Work? The Global Politics of Domestic Labour* (2000), and *Us and Them? The Dangerous Politics of Immigration Controls* (2013). The piece below was excerpted from an article published in *Social Research*, a scholarly journal, in 2017.

The Politics of Pests: Immigration and the Invasive Other

The United Nations High Commissioner for Refugees (UNHCR) estimates that more than one million people crossed into Europe by sea in 2015. At least 3,700 of those attempting to enter drowned. The vast majority of these travellers were from the world's top 10 refugee-producing countries, including Syria, Iraq, and Afghanistan. Like the apocryphal story about the Haitian slave revolutionaries who greeted the repressive French army by singing "La Marseillaise," so some people walking along the motorways of Hungary and Austria were carrying the European flag, as if to say "We share your respect for justice, freedom, and human rights, and here we are! We belong!"

This situation was labelled a "crisis," and the responses were schizophrenic. Widespread "Refugees Are Welcome" demonstrations were met with nationalist counterdemonstrations and fire-bombings. As autumn arrived amidst mutual recriminations of xenophobia and hypocrisy, Europe rebordered: checkpoints were instituted between Austria and Germany, Italy and France, Sweden and Denmark, Croatia and Austria, Macedonia and Greece. Thus the crisis brought into question not only the principles of asylum and free movement within the European Union, but also Europe's very idea of itself as a space of liberal values, freedom, moral equality, and human rights. As well as a migration crisis confronting Europe, what started to unfold was a *European* crisis confronting migrants: a multidimensional crisis of solidarity between member states, many of which are struggling with austerity and rapidly diminishing state capacity. This crisis was effectively called out by migration (Kriss 2015).

The media coverage of these events and their consequences reflected these tensions. Hostility toward mobile people, concerns about security, and demands on resources collided with the unavoidably human face of catastrophe, and for a time negative responses were mitigated by the photograph of drowned toddler Alan Kurdi. This contradiction was encapsulated in an editorial in *The Times* of January 21, 2016: "compassion is the right response but unconditional welcome is the wrong way to express it."

The relation between media coverage, policy, and public opinion is highly complicated, particularly in cases that are depicted as some kind of "crisis." Press coverage is not a neutral mirror of public opinion, nor does it simply shape public attitudes — news organizations are businesses, concerned with building relationships with their readers rather than challenging their views. The relation between media, public attitudes, and policymaking is complex and mutually constitutive, and there is a growing interest in this triangular relation in the case of how migration and asylum are covered (Matthews and Brown 2012). This question has received more attention post-2015, and there continues to be considerable debate about the role of the media in the representation of migrants/refugees, and its relation to public opinion. . . .

The use of imagery and metaphor of natural disasters permeates the coverage of migration. The particular ways in which migrants are portrayed offer insights into the nature of popular anxieties about the foreigner as invasive other and clues as to the political responses that can help to counter these anxieties. One metaphoric trope that has emerged as particularly powerful in the coverage of the 2015 events is the migrant as invasive insect, a metaphor that has been deployed by politicians as well as press commentators and reporters. . . .

However, metaphors are at their most effective when they are surreptitious and uncontested — not when they are applauded or called out, but when they pass unremarked into our language, when they shift from simile to metaphor suggesting the horror lurking beneath reason. In the press, migrants routinely scurry, scuttle, sneak, and they often swarm, too. Migrants are invaders, but invasion usually suggests a state or at least an authority that controls the invasion. In the case of migrants this invasion is a force of nature, of war without sovereignty and of agency without individuality.

ANIMAL MAGIC

Metaphors matter. "They are figures of thought as much as they are figures of speech" (Steuter and Wills 2008, 7), or to paraphrase Otto Santa Ana (1999), they do not simply color the poetic but shape the prosaic. They are a crucial element in the structuring of our conceptual systems, providing cognitive frames that make issues understandable. They bridge the gap between logic and emotion, exposing and shaping our feelings and responses and acting as both expression and legitimation (Mio 1997).

The comparison of foreigners and outsiders with animals has a long history. Noncitizens and those regarded as outsiders or subhuman have been called animal names, treated like animals, and forced to behave like animals. This has contemporary twists — in 2013, the Tripoli Zoo was turned into an immigration detention center — but it is not new. In Ancient Greece, Herodotus compares slaves to cattle, while more recently in the American South, slaves were commonly equated with domestic animals — oxen, hogs, calves, and colts (Jacoby 1994). Santa Ana analyzed the coverage in the *Los Angeles Times* of the referendum on Proposition 187 and found the key metaphor discerned to be "immigrants are animals" (1999), while O'Brien (2003) describes the metaphors deployed during the immigration debate in the United States of the early twentieth century, showing that the immigrant as invader and as animal were even then common tropes. O'Brien's analysis finds that in contrast to the depiction of slaves — who were imagined as beasts of burden to be whipped, branded, and controlled — migrants, whose entry must be controlled, are compared to "parasites or 'low animals' capable of infection and contamination" (243). Similarly, those seeking to enter Europe are not depicted as beasts or brutes but as vermin, forms of nonvital life, low down on the animal phyla.

Rats, cockroaches, and insects are urban — they are not considered wild animals. Unlike beasts of burden, these are not perceived as productive animals. They are alive but not perceived as truly sentient. Considered more closely, there are three interrelated connotations of invasive vermin that are of relevance to anxieties about asylum: waste, numbers, and threats to the home. . . .

Vermin are ubiquitous, and cockroaches, 10 rats, and "swarms" are everywhere indigenous. The horror is not simply that the "sneaky little creatures" do not respect borders or boundaries. They are not invasive of a *territorial* space.[1] What vermin are invasive of is the civilized space of the home. Thus comparing migrants to insects and vermin invokes what Walters (2010) has called "domopolitics," the aspiration to govern the state like a *home*. Indeed, Merkel's policy has been dubbed

---

[1] The Israeli army has opened small tunnels in the separation wall to allow migration, in part because of the separation of animal families caused by the wall (http://www.dw.com/en /israeli-army-opens-west-bank-barrier-for-animals/a-16351700). This of course is not deemed necessary for vermin like rats who live on both sides of the wall.

her "open door" policy and is in contrast to Cameron's stance that we need to stop migrants "breaking into Britain," both metaphors associated with the home. The home is our place, the space where "we" are native. In recent years in Europe there has been a striking resurgence of language of nativity and indigeneity. . . .

When they are in the home, insects must be dealt with, and while "exterminate all the brutes" is not acceptable, "exterminate all the bugs" is. Indeed, this is the solution to an infestation of pests. The lives of insects do not matter — they are not "grievable" (Butler 2009). Indeed, the relation between the development of pesticides for agricultural and domestic use and chemical technologies for the mass killing of humans has been well documented. During the Second World War, for example, the German chemical company IG Farben bought the patent for Zyklon B, which was used in the extermination camps of the Holocaust. Its original use was as an insecticide, and it had previously been licensed for delousing Mexican migrants to the United States in the 1930s.

There is no proposal to exterminate people at the borders of Europe (though Katie Hopkins' piece titled "Rescue Boats? I'd Use Gunships to Stop Migrants" came perilously close). However, "letting die" is a different matter. . . .

The etymological origin of "exterminate" is to put beyond the boundary or the frontier. The question is: where shall they be removed to? What to do with Bauman's "human waste," the "collateral casualties of progress" (Bauman 2003, 15)? . . .

Perhaps we can look to metaphor for political inspiration, for ways of reframing the relationship between embedded citizens and mobile populations. Teiko Tomita was a Japanese woman who came to the United States in 1921. Throughout her life she wrote beautiful *tanka*, a particular form of Japanese short poetry, expressing her struggles and hopes. When her poetry was published as part of a collection of Issei poetry, she entitled her section "Tsugiki," meaning "graft" or "grafted tree," a depiction of her and her children's relation to their lives in the United States (Nomura 2005).

> Carefully grafting
>
> Young cherry trees
>
> I believe in the certainty
>
> They will bud
>
> In the coming spring
>
> (Teiko Tomita)

REFERENCES

Bauman, Z. 2003. *Wasted Lives: Modernity and Its Outcasts*. Oxford: Wiley.

Butler, Judith. 2009. *Frames of War: When Is Life Grievable?* London: Verso.

Hopkins, Katie. 2015. "Rescue Boats? I'd Use Gunships to Stop Migrants." *The Sun*, April 17.

Jacoby, Karl. 1994. "Slaves by Nature? Domestic Animals and Human Slaves." *Slavery & Abolition* 15 (1): 89–99.

Kriss, Sam. 2015. "Building Norway: A Critique of Slavoj Žižek." https://samkriss.wordpress.com/2015/09/11/building-norway-a-critique-of-slavoj-zizek/.

Matthews, J., and A. R. Brown. 2012. "Negatively Shaping the Asylum Agenda? The Representational Strategy and Impact of a Tabloid News Campaign." *Journalism Criticism, Theory and Practice* 13 (6): 802–17. http://jou.sagepub.com/content/13/6/802.

Mio, J. S. 1997. "Metaphor and Politics." *Metaphor and Symbol* 12 (2): 113–33.

Nomura, Gail M. 2005. "Tsugiki, a Grafting: The Life and Poetry of a Japanese Pioneer Woman in Washington." *Columbia Magazine*, Spring, 19:1.

O'Brien, G. 2003. "Indigestible Food, Conquering Hordes and Waste Materials: Metaphors of Immigrants and the Early Immigration Restriction Debate in the United States." *Metaphor & Symbol* 18 (1): 33–47.

Santa Anna, Otto. 1999. " 'Like an Animal I Was Treated': Anti-immigrant Metaphor in US Public Discourse." *Discourse & Society* 10 (2): 191–224.

Steuter, Erin, and Deborah Wills. 2008. *At War with Metaphor: Media, Propaganda, and Racism in the War on Terror*. Plymouth: Lexington Books.

The Times. 2016. "Reality Check: Expecting European Union States to Accept Refugee Quotas Is Wishful Thinking. Brussels Must Focus on its External Borders and on the Territories Beyond." Editorial, January 21. http://www.thetimes.co.uk/article /reality-check-c7t930g5j7g.

Walters, William. 2010. "Secure Borders, Safe Haven, Domopolitics." *Citizenship Studies* 8 (3): 237–60.

Topics for Critical Thinking and Writing

1. In paragraph 3, Bridget Anderson refers to "hostility toward mobile people." Do you think, in general, that people have negative attitudes toward mobile people? Provide an example of a mobile population and examine the challenges they encounter.

2. Describe Anderson's understanding of the relationship between media portrayals of immigrants and public opinion about immigrants. Then consider the ways some group — an immigrant or a minoritized group, in any place or time — was affected by the way that group was portrayed in the media. What do you think is the best way to counteract stereotypical or misleading representations of people?

3. Paragraph 7 begins with a claim, "Metaphors matter." Think of some instances in the United States today in which a metaphor or figurative language is used to describe a group or class of people. What is suggested by the language — that is, what feelings are associated with the words used? What do you think are the consequences of such language use?

4. Construct two definitions of "civil disobedience" and explain whether and to what extent it is easier (or harder) to justify civil disobedience, depending on how you have defined the expression.

5. Imagine that someone your age from Syria, Iraq, or Afghanistan were moving into your hometown or starting classes at your school. Write a letter to the imagined person telling them what to expect, what to look forward to, and what to look out for.

6. In a previous selection, W. E. B. Du Bois, writing about a typical African American man, says that he would not want to "Africanize America," but neither would he wish to "bleach his Negro soul in a flood of white Americanism." Consider this idea from the perspective of immigrants to the United States: Should they be expected to "assimilate" by ridding themselves of the language and customs of their culture, or should they be appreciated for bringing more diversity to the nation?

JOHN BARTH

John Barth (b. 1930) is an American novelist decorated with numerous major writing awards and honors, including three nominations for the National Book Award for his novels *The Floating Opera* (1956), *Lost in the Funhouse* (1968), and *Chimera* (1972), the last of which shared the prize. The author of over twenty books and story collections, Barth is recognized as one of the most important postmodern literary writers, whose experiments in style and form expanded the boundaries of creative expression in the twentieth century. Some of his theories are present in the landmark essays "The Literature of Exhaustion" (1967) and "The Literature of Replenishment" (1980), both considered manifestos of postmodern literature. Barth is also a literary scholar who taught at Penn State University, SUNY–Buffalo, Boston University, and Johns Hopkins University. His latest books include *Every Third Thought: A Novel in Five Seasons* (2011) and an anthology of stories, *Collected Stories* (2015). The short story included here is from *The Development* (2008), a collection of nine interlocking stories set in a fictional Chesapeake Bay gated community, Heron Bay Estates.

Us/Them

To his wife, his old comrades at the *Avon County News*, or his acquaintances from over at the College, Gerry Frank might say, for example, "Flaubert once claimed that what he'd *really* like to write is a novel about Nothing." In his regular feature column, however — in the small-town weekly newspaper of a still largely rural Maryland county — it would have to read something like this:

> FRANK OPINIONS, by Gerald Frank
> Us/Them
>
> The celebrated 19th-century French novelist Gustave Flaubert, author of *Madame Bovary,* once remarked that what he would *really* like to write is a novel about Nothing.

After which he might acknowledge that the same was looking to be the case with this week's column, although its authors still hoped to make it not quite about Nothing, but rather ("as the celebrated Elizabethan poet/playwright William Shakespeare put it in the title of one of his comedies") about Much *Ado* About Nothing.

There: That should work as a lead, a hook, a kick-start from which the next sentences and paragraphs will flow (pardon Gerry's mixed metaphor) — and voilà, another "Frank Opinions" column to be e-mailed after lunch to Editor Tom Chadwick at the *News* and put to bed for the week.

But they *don't* come, those next sentences — *haven't* come, now, for the third work-morning in a row — for the ever-clearer reason that their semiretired would-be author hasn't figured out yet what he wants to write about, namely: Us(slash)Them. *In Frank's opinion,* he now types experimentally in his column's characteristic third-person viewpoint, *what he needs is a meaningful connection between the "Us/Them" theme, much on his mind lately for reasons presently to be explained, and either or all of (1) a troubling disconnection, or anyhow an increasing distinction/difference/ whatever, between, on this side of that slash, him and his wife — Gerald and Joan Frank, 14 Shad Run Road #212, Heron Bay Estates, Stratford, MD 21600 — and on its other side their pleasant gated community in general*

and their Shad Run condominium neighbor-
hood in particular; (2) his recently increasing
difficulty — after so many productive decades
of newspaper work! — in coming up with fresh
ideas for the F.O. column; and/or (3) the irre-
sistible parallel to his growing (shrinking?)
erectile dysfunction [but never mind *that* as a
column topic!].

Maybe fill in some background, to
mark time while waiting for the Muse of
Feature Columns to get off her ever-lazier
butt and down to business? Gerry Frank
here, Reader-if-this-gets-written: erstwhile
journalist, not quite seventy but getting there
fast. Born and raised in a small town near the
banks of the Potomac in southern Maryland
in World War Two time, where and when
the most ubiquitous Us/Them had been Us
White Folks as distinct from Them Coloreds,
until supplanted after Pearl Harbor by Us
Allies versus Them Japs and Nazis (note the
difference between that "versus" and the earlier, more ambivalent "as distinct from," a
difference to which we may return). Crossed
the Chesapeake after high school to Stratford
College, on the Free State's Eastern Shore (B.A.
English 1957), then shifted north to New Jersey
for the next quarter century to do reportage
and editorial work for the *Trenton Times*;
also to marry his back-home sweetheart,
make babies and help parent them, learn a
few life lessons the hard way while doubtless
failing to learn some others, and eventually —
at age fifty, when those offspring were off to
college themselves and learning their own life
lessons — to divorce (irreconcilable differences). Had the immeasurably good fortune
the very next year, at a Stratford homecoming,
to meet alumna Joan Gibson (B.A. English
1967), herself likewise between life chapters
just then (forty, divorced, no children, copy-
editing for her hometown newspaper, the
Wilmington [Delaware] *News Journal).* So

hit it off together from Day (and Night) One
that after just a couple more dates they were
spending every weekend together in her town
or his, or back in the Stratford to which they
shared a fond attachment — and whereto, not
long after their marriage in the following year,
they moved: Gerry to associate-edit the *Avon
County News* and Joan ditto the College's
alumni magazine, *The Stratfordian.*

And some fifteen years later here they are, s
happy with each other and grateful to have
been spared not only direct involvement in
the nation's several bloody wars during their
life-decades, but also such personal catastro-
phes as loss of children, untimely death of
parents or siblings, and devastating accident, disease, or other extraordinary misfortune. Their connection with Gerry's pair of
thirty-something children, Joan's elder and
younger siblings, and associated spouses and
offspring is warm, though geographically
attenuated (one couple in Oregon, another
in Texas, others in Vermont and Alabama).
Husband and wife much enjoy each other's
company, their work, their modest TINK
prosperity (Two Incomes, No [dependent]
Kids), and their leisure activities: hiking,
wintertime workouts in the Heron Bay Club's
well-equipped fitness center and summertime
swimming in its Olympic-size pool, vacation
travel to other countries back in more U.S.-
friendly times, and here and there in North
America since 9/11 and (in Gerald Frank's
Frank Opinion) the Bush administration's
Iraq War fiasco (U.S./"Them"?). Also their,
uh . . . friends?

Well: No F.O. column yet in any of *that,*
that Gerry can see. While typing on from pure
professional habit, however, he perpends that
paragraph-ending word above, flanked by
suspension points before and question mark
after: something to circle back to, maybe, after
avoiding it for a while longer by reviewing

some other senses of that slash dividing Us from Them. Peter Simpson, a fellow they know from Rockfish Reach who teaches at the College and (like Joan Frank) serves on the Heron Bay Estates Community Association, did a good job of that at one of HBECA's recent open meetings, the main agenda item whereof was a proposed hefty assessment for upgrading the development's entrance gates. As most readers of "Frank Opinions" know, we are for better or worse the only gated community in Avon County, perhaps the only one on Maryland's Eastern Shore. Just off the state highway a few miles south of Stratford, Heron Bay Estates is bounded on two irregular sides by branching tidal tributaries of the Matahannock River (Heron and Spartina Creeks, Rockfish and Oyster Coves, Blue Crab Bight, Shad Run), on a third side by a wooded preserve of pines, hemlocks, and sweet gums screening a sturdy chain-link fence, and on its highway side by a seven-foot-high masonry wall atop an attractively landscaped berm, effectively screening the development from both highway noise and casual view. Midway along this side is our entrance road, Heron Bay Boulevard, accessed via a round-the-clock manned gatehouse with two exit lanes on one side, their gates raised and lowered automatically by electric eye, and two gated entry lanes on the other: one on the left for service vehicles and visitors, who must register with the gatekeeper and display temporary entrance passes on their dashboards, and one on the right for residents and nonresident Club members, whose cars have HBE decals annually affixed to their windshields. So successful has the development been that in the twenty-odd years since its initial layout it has grown to be the county's second-largest residential entity after the small town of Stratford itself — with the consequence that homeward-bound residents these days not infrequently find themselves backed up four or five cars deep while the busy gatekeepers simultaneously check in visitors in one lane and look for resident decals in the other before pushing the lift-gate button. Taking their cue from the various E-Z Pass devices commonly employed nowadays at bridge and highway toll booths, the developers, Tidewater Communities, Inc., suggested to the Association that an economical alternative to a second gatehouse farther down the highway side (which would require expensive construction, an additional entrance road, and more 24/7 staffing) would be a third entry lane at the present gatehouse, its gate to be triggered automatically by electronic scansion of a bar-code decal on each resident vehicle's left rear window.

Most of the Association members and other attendees, Joan and Gerry Frank included, thought this a practical and economical fix to the entrance-backup problem, and when put to the seven members for a vote (one representative from each of HBE's neighborhoods plus one at-large tie-breaker), the motion passed by a margin of six to one. In the pre-vote open discussion, however, objections to it were raised from diametrically opposed viewpoints. On the one hand, Mark Matthews from Spartina Pointe — the recentest member of the Association, whose new weekend-and-vacation home in that high-end neighborhood was probably the grandest residence in all of Heron Bay Estates — declared that in view of HBE's ongoing development (controversial luxury condominiums proposed for the far end of the preserve), what we need is not only that automatic bar-code lane at the Heron Bar Boulevard entrance, but the afore-mentioned second gated entrance at the south end of the highway wall as well, and perhaps a third for service and employee vehicles only, to be routed discreetly through the wooded preserve itself.

In the bluff, down-home manner to which he inclined, even as CEO of a Baltimore investment-counseling firm, "Way it is now," that bald and portly, flush-faced fellow complained, "we get waked up at six a.m. by the groundskeepers and golf course maintenance guys reporting for work with the radios booming in their rusty old Chevys and pickups, *woomf woomf woomf,* y'know? Half of 'em undocumented aliens, quote unquote, but never mind *that* if it keeps the costs down. And then when we-all that live here come back from wherever, the sign inside the entrance says Welcome Home, but our welcome is a six-car backup at the gate, like crossing the Bay Bridge without an E-Z Pass. I say we deserve better'n that."

"Hear hear!" somebody cheered from the back of the Community Association's open-meeting room: Joe Barnes, I think it was, from Rockfish Reach. But my wife, at her end of the members' table up front, objected: "Easy to say if you don't mind a fifty percent assessment hike to build and staff those extra entrances! But I suspect that many of us will feel the pinch to finance just that automatic third entry lane at the gatehouse — which I'm personally all for, but nothing beyond that unless *it* gets backed up."

A number of her fellow members nodded 10 agreement, and one of them added, "As for the racket, we just need to tell the gatekeepers and the maintenance foremen to be stricter about the no-loud-noise rule for service people checking in."

Mark Matthews made a little show of closing his eyes and shaking his head no. The room in general, however, murmured approval. Which perhaps encouraged Amanda Todd — a friend of Joan's and an Association member from Blue Crab Bight — to surprise us all by saying "Gates and more gates! What do we need *any* of them for, including the ones we've got already?"

Mild consternation in the audience and among her fellow members, turning to relieved amusement when Joan teased, "Because we're a gated community?" But "Really," Ms. Todd persisted, "those TCI ads for Heron Bay are downright embarrassing, with their 'exclusive luxury lifestyles' and such. Even to call this place Heron Bay *Estates* is embarrassing, if you ask me. But then to have to pass through customs every time we come and go, and phone the gatehouse whenever we're expecting a visitor! Plus the secondary nighttime gates at some of our neighborhood entrances, like Oyster Cove, and those push-button driveway gates in Spartina Pointe . . . Three gates to pass through, in an area where crime is practically nonexistent!"

"Don't forget the garage door opener," Mark Matthews reminded her sarcastically. "That makes *four* entrances for some of us, even before we unlock the house door. Mindy and I are all for it."

"Hear hear!" his ally called again from the back of the room, where someone else reminded all hands that we weren't *entirely* crime-free: "Remember that Peeping Tom a few years back? Slipped past the main gatehouse and our Oyster Cove night gates too, that we don't use anymore like we did back then, and we never did catch him. But still . . ."

"You're proving my point," Amanda argued. 15 Whereupon her husband — the writer George Newett, also from the College — came to her support by quoting the Psalmist: "Lift up your heads, O ye gates! Even lift them up, ye everlasting doors, and the King of Glory shall come in!"

"Amen," she said appreciatively. "And *leave* 'em lifted, I say, like those ones at Oyster Cove. No other development around here has gates. Why should we?"

"Because we're *us,*" somebody offered, "with a community pool and tennis courts and bike paths that aren't for public use. If you like the other kind, maybe you should move to one of *them*."

Mark Matthews seconded that suggestion with a pleased head-nod. But "All I'm saying," Ms. Todd persisted, less assertively, "— as Robert Frost puts it in one of his poems? — is, quote, 'Before I built a wall, I'd ask to know what I was walling in and walling out, and to whom I'm likely to give offense,' end of quote. Somebody just mentioned *us* and *them:* Who exactly is the Them that all these walls and gates are keeping out?"

To lighten things a bit, I volunteered, "That Them is Us, Amanda, waiting at the gate until we get our Heron Bay E-Z Pass gizmo up and running. Shall we put it to a vote?"

"Not quite yet, Gerry," said Peter Simpson — 20 also from the College, as has been mentioned, and chairman of the Association as well as its member from Rockfish Reach. "Let's be sure that everybody's had his/her say on the matter. Including myself for a minute, if I may?"

Nobody objected. A trim and affable fellow in his fifties, Pete is popular as well as respected both in the Association and on campus, where he's some sort of dean as well as a professor. "I'll try not to lecture," he promised with a smile. "I just want to say that while I understand where both Mark and Amanda are coming from, my own inclination, like Joan's, is to proceed incrementally, starting with the bar-code scanner gate and hoping that'll do the trick, for a few years anyhow." He pushed up his rimless specs. "What's really on my mind, though, now that it's come up, is this Us-slash-Them business. We have to accept that some of us, like Amanda, live here because they like the place *despite* its being a gated community, while others of us, like Mark, live here in part precisely *because* it's gated, especially if they're not fulltime residents. The great

majority of us, I'd bet, either don't *mind* the gate thing (except when it gets backed up!) or sort of like the little extra privacy, the way we appreciate our routine security patrols even though we're lucky enough not to live near a high-crime area. It's another Heron Bay amenity, like our landscaping and our golf course. What we need to watch out for (and here comes the lecture I promised I'd spare you) is when that slash between Us and Them moves from being a simple distinction — like Us Rockfish Reach residents and Them Oyster Cove or Spartina Pointers, or Us Marylanders and Them Pennsylvanians and Delawareans — and becomes Us not merely *distinct* from Them, but more or less *superior* to Them, as has all too often been the case historically with whites and blacks, or rich and poor, or for that matter men and women."

Up with the glasses again. Mark Matthews rolled his eyes, but most present seemed interested in Pete's argument. "At its worst," he went on, "that slash between Us and Them comes to mean Us *versus* Them, as in race riots and revolutions and wars in general. But even here it's worth remembering that *versus* doesn't always necessarily mean inherently superior: It can be like Us versus Them in team sports, or the Yeas versus the Nays in a debating club, or some of the town/gown issues at the College that we try to mediate without claiming that either side is *superior* to the other."

Here he took the glasses off, as if to signal that the sermon was approaching its close. "I'm sure I'm not alone in saying that some of Debbie's and my closest friends live outside these gates of ours."

"Amen," Joan said on his behalf. After which, and apologizing again for nattering on so, Pete called for a vote authorizing the Association to solicit bids and award a contract for construction of an automatically gated HBE Pass third lane at our development's entrance. When the motion passed, six to one, Amanda Todd good-naturedly reminded Mark Matthews, the lone dissenter, that "Us versus You doesn't mean we don't love you, Mark." To which that broad-beamed but narrow-minded fellow retorted, "You College people, I swear."

"Objection!" Amanda's husband called out. 25

"Sustained," declared Peter Simpson, rising from his chair and gathering the spec sheets and other papers spread out before him. "No need to pursue it, and thank you all for coming and making your opinions known." Offering his hand to Matthews then, with a smile, "Here's to democracy, Mark, and parliamentary procedure. Agreed?"

"Whatever."

And that had been that, for then. But en route back along sycamore-lined Heron Bay Boulevard to our condominium in "Shad Row," as we like to call it (punning on that seasonal Chesapeake delicacy), we Franks had tsked and sighed at Mark Matthews's overbearing small-mindedness versus Pete Simpson's more generous spirit and eminently reasonable review of the several senses of Us/Them. "Like when people born and raised in Stratford talk about 'us locals' and 'them c'meres,'" Joan said, using the former's term for out-of-towners who "come here" to retire or to enjoy a second home. "Sometimes it's a putdown, sometimes it's just a more or less neutral distinction, depending."

"And even when it's a putdown," her husband agreed, "sometimes it's just a good-humored tease between friends or neighbors — unlike Lady Broad-Ass's Us/Thems in our condo sessions," he added, referring to his Shad Run Condominium Association colleague Rachel Broadus, a hefty and opinionated widow-lady who, two years ago, had vehemently opposed the sale of unit

117 to an openly gay late-middle-aged couple from D.C., early retired from careers in the federal government's General Services Administration — even letting the prospective buyers know by anonymous letter that while it was beyond the Association's authority to forbid the sale, homosexuals were not welcome in Heron Bay Estates. A majority of the Association shared her feelings and had been relieved when the offended couple withdrew their purchase offer, although most agreed with Gerry that the unsigned letter was reprehensible; he alone had spoken on the pair's behalf, or at least had opposed the opposition to them. When in the following year Ms. Broadus had similarly inveighed against the sale of unit 218 to a dapper Indian-American pharmacist and his wife ("Next thing you know it'll be Mexicans and blacks, and there goes the neighborhood"), he'd had more company in objecting to her objection, and the Raghavans had come to be well liked by nearly all of their neighbors. "Even so," Gerry now reminded his wife, "Broad-Ass couldn't resist saying 'Mind you, Ger, I don't have anything against a nice Jewish couple like you and Joan. But *Hindus*?'"

Joan groaned at the recollection — who on 30 first hearing from Gerry of this misattribution had said, "You should've showed your foreskinned shlong already. Oy." Or, they'd agreed, he could have quoted the Irish-American songwriter George M. Cohan's reply to a resort-hotel desk clerk in the 1920s who refused him a room, citing the establishment's ban on Jewish guests: "You thought I was a Jew," said the composer of "The Yankee Doodle Boy," "and I thought you were a gentleman. We were both mistaken." Rachel Broadus, they supposed, had heard of Anne Frank and had readily generalized from that famed Holocaust victim's last name, perhaps pretending even to herself that the Them to which she assigned the Shad Run Franks was not meant pejoratively. It was easy to imagine her declaring that "some of her best friends," et cetera. Gerry himself had used that edged cliché, in quotes — "Some of Our Best Friends . . ." — as the heading of a "Frank Opinions" column applauding the progress of Stratford's middle-class African Americans from near invisibility to active representation on the Town Council, the Avon County School Board, and the faculties not only of the local public schools but of the College and the private Fenton Day School as well.

All the above, however, is past history: the HBECA lift-gate meeting and us Franks' return to Shad Run Road for a merlot nightcap on our second-story porch overlooking the moonlit creek (where no shad have been known to run during our residency) before the ten o'clock TV news, bedtime, and another flaccid semi-fuck, Gerry's "Jimmy" less than fully erect and Joan's "Susie" less than wetly welcoming. "Never mind that pair of old farts," Joan had sighed, kissing him goodnight before turning away to sleep: "They're Them; we're still Us." Whoever *that's* getting to be, he'd said to himself — for he really has, since virtual retirement, been ever more preoccupied with his approaching old age and his inevitable, already noticeable decline. To her, however, he wondered merely, "D'you suppose they're trying to tell us something?"

"Whatever it is," she answered sleepily, "don't put it in the column, okay?"

The column: Past history too is his nattering on about all the above to his computer for four work-mornings already, and now a fifth, in search of a "Frank Opinions" piece about all this Us/Them stuff. By now he has moved on from Joan's "Us Franks" as distinct from "Them body parts of ours," or the singular "I-Gerry/Thou-'Jimmy,' " to Gerry's-Mind/Gerry's-Body and thence (within the former) to Gerry's-Ego/Gerry's-Id+Superego, and

while mulling these several Us/Thems and I/Thous of the concept Mind, he has duly noted that although such distinctions are *made* by our minds, it by no means follows that they're "all in our minds."

Blah blah blah: Won't readers of the *Avon County News* be thrilled to hear it?

Yet another Us/Them now occurs to him (just what he needed!): It's a standing levity in Heron Bay Estates that most of its male inhabitants happen to be called familiarly by one-syllable first names and their wives by two-: Mark and Mindy Matthews, Joe and Judy Barnes, Pete and Debbie Simpson, Dave and Lisa Bergman, Dick and Susan Felton — the list goes on. But while we Franks, perhaps by reflex, are occasionally fitted to this peculiar template ("Ger" and "Joanie"), we're normally called Gerry and Joan, in exception to the rule: an Us distinct from, though not opposed to, its Them.

So? So nothing. Has Gerald "Gerry" Frank mentioned his having noticed, years ago, that his normal pulse rate matches almost exactly the tick of seconds on his watch dial, so closely that he can measure less-than-a-minute intervals by his heartbeat? And that therefore, as of his recent sixty-eighth birthday, he had lived for 24,837 days (including 17 leap days) at an average rate of 1,400 pulses per day, or a total of 34,771,800, give or take a few thousand for periods of physical exertion or unusual quiescence? By which same calculation he reckons himself to have been mulling these who-gives-a-shit Us/Thems for some 7,200 heartbeats' worth of days now, approaching beat by beat not only his ultimate demise but, more immediately, Tom Chadwick's deadline, and feeling no closer to a column than he did five days ago.

Maybe a column about that? Lame idea.

Tick. Tick. Tick. Tick. Tick.

He believes he did mention, a few thousand pulses past, that the Shad Run Franks, while on entirely cordial terms with their workmates and with ninety-nine percent of their fellow Heron Bay Estaters, have no *friends*, really, if by friends one means people whom one enjoys having over for drinks and dinner or going out with to a restaurant, not to mention actually vacation-traveling together, as they see some of their neighbors doing. They used to have friends like that, separately in their pre-Us lives and together in the earliest, pre-Stratford period of their marriage. Over the years since, however, for whatever reasons, their social life has atrophied: annual visits to and from their far-flung family, lunch with a colleague now and then (although they both work mainly at home these days), the occasional office cocktail party or HBE community social — that's about it. They don't particularly *approve* of this state of affairs, mildly wish it were otherwise, but have come to accept, more or less, that outside the workplace that's who they are, or have become: more comfortable with just Us than with Them.

As if his busy fingers have a mind of their own, *To be quite frank, Reader,* he now sees appearing on his computer screen, *old Gerry hasn't been being quite Frank with you about certain things. E.g.:* 40

— He and his mate share another, very different and entirely secret life, the revelation whereof would scandalize all Stratford and Heron Bay Estates, not to mention their family.

— Or they *don't,* of course, but could sometimes half wish they did, just for the hell of it.

— Or they *don't* so wish or even half wish, for God's sake! Who does this nutcase columnist take us for, that he could even *imagine* either of them so wishing?

— Or he has just learned that the precious, the indispensable Other Half of our Us has been diagnosed with . . . oh, advanced, inoperable pancreatic cancer? While *he* sits scared shitless on his butt counting his heartbeats, her killer cells busily metastasize through that dearest of bodies. Maybe a dozen thousand ever-more-wretched tick-ticks to go, at most, until The End — of her, therefore of Us, therefore of him.

— Or he's just making all this crap up. Trying it out. Thinking the unthinkable, perhaps in vain hope of its exorcism, or at least forestallment. But such tomfoolery fools no one. While his right hand types *no one,* his left rummages in a "drawer of the adjacent inkjet-printer stand for the reassuring feel of the loaded nine-millimeter-automatic pistol that he keeps in there for "self-defense": i.e., for defending Joan and Gerry Frank yet a while longer from murder/suicide — which they agree they'd resort to in any such scenario as that terminal-cancer one above-invoked — by reminding himself that they have the means and the will to do it, if and when the time comes. 45

But they don't — have the means, at least; at least not by gunfire. There is no pistol, never has been; we Franks aren't the gun-owning sort. Should push come to shove *chez nous,* in our frank opinion we'd go the route that Dick and Susan Felton went last year: double suicide (nobody knows why) by automobile exhaust fumes in the closed garage of their empty-nest house in Rockfish Reach, with not even a goodbye note to their traumatized, life-disrupted offspring.

Well, we guess we'd leave a note.

Maybe this is it?

Nah. Still . . .

Deadline a-coming: Tick. Tick. 50

Deathline? Tick.

FRANK OPINIONS: Us/Them

or

Much Ado About

Topics for Critical Thinking and Writing

1. What do you think is the point of distinguishing at the start of the story the differences between how Gerald Frank would speak to his friends compared to his audience? What does the difference tell you?

2. John Barth is famous for his language games and unique grammar and syntax. Locate three moments in the story that were most unique to you. What effect did the language have on you?

3. Examine some of the self/other dualities in Barth's story and extrapolate how groups define and divide themselves through the processes of inclusion and exclusion. Draw on any of the theories of "othering" from other selections in this chapter to assist in your description.

4. When Barth published "Us/Them," he was eighty-eight years old. Discuss the significance of the author's age, the age of the characters, and your own experience living and reading this story. Is there an "us/them" division — an othering process — at work between the young and old in the United States today? Explain.

5. Examine your own neighborhood, town, or school, and attempt to understand how the people who are "insiders" (neighbors, residents, or students) define themselves against "others." Describe the dynamic: Is it hostile or friendly, part of a long tradition or something new, something at the forefront of awareness or more subtle? Now, describe an experience you had in encountering the other. What was it like? What did you learn — about yourself or about the other, or about the othering process?

6. Consider the "edged cliché" (para. 30) commonly used by people insisting that they do not disparage the other because "some of my best friends are X." Is it possible to have prejudice or bias against a racial, cultural, or ethnic group despite having "friends" who are of that origin? Explain.

JACOB RIIS

Jacob Riis (1849–1914) was a social reformer, journalist, and photographer who emigrated to the United States from Denmark in 1870 in one of the first waves of European immigration that brought around 12 million people to the country in the following three decades. After working as a carpenter, miner, and farmhand in western Pennsylvania and New York, Riis moved to New York City, where he trained as a journalist and eventually became the city editor of the *New York Tribune*. Riis, having lived among the swelling immigrant communities in lower Manhattan, witnessed the abject poverty and dire living conditions in the tenements of New York City where, according to one report, more than 335,000 people were crammed into a single square mile on the Lower East Side, making it the most densely populated place in the world. Conditions in the tenements — or slums — were abhorrent. Immigrants were packed into buildings whose interiors, modified to maximize the number of tenants, were often dark, dank, and disease-ridden, left to fester by mostly indifferent landlords who viewed the occupants as inferior races whose squalor was largely seen as their own responsibility. Riis became a crusader in exposing these conditions to the general public and working with other reformers to improve the conditions of the tenements. He was among the first Americans to use flash photography, and he included disturbing photographs of his subjects alongside the articles and books he wrote advocating for humanitarian responses to poverty in New York City. In 1890, he published his most famous work, *How the Other Half Lives*, a lurid account of tenement living conditions and an argument for philanthropic, legislative, and tax-based solutions to the public housing crisis. The images presented here are from that work.

Street Arabs in "sleeping quarters" [Original caption from *How the Other Half Lives* (1890)]

"Five Cents a Spot" — Lodgers in a crowded Bayard Street tenement

Topics for Critical Thinking and Writing

1. Explain how the first image of children sleeping an alley makes an argument. What kind of appeal does it make? To whom does it make the appeal?

2. It is known that Jacob Riis asked the boys in the first photograph to pose for this photograph. (Consider the similar concerns raised around the staged photograph "Home of a Rebel Sharpshooter" discussed in the section "Do Photographs Always Tell the Truth?" in Chapter 5, p. 163.) Do you think that the staging of these photographs undermines their integrity as a factual source? Why or why not?

3. Examine the second image, which shows lodgers who rented space in a tenement, and account for the denotative and connotative meanings of the elements within the frame (see the section "Seeing versus Looking" in Chapter 5, p. 153). How do the literal elements of the images communicate symbolic or figurative meanings?

4. An exposé is a type of representation that "exposes" a certain truth or reality to people who might not otherwise be aware of it. Think of an instance when photography has been used today to expose something. Was it effective? Explain your answer.

SIMONE DE BEAUVOIR

Simone de Beauvoir (1908–1986) was a French writer and philosopher whose work had a significant impact on feminist thought and social thought. Her dictum, "One is not born but becomes a woman," from her 1949 tome, *The Second Sex*, is one of the most quotable instances of the social constructionist perspective of gender development. She defined women as the second sex in a bivalent, or dualistic, symbolic system that relegated women to the status of "other." This symbolic system, spanning myth, language, and culture, resulted in the disenfranchisement of women in political, economic, and material realms. Her work is a foundational feminist tract and remains in print now seventy years since its initial publication. "The Woman as Other," excerpted below, is from *The Second Sex*.

The Woman as Other

Throughout history [women] have always been subordinated to men, and hence their dependency is not the result of a historical event or a social change—it was not something that *occurred*. The reason why otherness in this case seems to be an absolute is in part that it lacks the contingent or incidental nature of historical facts. A condition brought about at a certain time can be abolished at some other time, as the Negroes of Haiti and others have proved: but it might seem that natural condition is beyond the possibility of change. In truth, however, the nature of things is no more immutably given, once for all, than is historical reality. If woman seems to be the inessential which never becomes the essential, it is because she herself fails to bring about this change. Proletarians say "We"; Negroes also. Regarding themselves as subjects, they transform the bourgeois, the whites, into "others." But women do not say "We," except at some congress of feminists or similar formal demonstration; men say "women," and women use the same word in referring to themselves. . . . They have gained only what men have been willing to grant; they have taken nothing, they have only received.

The reason for this is that women lack concrete means for organizing themselves into a unit which can stand face to face with the correlative unit. . . . Male and female stand opposed within a primordial *Mitsein*,[1] and woman has not broken it. The couple is a fundamental unity with its two halves riveted together, and the cleavage of society along the line of sex is impossible. Here is to be found the basic trait of woman: she is the Other in a totality of which the two components are necessary to one another.

---

[1]*Mitsein* A concept developed by twentieth-century German philosopher Martin Heidegger meaning "being-with," or the essential characteristic of humanity that is the need to be with other humans, a social fact that influences our individual behavior.

Topics for Critical Thinking and Writing

1. Leading up to this passage, Simone de Beauvoir writes in *The Second Sex* that the category of the Other is "a fundamental category of human thought." If that is true — if otherness is a natural condition in human cultures — does it justify or excuse forms of devaluing other racial, cultural, or ethnic groups? Explain your response.

2. De Beauvoir wrote this piece in 1949. Do some research into the balance of rights and privileges of women, men, and nonbinary people during that time and explain if you agree with her that there was a condition of "male sovereignty."

3. Part of the problem with the empowerment of women, de Beauvoir suggests, is that women "do not say 'We' " (para. 1). What does she mean? How is the "We" spoken by other cultural and ethnic groups different from the ways women think of themselves collectively?

4. Research the concept of "intersectionality" and describe what challenges it poses to the notion of otherness as put forth by de Beauvoir.

5. Think of another group of people who do, or do not, have a strong sense of a collective "We." How did it develop or disintegrate — or was it ever present at all?

6. What are the benefits of unity within a group and what are the drawbacks? Explain using examples of more cohesive and less cohesive identity categories.

RUDYARD KIPLING

Rudyard Kipling (1865–1936) was an English journalist, poet, and writer of fiction. His most well-known work, *The Jungle Book* (1894), has been adapted in a wide variety of literature, music, and film, including the Walt Disney films of the same name. In his lifetime, Kipling was one of the most popular writers in the United Kingdom, publishing poems such as "Gunga Din" and "The White Man's Burden" in addition to short stories, children's books, travel books, military histories, and two autobiographies. In 1907, he won the Nobel Prize in Literature.

As an Englishman born in India, Kipling's work is suffused with Indian culture; as such, it has been criticized for representing India through the eyes of the colonialist. Indeed, Kipling's views were imperialistic. They accorded with attitudes of the time about the civilizing effects of empire — to many, a moral justification for exploitation in the colonies. In these views, natives of India were seen as backward, naïve, and almost childlike — beneficiaries, not victims, of colonization. This poem, "We and They," was published in 1926.

We and They

Father, Mother, and Me,
    Sister and Auntie say
All the people like us are We,
    And every one else is They.
And They live over the sea,   5
    While We live over the way,
But—would you believe it?—They look upon We
    As only a sort of They!

We eat pork and beef
    With cow-horn-handled knives.   10
They who gobble Their rice off a leaf,
    Are horrified out of Their lives;
While they who live up a tree,
    And feast on grubs and clay,
(Isn't it scandalous?) look upon We   15
    As a simply disgusting They!

We shoot birds with a gun.
    They stick lions with spears.
Their full-dress is un-.
    We dress up to Our ears.   20

They like Their friends for tea.
    We like Our friends to stay;
And, after all that, They look upon We
    As an utterly ignorant They!

We eat kitcheny food.   25
    We have doors that latch.
They drink milk or blood,
    Under an open thatch.
We have Doctors to fee.
    They have Wizards to pay.   30
And (impudent heathen!) They look upon We
    As a quite impossible They!

All good people agree,
    And all good people say,
All nice people, like Us, are We   35
    And every one else is They:
But if you cross over the sea,
    Instead of over the way,
You may end by (think of it!) looking on We
    As only a sort of They!   40

Topics for Critical Thinking and Writing

1. Do you think the "We" and "They" in this poem are presented equally and relatively, or is there an implied superiority in the speaker's words or tone? Using evidence from the poem, argue one way or the other.

2. In Chapter 5, we talked about accommodating, resisting, and negotiating the meanings of images. Apply those concepts to this poem: Determine what kind of approach to take and write an analysis in which you accommodate, resist, or negotiate the meaning of this poem.

3. Write about an practice in United States culture that "we" assume to be a typical, reasonable, right, or correct practice and then compare the practice of a different culture that "we" might (at least at first) consider to be inferior in some way. Now, assess the question of which practice is "better." What standards are you using? Do you have a basis for evaluating which is better or worse? What would an opponent say? How would you respond?

EMARI DIGIORGIO

Emari DiGiorgio is a poet and professor of writing at Stockton University. She is a Geraldine R. Dodge Foundation Poet and the author of two poetry collections, *The Things a Body Might Become* (2017) and *Girl Torpedo* (2018), which won the Numinous Orison, Luminous Origin Literary Award. DiGiorgio has received many poetry prizes including, in 2016, the Auburn Witness Poetry Prize and a New Jersey State Council on the Arts poetry fellowship. She is also the senior reviews editor for *Tupelo Quarterly*. In "The Brownest White Girl," DiGiorgio, an Italian American woman, explores the intersectional aspects of racial, ethnicity, and identity.

When You Are the Brownest White Girl

Someone will call you spic. And you won't
    know what to say
because you're a Ferrucci-DiGiorgio from the
    region of Molise

where olives become oil, and there are slurs
    for your kind, too:
Guinea, WOP, grease ball, so maybe, the sting
    is being slapped

with another's epithet. When you're the 5
    brownest white girl
at CCD, no one lets you play the Virgin Mary,
    even if you

look the most like her and have memorized all
    the prayers.
When you're the brownest white girl, you
    know you need

to run fast, leave their pink tongues flapping.
    Though you're

not as dark as the girl who just moved from 10
    Queens, or Javi

and Nando, and Keisha and Tasha have made
    it quite clear
that *you're a white girl, white girl*. Though
    someone tugs

at your kinky hair and says, *Mami, you got a
little black in you.*
And if there was, some big reveal on the
    Maury show, what

would it change? When you are the brownest 15
    white girl
at field day, you're a piñata and the blind-
    folded stick swinger.

One minute you use your hands to block their
    wild swings,
the next, you beg for your turn to beat on
    someone else.

Topics for Critical Thinking and Writing

1. Research the terms "intersectionality" and "intersectional identity." How do these conceptions challenge the We/They, Us/Them, Self/Other constructions? Explain your response.

2. Why do you think "fitting into" a racial category is important to the speaker in the poem?

3. Why do you think Emari DiGiorgio uses the piñata as an image in this poem? Is the usage ironic in any way? If yes, explain.

4. Have you ever been mistaken for a different identity group? If so, tell about the circumstances and how it made you feel. If not, what is it about you that made such an experience unlikely?

5. When the poet is told that she looks like she's "got a little black" in her (l. 13), she wonders — if she had, what would it change? Why do you think this is an important question for the poet?

28

What Is Happiness?

Thoughts about Happiness, Ancient and Modern

Here are some brief comments about happiness, from ancient times to the present. Read them, think about them, and then write on one of the two topics that appear after the last quotation.

Happiness is prosperity combined with virtue.   — ARISTOTLE (384–322 BCE)

The knowledge which you need to possess is, to know what you are; how you are created; whence you are; for what you are here; whither you are going; in what your happiness consists, and what you must do to secure it; in what your misery consists, and what you must do to avoid it.   — AL-GHAZALI (1058–1111)

Society can only be happy and free in proportion as it is virtuous.
                    — MARY WOLLSTONECRAFT SHELLEY (1759–1797)

The supreme happiness of life is the conviction that we are loved.   — VICTOR HUGO (1802–1885)

Ask yourself whether you are happy, and you cease to be so.   — JOHN STUART MILL (1806–1873)

Anguish and grief, like darkness and rain, may be described, but joy and gladness, like the rainbow of promise, defy alike the pen and pencil.   — FREDERICK DOUGLASS (1817–1895)

I have heard you intend to settle us on a reservation near the mountains. I don't want to settle. I love to roam over the prairies. There I feel free and happy, but when we settle down we grow pale and die.   —SATANTA (WHITE BEAR), KIOWA CHIEF (1820–1878)

A lifetime of happiness! No man alive could bear it: it would be hell on earth.
                    — GEORGE BERNARD SHAW (1856–1950)

If only we'd stop trying to be happy, we could have a pretty good time.

— EDITH WHARTON (1862–1937)

Happiness makes up in height for what it lacks in length.

— ROBERT FROST (1874–1963)

Point me out the happy man and I will point you out either egotism, selfishness, evil — or else an absolute ignorance.

— GRAHAM GREENE (1904–1991)

Those who are unhappy have no need for anything in this world but people capable of giving them their attention.

— SIMONE WEIL (1909–1943)

Happiness is always a by-product. It is probably a matter of temperament, and for anything I know it may be glandular. But it is not something that can be demanded from life, and if you are not happy you had better stop worrying about it and see what treasures you can pluck from your own brand of unhappiness.

— ROBERTSON DAVIES (1913–1995)

Don't wait around for other people to be happy for you. Any Happiness you get you've got to make yourself.

— ALICE WALKER

Topics for Critical Thinking and Writing

1. If any one of these passages especially appeals to you, make it the thesis of a brief essay.

2. Take two of these passages — perhaps one that you especially like and one that you think is wrong-headed — and write a dialogue in which the two authors converse. They may each try to convince the other, or they may find that to some degree they share views and they may then work out a statement that both can accept. If you do take the position that one writer is on the correct track but the other is utterly mistaken, try to be fair to the view that you think is mistaken. (As an experiment in critical thinking, imagine that you accept it and make the best case for it that you possibly can.)

HENRY DAVID THOREAU

Henry David Thoreau (1817–1862) was born in Concord, Massachusetts, where he spent most of his life ("I have travelled a good deal in Concord"). He taught and lectured, but chiefly he observed, thought, and wrote. From July 5, 1847, to September 6, 1847, he lived near Concord in a cabin at Walden Pond, an experience recorded in *Walden* (1854). He is also the author of the renowned essay "Resistance to Civil Government" (1849), sometimes called "Civil Disobedience," in which he forcefully argued against the institution of slavery with ideas later adopted by social reformers such as Mahatma Gandhi and Martin Luther King Jr.

This selection below, "As for Clothing" (the editors' title), comes from *Walden*, Chapter 1. "We Do Not Ride on the Railroad; It Rides upon Us" (also the editors' title) is from *Walden*, Chapter 2.

Selections from Walden

AS FOR CLOTHING

As for Clothing, to come at once to the practical part of the question, perhaps we are led oftener by the love of novelty and a regard for the opinions of men, in procuring it, than by a true utility. Let him who has work to do recollect that the object of clothing is, first, to retain the vital heat, and secondly, in this state of society, to cover nakedness, and he may judge how much of any necessary or important work may be accomplished without adding to his wardrobe. Kings and queens who wear a suit but once, though made by some tailor or dressmaker to their majesties, cannot know the comfort of wearing a suit that fits. They are no better than wooden horses to hang the clean clothes on. Every day our garments become more assimilated to ourselves, receiving the impress of the wearer's character, until we hesitate to lay them aside, without such delay and medical appliances and some such solemnity even as our bodies. No man ever stood the lower in my estimation for having a patch in his clothes; yet I am sure that there is greater anxiety, commonly, to have fashionable, or at least clean and unpatched clothes, than to have a sound conscience. But even if the rent is not mended, perhaps the worst vice betrayed is improvidence. I sometimes try my acquaintances by such tests as these, — Who could wear a patch, or two extra seams only, over the knee? Most have as if they believed that their prospects for life would be ruined if they should do it. It would be easier for them to hobble to town with a broken leg than with a broken pantaloon. Often if an accident happens to a gentleman's legs, they can be mended; but if a similar accident happens to the legs of his pantaloons, there is no help for it; for he considers, not what is truly respectable, but what is respected. We know but few men, a great many coats and breeches. Dress a scarecrow in your last shift, you standing shiftless by, who would not soonest salute the scarecrow? Passing a cornfield the other day, close by a hat and coat on a stake, I recognized the owner of the farm. He was only a little more weather-beaten than when I saw him last. I have heard of a dog that barked at every stranger who approached his master's premises with clothes on, but was easily quieted by a naked thief. It is an interesting question how far men would retain their relative rank if they were divested of their clothes. Could you, in such a case, tell surely of any company of civilized men which belonged to the most respected class? When Madam Pfeiffer,[1] in her adventurous travels round the world, from east to west, had got so near home as Asiatic Russia, she says that she felt the necessity of wearing other than a traveling dress, when she went to meet the authorities, for she "was now in a civilized country, where . . . people are judged of by their clothes." Even in our democratic New England towns the accidental possession of wealth, and its manifestation in dress and equipage alone, obtain for the possessor almost universal respect. But they who yield such respect, numerous as they are, are so far heathen, and need to have a missionary sent to them. Beside, clothes introduced sewing, a kind of work which you may call endless; a woman's dress, at least, is never done.

A man who has at length found something to do will not need to get a new suit to do it in; for him the old will do, that has lain dusty in the garret for an indeterminate period.

---

[1] **Madame Pfeiffer** Ida Pfeiffer (1797–1858), author of travel books.

Old shoes will serve a hero longer than they have served his valet — if a hero even has a valet — bare feet are older than shoes, and he can make them do. Only they who go to soirées and legislative halls must have new coats, coats to change as often as the man changes in them. But if my jacket and trousers, my hat and shoes, are fit to worship God in, they will do; will they not? Who ever saw his old clothes — his old coat, actually worn out, resolved into its primitive elements, so that it was not a deed of charity to bestow it on some poor boy, by him perchance to be bestowed on some poorer still, or shall we say richer, who could do with less? I say, beware of all enterprises that require new clothes, and not rather a new wearer of clothes. If there is not a new man, how can the new clothes be made to fit? If you have any enterprise before you, try it in your old clothes. All men want, not something to *do with*, but something to *do*, or rather something to *be*. Perhaps we should never procure a new suit, however ragged or dirty the old, until we have so conducted, so enterprised or sailed in some way, that we feel like new men in the old, and that to retain it would be like keeping new wine in old bottles. Our moulting season, like that of the fowls must be a crisis in our lives. The loon retires to solitary ponds to spend it. Thus also the snake casts its slough, and the caterpillar its wormy coat, by an internal industry and expansion; for clothes are but our outmost cuticle and mortal coil. Otherwise we shall be found sailing under false colors, and be inevitably cashiered at last by our own opinion, as well as that of mankind.

We don garment after garment, as if we grew like exogenous plants by addition without. Our outside and often thin and fanciful clothes are our epidermis, or false skin, which partakes not of our life, and may be stripped off here and there without fatal injury; our thicker garments, constantly worn, are our cellular integument, or cortex; but our shirts are our liber,[2] or true bark, which cannot be removed without girdling and so destroying the man. I believe that all races at some seasons wear something equivalent to the shirt. It is desirable that a man be clad so simply that he can lay his hands on himself in the dark, and that he live in all respects so compactly and preparedly, that, if an enemy take the town, he can, like the old philosopher, walk out the gate empty-handed without anxiety. While one thick garment is, for most purposes, as good as three thin ones, and cheap clothing can be obtained at prices really to suit customers; while a thick coat can be bought for five dollars, which will last as many years, thick pantaloons for two dollars, cowhide boots for a dollar and a half a pair, a summer hat for a quarter of a dollar, and a winter cap for sixty-two and a half cents, or a better be made at home at a nominal cost, where is he so poor that, clad in such a suit, *of his own earning*, there will not be found wise men to do him reverence?

When I ask for a garment of a particular form, my tailoress tells me gravely, "They do not make them so now," not emphasizing the "They" at all, as if she quoted an authority as impersonal as the Fates, and I find it difficult to get made what I want, simply because she cannot believe that I mean what I say, that I am so rash. When I hear this oracular sentence, I am for a moment absorbed in thought, emphasizing to myself each word separately that I may come at the meaning of it, that I may find out by what degree of consanguinity *They* are related to *me*, and what authority they may have in an affair which affects me so nearly; and finally, I am inclined to answer her with equal mystery, and without any more

---

[2] **liber** Inner bark of a tree.

emphasis of the "they" — "It is true, they did not make them so recently, but they do now." Of what use this measuring of me if she does not measure my character, but only the breadth of my shoulders, as it were a peg to hang the coat on? We worship not the Graces,[3] nor the Parcæ,[4] but Fashion. She spins and weaves and cuts with full authority. The head monkey at Paris puts on a traveller's cap, and all the monkeys in America do the same. I sometimes despair of getting anything quite simple and honest done in this world by the help of men. They would have to be passed through a powerful press first, to squeeze their old notions out of them, so that they would not soon get upon their legs again; and then there would be some one in the company with a maggot in his head, hatched from an egg deposited there nobody knows when, for not even fire kills these things, and you would have lost your labor. Nevertheless, we will not forget that some Egyptian wheat was handed down to us by a mummy.

On the whole, I think that it cannot be 5 maintained that dressing has in this or any country risen to the dignity of an art. At present men make shift to wear what they can get. Like shipwrecked sailors, they put on what they can find on the beach, and at a little distance, whether of space or time, laugh at each other's masquerade. Every generation laughs at the old fashions, but follows religiously the new. We are amused at beholding the costume of Henry VIII, or Queen Elizabeth, as much as if it was that of the King and Queen of the Cannibal Islands. All costume off a man is pitiful or grotesque. It is only the serious eye peering from and the sincere life passed within it which restrain laughter and consecrate the costume of any people. Let Harlequin be taken with a fit of the colic and his trappings will have to serve that mood too. When the soldier is hit by a cannon ball rags are as becoming as purple.

The childish and savage taste of men and women for new patterns keeps how many shaking and squinting through kaleidoscopes that they may discover the particular figure which this generation requires today. The manufacturers have learned that this taste is merely whimsical. Of two patterns which differ only by a few threads more or less of a particular color, the one will be sold readily, the other lie on the shelf, though it frequently happens that after the lapse of a season the latter becomes the most fashionable. Comparatively, tattooing is not the hideous custom which it is called. It is not barbarous merely because the printing is skin-deep and unalterable.

I cannot believe that our factory system is the best mode by which men may get clothing. The condition of the operatives is becoming every day more like that of the English; and it cannot be wondered at, since, as far as I have heard or observed, the principal object is, not that mankind may be well and honestly clad, but, unquestionably, that the corporations may be enriched. In the long run men hit only what they aim at. Therefore, though they should fail immediately, they had better aim at something high.

WE DO NOT RIDE ON THE RAILROAD; IT RIDES UPON US

Still we live meanly, like ants; though the fable tells us that we were long ago changed into men; like pygmies we fight with cranes; it is error upon error, and clout upon clout, and our best virtue has for its occasion a superfluous and evitable wretchedness. Our life is frittered away by detail. An honest man has

---

[3] **Graces** In Greek mythology, the Graces were three minor goddesses who were patrons of earthly pleasures such as happiness, creativity, beauty, and fertility.
[4] **Parcæ** Goddesses of fate in Roman mythology.

hardly need to count more than his ten fingers, or in extreme cases he may add his ten toes, and lump the rest. Simplicity, simplicity, simplicity! I say, let your affairs be as two or three, and not a hundred or a thousand; instead of a million count half a dozen, and keep your accounts on your thumb nail. In the midst of this chopping sea of civilized life, such are the clouds and storms and quicksands and thousand-and-one items to be allowed for, that a man has to live, if he would not founder and go to the bottom and not make his port at all, by dead reckoning, and he must be a great calculator indeed who succeeds. Simplify, simplify. Instead of three meals a day, if it be necessary eat but one; instead of a hundred dishes, five; and reduce other things in proportion. Our life is like a German Confederacy, made up of petty states, with its boundary forever fluctuating, so that even a German cannot tell you how it is bounded at any moment. The nation itself, with all its so-called internal improvements, which, by the way are all external and superficial, is just such an unwieldy and overgrown establishment, cluttered with furniture and tripped up by its own traps, ruined by luxury and heedless expense, by want of calculation and a worthy aim, as the million households in the land; and the only cure for it as for them is in a rigid economy, a stern and more than Spartan simplicity of life and elevation of purpose. It lives too fast. Men think that it is essential that the *Nation* have commerce, and export ice, and talk through a telegraph, and ride thirty miles an hour, without a doubt, whether *they* do or not; but whether we should live like baboons or like men, is a little uncertain. If we do not get out sleepers,[5] and forge rails, and devote days and nights to the work, but go to tinkering upon our *lives* to improve *them*, who will build railroads? And if railroads are not built, how shall we get to heaven in season? But if we stay at home and mind our business, who will want railroads? We do not ride on the railroad; it rides upon us. Did you ever think what those sleepers are that underlie the railroad? Each one is a man, an Irishman, or a Yankee man. The rails are laid on them, and they are covered with sand, and the cars run smoothly over them. They are sound sleepers, I assure you. And every few years a new lot is laid down and run over; so that, if some have the pleasure of riding on a rail, others have the misfortune to be ridden upon. And when they run over a man that is walking in his sleep, a supernumerary sleeper in the wrong position, and wake him up, they suddenly stop the cars, and make a hue and cry about it, as if this were an exception. I am glad to know that it takes a gang of men for every five miles to keep the sleepers down and level in their beds as it is, for this is a sign that they may sometime get up again.

---

[5] **sleepers** The woody ties beneath railroad rails.

Topics for Critical Thinking and Writing

1. What, according to Henry David Thoreau, are the legitimate functions of clothing? What other functions does he reject or fail to consider?

2. Many of Thoreau's sentences mean both what they say literally and something more; often, like proverbs, they express abstract or general truths in concrete, homely language. How might these sentences be interpreted? After explaining the sentences, consider: is this style effective or not? Explain.

   a. We know but few men, a great many coats and breeches.

b. Dress a scarecrow in your last shift, you standing shiftless by, who would not soonest salute the scarecrow?

c. If you have any enterprise before you, try it in your old clothes.

d. Every generation laughs at the old fashions, but follows religiously the new.

e. The head monkey at Paris puts on a traveller's cap, and all the monkeys in America do the same.

3. Notice that Thoreau writes in long paragraphs. (The first of them runs to more than 450 words — the length of many respectable essays.) Can such long paragraphs do their job effectively? What is the job of a paragraph? Or is there no one such job? Explain your response.

4. Toward the end of paragraph 2, we meet the cliché "new wine in old bottles." Do you think this sentence is effective? Why or why not? Was this expression already a cliché in Thoreau's day? Complete the following definition: "A word or phrase is a cliché if and only if . . ."

5. In paragraph 7, Thoreau criticizes "the factory system . . . by which men get clothing." What are his complaints? How do they relate to his other criticisms related to fashion? Could the same complaints be lodged today? Explain.

6. In paragraph 8, Thoreau asserts that "Our life is frittered away by detail." Is it possible to argue that "Yes, our life is frittered away by detail, but, perhaps oddly, attention to detail — studying for examinations, grading papers, walking the dog — is largely responsible for human happiness"? Explain your response.

GRETCHEN RUBIN

Gretchen Rubin is an author, podcaster, blogger, and speaker who has written a series of best-selling books on happiness, including *The Happiness Project* (2009), *Better Than Before* (2015), *The Four Tendencies* (2017), and, most recently, *Outer Order, Inner Calm* (2019). She created the Happier app and podcast, which has over one hundred million downloads (and counting), and offers courses on fulfillment and self-realization through her website. This selection is from *The Happiness Project*.

July: Buy Some Happiness

The relationship between money and happiness was one of the most interesting, most complicated, and most sensitive questions in my study of happiness. People, including the experts, seemed very confused.

As I did my research, Gertrude Stein's observation frequently floated through my mind: "Everyone has to make up their mind if money is money or money isn't money and sooner or later they always do decide that money is money." Money satisfies basic material needs. It's a means and an end. It's a way to keep score, win security, exercise generosity, and earn recognition. It can foster mastery or dilettantism. It symbolizes status and success. It buys time — which can be spent on aimless drifting or purposeful action. It creates power in relationships and in the world. It often stands for the things that we feel are lacking: if only we had the money, we'd be adventurous or thin or cultured or respected or generous.

Before I could figure out my resolutions for the month, I had to clarify my thinking about money. I was skeptical of much of what I read. In particular, I kept seeing the argument "Money can't buy happiness," but it certainly seemed that people appear fairly well convinced about the significance of money to their happiness. Money is not without its benefits, and the opposite case, though frequently made, has never proved widely persuasive. And in fact, studies show that people in wealthier countries *do* report being happier than people in poorer countries, and within a particular country, people with more money *do* tend to be happier than those with less. Also, as countries become richer, their citizens become less focused on physical and economic security and more concerned with goals such as happiness and self-realization. Prosperity allows us to turn our attention to more transcendent matters — to yearn for lives not just of material comfort but of meaning, balance, and joy.

Within the United States, according to a 2006 Pew Research Center study, 49 percent of people with an annual family income of more than $100,000 said they were "very happy," in contrast to 24 percent of those with an annual family income of less than $30,000. And the percentages of reported happiness increased as income rose: 24 percent for those earning under $30,000; 33 percent for $30,000 to under $75,000; 38 percent for $75,000 to under $100,000; and 49 percent for more than $100,000. (Now, it's also true that there may be some reverse correlation: happy people become rich faster because they're more appealing to other people and their happiness helps them succeed.)

Also, it turns out that while the *absolute* 5 *level* of wealth matters, *relative ranking* matters as well. One important way that people evaluate their circumstances is to compare themselves with the people around them and with their own previous experiences. For instance, people measure themselves against their age peers, and making more money than others in their age group tends to make people happier. Along the same lines, research shows that people who live in a neighborhood with richer people tend to be less happy than those in a neighborhood where their neighbors make about as much money as they do. A study of workers in various industries showed that their job satisfaction was less tied to their salaries than to how their salaries compared to their coworkers' salaries. People understand the significance of this principle: in one study, a majority of people chose to earn $50,000 where others earned $25,000, rather than earn $100,000 where others earned $250,000. My mother grew up feeling quite well-to-do in my parents' little hometown of North Platte, Nebraska, because her father had a highly coveted union job as an engineer on the Union Pacific Railroad. By contrast, a friend told me that he had felt poor growing up in New York City because he lived on Fifth Avenue above 96th Street — the less fashionable section of a very fashionable street.

The proponents of the "Money can't buy happiness" argument point to studies showing that people in the United States don't rate their quality of life much more highly than do people living in poverty in Calcutta — even though, of course, they live in vastly more comfortable circumstances. Most people, the world over, rate themselves as mildly happy.

It's admirable that people can find happiness in circumstances of poverty as well as in circumstances of plenty. That's the resilience of the human spirit. But I don't think that a particular individual would be indifferent to the disparities between the streets of Calcutta and the ranch houses of Atlanta. The fact is, people aren't made deliriously happy by the luxuries of salt and cinnamon (once so precious) or electricity or air-conditioning or cell phones or the Internet, because they come to accept these once-luxury goods as part of ordinary existence. That doesn't mean, however, that because people have learned to take clean water for granted, it no longer matters to their quality of life. Indeed, if that were true, would it mean it would be pointless to bother to try to improve the material circumstances of those folks in Calcutta?

But as I went deeper into the mystery of money, I was pulled toward research and analysis suitable for an entirely different book, away from my most pressing interest. Sure, I wanted to "Go off the path" to a point, and maybe one day I would devote an entire book to the topic, but for the moment, I didn't have to solve the enigma of money. I just needed to figure out how happiness and money fit together.

So was I arguing that "Money *can* buy happiness"? The answer: no. That was clear. Money alone can't buy happiness.

But, as a follow-up, I asked myself, "Can 10 money *help* buy happiness?" The answer: yes, used wisely, it can. Whether rich or poor, people make choices about how they spend money, and those choices can boost happiness or undermine it. It's a mistake to assume that money will affect everyone the same way. No statistical average could say how a particular *individual* would be affected by money — depending on that individual's circumstances and temperament. After a lot of thinking, I identified three factors that shape the significance of money to individuals:

It depends on what kind of person you are.

Money has a different value to different people. You might love to collect modern art, or you might love to rent old movies. You might have six children and ailing, dependent parents, or you might have no children and robust parents. You might love to travel, or you might prefer to putter around the house. You might care about eating organic, or you might be satisfied with the cheapest choices at the grocery store.

It depends on how you spend your money.

Some purchases are more likely to contribute to your happiness than others. You might buy cocaine, or you might buy a dog. You might splurge on a big-screen TV, or you might splurge on a new bike.

It depends on how much money you have relative to the people around you and relative to your own experience.

One person's fortune is another person's misfortune.

Developing and applying a three-factor test brought back pleasant memories of being a law student, and it was a helpful framework, but it was complex. I wanted a more cogent way to convey the relationship between money and happiness.

As I was mulling this over, one afternoon I picked up Eleanor the wrong way as I leaned over her crib, and the next morning, I woke up with agonizing back pain. For almost a month, I couldn't sit for long, I found it hard to type, I had trouble sleeping, and of course I couldn't stop picking up Eleanor, so I kept reaggravating the injury.

"You should go see my physical therapist," urged my father-in-law, who had suffered from back problems for years. "There's a lot they can do."

"I'm sure it will get better on its own," I kept insisting.

One night as I struggled to turn over in bed, I thought, "Ask for help! Bob says that physical therapy works; why am I resisting?" 15

I called Bob at work, got the information, made an appointment at the physical therapist's office, and two visits later, I was 100 percent better. It felt like a miracle. And one day after my pain was gone, I took my health for granted once again — and I had the Epiphany of the Back Spasm. *Money* doesn't buy happiness the way *good health* doesn't buy happiness.

When money or health is a problem, you think of little else; when it's not a problem, you don't think much about it. Both money and health contribute to happiness mostly in the negative; the lack of them brings much more unhappiness than possessing them brings happiness.

Being healthy doesn't guarantee happiness. Lots of healthy people are very unhappy. Many of them squander their health or take it for granted. In fact, some people might even be better off with some physical limitation that would prevent them from making destructive choices. (I once went on vacation with a group that included the most wild and reckless guy I'd ever met, and I was quite relieved when he broke his foot during an early escapade, because the mishap prevented him from getting up to much more mischief.) Ditto, money. But the fact that good health doesn't *guarantee* happiness doesn't mean that good health doesn't *matter* to happiness. Similarly, money. Used wisely, each can contribute greatly to happiness.

The First Splendid Truth[1] holds that to think about happiness, we should think about *feeling good, feeling bad, and feeling right, in an atmosphere of growth*. Money is most important for happiness in the "feeling bad" category. People's biggest worries include financial anxiety, health concerns, job insecurity, and having to do tiring and boring chores. Spent correctly, money can go a long way to solving these problems. I was extremely fortunate to be in a position where money wasn't a source of *feeling bad*. We had plenty of money to do what we wanted — even enough to feel secure, the toughest and most precious thing for money to buy. I resolved to do a better job of spending money in ways that could boost my happiness by supporting the other three elements of happiness.

INDULGE IN A MODEST SPLURGE

I didn't spend enough time thinking about how money could buy me happiness. 20

I'd always had a vague sense that spending money was self-indulgent and that I should avoid spending money whenever possible. I once spent six very satisfying months living in San Francisco on $5 a day (except when I had to use the Laundromat). Now, however, I decided to find ways to spend to further my happiness goals. Studies show that people's basic psychological needs include the need to feel secure, to feel good at what they do, to be loved, to feel connected to others, and to have a strong sense of control. Money doesn't *automatically* fill these requirements, but it sure can help. People at every level of income can

---

[1] **The First Splendid Truth:** Earlier in her book Rubin defines the First Splendid Truth: *To be happy, I needed to think about feeling good, feeling bad, and feeling right, in an atmosphere of growth*" (67). [Editors' note]

choose to direct their spending in ways that take them closer to happiness — or not.

I wanted to spend money to stay in closer contact with my family and friends; to promote my energy and health; to create a more serene environment in my apartment; to work more efficiently; to eliminate sources of boredom, irritation, and marital conflict; to support causes that I thought important; and to have experiences that would enlarge me. So, category by category, I looked for ways to spend money to support my happiness goals — within reason, of course.

For health and energy: in January, I'd already found a way to spend money to get better exercise. My strength-training workouts were expensive, but I was happy to know that I was doing something important for my long-term health. I also started spending more for food when I had to grab lunch outside our apartment. I'd always congratulated myself when I ducked into a deli to buy a bagel, because it was such a cheap and quick meal, but I stopped that. Instead, I gave myself a mental gold star for getting a big salad or soup and fruit, even though those choices were much more expensive.

For relationships: I'd give a party for my sister's wedding. It would be a major expenditure but also a major source of happiness. My relationship with my sister — and now with her fiancé — were among the most important in my life, but the fact that they lived in Los Angeles was a challenge. Hosting a party would be a way to make my own contribution to the wedding weekend.

For work: I bought some pens. Normally, 25 I used makeshift pens, the kind of unsatisfactory implements that somehow materialized in my bag or in a drawer. But one day, when I was standing in line to buy envelopes, I caught sight of a box of my favorite kind of pen: the Deluxe Uniball Micro.

"Two ninety-nine for one pen!" I thought. "That's ridiculous." But after a fairly lengthy internal debate, I bought four.

It's such a joy to write with a good pen instead of making do with an underinked pharmaceutical promotional pen picked up from a doctor's office. My new pens weren't cheap, but when I think of all the time I spend using pens and how much I appreciate a good pen, I realize it was money well spent. Finely made tools help make work a pleasure.

For others: I wrote a check to the New York Public Library's Library Cubs program. I was already donating my time and energy to helping form this group, which supports the children's rooms in library branches. Time and energy helped the library; money was also useful.

For happy memories: I bought those file boxes in April — an excellent modest splurge. Also, I've never forgotten an older friend's observation: "One of my regrets about my children's childhoods is that I didn't have more professional photographs taken." As luck would have it, I know a terrific photographer. I arranged to have pictures taken of our children, and I was thrilled with the results. These photographs were far better than any snapshot I could take, and I bought several for us and for the grandparents, too. Remembering happy times gives a big boost to happiness, and looking at photographs of happy times helps make those memories more vivid. The money I spent on the photographs will strengthen family bonds, enhance happy memories, and capture fleeting moments of childhood. That's a pretty good return on the happiness investment.

I pushed a friend to "Buy some happiness" 30 when I stopped by her apartment to admire her new baby (in keeping with my June resolution to "Show up").

"One thing is really bothering me," she said. "As a child, I was close to my grandparents, but my in-laws, who live nearby, aren't very interested in the baby. They already have seven grandchildren. My mother would love to see the baby all the time, but she lives in Cleveland and only comes to New York once a year."

"Well," I suggested, "at least until your son is in school, why don't you go to Cleveland every few months?"

She laughed. "That's way too expensive."

"It's a lot of money, but it's important to you. Could you afford it?" I knew she could.

"Well, yes, I guess," she admitted, "but it 35 would be such a hassle to fly with a baby."

"You could tell your mother you'll buy her plane tickets if she'll come to New York more often. Would she come?"

"You know . . . I bet she would!" my friend said. This solution shows both the importance of thinking about how money can buy happiness and also the importance of my Eighth Commandment: "Identify the problem." What was the problem? Finding a way for grandmother and grandson to spend time together.

Money, spent wisely, can support happiness goals of strengthening relationships, promoting health, having fun, and all the rest. At the same time, the emotions generated by sheer buying, by acquisition, are also powerful. Happiness theory suggests that if I move to a new apartment or buy a new pair of boots, I'll soon become accustomed to my new possession and be no happier than I was before. Nevertheless, many people make purchases for the fleeting jolt of happiness they get from the very act of gain.

Now, you might say — that's not true happiness; true happiness comes from doing good for others, being with friends and family, finding flow, meditating, and so on. But when I look around, I certainly see many people who look and act happy as they do their buying. The fact that the happiness boost that hits at the cash register isn't particularly admirable doesn't mean that it's not real — or that it doesn't shape people's behavior. Research and everyday experience show that receiving an unexpected present or being surprised by a windfall gives people a real boost; in one study, in fact, when researchers wanted to induce a good mood in their subjects to study the effects, the way they accomplished this good mood was to arrange for those subjects to find coins in a telephone booth or to be given bags of chocolates. For some people, the rush of happiness that accompanies gain is so seductive that they spend more money than they can afford and are hit by remorse and anxiety once they get their bags home. The quick fix of happiness turns into a longer-lasting unhappiness.

The happiness that people get from buy- 40 ing stuff isn't attributable only to consumerist indulgence. Any kind of gain creates at least a momentary atmosphere of growth, and there are a lot of reasons why people love to make a purchase: to keep their home in good repair, attractive, and well stocked; to provide for loved ones or strangers; to master something new (such as the latest gadget); to possess an admired object; to teach their children; to live as their peers live; to live differently from their peers; to beautify themselves; to maintain a collection; to keep up with fashion; to defy fashion; to support a hobby or expertise; to benefit others; to justify the enjoyment of shopping as an activity; to offer and return hospitality; to give gifts and support; to win or maintain status; to establish dominance and control; to express personality; to celebrate; to maintain traditions; to break traditions; to make life more convenient, healthier, or safer; to make life more challenging, adventurous, or risky.

I myself rarely feel cash register happiness. Quite the opposite. I'm usually hit by buyer's remorse when I spend, a feeling that I call "shop shock." Perhaps that's why I really notice other people's enthusiasm. Nevertheless, even for me, indulging in a modest splurge could bring a lot of happiness, if I made my purchases wisely. . . .

[O]ne of my favorite "modest splurges" was something that wouldn't appeal to most people — but for me meant getting my hands on something I'd coveted for years. I called Books of Wonder, a famous children's bookstore in Manhattan, and ordered the "Wizard's Super Special," the complete set of the fifteen Oz books by L. Frank Baum. Two weeks later, I got a huge thrill when I opened the large box. The hardback set had a unified design, with matching spines, gorgeous covers, and the original color illustrations.

Now, positive psychologists might argue that I'd adapt to my purchase. Soon I'd be accustomed to owning these books, they'd sit on a shelf and gather dust, and I'd be no better off than I was before. I disagree. Because I have a real passion for children's literature, I knew these books would give me a boost every time I saw them. After all, I keep a big stack of the old, beat-up *Cricket* magazines I had as a child, and just seeing them on the shelf makes me happy.

As always, the secret was to "Be Gretchen" and to choose wisely. What makes me happy is to spend money on the things *I* value — and it takes self-knowledge and discipline to discover what *I* really want, instead of parroting the desires of other people. One of the purchases that made my father happiest was a pinball machine. He'd played hours of pinball as a boy, and one of his childhood dreams was to have his own so he could play whenever he wanted, for free. This isn't a purchase that would have made everyone happy, but it made him extremely happy.

While I was thinking hard about the relationship between money and happiness, I struck up a conversation with a fellow guest at a bridal shower. I told her that I was trying to figure out ways to "Buy some happiness." (As I explained the issue, it began to dawn on me, dimly, that I might be becoming a happiness bore.)

She became quite indignant at my suggestion. "That's so wrong!" she said. "Money can't buy happiness!"

"You don't think so?"

"I'm the perfect example. I don't make much money. A few years back, I took my savings and bought a horse. My mother and everyone told me I was crazy. But that horse makes me incredibly happy — even though I end up spending all my extra money on him."

"But," I said, confused, "money *did* make you happy. It makes you so happy to have a horse!"

"But I don't have any money," she answered. "I spent it all."

"Right, because you used it to *buy a horse*."

She shook her head and gave up on me.

In some cases, though, when I tried to "Buy some happiness," it didn't work. I'd call this the "expensive-gym-membership effect," after the futile tendency to pay a lot for a gym membership with the thought, "Gosh, this costs so much, I'll feel like I have to go to the gym!"

I see the expensive-gym-membership effect when I pay money for something as a way to encourage myself to make time for something fun. For example, I went to three stores to hunt down the combination glue/sealer/finish Mod Podge, because I wanted to experiment with découpage. I really want to do it. But I bought that Mod Podge ages ago, and I've never used it. I want to take time for creative projects, but merely spending money on an art supply won't make it a priority. I have to decide to make time — and apparently I haven't. (Using Mod Podge can be another resolution for Happiness Project II.) Along the same lines, a workaholic friend of mine bought a fancy new tennis racquet because he wants to play more tennis, but he still hasn't used it. The tennis racquet is an expression of his desire to change something in his life, but just making a purchase won't accomplish that. He should have concentrated on fixing his calendar, not on finding the right racquet.

"Buy some happiness," of course, has its lim- 55 its. I knew I'd better not overlook the effects of the hedonic treadmill, which quickly transforms delightful luxuries into dull necessities. Indulging in a modest splurge would give me a happiness jolt only if I did it rarely. Take room service. Until my honeymoon, I'd never had room service in my life — and it was a thrill. But if I traveled for business and got room service frequently, it wouldn't be a treat anymore.

Because money permits a constant stream of luxuries and indulgences, it can take away their savor, and by permitting instant gratification, money shortcuts the happiness of anticipation. Scrimping, saving, imagining, planning, hoping — these stages enlarge the happiness we feel.

Even a modest pleasure can be a luxury if it's scarce enough — ordering coffee at a restaurant, buying a book, or watching TV — which is why deprivation is one of the most effective, although unenjoyable, cures for the hedonic treadmill. A friend told me that when she lived in Russia in the 1990s, the hot water would periodically stop working for weeks at a time. She said that very few experiences in her life have matched the happiness

she felt on the days when the hot water started working again. But now that she's back in the United States, where her hot water has never failed, she never thinks about it.

The hedonic treadmill means that spending often isn't a satisfying path to happiness, but nevertheless, money can help. My father still talks about the day he realized that he could afford to pay someone to mow the lawn. Some of the best things in life aren't free.

Another way to think about money's effect is in terms of the First Splendid Truth, as part of the "atmosphere of growth" that's so important to happiness. We need an atmosphere of *spiritual* growth, and as much as some people deny it, *material* growth is also very satisfying.

We're very sensitive to change. We mea- 60 sure our present against our past, and we're made happy when we see change for the better. In one study, people were asked whether they'd rather have a job that paid $30,000 in year one, $40,000 in year two, and $50,000 in year three or a job that paid $60,000, then $50,000 then $40,000. In general, people preferred the first option, with its raises — despite the fact that at the end of the three years, they would have earned only $120,000 instead of $150,000. Their decision might seem irrational, but in fact, the people who chose the first option understood the importance of *growth* to happiness. People are very sensitive to relative changes in their condition, for better or worse.

A sense of growth is so important to happiness that it's often preferable to be progressing to the summit rather than to be at the summit. Neither a scientist nor a philosopher but a novelist, Lisa Grunwald, came up with the most brilliant summation of this happiness principle: "Best is good, better is best."

One challenge of parenthood that I hadn't tackled in April, though perhaps I should have, was setting limits on buying treats for my children. For example, as a surprise, I bought Eliza a big book of optical illusions. As I expected, she loved the book — pored over it, looked at it with her friends, kept it out on her bedside table. I was so pleased with myself for choosing it for her. One day, not long after, I was in a drugstore that had a rack of cheap children's books. I spotted a book of optical illusions and almost bought it for Eliza; she'd enjoyed the other book so much. Then I stopped myself. She already had a book with three hundred illusions; this book probably didn't have much new. But even beyond that, I wondered if having two books of optical illusions might, in fact, dim Eliza's pleasure in the first book. It wouldn't seem as magical and definitive.

The head of Eliza's school told a story about a four-year-old who had a blue toy car he loved. He took it everywhere, played with it constantly. Then when his grandmother came to visit, she bought him ten toy cars, and he stopped playing with the cars altogether. "Why don't you play with your cars?" she asked. "You loved your blue car so much." "I can't love lots of cars," he answered.

It's easy to make the mistake of thinking that if you have something you love or there's something you want, you'll be happier with more.

BUY NEEDFUL THINGS

When I began to pay attention to people's relationship to money, I recognized two different approaches to buying: "underbuying" and "overbuying." I'm an underbuyer.

As an underbuyer, I delay making purchases or buy as little as possible. I buy saline solution, which I use twice a day, one little bottle at a time. I scramble to buy items like a winter coat or a bathing suit after the point at which I need them. I'm suspicious of buying things with very specific uses — suit bags, hand cream, hair conditioner, rain boots, Kleenex (why not just use toilet paper to blow your nose?). I often consider buying an item, then decide, "I'll get this some other time" or "Maybe we don't really need this." As an underbuyer, I often feel stressed because I don't have the things I need. I make a lot of late-night runs to the drugstore. I'm surrounded with things that are shabby, don't really work, or aren't exactly suitable.

I gaze in wonder at the antics of my overbuyer friends. Overbuyers often lay in huge supplies of slow-use items like shampoo or cough medicine. They buy things like tools or high-tech gadgets with the thought "This will probably come in handy someday." They make a lot of purchases before they go on a trip or celebrate a holiday. They throw things away — milk, medicine, even cans of soup — because they've hit their expiration date. They buy items with the thought "This will make a great gift!" without having a recipient in mind. Like me, overbuyers feel stressed. They're oppressed by the number of errands they feel obliged to do and by the clutter and waste often created by their overbuying. . . .

I knew that I'd be happier if I made a mindful effort to thwart my underbuying impulse and instead worked to buy what I needed. For instance, I ended my just-in-time policy for restocking toilet paper. One of my Secrets of Adulthood is "Keep a roll of toilet paper tucked away someplace," so we never actually ran out, but we teetered on the dreary brink.

I mentioned this problem to Jamie. "We're like Walmart," he said. "We keep all our capital working for us instead of sitting on a lot of inventory."

"Well," I said, "now we're going to invest in some redundant supply." Moderation is pleasant to the wise, but toilet paper was something

I wanted to keep on hand. This kind of little annoyance puts a surprisingly big drag on happiness. As Samuel Johnson remarked, "To live in perpetual want of little things is a state, not indeed of torture, but of constant vexation."

Another thing that I really needed was white T-shirts, because I wear them practically every day. I enjoy shopping only when I'm with my mother, so I waited to buy my T-shirts until my mother was visiting from Kansas City. I wanted T-shirts that were soft, stretchy, not too thin, V-necked, and long-sleeved, and to me, tracking down and buying such shirts seemed like an overwhelming challenge. My mother was undaunted. "We'll go to Bloomingdale's," she decided.

Though I felt dazed the minute I entered the store, my mother walked purposefully from one area to the next. As she began her systematic inspection, I trailed along behind her and carried the shirts she'd pulled out. After she'd considered every white shirt on the floor, I tried on — conservative estimate — twenty shirts. I bought eight.

My mother had joined with zeal my quest for the perfect white T-shirt, but when she saw the stack of monochrome cotton at the cash register, she asked, "Are you sure you don't want any other colors or styles? This is a lot of white shirts."

"Well . . ." I hesitated. Did I really want this many white shirts? Then I remembered a study showing that people think they like variety more than they do. When asked to pick a menu of snacks for the upcoming weeks, they picked a variety, but if they chose week to week what to eat, they picked their favorite snack over and over.

In the store, it seemed like a good idea to have a variety of colors. But I knew from experience that when I stood in front of my closet, I always wanted to pull out the same things:

white V-neck T-shirt; black yoga pants or jeans; and running shoes.

Buy needful things. "Yes, I just want white," I said firmly.

Inspired by my shirt success, I replaced our leaky blender. I bought a personalized return-address stamp. I'd realized that the paradoxical consequence of being an underbuyer was that I had to shop *more often*, while buying extras meant fewer trips to the cash register. I bought batteries, Band-Aids, lightbulbs, diapers — things I knew we would need eventually. I finally ordered business cards, which I'd been putting off for years. I was inspired when, at a meeting, someone handed me the best-looking business card I'd ever seen. I got all the information so I could order a copycat version for myself.

My decision-making process for ordering a business card showed me that not only was I an "underbuyer," I was also a "satisficer" — as opposed to a "maximizer." *Satisficers* (yes, satisficers) are those who make a decision or take action once their criteria are met. That doesn't mean they'll settle for mediocrity; their criteria can be very high, but as soon as they find the hotel, the pasta sauce, or the business card that has the qualities they want, they're satisfied. *Maximizers* want to make the optimal decision. Even if they see a bicycle or a backpack that meets their requirements, they can't make a decision until after they've examined every option, so they can make the best possible choice.

Studies suggest that satisficers tend to be happier than maximizers. Maximizers spend a lot more time and energy to reach a decision, and they're often anxious about whether they did in fact make the best choice. As a shopper, my mother is a good example of what I'd call a "happy limited maximizer." In certain distinct categories, she's a maximizer, and she loves the very process of investigating every possibility. Now that Eliza and Eleanor were going to be flower girls in my sister's wedding, I knew my mother would love nothing more than to examine every possible dress, just for the fun of it. But too often maximizers find the research process exhausting yet can't let themselves settle for anything but the best. The difference between the two approaches may be one reason some people find a big city like New York disheartening. If you're a maximizer in New York City, you could spend months surveying your options for bedroom furniture or even wooden hangers. In Kansas City, even the most zealous maximizer can size up the available options pretty quickly.

Most people are a mix of both. In almost 80 every category, I was a satisficer, and in fact, I often felt guilty about not doing more research before making decisions. In law school, one friend interviewed with fifty law firms before she decided where she wanted to go as a summer associate; I think I interviewed with six. We ended up at the same firm. Once I learned to call myself a "satisficer," I felt more satisfied with my approach to decision making; instead of feeling lazy and unconscientious, I could call myself prudent. A great example of reframing.

SPEND OUT

I tend to cling to things — to stuff, to ideas. I reuse razor blades until they're dull, I keep my toothbrushes until they're yellowed and frayed. There is a preppy wabi-sabi to soft, faded khakis and cotton shirts, but it's not nice to be surrounded by things that are worn out or stained or used up. I often found myself saving things, even when it made no sense. Like those white T-shirts I bought. I'd surmounted the challenge of buying them; then came the challenge of *wearing* them. When I took them out of the shopping bag and laid

them on my shelf — perfectly folded by the salesclerk as I've never learned to do — I could feel myself wanting to "save" them in their pristine glory. But not wearing clothes is as wasteful as throwing them away.

As part of my happiness project I wanted to stop hoarding, to trust in abundance, so that I could use things up, give things away, throw things away. Not only that — I wanted to stop worrying so much about keeping score and profit and loss. I wanted to *spend out.*

A few years ago, my sister gave me a box of beautiful stationery for my birthday. I loved it, but I'd never used it. When I was mailing some photos to the grandparents, I hesitated to use the new stationery because I was "saving" it; but to what better use could it be put? Of course I should use those notes. Spend out.

I looked through my apartment for ways to spend out. The toughest choices I made concerned things that sort of worked: the camera that had lost its zoom function, the label maker that didn't print properly. I hate waste, but it would probably have cost me as much money (and far more time) to repair these items as to replace them — and using them in their crippled states weighed me down. I replaced them.

My goal wasn't limited to my treatment 85 of my possessions; it also involved my ideas. For example, when I thought of a great subject for a blog post, I often found myself thinking "That's a good idea, save it for another day." Why? Why delay? I needed to trust that there would be more, that I would have great ideas in the future and so should use my best stuff *now.* Pouring out ideas is better for creativity than doling them out by the teaspoon.

"Spending out" also meant not being rigidly efficient. The other night, Jamie and I rented *Junebug* — an extraordinary movie, all about the nature of love and happiness. I was tempted to watch a few of my favorite scenes again after we saw it the first time, but I decided that would be a "waste" of time. Then I remembered my resolution, which included spending out my time. After all, I know that sometimes the things I do when I'm wasting time turn out to be quite worthwhile. I went to "Scene Selection" to rewatch the scene at the church social.

The most important meaning of "Spend out," however, is not to be a scorekeeper, not to stint on love and generosity. This was related to my February resolution, "Don't expect praise or appreciation." I wanted to stop constantly demanding praise or insisting on getting paid back. Saint Thérèse of Lisieux wrote, "When one loves, one does not calculate." I'm a big calculator, always looking for a return, especially with Jamie.

"I gave Eleanor a bath last night, so you . . ."

"I let you take a nap, so you . . ."

"I had to make the plane reservations, so 90 you . . ."

No! Spend out. Don't think about the return. "It is by spending oneself," the actress Sarah Bernhardt remarked, "that one becomes rich." What's more, one intriguing study showed that Sarah Bernhardt's pronouncement is *literally* true: people who give money to charity end up wealthier than those who don't give to charity. After doing complex number crunching to control for different variables, a researcher concluded that charitable giving isn't just correlated with higher income; it actually *causes* higher income. Some explanations for this surprising effect include the brain stimulation caused by charitable activity and also the fact that those who are seen behaving charitably are likely to be elevated to leadership positions.

It's certainly true in my household that spending out creates a wealth of love and tenderness, while calculation and scorekeeping build resentment.

To keep this important yet elusive resolution uppermost in my mind, I maintained a relic. In one of my last visits to my grandmother before she died, I picked up the My Sin perfume that had been sitting on her bureau for as long as I could remember. The bottle was still in its box, and when I opened it, I saw that it was still full to the top. I didn't ask her about it, but I'm sure someone, many years ago, gave her that bottle of perfume and she was "saving it." For what? After she died, I took the box home with me, and I keep it in my office to remind me to "Spend out."

Topics for Critical Thinking and Writing

1. Is Gretchen Rubin's "study of happiness" (para. 1) an example of deductive or inductive research? Explain, pointing to how her reasoning and uses of evidence indicate her methods. (For a reminder of inductive and deductive methods, see Chapter 4, "Types of Reasoning," beginning on p. 104.)

2. Is the evidence Rubin provides in paragraphs 4–5 reliable proof that money can in fact buy happiness? Why or why not?

3. Consider the role of qualifications in an argument (see "Modal Qualifiers" in Chapter 9, p. 338). Then, offer at least three qualifications to the argument that money *can* in fact buy happiness.

4. Reread paragraph 40, in which Rubin discusses ways that spending money can "buy happiness." Are there assumptions embedded in her explanation and reasoning? Do you think her list is adequate, or are there things left out? How does saving money factor into Rubin's argument?

5. Compare the last section of Rubin's essay on "spending out" to Henry David Thoreau's selections from *Walden* in this chapter. How might Thoreau respond to Rubin's "trust in abundance" (para. 82)?

6. Do you think that Rubin's ideas about finding a way to happiness through spending is an acceptable guideline for readers to follow, or that Rubin is really speaking to the self-interests of her audience? Explain. Then, write an essay on the role of self-interest in critical thinking and decision-making. What are some of the benefits and dangers of prioritizing self-interest in any specific political, social, or economic affairs?

HORACE

Born in Italy in 65 BCE, the Roman poet Horace studied literature and philosophy in Athens at the Academy founded by Plato. Following the assassination of Julius Caesar, he was recruited by Brutus to help overthrow Rome. After the defeat of Brutus's army by Octavian (later Caesar Augustus), Horace accepted a general amnesty and returned to Rome dispossessed of his land and station. His connections to the elite, however, helped him secure a position in government and an estate in the Sabine Hills outside of Rome. There, Horace wrote some of the most influential works of Roman literature, including satires, epistles (letters), and lyric verse. Among the latter, *Odes (Epodes)* includes seventeen poems that represent Horace's familiarity with Greek traditional verse and Epicurian philosophy, which emphasized natural pleasures in the context of a simple life as the greatest priority — pleasures of the mind and body, in moderation, including, joy, friendship, love, sex, food, and other comforts of life. While classical texts virtually ceased being reproduced between the sixth and eighth centuries AD, Horace's writings are among a few Roman texts to remain familiar to literate Europeans from as early as the ninth century. "Ode 1.11," included here, contains perhaps Horace's famous dictum, *carpe diem*, or "seize the day."

Ode 1.11

Translated by John Conington in The Odes and Carmen Saeculare of Horace (1882)

Ask not ('tis forbidden knowledge),
    what our destined term of years,
Mine and yours; nor scan the tables of
    your Babylonish seers.
Better far to bear the future, my Leu-
    conoe, like the past,
Whether Jove has many winters yet to
    give, or this our last;

This, that makes the Tyrrhene billows   5
    spend their strength against the
    shore.
Strain your wine and prove your wis-
    dom; life is short; should hope be
    more?
In the moment of our talking, envious
    time has ebb'd away.
Seize the present; trust tomorrow e'en as
    little as you may.

Topics for Critical Thinking and Writing

1. Horace's famous injunction, *carpe diem*, commonly translated as "seize the day," in this version is translated as "seize the present." In other places it has been translated as "pluck the day," "snatch the day," "gather the day," or "hold on to the day." Consider these alternative translations. Do they change the meaning of the poem? How?

2. Critics have proposed that Leuconoe may be a real person or an imagined person, perhaps a lover of Horace, a friend, or a servant. Does changing Leuconoe's status affect how you read the poem and interpret what its message might be?

3. Do you think this poem is optimistic or pessimistic? Explain by citing the lines that indicate the reasons for your interpretation.

4. Consider Horace's poem and John Martin Fischer's essay "The Problem of Now" together. If Fischer were to analyze Horace's poem, what might he say about it or the advice it gives?

JOHN MARTIN FISCHER

John Martin Fischer, a distinguished professor philosophy at the University of California–Riverside, has written scores of articles and authored many books on the subjects of free will and moral responsibility, including *The Metaphysics of Free Will* (1994), *My Way: Essays on Moral Responsibility* (2006), and *Death, Immortality and Meaning in Life* (2019). He is best known for his theory of *semicompatibilism*, a theory of moral responsibility that challenges prevailing ideas that determinism and moral responsibility are logically incompatible. If all things are predetermined, incompatibilists hold, then moral responsibility cannot be conceived as an act of conscious choice or freedom. Fischer's ideas introduced the plausibility of moral freedom within a deterministic outlook, thus "semicompatibilism."

In the essay included here, "The Problem of Now" (2021), Fischer poses a philosophical challenge to the notions of "seizing the day" — or considering the present moment as having privileged meaning or significance in our lives. "The Problem of Now" was published in *Aeon*, a digital magazine featuring leading thinkers in science, philosophy, society and the arts.

The Problem of Now

Many spiritual teachers have emphasised the notion of being fully present "in the now". Proponents of meditative practices of various sorts tout meditation as a way of immersing oneself fully in the present moment, and not attending to the past or future. The spiritual teachers (including prominent authors) and proponents of meditation typically point to many benefits of being fully present in the now. As the influential contemporary author Eckhart Tolle puts it in his book *The Power of Now* (1997):

> Since ancient times, spiritual masters of all traditions have pointed to the Now as the key to the spiritual dimension.

Some, however, don't leave it at that. They don't simply argue for the advantages of presence in the current moment on the basis of psychological or other practical benefits.

Rather, they point to the "singularity" of the present moment: the idea that the *now* is all we have (temporally). I will use *singular*, in the claim "The present moment is singular", to refer to this idea of "being the one and only". The "singularity thesis" is the idea that the present moment is all we have — the one and only time. The Flaming Lips remind us of this in their song *All We Have Is Now* (2002). What I will dub the "connection thesis" is a central claim of various spiritual practitioners, authors, lecturers and workshop leaders; it's the contention that we should focus our full attention on the present moment precisely because of its singularity.

The view being considered is that, although it might seem to us that other times — past and future — are appropriate targets of attention, we can come to understand (intellectually and affectively) that in a fundamental sense (perhaps difficult to specify), there is only the *now*, and thus our attention should be focused on it. Our appropriate target of full attention, then, depends on and arises from singularity.

The importance of the *now* is arguably a key idea in various religious, mystical traditions. Many spiritual teachers, including Ram Dass, Jiddu Krishnamurti, Jon Kabat-Zinn and Alan Watts, have emphasised it. Some have even articulated the singularity thesis. Perhaps the most salient contemporary spiritual teacher who emphasises both the ontological uniqueness of the present and also the connection thesis is Tolle, who collates and reworks many of the insights of a wide variety of thinkers. He not only highlights what he takes to be the fact that the present is the one and only moment, but he also explicitly contends that we ought to give our full attention to the present precisely because of this singularity.

Through various media, including many widely read books, Tolle has brought ideas about spirituality, mindfulness and meditation to many millions of people. At the very centre of it all is his advocacy of the connection thesis.

For example, in *The Power of Now*, Tolle writes:

Realise deeply that the present moment is all you ever have. Make the Now the primary focus of your life . . . Always say "yes" to the present moment. What could be more futile, more insane, than to create inner resistance to something that already *is*? What could be more insane than to oppose life itself which is now and always now? Surrender to what *is*. Say "yes" to life — and see how life suddenly starts working *for* you, rather than against you.

And:

the Now [is] the most precious thing there is. Why is it the most precious thing? Firstly, because it is the *only* thing . . . Life is now. There was never a time when your life was *not* now, nor will there ever be.

I am interested in the ideas that are clearly suggested by Tolle's remarks, as quoted above, but not in engaging in an exegetical exercise. The claims are very prevalent and influential, whether or not they are fully accurate interpretations of Tolle's overall views, when analytically reconstructed. Such a reconstruction would contrive to render the total set of views consistent — not an easy task.

Let's begin by considering the claim that the present moment is ontologically unique — the one and only time, and thus all we have. This claim of the singularity of the present can be put in various ways, including "it is always now". The idea is that if it is always the *same* time, i.e. now, there is just *one* time—the *now*. It was that same time yesterday, it is that time in the current moment, and it will be that time tomorrow: we never have had or will have any other time than the *now*.

The singularity of the *now* might appear to be a deep and profound insight. It's the springboard for various more practical strategies for achieving enlightenment and self-enhancement. But the claim that it is always *now* is so trivial that it can't support any interesting inference, and there are other ways of justifying these same strategies and practices.

What exactly does it mean that it is always *now*? I think that the best way to interpret the claim is first to note that the term *now* is an indexical term. That is, it's employed flexibly to point to the particular time when it's used, not the same time every time it's used. Similarly, the term *here* is an indexical term, employed flexibly to refer to the place where it's uttered, not the same place wherever it's uttered. *Now* is a temporal indexical, and *here* is a spatial indexical.

What is thus indisputably true is that if anyone were to think or utter "It is now", the proposition expressed would be true. Seeing that *now* is a temporal indexical explains why "It is now" is always true and, in this sense, it is always *now*. If I were to say or think "It is now Monday" on Monday, *now* would refer to a time on Monday. If I were to say or think "It is now Tuesday" on Tuesday, *now* would refer to a time on Tuesday. And so forth, for every statement or thought to the effect that "It is now . . ." on subsequent days.

By the linguistic rules of usage, *now* helps to specify a proposition expressed by the statement in which it occurs, contributing a different time on different occasions of usage. So, whereas "It is now" is always true, it does not follow, and it is not true, that the locution always expresses the same proposition. It's thus not true that it's always *now*, in the sense

that it's always the same time—the only time we have.

So the initial insight, rendered true by the semantic rules pertaining to the temporal indexical *now*, is too trivial to imply the substantive and important claim: the connection thesis. Interpreted so that it's correct, the intuitive idea that it's always *now* doesn't support the crucial inference that we should focus on the present because of its singularity—because it's all we have.

Is the claim of the singularity of the present a truth accessible via a mystical experience or through meditation? Since meditation typically involves full immersion in the here and now, this proposed interpretation would begin with full attention to the *now*, and this would lead to the singularity insight. This, however, gets the logic of the view backward, since the main idea is that we start with the singularity point and then infer the appropriateness of full immersion.

We noted above that *here* is a spatial indexical, just as *now* is a temporal indexical. Whenever one thinks or asserts "I am here now", it is true. Similarly for "I am here". It doesn't, however, follow that there is just one place, or that our current place is the one and only place—the only place we have. This would be a spurious transition, a fallacious inference of the sort we identified above with respect to *now*.

In the philosophy of time there are two main views: "presentism" and "eternalism". The presentist holds that only the present moment is real or exists, whereas the eternalist holds that every moment is equally real or extant. It's clear that one cannot propound the singularity thesis (or the connection thesis) on the assumption of eternalism. After all, eternalism holds that all times are equally real.

Perhaps the proponent of the connection thesis embraces the doctrine of presentism, on the basis of which he goes on to argue that our full attention should be focused on the only extant time — the *now*. Note, however, that presentism doesn't entail that we should focus only on the present moment. It's possible to attend to nonexistent entities, such as fictional characters; I can focus my attention on Macbeth, for example. It's possible to focus our attention on imaginary creatures, such as unicorns or hobbits and also on not-currently existing individuals, such as Aristotle or Kant. (I've taken philosophy classes!) We can also consider possibilities for our future — different paths our lives could take going forward. Eternalism and presentism are views about metaphysics, not psychology or practical reasoning. Echoing this point, Fleetwood Mac counter the Flaming Lips in their 1977 song lyric: "Don't stop thinking about tomorrow."

My point is not that the mere fact of these possibilities entails that we should fully and solely attend to any of them. Rather, it's that there's no necessity or inevitability to focusing only on the present moment, based on the fact (if it is a fact) that it's the only moment that exists or is real.

Here is a way one might seek to defend the connection thesis, building on (or at least presupposing) presentism. On this view, the current moment is all we have, because only the present exists or is real; thus our actions can take place only in the present. Recall that Tolle has pointed out (as quoted above) that nothing can either be or happen outside of the *now*. Similarly, one cannot act except in the *now*, given that the present is all we have. *Now* is where the action is.

This is, however, unconvincing. To see 20 why, we need to distinguish "basic" from "non-basic" actions. Roughly speaking, a basic action is an action one performs, but not by performing any other action. Some think of basic actions as mental – perhaps acts of will, choices or decisions. Others think of them as bodily movements (where this can include keeping still). For example, pulling the trigger (or perhaps choosing to pull the trigger) would be a basic action. You might say that an agent performs a basic action "directly": you do not, say, choose to pull the trigger by performing some other action. In contrast, a non-basic action is performed by performing another action. For example, assuming that you kill the mayor by shooting her, killing the mayor is non-basic.

We can perform basic actions only in the present moment — other times are not directly available. You pull the trigger now. It's important, however, that a basic action can have consequences for other times, and that in performing a basic action we might also be performing a non-basic one. Your killing the mayor is an extended process (a non-basic action) that takes place over time. In selecting my action now, I should (or, at least, might) consider the consequences of various actions for future times (that don't yet exist), and the consequences of my actions. *Now* is only where the basic actions are.

Neither presentism nor eternalism is helpful to the proponent of the connection thesis. Even if the present is singular — the one and only extant time — it doesn't follow that we should fully and solely attend to it. Additionally, the connection theorist cannot accept eternalism, as it straightforwardly denies the singularity of the present.

It's not even clear that we are ever given a pure experience of the *now*. In James Joyce's novel *Ulysses* (1922), Stephen Dedalus laments that history is "a nightmare from which I am trying to awake". It's doubtful that he — or anyone — can. This point is a staple of psychoanalysis, as well as a broad range of psychotherapies, particularly those that are psychodynamically informed, that is, informed by facts about one's family relationships — especially, but not exclusively, in one's early years. Additionally, the phenomenological tradition (developed in the work of Edmund Husserl, Martin Heidegger and Maurice Merleau-Ponty) holds that the *now* is necessarily structured by horizons of the past and the future. So every way of inhabiting the *now* (including "being here now") is also a way of taking up the past and orienting ourselves to the future.

"Be here now." I've argued that this recommendation cannot be supported by the singularity of the *now*. Two of the most salient alternative ways of justifying it are psychological health and enlightenment. Very broadly and roughly, one might distinguish meditation for serenity (Samatha) and meditation for insight (Vipassana). These are compatible approaches and one could, of course, have more than one reason for meditation.

Enlightenment can be gained through 25 Vipassana meditation and, in the Buddhist view, this consists in some version of the "no-self" view. Where gaining this sort of enlightenment would lead us is an open question. Some will find it comforting, especially as one considers one's own death, which loses its status as a fundamental and daunting change in metaphysical status. I am not what I thought I was — an enduring, substantial self — and thus my going out of existence isn't a matter for concern. Others will find this insight existentially disorienting: adopting the no-self view implies a potentially significant disruption of our metaphysical proprioception.[1] Even some Zen monks fear their own deaths.

Although insight meditation won't necessarily be a welcome therapeutic tool, serenity is possible through certain meditative practices. Many, especially in the contemporary self-help literature, including proponents of mindfulness meditation, point to the considerable therapeutic benefits of certain kinds of meditation. There are specific sorts of meditations for the relief of fear and anxiety in the Buddhist tradition.

Insight and serenity are compelling justifications for meditation, but there is another, which can go unnoticed. A good reason to meditate is to cultivate and sustain a certain kind of attentiveness. The idea here is to calm the mind and to free it from undue identification with particular thoughts and feelings. Thus the mind isn't scattered or captured, but is free to fully take in the unfolding reality in front of one. (These ideas are present in the work of the philosopher and spiritual teacher George Gurdjieff and his followers, including Jean Vaysse.) This isn't a passive reception of one's environment, nor does it issue solely in a cognitive apprehension. An attention that is active and open to what is unfolding in front of one is rare, but it can be cultivated. On this view, when one says "Be here now", the emphasis is on "be". "*Be* here now", not "Be here *now*." The norm encourages the development of a kind of being that involves unmediated openness to the unfolding world. It's the power of *be*.

Unlike the typology considered above (with two options), we might then distinguish between (at least) three kinds of meditation: serenity, insight and what I'll call "awareness" meditation. Insight meditation can lead to enlightenment, in the sense of a recognition (both cognitively and affectively) of certain basic truths about us and our relationship to the broader world. Serenity meditation seeks a peaceful affective homeostasis. Awareness meditation does not seek, in the first instance, the acquisition of truths, or even of serenity, but an active and clear-minded attention to

---

[1]**Proprioception** The body's ability to sense movement, action, and location.

(but not absorption in) what is unfolding in the here and now. "Be here now" can thus be construed as commending a certain quality of attentiveness — a certain way of being.

Our everyday consciousness is typified by a poor quality of attention. Either (1) our attention is captured, utterly absorbed, caught up in what is happening, where our sense of self is absent, and we are identified with our thoughts and feelings, having no distance from them; or (2) our attention is scattered, rushing associatively from one surface to another. *Being* here now requires (3) an open, active attention. A key idea, actually found in Tolle's work, is that we're not identical to our thoughts, but can instead separate ourselves from our mind and reflect on it. We are the watcher, not the mind. This recognition can help us to free ourselves from total absorption in the passing scene and the loss of self, but also to remain attentive and focused.

I have not challenged or impugned the desirability of achieving greater presence in the moment. I find this persuasive and important. I am, however, calling into question the connection thesis — the contention that we can defend an immersion in the present by noting that the present is the only time we have.

The singularity of the present is emphasised by influential spiritual teachers and it appears, at first, to be a profound truth. It is, however, superficial and not substantive enough to support the inference to immersion in the now. From the perspective of philosophy of language, we can see the impotence of *now*. From that of philosophy of time, we see that presentism doesn't, in itself, have any implication for psychology, and eternalism is a nonstarter. The connection thesis can be interpreted as linking focus on the present to a kind of necessity: the present is all there is. It's not surprising, then, that Tolle calls it a kind of "surrender" — a surrender to the *now*. The thrust of my argument can be construed as rejecting the surrender model and plumping for a "choice" model. We have a choice about what we focus on, a choice not dictated by the unique present, if there is one. We are free to choose how we wish to *be*. We should indeed be here now, but not because the *now* is all we have.

Topics for Critical Thinking and Writing

1. How does John Martin Fischer question the importance of "now" as a singularly important moment deserving of our special attention and focus (para. 1)? What does he mean by the "singularity thesis" (para. 4), and what kinds of problems does he introduce to the thesis?

2. The idea that the now — the present moment — is "all we have" (para. 2) can be (and is) commonly used as a persuasive appeal. Think of one or two truisms, sayings, song lyrics, or other cultural messages that encourage people to conceive the present moment as exceptional as a source of happiness or contentment. Then, discuss whether or not such appeals are rational or irrational, providing real or invented examples as you write.

3. Fischer begins paragraph 11 with the statement, "What is thus indisputably true is that if anyone were to think or utter 'It is now,' the proposition expressed would be true." However, he ends paragraph 12 with the statement, "[W]hereas 'It is now' is always true, it does not follow, and it is not true . . . that it's always *now*, in the sense that it's always the same time — the only time we have." Explain his logic in arriving at this conclusion. How can the statement "It is now" be both true and untrue?

4. Examine the metaphors Fischer uses throughout his essay. How do they contribute to his argument? Choose the most effective example and explain the claim Fischer is trying to support in using it.

5. What distinction does Fisher draw between insight meditation and serenity meditation? Why does he add "awareness meditation" as offering something additional (para. 28)?

6. We are often advised to "seize the day" and, at the same time, to "plan for the future." We often hear "beauty is only skin deep," but also "first impressions are everlasting." "Clothes don't make the person," but be sure to "dress for success." "Don't sweat the small stuff," but also be sure "pay attention to detail." Consider one of these mixed messages, or another you can think of, and identify sources where the messages are typically encountered. Do these mixed messages pose any kind of social or psychological challenges to you or to other people?

EPICTETUS

Epictetus (pronounced Epic-TEE-tus) was born in Phrygia (now southwestern Turkey) about 135 CE. His mother was enslaved, and he was enslaved when he was brought to Rome. At an uncertain date, Epictetus was given his freedom, and he went to Nicopolis in northwestern Greece, where he taught philosophy. One of his students, a Roman named Flavius Arrian, recorded the teachings of Epictetus in two books written in Greek, the *Discourses* (or *Lectures*) and the *Handbook* (or *Manual*, often known by its Greek title, *Enchiridion*). Our selection is from a translation by Helena Orozco.

The doctrine that Epictetus taught is stoicism, which can be briefly characterized thus: The goal of life (as other philosophers of the period would agree) is "happiness" or "a flourishing life" (*eudaimonia*). The way to achieve this condition is to understand the nature of the good. Such things as health, wealth, and rank are not good because they do not always benefit those who possess them. True, such things are "preferred," and sickness, poverty, and low social status are "not preferred," but all of these are "indifferent" when it comes to being good or evil. The only true good is virtue. Yes, wealth can be useful, but it is not good or bad. What is good or bad is the way in which one makes use of what one has. The life that is happy or fruitful (*eudaimôn*) is the virtuous life. Of course, some things are beyond our power, but we are able to judge whatever comes to us, to see that what is "not preferred" — for instance, poverty — is not bad but is morally indifferent (just as wealth is morally indifferent). And we also have the power to adapt ourselves to whatever comes our way. A slightly later contemporary reported that Epictetus said that if one wanted to be free from wrongdoing and wanted to live a peaceful life, then one should endure and abstain.

From The Handbook

1. Some things are in our control, and some are not. Our opinions are within our control, and our choices, our likes and dislikes. In a word, whatever is our own doing. Beyond our control are our bodies, our possessions, reputation, position; in a word, things not our own doings.

Now, the things that are within our control are by nature free, unhindered, unimpeded, but those beyond our control are weak, slavish, hindered, up to others. Keep in mind, then, that if you think things are free that by nature are slavish, and if you think that things that are up to others are yours, you will be hindered, you will suffer, you will complain, you will blame the gods and your fellows. But, on the other hand, if you take as yours only what in fact is yours, and if you see that what belongs to others belongs to others, nobody will compel you, nobody will restrict you; you will blame nobody, and you will do nothing against your will. No one will harm you, you will have no enemies.

5. People are not disturbed by what happens but by the view they take of what happens. For instance, death is not to be feared; if it were to be feared, Socrates would have feared it. The fear consists in our wrong idea of death, our idea that it is to be feared. When, therefore, we are disturbed or feel grief, we should not blame someone else, but our [false] opinion. An uneducated person blames others for his misfortunes; a person just starting his education blames himself; an educated person blames neither others nor himself.

6. Do not take pride in any excellence that is not your own. If a horse could be proud, it might say, "I am handsome," and such a statement might be acceptable. But when you proudly say, "I have a handsome horse," you should understand that you are taking pride in a horse's good. What has the horse's good to do with you? What is yours? Only your reaction to things. When you behave in accordance with nature, you will take pride only in some good that is your own.

7. As when on a voyage, when the ship is at anchor, if you go ashore to get fresh water, you may amuse yourself by picking up a seashell or a vegetable, but keep the ship in mind. Be attentive to the captain's call, and when you hear the call, give up the trifles, or you will be thrown back into the ship like a bound sheep. So it is in life: If instead of a seashell or a vegetable, you are given a wife or child, fine, but when the captain calls, you must abandon these things without a second thought. And if you are old, keep close to the ship lest you are missing when you are called.

9. Sickness impedes the body but not the ability to make choices, unless you choose so. Lameness impedes the leg, but not the ability to make choices, unless the mind chooses so. Remember this with regard to everything that happens: Happenings are impediments to something else, but not to you.

15. Remember, behave in life as though you are attending a banquet. Is a dish brought to you? Put out your hand and take a moderate share. Does the dish pass you by? Do not grab for it. Has it not yet reached you? Don't yearn for it, but wait until it reaches you. Do this with regard to children, a spouse, position, wealth, and eventually you will be worthy to banquet with the gods. And if you can forgo even the things that are set before you, you are worthy not only to feast with the gods but to rule with them.

17. Remember: You are an actor in a play that you did not write. If the play is short, then it is short; if long, then it is long. If the author has assigned you the part of a poor man, act it well. Do the same if your part is that of a lame man or a ruler or an ordinary citizen. This is yours to do: Act your part well (but picking the part belongs to someone else).

21. Keep in mind death and exile and all other things that appear terrible — especially death — and you will never harbor a low thought nor too eagerly covet anything.

36. At a feast, to choose the largest portion 10 might satisfy your body but would be detrimental to the social nature of the affair. When you dine with another, then, keep in mind not only the value to the body of the dishes set before you, but the value of your behavior to your host and fellow diners.

43. Everything has two handles, one by which it can be carried and one by which it cannot. If your brother acts unjustly, do not take up the affair by the handle of his injustice, for it cannot be carried that way. Rather, take the other handle: He is your brother, he was brought up with you. Taken this way, it can be carried.

Topics for Critical Thinking and Writing

1. Consider Epictetus's words in paragraph 1: "Our opinions are within our control, and our choices, our likes and dislikes." Does Epictetus exaggerate the degree to which these things are under our control? Do we, in fact, control opinions, choices, likes, and dislikes? Explain.

2. Epictetus advises us not to fear death. What is his argument?

3. It is often said when bad, wrongful, or immoral actions are taken, even for a good cause, that "the ends do not justify the means." Think of an instance that makes this claim concrete and explain why the ends do not justify the means.

4. Choose one from among the eleven paragraphs by Epictetus that best expresses your own view of life — or are you entirely at odds with what Epictetus believes? Explain your response.

5. What does the cartoon say about happiness? How would Epictetus respond to the cartoon's message?

Mischa Richter The New Yorker Collection/The Cartoon Bank

"If I won the lottery, I would go on living as I always did."

BERTRAND RUSSELL

Bertrand Russell (1872–1970), British mathematician and philosopher, was born in Wales and educated at Trinity College, Cambridge, where he later taught. His pacifist opposition to World War I cost him this teaching appointment and earned him a prison sentence of six months. In 1940, an appointment to teach at the College of the City of New York was withdrawn because of his unorthodox moral views. But he was not always treated shabbily. He won numerous prizes, including a Nobel Prize in Literature in 1950. Much of his work is highly technical, but he also wrote frequently for the general public. The following passage comes from one of his most widely read books, *The Conquest of Happiness* (1930).

The Happy Life

The happy life is to an extraordinary extent the same as the good life. Professional moralists have made too much of self-denial, and in so doing have put the emphasis in the wrong place. Conscious self-denial leaves a man self-absorbed and vividly aware of what he has sacrificed; in consequence it fails often of its immediate object and almost always of its ultimate purpose. What is needed is not self-denial, but that kind of direction of interest outward which will lead spontaneously and naturally to the same acts that a person absorbed in the pursuit of his own virtue could only perform by means of conscious self-denial. I have written in this book as a hedonist, that is to say, as one who regards happiness as the good, but the acts to be recommended from the point of view of the hedonist are on the whole the same as those to be recommended by the sane moralist. The moralist, however, is too apt, though this is not, of course, universally true, to stress the act rather than the state of mind. The effects of an act upon the agent will be widely different, according to his state of mind at the moment. If you see a child drowning and save it as the result of a direct impulse to bring help, you will emerge none the worse morally. If, on the other hand, you say to yourself, "It is the part of virtue to succor the helpless, and I wish to be a virtuous man, therefore I must save this child," you will be an even worse man afterwards than you were before. What applies in this extreme case, applies in many other instances that are less obvious.

There is another difference, somewhat more subtle, between the attitude toward life that I have been recommending and that which is recommended by the traditional moralists. The traditional moralist, for example, will say that love should be unselfish. In a certain sense he is right, that is to say, it should not be selfish beyond a point, but it should undoubtedly be of such a nature that one's own happiness is bound up in its success. If a man were to invite a lady to marry him on the ground that he ardently desired her happiness and at the same time considered that she would afford him ideal opportunities of self-abnegation, I think it may be doubted whether she would be altogether pleased. Undoubtedly we should desire the happiness of those whom we love, but not as an alternative to our own. In fact the whole antithesis between self and the rest of the world, which is implied in the doctrine of self-denial, disappears as soon as we have any genuine interest in persons or things outside ourselves. Through such interests a man comes to feel himself part of the stream of life, not a hard separate entity like a billiard ball, which can have no relation with other such entities except that of collision. All unhappiness depends upon some kind of disintegration or lack of integration; there is disintegration within the self through lack of coördination between the conscious and the unconscious mind; there is lack of integration between the self and society, where the two are not knit together by the force of objective interests and affections. The happy man is the man who does not suffer from either of these failures of unity, whose personality is neither divided against itself nor pitted against the world. Such a man feels himself a citizen of the universe, enjoying freely the spectacle that it offers and the joys that it affords, untroubled by the thought of death because he feels himself not really separate from those who will come after him. It is in such profound instinctive union with the stream of life that the greatest joy is to be found.

Topics for Critical Thinking and Writing

1. In paragraph 1, Bertrand Russell says, "The happy life is to an extraordinary extent the same as the good life." First, how do you suppose Russell knows that? How might one confirm or refute the statement? Second, do you agree with Russell? Explain in detail.

2. In his final paragraph, Russell says that it is through their interests that people come to feel that they are "part of the stream of life, not a hard separate entity like a billiard ball, which can have no relation with other such entities except that of collision." Does this sentence strike you as (a) effective and (b) probably true? Why or why not?

3. In the final paragraph, Russell says that happy people feel connected to themselves (do not feel internally divided) and connected to society (do not feel pitted against the world). Describe in some detail a person who seems to you connected to the self and to society. Do you think that person is happy? Explain. Describe two people, one of whom seems to you internally divided and one of whom seems to you separated from society. Now think about yourself. Do you feel connected to yourself and to the world? If so, are you happy? Why or why not?

THE DALAI LAMA AND HOWARD C. CUTLER

The fourteenth Dalai ("ocean-wide") Lama ("superior person"), Tenzin Gyatso, is the spiritual leader of the Tibetan people but has lived in exile in Dharamshala, India, since 1959, when China invaded Tibet. In 1989, he was awarded the Nobel Peace Prize. In 1982, Howard C. Cutler, a psychiatrist who practices in Phoenix, Arizona, met the Dalai Lama while visiting India to study Tibetan medicine. Cutler and the Dalai Lama had frequent conversations, which Cutler later summarized and submitted to the Dalai Lama for approval. The material was then published in *The Art of Happiness* (1998). Here is one selection from that book.

Inner Contentment

Crossing the hotel parking lot on my way to meet with the Dalai Lama one afternoon, I stopped to admire a brand-new Toyota Land Cruiser, the type of car I had been wanting for a long time. Still thinking of that car as I began my session, I asked, "Sometimes it seems that our whole culture, Western culture, is based on material acquisition; we're surrounded, bombarded, with ads for the latest things to buy, the latest car and so on. It's difficult not to be influenced by that. There are so many things we want, things we desire. It never seems to stop. Can you speak a bit about desire?"

"I think there are two kinds of desire," the Dalai Lama replied. "Certain desires are positive. A desire for happiness. It's absolutely right. The desire for peace. The desire for a more harmonious world, a friendlier world. Certain desires are very useful.

"But at some point, desires can become unreasonable. That usually leads to trouble. Now, for example, sometimes I visit supermarkets. I really love to see supermarkets, because I can see so many beautiful things. So, when I look at all these different articles, I develop a feeling of desire, and my initial impulse might be, 'Oh, I want this; I want that.' Then, the second thought that arises, I ask myself, 'Oh, do I really need this?' The answer is usually no. If you follow after that first desire, that initial impulse, then very soon your pockets will empty. However, the other level of desire, based on one's essential needs of food, clothing, and shelter, is something more reasonable.

"Sometimes, whether a desire is excessive or negative depends on the circumstances or society in which you live. For example, if you live in a prosperous society where a car is required to help you manage in your daily life, then of course there's nothing wrong in desiring a car. But if you live in a poor village in India where you can manage quite well without a car but you still desire one, even if you have the money to buy it, it can ultimately bring trouble. It can create an uncomfortable feeling among your neighbors and so on. Or, if you're living in a more prosperous society and have a car but keep wanting more expensive cars, that leads to the same kind of problems."

"But," I argued, "I can't see how wanting 5 or buying a more expensive car leads to problems for an individual, as long as he or she can afford it. Having a more expensive car than your neighbors might be a problem for them — they might be jealous and so on — but having a new car would give you, yourself, a feeling of satisfaction and enjoyment."

The Dalai Lama shook his head and replied firmly, "No. . . . Self-satisfaction alone cannot determine if a desire or action is positive or negative. A murderer may have a feeling of satisfaction at the time he is committing the murder, but that doesn't justify the act. All the nonvirtuous actions — lying, stealing, sexual misconduct, and so on — are committed by people who may be feeling a sense of satisfaction at the time. The demarcation between a positive and a negative desire or action is not whether it gives you an immediate feeling of satisfaction but whether it ultimately results in positive or negative consequences. For example, in the case of wanting more expensive possessions, if that is based on a mental attitude that just wants more and more, then eventually you'll reach a limit of what you can get; you'll come up against reality. And when you reach that limit, then you'll lose all hope, sink down into depression, and so on. That's one danger inherent in that type of desire.

"So I think that this kind of excessive desire leads to greed — an exaggerated form of desire, based on overexpectation. And when you reflect upon the excesses of greed, you'll find that it leads an individual to a feeling of frustration, disappointment, a lot of confusion, and a lot of problems. When it comes to dealing with greed, one thing that is quite characteristic is that although it arrives by the desire to obtain something, it is not satisfied by obtaining. Therefore, it becomes sort of limitless, sort of bottomless, and that leads to trouble. One interesting thing about greed is that although the underlying motive is to seek satisfaction, the irony is that even after obtaining the object of your desire, you are still not satisfied. *The true antidote of greed is contentment.* If you have a strong sense of contentment, it doesn't matter whether you obtain the object or not; either way, you are still content."

So, how can we achieve inner contentment? There are two methods. One method is to obtain everything that we want and desire — all the money, houses, and cars; the perfect mate; and the perfect body. The Dalai Lama has already pointed out the disadvantage of this approach; if our wants and desires remain unchecked, sooner or later we will run up against something that we want but can't have. The second, and more reliable, method is not to have what we want but rather to want and appreciate what we have.

The other night, I was watching a television interview with Christopher Reeve, the actor who was thrown from a horse in 1994 and suffered a spinal cord injury that left him completely paralyzed from the neck down, requiring a mechanical ventilator even to breathe. When questioned by the interviewer about how he dealt with the depression resulting from his disability, Reeve revealed that he had experienced a brief period of complete despair while in the intensive care unit of the hospital. He went on to say, however, that these feelings of despair passed relatively quickly, and he now sincerely considered himself to be a "lucky guy." He cited the blessings of a loving wife and children but also spoke gratefully about the rapid advances of modern medicine (which he estimates will find a cure for spinal cord injury within the next decade), stating that if he had been hurt just a few years earlier, he probably would have died from his injuries. While describing the process of adjusting to his paralysis, Reeve said that while his feelings of despair resolved rather quickly, at first he was still troubled by intermittent pangs of jealousy that could be triggered by another's innocent passing remark such as, "I'm just gonna run upstairs and get something." In learning to deal with these feelings, he said, "I realized that the only way to go through life is to look at your assets, to see what you can still do; in my case, fortunately I didn't have any brain injury, so I still have a mind I can use." Focusing on his resources in this manner, Reeve has elected to use his mind to increase awareness and educate the public about spinal cord injury, to help others, and has plans to continue speaking as well as to write and direct films.[1]

---

[1] Christopher Reeve died on October 10, 2004.

Topics for Critical Thinking and Writing

1. In paragraph 1, Howard Cutler says that he had long wanted a Toyota Land Cruiser. Exactly why might a person want such a vehicle? Do you think most people buy vehicles for the purpose of efficient transportation or as status symbols? How do you think identity is linked to the kind of car you drive?

2. At the end of paragraph 8, Cutler reports that the Dalai Lama suggests that the best way to achieve inner contentment "is not to have what we want but rather to want and appreciate what we have." In the next (final) paragraph, Cutler cites the example of Christopher Reeve. Drawing on your own experiences — which include your experience of persons whom you know or have heard about — can you offer confirming evidence? Explain your response.

3. The Dalai Lama refers several times to the ways satisfying certain desires can lead to "trouble" (paras. 3, 4, and 7) or "danger" (para. 6). What kinds of trouble and danger does he mean? What other kinds of trouble or danger can come from materialism or with "keeping up with the Joneses"? Think of examples — real or imagined — of such trouble or danger.

4. Compare the Dalai Lama's views with those of Epictetus. Would you say they are virtually the same? Why, or why not?

DANIEL GILBERT

Daniel Gilbert is the author of *Stumbling on Happiness* (2006), a book that has sold six million copies worldwide and that won the prestigious Royal Society Prize for Science Books. Hearing of the award, Gilbert said, "There are very few countries (including my own) . . . where a somewhat cheeky book about happiness could win a science prize — but the British invented intellectual humor and have always understood that enlightenment and entertainment are natural friends."

A high school dropout, Gilbert was nineteen when he visited a community college, intending to take a writing course but enrolling instead in the only course still open — a psychology course. He is now a professor of psychology at Harvard University and has shared his views on happiness in various essays and television appearances. In 2010, he co-wrote a six-hour television series for *NOVA*, "This Emotional Life," and in 2013, he gave one of the twenty most-viewed TED talks, "The Surprising Science of Happiness."

The following essay originally appeared in *Time* a few days before Father's Day in 2006.

Does Fatherhood Make You Happy?

Sonora Smart Dodd was listening to a sermon on self-sacrifice when she decided that her father, a widower who had raised six children, deserved his very own national holiday. Almost a century later, people all over the world spend the third Sunday in June honoring their fathers with ritual offerings of aftershave and neckties, which leads millions of fathers to have precisely the same thought at precisely the same moment: "My children," they think in unison, "make me happy."

Could all those dads be wrong?

Studies reveal that most married couples start out happy and then become progressively less satisfied over the course of their lives, becoming especially disconsolate when their children are in diapers and in adolescence, and returning to their initial levels of happiness only after their children have had the decency to grow up and go away. When the popular press invented a malady called "empty-nest syndrome," it failed to mention that its primary symptom is a marked increase in smiling.

Psychologists have measured how people feel as they go about their daily activities, and have found that people are less happy when they are interacting with their children than when they are eating, exercising, shopping, or watching television. Indeed, an act of parenting makes most people about as happy as an act of housework. Economists have modeled the impact of many variables on people's overall happiness and have consistently found that children have only a small impact. A small negative impact.

Those findings are hard to swallow because they fly in the face of our most compelling intuitions. We love our children! We talk about them to anyone who will listen, show their photographs to anyone who will look, and hide our refrigerators behind vast collages of their drawings, notes, pictures, and report cards. We feel confident that we are happy with our kids, about our kids, for our kids, and because of our kids — so why is our personal experience at odds with the scientific data?

Three reasons.

First, when something makes us happy we are willing to pay a lot for it, which is why the worst Belgian chocolate is more expensive than the best Belgian tofu. But that process can work in reverse: When we pay a lot for something, we assume it makes us happy, which is why we swear to the wonders of bottled water and Armani socks. The compulsion to care for our children was long ago written into our DNA, so we toil and sweat, lose sleep and hair, play nurse, housekeeper, chauffeur, and cook, and we do all that because nature just won't have it any other way. Given the high price we pay, it isn't surprising that we rationalize those costs and conclude that our children must be repaying us with happiness.

Second, if the Red Sox and the Yankees were scoreless until Manny Ramirez[1] hit a grand slam in the bottom of the ninth, you can be sure that Boston fans would remember it as the best game of the season. Memories are dominated by their most powerful — and not their most typical — instances. Just as a glorious game-winning homer can erase our memory of eight and a half dull innings, the sublime moment when our three-year-old looks up from the mess she is making with her mashed potatoes and says, "I wub you, Daddy," can erase eight hours of no, not yet, not now, and stop asking. Children may not make us happy very often, but when they do, that happiness is both transcendent and amnesic.

Third, although most of us think of heroin as a source of human misery, shooting heroin doesn't actually make people feel miserable. It makes them feel really, really good — so good, in fact, that it crowds out every other source of pleasure. Family, friends, work, play, food, sex — none can compete with the narcotic experience; hence all fall by the wayside. The analogy to children is all too clear. Even if their company were an unremitting pleasure, the fact that they require so much company means that other sources of pleasure will all but disappear. Movies, theater, parties, travel — those are just a few of the English nouns that parents of young children quickly forget how to pronounce. We believe our children are our greatest joy, and we're absolutely right. When you have one joy, it's bound to be the greatest.

Our children give us many things, but an increase in our average daily happiness is probably not among them. Rather than deny that fact, we should celebrate it. Our ability to love beyond all measure those who try our patience and weary our bones is at once our most noble and most human quality. The fact that children don't always make us happy — and that we're happy to have them nonetheless — is the fact for which Sonora Smart Dodd was so grateful. She thought we would all do well to remember it, every third Sunday in June.

---

[1]**Manny Ramirez** (b. 1972), a former professional baseball player, played for the Boston Red Sox from 2001 to 2008.

Topics for Critical Thinking and Writing

1. How would you define the "empty-nest syndrome" (para. 3), and how do you respond to Daniel Gilbert's suggestion that it was "invented"?

2. Do you believe the "studies" that Gilbert mentions in paragraph 3? Why or why not? Similarly, do you believe the "psychologists" of paragraph 4? Explain your response.

3. What does Gilbert mean when he describes the happiness that children cause their parents as "transcendent" (para. 8)? Are there other, nontranscendent kinds of happiness that parents experience? Explain your response.

4. Let's assume that even if you don't fully accept Gilbert's view about fatherhood and happiness, you're willing to grant that it is just possible that there may be something to what he says. Are you willing to take the next step and say that what he says of fatherhood may also be true of motherhood? Why or why not?

5. What do you think Gilbert's chief purpose is in this essay? To inform? To persuade? To entertain? Something else? Support your answer with evidence.

6. You may have been told not to write paragraphs consisting of only a sentence or two, but Gilbert's essay includes two such paragraphs, 2 and 6. Should Gilbert have revised these paragraphs? Or does their brevity serve a purpose? Explain your response.

TEXT CREDITS

Sohrab Ahmari, "Porn Isn't Free Speech — on the Web or Anywhere," *New York Post,* 9 Dec. 2019. Copyright © 2019 by New York Post. All rights reserved. Used under license. https://nypost.com/

Bridget Anderson, "The Politics of Pests: Immigration and the Invasive Other" (excerpt), *Social Research: An International Quarterly* 84.1, Spring 2017, pp. 7–8, 14–16, 18–19, 25, 26–28. Copyright © 2017 by Bridget Anderson. Reproduced with permission of Graduate Faculty of Political and Social Science at the New School for Social Research. Republished with permission of Bridget Anderson. permission conveyed through Copyright Clearance Center, Inc.

Anne Appelbaum, "The My Pillow Guy Really Could Destroy Democracy," *The Atlantic,* 29 July 2021. Copyright © 2021 The Atlantic Monthly Group, Inc. All rights reserved. Distributed by Tribune Content Agency, LLC.

Kwame Anthony Appiah, "Go Ahead, Speak for Yourself," *The New York Times,* August 10, 2018. Copyright © 2018 by The New York Times. All rights reserved. Used under license. https://nytimes.com/

Kristin Arola, "Indigenous Interfaces," University Press of Colorado from *Social Writing/Social Media: Pedagogy, Presentation, and Publics.* Eds. Douglas Walls and Stephanie Vie. WAC Clearinghouse Perspectives on Writing Series. Copyright © 2017 by University Press of Colorado. Used with permission.

Reyna Askew and Margaret A. Walls, "Diversity in the Great Outdoors: Is Everyone Welcome in America's Public Parks and Lands?" *Resources,* 24 May 2019. Copyright © 2019 by Resources for the Future. Used with permission. All rights reserved.

John Barth, "Us/Them," from *The Development: Nine Stories* by John Barth. Copyright © 2008 by John Barth. Reprinted by permission of Mariner Books, an imprint of HarperCollins Publishers and by permission of The Wylie Agency LLC.

Jennifer Bartlett, "Disability and the Right to Choose," *The New York Times,* 10 May 2017. Copyright © 2017 by The New York Times. All rights reserved. Used under license. https://nytimes.com/

Touria Benlafqih, "Has Social Media Made Young People Better Citizens?" from *World Economic Forum,* January 16, 2015, https://www.weforum.org/agenda/2015/01/social-media-made-young-people-better/. Reprinted by permission of the author.

Richard Blanco, "One Today: A Poem for Barack Obama's Presidential Inauguration," January 21, 2013. Copyright © 2013 by Richard Blanco. Reprinted by permission of the University of Pittsburgh Press.

Ariel Bogle and Jane Lee, "Children feature in COVID-19 and QAnon conspiracies, but these just most recent examples of a 'very old, powerful fear,'" *ABC,* 31 Oct 2020. Copyright © 2020 by ABC. Reproduced by permission of the Australian Broadcasting Corporation.

K. Tempest Bradford, news report titled "Commentary: Cultural Appropriation Is, in Fact, Indefensible," as originally published on npr.org on June 28, 2017. Copyright © 2018 K. Tempest Bradford for National Public Radio, Inc. Used with the permission of Jill Grinberg Literary Management LLC. Any unauthorized duplication is strictly prohibited.

Jeffrey T. Brown, "The Yelling of the Lambs," 23 Feb. 2018. Copyright © 2018 by American Thinker. Used with permission. All rights reserved.

Dana Brownlee, "Is 'Cancel Culture' Really Just Long Overdue Accountability for the Privileged?" *Forbes,* July 1, 2021. Copyright © 2021 by Forbes. All rights reserved. Used under license. https://forbes.com/

Marianna Cerini, "Why Women Feel Pressured to Shave," *CNN.com,* March 3, 2020. Copyright © 2020 by Turner Broadcasting Systems, Inc. All rights reserved. Used under license. https://CNN.com/

Ed Conard, "We Don't Need More Humanities Majors," *Washington Post,* July 30, 2013. Copyright © 2013 Ed Conard. Used with permission.

Tressie McMillan Cottom, excerpt from *Thick: And Other Essays.* Copyright © 2019 by Tressie McMillan Cottom. Reprinted by permission of The New Press. www.thenewpress.com.

Ben Crair, "Why Do So Many People Still Want to Believe in Bigfoot?" *Smithsonian Magazine,* Sept. 2018. Copyright © 2018 by Smithsonian Institution. Reprinted with permission from Smithsonian Enterprises. All rights reserved. Reproduction in any medium is strictly prohibited without permission from Smithsonian magazine.

Justin Cronin, "Confessions of a Liberal Gun Owner," *The New York Times,* January 28, 2013. Copyright © 2013 by The New York Times. All rights reserved. Used under license. https://nytimes.com/

Dalai Lama and Howard C. Cutler, "Inner Contentment," from *The Art of Happiness: A Handbook for the Living* by Dalai Lama and Howard C. Cutler. Copyright © 1998 by His Holiness the Dalai Lama and Howard C. Cutler, M.D. Used by permission of Riverhead, an imprint of Penguin Publishing Group, a division of Penguin Random House LLC and Howard C. Cutler.

Andrew Delbanco, "3 Reasons College Still Matters," first published in the *Boston Globe,* March 4, 2012, is reprinted from *College.* Copyright © 2012 Princeton University Press; Republished with permission of Princeton University Press. permission conveyed through Copyright Clearance Center, Inc. All rights reserved.

Tracy Deonn, "Every King Arthur Retelling Is Fanfic about Who Gets to Be Legendary." Originally appeared in *Tor,* 23 March 2021. Copyright © 2021 by Tracy Deonn. Used with permission.

Hossein Derakhshan, "How Social Media Endangers Knowledge," *Wired,* October 19, 2017. Copyright © 2017 Condé Nast. Reprinted by permission. All rights reserved.

Emari DiGiorgio, "When You Are the Brownest White Girl," from *Rattle* 58 (Winter 2017), https://www.rattle.com/print/50s/i58/. Copyright © 2017. Reprinted by permission of the author.

Nora Ephron, "The Boston Photographs," copyright © 1975 by Nora Ephron. Reprinted by permission of ICM Partners.

John E. Finn, "The Constitution Doesn't Have a Problem with Mask Mandates," *The Conversation,* 22 July 2020. This work is licensed under a Creative Commons Attribution-NoDerivatives 4.0 International (CC BY-ND 4.0).

John Martin Fischer, "The Problem of Now," *Aeon,* 8 Jan. 2021. Copyright © 2021 by Aeon Media. Used with permission. All rights reserved. This article was first published on Aeon (aeon.co).

Jonathan Safran Foer, "Show Your Hands" from *We Are the Weather: Saving the Planet Begins at Breakfast.* Copyright © 2019 by Jonathan Safran Foer. Reprinted by permission from Farrar, Straus and Giroux, Hamish Hamilton Canada, a division of Penguin Random House Canada Limited and Penguin Books Limited. All rights reserved.

Kmele Foster, David French, Jason Stanley, and Thomas Chatterton Williams, "We Disagree on a Lot . . . Except for the Dangers of Anti-Critical Race Theory Laws." *The New York Times,* 5 July 2021. Copyright © 2021 by The New York Times. All rights reserved. Used under license. https://nytimes.com/

Conor Friedersdorf, "A Food Fight at Oberlin College," *The Atlantic,* December 21, 2015. Copyright © 2015 The Atlantic Monthly Group, Inc. All rights reserved. Distributed by Tribune Content Agency, LLC.

Roxane Gay, "The Price of Black Ambition," *The Virginia Quarterly Review,* Fall 2014, Volume 90, Number 4. Copyright © 2014 by The Virginia Quarterly Review. Used with permission.

Evan Gerstmann, "Cancel Culture Is Only Getting Worse," *Forbes,* September 13, 2020. Copyright © 2020 by Forbes. All rights reserved. Used under license. https://forbes.com/

Daniel Gilbert, "Does Fatherhood Make You Happy?" from *Time* magazine, June 11, 2006. Reprinted by permission of the author.

Kenneth Goldsmith, Excerpt from *Uncreative Writing: Managing Language in the Digital Age.* Copyright © 2011 by Columbia University Press. Reprinted with permission of Columbia University Press.

Aubrey Gordon, from "Into Thin Air" from *What We Don't Talk About When We Talk About Fat.* Copyright © 2020 by Aubrey Gordon. Reprinted by permission of Beacon Press, Boston.

Index of Authors, Titles, and Terms

Syllogisms, 106–107, 350–351, 352–353, 354
Symbolism, 170
Synonym, 116–117
Synthesis, 291

Tables, 178
Tautology, 371
Technical language, 420
Technological industry, 443–443
Term, defined, 114
Testimony
    appeals, 160
    as classical topic, 23, 24
    as evidence, 289
Text-centered interpretation, 396, 397, 398
Theorizing, in literary criticism, 403
"The Price of Black Ambition" (Gay), 217–223
Thesis and thesis statement, 42
    of an analysis, 198–199
    checklist for, 232
    for different target audiences, 232–233
    examining, 192–193, 205
    in opening paragraphs, 239
    in oral presentations, 417–418
    stakes of, 231–233
    support for, 193
Thinking Critically. *see also* Critical thinking
    analysis of a political cartoon, 173
    constructing a Toulmin argument, 340
    eliminating *we*, *one*, and *I*, 250
    examining language to analyze an author's
        argument, 204
    generating ideas with topics, 28
    identifying *ethos*, 78
    identifying fallacies, 376
    previewing, 44
    using search terms, 271
    using signal phrases, 299
    using transitions in argument, 244
    "Walking the Tightrope," 233
Thinking process, 4, 16
**"13 Thoughts on Reparations, Afropessimism
    and White Supremacy" (Laomina),** 142–149
Thoreau, Henry David, Selections from *Walden*,
    730–735
Tierney, John, "The Reign of Recycling,"
    134–139
**Timmerman, Lesley, "An Argument for
    Corporate Responsibility,"** 313–318
Title, 41, 44, 237–238
Tolentino, Jia, "The I in the Internet," 556–561

Tone
    addressing opposition and, 248–249
    of author, 194–195, 200
    in oral presentations, 420
    and persona, checklist for establishing, 250
    writer's persona and, 246–248
Topics
    classical, 16–17
    in library databases, 269
    manageability of, 263
    in opening paragraphs, 239
Topoi. see Topics
Toulmin, Stephen, 334
Toulmin method, 333–347
    backing, 335, 337–338, 347
    checklist for using, 347
    claims, 335, 345–347
    example of, 341–345
    grounds, 335, 336, 345–347
    modal qualifiers, 335, 338–339, 347
    rebuttals, 335, 339–340, 347
    visual guide to, 335
    warrants, 335, 336–337, 345–347
Trade publications, 273–275, 287
Transitions, 193, 243, 244, 418
Transitivity, 351
"Trolls" (Lanier), 576–580
Trustworthiness, 247
Truth, 107–108, 355
Tu quoque fallacy, 366, 372

"Uncreative Writing" (Goldsmith), 534–540
Underlining, 48–49
Unfamiliar issues, 21
**"Unity in Times of Division: An Analysis of
    Richard Blanco's 'One Today'" (DiPiero),**
    407–412
Unreliable statistical evidence, 127–128
URLs, 268, 278
"Us/Them" (Barth), 714–721
Utopia, **from (More),** 655–666
**"Utopia Is a Dangerous Ideal: We Should Aim for
    'Protopia'" (Shermer),** 670–673

**Vaidya, Anand Jayprakash "The Inclusion
    Problem in Critical Thinking: The Case of
    Indian Philosophy,"** 31–35
Validity, 107–109, 350, 351–352
Venn diagrams, 351
Verbal irony, 84
Verbs that imply proof, 193